Also by John Updike

ODD JOBS

John Updike

ODD JOBS

ESSAYS AND CRITICISM

New York: Alfred A. Knopf

1991

THIS IS A BORZOI BOOK
PUBLISHED BY ALFRED A. KNOPF, INC.

Library of Congress Cataloging-in-Publication Data

Updike, John.
　Odd jobs : essays and criticism / John Updike.—1st ed.
　　p.　　cm.
　Includes bibliographical references and index.
　ISBN 0-679-40414-7
　I. Title.
PS3571.P403　1991
814'.54—dc20　　　　　　　　　　　　　　　　91-52738
　　　　　　　　　　　　　　　　　　　　　　　CIP

Manufactured in the United States of America

First Edition

Acknowledgments

Grateful acknowledgment is made to the following magazines and publishers, who first printed the pieces specified, sometimes under different titles and in slightly different form:

THE NEW YORKER: "Five Days in Finland at the Age of Fifty-five," "First Wives and Trolley Cars," "Mr. Volente," "John Cheever — I," "Emersonianism," "Howells as Anti-Novelist," "Many Bens," the introductions to Mikhail Prishvin's *Nature's Diary* and to Franz Kafka's *Complete Stories*, the two pieces of "Notes and Comment" in the appendix, and eighty-eight of the book reviews, including sixteen first published as "Briefly Noted."

THE NEW YORK TIMES BOOK REVIEW: "Hymn to Tilth," "Was B.B. a Crook?", "The Bimbo on the Barge," "Bull in a Type Shop," the introduction to Isak Dinesen's *Seven Gothic Tales*, and the material on pages 848 and 849–51.

THE NEW YORK TIMES: "Books into Film."

THE BOSTON GLOBE: "Overboard on *Overboard,*" "The Boston Red Sox, as of 1986," and "Can Architecture Be Criticized?"

THE NEW YORK REVIEW OF BOOKS: "How Does the Writer Imagine?", "Should Writers Give Lectures?", and the introductions to William Dean Howells's *Indian Summer* and to Graham Greene's *The Power and the Glory*.

THE NEW REPUBLIC: Introduction to *Appointment in Samarra*, by John O'Hara.

THE ONTARIO REVIEW: "The Parade."

ARCHITECTURAL DIGEST: "Fictional Houses," "A Sense of Transparency," and "Is New York City Inhabitable?"

ESQUIRE: "Edmund Wilson," "Popular Music," "The Importance of Fiction," and the response on page 847–48.

HARPER'S MAGAZINE: "Twisted Apples."

VOGUE: "Mother" and "High Art Versus Popular Culture."

COSMOPOLITAN: "Women."

LEAR'S: "Spirituality."

"W": "Beauty."

SPORT: "Ted Williams, as of 1986."

POPULAR MECHANICS: "Our National Monuments," titled "Sacred Places."

NEW ENGLAND MONTHLY: "A Short and Happy Ride" and "The Fourth of July."

MICHIGAN QUARTERLY REVIEW: "The Female Body" and the response on page 849.

TV GUIDE: "Being on TV — I" and "Being on TV — II."

CORRIERE DELLA SERA: "A Nameless Rose" and "Mr. Palomar."

LIBÉRATION: Answer to *"Pourquoi écrivez-vous?"*

LIFE: "John Cheever — II"

PENGUIN BOOKS USA INC.: Introduction to *Nature's Diary*, by Mikhail Prishvin. Introduction copyright © 1987 by John Updike. Reprinted by permission of Viking Penguin, a division of Penguin Books USA Inc. "The Gospel According to St. Matthew" and Introduction to *The Power and the Glory*, by Graham Greene. Introduction copyright © 1990 by John Updike.

THE BOOK-OF-THE-MONTH CLUB: Introductions to *Seven Gothic Tales*, by Isak Dinesen, and *Appointment in Samarra*, by John O'Hara.

VINTAGE BOOKS: Introduction to *Indian Summer*, by William Dean Howells. Introduction copyright © 1990 by John Updike. Reprinted by permission of Vintage Books, a division of Random House, Inc.

SCHOCKEN BOOKS: Foreword to *Franz Kafka: The Complete Stories* edited by Norm Nahum and N. Glatzer. Originally published in *The New Yorker* in 1983. Foreword copyright © 1983 by John Updike. Reprinted by permission of Schocken Books, published by Pantheon Books, a division of Random House, Inc.

WILLIAM B. EERDMANS PUBLISHING CO.: Introduction to *Wolfgang Amadeus Mozart*, by Karl Barth. Copyright © 1986 by William B. Eerdmans Publishing Company.

ADDISON-WESLEY CO.: "The Fourth of July," in the anthology *Summer*, copyright © 1990 by Addison-Wesley Publishing Company Inc.

LORD JOHN PRESS: Foreword to *Jester's Dozen*. Reprinted by permission of the publisher.

SYLVESTER & ORPHANOS: "John Cheever — III"

POETS & WRITERS MAGAZINE: "Writers as Progenitors and Offspring."

BOOKENDS: "I Was a Teen-Age Library User."

THE INDEPENDENT ON SUNDAY: "A Book That Changed Me."

SPECIAL REPORT: "Harvard Yard."

HARVARD GAZETTE: "I had a lot to learn when I came . . . "

HARVARD MAGAZINE: Answer to "What is your favorite spot in and around Harvard?"

HARVARD UNIVERSITY: Preface to the catalogue of an exhibit of my own papers in Houghton Library.

THE FRANKLIN LIBRARY: The forewords for *The Witches of Eastwick*, *Roger's Version*, and *Rabbit at Rest* are copyrighted 1984, 1986, and 1990 respectively by The Franklin Library, Franklin Center, PA, for exclusive use in its Signed First Editions of those books. The Forewords have been reprinted in this edition by special permission of The Franklin Library.

THE WALL STREET JOURNAL: Expanded version of remarks on artistic free-dom. Shorter version published in the PROCEEDINGS OF THE AMERICAN ACAD-EMY OF ARTS AND LETTERS (Second Series, No. 40).

Grateful acknowledgment is made to the following for permission to reprint previously published material:

HARPERCOLLINS PUBLISHERS INC.: Excerpt from "Traveler's Song" from *The Fox from Peapack* by E. B. White. Copyright 1938 by E. B. White. Re-printed by permission of HarperCollins Publishers Inc.

PENGUIN BOOKS USA INC.: "Résumé," copyright 1926, renewed 1954 by Dorothy Parker, "Garden Spot," copyright 1931, renewed 1959 by Dorothy Parker, from *The Portable Dorothy Parker* edited by Brendan Gill. Reprinted by permission of Viking Penguin, a division of Penguin Books USA Inc.

JOEL WHITE: "A Forward Glance O'er the Obituary Page" by E. B. White. *The New Yorker*, August 28, 1948. Reprinted by permission of Joel White.

To Martha

Contents

ESSAYS ON ASSIGNED TOPICS

Mostly Literary

TRIBUTES

SPEECHES

INTRODUCTIONS

Preface

NOT LONG AFTER ASSEMBLING my last eight-years' accumulation of
essays and criticism, *Hugging the Shore,* I acquired a word processor,
a writing instrument so dazzling that I composed a poem to it, on it,
beginning

> Wee.word.processor,.is.it.not
> *De.trop.*of.you.to.put.a.dot
> Between.the.words.your.nimble.screen
> Displays.in.phosphorescent.green?

and ending

> My.circuits.have.been.scrambled.by
> Your.being.brighter,.far,.than.I.

In fact the machine does have a staring quality that introduces an element
of social embarrassment into the prolonged, tenuous intimacy of composing a novel, and that drives one back to pencil on paper. But for odd jobs,
the odd literary jobs—the prefaces and puffs, the "few paragraphs" on
beauty or baseball—that a persevering writer, aging into a shaky sort of
celebrity, gets increasingly asked to do, the machine is ideal, rattling off
clean copy at the stab of a switch, accommodating revisions in a seamless
electronic twinkling. An element of technological suavity is introduced
into one's hitherto clumsy literary labors, with their bleary carbons and
slow-drying whiteout and anxious marginalia. Almost irresistible become
the seductive invitations on the perfumed stationery of ad-chocked ladies'
magazines for a feuilleton on femininity, the brisk demands from con-
glomerate-owned publishers for a fresh introductory slant onto their new
printing of an alleged classic, the charmingly hand-penned notes from the
guiding spirits of highbrow quarterlies, the disarmingly misspelled and

dot-matrixed pleas for a credo from college monthlies, the imperious phone calls from the English-accented secretaries of editorial power-brokers in their Manhattan aeries, the urgent requests that bring the white Federal Express trucks roaring up the driveway and once again over the freshly seeded edges of the lawn. With his wonderful new tool of ease how can a writer say No?

Clearly, the present writer said Yes not infrequently. In one especially affirmative phase, toward the end of 1988, as I was trying to muster my scattered resources and commence a novel, I found myself obligated to write an introduction to an album of *New Yorker* covers, a study of our national monuments from the engineering angle for *Popular Mechanics*, a hymn to winter golf for *Golf Digest*, and an essay upon the Gospel of St. Matthew for a book on the New Testament—an anthology of amateur exegeses called *Incarnation*, a wispy Christian sequel to an Old Testament bodice-ripper titled *Congregation*—not to mention an adaptation of an old short story of mine into a brief play, a commentary upon a poem of mine for a children's anthology, a speech on computers to be given at M.I.T., and definitive reviews of a Chinese Communist sex novel, a historical treatise upon a certain John Hu who happened to go crazy in eighteenth-century France, and two giant tomes devoted to the further glory of George Bernard Shaw. Except for the tiny commentary on the poem, written in kiddy-talk, and the cover introduction, senseless without the covers themselves, and the golf piece, saved for some more sporty collection, all these efforts are contained in *Odd Jobs*, including the *Popular Mechanics* article, which I had considered leaving out but which on being reread held my interest, with its piquant nuts and bolts, its saga of lever-aged heft and large-scale chiselling in the cause of patriotic symbolization. Do not think, however, that I have lazily included every odd job performed since mid-1982: I left out forewords to the collected lyrics of Cole Porter and the supposedly best short stories of 1984, several essays on photographs, a number of pedagogic textbook commentaries, two funeral orations, a few *New Yorker* "Notes and Comments," all essays on golf and art, and more than a few saucy little speeches, including one jovially introducing George Plimpton so he could as jovially present the Mac-Dowell Medal to a slightly less jovial William Styron.

The very first item, the account of my five days in Finland, came about curiously: a new Condé Nast magazine, *Traveler*, invited me to contribute, and, since I had already scheduled my sentimental visit to Finland, I thought to write for them a kind of parody of a travel piece. But *The New Yorker*, to whom, in obedience to my contractual obligations, I showed the result first, surprisingly accepted it, and thus my nonevents and angst-ridden excursion popped up in its deadpan pages, under the commodious heading "Our Footloose Correspondents." Several Finnish schoolchildren, thinking I was attacking their excellent country, sent me indignant postcards. My travel confidences are followed herein by two stray pieces of semi-fiction, to give them a home between covers, and the wee self-plagiarized play. In the cases of "The Importance of Fiction" and "Can Architecture Be Criticized?" an irritation with myself for accepting the assignments may have galvanized my style and hyperbolized my assertions. Otherwise, my conscience is clear enough. After all, what is a writer for but to write? Some novelists—Bellow, Styron, Pynchon—seem able to confine themselves to well-spaced presentations of book-length works to a grateful public; I, even though (or perhaps because) I have lived most of my life in small towns, need a certain frequent reassurance of proofs coming and going, of postage and phoning, of input and output. The discreet fuss of periodical publication gives me citizenship in the corporate world and connects me, not too bindingly, with a network of literary colleagues. I cannot live within the anchorite's cell of a novel all the time. And, raised in a Depression atmosphere of financial anxiety, I have trouble turning money from the door; today's eager profferer of two dollars a word may be tomorrow's bankrupt venture in targeted marketing. Just now, as I write these words, *New England Monthly,* which ran several of the frothier concoctions below, has its folding noted in the morning paper, and an hour later a Federal Express truck huffs and puffs to my door with a billet-doux from *Gentlemen's Quarterly:* "We would very much like to have something by you in the magazine. We had thought of a couple of essay ideas—art, the business of art, galleries, museums, etc.—but we wonder if you might not rather write a piece on golf?" Alas, even the courteously cajoling editor seems to sense that I may have said my fill on these thoroughly stroked pet topics. My best defense, in fending off odd jobs, remains a widespread ignorance.

One accepts editorial invitations in the hopes of learning something, or of extracting from within some unsuspected wisdom. For writing educates the writer as it goes along. "I always write a thing first and think about it afterwards," E. B. White wrote, "because the easiest way to have consecutive thoughts is to start putting them down." The pieces herein that I feel fondest toward are, perversely, those prodigals that gave me most trouble: the eye-grinding forays into vast prose tracts of Emerson and Howells, of Tolstoy and Shaw and Ben Franklin. I returned with a piece of the boundless kingdom of the written word a little better mapped in my mind. Without being a reader the way some professors, editors, and chairbound agoraphobes are readers, I am shyly happy among texts. Quotations, and even quotations within quotations, please me. How nicely, it seems to me, "Fictional Houses" frames up its topic, of the real within the imaginary! How real, to me, became, in Stephen Gould's exposition, the precipitous, layered terrain where Victorian theology and geology collide! My ability to get excited by such verbal constructs perhaps goes back to my childhood cartooning—my yen to draw talk balloons in ruled-off panels. Then I became a college English major. Now, having shied from graduate school and the conventional literary sideline of teaching, I feel a need for quick-fix seminars, and write term papers for pay instead of for grades.

Of the odd jobs I do, writing *New Yorker* reviews feels the least odd; the generous space the magazine provides, the weight of attention its editors and fact-checkers selflessly bring to bear upon the columns my name alone claims, the cheerful welcome granted to a little fun and free-style generalization in the prose all make the reviews feel like a profitable subdivision of creativity. To date I have written two hundred and one signed reviews for the magazine, plus dozens of "Briefly Noted"s. In my four collections of non-fictional prose, I count (not including introductions) three hundred sixty-nine books reviewed. At the modest estimate of ten hours per book, that comes to 3,690 hours, or 461.25 eight-hour days, amounting to ninety-two five-day weeks, or, less holidays and vacations, just about two working years. I consider it time not ill spent. At this task I have been allowed to create an alter ego, a kind of sage younger brother, urbane and proper, with none of the warts, tics, obsessions, and compulsions that necessarily disfigure an imaginative writer, who must project a world out of a specific focus and selected view—whose peculiarities, indeed, *are* his style, his personality, his testimony, his peculiar value. It is reassuring, not only to such a monster but to his ideal readers, to be able to claim as kin a business-suited, levelly judgmental critic—a kind of lawyer in the family. The establishment and certification of this figure (no more or less fictional, somehow, than the heroes of *Rabbit, Run* and *The Coup* and *Self-Consciousness*) has given me much methodical pleasure over the decades and lent the comfort of respectability to my near and dear.

Respectability, however, comes with a price for a would-be artist. As eminent a critic as Malcolm Cowley once, after some kind words about a review of mine of James Joyce's letters, wondered if I ought to be doing this sort of thing at all. I wondered, too. Creativity is a delicate imp; it should dwell under toadstools and garb itself in cobwebs and not be smothered beneath a great load of discriminatory judgments. Too much left-brained control takes the emptiness, as a Zen golf instructor might say, out of your swing. And there is a rhythm, of artful qualification—a scorpion circling, sting poised above his back—that critical sentences acquire, and which can infect descriptive prose with a circumlocutory smugness. It is almost impossible to avoid, in writing a review, the tone of being wonderfully right; whereas any creative endeavor launches itself on the winds of uncertainty and accident, and will certainly go wrong in some drifts and be judged wrong in others. I found the writing of these reviews a bit hectic—locating the quote you want, patching up the transitions, rushing along before the book quite fades from memory—but reprehensibly safe from the fear of blasphemy, the fear of doing a great thing poorly that makes every venture into fiction and poetry a tentative and fretful affair, rife with delaying maneuvers and second cups of fortifying tea. How much better to do a great thing worthily than to do many things well enough! "Man of letters" is not, to me, a term of much praise; it suggests the uniform yet lightweight solidity of a mannequin, a humanoid artifact posed in the big windows of cultural display, crisply dressed in this season's fashions but its body consisting, from toeless feet to alertly tilted head, of a single plastery substance, ground-up letters. A mannequin's eyes are dead; there is nobody home; men of letters live in limbo. So I am relieved to see that, under *The New Yorker*'s new management, fresh young untamed blood is being infused into the Books Department and my dutiful reviewing pace can at last be slackened. Though the present editor, Robert Gottlieb, and the editor for my Books pieces, Ann Goldstein, are as hospitable and assiduous as their predecessors, William Shawn and Susan Moritz, and though Edith Oliver, the Books dispatcher, is as recklessly on-cheering as ever, the heat is somehow off. In keeping with the valedictory mood of my late fifties (see page 872), the bulk of my reviewing feels behind me, and a perspective looms from which all of it was, if not a mistake, an aberration. My purpose in reading has ever secretly been not to come and judge but to come and steal.

Though it is hard to believe that even that chairbound agoraphobe will read this collection straight through, I have tried to arrange its over one hundred and sixty items along an encouraging curve. The book arches from the fairly personal into the wide heavens of other people's books and then back to the grassy earth of the personal again, in the form of salvaged bits of autobiography and autocriticism. It became my habit to review, for *The New Yorker*, two or more books together, aggregation providing a pleasant reinforcing effect. Where the pairing was but lightly secured, I have separated the titles, but in most cases the glue of joint argumentation resisted, and the bond was allowed to stand. Hence only one author, Philip Roth, has a section all to himself, and some, like Umberto Eco and Mario

Vargas Llosa and Robert Pinget, are repeatedly considered but in widely separated places. Where a miniature review, written anonymously for *The New Yorker*'s "Briefly Noted" section, fit handily, I slipped it in. Laughably loose categories like "Other Countries Heard From" and "Odd Couples" catch the otherwise unclassifiable. Most of the books reviewed are novels and most of these, by my preference, are from across the Atlantic or south of the border. The innovative power of American realism isn't what it was for Hemingway and Faulkner, and foreign solutions to the puzzle that fiction poses in this post-print, anti-teleological era held out to me hope of some magical formulae that wouldn't occur to my fellow countrymen.

The reviews are undated but were generally written the years the books were published, which is given in the subheadings. An effort has been made to reproduce the numerous quotations accurately, even to paragraph indentations and English spellings. Franklin, Emerson, and Howells are as they appear in the Library of America texts, quaint punctuation and all. The problem of how to address authors in the course of a piece, where their names arise as faithfully as a drumbeat, has been relegated to the inconsistencies of social instinct: simple last names sit less rudely on men than on women; in the case of a female author known to use a married name, "Mrs." is used, and "Miss" for maiden-name users old enough not to find the usage curious. Mrs. Spark, Miss Murdoch, Ms. Tyler: please don't be offended. But for a few brief footnotes, no attempt has been made to bring the historical background—the contemporary temperature of the Cold War, the political condition of Chile and Germany and Albania—up to date. Most of the pieces belong to an already slightly bygone era when Ronald Reagan reigned over the United States and William Shawn over *The New Yorker*, and it seemed important to quote from Calvino and Borges at length. The presiding term was "postmodern," yet, though the concept of postmodernism comes in for a grapple several times, I remain uncertain whether it means anything more than a bored playfulness and a nagging sensation of déjà vu. It is perhaps in the nature of Nineties to be mauve decades, silted-up *fins de siècles*. These assembled critical considerations muster, it seems, their stoutest enthusiasm for the products of decades early in the century, when even Kafka's terrible vision had an edge of naïveté to it, an awareness undulled by an accumulated and still-accumulating muchness. My diffident title for this high heap of work is, I suppose, postmodern in itself. But honest labelling never goes out of date, and an honest laborer usually gets his due.

J.U.
September 1990

Fairly Personal

FIVE DAYS IN FINLAND
AT THE AGE OF FIFTY-FIVE

As I GET OLDER, my childhood self becomes more accessible to me, but selectively, in images as stylized and suspect as moments remembered from a novel read years ago. In one of my first memories, I am lying on the floor reading newspaper headlines to my grandfather, who has been temporarily blinded by a cataract operation, and the cartoon on the editorial page shows a little fellow on skis defiantly standing up to a huge bear, who is wearing bandages and has the cartoon symbols signifying dizziness and pain scattered about his head. The bear is Russia, and this must be the Russo-Finnish "Winter War" of 1939–40, when I am seven. At some later moment in my childhood, I am pondering a photograph of Jean Sibelius, perhaps in *Life*. His head is spectacularly bald, whereas all the other composers I have seen depicted are very hairy. His eyes are shut, as if he were intently listening or having a headache, perhaps from the veins that stand out on his bald head. He lives in Finland, the caption tells me, among lakes and forests. Finland: a cold, shaggy place, far away. To me at that age the world is like a coloring book, full of outlined spaces. When one visits such a space, that colors it in.

Although, by the age of fifty-five, I had been to Norway, Sweden, Denmark, and, on the far side of Scandinavia, the Soviet Union, I had never been to Finland. All I had added to my images of Sibelius and Finnish valor were yards of splashy Marimekko fabric, with which my first wife had draped our windows and herself. Then an opportunity arose: I was asked to come to Sweden, for a conference, and agreed if I could also spend five days in Finland, for fun. People seemed amused. Finland? A number of my professional acquaintances had attended conferences in Helsinki, much as they had in Tokyo, Aspen, and Atlantic City. Helsinki to them was a set of hotel rooms, a city without qualities.

But I take an interest in hotel rooms. To the man travelling alone, his hotel room, first entered in rumpled clothes, with a head light from

sleeplessness, looms as the arena where he will suffer insomnia, constipa-
tion, loneliness, nightmares, and telephone calls; his room will become
woven into the deeper, less comfortable self that travel uncovers. My room
in Helsinki was shaped like a triangle with a tip cut off, and in the
truncated corner was fitted a long wooden tray that would be my bed.
Pieces of upright varnished wood were spaced about on the walls, notched
as if for some utilitarian purpose but revealing to inspection no other
purpose than to look Finnish. Wood, it seemed, was the Finnish look—
wood, and a certain determined stylishness of design. The closet coat
hangers were especially progressive—abstract sculptures of white plastic
it took some practice to manipulate. One's hotel room is a place one is
always trying to leave and yet always returning to. Staying in it, alone
with the television set, seems cowardly and a waste of the airplane ticket,
and yet leaving it—stepping into the long, windowless, carpeted hall,
letting the door click shut as you tap your pocket to make sure the key
is there—has a sadness, too, the sadness of rejecting a symbolic mother,
a place that would serve as home.

It was raining when I arrived in Finland, in mid-August of what people
told me had been the coldest and rainiest summer in a hundred years. I
set out from the hotel room to walk around Helsinki, but the rain defeated
me. I found a handsome esplanade, of unoccupied benches and tightly
shut kiosks, but there was no place, at six o'clock on a Saturday evening,
where I could buy an umbrella. In an American city, some capacious
all-night drugstore would have had a basket of umbrellas tucked away over
in a corner by the discounted bathing caps and welcome mats, or some
boutique would have hungrily kept open an extra hour to catch the stray
tourist, but here a grave mercantile decorum had shut up everything
except for a bright-yellow *hamburgerrestaurant* called Clock. The Finns
had umbrellas, most of them, and some even wore boots—ankle-high
wading boots with pale soles—but others, the younger ones, walked along
as if the rain were all in my mind. I ducked from doorway to doorway
along the esplanade until I arrived at a harbor where a towering white
ferryboat was slowly turning its stern upon the city and heading out
through a misty maze of islands. Destinations that are not ours always
seem romantic. I was in Finland, but sitting on it like a raindrop that,
unlike the drops on my scalp and raincoat, had not begun to soak in.

Next day, a Sunday, I took a train to Savonlinna, the heart of the region
of lakes and forests. In the railroad station (designed by Eliel Saarinen),
a brilliant arcade of food shops contrasted with the abandoned gloom of
most American terminals, and I attempted to start soaking into Finland

by making a purchase. In a candy store I spotted a bag of what in England are called "licorice all-sorts." I read on the label ENGLANNIN LAKRITSI; these words seemed within my capacity to pronounce but the woman at the counter stared at me with alarmed incomprehension, and even my pointing gestures took her some time to decipher. She counted out my change for me in a mincing, rebuking English. The Finnish language, a non-Indo-European tongue related to Hungarian and Estonian and a number of minor variants like Karelian, Olonets, Lude, Vepse, and Vote, yields few clues to an American. As a focus of Finnish nationalism through centuries of domination by Sweden and, after 1809, Russia, it resists loan-words, though APTEEKKI identifies an apothecary, POSTI a post office, POLIISI the police, and ESPLANADI and MOOTORI what you might imagine. POSTIPANKKI is a postal bank, but PÄIVÄRANNAN RUUSU is the name of a flower shop and not a Russian restaurant. During the six-hour train ride to Savonlinna, I kept seeing on other railway cars AIDS ON TAPPAVA TULIAINEN: I thought the first word could not be what it seemed but it turns out that indeed the Finns have borrowed the English acronym and were publicizing a campaign against the disease. There is a certain bliss in being surrounded by a language that no one expects you to know. Nevertheless, it annoyed and even frightened me that for five days I was unable to recall so much as the word for "thank you," which is *kiitos*. The double "i" would come to mind but the consonants kept scrambling.

Through the train windows, the Helsinki suburbs fell away, and lakes and forests began. Relatively few species dominated—pine (*Pinus sylvestris*, Scotch pine, the trunk pinkish, as if rubbed raw, above the lower portion), spruce, and white birch—with here and there silvery willows, twinkling aspens, rowan trees decked out in their bright-orange berries, and alders clogging the drainage ditches. The fields, irregular in shape, were all drained by ditches, and the stands of rye and wheat were flattened in ragged patches, as if by rambling dogfights. It seemed a restless, struggling agriculture: some fields were being reclaimed by the forest, and others had been recently cleared, with heaps of stumps left to dry and blanch in grisly bone-colored tangles. Muddy cabbage-patches near the tracks flicked past, and towns hurriedly assembled and dispersed. The traditional wooden architecture mingled vertical and horizontal boards in a way that looked faintly barbaric, like the hatching in a Steinberg drawing; the older houses showed a complex abundance of gables and dormers. These domestic fortresses, whose prominent double-casement windows bespoke winter's long siege, were roofed mostly with ridged tin, and sometimes with tile, rather than with the battened planks of earlier centuries. A picture-book farm whose manse and outbuildings bore matching red sides and minty-green roofs—Christmas colors—made me realize how few of these habitations could be called pretty. Like the Finns themselves, they seemed more sturdy than ornamental.

The landscape, with its rubbed-looking pines and low granite outcroppings, didn't much vary. Monotonous landscapes, perhaps, are the most penetrating, and inspire the most intense nostalgia: we love countries that dare to bore us. As the train looped north, it passed, I could see by the map, very close to the Russian border, but I failed to spot, above the bristling tree-line, the watchtowers I was told were there. Lakes opened up the vista on one side of the tracks or the other and then on both sides as we rolled along the famous, photogenic Punkaharju ridge—Finland's postcard icon, its Mount Rushmore, its Eiffel Tower. The morning's windy bits of blue sky had disappeared and it was raining again, and the lake water looked black and bitter, slapping the embankment with little dirty waves. I still had no umbrella.

Savonlinna itself, where I found my hotel by crossing a narrow bridge in a drenching rain, had the wistful melancholy of a summer place out of season—empty balconies and outdoor tables, deserted docks and diving boards, boats moored in waterlogged rows. European vacation places always seem a bit slick and tinny to me, perhaps because they awaken no memories of my own childhood holidays. Yet, after eliciting tea from a waitress in the bar and letting my raincoat dry for an hour, I borrowed an umbrella at the hotel desk and set out to see what wet sights there were. It reminded me of, years ago, my venturing up Wilshire Boulevard, in another Sunday twilight, to fulfill a lifelong ambition to view the La Brea Tar Pits. On the old Jack Benny program, they used to crack jokes about the tar pits, and though I was in Los Angeles for only a night, and had a worrisome toothache, I had waited much of my life for this opportunity. Oddly, though I could only peek through a fence, and a tar pit in the dark is not much to see, I was not disappointed. A sight is composed, in large part, of our desire to see it. And, as we say on a golf course when it rains, "At least it's kept the crowds away." Savolinna was not crowded.

Cozy and dizzy with jet lag beneath my borrowed umbrella, I walked along the lakeside, under dripping linden trees, past pastel holiday homes and shop windows hopefully displaying images of bronzed beauties. A beach that had, in the tourist brochure I had studied, extensively brimmed with basking flesh seemed in reality no bigger than a hall rug, set out to soak. Olavinlinna Castle, approached across a little bridge where my umbrella nearly blew inside out, was closed. The floating walk to it was rather gleefully tied up on the other side of a kind of moat, and a trio of German hikers clowned away their disappointment in the small green park here, like sparrows frisking in a birdbath. But the civic museum nearby, quite surprisingly, was open. Just as a toothache almost justifies itself in the relief of its ceasing, our trips to Europe pay off with these unexpected admissions.

Inside, it was dry, and dim, and almost deserted. On the first floor, primitive Finland explained itself in terms of geological maps, Neolithic artifacts, rock paintings executed at heights that indicated shifting lake levels, agricultural tools of a touching cleverness and gawky beauty, a reconstructed peasant's house with one dummy in a rocking chair and another tucked asleep up in a high nook against the whitewashed fireplace chimney. Finland's land, I read, had emerged from the sea less than twenty thousand years ago, and was still rising, a centimeter a year. On the museum's second floor, a new exhibit revelled in the ingenuity with which the nation's proud and perennial harvest of trees was conducted: logs used to herd logs, logs lashed into chutes and bumpers and, when wide lakes were reached in the logs' watery descent toward the sawmill, into great floating corrals pulled to the next river by oared or steam-driven boats. The chains of logs had been tied together with knotted withies, and snow as well as water had been employed to skid the trees out. The tools of this epic labor, the axes and grapples and the marking sledges that branded the logs like heads of cattle, the antique measuring calipers and early chain saws and the long files that restored metal's virginal edge composed that solidest type of poetry, the shapes of fact and necessity. The poetry sang without words to me, for the only words in English were DON'T TOUCH THE OBJECTS, PLEASE, a command which in Finnish was even more forbidding: NÄYTTELYESINEISIIN KOSKEMINEN KIELLETTY!

As if worn out with all this vicarious logging labor, I fell asleep easily after dinner in the hotel; but I awoke at two, and stayed awake until six, when it would have been eleven at night at home. The bone-deep self-estrangement of jet lag: is it for this racking existential confrontation that we travel? In the wrestle with insomnia, my heart felt stuffed with tremulous agitation, and my head seemed a bundle of electricity irrepressibly twitching my body. All the people of my life, from my eighty-three-year-old mother to my three-month-old grandson, passed through my consciousness in a murky, nebulous cloud of unfulfilled responsibility. Dread crystallized as a strange, periodic, unlocated clicking from the direction of the bathroom. The hotel room was paler and more modern than the one I had left in Helsinki and to which I would return; but the bed also suggested a tray—a tray on which I was being offered to Morpheus, who turned up his nose.

In the vain effort to escape myself, I shifted my pillow and my head to the bed's other end, and, that failing, I stepped onto the balcony and gazed at the sleeping resort city. The names of hotels and stores were spelled in light, but nothing moved. Not even the clouds moved—yellowish strips of nimbus that seemed the hellish underside of something else. I had never before been—not in Leningrad, not in the Orkney Islands—this far north on the planet, and the arrangement of reservations and obligations whereby I would make my way home seemed impossibly rickety and precarious. The precariousness of being alive and human was no longer hidden from me by familiar surroundings and the rhythm of habit. I was fifty-five, ignorant, dying, and filling this bit of Finland with the smell of my stale sweat and insomniac fury.

But in the morning, a Monday morning, the stores were open, and it was so blowy and cold the people in the market were wearing gloves and wool caps. For twenty finnmarks—a bargain, less than five dollars—I bought an umbrella from a girl in a market stall. "Cold," I said. She laughed: "Very cold!" The joys of exchange. Because it was so comically cold, I bought a hat and some candy along a main street of stores that reminded me of one in a busy English tourist town, like Windsor—especially the sweetshop down a few steps off the street, with candies and nuts loose in jars, and a bored girl weighing the purchases on a computerized scale. At times, as when I had watched on television an earnest Algerian documentary about nation-building, or observed the elderly, slightly shabby Finns around me in the hotel, I had felt I was in a Socialist country—a relatively liberated one, like Yugoslavia—but Monday morning banished any doubt that consumerism reigned in Finland. The department store, in its layout and contents, spelled out an intelligible code, even to the word KASSA for cashier; the language of buying and selling, of displays and price tickets and receipts and correct change, was one I could speak, though I couldn't manage to say "*kiitos.*" At an APTEEKKI, I bought a little round, drum-shaped box of Oropax, those fuzzy wax earplugs available only in Europe. They seemed smaller than the Oropax you get in Italy—there was less noise, possibly—and cost only twelve finnmarks. On second thought I went back into the drugstore and bought another box. Our attitude to spending foreign currency goes through two stages: at first, one is reluctant to part with it, as if its uncertain value makes it immeasurably precious; then one begins to spend quite freely, as if it is play money, and one is playing a trick by getting real goods for it.

The rain, once my own umbrella was in hand, ceased to fall. Perhaps it *had* been all in my mind.

Back in the hotel room, a newspaperwoman called, asking for an interview, and this, too, like shopping, was familiar, friendly territory. I swapped an interview for a ride to Retretti, the partially subterranean art center twenty-three kilometres away. Vast underground caverns had been supposedly blasted out of the bedrock by a young entrepreneur, Pekka Hyvärinen, to serve as art galleries, a concert hall, a restaurant, and a nightclub; but it was hard for me to believe that the caves hadn't been already there, carved for some more governmental purpose like the storage of armaments or of nuclear wastes. But no Finn I talked to admitted that this was the case. Finns seem to cherish the aesthetic uses of dynamite: one of the few sights I was taken to in Helsinki was the Temppeliaukio Church, a large round church blasted out of rock in 1969, with a skyey roof suggesting a hovering spaceship. In the towering, dripping Retretti caves, chunks and hardened puddles of glass, by Timo Sarpaneva, were displayed. I ascended from this mineral world into miles of surreal art— Belgian, Austrian, Romanian—hung in a huge shed. Surrealism, I began to feel, had only two ideas, blasphemy and pornography. Outdoors, lumps of cracked stone and grassed-over earth, by Olavi Lanu, defied recognition as sculptures.

Retretti boasts of being the largest art center in Finland, and it was certainly too large for me. Not many miles away, at Kerimäki, stands the largest wooden church in the world. I did not visit it. I did visit, however, in Helsinki, what was alleged to be the largest bookstore in Europe, the Akateeminen Kirjakauppa. This yen for largeness may be a mark of young countries; Finland achieved national independence only in 1917. I was assured that other countries consider it "the America of Europe." I suppressed my incredulity: the Minnesota of Europe, at most. But the Finns are proud of the independence they managed to salvage from two world wars fought on the losing side, and of the enterprise that has enabled them to exploit to their economic advantage their potentially oppressive closeness to Russia. More than once, I heard the joke that Finland treats the Soviet Union as its colony—importing raw materials (oil and natural gas, above all) and exporting manufactured goods. But the Soviets, I was also told, are beginning to want not Finnish shoes but Italian shoes, and the Finns must improve their trade relations with Western Europe in order to preserve the prosperity that their endless forests and special Russian connection have given them since the war. They hope, specifically, that the Soviets will build a highway south from Leningrad to Poland, which would enable the Finns to drive their cars and trucks into Europe instead of, as now, shipping them by ferry across the Baltic to Sweden, driving down through Sweden, and ferrying them again to the European mainland.

Helsinki is a handsome city—not playful like Copenhagen, or elegant like Stockholm, or crabbedly picturesque like Oslo, but with a certain somber massy grandeur in its center and a fragrant woodsy looseness in its parks and suburbs. I was taken to one of its four "tourist islands," Seurasaari, where antique buildings from all over Finland have been assembled, so that one can experience the space and the furniture and even the aromas of a village parsonage, a sod-roofed hut from Lapland, and a low-ceilinged farmhouse from the time of Napoleon. It was Napoleon who, to bring pressure on Sweden, persuaded the Czar to annex Finland. Down near the South Harbor stand the prodigious Russian Orthodox Cathedral and, at the top of the St. Petersburg–like Senate Square, the pale-gray Lutheran Cathedral. Though raised as a Lutheran, I had never seen a Lutheran cathedral before, and was charmed by the unexpectedly austere and symmetrical interior—its bare walls, its box pews, and its square nave, which had at its four corners, counterclockwise, a cylindrical marble pulpit and statues respectively of Melanchthon, Luther, and Michael Agricola, whose translations from the Bible created literary Finnish much as Luther's Bible established written German. Senate Square, rimmed by Italianate Empire façades housing government, university, and police offices, has in its center one of the few statues of a czar left standing anywhere in the world—of Alexander II, whose government granted Finland, organized as a grand duchy with its own language and institutions, more autonomy than had the Swedes. When, in 1917, the czarist regime in Russia collapsed, the Finnish Parliament declared first limited, and then total independence. In the course of a brief but bloody civil war between Reds and Whites, the Germans came in to help drive the Russians out. After the Winter War, Finland was dragged into World War II as a reluctant co-belligerent with the Germans; in 1944, as part of the terms of their separate truce with the Russians, the Finns were compelled to drive the Germans out, and they did, up through Lapland into Nazi-occupied Norway. Such are the shifts of keeping intact a small nation among mighty ones. As part of the price of their peace with the Soviet Union, the Finns paid immense reparations and ceded the long-disputed Karelian region west and north of Lake Ladoga, which meant that one in ten Finns had to be relocated, and that the homeland of the Finnish epic the *Kalevala* was lost.

It is a fashion, now, in Scandinavian countries for blond girls to dye their hair shoe-polish black, and to dress in black jumpsuits, so they suggest a race of lissome trolls. Punk goes well with the mischievous Finnish looks. The English language sweeps in all day long, as English and American rock throbs over the radio and from restaurant walls, and as American television serials play, with subtitles, on state-run Finnish television. Whatever the makers of *Dallas* and *Dynasty* and *Falcon Crest* intended, it was probably not to give English lessons to millions of European children. This is, however, what such programs do. With a Swedish-speaking minority of about six percent, Finland is officially a bilingual country, and has signs in two languages, as Canada does; yet in its schools English has thumpingly replaced Swedish as the second language of choice. My publisher, Matti Snell, who knows Swedish as well as English and Russian and French and German, lamented to me that younger Finns can talk to the Swedes in English only, and that Finland is generally losing its old cultural contacts with the Continent, as the electronic winds blow in from London and Los Angeles. Three-quarters of the books used by college students are in the English language, and four-fifths of all works translated are American or English titles. American-style football, even, has caught on here, and the Finns were hosts of the European championships at the time of my five-day visit.

On my last night, I was free in Helsinki, and took a looping trolley-car ride that my guidebook had recommended, promising that it would return me to where I began. In my Finnish hat I sat disguised as a workaday passenger and let the city glide by. Some of the neighborhoods looked rather sullen, architecturally, but none of them looked poor, and there were streets that still had wooden houses, in the complicated gabled style. The trolley passed the stadium for the 1952 Olympic games, its entrance marked by a quite naked statue of the other Finn (besides Sibelius) who won global name-recognition, the great runner Paavo Nurmi. I had read in my guidebooks about Finnish drunkenness but in fact had seen only sobriety, and been sober myself. Ordering mineral water *(kivennäisvesi)* is easier than in America, where the waiters sometimes refuse to believe their ears and generally condescend to you as a party poop. In Europe, water, internally and externally applied, has an honored place in ancient health regimens linked to witchcraft and miracle-cures. But onto the trolley car unsteadily climbed a number of men who, in response to the white summer nights or the gray winter days, to Russian fallout or American popular culture, were still self-administering the alcohol-cure, and who sat with the uncanny stillness of those who, like pregnant women, are holding a wondrous world inside themselves. A dating couple side by side across the aisle, in a fine sweat already, took alternating pulls at a beer bottle, and the girl began to roll a mysterious cigarette while still on the tram. ALL YOU NEED IS LOVE, said the marquee of the Svenska Teatern, the Swedish Theatre. On the façade of the railroad terminal four stone giants held globular lamps in two stone hands each. I was back in the middle of town.

Almost at home in Helsinki, I went, at last, to the Clock *hamburgerres-*

taurant and, surrounded by denim-clad patrons less than half my age, watched Finland get beaten by West Germany in American-style football. It looked much like the real thing, even to zoom shots of the frowning Finnish coaches, both black Americans; but the European players had a disconcerting way of carrying the ball in two hands, like the statues on the railroad terminal, and swinging it daintily back and forth as they ran. They seemed lighter and bouncier than their American counterparts, so that long unimpeded runs occurred, on a somehow more spacious field. They hadn't yet learned how to invest the game with our lumbering, obstructive passion.

I had been warned that the Finns put ground-up fish in their hamburgers, but mine, under its burden of obligatory condiments, tasted remarkably like those being served up four thousand miles away. The planet Earth is like our allotted span of life—ample but finite. Seven continents, seven decades. As a child, I used to wonder whether or not I would live to the year 2000. It seemed incredibly far away. Now, here in Finland, I sat gray-haired among unintelligibly chatting teen-agers who had every expectation of entering the twenty-first century. I was happy in their company. The two national treats tourists are expected to savor—taking a sauna and eating reindeer meat—I had managed to avoid, but I had survived my nights in hotel rooms, and I had brought sunlight to this waterlogged land by the simple act of buying an umbrella. I had seen the lakes and forests. I had filled in another blank space in the coloring book of the world.

1987

THE PARADE

I HAD NOT EXPECTED the parade to be such agony. At the pace of a constrained walk, it threaded back and forth through the neat brick blocks of Hayesville's square mile. I was reminded of those mazelike mathematical puzzles that call for connection of all possible dots of a set. There was scarcely a block we did not crawl past, the fire sirens up ahead wailing as if in attendance upon some peculiarly static disaster. The borough was celebrating the seventy-fifth anniversary of its incorporation; I, as a prominent former resident, had been invited, by mimeographed form letter, to ride in one of the limousines. I had been a fool to accept.

In what way prominent? In alien cities and universities, where the dialect spoken would be unintelligible in Hayesville, I have scaled certain immaterial heights, with no company save the icy winds of truth and the whispering voices of the mighty dead. For twenty years my achievements were obscure, buried in technical journals; in the last decade the medium of the television talk show, in which I proved to have a certain aptitude—provocative yet genial, relaxed yet not at the sacrifice of accuracy or intellectual passion—has given me a celebrity which I welcomed at first but which has become, as far as my actual work goes, a burden upon both my time and imagination.

They had put my name and the simultaneously empty and pregnant word "Celebrity" on a paper banner on the side of the limousine. I was to ride with the local Congressman, who was running for re-election and who said he had been one of my supervisors at the old Hayesville playground. I didn't remember him, but, then, as a child I had rarely looked up at those adults whose gargoylish heads loomed at the level of the sun and the moon. Even then my focus had been on the transpersonal, my gaze stubbornly fixed on the pavement, the pebbles, the grass, the dirt. The dirt at the playground had been a pale ochre, beaten by innumerable pairs of energetic sneakers to the fineness of milled flour and given therefore to rising up in little eye-stinging clouds at the merest stir of breeze. The same breeze would bring out from under the open-sided shelter of the pavilion the lonely, banana-ish smell of the shellac we used to solidify the tablemats and little striped bowls we "crafted" of multi-colored gimp, and the desolate sound, the hesitant clickclack, of checkers being played. I had spent summer after summer there, never believing there would be a last summer. Obscene incredible things were written and drawn on the back of the equipment shed, and I never believed that such things—such blooms of hidden flesh, such violent conjunctions—would become on the larger playground of life not only credible but commonplace.

Besides the Congressman and myself, there were to be fourteen marching bands, thirty-seven fire engines, three probate judges, a Hollywood stunt man whose father used to peddle pretzels door to door, Miss Junior Pennsylvania, Mr. Gay Pennsylvania, and a flatbed truck of supposed Delaware Indians—real survivors, those. But when, before the parade mustered, I made anthropological inquiries of them, they turned out to be all brothers and uncles in the fuel-oil business, operating out of Chester County.

On the mustering-field—the parking lot of the newly enlarged regional high school—the personality I had created for use in the world outside Hayesville began to disintegrate. With downcast head I sensed from all sides a certain irradiation, as if the television sets out of which I had so urbanely expressed myself had reversed their currents and now were burning my reality away. In the tangle of assembled marching units and minor dignitaries I became obsessed with avoiding contact, and slithered back and forth in my inappropriate seersucker suit like a pariah or like a gossip reporter from some universally loathed but, because this is America, tolerated journal. The lead car of the parade, I observed, contained the burgess—an irrepressible bully, my contemporary, once nicknamed, because of his multiple warrior wounds, Scabs, and still, after forty years, called that. Also in this car rode the four borough aldermen, all wearing uniformly black suits as if to emphasize their remarkably distributed disparity in size, like a set of toys. The smallest was a virtual dwarf, a tailor called Runt Miller, and the tallest Gus Horst, a six-foot-eight-inch giant famous, in my high-school years, not only for his basketball prowess but for his skill at the discus, which flew from his long hairless arm as from a sling. The limousine behind theirs was to hold four beribboned veterans, one each from the two world wars and the two Asian involvements. Then some fire engines festooned with tricolor bunting, and a marching band led by stocky-legged young twirlers in white plastic boots and silver

sequinned miniskirts, and the truckload of Indians, some more fire engines, and a limousine holding a probate judge, and the flower-banked
float holding Miss Junior and Mr. Gay Pennsylvania, both gorgeous in
chiffon, and another marching band. Our open limo, a '68 Caddy with
corrosion-speckled chrome, came toward the end.

The streets were lined with faces, unfamiliar most of them, hatched
since "my time," yet all of them in another sense profoundly familiar, with
that Hayesville look, a doughy solidity, a way of sitting, "just so," on the
curbs and porches and aluminum folding chairs brought out to the sidewalk, and with that Hayesville accent in their singsong voices, those
voices with always something sardonic and something kindly about them,
that small-town mix of street slyness and barnyard slyness, with love in
the slyness, and menace in the love. Block after block was lined with these
faces; they called my name, they pointed and laughed at my banner. I was
trapped and had no idea how to act. My fellow limousine passenger, the
Congressman, kept gladly waving, gathering votes; he called out people's
names; he bounced back to these sidewalk crowds their own belief that
by being born in a place and staying there year after year they had performed a great and cherishable feat.

When I tried to imitate the Congressman's waving, my hands felt like
lead. My face seemed imposed from afar, a mask stiff with fear. I had
traversed every inch of these streets, as a child, in all weathers, dragging
a sled in winter, bouncing a basketball in summer, sashaying in a noisy
group of semi-delinquent, cigarette-puffing buddies, or clinging awkwardly to the fragrant body of a solid local girl; but never had I moved
as slowly as in this infernal siren-plagued inane caravan. I would have
screamed, as one screams in a stalled elevator, but for the illusion that I
was in a narrow glass display box and a scream would use up all my air.

An old classmate, now a beefy master plumber in a denim leisure suit,
capered to the side of the limousine and offered me a beer. A middle-aged
woman in purple slacks held aloft a sign upon which my face, torn from
the cover of a sensational magazine, had been pasted and captioned in
Magic Marker with the words NOT THIS BUT JESUS. The parade was
heading down Filbert Street now; at its corner with Elm lived a woman
who had been kind to me, who had let me sit in her kitchen while her
daughter entertained more amusing boys in the parlor—a disconsolate
paranoid widow who had always been fighting with her neighbors but
who had served me Ovaltine on her porcelain kitchen table and let me
shell peanuts into her wastebasket while she told me the plots of the
cellophane-wrapped novels she read all day in her dark and manless house.
(She rented those novels from the Hayesville Drugstore's lending library;

how gaudy and dynamic and precious books seemed then, well worth a nickel a day!) At her corner the crowd was thick but she, who had seemed old then and would be ancient now, was not present among her neighbors—still fighting with them, I supposed. I looked toward her big front window and, indeed, a watching shadow lurked within, not close to the glass, where she might have attracted hostility, but deep in the aquarium gloom of that living room in whose brown, nappy, welcoming furniture I had once sunk so gratefully, as respite from the exhausting furniture of my own home. I waved, and the shadow in that dim parlor waved back. "Now you're cooking," the Congressman told me. "Give 'em the high five."

Hayesville tots in strollers clutched balloons and flags. Some tots looked like candy apples, big heads on sticks, their faces smeared with sugar. Older boys raced in and out of the crawling parade, taunting it as they would tease a half-crushed snake. I saw a young father lift an infant to his shoulders, and I remembered my own father's shoulders under me, and my panicked grip on his high unsteady head, on that brown straight hair of his, hair so fine that in the coffin, while the minister was doing the eulogy, some strands of it had riffled in an imperceptible draft. That infant being lifted now would never forget his glimpse of this parade. History's grind was beginning in his poor soft brain.

The parade rounded a corner where a Buddha of a man sat surrounded by devotees. An aluminum chair was folded into his fat like spit into chewing gum. It was Lefty Reisenbach, the only major leaguer Hayesville has ever produced. I had seen him play shortstop for the playground team, slim as a knife, and as flashing. Then, on rudimentary Fifties television, as a blur of gray sparks, cocking his bat, squinting toward third base for the sign. Now he was back home and bloated on fifteen years' worth of local beer. Old ballplayers are like ruined temples: their gifts have blown through them and left not a trace, just a hollow inscrutable pomp.

The secretary of my high-school class broke from the crowd and ran along beside us. She had been lithe and wasp-waisted, a cheerleader and a wing on our undefeated girls' hockey team. Her weight had doubled since then, but she still moved athletically, matching the limousine's pace with easy strides. Her chest, her bouffant hairdo, the upper parts of her arms all bounced. "Bobby!" she called. "Are you married?"

The sirens, and a marching band from the coal regions hitting hard on "The Marine Hymn," made it difficult to hear. "We're divorced!" I shouted.

"I *know* that," she called impatiently, beginning to be winded. "It was in *People!* Have you married *again?*"

"No," I called back, as the limousine jerkily accelerated. "I'm living with a woman! Everybody's doing it!"

"Not around here . . . they're not," she responded faintly, curling up and falling away like an autumnal leaf. There was something amiss, some secret, as always in Hayesville, I was not privy to. The day, which had mustered itself under one of those white hazed skies that represent sunshine in these humid parts, was clouding; large ragged scraps of cloud, with plum-colored centers, had gathered above the dark green crowns of the Norway maples that line the borough's straight streets. The horse-chestnut trees—the guardians of my childhood with their candles of bloom, splayed fingerlike leaves, and glossy, inedible, collectible nuts—had been mostly cut down.

The parade ended way over on Buttonwood Avenue, where the sycamores form an allée and the trolley tracks used to head out of town. The parade did not disperse but had become a vast collapsed mob. Jostling tubas and glockenspiels uttered random notes and leggy twirlers in their white boots and braid-encrusted jackets giggled in anticipation of what came next. What did come next? The four aldermen had gathered, making a single black sloping mass, Gus Horst foremost and leaning dolefully forward. Behind them rose a temporary structure of raw new pine—a platform for speeches, I guessed at a glance. With a shudder of its gummy carburetor, our limousine at last stopped. When I opened the door and tried to step from it into freedom, Scabs's steel-hard, bullying hands seized my arms. Several of Hayesville's sleepy-eyed young policemen moved in to back him up.

A certain reverential hush overtook the crowd as it parted for us. Drawing nearer, near enough to smell the resinous fresh lumber, I saw the structure to be a gallows. Of course. It was for me. It was what I deserved. Terror thickened in my throat and then vanished. By ever leaving Hayesville, I had as good as died anyway.

1976

FIRST WIVES AND TROLLEY CARS

WILLIAM FARNHAM, though as tough and flip as most denizens of this eighty-two-percent-depleted century, was sentimental about first wives and trolley cars. A trolley line had been threaded down the center of the main street of Wenrich's Corner, his home town, leading one way to the minor-league metropolis of Alton and in the other direction to a town so small and rural that its mere name, Smokeville, was enough to make the boy Farnham and his flip pals laugh. Yet it was the ride toward Smokeville that lingered sentimentally in his memory.

For several years he delivered free movie-circulars for the Wenrich's Corner Movie Theatre, walking up and down the rectilinear maple-shaded streets on Saturday mornings, darting up cement walks and tossing the leaflets onto porches as if playing Halloween pranks in broad daylight. The leaflets announced the week's coming attractions and were distributed not just throughout Wenrich's Corner but in the neighboring towns as well. Some Saturdays, Farnham was assigned Smokeville and given the two dimes' trolley fare there and back by the tall bald man, the town's only Jew, who owned the movie theatre. The shows changed three times a week, with B-movie double features on Mondays and Tuesdays, free dishes to the ladies on Thursday nights, and free Hershey bars to children after the Saturday matinée. All Hollywood's produce poured through that little theatre, with its slanted cement floors and its comforting smells of steam heat and bubble gum. There were some minimal wall decorations in what Farnham thought of as Egyptian style but he now knew to have been Art Deco, reduced at this remote provincial level to a few angular stripes of beige and silver paint.

Farnham was eleven, twelve. He believed in the movies, and in the Sunday-night radio shows broadcast from Hollywood, where Jack Benny would drop by at Ronald Colman's house to borrow a cup of sugar, just like neighbors in Wenrich's Corner. The boy Farnham's simple joy in the

Jack Benny program was only slightly troubled by certain paradoxes. If Benny and Mary Livingstone were married, as the newspapers all said, why didn't they live together and why was her last name different? And why, when Dennis Day sang his song, was it always to show Jack and Rochester what it *would* sound like when he did it *really* on the Sunday-night show, which they all admitted existed but which never, on the air, arrived, except in the form of rehearsal? These were mysteries, like what girls were thinking and why all heroes in comic books wore capes.

The movies as well as trolley cars and comic books cost a dime, if you were twelve or under. When admission went up by a penny tax for the war effort, this tiny increase drove Farnham, whose weekly allowance was thirty-five cents, to deliver circulars in exchange for a week's free pass. Otherwise he wouldn't have a nickel for the Sunday-school collection. He often went to the movies three times a week, walking, unaccompanied by a parent, in these far-off days before television and R ratings, when Hollywood's fantasies were as safe as the family living room.

On the way to Smokeville, the tracks rounded the eponymous but no longer central corner—the town had grown east, toward Alton. Wenrich's Inn had stood here until Prohibition. Throughout Farnham's boyhood, the building, stuccoed sandstone with a long second-story porch rimmed in peeling jigsaw carpentry, had been dismally boarded up; after the war, it opened as a camera store at one entrance and a bakery at the other, with two dentists and a chiropractor upstairs. On his last sentimental visit to the town, Farnham, an art historian who had found tenure in southern California, saw that the inn had been re-established as an eating place, with exposed beams and fancy prices. The streetcars had negotiated this corner with much plaintive friction of metal on metal and sometimes a shower of sparks that indicated the trolley had lost its electrical connection overhead. The motorman, generally a rude and overweight Pennsylvania Dutchman, would shove off from his high metal stool, let himself out of the clattery folding doors, step on a step that flopped magically into place, and run to the rear of the stalled car, where with a single angry thump he would set things right. The motor resumed its throb, that incessant mechanical pulsing as of a heart trapped beneath the long, dirt-blackened floorboards.

Past the corner, the tracks, which had hogged the center of Alton Avenue all through town, now moved to one side, so the trolley car skimmed and swayed along in the shade of old buttonwood trees, on the edge of front yards where men in suspenders were trimming their hedges and fat women in cotton dresses were bending to their flowerbeds. The last brick rows of Wenrich's Corner were left behind, and a ragged area of open fields and scattered stone farmhouses was traversed, with relatively few stops. The tracks seemed to give the car a livelier ride; the shiny straw seats and the stiff porcelain hand-loops glittered in the shuttling, slanting sunlight, and the air that rushed in through the window grates of crimped black wire had the smell of moist hay. Farnham was always thrilled by a spot where the trolley car, on Smokeville's outskirts, leaned into a long curve and deftly rattled across a spindly wooden trestle bridge at a sudden scary height above a stagnant brook; from its glaring black surface a few white ducks would thrash up in alarm. These ducks would resettle while still in sight, making concentric circles on the water. The wire grate was always dirty, and dust came off in squares on Farnham's face as he pressed to see.

An isolated row of asbestos-shingled houses, gaunter and meaner somehow than those in Wenrich's Corner, would fling into view, and then a long brick building that people said was a hat factory, and more drab houses, while the irritable conductor moved along the aisle slamming seat backs into the other position. Smokeville was the end of the line, where the cars reversed direction. Farnham and his partner would hoist up their packets of circulars and step into the town; the boys were sent out in pairs because two could work both sides of a street and one could watch that the other didn't dump his leaflets down the sewer. This had happened more than once, it was said, though Farnham could scarcely believe such evil existed in the world. Smokeville was considered undesirable duty by the movie-circular boys, because of its steep streets and the long cement stairs up to the porches. Yet often, Farnham remembered, he and his companion, when their circulars were at last all gone, would agree to buy candy bars with their trolley dimes and in the resilience of youth walk the three miles back, along the tracks. Milk-white water trickled in the ditches near the hat factory, and the gaps between the ties of the rickety trestle were giddying if you looked down at the white ducks hiding in the reeds.

Three miles the other way from Wenrich's Corner, along an avenue whose general slope was downward as it passed between tall tight rows of houses with octagonal cupolas roofed in slates like fish scales, lay Alton, where Farnham's father worked and his mother shopped. When Farnham reached high-school age, in that era before the century was even half depleted, he and his pals would take the trolley to town just for the nightlife—for the bowling alleys and the packs of strange girls roaming the wide pavements and the big first-run movie theatres, with names like Majestic and Orpheum, where the same show played for weeks at a time and plush curtains lifted in thick crimson festoons to reveal the lightstruck screen. The trolley cars had run all through the war and it seemed they must last forever. But while Farnham was at college they were phased out and replaced by belching, dark-windowed buses, and by the time he was married and living far away, even the old tracks were torn up and buried, buried everywhere but at Wenrich's Corner itself, where a few yards of track glinted through the asphalt like the spine of a dinosaur drowned in tar, or like a silver version of those curved lines whereby cartoonists indicate swift motion, with a word like *"Zip!"* or *"Zoom!"*

Farnham in his middle age was susceptible to images of trolley cars in old photographs of city streets. To think that Manhattan, and Bangor, and Kansas City were all once webbed with their inflexible, glinting paths! He was moved by glimpses of them in fiction, such as Augie March's recalling "those leafy nights of the beginning green in streets of the lower North Side where the car seemed to blunder as if without tracks, off Fullerton or Belmont" or, in *Ulysses,* the onomatopoetic sentence "Right and left parallel clanging ringing a doubledecker and a singledeck moved from their railheads, swerved to the down line, glided parallel" or Bellow's description, in "The Silver Dish," of "an old red Chicago streetcar, one of those trams the color of a stockyard steer" as it heroically battered north against a blizzard on the Western Avenue line. Glimpses of first wives, in fiction, moved him also: often discarded before the author found his full voice, they figure as shadows in those first, awkwardly tactful and conventional novels; as marginal obstacles to the narrator's slowly unfolding, obscurely magnificent quest; as tremulous rainbows cast by the prism of his ego, bound at a cloud's passing to pale and wink out. Yet they return, vividly. In John Barth's *Sabbatical,* the first wife returns in malevolent triumph as a CIA operative and withers with a few stern words the ingenious hero's eager foliage of invention and lovableness. And Hemingway's Hadley, seen so wispily in those early short stories, returns in *A Moveable Feast* to dominate his dying imagination.

In memory's telephoto lens, far objects are magnified. First wives grow in power and size, just as the children we have had by them do. They knew you when, and never let that knowledge go. Their very ability to survive the divorce makes them huge, as judges and public monuments are huge. Tall and silent, they turn at the head of the stairs, carrying a basket of first-family laundry, and their face is that of Vermeer's girl with the pearl earring, of Ingres's Grande Odalisque, of all the women who look at us over their shoulders in endless thoughtful farewell.

They were so young. They were daughters. Captured from their still vigorous and menacing parents, carried off trailing ribands and torn threads of family connection, some clasped teddy bears and dance cards with all but the tangos filled in. Some still smelled faintly of their fathers' shaving lotion. Their bodies were so fresh and smooth, it was hard to make a dent in them. Tomboyish, they stuck out their chins and kept their legs under them; later wives by comparison crumple like wastepaper, and bruise easy as peaches. Of course, a first husband is young too, and perhaps his wallop lacks substance. They looked at us level, our firm-bodied Eves, and demanded, "O.K., show me this apple."

A quality first wives bestow, of dismissability, turns out to be precious, as the aging world needs us more and more and lets our traces deepen, like initials carved in the expanding bark of a beech tree. We sat light on the world once; the keys to this lightness first wives have taken with them, along with the collected art books so thriftily budgeted for, the lithographs carefully selected at the gallery together, the *objets* nested in the excelsior of remembered lovemaking, the slide projector, the ground-glass screen that unfurled, the card table the projector sat upon, and the happy pink infants cradled in their Kodak Carousels. With a switchy swiftness, in bikinis daring at the time, with narrow tan hands and feet, they move as fledgling mothers through home movies taken at poolside or by the back lawn swings, movies we will never see again, movies they will show their second husbands, who will be polite but bored.

The night of the day when Farnham's first wife remarried, he had a vivid dream. She was crouched by a wall naked, and he, fully dressed, was trying to extend a measure of protection. There was, out in the center of the street or room, a crowd that her nakedness must confront and pass through, as through a sieve. Farnham was alive simultaneously to the erotic appeal of her nudity and to the social embarrassment of it. She was not quite naked; a thin gold ring glinted on the third finger of one hand. He conferred urgently with her, pouring down advice from above, from within the armor of his clothes, while still revolving within himself the puzzle of how to get her, so vulnerable and luminous, through that gathering. The problem being insoluble, he awoke, with an erection of metallic adamancy.

Mournfully the palms outside his window rattled. Southern California was soaked in moonlight. The woman asleep beside him was pale and, like a ghost, transparent. Everything was black and white. Only his dream had been in color.

In those far days before suburban shopping malls and inner-city decay, the more enterprising people of Wenrich's Corner took the trolley car into Alton to shop, to be entertained, to seek refinement. Farnham's mother enrolled him in a futile series of lessons there—piano, clarinet, and, worst of all, tap dancing. Such metropolitan skills were thought to be a possible way out of the region; the assumption was in the air, like the hazy high humidity, that one would want to get out. But instead of being taught how to fly in white tie and tails across a heavenly sound stage with an effortless clatter of taps, the child was set in a line with others and put through a paramilitary exercise whose refrain was "Shuffle *one*, shuffle *two*, kick, kick, kick." His mother amused herself in the stores, rarely buying anything, during this hour of torture. When they were reunited, his noon reward and weekly treat was a sandwich—bacon, lettuce, and tomato, cut into quarters, with each triangular fourth held together by a tasselled toothpick—and a pistachio ice-cream soda in a drugstore with a green marble counter that seemed, with its many chrome faucets, the epitome of luxury. It was in such Forties drugstores, redolent of beauty aids, that Hollywood stars were discovered. Farnham was surprised to learn, years later, at about the same time that the trolley cars were replaced by buses, that this drugstore, Alton's finest, had closed and been replaced by a gloomy outlet that sold name-brand clothes at factory prices.

On the trolley ride home, the car clanged and bucked its way through the dense blocks of Alton's south side and up over a big bridge whose concrete had the texture of burned coconut cookies. Tough local boys swaggered and hooted from the broad wall of this bridge; unlike Farnham, they would never get out. The ill-tempered motorman pounded the warning bell with the heel of his black shoe, and there was a smell of something, like oily rags burning, that Farnham years later was told must have been ozone. Cumbersomely the car halted and started, bunching auto traffic behind it, and swung its bulky long body into the double-track turnouts, where one car waited for another, coming in the opposite direction, to pass. The row houses with their turrets and fish-scale slates slid by, mixed with used-car lots and funeral parlors and florist's greenhouses and depressing brick buildings that manufactured Farnham didn't know what. He felt sorry for these factories; they looked empty and shabby and hopeless.

The return trip sloped slightly uphill, which made it seem longer and more obstructed. The distance to the stop in Wenrich's Corner where he and his mother could most conveniently alight was now two miles away, less than fifteen minutes; but minutes and miles can seem infinite to a child, and nausea was creeping up from underneath the grooved and blackened and throbbing floorboards, the ozone mixing with the tastes of bacon and pistachio and the oppressive monotony of shuffle *one*, shuffle *two*.

His mother was watching his face grow paler. She squeezed his hand, so he felt how damp his palm was. "Only seven more stops," she promised him.

"Seven," he repeated. The number had no end to it, it had curves and plateaus within it, which doubled and redoubled.

Amid his discomforts was a wish not to spoil this outing for his mother. He felt her life had few pleasures, and a Saturday excursion to Alton was one of them. He was eight, nine. She was, he realized now, herself young. The hand of hers not holding his rested gracefully in her lap, wearing its thin gold wedding ring. It was sad, he thought, the way she never bought anything in the stores. There was a poverty in her life that pained him.

(Years later, Farnham's first wife was told by a doctor that she suffered from depression. This, too, pained Farnham. They were not poor, and he could not imagine any other reason for depression.)

The trolley car struggled and swayed. Shapeless nameless trees, houses with drawn front curtains, front yards he would never play in crawled past in fitful starts that he timed with held breath, willing the contents of his stomach to stay down. The air on the outside of the window grate seemed a precious clear fluid, the transparent essence of freedom. The things to see inside the car—the sun-faded curved advertisements and the old faces of the other passengers and the pale-green pamphlets the trolley company gave out free from a little tin box behind the motorman's head— had all become a kind of poison; if he rested his eyes on them even a second, he grew sicker.

(Years later, the idea very slowly grew upon him that *he* might be the reason for his wife's depression.)

There was a long wait at a turnout while the motor throbbed like a trapped thing. The woman beside him kept glancing down at the side of his face, and her concern joined the other pressures afflicting him. The worn straw seats repeated and repeated their pattern of tiny, L-shaped shadows in the sunlight that slanted in through the dust; her wedding ring glinted in her lap.

(Yet when he first suggested the possibility of separation her reaction had been fear and tears.)

His trolley-car stomach now was riding high in his chest, and swallowing only made it bob lower for an instant, like a hollow ball in water. His whole skin under his clothes was sweating like his palms.

"Just four more stops," his mother said brightly. "See—there's the poorhouse lane."

Four: the number multiplied within him, enormous, full of twos. The idling motor throbbed. Farnham stared rigidly at the motionless world outside, a kind of paradise that could be attained only through dishonor.

Beyond the poorhouse lane, the grassy open acres of the school grounds began, and it was possible to get off here and walk diagonally across them the half-mile to his home. Each trip, each Saturday, the boy vowed not to make his mother get off the trolley car early.

The motorman, the back of his neck in thick folds above the sweat-blackened collar of his uniform, pounded the floor gong and swung a burnished brass handle back and forth in a fury. The long inside of the car lurched, and the other passengers lost their faces. The smell and the throbbing and the vow to hold on had rubbed them out.

Her voice tugged at him gently. "Willy, let's get off here. We can walk across the school grounds."

"No. I can make it."

But she had decided. She had become girlish and animated, insisting, "Come on, I *want* to. It'll be *good* for us." She pushed the bell. The old trolleys did not have pull cords; instead there were porcelain buttons like doorbells above each seat.

The double-hinged door flapped open. The little step magically flopped down. His feet firm on the concrete road, Farnham inhaled real air. His relief overwhelmed his guilt. The trudge across the fields, with their cinder track and wooden bleachers and the bucking sled for the football players, was long enough for his stomach to settle and his color to return. He put away his mother's hand as something he no longer needed, and raced ahead. When, having reached the hedge at the bottom of their own yard, he turned, she seemed a distant stranger, a woman walking alone.

1982

YOUR LOVER JUST CALLED
A Playlet

*Adapted from the Short Story of the Same Name
for an Evening of Fifteen-Minute Plays at the Blackburn Theatre,
in Gloucester, Massachusetts, on April 10, 1989*

DRAMATIS PERSONAE: *Richard and Joan Maple, in their thirties*
SCENE 1: *An upstairs hall, Friday morning, ten o'clock*
SCENE 2: *Same place, next day, same time*

(Stage set: A table with a telephone on it. Chair. Door left leads to bedroom.)

PHONE: *(Rings. Rings twice. Thrice.)*
RICHARD *(sniffing, coughing, in pajamas, emerges from bedroom door):* Hello? *(Listens, then sings musically)* Hello hello? *(Hangs up. Stands there puzzled.)*
JOAN *(coming upstairs, carrying a blanket, a jar of vitamin C, a glass of apple juice, a book):* Richard, you *must* stay in bed if you want to get well enough to entertain Mack tonight.
RICHARD: Your lover just called.
JOAN: What did he say?
RICHARD: Nothing. He hung up. He was amazed to find me home on a Friday.
JOAN: Go back to bed. Here's an extra blanket, some chewable vitamin C, a glass of apple juice, and that book you wanted from the library. It took me the *long*est time to find it. I didn't know whether to look under "L" for "Laclos," "d" for "de," or "C" for "Choderlos."
RICHARD *(taking book):* Great. *(Reads title)* Les Liaisons dangereuses.
JOAN: How do I know it wasn't *your* lover?
RICHARD: If it was my lover, why would she hang up, since I answered?

JOAN: Maybe she heard me coming up the stairs. Maybe she doesn't love you any more.

RICHARD (*after blowing his nose*): This is a ridiculous conversation.

JOAN: You started it.

RICHARD: Well, what would *you* think, if you were me and answered the phone on a weekday and the person hung up? He clearly expected you to be home alone like you always are.

JOAN: Well, if you'll go back to bed and fall asleep I'll call him back and explain what happened.

RICHARD: You think *I'll* think you're kidding but I know that's really what *would* happen.

JOAN: Oh, come on, Dick. Who would it be? Freddy Vetter?

RICHARD: Or Harry Saxon. Or somebody I don't know at all. Some old college sweetheart who's moved to West Gloucester. Or maybe the milkman. I can hear you and him talking while I'm shaving sometimes.

JOAN: We're surrounded by hungry children. He's sixty years old and has hair coming out of his ears.

RICHARD: Like your father. You *like* older men. There was that section man in Chaucer. You and he were always going out for coffee together after the lecture.

JOAN: Yes, and he gave me a C for the course. C for coffee.

RICHARD: Don't try to change the subject. You've been acting awfully happy lately. There's a little smile comes into your face when you think I'm not looking. See, there it is!

JOAN: I'm smiling because you're so ridiculous. I have no lover. I have nowhere to put him. My days are consumed by devotion to the needs of my husband and his numerous children.

RICHARD: Oh, so I'm the one made you have the children? While you were hankering after a career in fashion or in the exciting world of business. You could have been the first woman to crack the wheat-futures cycle. Or maybe aeronautics: the first woman to design a nose cone. Joan Maple, girl agronomist. Joan Maple, lady geopolitician. But for that patriarchal brute she mistakenly married, this clear-eyed female citizen of our milder, gentler republic—

JOAN: Dick, have you taken your temperature? I haven't heard you rave like this for years.

RICHARD: I haven't been wounded like this for years. I hated that *click.* That nasty little I-know-your-wife-better-than-you-do *click.*

JOAN: It was some child, playing with the phone. Really, if we're going to have Mack for dinner tonight, you better convalesce now.

RICHARD: It *is* Mack, isn't it? That son of a bitch. His divorce isn't even finalized and he's calling my wife on the phone. And then proposes to gorge himself at my groaning board.

JOAN: The board won't be the only thing groaning. You're giving me a headache.

RICHARD: Sure. First I foist off more children on you than you can count, then I give you a menstrual headache.

JOAN: Darling. If you'll get into bed with your apple juice, I'll bring you cinnamon toast cut into strips the way your mother used to make it.

RICHARD: You're lovely. *(Kisses her brow, takes blanket, pills, and juice, and goes into bedroom. She turns to head downstairs.)*

PHONE: *(Rings.)*

JOAN: Hello . . . yes . . . no . . . no . . . sorry.

RICHARD *(shouting from behind door)*: Who was it?

JOAN: Somebody wanting to sell us the *World Book Encyclopedia.*

RICHARD*'s voice, after pause, with obscure satisfaction:* A very likely story.

(Blackout to indicate lapse of time. Next morning.)

PHONE: *(Rings.)*

JOAN *(entering from downstairs in tennis dress)*: Hello . . . oh, pity . . . don't worry about it . . . I'll be there.

RICHARD *(coming out of bedroom still in pajamas)*: Who was that?

JOAN: Nancy Vetter. Francine has had to take little Robbie to the orthodontist this morning because Harry's plane got fogged in in Denver. So our tennis won't be until eleven.

RICHARD: Mmh *(the noise indicating slight surprise: not* Hmm *or* Humph*)*. One good thing about a hangover, it makes a cold feel trivial.

JOAN: I don't know why you drank so much. Or why Mack stayed until one in the morning.

RICHARD: It's obvious why. He had to stay to make sure there were no hard feelings.

JOAN: Why would there be? Just because you were sneaking around outside your own kitchen windows and saw him giving me a friendly peck?

RICHARD: Friendly peck! That kiss was so long I thought one of you might pass out from oxygen deprivation!

JOAN: Don't try to be funny about it. It was shockingly sneaky of you, and we were both embarrassed on your behalf.

RICHARD: *You* were embarrassed! You send me out for cigarettes in the dark of the night, and stumbling back through my own backyard what do I see all lit up in the kitchen but you two making like a blue movie!

JOAN: You could have coughed. Or rattled the screen door or something.

RICHARD: I was paralyzed with horror. My first primal scene. My own wife doing a very credible impersonation of a female spider having her abdomen tickled. Where did you learn to flirt your head like that? It was better than finger puppets.

JOAN: Really, Richard, how you go on. We were hardly doing anything. Mack always kisses me in the kitchen. It's a habit, it means nothing. You know for yourself how in love with Eleanor he is.

RICHARD: So much he's divorcing her. His devotion borders on the quixotic.

JOAN: The divorce is her idea, you know that. He's a lost soul. I feel sorry for him.

RICHARD: Yes, I saw that you do. You were like the Red Cross at Verdun.

JOAN: What I'd like to know is, why are you so pleased?

RICHARD: Pleased? I'm annihilated.

JOAN: You're delighted. You should see your smile.

RICHARD: You're so incredibly unapologetic about it, I guess I keep thinking you're being ironical.

PHONE: *(Rings.)*

JOAN: Hello? *Hello? (Hangs up, stares at him.)* So. She thought I'd be playing tennis by now.

RICHARD: Who's she?

JOAN: You tell me. Your lover. Your loveress.

RICHARD: Honey, quit bluffing. It was clearly yours, and something in your voice warned him off.

JOAN *(with sudden furious energy):* Go to her! Go to her like a man and stop trying to maneuver me into something I don't understand! I have no lover. I let Mack kiss me because he's lonely and drunk! Stop trying to make me more interesting than I am! All I am is a beat-up housewife who wants to go play tennis with some other beat-up victims of a male-dominated society!

RICHARD *(studying her as if for the first time):* Really?

JOAN *(panting):* Really.

RICHARD: You think I want to make you more interesting than you are?

JOAN: Of course. You're bored. You left me and Mack alone last night deliberately. It was very uncharacteristic of you, to volunteer to go out for cigarettes with your cold.

RICHARD: My cold. I feel rotten, come to think of it.

JOAN: You want me to be like that woman in the book, in the movie. The

Marquise de Whatever. Glenn Close. All full of wicked schemes and secrets.

RICHARD *(putting hand to forehead):* I think I do have a fever now.

JOAN: When I'm really, sad to say, that other woman. Poor Madame Something. Too good to live.

RICHARD: You are? You're Michelle Pfeiffer?

JOAN: Exactly. Without you, I'd just go back to the convent and curl up and die.

RICHARD: Feel. *(Puts her hand to his forehead.)*

JOAN: A *teeny* bit warm.

RICHARD: Would you . . . ?

JOAN *(sharply, on her mettle):* Would I what?

RICHARD: If I went back to bed would you come tuck me in before you go off to tennis?

JOAN: I'll tuck you in. No toast, though.

RICHARD: No nice sliced cinnamon toast. It's sad, to think of you without a lover.

JOAN: I'm sorry. I'm sorry to disappoint you.

RICHARD: You don't, entirely. I find you pretty interesting anyway. *(They move toward the door and through it. From behind the door)* You're interesting here, and here, and here.

JOAN's *voice:* I said I'd just tuck you in.

(Silence. Empty stage.)

PHONE: *(Rings. Twice. Thrice. Four times. Stops. Then a little questioning pring, as when someone in passing bumps the table. Then, perhaps, more rings, as many as the audience can stand, unanswered.)*

MEDIA

Being on TV — I

I WELL REMEMBER my first experience of being on TV. It was in 1962, and I had contributed to a book of five boyhood reminiscences; the other contributors were a revered playwright, a best-selling writer, a celebrated cartoonist, and an esteemed critic.* I was the youngest of the five. Thanks no doubt to the celebrity of my elders, a group interview was arranged at a New York station, for a half-hour live show. There was a dry run; while the others, especially the cartoonist and the best-seller writer, irrepressibly sparkled and effervesced, I sat there demurely in my chair, wondering at the shabby, cluttered surroundings from which our electronic marvel was to emanate. A break was declared before the real broadcast, and the cartoonist and the writer excused themselves and visited, it turned out, a bar on the street downstairs. When they returned, and the cameras began to roll, the two were companionably silent, and sat back in their chairs with imperturbable smiles. It dawned on me that theirs had been the opposite of a dry run, that a conversational vacuum had been created, that air time was rushing by, and that *I must talk.* I opened my mouth; words came out, any words. They sounded good. I gestured with my hand, and I could see the gesture flicker on a half-dozen monitors. The klieg lights were burning brighter than midday, and, as the cameras rolled, little red bulbs glowed above their great lavender lenses like rubies in the brows of dragons. They were feeding on me; I was being lapped up and broadcast into thousands and thousands of sets. *I was on TV.*

The feeling was scary and delicious, of an impalpable multiplication and widespread scattering of the self. Stammer, warts, miscombed hair,

*Why not name them, nearly three decades down the road? Howard Lindsay, Harry Golden, Walt Kelly, and William K. Zinsser. Only Zinsser and I still live.

crooked necktie—out it all went, over the airwaves. From within this messy room, with its floorful of snaking gray cables and its invisible scurry of behind-the-camera technicians, reality was being reprocessed and re-born; millions of jittery images, refreshed thirty times a second, flowed from my face, my voice. It was as if I had spent all of my life previous to this moment in a closet, and at long last proper attention was being paid.

Americans, once a shy and dry-voiced race away from the intimacy of their own work sheds and back porches, have certainly, in these last thirty years, become better at being on TV. Game shows turn hundreds of them into momentary stars every week. On the news, witnesses to shootings, victims of floods, debunked economists, and freshly traded quarterbacks all now gaze into the camera levelly and speak in shapely sentences. Golfers are expected to have a few words for the camera between shots, and do; local police chiefs never know when they'll have to supply a twenty-second statement for the national news, and when their moment comes they enunciate as sonorously as Raymond Burr playing Perry Mason, if not John Housman urging the praises of Smith Barney. Televi-sion has so interpenetrated our daily lives we are no more shy of it than of the family cat. It comes into our homes, and our homes go into it. During the last hostage crisis [TWA, Athens-Tunis-Beirut, July 1985], families were shown on television watching television, where the kid-napped were being interviewed by their kidnappers, and then were in turn, the families, interviewed by the local television news team.

We love being on TV. Passersby mug and wave behind the on-the-street reporter. Spectators go to sports events wearing funny hats and purple hair to court their death-defying second of electronic multiplica-tion. People in ballparks drape banners from the railings to attract the camera to themselves. "The wave"—the successive standing up of section after section—is folk art invented for television, a stadium full of hams performing as one huge telegenic creature. Television need not focus any longer on the famous; its focus *is* fame, and throughout the Western world the nightly news commentators are better known and more trusted than the political leaders.

In my very slight TV career, I have waited for my six-minute morning-interview stint in company with Muhammad Ali and Peter, Paul, and Mary, with a ninety-nine-year-old beekeeper and a seven-year-old chess player. The latter showed no less aplomb than the former. Radio and the cinema in their heyday tended to create an elite of the golden-voiced and the silver-skinned; almost anybody can be on TV, once the switches are thrown. Being natural beats any performing skill, and a German inter-viewer recently explained to me that, on television, being a bit ugly helps.

Everything, in a sense, helps. There is no hiding from the camera; but, then, in this laid-back era of the global village, why hide? The studios themselves tend to be cozy places, with coffee and doughnuts in the green room, cheerful confusion on the set, and tinselly cardboard props leaning against the walls. The atmosphere is that of an underrehearsed high-school play: no matter how badly things go, it's only our parents out there and we'll meet at the sub shop afterwards to laugh about it.

Once I found myself enmeshed in a televised spectacular. Three hundred "stars" were assembled, many of them nouveaux novas but all of them with an undeniable lustre, even a detectable radioactivity; the women had eyelashes like receiving antennae, and teeth shaped by laser beam. The taping of the unwieldy show, in the Radio City Music Hall, dragged on and on, through mistakes and retakes; the saintly patience of professional performers was amazing to a short-fused print-media type like me. Elderly actors and actresses (Jimmy Stewart, Ginger Rogers) already deep into apotheosis gamely went through their paces, and went through them again. The ordeal began in the morning and finished at two the next morning, when the grand finale was staged. We all assembled to sing a song whose words were flashed on cards behind the central camera. Most of the audience had melted away or was milling about in the hysteria of advanced fatigue. The moon was sinking over Manhattan. But were we in front of the cameras tired? No. We were on TV. Lillian Gish was in front of me, Cesar Chavez to the left, Dinah Shore and Raquel Welch somewhere in the vicinity. On my right, a tall enamelled female, unknown to me but no doubt known to millions, had a throat of steel as she warbled from the cards. A retake was called for; she and the others all sang louder, even more thrillingly, so that I felt lifted on wings of unnatural energy, pouring my miserly old scribbler's heart into that lavender lens at two in the morning.

Being on TV is like being alive, only more so.

Being on TV — II

IN THIS MEDIA-MAD AGE, one of the few questions that people still ask an old-fashioned word writer is how he feels about film adaptations of his work. My answer is, "Embarrassed." I feel embarrassed, watching the gifted and comely actors writhing and grimacing within my plot, heaving away at lines of dialogue I put down in a few minutes' daze years before, and straining to bring to life some tricky moral or social issue that once bemused me. I feel I have put them (along with the director and camera-men and set designers) in a glass box; like wide-eyed fish in an aquarium they bump their noses on the other side of the screen and ogle me help-lessly. I yearn to break the glass, to set them free to do their own thing—juggle, jog, take off their clothes, put *on* some clothes, tell us what be-muses *them* these days, cook up their *own* story.

For me, it is an act sufficiently aggressive to take pencil and paper in hand (or to switch on the word processor with its mind-curdling hum) and to forge sentences and paragraphs out of my flitting fancies and dimming memories. That these words are then turned, by a large and highly paid crew, into photogenic, three-dimensional, *real* furniture, bod-ies, and conversational tussles strikes me as rather horrible, in the way that an elephant tusk patiently carved and filed into many tiny interlocking figures, pagodas, and ginkgo trees is horrible.

In the late Sixties two youngish men full of energy and flattery ap-proached me about making a motion picture of my novel *Rabbit, Run*, and a deal was arranged. After some time, in 1970, I was invited to attend a showing of the result. My wife and I went to the appointed theatre in Boston and found ourselves the only audience in all the rows and rows of seats; an author, it suddenly dawned on me, was expected to organize a viewing party of agents, editors, and well-wishers. In lonely splendor, then, after a nervous consultation with the projectionist, we watched a giant flickering that began with my title and ended with the concluding sentence of my text flashed onto the screen, over the figure of a man running. In between, everything was mine yet not mine, and intensely embarrassing.

Not that the film lacked good qualities or surface fidelity to the novel. There were admirable performances by James Caan and Carrie Snodgress and stunning views of Reading, Pennsylvania, whose steep streets of row houses had been in my mind as I wrote. But the voice of the novel, and the cogency of its implied argument, had vanished in a hash of visual images and coarse simplifications. The movie often failed, it seemed to me, to make sense. For instance, in a central early episode, my hero impul-sively gets into a car and drives away from his wife and his life; within twelve hours he gets lost somewhere in West Virginia and realizes he has nowhere to go but back to Pennsylvania. The basic movement, out and back in, was rendered in the movie by an unintelligible montage of speed-ing automobiles and highway signs; when I mentioned this muddle in a telephone conversation with the director, he admitted that, when they returned from Pennsylvania to Hollywood, they discovered they had no "night footage." You make a film, of course, out of footage, and if in some sequences you have nothing but, in another phrase of his, "deplorable footage," you use that, or else leave holes that only the author, let's hope, will notice.

Since 1970, as of 1986, only television movies have been made of my stubbornly verbal works: two short stories, "The Music School" and "The Christian Roommates," were produced for public television, and a two-hour film, given the title *Too Far to Go,* was fashioned from a set of linked short stories. In the first two instances, the choices struck me as strange. "The Music School" is a monologue whose principal action lies in the leaps of the narrator's voice, and "The Christian Roommates" attempts to render the nuances of relationship within a group of Harvard dormitory-mates in the early 1950s. Both adaptations appeared, as I watched them on television, lugubrious. My hero in "The Music School" is troubled by guilt but on film he is positively sodden with it; on film the roommates' jittery antipathy turns downright pathological. As I watched, my attention gratefully flew to bits that weren't in the story, or were a matter of a word or two: in *The Music School,* a science-fiction episode eerily emerges through a violet filter, and we witness the lively industrial process, staffed by nuns in full habit, of the baking and cutting of communion wafers; in *The Roommates* (my "Christian" was dropped, as perhaps too provocative), the hero's sketchy home-town romance is elaborated with a delightful wealth of period make-out music and exposed underwear. Many details, indeed, in "The Roommates," which was spun out to two hours, were admirably full and careful. The college students glowed with health and beauty, and Northwestern's buildings (not Harvard's) posed handsomely. But of my short story the point itself—that one of the Christian roommates was so distressed by the other that he lost his faith—was serenely omitted.

In fairness, can any film adaptation fail to seem, to the author of the original, heavy on detail and light on coherence? Would any representation of the troubled married couple in *Too Far to Go* have failed to embarrass me? Perhaps inevitably, the suburbia became a movie suburbia, free of peeling paint and crabgrass, and the adulteries movie adulteries, skinny plot-turns as predictable as, in other cinematic contexts, pratfalls and shootouts. Footage problems arose when a car accident that I had located in a snowstorm was implausibly transferred (because of seasonal filming, or a studio shortage of soap flakes) to a rainstorm; not even a monsoon could have sloshed so many buckets of water across the windshield behind the entangled couple.

Words have a merciful vagueness wherein readers can—nay, *must*—use their imaginations. Movies are, like sharp sunlight, merciless; we do not imagine, we view. Written images perforce draw upon imagery our memory has stored; no one reads the same book, and each reader is drawn into an individual exchange with the author's voice. A seductive relationship is in progress, which the reader can terminate more easily than involvements in real life. Film, instead, breaks upon us like a natural phenomenon—ungainsayable, immediate, stark, marvellous, and rather bullying. My exposures to adaptation, it should be said, were the work of talented people who were fond of my writing; my impulse was all the stronger, then, to break the glass box and let them out, to do their own things, while my text, safe between covers, did its.

Books into Film

MOVIEMAKERS, like creative spirits everywhere, must be free; they owe nothing to the authors of books they adapt except the money they have agreed to pay them. In the case of the first book to be made into a film, *Ben Hur,* not even a financial indebtedness was acknowledged; the movie would be good publicity for the book, it was argued, and General Wallace should be acquiescently grateful. He and his lawyers disagreed, establishing a happy precedent for those of us who, as the saying goes, take the money and run. And hide, ideally. For the author owes, at least, his Hollywood benefactors a tactful silence.

A film adaptation of a novel of mine* is about to be released. It bears the book's title, and my own name will presumably scurry by in the credits. One would have to have an ego of steel not to be pleasantly dented, or dimpled, by such attentions. Otherwise, the movie will bear, indications all agree, little resemblance to my text—which exists, however, in hardcover and paperback editions and even in a large-print edition for the

---

The Witches of Eastwick, concerning which I wrote the agent responsible for the deal, on July 10, 1987, "I have seen the movie and after surviving the bursts of grossness in the beginning, and the echoes of my own dialogue, I settled into the incoherent fantasy of it all and especially admired the skating around in pink balloons and the very vivid pomegranate chewing [an episode, owing nothing to the novel, in which Jack Nicholson, as the devil-figure Darryl Van Horne, torments the excessively fertile Michelle Pfeiffer by biting into a ripe pomegranate that, in perfect illustration of the principle of sympathetic magic, transfers a griping agony to her uterus]. The less it resembled my book, the better I felt. And something about the war between the sexes did carry over, in quite different form. It is not a movie I would see twice but I did sit through to the end, whereas I couldn't make myself read the script at all."

dimsighted. That is one of the charms of the authorial business—the text is always there, for the ideal reader to stumble upon, to enter, to reanimate. The text is almost infinitely patient, snugly gathering its dust on the shelf. Until the continental drift of language turns its English as obscure as Chaucer's, the text remains readily recoverable and potentially as alive as on the day it was scribbled by one's own hand. Not so film: its chemicals fester in the can, it grows brittle and brown, its Technicolor bleaches, it needs a projector and a screen, it is scratched and pocked and truncated by the wear and tear of its previous projections. So let's not begrudge it its moment in the sun—the moment when, in the darkened theatre, the movie bursts upon us as if it *were* the sun.

Let's hear it for filmmakers. They bring their visions to market through a welter of props and egos, actors and bankers that a mere wordmonger would be overwhelmed by. Considering the vast number of fingers in the pot, and the amount of financial concern that haunts the sound stage, it's a wonder any motion picture comes out halfway coherent. Lack of coherence—the inner coherence works of art should have, the ultimate simplicity of one voice speaking—is surely a failing especially of today's films, in the absence of studio control and of the adult, bourgeois audience that filled the movie palaces in the palmy Depression days. Now only adolescents have strong and recurrent reason to get out of the house with its lulling television sets, and films are inexorably juvenile. Maybe they always were, and I was too juvenile to notice. In the backward glance there is a dignity—a rather religious stateliness and intensity—to the Gary Cooper–Rita Hayworth–Fred Astaire black-and-white movies that seems oddly lost in videotape rerun. Those barking men, those vaudeville gags, those plainly fake backdrops—weren't we pained by them the first time around? Still, there was not that jittery prurience, that messy something-for-everybody grabbiness which reaches out now from the curtainless screens of the shopping-mall complexes, where, as I write, *Creepshow II* is competing with *Meatballs III*.

Even a very lame movie tends to crush a book. When I try to think of *The Great Gatsby,* I get Robert Redford in a white suit, handsomely sweating in a pre-air-conditioning room at the Plaza, and Mia Farrow in a floppy pastel hat, or Alan Ladd floating dead in an endless swimming pool, before I recover, via Fitzgerald's delicate phrasing, Daisy's little blue light or the hair in the gangster Wolfsheim's nostrils. *Ulysses,* which one might have thought impervious to non-verbal invasion, is blighted for me by the pious film adaptation and its disconcertingly specific and youthful Bloom. Who can now read *For Whom the Bell Tolls* and not visualize its fellow-travelling hero as an avatar of Sergeant York, or its Spanish virgin as a Swedish beauty? Once I had a dream in which I was sitting high in the balcony of a vast movie theatre watching the film adaptation of *Remembrance of Things Past;* it consisted of, on a wide screen, Proust's pale fastidious face, his eyelids closed as if in sleep. I prefer my version to the Harold Pinter script for Joseph Losey, which was written and published but never produced.

Successful movies tend to take off from the book, rather than take it too seriously. *One Flew over the Cuckoo's Nest,* for example, or the impudent version, in which Faulkner had a hand, of *To Have and Have Not.* When the author gets too involved, and out of proprietary anxiety or love of the cinematic art strives to assert too much control, the result may be merely an unshot script and a batch of threatened lawsuits. What ever happened to the film adaptations of *Fear of Flying* and *The Confessions of Nat Turner?* On the other hand, it must be admitted that Jerzy Kosinski, with some help from Peter Sellers, did succeed in making *Being There* a better movie than it was a book. But, then, Kosinski, as he showed in *Reds,* is a natural film performer. He gets, over Norman Mailer in *Ragtime* and George Plimpton in *Volunteers,* the Eighties Authorial Cinemacting Prize.

In a novel, the prose is the hero, the human thing; the author's voice is our foremost point of contact and upholds one side of the shifting, teasing relationship we as readers are invited into. In a movie, the actors and actresses are what win us—these giant faces, all but impassive, like the faces of gods. As Wolcott Gibbs wrote some forty years ago, the movies are "an art form fundamentally based on the slow, relentless approach and final passionate collision of two enormous faces." The mounting of these faces and their collision can be more or less elaborate, and more or less impressive, as directors, scriptwriters, cameramen, grips, costumers, and set designers labor at it, but a bad mounting will not altogether defeat the box-office magic of, say, Marilyn Monroe or Eddie Murphy, and no amount of skillful mounting will make Meryl Streep as winning as Diane Keaton. This visceral simplicity of the cinema embarrasses criticism: Gibbs, in his definitive if unabashedly class-conscious essay, "The Country of the Blind," described his short-term stint as a film critic as attempting "to write . . . for the information of my friends about something that was plainly designed for the entertainment of their cooks."

Now and then, in watching a movie, we are troubled by awareness of something caught inside and trying to get out, trying to make more sense than the colliding faces that we see. On a recent evening while visiting New York, I walked up Fifth Avenue to view, at the convenient Paris Theatre, a French film called *L'Année des méduses,* starring Valérie Kaprisky. The frisky, risqué picture, located on the French Riviera, devoted itself almost exclusively to the photography of young women's bare breasts and, when the plot needed thickening, their buttocks. But toward the end, the characters abruptly began to speak in lengthy speeches, and there was a sudden ugly splash of attempted resolution, and I realized that the movie had been based upon a book, and that the book was still in there, still fighting to impose a plot and a moral and even a twist of suave irony upon this pageant of Gallic bathing beauties, which we of the audience had been gazing at in blissful ignorance of any such darkly clever, print-inspired designs. It turns out that the director of the film was also the author of the book. He did not feel free; he felt he owed himself something. Seeing the movie made me, with an impulse of pity such as all tourists must learn to resist as they thread their way among the importunities of Fifth Avenue, want to read the book.

A Nameless Rose

THE NAME OF THE ROSE was an unlikely book to adapt for the cinema—intensely literary, bleak in mood and moral, and loaded with in-jokes only a semiotician who was also a medievalist could love. Yet the film's makers, a mix of European names, have done an honorable and at moments moving job of converting one thing—an obdurately textual text, abstruse and challenging—into another, a succession of filmed images ultimately conforming to a moviegoer's conventional expectations.

Movie and novel alike boldly ask us to conceive of the Middle Ages *intellectually,* as an arena of contesting ideas rather than the hackneyed site of tourney and Crusade, of flying pennants and glinting armor, of picturesque battles clouding the sky with arrows and colorfully gowned beauties exciting the clash of heraldry-laden combatants. The motion-picture version of *The Name of the Rose,* but for a recurrent splash of blood, is relentlessly dull in color, all gray and brown. The cast, but for a single besmudged and silent young female, is all male, and most of the men are ugly. The scene is a masterpiece of desolation, an abbey in the wintry remoteness of mountains in the North of Italy; the opening and closing shots panoramically establish something we tend to forget about the Middle Ages—how relatively empty their Europe was, a continent of populated islands connected by thin and perilous paths. Desolation without, desolation within: the stony walls and slanting courtyards of the abbey look cold, and as the actors speak their breath is white. Only the wandering Franciscan William of Baskerville and his accompanying novice,

Adso, do not appear grotesque; the rest are robed, eye-rolling residents of a frosty hell claiming to be a path to heaven. Such a gloomy, almost sardonic bleakness lifts the film into the realm of intellectual enterprise.

One of the pleasant surprises of the picture is how Sean Connery, the swashbuckling 007 of the James Bond soft-porn thrillers, carries off the difficult lead part, bodying forth our detective-hero's necessary dignity and trustworthiness while conveying also the something troubled and flawed about him, a rational man in a century, the fourteenth, dominated by murderous superstition and a tortuous church-state rivalry. Eco's fascinating and sometimes fatiguing explication of late-medieval theological debates—the wild heresies, the incipient rebellion against a totalitarian church, the precarious position of the Franciscan movement itself—is necessarily skimped, but not ignored. The shudder of a rotten world on the verge of upheaval is felt. The extravagant costuming of the Pope's emissaries, when they erupt upon the bleak monastic scene, constitutes visual farce worthy of Brecht.

Umberto Eco's text is full of ironies, and motion pictures do not have leisure, generally, to be ironical. What in the novel is mandarin parody—two travelling monks as Sherlock Holmes and Watson, the isolated abbey as a closed "country house" for a classic murder mystery—the movie takes more or less straight; the clichés simply excite us, as they often have before. The plot is rather clearer than in the novel, because less surrounded by exposition and Latinate discourse, and the book's central irony—a succession of murders that do not link up but turn out to be, like the Godless universe itself, the work of many chancy happenings—is lost in the visual tumble, one fright after another, that we as moviegoers expect. The movie makes less sense than only the most artful of suspense films, and we do not begrudge it its strain of incoherence, even to the miraculous escape of William from the burning library; he must have used the secret stairway carefully diagrammed in the novel but scarcely mentioned in the film, whose makers must have concluded that one secret passageway—the one leading from the chapel altar, with a carved skull's eyes as its door latch—was enough. In place of diagrams and deductive brilliance, we have the brilliance of the set designers who constructed the labyrinthine library with its big pale vellum-bound volumes, its musty angled surfaces, and its Piranesiesque tangle of staircases. The set is splendid but its conflagration is relatively perfunctory; the scholarly Eco's vision of a massive and sickening loss of historic texts cannot be shared by the makers of films, for whom waste—of "takes," of abandoned and ruthlessly revised scripts, of time, of money—is inextricable from the artistic process. A movie is itself a flickering flame, a piece of visible consumption.

Yet movies have their rigors: in a book, with its negligible budget, the author's wishes dominate; but in a motion picture the wishes of the audience shape the product. What we wish to happen, will happen. As film-goers we know that the abbey must burn, because it is hopelessly polluted, and its confusions can be satisfyingly dealt with only through destruction. The primitive ethical logic of film demands, too, that the villain of the piece, in this case the inquisitor Bernard Gui, be dealt a bloody death. The torturer falls from a great height and is many times pierced by a hay rake. The book, on the other hand, merely lets Gui sink back into the morass of history, which is so replete with villains that none can be dignified with punishment.

Movie logic demands as well that the nameless peasant girl who impulsively and wordlessly (for she speaks a dialect remote from Latin) bestows herself upon young Adso be spared the death on the pyre to which Eco, with historically correct heartlessness, casually and irrevocably consigns her. But in the rigid ethical system, based upon wish-fulfillment, that controls the myth-making operations of the cinematic art, she must be saved and glorified, not just because Adso loves her. It is *we* who love her: how, once she has, in the movie's one sex scene, so charmingly shown us her breasts and buttocks, can we watch her burn, or think of her burning? Even the ferocity of Bergman's films, wherein animals and fish are killed before the camera, balks at the sacred inviolacy of the bared female form; in *The Seventh Seal,* the condemned young witch survives. Further, Adso prays to the Madonna that the girl be spared, and in our cinematic universe not only is sexual energy always conserved but prayers are always answered. We viewers of *The Name of the Rose* can scarcely withhold tears of gratitude and religious hysteria at the sight, appropriately phallic, of the deserted stake where the movie's lone heroine has been somehow saved. Saved, the movie tentatively suggests, by a peasant uprising, in behalf of lovely young witches and the chthonian fertility they represent.

After touch, the visual is the supreme erotic sense, and there is no keeping sex marginal in a motion picture. If it is there at all, it will overflow the screen, and demand to rule the plot. An erotic incident minor (and pedantically overwritten) in the novel irresistibly becomes central in the movie, and though Adso in the end rejects the live girl in favor of monkish celibacy, this is movie logic also, for thus he enshrines her forever in his memory. He even, in the most surprising twist given the novel by the moviemakers, makes her illiterate silence the point of the title: she is the rose who never acquired a name. And perhaps Adso's typical romantic deferral of perishing actuality, this heretical (according to Denis de Rougemont) act of eternalization through denial, is not unfairly read into the novel's title, taken from the Latin "stat rosa pristine nomine, nomina nuda tenemus." The rose remains pristine in name; we hold (keep) her name (the idea of her) naked (pure).

Overboard on Overboard

I SAW A NUMBER of last season's well-reviewed movies, and some, like *Moonstruck* and *The Last Emperor,* lived up to their notices, and others, like *Broadcast News* and *My Life as a Dog,* seemed to me to misfire, though their good intentions were obvious. But the motion picture I liked best was one I went to impulsively, at the local second-run house, with no memory of its reviews save the dismissive observation, somewhere, that Goldie Hawn should pick her material better. I went to *Overboard* expecting only that it would contain Goldie Hawn and would attempt to be funny and at least wouldn't depress me. In the event, it moved me, and I feel I should, apologetically, try to explain why.

First, Goldie Hawn. I used to love her on *Laugh-In,* which was one of the Vietnam era's few light-hearted spots. She and Judy Carne would revolve their bikini-bared bodies, painted with slogans in that heyday of angry graffiti, and it would seem that anger wasn't everything, and that thanks to laughter and bimbos we might survive. Her face, on the verge of pop eyes and buck teeth, was a semi-comic valentine, surrounded by tumble-dried blond hair. We go to movies to see a star, just as they did in the Thirties—a dependably familiar presence mounted in some new, but not disturbingly novel, vehicle.

Next, the theatre. The Cabot Theatre in Beverly is a consciously preserved and considerably restored old-fashioned small-city movie palace, with a stage, a balcony, a uniformed doorman, and a player piano in the lobby; it puts anybody over fifty in a nostalgic, tolerant frame of mind. Admission costs three dollars and the smallest size of popcorn only a dollar, as opposed to twice that at the malls. The floor doesn't stick to your shoes, an usher will lead you to your seat with a flashlight, and you sit there with the simple heart of a child.

Then the movie. Goldie Hawn, an impossibly spoiled rich bitch, falls off her yacht and, when rescued, is suffering from amnesia so total that a lowly beer-swilling carpenter (played by Kurt Russell) whom she has recently offended persuades her that she is his wife and must come keep his house and raise his four sons by (in fact) a wife three years dead. The joke and miracle of it is that, though equipped with an incongruously tony accent and a total innocence of housekeeping skills, she gradually submits to the assigned role, falls in love with her false husband, and finds happiness.

Sound familiar? The story touches timeless themes—the taming of the shrew, and the war of the sexes. It concerns, like the classic romantic comedies of the Thirties, education—the thawing, through a man's rough care, of a Hepburnesque ice princess. Hawn, cuddly and woozy, is no Hepburn, which makes the transformation rather more affecting: it is her real self she is restored to. When we see her on the yacht, swaggering about with her hair pulled in a tight chignon and her lips twisted in an upper-class sneer, we do not recognize her as Hawn—at least I didn't, though I knew I had paid three dollars to see her in a movie. As soon as she falls overboard, and is found with scraggly hair half-hiding her face, we know who she is, even if she does not.

Considerable cruelty attends her initiation into being the carpenter's house-slave. He and his four sons, who all seem to be crowding adolescence, spatter her with food and fire-extinguisher foam, dunk her in a rain barrel, dress her in grotesquely ill-fitting clothes, and wear her to a delirious frazzle. The abuse is drastic, but, then, her sins, as a rich bitch, have been shown as extreme; when still in her right mind she refused to pay Russell for a cunning shoe-closet he has built for her on the yacht, pushed him overboard, and, worst of all, threw his tools after him into the ruinous saltwater. His revenge has limits, however: he shows his basic decency by not forcing the sexual side of her wifely services, and thereby the film keeps its own honor; a rape, however finagled, would put the moral onus on the poor rather than the rich. Also, Hawn has a legitimate husband (played by Edward Hermann, fresh from his husbandly stint in *Mrs. Soffel*), who, though a callow snob, must be figured into the final moral accounting.

Her basic decency comes into play when, against all her pre-amnesia conditioning, she takes hold in the house and becomes a mother to the motherless boys, defending them from a shrewish schoolteacher, rubbing calomine lotion on their poison-oak rash, and teaching the illiterate youngest to read. The slovenly widower's shack yields to the ordering, cleansing female touch; her own costumes move from grotesque misfit to K-Mart *chic*. Russell, too, suffers some changes: he is surprised into a decent embarrassment as she makes his lies come true, and then into real affection as she settles at his side. His attempts to confess the truth are frustrated by his sons, who have come to need the mock mother, and by a buddy, who tells him the mock marriage is a good one. Her real husband belatedly appears, and her amnesia simultaneously falls away, but we have no doubt that nature, now that it is aroused, will triumph over nurture and come to true love's rescue.

Hollywood has always voted for nature over nurture, for love over social position. In this it confirms us in our wishes, and assures us of the soundness of our instincts. *Overboard* is about bad nurture: Russell, in being wifeless and permissive, is a bad father, and Hawn's mother a bad mother in raising a little rich bitch. This mother—a New Yorker shown in her outrageously posh apartment surrounded by pillows and dog manicurists—figures not so much in the plot as in the moral equation. For raising her daughter poorly, she must be punished, albeit lightly; twice she is shown being thrown out of bed by the swervings of the yacht as the plot zigzags toward resolution. The husband, on the other hand, has his punishment foreordained, in the loss of his star of a wife; therefore he must be established as deserving punishment. So we see him decline to rescue her on the day after she fell overboard, and instead embark on months of floating orgy with some Los Angeles tarts. He deserves to be left, the mother deserves her lumps, the boys deserve a mother, the lovers deserve each other, and we the audience deserve to congratulate ourselves for feeling so pleased about it all.

All this moral rigor would be merely mechanical, of course, if Hawn and, to a lesser extent, Russell, who in *real* real life lives with her, did not bring warmth to the acting, and give their educations—their transformation into loving adults—a rounded-out, on-screen reality. In *Broadcast News*, by contrast, the educations of the romantic principals feel incomplete, and we are frustrated by the heroine's inability to find happiness with either man. In *My Life as a Dog*, the boy's education or maturation is anticipated but never arrives through the odd muddle of a dying, receding mother and repeated sexual assaults by too many pubescent girls. Instead of becoming human, he becomes a dog, barking crazily.

Moonstruck balances its accounts and gives us our way, but with its tongue in its cheek; it is a consciously old-fashioned—charmingly so— movie. *Overboard*, for all of its slapstick, takes itself more seriously, and moves us without a wink, especially at the moment when the heroine, suddenly faced with two husbands and two lives, tries to puzzle her way to the truth of who she is. We allow confusion-of-identity plots their implausibilities because they bring to life, in a world that tends to lock us in, the possibilities of reversal and renewal. Like *The Last Emperor*, *Overboard* deals with the poignant mystery of being oneself: a puzzled tot thrust into the condition of emperor and buffeted by post-imperial history, and a young woman born into blood-curdling privilege and then dumped for her salvation into the lower middle class. We are so persuaded, in *Overboard*, of the moral and sexual superiority of beer over champagne that it comes as a shock, at the end, to learn that the money belongs to

Goldie Hawn's Cinderella, and that she will bestow it upon her carpenter-prince. How will he avoid, then, becoming as fatuous and effete as the former husband? Already, one of his sons is heard demanding a Porsche. This final fillip, perhaps intended as a casual sop to our notorious Eighties greed, disturbs the fable so nicely constructed. How can she, now knowing herself to be rich, slip back into the healthy rigors of wifely servitude? Money is the root of all evil in *Overboard,* and its final overthrow needs a Nineties sequel, in which the money goes overboard.

ENVIRONS

Fictional Houses

NOT ONLY do fictional characters have to be supplied with faces and life histories, speech rhythms and psychologies; they must have houses to live in:

> By daylight, the bower of Oak's new-found mistress, Bathsheba Everdene, presented itself as a hoary building, of the early stage of Classic Renaissance as regards its architecture, and of a proportion which told at a glance that, as is so frequently the case, it had once been the manorial hall upon a small estate. . . . Fluted pilasters, worked from the solid stone, decorated its front, and above the roof the chimneys were panelled or columnar, some coped gables with finials and like features still retaining traces of their Gothic extraction.

Hardy had been trained as an architect, and in *Far from the Madding Crowd* has no trouble embowering his heroine with a solidity subtly proportionate to her worth as a mate, and in agreeably animating her inherited home's interior: "Lively voices were heard this morning in the upper rooms, the main staircase to which was of hard oak, the balusters, heavy as bed-posts, being turned and moulded in the quaint fashion of their century, the handrail as stout as a parapet-top, and the stairs themselves continually twisting round like a person trying to look over his shoulder." Our story takes place, we are made certainly to feel, in enduring settings that long predate and will long outlast these momentary actors; Hardy's most ardent evocation is of the stone barn, four centuries old:

> Standing before this abraded pile, the eye regarded its present usage, the mind dwelt upon its past history, with a satisfied sense of functional continuity throughout. . . . The lanceolate windows, the time-eaten archstones and

chamfers, the orientation of the axis, the misty chestnut work of the rafters, referred to no exploded fortifying art or worn-out religious creed. . . .

To-day the large side doors were thrown open towards the sun to admit a bountiful light to the immediate spot of the shearers' operations, which was the wood threshing-floor in the centre, formed of thick oak, black with age and polished by the beating of flails for many generations, till it had grown as slippery and as rich in hue as the state-room floors of an Elizabethan mansion.

History of a more hurried, borrowed sort shapes the home of Mrs. Manson Mingott, so daringly located (in the 1870s) above New York's 34th Street: "The house in itself was already a historic document, though not, of course, as venerable as certain other old family houses in University Place and lower Fifth Avenue. Those were of the purest 1830, with a grim harmony of cabbage-rose-garlanded carpets, rosewood consoles, round-arched fireplaces with black marble mantels, and immense glazed book-cases of mahogany; whereas old Mrs. Mingott, who had built her house later, had bodily cast out the massive furniture of her prime, and mingled with the Mingott heirlooms the frivolous upholstery of the Second Empire." Edith Wharton's splendid eye for decor was not blind to the potential oppression of the correct and the expected; Mrs. Mingott, though immobilized by obesity, is one of the few free spirits in *The Age of Innocence*. The novel's hero, Newland Archer, nearly swoons at the Countess Olenska's unconventional room appointments, her "small slender tables of dark wood" and stretch of red damask: "The atmosphere of the room was so different from any he had ever breathed that self-consciousness vanished in the sense of adventure." His mind casts ahead to the house his prospective father-in-law has lined up for him:

> . . . the house was built in a ghastly greenish-yellow stone that the young architects were beginning to employ as a protest against the brownstone of which the uniform hue coated New York like a cold chocolate sauce; but the plumbing was perfect. . . . The young man felt that his fate was sealed: for the rest of his life he would go up every evening between the cast-iron railings of that greenish-yellow doorstep, and pass through a Pompeian vestibule into a hall with a wainscoting of varnished yellow wood.

Nor does his betrothed, the too-perfect May, promise rescue from the ordained environment; a dutiful daughter of privilege, she has "submitted cheerfully to the purple satin and yellow tuftings of the Welland drawing room, to its sham buhl tables and gilt vitrines full of modern Saxe."

Innumerable other novels could be cited, though Hardy and Wharton are especially lavish, shrewd, and tender, I think, in the building and furnishing of imaginary houses. A fiction can scarcely exist, however surreal and minimal, that does not involve some construction business; Samuel Beckett, the son of a professional quantity surveyor, provides rigorous dimensions for his shadowy hells. Hardy's Wessex architecture merges into English history, giving his settings a largeness of time as well as space; nostalgia animates Wharton's specification of the New York she remembered, but also a satiric impulse is at work, and a vivid claustrophobia. *Lolita* was inspired, Nabokov claimed, by the newspaper story of an ape who, "after months of coaxing by a scientist, produced the first drawing ever charcoaled by an animal: the sketch showed the bars of the poor creature's cage." Architecture confines and defines us. Our human world speaks to us, most massively, in its buildings, and a fiction writer cannot make his characters move until he has some imaginative grasp of their environment. Nearly thirty years later I can still feel the thrill of power with which, in my first novel, *The Poorhouse Fair,* I set characters roaming the corridors of an immense imaginary mansion which I had based upon an institutional building, for the poor and homeless, that had stood at the end of our street in Pennsylvania but that I had never once, as a child, dared enter. Now, as an author, I climbed even to the cupola, and chased a parakeet down long halls, "channels of wood and plaster" where a crossing made "four staring corners sharp as knives."

In my second novel, *Rabbit, Run,* an entire street—a steep street of row houses, "covered with composition shingling varying in color from bruise to dung"—had to be constructed to give my young couple housing, and then the fleeing husband had to be followed through the labyrinth of Brewer, based upon a city, Reading, where I had never in fact lived. Truly, the hollowing-out of these habitable burrows, assigning wall tint and texture, visualizing fanlight and doorbell, shag rug and windowsill, constitutes a primary adventure of the fiction-generating mind. (And the fiction-enjoying mind, too: with what delight, in my mystery-novel-consuming days, did I ponder the ominous diagram of the sequestered country house, and the clue-bearing map of the murder-haunted village.) The firmest house in my fiction, probably, is the little thick-walled sandstone farmhouse of *The Centaur* and *Of the Farm;* I had lived in that house, and can visualize every floorboard and bit of worn molding. But many houses I have lived in have sheltered little of my fiction, and the various domiciles of the Rabbit books are based upon scanty glimpses, in boyhood, of other people's mysteriously enviable homes.

Seeing the (unsuccessful) movie of *Rabbit, Run,* I was struck by how painstakingly the moviemakers had reconstructed the details of, say, Rabbit's apartment, setting forth for the camera many more furnishings, faithful as to sociology and period, than I had dreamed of. Yet these conscientiously assembled sets were relatively meaningless; they flickered past and could be ignored. They did not pass through, one observed detail at a time, the minds of characters, and become bonded with states of mind and emotion.

The substance of fictional architecture is not bricks and mortar but evanescent consciousness. Sometimes, therefore, a door opens into a hallway impossibly, and the placement of our heating ducts and storage space borders on the irresponsible. I have great trouble, myself, in imagining the floor plans of split-level homes, though I feel they are important sites of the American condition; I spent many words in *Rabbit Is Rich* in laying out the Murketts' garrison colonial tract house, which in my hero's mind environed such intense domestic happiness. With a workman's simple pride I remember the living-room ceiling that Rabbit covetously observes—the "little sparkles, like mica on a beach, in the overlapping arcs of the rough-plastered ceiling." Writing American fiction forces us to think about our virtually unthinkable mass architecture, with its murky manufactured substances (Celotex? polyurethane?) and the hodgepodge styles decreed by forgotten developers. The ordinarily ersatz comes to border on the monstrous, as with this California cottage in Nathanael West's *The Day of the Locust:*

> The house was queer. It had an enormous and very crooked stone chimney, little dormer windows with big hoods and a thatched roof that came down very low on both sides of the front door. This door was of gumwood painted like fumed oak and it hung on enormous hinges. Although made by machine, the hinges had been carefully stamped to appear hand-forged. The same kind of care and skill had been used to make the roof thatching, which was not really straw but heavy fireproof paper colored and ribbed to look like straw.

Less grotesquely, how does one convey the cozy quality of the brick rows of Pennsylvania small towns, with their square porch pillars and tiny terraced front lawns, or discriminate, in New England, among the many subtle styles, much patched and revised, of wooden farmhouse? To describe these houses is halfway to describe the life lived in them. My novel *Couples* was originally titled *Couples and Houses and Days* and was all about our entry into other people's homes, as guests and lovers, and ultimately about one couple's escape from the "low-ceilinged colonial room whose woodwork was painted the shade of off-white commercially called eggshell" in which they are seen on page one, naked and captive and struggling to be hatched.

The dwelling places of Europe have an air of inheritance, of cumulative possession—hives occupied by generations of bees. In America, the houses seem privately ours, even when we have not built them up, in pine two-by-fours and four-by-eight sheets of plywood, from a poured-cement foundation. Houses are, as Newland Archer sensed, our fate. The residences we build in our fiction need not conform to a floor plan—indeed, the reader's capacity for visualizing spatial relations is feeble—but they must conform to a life plan, feeding the characters' senses whenever these turn outward, confirming social place with their walls and accoutrements, echoing in authentic matter the spiritual pattern the author intends to trace. Houses, having been willfully purchased and furnished, tell us more than bodies do, and their description is a foremost resource of the art of fiction. Every novelist becomes, to a degree, an architect—castles in air!— and a novel itself, of course, is a kind of dwelling, whose spaces open and constrict, foster display or concealment, and resonate from room to room.

Can Architecture Be Criticized?

I AM SOMETIMES VISITED by the heretical thought that there is no such thing as good and bad architecture, any more than there is good and bad nature. It is all in where you stand at the time. Victorian domestic architecture, for instance, was thought in the heyday of less-is-more modernism to be simply atrocious: wasteful, decorative, asymmetrical, patchy, heavy, sentimental. But now how oddly charming seem the neo-Gothic, gingerbreaded mansions of, say, Newton, Massachusetts, with their fish-scale shingles, corner towers and bristling gables, long wide porches, busy spindles and brackets, hodgepodge fenestration, and outward air of inward secret passageways and cozy illogic. A lost abundance of materials and richness of household arrangements speaks now in these confident, innocent, ample buildings. Time deposits upon even the satanic mills of Lowell a nostalgic patina.

I live, as it happens, in an area of old North Shore estates, big summer places built, for the most part, by quiet Boston money, though Mr. Frick and Mr. Crane came in from Pittsburgh and Chicago respectively and erected monuments of conspicuous construction. The most modest of the old summer houses encompassed large breezy rooms for the owners and numerous small rooms for the servants; this was sound architecture in an era of cheap domestic labor and for a season when coolness, not heat, was desired. As the upper classes learned to do without live-in servants, and as air-conditioning and modern medicine lessened the terrors of summer in the city, the houses have become all-year residences, hard to heat and awkward to maintain, for all their enduring amenities of site and style. Good architecture has become less good, and its most extravagant examples are torn down as uninhabitable (the Frick mansion), converted to public wards (the Crane "castle"), or ignominiously condominiumized.

Row houses, built by developers block by block, were the metropolitan norm in my native Pennsylvania, famously so in Philadelphia but in small towns, too, right to the edge of cornfields. In the postwar period of explosive suburbanization and one-home-to-a-lot tract development, even the most elegant row wore a distasteful aura of compromised privacy and potential squalor. Then, with the rise of fuel and land prices and the return to the inner city, row houses were freshly admired for their efficiency, their close communal witness to the life of the street. They became good architecture.

And what, indeed, of Levittowns? Deplored as ticky-tacky boxes when freshly imposed upon the acres of scraped earth, the uniform units in many areas turned, decade by decade, less tacky and boxlike as proud owners made additions and improvements, and trees and shrubs matured in a pervasive softening. Caring occupancy can redeem unpromising architecture, and impoverished, uncaring occupancy has destroyed many a thoroughly planned and well-intentioned project, in East St. Louis and elsewhere. What we see, in looking at most domestic architecture, is less the spirit of the architect than that of the occupants. The unlovely three-decker, New England's special contribution to urban design, looks lovely to someone who has had a happy childhood in one, or is moving up to his generous floor-through from a single basement room. The best urban plan, Jane Jacobs and others seem to say, is Topsy's: let cities just grow, and they will fall into neighborhoods of shops, services, and solicitous mutual awareness. The best plan is the least, the loosest, allowing most scope to human powers of accommodation.

Insofar as we are all architectural critics, we tend to admire either grand gestures (the Pyramids, Salisbury Cathedral, the Seagram's Building, the Hancock Tower) or else buildings that blend into the landscape. We are fond, exteriorly, of habitations—thatched cottages, pueblos, yurts, igloos—in which we would not care to spend a night. We like buildings that appear to merge with nature, but when the merger involves our sleeping on a dirt floor, or consorting with the rodents that live in the thatch, we opt out. The American psyche is ambivalently pro-wilderness; once we have secured and insulated our own sanitized, electrified Cape Cod ranch, we dislike all further building. Nothing looks uglier than a construction site, with its bulldozer-scarred boulders and tangled stumps and muddy cellar holes where a few days ago green woods sheltered a few frolicking squirrels and raccoons. There is no downward statistic as pleasing as a slump in the number of housing starts.

A healthy hatred of our own species animates, I believe, the most spirited architectural criticism. Faithful readers of *The New Yorker* have for decades nodded agreement with the witty fulminations of the late Lewis Mumford and now of Brendan Gill against those two inevitable manifestations of a burgeoning metropolis, skyscrapers and expressways. Gill sees nefarious developers conspiring with imbecilic city officials to obliterate the human-scaled charms of the X-rated blocks of 42nd Street, and Mumford saw in Boston's own Storrow Drive a ruinous sacrifice of riverbank to that vile creature from outer space, the automobile. As if people were not in those automobiles, and had not irrevocably demonstrated their preference for driving over walking.

Are superhighways good or bad architecture? Photographed from above, surely, they have their cloverleafy beauty, though a lot of real clover got paved over. Was Baron Haussmann the creator of the City of Light as we know it, or was he the ruthless razer of vast irreplaceable tracts of medieval Paris? He was both. Is the skyline of New York City any less deserving of romantic rhapsodies than another product of blind upthrust like the Himalaya Mountains? Only if a mud hut is less deserving than an anthill. Is architecture, finally, in the mass (as distinguished from the leaky, inconvenient set pieces of tyrannical maestros like Wright or Le Corbusier), too big, too brute, too tied to money and the popular will, to be judged? I recently saw on television some aerial photographs of a giant futuristic hive of streets and houses in Arizona called Sun City. There it sat, a huge human excrescence sucking water out of the ground and pouring carbon dioxide into the air. It was monstrous. It was beautiful.

Speaking of Wright, is the Guggenheim Museum good or bad architecture? Its shape—a top, in layers, of the ugliest of materials, poured concrete—affronts sedate Fifth Avenue. A spiralling ramp within, it is like no other museum. This singularity can be both admired and deplored. It sticks in the mind; it wakes us up. Within, the viewing space, at a perpetual tilt and open on one side to a man-made abyss, quite fails to give us and the works on display the sense of hushed enclosure, of a casketlike eternal preservation, that the rooms of the Metropolitan Museum and the Frick do. The problems of mounting and lighting weren't solved in Wright's design and all the doctoring since has left the paintings still wallflowerish. And yet, we see them twice—once up close, within the limits of the guard wall, and again across the great round atrium, where they take on the intense brightness of miniatures. We slowly spiral along, dazed and amused. Though poor in treasure, the museum attracts tourists. It is a stunt, but why shouldn't architecture be a stunt? What are Baroque churches but an accretion of stunts? Isn't one duty of architecture, as of fashion in clothing, simply to be different—to give us a sense of change and renewal in our lives? Showmanship would seem to be part of the architect's equipment, along with a careless faith that the accomplished work will be viewed from a variety of angles. Architecture does not imitate nature, it adds to it, and, as with nature, the aesthetic effect lies with the beholder. Once a thing exists, especially if it is big, we learn to live with it, and judge it as leniently as we judge ourselves.

Is New York City Inhabitable?

NEW YORK is of course many cities, and an exile does not return to the one he left. I left, in April of 1957, a floor-through apartment on West Thirteenth Street, and return, when I do, to midtown hotels and the Upper East Side apartments of obliging friends. The Village, with its bookstores and framer's shops, its bricked-in literary memories and lingering bohemian redolence, is off the track of a professional visit—an elevator-propelled whirl in and out of high-rise offices and prix-fixe restaurants. Nevertheless, I feel confident in saying that the disadvantages of New York life which led me to leave have intensified rather than abated, and that the city which Le Corbusier described as a magnificent disaster is less and less magnificent.

Always, as one arrives, there is the old acceleration of the pulse—the mountainous gray skyline glimpsed from the Triboro Bridge, the cheerful games of basketball and handball being played on the recreational asphalt beside the FDR Drive, the startling, steamy, rain-splotched intimacy of the side streets where one's taxi slows to a crawl, the careless flung beauty of the pedestrians clumped at the street corners. So many faces, costumes, packages, errands! So many preoccupations, hopes, passions, lives in progress! So much human stuff, clustering and streaming with a languid colorful impatience like the pheromone-coded mass maneuvers of bees!

But soon the faces and their individual expressions merge and vanish under a dulling insistent pressure, the thrum and push of congestion. As ever more office buildings are heaped upon the East Fifties—the hugest of them, the slant-topped white Citicorp building, clearly about to fall off its stilts onto your head—and an ever-greater number of impromptu

merchants spread their dubiously legal wares on the sidewalks, even pedestrian traffic jams. One is tripped, hassled, detoured. Buskers and beggars cram every available niche. The sidewalks and subway platforms,
generously designed in the last century, have been overwhelmed on both
the minor and major entrepreneurial scales. The Manhattan grid, that fine
old machine for living, now sticks and grinds at every intersection, and
the discreet brownstones of the side streets look down upon a clogged
nightmare of perpetual reconstruction and insolent double parking. Even
a sunny day feels like a tornado of confusion one is hurrying to get out
of, into the sanctum of the hotel room, the office, the friendly apartment.
New York is a city with virtually no habitable public space—only private
spaces expensively maintained within the general disaster. While popular
journalism focuses on the possible collapse of Los Angeles and San Francisco into chasms opened by earthquakes, here on the East Coast, on its
oblong of solid granite, the country's greatest city is sinking into the
chasm of itself.

Hardened New Yorkers will sniff, What else is new? Their metropolis
has been a kind of vigorous hell since the days of the Five Points and the
immigrant-packed Lower East Side. Its vitality and glamour are ironically
rooted in merciless skirmish and inconvenient teeming; a leering familiarity with crowdedness and menace is the local badge of citizenship, and the
city's constant moral instruction features just this piquant proximity of
rich and poor—the Park Avenue matron deftly dodging the wino on his
grate, the high-skirted hooker being solicited from the black-windowed
limousine. In a city that rises higher and digs deeper than any other,
unchecked ascents and descents rocket side by side, exhilaratingly. In the
noonday throng on Fifth Avenue near Forty-second Street, I once saw a
nearly naked man, shirtless and barefoot and sooty from his place of
subterranean rest, scuttle along in a pair of split overalls that exposed his
buttocks, and everyone's eyes but mine were expertly averted. Mr.
Sammler reflects, in Saul Bellow's late-Sixties novel of Manhattan, "You
opened a jeweled door into degradation, from hypercivilized Byzantine
luxury straight into the state of nature, the barbarous world of color
erupting from beneath."

My complaint, as an exile who once loved New York and who likes to
return a half-dozen times a year, is not that it plays host to extremes of
the human condition: there is grandeur in that, and necessity. For the
Korean grocer and the Ukrainian taxi-driver, the apparent turmoil holds
out opportunity and hope. The chaos is not quite complete; food is
trucked in through the tunnels and purveyed in epic daily amounts,
Bloomingdale's brightly peddles kitchen wares to young couples who

have somehow found an apartment they can afford, the museums continue to expand, Central Park still offers patches of grass for a sunbath and a doze in the bosom of humanity. But the price of those delights, in the three decades of my exile, has gone from steep to exorbitant. Archibald Mac-Leish, toward the end of his long life, told me, "New York used to be a giving place, a place that gave more than it took. Now it takes more than it gives." Even for those with access to the right side of the jewelled door, the city teeters on the edge of dysfunction. Something as simple and, elsewhere, as comfortable as a rainy day tips it over the edge.

I heard the rain beginning at my back as I sat at one of those late dinner parties (we sat down at ten) with which the Manhattan rich prove their fortitude. The rain made a lyrical sound, ticking off the fire escapes and deepening the swish of cars on the street far below and forming a soothing undercurrent to the name-dropping and scarcely veiled financial bragging and media exegesis. (I am struck by how seriously—religiously, indeed—New Yorkers watch television. In other parts of the country, television is taken as an escape from reality; in New York, all things being relative, it is considered a window *into* reality, and no doubt its phantoms do have more substance than the doormen downstairs, and the neighbors behind the apartment wall, and the mugger waiting around the corner.) Rain in New York seems to arrive from so great a distance, picking its way through so many intervening obstacles, as to be a friend bearing a private message. But the next day, having allowed plenty of time to reach my appointment, I found my host's doorman overwhelmed with taxi requests on an avenue of cabs already taken, hurrying heedlessly past with their doused FOR HIRE lights. In the meantime, I and several other mature citizens who had miles to go and promises to keep tiptoed among the rivers that ran under the canopy and watched the minutes pour by. As frequently (but not inevitably) happens, a few empty cabs did at last wink into view and, as grateful as elderly Eskimos who at the last minute were *not* abandoned to starve in the snowfields, we were damply bundled off to our destinations, shedding tips like dandruff.

But at the end of my day, spent at an anachronistic ceremony held at a site, on West 155th Street, where no taxi-driver believes you want to go if you're white, the rain had intensified, and the taxi dearth was complete; I found myself up to my ankles in a babbling gutter, waving at ships that passed in the night and thinking that my best option might be painlessly to drown. As luck would have it, in this town of hairbreadth rescues, a limousine at loose ends offered me a ride to the airport for (the driver was very clear) "thirty-five dollars—cash." Beggars can't be choosers, and drowning exiles can't be thrifty, and so off we went, weaving jubilantly, only to bog down in a solid hour of stop-and-go traffic on 125th Street and another hour of trying to nudge our way onto the Triboro Bridge. The escape routes from the city were all but impenetrably jammed, and, reaching the airport, where planes not uncommonly sit on the runway for six hours waiting for their turn to fly, I tipped my driver, who had become my comrade in misery, five dollars. In his agitation at wasting so much of his time on me, he had cracked the taillight of another auto, whose protesting driver, a young Hispanic, he silenced by offering to trade insurance-company names. He knew, he explained confidentially to me, that his victim's car would be uninsured, illegally. Thus the have-nots get their taillights raped. The little incident, one no doubt of a thousand bits of preëmptory maneuver in that hour of urban squeeze, saddened me, but instead of standing up for justice I sat back for greater ease, in the only transportation the rain-soaked jungle seemed likely to provide.

The emergency atmosphere of this most recent visit is typical, and by no means as bad as it can get: I have not yet been mugged, knocked down by a bicycling messenger, crushed by a falling construction crane, or poisoned by a handcart hot dog. The few friends of mine still toughing it out in the city assure me that such inconveniences scarcely threaten residents, who have their cozy digs, their settled ways, their familiar routes and haunts, their terms of accommodation with the state of nature. Of course I remember how one does, over the weeks and months, pull a kind of friendly village—grocery store, newsstand, flower shop, laundry, dentist—out of New York's ghastly plenitude, its inexhaustible and endlessly repeated urban muchness. But the friendliness lies more in our wishing it to be so than in any confirming reality; returning only a little later, one finds the shops have changed names, the chummy clerks are gone, and one's name has been erased from the computer.

Toward the end of each of my by now countless trips to New York, I must still fight a rising panic that I won't be able to get out. The city, like the Soviet Union, has this constant usefulness: it makes you glad you live somewhere else. As in the Soviet Union, nothing is easy: there are lines at the bank and the post office, there is nowhere to park, everything is an exhausting walk away, the restaurant has no tables, the theatre has no seats, and carbon monoxide ubiquitously offers an invitation to succumb. Time has only strengthened my impelling perception of thirty years ago: being in New York takes so much energy as to leave none for any other kind of being.

A Sense of Transparency

Most Americans haven't had my happy experience of living for thirteen years in a seventeenth-century house, since most of America lacks seventeenth-century houses. But not New England, and especially not Ipswich, Massachusetts, which, thanks to an early boom and a long stagnation, has more so-called seventeenth-century houses still standing than any other town in the nation. "So-called" because old wooden houses aren't simple to date: the early Yankees, thrifty and handy, reused and transposed major worked timbers without any consideration for the antiquarians of the future. A noble chamfered summer beam, for instance, may certainly date from before 1680, but be worked in with structural members from several decades later, in a room with raised-field panelling from 1750, in a house fitted with new windows and staircases in the nineteenth century, and most recently clapboarded in 1950. The old frameworks were sometimes completely swallowed in later renovations, and the original shape of the place was detectable only in the attic and around the cellar stairs. The foundation itself may have belonged to an earlier, quite vanished house. Architectural historians use the term "first-period," signifying a date before 1720. The house I and my wife and four children lived in was called, on a plaque beside the front door, the Polly Dole House and given a date of 1686, though one visiting expert sneeringly said that dating it prior to 1725 would compromise his integrity.

A seventeenth-century house can be recognized by its steep roof, massive central chimney, and utter porchlessness. Some of these houses have a second-story overhang, emphasizing their medieval look. The gables are on the sides. The windows were originally small, with fixed casements and leaded diamond panes. The basic plan called for two rooms over two, the fireplace opening into each room; a later plan added half-rooms behind, creating the traditional "saltbox" shape. Inside the front door—at least our front door—a shallow front hall gave onto an exiguous staircase squeezed into the space left by the great brick core at the heart of the house. The fireplace, with its cast-iron spits and recessed bake ovens, had been the kitchen. The virgin forests of the New World had contributed massive timbers, adzed into shape and mortise-and-tenoned together, and floorboards as much as a foot wide.

The Polly Dole House had a living room so large that people supposed the house had originally been an inn, on the winding old road to Newburyport, which ran right by. Polly Dole was a shadowy lady who may have waited on tables; we never found out much about her, though local eyebrows still lifted at her name. The big room, with its gorgeous floor-boards, was one you sailed through, and the furniture never stayed in any one place. The walk-in fireplace, when the three-foot logs in it got going, singed your eyebrows and dried out the joints of any chair drawn up too cozily close. In the middle of the summer beam, a huge nut and washer terminated a long steel rod that went up to a triangular arrangement of timbers in the attic; at one point in its history the house had been lifted by its own bootstraps. I used to tell my children that if we turned the nut the whole house would fall down. We never tried it.

The decade was the Sixties, my wife and I were youngish, and the house suited us just fine. It was Puritan; it was back-to-nature; it was less-is-more. A seventeenth-century house tends to be short on frills like hallways and closets; you must improvise. A previous owner had put a pipe and a pole in a small upstairs room to make a walk-in closet; fair weather or foul, I would hike from our bedroom to my clothes every morning. I discover I have no memory at all of where my wife kept hers. Perhaps, it being the Sixties, she only needed a miniskirt and a lumberjack shirt. Our children, four of them, slept in four little rooms in a row above the long kitchen, which for a time had been two kitchens, a partition intervening. There had been only two children when we moved in, and if there had been six little rooms, we might have felt obliged to produce six little tenants. When they were awake and downstairs, the children raced around and around the central brick mass with its four fireplaces on a counterclockwise route that went front hall, living room, kitchen, dining room, front hall.

The living room, beneath its low smoky-beamed ceiling, cheerfully accepted our butterfly chairs and Danish modern and glass-and-chrome coffee table. Such austere furniture looked in tune, on the broad old boards, under the slightly sway-backed beams. The ancient house felt oddly up-to-date in its serene lack of Victorian complications. Around 1940, an Ipswich eccentric (one of many), a bachelor antiquarian whose quest for religious authenticity eventually took him from the Anglican priesthood into that of Russian Orthodoxy, had rescued the place from tenement status. At the Depression nadir of its fortunes, we were told, not only too many people had inhabited the rooms but a flock of chickens as well. The architect-priest had in his renovations installed generous, twelve-over-twelve sash-hung windows, and this fenestration dispelled any lingering gloom. One felt Puritan claustrophobia only in the cellar, among the fieldstone foundation walls, piled up without much benefit of mortar, and threaded with a worrisome inheritance of deteriorating pipes and wires. There was no sewer connection, only a cesspool in the back-yard which, by the inexorable laws of hydraulics, would sometimes overflow into our kitchen sink. In the attic, as I recall, there were many loose boards, some pink fluff pretending to be insulation, a fine view over the rooftops toward the town wharf, a ramshackle TV aerial, and, in the end, tons of stacked *New Yorkers*.

How did inhabiting such an antique affect our lives? We joined the local historical society, for one thing. We worked up, for benefit of our fellow first-period owners, a smattering of small talk about gunstock posts, clam-shell plaster, purlin-type roof construction, and original brick nogging. First-period houses, mixed in with creditable specimens of the Georgian and Federal styles, were strung up and down our street, called High at one end and East at the other. Architectural conservation was freshly in the air; Ipswich's old houses, left for centuries to fend for themselves, were no longer being torn down and, rather, were being taken in hand and fixed up by newcomers to the town—commuters and artisans with beards, pigtails, and a regard for history. We ourselves felt part, deeply and effortlessly, of the community because we owned a piece of its past, sleeping and eating in rooms where fourteen or so previous generations had left their scuff-marks.

The straightforward, hearth-centered architecture of our house must have strengthened our family sense. Once we moved, the fact is, things fell apart. The big nut and bolt were holding us together as well. Erwin Panofsky, in his elegant monograph *Gothic Architecture and Scholasticism*, describes the architectural spirit of the medieval cathedrals as one of *manifestatio*—the principle of elucidation and continuous clarification that informs scholastic philosophy. Each rib of the ceiling vault, for example, can be followed down into the compound columns that line the nave. Abbot Suger, the first known architectural theorist of the Middle Ages, wrote of the "principle of transparency." "And so," Panofsky tells us, "did High Gothic architecture delimit interior volume from exterior space yet insist that it project itself, as it were, through the encompassing structure; so that, for example, the cross section of the nave can be read off from the façade." So, too, the layout of the rooms—two above, two below—can be read off the façades of the houses the Puritans built, and a certain transparency quickens the life within. The beams are plain to see in the rooms; organic grains and irregularities animate the floors and walls; there are no hidden passageways, no cunning closets, no dumbwaiters, no cubbyholes for servants. To wake and work in such a house felt like an honor—a privileged access to the lucid spirit of the New World's Puritan settlements.

A Short and Happy Ride

THE STRANGE EXPECTANCY that getting on any train gives us quite outshines whatever pleasurable sensations may accompany climbing into a car or onto an airplane. It is, perhaps, the *threading through* of train travel, the knowledge that its path is inflexibly fixed in steel and spalls and oil-soaked ties, which makes the traveller tingle; or perhaps it is the largeness and throbbing, chuffing power of the vehicle, quite disproportionate to our simple need to get from here to there, that, as with the great steamships of the pre-jet era, spikes the trip with a dash of extravagance, of holiday. One of the cherishable distinctions of the Boston area's North Shore (as opposed to the South, whose Old Colony Railroad shut down in 1959) remains its possession, through thick and thin, of a working commuter-train.

The line, long under the management of the Boston and Maine and now part of the Massachusetts Bay Transportation Authority, has two branches, which part at Beverly. One, the Gloucester or Rockport branch, continues northeast, up the shaggy middle of Cape Ann, and ends behind a gas station in Rockport, a ten minutes' winding, downhill walk from a public beach; the other bears due north through the coddled greenery of Wenham and Hamilton and at one time continued on past Ipswich to Newburyport and Salisbury. I was present, over twenty years ago, at a town meeting in Ipswich which debated a motion to subsidize continued train service, or else see it cease. Commuters were much a minority at that time, but the vote carried, and the Ipswich branch did not wither away, as did its continuation up the coast. Now, I believe, at a time when the automotive passageways to Boston are increasingly congested and bound to get worse as new highways and tunnels are being desperately constructed, the railroad is prized as a regional asset, as precious to the milieu as granite outcroppings, wild blueberries, and lobster boats bobbing offshore. Suave and smooth-rolling new cars made in Canada are replacing the battered Budd coaches with their fractured windows and tattered slam-back seats, and the decaying, abandoned stations are refurbished and decorated with bright metallic maps proclaiming these once-remote outposts part of the metropolitan "T."

Nahant, a breezy square mile of pasture and cliff connected to Lynn by a thin curve of beach, was America's first summer resort, and the Eastern Railroad by 1838 was ferrying passengers across the harbor to East Boston and thence by rail to Nahant and Salem. The rails were extended to Beverly and Ipswich and New Hampshire; in 1847 the Gloucester branch came into existence, and seven years later the ferry was rendered obsolete by an overland link, and Gloucester found itself a mere hour from Boston. Joseph Garland's *Boston's Gold Coast* reports a native of the time poetically complaining, "A hand of iron had been laid upon the bosom of Essex County." In his own amply poetic voice, Garland describes the subsequent invasion of the Boston rich:

> Sowing the merest chaff from their bank accounts among the knowing natives, they reaped mile after priceless mile a harvest of salt water farms regarded by father unto son of shrewd Yankee owners as so many worked-out birthrights that looked out on nothing more promising or profitable than the heaving emptiness of the Atlantic Ocean. The wooing and the winning, not to say the seduction, of that virginal coast between Boston Harbor and Cape Ann followed the railroad as surely as did the opening of the West.

This proto-West has by now been thoroughly won and tamed. The trains on weekdays sternly carry commuters and shoppers into the city's dusky, well-worn North Station. On summer weekends, the cars are almost orgiastic with lightly clad city-dwellers being hauled back, coated with salt and sand and sunburn, at the end of a day by the sea. Celtics and Bruins fans have a most convenient time of it, since the arena where both teams play is physically part of the terminal. But even those who rarely take the train get something out it—a rumor of motion, a suggestion of potential escape. The first locomotive noisily moves before six; the last sounds its whistle long after midnight. A string of crossings excitingly ding their warning bells and lower their gates. Between the hourly passings, the empty tracks are strolled by schoolchildren, as shortcuts to here and there. Where the rails run west, they reflect the orange sunset; east, the pink sunrise. The tracks' proximity, at least in the outer reaches, does not seem to depress property values. My own house, up a wooded hill, trembles when the train passes, and the effect is as of a caress, a gentle reminder, like the sight of airplane lights circling in over Massachusetts Bay toward Logan Airport, that an urban congeries lurks over the arboreal horizon.

From either terminus, at Ipswich or Rockport, the train scuds through bucolic landscape for a while, the rocks and trees permitting glimpses of Appleton Farm and the Wenham Golf Course, Lily Pond and Manchester Harbor. Then, on the fringes of Beverly, the houses irrevocably thicken, and a grit of warehouse backs and commercial outlets flies into the eyes. Beverly Station is an ambitious yellow-brick structure that now serves the public only as a restaurant. On the coldest of winter days, with the wind-chill off of the Bass River bitter beyond factoring, the commuters huddle within the doorway to the bar or else in the lee of one of the obsolete baggage-carts that decorate the platform, cemented fast. Once mounted into the train, however, passengers are greeted with a warmth so steamy as to induce instant sleep. Forthwith, there is the sudden adventure of crossing a wide estuary on a railroad bridge narrow enough to give the illusion of riding a Hovercraft. The old oil-soaked wooden bridge burned down a few years ago, and two trains trapped north of Salem for some weeks buzzed back and forth on Cape Ann, like hornets in a bottle, until they were captured and barged back to Boston. The bridge has been rebuilt in concrete.

After the sunny dazzlement of the open water and its scenic flock of boats and its fringe of shingled condominiums, the train takes a dark plunge into the earth beneath Salem, depriving us of the sight of the town's handsome old heart—the pillared brick mansions the China trade financed, and the civic buildings that have succeeded to the Old Custom House, which gave employment to Hawthorne and a starting point to *The Scarlet Letter.* Perhaps the ominous darkness fittingly memorializes Hawthorne and his ancestor Judge Hathorne, who sat in on the notorious witchcraft trials of 1692. The tunnel ends in a graffiti-rich concrete trough which was, until recently, the Salem waiting platform—now mercifully replaced by a tidy pair of postmodern pavilions on the side of the tunnel toward Beverly.

Salem's outskirts shudder into those of Swampscott, a city of dentists, which until recently boasted the most dilapidated station on the line. Then the train takes wing into Lynn, which it enters on high, on an elevated iron platform at the level of the upper windows of the boarded-up factories. So desolate, so scratched and rusted and spray-painted is this spot that one might be in the gutted sections of the Bronx; yet between here and Boston intervenes a spacious prairie of marsh grass and winding saltwater inlet. Nothing—not the car dumps or the gravel yards of Revere, not the swamped sand barges or the skeletal carcasses of abandoned dories—can quite hide the basic grandeur of this amphibious domain, which in summer puts on a dress of shimmering green and in winter entertains a glittering clash of ice and tide. It seems ages until the Chelsea stop, which some trains ignore, and ages more of sidling superhighway stanchions and factory flanks (one advertises ARISE FUTON, *The Original Futon Company*) before the train slows its swaying glide through the multiplying tracks and comes to a stop, with a tremendous shout from the conductor, in North Station.

I am always astonished, disembarking from the train, by how many others have accompanied me on the trip, which seems such a solitary, meditative hour of shifting scenery. We are a multitude, all marching in the same direction alongside the train, like a sleeve that floppily follows the direction of a halted fist. We are motley, of all hairdos and ages; at peak hours there are plenty of men in gray suits, but also sturdy working women wearing white socks and sneakers and carrying their heels in their briefcases. Two-tone L. L. Bean rubbers are not uncommon, nor tatty collegiate parkas festooned with dead ski-lift tickets. The train-shed roofs are usually dripping rain or melted snow, and there is always the same red-faced man selling paper cones of roses, and another peddling soft pretzels *à la moutarde*. When a trestle bridge nearer the city burned, in that era of burning bridges, and the short and happy ride ended in a dusty improvised parking lot in easternmost Cambridge, these two small merchants appeared with their carts, without missing (to my knowledge) a single day. We avoid their importunities expertly, walking with a stride simultaneously brisk, wary, and bored; we have become, by a miracle of transportation, city folk.

ESSAYS ON ASSIGNED TOPICS

Women

THE TOPIC appeals, appalls, dizzies, delights. It dwarfs the male pen by much the same scale as the human ovum dwarfs the spermatozoon; that is, by 1,400,000 cubic microns to seventeen, or over eighty thousand to one. If life is a forest, women are the trees. Mothers, grandmothers, aunts, cousins, teachers, classmates, playmates, dates, mates, daughters, editors, reviewers both hostile and friendly—my goodness, how can one generalize about faces and voices whose sum leaves almost nothing of one's earthly existence unaccounted for? Further, the topic is not only vast but hot, and any word a male ventures upon it will be as inevitably suspect as an accused murderer's testimony in his own behalf.

Let me, testing the thin ice, begin as far back in time as my memory can reach, with my maternal grandmother, whose beautiful full name was Katherine Ziemer Kramer Hoyer. I grew up in the house she kept. Always serving, serving others: that was the image she projected. She cooked the meals and then herself ate standing up, while the rest of us sat at the table. Her very shape had become bent by slaving; she was a small thin woman in a cotton dress bent over as if constantly peering into a pot. I still remember the strain on her sharp-nosed face as she stared upward at me while I crouched on a lower branch of a tree. That was one of the things women did, I early concluded: they tried to get you to come down out of a tree. She was afraid I would fall, and that possibility had occurred to me also, so I was half grateful to be called down. But the other half, it seemed, needed to climb higher and higher, in defiance of the danger. Society and God wanted me to keep climbing, however much my heart was on the ground with my grandmother. This ambiguity is with me yet. Dare it, don't dare it. What do women want? Some of the girls I grew up with climbed higher than I dared, showing their underpants as they ascended.

The girls at school both did and did not want attention—to be teased, chased, bumped, have their pigtails pulled, and all the rude clumsy rest up through kissing to the fabled ultimate discourtesy over the horizon, from whence only pornographic comic books returned to tell the tale. I, timid and thin-skinned, hung back waiting for a moment of unambiguously signalled receptivity, which never came. It was the boy's duty to project and act, it seemed, and the girl's privilege to select from the circumambient field of disorganized male activity and thrustingness those instances which it pleased her to cultivate, to take into herself. She was desired, he the desirer. She was the center, he the arrow; by this formulation motionlessness was her essence, and part of the male job was, through dazzling and bemusing display, to reduce her to the stillness that permits possession. And indeed, now, thanks to the miracles of nature photography whereby educational television fills what little of its program time is not consumed by borrowings from the BBC, we can see that this is just how, say, the male spider fulfills his biological assignment. With his eight-legged antics and ticklings he hypnotizes the great female at the center of her web, then skitters away before, fertilized and hungry, the betranced wench awakens.

Sometimes I do wonder if women are not more territorial than men. Perhaps I have just happened to know women who took comfort in acreage; but I have known a number, who have clung to their piece of weed-infested land even when circumstances conspired to make their tenacity quixotic. More vulnerable on the road than men and less well trained by society for the free-lance life, women must make their assets out of what they can hold. Men, with the superior earning ability they have bestowed upon themselves, are territory of a kind, and a cocktail party is threaded with invisible trip-wires and barbed demarcation lines. Like birds chirping their friendly-sounding songs, like impala marking bushes with scent rubbed off their dear faces, women subtly signal a turf, and become fierce in defense of it. "I will greatly multiply thy sorrow," the Lord said to Eve upon expelling her from the turf called Eden. Adam doubtless took it less hard; he was about to mosey out the gate into the wilderness anyway.

It's a man's world, they say; but in its daily textures it is a world created by and for women. Men dress to please women, and women dress for women also. Our furniture and cuisine, our gardens and carpets and wallpaper are selected and tended by the eyes and hands, generally, of women. Even such an originally masculine artifact as the automobile has been progressively feminized in its shape and tint and in the silky way it "handles." In a movie theatre, scientific tests have shown, the eyes of men and women both are attracted to the giant silver face of the actress; a woman does not look like a half of the human race but a more refined and animated, more magnetic version of it. In a female face, the things that can open, the eyes and the mouth, open wider. Women talk, women see. Men, comparatively, are laced shut. They inhabit a world too delicate and finely tuned for them, where they miss many of the signals and blunder through cunning patterns of fabric and ornament as through a tinted fog.

I fancy myself a not untypical male in feeling that, when there is no woman in the room, the effort of making conversation is quite unnecessary; a few grunts will do. Social cohesion and civilization, mundane safety and comfort are female inventions. Basically, men fear other men— competitive killers, sadistic louts whose idea of a good time is to squat in some icy reeds and blast away with shotguns at downy goslings.

But when a woman comes into the room, or the cave or teepee, the possibilities of law, mercy, wit, and affection arise. One's stutter melts, one's blood takes on a champagne simmer and sets the brain to scintillating. This is, I will be told, male-chauvinist romanticism. Women can be just as brutal and murderous as men. They are in the hunt, too, as we can see with just a glance at *Cosmopolitan*. There is, I learned from Donald Barthelme's great early story "Me and Miss Mandible," something called "woman's disguised aggression." The phrase made me stop, years ago, in my innocence. Women? Aggressive? Think of Lizzie Borden. Of Martina Navratilova. Of Ulrike Meinhof. Of Sally Ride. Women are no stationary bull's-eye, painted red; they are on the move, and their trim hard figures express it, and their roller skates, and their punk haircuts and parachute pants.

My grandmother, as a matter of fact, was also on the move, between the stove and the table, and the back door and the chicken yard. My mother's theory, now and then expressed aloud, went that her mother had waited upon her father until he was helpless without her; thus she had enslaved him. This was woman's aggression in its old-fashioned form.

A woman of my acquaintance wrote her doctoral thesis on female masochism. She was a young woman, young enough to take nothing about womanhood for granted, and had concluded on the basis of statistical and laboratory studies that female masochism did indeed exist. Under some grilling from me as to gritty details of the case, she went on to say that women, these same studies reveal, are not perverse. They just aren't. She shrugged, and batted her lashes, like "stout Cortez when with eagle eyes / He star'd at the Pacific—and all his men / Look'd at each other with a wild surmise."

Women are not perverse. What can that mean? It rings oddly true: women, though invited to be partners in so-called perversity every minute all over the turning globe, are themselves exempt from being perverse, which the dictionary defines as "obstinate in opposing what is right, reasonable, or accepted." Perversity must be, then, an exclusively male protest against the given, the unavoidable, the Nature which is so free with death and whose atrocities the Marquis de Sade claimed he was merely palely imitating. The love of killing (*vide* Hemingway) springs from the fear of being killed: a counterblow, as it were, delivered against the encircling dark. Perhaps women have not traditionally been allowed the luxury of cosmic protest. Perhaps they deflect it inward, and make it into suicide or churchgoing or anorexia. Perhaps in their bones and wombs they feel no need to go against the larger grain, to do more than battle against mismanagement in the immediate vicinity, against invasions of the territory at hand. If women are not perverse, then by definition they are right and reasonable. So I have, in my three and fifty years of suckling and listening, adoring and cohabiting, found them. Women are reasonable and right. More power to them.

Mother

ANY PREGNANT WOMAN, be she young or old, silly or wise, is very apt, in nine months' time or less, to become a mother. When I see girls in the supermarket pushing their swaddled tots along in wire grocery carts, I remind myself with difficulty that in the groggy eyes of these infants what looms above them is not a gum-chewing ex-adolescent but Mother. For the undoubted feat of achieving a biological split women receive much praise and some flak. The solemn infant psyche brings a terrible focus upon the psychological matrix—the *alma* or *saeva mater,* as the case may be; the dawning psyche's first and everlastingly internalized encounter; "The Most Unforgettable," to quote Alexander Portnoy's autobiography, "Character I've Met." The first sentence of that notorious confession runs, you will remember, "She was so deeply embedded in my consciousness that for the first year of school I seem to have believed that each of my teachers was my mother in disguise." Men succeed, Freud tells us, because their mothers love them; men become homosexuals, some lesser psychologists have theorized, because they cannot bear to betray their mothers with another woman. Such a powerful personage must shoulder, like God, a lot of blame. Prince Hamlet greatly resents that his mother is anything *but* a mother, and feels entitled to scold her and commit murder in her boudoir. The largeness of our mother-myth has a paradoxically dwindling effect upon the women concerned: they must be in all things motherly and become therefore natural processes rather than people. Few things are harder, in this era so preoccupied with the monitoring of human relations, than to get to know one's mother as a person—to forgive her, in effect, for being one's mother.

My own is now eighty. She has just renewed her driver's license and has upwards of twenty cats to feed—to feed and to kill, for, in motherly fashion, her responsibilities toward her adopted dependents are conflicted. She began feeding a stray cat to spare the birds around the place; more and more cats appeared at her back door; and now the perplexities of mercy ask that she keep their feline herd thinned. It is a bind, and not the first she has been in. She was, for the twenty-one years in which she and I shared the same address, not only a mother but a daughter. We lived, my mother and father, her parents, and me, in a household with a strong undertow of Depression, a historical event that had happened to hit both my father and grandfather hard. One lost his job, the other his money. She helped out by working in a department store three miles away, in the fabrics department, for fourteen dollars a week. Later, in the war, she worked in parachute factories. But most of the time she was home writing, sitting in the front bedroom, with its view of horse-chestnut trees and telephone wires, and tapping out pages to send to New York magazines in brown envelopes. The brown envelopes always came back. Ours was a big white brick house but much cramped by worry and need. At its center, squeezed from all sides, my mother held forth and held out, and pulled us through. Or maybe we pulled her through. In any case, she and I are now the only survivors of that five-sided family, and these last twelve years, in which she has been a widow, have been pleasant ones for me, of getting to know her, of tuning her in without the static of kindred broadcasting stations.

Her intelligence and humor, as she fends off the perils of old age, are startling. Though with a son's luck I have reaped most of the benefits, it was she who made the great leap of imagination up, out of the rural Pennsylvania countryside—German in accent and practical in emphasis—into the ethereal realm of art. I glimpse now how bright that little girl must have been to skip all those grades in her one-room schoolhouse and head off to normal school so painfully young. At college, she was four years younger than her classmates, of whom my father was one. This simple brightness comes in handy, as in solitude she calculates her taxes, administers her acres, operates her machinery, retypes her manuscripts, and entertains her grandchildren as they breeze in, not always unaccompanied, from their strange new world. She and I used to write letters; now, grown spendthrift and lazy, we talk on the telephone, and I hear how festive and limpid her wit is, and with what graceful, modest irony she illuminates every corner of her brave life. All this for decades was muffled for me behind the giant mask of motherhood.

When I try to pull "mother" from my childhood memories, I come up with two images, both of them, I fear, already embedded in some work of fiction or another. In one, my mother, young and rather formally dressed, is sitting opposite me on the floor, coloring at the same page of a coloring book. I marvel at how neatly she does it, even though from her vantage the page is upside down. She seems calm and comely and I am so proud it makes me shy. In the other, we are both somewhat older, and I see her, while standing at the ironing board, jump slightly and touch her jaw with her hand: a twinge of toothache, and my first unsolicited empathy into the pain of another human being. And this vision merges with the pathetic remedy our family used to apply to aches of all sorts, toothaches and earaches and eye-aches—a folded dishtowel, warmed by the iron. How many, in those pre-antibiotic years, sugar pills and dabs of ointment and spoonfuls of syrup went into the nurture of a sickly child, like those little pats of wind and rain that reassure a seedling and embolden it to lengthen its roots.

As I get older, her genes keep sprouting in me. We eat alike, with a steady, enchanted absorption in the food. We laugh alike, and evade awkward questions with similar flurries of fancy; I hear her voice flirtatiously pop from my mouth. My hair, fine like my father's, went gray early like hers. Her old hobbies, which I thought eccentric—organic gardening, natural foods, conservation—now seem to me simple good sense. More deeply than any patriarchal religion, I believe what she instilled: the notions that we should live as close to nature as we can, and that in matters of diet and behavior alike we should look to the animals for guidance.

She can name all the trees and flowers and birds in her woods; I wish I could, and try to learn the names from her now, since I paid scant attention when young. As we walk carefully through these woods, with their treacherous footing of boulders and mossy logs (both of us grown too brittle to relish a tumble), the biological event that linked our two bodies seems further and further away—the mere beginning of a precious companionship.

The Female Body

"THY NAVEL is like a round goblet, which wanteth not liquor," says the male voice in the Song of Solomon, "thy belly is like a heap of wheat set about with lilies. Thy two breasts are like two young roes that are twins." Robert Graves, in *Watch the Northwind Rise*, quotes a vernacular rendering of these verses which goes, "Your belly's like a heap of wheat, / Your breasts like two young roes. / O come to bed with me, my sweet, / And take off all your clo'es!" A naked woman is, for most men, the most beautiful thing they will ever see. On this planet, the female body is the prime aesthetic object, re-created not only in statuary and painting but in the form of door knockers, nutcrackers, lamp stands, and caryatids. For the Victorians, it was everywhere, naked in brass, while their real women were swaddled and padded and reinforced like furniture; in this century, the female body haunts merchandising from top to bottom, from the silky epidermal feel of a soft cigarette pack to the rumpy curves of a Porsche. The female body is a masterpiece of market design, persuading the race to procreate generation after generation, extracting semen from mesmerized men with the ease of a pickpocket at a girlie show.

This captivating mechanism pays a price for its own complexity: cancer attacks breasts and ovaries, menstrual cramps and hysteria impair performance. Its season of bloom, of potential fertility, is shorter than that of the male body, though more piquant and powerful. Kafka, in a letter to Max Brod, unchivalrously remarked of women, "Not until summer does one really see their curious kind of flesh in quantities. It is soft flesh, retentive of a great deal of water, slightly puffy, and keeps its freshness only a few days." He goes on, with his scrupulous fairness: "Actually, of course, it stands up pretty well, but that is only proof of the brevity of human life." Just so, the actuarial longer-lastingness of the female body demonstrates the relative biological disposability of the male, and the salubrious effects of lifelong exercise in the form of housework.

If the main social fact about the female body is its attractiveness, the main political fact is its weakness, compared with the male body. There may be some feminists ardent enough to dispute this, but the truth is elemental. As Elizabeth Hardwick, reviewing Simone de Beauvoir's *The Second Sex*, put it with admirable firmness, "Women are certainly physically inferior to men and if this were not the case the whole history of the world would be different. . . . Any woman who ever had her wrist twisted by a man recognizes a fact of nature as humbling as a cyclone to a frail tree branch." This fact lies behind many facts of feminine circumstance, such as the use of women as domestic drudges and beasts of burden in the world's fundamental economy, and the superior attentiveness and subtlety of women in the private maneuvers of advanced societies. "The fastidiousness of women," Stendhal wrote in *On Love,* "is the result of that perilous situation in which they find themselves placed so early, and of the necessity they are under of spending their lives among cruel and charming enemies."

This physical weakness and the cruelties that result are the truth but not all the truth, and from the standpoint of the species not even the main truth. An interesting thought-experiment, for an adult male, is to try to look at a prepubescent girl, one of ten or eleven, say, with the eyes again of a boy the same age. The relative weakness, the arresting curves, the female fastidiousness are not yet in place, but the magic is—the siren song, the strange simultaneous call to be kind and to conquer, the swooning wish to place one's life *beside* this other. To be sure, cultural inducements to heterosexuality bombard us from infancy; but they fall, generally, upon terrifically receptive ground.

The female body is, in its ability to conceive and carry a fetus and to nurse an infant, our life's vehicle—it is the engine and the tracks. Male sexuality, then, returning to this primal source, drinks at the spring of being and enters the murky region, where up is down and death is life, of mythology. The paradoxical contradictoriness of male attitudes toward the female and her body—the impulses to exalt and debase, to serve and enslave, to injure and comfort, to reverence and mock—goes back to some point of origin where emotions are not yet differentiated and energy has no distinct direction. The sex act itself, from the male point of view, is a paradox, a transformation of his thrusts into pleasure, a poke in the gut that is gratefully received. Sadism and masochism naturally flirt on the edges of our, as Katherine Mansfield said, "profound and terrible . . . desire to establish contact."

And naturally modern women feel a personal impatience with being mythologized, with being envisioned (talk about hysteria!) as madonnas and whores, earth-mothers and vampires, helpless little girls and implacable dominatrices, and with male inability to see sex simply for what it is. What is it? A biological function and procedure, presumably, on a plane with eating and defecation, just as women are, properly regarded, equally entitled human beings and political entities with minds of their own. Well, men *have* been known, inadvertently, in lapses of distraction or satiety, to see the female body as just a body, very like their own, built for locomotion as well as procreation, an upright watery stalk temporarily withstanding, with its miraculous molecular chain reactions, the forces of gravity and entropy. It is a lucid but dispirited moment, seeing a nude woman as a kind of man, only smaller, lighter-framed, without a beard, but matching men tuft for tuft otherwise, and with bumps, soft swellings, unmale emphases stiffened with fat, softly swayed by gravity . . . a heap of wheat set about with lilies . . . those catenary curves, that curious, considerate absence . . . the moment of lucid vision passes.

In asking forgiveness of women for our mythologizing of their bodies, for being *unreal* about them, we can only appeal to their own sexuality, which is different but not basically different, perhaps, from our own. For women, too, there seems to be that tangle of supplication and possessiveness, that descent toward infantile undifferentiation, that omnipotent helplessness, that merger with the cosmic mother-warmth, that flushed pulse-quickened leap into overestimation, projection, general mix-up.

The Song of Solomon has two voices; there is a female extoller as well. She claims, "My beloved is white and ruddy, the chiefest among ten thousand. His head is as the most fine gold, his locks are bushy, and black as a raven. . . . His belly is as bright ivory overlaid with sapphires," etc. Can it be that the male body—its bulky shoulders, its narrow hips, its thick-veined feet and hands, its defenseless boneless belly above the one-eyed priapic oddity—may also loom as a glorious message from the deep? In Margaret Atwood's last novel, *Cat's Eye,* the heroine, in one of the many striking passages about growing up female and human, reflects upon the teen-aged boys she talks to on the telephone: "The serious part is their bodies. I sit in the hall with the cradled telephone, and what I hear is their bodies. I don't listen much to the words but to the silences, and in the silences these bodies re-create themselves, are created by me, take form." Some of this is sexual, she reflects, and some is not. Some is purely visual: "The faces of the boys change so much, they soften, open up, they ache. The body is pure energy, solidified light." For male and female alike, the bodies of the other sex are messages signalling what we must do—they are glowing signifiers of our own existence.

Beauty

SOME SAY beauty is use, and others say energy is beauty. In either case beauty appears as a side product of activity: a static expression of kinetic potential, usually characterized by high gloss and smooth rounded forms. The ancients tried to bring the concept of beauty mathematically into line with diagrams of harmony and a set of Platonic crystals somewhere behind the sky. What, then, of those vague landscapes, those misty watery vistas, that relax us into a sensation we call beautiful? I think, perhaps, we feel ourselves in the presence of beauty whenever we are lifted friction-lessly out of self-concern, whether a mountain or a watchworks does it. Beauty surprises us out of our egos, and like happiness must come around the corner unexpectedly—a miniskirted Japanese model carrying a parasol the shades of cinnamon and jade, with rice-white face but long, long legs, not necessarily followed by a *Vogue* photographer with his silver flash-reflectors.

Spirituality

THE WORD "SPIRITUALITY" comes, by way of "spirit," from the Latin verb for the act of breathing, *spirare.* Spirit, then, is the principle of life within us, our invisible essence. A parallel derivation took a rather differ-ent turn in French, becoming the noun *esprit,* which came to signify the mind, the rarefied human gift of understanding. In English the word remains brainless, and it has diminished over the decreasingly metaphysi-cal decades to a semi-comic ghost, as when we say "evil spirits," which are not to be confused with spirits of alcohol or turpentine. The concept of spirituality retains connotations of the volatile, the impalpable, the immaterial, the dispensable. It suggests the vapors, the heavenward hys-teria of St. Teresa or a Victorian spiritualist, a tricky dependence upon the unseen that any man or sensible woman can do without. Myself, I associate spirituality with intuition, which is often labelled "feminine." The ability to make one's way among the unseen currents, to arrive at the truth while bypassing induction and deduction, to pluck things out of the air—a gender tilt in this area would help account for the female prepon-derance of fortune-tellers and churchgoers. A spiritual person of either sex embodies an alternative to the obvious—to bank accounts and syllogisms, to death and taxes. Pressed, I would define spirituality as the shadow of light humanity casts as it moves through the darkness of everything that can be explained. I think of Buddha's smile and Einstein's halo of hair. I think of birthday parties. I think of common politeness, and the breath-taking attempt to imagine what someone else is feeling. I think of spirit lamps.

The Fourth of July

IT IS A HUMAN PROVIDENCE that scatters the holidays around so conveniently on the calendar. The American summer has three days to mark its phases—Memorial Day to signal its beginning, the Fourth of July to mark the start of high summer, and Labor Day to bring it to a gentle close. Of these three, the first and third were invented and bestowed upon the year by governmental fiat, and even the Fourth is somewhat arbitrary. The Continental Congress actually declared that "these United Colonies are, and of right ought to be Free and Independent States" on July 2, 1776, and on the fourth merely voted to adopt the Declaration of Independence, which was publicly read in the yard of the Pennsylvania statehouse in Philadelphia on July 8. It was not copied onto parchment and signed by the delegates in attendance until August 2, and the last of the fifty-six signatories, Thomas McKean of Delaware, did not affix his name before 1777. The first anniversary of July Fourth was celebrated that year in Philadelphia, with parades and oratory and fireworks and the ringing of bells, and the custom spread and has lasted. This most American of holidays serves to remind us, if we care, that our founding fathers, wearing wigs and jabots and lace-trimmed frock coats, met and debated in a fearful sweat, and delicately and artfully stitched together our national fabric amid the muggy, buggy heat of a Philadelphia summer before air-conditioning and pesticides.

The northern Europeans who came here encountered hotter summers than they had known, and they were slow to compromise their costumes. For most of the nineteenth century, the middle class kept buttoned up and voluminously swathed in dark colors, and only the underprivileged enjoyed the privilege of dressing light. The Fourth of July still reminds us of that end-of-the-century loosening up—the arrival of straw hats and cambric dresses, the resort to wide-porched summer hotels and sandy cliffs climbed by flights of wooden stairs, the discovery of the American summer as another continent, a land of ice and ice cream and baseball and beach picnics and outdoor concerts, of freedom felt in the body itself. We have brought forth a new world of nearly naked red men and brown women camping out and cooking out by seaside and lakeside. Sea and lake and mountain are where King Summer reigns, and the Fourth of July fireworks are his coronation jewels.

Yet fireworks have a sadness. They are expensive, somewhat dangerous, and soon over. Quickly subsiding into their final shreds and sparks, they impose our passion and mortality on the night sky. Though the Fourth marks the beginning of true summer warmth, already the long June evenings are drawing in, and by the end of the month the shimmering days have been perceptibly nipped shorter. The holiday has an undertow of perfect ripeness; it reaches its climax in the dark, not long before bedtime—in contrast to Easter and Christmas, whose glad tidings arrive in the morning, and Thanksgiving, which sluggishly crests in mid-afternoon. Slightly melancholy, too, seems the Fourth's great show of red, white, and blue, harking back to a primitive patriotism that can only make us feel a bit inadequate, as Washington's Birthday used to before it was unceremoniously lumped into Presidents' Day.

Bonfires, perhaps, more than fireworks capture the basic flavor of the Fourth. The initial event had the acrid taste of political defiance, the crackle of the violent cleansing that a revolution intends. The men whose prim and flossy signatures are aligned on the Declaration of Independence were risking their necks, and for eight years men of many nationalities died so that one more nation could be born. Our Revolution seems, in the attic of our shared imagery, a kind of popgun war, with chorus lines of redcoats and Minutemen; even the tatters of Washington's troops at Valley Forge and his icy crossing of the Delaware feel stylized and mock-heroic. Bonfires, which in some towns are still heaped up building-high on the main square, remind us, as Bastille Day and Guy Fawkes Day remind the citizens of other sovereignties, that conflagrations and constitutions keep close company, and that established statehood rests upon triumphant violence. It is grimly appropriate that every year, as fireworks misfire and canoes overturn, the Fourth of July is marked with a few more American deaths. Independence is risky. Strangely, high summer's only other significant national anniversary is V-J Day, celebrating Japan's surrender to our atomic bombs.

One's own memories of the Fourth tend to blend, much as summer days blend one into the next. My father, in the firefly-rife backyard of my first home, lights a bundle of little firecrackers and darts dramatically back, and we all stand around in an awed circle, at what we hope is a safe distance, as the device twists and jumps and shouts its furious, frustrated noise. It wants to kill us, and can't. I hold a sparkler at arm's length, marvelling that its sparks do not burn. Then there is something we children call a "snake," which combustively turns itself into a coil of gray ash. How one acquires such things is at least as fascinating as their ignition: they are illegal in Pennsylvania and have been smuggled in from other, more permissive states; the illicit traffic in fireworks is as signal a feature of our national life as the different-colored license plates, the drinking ages that go up and down as state borders are crossed, and, for real grown-ups, the patchwork of statutes controlling divorce and abortion. These discrepancies help make the United States an interesting place to inhabit, and hint at what the original uniters were contending with.

Later, myself a father, I drove station wagons full of sleepyheads to towns and beaches and country clubs where firework displays, ever threatened by local regulations and limited budgets, still occurred. Once, off the Edgartown dock, we watched fireworks in a dense fog—subtle tints appeared in the mist above us, and explosive noises tardily descended. At the Essex County Club, in Manchester-by-the-Sea, a golf course was the site, and members, in summer tuxedos and full-length dresses, watched from within a roped-off enclave while we non-members huddled in the sand traps. In 1976, on the two-hundredth anniversary of our independence—a beautiful day all across the country—my wife and I flew from Chicago, and under us, from Indiana to Massachusetts, fireworks silently expanded and vanished like small soft radiant dandelion polls. A few years later, she and I were part of the immense throng that observes July Fourth in Washington, D.C., filling the Mall from the Lincoln Memorial to the Capitol lawn; the fireworks, in the vicinity of the Washington Monument, seemed very far away, as most things are in this grandly diffuse city. And recently, just last summer, returning to my own yard after wearying of a local display, I discovered that fireworks look biggest and most astonishing when seen above and through trees—like the moon (that old dud that won't quite wink out) they take impressiveness from a near horizon. These giant chrysanthemums and jellyfish seemed, thrusting and pulsing just above the silhouettes of my arbor vitae and hickory tree, visitations from space, from beyond our shadowy three dimensions.

Of course there is more to the Fourth of July than fireworks. There are, or used to be, parades and footraces, clambakes and corn-on-the-cob, doubleheaders and sunburn and beer and dyspepsia. Its virtue as a holiday is that one is not expected to give any gifts or eat any large bird; its disadvantage is its delayed climax. It goes on all day. An enormous novel once of some fame, Ross Lockridge's *Raintree County*, took place entirely (with flashbacks) on July 4, 1892. At some moment during the day one has the sensation of being in Kansas. July Fourth is as close to the center of the year as Topeka is to the geographical center of the forty-eight conterminous states. It is the unmoving pivot, a little frightening in its stillness, a stillness we hear between the bursts of firecrackers, the crashing advance and pebble-rattling retreat of waves, the roar of powerboats, the radios in the sand, the hiss of pop-tops being pulled. Not all our deliberate and defiant fun can quite hide the long day's dry American silence. The clouds are high wisps of icy cirrus; it's cold up there. The tops of your feet and tip of your nose hurt from too many ultraviolet rays, and even after a shower, sand keeps trickling down your neck. The grand set-piece finale, with its starlike spinning rockets and undulating red and white stripes and grimacing eagle outlined in phosphorus, rather fizzles, even though the Independence Day Observance Committee invested a fortune in it and the fireworks contractor (a Japanese company, as it happens) virtually guaranteed success. Like most birthday parties, the Fourth of July makes us a little wary, a touch cranky. We want to go to bed. Tomorrow, let high summer dawn.

Our National Monuments

THIS DEMOCRACY'S FAVORITE MONUMENTS have evolved through processes that in retrospect seem random and chancy, out of seeds of inspiration in one or two determined individuals, under clouds of debate and delay and budget shortfall, into an impalpable rapport with the masses. In 1987 the seven most visited national sites were, in order—according to the statistics of the U.S. Park Service—the Lincoln Memorial, the Vietnam Veterans Memorial, the Statue of Liberty, the St. Louis Arch, the Jefferson Memorial in Washington, Mount Rushmore, and the Washington Monument. The poor showing of the last-named seems surprising; but one has to stand in a three-hour line, on a summer day, to ride to the top of the monument, whereas the Lincoln Memorial is an easy walk-through at the end of the Reflecting Pool. The nearby Vietnam Veterans Memorial is undoubtedly the nation's most emotional spot now, its eloquent starkness of engraved black panels crowded with the written and floral tributes of wives and parents and sweethearts and fellow soldiers for whom the war and its wounds are still fresh memories. But such warm-blooded immediacy is rare in major monuments; Washington was dead for seventy-seven years, Lincoln for fifty-seven, and Jefferson for well over a century when their monuments were at last dedicated.

At the time of his death in 1885, Ulysses S. Grant was, we are assured, "undoubtedly the most popular man in America." A crowd of over one million attended his funeral and, twelve years later, the dedication, in New York City, of the Grant Monument, popularly known as "Grant's Tomb"—a classical mausoleum comparable in sheer size and costliness only, in nineteenth-century America, to the Washington Monument and the Statue of Liberty. But over the years the crowds who came to this vast shrine thinned, the last veteran in the Grand Army of the Republic passed away, and Grant's heroic generalship became diluted, in our shifting historical memory, by our awareness of his weaknesses and the sad corruption of his Presidential administrations. Warmth has ebbed from Grant's memorial, though its park is still gratefully used. The eventual fate of all monuments is to become, like the Sphinx, a riddle.

The word "monument" derives from the Latin *monere*, "to advise or remind." To achieve its monitory, mnemonic objective, the monument should be striking in some way, usually in its great size, from which comes the secondary meaning of "monumental." The Washington Monument was and still is the world's tallest masonry structure, the Statue of Liberty its largest freestanding statue, the faces of Mount Rushmore its grandest examples of sculpture, the St. Louis Arch—properly, the Jefferson National Expansion Memorial—its highest arch by far, containing more stainless steel than any other human project. To erect these symbolic marvels, engineers must cope with unprecedented challenges and create inventive solutions.

For instance, the Bunker Hill Monument, a granite obelisk two hundred twenty-one feet high in the Charlestown section of Boston, occasioned, in 1826, the building of the first railway in the United States. The monument, which, in the words of a fund-raising flier, "As it will commemorate the *Greatest Event* in the history of civil liberty [the battle of June 17, 1775], should be, and *shall be*, the grandest Monument in the world," required large blocks of gray granite from a quarry in Quincy that thenceforth was named Bunker Hill Ledge. A three-mile rail line from the quarry to the shore was constructed, with granite sleepers, wooden rails topped by iron plates, and a continuous chain that enabled the loaded cars, travelling downhill, to pull up the empty ones. Yet the loading and unloading at the Quincy and Charlestown wharves proved troublesome, and the Granite Railway Company, failing to justify its disproportionate expense, was replaced by the time-honored method of ox teams, which pulled the blocks the twelve overland miles to Bunker Hill. The original design called for courses of stone eighteen inches high; the final architect, Solomon Willard, asked for blocks two and a half feet wide, and twelve feet long. The extraction and handling of such massive stones prompted the invention of a number of ingenious hoisting jacks, with worm gears and lifting wedges. Most important, a steam-driven crane was designed by the Boston seaman Almoran Holmes; its boom had a range of fifty feet and could be rotated through three hundred sixty degrees. The latter stages of construction were greatly eased and speeded by this improvement over ox-powered hoisting. Willard wrote admiringly, "This hoisting apparatus is remarkable for its compass, and for the ease and grace with which it performs its work. . . . This apparatus, with some variation, has come into general use, and is so well contrived for the purpose intended, as to leave little to be wished for, in regard to apparatus for hoisting." Also, marvels of stone carving were achieved to fit inside the obelisk a center core, in exactly twice as many courses as the exterior, with a curved stair and a conical air space.

An obelisk manages to combine, in its form, aggressiveness and eternity, peace and a spear. Obelisks in ancient Egypt, appearing first as grave markers, came to be used to celebrate pharaonic jubilees and, their pyramidal summits plated with shiny electrum, as symbols of sun worship. Despite their immense weight, a number were taken to Europe, and one such "Cleopatra's needle" adorns New York City's Central Park. The obelisk became a popular nineteenth-century motif of tombstones and a monumental rival to the triumphal column, a Roman form found in the Place Vendôme, in Trafalgar Square (Nelson's column), and in Baltimore, as a monument to George Washington. The idea of a monument to Washington is as old as the Continental Congress, which in 1783 passed a resolution in favor of an equestrian statue of the toga-clad general. Washington himself objected to the expense and the matter was dropped. No sooner was he dead, however, in 1799, than the matter revived; the jurist John Marshall proposed a marble mausoleum in the form of a pyramid one hundred feet square at the base. Three decades later, Henry Clay cried in Congress, "As a monument, rear it; spend on it what you will; make it as durable as the Pyramids, eternal as the mountains!" In 1836 a competition was held, and the contending entries included Italian campaniles, English Gothic towers, and, most grotesquely, a structure, proposed by a California architect, showing "affinity with some of the better Hindu pagodas" and featuring a giant statue of Washington "attended by ladies gracefully leaning on their elbows." Even the winning entry, by Robert Mills, called for gigantic stars on the obelisk, at its six-hundred-foot-high tip a statue of Washington in a Roman chariot driving four horses, and around the base a colonnaded Greek temple one hundred feet high with thirty columns twelve feet across. All these elaborate features were fortunately dropped during the actual construction, one of the most prolonged and tortuous labors in the history of America's sacred places.

In the three decades after Washington's death, Congress had proved readier to come up with florid praise of the first President than with funds and legislation enacting a monument. In 1833, private citizens formed the Washington National Monument Society, which held a competition for the design and attempted to raise money by way of the 1840 census, awarding lithographs to contributors. By 1847, $70,000 had been collected, enough to finance the commencement of construction; on July 4, 1848, with impressive Masonic rites, a cornerstone was laid, though no one now knows which stone it was. By 1854, $300,000 had been raised, and the shaft had been raised to the height of a hundred fifty feet. There it stopped for over twenty years. The approaching War Between the States and its aftermath extended the interruption, but the affair of the "Pope's Stone" was the immediate cause. As anyone who has walked up the steps inside the Washington Monument realizes, the interior walls hold about two hundred memorial stones donated by states, cities, organizations, Indian tribes, and foreign states. Pope Pius IX sent a block from the Temple of Concord in Rome, and the Know-Nothings, a xenophobic secret society especially antagonistic to Roman Catholicism, attacked the watchman on the night of March 5, 1854, carried off the "Pope's Stone," and presumably dumped it in the Potomac. The next year, on the eve of a substantial congressional appropriation for completion of the great shaft, the Know-Nothings broke into the office of the society, stole all the books and records, and claimed to be in possession of the monument, which they promised to complete as "an American institution, supported by all Americans."

But the easily observed change of color about a third of the way up the obelisk does not relate, as is sometimes thought, to a change from imported Italian to native marble. Up to 1854, the monument was faced with marble from a quarry at Texas, Maryland, just north of Baltimore. Upon resumption in 1879, four courses were laid with marble from Lee, Massachusetts; but this proved too expensive, and the remainder of its five-hundred-fifty-five-foot height was finished with marble from Cockeysville, in the Piedmont section of Maryland. In late December of 1884, thirty-six years after its unknown cornerstone had been laid, the monument was capped with a stone weighing a ton and a half and topped by a hundred-pound pyramid of pure aluminum. The giant obelisk was at this time the tallest structure in the world, and it remains, by civic decree, the tallest building in the nation's capital.

Before the era of skyscrapers and airplane travel, such vertical monuments and mountaintops were the only means whereby men could view their world from above. Now that aerial views are commonplace, sacred places tend to hug the earth; indeed, the Vietnam Veterans Memorial descends into it, to the depth of ten feet. The most heroically high American monument is the Jefferson National Expansion Monument, designed by Eero Saarinen and erected to symbolize the city of St. Louis's historical role as gateway to the West; it would arch over the Washington Monument with more than sixty feet of clearance. The construction of this great parabola of stainless steel, from 1962 to 1965, with the MacDonald Construction Company as general contractor, involved prodigies of improvisatory engineering. The arch was assembled of one hundred forty-two non-interchangeable segments, equilaterally triangular in cross-section. Prefabricated in Pittsburgh, they consisted of an outer skin of quarter-inch stainless steel and an inner skin of carbon steel; the gap between the skins, three feet at the bottom of the arch and less than eight inches at the top, was filled with reinforced concrete up to the three-hundred-foot mark and then left hollow but for interconnecting braces. The first six sections, to a height of seventy-two feet, were stacked by crawler cranes on the ground; for the rest, a kind of twin railroad into the sky was devised. Eighty-ton work platforms climbed the two legs of the arch on tracks of thirty-inch steel beams spaced twenty-four feet apart. Telescoping supports kept the work platforms, with their own heated shacks, tool sheds, and sanitary facilities, level as they climbed the arch. When a height of five hundred thirty feet was reached, the original plan to use guy cables for stability was scrapped in favor of that of a sixty-ton steel stabilizing truss nearly as long as a football field. Yet amid all these dimensions and tonnages an almost microscopic precision had to be maintained: an error of as little as a sixty-fourth of an inch would cause trouble at the top, when the two segments met. The steel walls were cambered one and a half inches every thirty-five feet to allow for welding deformation, and geometry control readings were taken at night, to eliminate the factor of uneven expansion in the sun's heat. The last segment fit perfectly.

Heat expansion also figured in the construction of the Statue of Liberty nearly a century before. The outside of the one-hundred-fifty-one-foot-high statue consists of copper sheets three-thirty-seconds of an inch thick—a hair thicker than a penny—beaten into shape over wooden forms; its interior structure was designed by the great French engineer Gustave Eiffel. Eiffel concocted a gridwork of iron bars shaped to follow the convolutions of Frédéric Bartholdi's statue; the armature bars were not directly attached to the copper skin but were fitted loosely into U-shaped saddles riveted to it, thus enabling the great sheets of shaped copper to expand and contract in the weather. In preparation for the renovation of the Statue in the 1980s, a team discovered that all 1,705 of these bars were frozen into place by corrosion; the replacement of 1,699 of them was one of the most painstaking and crucial, though unspectacular, aspects of the renovation, whose most prominent improvement was the de-electrification of the torch and a return to Bartholdi's original concept of a gilded, reflective flame. The entire renovation, in passing, generated another monumental "most": the scaffolding at no point touched the statue and was therefore the largest freestanding scaffolding ever built.

News stories about the heavily publicized restoration spoke of the pride and *esprit de corps* among the workmen. The quixotic actualization of these enormous symbols does seem to inspire the work crews. Our monuments generally have good safety records: the construction of the St. Louis Arch, calculated to cost the lives of thirteen workmen, in fact proved fatality-free, and the Mount Rushmore sculptures, though carved at a perilous height amid a number of mishaps, caused injuries but no deaths in their fourteen years of creation, from 1927 to 1941. Not the least accomplishment of Gutzon Borglum, the headstrong creator of the gigantic sculptures, was his uniting of a crew of mostly local South Dakota mine workers and roughnecks into an artistic instrument that, with dynamite and jackhammers, sensitively translated his vision to a granite mountaintop. One of the crew, Red Anderson, said shortly before his death thirty-six years after work stopped, "I think now that Rushmore has been ninety percent of my life." Borglum himself devised the sling-seats that held the men secure as they drilled at the cliff-face. And Borglum, who had previously worked on Stone Mountain near Atlanta and there used a photo-projector for his aborted bas-relief, invented for Mount Rushmore a boom-and-plumb-bob arrangement whereby points could be transferred, at the enlargement of an inch to a foot, from his three-dimensional models to the rugged volumes of the mountain. Studying photographs of the plaster models, one is struck by how much more aesthetically successful the actual full-scaled heads are, emerging in their giant sunstruck simplicity from the natural mass of white granite. The monument, because of Borglum's death and the advent of World War II, was left uncompleted; Borglum's last model calls for the four Presidents to be carved down to the hems of their coats, with Lincoln's hand clutching his lapel. A comic effect of crowding might have been produced among the mountainous half-giants, where the bodiless but finished heads have a surreal dignity in their close placement and abstract union with the natural rock.

A happy providence, it may be, has watched over our foremost national monuments, stopping them short at a grand simplicity. The Vietnam Veterans Memorial, we are surprised to learn, was first designed by Maya Lin with a row of toppling stone dominoes in front of the wall of names—an obstructing pun her Yale classmates persuaded her to eliminate. We are moved, often, by effects that can scarcely have been planned—the sheer loneliness, for example, of the Washington Monument on its bare knoll and the slight tilt of the round plaza of the United States Navy Memorial on Pennsylvania Avenue, a tilt that makes us feel we are on the deck of a ship with the statue, just a bit greater than life size, of the Lone Sailor and his duffle bag. This plaza, a map of the world carried out in two tones of granite, embodies a new breakthrough in stone cutting, a method of cutting an irregular line with a high-powered, computer-directed jet of water and silica slurry. Without this technique, which can slice two-inch granite a half-inch per minute on intricately curved cuts, the tightly fitting coastlines of the map could not have been carved. Advanced stoneworking techniques contributed as well to the emotional impact of the black granite tablets—imported from India, since all American granite was streaked with gray—that make up the Vietnam Veterans Memorial; the mirroring polish was imparted, in the final stage, by a felt buffer covered with tin oxide, which is finer than talc. The beauty and legibility of the lettering were finely calibrated; they are precisely thirty-eight thousandths of an inch deep, and were grit-blasted from the front, giving a central valley that minimizes shadow, with a fine aluminum oxide.

The newest major American monument, the planned Astronauts' Memorial in Florida, also employs highly polished granite—a mirror-finished sheet, fifty feet wide and forty high, which will reflect the sky while angled mirrors behind it shine sunlight through the dead astronauts' names, which are perforated in the stone and filled with glass or a light-diffusing epoxy. The names—twelve men and two women have died so far in the space program—will thus appear to float in a reflected sky; the slab is mounted and motorized to track the sun through the day, and at night electric light will shine through the names. The emotional effect of this apparatus must wait upon its construction; in its depictions the memorial seems possibly too glitzy and tricky. Its designers claim that a technological venture warrants a technological memorial; but technology can outrace our aesthetic sense and trivialize perduring matter. We expect our monuments to be simple and still—emblems of permanence to which we bring the living, changing flowers of homage.

We expect monuments, too, to be low-maintenance and relatively immune to the erosions of time. In fact, nothing material is totally immune; even the giant faces of Mount Rushmore are constantly inspected for fissures and repaired. Rust and corrosion attack metal, frost and spalling attack stone, and vandalism and acid rain are on the rise. Frequent repairs of the Saratoga Battle Monument, a Gothicized obelisk erected over a century ago along the Hudson, cannot keep pace with the "structural distress" wrought by climatic dampness and cold. New York City, embarrassed by its plethora of ill-maintained monuments, has enlisted the private sector in an "Adopt a Monument" program. And there is a danger, even in our spacious capital city, of too many monuments; the long delay in building the Franklin Delano Roosevelt Memorial, though its funds have been already voted by Congress, shows a traditional American reluctance to monumentalize individuals. The severely simple horizontal monolith that Roosevelt himself designed to mark his grave at Hyde Park perhaps is already a perfect sufficiency. A monument needs space around it, and time as well. A clutter and proliferation of sacred symbols and sites is a sign of decadence in religion, including the secular religion of patriotism. A monument should be singular. It should be somewhat blank, like a battlefield long afterwards. Fate and happenstance have endowed this democracy with a constellation of remarkably varied and aesthetically impressive representations of our national adventure, and this endowment should be enlarged with care.

The Importance of Fiction

WELL, when the importance of something has to be proclaimed, it can't be all that important. And certainly most of the people in the United States get along without reading fiction, and more and more magazines get along without printing it. Even *Esquire,* which used to run short stories as automatically as he-men smoked unfiltered cigarettes, has to whip itself up and cheer itself on to give us an issue like this one [its August 1984 Special Fiction Issue].

The old throwbacks still producing fiction should be grateful, and we are. It's hard to believe that this fragile business ever had any muscle, but it did. In Gutenberg's Gymnasium, Dickens and Balzac worked out on the high rings and the Brontë sisters did the backward flip in unison on the balance beam and Harriet Beecher Stowe bench-pressed more kilos than Herman Melville, while Flaubert and Mark Twain were just a double blur on the parallel bars and the bourgeoisie in the bleachers went wild. Even in the days of network radio, fiction put hair on Hemingway's chest and gin in Fitzgerald's glass and that far-off starry look in Faulkner's eye, those days when the mules weren't running. But after Hitler's coonskin was nailed to the barn door and the boys came back to make babies and put on gray flannel suits, something went out of fiction. Those good folks who sat around in the kitchen near the wood stove reading about Mr. Tutt and Perry Mason in the *Saturday Evening Post* had slipped out the back door and bought oil burners and television sets, and the aura of the party being over was so pervasive that Norman Mailer tried to be a party all by himself. Saul Bellow kept winning the prizes but there was something effete and professorial about his appeal, compared with the way Sinclair Lewis and John Steinbeck had reached down and given Main Street a shake, and the way those two-dollar books of theirs had stood on the windowsills of every small-town piano teacher's front parlor.

The Sixties were when the demise of fiction became something to crow about. Philip Roth told us that life in America had become so barbaric and bizarre that no fiction could hold a candle to the grotesque truth. Truman Capote allowed as how he had invented a new kind of narrative treat, the non-fiction novel, that made the un-non kind as obsolete as hand-churned ice cream. Tom Wolfe (the younger) let us ineluctably know that his new journalism was zippier, grabbier, funnier, wilder, and truer-to-life than any old wistful bit of fiction published by, say, those tiny giants over at *The New Yorker*. Even in *The New Yorker*, as the old two-column departments died off and were replaced by learned specialists whose exhaustive poop overflowed the narrow columns like freshly singed popcorn, there was less space for fiction than there had been in the days of Bob Benchley or even the days of Nat Benchley. The revolution had little use for fiction: fiction was sublimation, it was Leavis and Trilling, it was graduate school; it was civilization and its discontents, it was the lonely crowd. Fiction was how you consoled yourself in the dark ages before love beads and Lucy in the Sky with Diamonds. A revolution sings songs and trashes chain-store windows; it does things in a bunch, and nothing is more antisocial and non-tribal than one individual sitting in a quiet room coding make-believe for another individual to decipher in a quiet room maybe tens of years and thousands of miles away.

Accordingly, the revolution left us rock music and co-ed dormitories but not much in the way of fiction. Who now remembers Marge Piercy's *Dance the Eagle to Sleep* and Gurney Norman's *Divine Right's Trip?* I do, because I reviewed them. Otherwise, there were Pynchon and Kesey, who have subsequently tended to imitate the sound of one hand clapping. The post-revolutionary anticlimax, though, has not lacked for bards, beginning with Ann Beattie, who found the right filtered tone to let the lack of sunshine in, and who, young as she is, has played dearth mother to a vast fresh bevy of tender/tough female talents, such as Mary Robison, Laurie Colwin, Elizabeth Tallent, T. Gertler, Andrea Lee, Deborah Eisenberg, to name but a few. The young males aren't quite so vivid, since, having made their entry splash, they tend to sink into full-time extra-literary employment or to sidestroke toward Hollywood, like John Sayles. But, however the generations take them, fiction's magnificent opportunities, as demonstrated in the classics, abide.

Fiction is nothing less than the subtlest instrument for self-examination and self-display that Mankind has invented yet. Psychology and X-rays bring up some portentous shadows, and demographics and stroboscopic photography do some fine breakdowns, but for the full *parfum* and effluvia of being human, for feathery ambiguity and rank facticity, for the air and iron, fire and spit of our daily mortal adventure there is nothing like fiction: it makes sociology look priggish, history problematical, the cinema two-dimensional, and *The National Enquirer* as silly as last week's cereal box.

In fiction, everything that searchers for the important tend to leave out is left in, and what they would have in is left out. Stendhal had served devotedly under Napoleon and was one of the most lucid thinkers in Europe, but what Fabrizio, in *The Charterhouse of Parma*, makes of Waterloo is sheer confusion, highlighted by a running conversation with a *cantinière* steering her cartful of brandy through the thick of the battle. For Tolstoy, Napoleon was an excuse for the Moscow aristocrats to gossip and to push on with their spiritual searches; for Jane Austen, Napoleon was the reason the English countryside was so sparsely equipped with prospective husbands. Thus a vast historical presence refracts down into little lives which are precious only because they resemble our own. Kutuzov, Tolstoy's splendidly fictionalized version of an actual Russian general, reads French romances while the steppes around him tremble at the approach of the superman, the master strategist, the general of supreme genius. Romances safeguard the importance of our sentiments amid the uncontrollable large-scale surges that constitute history; the inner lives of the obscure, as Erich Auerbach points out in his *Mimesis,* have been, from the New Testament on, the peculiar and precious burden of the Western narrative imagination.

The fiction writer is the ombudsman who argues our humble, dubious case in the halls of eternal record. Are defecation, tipsy bar babble, days of accumulating small defeats, and tired, compromised, smelly connubial love part of our existence? Then put them into literature alongside of Homer, says *Ulysses.* Has a life been ill-spent in snobbery, inaction, neurasthenia, and heartache? Then make that life into a verbal cathedral, says *Remembrance of Things Past.* Do pathetic and senseless-seeming murders appear daily in the newspapers? Then show the humble aspirations and good intentions and small missteps that inexorably lead to such ruin, say *Tess of the D'Urbervilles* and *An American Tragedy.* Feeling nervous, and as though things don't quite add up? Then write like Virginia Woolf, and give us actuality in its sliding, luminous increments. Feeling worse than nervous, and certain that the world is a mess? Then write like Céline, and wake up the French language. Want a taste of Latin American back-country blues? Try Graham Greene or Gabriel García Márquez. Want to know what goes on in those tacky developments across the highway? Let Raymond Carver or Bobbie Ann Mason tell you. Curious about the condo life in the new, homogenized Deep South? Here comes Frederick Barthelme. No soul or locale is too humble to be the site of entertaining and instructive fiction. Indeed, all other things being equal, the rich and glamorous are *less* fertile ground than the poor and plain, and the dusty corners of the world of more real interest than its glittering, already sufficiently publicized centers.

Yet we do not read fiction for information, informative though it can be. Unlike journalism, history, or sociology, fiction does not give us facts snug in their accredited truth, to be accepted and absorbed like pills, for our undoubted good; we *make* fiction true, as we read it. Fiction can poison our minds, as it did those of Madame Bovary and Don Quixote. It offers to enlarge our sense of possibilities, of potential freedom; and freedom is dangerous. The bourgeois, capitalist world, compared with the medieval hierarchies it supplanted and with the Communist hierarchies that would supplant it, *is* a dangerous one, where failure can be absolute and success may be short-lived. The novel and the short story rose with the bourgeoisie, as exercises in democratic feeling and in individual adventure. *Pamela, The Pilgrim's Progress, Robinson Crusoe*—what do they tell us but that our entrepreneurism, on one level or another, may succeed? If fiction is in decline, it is because we have lost faith in the capacity of the individual to venture forth and suffer the consequences of his dreams. Myself, I feel that this most flexible and capacious of artistic forms still holds out its immense space to our imaginations, still answers to a hope within us of more adventure. What is important, if not the human individual? And where can individuality be better confronted, appraised, and enjoyed than in fiction's shapely lies?

High Art Versus Popular Culture

LIKE MANY ANOTHER would-be practitioner in the arts, I caught the bug from popular culture: coloring books, animated cartoons, comic books, songs on the radio, radio drama and comedy, the so-called slick magazines, and the movies. These, in the era before television, filled my waking and dream life with images of glamour, heroism, grace, droll resilience, and doomed beauty. To get on the mysterious other side of this veil of illusion and become, like Frank Morgan's foxy Wizard of Oz, a producer of it, seemed self-evidently worth aspiring to. I began by copying comic-strip characters from the daily newspaper and have ended up by writing novels and book reviews, but the causes of this deflected career—opportunity, aptitude—seem merely accidental compared with the seminal impulse toward pretense and performance; I would not have minded becoming a movie star like Errol Flynn or a pop comedian like Jack Benny or a dancer like Ray Bolger. Just as long as it wasn't a real job, that took place in the world I could see around me, where my father and the fathers of my friends labored.

Since popular culture nurtures us as children and serves lifelong as culture enough for the majority of our fellow countrymen, it seems ungrateful to seek out what distinguishes it from "high" art. In the field of fiction, the distinction seems especially elusive, since all fiction is designed to be read and, before that, to be bought. Producing a best-seller does not utterly disgrace a "serious" novelist—Nabokov, Pasternak, Philip Roth, E. L. Doctorow have all done it—but a consistent best-seller producer like James Michener and Stephen King makes us uneasy; there must be something wrong with him. The novel, but a few centuries old, began as a form of popular culture, and the large and weepy publics of Dickens and Dostoevsky are part, though not the "highest" part, of their greatness. This century brought with it a disdain for the crowd-pleasers of the previous, and if Henry James never quite realized that the price of excellence is a large neglect, James Joyce and Marcel Proust certainly did; the publication of their masterpieces required, respectively, heavy patronage and a private income. Yet Mann's *Buddenbrooks* was widely enjoyed, and the taint of popular success clung to Hemingway, for all his purism, and commercial dealings pursued the hectically modernist Faulkner.

No convenient market distinction exists in fiction like that in art between commercial illustration, created for reproduction, and easel painting, created for single sale and museum display. Chester Gould's Dick Tracy is popular culture; Andy Warhol's copy of Gould's Dick Tracy is high art. A more complicated appeal is essayed by the latter—ironical, self-referential, and aimed at connoisseurs. High art, we might say, is art which presumes knowledge of other art; popular culture is prepared to deal with the untutored. The difference is not very deep, it seems to me, and crossovers and problematical instances are not hard to find. The thrust—the basic exploitation of our human weakness for color and rhythm, story and spectacle—is the same, and while popular culture need know nothing of high art, a high art entirely detached from popular culture would be as sterile as Esperanto or the Enlightenment religion invented by the *philosophes*.

Popular Music

FOR MANY, popular music is more pain than pleasure, and any of us, trapped on a subway car with a ghetto blaster or in an elevator leaking old Montovani, might admit there is much too much of it. That hypothetical visitor from Mars we used to talk about, before Mars was exposed as a spherical pink desert lightly frosted at the poles, would surely be struck by this incessant and apparently inutile accompaniment to earthly lives, as we move from musical alarm clock to car radio to a workplace insidiously saturated with psychologically programmed Muzak through a lunchtime stroll amid mendicant buskers and break-dancers and, after work, to a tinkling drink in a bar with an old-fashioned jukebox and, if not home to a suburban house where teen-age children have their tapes turned way up, then on to a romantic rendezvous orchestrated by a gypsy band at the restaurant, a cocktail pianist with the nightcap, and sleepy old Sinatra records in the dimmed apartment. What do they *mean*, all these tunes, as miraculously as snowdrops no two quite alike but again like snowdrops melting over the days into gray slush and then into air, thin air?

Hormones, the answer must be. Popular music, save for the small fraction designed to excite martial or religious ardor, has to do with mating and break-up, with love and its losses, with the anticipation of love reaching deep into childhood (Lollypop Pop) and its recollection extending far into senescence (Golden Oldies). We dance, we touch, we shut our eyes, we become the song. From the decades' massive flow of technologically broadcast songs we each extract an emotional autobiography. The first popular songs that memorably impinged upon my evolution were "Playmates," with its oddly thrilling invitation to "look down my rain barrel, slide down my cellar door," and, in 1939, "Oh, Johnny!" The little girls chanted "How you can love!" at me on the way to second grade and back, my ears and cheeks burning and all my conscious desires simply bent upon getting to my next balsa-wood model airplane.

Then came the Great Patriotic War, and "Sleepy Lagoon" and "Paper Doll" and "That Old Black Magic" (icy fingers up and down my spine!) along with the relatively asexual "Mairsy Doats" (but what did it *mean*, to "kiddley-divey, too"?) and "Praise the Lord and Pass the Ammunition." Postwar, there was high school, and dances in the gym, and drooping crêpe paper affixed to the basketball backboard, and plump white strapless shoulders in the violet lights, and "Tenderly," and "They Say It's Wonderful," and six boys on the stage doing our local small-band version of the big-band sound, saving (what else?) "Star Dust" for last.

The hormones had the tune down pat, though the lyrics still wondered why they spent the lonely nights dreaming of a song. The big-band sound was an erotic engine, a soft machine of sax-throb and phallic clarinet moving down its tracks as irresistibly as the Chattanooga choo-choo. That certain party at the station, in old satin and lace, we used to call Funny Face turned into Doris Day announcing a sentimental journey ("never thought my heart could be so yearny") whose final prolonged syllable "ho-o-o-ommmmme" pulled open a delicious abyss of female power. On the jukebox at Stephens' Sweet Shop, the sly laid-back melodiousness of Bing Crosby and the Ink Spots gave way to big, twanging voices: Frankie Laine and Patti Page, "That Lucky Old Sun" and "Tennessee Waltz." Laine was especially thrilling, hollering to his mules and his ghost riders in the sky and wanting to go where the wild goose went and mincing out the exact specifics of his "dee-zy-yuh" ("we'll sip a little glass of wine, I'll gaze into your eyes divine, I'll feel the touch of your lips, press-*sing* on mi-yun"). His voice was gutsy; it rubbed those secret spots within.

The popular music of the late Forties and early Fifties, falling between the fading of the big bands and the beginning of rock, is generally forgotten; no jazzomaniacs or rock addicts or show-tune nuts visit its files, and Golden Oldie disc jockeys rarely touch it. But it has preëmpted millions of my neurons with half-remembered titles and lyrics. Girls' names: "Peg o' My Heart" and "Amy" and "Laura" and "Linda" ("when I go to sleep, I never count sheep, I count all the charms about Linda"). Strange little men: "The Old Lamplighter" and "Nature Boy" and that old master painter from the faraway hills whom we teen-agers so inevitably recast as the old masturbator. Who could get moony over "Golden Earrings" or "Tree in the Meadow"? We could, that's who. In 1948 James C. Petrillo called every orthodox musician out on strike and left us to dream along with ununionized sweet potatoes, banjos, bones, whistling choruses ("Heartaches"), and musical saws; we dreamed on anyhow. "So Tired," made great in Russ Morgan's arrangement, was, with "Star Dust," the epitome of violet-spotlight chic, the draggy end of the high-school dance, the fag end of our sophisticated smoky days—"so tired, so tired of living" and all of seventeen.

Then came college and, for me, a kind of pop silence. There was no music in the libraries then, and little in the dorms—it was believed to interfere with thought processes, rather than (as now) to be essential to them. I do seem to recall, from those four lost years, incredulously auditing in a humble Cambridge eatery Johnny Ray's "The Little White Cloud That Cried." I knew it was the end of something, but I didn't know of how very much. Rock 'n' roll began to shake the Eisenhower chapel; Elvis

Presley suddenly achieved divinity—but all out of my earshot. The first song I remember distinctly getting to me, post-grad, was "Blueberry Hill," where Fats Domino claimed to have found his thrill. Was finding your thrill anything like kiddley-diveying? No matter: I knew in my hormones what he meant, and just why Chubby Checker wanted to twist again like we did last summer. We had become suburbanites and wage-earners and parents, but our glands were less quiescent than they should have been: the sounds of revolution (Baez and Dylan; Peter, Paul, and Mary; Sonny and Cher) trickled through the Marimekko curtains, and our children taught us to frug. Oh, those glorious piping sugar-harmonied Supremes records before Diana Ross became a law unto herself! And of course the Beatles, who were intellectually ambitious even, and kept going deeper, just like Beethoven. I suppose my heartfelt farewell to popular music came in England, at the end of the Sixties, crooning and thumping and blinking back tears through the endless chorus of "Hey Jude," in which the Beatles could be heard dissolving. Take a sad song and make it better.

But you never really say goodbye; popular music is always there, flavoring our American lives, keeping our mortal beat, a murmuring subconscious sneaking up out of the car radio with some abrupt sliding phrase that hooks us into jubilation, into aspiration. I like it when, say, Madonna's "True Blue" comes on: catchy. Long ago, driving to school with my father on cold winter mornings, I would lean into the feeble glow of the radio dial as if into warmth: this was me, this yearniness canned in New York and beamed from Philadelphia, beamed through the air to guide me, somehow, toward a wonderful life.

The Boston Red Sox, as of 1986

FORTY YEARS AGO and four hundred miles from Boston, I sat in my father's Chevrolet, in the Shillington (Pennsylvania) High School parking lot, and listened to the seventh game of the 1946 World Series, the Red Sox versus the Cardinals. Eighth inning, score 3–3, Cardinals up, Enos Slaughter on first base, Harry Walker at the plate; there's a hit to center field, Culberson (substituting for the injured Dom DiMaggio) throws to the infield, shortstop Johnny Pesky cuts it off—Slaughter is being waved around third! Pesky hesitates, the throw is late, Slaughter scores!! The Cardinals hold on to win the game and the World Series. I don't know if I cried, sitting alone in that venerable Chevrolet, but I was only fourteen and well might have. Dazed and with something lost forever, I emerged into the golden September afternoon, where my classmates were nuzzling their steadies, sneaking smokes, and shooting baskets in a blissful animal innocence I could no longer share.

What had led me, who had never been north of Greenwich, Connecticut, and didn't know Beacon Hill from Bunker Hill or Fenway Park from the Public Garden, to attach my heart to that distant aggregation? Ted Williams had made a dent in my consciousness before the war, but it was the '46 Sox that made me a passionate fan. What a team that was!—Ted in left, Dom in center, Doerr at second, Pesky at short, big Rudy York having a great twilight season at first, Boo Ferriss and Tex Hughson on the mound. Though the Cardinals squeaked by them in that series, the Sox looked sure to cruise to pennants at least until I got out of high school in 1950. But in fact they didn't, coming perilously close in '48 and '49 but not quite having it in the clutch. The postwar pattern of thrills and spills was set, and whenever they came to Philadelphia, there I was, hanging by the radio.

With its nine defensive men widely spaced on the field, baseball is an easier game to visualize than a fast shuffle like basketball and hockey, and until girls and a driver's license got me by the throat I spent many an idyllic summer day indoors huddled on the easy chair next to the hoarse little family Philco. The announcers' voices in their granular shades of excitement, and the wraparound crowd noise, and the sound in the middle distance of the ball being hit, not to mention the uproarious clatter when a foul ball sailed into the broadcast booth, made a vivid picture in ways superior to what I would see when, once or twice a summer, I was bused the fifty miles to Shibe Park's bleachers. I even kept box scores of my audited games, and listened on the rainout days when the play-by-play of some remote and feeble contest like the Browns against the Senators would be verbalized from a teletype whose chattering could be heard in the lulls. The two Philadelphia teams were pretty feeble themselves, and created the vacuum into which my irrational ardor for the Red Sox nicely filled.

My barber was a Yankee fan; that was the other choice in Pennsylvania. As his scissors gnashed around my ears and his hair tonic ate into my scalp he would patiently again explain why Joe DiMaggio was a *team* player, and why as a team the Yankees would always *win*. But they didn't like Roosevelt or Truman at the barbershop, either, and I would rather lose with Boston than win with New York. When my college choices came down to Cornell or Harvard, the decision was obvious. And yet, those four years in Cambridge, it seems to have dawned on me rather rarely that the Red Sox were only two ten-minute subway rides (or, on a sunny day, a nice walk along the river) away. Living in New York, though, I would brave the West Side IRT up to the Bronx and from within the cavernous shadows of the Stadium admire the aging Williams as he matched strokes with Mickey Mantle, who had replaced DiMaggio as the hood ornament of the onrolling Yankees. The Fifties Red Sox didn't leave much of a mark on the record book, but they seem to have inspired an unflagging loyalty in me. While it is not entirely true that I moved from New York to New England to be closer to the Red Sox, it is not entirely false either. I wanted to keep Ted Williams company while I could.

Lying in backyards or on the beach, driving in the car or squinting into a book, I listened to the games, and internalized Curt Gowdy. That ever so soothing and sensible voice, with its guileless hint of Wyoming twang, relayed pop-ups and bloop hits, blowouts and shutouts; passing heroes like Clyde Vollmer and Ellis Kinder and Walt Dropo and Sammy White flitted across the airwaves, and Jackie Jensen and Jimmy Piersall glimmered in Williams's lengthening shadow. My wife's parents had a retreat on a far hill of Vermont, without electricity or telephone but with plenty of pine cones and bear turds in the woods. We parked our car on the edge of that woods, and there I would go, many an afternoon, to sit in the front seat and tune in the Red Sox. Curt's voice came in strong from (I think) Burlington—so strong that one day the car battery wouldn't turn the starter over, and we were stranded. I must have been the only man in New England who, rather than lose touch with the Red Sox, marooned his near and dear in a forest full of bears.

The older you get, the stranger your earlier selves seem, until you can scarcely remember having made their acquaintance at all. Whatever held me there, rapt by the radio, all those precious hours? Ted, of course, who was always doing something fascinating—getting injured, going off to Korea, vilifying the press, announcing his retirement, hitting .388, hitting Joe Cronin's housekeeper with a tossed bat, spitting at the stands, going fishing when he shouldn't, etc. But the Red Sox around him had a fascination, too; generous-spending Yawkey saw to it that there were always some other classy performers, and some hopeful passages in every season. Yet the wheels inevitably came off the cart, or were lubricated too late in the summer, and the Red Sox—like Mercutio, Scott Fitzgerald, and Adlai Stevenson—had that ultimate charm, the charm of losers.

All men are mortal, and therefore all men are losers; our profoundest loyalty goes out to the failed. Chris Evert, for example, did not win our hearts until Navratilova began to push her around, and I know a man who, to his own evident satisfaction, has been a Chicago Cubs fan for fifty years.

Are the killer Mets of today nearly as much fun as those hapless teams of post-expansion days, the "Amazing Mets" that New Yorkers, bored by the Yankees, clasped to their sardonic hearts? As a boy in Pennsylvania I felt sorry for Mr. Yawkey, that all his financial goodness couldn't buy a World Series. I felt sorry for Williams, that he didn't go five-for-five every day and that spiteful sportswriters kept cheating him of the MVP award. The Red Sox in my immature mind were like the man in the Hollywood movie who, because he's wearing a tuxedo, is bound to slip on a banana peel. They were gallantry and grace without the crassness of victory. I loved them. I might have loved some other team just as well—an infant gosling, if caught at the right moment, will fall in love with a zoologist instead of its mother, and a German, if kicked often enough, will fall in love with a shoe—but the Red Sox were the team I had chosen, and one's choices, once made, generate a self-justifying and self-sustaining inertia. All over the country, millions of fans root and holler for one team against another for no reason except that they have chosen to. Fanship is an *acte gratuit*, hurled into the face of an indifferent (or at least a preoccupied) universe.

Since Williams retired—dramatically, as usual—in 1960, my Red Sox ardor, with its abuse of car batteries, has cooled. But I have not been unaware, in the quarter-century since, of the pennants of 1967 and '75, and, just as in 1946, the subsequent seventh-game disappointments in the World Series. I remember, in fact, on a late-September Sunday of 1967, crouching with some other suburban men, in an interruption of a touch-football game, around a little radio on the grass as it told us that the Twins were losing to the Red Sox while the White Sox were beating the Tigers, thus allowing our Yastrzemski-led boys to back into their first pennant in twenty-one years. And I remember, as well, at the end of another season, in 1978, when my wife and I, heading for a Cambridge dinner party, parked along Memorial Drive and listened to the last inning of the Yankees–Red Sox playoff. We heard about the pokey Bucky Dent home run, and we heard in living audio the foul Yastrzemski pop-up. It was Slaughter rounding third all over again.

The memoirs of a Red Sox fan tend to sound sour, a litany of disappointments and mistakes going back to the day when Babe Ruth was traded. But the other side of this tails-up coin is that time and again the team, as its generations of personnel yield one to another, has worked its way to the edge of total victory. Yaz's famous pop-up, for instance, was preceded by a heroic week of solid victories, forcing the Yankees to a playoff, and in the game itself we (notice the reflexive-possessive pronoun) had fought back from a 5–2 deficit to 5–4 with the tying run on third. In sports, not only do you win some and lose some but twenty-five competitors, in a twenty-six-team sport, are going to come in lower than first. What makes Boston—little old Boston up here among the rocky fields and empty mills—think it deserves championship teams all the time? Having the Celtics may be miracle enough, not to mention a Patriots team that finally won in Miami. The founding Puritans left behind a lingering conviction that divine election is reflected in earthly success, and that this so-called city built upon a hill has hosies on a prime share. The scorn heaped in the Boston columns upon imperfect Red Sox teams is nothing if not self-righteous.

Now this summer's team, casually relegated by most April prophets to a fourth- or fifth-place finish, has made it to the playoffs. It seems a strange team to us veteran Red Sox watchers—solid, sometimes great pitching, and fitful, even anemic hitting. Where are the home runs of yesteryear? Wade Boggs singled his way to some batting championships, and now Jim Rice has choked up on the handle and is hitting for average, too. Only Baylor and Armas seem to be swinging from the heels any more. Heroism has moved from the plate to the pitchers' mound: Clemens so full of the Right Stuff his uniform fairly pops its buttons, and Hurst and Seaver looking just as resolute. Oil Can Boyd emerged from his month in the doghouse with an enhanced charisma; the one thing made clear in that murky episode* was how much we need him, his arm and his twitchy self-exhortations and his terrific name. And Sambito and Schiraldi staggered out of nowhere to help the much-abused Stanley nail the slippery games down. This nervous-making crew, with its gimpy veterans and erratic infield, has shown toughness and courage and internal rapport, and like last year's Patriots did better than anyone dared hope. These Sox were spared the burden of great expectations carried by so many of their star-crossed predecessors; now they have nothing to lose but the marbles. Once again, I'm tuned in.

Postscript: Well, the team was overwhelmed in the end by historical precedent. In the fifth game of the league playoffs against the California Angels, it came back to win after being one strike away from defeat, 5–4, and elimination, four games to two. After this miracle, it easily beat the

---

*The episode has become murky in my memory—something involving erratic attendance, sudden hospitalization, and rumors of drug use by the sometimes lustrous Oil Can. This piece was written for the Boston *Globe* at the end of the 1986 regular season and rosters come, rosters go. *Où sont les brouhahas d'antan?*

Angels twice more, and began the World Series by taking two from the New York Mets in Shea Stadium. Then the spell wore off, to be replaced by the hoary jinx. Two losses to the Mets at Fenway evened the series; Hurst, the winner of the first game, a shutout, valiantly won the fifth game, and back in Queens the Red Sox seemed to have the sixth game and the World Series sewed up. They went into the bottom of the tenth leading 5–3, and Schiraldi, having replaced Clemens in the eighth, retired two batters and got two strikes on Gary Carter. Then ensued, amid the tumult of a stadium of fans called back from the dead, a nightmare to cap all Sox fans' nightmares: three successive singles, a wild pitch (by Stanley), and an error (by Bill Buckner, the hobbling first baseman) that let in the third and winning run of the inning. All over New England, people stared incredulous at their television sets. Three times in that inning the Red Sox were within one strike of winning the World Series for the first time since 1918. After such an epic collapse (or miraculous comeback, from the Mets' point of view) not even Hurst could win the next game, though he took a 3–0 lead into the sixth inning. For the fourth time in forty years, the Red Sox lost the World Series in the seventh game.

Ted Williams, as of 1986

HE APPEARS in television commercials now, but seems sheepish saying the lines, a leathery-faced old gent whose eyes look a bit menacing even as they strive to twinkle. For a long time, as Joe DiMaggio urbanely peddled coffee machines on the little round-cornered screen, Ted Williams was conspicuous for his absence from the public eye, save when he peeped out of the dugout while managing the overlookable Senators/Rangers of 1969–72. The last time he appeared in an old-timers game at Fenway Park, he made a valiant shoestring catch but could hardly get his bat on the ball, though he was given an extra, out-of-turn "ups." His recent interviews are eerily good-natured, as he blesses the newest version of the Red Sox or the newest unsuccessful attempt—by Rod Carew, George Brett, Wade Boggs—to supplant him as the last .400 hitter.

It is now forty-five years since the cocky, lanky kid from San Diego closed out the season with an average of .406. That statistic has emerged from the shadows of 1941 (when Jolting Joe hit in fifty-six straight games and the Japanese hit Pearl Harbor) to become Williams's most famous feat, the tarnish-proof polish on the silver of his reputation; but it really is the fifteen postwar years of his career, harassed though they were by injuries, sportswriters, boos, disappointments on the field and marital misadventures off it, the Korean War, and the Williams Shift, that established him as a steady wonder, the best hitter of his era and a kind of link between the highly technological players of today and the rough-hewn statistical giants (Cobb and Hornsby, Sisler and Ruth, Napoleon Lajoie and Shoeless Joe Jackson) of a virtually mythological time whose living witnesses are increasingly few.

By 1986 more than a generation of baseball fans and players has grown up who never saw Williams play—never saw him *hit,* one should say, for though he was a dutiful outfielder with a strong arm when young, and a baserunner who went through the motions and stole as much as four bases a season, he always looked as if his heart was at the plate, which it was. Hitting was his thing, and even when the Red Sox, in the late Forties, had stars at almost every position, the crowd waited through the line-up to see Ted's turn at bat. A tall man with broad shoulders, he towered over the plate, and seemed greedy while there, wringing the bat handle with his fists, switchily moving it back and forth as if showing the pitcher exactly where he wanted the poor ball placed. He had a wide stance with nothing contorted about it, no peek-a-boo around his shoulder like Stan Musial, no funny work with the feet like so many of today's overcoached fusspots.

In Williams's day baseball still savored of its cow-pasture beginnings—the East still held a few actual cow pastures—and the uniform was baggy, and no hitter wore a golf glove, let alone two, and the batting helmet was viewed (at least by Williams) as an encumbering innovation. His swing was long, much longer than Ruth's (how *did* Ruth hit all those home runs out of that chop?), and beautiful the way Sam Snead's swing is beautiful, all body parts working together and the ball just an incident in the course of the arc. *Pop the hips* was his theory, just like a golf pro's; but the golf ball isn't coming at you at ninety miles an hour with English on it, out of a mess of billboards. He says he swung slightly upwards, to compensate for the pitcher being raised above the batter; but it didn't look like that. His swing looked level. The first Williams homer I remember, seen from the bleachers of old Shibe Park in Philadelphia, was a line drive that was still rising as it cleared the right-field fence. There was something very pure and uncontrived about the way he hit, and though his power totals and his averages are not the best, nobody ranks so high in both departments of hitting. To put it another way, nobody else with over five hundred homers (521) has so high a lifetime average (.344). He was the strongest good hitter, or the finest-tuned slugger, the game has seen. Temperamental and injury-prone, he yet showed an impressive durability; he won his fifth batting championship in 1957 by hitting .388, and won his sixth the next year at the age of forty.

He came from California to a dowdy New England metropolis with too many newspapers, and was instant news. The Williams excitement had to do with his personality as well as his prowess; the former was as complex as the latter seemed transparent. He was, like Ty Cobb, a deprived man, hungry for greatness; but, unlike Cobb, he had a sweet smile. The smile can be seen on the old pre-war photos, and in televised interviews now, as the philosophical fisherman from Islamorada fields an especially cute question. Boston wanted to love the Kid, but he was prickly in its embrace. He was hot-tempered and rabbit-eared and became contemptuous of sportswriters and too proud to tip his hat after hitting a home run. And the teams he ornamented didn't win all the marbles; the spectacular Sox of 1946 lost the World Series, and after that pennants just slipped away, while Williams sulked, spat, threw bats, and threatened retirement. In the end, the city loved him all the more because the relationship had proved so complex; "some obstacle," as Freud wrote, "is necessary to swell the tide of libido to its height." No sports figure—not Bobby Orr or Larry Bird or Rocky Marciano—had a greater hold over the fans of New England than Ted Williams. From the generous team owner Tom Yawkey he received top dollar—what now seems a paltry $125,000 a season—but he was one of the few ballplayers who all by themselves brought people out to the park. In 1957 the third-place Red Sox drew 1,187,087, and the sportswriter Harold Kaese wrote, "The Red Sox drew 187,087 and Ted Williams drew the other million."

He had talent: a big man with great eyes. He had intensity, and nobody practiced longer or thought harder about the niceties of the little war between pitchers and hitters. But he also had poignance, a flair for the dramatic. His career abounds with thunder that remained etched on the air: the last-day six-for-eight that lifted his average in 1941 up from .3995; the home run that same year that won the All-Star Game in Detroit; the home run he hit in 1946 off of a Rip Sewall blooper pitch; the home run with which he went off to Korea (he flew thirty-nine missions, crash-landed a bullet-riddled plane, and hit .407 in the two baseball months after he returned); and the one that concluded his career. But behind that thunder stood a multitude of hot days and wearisome nights, games that didn't mean much beyond the moment, to which Williams brought his electric, elegant best. We loved him because he generated excitement: he lifted us out of our own lives and showed us, in the way he stood up at the plate, what the game was all about.

Mostly Literary

TRIBUTES

Edmund Wilson

IN THE LAST FIFTY YEARS, literary criticism, and for that matter literary consumption, has become increasingly academic. Who would read good books if college students were not compelled to read them? And who would write about them if professors were not obliged, for reasons of career advancement, to publish something from time to time? Yet the leading American critic of this era was a man, Edmund Wilson, who held no more advanced degree than a bachelor of arts from Princeton and whose stints of teaching were brief and few. He once wrote that "after trying to do something with teaching and rather enjoying it at first ... I've decided that the whole thing, for a writer, is unnatural, embarrassing, disgusting, and that I might better do journalism, after all, when I have to make money." Not that he was against education. Indeed, he seems to have enjoyed and cherished his own more than most. He maintained until the older man's death an affectionate correspondence with Christian Gauss, the favorite of his Princeton professors, and wrote an admiring and grateful memoir of his prep-school instructor in Greek: "The thing that glowed for me through Xenophon and Homer in those classrooms of thirty years ago has glowed for me ever since." To Greek and Latin, French and Italian, Wilson added self-taught German, Russian, Hebrew, and Hungarian. One of his complaints about academicians, indeed, was that they were too lazy to read much, and hence elevated the reputations of unprolific writers like T. S. Eliot. Wilson was a great reader who communicated on almost every one of his thousands of pages of criticism the invigorating pleasure—the brisk winds and salubrious exercise—to be had in the landscape of literature.

There was a musty, walled-in quality about his childhood. He was born in 1895 in Red Bank, New Jersey. His father, Edmund Wilson, Sr., was a brilliant and successful lawyer, attorney general for the state of New Jersey under two administrations, yet with something eccentric and delicate about him; he was often, his son tells us in his memoir *A Prelude,* "in eclipse in some sanitorium for what were then called 'neurasthenics.'" The mother of the household, the former Helen Mather Kimball, was hard to get at in another way; she was deaf (she went deaf, in fact, shortly after being told that her husband was mad) and devoted herself to her gardens. Wilson was an only child. His solitude found relief in the array of aunts and uncles that his genteel Presbyterian background provided, and in books. He early pointed himself toward literature. Before he was able to read, he tells us in another memoir, *Upstate,* he suddenly said to himself, "I am a poet," and then corrected this to "No: I am not quite a poet, but I am something of the kind." By the age of seventeen he was exchanging with his friend Alfred Bellinger precocious literary opinions upon Kipling, Meredith, Shaw, and Pater. At Princeton he fell in with Scott Fitzgerald and John Peale Bishop and remained ever after their enthusiastic, if sometimes chastening, comrade in the pursuit of literary immortality. Though he could be brusque and was invariably frank, loyalty and friendship were among the gifts and appetites the shy boy from Red Bank developed. The Princeton idyll ended in 1916; he got a job as a reporter with the New York *Evening Sun* and extended his collegiate life pleasantly into Manhattan's bohemia. But all pleasantness ended as America entered the war; though he had "never really felt it [his] duty to fight in this war," he enlisted in a hospital unit and served as a stretcher-bearer in France. Like Hemingway, though he made much less of it, Wilson handled the mustard-gas-blinded, the mutilated, and the dead. World War I was the rite of passage for the "lost" generation, from which it emerged wiser than its years and furious to live and to achieve.

Wilson did not set out to be a critic. He settled into New York in 1919 to be a free-lance writer, and some of his projects during the Twenties sound Dadaesque: a letter of 1922 gleefully announces a "tremendous burlesque . . . which will deal with the expedition to capture the glyptodon or plesiosaurus or whatever it is in Patagonia," and in 1924 he travelled to California in hopes (vain) of persuading Charlie Chaplin to take a role in a "great super-ballet" he had written. Wilson composed much poetry, for which he had an indifferent ear, and wrote plays, one of which, *The Crime in the Whistler Room,* was produced in New York by the Provincetown Players. (The leading actress, Mary Blair, became the first of his four wives.) He served as theatre critic for *The Dial,* as managing editor for *Vanity Fair,* and as literary editor for *The New Republic;* he wrote reviews for the latter but the three books he published in this decade were all belles lettres: *The Undertaker's Garland* (poems and stories, with John Peale Bishop, 1922); *Discordant Encounters* (plays and dialogues, 1926); and *I Thought of Daisy* (a novel, 1929). The novel, which cost Wilson much Proustian cerebration, now seems a somewhat crabbed valentine to the Greenwich Village of bootleg gin and Edna St. Vincent Millay. Wilson as a fiction writer is far from contemptible: he creates a solid world, has an unforced feel for the macabre and for moral decay, and allows eroticism its centrality in human doings. But away from the erotic episodes, something leaden and saturnine depresses our attentiveness; Wilson could never skim along the way a story-teller must, simply delighted by surfaces.

The truth may be that the personalities he encountered in life meant less to him than those he met in print. After 1930 his biography becomes largely bibliography. While revising, with much difficulty, *I Thought of Daisy*, Wilson was with relative ease enlarging some essays on Symbolism and its successors into a critical work, *Axel's Castle* (1931): here his indispensable oeuvre begins. Though the individual chapters on Yeats, Valéry, Eliot, Proust, Joyce, Stein, and Rimbaud might be faulted, the sum portrait of modernism was vivid, appreciative, historically informed, justly balanced, and unprecedented: authors and writings still little more than rumors or jokes to the general public (and the academic establishment) were, without a trace of popularizing tendency, placed in clear perspective. Wilson was an exemplary animator of authors; his ability to distill out of a mass of reading the personality and bias of an oeuvre showed a strength of the earth-moving kind and a confidence we might call patrician. A. E. Housman and Henry James would never be the same for those who read the essays on them in *The Triple Thinkers* (1938). The long essays on Dickens and Kipling in *The Wound and the Bow* (1941), which added a phrase to the language, excite us like detective stories as Wilson probes the works for the wounded psyche behind them. He was fearless in judgment; who else in 1938 was praising Henry Miller and panning Louis Bromfield? He would tackle anything; it occurred to him one day "that nobody had ever presented in intelligible human terms the development of Marxism and the other phases of the modern idea of history. . . . I knew that this would put me to the trouble of learning German and Russian and that it would take me far afield . . . but I found myself excited by the challenge." The result was his magnum opus of the Thirties, *To the Finland Station* (1940).

He faithfully and with confessional honesty kept journals, which toward the end of his life he had begun to edit for publication and which Leon Edel has posthumously ushered into print. Wilson's life did seem to fall into decades; he caroused and clowned with the Twenties and brooded over Socialism with the Thirties. In 1941, he withdrew from metropolitan life, buying a home in Wellfleet, on Cape Cod, and a few years later he found in *The New Yorker* the ideal sponsor for his physical and mental travels. In 1946, he published his one best-seller, *Memoirs of Hecate County*, and married the last of his four wives, Elena Mumm Thornton. His second wife, Margaret Canby, had died of a fall in Santa Barbara in 1932; his third, Mary McCarthy, recorded her own impressions of the early Wellfleet years in her novel *A Charmed Life* and some brilliant short stories. Without forsaking Wellfleet, Elena, or *The New Yorker*, Wilson was drawn in his later decades more and more to the old family summer estate in Talcottville, New York, and to reflections upon family history and his own past. His once-vivacious interest in contemporary writing settled instead upon such subjects of recondite research as Indian land claims and the Dead Sea Scrolls. But to the end of his life in 1972 he remained a lodestar—an American mind European in its scope and its delight in its own play. One of his late collections is entitled *A Piece of My Mind*; an irreverent friend of mine suggested it should have been called *Kiss My Mind*. Wilson might have appreciated the joke; he tolerated the undignified nickname of "Bunny," wrote limericks in letters to his friends, was an amateur magician who put on shows for children, and to the end of his days showed a cheerful capacity for liquor.

His virtues were old-fashioned American ones: industriousness, enthusiasm, directness, integrity. Among his books is an invaluable anthology, *The Shock of Recognition* (1943), subtitled *The Development of Literature in the United States Recorded by the Men Who Made It*. He urged the creation of a definitive series of the classic American literary texts, like the French Pléiade editions—an idea now being handsomely realized by The Library of America. If in Wilson's last decade he soured on the official United States, it was a possessive grandee sourness in the style of Thoreau and Henry Adams. Tax difficulties over his *Hecate County* royalties led to the self-serving fulminations of *The Cold War and the Income Tax* (1963) and the Swiftian preface to the mockingly titled *Patriotic Gore* (1962). Yet *Patriotic Gore* itself is a masterpiece of appreciation of nineteenth-century minds and moral struggle and constitutes a substantial bequest to Wilson's native ethical tradition. In even the quirkiest corner of his production, he enriched the American scene as a paragon of intellectual energy and curiosity.

Mr. Volente

How many times I've said to my wife
  As I scanned the morning paper,
"I see that So-and-So is dead."
My wife looks up and nods her head.

How oft I've thought of him who'll say
  As he scans the morning paper,
"I see that E. B. White is dead."
His wife looks up and nods her head—
  Such queer, insensible people!
  Ah, lucky, loathsome people!

This poem by E. B. White, entitled "A Forward Glance o'er the Obituary Page," appeared in *The New Yorker* in 1948 but, judged perhaps too morbid or too slight, was never placed by the poet in a collection. As prophecy it has proved its worth, for White has died, on the first day of October 1985, in Maine, at the age of eighty-six, leaving the world a perceptibly less classy place. He possessed abundantly that most precious and least learnable of writerly gifts—the gift of inspiring affection in the reader. Affection and trust: for why should we like a writer who gives us anything less than the trustworthy truth, in his version of it, delivered up without fuss or shame? In White's version of his own career, transparently fictionalized for a "Mr. Volente" in a story called "The Hotel of the Total Stranger," it all began when a waitress, in a Childs restaurant, spilled a glass of buttermilk down his blue serge suit: "Mr. Volente had written an account of the catastrophe at the time and sold it to a young and inexperienced magazine, thus making for himself the enormously important discovery that the world would pay a man for setting down a simple, legible account of his own misfortunes." The magazine, of course, was *The New Yorker,* and for more than half a century after that spilled buttermilk White's confessions, comments, poems, and stories awakened the laughter and enhanced the alertness of *New Yorker* readers. Elsewhere, too, in other magazines and in surprising forms—in three classic small novels for children and in the revision of a Cornell professor's guide to English usage—his intensely graceful and lucid brand of simple legibility sparkled. He would try anything, from a rondeau to a cartoon caption, from collaborating with James Thurber on a book ostensibly about sex to collaborating with his goddaughter on a non-posthumous volume of his own letters, and his widely assorted oeuvre is lit from within by a certain jaunty restlessness. Though timid of air travel, he moved nimbly on land and, in one of his series of essays, dispatched letters from all points of the compass. He ranged far, in his quest for artistic freedom. His young life was animated by a number of sudden excursions and departures. Mr. Volente recalls with pleasure "the renewal of liberty" that comes with quitting a job: "the sense of the return of footlooseness, the sense of again being a reporter receiving only the vaguest and most mysterious of assignments, was oxygen in his lungs." Young and aspiring in an era when urban gaiety was plentiful and witty humorists were common, he became a humorist, and, with his fastidious verbal timing and frequent sensations of bemusement, one of the best; but he was a humorist with broad perspectives, a light-verse writer who could also ask, in the poem "Traveler's Song," "Shall I love the world / That carries me under, / That fills me full / Of its own wonder / And strikes me down / With its own thunder?" White was a man attached to beauty, to nature, and to human freedom, and these concerns lifted his essays to an eloquence that could be somber and that sets them on the shelf with those of Thoreau. The least pugnacious of editorialists, he was remarkably keen and quick in the defense of personal liberty and purity of expression, whether the threat was as overt and ugly as McCarthyism or as seemingly innocuous as Alexander Woollcott's endorsement of Seagram's whisky and the Xerox company's sponsorship of an article in *Esquire*. American freedom was not just a notion to White, it was an instinct, a current in the blood, expressed by his very style, his efficient and engaging informality, his courteous skepticism, his refusal to be held within accepted genres, his boundless, gallant capacity for seeing the world afresh.

Mr. Palomar

THE SUDDEN DEATH of Italo Calvino, scarcely into his sixties, deprives the world of one of its few master artists, a constantly inventive and experimental writer who nevertheless brought to his work a traditional elegance, polish, and completeness of design. Twenty years ago, he was little known in the United States; it was John Barth, himself an avant-garde writer with a strong admixture of aesthetic conservatism, who first mentioned him to me, as someone urged upon him by his own writing students. These students had met him, primarily, in the science fiction of *Cosmicomics* and *t zero*. I began to read Calvino, with admiration and delight, and had the pleasure of reviewing at length his beautiful *Invisible Cities*. What struck me, along with the rigor of the book's intricate scheme and the inventiveness that filled out the scheme with a dazzling plenitude, was the tenderness of the civic concern that showed in his fantasy of many cities. The modern writer has often taken a mordant and hostile attitude toward human institutions; Calvino by contrast was a respectful sociologist, an amused and willing student of things as they are.

He was willing, in his basic reverence toward the human honeycomb, to submerge himself for years in his massive anthology, *Italian Folktales*, whose pattern of numerous interwoven tales influenced the form of *The Castle of Crossed Destinies* and, to a lesser extent, that of *If on a winter's night a traveler*. Plurality became the method of his fiction, most recently reflected in the twenty-seven symmetrical facets of *Mr. Palomar*. His taste for complex patterns of little tales perhaps prevented his acceptance by that large public which likes the long and involving sweep of the novel, and which took Umberto Eco's *Name of the Rose* to its bosom. But nevertheless, within the last twenty years, Calvino had become at least in American academic circles the best-known living Italian writer, whose name, along with those of Nabokov and Borges and Günter Grass, figured in the inventories of any who tried to compile the "postmodernist" masters. Calvino was an artist in whom the intellectual and revolutionary passions of the modernists had been transmuted to a marvellously knowing if relatively detached meditation upon the oddities and bemusements of the postwar world. Born in Cuba of agronomist parents, Calvino grew up in San Remo and fought with the Italian partisans as a young man. His war stories, written in the late Forties and available in English in *Difficult Loves*, are like little else he wrote, in that the material outweighs, in interest, the form. His first novel, *The Path to the Spiders' Nest*, deals, from a boy's point of view, with the same material. Calvino began his literary career as a member of the Communist Party and of the neorealist movement, but by the Fifties had withdrawn from both and worked, as he would for the rest of his life, as an editor for the Turin publishing house of Einaudi. A state of philosophical suspension and political coexistence seems to be declared in his good-humored, exquisitely imagined fables. Speaking at Columbia University in New York a few years ago, he described the Italian writer's need for elaborate schemata as a way of coping with the quicksand upon which he stands. Certainly no fiction writer of his time perpetrated designs more elaborate, more rigorous in their geometry.

With all due homage to the insights and harmonies of his later work, the trilogy of early fanciful novels with parallel titles remains in my mind as perhaps the liveliest and blithest items of his production. All three begin with premises that seem impossible: a knight who is nonexistent, an empty suit of armor; a viscount who is half a man, with one eye, arm, and leg; and a baron who decides to live among the trees, vowing never to set foot on the ground. Calvino's inexhaustible fancy and his great literary tact breathe life into these grotesques, and use them not only to illustrate metaphysical and psychological ideas but to illumine various historical epochs. The learning behind his flights of fancy was always solid and extensive; his make-believe was spun from the real straw of scholarship. Of the three novels, the most extended and the most charming is *The Baron in the Trees,* which serves as a metaphor for the Enlightenment and for the life of the mind. Moving from limb to limb like a bird, concocting for himself many ingenious arboreal amenities, Cosimo avoids the earth even in death, when the dying old man sails skyward in a balloon. Calvino, too, seemed to live well off the ground—though of course the trees he so agilely explored were rooted in reality. The son of scientists, he is never loose or vague in his inventions, even when they have the luxuriance of tropical plants. His creative impulse, if a single one can be discerned behind an oeuvre so variously antic, so tirelessly infused with intellectual play, was a curiosity concerning how men live with one another, in this crowded and paved-over world that they have made. His death removes from the global literary scene its most urbane star, its most civilized voice.

John Cheever — I

June 1982

INTRODUCING his collected stories, John Cheever wrote:

> My favorite stories are those that were written in less than a week and that were often composed aloud. I remember exclaiming: "My name is Johnny Hake!" This was in the hallway of a house in Nantucket that we had been able to rent cheaply because of the delayed probating of a will. Coming out of the maid's room in another rented house I shouted to my wife: "This is a night when kings in golden mail ride their elephants over the mountains!"

The gusto, the abrupt poetry, the clear consciousness of which room is the maid's room are all Cheeveresque. From somewhere—perhaps a strain of sea-yarning in his Yankee blood—he had gotten the authentic archaic storytelling temper, and one could not be with John Cheever for

more than five minutes without seeing stories take shape: past embarrassments worked up with wonderful rapidity into hilarious fables, present
surroundings made to pulse with sympathetic magic as he glanced around
him and drawled a few startlingly concentrated words in that mannerly,
rapid voice of his. He thought fast, saw everything in bright, true colors,
and was the arena of a constant tussle between the bubbling *joie de vivre*
of the healthy sensitive man and the deep melancholy peculiar to American Protestant males. He wrote, in *Bullet Park,* of a hero pursued by a
cafard—"the blues" would be a translation—and he kept a little ahead of
his own by means of beautiful sprints of art. His face always looked
reddened and polished, as if by a brisk wind, though his hair was perfectly
combed and his necktie tightly knotted. His characters cry out for the
old-fashioned virtues—"Valor! Love! Virtue! Compassion! Splendor!
Kindness! Wisdom! Beauty!"—while living lives exemplary in their modern muddle of emotional greed and misplaced aspiration. "Truly nostalgic
for love and happiness" is how he described his generation. Though he
was as alertly appreciative of contemporary details as any writer—his last
novel breaks into a paean to supermarkets—he was born and bred on
Boston's South Shore, a pleasant, long-settled stretch that, like much of
Massachusetts, has kept a visible residue of earlier centuries. From its
steepled, shingled, sandy landscape Cheever distilled the lovely town of
St. Botolphs in the two Wapshot novels, and it was there, in the First
Parish Cemetery of Norwell, with its grassy hillocks and overarching
trees, that he was laid to rest, alongside the traditional slate tombstones of
his parents.

He was often labelled a writer about suburbia; but many people have
written about suburbia, and only Cheever was able to make an archetypal place out of it, a terrain we can recognize within ourselves, wherever we are or have been. Only he saw in its cocktail parties and
swimming pools the shimmer of dissolving dreams; no one else satirized
with such tenderness its manifold distinctions of class and style, or felt
with such poignance the weary commuter's nightly tumble back into
the arms of his family. He made of the suburbs another episode in the
continuing New World epic of Man's encounter with Nature. Natural
grandeur and human ignominy and dissatisfaction mingle in the haze
from the cookout grill:

> We have a nice house with a garden and a place outside for cooking meat,
> and on summer nights, sitting there with the kids and looking into the front
> of Christina's dress as she bends over to salt the steaks, or just gazing at the
> lights in heaven, I am as thrilled as I am thrilled by more hardy and danger-

ous pursuits, and I guess this is what is meant by the pain and sweetness of life.

Thus spoke Johnny Hake, in "The Housebreaker of Shady Hill," before telling the reader how his quest for the good life led him to crime and repentance. It took an effortlessly moral nature to imagine fall and redemption in that realm of soft lawns and comfortable homes; Cheever's sense of the human adventure lay squarely in the oldest American vein. Like Hawthorne's, his characters are moral embodiments, rimmed in a flickering firelight of fantasy. Like Whitman, he sang the common man, the citizen average in his sensuality, restlessness, lovingness, and desperation. A suburban man infatuated with his babysitter should make a sad and squalid story, but in "The Country Husband" the story ends with a glad shout of kings in golden mail riding their elephants over the mountains.

John Cheever — II

November 1982

HE WAS a courteous fidgety man with a rapid laugh that ended in a blend of hum, snort, and sigh, as jazz singers used to end a chorus with "Oh, yeass." He was wonderfully quick—quick in apprehension, quick to find the words he wanted, quick to move on. The prose reflected the man, except that what in the man sometimes seemed impatience was in the prose all golden speed and directness. In his first short story, written when he was seventeen and published in *The New Republic,* he wrote: "In the spring I was glad to leave school. Everything outside was elegant and savage and fleshy. Everything inside was slow and cool and vacant. It seemed a shame to stay inside." The mature Cheever is already here, in these definite declarative rhythms, the unexpected but *echt* adjectives, the love of the outdoors. He loved air and light and smells and weather and flesh; he had, like his character Moses Wapshot, "a taste for the grain and hair of life." If his novels and even some of his longer short stories surprise us with the directions they take, and lose thereby something of momentum, blame his very acuity and ardor, which were excited by any scent and found the heart's prey trembling in every patch of experience. He was of an ever-rarer breed, a celebrant.

His life, which began in late May of 1912, in Quincy, Massachusetts, followed a classic tripartite pattern: the provincial, sheltered home territory (Boston's South Shore); the years of adult initiation in the big city

(New York, from the early 1930s to 1950, with time out for war); and eventual settlement in suburbia (Westchester County and, from 1956 on, Ossining, in an eighteenth-century Dutch farmhouse). The major decision of his young life would seem to have been leaving New England and the company of his brother, Frederick, who was almost seven years older; versions of the break figure in his early short story "The Brothers" (1935) and in that splendid monument to his youth *The Wapshot Chronicle* (1957). By quitting the sleepy tidal land where his ancestors presided, Cheever created for himself a changeless paradise, to whose skating pond and steepled village profile his imagination recurred in his last extended work, a valedictory novelette disjointed by the pain in which it was composed but overall as luminous and rapt as its title, *Oh What a Paradise It Seems*.

Inherited Yankee notions of virtue and rectitude gave edge and shadow to the Manhattan short stories of which "The Enormous Radio" is the best known. At the age of twenty-two Cheever had become a contributor to the also youthful *New Yorker*. For three decades his short stories stood out, in that crowded display case, in a heyday of the genre, as the most trenchant, being at the same time strikingly lyrical, frequently comic, and overtly tender. He was a fine observer and, better yet, a brave inventor. He became typecast as a laureate of the comfortable suburbs, but in truth Shady Hill and Bullet Park were as much states of a religious mind as paradisaical St. Botolphs, the site of the Wapshot tales. His suburbs were anything but comfortable: vastly uneasy, rather, and citadels of disappointment, vain longing, disguised poverty, class cruelty, graceless aging, and crimes ranging from adultery and theft to murder. He sniffed out corruption with the nose of a Cotton Mather or a Hawthorne. The Puritan admonition to look into the darkness of our hearts was not lost on him. Though a great evoker of lust, he does not show it as a simple force, or love as an unmixed blessing; Rosalie, the nymph who brings sex into St. Botolphs, grows "weary of trying to separate the power of loneliness from the power of love" and, looking at a lover, sees that "Lechery sat like worry on his thin face." When Rosalie is spied naked, Moses Wapshot, the spier, feels "shamefaced, his dream of simple pleasure replaced by some sadness, some heaviness that seemed to make his mouth taste of blood and his teeth ache." Alcohol, another two-edged pleasure, figures on the whole benignly in Cheever's vision of mundane happiness; yet as he aged it was eroding his life. It testifies to his strength as an artist and to the irrepressibility of his wits that as things fell apart he was able to make of his sliding sensations such poetic and universal stories as "The Ocean" and "The Swimmer"—this last a counterpart in nightmare to "The Enormous Radio" a generation earlier.

*   *   *

I had known John as a reader knows a writer for some fifteen years before we met, in 1964, in Russia. He and I were both guests of the state, and his lively fancy and brave ebullience lit up those potentially glum Soviet surroundings and made our days of touring catacombs and classrooms and speaking to wary clusters of writers and students as gay as an April in Paris. Ten years later, we lived for a time on opposite ends of Boston's Back Bay. He had almost ceased to write. He taught and, living alone on Bay State Road as a Boston University faculty member, touched what looked like bottom. Being back in New England had activated dormant devils in him; the hellish atmosphere of *Falconer* contains those strange penitential months. He performed his duties in a daze and suffered cardiac seizures that might have proved fatal. His brother, who lived on Cape Cod, called his apartment every morning to see if he was still alive. Miraculously, he was. At last, in April, John returned to New York and signed himself into a hospital to be cured of alcoholism. He never took another drink, not even in the last days, seven years later, of terminal cancer. With sober dispatch he wrote his long-deferred prison novel, *Falconer*. With even greater success he collected his short stories, in a big shiny red book that appeared under everyone's Christmas tree. Those old *New Yorker* stories had put on weight since their first printing: they had become the imperishable record of an American moment; the glowing windows of suburban houses would never again seem so beaconlike. If Cheever did not, like Hemingway, create a life-style, he did, like Faulkner, give a style of life its definitive fictional locale.

He was a gentleman, with a gentleman's graces and scruples and sometimes a gentleman's testiness. Expelled from prep school, he educated himself in the "elegant and savage and fleshy" world. He travelled widely and keenly and set some of his best later stories in Italy, where he lived for several periods with his family. He had one wife and often described connubial love. His books preach paternal nurture, and he practiced it with his three children. He served four years in the Army in World War II and wrote almost nothing about it. He could not, it seemed, write about people without imagining a town, without painting a backdrop of community. In a profession for loners, he was generous with praise and practical encouragement. His letters were as deft, kind, and droll as they were brief. In conversation he could be immensely, cascadingly funny. Like any quest of old, modern life for him was rimmed with the marvellous; his adventurers and adventuresses are beset by enchantments, monsters, sirens, strange lights. He himself, in his reasserted career, lived a redemptive fable. His never-gray hair burned away by cancer therapy, his trim outdoorsman's frame softened and leaning on a cane, he accepted the

National Medal for Literature on the stage of Carnegie Hall two months before his death with a speech that said, "A page of good prose remains invincible." All the literary acolytes assembled there fell quite silent, astonished by such faith.

John Cheever — III

July 1985

THOSE OF US even modestly acquainted with the work and life of John Cheever had heard of his first published short story, "Expelled," written when he was seventeen and accepted by Malcolm Cowley at *The New Republic;* but it is still an invigorating shock to read it now, and to see so many elements of the Cheeverian genius firmly in place at an adolescent age: the declarative swiftness of the prose; the dashes of unexpected color ("the gravy-colored curtains"); the matter-of-factly mordant social eye ("Her skirt was askew, either too long in front or hitching up on the side"); the casually surreal detail ("He was a thin colonel with a soft nose that rested quietly on his face"); and the air of expectancy, a vibrant translucence wherein the momentarily disarmed narrator prepares to yield to the next tug of enchantment.

What happened to Cheever at Thayer is not here (and never was elsewhere) made clear: the circumstances that led the fictional Charles, with his manifest intelligence and precocious sense of style, to be expelled by his school are not explained by the story's murmurs of leftist protest, of sympathy for Sacco and Vanzetti and their champion Laura Driscoll, dismissed from a "faculty [who] all thought America was beautiful." Charles truthfully, five months after his expulsion, finds it "strange to be so very young and to have no place to report to at nine o'clock." As Malcolm Cowley has described, the young Cheever had a hard row to hoe—on his own in New York in the depths of the Depression, trying to begin as a writer in a world of failing magazines, living in a three-dollar-a-week room on Hudson Street, making do on a weekly ten dollars supplied by his older brother, Fred. Within a few years, Yaddo and *The New Yorker* took him up, but in the meantime the school of hard knocks proved to be the alternative to Thayer; the adult Cheever—a superb, quick learner—was always somewhat embarrassed by the aborted nature of his formal education. A violence of indiscipline is implied by "Expelled" but not pictured, much as the vintage Cheever short stories were written around, but never openly confessed, a central problem of alcoholism. Curious circumstances and specifics are from the start sublimated into a quasi-religious imagery of stark and simple contrasts: "I wanted to feel and taste the air and be among the shadows. That is perhaps why I left school. . . . It seemed a shame to stay inside."

The contrasting portraits of the two female teachers, the satiric sketch of the colonel's inconvenient chapel address, and even the brilliantly wry opening section (similar, but for Charles's unexpected dream of "dry apple trees and a broken blue egg cup," to the beginning of *Catcher in the Rye*) are all in their material schoolboyish; it is the electric presentation that is alarmingly mature, with a touch of the uncanny, as the rare examples of literary precocity—Rimbaud, Chatterton, William Cullen Bryant, Henry Green—tend to be. True, the young Cheever had borrowed a bit from Hemingway and Dos Passos, and some of the sentiments were taken from their time; an enlightened liberalism generates an image of untypical ugliness and strain: "Because the tempered newspaper keeps its eyes ceilingwards and does not see the dirty floor." But we feel, as we feel reading Thoreau and Lawrence, that the author has primarily put himself to school with the brooks and the wind, that a miraculously direct access to the actual has been established, in a language as solid as wood, and as quirkily grained. Cheever spoke as he wrote, with a rapid humorous poetic fancy and an ardor of intuition that did not invite revision; his voice is already here, and his keen and careless eye, and his gallant love of a world both magical and out of joint. It is touching and amazing to find these gifts in the possession of a self-proclaimed "lost" boy who, as he puts it, "lacks a place to stand where [he] can talk." He was to find a place, and to talk enduringly; but something of the nervous radiance and careening momentum of this first published effort was to follow him all the way to the grave.

John Cheever — IV

July 1990

IT WAS WITH SOME SURPRISE that I read, in *The Letters of John Cheever* (edited by Benjamin Cheever, 1988), "Updike, whom I know to be a brilliant man, traveled with me in Russia last autumn and I would go to considerable expense and inconvenience to avoid his company. I think his magnaminity [*sic*] specious and his work seems motivated by covetousness, exhibitionism and a stony heart." This was to Frederick Exley in

June of 1965; somewhat later in the month he wrote Exley, of the same trip to Russia, "Updike and I spent most of our time back-biting one another. I find him very arrogant but my daughter tells me that I'm arrogant. We dined together at the White House last Tuesday and I did everything short of putting a cherry bomb in his bug juice. It made me feel great."

These passages, lively and unhesitant in the usual Cheever style, cast a new light upon the time we shared, in the fall of 1964, in the Soviet Union, a time I recalled so affectionately in the words I spoke at his burial service: "The Russians were drawn to his courage and ebullience and became more themselves in his presence. John was a great spirit, and these connoisseurs of the spirit knew it, and loved him." The impression that I made upon him, it saddens me to realize, was less favorable. I arrived when he was midway in his own month of cultural exchange, just after Nikita Khrushchev had been, in the grand tradition of Kremlin skulduggery, mysteriously removed from office. I came with my wife, where Cheever was alone—insofar as one could be alone amid the ubiquitous Soviet escorts and translators and their jealously watchful American counterparts. Though I was twenty years younger than Cheever, a bit more of my work had been translated into Russian, and my relative youth—I was thirty-two, about the same age as Yevtushenko and Vosnesensky, the glamour boys of Russian poetry and of the momentary Khrushchevian thaw—was perhaps endearing to our hosts; in the Communist world my eager middle-American naïveté may have been more intelligible than Cheever's wry East Coast diffidence. I led a rather sheltered existence back home but as a cultural emissary, in a culture full of strangeness and menace and flattery, I became, on stage, quite talkative. At one of our joint appearances, I blush to remember, observing our audience's total ignorance of Cheever's remarkable work, I took it upon myself to stand up and describe it, fulsomely if not accurately, while my topic sat at my side in a dignified silence that retrospectively feels dour. Perhaps it felt dour at the time: the thought that I might have seemed officious flitted, batlike, through my mind as the limousine hauled us on to the next exposure.

John Cheever was a golden name to me—a happy inhabitant of *The New Yorker* penthouse all those years I was staring up from the sidewalk. In fact, it was my covetous dissatisfaction with one of his most assured and sardonic tales of suburban life, "O Youth and Beauty!," that goaded me to write a contrastingly benign story, "Friends from Philadelphia," which *The New Yorker*, to my undying gratification, accepted. In my youthful innocence I had mistakenly misread Cheever, one of the most celebratory of writers, as a misanthropic satirist. Never mind—my misapprehension gave me the needed push, the crystallizing spark; my debt to him was real. My appreciation of his prose, in the next ten years, as I ripened into a suburban householder myself, had deepened and widened. It is very hard for a young writer to imagine that an older, with a famous name and his books deathless on the shelf, might be unhappy or have feelings that can be hurt. Incredulously I heard Cheever confide, on a night when—our cultural duties for the day behind us—my wife and I and he sat up talking in the hotel, that it had been three years since he had had a story accepted at *The New Yorker.* He found it, he said, a considerable relief. It seemed very obvious to me at the time that *The New Yorker* knew best, *was* best, and that, for all the editors' sometimes meddlesome perfectionism and, in that era, anachronistic nice-nellyism, its pages were far above all other possible display cases. Cheever's confession made me sad and, yes, exultant: one less competitor for that delicious glossy space between the cover and the back-page whisky ad. I was so ardent a contributor that even amid the rigors of the Soviet trip, in one neo-czarist hotel room after another, I managed to write and send off, in pencilled copy, a few poems, which Cheever in a letter to Tanya Litvinov that June, when I evidently weighed on his mind, described as "some assinine [*sic*] poems on Russian cities in the last New Yorker."

I have read wonderingly, as the rapid posthumous invasion of his privacy has proceeded, of his discontents with *The New Yorker* even in the decades of his prime there, of his financial straits and ruinous drinking, of his sexual straying and ambivalence, of his inconsolable insecurity. Looking back, I can almost see how he might have envied me not only my twenty years' juniority and my Harvard education and my translated *Centaur* but the companionship, in Russia, of my wife—named, like his own, Mary and, during that excursion, a kind of Russian beauty, with a friendly dimple and a sturdy capacity for vodka. Another of his letters to Exley cooks up a fantastic triangle, in gaudy Cheeverian colors:

> Our [his and my] troubles began at the Embassy in Moscow when he came on exclaiming: "What are you looking so great about? I thought you'd be dead." He then began distributing paper-back copies of the Centaur while I distributed hard-cover copies of The Brigadier [*and the Golf Widow,* his latest collection of short stories]. On the train up to Leningrad he tried to throw my books out of the window but his lovely wife Mary intervened. She not only saved the books; she read one. She had to hide it under her bedpillow and claim to be sick. She said he would kill her if he knew. At the University of Leningrad he tried to upstage me by reciting some of his nonsense verse but I set fire to the contents of an ashtray and upset the water carafe. But when I pointed out to President and Mrs. Johnson that the

bulkiness of his appearance was not underwear—it was autographed copies of The Centaur—he seemed deeply wounded.

The allusion to the Johnsons harks back to the same White House event where he almost put a cherry bomb in my bug juice—a gala for National Honor Students, including an entertainment in which I read. Cheever is cited as an authority on my performance, in a letter by S. J. Perelman* to Ogden Nash: "The very next morning I had to fly to Washington to a reception for Presidential scholars at which J. Cheever was a great help. Also present at this was that eminence gris, J. O'Hara, and that somewhat younger eminence & literatus, J. Updike. The latter read extracts from three works of his to the assembled scholars, which I couldn't personally hear as I was overtaken by the characteristic nausea that attacks me when this youth performs on the printed page. But Cheever brought me tidings that all three extracts dealt with masturbation, a favorite theme of Updike's. When I asked Cheever whether Lady Bird was present, he informed me that she was seated smack in the middle of the first row. What are we coming to?"

In truth, only one of the passages, from the end of the fourth chapter of The Centaur, touched upon (so to speak) masturbation, and so deftly I had assumed only the most sensitive and corrupt of the honor students would get it. The effect, of finding myself discussed with such gleeful malice in the letters of men whom I idolized, and whose works I had pondered in my teens as gifts from above and signposts to heaven, is chastening, perhaps edifyingly so. Aspiring, we assume that those already in possession of eminence will feel no squeeze as we rise, and will form an impalpable band of welcoming angels. In fact, I know now, the literary scene is a kind of Medusa's raft, small and sinking, and one's instinct when a newcomer tries to clamber aboard is to stamp on his fingers. I met Perelman on a few occasions—most memorably at Lillian Hellman's on the Vineyard, where his pink face, pince-nez, impeccable dress, and dignified bearing, as of a well-established West 47th Street diamond merchant, made an entirely favorable impression—but I really associate him with the comfort his Acres and Pains brought me as an adolescent transplanted to some Pennsylvania acres even more weedy than his own, with the admiration we young quipsters at the Harvard Lampoon felt for his New Yorker contributions, and with the actual hard laughter his amazingly ornate and cunningly adjusted sentences faithfully sprang from my voice box. He was the last humorist of his droll generation to keep practicing, and to

*From Don't Tread on Me: The Selected Letters of S. J. Perelman, edited by Prudence Crowther (Viking, 1987).

think that I was, however modestly, an irritant to his exquisite sensibility is almost a source of pride. To those who yearn to join the angels, even the sound of angelic mockery is music. And dead men shouldn't be blamed for having their private letters published.

In reality, Cheever was always courteous to me and increasingly friendly and kind. He took to writing me impulsive, complimentary notes, such as one saying of a book review of mine, "You speak of literature as if it played some part in civilization and I feel briefly that perhaps I'm not ironing shirts in the back of a Chinese laundry." The year before he died, looking unwell, he had himself driven down to New York so he could appear on the *Dick Cavett Show* with me and tell the world that my new novel was "important"—a word he kept using, with an effect of litany. That same last year of his, he and Mary gave me and my second wife lunch at Ossining; though he had no appetite, he sat at the table, courtly and witty, and then took us on a brief excursion to his favorite local sight, the Croton Dam. My wife took a photograph of the two of us there, and John is visibly in pain, yellowish and compressed and frowning. Yet such was his vitality, and the dazzling veil of verbal fun he spun around himself, that only the photograph made me realize how bravely ill he was that day.

For eight months, ten years after our Russian episode, he and I lived at opposite ends of Boston's Back Bay, both estranged from our Marys, both in a brick-lined limbo. He had come to teach at Boston University in bad shape, and got no better. Boston and its settings from his youth weighed on him heavily, and alcohol had reduced his mind to a mumble. I seem to remember seeing the first sentences of *Falconer* on a piece of paper in his typewriter, but the page and the platen never moved, nor did food appear in his refrigerator or books on his bookshelves. The apartment the university had given him on Bay State Road looked no more lived-in than a bird perch. My attempts to entertain him generally misfired. The old Garbo film at the Museum of Fine Arts was sold out when we arrived, and our main adventure of the night was my getting us lost in Roxbury and his jumping from the car to buy a pack of cigarettes at a dark and heavily grated corner emporium. When I came to take him to Symphony Hall one Tuesday night, he was standing naked on the third-story landing outside his door; his costume indicated some resistance to attending symphony but I couldn't imagine what else, and I primly concentrated on wedging him into his clothes. We arrived late and lasted until intermission, when he felt compelled to leave and go buy a bottle of gin around the corner, from a surly salesman who failed to realize he was dealing not with an old rummy but with one of America's most distinguished authors. John pulled his Brahmin accent on him, showed him his ready cash, and got the gin. He had the distracted air of a man convinced that the real fun was elsewhere. Some of the bizarre things he saw in the students' windows on Bay State Road (which he indignantly called "a slum") worked their way into the prison milieu of *Falconer*. B.U. to him was prison.

My scattered memories of those eight months—which ended when, having rather miraculously failed to kill himself with alcohol, he took himself to New York City and dried out for good, finished *Falconer*, and embarked upon seven years of sobriety and celebrity—seem to center on his acts of consumerism. Our first meeting occurred by accident, in the dry sunshine of September 1974, outside of Brooks Brothers, where he had come to buy shoes. He invited me to follow him in. He was somewhat satirical about the tassels on the footwear the salesman offered him, but he bought two pairs anyway. I was struck by that, his carefreely buying two pairs at once, and by the way, in the Kon-Tiki bar of the Park Plaza, where we repaired afterward to renew old acquaintance, he insisted to the waiter that the drinks he was brought be doubles. His insistence was anxious, as if a drink that was merely single might in its weakness poison him. Yet when, after three or so of these, John stood up to go, he exclaimed, in a drawl of surprise, "God—I'm drunk!!"

He did seem a bit wobbly. We walked a few blocks together. I asked him if he could make it back to his place, the shimmering length of Back Bay away. He assured me he could and, holding the blue Brooks Brothers shopping bag full of tasselled shoes, his small figure dwindled down the green and monumental perspectives of Commonwealth Avenue. Rather callously, I figured he would be all right. To me he was less a mortal man than an enviable prose style.

The Letters of John Cheever is to be valued for its outpouring of that style, for the tender, puzzled notes by his son Ben, and for the jesting gallantry of his last death-defying letters. In one of them, to me, he awards me the magnanimity he had doubted earlier: apropos of a published review of his last novel, *Oh What a Paradise It Seems*, he wrote, "Your magnaminity is overwhelming." Fifteen years had gone by and he still couldn't spell the word, but it meant something real and important to him. Evidences of an impulsive, plaintive, insecure, and haughty nature have quickly accumulated, in his daughter's memoir *Home Before Dark*, in Scott Donaldson's biography, and in the volume of letters, with some frank, abysmally depressed journals to come. For all that, those who knew him can testify, he was a gem of a man, instantly poetic and instinctively magnanimous— one of those rare persons who heighten your sense of human possibilities.

SPEECHES

How Does the State Imagine?

OUR ASSIGNED TITLE challenges the literary man's traditional duty to be specific. Like almost everybody else in the world I was born into a tribe, with its rites and obligations and mystic signs. I was early introduced to the flag called the Stars and Stripes, and to the eagle with his claws full of arrows, and the symbols for dollars and cents, and the map showing our national westward expansion. The place where my personal hopes and dreams and the intentions and provisions of the state intersected was the postal system. Its workers, whom in my small town I knew all by name, brought to the house the printed journals—the newspapers and magazines—that represented to me a world where I wished to locate my future. In those days when a postage stamp cost three cents, I sent letters to great and distant men, cartoonists and writers, some of whom deigned, to my eternal gratitude, to respond. Each day's mail brought potential treasure. This is still true for me. I send manuscripts away, I sometimes get praise and money in return. It is the United States mails, with the myriad routes and mechanisms that the service implies, not to mention the basic honesty and efficiency and non-interference of its thousands of employees, that enable me to live as I do, and to do what I do. I never see a blue mailbox without a spark of warmth and wonder and gratitude that this intricate and extensive service is maintained for my benefit.

Now, what do these hollow blue monuments on street corners from here to Hawaii tell of how the state imagines? It desires, we must conclude, its citizens to be in touch with one another; the tribe seeks interconnection and consolidation. The state imagines solidarity, and resists

My contribution to a panel, "How Does the State Imagine?," conducted on January 13, 1986, as part of the 48th International PEN Congress, held in New York City with the overall theme of "The Writer's Imagination and the Imagination of the State."

secession and nonconformity, which is secession on the personal scale. Its instinct is conservative, I would say, more than, as is often charged, expansionist; only when the territorial enlargement is made to seem necessary to conserving what already exists is the effort of tribal aggression enthusiastically undertaken.

However, a state will almost never, without a fight, submit to its own diminishment; this is true of its government as well. Compared with a human individual, the state is a relatively rudimentary organism. The individual options of altruism and self-sacrifice and weary withdrawal and anorexia are too intricate and perverse for it. It can imagine only a continual health, the vigor of a gently inflationary status quo; this is because its imagination is composed of the wills of thousands of its administrators, almost none of whom wishes to lose his or her job. A democracy wisely provides an electoral process whereby most of the top officials must periodically run the risk of replacement; but the numerous workers beneath them are no longer subjected to such a risk. It is an awesome sight, in Washington, D.C., around five o'clock, to see the armies of government workers swarm like locusts into the mellowing sunlight. Just as bone counters every injury with the production of more calcium, more bone, so government tends, under every stimulus, to extend its connections with its citizens and the services it proposes to render them. Automobile seatbelts become mandatory by law and by law warnings from the surgeon-general are printed on cigarette packages. All this, of course, for the cause of tribal well-being.

The imagination of the modern artist, on the contrary, is committed not to conservation, which is carried on by the libraries and museums devoted to his art, but to exploration and danger, to expansion. It was not always so; the artist for millennia has been in league with the state, and has chiselled its propaganda and its gods on the appropriate temples and mausoleums. But an alternative patron to autocratic government, an affluent and varied popular audience, has arisen, and after it the notion of a perpetual avant-garde—the notion of an art wherein change, like change in fashion or the climate, is amusing and desirable in itself. The state, like a child, wishes that each day be just like the last; art, like a youth, hopes that each day will bring something new.

It seems to me that the writer's imagination and the imagination of the state have opposite tendencies and should keep a respectful distance from one another. Myself, I ask mainly that my tribal officials keep the mails operating—no small task, and one where many tribes fail—and continue to safeguard the freedom of expression that my particular state's founders rashly promised its citizens. This is plenty, and this is enough. I do not know why, in 1965, the United States government felt obliged to create endowments to encourage and fund the arts and the humanities. Government money in the arts, I fear, can only deflect artists from their responsibility to find an authentic market for their products, an actual audience for their performance. This is above all true for writing, which, requiring only pen and paper and a solitary author's time, can be cheaply produced and has been, since the invention of printing, a popular art, an art that seeks to draw its support from below and not from above.

P.S.: Brief as it is, this speech, addressing the stated question with all the honesty and good nature at my command, sticks in my mind as an epitome of discomfort in its delivery. The audience—writers and workers in the literary vineyard, assembled from many countries but predominantly New Yorkers—seethed with barely suppressed anger and was audibly impatient with any utterance other than a straightforward condemnation of the Reagan administration. The common-law wife of Daniel Ortega, the then President of Nicaragua, spoke from the floor in impassioned English about American "genocide" in her country and asked the panel, which included a German and a Pole, what we were going to do about it. The panel's chairman, E. L. Doctorow, after hearing my remarks, acknowledged the existence of blue mailboxes but said that if you looked carefully you could find a missile site around the corner; the fact of the United States possessing missiles, even unlaunched in their silos, was so self-evidently evil to him as to admit no counter-comment. Rhoda Koenig, reviewing the PEN Congress in *New York,* called my speech "a fairy tale," but what seemed fabulous to me was the goblin air of fevered indignation and reflexive anti-Americanism that may, for all I know, poison the atmosphere whenever the New York literary community gathers in numbers larger than two or three. If, for most of those citizens present, the United States had proved to be a land of educational and economic opportunity, with almost unparallelled guarantees of free expression, there was, once my mouth shut, not a whiff of acknowledgment, let alone gratitude.

How Does the Writer Imagine?

THE CAREER OF HERMAN MELVILLE, whose name adorns our lecture series and the history of Albany, invites us to reflect upon the vicissitudes

The inaugural annual Herman Melville Lecture on the Creative Imagination, sponsored by The Writers' Institute at Albany, New York, and given in that city on April 25, 1985.

of literary creation. He was born in the summer of 1819 on Pearl Street in lower Manhattan, into those circumstances so frequent in the biographies of writers—circumstances of fallen gentility. His father, Allan Melvill, was the younger of the two sons of a formidable orphan, Thomas Melvill, who participated in the Boston Tea Party and was appointed Collector of the Port of Boston by George Washington. Major Melvill, as he was called, held this sinecure for forty years, and shrewdly accumulated a fortune while doing so. His sons, however, inherited the habits, the good self-regard, and the optimism that money bestows without inheriting the gift of making more of it themselves. Allan as a youth went to Europe on the then-obligatory Grand Tour, and stayed for some years; he learned French, collected books and prints, and posed for a dandified portrait. Returning, he entered the import business and for all of his unfortunate commercial life was associated with the clothing trade. In 1814 he married Maria Gansevoort, of a prominent and wealthy family of this city. For four years the young couple lived in Albany, sharing a house with her mother and brother, and their first two children were born here. Allan's rich relations had set him up in the dry-goods business, but he managed to find the attractions of Albany resistible, and in 1818 moved to New York, where he fathered Herman and five more children, moved from house to house, lived and invested beyond his means, and borrowed heavily against his expectations from both his father and his wife's family. Sued by creditors, he took refuge back with the Gansevoorts in Albany; returning from a trip to Boston and New York in search of more credit, he walked across the iced-over Hudson in below-zero weather, took ill, and died early in the year 1832, when Herman was twelve. Throughout January, the dying man had raved like a maniac; this sad spectacle made a lasting impression upon his second son, whose work and career were both to be ever haunted by the fear of madness.

The years that Herman spent in the Albany area after his father's death could not have been very happy ones. The tangled reins of the family affairs had passed into the widow's rather frantic hands; she moved the family to nearby Lansingburgh, and added an "e" to the name of Melvill. Within a month of Allan's burial, Herman and his older brother, Gansevoort, were taken out of Albany Academy; the older boy was to assume management of the father's bankrupt business, and Herman was set to work as a clerk at the New York State Bank. Though his education was fitfully resumed at the Academy and at Albany Classical School, his adolescence was basically spent at labor; after the bank, he worked as a bookkeeper for his brother, and worked on his uncle Thomas Melvill's farm in Pittsfield, Massachusetts, and later taught school near there. His other uncle, Peter Gansevoort, assisted the dishevelled Melvilles as best he could, but, after a deceptive period of success, young Gansevoort Melville ran matters into bankruptcy again, and headed, as his father had done a decade before, for New York City. Herman, who as a child had been described by his father as "very backward in speech & somewhat slow in comprehension, but . . . of a docile & amiable disposition," in 1838 studied surveying to qualify as an engineer; but nothing came of this, and in the summer of 1839, by his older brother's arrangement, he shipped out as a crew member on a ship to Liverpool. Returning four months later, he taught school in Greenbush, New York, visited his uncle Thomas in Illinois, and, failing to find a job in New York City, shipped out from New Bedford on the whaling ship *Acushnet* early in 1841. For the next four years he was at sea or, having deserted one ship and mutinied on another, adventuring in the South Seas.

On his return to Lansingburgh, Melville, whose previous literary activity had consisted of a few pseudonymous articles for the local newspaper, sat down and wrote a book, *Narrative of a Four Months' Residence Among the Natives of a Valley of the Marquesas Islands*, now known under its American title of *Typee*, which became a great success in both England and the United States. He followed it with a sequel, *Omoo*, which also enjoyed a significant, if lesser, success, and then a third book, *Mardi*, which, though beginning in the same ebullient and popular manner as the others, branched hugely into fantasy, allegory, and intellectual extravagance. The fat volume, in one hundred ninety-five chapters, did not please critics or readers, and Melville, seeking to recapture his public, very rapidly wrote *Redburn* and *White-Jacket*, two more accounts based upon portions of his ocean venturing. His sixth book, *Moby-Dick*, like *Mardi*, diverged from its surface narration of a sea-tale to include philosophic and poetic digressions and, like *Mardi*, was generally accounted a disappointment, though it found some enthusiastic readers. Universally deplored and mocked, however, was Melville's next book, his seventh in seven years, the novel *Pierre*, and its harsh failure left wounds that never healed; his family became concerned about his health, and his search for a way out of financial insecurity began. From 1853 to 1856 Melville wrote a number of sketches and short stories for magazine publication, and a kind of novella, *Israel Potter*, based upon an old document. In 1856 he composed what was to be his last attempt to wrest a living from authorship, the novel *The Confidence-Man*, and undertook a therapeutic trip to Europe and the Holy Land. He was at his return not yet thirty-eight years old; except for some Civil War poems published in *Harper's Magazine* and later collected in a volume, his public career as an author was over.

For three seasons Melville attempted the lecture circuit, with indifferent success; in 1863 he sold the farm in Pittsfield where the bulk of his oeuvre had been written, and moved to New York City. For twenty years, until 1885, he worked as a customs inspector in that port, and sank into nearly total obscurity, he who had once been famous as the "man who lived among cannibals." He read widely, leaving a library full of interesting marginalia, and privately published two small volumes of poetry and a long poem, *Clarel*, whose expense was covered by his Albany uncle Peter Gansevoort. He died in 1891, leaving *Billy Budd* in manuscript; his reputation, totally eclipsed but for a few scattered admirers and a dim historical recall of *Typee*'s old splash, was revived in the 1920s, and Melville's name now presides at or near the very summit of American literary renown.

What does Melville's story tell us of the creative imagination but that it lies at the mercy of earthly circumstances? He wrote, in his dozen productive years, with extraordinary intensity, spending such long hours at his writing table that his health and sanity were feared for and his eyes became, in his words, "tender as young sparrows." Yet his youth held few hints of precocity or of literary concern; in 1850 he told Hawthorne, "Until I was twenty-five, I had no development at all. From my twenty-fifth year I date my life. Three weeks have scarcely passed, at any time between then & now, that I have not unfolded within myself." The pre-*Typee* silence of this "amiable and docile" youth—compare Poe and Hawthorne and Bryant, all scribbling and published by their very early twenties—foreshadows the eventual return to silence, when Melville again succumbed to fatalism and intellectual passivity. At the age of twenty-five, however, he found himself brimming with the exotic material of his recent adventures, and sensed a public eager for the kind of adventure tale that he could provide. "The book is certainly calculated for popular reading, or for none at all," he wrote the publisher of *Typee*. The English edition coming first, he permitted the American text to be bowdlerized of "all passages . . . which offer violence to the feelings of any large class of readers." These included not only "indelicate" sexual passages quite appropriate to the Polynesian setting but unflattering accounts of the South Seas missionaries: "I have rejected every thing, in revising the book, which refers to the missionaries," Melville wrote his publisher. "So far as the wide & permanent popularity of the book is concerned, their exclusion will certainly be beneficial." A certain Walter Whitman, reviewing the book in the Brooklyn *Eagle*, praised it as summer fare: "A strange, graceful, most readable book this . . . As a book to hold in one's hand and pore dreamily over of a summer day, it is unsurpassed." Its successor, *Omoo*, was even more consciously shaped to avoid offending the prejudices of a large audience, and to at least one reader, the wife of Henry Wadsworth Longfellow, seemed "very inferior to *Typee,* being written not so much for its own sake as to make another book apparently."

In writing *Mardi,* Melville himself began to chafe against the requirements of making yet another book. Writing his English publisher, John Murray, he confessed, "Proceeding in my narrative of *facts* I began to feel an incurable distaste for the same; & a longing to plume my pinions for a flight, & felt irked, cramped & fettered by plodding along with dull common places." Chastened by the self-indulgent book's failure, he returned to facts and commonplaces in *Redburn* and *White-Jacket,* but with a good deal of resentment and bitterness and self-scorn. He wrote his father-in-law that the books were "two *jobs,* which I have done for money—being forced to it, as other men are to sawing wood." To Richard Henry Dana, Jr., whose *Two Years Before the Mast* was a classic of the genre in which Melville first composed, he claimed to have turned out these books "almost entirely for lucre" and in his journal marvelled that a favorable reviewer of *Redburn* should "waste so many pages upon a thing, which I, the author, know to be trash, & wrote it to buy some tobacco with." And he told Evert Duyckinck that he hoped never to write another book like it, though it "puts money into an empty purse." When an author, he goes on, "attempts anything higher—God help him & save him! for it is not with a hollow purse as with a hollow balloon—for a hollow purse makes the poet *sink*—witness 'Mardi.' "

Yet his spirits and energy remained high, and in the middle of writing the next sea-adventure, *Moby-Dick,* he met Hawthorne, whose example and presence, for the year that they lived as neighbors in the Berkshires, emboldened Melville to plume his pinions for another flight, and to rewrite his text into an exuberant, exfoliating, exhaustive masterpiece. However, as with *Mardi,* the reviews were sour and the receipts meagre, and he settled again to court a popular audience. To his publisher he promised, "My new book [is] very much more calculated for popularity than anything you have yet published of mine—being a regular romance, with a mysterious plot to it, & stirring passions at work, and withall, representing a new & elevated aspect of American life." Alas, *Pierre,* weirdly fetching up all the resentments and tribulations he had endured in the households of his mother and his wife, disastrously miscarried, as did *The Confidence-Man,* its attempt to convey riverboat atmosphere and frontier humor all but smothered beneath a misanthropy that verges on pathology. Rage had overtaken the sunny-humored natural stylist of *Typee* and *Omoo,* and he ceased to court an audience that had ceased to respond.

The spectacle of an artist at war with an audience's expectations was, by Melville's time, still uncommon. His contemporary Dickens appeared to enjoy the give-and-take with readers that periodical serialization had opened up, and with no strain upon his artistic conscience sometimes trimmed his plot in response to letters he received. This same Dickens undertook extensive tours of dramatic readings from his own work, weeping with his audience over the death of little Nell and indeed putting so much of himself into these performances that he shortened his life—a crowd-pleaser, as well as a genius, to the end. Pleasing the audience, for writers as well as for other sorts of Victorian entertainer, *was* the art, and, though Stendhal claimed to be writing for an audience of the future, not until Flaubert was the notion formulated of a novelistic art that existed in independence of and even in defiance of the bourgeois public.

The idea of an artist arose, we may surmise, in tribal environments where the distinction between art's producers and its consumers was shadowy at best. All tribal members collaborated in the dance, in the enactments of ritual, and the tale-teller and mask-maker were exemplary performers within a rite created by the group. The social function of art could scarcely be an issue when all function was social, when individual gratification was inconceivable apart from the aggregate health and spiritual soundness. The oldest surviving art objects are votive and totemic; sculptural and graphic representation began in service to religion; and an awesome submissiveness underlies the serene monotony of Egyptian and Chinese representational conventions. It should be noted, though, that even in immensely static Egypt, when a revolutionary pharaoh, Akhenaten, proclaimed a new theology—a kind of anti-clerical sun-worship—the artists of his time responded with a new, slightly more supple and naturalistic style. Furthermore, in the tombs of the lesser nobles, Egyptian mural art becomes less pharaonic, more playful and attentive to the tender details of life, to the birds and reeds, in the Nile Valley. Artistic creativity, that is, tends to frolic in the margins of its hieratic assignments, and a perennial skirmishing exists between received conventions and unstructured impressions.

At the dawn of Western literature, with Homer, the Old Testament writers, and the bards and balladeers whose oral compositions have descended from the smoky throne rooms of northern Europe, it is difficult to discern any chink between the assignment and the execution, between the assumptions of the performer and those of the audience. A seamless intention seems bound up in these old masterworks; as in today's symbiosis between the yelling youthful rock star and his screaming adolescent fans, the artist enunciates the inner impulses of all, and his poetry has little more personal taint than that of the jokes and riddles which mysteriously arise and circulate among schoolchildren even today. The bard proclaims the tribal record; he speaks, or so we imagine at this great distance, for all.

So, too, the great playwrights of ancient Greece descend to us as synonymous with their culture, their popularity certified by the very survival of their texts and by their many first prizes at the Dionysia, the spring festival of Dionysius at Athens—thirteen first prizes for Aeschylus, about twenty for Sophocles (who never placed less than second in these competitions), and only four for Euripides. With Euripides, the youngest of the three, we have hints of author-audience tension in the modern style: the relative paucity of his prizes, his irreverent and even hostile treatment of the gods and their myths, his cursory handling of the conventional *deus ex machina* ending—as if the playwright is impatiently bowing to convention—and the something morbid and quarrelsome in the psychology of his characters all suggest an artist more intent upon saying what interests him than saying what people ought to hear. The improprieties of realism, which are to close English theatres under the Puritans and to scandalize readers of Flaubert and Zola, Dreiser and Joyce, first arise with Euripides, who is said to have been tried for impiety and to have gone to live in the court of the King of Macedonia because of his unpopularity in Athens.

The Middle Ages enlisted artists, usually anonymously, in the praise and service of God; we do not hesitate to credit the inner life of the age, rather than the genius of the individual stone-carver, with the sublime sculptures at Chartres and Rheims. Dante is the first writer since St. Augustine to whom we easily ascribe a personality, a personal history unmistakably embedded in his work. Shakespeare is our classic folk artist, who disdained no extremity of farce or fustian to keep the groundlings at the Globe entertained. He cobbled up coarse old plots, turning their absurdities into profundities and their carpentry into poetry; he concocted roles for whatever actor needed one, such as the company clowns William Kempe and Robert Armin; he casually collaborated with lesser talents and merged the proverbial wisdom of the time with his own prodigious originality. To think of Shakespeare as so immensely obliging and yet the glory of our language flatters us, of course, and suggests that being a great writer isn't something to get all fussy and truculent about. Since he left so little biographical trace that men still write serious books maintaining he was somebody else, we have only the work as a record of the man. To those who believe this record reveals nothing, I recommend an, I fear, out-of-print book by the late Irish short-story writer Frank O'Connor, called

Shakespeare's Progress; O'Connor, with many a bold reading and pugnacious opinion, sketches a turbulent, conflicted, and resentful life behind the oeuvre. O'Connor quotes the quatrain from Sonnet 111—

> O for my sake do you with Fortune chide,
> The guilty goddess of my harmful deeds,
> That did not better for my life provide
> Than public means, which public manners breeds—

and adds this comment: "All the tragedy of the fastidious man who has to make his living in the theatre is in that last unforgettable line."

Perhaps it needed the rise of a bourgeois audience to generate a fully conscious conflict between the artist's needs and manners and his public's. While we are aware that the genius of Leonardo da Vinci and, to a lesser extent, that of Michelangelo were led into many aborted and ephemeral projects by their aristocratic and papal patrons, it is not until Rembrandt that an artist pursues and improves his art at the distinct price of leaving his patronage behind. As Rembrandt's painting became broader, rougher, more daring, and ever more deeply humane, his commissions from the solid Dutch burghers dried up. What did they want with these light-encrusted portraits of wrinkled Amsterdam Jews, these Biblical scenes featuring big-bellied, unmistakably middle-aged women? They wanted, very sensibly, idealized portraits of themselves, with no more psychological depth than was needed to make the likeness vivid.

Another writer with distinguished Albany connections, Henry James, enjoyed the most sustained and rounded career of any American novelist, yet he, too, could be said to have outdistanced his public. Though his fluent style and tireless intelligence won him in his early twenties the loyalty of editors, his audience was at best limited, and his efforts to widen it proved futile; his attempt, for five years, to write for the London theatre ended in disaster—he came onto the stage after the premier performance of *Guy Domville* in 1895 and was unmistakably booed—and as his style became more ornate and his plots more rarefied his novels passed in many quarters for curiosities, the butt of parodies and patronizing reviews. The New York edition of his fiction, whose prefaces and revisions formed a labor of literary love and self-summation without parallel in the annals of the novel, was described by James in the last year of his life as "really a monument (like Ozymandias) which has never had the least intelligent critical justice done to it—or any sort of critical attention at all paid to it." As to his material rewards, James added, "No more commercially thankless job of the literary order was (Prefaces and all—*they* of a thanklessness!) accordingly ever achieved." Throughout his magnificently productive and thoughtful career, he needed for sustenance his share of the fortune amassed here in Albany by his Irish immigrant grandfather.

But at least James had no difficulty getting published; William Kennedy, who is among us tonight as this city's foremost literary exponent and ornament, whose novel *Ironweed* won two of its year's three main prizes for fiction, has confided in accepting one of them that this novel was rejected by publishers thirteen times. The annals of modernism abound in such horror stories: no less a first reader than André Gide turned down, for Éditions Gallimard, *Swann's Way,* the first volume of Proust's sublime *Remembrance of Things Past,* whose publication Proust then undertook to finance himself; and not only did James Joyce's *Ulysses* have to be privately printed in France, but his exemplary book of short stories, *Dubliners,* now standard fare for high-school students, went unpublished for ten years while Irish and English printers dithered over a few of its excessively accurate details.

Now, how does this make us feel, here in 1985? Superior, I think, and anxious. Superior because obviously *we,* had we been in the audience, would not have booed poor Henry James; *we,* had we been editorially empowered, would have accepted *Ironweed,* and *Swann's Way; we,* had we been alive in 1851, would have recognized *Moby-Dick* to be the great American epic it is. And anxious because we naturally wish to shelter authors, in their selfless delicacy and rapture, from the crass vagaries of obtuse editors, obtuser reviewers, and still obtuser book-buyers. One approach is to fund governmental and academic sponsorship of the arts. In 1965 Lyndon Baines Johnson signed into being the National Endowments for the Arts and for the Humanities; in 1984 the Senate-Assembly of your great state of New York, Governor Cuomo assenting, passed an act stating that "the general welfare of the people of the state will be enhanced by the establishment of a center devoted to writing and the allied arts," some specified objectives of which center are to hire writers, offer scholarships, foster coöperation among writers' programs and workshops, offer programs for the teaching of the craft of writing, and, even, to "offer at least one lecture annually by a distinguished writer on an aspect of the creative imagination which will further the objectives of the institute's programs and which will enrich the community's exposure to the arts."

One wonders, really, whether such a proposed whirlwind of worthiness will ever do more than provide a few sinecures and some cheerful fellowship for writers who otherwise might have to develop a new profession. The more widespread solution, to bourgeois pro-art anxiety in the wake of modernism, has been academic patronage. On this recourse, as it pertains to the art of music, Mr. Richard Sennett was recently eloquent in last year's December *Harper's* magazine:

> The emergence of the university as the primary patron of and shelter for the artist, a transformation that occurred in America, Great Britain, and, to a lesser degree, the rest of Western Europe after the Second World War, profoundly changed the conditions under which artistic experimentation occurred. This was true not only in music but also in dance and theatre, as well as in literature and the visual arts. It represented a new stage in the social history of art: the artist was protected from the stupidity, the desire for pleasure, tears, and amusement, the wavering attention and sudden, unpredictable enthusiasms of an audience—which is no more and no less than a spoiled mixture of humanity itself. In 1958 the composer Milton Babbitt wrote an article for *High Fidelity* that the magazine decided to call "Who Cares If You Listen?" The title was an apt, unvarnished description of the mentality of tenured art: the artist should be thought of as a researcher, and his listeners, if any, should feel the same thrill that people at a dinner party feel when an honored guest deigns to explain what earned him the Nobel Prize in physics.

Mr. Sennett goes on to doubt that the results of such a tenured art have been, at least in music, very wonderful, or even, as one might expect, very adventurous: "Security brought about a new kind of provincialism, the provincialism of the college town. . . . And so avant-garde became predictable. It was a logical turn of events, once the campus salon replaced the music hall."

The situation as described is perhaps an extreme one. The homely art of fiction, with its roots in penny journalism and the common coin of spoken language, could never become so sequestered; nor, in my opinion, should it. The creative imagination is not born in a vacuum. Its first impulses bloom under the stimulus of parental and institutional praise, and even the most precocious musical genius needs a piano in the house and, now, records and tapes. Creativity, as I construe it, is a tripartite phenomenon. There is the artist, keen to express himself and make an impression. But there also has to be a genre, a pre-existent form or type of object to which the prospective artist's first relation was that of consumer, the pleasure of his consumption extending itself into the ambition to be a producer. And attached to that genre and inextricable from its growth is the audience that finds in the contents of this form some cause for consolation, amusement, or enlightenment. In Pompeii, racy frescoes served a purpose; in seventeenth-century Amsterdam, wall paintings became necessary furniture. In the nineteenth century, novels developed a wide public, and Mr. Sennett's description of the plight and progress of classical music affords an interesting parallel: he says, "In the nineteenth century, problems in communication arose because of the moral expectations the bourgeoisie had of art. Art, it was held, could refine taste, could remove one from the sordid world of small-mindedness and material striving. The Romantic musicians struggled constantly against these restraints of 'good taste.' "

Art, then, became, for the hard-working bourgeoisie, a relief from life rather than, as for pre-capitalist tribesmen, an explanation and intensification of it. To an extent, the arts survive as an instrument and emblem of social improvement: one goes to the museum, and concerts, and reads books, because other nice people do. One attends college partly to get the knack of the arts, so one will move at ease among other people who have mastered the same knack. Art functions as grease in the social wheels. Banks and corporations are now among the chief purchasers of contemporary paintings, which hang in their offices not only as a possibly sound investment for themselves but as a kind of soothing visual Muzak to lull the customers, to create an atmosphere of play that alleviates the terrible seriousness with which money offers itself to our management. The theatrical arts serve now as they have done for centuries as backdrop to courtships and seductions on the private as well as the business level. Art is associated with refinement, and refinement with wealth, and wealth with power.

People once read Fanny Burney and Thackeray to learn about manners and decorum in the social class a notch or two above their own; one of the charms, certainly, of going to the movies in the Thirties and Forties was seeing how the rich lived, in their penthouses, with their tuxedos and butlers and silver cigarette cases. The recent success on television of *Dynasty* again demonstrates that the rich, who always look well in their clothes and always find parking places in front of hotels, remain fascinating—supermen and wonder women of the consumer society. But people who read novels now do so, I suspect, more to learn how other people act in bed than at the table; our fantasies run less toward palaces and penthouses than toward the violence and paranoia of the international thriller.

People look to the arts, in any case, to supplement their lives, and when a genre ceases to provide supplements self-evidently desirable, then uneasy philanthropic and legislative effort to encourage the art, to foster its perpetuation and ensure its survival, enter in. Why does one never hear of government funding for the preservation and encouragement of comic strips, girlie magazines, and TV soap operas? Because these genres still hold the audience they were created to amuse and instruct; they exist in our culture unaccredited, unrespectable, and unsponsored, except by popular demand, like the novel in the nineteenth century, like the drama in the reign of Queen Elizabeth. An art form does not determine itself from abstract or intrinsic causes; it is shaped by the technology and appetite of the time. Very quickly, a dust of nostalgia and scholarship can deceptively accumulate upon a form, so that it seems to have been always dusty. Already, learned societies devote themselves to the early history of the comic strip, and the Hollywood movies of the studio era, turned out as giant artifacts by so-called film factories, can now be seen to have artistic qualities and, more surprisingly, an artistic integrity lacking in the much more artistically self-conscious movies of today. There comes a moment in the evolution of art when a certain thing cannot any more be done; Busby Berkeley musicals could not be produced at contemporary wagerates, and we cannot now, except with a great effort of mimicry, produce images with the texture of those Victorian block-prints that, until the invention of photogravure, were turned out by the tens of thousands. So, in the collage-narratives of Max Ernst and Donald Barthelme, these prints become art. Qualities that once seemed neutral and inevitable are the second time around revealed as full of the passion of the time, as declared by a style that in retrospect brims with strangeness.

Now, where does this rather fatalistic and determinist overview of art leave the individual creative imagination? The creative imagination, I would say, functions with a certain indispensable innocence within its implacable context. Ever renewed as each generation emerges from childhood, it wants to please. It wants to please more or less as it has been pleased, by the art that touched it in its formative years. Already, a generation of novelists flourishes, Stephen King foremost, that has been deeply penetrated by the narrative vocabulary of television; I cannot feel more than mildly alarmed, since my own generation was enslaved to the movies. The creative imagination wants to please its problematical audience, and it does so by sharing what is most precious to it. A small child's first instinct vis-à-vis possessions is to hug what it has tight to itself; its socialization and its creativity begin when it pushes a lima bean or a slobbered toy truck toward a sibling or playmate. Perhaps we can take this development a step further back: Freud somewhere claims that a child's first gifts, to its parents, are its feces, whose presentation (in the appropriate receptacle) is roundly praised. And, as in this primal benefaction, the writer extrudes his daily product while sitting down, on a healthy basis of regularity and avoidance of strain. The artist who works in words and anecdotes, images and facts wants to share with us nothing less than his digested life, his life as he conceives it, in the memories and fantasies most precious, however obscurely, to him. Let me illustrate all this with a brief example from the creative process I know best, my own.

In 1958 I was a young man of twenty-six who had recently presumed to set himself up in a small New England town as a free-lance writer. My obligations to my career and my family, as I had framed them, were to sell six short stories a year to *The New Yorker* magazine. I had already written and sold a number based upon my Pennsylvania boyhood and my young married life in New York City; one winter day I happened to remember, with a sudden simultaneous sense of loss and recapture, the New Year's Eve parties my old high-school crowd used to have at a certain home, and how even after most of us had gone off to college we for several years continued the custom, which now served as a kind of reunion. The hero of my story is a college sophomore, already committed to a college girlfriend and to aspirations that will take him forever away from his home town. He tells us of a moment in this hectic gathering of nineteen- and twenty-year-olds:

The party was the party I had been going to all my life, beginning with Ann Mahlon's first Hallowe'en party, that I attended as a hot, lumbering, breathless, and blind Donald Duck. My mother had made the costume, and the eyes kept slipping, and were further apart than my eyes, so that even when the clouds of gauze parted, it was to reveal the frustrating depthless world seen with one eye. Ann, who because her mother loved her so much as a child had remained somewhat childish, and I and another boy and girl who were not involved in any romantic crisis went down into Schuman's basement to play circular ping-pong. Armed with paddles, we stood each at a side of the table and when the ball was stroked ran around it counter-clockwise, slapping the ball and screaming. To run better the girls took off their heels and ruined their stockings on the cement floor. Their faces and arms and shoulder sections became flushed, and when a girl lunged forward toward the net the stiff neckline of her semi-formal dress dropped away and the white arcs of her brassiere could be glimpsed cupping fat, and when she reached high her shaved armpit gleamed like a bit of chicken skin. An earring of Ann's flew off and the two connected rhinestones skidded to lie near the wall, among the Schumans' power mower and the badminton poles and empty bronze motor-oil cans twice punctured by triangles. All these images were immediately lost in the whirl of our running; we were dizzy before we stopped. Ann leaned on me getting back into her shoes.

The story is called "The Happiest I've Been." It was accepted and paid for, and has been reprinted in a few anthologies. While writing it, I had a sensation of breaking through, as if through a thin sheet of restraining glass, to material, to truth, previously locked up. I was excited, and when my wife of those years read the first draft, she said, "This is exciting." Now, what was exciting? There is no great violence or external adventure in the story, no extraordinary characters. The abrupt purchase on lived life, I suggest, is exciting. In 1958 I was at just the right distance from the night in Shillington, Pennsylvania, when 1952 became 1953; I still remembered and cared, yet was enough distant to get a handle on the memories, to manipulate them into fiction.

That is part one of creativity: the ego and its self-expression. For part two, the genre, there was the American short story, *The New Yorker* short story indeed, of which many had been written in the decades preceding 1958, but none, my happy delusion was, quite in this way about quite this sort of material. Non-Southern small towns and teen-agers were both, my impression was, customarily treated with condescension, or satirically, in the fiction of the Fifties; the indictments of provincial life by Sinclair Lewis and Ring Lardner were still in the air. My mission was to stand up and cry, "No, here is life, to be taken as seriously as any other kind." By this light tiny details, such as the shaved armpit gleaming like a bit of chicken skin or the two triangular punctures in an empty oil can, acquire the intensity of proclamation. Things turn symbolic; hidden meanings emerge. The blurred sexuality of this playful moment is ominous, for it is carrying the participants away from their childhoods, into the dizzying mystery of time.

As to the third part of the creative process, the audience beyond the genre, there was *The New Yorker* reader of my imagination, pampered and urban, needing a wholesome small-town change from his then-customary diet of Westchester-adultery stories and reminiscences of luxurious Indian or Polish childhoods. I believed, that is, that there was a body of my fellow Americans to whom these modest doings in Pennsylvania would be news.

Such was the state of my imagination as I wrote this story; actually, many stories not unlike it appear in the magazine now, and perhaps always have: but in my possibly mistaken sense of things the material was fresh, fresh to me and fresh to the world, and authentic. By authentic I mean actual. For the creative imagination, as I conceive it, is wholly parasitic upon the real world—what used to be called Creation. Creative excitement, and a sense of useful work, has invariably and only come to me when I felt I was transferring, with a lively accuracy, some piece of experienced reality to the printed page. Those two triangular holes and that bit of chicken skin are pearls of great price, redeemed from the featureless sweep of bygone experience. The wish to do justice to the real world compels language into those semi-transparent layers that make a style. No style or form exists in the abstract; whatever may be true in painting or music, there is no such thing as abstract writing. Words even when shattered into nonsense struggle to communicate meanings to us; and behind the most extreme modernist experiments with the language of fiction—Joyce's *Finnegans Wake;* the late writing of Gertrude Stein; the automatic writing of Dada—some perception about the nature of reality seeks embodiment.

The creative imagination, then, has a double interface: on the output side, with some kind of responsive audience, and on the input side, with reality itself. If either connection breaks down, the electricity ceases to flow. Both sides of the creative event demand trust: on the output side, we must hope an audience is there, or will be there. On the input, we must sit down in the expectation that the material will speak through us, that certain unforeseeable happinesses of pattern and realization will emerge out of blankness as we write.

We began with Melville. His audience, in that England-oriented, romance-minded America of a hundred forty years ago, was wandering away, but something was frazzling as well in his relation with his raw material. Melville was interested—turned on, we might say—by the sea, and by male interchange, and toward the end of his long-silent life wrote in his obscurity one more masterpiece, *Billy Budd,* along the lines of these concerns. The vast land of America and the complexities of family life depressed rather than fired his imagination. So, his attempts to abandon his oceanic material rebuked, he abdicated the professional writer's struggle and has probably made a stronger impression on posterity for it. He seems, at this distance, unencumbered by facile prolixity or mere professionalism; the lack of public means spared him public manners. In his professional defeat his imagination remained his own.

In this present age of excessive information and of cheerful inaccuracy, where six shrewd or at least intimidatingly verbal critics exist for every creative spirit, the writer has no clearer moral duty than to keep his imagination his own. In doing so, he risks becoming offensive. Listen, if you will, to the tone of this contemporary review of *Moby-Dick:*

> Mr. Melville is evidently trying to ascertain how far the public will consent to be imposed upon. He is gauging, at once, our gullibility and our patience. Having written one or two passable extravagances, he has considered himself privileged to produce as many more as he pleases, increasingly exaggerated and increasingly dull. . . . The truth is, Mr. Melville has survived his reputation. If he had been contented with writing one or two books, he might have

been famous, but his vanity has destroyed all his chances of immortality, or even of a good name with his own generation.

"O generation of vipers" runs through the mind. All generations, each in their time, are viperish, and how the artist survives and makes his way in his own lifetime is fundamentally a personal problem, with many solutions, none of them ideal. But this much seems certain: what we end by treasuring in the creative imagination is the freedom it manages to keep, regardless of contemporary response. Or, rather, the degree to which it, imagining an ideal audience, succeeds in creating an audience with an enhanced capacity for response.

Should Writers Give Lectures?

THE VERY FIRST PEOPLE whom we consider authors—the minds and voices behind the tribal epics, the Bible and Homer, the Vedas and the sagas—were, it would seem, public performers, for whom publication took the form of recitation, of incantation, of (we might say) lecturing. The circumstances wherein these primal literary works were promulgated are not perfectly clear, nor are all examples of oral literature identical in purpose and texture; but we could risk generalizing that the bard's function was, in the Horatian formulation, to entertain and to instruct, and that the instruction concerned the great matter of tribal identity. The poet and his songs served as a memory bank, supplying the outlines of the determinative tribal struggles and instances of warrior valor. Who we are, who our heroic fathers were, how we got where we are, why we believe what we believe and act the way we do—the bard illuminates these essential questions, as the firelight flickers and the mead flows and the listeners in their hearts renew their pact with the past. The author is delivering not his own words but his own version of a story told to him, a story handed down in an evolving form and, at a certain point, fixed into print by the written version of a scribe. The author is not only himself but his predecessors, and simultaneously he is part of the living tribal fabric, the part that voices what all know, or should know, and need to hear again.

The mnemonic function of poetry weakly persists: American schoolchildren remember a certain epic date with the rhyme "In fourteen hundred ninety-two / Columbus sailed the ocean blue," and verses exist that

---

Delivered at the Gothenburg Book Fair, in Gothenburg, Sweden, on August 20, 1987.

enable one to recall the Kings of England and which months of the year contain thirty days or, in the case of February, even fewer. The nineteenth century abounded in ballad versions of such historical events as the midnight ride of Paul Revere and the bravery, in the midst of the Civil War, of a certain elderly Barbara Frietchie, who brandished the Union flag at rebel soldiers and inspired this famous couplet:

> "Shoot, if you must, this old gray head,
> But spare your country's flag," she said.

As recently as a decade ago, consumers of popular music were startled by a hit that rousingly set forth the facts of the Battle of New Orleans, which was fought in 1814.

And the traditional, even sacred centrality of the bard at the tribal conference is remembered, I think, by the widely held notion that authors can "speak"—that their vocation includes an ability and a willingness to entertain and instruct, orally, any gathering where the mead flows and ring-gold forthcomes in sufficient quantities. The assumption is flattering but in truth the modernist literary tradition, of which we are all, for lack of another, late and laggard heirs, ill prepares a writer for such a performance. James Joyce, evidently, had a fine tenor voice and loved to sing, and he also, inspired by enough mead, could kick as high as the lintel of a doorway; but Proust was of a thoroughly retiring and unathletic nature, and murmured mostly to himself. "Authentic art has no use for proclamations, it accomplishes its work in silence," he wrote, in that massive meditation upon the writer's task which concludes *Remembrance of Things Past.* "To be altogether true to his spiritual life an artist must remain alone and not be prodigal of himself even to disciples" is another of Proust's strictures. The artist, he repeatedly insists, is not another citizen, a social creature with social duties; he is a solitary explorer, a pure egotist. In a great parenthesis he explains that "when human altruism is not egotistic it is sterile, as for instance in the writer who interrupts his work to visit an unfortunate friend, to accept a public function, or to write propaganda articles."

In almost the exact middle of *Time Regained,* Marcel contemplates his task—the huge novel we have at this point almost read through—and quails at a prospect so grand and exalted. He has stumbled upon the uneven paving stones that have recalled Venice to him, has heard the clink of the spoon upon glass that has reminded him of the train journey in which he had observed the steeples of Martinsville, has felt the texture of the stiff napkin that has reminded him of Balbec and its beach and ocean;

he has tasted the madeleine out of which bloomed all Combray, and sees that these fragments involuntarily recovered from the abyss of Time compose the truth he must deliver:

> Beneath these signs there lay something of a quite different kind which I must try to discover, some thought which they translated after the fashion of those hieroglyphic characters which at first one might suppose to represent only material objects. No doubt the process of decipherment was difficult, but only by accomplishing it could one arrive at whatever truth there was to read. For the truths which the intellect apprehends directly in the world of full and unimpeded light have something less profound, less necessary than those which life communicates to us against our will in an impression which is material because it enters us through the senses but yet has a spiritual meaning which is possible for us to extract.

This extraction of meaning from hieroglyphs becomes on the next page an underwater groping:

> As for the inner book of unknown symbols (symbols carved in relief they might have been, which my attention, as it explored my unconscious, groped for and stumbled against and followed the contours of, like a diver exploring the ocean-bed), if I tried to read them no one could help me with any rules, for to read them was an act of creation in which no one can do our work for us or even collaborate with us. How many for this reason turn aside from writing! What tasks do men not take upon themselves in order to evade this task! Every public event, be it the Dreyfus affair, be it the war, furnishes the writer with a fresh excuse for not attempting to decipher this book: he wants to ensure the triumph of justice, he wants to restore the moral unity of the nation, he has no time to think of literature. But these are mere excuses, the truth being that he has not or no longer has genius, that is to say instinct. For instinct dictates our duty and the intellect supplies us with pretexts for evading it. But excuses have no place in art and intentions count for nothing: at every moment the artist has to listen to his instinct, and it is this that makes art the most real of all things, the most austere school of life, the true last judgement.

Now, perhaps in this audience there have been some smiles at Proust's enthusiasm over the still-fresh discovery of the unconscious and at his virtually religious exaltation of the private over the public—of instinct, which can be expressed only through concrete images impressed upon us by reality and re-created in works of art, over intellect, which can speak the language of men, of social commerce. Is not a bustling book fair the silliest place in the world to suggest that literature is an activity apart, an activity of the spirit as intimate as prayer, an activity for whose sake we must renounce deeds as praiseworthy and socially useful as helping sick friends, propagandizing for worthy causes, and accepting public functions such as the one I am now fulfilling? The religious tone of classic modernism, breathing austerity and fanaticism, strikes us as excessive. Its close imitation of European Catholicism seems puzzling, now that the vessel of Christianity is a century more depleted. Austerity and fanaticism are now given over to the Muslims, who alarm us each night on the televised news. What do the emanations from the ivory tower count against those from the television transmitting tower?

This phrase "ivory tower" was proposed by Flaubert, the first modernist novelist, when he wrote,

> Between the crowd and ourself, no bond exists. Alas for the crowd; alas for us, especially. But since the fancy of one individual seems to me just as valid as the appetite of a million men, and can occupy an equal place in the world, we must (regardless of material things and of mankind, which disavows us) live for our vocation, climb up our ivory tower and there, like a bayadere with her perfumes, dwell alone with our dreams.

The artist's only possible camaraderie, Flaubert elsewhere asserts, can be with other artists. "Mankind hates us: we serve none of its purposes; and we hate it, because it injures us. So let us love one another 'in Art,' as mystics love one another 'in God.' " God much haunts his mind, as in the famous dictum "An author in his book must be like God in the universe, present everywhere and visible nowhere." God does not lecture, except to the Old Testament Israelites, who did not always listen. The modernist writer does not lecture; he creates, he dreams, he deciphers his hieroglyphs, he exists in a state of conscious antagonism to the busy bourgeois world. The lecture is an instrument of the bourgeoisie, a tool in the mass education essential to modern democracies. Though Flaubert says that no bond exists between the crowd and literary artists, the crowd offers to make one and invites the writer to lecture. "Descend from your ivory tower," the crowd cries, "and come share, O bayadere, your fabulous perfumes with us." Godlike and savage in his purest conception of himself, the author is thus brought back into society, into the global village, and trivialized into being an educator and a celebrity.

I am thinking primarily of my own country in offering this last image. Lectures by authors go back, in the United States, to the so-called lyceum circuit, which, beginning in the 1830s, brought to the scattered American provinces inspirational and educational speakers. Ralph Waldo Emerson was such a star, hitting the road with secular sermons culled from his journals, and then collecting these oral gems into the volumes of essays that are among the classic texts of American style and thought. Mark Twain, a generation and a half later, began as a comic lecturer, a stand-up comedian without a microphone, and his best-selling novels and travel accounts retained much of his crowd-pleasing platform manner. Even writers relatively abstruse and shy followed the lecture trail; Henry James toured the States coast to coast in 1904–5 lecturing on "The Lesson of Balzac," and Melville for a time in the late 1850s, when he was still somewhat famous as "the man who had lived among cannibals," sought to generate the income that his books were failing to supply by speaking, at fifty dollars a lecture, on "Statues in Rome" and "The South Seas." Even a figure as eccentric and suspect as Whitman travelled about, evidently, with a lecture on Lincoln. Yet in its very heyday the lyceum style of bardic enterprise had its detractors among literary men: Hawthorne wrote in *The Blithedale Romance* of "that sober and pallid, or, rather, drab-colored, mode of winter-evening entertainment, the Lecture," and Oliver Wendell Holmes returned from a tour reporting that "a lecturer was a literary strumpet."

Still, as one tries to picture those gaslit auditoriums of the last century, with the black-clad lecturer and his oaken lectern framed by velvet curtains heavy with gold tassels—curtains that the next night might part to reveal a scuffed and much-travelled opera set or the chairs of a minstrel show—one imagines an audience and a performer in sufficient agreement as to what constituted entertainment and edification; the bonds between the culture-hungry and the culture-dispensing were stretched thin but not yet broken in the innocence of the New World wilderness. One thinks of the tremendous warmth Emerson established with his auditors, to whom he entrusted, without condescension or clowning, his most profound and intimate thoughts, and who in listening found themselves discovering, with him, what it was to be American.

Like book clubs and other movements of mass uplift, the lecture circuit gradually gravitated toward the lowbrow. The famous Chautauqua Movement, which persisted into the 1920s, blended with camp meetings and tent revival meetings—each a high-minded excuse to forgather, with the usual mixed motives of human gatherings. The writers most admired in my youth did not, by and large, lecture, though some of the less admired and more personable did, such as the then-ubiquitous John Mason Brown and Franklin P. Adams. But Hemingway and Faulkner and Fitzgerald and Steinbeck were rarely seen on stages; their advice to humanity was contained in their works, and their non-writing time seemed amply filled with marlin fishing, mule fancying, skirt chasing, and recreational drinking. They were a rather rough-hewn crew, adventurers and knockabouts who had trained for creative writing by practicing journalism. Few were college graduates, though Fitzgerald's years at Princeton were important to him and Sinclair Lewis and Thornton Wilder did hold degrees from Yale. But doing was accepted as the main mode of literary learning. Hemingway began as a reporter for the Kansas City *Star* at the age of eighteen, and at the age of nineteen Eugene O'Neill quit Princeton and shipped out to sea. The world of print was wider then: a major American city might have as many as eight or ten daily newspapers, and a number of popular magazines paid well for short stories. The writers of this pre-television generation, with their potentially large bourgeois audience, yet were modernist enough to shy from crowd-pleasing personal appearances; nor, in the matter of lecturing, is there much reason to suppose that they were often invited. Why would the citizens of Main Street want to hear what Sinclair Lewis thought of them? Gertrude Stein, of all people, did go on a nationwide lecture tour in 1934, speaking in her complacently repetitive and cryptic style on such topics as "What Is English Literature," "The Gradual Making of the Making of Americans," and "Portraits and Repetition." One suspects, though, that the audiences came to hear her much as they had flocked to hear Oscar Wilde in 1882—more for the spectacle than the sense, and to be titillated by the apparition of the writer as an amusing exotic.

It is true that, in the early decades of the twentieth century, such very estimable literary artists as Shaw, Eliot, and Mann did not infrequently lecture. Shaw, however, was a man of the stage, with something political—Fabian Socialism—to sell. Eliot was a critic as much as he was a poet, with an excellent formal education in his possession and a considerable financial need to urge him to the lectern. And Mann, well, was German, and in the mighty role of *Dichter* rather close to the primeval bard. By lecturing, with authority and aplomb, on Freud, Goethe, and Wagner, Mann was, besides acknowledging sources of his own inspiration, paying homage to tribal gods, to exemplary heroes of German culture. The French, too, one might observe in passing, now and then cast up literary figures whose magisterial presence consists of the sum of their work with something added from before and beyond. Figures like Valéry and Sartre even in their silences and refusals lecture, reminding their publics of the ancient glories of Gallic acumen. When one tries to think of who in recent French culture has projected the most vital images outward to the non-French world, one comes up with lecturers—Barthes, Derrida, Lévi-Strauss, Lacan, Braudel.

But in my own country, in the four decades since the end of World War II, one sees not the elevation of analysis and thought to the animated and brightly visible level of creative art, but the reduction of literary artists to the status of academic adjuncts. Where creation is taken as a precondition for exposition, the creator is expected to be, in Proust's phrase, "prodigal of himself." It is not merely that poets out of economic necessity teach in colleges and read their works in other colleges and in time understandably take as a standard of excellence a poem's impact upon a basically adolescent audience, or that short-story writers move from college writing program to summer workshop and back again and consider actual publication as a kind of supplementary academic credential, while a karmic turnover of writing students into graduate writing students into writing teachers takes place within an academic universe sustained by grants and tax money and isolated from the marketplace. It is not merely that contemporary novels are studied for course credit and thus given the onus of the compulsory and, as it were, the textbook-flavored—a modernization of the literary curriculum, one might remark, that displaces the classics and gives the present a kind of instant fustiness. It is that American society, generously trying to find a place for this functionary, inherited from other epochs, called a writer, can only think to place him as a teacher and, in a lesser way, as a celebrity.

He is invited to come onto television and have his say, as if his book, his poor thick unread book, were *not* his say. He is invited to come into the classroom and, the meagrest kind of expert, teach himself. Last century's lyceum circuit has moved indoors, from the open air of a hopeful rural democracy to the cloistered auditoriums of the country's fifteen hundred accredited colleges and universities; the circuit has been, as it were, miniaturized. Though the market for actual short stories is down, in the vastness of the United States, to a half-dozen or so paying magazines, the market for fiction writers, as adornment to banquets and conferences and corporate self-celebrations, is booming. Kurt Vonnegut has observed that an American writer gets paid more for delivering a speech at a third-rate bankrupt college than he does for writing a short-story masterpiece.

I do not wish to complain or to exaggerate. Sociological situations have causes that are not altered by satire or nostalgia. The university and the printshop, literature and scholarship have been ever close, and the erratic ways in which writers support themselves and their books seek readers have changed a number of times since the Renaissance days when poets sought with fulsome dedications to win the support of noble patrons. The academization of writing in America is but an aspect, after all, of the academization of America. The typical writer of my generation is college-educated; in fact I am rather a maverick in having avoided graduate school.

Academically equipped and habituated, it is natural for, say, John Barth and Joyce Carol Oates to teach and to lecture. They know a lot, and the prestige of their authorship adds a magic twinkle, a raffish spin, to their knowledge. Writers such as they stand ready to participate in the discourse of civilized men and women, just as, in pre-war Europe, writers like Mann and Valéry and Eliot could creditably perform in the company of scholarly gentlemen. Until the arising, not so many centuries ago, of a large middle-class audience for printed material and with it the possibility of professional writers supported by the sales of their works, writers had to be gentlemen or daughters of clergymen or courtiers of a kind; like jesters, writers peeked from behind the elbow of power. If, in a democracy without a nobility or much of a landed gentry, the well-endowed universities step in and act the part of patron, where is the blame? Who longs for the absinthe-soaked bohemia that offered along with its freedom and excitement derangement and despair, or for the barren cultural landscape that so grudgingly fed the classic American artists? Is not even the greatest American writing, from Hawthorne and Dickinson to Hemingway and Faulkner, and not excluding Whitman and Mark Twain, maimed by the oddity of the native artist's position and the limits of self-education? Perhaps so; but we suspect in each of the cases named that the oddity is inextricable from the intensity and veracity, and that when the writer becomes a lecturer, a certain intensity is lost.

Why should this be? To prepare and give a lecture, and to observe the attendant courtesies, takes time; but time is given abundantly to the writer, especially in this day of antibiotics and health-consciousness, more time than he or she needs to be struck by his or her particular lightning. There was time enough, in the life of Wallace Stevens, to put in eight-hour days at his insurance company in Hartford; time enough, in the life of Rimbaud, to quit poetry at the age of nineteen; time enough, in the life of Tolstoy, to spurn art entirely and to try to educate the peasants and reinvent religion. We feel, in fact, that if a writer's life does not have in it time to waste—time for a binge or a walk in the woods or a hectic affair or a year of silence—he can't be much of a writer. In a sense none of his time is wasted except that in which he turns his back on nature, shuts down his osmotic function, and tries to lecture. Mann, in his lecture on Freud—given at the celebration of Freud's eightieth birthday, in Vienna in 1936—warned his audience, "An author, my friends, is a man essentially not bent upon science, upon knowing, distinguishing, and analysing; he stands for simple creation, for doing and making, and thus may be the object of useful cognition, without, by his very nature, having any competence in it as subject." The artist, in his experiences, passions, prejudices, and ignorances, is a delegate from reality, a distillation or an outgrowth of it, and in all humility offers himself as an object of study rather than as an expert, even on the topic of himself. Decipherment of the inner hieroglyphics that reality has stamped upon him, to use Proust's metaphor, is his business, and he should undertake no task that might impair his deciphering. Asking a writer to lecture is like asking a knife to turn a screw. Screws are necessary to hold the world together, the tighter the better, and a screwdriver is an admirable tool, more rugged and less dangerous than a knife; but a knife with a broken tip and a dulled or twisted edge serves all purposes poorly. Of course, if a knife is repeatedly used as a screwdriver, it will get worn into the shape of one; but then don't expect it to slice any more apples.

Perhaps, in this electronic age, one should attempt to speak in terms of input and output and static. Invited to lecture, the writer is flattered. He feels invited up, after years of playing on the floor with paper dolls and pretend castles, into grown-up activity, for which one wears a suit, and receives money or at least an airplane ticket. He furthermore receives society's permission, by the terms of the contract, to immobilize an audience of some hundreds or at least dozens of fellow human beings. I must be, he can only conclude, an interesting and worthy person. With this thought, on this particular frequency, static enters the wave bands where formerly he was only hearing the rustle of paper dolls—static, alas, that may be slow to clear up. Input and output are hard to manage simultaneously. A writer on show tends not to see or hear much beyond his own performance. A writer whose thinking has become thoroughly judgmental, frontal, and reasonable is apt to stop writing.

For a work of fiction is not a statement about the world; it is an attempt to create, out of hieroglyphs imprinted by the world upon the writer's inner being, another world. The kind of precision demanded concerns how something would be said, how someone or something would look, or how closely the rhythm of a paragraph suggests the atmosphere of a moment. The activity—if I may confess this without offending our secular fair—feels holy; it is attempted with much nervousness and inner and outer circling, and consummated with a sense of triumph out of all apparent proportion to the trivial or even tawdry reality that has been verbally approximated. Compared with such precision, everything that can be said in a lecture feels only somewhat true, and significantly corrupt. Lecturing deprives the author of his sacred right to silence, of speaking only on the firm ground of the imaginary. To the mind whose linguistic habits have been shaped by the work of mimesis, assertions and generalizations, however subtly and justly turned, seem a self-violation; and if the violation is public, as a lecture is, the occasion partakes of disgrace—one has deserted one's post and forsaken one's task for a lesser, however richly society has wrapped the occasion in plausibility and approval.

But how understandable it is, after all, for society to assume that the writer has something to say. To assume the opposite—that the writer has nothing to say—seems scandalous, though it is somewhat true, at least to the degree that we all have nothing to say, relative to the immense amount of saying that gets done. Most human utterance is not communication but a noise, a noise that says, "I am here," a noise that says, "You are not alone." The value, for the author, of a lecture is that he confesses, by giving one, that he, too, needs to make this noise. The Flaubertian pose of God the creator ("paring his fingernails," James Joyce added in a famous specification—"within or behind or beyond or above his handiwork, invisible, refined out of existence, indifferent, paring his fingernails") yields in these post modern times to the pose of a talkative good fellow, a fellow speaker, contributing his bit to the chatter that holds the surrounding silence at bay.

Giving a lecture gets the writer out into the world, and in its moment of delivery enables him to savor the ancient bardic role. It confronts him with an audience, and healthily deprives him of the illusion that he is his own audience—that his making, like the Lord's, takes place in a void. In the literary art, however abstruse or imagist, surreal or impersonal, communication is hoped for, and communication implies the attempt to alter other minds. This is the shameful secret, the tyrannical impulse, hidden behind the modernist pose of self-satisfying creation. A Western writer who has travelled even a little in the Third World has encountered the solemn, aggressive question "What is the writer's social purpose?" In other words, "How do you serve your fellow men?" It seems embarrassing and inadequate to reply honestly that—if one is a fiction writer—one serves them by constructing fantastic versions of one's own life, spin-offs from the personal into the just barely possible, into the amusingly elaborated. Giving a lecture reminds the writer of another dimension of his task, that of making contact with his nation. His work in a sense is one long lecture to his fellow countrymen, asking them to face up to his version of what his life and their lives are like—asking them, even, to do something about it.

The very book, *Portrait of the Artist as a Young Man,* that contains the description of the Godlike artist paring his fingernails ends with this altruistic vow of the hero, Stephen Dedalus, Stephen the artificer: "Welcome, O life! I go to encounter for the millionth time the reality of experience and to forge in the smithy of my soul the uncreated conscience of my race." The authorial service, by this formulation, connects the experience and the race, whose conscience and consciousness must be, repeatedly, created. Joyce's emotional and aesthetic loyalty to an Ireland where he couldn't bear to live is heroic, as is his attempt, in the two long and unique novels which succeeded *Portrait of the Artist,* to re-create the bardic persona—to sing, that is, in epic form, the entire history of his city and nation. And Proust, too, amid the magnificent unscrolling of his own snobbish and hyperesthetic life, sings hymns to French cathedrals, French place-names, and the visions of French history. Kafka, doubly alien, as a German-speaking Jew within a Czech-speaking province of the Austro-Hungarian Empire, and a writer furthermore for whom publication was a kind of desecration, yet had the epic touch; his parables of rootlessness are securely rooted in the landscape and civic machinery of Bohemia and Prague, where, in spite of the dreariness and caution of the present Communist regime, he is revered as a national prophet.

One could go on with this catalogue of tribal resonances, for a mark of a great writer, as Walt Whitman observed, is that a nation absorbs him, or her, in its self-knowledge and self-image. The confident writer assumes that his own sensibility is a sufficient index of general conditions, and that the question "Who am I?," earnestly enough explored, inevitably illuminates the question "Who are we?"

But if giving a lecture calls the writer down from his ivory tower and administers a healthy dose of humanity, what benefit does the audience receive? Why invite this person to give a type of performance he is instinctively reluctant to give, and does not give very well? His expertise, as we have said, is nebulous, and his public manner is owlish and shy. Thomas Mann, in preparing the way for his own lecture on Freud, gracefully suggested that the author is especially called to celebrations, for "he has understanding of the feasts of life, understanding even of life as a feast." I would suggest, furthermore, that feasts traditionally require, within their apparatus, a figure of admonition, a licensed representative, sometimes costumed as a skeleton and wearing a grinning skull-mask, of those dark forces that must be invoked and placated before the feast can be wholly enjoyed. It used to be that in America, at even the blithest of celebrations—at weddings, say, or at the opening of a new automobile agency—a clergyman, dressed in chastening black, would stand and, with his few words and declared presence, like a lightning rod carry off all the guilt and foreboding that might otherwise cloud the occasion.

As the church's power to generate guilt fades, the writer, I suggest—the representative of the dark and inky realm of print—has replaced the priest as an admonitory figure. In this electronic age, when everyone is watching television and even book critics (as Leslie Fiedler has confided) would rather go to the movies, books make us feel guilty—so many classics gathering dust unread, so many new books piling up in bright heaps, and above this choking wasteland of print the plaintive cries of sociologists waving fistfuls of tabulated high-school tests and telling us how totally illiterate we are all becoming. Gutenberg is dead, but his ghost moves among us as a reproachful spectre. What better exorcism, that the feast of life may tumble on untroubled, than to invite a writer to lecture? The rite is now complete; my role has been discharged. Book-fair celebrants, consider now banished all spiritual impediments to your barter and display; your revels may begin.

Emersonianism

THE CRITIC WARNER BERTHOFF, in his essay "American Literature: Traditions and Talents," concedes that "the American circumstance has indeed managed to yield its originating masters," then challenges himself to name them. As if slightly surprised, he responds, "I should speak at once of Melville, or Whitman, and of Emerson, who remain, in their several ways, the freshest of our writers, as well as the most provocatively intelligent; their wit, so to speak, is still the liveliest potential cause of wit in others."

One searches one's own wits, reading this. Melville and Whitman, of course. *Moby-Dick* and *Leaves of Grass,* both published in the 1850s to a reception of mockery and indifference, are American classics if any exist. Or so, at least, we feel now, having inherited our high opinion from the modernist critics of this century, who in Melville's case had to perform a considerable work of resurrection. But our received opinion, tested against the texts themselves, does seem just: the words sing, burn, and live; they have the stimulating difficulty of reality itself, and the pressure and precision of things that exist. With something like rapture, each author's voice makes solid connections, and however widely their raptures range Melville and Whitman persuasively strive to give us the substance promised by their titles: grass and a whale, earth and the sea are delivered.

But Emerson? Is there not something dim at the center of his reputa-

---

An address given at the Davis campus of the University of California on October 25, 1983, and then, somewhat revised, at the 1,644th stated meeting of the American Academy of Arts and Sciences, in Cambridge, Massachusetts, on November 9, 1983.

tion, something fatally faded about the works he has left us? When, I ask myself, did I last read one of his celebrated essays? How much, indeed, are Emerson's works even assigned in literary courses where the emphasis is not firmly historical? I sometimes receive in the mail anthologies designed for instruction in colleges and high schools, and a check of their indices reveals little Emerson, and then often no more than one or two of his shorter poems, or a paragraph or two quoted in explication of *Walden*, or a footnote explaining how the living writer Ralph Ellison's middle name came to be Waldo. *An Approach to Literature*, a massive double-column anthology edited by Cleanth Brooks, John Thibaut Purser, and Robert Penn Warren, contains not a word by Emerson, nor does Donald Hall's fifteen-hundred-page assemblage, *To Read Literature*. The countercultural wave which lifted Thoreau and Whitman into renewed fashionability left Emerson scarcely touched; he was not revolutionary, or ecological, enough. Recessive, fantastical Hawthorne is an indispensable anthology presence in a way Emerson is not; even Longfellow and Whittier, it may not be reckless to say, left texts more vivid in the communal memory than the literary remains of Emerson, who, so dominant and dignified a presence among his contemporaries, now clings to immortality almost because he cannot be extricated from them.

For, however much a cause of wit he has proved or will prove to be among ourselves, he was undoubtedly in his living prime a most fertile cause of wit in others. He was a great encourager and inspirer, a center of excitement in Concord and Boston and a bestower of boldness and energy wherever he spoke. In 1842 the twenty-three-year-old Walter Whitman heard him lecture in New York: "I was simmering, simmering, simmering," the poet said;* "Emerson brought me to a boil." And when in 1855 Whitman sent the busy Emerson a privately published sheaf of poems, a booklet in its eccentric appearance begging to be tossed aside as the work of a crank, Emerson astoundingly read it and recognized its epochal worth, as the answer to his platform prayers for a new literature and an untrammelled new consciousness. "I am not blind to the worth of the wonderful gift of 'Leaves of Grass,' " he wrote Whitman. "I find it the most extraordinary piece of wit & wisdom that America has yet contributed. . . . It has the best merits, namely, of fortifying & encouraging." The unstinting tone of this praise, volunteered to a stranger, is generous; the terms of the praise reflect back upon the giver. Emerson was too bent upon the business of encouraging and fortifying others to feel

---

*To John Townsend Trowbridge, as reported in Trowbridge's "Reminiscences of Walt Whitman," *The Atlantic Monthly*, LXXXIX (February 1902).

envy. His long and patient patronage of Henry David Thoreau is well known. Less well known is Emerson's kindness to the half-mad, religiously obsessed Jones Very of Salem; for all the young man's eccentricities, Emerson not merely held frequent discourse with him but himself edited and saw to the publication of Very's *Essays and Poems* in 1839. The volatile, brilliant Margaret Fuller also presented a troublesome friendship to Emerson. "I want to see you, and still more to hear you," she wrote him in 1838. "I must kindle my torch again." She taxed him with "a certain inhospitality of soul" toward her and provoked him to address her in his journals with an imaginary rebuff that began, "You would have me love you. What shall I love?" But he fended off her appeals for more than he could provide and made something positive of their intellectual association in the so-called Hedge's Club and her editorship of the Transcendentalist magazine *The Dial*. Many others, men and women, basked in the Emerson circle at Concord; though he complains in his journals of the constant infractions upon his time, it was not only his nature but his mission to be encouraging. His address in Boston on "Man the Reformer" proclaimed a "new spirit" and called upon men to "begin the world anew." Books, he had asserted in his famous address on "The American Scholar," "are for nothing but to inspire." In his call for renewal, in his capacity for appreciation and for generating excitement, Emerson stands in catalytic relation to the classic period of American letters as Ezra Pound does to the modernism of the early twentieth century. "A village explainer," Gertrude Stein called Pound, and the Sage of Concord was that *par excellence*. He lectured everywhere, and knew everybody. In New York, one of his best friends was the senior Henry James, and on his last European jaunt in 1872 the young Henry James was one of his escorts in Paris. Twenty years earlier, having travelled by railroad and steamboat to speak in St. Louis, he especially enjoyed the companionship of the Unitarian minister William Greenleaf Eliot, the grandfather of T. S. Eliot. Our impression that Emerson laid benedictory hands upon all the heads of at least the Northeast American literary tradition is compounded by the fancy that Emily Dickinson is Emerson's spiritual daughter: like him she wrote poems to bumblebees and felt herself drunk upon the intoxicating light of the divine sun. Her accomplishment proves the truth of his assertion, in "The Poet," that "Day and night, house and garden, a few books, a few actions, serve as well as would all trades and all spectacles." What better encapsulation of his doctrine of "Self-Reliance" than this stanza of hers:

> The soul selects her own society,
> Then shuts the door;

> On her divine majority
> Obtrude no more.

In the two great poets Emerson's influence seems to bifurcate: his boastful all-including optimism trumpeted by Whitman, his more playful, skeptical quizzing of God and Nature intensified by the Amherst recluse.

We should not, however, imagine that all the great names of the American Renaissance obediently constellate around Emerson's. Hawthorne, a year younger than he, and of the same upper-class Yankee stock, shared Concord and a long acquaintanceship with him, and lies buried a few paces away; but in life there was always between them a certain distance and coolness of appreciation. When the author of *The Scarlet Letter* died in 1864, Emerson wrote in his journal:

> I have found in his death a surprise & a disappointment. I thought him a greater man than any of his works betray. . . . Moreover I have felt sure of him in his neighborhood, & in his necessities of sympathy & intelligence, that I could well wait his time—his unwillingness & caprice—and might one day conquer a friendship. It would have been a happiness, doubtless to both of us, to have come into habits of unreserved intercourse. It was easy to talk with him—there were no barriers—only, he said so little, that I talked too much, & stopped only because—as he gave no indications—I feared to exceed.

Amid the quiet ghosts of Salem, Hawthorne had worked out his artistic and personal credo with no assistance from Transcendentalism; he took a generally satiric view of enthusiasm, Unitarianism, *The Dial,* and Margaret Fuller, and remained at heart loyal to the Puritan sense of guilt and intrinsic limitation which Emerson so exultantly wished to banish. Melville loved Hawthorne and his "power of blackness"; he is the second great member of what we might call the anti-Emerson party. "I do not oscillate in Emerson's rainbow," he wrote. After reading some essays by "this Plato who talks through his nose," he pronounced, "To one who has weathered Cape Horn as a common sailor what stuff all this is." In that scarcely coherent voyage of rage called *The Confidence-Man* Melville planted a caricature of Emerson called Mark Winsome, who is travelling on the Mississippi with a Thoreau-like disciple named Egbert. Winsome is portrayed as "with such a preternaturally cold, gemmy glance out of his pellucid blue eye, that he seemed more a metaphysical merman than a feeling man." As "coldly radiant as a prism," Winsome spouts Plato and mocks consistency. The author, represented by his hero "the cosmopolitan," seems to find double fault with Winsome: he is too mystical and also too practical. His philosophy is unreal, yet at the same time it serves the world's base purposes. "Mystery is in the morning, and mystery in the night, and the beauty of mystery is everywhere," Winsome is made to say; "but still the plain truth remains, that mouth and purse must be filled. . . . Was not Seneca a usurer? And Swedenborg, though with one eye on the invisible, did he not keep the other on the main chance?" The disciple Egbert appears "the last person in the world that one would take for the disciple of any transcendental philosophy; though, indeed, something about his sharp nose and shaved chin seemed to hint that if mysticism, as a lesson, ever came in his way, he might, with the characteristic knack of a true New-Englander, turn even so profitless a thing to some profitable account." In the end the two are dismissed as professors of an "inhuman philosophy"—"moonshine" suited to "frozen natures."

It is high time to let Emerson speak for himself. His first book, *Nature*—published in 1836 and the only one of his major prose writings that did not first exist in the form of public utterance—proposed some remarkable inversions of the common way of seeing things:

Nature is the symbol of spirit. . . . The use of natural history is to give us aid in supernatural history: the use of the outer creation, to give us language for the beings and changes of the inward creation. . . . Man is conscious of a universal soul within or behind his individual life, wherein, as in a firmament, the natures of Justice, Truth, Love, Freedom, arise and shine. This universal soul, he calls Reason: it is not mine, or thine, or his, but we are its; we are its property and men. . . . That which, intellectually considered, we call Reason, considered in relation to nature, we call Spirit. Spirit is the Creator. Spirit hath life in itself. And man in all ages and countries embodies it in his language, as the FATHER. . . . There seems to be a necessity in spirit to manifest itself in material forms; and day and night, river and storm, beast and bird, acid and alkali, preëxist in necessary Ideas in the mind of God, and are what they are by virtue of preceding affections, in the world of spirit. A Fact is the end or last issue of spirit. The visible creation is the terminus or the circumference of the invisible world.

Such thought is called Idealism, and has long roots in Plato and the Neoplatonists, in Christian metaphysics, in Berkeley and Kant and Swedenborg. Hegel, whom Emerson read only late in life and then without enthusiasm, made Idealism the dominant mode of nineteenth-century philosophy; it came to America through the writings of Coleridge and Carlyle and Goethe, whom Emerson did read. This way of construing reality awakens resistance in us, but a hundred and fifty years ago the men and women of Christendom were imbued with notions of an all-determining, circumambient invisible Power around them. Insofar as Idealism expresses the notion of repeating laws and analogies and interchanges permeating the universe, it is modern, and scientific; and Emerson was quite scientific-minded. In *Nature* he wrote:

> Not only resemblances exist in things whose analogy is obvious, as when we detect the type of the human hand in the flipper of the fossil saurus, but also in objects wherein there is great superficial unlikeness. . . . A rule of one art, or a law of one organization, holds true throughout nature. So intimate is this Unity, that, it is easily seen, it lies under the undermost garment of nature, and betrays its source in Universal Spirit.

Except for the use of the term "spirit," this search for a Grand Unified Theory is familiar enough. And Idealism does locate a real cleavage in our consciousness: "Idealism acquaints us with the total disparity between the evidence of our own being, and the evidence of the world's being." The two types of evidence, indeed, are so disparate that only moments that savor of mysticism fuse them:

> In the woods, we return to reason and faith. There I feel that nothing can befall me in life,—no disgrace, no calamity (leaving me my eyes), which nature cannot repair. Standing on the bare ground,—my head bathed by the blithe air, and uplifted into infinite space,—all mean egotism vanishes. I become a transparent eyeball; I am nothing; I see all; the currents of the Universal Being circulate through me; I am part or particle of God.

Now, our concern is less to explicate Emerson's philosophy than to test whether it, and the elaborations that followed from it, still might serve as the cause of wit in others. That the Idealism set forth in *Nature* served to guide Emerson himself through a productive life of exceptional serenity is a matter of biographical record. In 1871, when he was late in his sixties, he visited northern California, descending even into the opium dens of San Francisco; a travelling companion, Professor James B. Thayer, wrote this of a trip to Yosemite:

> "How *can* Mr. Emerson," said one of the younger members of the party to me that day, "be so agreeable, all the time, without getting tired!" It was the *naïve* expression of what we all had felt. There was never a more agreeable travelling companion; he was always accessible, cheerful, sympathetic, considerate, tolerant; and there was always that same respectful interest in those with whom he talked, even the humblest, which raised them in their own estimation. One thing particularly impressed me,—the sense that he seemed to have of a certain great amplitude of time and leisure. It was the behavior of one who really *believed* in an immortal life, and had adjusted his conduct

accordingly; so that, beautiful and grand as the natural objects were, among which our journey lay, they were matched by the sweet elevation of character, and the spiritual charm of our gracious friend.

Though he never again stated the tenets of Idealism at such length, and with as near an approach to system, as in *Nature,* they remained at the core of his thought, and all his lectures circle around the reassuring assertions that spirit is the author of matter and that our egos partake of the benign unity of Universal Being. "I have taught one doctrine," he wrote in his journals, "the infinitude of the private man."

The year after publishing *Nature,* Emerson was invited to give the annual Phi Beta Kappa oration at Harvard, since the society's first choice, a Dr. Wainwright, had declined. Emerson's address that last day of August made his fame. Oliver Wendell Holmes was present on the platform, and called it at the time "our intellectual Declaration of Independence." In it Emerson told the young scholars of his audience that "We have listened too long to the courtly muses of Europe," and that "if the single man plant himself indomitably on his instincts, and there abide, the huge world will come round to him." Not books but nature—with which North America, amid many deficiencies, was well supplied—shall be the foremost shaper of these indomitable instincts. Emerson describes education by osmosis, out-of-doors:

> Thus to him, to this school-boy under the bending dome of day, is suggested, that he and it proceed from one root; one is leaf and one is flower; relation, sympathy, stirring in every vein. . . . He shall see, that nature is the opposite of the soul, answering to it part for part. One is seal, and one is print. Its beauty is the beauty of his own mind. Its laws are the laws of his own mind. . . . So much of nature as he is ignorant of, so much of his own mind does he not yet possess. And, in fine, the ancient precept, "Know thyself," and the modern precept, "Study nature," become at last one maxim.

Can this, we wonder now, and his audience then must have wondered, be true? In what sense can nature, that implacable *other* which our egos oppose, whose unheeding processes make resistance to our every effort of construction and husbandry, and whose diseases and earthquakes and oceans extinguish us with a shrug, be termed identical with our own souls? Is not a world of suffering scandalously excluded from such an equation? Emerson's next address, to the graduating seniors of the Harvard Divinity School in July of 1838, takes up again the theme of nature as the end and means of education:

> The child amidst his baubles, is learning the action of light, motion, gravity, muscular force; and in the game of human life, love, fear, justice, appetite,

man, and God, interact. These laws refuse to be adequately stated . . . yet we read them hourly in each other's faces, in each other's actions, in our own remorse. . . . The intuition of the moral sentiment is an insight of the perfection of the laws of the soul. These laws execute themselves. They are out of time, out of space, and not subject to circumstance. Thus; in the soul of man there is a justice whose retributions are instant and entire. . . . See how this rapid intrinsic energy worketh everywhere, righting wrongs, correcting appearances, and bringing up facts to a harmony with thoughts. Its operation in life, though slow to the senses, is, at last, as sure as in the soul. . . . Character is always known. Thefts never enrich; alms never impoverish; murder will speak out of stone walls.

Do we, in late 1983, believe this? I suggest we do not: it is part of our received wisdom to believe that stone walls often conceal murder very well; that character is obscure and deceptive; that whatever harmony we enjoy with nature is the cruel and monstrously slow haphazard work of adaptive evolution; that our moral dispositions are bred into us by the surrounding culture; and that no great soul is shared by our own greedy egos and the ravenous natural forces at bay around us. In so believing, if Emerson is correct, we differ from all mankind hitherto, which has conceded the "facts" of indwelling moral sentiment. "These facts," he claims,

have always suggested to man the sublime creed, that the world is not the product of manifold power, but of one will, of one mind; and that one mind is everywhere active, in each ray of the star, in each wavelet of the pool; and whatever opposes that will is everywhere balked and baffled, because things are made so, and not otherwise. Good is positive. Evil is merely privative, not absolute: it is like cold, which is the privation of heat. All evil is so much death or nonentity. Benevolence is absolute and real. So much benevolence as a man hath, so much life hath he. . . . Whilst a man seeks good ends, he is strong by the whole strength of nature.

These assertions, too, we tend to doubt, though our popular arts, as recently exemplified by the *Star Wars* saga, join Emerson in proposing that a good man is naturally strengthened and evil is in the end an illusion that dissolves. To many of Emerson's audience (raised, after all, not only in the hard world but in a religious orthodoxy whose central figure was a suffering God) his optimistic cosmology must have seemed moonshine, to use Melville's word. His assertion that nature and our souls are one is a deliberate affront to our common assumptions, as is Jesus's that the meek shall inherit the earth, or Luther's that men are saved by faith alone, or Buddha's that the craving for existence and rebirth is the source of pain:

such affrontive assertions mark the creation of a new religion. And have no doubt that Emerson thought a new one was needed. He was, we must remember, a radical, whose negative views of the Christian church were considered extreme even in Transcendentalist circles. In middle life, he told a visitor,* "I cannot feel interested in Christianity; it is deplorable that there should be a tendency to creeds that would take us back to the chimpanzee." Even the mild and minimal Unitarian faith—"the ice house of Unitarianism," he called it in his journals—had so strained his credence that he had resigned the ministry. He did not mince words to the Harvard Divinity School students:

> . . . it is my duty to say to you, that the need was never greater of new revelation than now. From the views I have already expressed, you will infer the sad conviction, which I share, I believe, with numbers, of the universal decay and now almost death of faith in society.

To those of us whose religious views have been formed by the crisis theology of Kierkegaard and Barth, which predicates a drastic condition of decay and collapse within so-called Christendom, it is an eerie sensation to apprehend, in the young life and thought of Emerson, the collapse arriving, as the geology, the paleontology, and the Biblical criticism of the early nineteenth century pile in upon thinking men with their devastating revelations. Emerson was well aware of the historical situation: "The Puritans in England and America," he said in his Divinity School address, "found in the Christ of the Catholic Church, and in the dogmas inherited from Rome, scope for their austere piety, and their longings for civil freedom. But their creed is passing away, and none arises in its room. I think no man can go with his thoughts about him, into one of our churches, without feeling, that what hold the public worship had on men is gone, or going. It has lost its grasp on the affection of the good, and the fear of the bad. In the country, neighborhoods, half parishes are *signing off*,—to use the local term."

Yet there is, he feels, great need for *a* religion:

> What greater calamity can fall upon a nation, than the loss of worship? Then all things go to decay. Genius leaves the temple, to haunt the senate, or the market. Literature becomes frivolous. Science is cold. The eye of youth is

---

*Moncure Conway, a young Virginian ordained as Methodist minister and subsequently liberalized by Emerson's *Essays*. Emerson also told him that he kept a local pew for his wife and children and to that extent supported the minister because it was useful to have "a conscientious man to sit on school committees, to help at town meetings, to attend the sick and the dead."

not lighted by the hope of other worlds, and age is without honor. Society lives to trifles, and when men die, we do not mention them.

What is to be done, then? Emerson invokes the soul: "In the soul, then, let the redemption be sought." What does this mean, exactly? It means, I think, what Karl Barth warned against when he said, "One can *not* speak of God by speaking of man in a loud voice." Emerson defined "the true Christianity" to the divinity students as "a faith like Christ's in the infinitude of man." An infinitude, in Emerson's if not in Jesus's terms, based upon an understanding of each man's soul as a fragment and mirror of the Universal Soul, the Over-soul, whose language is nature. A special beauty of this new religion is that, new wine though it is, it can be poured into the old bottles of the existing churches. Emerson concludes with a peroration that touches upon practical concerns:

> The evils of the church that now is are manifest. The question returns, What shall we do? I confess, all attempts to project and establish a Cultus with new rites and forms, seem to me vain. Faith makes us, and not we it, and faith makes its own forms. All attempts to contrive a system are as cold as the new worship introduced by the French to the goddess of Reason,—to-day, pasteboard and fillagree, and ending to-morrow in madness and murder. Rather let the breath of new life be breathed by you through the forms already existing. For, if once you are alive, you shall find they shall become plastic and new. The remedy to their deformity is, first, soul, and second, soul, and evermore, soul. . . . Two inestimable advantages Christianity has given us; first; the Sabbath, the jubilee of the whole world. . . . And secondly, the institution of preaching,—the speech of man to men,—essentially the most flexible of organs, of all forms.

And so the young divinity students of the class of 1838, shaken but, let us hope, inspired, were sent forth to take their places behind the rotten pulpits, to fill the hollow creed and exhausted forms of Christianity with the life of their own souls, somehow; the Harvard faculty did not invite Emerson to speak at Harvard again for thirty years.

Emerson had renounced his own ministry in 1832. At that time the secular profession of lecturer was making its beginnings with such speakers as Edward Everett, Daniel Webster, and Horace Mann; within a decade Emerson was a star of the lyceum circuit.* His lectures, many of

---

*Hawthorne, in "The Celestial Railroad" (1843), ridiculed the "innumerable lecturers, who diffuse such a various profundity, in all subjects of human or celestial science, that any man may acquire an omnigenous erudition, without the trouble of even learning to read."

which became the essays collected in two volumes in 1841 and 1844, from their titles could seem to be about anything—"History," "Heroism," "Circles," "Gifts," "Manners," "Experience"—but all were sermons of a sort in behalf of the Emersonian religion, "the speech of man to men," demonstrating in themselves and urging upon others the free and generous action of a mind open to the inspirations and evidences of the Universal Soul. They were all exhortations to be brave and bold, to trust the universe and oneself. Their supernaturalist content in general, after *Nature,* tends to fade, but is never disavowed, and usually becomes the final recourse of the exhortation. "Let a man fall into the divine circuits, and he is enlarged," concludes Emerson's disquisition on "New England Reformers." "We are escorted on every hand through life by spiritual agents, and a beneficent purpose lies in wait for us," states the essay entitled "Nature." "Nature is the incarnation of a thought, and turns to a thought again, as ice becomes water and gas. The world is mind precipitated, and the volatile essence is forever escaping again into the state of free thought. . . . Every moment instructs, and every object: for wisdom is infused into every form."

Of all the essays, the one entitled "Self-Reliance" is perhaps the best known, and has entered most deeply into American thinking. It offers a curious counsel of fatalism couched in the accents of activism:

> Trust thyself: every heart vibrates to that iron string. Accept the place the divine providence has found for you, the society of your contemporaries, the connection of events. Great men have always done so, and confided themselves childlike to the genius of their age, betraying their perception that the absolutely trustworthy was seated at their heart, working through their hands, predominating in all their being.

The society of one's contemporaries, however, would seem not to be entirely acceptable, for, we learn a page later, "Society everywhere is in conspiracy against the manhood of every one of its members. . . . The virtue in most request is conformity. Self-reliance is its aversion. . . . Whoso would be a man must be a nonconformist."

Emerson had refused to conform when he resigned the ministry that his ancestors had honored, and did so furthermore at a moment when his widowed mother and a quartet of brothers were all looking to him for stability. At the price of breaking up their Boston home, and with no financial prospects but his eventual inheritance from his recently dead young wife, Ellen, he set sail for the first of his three excursions to Europe. Frail as a young man, he had developed the gift of taking it easy on himself; unlike his three brilliant brothers, William, Edward, and

Charles,* he compiled a mediocre record at Harvard, and he outlived them all, into a ripe old age. His third European trip was undertaken as he neared seventy, in order to escape the renovation of his house in Concord, which had suffered a fire. There was something a touch cavalier about his second trip, too—nine months of lionization in England while his second wife, Lidian, coped in Concord with three small children and straitened finances. Emerson's great discovery, amid the ruins of the Puritan creed, was the art of relaxation and of doing what you wanted. In "Self-Reliance" he proclaims:

> I shun father and mother and wife and brother, when my genius calls me. I would write on the lintels of the door-post, *Whim*. I hope it is somewhat better than whim at last, but we cannot spend the day in explanation.

The importunities of philanthropy—a real menace in the New England of this time, especially for the foremost proponent of Idealism—must be repelled:

> Do not tell me, as a good man did to-day, of my obligation to put all poor men in good situations. Are they *my* poor? I tell thee, thou foolish philanthropist, that I grudge the dollar, the dime, the cent, I give to such men as do not belong to me and to whom I do not belong.

A doctrine of righteous selfishness is here propounded. The Biblical injunction "Love thy neighbor as thyself" is conveniently shortened to "Love thyself":

> I must be myself. I cannot break myself any longer for you, or you. If you can love me for what I am, we shall be the happier. . . . I will so trust that what is deep is holy, that I will do strongly before the sun and moon whatever inly rejoices me, and the heart appoints.

As the Yippies were to say: "If it feels good, it's moral." Or, in the nineteenth-century idiom of William Henry Vanderbilt, "The public be damned!" The American Scholar being advised to "plant himself indomitably on his instincts" shades, in "Self-Reliance," into the entrepreneur; the great native creed of Rugged Individualism begins to find expression. After deriding feckless college men who lose heart if "not installed in an office within one year afterwards in the cities or suburbs of Boston," Emerson asserts:

---

*Edward and Charles both died before the age of thirty. William lived to be sixty-seven. The fifth brother who lived to adulthood, Robert Bulkeley, was mentally retarded and resided in institutions or foster homes until his death at the age of fifty-two.

A sturdy lad from New Hampshire or Vermont, who in turn tries all the professions, who *teams it, farms it, peddles,* keeps a school, preaches, edits a newspaper, goes to Congress, buys a township, and so forth, in successive years, and always, like a cat, falls on his feet, is worth a hundred of these city dolls. He walks abreast with his days, and feels no shame in not 'studying a profession,' for he does not postpone his life, but lives already.

Emerson wished to give men courage to be, to follow their own instincts; but these instincts, he neglected to emphasize, can be rapacious. A social fabric, he did not seem quite to realize (and in the security of pre–Civil War America, in the pretty farm-town of Concord, what would insist he realize it?), exists for the protection of its members, as do the laws and inhibitions such a fabric demands. To be sure, he did not create American expansionism and our exploitive verve; but he did give them a blessing and a high-minded apology. Are we afraid the rich will oppress the poor? In his essay on "Compensation" Emerson assures us, "There is always some levelling circumstance that puts down the overbearing, the strong, the rich, the fortunate, substantially on the same ground with all others." Do our hearts bleed for the manacled slave? "Most suffering is only apparent," he informs us in his uncollected but fascinating essay upon "The Tragic":

A tender American girl doubts of Divine Providence whilst she reads the horrors of "the middle passage:" and they are bad enough at the mildest; but to such as she these crucifixions do not come: they come to the obtuse and barbarous, to whom they are not horrid, but only a little worse than the old sufferings.

Do the dirtiness and noise of the railroad and factory affront us? "Readers of poetry," Emerson says in his essay on "The Poet," "see the factory-village, and the railway, and fancy that the poetry of the landscape is broken up by these; for these works of art are not yet consecrated in their reading; but the poet sees them fall within the great Order not less than the bee-hive, or the spider's geometrical web." Are we afraid, in a land so carelessly given over to youth and its divine instincts, of growing old? No problem, says Emerson in effect, in his essay on "Circles": "Nature abhors the old, and old age seems the only disease. . . . I see no need of it. Whilst we converse with what is above us, we do not grow old, but grow young." Death, too, is eloquently fudged away: "And the knowledge that we traverse the whole scale of being, from the centre to the poles of nature, and have some stake in every possibility, lends that sublime lustre to death, which philosophy and religion have too outwardly and literally striven to express in the popular doctrine of the immortality of the soul. The reality is more excellent than the report. . . . The divine circulations never rest nor linger" ("Nature"). Are we vexed, depressed, or indignant? Emerson tells us "that there is no need of struggles, convulsions, and despairs, of the wringing of the hands and the gnashing of the teeth; that we miscreate our own evils. We interfere with the optimism of nature. . . . Nature will not have us fret and fume" ("Spiritual Laws").

Understood in relation to Emerson's basic tenets, these reassurances are not absurd. Further, amid the fading of other reassurances, they were urgently useful, and have been woven into the created, inherited reality around us. The famous American pragmatism and "can do" optimism were given their most ardent and elegant expression by Emerson; his encouragements have their trace elements in the magnificent sprawl we see on all sides—the parking lots and skyscrapers, the voracious tracts of single-family homes, the heaped supermarket aisles and crowded ribbons of highway: the architectural manifestations of a nation of individuals, of wagons each hitched, in his famous phrase, to its own star. Like balloon-frame house construction—another American invention of the 1840s—Emersonianism got the job done with lighter materials. In his journals he struck the constructive note: "It is greatest to believe and to hope well of the world, because he who does so, quits the world of experience, and makes the world he lives in."

And, reading Emerson, one wonders if the American style is so much a matter of energy and enterprise as of insouciance, of somewhat reckless relaxation into the random abundance of opportunities which a plenteous Nature has provided. The American accent is a drawl, and Emerson, in his collection *English Traits,* more than once marvels at the vigor and force and ruddiness of the English, as if in contrast to a languid, lazy, and pallid race he has left behind. Can it be true that, along with our sweet independence and informality, there is something desolate and phantasmal, a certain thinness of experience that goes with our thinness of civilization? As an introspective psychologist, Emerson is nowhere more original than in his baring of his own indifference. "I content myself with moderate, languid actions," he wrote in his journal of November 3, 1838. "I told J[ones] V[ery] that I had never suffered, & that I could scarce bring myself to feel a concern for the safety & life of my nearest friends that would satisfy them: that I saw clearly that if my wife, my child, my mother, should be taken from me, I should still remain whole with the same capacity of cheap enjoyment from all things." This was written before the death of his beloved five-year-old son, Waldo. After it, in his uncharacteristically somber essay "Experience," Emerson confessed:

Grief too will make us idealists. In the death of my son, now more than two years ago, I seem to have lost a beautiful estate,—no more. . . . It does not touch me: something which I fancied was a part of me, which could not be torn away without tearing me, nor enlarged without enriching me, falls off from me, and leaves no scar. . . . The Indian who was laid under a curse, that the wind should not blow on him, nor water flow to him, nor fire burn him, is a type of us all. The dearest events are summer-rain, and we the Para [rubber] coats that shed every drop.

Which brings us back to Melville's charge of coldness, his picture of Mark Winsome "coldly radiant as a prism." Emerson in his lifetime was accused of coldness, by Margaret Fuller and Thomas Carlyle among others, and in "Experience" addresses the issue: "The life of truth is cold, and so far mournful; but it is not the slave of tears, contritions, and perturbations. It does not attempt another's work, nor adopt another's facts. . . . I have learned that I cannot dispose of other people's facts. . . . A sympathetic person is placed in the dilemma of a swimmer among drowning men, who all catch at him, and if he give so much as a leg or a finger, they will drown him." The practical ethics of Idealism, then, turn out to be seclusion and stoicism. "We must walk as guests in nature—not impassioned, but cool and disengaged," Emerson says in "The Tragic." Is there possibly, in this most amiable of philosophers, a preparation for the notorious loneliness and callousness and violence of American life which is mixed in with its many authentic and, indeed, unprecedented charms?

Emerson was the first American thinker to have a European influence; Carlyle sponsored him, and Matthew Arnold once said that no prose had been more influential in the nineteenth century than Emerson's. He was, in German translation, a favorite author of Friedrich Nietzsche, who copied dozens of passages into a notebook, borrowed the phrase "the gay science" for philosophy, and wrote of the *Essays,* "Never have I felt so much at home in a book, and in *my* home, as—I may not praise it, it is too close to me." Both men were ministers' sons exultant in the liberation that came with the "death" of the Christian God; both were poets and rhapsodists tagged with the name of philosopher. Almost certainly Emerson's phrase "Over-soul" influenced Nietzsche's choice of the phrase "*Übermensch,*" even though "Over-soul" in the edition that Nietzsche read was translated "*Die höhere Seele,*" the higher soul, which is echoed by Nietzsche's talk of "the higher men." From the Over-soul to the *Übermensch* to the Supermen of Hitler's Master Race is a dreadful progression for which neither Emerson nor Nietzsche should be blamed; but Emerson's coldness and disengagement and distrust of altruism do become, in

Nietzsche, a rapturous celebration of power and domination and the
" 'boldness' of noble races," and an exhilarated scorn of what the German
called "slave morality." Not just the mention of Zoroaster seems Nietzschean in this passage from "Self-Reliance":

> Welcome evermore to gods and men is the self-helping man. For him all
> doors are flung wide: him all tongues greet, all honors crown, all eyes follow
> with desire. Our love goes out to him and embraces him, because he did not
> need it. We solicitously and apologetically caress and celebrate him, because
> he held on his way and scorned our disapprobation. The gods love him
> because men hated him. "To the persevering mortal," said Zoroaster, "the
> blessed immortals are swift."
>
> As men's prayers are a disease of the will, so are their creeds a disease of
> the intellect.

The essay approvingly quotes Fletcher's "Our valors are our best gods"
and bluntly states, "Power is in nature the essential measure of right."
Totalitarian rule with its atrocities offers a warped mirror in which we can
recognize, distorted, Emerson's favorite concepts of genius and inspiration and whim; the totalitarian leader is a study in self-reliance gone amok,
lawlessness enthroned in the place where law and debate and checks and
balances should be, and with no obliging law of compensation coming to
the rescue. The extermination camps are one of the developments that
come between us and Emerson's optimism.

Another is modern science, as it has developed. "Our approach now,"
my dermatologist told me the other day, "is that nature is utterly stupid."
The same chemical mechanisms, he went on to explain, will destroy as
blindly as they heal, and a goal of contemporary medicine is to block the
witless commands that unleash harmful reactions in the body. Where, in
this molecular idiocy, can we find indication that "acid and alkali preëxist
in necessary Ideas in the mind of God, and are what they are by virtue
of preceding affections, in the world of spirit"?

Also, we find aesthetic difficulty in a disconnected quality of Emerson's
discourse that in the actual lectures must have been greatly masked and
smoothed by his handsome manner and appealing baritone voice. We are
left with his literary voice, which (unlike Thoreau's similar voice) seems
pitched a bit over our heads, toward the back rows, and too much partakes
of what he himself called "the old largeness." Knut Hamsun, in his own
lectures on *The Cultural Life of Modern America*, expressed what many a
student has groped to say since:

> One reads all his excellent comments; one reads while awaiting a conclusion
> relevant to the subject itself. One awaits the third and final word that can

draw a figure or cast a statue. One waits until the twentieth and final page—one waits in vain: at this point Emerson bows and departs. And the reader is left with a lapful of things said; they have not formed a picture; they are a brilliant welter of small, elegant mosaic tiles.

I myself found, preparing for this talk, that the essays melted and merged in my mind; so exciting in their broad attack and pithy sentences, they end, often, disconcertingly in air, and fail to leave an imprint of their shape in the mind. This need not have been so: the one sermon of Emerson's commonly reprinted is his farewell sermon in the Second Church of Boston, explaining why he could not in good faith administer the Lord's Supper and therefore must resign.* It moves dramatically from careful examination of the relevant Biblical and patristic texts to the speaker's own conclusions and thence to his beautifully understated but firm farewell. We remember it; its segments are articulated in a single gesture of argument. Of few of his essays can this be said. With his belief in inspiration and what he called *"dream-*power" and in patterns that all nature would conspire to express once a sufficiently pure surrender to the Over-soul was attained, Emerson read in his Concord study as his whim and his interest dictated and wrote in his celebrated journal, maintained since his college years, such quotations and paragraphs of independent thought as came to him. He assembled his lectures from this lode of intellectual treasure and, though the joinery is cunning and the language often brilliantly concrete, the net effect is somewhat jumbled and vague. We have been superbly exhorted, but to what effect? A demonstration of wit has been made, but somewhat to the stupefaction of our own wits. Modern critics, my impression is, are additionally embarrassed by the Neoplatonic, supernaturalist content of the early essays, and prefer the later, more factual considerations and the journals themselves, where the discontinuity is overt and the tone is franker and more intimate. Yet would the journals and even the excellent *English Traits*—the centerpiece of Mark Van Doren's *Portable Emerson*—make a major claim on our attention had they not been hoisted into prominence by the celebrated, evangelical early addresses and essays? There is this awkwardness, I believe, in Emerson's present reputation: what we like about him is not what is important, and what *is* important we do not much like. Emerson the prophet of the new American religion

---

*One hundred seventy-nine sermons by the young Emerson survive in Houghton Library at Harvard and are to be published eventually, in four volumes, by the University of Missouri Press. In 1938, twenty-five of them, selected by Arthur Cushman McGiffert, Jr., appeared under the ambiguous title *Young Emerson Speaks: Unpublished Discourses on Many Subjects.*

seems cranky and dim; what we like is the less ethereal and ministerial Emerson, the wry, observant, shrewd, skeptical man of this world.

Emerson was always such, of course; as Oliver Wendell Holmes said of him, "He never let go the string of his balloon." The founder of Emersonianism was not its ideal practitioner; his extraordinary loyalty to the exasperating Bronson Alcott must have resided, it seems to me, in his awe of Alcott's greatly superior impracticality. Thoreau, too, appeared to Emerson a kind of saint, who, he said in the beautiful eulogy delivered at Thoreau's funeral in 1862, "lived extempore from hour to hour, like the birds and the angels." Thoreau even worked miracles: "One day walking with a stranger who inquired, where Indian arrowheads could be found, he replied, 'Every where,' and stooping forward, picked one on the instant from the ground." More amazing still, "From a box containing a bushel or more of loose pencils, he could take up with his hands fast enough just a dozen pencils at every grasp."* No such magical sureness, his self-doubting journals reveal, had been granted Emerson; he felt skeptical about his own enthusiasms, mocking himself, in the essay "Illusions," as susceptible to any new style or mythology. "I fancy," he wrote, "that the world will be all brave and right, if dressed in these colors, which I had not thought of. Then at once I will daub with this new paint; but it will not stick. 'Tis like the cement which the peddler sells at the door; he makes broken crockery hold with it, but you can never buy of him a bit of the cement which will make it hold when he is gone."

I found the preparation of this lecture a somewhat recalcitrant process, especially since Emerson himself, as I read him, seemed to be advising against it. Such a performance by a would-be creative writer goes against my own instincts; it is something done to please society, that society which, we have just learned, is a "conspiracy against the manhood of every one of its members." And I did not even have the excuse, which Emerson had, of making a living by lectures. Further, the subject himself proved elusive and problematical, in the manner I have tried to describe; as I read, a hundred stimulated thoughts would besiege me, but all in the nature of paint that would not stick. What notes I took became scrambled; seeking to refer back to a key passage, I would find the words had quite vanished from Emerson's pages. So, one morning, I decided to take leave of my bookish responsibilities and work in my cellar upon some modest carpentry project that had been long left hanging. While happily, brainlessly planing away, I turned on the radio—an "educational" station, to be

---

*See page 804.

sure—and was treated to a lengthy "Earth Mass" employing not only human voices and conventional musical instruments but tapes of howling wolves, whales conversing in their mysterious booms and groans, and the rushing sound of the Colorado River. How very Emersonian, I thought: and felt his ghost smile within me. For have we not late in this century come to see how it is that "the mind is One, and that nature is its correlative"? Amid all our materialism, have not sheer crowding and shared peril merged nature with our souls?

Then I had to make haste, for I was to take a train from my suburban town into Boston; I was to have a painless session at Massachusetts General Hospital, where anesthesia was first demonstrated in this country and where my dermatologist stood ready to tell me that nature was utterly stupid. I walked down to the tracks through my own woods and in my transcendental humor perceived the oddity of owning woods at all, of legally claiming a few acres of forest that so plainly belong to the trees themselves, and to the invisible creatures that burrow and forage among the trees and will not mark with even a minute's respectful pause their ostensible owner's passing from this earth. Emerson, expanding his holdings in Concord, in 1844 bought fourteen wooded acres by Walden Pond; but it was Thoreau who built a cabin and lived there, and Thoreau who wrote the masterpiece called *Walden*. We possess, that is, by apprehension and not by legal fiat; the spirit *does* create matter, along its circumference of awareness.

Emerging from my own neglected woods, I crossed the railroad tracks and bought at a so-called Convenient Food Mart a can of ginger ale and, after much hesitation, a bag of peanuts in the shell. Most of my life has been lived with women who find peanut shells a trial, especially those papery inner husks that elude every broom; I have associated shelling peanuts with the exercise of personal freedom ever since, as a boy, left alone to wander for an hour in the Pennsylvania city three miles from my home, I would buy a half-pound bag and eat the peanuts as I wandered, dropping the shells into what trash cans and gutters and hedges and sewer grates presented themselves during my carefree stroll. Buying and eating so whimsical a lunch as peanuts and ginger ale appeared to me, obsessed with preparations for this address, as a peculiarly national opportunity and an appropriate celebration of the American insouciance that Emerson had labored to provide with a philosophical frame.

The train, I should say, was equipped with plastic windows, since younger Americans than I had been long celebrating their own insouciance and yielding to their own inspirations by tossing rocks at the windows as they flew past and shattering them if they were glass. Substituted plastic solved that problem, but in time the plastic has clouded to near-perfect opacity, so that as I hurtled to Boston the trees and houses and vistas on the way were vaguer and less to be guessed at than the shadows flickering in Plato's famous cave, the womb out of which both Emersonianism and the Gospel of St. John were born.

I arrived, still cracking peanuts, at the hospital. What better exemplifies modern-day America than a hospital! Here a true cross-section of colors and creeds, ages and classes mingles, united by our physical fallibility and our hope that science will save us. Though it was autumn, the weather in New England was lingeringly warm, so the crowd summoned to the hospital was lightly dressed, in bright colors, in sandals and jogging shorts. Nubile, merciful nurses and brisk, sage physicians moved in angelic white through the throng of the infirm and their visitors. There were limping young athletes called in from their game by some injury they would forget in a week, young women pushing delicate bug-eyed babies in strollers or lugging them on their hips, elderly couples with an air of having long harbored a single complaint between them. "Life is an ecstasy," Emerson tells us in "Illusions." "Life is sweet as nitrous oxide; and the fisherman dripping all day over a cold pond, the switchman at the railway intersection, the farmer in the field, the negro in the rice-swamp, the fop in the street, the hunter in the woods, the barrister with the jury, the belle at the ball, all ascribe a certain pleasure to their employment, which they themselves give it." Now a multitude of such as these had been fetched here, smelling of nitrous oxide, bearing the rainbow auras of their lives and their employments; to be among them was happiness.

I noticed a man about my age with a bald head—not a healthy, luminous baldness but the unnatural, gauzy baldness that chemotherapy induces. On Emerson's advice, I checked the presumptuous motion of pity in my heart, my officious inner attempt to adopt and dispose of other people's facts; for, sitting there in the waiting lounge somewhat like a sultan, the man was not asking for pity but instead was calmly wrapped in his own independent and perhaps triumphant thoughts. I sat down myself and read—who else?—Emerson. Emerson it was my own whim to peruse in the little old uniform edition of brown leather and marbled endpapers I had bought at a church fair for five dollars and most of whose pages had never been cut. To slit these pages I used my bookmark, the joker of an old deck of cards—another whim, and yet efficient. "The way of life is wonderful," I read; "it is by abandonment." Looking up, I noticed a man in a chair opposite me reading a book also. He was reading a novel called *The Coup,* which I had once written. He was a stout cigar-smoking man who slowly turned the pages with a terrible steady frown; he was not at all my image of the Ideal Reader. Yet there he was, in front of me; who was I to doubt now that, as Emerson promised, "Every proverb, every book, every byword that belongs to thee for aid or comfort, shall surely come home through open or winding passages"? And that, as the same page of "The Over-Soul" states, "The heart in thee is the heart of all; not a valve, not a wall, not an intersection is there anywhere in nature, but one blood rolls uninterruptedly an endless circulation through all men, as the water of the globe is all one sea, and, truly seen, its tide is one." Was not this day of mine—October 4, 1983—demonstrating at every emblematic turn that "a thread runs through all things: all worlds are strung on it, as beads; and men, and events, and life, come to us, only because of that thread"?

A man within unavoidable earshot was making a call on a pay phone. His side of the conversation went: "Stella? Any news?" A pause, and then, "Isn't that great? It so easily could have been different. I'm so happy for him." How much, indeed, I could not help thinking, of the news we receive *is* good. "We are natural believers," Emerson says in his essay on Montaigne. "Belief consists in accepting the affirmations of the soul; unbelief, in denying them." It was Emerson's revelation that God and the self are of the same substance. He may have been wrong, too blithe in Mankind's behalf, to think that nature—which he called the *"other me"*—is possessed of optimism and always answers to our soul; but he was immensely right in suggesting that the prime *me*, the ego, is perforce optimistic.

Howells as Anti-Novelist

THIS YEAR is the one-hundred-and-fiftieth anniversary of William Dean Howells's birth, and the fact has been celebrated but quietly. Few writers filled the American literary sky as amply as Howells in his prime; few have fallen so relatively far into disesteem. We remember Howells, if we do, as a genial broad valley between Mark Twain and Henry James—a cultivated and well-travelled Ohioan able to appreciate two great writers who could not at all appreciate each other. And then there was something about his calling himself a "realist," and depicting "the American girl," and turning toward socialism in middle age. As a poet, playwright, and short-

Given on May 1, 1987, at Harvard University, in Emerson Hall, as part of a two-day birthday party for Howells.

story writer, he has left no impression, and as a novelist a diminished one; but as a critic and an editor he cannot be eradicated from the high annals of the literature of the long period between the end of the Civil War and America's entry into World War I. Affectionate correspondent and zealous promoter of James and Twain, vivacious intimate of the New England worthies Longfellow, Lowell, Holmes, and Whittier, a tireless fosterer of younger realists such as Hamlin Garland, Frank Norris, and Robert Herrick, he boldly pushed the young Stephen Crane's *Maggie: A Girl of the Streets* at a time when bookstores were too scandalized to carry it, urged Swedish and Spanish and Russian novelists upon American readers, and welcomed to native letters the first Jewish-American novelist, Abraham Cahan. Theodore Dreiser called Howells our " 'lookout on the watch-tower,' straining for a first glimpse of approaching genius"; Edmund Wilson summed him up as "our always tactful toastmaster, our clearing-house, our universal solvent, our respecter of the distinguished veteran, our encourager of the promising young." His wife, Elinor Mead Howells, was a cousin of President Rutherford B. Hayes, and President William Howard Taft attended Howells's seventy-fifth birthday party, in 1912, to which not only Henry James but H. G. Wells and Thomas Hardy sent warm greetings; seventy-five years after that gala event, which four hundred guests thronged at Sherry's Restaurant in Manhattan, we can still find traces of Howells's tremendous charm and prestige fossilized at the head of lists: in Boston, he was the first president of the Tavern Club, and in New York, of the American Academy of Arts and Letters.

As a novelist, he was, after Twain, the most financially successful American of his time. His novels, few of them short, were serialized in magazines and then purchased and admired again in book form. The critical terms of the admiration were, to an extent, ones he himself set in his own criticism—his book reviews and literary columns in *The Atlantic Monthly, The Century,* and *Harper's Magazine.* Howells had what very few American novelists have had: a theory of the novel—how it should be written, and what it should be about. Its method should be realism, which he once defined as "nothing more and nothing less than the truthful treatment of material," and its subject should be the common life of ordinary Americans. In 1899, at the peak of his prestige, he enunciated a radical aesthetic agenda for the audience of a lecture, "Novel-Writing and Novel-Reading." The ideal novelist of the future, he proposed,

> will not rest till he has made his story as like life as he can, with the same mixed motives, the same voluntary and involuntary actions, the same unaccountable advances and perplexing pauses, the same moments of rapture, the

same days and weeks of horrible dullness, the same conflict of the higher and lower purposes, the same vices and virtues, inspirations and propensities. . . . As it is now the representation of life in novels, even the most conscientious in its details, is warped and distorted by the novelist's anxiety to produce an image that is startling and impressive, as well as true. But if he can once conceive the notion of letting the reader's imagination care for these things; if he can convince himself that his own affair is to arrange a correct perspective, in which all things shall appear in their very proportion and relation, he will have mastered the secret of repose, which is the soul of beauty in all its forms.

This vision, of bringing dullness and mixedness out of the rain of actuality into the house of fiction, had been with Howells from the start. In the first book of his which might be called a novel, *Their Wedding Journey* (1871), the author, while describing conversations his honeymooners overhear on a night boat up the Hudson, suddenly exclaims, "Ah! poor Real Life, which I love, can I make others share the delight I find in thy foolish and insipid face?" A dozen pages farther on, his married couple, Isabel and Basil March—alter egos who are to reappear in Howells's novels in the decades ahead—sit alertly in a railway carriage and their loquacious companion the author confides to us:

It was in all respects an ordinary carful of human beings, and it was perhaps the more worthy to be studied on that account. As in literature the true artist will shun the use even of real events if they are of an improbable character, so the sincere observer of man will not desire to look upon his heroic or occasional phases, but will seek him in his habitual moods of vacancy and tiresomeness. To me, at any rate, he is at such times very precious; and I never perceive him to be so much a man and a brother as when I feel of the pressure of his vast, natural, unaffected dullness. Then I am able to enter confidently into his life and inhabit there, to think his shallow and feeble thoughts, to be moved by his dumb, stupid desires, to be dimly illumined by his stinted inspirations, to share his foolish prejudices, to practice his obtuse selfishness.

Howells's next book, *A Chance Acquaintance* (1873), may unambiguously be called a novel, though it also makes extensive use of travel impressions and takes up a character, Kitty Ellison of Eriecreek, New York, whom the Marches had encountered in their wedding journey; their paths diverged, and the reader of *A Chance Acquaintance* follows Kitty and her uncle and aunt into the province and city of Quebec, where she enjoys a romantic encounter with a young traveller from Boston, Mr. Arbuton. In the course of deepening their acquaintanceship they several times discuss the problem of making the American reality—North American, in this instance—accessible to the imagination. They take a boat cruise up and down the Saguenay River, amid scenery of grand emptiness:

> On either hand the uninhabitable shore rose in desolate grandeur, friendless heights of rock with a thin covering of pines seen in dim outline along their tops and deepening into the solid dark of hollows and ravines upon their sides. The cry of some wild bird struck through the silence of which the noise of the steamer had grown to be a part, and echoed away to nothing.

Mr. Arbuton, who has travelled much in Europe and has the air of a Harvard man, observes, "The great drawback to this sort of thing in America is that there is no human interest about the scenery, fine as it is."

Kitty loyally protests, "Why, I don't know, there was that little settlement round the saw-mill. Can't you imagine any human interest in the lives of the people there? It seems to me that one might make almost anything out of them. Suppose, for example, that the owner of that mill was a disappointed man who had come here to bury the wreck of his life in—sawdust?"

Our Boston swain answers politely, "O, yes! That sort of thing; certainly. But I didn't mean that, I meant something historical. There is no past, no atmosphere, no traditions, you know." And, later, continuing this flirtatious debate, Kitty says, "If I were to write a story, I should want to take the slightest sort of plot, and lay the scene in the dullest kind of place, and then bring out all their possibilities." Indeed, she has read a book just like that, called *Details*, with the texture of Howells's ideal fiction: "Nothing extraordinary, little, every-day things told so exquisitely, and all fading naturally away without any particular result, only the full meaning of everything brought out." Mr. Arbuton's rejoinder is weak but with something, surely, in it: "And don't you think," he asks, "it's rather a sad ending for all to fade away without any particular result?"

The issue of whether or not this continent could nurture and sustain a serious literary artist was much discussed in the post-bellum United States. Howells and Henry James discussed it, on long walks in Cambridge in the late 1860s, when both young men had their careers before them,* and before James had voted, as it were, with his feet, and taken up

---

*The two young Americans did not have many acknowledged American masters of prose fiction to serve as concrete exemplars. Melville's achievements were quite unappreciated, and Poe, whom Emerson had called "the jingle man," was lightly regarded in New England. There was Washington Irving and James Fenimore Cooper and *Uncle Tom's Cabin* and Hawthorne; and of those Hawthorne was the greatest—"he has the importance," James was to write a decade later, in his small book on Hawthorne, "of being the most

permanent European residence. Howells in 1866 wrote to Edmund Clarence Stedman, "Talking of talks: young Henry James and I had a famous one last evening, two or three hours long, in which we settled the true principles of literary art." In the last year of his life, 1920, Howells recalled in an unfinished memoir, "We seem to have been presently always to-

---

beautiful and most eminent representative of a literature. The importance of the literature may be questioned, but at any rate, in the field of letters, Hawthorne is the most valuable example of American genius." In this remarkable little volume's most famous, and perhaps most heartfelt, passage, the now thoroughly expatriated James pities Hawthorne for "the coldness, the thinness, the blankness" of the American world he looked out upon, and asserts, "It takes so many things, as Hawthorne must have felt later in life, when he made the acquaintance of the denser, richer, warmer European spectacle—it takes such an accumulation of history and custom, such a complexity of manners and types, to form a fund of suggestion for a novelist. . . . The negative side of the spectacle on which Hawthorne looked out, in his contemplative saunterings and reveries, might, indeed, with a little ingenuity, be made almost ludicrous; one might enumerate the items of high civilization, as it exists in other countries, which are absent from the texture of American life, until it should become a wonder to know what was left. No State, in the European sense of the word, and indeed barely a specific national name. No sovereign, no court, no personal loyalty, no aristocracy, no church, no clergy, no army, no diplomatic service, no country gentlemen, no palaces, no castles, nor manors, nor old country-houses, nor parsonages, nor thatched cottages nor ivied ruins; no cathedrals, nor abbeys, nor little Norman churches; no great Universities nor public schools—no Oxford, nor Eton, nor Harrow; no literature, no novels, no museums, no pictures, no political society, no sporting class—no Epsom nor Ascot!"

This list of negatives has become, at least among American-lit majors, famous; less well known is Howells's rejoinder, in a basically friendly review of the biography in *The Atlantic Monthly* in early 1880. He says of Hawthorne: "As a romancer, the twelve years of boyhood which he spent in the wild solitudes of Maine were probably of greater advantage to him than if they had been passed at Eton and Oxford. At least, until some other civilization has produced a romantic genius at all comparable to his, we must believe this. After leaving out all those novelistic 'properties,' as sovereigns, courts, aristocracy, gentry, castles, cottages, cathedrals, abbeys, universities, museums, political class, Epsoms, and Ascots, by the absence of which Mr. James suggests our poverty to the English conception, we have the whole of human life remaining, and a social structure presenting the only fresh and novel opportunities left to fiction, opportunities manifold and inexhaustible. No man would have known less what to do with that dreary and worn-out paraphernalia than Hawthorne."

However, by insisting, as he often did, on Hawthorne as a "romancer" and his full-length fictions as "romances," Howells rather concedes James's point: America had yet to produce its true novelists. And James, it should be remembered, went on to say, his list completed: "The natural remark, in the almost lurid light of such an indictment, would be that if these things are left out, everything is left out. The American knows that a good deal remains; what it is that remains—that is his secret, his joke, as one may say." What remains, James pleasantly leaves it to us to conjecture, is the American's freedom, his space, his gun, his home-grown food, and his right to look every other (male, white) citizen square in the eye—what de Tocqueville called "the general equality of condition among the people."

gether, and always talking of methods of fiction, whether we walked the streets by day or night, or we sat together reading our stuff to each other. I was seven years older than James, but I was much his junior in the art we both adored. Perhaps I did not yet feel my fiction definitely in me." James's tribute to Howells on his seventy-fifth birthday remembered this time "when we knew together what American life *was*—or thought we did. . . . You knew and felt these things better than I; you had learned them earlier and more intimately, and it was impossible, I think, to be in more instinctive and more informed possession of the general truth of your subject than you happily found yourself. The *real* affair of the American case and character, as it met your view and brushed your sensibility, that was what inspired and attached you, and . . . you gave yourself to it with an incorruptible faith. You saw your field with a rare lucidity: you saw all it had to give in the way of the romance of the real and the interest and the thrill and the charm of the common. . . ." In his letters to others, however, James spoke in less courtly fashion of Howells's commitment to the American substance: as *Their Wedding Journey* was being serially published, he wrote to Grace Norton, "Poor Howells is certainly difficult to defend, if one takes a stand-point the least bit exalted; make any serious demand, and it's all up with him. He presents, I confess, to my mind, a somewhat melancholy spectacle—in that his charming style and refined intentions are so poorly and meagerly served by our American atmosphere. There is no more inspiration in an American journey than *that!*" In reviewing Howells's novel *A Foregone Conclusion* (1874) for *The Nation*, James nicely described the cultural situation as he saw it: "[Howells] reminds us of how much our native-grown imaginative effort is a matter of details, of fine shades, of pale colors, a making of small things do great service. Civilization with us is monotonous, and in the way of contrasts, of salient points, of chiaroscuro, we have to take what we can get. We have to look for these things in fields where a less devoted glance would see little more than an arid blank, and, at the last, we manage to find them. All this refines and sharpens our perceptions, makes us in a literary way, on our own scale, very delicate."

By the time of their Cambridge walks James had already formed that exalted conception of the novel which was to carry him through his life of triumphant single-mindedness; Howells had come more gingerly to the temple of prose fiction, by way of journalism and travel sketches. His first book with an American setting, *Suburban Sketches* (1870), attempts to treat the neighborhoods and incidents of Cambridge in terms of local color, much as he had treated those of Venice in his first book, *Venetian Life* (1866). Howells's first two novels were elaborated books of travel; and he himself had travelled a long way to reach the threshold of what was to become an impressively productive career not only as a novelist but as a propagandist for the novel—the novel as a means of seizing reality, monotonous and delicate though it be.

He was born in Martins Ferry, Ohio, in 1837, the son of a country-newspaper editor; the political and financial hazards of his father's profession took Howells's family to many Ohio towns, of which he lived longest in Hamilton, where he passed the eight years of childhood recalled in his memoir *A Boy's Town* (1890), and Jefferson, where the now adolescent boy undertook a program—rigorous to the point of inducing nervous breakdown—of self-education, teaching himself Latin, Greek, Spanish, French, and German, in addition to reading voluminously in English. He had been setting type at age nine and delivering papers earlier still, and his actual formal schooling amounted at most to two years. In Jefferson, he set type from seven to lunch hour, read proof and distributed his case after lunch, and came home at about two or three to devote himself to reading or writing, in his little study beneath the stairs, until the rest of his family were in bed. He had conceived a fierce literary ambition, in an era when, as he wrote forty years later, "almost all the literary men in the country had other professions . . . or they were men of wealth; there was then not one who earned his bread solely by his pen in fiction, or drama, or history, or poetry, or criticism, in a day when people wanted very much less butter on their bread than they do now."

Howells often wrote reminiscently of his Ohio years, with the feeling and liveliness that attaches to formative experience. Among his memoiristic works is *My Literary Passions* (1895), which has the multiple value of being a sketchy autobiography, a record of his reading, and evidence of what books offered themselves to a Midwestern autodidact in the decades before the Civil War. His first passion, he tells us, was Goldsmith, and in the long backward glance Howells commends his kindly style: "The style is the man, and he cannot hide himself in any garb of words so that we shall not know somehow what manner of man he is within it; [Goldsmith's] spiritual quality, his essential friendliness, expressed itself in the literary beauty that wins the heart as well as takes the fancy in his work." The supreme reading experience of Howells's childhood was *Don Quixote,* translated by him into hundreds of Spanish daydreams and boyish games; from Cervantes and the other authors to whom his Spanish passion led, Howells drew this lesson: "I am sure that the intending author of American fiction would do well to study the Spanish picaresque novels; for in their simplicity of design he will find one of the best forms for an

American story. The intrigue of close texture will never suit our conditions, which are so loose and open and variable; each man's life among us is a romance of the Spanish model." Shakespeare and Dickens and Thackeray and Macaulay and Chaucer and Tennyson took their turns in his affections and his attempts at mimicry; for a time, he indentured himself to the tight heroic couplets of Pope: "What I liked then was regularity, uniformity, exactness," he says, going on to tell us in the tones of the mature aesthetic radical, "I did not conceive of literature as the expression of life, and I could not imagine that it ought to be desultory, mutable and unfixed, even if at the risk of some vagueness."

It was the poet Heine, for whose sake he submitted to the rigors of German grammar, who showed him that "the life of literature was from the springs of the best common speech, and that the nearer it could be made to conform, in voice, look, and gait, to graceful, easy, picturesque and humorous or impassioned talk, the better it was." Howells says, "He undid my hands, which I had taken so much pains to tie behind my back." Howells's first acceptance from *The Atlantic Monthly*, in 1858, was a poem so much in his idol's manner that it was held from publication for a year, until the editors had satisfied themselves it was not a translation; the magazine's editor, James Russell Lowell, advised him years later, "You must sweat the Heine out of your bones as men do mercury." In his life after leaving Ohio, Howells received especially strong impressions from such varied authors as the Italian playwright Goldoni, the Russian writer Turgenev, and the Norwegian novelist Bjørnson, from whom he learned that "the finest poetry is not ashamed of the plainest fact [and] that telling a thing is enough, and explaining it too much." All three writers impressed him with what were, broadly speaking, the same virtues: naturalness of manner, a tact of presentation that allows the story to seem to tell itself, and a willingness to deal with common material and to suppress the author's personality, which yet makes itself felt in the "essential friendliness" of style—the virtues, in short, that Howells was himself to manifest.

When Howells was twenty-one, he tells us, "the whole world opened to me through what had seemed an impenetrable wall." He was offered a job as editor and reporter with a Republican newspaper, the *Ohio State Journal,* in Columbus; he was a success at it and in this state capital's active society. In 1860 he was invited to write a campaign biography of Abraham Lincoln, and with the proceeds travelled east, where, at the age of twenty-three, he was received by the major intellectual figures of New England, even the reclusive Hawthorne and Thoreau, at a time when American literature was almost solely in Yankee hands. On this same excursion he went north to Brattleboro, to meet the family of Elinor Mead, the artistic and spirited young woman he was to marry. Lincoln won the election, and his administration awarded Howells, after some haggling, the U.S. consulship in Venice, where he was to remain for the four years of the Civil War. His first letters home overflow with a heightened sense of what a blessing it is to be an American: "Ah! come abroad, anybody that wants to know what a dear country Americans have!" and "There is no life in the world so cheerful, so social, so beautiful as the American" and "No one knows how much better than the whole world America is until he tries some other part of the world. Our people are manlier and purer than any in Europe; and though I hope to stay here my full four years, and know I shall profit by my experience and enjoy it, I still hope to go back and engage in the strife and combat, which make America so glorious a land for individuals."

In 1865 he returned to the strife and combat with his armor of culture considerably thickened and polished; if Ohio printshops had formed his secondary education, Venice was his college. A sojourn abroad not only enhances the home country; it reduces it and places it in a context. Howells's sense of American life as a literary subject would not have been so vivid had he stayed in the Midwest, where he was immersed in this reality without boundary. He returned to the United States but did not wish to return home. A certain gloom, in fact, attached to his youth in Ohio, where he had been, he once wrote, "proud, vain, and poor." He had suffered phobias and depression there, as well as overwork, and in 1864 he wrote his father, "I do not conceal from you that I have not yet in three years shaken off my old morbid horror of going back to live in a place where I have been so wretched." "Morbid" is the striking term. His boyhood was characterized, he wrote in *A Boy's Town,* by "more fears than hopes." The central figure of his last novel, *The Leatherwood God* (1916), is said to be "so miser'ble, all the time, and so—well—scared." The stanza of a poem from 1860 runs,

> Once on my mother's breast, a child, I crept,
>   Holding my breath;
> There, safe and sad, lay shuddering, and wept
>   At the dark mystery of Death.

According to Leon Edel's biography of Henry James, Howells once confided to Grace Norton his feeling "that he had lived his life under the dominion of fear." Edel continues:

James, commenting on this, said he had always felt the depression in Howells, but believed he was able to disconnect it from his *"operative* self." It had never been, said James, "the least paralysing, or interfering, or practically depressing." On the contrary, Howells had arrived at compensations "very stimulating to endeavor."

One wonders if Howells's tenacious artistic clinging to the surface of things doesn't show a fear of falling back into an abyss. Ohio had depths he did not wish to re-explore. He was no less than Henry James an expatriate, refusing to return to Jefferson, where his Swedenborgian father lived, much as James spurned Cambridge, where *his* Swedenborgian father lived.

The East became Howells's place of happy exile. He worked for four months in New York, as a columnist with *The Nation,* and then was asked by James T. Fields, who had succeeded Lowell as editor of *The Atlantic,* to come to Boston as his assistant. He accepted, and he and his wife soon moved to Cambridge, then considered a suburb, where his friendship with Lowell led to others with such literary Brahmins as Longfellow and Oliver Wendell Holmes and Charles Eliot Norton. His social and family life were active, his editorial duties many; yet he was no stranger to work, and had energy enough to continue worrying the curious problem of how to write fiction worthy of America, how to render his mystical sense of "poor Real Life" and of the something glorious in the average American's "vast, natural, unaffected dullness." He stated in retrospect, "Early in the practice of my art I perceived that what I must do in fiction, if I were to do anything worth while, was to get into it from life the things that had not been got into fiction before."

Over the years to come, Howells wrote a great deal of criticism, stating in sometimes pugnacious and controversial terms his increasingly firm views on the novel and on "realism"—a word he did much to promote. But we would seek, in the time remaining this afternoon, to focus more on the practice than on the preachments, and to touch on three of the features that distinguish his fiction and make it, even now, unsettling to our readerly expectations and irreducibly, as it were, avant-garde.

The first of these truth-seeking, realistic features we might call the Not Quite Likable Hero. In his very first review of a novel for *The Atlantic,* Howells in 1866 complained of Bayard Taylor's *The Story of Kennett:* "The hero of the book, we find a good deal like other heroes,—a little more natural than most, perhaps, but still portentously noble and perfect. He does not interest us much." And seven years later, reviewing Ivan Turgenev's *Dimitri Roudine* positively, he stated, "We are not quite sure whether we like or dislike the carefulness with which Roudine's whole character is kept from us, so that we pass from admiration to despite before we come finally to half-respectful compassion; and yet is this not the way it would be in life?" This effect, of a hero whose moral aspect alters as we read about him, thus stirring up and challenging our preconceptions,* was always striven after by Howells, and helps produce our sensation, in his mature fiction, of not quite knowing which side we are on.

There is no question, in *Their Wedding Journey,* of our not liking Basil March; he is so close to the author in temperament and intelligence that if we disliked him we would be obliged to close the book. But in *A Chance Acquaintance,* Arbuton, the very type of upper-class Boston rectitude—a "simulacrum," Howells wrote to James, and a "stick"—is clearly not meant to be entirely likable; his faults of stiffness and snobbery are spelled out by the author and perceived by the sensitive heroine. For all of that, he has admirable traits, and is to be pitied in his final defeat, and in the ghastly comic scene where two proper Boston acquaintances surprise him into snubbing his own fiancée. In short, Arbuton is a created character; we can walk clear around him and see his several sides without confusion. *A Chance Acquaintance,* indeed, slight little vehicle as it is, seems to me to hold the Howells essence pure; there is nothing spun-out in it, nothing limp; Howells's strong suit, his insight into the intricacy of male-female relations, is played with a crispness that amuses and affects us; the whole thing is as tonic and lucid as a dipperful of country spring water. Howells's idol Turgenev, in Paris, read this little novel, and said, "Now I should like to visit a country where there are girls like the heroine."

But what are we to think of the hero of the next novel, *A Foregone Conclusion*? Henry Ferris, a rather dabbling painter who occupies the post Howells did, of American consul in Venice, seems an unmarried Basil March, yet with a passive and churlish streak that makes him appear inadequate in dealing with the spirited American girl Florida Vervain, and distinctly ungracious in responding to his unfortunate rival, the priest Don Ippolito, who on his deathbed vainly reaches out to the cold-hearted American. Ferris's eventual triumph, in marrying the rich and beautiful Florida, is celebrated with sour notes:

> People are never equal to the romance of their youth in after life, except by fits, and Ferris especially could not keep himself at what he called the operatic pitch of their brief betrothal and the early days of their marriage. . . . It was fortunate for Ferris, since he could not work, that she had money;

---

*He once described the novelist's function as that of "dispersing the conventional acceptations by which men live on easy terms with themselves and obliging them to examine the grounds of their social and moral opinions."

in exalted moments he had thought this a barrier to their marriage; yet he could not recall any one who had refused the hand of a beautiful girl because of the accident of her wealth, and in the end, he silenced his scruples.

In this novel the heroine, too, with her erratic and imperious temper, is not entirely likable; Howells's dampening psychological reductions, on behalf of realism, were not confined to the male sex. But his females tend at least to be dynamic; their sins are ones of commission rather than omission, and the author asks the reader to excuse much that happens within, as he puts it here, "the whole mystery of a woman's nerves."

Indian Summer (1886) also takes place in Italy, and its hero, Theodore Colville, like an older and plumper but not much wiser Ferris, also finds himself at the mercy of uncomprehended sexual maneuvers by the fair sex. Seventeen years ago, in Florence, he had vainly wooed an American girl; returning to this city as a tourist, he fails to realize that he is in love with her companion of old, now a handsome widow, and permits a girl of very tender years and slight experience to attach herself to him romantically. He goes about "feeling like some strange, newly invented kind of scoundrel—a rascal of such recent origin and introduction that he had not yet had time to classify himself and ascertain the exact degree of his turpitude. . . . He was the betrothed lover of this poor child, whose affection he could not check without a degree of brutality for which only a better man would have the courage." Though the women of the novel, including the girl's mother and the widow's small daughter, eventually straighten things out for him, we remain somewhat resentful of his muddled behavior, of his idle-rich complacency, and of his relentless facetiousness and bemused detachment. Basil March, the charming travel companion and enraptured witness to human dullness, cuts an equivocal figure when cast as a romantic protagonist.

But it is Bartley Hubbard, in *A Modern Instance* (1882), who lifts unlikability to something like the sublime—he is so bad, one might say, he is good. In a typically Howellsian daze of vanity and drifting good nature, he yields to the sexual aggression, in a small Maine town, of Marcia Gaylord, marries her when she chases him, and then acts out his wedded discontent in Boston. The novel, perhaps Howells's strongest overall performance, made a sensation in its day with its depiction of a divorce; but its verity and power lie in its portrait of a marriage insecurely based upon unequal loves. Bartley's beautifully slippery yet never downright ill-intentioned stream of self-advocacy, as it works within his unstable marriage and within his declining journalistic career, is of a psychological subtlety as humorous as it is accurate. For example, in the superb reconciliation scene the day after Bartley, in the wake of a bitter marital quarrel, was brought home dead drunk, many small motions of the husband's mind, as it oscillates between apology and advantage-seeking, are registered. Albeit repentant, "he was not without a self-righteous sense of having given her a useful and necessary lesson." She acts more repentant than he, and bursts into tears: "The sight unmanned Bartley; he hated to see any one cry, even his wife, to whose tears he was accustomed." In promising it will never happen again, "he felt the glow of virtuous performance." Her extreme innocence about alcohol and its effects gives him more leeway than he had expected; he explains to her that "If I'd had the habit of drinking, I shouldn't have been affected by it. . . . I took what wouldn't have touched a man that was in the habit of it." Marcia eagerly pounces on this self-justification, and gazes upon him as the "one habitually sober man in a Boston full of inebriates." She resumes her sewing "with shining eyes," and "Bartley remained in his place on the sofa, feeling, and perhaps looking, rather sheepish. He had made a clean breast of it, and the confession had redounded only too much to his credit. To do him justice, he had not intended to bring the affair to quite such a triumphant conclusion; and perhaps something better than his sense of humor was also touched when he found himself not only exonerated but transformed into an exemplar of abstinence."

Mark Twain, reading this novel as it was serialized, jubilantly wrote Howells, "You didn't intend Bartley for me, but he *is* me, just the same." Years later Howells told Brander Matthews that he had drawn Bartley, "the false scoundrel," from himself. Certainly this flawed man and his flawed marriage are depicted with an unblinking scrutiny the opposite of sentimental. The scene summarized above is ironically refracted within the idealism of Ben Halleck, one of Howells's hypermoralistic Bostonians, who finds the Hubbards' reconciliation after "such beastliness" incredible, and has to be told of the married couple, "They can't live together in enmity, and they must live together. I dare say the offense had merely worn itself out between them."

When Bartley at last deserts Marcia, he becomes, by the light of her lonely vigil and proud agony, a villain; and the desperate trip to Indiana that Marcia and her father and child and Halleck and his sister undertake to forestall Bartley's divorce proceedings is thrilling like little else in Howells. The reader's pulse races as the party descends by train from the chill of Boston in early April into the softer, warmer Midwest from which Howells had sprung:

> It is a beautiful land, and it had, even to their loath eyes, a charm that touched their hearts. . . . They had now left the river-hills and the rolling country

beyond, and had entered the great plain which stretches from the Ohio to the Mississippi; and mile by mile, as they ran southward and westward, the spring unfolded in the mellow air under the dull, warm sun.

The novel, in this heartland, becomes an old-fashioned novel, melodramatic and sentimental; Marcia's father, a Maine lawyer known as the Squire—as was Howells's own father-in-law, in Brattleboro—arrives in the nick of time to deliver an old-fashioned peroration, much admired in the sleepy Indiana courtroom, in order to "bring yonder perjurer to justice." But Marcia cries out that she means Bartley no harm; the Squire, thus arrested in his vengeance, collapses of a stroke; and the next day Bartley reveals himself to Halleck as much his old self—jocose, insouciant, not particularly repentant, with a self-justifying story to tell. He even has a happy ending to suggest: that Halleck, who loves Marcia, now marry her. But the Bostonian is too priggish, too tortured in his moralism, to accept, and by inaction condemns her to shrewish loneliness. Judged by standards derived not from novels but from American reality, the blithe deserter is not entirely unlikable, and the scrupulous man is far from admirable.

The muted, ambiguous ending of *A Modern Instance* brings us to the second peculiarity of Howells's novels: their tendency to defuse themselves, to avert or mute their own crises. No book illustrates this tendency better than the one we are most likely to have read, *The Rise of Silas Lapham* (1885). The opening pages show Lapham, a blustering Vermonter who has made a fortune in the manufacture of paint, being interviewed by none other than Bartley Hubbard, in his better days. We prepare ourselves for a more or less painful tale of misdirected social aspiration—the loutish new capitalist thrusting himself and his modest wife, for the sake of their two marriageable daughters, upon the gentry of old Boston. From the start we are imbued with suggestions that Lapham, a coarse good fellow, is bound to overreach and arrive at ruin; an old financial sin—forcing out a partner at the point when his business began to prosper—is bound, by the logic of novels, to catch up with him. But, as the events unfurl, the representatives of Boston society, the Coreys, are too ironical and realistic to stage a confrontation or offer much resistance. When Mrs. Corey raises the dreadful possibility of their son's marrying a "paint princess," her husband, a dilettante painter (he works on a smaller scale than Lapham, who has surreally painted whole Vermont boulders in advertisement of his product), says breezily, "If money is fairly and honestly earned, why should we pretend to care what it comes out of, when we don't really care? That superstition is exploded everywhere."

And the son, Tom Corey, actually *wants* to get into the paint business, and is level-headed enough to overlook Lapham's bad points in behalf of the good ones and the opportunities for himself. There is an obligatory scene of social gaucherie, when new money mixes with old and the self-made Vermonter gets drunk on Beacon Hill spirits; but the scene is tenderly, lightly done, with something of nobility emerging from Lapham's Civil War reminiscences and something of graciousness from the Coreys' well-bred politeness.

Again, the wrong paint princess imagines that Tom is in love with her, but when this prolonged misunderstanding arrives at its denouement, the forsaken sister sensibly and stoically takes herself upcountry and doesn't return to the novel until her wound is healed. In a piquing little subplot, a mysterious and ominously pretty girl working in Lapham's Boston office appears to be under his special protection. An illegitimate daughter? God forbid, a mistress? The answer, when it comes, does Lapham nothing but credit and makes Mrs. Lapham ashamed of her wicked suspicions. Most benignly of all, the long-anticipated financial reverses turn out to be a blessing in disguise, involving Lapham's moral regeneration and sending him back to Vermont, where he belongs. When the splendid house in Back Bay, whose construction has served as the very symbol of Lapham's urban aspirations, burns to the ground uninsured, his wife exclaims, "Oh, thank the merciful Lord!" and Lapham coolly calculates that, "having resolved not to sell his house, he was no more crippled by its loss than he would have been by letting his money lie idle in it." Indeed, Howells's presiding comedic spirit contrives such a virtually irresistible opportunity for Lapham to recoup his fortunes that only a very elaborate exercise of fine scruple—as fantastically fine, to this reader, as Ben Halleck's in *A Modern Instance*—enables him to escape renewed prosperity.

It is as if two men were busy in the composition of *Silas Lapham*—a plot deviser mapping out conflicts and points of explosion, and an agile underminer who knows that misunderstandings don't last forever, that in this genial democracy social differences get easily bridged, that people or at least Americans are basically reasonable and make the best of their disappointments, and that things generally work out if not for the best then for the second best. Howells says as much: "Our theory of disaster, of sorrow, of affliction, borrowed from the poets and novelists, is that it is incessant; but every passage in our own lives and in the lives of others, so far as we have witnessed them, teaches us that this is false. . . . Lapham's adversity . . . was not always like the adversity we figure in allegory; it had its moments of being like prosperity."

Realism for Zola and Frank Norris and Sinclair Lewis meant the exposure of something unpleasant; for Howells, it meant fidelity to the mild, middling truth of average American life. Chastised for tameness, he answered, "The manners of the novel have been improving with those of its readers; that is all. Gentlemen no longer swear or fall drunk under the table, or abduct young ladies and shut them up in lonely country-houses, or so habitually set about the ruin of their neighbors' wives, as they once did." In defending the American novel, compared with the French, for its lack of sexual frankness, he argued, "No one will pretend that there is not vicious love beneath the surface of our society; if he did, the fetid explosions of the divorce trials would refute him; but if he pretended that it was in any just sense characteristic of our society, he could be still more easily refuted." Even Howells's much-mocked phrase "the smiling aspects of American life" in its context argues from the perceived local reality: "Our novelists . . . concern themselves with the more smiling aspects of life, which are the more American. . . . It is worth while, even at the risk of being called commonplace, to be true to our well-to-do actualities; the very passions themselves seem to be softened and modified by conditions which formerly at least could not be said to wrong any one, to cramp endeavor, or to cross lawful desire."

Men and circumstances are mightily mixed, and crises are generally averted or deflected, and life does not fall into plots: Howells's novels press these truths upon us, in defiance of novelistic convention, which asked for heroes, crises, and elaborate plots. Like Kitty Ellison, he wanted "to take the slightest sort of plot, and lay the scene in the dullest kind of place, and then bring out all their possibilities." In 1871, while working on his first novel, Howells wrote a friend, "There's nothing like having railroads and steamboats transact your plot for you." Decades later, in writing of Dickens, he stated, "The true plot comes out of the character. . . . Plot aforethought does not characterize. But Dickens believed it did, and all the romantic school of writers believed it did. Bulwer, Charles Reade, and even George Eliot, in some measure, thought so; but for all that—all that faking, that useless and false business of creating a plot and multiplying incidents—Dickens was the greater artist, because he could somehow make the thing transact itself." All that faking, that useless and false business, Howells found a name for in an essay by a Spanish novelist, Armando Palacio Valdés, who assigned the term "effectism" to "the awaking at all cost in the reader vivid and violent emotions" with "a complicated plot, spiced with perils, surprises, and suspenses." In opposition to "effectism" stood the simple, direct novels of Bjørnson, from which, according to Howells, we learn "that the lives of men and women, if they be honestly studied, can, without surprising incident or advantageous circumstance, be made as interesting in literature as are the smallest private affairs of the men and women in one's own neighborhood."

Howells's books have plots, but the author—this is the third strange feature—does not seem to get whole-heartedly behind them, and leaves us with an impression of outlines not filled in, of developments not permitted. His characters strain against a leash that is not entirely in the hand of circumstance. Howells distrusted exaggeration and, insofar as exaggeration would seem to be intrinsic to fiction, he distrusted fiction. His long early training, remember, was in journalism, and his favorite novel, *Don Quixote*, warned of a man who had been deranged by reading the novels of his day, medieval romances. In *My Literary Passions*, Howells admits that he is not sure he doesn't prefer history to fiction, and tells of a long sickness in his middle years when for seven or eight weeks "the mere sight of the printed page, broken up in dialogue, was anguish": "it was the dramatic effect contrived by the playwright or novelist, and worked up to in the speech of his characters that I could not bear." And it is a rare novel by Howells where the characters do not at some point sardonically contrast their behavior to that of people in novels.

The issue of plot goes deeper than melodrama or effectism; in subordinating action to character, Howells set himself against the greatest theoretician of narrative, Aristotle. In his 1899 lecture on the novel, Howells stated, "The old superstition of a dramatic situation as the supreme representation of life must be discarded, and the novelist must endeavor to give exactly the effect of life. I believe he will yet come to do this. I can never do it, for I was bred in a false school whose trammels I have never been quite able to burst; but the novelist who begins where I leave off, will yet write the novel which has been my idea." Henry James, in one of his graceful yet guarded tributes, spoke of Howells as having transcended "the superstition of 'form.' "

Why "superstition"? What does "form" mean, applied to narrative? For Aristotle—who was a physician's son, and a keen student of physiology and zoology—the form of a play or narrative derives from its human use: the course of action in a tragedy "through pity and fear effecting the proper purgation of these emotions." This is primary effectism: our hearts, entering into the complication and unravelling of the drama, achieve catharsis. A plot is a kind of machine that works upon us a beneficial, purgative effect, an effect of heightened tension which is then relieved; and so can most popular novels, movies, and television dramas be described: they are devices which more or less mechanically and cynically process our emotions and our capacity for caring about phantoms.

But what if a story is not a therapy—not an antidote to life but a clarification of it? What if you think that the narrative art derives its value and importance from its patient truthfulness to our mundane human condition? Then plot is justifiable only to the extent that reality itself can be said to have a plot, a design—plot becomes a philosophical and indeed a theological question. For the Greeks, plot traces the vengeance of the gods, often working their will through human passions. For Christians, plot bares divine Providence and its ultimate justice. In *My Literary Passions*, Howells recalled his youthful reading of Dickens:

> While I read him, I was in a world where the right came out best . . . and where merit was crowned with the success which I believe will yet attend it in our daily life. . . . In that world of his, in the ideal world, to which the real world must finally conform itself, I dwelt among the shows of things, but under a Providence that governed all things to a good end, and where neither wealth nor birth could avail against virtue or right.

Howells's fiction, however, reveals little instinctive belief that merit will in fact be crowned with success and that the real world must conform itself to the ideal. Reared rather haphazardly as a Swedenborgian, in an Ohio saturated with Protestant piety, he slowly but thoroughly became an agnostic, and in his middle life turned to Tolstoy and Socialism in lieu of a supernatural faith. Purposefully, then, and not from any mere aesthetic disdain of flashy effectism, his fiction is formless, and was sensed as such by his contemporaries. A reviewer wrote that "Mr. Howells is more than democratic, he is anarchical." Howells admired the aesthetic anarch in Mark Twain: "So far as I know Mr. Clemens is the first writer to use in extended writing the fashion we all use in thinking, and to set down the thing that comes into his mind without fear or favor of the thing that went before, or the thing that may be about to follow. . . . He saunters out into the trim world of letters, and lounges across its neatly kept paths, and walks about on the grass at will." And Henry James, writing to his brother William concerning Howells's novel of 1890, *A Hazard of New Fortunes*, complained, "His abundance and facility are my constant wonder and envy—or rather not, perhaps, envy, inasmuch as he has purchased them by throwing the whole question of form, style and composition overboard into the deep sea—from which, on my side, I am perpetually trying to fish them up."

When we look into ourselves on this question of form in fiction, we find an instinctive expectation that the events and characters presented to us will all prove part of a unified field, that a certain economy will limit their number and distribution, and that the story will end with everybody, in some sense, paid off—a villain like Iago brought to justice, a tormented soul like Othello laid to rest, and an innocent like Desdemona, if not rescued, at least vindicated. This sense of ultimately balanced accounts, still forceful in Dickens, rules the classic European novel, and oddly enough persists in Henry James, like Howells raised as a Swedenborgian and like Howells thoroughly lapsed. But, as no less an expert on matters of faith than Graham Greene has pointed out, James retained a religious sense; without any reference to God, it permeates his novels and gives their moral struggles an ominous grandeur, and their characters' fates an air of just punishment.* Howells, though he sometimes tries to administer some heavenly justice—Bartley Hubbard, for instance, is perfunctorily shot and killed in Arizona, and Ben Halleck upbraids himself for having dared love Marcia while she was married to this cheerful rotter—really seems to have no heart for it; he was a moral anarch in his art, while observing all the proprieties as husband, concerned citizen, neo-Tolstoyan social moralist, and exemplary dean of the literary community. His dependence upon the received code of the proprieties helps account for his excessive prudery. His realism stopped sharply short of sexual realism,† and he condemned it in others, going back to Chaucer. Prudery may be to blame for his one outstanding critical failure, in a life so strikingly

---

*His characters suffer for their sins, however hedged and slight: in *The Wings of the Dove*, things will never be as they were for Kate Croy and Merton Densher as a result of their deception of Milly Theale, and in *The Golden Bowl* Charlotte Stant is not just punished but tortured for loving a man she does not have the money to buy. In even a relatively light-hearted short novel like *The Spoils of Poynton*, the calculated reticences and elaborate scruples ramify restrictingly. "You'll be happy if you're perfect!" Fleda Vetch tells Owen Gereth, who is doomed to be imperfect, an injunction oddly echoed at the end, when, in response to her incredulous query, "Poynton's *gone?*," the stationmaster tells her, "What can you call it, miss, if it ain't really saved?" Such absolutism—such a sense of life as a set of irreparable moral crystals—is quite alien to Howells's elastic world. It must be admitted that the rotation of these crystals generates a degree of heat, a heat of old hellfire that in Howells rather leaks away.

†Not that there is no sex in Howells's novels; but it surfaces in sudden small gestures or objects of a fetishistic intensity: in *Lapham*, Tom Corey presents Irene Lapham with a wood shaving she had playfully pierced with her parasol, and when she gives the souvenirs of her love over to Penelope, the pine-shaving, "fantastically tied up with a knot of ribbon," is among them; in *A Modern Instance*, Marcia Gaylord, after Bartley Hubbard goes out the door, stoops and kisses the doorknob "on which his hand had rested"; in *The Landlord at Lion's Head*, Jeff Durgin, as he walks along with Bessie Lynde, whose mouth has been previously described as "beautiful and vividly red," notices "the gray film of her veil pressed softly against her red mouth by her swift advance" and keeps "seeing the play of the veil's edge against her lips as they talked." These concentrated, veiled images stay impressed in the mind where a fuller and less inhibited treatment might fade.

generous in its recognition of the various talents of others—his failure to appreciate *Sister Carrie* and to see that Dreiser, far more helplessly immersed than he in the new American reality of godless competition, had written, in this matter-of-fact account of a fallen woman's rise, the untrammelled novel Howells wanted to write, a novel as realistic in its amorality as in its urban details.

A Hazard of New Fortunes strives to be a novel of the modern city. One begins to read it exhilarated that Howells's powers of observation have been released from the rather narrow, backward-looking world of Boston into the ethnic breadth and gritty energy of New York. Howells's life-journey had taken him from Ohio to Italy, from Italy to New England, and in 1888, by gingerly half-steps, from Boston to New York. By moving, it has been said, he took the literary center of the United States with him, but the New England giants whom he had adored from afar and catered to in Cambridge were dead or senescent, and vitality had already passed from Boston, with its (as Howells put it) "idealizing tendency," to New York, with its "realizing tendency." His instincts for where his career should take him were ever sound.

In *A Hazard of New Fortunes,* a whole new world of novelistic possibilities opens up; but these possibilities are exploited piecemeal, in an attenuated chain. The early pages, following our old friends Basil and Isabel March in their search for an apartment, take us back to the light atmosphere of *Their Wedding Journey*—picaresque comedy and droll encounter on American soil. But as other characters are introduced, and various lines of tension and possibility established, we feel the lack of a unifying field, some equivalent of Napoleon's invasion in *War and Peace* or the fog in *Bleak House.* There appear to be altogether too many of Howells's young ladies, with not near enough swains to carry them off, and the literary journal *Every Other Week* does not seem a massive enough central switchboard to connect the many human specimens, from raving Socialist to crusty millionaire, that the novel introduces. We are reminded of the author's own warning that "the intrigue of close texture will never suit our conditions, which are so loose and open and variable." We are conscious of the wide spaces, psychological and even geographical, between the characters—almost none of them native New Yorkers—that Howells has dotted about on Manhattan's grid, and of the artificial coincidences whereby he brings them together to give off a few sparks. The Dryfooses, from the dark and fiery oil fields of northern Ohio, are vivid enough, but vivid in isolation, as are the charming Southerners the Woodwards, and the plucky protofeminist Alma Leighton, and the vacuous artist Beaton, an especially unlikable recruit in Howells's long line of passive and foppish highbrow drifters. In short, where Howells needs a plot, to activate so large a field and give it overall momentum, he comes up instead with descriptions of New York, and honorably shrewd and concerned remarks about poverty and wealth, and isolated brilliant scenes, and characters too numerous and sharply distinct to disarm a feeling of caricature.

A better novel from the Nineties, in my view, is *The Landlord at Lion's Head* (1897), which returns to New England and tries to face the ancient issue of why bad men succeed—though in truth Jeff Durgin strikes one as not only more likable but even more sensitive than his stern critic, the fastidious painter Westover. It turns out, quite charmingly, that underneath everything the two men have been competing for a girl, Cynthia, whom Westover first sees as a child, and whom Durgin bravely recognizes as too fine for him. The book has the ghostly flavor of a romance, with an alcoholic brother and a tubercular family out of Poe, and shows how little an author can will Tolstoyan solidity in a land where the monotonous civilization of a democracy imposes fine shades and pale colors.

The slim Ohio youth who in 1860 was recommended to Emerson by Hawthorne with the laconic note "I find this young man worthy" lived to see himself sneered at by Ambrose Bierce and H. L. Mencken as the portly symbol of an outworn genteel tradition. Posterity tends to be hard upon those who have served their own times too well. If we imagine Howells and Henry James, as they paced the streets not far from here in Harvard Yard, to be competing in setting forth "the true principles of literary art," we must admit that James won the race. His titles thrive in paperback; in the divagational difficulty of his sentences and the proud passion of his increasingly abstract pattern-making he looms as the first great American modernist. Gertrude Stein, in her *Lectures in America*, differentiated him from his English contemporaries: "The others all stayed where they were, it was where they had come but Henry James knew he was on his way. That is because this did connect with the American way. And so although they did in a way the same thing, his had a future feeling and theirs an ending." Yet, as we look about, could we not say that James has many academic idolaters but few imitators—Peter Taylor and Cynthia Ozick in their youths are the last I can think of—whereas the Howells faith in "poor Real Life" relayed with a "poetry . . . not ashamed of the plainest fact" is on all sides put to the test, and "effectism" banished to the drugstore racks and the best-seller lists? Howells's heirs include not only Hamlin Garland and Booth Tarkington, who wrote and thanked him, but Sinclair Lewis, who devoted part of his Nobel Prize acceptance speech to attacking him, and John O'Hara and Raymond

Carver, who may not have read him. Today's fiction, the vein of modernist formal experimentation exhausted, has turned, with an informal—a minimalist—bluntness of style, and with a concern for immediate detail that has given regionalism new life, to the areas of domestic morality and sexual politics that interested Howells. "Even if at the risk of some vagueness," our "desultory, mutable, and unfixed" narratives of private conscience and crisis illumine the "vast, natural, unaffected dullness" of middling American life.

It is, after all, the triumph of American life that so much of it should be middling. Howells's agenda remains our agenda—for the American writer to live in America and to mirror it in writing, with "everything brought out." In 1903, I know not why, Charles Eliot Norton showed Howells some letters that Henry James had written him, likening Howells with his fine style to "a poor man holding a diamond and wondering how he can use it." Howells's response was equable and defiant: he wrote Norton, "I am not sorry for having wrought in common, crude material so much; that is the right American stuff. . . . I was always, as I still am, trying to fashion a piece of literature out of the life next at hand." It is hard to see, more than eight decades later, what else can be done.

INTRODUCTIONS

To Indian Summer, *by William Dean Howells*

THOUGH IT PRESENTS not so broad and conscientiously loaded a canvas as such important Howells novels as *A Modern Instance, The Rise of Silas Lapham,* and *A Hazard of New Fortunes, Indian Summer* has faded less than most of this author's immense and once immensely admired oeuvre. It was completed by March of 1884, when the impressions of an extended European trip with his family were fresh in his mind, but was held for sixteen months while *The Rise of Silas Lapham,* composed after *Indian Summer,* ran as a serial in *Century* magazine; accordingly, Howells had more time to polish this novel than he usually allowed himself, and in its text as serialized in *Harper's Monthly* from July 1885 through February 1886 he found little to improve for book publication. In one inscribed copy of the book, Howells called it "the one *I* like best." As it happens, I have read *Indian Summer* twice in the last three years, and found it even better on the second reading than at the first. Knowledge of the denouement enhances one's appreciation of Howells's foreshadowings and fine shadings. His determined—nay, doctrinaire—fidelity to the inconclusive texture of quotidian life, which can leave his novels diffuse and tepid, here attaches to a colorful locale and a classic situation. The novel examines a sexual triangle, with variations on the Oedipal triangle. Its unity of place, its small cast of characters, its precise evocation of the sights and seasons of Florence, its exceptionally well-honed prose, and something heartfelt in its basic concern with aging combine to give it the formal concentration whose absence is usually cited as one of Howells's chief faults.

Indian Summer is the culmination of Howells's transatlantic, Jamesian mode. It might be imagined to hold a touch of friendly challenge, of riposte to the narratives of Americans abroad that had brought Henry James his one strong dose of popular success. *Daisy Miller,* when it appeared in *Cornhill Magazine* in 1878, made a considerable sensation, and *Indian Summer*'s young heroine, Imogene Graham, even without the teasing dialogue that openly names James and Howells toward the end of Chapter XIV, would have been recognized as one of Daisy's sisters, another heartbreakingly uncautious cornfed beauty—an, in James's phrase, "inscrutable combination of audacity and innocence." Though Howells was six years older than James and during his lifetime came to enjoy the securer hold on the American reading public, he was slower to make his start in fiction, staunchly loyal to James in his capacity of magazine editor, and never averse to learning from other writers. Not only *Daisy Miller* but *The American* (1877) and *The Portrait of a Lady* (1881) may have been in his mind as he settled to the glamorous scenes of *Indian Summer*.

Americans of apparently unlimited means established in foreign apartments; teas and balls in the expatriate community; the rustle of long dresses and insular gossip; exotic customs and colorful native populations gaily viewed from the height of a rattling carriage; meetings in museums; pagan and Catholic monuments somewhat sinisterly redolent in Puritan nostrils—such, since Hawthorne's *The Marble Faun,* composed a comfortable ground for a romantic novel. Howells was well qualified to write one: he had spent the years of the Civil War as the American Consul in Venice and was a natural cosmopolitan, a learner of languages and a reader of European literature even as a boy in Ohio. What strikes us, however, in *Indian Summer* are its *un-*Jamesian elements, beginning with the American colloquialism of the title. Though Florence and the Italian landscape are described with guidebook thoroughness, it is the fragmentary memories of America that are truly poetic—workaday Des Vaches, Indiana, and its Main Street bridge overlooking a "tawny sweep of the Wabash"; the "untrammelled girlhood" America offers its young females, with strolls and picnics "free and unchaperoned as the casing air"; and the Spartan New England village of Haddam East Village, whose winter snows still visit the Reverend Mr. Waters in his dreams: "I can still see the black wavering lines of the walls in the fields sinking into the drifts! the snow billowed over the graves by the church where I preached! the banks of snow around the houses! the white desolation everywhere!" Even the old clergyman's vanished faith—"pale Unitarianism thinning out into paler doubt"—has in the description an affectionate, nostalgic ring. James's expatriates rarely strike this note of fond specificity in their memories of the mother country: Fanny Assingham, in *The Golden Bowl,* speaks shudderingly of return to "the dreadful great country, State after State." Howells's hero, the dilettante architect Theodore Colville, is credited with the author's own passionately professional interest in the United States as a site of mental exploration: "It was the problem of the vast, tumultuous American life, which he had turned his back on, that really concerned him." James's expatriates are seeking and losing their souls abroad; Howells's are on holiday.

Nor is the attitude toward the basic issue, the sexual core of romantic maneuver and plot, the same. James regards sex as a force, all right, and concedes it its power to inspire betrayal and social disruption, but he shows little interest in sex itself and little pleasure in tracing its living currents and contradictions; whereas Howells, in spite of the prudery that led him to deplore Chaucer and disdain Dreiser, is fascinated and truthful. The attraction between the forty-one-year-old Colville and the twenty-year-old Imogene is not purely a misunderstanding or piece of folly. Such matings were common enough in an age when men were expected to offer their brides an achieved social substance, and when for respectable women the only permissible sexual experience occurred within marriage. The former could hardly come to the altar too late, or the latter too early.

When Colville, renewing old acquaintance and attending Mrs. Bowen's soirée, first sees Imogene, dressed in ivory white, he asks his hostess, "Who is that Junoian young person at the end of the room?" Imogene, as their shadow-engagement takes hold, becomes indeed Junoian. She adopts an undeviating stance of cold enmity to her sexual rival, Mrs. Bowen, so recently her surrogate mother, and she begins to explore her new sexual rights with a speed that alarms Colville: "She pulled him to the sofa, and put his arm about her waist, with a simple fearlessness and matter-of-course promptness that made him shudder." At the basic biological level, a girl of twenty can be a *match* for a man of over forty. Only Colville's fastidious, facetious distancing and the fortuitous appearance of the attractive young Reverend Morton dampen the spark. Society's complicity—Imogene's mother, it turns out, is prepared to approve the match—combines with Colville's instincts: "He felt sure, if anything were sure, that something in him, in spite of their wide disparity of years, had captured her fancy, and now in his abasement he felt again the charm of his own power over her. They were no farther apart in years than many a husband and wife; they would grow more and more together; there was youth enough in his heart yet; and who was pushing him away from her, forbidding him this treasure that he had but to put out his hand and make his own." To an extent of which the author is perhaps unaware, Mrs. Bowen, heaped high though she is with tender epithets, has Juno's place as the jealous wife forbidding her consort (no Zeus, but a Theodore) his death-defying conquest of a younger woman.

Howells excelled in his portrayals of men in their normal moral indolence. Colville is shown "struggling stupidly with a confusion of desires which every man but no woman will understand." He passively wallows in polymorphous sexuality as not two but three females compete in lavishing love upon him. The triangle has a fourth corner, the child Effie, whose wish to make him her father exerts the force that tips the balance. The vividness with which this ten-year-old makes her presence felt may be traced to the presence of an actual ten-year-old girl, Howells's younger daughter, Mildred, on the European trip, of 1882–83, that gave him the refreshed Italian background of *Indian Summer*. If Imogene usurps the consortial love to which Mrs. Bowen feels entitled, Effie seizes the paternal attention for which Imogene pleads when she says: "If I am wrong in the least thing, criticise me, and I will try to be better. . . . Wouldn't you like me to improve?"

Colville's evasive banter is least jarringly tuned to Effie's prepubescent mentality. An unaccountable gap exists in his masculine make-up—the seventeen celibate and apparently chaste years spent in Des Vaches, with not a whisper of heterosexual involvement, leaving him free to take up his Florentine romance right where he left it, only this time with the alter ego of the original inamorata. Imogene, naïve or not, seems right in divining that Colville's real love-object is his own youth, and shrewd in offering herself as an embodiment of it: "I want you to feel that *I* am your youth—the youth you were robbed of—given back to you." Her "sentimental mission" is not misconceived, except in her estimate of Colville's robustness. She is a match for him, but not he for her.

With all his energy and breadth of interest, there was a nervous delicacy in Howells, a tendency toward depression and breakdown. His novels invite us to dabble in psychological waters because they are his chosen element, where only partly disclosed elements of his own unresolved psychology float. There is something in process, something not precisely formed about his characters, like—as Dorothy Parker said of the men and women drawn by Howells's fellow Ohioan James Thurber—"unbaked cookies." Here the contrast with Henry James tends to be in the other man's favor, for James's characters are nothing if not baked—finished, angular, crisp. They jab and scrape against one another where Howells's characters tend to slide around their oppositions. James had a judgmental sharpness that readily becomes satire. The run-on chatter of his Daisy Miller, for instance, is startling and caricatural and coolly observed and in the end touching. She is full of herself, which makes her courted doom poignant, while Imogene Graham, not quite full and not quite empty, is created to be rescued and consigned to a vague future. Howells's world may be more lifelike in its ambiguity and inconclusiveness, but James's feels livelier, for being more aggressively imagined, with more than a glint of snobbery.

Howells's first imitative enthusiasm was for Heine, and he broke into print—aside from his youthful journalism—as a poet, in *The Atlantic Monthly*. A poet's light touch and trust in the vagaries of rendering was ever to flavor his approach as a novelist, along with a prose style that remained lucid, nimble, and youthful. Again and again in *Indian Summer*, the felicity of the writing makes us pause in admiration: the brimful inventory of Florentine "traits and facts" at the end of the first chapter; the complex activity of adverbs in such a social image as "some English ladies entered, faintly acknowledging, provisionally ignoring, his presence"; the charming period detail of how the two heroines "stood pressing their hands against the warm fronts of their dresses, as the fashion of women is before a fire"; Colville's first appraisal of Mrs. Bowen with its culminating simile: "She had, with all her flexibility, a certain charming stiffness, like the stiffness of a very tall feather." The ubiquitous horses of this premotorized Italy are observed with a sympathy that readies us for the novel's only incident of physical violence. Colville, having just appraised Mrs. Bowen, notices how the cab that takes her away is pulled by a "broken-kneed, tremulous little horse, gay in brass-mounted harness, and with a stiff turkey feather stuck upright at one ear in his headstall." In the line of cabs at Madame Uccelli's, "the horses had let their weary heads droop, and were easing their broken knees by extending their forelegs while they drowsed." When the horses bringing them back from their tense journey to Fiesole bolt at the sight of a herd of black pigs, and drag the carriage off the road, it is as if the abused equine species at last claims its revenge.

The natural world with its animal surges is not far from these prim drawing rooms. In the aftermath of a heated exchange between Imogene and Mrs. Bowen, "They looked as if they had neither of them slept; but the girl's vigil seemed to have made her wild and fierce, like some bird that has beat itself all night against its cage, and still from time to time feebly strikes the bars with its wings." In contrast, "Mrs. Bowen was simply worn to apathy." The moods of these two competing women, caught in the entangling wraps of genteel late-Victorian propriety and social duty, are beautifully searched out, and their differences in social wisdom and natural vitality scrupulously kept in account. Howells feels sufficiently master of the feminine heart to dare present, as in the fine tenth chapter, conversation between the two of them, in female intimacy. On the level of manners, Imogene is a Mrs. Bowen in bud, an apprentice society woman, and Colville, as a specimen man, the somewhat erratic instrument of her education:

He got himself another cup of tea, and coming back to her, allowed her to make the efforts to keep up the conversation, and was not without a malicious pleasure in her struggles. They interested him as social exercises which, however abrupt and undexterous now, were destined, with time and practice, to become the finesse of a woman of society.

These expatriate gentry have little to do but talk and improve their finesse as they drift across a Europe whose exchange rate favors the Gilded Age American dollar, and this leisure, this exclusive labor in human relationships, supplies a stately languor to the developments—to the exquisitely modulated evolution, conversation by conversation, of the characters toward their proper romantic fate. As subjects for a novel, they are rather too ideal, too complacently and volubly self-concerned. Howells would not write about Americans abroad again, turning to New York and a more muscular, Tolstoyan, socially challenging, economically panoramic style of fiction. James, on the other hand, never wearied of his Americans freed of the vacuous coarseness of America, and refined their scruples and disappointments into fictions so spectacularly finespun as to be modernist. No such late blooming awaited Howells; he never wrote better than in *Indian Summer*, though he wrote much more, and for decades admirably acted the part of Foremost American Man of Letters. His talent was very American in needing an injection of youth, of youth's suppleness and careless rapture; his casual charm and vivacious accuracy of observation were definitively displayed in his very first novels, *Their Wedding Journey* and *A Chance Acquaintance*, not so much novels as elaborations of trips he and Mrs. Howells had taken.

Indian Summer, too, has a trip at its heart, a return to Italy, and its hero, at the age of forty-one, is saying goodbye, on behalf of an author in his mid-forties, to youth. A midlife crisis has rarely been sketched in fiction with better humor, with gentler comedy, or more gracious acceptance of life's irreversibilty. This comedy's curious Virgil, godless old Mr. Waters from Haddam East Village, states the optimistic, Emersonian principle that makes Howells's novels so strangely delicious and diffident: "the wonderful degree of amelioration that any given difficulty finds in the realization." Elsewhere, Mr. Waters avows that "men fail, but man succeeds." Colville, amid the "illogical processes" of amorous tendency, somehow fails to evade an "affection he could not check without a degree of brutality for which only a better man would have the courage." But mankind, in the form of a predominantly feminine polite society, succeeds in straightening out the tangle. Howells's tropism toward "the smiling aspects of life" finds, in the microcosm of these few amiable tourists in Florence, a world where smiling does not deny the deeper intuitions of his realism.

To Nature's Diary, *by Mikhail Prishvin*

THE RUSSIAN LANDSCAPE surprises the American visitor with an impression of feminine gentleness. Rollingly flat and most conspicuously marked by the wavering white verticals of the ubiquitous birches, it lacks the shaggy, rocky assertiveness a North American is used to. It seems a young and tender landscape, without defenses. When the single-station radio in the hotel room croons and wails its state-approved folk song, there is no mistaking what the song is about: the motherland. In the fall of 1964 I spent a month in the Soviet Union, and at the end of it my constant companion and weariless interpreter, Frieda Lurie, presented me with a copy of Prishvin's *Nature's Diary*. The volume, printed in slightly ragged type by Moscow's Foreign Languages Publishing House, was small enough to fit into a coat pocket and decorated with a few line drawings in the innocent Soviet style. Frieda could have chosen no nicer souvenir of her country. From its first pages—from Prishvin's sighting of the first cloud of spring, "huge and warm, smooth and gleaming, also like the unruffled breast of a swan"—I felt drawn back into that maternal immensity, into a stately progress of weather and vital cycle upon a colossal stage, as related in a prose now limpidly transparent and now almost gruff, a foxy prose glistening with alert specifics and with *joie de vivre*.

Nature's Diary records a Russian's love of his land, particularly of the swampy, almost featureless, virtually endless taiga that stretches, south of the tundra, from the Gulf of Finland to the Sea of Okhotsk. Most of Siberia is taiga, but great tracts of European Russia also hold these subarctic forests of spruce and fir and birch and aspen, abounding in wildlife; the observations and adventures recorded in Prishvin's *Diary* stem from a year, the author's fiftieth, spent in deliberate nature study at a rudimentary research station near Lake Pleshcheyevo, less than a hundred miles northeast of Moscow. This was the time of Lenin's dying and the murderous struggles for power from which Stalin emerged triumphant and Trotsky an exile; but Communism intrudes rarely into the texture of life by Lake Pleshcheyevo, and when it does it takes the innocuous form of some raggle-taggle and self-important young Komsomol members. The youthful Socialist republic was still a world where one could get away from it all. "My love for nature," Prishvin boasts, "has never prevented me from liking beautiful cities and their complex and fascinating world. But when I tire of city life I take a tram and within twenty minutes am out in the open again. I must have been cut out for a free existence. I can live for years in the huts of fishermen, hunters and peasants."

Mikhail Mikhailovich Prishvin, the son of a rich merchant, was born in 1873 on the family estate in the north of Russia. While a student at Riga, he was arrested for revolutionary activity. After his release, he studied in Leipzig and in 1902 received a degree in agronomy. As young gentlemen were in those years, Prishvin was free to indulge his interests, and he travelled throughout Russia, Central Asia, and the Far East, educating himself in ornithology, linguistics, folklore, and ethnography. His first two books—*In the Land of Unfrightened Birds and Animals* (1907) and *Small, Round Loaf* (1908)—dealt with northern Russia and the customs and legends of its peasants. According to the literary historian D. S. Mirsky, "These studies taught Prishvin to value the originality of the uneducated Russian and the native force of 'unlatinized' Russian speech." Mirsky claims Prishvin to have been further influenced along these lines by a younger writer, the Symbolist Alexey Remizov, whose greatly varied production was "unified by one purpose—which is to delatinize and defrenchify the Russian literary language and to restore to it its natural Russian raciness." While such linguistic nuances can scarcely be conveyed in translation, this rendering by Lev Navrozov does permit us to feel a raciness in the highly informal organization—an impulsiveness of movement that keeps the reader constantly and pleasantly off-balance as he moves with Prishvin through the year. Almost half the book, for instance, is taken up with spring, and the summer section is monopolized by the author's hunting dogs, and the final pages are concerned with a bear hunt that took place nowhere near Lake Pleshcheyevo. *Nature's Diary*, and Prishvin's other rural sketches, achieved considerable popularity with an increasingly urbanized Soviet public; he maintained, we are told, his artistic independence throughout the Stalin era, and died in 1954, at the age of eighty-one.

The nature he contributes to the Penguin Nature Library seems familiar; we have already met it in the scenery of Turgenev and Tolstoy, Chekhov and Nabokov. The continental cold is slow to relinquish the land—we read of frost in May—and quick to reclaim it, with flurries of snow and a film of morning ice on the autumnal marshes. But the fauna, above all the birds, begins its cycles of procreation in the depths of winter, and Prishvin's swift eye sees life everywhere. Carrion crows somersault in their love frenzy, the blackcocks sing and mate as the icy creeks thaw into song, the cranes and kestrels return, and ducks fill the air with noise. Man, too, is active in the cold landscape: "The snow was frozen hard and powdered by the latest fall. The going was pure joy whichever way we turned." And then, gradually, the frogs stir, the finches arrive, grass appears, and the first mushrooms and the early flowers, the blossoms of

aspen and lungwort; the first cuckoo is heard, and then the first nightingale. These manifestations of thaw and revival are intermixed, in Prishvin's diary entries, with the comings and goings of men—with local gossip
and the lore of pike fishermen, with an archaeological expedition and an
ethnological excursion to see a pre-Christian village rite, the Nettle Feast.
Nature, which to an American instinct looms as purely and grandly
inhuman as an Ansel Adams photograph, is for the Russian interwoven
with humanity; this North Russia is a vast and forbidding but long-
inhabited terrain, warmed in its remotest corners by the traces of men. In
the dead cold of a winter night, a hunter in pursuit of a marten burns an
anthill to make himself a warm bed of ashes, and the charred ruins remember him. On a desolate marsh, Prishvin (to his annoyance) suddenly spots
another man walking. He participates in an archaeological dig, which
finds evidence of long habitation, the skull of a prehistoric predecessor—
"more impressive" than he had expected, the skull's color "not the colour
of bone but almost that of copper or burnt clay," the teeth and forehead
perfectly white. Everywhere in this wild landscape, people pop up, more
than we can keep track of. The peasantry seems ubiquitous, like walking
tummocks or another species of animal, part of the land's furniture and
casually included in this inventory:

> The trees, grass and flowers wore their most sumptuous garb. The birds of
> early spring grew silent: the cocks had hidden themselves away, moulting,
> and the hens were fasting on their nests hatching their eggs. The animals
> were busy seeking food for their young. What with sowing and ploughing,
> the peasants were more harassed than ever.

Some of the peasant lore—frogs are woken from hibernation by thunder,
a mushroom detected by the human eye will cease to grow—is perhaps
open to scientific refutation, but the observations that the roach is a lonely
fish and that roach soup makes people brood would seem hard to argue.
Prishvin himself asserts with mystic authority: "The orioles are very fond
of choppy weather. They like the sun to come and go, and the wind to
play with the leaves as with waves. Orioles, swallows, gulls and martins
have a kinship with the wind."
   Man's interpenetration with nature takes many forms: superstition,
lore, and annual rite, as in the Nettle Feast; scientific probing and investigation, as in Prishvin's research; pantheistic communion ("I . . . sat down
on a soft mossy hillock under a pine-tree and began to sip the tea slowly,
musing and gradually merging with the life around me"); and hunting.
There is a great deal of hunting and killing here—more than a modern
nature-lover expects. Prishvin at one point steps forward to reassure the

squeamish: "There is no need to pity the animal, my kind-hearted readers, we're all due for it sooner or later, I for one am almost ready. . . ." To hunt successfully, one must empathize with the animals, think like them; in this immemorial way Man draws close to his fellow creatures. The strategies of foxes, the scruples of wolves are fascinatingly noted. And the minds of the dogs trained to hunt at Man's side are wonderfully well explored. With Olympian humor Prishvin explicates the urinary truce agreements of competing dogs; he triumphantly psychoanalyzes the feminine pretenses of his disappointing pointer, Kate, her nose dulled by two housebound years in Moscow, and rejoices when her nose revives in the country wind. Nature for Prishvin not only spreads itself externally but lies within the mind of a dog, a fox, even a fish or mayfly. He tiptoes toward the mysteries of the woods; he marvels at the snoring sound that emerges from a tree holding a sleeping wood-grouse and speculates on its source:

> I suppose that the sound comes from the fluttering feathers when a large bird breathes under its wing in sleep. However, I shouldn't swear to it that wood-grouse do sleep with their heads under their wings. I am judging by the domestic fowl. It's all surmises, stories and speculation, whereas the real world of the woods is little known.

Though he was something of a scientist, there is little in Prishvin's grasp of nature that corresponds to Loren Eiseley's paleontological perspective or Joseph Wood Krutch's biological microscopy. He is, like Thoreau and John Muir and Annie Dillard, confrontational in his dealings with the outdoors, and existential, his own consciousness his keenest exploratory tool. Nature to Prishvin appears "little known," and the riddles that concern him—how do wood-grouse snore? why do the jackdaws come to see off the migrating rooks?—are ones that a closely observant child might ask. He restores us, in an anecdote like that of the old itinerant nurse who successfully pleaded for mercy with the wolves, to the pre-medieval Europe of the fairy tales, when animals spoke with dignity on behalf of their own societies and men shared with all life a single network of sensation and motive. The semi-centenarian is thrilled to be alive, he tells us more than once. His descriptions of days—especially of that magical hour before dawn, which he is always avid to witness—have a sublime freshness:

> There was a morning moon. The eastern sky was clouded. At long last a strip of dawn showed from under the heavy blanket, and the moon floated in deeper blue.

The lake seemed to be covered with floes, so queerly and abruptly had the mist broken up. The village cocks and swans gave voice.

An Adamic freshness of earliest morning is what one finds in Prishvin; we see the earth being created, and its elemental patterns established:

The most exquisite and mysterious time of the day is that between the first streak of light and sunrise, when the pattern of the leafless trees just begins to be outlined. The birches seem to have been combed downwards, the maples and aspens upwards. I witnessed the birth of the hoar-frost, saw it shrivel and whiten the old yellow grass and glass the puddles with the thinnest film of ice.

The vibration of our animal existence is in him, as well as those tentative motions of mind whereby Man began to subdue his magnificent, riddle-filled environment. The first inklings of morality, of conscious manliness, issue from a hunter's encounters: facing a bear, Prishvin experiences the click of courage, perceiving that "the struggle between the proud free man and the coward was inevitable and needful for it's the coward in us that puts us to the test. One could not talk oneself into bravery as one could not stop the heart from thumping more and more violently. I thought it would burst in a moment, but then came the line beyond which there was no struggle, the coward was vanquished and I turned into a mechanism with the precision of a steel spring in a clock." And death, awareness of which separates us from our fellow animals, is banished by natural busy-ness: "I am no longer young, that's true, but I am as busy as ever and keep my cup brimming full. And as long as I can keep it so, all thoughts of death are empty." Handed down by a more academic stoicism, such consolation might ring hollow; but Prishvin speaks in the unforced voice of nature herself and, with a characteristically Russian blend of fatalism and exuber-ance, imparts to us her ageless imperatives.

To The Complete Stories, *by Franz Kafka*

Published on the Centennial of his Birth

All that he does seems to him, it is true, extraordinarily new, but also, because of the incredible spate of new things, extraordinarily amateurish, indeed scarcely tolerable, incapable of becoming history, breaking short the chain

of the generations, cutting off for the first time at its most profound source
the music of the world, which before him could at least be divined. Sometimes in his arrogance he has more anxiety for the world than for himself.

—KAFKA, "He" (Aphorisms)

THE CENTURY since Franz Kafka was born in 1883 has been marked by
the idea of "modernism"—a self-consciousness new among centuries, a
consciousness of being new. Sixty years after his death, Kafka epitomizes
one aspect of this modern mind-set: a sensation of anxiety and shame
whose center cannot be located and therefore cannot be placated; a sense
of an infinite difficulty within things, impeding every step; a sensitivity
acute beyond usefulness, as if the nervous system, flayed of its old hide
of social usage and religious belief, must record every touch as pain. In
Kafka's peculiar and highly original case this dreadful quality is mixed
with immense tenderness, oddly good humor, and a certain severe and
reassuring formality. The combination makes him an artist; but rarely can
an artist have struggled against greater inner resistance and more sincere
diffidence as to the worth of his art.

This volume holds all of the fiction that Kafka committed to publication
during his lifetime:* a slender sheaf of mostly very short stories, the
longest of them, "The Metamorphosis," a mere fifty pages long, and only
a handful of the others as much as five thousand words. He published six
slim volumes, four of them single stories, from 1913 to 1919, and was
working on the proofs of a seventh in the sanatorium where he died on
June 3, 1924, of tuberculosis, exactly one month short of his forty-first
birthday. Among his papers after his death were found several notes
addressed to his closest friend, Max Brod. One of them stated:

> Of all my writings the only books that can stand are these: *The Judgment,
> The Stoker, Metamorphosis, Penal Colony, Country Doctor* and the short story:
> *Hunger-Artist.* . . . When I say that those five books and the short story can
> stand, I do not mean that I wish them to be reprinted and handed down to
> posterity. On the contrary, should they disappear altogether that would
> please me best. Only, since they do exist, I do not wish to hinder anyone
> who may want to, from keeping them.

The little canon that Kafka reluctantly granted posterity would, indeed,
stand; "The Metamorphosis" alone would assure him a place in world
literature, though undoubtedly a less prominent place than he enjoys

---

*The single exception is "The Stoker," published as *Der Heizer, Ein Fragment* in 1913
but now incorporated, in German and in English, as the first chapter of Kafka's unfinished
novel, *Amerika.*

thanks to the mass of his posthumously published novels, tales, parables, aphorisms, and letters. The letter quoted above went on to direct Brod to burn all of Kafka's manuscripts, "without exception and preferably un-read." Another note, written later, reiterated the command even more emphatically; and Dora Dymant, the young woman with whom Kafka shared the last year of his life, obediently did destroy those portions of the Kafka hoard within her keeping. But Brod disobeyed. Predictably: while Kafka was alive Brod had often elicited manuscripts from his excessively scrupulous friend and was instrumental in the publication of several of them. In Brod's words: "he knew with what fanatical veneration I listened to his every word. . . . During the whole twenty-two years of our un-clouded friendship, I never once threw away the smallest scrap of paper that came from him, no, not even a post card." In a conversation of 1921 he warned Kafka he would burn nothing. And so with good conscience the executor issued to the world *The Trial* and *The Castle*—both novels unfinished and somewhat problematical in their texts but nevertheless stunningly realized—and a host of lesser but still-priceless fragments, painstakingly deciphered and edited. Kafka and Shakespeare have this in common: their reputations rest principally on texts they never approved or proofread.

This volume, then, holds as well many stories in various states of incompletion. Some, like "The Village Schoolmaster" and "Blumfeld, an Elderly Bachelor," seem fatally truncated, their full intentions and final design destined to remain mysterious. In some others, notably "Investiga-tions of a Dog," the author appears to have played out his inspiration without rounding out the story; Kafka's need to explore this conceit of philosophical speculation in a canine world where human beings are somehow unseen ("a sort of canine atheism" one commentator has called the phenomenon) has been happily exhausted before an end is reached. The failure is purely mechanical and we do not feel cheated, since the story's burden of private meaning has been unloaded—there are scarcely any pages in Kafka more sweetly and winningly autobiographical than these. In still other of these uncompleted stories, such as "The Great Wall of China" and "The Burrow," the end is even nearer, and we do not wish for any more. According to Dora Dymant, "The Burrow" had been concluded, in a version she destroyed, with a "scene describing the hero taking up a tense fighting position in expectation of the beast, and the decisive struggle in which the hero succumbs"; though there is poignance in this—"the beast" was Kafka's nickname for his disease, to which he was to succumb within a few months—we are glad to leave the burrowing hero, fussily timorous and blithely carnivorous, where he is, apprehensively poised amid menaces more cosmic and comic than anything his claws could grapple with.

"The Burrow" and "The Great Wall of China" belong with the best of Kafka's creations; their fantastic images are developed with supreme elegance and resonance. The German titles of both contain the word *Bau*. Kafka was obsessed with building, with work that is never done, that can never be done, that must always fall short of perfection. His manuscripts show Kafka to have been a fervent worker, "scribbling" (as he called his writing) with a stately steadiness across the page, revising rather little, but ceasing when authenticity no longer seemed to be present, often laying down parallel or even contradictory tracks in search of his prey, and content to leave his works in an "open" state like that of his Great Wall—their segments uncertainly linked, strange gaps left, the ultimate objective shied from as if too blindingly grand. Not to write for money or the coarser forms of glory is common enough among modern avant-gardists; but to abjure aesthetic "finish" itself carries asceticism a step further, into a realm of protest where such disparate modernists as Eliot and Pound (in the intrinsically fragmentary nature of their poetry) and Rilke and Salinger (in their capacities for silence) keep Kafka company. Incompletion is a quality of his work, a facet of its sincerity.

Hearing Kafka read aloud from his youthful works "Description of a Struggle" and "Wedding Preparations in the Country" instantly convinced Max Brod that his friend was a genius: "I got the impression immediately that here was no ordinary talent speaking, but a genius." You who are picking up this volume in innocence of the author, however, might do well to skip these first two titles and return to them when initiated. Repeated readings of these grouped fragments have left them, for me, not merely opaque but repellent. "Description" was composed no later than 1904–5, when Kafka was in his early twenties. It is full of contortions both psychological ("I had to restrain myself from putting my arm around his shoulders and kissing him on the eyes as a reward for having absolutely no use for me") and physical ("this thought . . . tormented me so much that while walking I bent my back until my hands reached my knees"; "I screwed up my mouth . . . and supported myself by standing on my right leg while resting the left one on its toes"). There is something of adolescent posturing here, or of those rigid bodily states attendant upon epilepsy and demonic possession. The conversation seems hectic, and the hero and his companions pass a mysterious leg injury back and forth like the ancient Graeae sharing one eye. Self-loathing and self-distrust lurk within all this somatic unease; the "supplicant" prays in church at the top of his voice "in order to be looked at and acquire a body."

A certain erotic undercurrent is present also, and in "Wedding Preparations" the hero, Eduard Raban, is proceeding toward his wedding in the country. This narrative at least boasts a discernible direction; but we strongly feel that Raban, for all his dutiful determination, will never get there. The typical Kafkaesque process of non-arrival is under way. And in truth Kafka, though heterosexual, charming, and several times engaged, and furthermore professing that "marrying, founding a family, accepting all the children that come [is] the utmost a human being can succeed in doing at all," never did manage to get to his wedding.

The charm that these disquieting, abortive early pieces exerted upon Brod and other auditors (for Kafka used to read his work aloud to friends, sometimes laughing so hard he could not continue reading) must have largely derived from the quality of their German. The lucid and fluent English versions by the Muirs and the Sterns can capture only a shadow of what seems to have been a stirring purity. "Writing is a form of prayer," Kafka wrote in his diary. Thomas Mann paid tribute to Kafka's "conscientious, curiously explicit, objective, clear, and correct style, [with] its precise, almost official conservatism." Brod likened it to J. P. Hebel's and Kleist's, and claimed that "its unique charm is heightened by the presence of Prague and generally speaking Austrian elements in the run of the sentence." The Jews of Prague generally spoke German, and thus was added to their racial and religious minority-status a certain linguistic isolation as well, for Czech was the language of the countryside and of Bohemian nationalism. It is interesting that of the last two women in Kafka's life—two who abetted the "reaching out" of his later, happier years—Milena Jesenská-Pollak was his Czech translator and helped perfect his Czech, and Dora Dymant confirmed him in his exploration of Judaism, including the study of Hebrew. He wrote to Brod of the problems of German: "Only the dialects are really alive, and except for them, only the most individual High German, while all the rest, the linguistic middle ground, is nothing but embers which can only be brought to a semblance of life when excessively lively Jewish hands rummage through them." Though fascinated by the liveliness of Yiddish theatre, he opted for what Philip Rahv has called an "ironically conservative" style; what else, indeed, could hold together such leaps of symbolism, such a trembling abundance of feeling and dread?

Kafka dated his own maturity as a writer from the long night of September 22–23, 1912, in which he wrote "The Judgment" at a single eight-hour sitting. He confided to his diary that morning, "Only *in this way* can writing be done, only with such coherence, with such a complete opening out of the body and the soul." Yet the story is not quite free of the undeclared neurotic elements that twist the earlier work; the connection between the engagement and the father seems obscure, and the old man's fury illogical. But in staring at, with his hero Georg, "the bogey conjured up by his father," Kafka broke through to a great cavern of stored emotion. He loved this story, and among friends praised—he who deprecated almost everything from his own pen—its *Zweifellosigkeit,* its "indubitableness." Soon after its composition, he wrote, in a few weeks, "The Metamorphosis," an indubitable masterpiece. It begins with a fantastic premise, whereas in "The Judgment" events become fantastic. This premise—that Gregor Samsa has been turned overnight into a gigantic insect—established in the first sentence, "The Metamorphosis" unfolds with a beautiful naturalness and a classic economy. It takes place in three acts: three times the metamorphosed hero ventures out of his room, with tumultuous results. The members of his family—rather simpler than Kafka's own, which had three sisters—dispose themselves around the central horror with a touching, as well as an amusing, plausibility. The father's fury, roused in defense of the fragile mother, stems directly from the action and inflicts a psychic wound gruesomely objectified in the rotting apple Gregor carries in his back; the progression of the sister, Grete, from shock to distasteful ministration to a certain sulky possessiveness and finally to exasperated indifference is meticulously sketched, with not a stroke too much. The terrible but terribly human tale ends with Grete's own metamorphosis, into a comely young woman. In a strange way this great story resembles a great story of the nineteenth century, Tolstoy's "The Death of Ivan Ilyich"; in both, a hitherto normal man lies hideously, suddenly stricken in the midst of a family whose irritated, banal daily existence flows around him. The abyss within life is revealed, but also life itself.

What kind of insect is Gregor? Popular belief has him a cockroach, which would be appropriate for a city apartment, and the creature's retiring nature and sleazy dietary preferences would seem to fit. But, as Vladimir Nabokov, who knew his entomology, pointed out in his lectures upon "The Metamorphosis" at Cornell University, Gregor is too broad and convex to be a cockroach. The charwoman calls him a "dung beetle" *(Mistkäfer)* but, Nabokov said, "it is obvious that the good woman is adding the epithet only to be friendly." Interestingly, Eduard Raban of "Wedding Preparations" daydreams, walking along, "As I lie in bed I assume the shape of a big beetle, a stag beetle or a cockchafer, I think." Gregor Samsa, awaking, sees "numerous legs, which were pitifully thin compared to the rest of his bulk." If "numerous" is more than six, he must be a centipede—not a member of the Insecta class at all. From evidence in the story he is brown in color and about as long as the distance between a doorknob and the floor; he is broader than half a door. He has a voice at first, "but with a persistent horrible twittering squeak behind it like an undertone," which disappears as the story evolves. His jaws don't work as ours do but he has eyelids, nostrils, and a neck. He is, in short, impossible to picture except when the author wants to evoke him, to bump the reader up against some astounding, poignant aspect of Gregor's embodiment. The strange physical discomfort noted in the earlier work is here given its perfect form. A wonderful moment comes when Gregor, having been painfully striving to achieve human postures, drops to his feet:

> Hardly was he down when he experienced for the first time this morning a sense of physical comfort; his legs had firm ground under them; they were completely obedient, as he noted with joy; they even strove to carry him forward in whatever direction he chose; and he was inclined to believe that a final relief from all his sufferings was at hand.

When "The Metamorphosis" was to be published as a book in 1915, Kafka, fearful that the cover illustrator "might be proposing to draw the insect itself," wrote the publisher, "Not that, please not that! . . . The insect itself cannot be depicted. It cannot even be shown from a distance." He suggested instead a scene of the family in the apartment with a locked door, or a door open and giving on darkness. Any theatrical or cinematic version of the story must founder on this point of external representation: a concrete image of the insect would be too distracting and shut off sympathy; such a version would lack the very heart of comedy and pathos which beats in the unsteady area between the objective and the subjective, where Gregor's insect and human selves swayingly struggle. Still half asleep, he notes his extraordinary condition yet persists in remembering and trying to fulfill his duties as a travelling salesman and the mainstay of his household. Later, relegated by the family to the shadows of a room turned storage closet, he responds to violin music and creeps forward, covered with dust and trailing remnants of food, to claim his sister's love. Such scenes could not be done except with words. In this age that lives and dies by the visual, "The Metamorphosis" stands as a narrative absolutely literary, able to exist only where language and the mind's hazy wealth of imagery intersect.

"The Metamorphosis" stands also as a gateway to the world Kafka created after it. His themes and manner were now all in place. His mastery of official pomposity—the dialect of documents and men talking business—shows itself here for the first time, in the speeches of the chief clerk. Music will again be felt, by mice and dogs, as an overwhelming emanation in Kafka's later fables—a theme whose other side is the extreme sensitivity to noise, and the longing for unblemished silence, that Kafka shared with his hero in "The Burrow." Gregor's death scene, and Kafka's death wish, return in "A Hunger Artist"—the saddest, I think, of Kafka's stories, written by a dying man who was increasingly less sanguine (his correspondence reveals) about dying. The nature of the hunger artist's abstention emerges in the opposing symbol of the panther who replaces him in his cage: "the joy of life streamed with such ardent passion from his throat that for the onlookers it was not easy to stand the shock of it." In 1920 Milena Jesenská-Pollak wrote to Brod: "Frank cannot live. Frank does not have the capacity for living. . . . He is absolutely incapable of lying, just as he is incapable of getting drunk. He possesses not the slightest refuge. For that reason he is exposed to all those things against which we are protected. He is like a naked man among a multitude who are dressed." After Gregor Samsa's incarnation, Kafka showed a fondness for naked heroes—animals who have complicated and even pedantic confessions to make but who also are distinguished by some keenly observed bestial traits—the ape of "A Report to an Academy" befouls himself, and his fur jumps with fleas; the dog of "Investigations" recalls his young days when, very puppylike, "I believed that great things were going on around me of which I was the leader and to which I must lend my voice, things which must be wretchedly thrown aside if I did not run for them and wag my tail for them"; the mouse folk of "Josephine the Singer" pipe and multiply and are pervaded by an "unexpended, ineradicable childishness"; and the untaxonomic inhabitant of "The Burrow" is the animal in all of us, his cheerful consumption of "small fry" existentially yoked to a terror of being consumed himself. An uncanny empathy broods above these zoö-morphs, and invests them with more of their creator's soul than the human characters receive. So a child, cowed and bored by the world of human adults, makes companions of pets and toy animals.

Kafka, in the long "Letter to His Father," which he poured out in November 1919 but that his mother prudently declined to deliver, left a vivid picture of himself as a child, "a little skeleton," undressing with his father in a bathing hut. "There was I, skinny, weakly, slight; you strong, tall, broad. Even inside the hut I felt a miserable specimen, and what's more, not only in your eyes but in the eyes of the whole world, for you were for me the measure of all things." Herrmann Kafka—"the huge man, my father, the ultimate authority"—was a butcher's son from a village in southern Bohemia; he came to Prague and founded a successful business, a clothing-and-notions warehouse selling wholesale to retailers in country towns. He was physically big, as were all the Kafkas (Franz himself grew to be nearly six feet*), and a photograph of Herrmann in 1910 shows arrogant, heavy features. No doubt he was sometimes brusque with his sensitive only son, and indifferent to the boy's literary aspirations. But Herrmann Kafka cannot be blamed for having become in his son's mind and art a myth, a core of overwhelming vitality and of unappeasable authority in relation to which one is hopelessly and forever in the wrong. It is Franz Kafka's extrapolations from his experience of paternal authority and naysaying, above all in his novels *The Trial* and *The Castle,* that define the word "Kafkaesque." Like "Orwellian," the adjective describes not the author but an atmosphere within a portion of his work. Kafka's reputation has been immeasurably enhanced by his seeming prophecy, in works so private and eccentric, of the atrocious regimes of Hitler and Stalin, with their mad assignments of guilt and farcical trials and institutionalized paranoia. But the seeds of such vast evil were present in the Europe of Emperor Franz Josef and Kaiser Wilhelm II, and Kafka was, we should not forget, a man of the world, for all his debilities. He attended the harsh German schools of Prague; he earned the degree of doctor of law; he had experience of merchandising through his father's business. He worked thirteen years for the Workmen's Accident Insurance Institute for the Kingdom of Bohemia—his speciality was factory safety, and his reports were admired, trusted, and published in professional journals. He retired as Senior Secretary, and a medal of honor "commemorating his contribution to the establishment and management of hospitals and rest homes for mentally ill veterans" was on its way to him as the Austro-Hungarian monarchy collapsed in 1918. Out of his experience of paternal tyranny and decadent bureaucracy he projected nightmares that proved prophetic. A youthful disciple, Gustav Janouch, who composed the hagiographic *Conversations with Kafka,* once raised with him the possibility that his work was "a mirror of tomorrow." Kafka reportedly covered his eyes with his hands and rocked back and forth, saying, "You are right. You are certainly right. Probably that's why I can't finish anything. I am afraid of the truth. . . . One must be silent, if one can't give any help. . . . For that reason, all my scribbling is to be destroyed."

Janouch also alleges that Kafka, as they were passing the Old Synagogue in Prague (the very synagogue Hitler intended to preserve as a mocking memorial to a vanished people), announced that men "will try to grind the synagogue to dust by destroying the Jews themselves." His ancestors had worn the yellow patch, been forbidden to own land or practice medicine, and suffered onerous residence restrictions under the

---

*His application for employment at the Assicurazioni Generali gives his height as 1.81 meters, or over five foot eleven.

emperors. Kafka lived and died in a relatively peaceful interim for European Jewry; but all three of his sisters were to perish in the concentration camps. The Kafka household had been perfunctorily observant. Herrmann Kafka had been proud of the degree of assimilation he had achieved, and the Judaism he had brought from his village was, his son accused him, too little; "it all dribbled away while you were passing it on." Kafka's mother, Julie Löwy, came from an Orthodox family and remembered her grandfather as "a very pious and learned man, with a long white beard." As if to assert himself against his father, Franz took a decided interest in Jewishness; his diary of 1911 records:

> Today, eagerly and happily began to read the *History of the Jews* by Graetz. Because my desire for it had far outrun the reading, it was at first stranger to me than I had thought, and I had to stop here and there in order by resting to allow my Jewishness to collect itself.

He studied Hebrew and, with Dora Dymant, dreamed of moving to Palestine. Yet churches loom larger than synagogues in Kafka's landscapes; he also read Kierkegaard. His diary of 1913 notes:

> Today I got Kierkegaard's *Buch des Richters* [*Book of the Judge*, a selection from *his* diaries]. As I suspected, his case, despite essential differences, is very similar to mine. At least he is on the same side of the world. He bears me out like a friend.

Kierkegaard's lacerating absolutism of faith would seem to lie behind the torture machine of "In the Penal Colony" and the cruel estrangements of *The Trial*, and to have offered Kafka a certain purchase on his spiritual pain. But in 1917 he wrote Oskar Baum, a fellow writer in Prague, "Kierkegaard is a star, although he shines over territory that is almost inaccessible to me." Kafka came to resign himself to this inaccessibility of faith; of his theology it might be said in sum that though he did not find God, he did not blame Him. The authority masked by phenomena escapes indictment. In his shorter tales an affinity may be felt with the parables of Hasidism, the pietist movement within Judaism which emphasized, over against the law of Orthodoxy, mystic joy and divine immanence. Certain of the parables share Kafka's relish in the enigmatic, his sublime shrug:

> A man who was afflicted with a terrible disease complained to Rabbi Israel that his suffering interfered with his learning and praying. The rabbi put his hand on his shoulder and said: "How do you know, friend, what is more pleasing to God, your studying or your suffering?"
>
> [Martin Buber, *Tales of the Hasidim*, Vol. II]

But there is little in the Hasidic literature of Kafka's varied texture, his brightly colored foreign settings, and the theatrical comedy that adorns the grimmest circumstances—the comedy, for instance, of the prisoner and his guard in the penal colony, or of the three bearded boarders in "The Metamorphosis." The Samsas, one should notice, are Christian, crossing themselves in moments of crisis and pinning their year to Christmas; Kafka, however unmistakable the ethnic source of his "liveliness" and alienation, avoided Jewish parochialism, and his allegories of pained awareness take upon themselves the entire European—that is to say, predominantly Christian—malaise.

Some of his shorter stories sparkle with country glimpses, with a savor of folk tale and of medieval festivity. They remind us that Kafka wrote in a Europe where islands of urban wealth, culture, and discontent were surrounded by a countryside still, in its simplicity, apparently in possession of the secret of happiness, of harmony with the powers of earth and sky. Modernity has proceeded far enough, and spread wide enough, to make us doubt that anyone really has this secret. Part of Kafka's strangeness, and part of his enduring appeal, was to suspect that everyone except himself had it. He received from his father an impression of helpless singularity: "I, the slave, lived under laws that had been invented only for me." A shame literally unspeakable attached itself to this impression. Fantasy, for Kafka even more than for most writers of fiction, was the way out of his skin, so he could precariously get back in. He felt, as it were, abashed before the fact of his own existence, "amateurish" in that this sensation had never been quite expressed before. So singular, he spoke for millions in their new unease; a century after his birth he seems the last holy writer, and the supreme fabulist of modern man's cosmic predicament.

To Seven Gothic Tales, *by Isak Dinesen*

WHEN THE YOUTHFUL Book-of-the-Month Club announced *Seven Gothic Tales* as its selection for April of 1934, its newsletter said simply, "No clue is available as to the pseudonymic author." But even then, with some detective work by the newspapermen of Denmark, this utterly obscure author was emerging into the spotlight as one of the most picturesque and flamboyant literary personalities of the century, a woman who had "style" as well as an anachronistically grave and luminous prose style, and whose works as they followed her veiled debut seemed successive enlargements of her dramatic persona. She relished what she called "the sweetness of fame" and the company of the great and glamorous; she received in her native Denmark and while travelling elsewhere the attention due a celebrity. In her frail last years, on her one trip to the United States, she went out of her way to meet Marilyn Monroe, and recently has herself become a movie heroine, as played by Meryl Streep in the scenic adaptation of *Out of Africa.* Since her death in 1962—stylishly, the cause of death was given as "emaciation"—the many-named woman known to the world as Isak Dinesen has been the subject of a number of biographies, including a truly excellent one by Judith Thurman, from which I have drawn most of the following facts.

Karen Christentze Dinesen was born in April of 1885, in a manor house near the coast fifteen miles north of Copenhagen. Her father, Wilhelm Dinesen, the younger son of a Jutland landowner who had once travelled through Italy with Hans Christian Andersen, was a soldier, an adventurer, and a writer; his epistolary memoir, *Letters from the Hunt,* ranks as a minor classic of Danish literature. Karen's mother, Ingeborg, came from a family of wealthy traders and merchants; hard-working, with social views both liberal and prudish, the family had attempted to discourage her liaison with the rakish, countrified, somewhat aristocratic Dinesens. Ingeborg, though reserved and domestic by nature, had travelled, spoke several languages, and described herself as a "free-thinker" and a "bookworm of the most gluttonous sort." She married Wilhelm in 1881 and within five years was the mother of three daughters, of whom Karen, nicknamed "Tanne," was the second; two more children, both sons, followed in the next decade. Tanne was her father's favorite and confidante; all the greater the blow, then, to the little girl when Wilhelm, whose careers in both politics and literature had taken discouraging turns, and who had a history of restlessness and "soul-sickness," committed suicide, by hanging, shortly before Tanne's tenth birthday.

Karen grew up, in the strongly feminine company of her mother and sisters and servants and aunts, as the family fantastic, who from the age of ten or eleven concocted plays that were performed within the domestic circle, the children and their friends taking the parts of Columbine and Harlequin, Blancheflor and Knight Orlando. Copenhagen's Tivoli Gardens held a carved and gilded pantomime theatre, and the stock figures of the commedia dell'arte and the emotionally charged artifice of masks and masquerades ever fascinated Isak Dinesen. As a child, she drew and painted, expertly and copiously, and several times in the course of her spotty education escaped her mother's house to study art. But like most upper-class girls she was being prepared principally for marriage, and except for excursions to improve a foreign language was kept sheltered and close to home. In adolescence she became obsessed with the figure of her dead father and the notion that his ideals and romantic spirit had descended into her. When, in her early twenties, she published a few tales in Danish magazines, it was under the pen name "Osceola." Osceola was the name of Wilhelm's dog, with whom the father and daughter used to take their walks; the name came from that of a Seminole chief born to an English father and a Creek mother. This allusion to a disparate parentage declares an allegiance to her father; he had travelled in America, written admiringly of the American Indians, and published under the pseudonym of Boganis, another Indian name. In 1934 Isak Dinesen explained to a Danish interviewer that she had taken a pen name "on the same grounds my father hid behind the pseudonym Boganis . . . so he could express himself freely, give his imagination a free rein. . . . In many things I resemble my father." And when, in early 1914, at the near-spinsterish age of twenty-eight, she married, it was to a Swedish aristocrat, her cousin Bror Blixen, who like her father was restless, impractical, and cavalier. Though he was to be an unfaithful husband, he gave her two wedding gifts faithful to her fantastic sense of herself: he made her a baroness, and he took her to Africa.

Baroness Blixen's time in Africa—1914 to 1931—has been much written about, most splendidly by her. Her main memoir, *Out of Africa*, published in 1937, has been called the greatest pastoral romance of modern times; it is a severely smoothed account of seventeen bumpy years, her prime as a woman, spent coping with a recalcitrant and ill-conceived coffee plantation, with her rich Danish relations as they reluctantly financed this losing venture, with an errant and often absent big-game-hunting husband and then a lover (also a big-game hunter) even more elusive, and with a painful and persistent case of syphilis contracted from Bror in the first year of their marriage. From the standpoint of her writing, two crucial developments might be noted. In British East Africa, English became her daily language; and in the person of her handsome, Etonian, Oxonian lover, Denys Finch Hatton, she for the first time encountered a fully involving intellectual partner, a brilliant and playful stimulant to her own intelligence and story-teller's gift. "When I was expecting Denys," she wrote, "and heard his car coming up the drive, I heard at the same time, the things of the farm all telling what they really were. . . . When he came back to the farm it gave out what was in it; it spoke." She liked to think of herself as Scheherazade, and in Denys she met her Sultan. In the Kenyan Highlands she encountered two societies, the African and the white settlers', colorfully imbued with the notions of honor, fatalism, and daring that had always attracted her. Many of the nineteenth-century exotics of *Gothic Tales* are based, in fact, upon originals met in the semi-feudal colonial society, simultaneously raffish and posh, rough and luxurious, around Nairobi.

Her situation, when at the age of forty-six she was at last compelled to return to Denmark, might be described as ignominious. Her marriage long ended, her farm bankrupt and sold to a real-estate developer, her lover recently dead in the crash of his airplane, her body tormented by the complications of *Tabes dorsalis,* she was received into her mother's household as a prodigal daughter, a middle-aged adolescent. Setting up shop in her father's old office, she picked up notebooks and ideas she had been toying with for ten years, while in Africa. Her method of writing was one of accretion, of retellings and fresh inspirations flowing one into the other. She wrote in English and placed her tales in the previous century for the same reason, she said, that she took a pseudonym: "Because . . . only in that way did I become perfectly free." The manuscript of *Seven Gothic Tales* was ready by the spring of 1933 but, rich and strange and free as it was, met difficulty getting into print. Several English publishers rejected it; Thomas Dinesen, however, had befriended an American writer, Dorothy Canfield Fisher, and sent his sister's manuscript to her in Vermont. Miss Canfield was impressed, and urged the book in turn upon her neighbor, Robert Haas, a publisher whose firm later merged with Random House. He published the book in January of 1934, with an introduction by Miss Canfield that memorably begins, "The person who has set his teeth into a kind of fruit new to him, is usually as eager as he is unable to tell you how it tastes."* The new fruit met critical acclaim and, unexpectedly, commercial success as well. The Book-of-the-Month Club printed fifty thousand copies, and was to select books by her five times in the future. This Danish woman who had lived among the English had her breakthrough in the United States, and a special warmth continued to exist between Isak Dinesen and her American audience. Not only were her American royalties much the most munificent, but the reviewers treated her without the note of cavil and suspicion often heard in England and Denmark. When at last the wraithlike author visited the United States in 1959, she told a Danish reporter, "When I compare the American and Danish reviews of my first book I cannot help but think how much better I have been understood and accepted in America than in Denmark."

That same year, she spoke to another interviewer with what he reported as embarrassment of *Seven Gothic Tales.* It was "too elaborate," she said,

---

*The full text of her description is preserved as an introduction to the Modern Library edition of *Seven Gothic Tales.*

and had "too much of the author in it." Now Pauline Kael has taken the occasion of the Meryl Streep movie to tell us, with her customary verve and firmness, that Isak Dinesen's "baroque stories are lacquered words and phrases with no insides. Some seem meant to be morality tales, but you never get the moral. And the supernatural effects in them aren't connected to any spirituality—they're a display of literary armature, of skill. As author, she's the teller of the tale; nothing is presented more passionately than anything else—she seems to refuse to draw from her own experience. . . . 'Seven Gothic Tales' are a form of distraction; they read as if she had devised them in the fevered atmosphere of all-night debauches." This verdict echoes the prim censoriousness of the young Danish reviewer Frederick Schyberg, who wrote when the book was new, "There are no normal human beings in *Seven Gothic Tales.* The erotic life which unfolds in the tales is of the most highly peculiar kind. . . . There is nothing, the reviewer finds . . . behind [the author's] veil, once it is lifted."

Well, as Dorothy Canfield Fisher advised fifty years ago, "Take a taste, yourself." Enter a deliciously described world of sharply painted, dramatically costumed heroes and heroines posing, with many a spectacular gesture and eloquent aria, in magnificent landscapes maintained as a kind of huge stage set. This operatic Europe, like opera itself, would call us into largeness. One character is "hurt and disappointed because the world wasn't a much greater place than it is," and another says of himself at a moment of crisis, "Too small I have been, too small for the ways of God." Although Isak Dinesen's leisurely and ornate anecdotes, which she furnishes with just enough historical touches to make the stage solid, have something in them of the visionary and the artificial, they are not escapist. From the sweeping flood of the first story to the casual and savage murder of the last, they face pain and loss with the brisk familiarity of one who has amply known both, and force us to face them, too. Far from hollow and devoid of a moral, the tales insistently strive to inculcate a moral stance; in this, her fiction suggests that of Hemingway, who thought well enough of her to interrupt his Nobel Prize speech with a regret that she had not received it. Both authors urge upon us a certain style of courage, courage whose stoic acceptances are plumed with what the old Cardinal, in the first Gothic Tale, calls "divine swank." Dinesen even called this quality "*chic,*" ascribing it to the costumed Masai warriors who, "daring, and wildly fantastical as they seem, . . . are unswervingly true to their own nature, and to an immanent ideal." She also admired, in Africa, the Muslims, whose "moral code consists of hygiene and ideas of honor—for instance they put discretion among their first commandments."

This admiration of the warrior's code surprises us in a woman. She was a feminist who included within her ideal of the energizing sexual trans-action what is heedless and even hostile in the male half of the sexual dichotomy.* The three men she most loved—her father, her husband, her lover—all conspicuously failed to shelter her; and she took their desertions as a call to her own largeness. This call, which reverberates throughout her tales in all their abrupt and sternly mysterious turnings, was, it would appear, more easily heard and understood in the land of Emerson and Whitman than in cozily inhabited England and Denmark. America played the role of Africa for an older Europe: a place of dangerous free-dom, of natural largeness and of *chic*, discreet natives. The discretion in Dinesen's writing, the serene and artful self-concealment even in her memoirs, is an aspect of the personal gallantry which, in the social realm, masked her frightful bouts of pain and debility with the glamorous, heav-ily made-up, in the end sibylline persona who sought to be entertaining.

The teller of tales would ennoble our emotions and our encounters with a divine fatality. Isak Dinesen wrote that we must take "pride . . . in the idea God had, when he made us." She was a theist of a kind (and was much twitted about this by her brother Thomas, a sensible Danish atheist). For there to be "divine swank," after all, there must be a divinity. She placed these Gothic Tales in the Romantic era, when God, no longer housed in churches and sacred institutions, was thought to be outdoors, in the moun-tains and sunsets. But even this evaporated divinity appears in the twen-tieth century too benign to be credible, too bland a guarantor of our inner sense of honor. In "The Dreamers," the story-teller Mira Jama asserts of

---

*She takes sex most seriously, and writes about it with a searchingness few fiction writers can match. The young hero of "The Roads Round Pisa," Count Augustus von Schimmel-mann, poses something like Freud's deplored question "What does a woman want?" Having newly met an arresting young woman, he expresses distress at her low opinion of men, and tells her, "It has happened to me many times that a lady has told me that I was making her unhappy, and that she wished that she and I were dead, at a time when I have tried hardest to make her happy. It is so many years now since Adam and Eve . . . were first together in the garden, that it seems a great pity that we have not learned better how to please one another."

The girl ponders and answers that God, when He created Adam and Eve, "arranged it so that man takes, in these matters, the part of a guest, and woman that of hostess. Therefore man takes love lightly, for the honor and dignity of his house is not involved therein." She goes on, "Now, tell me, Count, what does a guest want?"

He ventures that a guest wants "first of all to be diverted," then "to shine, to expand himself and impress his own personality upon his surroundings," and, lastly, perhaps "to find some justification for his existence altogether." Then he asks in turn, "What does a hostess want?"

"The hostess," said the young lady, "wants to be thanked."

God, "To love him truly you must love change, and you must love a joke, these being the true inclinations of his own heart." Such a deity feels pre-Christian—a vitality at the dark heart of things. One of the many magical atmospheric sentences in "The Poet" runs, "The stillness and silence of the night was filled with a deep life, as if within a moment the universe would give up its secret." The brand of stoicism which these tales invite us to share is not dispassionately Roman or of the pleasure-denying Protestant variety; it has Viking intoxication and battle-frenzy in it. Intoxication figures frequently in Isak Dinesen's work, and mercilessness was part of the story-teller's art as she construed it: the story must pursue its end without undue compassion for its characters. Combat lies closer than compassion to the secret of *Seven Gothic Tales,* and its exhilaration is their contagious mood.

To Appointment in Samarra, *by John O'Hara*

WHEN HE BEGAN TO WRITE THIS NOVEL in mid-December of 1933, John O'Hara was a twenty-eight-year-old, recently divorced journalist distinguished chiefly by the lateness of the hours he kept, the amount of liquor he could absorb, and the number of jobs he had been fired from. He had held and lost jobs with the Pottsville *Journal,* the Tamaqua *Courier,* the New York *Herald Tribune, Time* magazine, *The New Yorker, Editor and Publisher,* the New York *Daily Mirror,* the *Morning Telegraph,* the publicity department of Warner Brothers, the public-relations firm of Benjamin Sonnenberg, and a fledgling Pittsburgh magazine called the *Bulletin-Index,* of which he was editor for four months. In all of his positions O'Hara showed ability, but some combination of his irregular hours and innate abrasiveness produced an early departure. At *The New Yorker,* according to the "Talk of the Town" head, B. A. Bergman, O'Hara submitted "some excellent pieces—tightly written, graceful, revealing [but] for reasons I never discovered, Ross took a dislike to O'Hara from the day he was hired and rejected every O'Hara piece I turned in." The "Talk of the Town" job lasted one month. *The New Yorker,* however, was O'Hara's one area of sustained success, as a free-lance contributor; the editors had taken his first piece in 1928 and, thanks in part to Katharine Angell's fondness for his work, over a hundred pieces thereafter. In early January of 1934 O'Hara wrote Ross, with typical semi-ingratiating cockiness, "I think it would be nice if you were to have a medal struck, or did something else in the way of commemorating what I believe to be a fact:

that in the period beginning 1928 I have contributed more pieces to The New Yorker than any other non-staff man." But *The New Yorker*'s rates were not enough for anyone, let alone a man of O'Hara's bibulous and increasingly expensive tastes, to live on: he received fifteen dollars for his first contribution and the going rate was ten cents a word, which amounted to a few hundred dollars a year.

It was Dorothy Parker, evidently, who encouraged the young Pennsylvanian, back in New York after abruptly quitting the Pittsburgh editorship, to concentrate his energy on a full-scale novel about Pottsville. His home town had increasingly figured in O'Hara's fiction, and among his intended projects was a book of three long stories about it; he had already written "The Doctor's Son," based upon his childhood as the oldest son of the dedicated, pugnacious Dr. Patrick O'Hara, and "The Hoffman Estate," a tale of country-club types hastily written in an unsuccessful attempt to win the Scribner's Prize Novel award. He planned to add to these a third story about, he wrote his friend Robert Simonds in December of 1932, a "Schuylkill County gangster . . . a sort of hanger-on at a roadhouse which was occasionally visited by the Pottsville country club set." Instead, a year later, living in a small eight-dollar-a-week room at the Pickwick Arms Club Residence on East 51st Street near the Third Avenue el, scraping by on occasional free-lance sales, he began a novel with a working title that Parker had given him, having discarded it for a collection of her short stories—*The Infernal Grove,* after a poem by Blake. By February 12, 1934, he was able to write a synopsis to his brother Tom:

> The plot of the novel, which is quite slight, is rather hard to tell, but it concerns a young man and his wife, members of the club set, and how the young man starts off the Christmas 1930 holidays by throwing a drink in the face of a man who has aided him financially. From then on I show how fear of retribution and the kind of life the young man has led and other things contribute to his demise. There are quite a few other characters, some drawn from life, others imaginary, who figure in the novel, but the story is essentially the story of a young married couple and their breakdown in the first year of the depression. I have no illusions about its being the great or the second-great American novel, but it's my first. And my second will be better. All I care about now is getting it finished, written. I'll be able to edit and to polish off etc. after I've done the labor of setting down what I have to tell. I have done no rewriting up to now and very little editing.

Two months later, on April 9, O'Hara wrote Tom that he had finished the novel: "I'm afraid I've muffed the story, but I can't do anything about it now. Oh, I know there'll be more work. I know it because I haven't got the sense of relief that I thought I'd have on finishing it. I've been working on it since December, and doing nothing else, and now I have to bat out some New Yorker stuff."

It is hard to believe he ever got to do much more work—"to edit and to polish off etc."—for *Appointment in Samarra* was published with what seems, today, lightninglike speed. Submitted in April, it was out by August and went through three printings. Harcourt, Brace, the publisher, had asked for some cuts reducing sexual explicitness, but even so the novel was attacked for obscenity by Henry Seidel Canby and Sinclair Lewis ("nothing but infantilism—the erotic visions of a hobbledehoy behind the barn"). However, the book was praised by Scott Fitzgerald and Ernest Hemingway, who wrote in *Esquire*, "If you want to read a book by a man who knows exactly what he is writing about and has written it marvellously well, read Appointment in Samarra by John O'Hara." Dorothy Parker's praise was more epigrammatic and judicious: "Mr. O'Hara's eyes and ears have been spared nothing, but he has kept in his heart a curious and bitter mercy."

The "slight" novel, the "muffed" product of less than four months, has lasted. Though O'Hara wrote many more novels and produced amazing quantities of short stories, he never surpassed the artistic effect achieved by *Appointment in Samarra*. He belongs, with Hawthorne and Hemingway, to the distinguished company of American novelists whose first published novel is generally felt to be their best. Rereading *Appointment*, I was struck by the extent to which even it displays O'Hara's besetting weaknesses as a novelist—his garrulity and his indifference to structure. All sorts of irrelevancies stick up, almost like bookmarks, out of this saga of the fall of Julian English. The subplot involving Al Grecco and Ed Charney, for instance, seems a leftover from the earlier three-part intention, the unwritten "Schuylkill County gangster" story; it truly meshes with the rest only momentarily, in the scene at the Stage Coach, and not significantly, since Ed Charney's revenge upon Julian, like Harry Reilly's, never has time to arrive, and we don't know if there would have been any. Though Luther and Irma Fliegler open and close the novel, they virtually disappear in the middle and seem rather inertly to represent the conventional Lutheran middle class that lies in the social scale just below the high-living Englishes. A certain hurry toward the end nips off a number of threads: Harry Reilly, so thoroughly introduced, melts away as a character, and Al Grecco's provocative early premonition that Caroline English "might be a cheater" comes to nothing. On the other hand, at a number of spots the authorial voice suddenly decides to tell us more than we ask to know about how to drive from Philadelphia to Gibbsville, how a small-city bootlegger works, how the anthracite strike of 1925 affected the coal-region economy, what memberships Dr. William English holds, what Mrs. Waldo Wallace Walker wears, and who all does belong to the Gibbsville Club.

Yet none of this gratuitous detail is really deadening, for the complete social portrait of Gibbsville helps explain why Julian English, caught in this narrow world, so feebly resists destruction. Though O'Hara works up some details as to how to run a garage and car agency, Julian seems miscast as a Cadillac dealer, and indeed tells Monsignor Creedon, in the book's odd moment of Catholic confession, "I never was meant to be a Cadillac dealer or any other kind of dealer." The priest's shrewd suggestion that Julian might be a "frustrated literary man" is brushed aside, as it would bring Julian too close to his creator, who wants to see Gibbsville from afar, objectifying into sociological detail the frustrations and rage he experienced in Pottsville.

Appointment in Samarra is, among other things, an Irishman's revenge on the Protestants who had snubbed him, a book in which O'Hara had taken his own advice to his fellow Pottsville scribe Walter Farquhar: "If you're going to get out of that God awful town, for God's sake write something that will *make* you get out of it. Write something that automatically will sever your connection with the town, that will help you get rid of the bitterness you must have stored up against all those patronizing cheap bastards." Julian is named English and he throws a drink into Harry Reilly's "stupid Irish face" after hearing him tell one too many humorous Irish stories; since Julian is O'Hara's hero and a "high class guy," the Irish author restrains his animus* and gives English the benefit of his own sensitivity, observational powers, and (less attractively) impulsive bellicosity. In the treatment of Julian's father, Dr. William English, a regional aristocrat and the lord of local medicine, O'Hara's animus is unrestrained: the senior English is described as, beneath his veneer of correct memberships and public decorum, murderously incompetent. He loves performing surgery on the men injured in mine accidents, yet can safely do it only under the direction of his inferior at the hospital, Dr. Malloy—the name O'Hara gave his own father in the autobiographical "The Doctor's Son." Dr. English gets a nurse fired after he overhears her say, "Trephine this afternoon. I hope to God Malloy's around if English is going to try it." Though this firing alienates Dr. Malloy, Dr. English, we are dryly told,

---

*He bore some animus as well, an informant from Pottsville wrote me, against the Irish of the town; the O'Haras evidently felt snubbed by the Irish elite, headed by the McQuails, and Harry Reilly was supposedly modelled on Billy McQuail.

"continued to do surgery, year after year, and several of the men he trephined lived." Not only are many hospital deaths on his head, but when his only son commits suicide, Caroline, Julian's wife, with a brutality just barely in character, accuses him to his face, "You did it. . . . You made him do it." Dr. English's sin seems to consist of offering Julian a role model of small-city propriety and expressing regret—just like Dr. Malloy in "The Doctor's Son" and O'Hara's father in real life—that his son refused to follow him into medicine.

To the powerful stew of ethnic awareness and filial tension that simmered within O'Hara he added the distress of his brief marriage (1931–33) to Helen Petit, called "Pet." She came from a well-to-do Episcopalian family in Brooklyn; her mother had not approved of her liaison with this brawling, hard-drinking Irish-Catholic journalist, and indeed his drinking helped undo them. In 1932 he wrote Robert Simonds, "I wish I could take a vacation from myself. I have, of course, taken quite a number of overnight vacations; getting so cockeyed drunk that twenty hours elapse before I recover." Also, in these first years of the Depression, his writing career was faring little better than Julian English's Cadillac agency; he gave Julian his own quixotic chip on the shoulder and compulsion to offend those he should court. Yet before Caroline is finally alienated in one last shouting match of sarcasms and masked pleas, she shares Julian's terrible sudden slide, and a number of intimate touches show the tenderness that is being squandered:

> He walked slowly up the stairs, letting each step have its own full value in sound. It was the only way he knew of preparing Caroline for the news of Reilly's refusal to see him, and he felt he owed her that. It would not be fair to her to come dashing in the house, to tell her by his footsteps that everything was all right and Reilly was not sore, only to let her down.

So subtle a language of footsteps, with the elliptic conversation and the lovemaking that follow, could have been described only by a man with a marriage on his mind, and a real woman haunting it. The best passage of sociology in the book, which infuses its knowing with feeling and a remarkable empathy into female experience, is Chapter 5, telling of Caroline's life before marrying Julian; it seems unfortunate that later in the novel O'Hara chose to foist off upon her some relatively unpersuasive Joycean stream-of-consciousness. Nonetheless, the Englishes have a heterosexual relationship beside which those in *The Great Gatsby* and *A Farewell to Arms* are romantic and insubstantial. The repeated offense O'Hara gave to Mrs. Grundy lay mostly, I think, in his insistence on crediting his female characters with sexual appetites—with sturdy and even sweaty bodily and psychological existences independent of male desires.

For all its excellence as a social panorama and a sketch of a marriage, it is as a picture of a man destroyed by drink and pride that *Appointment in Samarra* lives frighteningly in the mind. Julian's disintegration, within this society whose many parts are so zealously particularized, takes place in three days—a kind of Calvary, whose stations progress from the tossed drink that we do not see (though we experience it as a vision in Julian's mind and then as a burst of aghast gossip in the country-club ballroom) to the almost comic drunken whirl and babble in which he spirits Helene Holman out to the Stage Coach parking lot and on to the unforgettable freak of the mammoth highball he mixes in a flower vase during his last earthly hour. When I first read this novel, as a teen-ager (because, I suppose, the scandal of it in Pottsville had stirred waves still felt in Reading, forty miles away, fifteen years later), this monstrous mad drink, and Julian's sodden retreat to the interior of his Cadillac, seemed overwhelmingly dreadful—a liquid vortex opening a hole in the workaday Pennsylvania world about me. How surprisingly brief, on rereading, the sentences are! Dorothy Parker correctly spoke of the book's "almost unbelievable pace."

Julian's choice of an automobile as his instrument of death is a brilliant stroke. In this intensely American novel, the ubiquitous automobile serves as status symbol, as love nest, as contemplation cell, as communal signal. Throughout, on these Gibbsville streets, people hear and see each other come and go in their cars. In the beginning Irma Fliegler hears the Newtons return, and at the end Julian hears Alice Cartwright leave, a sound Herbert Harley also hears. As the engines purr and the broken chain links clatter against fenders, an entire web of motion calls out to those in bed, bidding them to be out and doing, warning them not to fall behind, to miss out.

O'Hara was back in Pottsville for the Christmas of 1930, and we assume that the snowy weather is as authentic as the Ralph Barton cover on *The New Yorker* that Caroline is reading.* Authenticity of this small factual kind became the byword for his fiction, and something of a fetish for him; factuality was O'Hara's gruff way of telling the world he loved it. But

---

*"It was a Ralph Barton drawing, a lot of shoppers, all with horribly angry or stern faces, hating each other and themselves and their packages, and above the figures of the shoppers was a wreath and the legend: Merry Xmas." The date of the cover—the artist's only one—is December 13, 1930. Barton had committed suicide between then and the writing of this book, and perhaps this mention is O'Hara's tribute to a fallen fellow convivialist.

authenticity of a larger sort takes this novel almost, as it were, unawares: *Appointment in Samarra* is faithful to the way our fates sneak up on us and occur within a scattered social context that widens out to absolute indifference. In its centrifugal fashion the book is about Luther Fliegler's promotion (it seems likely, but is not nailed down), and Mary Manners's metamorphosis from a coal-region beauty to a New York floozy, and Al Grecco's career as Ed Charney's henchman, which appears to survive his failure to protect Ed's mistress from Julian English, though Al may be henceforth more treacherous. Most events don't come to anything much, but there is an accretion that can suddenly crush a life. O'Hara's short stories in their drifting motion catch a moment in this almost unnoticeable process, this transformation of what we do into what we are. And what we are is seldom what we think we deserve.

Most men lead lives of quiet desperation, according to Thoreau. John O'Hara, as a doctor's son, and as a newspaperman, and as a roisterer and the holder of many part-time jobs, saw exceptionally much of the seamy, disappointed side of American life, and part of his veracity was not to melodramatize it, or to forget that the human will gleams in even the dingiest folds of the social fabric. A curious cheerful toughness enlivens a loser like Pal Joey, and *Appointment in Samarra* does not leave us with the tragic sense of a rigorous destruction that, say, *Madame Bovary* does. Julian keeps a kind of jaunty, willful dignity. Caroline thinks, "He was drunk, but he was Julian, drunk or not." He goes out jokingly, with a last clock-smashing gesture for "the bastards." Like his jut-jawed creator, he gave as good as he got.

To The Power and the Glory, *by Graham Greene*

FIRST PUBLISHED FIFTY YEARS AGO in a modest English edition of thirty-five hundred copies, *The Power and the Glory* is generally agreed to be Graham Greene's masterpiece, the book of his held highest in critical as well as popular esteem. Based upon less than two months spent in Mexico in March and April of 1938, including five weeks of gruelling, solitary travel in the southern states of Tabasco and Chiapas, the novel is Greene's least English, containing only a few minor English characters. Perhaps it succeeds so resoundingly because there is something un-English about the Roman Catholicism which infuses, with its Manichaean darkness and tortured literalism, his most ambitious fiction. The three novels (as opposed to "entertainments") composed before and after *The Power and the*

Glory—Brighton Rock (1938), *The Heart of the Matter* (1948), and *The End of the Affair* (1951)—all have claims to greatness; they are as intense and penetrating and disturbing as an inquisitor's gaze. After his modest start as a novelist under the influence of Conrad and John Buchan, Greene's masterly facility at concocting thriller plots and his rather blithely morbid sensibility had come together, at a high level of intelligence and passion, with the strict terms of an inner religious debate that had not yet wearied him. Yet the Roman Catholicism, in these three novels, has something faintly stuck-on about it—there is a dreamlike feeling of stretch, of contortion. This murderous teen-age gang-leader with his bitter belief in hell and his habit of quoting choirboy Latin to himself, this mild-mannered colonial policeman pulled by a terrible pity into the sure damnation of suicide, and this blithely unfaithful housewife drawn by a happenstance baptism of which she is unaware into a sainthood that works posthumous miracles—these are moral grotesques, shaped in some other world; they refuse to attach to the worlds around them, the so sharply and expertly evoked milieux of Brighton, British West Africa, and wartime London.

In contrast, *The Power and the Glory*'s nameless whisky priest blends seamlessly with his tropical, crooked, anti-clerical Mexico. Roman Catholicism is intrinsic to the character and terrain both; Greene's imaginative immersion in both is triumphant. A Mexican priest in 1978 told Greene's biographer, Norman Sherry: "As a Mexican I travel in those regions. The first three paragraphs, where he gives you camera shots of the place, why it is astounding. You are *in* the place." In 1960 a Catholic teacher in California wrote Greene:

> One day I gave *The Power and the Glory* to . . . a native of Mexico who had lived through the worst persecutions. . . . She confessed that your descriptions were so vivid, your priest so real, that she found herself praying for him at Mass. I understand how she felt. Last year, on a trip through Mexico, I found myself peering into mud huts, through village streets, and across impassable mountain ranges, half-believing that I would glimpse a dim figure stumbling in the rain on his way to the border. There is no greater tribute possible to your creation of this character—he lives.

Greene's identification with his anonymous hero—"a small man dressed in a shabby dark city suit, carrying a small attaché case"—burns away the educated upper-middle-class skepticism and ennui which shadow even the most ardently spiritual of his other novels. Mr. Tench, the dentist, and the complicated Fellows family are English, and may have been intended to play a bigger part than they do; as it is, they exist marginally, like little figures introduced to give a landscape its grandeur. The abysses and heights of the whisky priest's descent into darkness and simultaneous ascent into martyrdom so dominate the canvas that even his pursuer and ideological antagonist, the fanatically atheistic lieutenant, is crowded out, flattened to seem a mere foil. Only the extraordinary apparition of the mestizo, with his yellow fangs and wriggling exposed toe and fawning, clinging, inexorable treachery, exists in the same oversized realm of transcendent paradox as the dogged, doomed priest.

Edith Sitwell wrote Greene in 1945 that he would have made a great priest. His conversion, in Nottingham at the age of twenty-two in 1926, was at the hands of a priest, Father Trollope, who, after his own conversion, had been—according to Greene's memoir *A Sort of Life*—"driven further by some inner compulsion to the priesthood." But Greene was in little such danger; he was converting in order to marry a Roman Catholic, and in any case, he wrote in 1938, "chastity would have been beyond my powers." Yet his serious novels usually have a priest in them, portrayed as fallibly human but in his priestly function beyond reproach. In his second book of autobiography, *Ways of Escape*, Greene writes, "I think *The Power and the Glory* is the only novel I have written to a thesis. . . . I had always, even when I was a schoolboy, listened with impatience to the scandalous stories of tourists concerning the priests they had encountered in remote Latin villages (this priest had a mistress, another was constantly drunk), for I had been adequately taught in my Protestant history books what Catholics believed; I could distinguish even then between the man and the office." The distinction between sinful behavior and sacramental function is clear also to the debased priests of *The Power and the Glory*. Father José, compelled by the state and his cowardice to marry, remembers "the gift he had been given which nobody could take away. That was what made him worthy of damnation—the power he still had of turning the wafer into the flesh and blood of God." The whisky priest can no longer find meaning in prayer but to him "the Host was different: to lay that between a dying man's lips was to lay God. That was a fact—something you could touch." Greene says of his hero what he might say of himself: "Curious pedantries moved him."

In the unrelenting succession of harrowing scenes as the hunted man tries to keep performing his priestly offices, none is more harrowing, more grisly in its irony and corrosive earthy dialogue, than the episode wherein he must watch a trio of local low-lifes, including the police chief, drink up a bottle of wine he had bought for sacramental purposes with his last pesos. But almost every stage of the priest's ragged pilgrimage, between Mr. Tench's two glimpses of him in the stultifying capital of the hellish state (Tabasco, but unnamed), grips us with sorrow and pity. Greene, as a reviewer, saw a lot of movies in the Thirties, and his scenes are abrupt, cinematic, built of brilliant, artfully lit images: the "big whitewashed building," for instance, which the priest does not recognize as a church and mistakes for a barracks, at the end of Part II, and the mountaintop grove of tall, crazily leaning crosses "like trees that had been left to seed," which marks the Indian cemetery and the boundary of the less intolerant, safe state (Chiapas, also unnamed). The preceding climb, in the company of the Indian woman carrying her dead child on her back, is as grandly silent as a pageant in Eisenstein, and there is a touch of surreal Buñuel horror in the priest's discovery, when he returns to the cemetery, of the dead child's exposed body, with a lump of sugar in its mouth. In *A Sort of Life*, Greene, thinking back upon his many novels for "passages, even chapters, which gave me at the time I wrote them a sense of satisfaction," named "the prison dialogue in *The Power and the Glory*," and indeed this scene, in which the priest, at the nadir of his abasement and peril, sits up all night in a crowded dark cell listening to the varied voices—the disembodied souls—of the other inmates, is, in its depth, directness, and strange comedy, worthy of Dostoevsky, another problematical believer.

Greene's conversion to Catholicism, as he describes it in *A Sort of Life*, was rather casual. He was walking his dog past a church that "possessed for me a certain gloomy power because it represented the inconceivable and the incredible. Inside, there was a wooden box for inquiries and I dropped into it a note asking for instruction. . . . I had no intention of being received into the Church. For such a thing to happen I would need to be convinced of its truth and that was not even a remote possibility." But, after a few sessions of his vigorously arguing the case for atheism with Father Trollope, something happened: "I can only remember that in January 1926 I became convinced of the probable existence of something we call God, though I now dislike the word with all its anthropomorphic associations." Early the next month, he made his first General Confession and was baptized and received. "I remember very clearly the nature of my emotion as I walked away from the Cathedral: there was no joy in it at all, only a sombre apprehension." The entire swift surrender reminds us of another, which occurred a bit earlier during his four months of living alone in Nottingham and being terribly bored.

> Once on my free day I walked over the hills to Chesterfield and found a dentist. I described to him the symptoms, which I knew well, of an abscess. He tapped a perfectly good tooth with his little mirror and I reacted in the correct way. "Better have it out," he advised.
> "Yes," I said, "but with ether."

> A few minutes' unconsciousness was like a holiday from the world. I had lost a good tooth, but the boredom was for the time being dispersed.

While still an Oxford undergraduate, he had repeatedly played Russian roulette, in search of a permanent holiday from the world. The world gets a grim report in his fiction. For Pinkie in *Brighton Rock*, "the world never moved: it lay there always, the ravaged and disputed territory between two eternities." In *The Power and the Glory*, the priest, looking at the stars, cannot believe that "this world could shine with such brilliance: it would roll heavily in space under its fog like a burning and abandoned ship." Looking at his illegitimate child, he sees that "the world was in her heart already, like the small spot of decay in a fruit." In the prison cell, he reflects, "This place was very like the world: overcrowded with lust and crime and unhappy love, it stank to heaven; but he realised that after all it was possible to find peace there, when you knew for certain that the time was short." An ascetic, reckless, life-despising streak in Greene's temperament characterized, among other precipitate ventures, his 1938 trip to Mexico.

He had been angling since 1936 for a way to travel on assignment to Mexico, to write about "the fiercest persecution of religion anywhere since the reign of Elizabeth." The persecution had peaked a few years earlier, under President Calles, elected in 1924, and the infamous atheist Governor of Tabasco, Garrido Canabal. Greene finally got his backing, from Longman's in England and Viking in the United States, survived his trip, and produced his book, called *The Lawless Roads* in England and *Another Country* here. (Such transatlantic title-changes were once common; *The Power and the Glory* was first issued by Doubleday under what Greene called "the difficult and misleading title of *The Labyrinthine Ways.*") *Another Country* still reads well, though episodic and in spots carelessly written. Greene has a charming way of tossing into its text passages from Trollope and Cobbett, as he was reading them on the move, and also accounts of his dreams. Many elements of the novel are easily recognizable: the geography, the vultures, the layout and torpor of Villa-hermosa, the amiably corrupt police chief, the officious village school-teacher trying to replace the banished priest, the European *finca* whose proprietors bathe in the stream with nibbling fish, the lump of sugar, the fanged mestizo (encountered behind a typewriter in the village of Yaja-lon), and the rumor of the whisky priest, even to his drunken insistence on baptizing a son Brigitta. But in *The Power and the Glory* it was all marvellously transposed and edited: the priest's mule-riding flights from capture in the Tabasco-like state were based upon agonizingly long mule-rides that Greene took in Chiapas, on the way to Las Casas, which his fictional priest never reaches. Had the air service between Yajalon and Las Casas not been cancelled by rain, his novel might have lacked its most memorable and Biblical mode of transportation.

The tone, too, is transformed; in *Another Country* Greene is very much the exasperated tourist, hating Mexican food, manners, hotels, rats, mosquitoes, mule rides, souvenirs, and ruins. He even inveighs against the "hideous inexpressiveness of brown eyes." In the novel, as it shows a Mexican moving among Mexicans, and these generally the most lowly and impoverished, all querulousness has vanished, swallowed by matters of life and death and beyond. There are hints of a redeeming mood even in *Another Country:* "What had exhausted me in Chiapas was simply physical exertion, unfriendliness, boredom; life among the dark groves of leaning crosses was at any rate concerned with eternal values." The whisky priest, who before *The Power and the Glory* opens has been stripped of his livelihood and the flattery of the pious, in the course of the novel loses his attaché case and suit; he is stripped down to his eternal value, or valuelessness. Greene, at a low ebb in his Chiapas travels, took shelter in a roadside hut, "a storehouse for corn, but it contained what you seldom find in Mexico, the feel of human goodness." The old man living there gave up his bed—"a dais of earth covered with a straw mat set against the mound of corn where the rats were burrowing"—to Greene, who wrote of the moment, "All that was left was an old man on the verge of starvation living in a hut with the rats, welcoming the strangers without a word of payment, gossiping gently in the dark. I felt myself back with the population of heaven." *Blessed are the poor in spirit: for theirs is the kingdom of heaven.*

Graham Greene's sympathy with the poor in spirit, with the world's underdogs, preceded his religious conversion and survives it, apparently: he doubted to Norman Sherry that he still believes in God and in *A Sort of Life* says, "Many of us abandon Confession and Communion to join the Foreign Legion of the Church and fight for a city of which we are no longer full citizens." His religious faith always included a conviction that, as he put it in an essay on Eric Gill in 1941, "Conservatism and Catholicism should be . . . impossible bedfellows." In 1980, reflecting upon Mexico in *Ways of Escape* (where he describes how *The Power and the Glory* was written, back in London, in the afternoons, slowly, on Benzedrine, after mornings of racing through *The Confidential Agent*), Greene complains that the contemporary Mexican government is not left-wing enough, compared with Cuba's. His sympathies have led him into a stout postwar anti-Americanism and a rather awkward pleading for the likes of Castro and Kim Philby. But the energy and grandeur of his finest novel derive from the same will toward compassion, an ideal Communism more

Christian than Communist. Its unit is the individual, not any class. The priest sees in the dark prison cell that "When you visualised a man or woman carefully, you could always begin to feel pity—that was a quality God's image carried with it."

To Wolfgang Amadeus Mozart, *by Karl Barth*

KARL BARTH'S INSISTENCE upon the otherness of God seemed to free him to be exceptionally (for a theologian) appreciative and indulgent of this world, the world at hand. His humor and love of combat, his capacity for friendship even with his ideological opponents, his fondness for his tobacco and other physical comforts, his tastes in art and entertainment were heartily worldly, worldly not in the fashion of those who treat this life as a way-station and testing-ground but of those who embrace it as a piece of Creation. The night of his death, he was composing a lecture in which he wrote, in a tremulous but even hand, that "God is not a God of the dead but of the living." Not long before this, Barth made notes foreseeing his death and the manifestation before "the judgment seat of Christ" of his "whole 'being' "—his being "with all the real good and the real evil that I have thought, said and done, with all the bitterness that I have suffered and all the beauty that I have enjoyed." Foremost for him in the ranks of beauty stood the music of Mozart, music which he placed, famously and almost notoriously, above the music of Bach and all others as a sounding out of God's glory. He began each day with the playing of a Mozart record, partook of Mozart celebrations and festivals, and conscientiously served as a member of the Swiss Mozart Committee, which included the government minister Carl Burkhardt and the conductor Paul Sacher. "If I ever get to heaven," he said, in the first tribute printed in this posthumous collection, "I would first of all seek out Mozart."

It is good to have together, in this slim volume, Barth's formal pronouncements upon his—so to speak—idol, not only for the charm and ardor with which he addresses the subject but for what light his praise sheds upon that question which, despite all the voluminous dogmatics and the superabundance of lectures, sermons, and incidental utterances that Barth's long and industrious life produced, remains a bit obscure in his version of Christianity: the question *What are we to do?** Granted that the

---

*"I hardly dare and yet I do dare to hope that no one will come to me now and say, Well, then, what shall we do about it?" Barth told the auditors of his brilliant exposé of Christian perplexity in "The Word of God and the Task of the Ministry." "*If* the situation is as I

situation of the world and of the individual life is as desperate as Barth paints it, and granted that the message of the Bible, and of the Pauline epistles in particular, is just as he explicates it, amid these radical truths how shall we conduct our daily lives? Does not God's absolute other-ness diminish to zero the significance of our petty activity and relative morality?

Yet Mozart's activity, his *playing,* is regarded by Barth as exemplary, and the intensity and the *freedom* of his playing exonerate, it would seem, Mozart's narrowness, his ignorance of his era's science, politics, and phi-losophy, and the disastrous naïveté with which he conducted his practical affairs. Barth's attitude toward Mozart puts me in mind, incongruously, of Walt Whitman's praise, in "Song of Myself," of animals:

> They do not sweat and whine about their condition,
> They do not lie awake in the dark and weep for their sins,
> They do not make me sick discussing their duty to God.

Like those beautiful and guiltless animals, Mozart's music says Yea; hearing it, Barth tells us, "one can live." By focusing so purely, so simply, upon the making of music, Mozart, like Whitman's panther who "walks to and fro on a limb overhead," gives us an example of tending to business, of channelling and reflecting, within the specialized talent, divine energy. Mozart, superb creature, "never knew doubt." His "ever present light-ness" exalts him above all other composers; Barth marvels at "how this man, while truly mastering his craft and always striving toward greater refinement, nevertheless manages never to *burden* his listeners—especially not with his creative labors!"

And yet a Yea, to have weight and significance for us, must overpower and contain a Nay, and so in Mozart's limpid outpouring Barth also hears "something very demanding, disturbing, almost provocative, even in the most radiant, most childlike, most joyful movements." "What he trans-lated into music was real life in all its discord." His music reflects the conflicts and passions of his time as fully as the omnivorous mind of Goethe. A tireless absorber of the musical currents around him, Mozart "moved freely within the limits of the musical laws of his time, and then later ever more freely. But he did not revolt against these laws; he did not break them." It is in his consideration of Mozart's freedom that Barth becomes most theological, most instructive, and even most musicological: this ideal man, Mozart, carrying the full baggage of human woe and of temporal convention and restraint, possesses his freedom through a "tri-

---

have described it," he goes on, "it seems to me that it is out of place to speak of what we ought to do. The question is simply or not whether we recognize this to be the situation."

umphant turn" out of Nay into Yea. This turn is construed as more admirable than Goethe's sovereign humanism or Schleiermacher's location of a neutral center whereon balance can be achieved: "What occurs in Mozart is rather a glorious upsetting of the balance, a turning in which the light rises and the shadows fall, though without disappearing, in which joy overtakes sorrow without extinguishing it, in which the Yea rings louder than the ever-present Nay."

"Though without disappearing"—thus the theologian acknowledges the inextinguishable problem of evil. He implies a cosmic paradigm in the way in which Mozart sweeps into his magnificent lightness everything problematical, painful, and dark. Mozart's music, for Barth, has the exact texture of God's world, of divine comedy. Hearing it, he is "transported to the threshold of a world which in sunlight and storm, by day and by night, is a good and ordered world." The order is, in Mozart, deeply assimilated and not a kind of exoskeleton, a message, as in Bach. Nor is Mozart engaged in personal confession, like Beethoven. Between the creedal and the personal, he embodies the vital, the "living God" so recurrent in Barth's phraseology: Mozart's music, like the teeming drama of the Bible and like good crisis theology, gives us permission to live. "With an ear open to your musical dialectic, one can be young and become old, can work and rest, be content and sad: in short, one can live": thus Barth speaks directly to Mozart, in a tone of profound gratitude. Those who have not felt the difficulty of living have no need of Barthian theology; but, then, perhaps they also have no ear for music.

MORALISTS

The Gospel According to St. Matthew

MATTHEW might be described as the workhorse of the four Gospel writers, the establishment man. His version of the story of Jesus traditionally begins the New Testament and continues to be placed first among the canonical four Gospels, even though Mark's has been recognized since the 1830s as most probably the earliest composed, and therefore (presumably) the most authentic and the least overlaid by wishful thinking and concealed doctrinal pleading. Mark has his electric compactness and swiftness of narrative, Luke has those tender human episodes (the annunciation, the birth of John, the nativity in the manger, the twelve-year-old Jesus in the Temple at Jerusalem, the story of Mary and Martha, the parables of the prodigal son and the pearl of great price, the good criminal on the cross, the appearances of the risen Jesus at Emmaus and Jerusalem) absent from the other Gospels, and John has his animated dialogues and Platonic outbursts. Compared with these writers, Matthew is a drab and not entirely appealing "safe man" who manfully handles Christian belief's awkward lumber—the threats of hellfire and outer darkness and the, to a modern reader, irksome insistence upon Christ's life as a detailed fulfillment of Old Testament prophecies. But one cannot speak of any of the Gospels as the exclusive product of a writer's personality and inspiration, for all drew upon the same body of oral tradition and contain numerous parallel if not identical passages.

Aside from a few glancing and problematical references in Josephus, Suetonius, and Tacitus, the biography related in the Gospels left no trace in contemporary non-Christian annals. However, Paul's epistles, which predate even Mark, and the Acts of the Apostles, composed by the author of Luke, verify that there was a historical Jesus, whose life and death exerted a transforming influence upon, first, an inner circle of disciples and followers and, within a generation of his death, groups of worshippers throughout Palestine and, by the next generation, much of the Roman world. The Gospel writers belong, it is likely, to the second generation of Christians after the apostles, though early church tradition claims Mark to have been dictated by Peter, and John to have been the actual work of one of the twelve, John son of Zebedee, "the disciple whom Jesus loved," recalling these events as a very old man in Ephesus around the year 100 A.D.

No other texts have suffered such a weight of analysis, yet there is still opportunity for scholars to disagree over such basics as the date, place, and order of their composition, and for significant flaws to be found in every theory. Nevertheless, venerable scholarly consensus dates Mark at about 65 A.D., and places Matthew ten or fifteen years later—certainly after the destruction of the Temple in 70, an event to which Jesus is made to allude in 23:38. Matthew follows, with some deviations and improvements of Greek, Mark's narrative, adding to it a wealth of sayings and teaching present also in Luke: the body of material in common constitutes the well-known hypothetical document Q, named from the German *Quelle* for "source." While Matthew and Luke did not have exactly the same Q in front of them, and small discrepancies abound, it is roughly true that Matthew = Mark + Q and that Luke = Mark + Q + the considerable body of narrative and preachment present only in Luke, called by some scholars S. And if these three "synoptic" gospels are thought of as thus progressively sedimentary, then the Gospel of John is like a metamorphic rock in which these strata have been violently annealed but in which recognizable veins remain. Nineteenth-century scholars, in working upon the Gospels, naturally thought in terms of men manipulating written texts. Many of the puzzles they formulated, concerning the inconsistencies and variations among the texts, disappear if we imagine the Gospel writers as independently drawing upon a lively body of oral history—a body that threatened, as the Christian community became more scattered and diverse, to become ever more distorted and open to inauthentic, notably Gnostic, incursions. By the last quarter of the first Christian century, a written testament was necessary if the movement was to remain coherent. Luke's dedication of his Gospel to Theophilus evokes a scene of growing confusion wherein "many have undertaken to arrange in narrative form such accounts of the momentous happenings in our midst as have been handed down to us by the original eye-witnesses and ministers of the Word."*

---

*This and all subsequent translations are taken from E. V. Rieu's 1952 translation *The Four Gospels,* for the Penguin Classics series.

Those of us who call ourselves Christians, then, look *through* the Gospels that did emerge from the first century as through a cloudy glass toward a brilliant light. But the Gospel writers, whether rememberers or editors of others' memories, themselves were looking through accretions of written and oral history toward events as distant from them as World War II is from us. Their thumbprints, as it were, cannot be rubbed off the glass; at the outset of this century Albert Schweitzer demonstrated in his book *The Quest of the Historical Jesus* that no pleasingly liberal Jesus—no purely political revolutionary stripped of superstitious accretions, no sweet Jesus who is all beatitude—can be extracted from the Gospel record, which is supernatural to its core. Yet Mark, by itself, is a rather cryptic storm of parable and miracle, which begins when Jesus appears, fully grown, "coming from Nazareth in Galilee," to be baptized, and which ends at the point where three of his female followers come to the tomb in search of his crucified body and are greeted by "a young man in a white robe" who tells them that Jesus "has risen: he is not here." Though he also tells the women, "Do not be afraid," the text of Mark judged to be authentic ends with the sentence "They said not a word to anyone, because they feared." The triumphant and redeeming end of the story, Christ's miraculous resurrection, is mysteriously muted in this ending, and a writer of the second century, in a style of Greek plainly not Mark's, appended twelve verses outlining some of Jesus's post-resurrection appearances to the apostles and containing his charge to them to "Go into every part of the world and preach the Gospel to the whole creation." These added verses, included in all Bibles, are canonical but not Marcan; in what survives of *echt* Mark, Jesus disappears from the tomb as casually as he appears at the Jordan to be baptized by John. There is no nativity story, and no follow-up of the empty tomb. Nor is there much explanation of Jesus's announcement, "The time has come, and the Kingdom of God is at hand. Repent and put your trust in the Good News." The news we are given concerns a young man, a paragon of vitality and poetic assertion, who after an indeterminate period of itinerant preaching and miraculous healing in Palestine is taken prisoner in Jerusalem by the Roman authorities at the request of the Jewish priesthood and ignominiously put to death, crying out on the cross, in his language of Aramaic, "*Eloi, Eloi, lama sabachthani*—My God, my God, why hast thou forsaken me?"

Matthew takes up the task of giving these events a cosmic context, by knitting them tight to the sacred texts of the Jewish people collected in what is now called the Old Testament. Matthew is viewed by tradition as the most specifically Jewish of the Gospel writers: Eusebius in his fourth-century *Historica Ecclesiastica* quotes Papias, the bishop of Hierapolis around 130, as saying that "Matthew compiled the oracles (or 'sayings') in the Hebrew language, but everyone translated them as he was able," and Eusebius cites Irenaeus as claiming that "Matthew published a gospel in writing also, among the Hebrews in their own language." The contemporary Biblical scholars who edited the Anchor Bible edition of Matthew, W. F. Albright and C. S. Mann, propose that the disciple Matthew, a former tax-collector identified elsewhere as Levi, in fact was Matthew the Levite, who as à Levite would have been "a Pharisee, educated, and from an orthodox . . . background." The author of the Gospel of Matthew, whatever his actual name, was, they believe, "a conservative-minded Jew" especially interested in the Law and aware of "Messianic titles (the Prophet, the Righteous One) already archaic in the time of Jesus." Without wishing to present Jesus as the new Moses, Matthew shows a "consuming interest in the spiritual history of Israel as a chosen people" and "in carefully preserving sayings of Jesus which re-establish the true principles of the Mosaic Law."

Certainly Matthew can be wearisomely legalistic, beginning with the badly stretched genealogy from David to Jesus that opens his Gospel. Ten times—and each time dampening credibility rather than, as in the original cultural context, creating it—he claims that something occurred in order to fulfill what the Lord had spoken through the prophets: the virgin birth, Bethlehem as the birth site, Herod's massacre of children under the age of two, the flight of Joseph and Mary with their infant son to Egypt, their eventual settling in Nazareth, Galilee as the site of Jesus's ministry, his healing of the sick, his modesty, his speaking in parables, his curious choice of both a donkey and a colt to enter Jerusalem upon, and Judas's acceptance of thirty pieces of silver all take their significance from having been foreshadowed by texts in Isaiah or Jeremiah. For the sake of a verse of the Psalms, "They gave me gall for food, and for thirst they gave me vinegar to drink" (Psalm 69:21), Matthew altered Mark's "They offered him wine mingled with myrrh" to "mingled with gall." It would appear that Jesus himself came to see his life in terms of Israel's hopes of a Messiah. In Mark 14:27, he quotes Zechariah, "I shall strike the shepherd and his sheep shall be scattered," to give the dignity of foreordainment to his disciples' coming abandonment of him. But it is hard not to feel that words are being put in Christ's mouth when Matthew has him, in 26:53–54, say to a disciple who has drawn a sword, "Do you suppose that I could not call upon my Father and that he would not in a moment have a greater force than fifty thousand Angels at my side? But then, how could the Scriptures be fulfilled which say, it shall be thus?" And a few verses farther on, Matthew's Jesus rebukes the crowd that has gathered at his arrest, "I see that you have come out with swords and sticks to capture me as though

I were a brigand. Day after day I sat in the Temple, teaching, and you did not arrest me. But all this has happened so that what the Prophets wrote may be fulfilled." This appeal to the prophets has a parallel in Mark (14:49) and in Luke, but in Luke assumes a quite different quality: "When I was with you in the Temple day after day, you did not raise a hand against me. But this is your hour. Night takes command" (22:53). In John, which names Peter as the disciple who took the sword and cut off the right ear of the high priest's servant, there is no parallel.

A legal passion peculiar to Matthew insists that "while heaven and earth remain, the Law shall not be docked of one letter or one comma* till its purpose is achieved" (5:18). Jesus assures his auditors, "Do not imagine that I came to abolish the Law and the Prophets. I came, not to annul them, but to bring them to perfection" (5:17). The parallel passage in Luke has no such assurance, nor does it contain Matthew's strictures on oath-taking or his stress upon inwardness and secrecy in performing acts of prayer, fasting, and almsgiving: "But when you practise charity, do not let your left hand know what your right hand is doing, so that your charity may be in secret; and your Father who sees in secret will render you your due" (6:3–4). And only Matthew's list of beatitudes ends with "Happy those that have been persecuted for righteousness; for theirs is the Kingdom of Heaven"; the young church was already suffering persecution, and hence Matthew speaks through Jesus to the imperilled faithful of 80 A.D. The threat of hell seems especially vivid in Matthew, and ready to hand, to brandish as a menace: in two separate places (5:29–30; 18:8–9) he repeats the ferocious admonishment found in Mark 9:43–48:

> If your hand leads you into evil, cut it off: it is better for you to come into Life maimed than, with both hands, to depart into hell, into the fire that cannot be put out. And if your foot leads you into evil, cut it off: it is better for you to come into Life crippled than, with both feet, to be cast into hell. And if your eye leads you into evil, pluck it out: it is better for you to come into the Kingdom of God with one eye than, with two, to be cast into hell, where their worm does not die and the fire is never quenched.

These are among the hardest of the not unnumerous hard sayings of Jesus, and Matthew brings them to the fore; his presentation delights in a moral perfectionism. "You then must be perfect, as your Father in Heaven is perfect" (5:48). The Kingdom of Heaven is very precarious of entrance,

---

*In Greek the words are *iota* and *keraia*, the latter being small horns attached to some letters of Hebrew; the King James translation has it "one jot or one tittle," and the Standard Revised "not a letter, not a stroke."

a matter of jots and tittles of the ancient Law: "The man who abolishes one of these little rules and teaches people to forget it shall count for little in the Kingdom of Heaven" (5:19).

What is this Kingdom of Heaven? At times it seems to be a revolutionized earth, an earth brought under the rule of God; at others a realm of an otherworldly afterlife, the opposite of hell and outer darkness. And yet again it seems a new state of inner being, a state of moral perfection that is not so much the ticket to the Kingdom but the Kingdom itself. In Luke, Jesus tells his disciples, "Watch as you may, you will not see it come. People will not be saying 'Here it is!' or 'There!' And the reason why is this—this Kingdom of God is within you" (17:20–21). The most extended statement concerning the Kingdom, and the longest compilation of Christ's instruction, comes in Matthew, Chapters 5 through 7, and it is this so-called Sermon on the Mount, or Great Instruction, that would be the sorest loss if Matthew's Gospel, in that precarious welter of first-century Christian testimony, had vanished along with Q and Matthew's supposed version in Hebrew. Luke's shorter version of the Sermon, delivered not on a mountain but on a plain, in 6:17–49, is less than half as long, and strikes a merry note peculiar to itself: "Happy, you that weep now; for you shall laugh." Matthew does not mention laughing, but his extended collection of the sayings of Jesus holds many touches of that sublime gallantry, that cosmic carefreeness which emanates from the Son of Man:

> Count yourselves happy when the time comes for people to revile you and maltreat you and utter every kind of calumny against you on account of me.

> Let your light so shine upon the world that it may see the beauty of your life and give glory to your Father in Heaven.

> If anyone strikes you on the right cheek, turn the left towards him also. If anyone sees fit to sue you for your tunic, let him have your cloak as well. If anyone impresses you to go a mile, go along with him for two.

> Love your enemies and pray to those that persecute you, so that you may become children of your Father in Heaven, who causes his sun to rise on the wicked and the good, and rains on the just and the unjust alike.

> Do not amass for yourselves treasure on earth, where moth and rust destroy, and thieves break in and steal.

> Learn from the lilies of the fields and how they grow. They do not work, they do not spin. But I tell you that not even Solomon in all his glory was robed like one of these.

Do not judge, lest you be judged.

Do not give holy things to dogs, nor scatter your pearls in front of swine, or they may trample them underfoot, and turn and tear you to pieces.

Ask and you shall receive. Seek and you shall find. Knock and the door shall be opened to you. For everyone that asks receives; every seeker finds; and to everyone that knocks the door is opened.

These commands do not form a prescription for life in this world. The auditors are described as "filled with amazement at his teaching; for he taught them like one with authority and not like the Doctors who usually taught them." The concept of amazement recurs in this part of Matthew. In the next chapter, the disciples are, in Rieu's translation, "amazed" at Jesus's stilling the wind and sea, and Jesus is "amazed" at the faith of the centurion who comes to Jesus to heal his paralyzed son.

Two worlds are colliding; amazement prevails. Jesus's healing and preaching go together in the Gospel accounts, and his preaching is healing of a sort, for it banishes worldly anxiety; it overthrows the common-sense and materially verifiable rules that, like the money-changers in the Temple, dominate the world with their practicality. Jesus declares an inversion of the world's order, whereby the first shall be last and the last first, the meek shall inherit the earth, the hungry and thirsty shall be satisfied, and the poor in spirit shall possess the Kingdom of Heaven. This Kingdom is the hope and pain of Christianity; it is attained against the grain, through the denial of instinctive and social wisdom and through faith in the unseen. Using natural metaphors as effortlessly as an author quoting his own works, Jesus disclaims nature and its rules of survival. Nature's way, obvious and broad, leads to death; this other way is narrow and difficult: "Come in by the narrow gate, for the way to destruction is a broad and open road which is trodden by many; whereas the way to life is by a narrow gate and a difficult road, and few are those that find it" (7:13–14).

Life is not what we think and feel it is. True life (sometimes capitalized "Life" in the Rieu translation, as in the quotation from Mark above) is something different from the life of the body: "He that wins his life will lose it, and he that loses his life for my sake shall win it" (10:39). Christ's preaching threatens men, the virtuous even more than the wicked, with a radical transformation of value whereby the rich and pious are damned and harlots and tax-collectors are rather more acceptable. The poor, ignorant, and childish are more acceptable yet: Jesus thanks God "for hiding these things from wise and clever men and revealing them to simple folk" (11:25). Even ordinary altruism is challenged, and decent frugality, in the incident of the woman who poured precious ointment over Jesus, to the amazement and indignation of the apostles. They object, "That might have fetched a good price, and so been given to the poor." The blithe, deathless answer is given: "You have the poor among you always; but me you have not always" (26:11). Over against human perspective stands God's perspective, from which even sparrows sold two for a farthing have value. Just so, each human soul, including those of women and slaves and gentiles, has value. From our perspective, the path of righteousness is narrow; but the strait gate leads to infinite consolation: "Put on my yoke and learn from me, who am gentle and humble in heart—and you will find rest for your souls. For my yoke is easy and my burden light" (11:28–30). Fulfillment of the old Law turns out to be close to lawlessness: circumcision, dietary restrictions, strict observance of the Sabbath, familial piety, Pharisaical scruples are all swept away by the new dispensation. Said John the Baptist: "He will baptize you in the Holy Spirit and fire. His winnowing-fan is in his hand. He will clear his threshing-floor and gather the grain into his barn" (3:11–12). Said Jesus: "The blind see once more; the lame walk; lepers are cleansed; the deaf hear; dead men are brought back to life, and beggars are proclaiming the Good News. Happy the man who finds no fault in me" (11:5–6).

Christ's easy yoke drew dozens and then thousands and millions into Christianity, which for the first three centuries of its existence was professed in the Roman Empire under penalty of death. Neither in terms of Judaic scripture and religious practice nor in the context of other world religions was the transformation of value Jesus introduced totally new, but it felt new to those who embraced it, in the aftermath of his brief ministry and alleged resurrection. He is the new wine, and of all the Gospel writers Matthew takes the most trouble to decant him from the old skin. The Judaic God had walked in the Garden with Adam, joked with the Devil, bullied Job, and wrestled with Jacob: still, it was a scandalous act to send His Son to earth to suffer a humiliating and agonizing death. The concept profoundly offended the Greeks with their playful, beautiful, invulnerable pantheon and the Jews with their traditional expectations of a regal Messiah. Yet it answered, as it were, to the facts, to something deep within men. God crucified formed a bridge between our human perception of a cruelly imperfect and indifferent world and our human need for God, our human sense that God is present. For nearly twenty centuries now, generations have found comfort and guidance in the paradoxical hero of the Gospels, the man of peace who brings a sword, the Messiah who fails and shouts his despair aloud, the perfect man who seems to drift, who seems in most of his actions to be merely reacting to others, as they beg him to heal them, or challenge him to declare himself the King of the Jews ("The words are yours," he replies), or ask him, as does his Father in heaven, to undergo crucifixion.

In the Lutheran Sunday school I attended as a child, a large reproduction of a popular painting in a milky Germanic Victorian style showed a robed Jesus praying in Gethsemane, his hands folded on a conveniently tablelike rock, his lightly bearded face turned upward with a melancholy radiance as he asked, presumably, for this cup to pass from him, and listened to the heavenly refusal. I was a mediocre Sunday-school student, who generally failed to win the little perfect-attendance pin in May. But I was impressed by the saying that to lust after a woman in your heart is as bad as actual adultery and deserving of self-mutilation, because it posited a world, co-existent with that of trees and automobiles and living people around me, in which a motion of the mind, of the soul, was an actual deed, as important as a physical act. And I took in the concept that God watches the sparrow's fall—that our world is everywhere, at all times, in every detail, watched by God, like a fourth dimension. Some of the parables—the one in which the prodigal son received favorable treatment, or those in which foolish virgins or ill-paid vineyard workers are left to wail in outer darkness—puzzled and repelled me, in their sketches of the dreadful freedom that reigns behind God's dispensations, but the parable of the talents bore a clear lesson for me: Live your life. Live it as if there is a blessing on it. Dare to take chances, lest you leave your talent buried in the ground. I could picture so clearly the hole that the timorous servant would dig in the dirt, and even imagine how cozily cool and damp it would feel to his hand as he placed his talent in it.

Like millions of other little citizens of Christendom I was infected with the dangerous idea that there is a double standard, this world's and another, and that the other is higher, and all true life flows from it. Vitality, perhaps, is the overriding virtue in the Bible; the New Testament, for all its legalisms, obscurities, repetitions, and dark patches, renews the vitality of the Old. From certain verbal prominences, burnished by ages of quotation like kissed toes on bronze statues of saints, and from certain refracting facets of the tumbled testamental matter a light shuddered forth which corresponded, in my consciousness as a child, to the vibrant, uncourted moments of sheer happiness that I occasionally experienced. I still have them, these visitations of joy and gratitude, and still associate them with the Good News. "Know too," Matthew's Gospel ends, "that I am with you every day to the end of time."

Many Bens

1. The Founding Father

THE LIBRARY OF AMERICA, in advertising their sixteen-hundred-page volume of Benjamin Franklin's writings, calls him "the most delightful Founding Father." We do not expect, and it is not certain that we desire, a founding father to be delightful. Sober cool white marble is what we have made of these men, and Houdon's bust of Franklin is almost unrecognizable; we miss the spectacles, and the twinkle behind them. The other founders looked at him a bit askance. Of Franklin as he seemed at the Constitutional Convention of 1787, one of the delegates from Georgia, William Pierce, wrote, "Dr. Franklin is well known to be the greatest philosopher of the present age. . . . But what claim he has to the politician, posterity must determine. It is certain that he does not shine much in public council; he is no speaker, nor does he seem to let politics engage his attention. He is, however, a most extraordinary man, and tells a story in a style more engaging than anything I ever heard. . . . He is eighty-two and possesses an activity of mind equal to a youth of twenty-five years of age." An observer from the other end of the newly united states, Manasseh Cutler of Massachusetts, visited Franklin at his Philadelphia home and found "a short, fat, trunched old man in a plain Quaker dress, bald pate and short white locks, sitting without his hat under the tree." Franklin was the oldest man in attendance, as he had been at the second Continental Congress, a dozen years before. There the dynamic orator John Adams had observed him "from day to day sitting in silence, a great part of the time fast asleep in his chair." At both epochal gatherings in Philadelphia the local sage, for so much of his life an ornament and a servant of the colonial establishment, and for most of the last thirty years a resident abroad, did not fit into the new aristocracy of lawyers and military men, Massachusetts merchants and Virginia planters who had led the young nation into revolution and independence.

Franklin's traceable contribution to the Declaration of Independence consists of a few emendations to Jefferson's prose—most notably, where Jefferson had written "We hold these truths to be sacred and undeniable" Franklin scratched the two adjectives and substituted the crisp "self-evident." At the signing of the document, he supposedly said to John Hancock, "We must indeed all hang together, or most assuredly we shall all hang separately"—but the early biographies make no mention of the remark; it first appeared in print in 1839. In regard to the U.S. Constitution, his ideas were generally voted down. He favored a single legislature and a plural executive branch whose officers would serve without salary. His speech warning of the dangers of "making our Posts of Honour Places of Profit" was read, in deference to his age and frailty, by his fellow Pennsylvanian James Wilson; Alexander Hamilton seconded, and the motion, James Madison noted, "was treated with great respect, but rather for the author of it than from any conviction of its expediency or practicability." When Franklin moved—rather surprisingly, for a man once notorious for his Deism and freethinking—that each session of the assembly begin with a prayer ("The longer I live, the more convincing proofs I see of this Truth, *that* GOD *governs in the Affairs of Men.* And if a Sparrow cannot fall to the Ground without his Notice, is it probable that an Empire can rise without his Aid?"), the delegates, but for three or four, said prayers were unnecessary, and one member claimed aloud that the Convention couldn't afford a minister. Franklin's view that the executive should not be allowed an absolute veto over the legislature did prevail, but not his arguments in favor of strictly proportional representation of each state in the federal legislature. His most useful performance was as the author of the compromise that settled upon a proportionally determined House of Representatives and a Senate in which states were equally represented—it carried narrowly, five states against four, with Massachusetts divided and not counted. In the two and a half remaining months of the Convention, Franklin spoke rarely, but on the liberal side: once, to defend the clause that would make the national executive impeachable; another time, to protest limiting suffrage to freeholders; again, to say that fourteen years of American residence was too long a time to require immigrants to qualify for public office; and yet again, to oppose a property qualification for officers of the government—"Some of the greatest rogues [I] was ever acquainted with were the richest rogues."

At the Convention's end, he rose to move a unanimous vote in favor of the plan hammered out with so much rancor and apprehension, and containing so few of his pet ideas. His speech breathes a benign democratic faith and the patient fatalism learned in his life of dealings with passive-aggressive Quakers, autocratic minions of the British monarchy, the adroit lords and ladies of the French court, and his testy fellow revolutionaries:

> I agree to this Constitution, with all its faults,—if they are such; because I think a general Government necessary for us, and there is no *form* of government but what may be a blessing to the people, if well administered; and I believe, farther, that this is likely to be well administered for a course

of years, and can only end in despotism, as other forms have done before it, when the people shall become so corrupted as to need despotic government, being incapable of any other.

This blessing, which did much to quiet popular resistance to the centralized form the Constitution had taken, was Franklin's last great gift to his nation. The unanimous vote carried, and the Constitution was eventually ratified. His attempts to place his grandson, William Temple Franklin, and his son-in-law, Richard Bache, in the new government were frustrated; the Congress voted him no reward, not even an address of thanks, for his eight years of invaluable diplomacy in France, and declined to settle the accounts of his mission. Franklin died in 1790. He had been of a different generation from the other founders—Washington was twenty-six years younger, John Adams thirty, Jefferson thirty-seven, Madison all of forty-five—and what they had needed from him was his potent presence, as the most celebrated American of the pre-Revolutionary time; they had needed his image.

This image is with us still—in the face on the hundred-dollar bill, in the name that attaches to The Franklin Mint and Franklin and Marshall College, in the Franklin Streets you can find in most Pennsylvania cities, in the twenty-five American counties called Franklin and the upwards of thirty towns, in the iconographic vignettes of the young man who walked into Philadelphia with loaves of bread under his arms and of the older man who went out with a kite to capture the lightning, in the living sayings of Poor Richard and the steady warmth of the Franklin stove. A Philadelphia actor called Ralph Archbold offers to impersonate Franklin at schools and conventions and advertises "more than 200 performances annually since 1973"; this is not inappropriate, since Franklin himself was an inveterate impersonator, preferring to write under pseudonyms and bringing to all his life roles a theatrical flair and good-humored adaptability. The image of himself that he projected was protean—at one point an embodiment of fanatic thrift and industry and at another of pagan rakishness, in one phase a substantial British clubman and in an earlier a lean and penniless journeyman. Reflecting back upon the bulky, farraginous, sometimes tedious and opaque volume which J. A. Leo LeMay has assembled for the Library of America, the reader seems to see many Franklins, one emerging from another like those brightly painted Russian dolls which, ever smaller, disclose yet one more, until a last wooden homunculus, a little smooth nugget like a soul, is reached.

The political patriarch, though the biggest, is in a sense the hollowest Franklin; it is not hard to feel, with Pierce of Georgia, that politics did not engage his attention, at least his deepest and most ardent attention. His non-ironical political writings in this collection are the heaviest going, and not just because the contextual circumstances and tensions are very lightly explained, in accordance with the Library's policy of presenting classic American texts with minimal apparatus. Franklin instinctively saw relations between men and nations as matters of competing self-interest, construed in material terms. Though he mustered a certain patriotic indignation as the American Revolution approached, there is little from his pen that has Thomas Paine's furious sense of an incubuslike British tyranny, or of Jefferson's fervid religious belief in a natural man with sacred rights. From Franklin's vantage in London, the conflict of the 1770s was brought on by "a corrupt Parliament, that does not like us, and conceives itself to have an Interest in keeping us down and fleecing us." It was a matter of markets and demographics in his analysis, and though a wiser king or less venal ministers might have made some difference, Franklin seems basically resigned, should reasonableness fail, to an inevitable historical process. He wrote to Samuel Mather in 1773, "But all these Oppressions evidently work for our Good. Providence seems by every Means intent on making us a great People." Two years earlier, he had confided to his sister Jane, "Upon the whole I am much disposed to like the World as I find it, and to doubt my own Judgment as to what would mend it." Such a doubt makes for a lacklustre inspirator but for a cool and flexible diplomat.

2. The French Franklin

From late 1776 to 1785, Franklin served the fledgling, embattled Congress as one of three commissioners to France and, after 1778, as sole minister plenipotentiary. The French took to him, and he to them, amazingly; years and cares seemed to fall from him. "Being arrived at seventy," he wrote from the Paris suburb of Passy to Thomas Bond in Philadelphia, "and considering that by travelling further in the same road I should probably be led to the grave, I stopped short, turned about, and walked back again; which having done these four years, you may now call me sixty-six." While periodically coaxing millions of livres from the French Foreign Minister, the Comte de Vergennes, for the tattered American cause, he fell in love with French ladies and printed flirtatious bagatelles for them, sometimes in French and sometimes in English, on his private press. The French, seeing in him a mixture of the sage Voltaire and the noble savage predicated by Rousseau, turned him into a knickknack of the Enlightenment. According to Carl Van Doren's biography, "Houdon and Jean-Jacques Caffieri modelled busts, in marble, bronze, and plaster. There

were other paintings and busts, miniatures, medallions, statuettes, drawings, and prints, endlessly reproduced, first on snuff-boxes and rings and
in time on watches, clocks, vases, dishes, handkerchiefs, and pocket-
knives. Probably no man before Franklin had ever had his likeness so
widely current in so many forms." His image, often in dark "Quaker"
garb and trimmings of fur, was rendered so often he complained, "I have
. . . sat so much and so often to painters and statuaries that I am perfectly
sick of it."

This image fascinated the French but the visible reality did not charm
his fellow negotiator John Adams, who complained to his journal:

> I found out that the Business of our Commission would never be done,
> unless I did it. . . . The Life of Dr. Franklin was a Scene of continual
> discipation. I could never obtain the favour of his Company in a Morning
> before Breakfast which would have been the most convenient time to read
> over the Letters and papers. . . . It was late when he breakfasted, and as soon
> as Breakfast was over, a crowd of Carriages came to his Levee . . . with all
> sorts of People; some Phylosophers, Accademicians and Economists . . . but
> by far the greater part were Women and Children, come to have the honour
> to see the great Franklin, and to have the pleasure of telling Stories about
> his Simplicity, his bald head and scattering strait hairs, among their Ac-
> quaintances.

This riot of "discipation" is not entirely out of character; Franklin had
always been sexy. His autobiography confesses how "that hard-to-be-
govern'd Passion of Youth, had hurried me frequently into Intrigues with
low Women that fell in my Way." Poor Richard, especially in the earlier
issues of his Almanack, offers some racy aphorisms: "After 3 days men
grow weary, of a wench, a guest, & weather rainy"; "Neither a Fortress
nor a Maidenhead will hold out long after they begin to parly"; "She that
paints her Face, thinks of her Tail." And his "Old Mistresses Apologue"
(1745), advising a young correspondent to resort to older women, startlingly combines medical misinformation with the wisdom of experience:

> Because in every Animal that walks upright, the Deficiency of the Fluids
> that fill the Muscles appears first in the highest Part: The Face first grows
> lank and wrinkled; then the Neck; then the Breast and Arms; the lower Parts
> continuing to the last as plump as ever: So that covering all above with a
> Basket, and regarding only what is below the Girdle, it is impossible of two
> Women to know an old from a young one. And as in the dark all Cats are
> grey, the Pleasure of corporal Enjoyment with an old Woman is at least
> equal, and frequently superior, every Knack being by Practice capable of
> Improvement.

By a gray cat whose name was never disclosed, Franklin had fathered an illegitimate son, William. The boy lived with him and his common-law wife, Deborah; a son of theirs, Francis Folger, died in 1736, at the age of four, and a daughter, Sarah, was born in 1743. Franklin's wife (whom he had once fondly likened to a "large fine Jugg for Beer") died two years before his departure to France, and the giddy widower lavished coquettish proposals upon his new female friends. He informed Madame Brillon that there were twelve Commandments, the extra two being "Increase & multiply & replenish the earth" and *"Love one another,"* and advised her that "the most effectual way to get rid of a certain Temptation is, as often as it returns, to comply with and satisfy it." From Madame La Freté he expected "half a Dozen of your sweet, affectionate, substantial, & heartily applied Kisses," and via the personae of the flies buzzing in his chambers Franklin expressed to Madame Helvétius the hope that she and he would combine households. Not just John Adams was disapproving; Adams's wife, Abigail, wrote to a friend a mordant description of Madame Helvétius, dressed in "a Chemise made of Tiffany, which she had on over a blue lute-string, and which looked as much upon the decay as her beauty, for she was once a handsome woman; her hair was frizzled; over it she had a small straw hat, with a dirty gauze half-handkerchief round it, and a bit of dirtier gauze, than ever my maids wore, was bowed on behind." This shabby temptress greeted Franklin with "a double kiss, one upon each cheek, and another upon his forehead," and during dinner was seen "frequently locking her hand into the Doctor's . . . then throwing her arm carelessly upon the Doctor's neck." Mrs. Adams indignantly goes on, "After dinner she threw herself upon a settee, where she showed more than her feet. She had a little lap-dog, who was, next to the Doctor, her favorite. This she kissed, and when he wet the floor she wiped it up with her chemise. This is one of the Doctor's most intimate friends, with whom he dines once every week, and she with him." The revered septuagenarian probably received from these lively Gallic women few favors more carnal than being petted and kissed and teased for his faulty French; but a "naughty" Franklin persisted in the American imagination, taking bawdy forms on the popular stage and figuring in Melville's *Israel Potter*. Melville, sixty-five years after Franklin had died, sums up the legend:

> Franklin was not less a lady's man, than a man's man, a wise man, and an old man. Not only did he enjoy the homage of the choicest Parisian literati, but at the age of seventy-two he was the caressed favorite of the highest born beauties of the Court; who through blind fashion having been originally attracted to him as a famous *savan,* were permanently retained as his admir-

ers by his Plato-like graciousness of good humor. Having carefully weighed the world, Franklin could act in any part in it. . . . This philosophical levity of tranquillity, so to speak, is shown in his easy variety of pursuits. Printer, postmaster, almanac maker, essayist, chemist, orator, tinker, statesman, humorist, philosopher, parlor man, political economist, professor of housewifery, ambassador, projector, maxim-monger, herb-doctor, wit:—Jack of all trades, master of each and mastered by none—the type and genius of his land. Franklin was everything but a poet.

In his French phase Franklin came closest to being a pure litterateur; in the delicious relaxation of his epicurean twilight, under the stimulus of feminine French wits, he produced bagatelles, parables, parodies of the Bible, and unclassifiable *oeuvrets* (a word of his coinage) that are to the run of his prose as silk is to serviceable muslin. His "Dialogue Between the Gout and Mr. Franklin" (imitating verses by Madame Brillon and annotated and corrected by her) has, for all its airy form, real midnight power; the former stern advocate of temperance is rebuked by the voice of pain as "a glutton and a tippler" and told, "You philosophers are sages in your maxims, and fools in your conduct." It ends on an eerie puritanical note as the Gout assures its sufferer that "my object is your good, and you are sensible now that I am your *real friend.*" Apparently unpersuaded, in this same period Franklin drew (or had one of his grandsons draw) for the freethinking Abbé Morellet some anatomical sketches inviting "your piety and gratitude to Divine Providence" for its having placed the elbow just where convenient for bringing a glass to the mouth: "Let us, then, with glass in hand, adore this benevolent wisdom;—let us adore and drink!" And in a earthy spoof of scientific research Franklin proposed experiments *"To discover some Drug wholesome & not disagreable, to be mix'd with our common Food, or Sauces, that shall render the natural Discharges of Wind from our Bodies, not only inoffensive, but agreable as Perfumes."* An epitome of Enlightenment amelioration.

3. The English Franklin

From 1757 to 1762, and—after a rather tumultuous and unsatisfactory interval back in Philadelphia—from 1764 to 1775, Franklin lived in London, as the agent of the Pennsylvania Assembly, to negotiate its longstanding and intractable differences with the Proprietors, Richard and Thomas Penn. Later, he was appointed the agent of the legislatures of Georgia, New Jersey, and Massachusetts as well. He did secure from the Privy Council in 1760 the concession that the lands of the Proprietors would be no longer exempt from taxation. His defense of the American position before the Committee of the Whole of the House of Commons in 1766 contributed to the repeal of the Stamp Act and established him as the preëminent representative of the Colonies. Though his fifteen years in England were fruitful of little else in the way of political agreement, and ended in bloody revolution and a hasty return, for him they were years rich in honors and sociability.

In France, he took on the fantastic, delicate coloration of a dream realm, an aristocratic world of powdered wigs and romantic intrigue, of balloon ascents and literary games enacted in the gossamer last days of the *ancien régime*—a regime bankrupted, in part, by the American aid Franklin had coaxed from it. Writing near the end of his life to Madame Helvétius, he talked of dreams: *"Et souvent dans mes Songes, je dejeune avec vous, je me place au coté de vous sur une de votre mille sofas, ou je promène avec vous dans votre belle jardin"* ("And often in my dreams, I dine with you, I sit beside you on one of your thousand sofas"—a touch of the poet, surely, in that—"or I walk with you in your beautiful garden"). In England, things were solid, sooty, burly, clamorous, and masculine. After a while, he stayed, it seemed, only because it suited him. The purpose of his second mission had been to petition the King to take over the government of Pennsylvania from the Penns, and to persuade the Ministry and Parliament to recognize the Assembly as the legislative authority of the province. In the words of Bernard Faÿ's biography, "Franklin walked from one anteroom to another, with his eternal petition in his hand, hearing nothing but words which were more and more vague, and receiving invitations to dinner which were more and more cordial." According to Faÿ, his position became increasingly equivocal, and eventually untenable: "He continued to serve with Foxcroft as the postmaster-general of America, which was a royal office; he was agent for the Pennsylvania Assembly, which was very moderate, for the New Jersey government of his son, which was very Tory, and for the Massachusetts Assembly, which was very radical." Yet even after his dismissal as deputy postmaster-general early in 1774, as punishment for his disclosure of some secret government letters to the Massachusetts Assembly, he lingered another year, while his wife lay dying in Philadelphia. Jug-shaped Deborah was afraid of sea voyages and had twice refused to accompany him abroad.

Within a few days of his London arrival in 1757, Franklin had found lodgings in Craven Street, Strand, with Margaret Stevenson, a widow his age, and her daughter Mary, called Polly. This surrogate household, echoing in composition that of the wife and daughter he had left behind in Philadelphia, remained his home for all his English years; when, in 1772, Mrs. Stevenson moved a few doors away, her distinguished lodger moved with her. She cooked for him and nursed him when he was sick. According to Claude-Anne Lopez and Eugenia W. Herbert in their lively *The Private Franklin*, "People fell into a habit of inviting them together or sending greetings to both." Were they, in his fifteen years beneath her roof, lovers? Some historians speculate that his amorous favor fell instead upon her daughter, who was eighteen when they first met. Before Polly Stevenson's marriage, to Dr. William Hewson, Franklin wrote long paternally instructive letters to her, and she was responsive enough to attempt communicating in the phonetic alphabet he invented, of which the Library of America volume includes three eye-boggling pages. After her husband's death, she came to Philadelphia at Franklin's invitation, stayed four years, until his death, then stayed five years more, until her own death, even though she had complained to her son, "Nothing but insignificance or slavery awaits a woman here."

In London, on the face of it, Franklin behaved as head of the Stevenson household and used it as the comfortable base of his flattering English life. An American friend, after visiting Craven Street, reported that "Doctor Franklin looks heartier than I ever knew him in America." He became a man-about-town. As earlier in Philadelphia and later in France, his devoted membership in the Masons opened doors and cemented friendships. While still in America, he had been elected a member of the Royal Society and of the Premium Society, or Society of Arts. He received awards and honorary degrees, and, summers, travelled in the British Isles and on the Continent, receiving more honors. He frequented taverns and coffeehouses, usually dining on Mondays at the George and Vulture with a group of scientists, and on Thursdays with the Club of Honest Whigs at St. Paul's Coffeehouse. "Conversation warms the mind," he wrote one of his many new friends, Lord Kames. Not only was Franklin's one of those reputations, like Poe's and Faulkner's, that the French have returned to us enhanced but he was one of those Americans, like Henry James and T. S. Eliot, who found refuge in England from the thinness of native cultural life. Temporarily back in Philadelphia in 1763, he wrote Polly, "Of all the enviable Things England has, I envy it most its People. Why should that petty Island . . . enjoy in almost every Neighbourhood, more sensible, virtuous and elegant Minds, than we can collect in ranging 100 Leagues of our vast Forests."

His renown as a scientist, especially as an "electrician," had preceded him and smoothed his way, and it is the scientific passages in the London pages of this bulky selection that form the easiest reading and best give the impression of a mind congenially engaged. These years began with his penning, on the boat across the Atlantic, the haranguing summary of

Poor Richard's cautionary sayings which, separately published as "Father Abraham's Speech" or "The Way to Wealth," was to enjoy wide circulation and many translations. During his Philadelphia hiatus, he wrote perhaps his fiercest and most eloquent pamphlet, decrying the slaughter of twenty friendly Indians living peaceably in Lancaster by a gang of Scotch-Irish farmers calling themselves the Paxton Boys, in reaction to Indian massacres along the Pennsylvania frontier. Franklin's passionate language still stings: "What had little Boys and Girls done; what could Children of a Year old, Babes at the Breast, what could they do, that they too must be shot and hatcheted?—Horrid to relate!—and in their Parents Arms! This is done by no civilized Nation in *Europe*. Do we come to *America* to learn and practise the Manners of *Barbarians?* But this, *Barbarians* as they are, they practise against their Enemies only, not against their Friends."

The bulk of the topical articles and ironical letters published in England, under a parade of pseudonyms—*A New Englandman*, A Briton, The Spectator, A Traveller, N.N., Pacificus Secundus, Homespun, F.B., Americanus, Arator, *A Friend to both Countries*—have rather outworn their complicated occasions. When his sister Jane asked him for a collection of his recent political pieces, Franklin wrote her, "They were most of them written occasionally for transient Purposes, and having done their Business, they die and are forgotten. I could as easily make a Collection for you of all the past Parings of my Nails." Only when the irony—aimed now from a British persona, now from an American— grows outrageous, do the pieces still throw off sparks, as when whales are alleged to leap up the Niagara Falls in the pursuit of cod ("one of the finest Spectacles in Nature!") or, in a hoax that was taken seriously in some quarters, the King of Prussia is supposed to be promulgating an edict demanding, since ancient Britain was a kind of German colony, that all British cargoes be unloaded and taxed in Köningsberg, on the analogy of regulations and duties imposed by the Crown upon the American Colonies. As Boston was blockaded and American blood shed, Franklin's satires became more savage and Swiftian. One of them provides a slogan that Jefferson proposed as a motto for the great seal of the United States: "REBELLION TO TYRANTS IS OBEDIENCE TO GOD."

The reader enters sweeter, less swift-flowing waters in those letters which deal with science, in lessons to Polly Stevenson or in consultation with such learned men as John Pringle, David Hume, Oliver Neave, Thomas Percival, Benjamin Rush, and William Brownrigg. Eighteenth-century science lay in the care of amateurs and permitted a vigorous-minded original like Franklin to roam productively across a wide range of basic phenomena. How and why evaporation cools, how raindrops accumulate, why oil calms water, why a low canal pulls harder than a full one, why rock strata are jumbled, what strange old teeth and tusks signify—such questions are attacked at the level of common sense and everyday life. Franklin describes an experiment in chromatic heat conduction charming in its simplicity, though rigorous and conclusive:

> My Experiment was this. I took a number of little Square Pieces of Broad Cloth from a Taylor's Pattern Card, of various Colours. There were Black, deep Blue, lighter Blue, Green, Purple, Red, Yellow, White, and other Colours or Shades of Colours. I laid them all out upon the Snow in a bright Sunshiny Morning. In a few Hours (I cannot now be exact as to the Time) the Black being warm'd most by the Sun was sunk so low as to be below the Stroke of the Sun's Rays; the dark Blue almost as low, the lighter Blue not quite so much as the dark, the other Colours less as they were lighter; and the quite White remain'd on the Surface of the Snow, not having entred it at all. What signifies Philosophy that does not apply to some Use? May we not learn from hence, that black Cloaths are not so fit to wear in a hot Sunny Climate or Season as white ones?

With the revelations of microscopy barely dawned upon them, Franklin and his contemporaries groped in the familiar macrocosm. He almost arrived at the germ theory of disease: "I have long been satisfy'd from Observation, that . . . People often catch Cold from one another when shut up together in small close Rooms, Coaches, &c. and when sitting near and conversing so as to breathe in each others Transpiration, the Disorder being in a certain State. I think too that it is the frowzy corrupt Air from animal Substances, and the perspired Matter from our Bodies, which . . . obtains that kind of Putridity which infects us." His Philadelphia experiments with electricity, demonstrating that lightning and static electricity were the same "Fluid" and leading to his invention of the lightning rod, made him celebrated in scientific circles and popularly regarded as something of a wizard, like Swedenborg and Cagliostro. On at least one occasion, Franklin acted the part. At Lord Shelburne's castle, while a large party was walking outdoors, Franklin volunteered that he could calm the waters quite as easily as Jesus Christ. Meeting general disbelief, he went to a pond that was being rippled in the breeze, raised the staff with which he had been walking, whirled it three times above the water, and signed the air with a magic hieroglyph. In a few minutes, the company was astonished to see, the pond became glassy as a mirror. The magician later revealed that his staff was hollow and had been filled with oil. Franklin had become interested in the calming effects of oil upon water while observing a swinging lamp on one of his eight trips across the Atlantic. And he also employed these long crossings to study and describe the Gulf Stream—the first scientist to do so. Worlds lay open to his endless curiosity, and he once wrote to Joseph Priestley, "The rapid Progress *true* Science now makes, occasions my regretting sometimes that I was born so soon."

4. The Philadelphia Franklin

Alone and almost penniless, Franklin came to Philadelphia at the age of seventeen. The next day, he had found work, as a journeyman printer, and within six years he and a partner owned their own press and newspaper, *The Pennsylvania Gazette.* His business, which included a shop that sold stationery, books, quills, ink, slates, parchment, sealing wax, foodstuffs, patent medicines, cloth, stoves, and even slaves and the unexpired terms of indentured servants, prospered to such an extent that in 1748, at the age of forty-two, he felt free to retire and to devote himself to scientific research and civic affairs. Though by 1725 Philadelphia was the second-biggest city in the New World, it seems to have been an institutional wasteland, wherein Franklin founded or was a prime mover in organizing the first self-improvement and mutual-aid society, the Junto (1727), the first subscription library (1731), the first German-language newspaper (1732), the first fire company (1736), the first citizen militia (1747), the Colonies' first learned society, The American Philosophical Society (1743), the city's first college, the Philadelphia Academy, which became the University of Pennsylvania (1749), the first hospital (1751), and the first American fire-insurance company (1751). He also proposed and supervised the first plans to sweep and light Philadelphia's streets, not to mention proclaiming the province's first fast day, on January 7, 1748. This Philadelphia Franklin, the tireless improver of self and surroundings, is the one most deeply settled in American legend, thanks mostly to himself. *The Autobiography of Benjamin Franklin* lists his "firsts," describes his rise, and contains a detailed prescription, with a handy checklist, for attaining "moral Perfection." It is this document, along with the repeated admonitions to thrift and prudence in Poor Richard's Almanacks, that goaded D. H. Lawrence to protest, "I am not a mechanical contrivance," and to sneer:

> The perfectibility of man, dear God! When every man as long as he remains alive is in himself a multitude of conflicting men. Which of these do you choose to perfect, at the expense of every other?

Old Daddy Franklin will tell you. He'll rig him up for you, the pattern American. Oh, Franklin was the first downright American. He knew what he was about, the sharp little man. He set up the first dummy American.

And yet Franklin's autobiography is a very unmechanical, elastically insouciant work, full of cheerful contradictions and humorous twists—a fond look back upon an earlier self, giving that intensely ambitious young man the benefit of the older man's relaxation. He loves his younger self—his strength,* his scrapes. He relates amusingly how the young man tried to seduce his friend's mistress, and how he gave up vegetarianism when confronted with some tasty cod: "When the Fish were opened, I saw smaller Fish taken out of their Stomachs:—Then, thought I, if you eat one another, I don't see why we mayn't eat you. . . . So convenient a thing is it to be a *reasonable Creature*, since it enables one to find or make a Reason for every thing one has a mind to do." The *Autobiography*'s first, and masterly, part was written in the form of a letter to his son William, in two weeks of a summer visit to the English countryside, at Bishop Shipley's residence in Twyford, when Franklin was sixty-five. It breaks off as the Philadelphia Franklin is founding the subscription library, and was resumed in 1784, in the idyll of Passy, without the earlier section's being at hand. It then breaks off in a discussion of how to subdue the natural passion of Pride, and was taken up again in 1788, and carried forward into the beginnings of the English mission in 1757, but breaks off a last time, as the by now very aged writer bogs down in the details of futile bygone negotiations. The details of his unheralded arrival in Philadelphia—the weary boy in dirty clothes, the unexpected type and quantity of bread he gets for three pennies, the two excess rolls carried one under each arm, the amused glance from the girl who was to become his wife, the involuntary nap in the Quaker meeting—have passed into American mythology, and have the advantage over Parson Weems's tale of Washington and the cherry tree of being possibly true. These pages by Franklin, from his Boston departure to his employment by the printer Samuel Kiemer, are a surpassingly vivid window into colonial life:

In crossing the Bay we met with a Squall that tore our rotten Sails to pieces, prevented our getting into the Kill, and drove us upon Long Island. In our

---

*He relates how, during his first London sojourn, while working at the Watts's Printing House, he "carried up & down Stairs a large Form of Types in each hand, when others carried but one in both Hands" and, to impress some acquaintances, he swam the Thames from near Chelsea to Blackfriars, a distance of five miles, "performing on the Way many Feats of Activity both upon & under Water." He considered opening a swimming school in London, and his thoughts on how to teach the skill, as confided in a letter to Oliver Neave, are typically ingenious and sound.

Way a drunken Dutchman, who was a Passenger too, fell over board; when he was sinking I reach'd thro' the Water to his shock Pate & drew him up so that we got him in again.—His Ducking sober'd him a little, & he went to sleep, taking first out of his Pocket a Book which he desir'd I would dry for him. It prov'd to be my old favourite Author Bunyan's Pilgrim's Progress in Dutch, finely printed on good Paper with copper Cuts, a Dress better than I had ever seen it wear in its own Language.

At a later stage of this long, damp journey, while walking fifty miles across New Jersey, Franklin encounters "an itinerant Doctor," who "was ingenious, but much of an Unbeliever, & wickedly undertook some Years after to travesty the Bible in doggrel Verse as Cotton had done Virgil."* Thus in the space of a few paragraphs the seventeen-year-old pilgrim meets types of drunkenness and unbelief, and has reason to remember the Puritan author who inspires his own progress. As his Philadelphia career evolves, other characters—Kiemer, gluttonous and disorganized; Governor William Keith, who out of empty vanity sends the boy on a fool's errand to England; James Ralph, who deserts his wife and child and wastes Franklin's money—serve as bad examples amid whose sinking the young hero, a fine swimmer, can be felt almost physically to be rising, toward Virtue and Happiness.

The close relation between virtue and happiness is his great perception. "I grew convinc'd that *Truth, Sincerity & Integrity* in Dealings between Man & Man, were of the utmost Importance to the Felicity of Life." "It was my Design to explain and enforce this Doctrine, that vicious Actions are not hurtful because they are forbidden, but forbidden because they are hurtful, the Nature of Man alone consider'd: That it was therefore every ones Interest to be virtuous, who wish'd to be happy even in this World." And this recognition is not itself enough: "I concluded at length, that the mere speculative Conviction that it was our Interest to be compleatly virtuous, was not sufficient to prevent our Slipping, and that the contrary Habits must be broken and good Ones acquired and established." Hence, the self-conditioning of his list of thirteen virtues and their daily checklist, detested by D. H. Lawrence and touchingly echoed in the journal of F. Scott Fitzgerald's aspiring bootlegger Jay Gatsby.

Franklin's criterion of utility works as well the other way: a Deist by fifteen, in rejection of his parents' strict Presbyterianism, and at nineteen the author of a published dissertation arguing that God sees no evil in the universe and that "since every Action is the Effect of Self-Uneasiness"

---

*Charles Cotton (1630–87), whose *Scarronides: or, Virgil Travestie* has lines that might also apply to our journeying hero: "Long wander'd he thro' thick and thin; / Half-roasted now, now wet to the Skin."

there can be no distinction between virtue and vice, Franklin at twenty-two (according to Franklin at sixty-five) "began to suspect that this Doctrine [Deism] tho' it might be true, was not very useful." Usefulness is all. "What signifies Philosophy that does not apply to some Use?" There is, he wrote in the *Gazette*, a "SCIENCE OF VIRTUE" that is "of more consequence to [a man's] Happiness than all the rest put together." "Virtue and Happiness are Mother and Daughter," Poor Richard said, and, most famously, "Early to bed and early to rise, makes a man healthy wealthy and wise"—the lack of serial commas emphasizing, perhaps, the interchangeability of health, wealth, and wisdom. Among the assertions of Poor Richard will *not* be found "Honesty is the best policy"; this saying dates from the sixteenth century and appears in the *Apophthegms* of Archbishop Whately of Dublin with an unexpected second thought: "Honesty is the best policy; but he who is governed by that maxim is not an honest man."

Those who would find Franklin's practical morality too hard-hearted and smugly anti-rational should try to imagine the profligate, besozzled, rather murderous New World it was meant to tame. The Library of America reprints a number of news items that Franklin is now believed to have written for *The Pennsylvania Gazette:*

> We hear from the Jersey side, that a Man near Sahaukan being disordred in his Senses, protested to his Wife that he would kill her immediately, if she did not put her Tongue into his Mouth: She through Fear complying, he bit off a large Piece of it, and taking it between his Fingers threw it into the Fire with these Words, *Let this be for a Burnt-Offering.*

> Last Monday Morning a Woman who had been long given to excessive Drinking, was found dead in a Room by her self, upon the Floor. . . . Her former Husband had many Times put several Sorts of odious Physick into her Drink, in order to give her an Aversion to it, but in vain; for who ever heard of a Sot reclaim'd?

> Saturday last, at a Court of Oyer and Terminer held here, came on the Tryal of a Man and his Wife, who were indicted for the Murder of a Daughter which he had by a former Wife, (a Girl of about 14 Years of Age) by turning her out of Doors, and thereby exposing her to such Hardships, as afterwards produced grievous Sickness and Lameness; during which, instead of supplying her with Necessaries and due Attendance, they treated her with the utmost Cruelty and Barbarity, suffering her to lie and rot in her Nastiness, and when she cried for Bread giving her into her Mouth with an Iron Ladle, her own Excrements to eat.

To be a civilizing force in such a world is no despicable achievement. If Poor Richard's advice "Get when you can, and what you get hold" is a long way from "Lay not up for yourselves treasures upon earth," his assertion "When you're good to others, you are best to yourself" is not far from the Golden Rule.

The writings from these Philadelphia years show an ebullient spirit. Franklin's parodies can be hilarious, as when he versifies the speech of Virginia's Governor William Gooch, whose capitol building had burned down early in 1747:

> L—d have Mercy on us!—the CAPITOL! the CAPITOL! is burnt down!
> O astonishing Fate!—which occasions this Meeting in Town. . . .
> Mean time the College and Court of Hustings our *Weight* may sustain,
> But pray let us speedily have our CAPITOL, our *important CAPITOL*
>   again.

In that same year, he printed the famous "Speech of Miss Polly Baker," in which, supposedly, a Connecticut woman, being for the fifth time prosecuted for bearing a bastard, argues her case with such spirited and persuasive rhetoric that one of the judges marries her the next day. "How can it be believed," she asks, "that Heaven is angry at my having Children, when, to the little done by me towards it, God has been pleased to add his divine Skill and admirable Workmanship in the Formation of their Bodies, and crown'd it by furnishing them with rational and immortal Souls?" Franklin's voice warmed to the feminist cause and its defiance of legislated Puritan morality, and made Polly Baker so real that for years she was thought to be an actual person, cited in debate both in the Colonies and abroad. But John Adams thought the jape one more of Franklin's "Outrages to Morality and Decorum."

The Philadelphia Franklin, one should not forget, had enemies. His satire could bite and his liberalism offend. The clergy and the pious distrusted him for impiety. The Scotch-Irish Presbyterians remembered that he had defended the Indians against the "Christian white savages" of the Paxton gang, and the German immigrants that he had called them, in one of his few outbursts of ethnic prejudice, "Palatine boors . . . [who] will never adopt our Language or Customs, any more than they can acquire our Complexion." To the Quakers, who had created in Philadelphia an atmosphere more congenial to him than the musty theocracy of Boston, he nevertheless must have seemed an upstart. One of two deputy postmasters-general since 1751, he used the office as a private fiefdom, staffing post offices up and down the coast with relatives and friends. And there was real enmity between him and the Penns and their deputies. In the Pennsylvania Assembly election of 1764, Franklin was defeated, though narrowly, on both the city and county lists, and the following year, after his return to England, Deborah was obliged to bring in guns and some male reinforcements to defend their house from a mob that believed Franklin to have been too soft on the Stamp Act. He did hold some political offices: clerk of the Assembly for fifteen years (he doodled at mathematical puzzles to relieve his boredom*), Assembly representative from Philadelphia from 1751 to 1764, and from 1785 to 1788 President of the Supreme Executive Council of Pennsylvania—in effect, state governor. But his standing was always better with the people at large than with the establishment. Democratic in his instincts, a publicist by trade, he projected a popular image, sometimes calculatedly. *The Autobiography* confides: "In order to secure my Credit and Character as a Tradesman, I took Care not only to be in *Reality* Industrious & frugal, but to avoid all *Appearances* of the Contrary. . . . To show that I was not above my Business, I sometimes brought home the Paper I purchas'd at the Stores, thro' the Streets on a Wheelbarrow."

5. The Boston Franklin

Franklin was born in January of 1706 in a rented house on Milk Street near Marlborough, opposite Old South Church. His father, Josiah, was a Nonconformist dyer from Northamptonshire who, rather than submit to the Church of England, had moved to the New World in his twenties and become a maker of candles and soap in Boston. Josiah fathered a total of seventeen children, ten by his second wife, Abiah Folger from Nantucket.

---

*Mr. Paul B. Beers, Legislative Historian for the Pennsylvania General Assembly, House and Senate, has genially informed me that "Franklin did a bit more than doodle." Exactly what is not easy to ascertain, however, since Franklin "might have been the most duplicitous lawmaker in 305 years of the General Assembly" and as chief clerk "edited the Legislative Journals, and edited references to himself out." "It was he who printed the 3 volumes of 'Votes and Proceedings of the Assembly'" and "he edited the journals so thoroughly that most years his name is mentioned once." It seems clear, however, that his ability to retire in comfort at the age of forty-two was related to his activities as clerk; he himself wrote in his autobiography, "The Place gave me a better Opportunity of keeping up an Interest among the Members, which secur'd to me the Business of Printing the Votes, Laws, Paper Money, and other occasional Jobbs for the Public that, on the whole, were very profitable." Though Franklin spoke against paying elected public officials, as President of the Supreme Executive Council of Pennsylvania he—Mr. Beers avers—"took a damn good expense account." At his death in 1790, the estate of Poor Richard was worth an estimated $500,000, not the largest fortune in the Commonwealth but twice the state's 1791 budget of $249,538. Considerable elisions in the records, evidently, make a thorough financial history of the public Franklin a smiling mystery.

Benjamin was the fifteenth of these seventeen, and the youngest son; though a few of his siblings died in infancy, and the oldest were gone by the time he appeared, he could remember thirteen children sitting down at one time at his father's table. His autobiography has a fair amount to say of his father—Josiah's trade, his musical ability, his mechanical skill, his "sound Understanding, and solid Judgment in prudential Matters," his improving discourse at meals—but only this of his mother: "My Mother had likewise an excellent Constitution. She suckled all her 10 Children. I never knew either my Father or Mother to have any Sickness but that of which they dy'd, he at 89 & she at 85 Years of age."

In an era when medical remedies for disease consisted mainly of deleterious purges and bleedings, a good constitution was to be treasured, and Franklin's memories of himself as a boy show him swimming and fishing in the Boston salt marshes, and, in one incident, inciting his friends to appropriate some building stones to make a wharf. He concocted artificial flippers to improve his swimming and once let himself be pulled along in the water by a kite. At the age of seven, he impulsively gave all his halfpence to another boy for a whistle he fancied and was mocked by his siblings for the extravagance; over sixty years later, he made of the memory a moralistic bagatelle to charm and edify Madame Brillon. Franklin could not remember a time when he couldn't read. In his one year at Boston Grammar School (which had a classical curriculum and became the Boston Latin School), he advanced to the head of the class. But his father, after placing him at George Brownell's English School for another year, brought him home to the candle-and-soap business. Yet Josiah Franklin was not entirely insensitive to the needs of his gifted Benjamin; registering the boy's distaste for chandlery, and fearful of his running off to sea as an older brother had, he shopped with him for a vocation: "He therefore sometimes took me to walk with him, and see Joiners, Bricklayers, Turners, Braziers, &c. at their Work, that he might observe my Inclination, & endeavor to fix it on some Trade or other on Land." At one point, Benjamin was to be apprenticed as a cutler to his cousin Samuel, but finally, out of deference to his passion for reading, he was apprenticed to his brother James, who in 1717 had returned from England to set up as a printer in Boston.

In discussing his childhood reading, Franklin first mentions *The Pilgrim's Progress,* from which he moved on to Bunyan's other works. His father's "little Library consisted chiefly of Books in polemic Divinity, most of which I read, and have since often regretted, that at a time when I had such a Thirst for Knowledge, more proper Books had not fallen in my Way." He read Plutarch's *Lives,* and "a Book of Defoe's called an

Essay on Projects and another of Dr Mather's call'd Essays to do Good, which perhaps gave me a Turn of Thinking that had an Influence on some of the principal future Events of my Life." Later, he came upon "an odd Volume of the Spectator," and fell under the spell of Addison and Steele:

> I thought the Writing excellent, & wish'd if possible to imitate it. With that view, I took some of the Papers, & making short Hints of the Sentiment in each Sentence, laid them by a few Days, and then without looking at the Book, try'd to compleat the Papers again, by expressing each hinted Sentiment at length & as fully as it express'd before, in any suitable Words that should come to hand.
>
> Then I compar'd my Spectator with the Original, discover'd some of my Faults & corrected them.

Such exercises brought him to a precocious proficiency; when James's press undertook to bring out a newspaper, *The New England Courant*, Benjamin slipped an epistolary contribution, ostensibly from a middle-aged widow called Silence Dogood, under the door at night; it was admired by his brother's literary friends and printed. Nor was this the first of Franklin's published writings; earlier still, when he was a mere twelve, he wrote and his brother printed and distributed a ballad called "The Light House Tragedy," based upon a misfortune that befell the keeper of the Boston light and his family in late 1718. Though it "sold wonderfully, the Event being recent, having made a great Noise," no copy survives, and Franklin's father, "by ridiculing my Performances, and telling me Verse-makers were generally Beggars," effectively discouraged his career in balladmongery.

The Silence Dogood letters, of which there were eventually fourteen, open the Library of America collection on a transsexual note. Asking the reader to "bear with my Humours now and then," Mrs. Dogood explains how "nothing is more common with us Women, than to be grieving for nothing, when we have nothing else to grieve for." Though the adolescent boy does not always succeed in maintaining the female persona—"her" satires on Harvard College and New England poetry have quite a masculine ring—the androgyny of Franklin's imagination, from the speech of Polly Baker to his literary gallantries among the ladies of Paris, is one of his surprising qualities. His appreciation of women must have begun with the one who suckled all ten of her children, and continued with his younger sisters, Lydia and Jane. The two children immediately older than he in the vast sibling constellation, both of them brothers, died young, leaving him the oldest child and only male in this last group of three. Jane, who became Jane Mecom, was his favorite, and letters passed between them to the year of his death. She survived him, and wrote his daughter, Sarah Bache, in condolence, "He while living was to me every enjoyment. Whatever other pleasures were, as they mostly took their rise from him, they passed like little streams from a beautiful fountain."

The phenomenal creative energy that was to produce a model citizen in Philadelphia burst its mold in Boston; Franklin broke with his brother, who beat him, "tho' He was otherwise not an ill-natur'd Man: Perhaps I was too saucy & provoking." Also, the *Courant* had several times offended the authorities, who had jailed James and prohibited him from publishing; in response Benjamin was listed as publisher. His ninth Silence Dogood letters began, "It has been for some Time a Question with me, Whether a Commonwealth suffers more by hypocritical Pretenders to Religion, or by the openly Profane? But some late Thoughts of this Nature, have inclined me to think, that the Hypocrite is the most dangerous Person of the Two, especially if he sustains a Post in the Government." In his autobiography, Franklin says he felt "the rather inclin'd to leave Boston, when I reflected that I had already made my self a little obnoxious, to the governing Party." Though, in the course of his far-ranging career, he seldom returned to his native city, he exchanged letters with his family, attempted to reassure them that he was not such an infidel as was rumored, supplied financial aid and patronage, and to his last days identified himself by the trade he had learned there: printer.

Arranging words letter by letter in metal is an intellectual form of manufacture, and fits a man for a life of careful making. Spoken words were not Franklin's métier; he tells of being bettered in eloquence as a child, and early in his Philadelphia years a friend said of him, "In his common Conversation, he seems to have no Choice of Words; he hesitates and blunders; and yet, good God, how he writes!" It is as a maker that he impressed his contemporaries, and impresses us. Franklin defined Man (according to Boswell, in his *Life of Samuel Johnson*) as a "tool-making animal." In the *Autobiography* he tells how, after his trade-seeking walks with his father, "it has ever since been a Pleasure to me to see good Workmen handle their Tools; and it has been useful to me, having learnt so much by it, as to be able to do little Jobs my self in my House, when a Workman could not readily be got; & to construct little Machines for my Experiments." His inventiveness never ceased; the "trunched old man" who received visitors during the Constitutional Convention would show them his mechanical arm for removing books from high shelves, his letter copier, his chair with a seat that became a ladder, his armchair with its mechanical fan. His enduring inventions range from his stove and lightning rod to bifocals and the glass harmonica. In the New World wilderness, man of necessity became *Homo faber,* and of all the improvising artificers of apple corers, gearboxes, and computer chips Franklin is the patron saint.

In a sense, too, his successive selves were artifacts—self-made men. He remade the Puritan in him into a zealous bourgeois, and certainly this is his main meaning for the American psyche: a release into the Enlightenment of the energies cramped under Puritanism, and a Middle Atlantic model of virtue distinct from the ossified pieties of the Mathers and Adamses. The step beyond Cotton Mather, himself a considerable dabbler in science and public works, was not a short one, but Franklin took it. Mather, though tainted by his involvement in the 1692 witch trials, was still the dominant intellectual presence in Franklin's Boston; young Benjamin heard him preach, and even enjoyed an audience with him in 1723. The preacher's home had a passage with a low beam, and when the young man hit his head, Mather advised him, in the hard accents of Poor Richard, "Let this be a Caution to you not always to hold your Head so high; Stoop, young Man, stoop—as you go through the World—and you'll miss many hard Thumps." Franklin's first pseudonym, Silence Dogood, mocked two of Mather's publications, *Silentarius* and *Bonifacius or Essays to Do Good,* and in a return courtesy Mather dubbed the *Courant* writers "the Hell-Fire Club." Mather and Franklin alike had indefatigably curious minds and active pens, but where the clergyman wrote of "the powers of the air," Franklin tried to analyze evaporation, whirlwinds, barometric pressure, and electrical discharge. Two of his early letters to his own *Gazette,* "Men are naturally Benevolent as Well as Selfish" and "Self-Denial Not the Essence of Virtue" deliberately overturn two basic Christian tenets— man's fall and intrinsic sinfulness, and the obligatory war upon the flesh and its appetites. He broke with Puritanism and orthodox theology, but kept considerable piety. His letters as he aged were full of cheerful and not entirely ironical talk of the next life, and his letter of condolence, in 1756, to Elizabeth Hubbart on the death of her stepfather, his brother John, emphatically embraces the supernatural: "It is the will of God and Nature that these mortal bodies be laid aside. . . . A man is not completely born until he be dead. . . . We are spirits."

The Puritan became a respectable, though church-avoiding bourgeois, and then went on to pose as an English gentleman, a French *savant,* and a philosopher-king with Promethean overtones. *Eripuit caelo fulmen sceptrumque tyrannis* ("He seized lightning from heaven and the sceptre from the tyrant") runs the grand Latin motto Anne-Robert Turgot coined for him, which Philip Freneau paraphrased in homely American verse in his "On the Death of Dr. Benjamin Franklin":

But, matchless Franklin! what a few
Can hope to rival such as you,
Who seized from kings their sceptred pride,
And turned the lightning's darts aside!

This apotheosized Franklin is the outermost shell; the innermost nugget can perhaps be found in the autobiographical passage where, discussing their English forebears, Franklin relayed to his son an anecdote he had heard from his uncle Benjamin: "This obscure Family of ours was early in the Reformation, and continu'd Protestants thro' the Reign of Queen Mary, when they were sometimes in Danger of Trouble on Account of their Zeal against Popery. They had got an English Bible, & to conceal & secure it, it was fastned open with Tapes under & within the Frame of a Joint Stool. When my Great Great Grandfather read in it to his Family, he turn'd up the Joint Stool upon his Knees, turning over the Leaves then under the Tapes. One of the Children stood at the Door to give Notice if he saw the Apparitor coming, who was an Officer of the Spiritual Court. In that Case the Stool was turn'd down again upon its feet, when the Bible remain'd conceal'd under it as before." A self-reliant piety yoked to an unembarrassed practicality—here, in this quintessential Protestant gadget, this seat with a Bible on its underside, we have Franklin in embryo, waiting to be born.

The Ugly Duckling

TOLSTOY'S DIARIES, edited and translated from the Russian by R. F. Christian in two volumes: *1847–1894* and *1895–1910*. 755 pp. Charles Scribner's Sons, 1985.

If all the formal works of, say, Emerson or Kierkegaard quite vanished, and only their journals remained, we would still have a good idea of their thought and sensibilities, and an adumbration of their achievements. In the case of, say, Edmund Wilson or Franz Kafka, the relative loss would be greater, but a fair sense of the man and the reach of his concerns and his imagination would remain. But in the case of Tolstoy, who kept a diary, off and on, from the age of eighteen to that of eighty-two and whose journals occupy thirteen volumes in the complete Russian edition, we would have hardly a clue to the generous-spirited, all-knowing author of *War and Peace, Anna Karenina, Family Happiness,* and "The Death of Ivan

Ilyich." A reading through of the two-volume abridgment of *Tolstoy's Diaries* is a claustrophobic experience, an intimate long sojourn with a mentality so morose and censorious, so puritanically perfectionist and dourly dissatisfied, that any significant creative achievement would seem to have been out of the question. The sunlight of Tolstoy's art scarcely penetrates into the monk's cell of his unremitting moralism and self-scorn; the artist's thoroughly illumined world, creating its characteristic Tolstoyan impression of simultaneous transparence and density, lies beyond the horizon of the diaries, which began as a schoolboy's notations on his strenuous self-improvement and ended as an old man's melancholy, oblique communications with his hysterical wife and an unseen host of more or less burdensome disciples. A note of unhealth sounds from beginning to end: the first entries are made in the Kazan University clinic, where the young law student was confined with a case of gonorrhea, and the last were scrawled on the internationally renowned sage's deathbed in the railroad depot at Astapovo, a few days after he had at last fled the conflicting claims of family and philosophy, of earthly existence and ideal goodness.

The Tolstoy we care most about, the man who between 1863 and 1877 wrote *War and Peace* and *Anna Karenina,* kept his journal least assiduously. Again, in the 1890s, when he composed his third full-size novel, *Resurrection,* there was a slacking off. The Tolstoy we might do with less of, the elderly prophet in baggy peasant shirt and forked white beard, who lived on and on into this uncongenial century, became quite attached to daily diary entries, and well over two-thirds of Mr. Christian's seven-hundred-page selection comes from the years between 1880 and 1910. The young Tolstoy, up to his marriage to Sonya Behrs at the age of thirty-four, accounts for one hundred and sixty-five pages. He priggishly announces to himself at the outset: "I have never kept a diary before, because I could never see the benefit of it. But now that I am concerned with the development of my own faculties, I shall be able to judge from a diary the progress of that development." Finding odd moments between bouts of dissipation and soldiering, of European travel, estate management, and educational theory tested upon peasant children, he takes note of his toothaches and losses at cards (both prodigious) and even now and then of his considerable literary successes, which began with "Childhood," composed when he was twenty-three. He is a tireless compiler of lists of rules for himself— "Rules for developing the physical Will," "Rules for developing the emotional will," "Rules for subordinating to the will the feeling of love of gain," "Rules for developing lofty feelings and eliminating base ones, or, to put it another way, rules for developing the feeling of love and eliminating the feeling of self-love." His was an ego determined to concoct a superego as powerful as itself: "I am beginning to acquire physical will-power, but my mental will-power is still very weak. With patience and application I am sure that I shall achieve everything I want." His program for himself was infinitely ambitious: "What is the purpose of a man's life? Whatever the point of departure for my reasoning, whatever I take as its source, I always come to the same conclusion: the purpose of a man's life is the furtherance in every possible way of the all-round development of everything that exists."

He never moderated that mighty sense of purpose. In these early pages he pays homage to Franklin and Rousseau and Sterne, and reminds us of how much Tolstoy himself remained rooted in the eighteenth century, a man of the Enlightenment to whom "man's primary faculty" is self-evidently "reason." We are also reminded that Tolstoy was an orphan from the age of nine, left with no conscious memory of his mother, who died when he was not quite two, and with no very directive image of his father. Nicholas Tolstoy, a dandified playboy whose own father had bank-rupted the family with such luxuries as sending his laundry across Europe to be washed in Holland, had married Leo's mother, Marya Volkonsky, as a way out of financial destitution; she was five years older than he and characterized in a contemporary letter as "an ugly old maid with bushy eyebrows." A shy, well-educated woman, she was the heiress to the rich estate of Yasnaya Polyana, which Leo, the youngest of the four sons that the couple bore, was eventually to inherit.

Although "Childhood" should not be taken (as Tolstoy himself in-sisted) as a purely autobiographical document, the sketch of the father surely conveys the emotional temperature of Nicholas's paternity: "He was a man of the preceding century and possessed the elusive nature blended of chivalry, initiative, self-confidence, amiability and rakishness characteristic of that century's youth. . . . His life was so full of all kinds of diversions that he had no time to form any convictions and, besides, he was so happy in life that he saw no necessity for it." Within a few years of his father's sudden death of apoplexy, the child's affectionate grand-mother and his aunt Aline, his official guardian, both died; though the prosperous family matrix provided more aunts (notably his father's distant cousin, Aunt Toinette) and tutors and servants to fill the void, Tolstoy's feeling, as recalled in *My Confession,* was that "I was alone, wholly alone, in my search after goodness. Every time I tried to express the longings of my heart to be morally good, I was met with contempt and ridicule, but as soon as I gave way to low passions, I was praised and encouraged." An unnamed "kind-hearted aunt" would tell him that "there was one thing above all others which she wished for me—an intrigue with a married woman." Tolstoy states of this nurturing time, "I cannot now recall those years without a painful feeling of horror and loathing." For all of his life, and in crisis proportion for the last thirty years of it, he was to feel, as a journal entry of 1891 puts it, "depressed by the evil life of the gentry of which I'm a part." A year later he wrote, "even the people who are always with me—my children, my wife. . . . In the midst of all these people I am alone, quite alone and isolated."

As alone as God, he created himself, and a clangor of resolve and self-rebuke rings through the early journals. "I'm tormented by the petti-ness of my life . . . but I still have the strength to despise both myself and my life. There's something in me that makes me believe that I wasn't born to be the same as other people. . . . I am old—the time for development has passed, or is passing; but I'm still tormented by thirst . . . not for fame—I don't want fame and I despise it—but to have a big influence on people's happiness and usefulness." The vagueness and largeness of "peo-ple" perhaps compensate for something more palpable, a social deficiency that Tolstoy describes as "my inability to get on with people." He asks, "Why are all people—not only those whom I don't like or respect and who are of a different bent from me, but all people without exception—noticeably ill at ease with me? I must be a difficult, unbearable person." The next year, at the age of twenty-four, he asks his journal, "Why does nobody love me? I'm not a fool, not deformed, not an evil man, not an ignoramus. It's incomprehensible." And the next year, a soldier now, he asks, "What am I?" and answers:

> One of four sons of a retired lieutenant-colonel, left an orphan at seven years of age [nine, really] in the care of women and strangers, having received neither a social nor an academic education and becoming my own master at the age of seventeen, without a large fortune, without any social position . . . without patrons, without the ability to live in society, without knowledge of the service, without practical talents—but with enormous self-love! . . . I am ugly, awkward, untidy and socially uneducated. I am irritable, boring to other people, immodest, intolerant and bashful as a child. I am almost an ignoramus. . . . I am intemperate, irresolute, inconstant, stupidly vain and passionate like all people who lack character. I am not brave.

In fact he was brave, and had citations to prove it, and if an ignoramus one who read widely all his life, not only in Russian and the foreign languages expectable among the aristocracy (French, German, and En-glish) but in, as occasion demanded, Dutch, Italian, Latin, and Greek. Ugliness is a self-accusation hard to pin down for rebuttal. Henri Troyat, in his biography of Tolstoy, does not give a source for his affecting word-picture of "little Leo" as he, having admired his face disguised with a turban and a burnt-cork mustache, became grieved to see that "when his make-up was washed off again there was the same old baby face, with its shapeless nose and thick lips and little gray eyes. A big, fat boy, a 'pata-pouf,' like Papa said." A few years later, according to Troyat, "he had hoped his features would improve with time, but at nine, at ten, he still had his cauliflower nose and little steely eyes set deep in their sockets." The hero of "Childhood," it seems safe to presume, speaks for "little Leo" when he confesses, "I thought there would be no happiness on this earth for someone with such a broad nose, thick lips and small gray eyes as mine. I prayed to God for a miracle that would transform me into a handsome man, and I would have given all I had and all I might ever have in the future for a handsome face." On the youthful photographs, he looks as handsome as most, and the face from "Childhood" that we remember is this one, after the hero, made bold by a little champagne, has energetically danced with the lovely little Sonya:

> Passing through Grandmother's boudoir I glanced at myself in the mirror: my face was bathed in sweat, my hair was mussed up and my cowlicks were sticking up worse than ever; but my general expression was so lively, healthy and good-natured that I was pleased with myself.

But what the mirror sees, or other people see, is less important than what the mind's eye conceives. "My shyness was aggravated by the conviction that I was ugly," states the narrator of "Boyhood." "I am quite certain that nothing has such a telling impact on a man's cast of thought as his appearance, and not his appearance itself so much as his conviction that it is attractive or unattractive." Tolstoy thought of himself, with a certainty as unusual as his sense of moral isolation, as physically ugly, and the mother, herself homely, who might have weaned him away from self-dislike on this score ("I am told," he noted in his "Recollections," "that she was very fond of me, and called me, 'mon petit Benjamin' "), died before he could remember her. In "Childhood" he constructs a mother who offers the rather stern consolation, "Remember, Nikolenka, that no one will ever love you for your face, so you must try to be a good and clever boy."

Try he did, becoming a cruelly demanding tutor to his own lazy and wayward pupil. "It's sad to know," he wrote, "that my mind is uneducated, imprecise and feeble (although supple), that my feelings lack constancy and strength, that my will is so wavering that the least circumstance destroys all my good intentions." "I lack perseverance and persistence in everything. As a result I've become unbearably repulsive to myself." This repulsiveness extends to his writing: "Got up early, got on with *Childhood;* it's become extremely repulsive." Of the same work, he wrote, "I'm absolutely convinced that it's no good at all. The style is too careless and there are too few ideas to make it possible to forgive the emptiness of content."

From the start, he was the most harshly self-critical of writers. Of *A Landowner's Morning,* which he had begun with considerable enthusiasm ("Feel positively ashamed to be devoting my time to such follies as my stories when I've begun such a wonderful thing"), he finally concluded, "It's definitely poor, but I'll publish it," just as, two months before in 1856, he had noted, "Finished *Youth;* poor, but sent it off." Self-condemnation marches in stride with his growing oeuvre. "I'm altogether dissatisfied with the Caucasian tale" (8/18/57). "Received *Family Happiness.* It's a shameful abomination" (5/9/59). "Corrected the proofs of *The Cossacks*— it's terribly weak" (1/23/63). During the years of his two great novels, the carping diary falls all but silent, and does not show Tolstoy disparaging *War and Peace.* His work on *Anna Karenina,* however, proceeded by surges of enthusiasm and indifference, and at the end, as the novel thrived at the bookstores, he grumbled to his family, "What's so difficult about describing how an officer gets entangled with a woman? There's nothing difficult in that, and above all, nothing worthwhile. It's bad, and it serves no purpose." In *My Confession,* begun in 1879, he dismissed his great creative period in a paragraph:

> Notwithstanding that during these fifteen years I looked upon the craft of authorship as a very trifling thing, I continued all the time to write. I had experienced the seductions of authorship, the temptations of an enormous pecuniary reward and of great applause for valueless work, and gave myself up to it as a means of improving my material position, and of stifling in my soul all questions regarding my own life and life in general. In my writings I taught what for me was the only truth,—that the object of life should be our highest happiness and that of our family.

Those around him were dismayed at the new direction he took at the end of the Seventies. Sonya wrote to her sister in November of 1879, "Leo is still working, as he calls it, but alas! all he is producing are philosophical disquisitions! He reads and thinks until it gives him a headache. . . . My only hope is that he will soon get over it, and it will pass, like a disease." Turgenev, visiting in 1880, wrote, "In contemporary European literature he has no equal. . . . But what is one to do with him? He has plunged headlong into another sphere: he has surrounded himself with Bibles and Gospels in all languages, and has written a whole heap of papers." The superego embodied in the diary has triumphed, and the journals greatly expand, singing the same conscience-stricken, self-hating song—religious self-mortification mixed in with exorbitant artistic standards and a dandy-ish *Weltschmerz*. "I often wish to die. Work doesn't absorb me" (9/2/81). "Shameful and vile. Terrible depression. Full of weakness. I must take care of myself, as though I were asleep, so as not to damage what I need when I'm awake. I'm being more and more dragged into the mire, and my convulsions are of no avail" (4/11/84). "I try to be serene and happy, but it's very, very hard. All that I do is bad, and I suffer terribly from it" (5/28/84). In his peculiar mire he devoted more energy to making boots, mingling with the peasants, urging chastity and poverty upon his un-receptive family, and reproaching his own laziness and sensuality than to writing: "I'm writing *The Kreutzer Sonata* and even *On Art*, and both are negative and evil, and I want to write something good" (7/24/89). "Thought about the fact that I'm fussing over my writing of *The Kreutzer Sonata* out of vanity; I don't want to appear in public as not fully finished, clumsy, even poor. And that's bad" (8/29/89). "In the morning I wrote a new variant of *The Kreutzer Sonata*—not badly, but sluggishly" (10/6/89). "Looked through the whole of *The Kreutzer Sonata*, made deletions, corrections and additions. I'm awfully fed up with it. The main thing is that it's artistically wrong and false" (12/6/89). "Read through all the works of fiction which I've begun. They're all bad" (6/14/94).

The year 1895 brings us, with a weary sigh, into the second volume of the journals. Tolstoy had fifteen more years to live. In this period he managed to finish *Resurrection*—"Finished *Resurrection*. It's not good. Not revised. Too hurried. But I'm free of it, and it doesn't interest me any more" (12/18/99). He also produced "Master and Man" ("pretty worth-less") and *Hadji Murád* ("stupid"), some fables, the play *The Light Shineth in Darkness,* several volumes of an anthology of the world's wisdom called *A Cycle of Reading,* and a large number of pamphlets and pronounce-ments. "But still I'm a disgusting, repulsive creature," he reassures his diary. "And how good it is to know this and remember it" (10/9/1900). "Thank God, I'm loathsome and worthless to the last degree" (12/21/09). His struggles with virtue's impossible demands, the world's intractable problems, his incorrigible family, his implacably clinging wife, and his own oppressive celebrity make for a hectic atmosphere. His diary seems to be read, almost like a bulletin board, as he writes it, and Sonya is keeping her own, which he in turn reads, while he hides his top-secret diary in his blouse or his boot. She rifles through his papers in the dead of the night and, at the height of her jealousy of Vladimir Chertkov, the chief apostle of the Tolstoyan creed, waves in her husband's face passages she has copied from his old diaries as proof of his homosexuality. It all seems childishly violent and repetitive, and had been going on for years. In the year 1889 Tolstoy recorded a dialogue with Sonya that captures the tone of their discussions, not entirely to his own advantage:

> *I.* "What wonderful articles about non-resistance." *She.* "Yes, but it's all talk. Everyone knows it and no one does it, because it doesn't pay." *I.* "That's because people don't drum it in." *She.* "However much you drum it in, they won't do it." *I.* "Why not, if it's drummed in in the same way as, say, the holiness of the sacrament? . . . You don't understand." *She.* "What is there to understand? I understand already what you're going to say next. You just keep on and on about the same old thing."

Tolstoy for all his self-flagellation and willed saintliness only rarely detects the tyrannical egoism of his determination to "drum in," to achieve the long-deferred "all-round development of everything that exists," beginning with his wife and recalcitrant, roistering sons. A few months after his dialogue with Sonya, he does confess that "the devil" assails him "in the form of a proud passion, a desire that everyone should immediately share my views." In 1891 he rather desperately concludes, in regard to the world's deplorable plight, "The only possible arrangement is to make all men good."

He often notes that he is depressed: "I'm depressed. I'm a worthless, pathetic, unnecessary creature, and moreover a self-centered one. The one good thing is that I want to die" (5/3/84). "I don't remember such depression for a long time" (5/13/95). "I can't sleep for depression" (1/12/97). He reads William James's *Varieties of Religious Experience* and finds that "in James' book it is said that I'm a melancholic, close to mental illness." Saturation in these melancholy diaries led this reader to conclude that Tolstoy suffered from the ailment of excessive clear-sightedness. He saw through everything to the hard truth, and art was the one realm where such clairvoyance could be utilized. Having had his spell of sexual adventuring and family happiness, he saw through these pleasures to their bottom of selfishness and transience. He saw the oppression and cruelty in the autocratic, capitalist system that prevailed, but also saw that Socialist revolution was no solution. His critiques of Marxism, two decades before it came to rule his country, are prophetic:

> Even if what Marx predicts were to happen, then the only thing that would happen would be that despotism would be transferred. Now the capitalists are in power, then the workers' bosses would be in power. . . . The main misjudgement, the main error of Marx's theory is the supposition that capital

will pass out of the hands of private individuals into the hands of the government, and from the government, representing the people, into the hands of
the workers. . . . It is a fiction, a deception, that the government represents
the people.

Tolstoy saw that life without a religion amounts to death and darkness and
Darwinian struggle; but he also saw orthodox Christianity as absurd and
had great trouble maintaining even a minimal faith: "Sonya has gone to
Kiev. An inner struggle. I don't much believe in God." His creed, when
stated, is stripped-down Kant, a hypothetical "law": "Does God exist? I
don't know. I know that there is a law governing my spiritual being. The
source of, and the reason for that law I call God." As a thinker, Tolstoy
belongs not with the Victorian rediscoverers of faith like Dostoevsky,
Kierkegaard, and Newman, but with the eighteenth-century *philosophes*
and Deists, and even with the cynical, reductionist court maximists like
La Rochefoucauld and Chamfort. He seeks the underlying principle, the
sweeping law, and at the end of *War and Peace* confounds the readers of
his momentous panorama of human activity and moral search with the
announcement that free will is as much an illusion as the stationariness of
the earth. Nowhere is Tolstoy more powerful as a writer than when, with
Ivan Ilyich and Anna Karenina, he sees through to the horror of things—a
horror he then attempts to cancel with a flash of light: for Ivan Ilyich, "in
place of death there was light," and, as the train wheel crushes Anna, "the
light . . . flared up more brightly than ever before, lighted up for her all
that had been in darkness." May it prove so; but Tolstoy's religiosity
usually seems somewhat strained, and his theories advocating a "moral,"
populist art self-woundingly reactionary and doctrinaire.

The journals contain many severe and downright dismissive comments
on other writers. "I've been reading Shaw. His triviality amazes me."
"Read Nietzsche's *Zarathustra*, and his sister's note about how he wrote
it, and am absolutely convinced that he was completely mad when he
wrote it." "Read Boccaccio. The beginning of ruling-class immoral art."
"Read Dostoyevsky and was astonished at his slipshod manner, artificial-
ity and fabrication." Goncharov's *Oblomov* provokes the exclamation
"How paltry!" and a sampling of Walt Whitman is summarized as "Some
stupid poems." Writers he partially admires elicit rather subtler judgments. "We spoke about Chekhov. . . . It became clear to me that he, like
Pushkin, has made an advance in form. And that's a great service. But, like
Pushkin, he hasn't any content." "Sat all evening alone, read Chekhov. He
has the ability to love as far as artistic insight goes, but as yet no reason
to." "Have just read Chekhov's story *On the Cart*. Excellent for its descrip-

tiveness, but rhetorical as soon as he wants to give a meaning to the story."
"Read Coleridge. A writer very sympathetic to me—precise, clear, but
unfortunately timid—an Englishman—the Church of England and redemption. Impossible . . ." When Tolstoy came, late in life, to express his
literary opinions in print, he proved to be one of the great scolds in the
history of criticism. He devoted pages of *What Is Art?* to condemning
Baudelaire, Verlaine, Mallarmé, and other "decadents" as "incomprehensible." He composed a lengthy, energetic essay in justification of the
"insuperable repulsion and tedium" aroused in him by the works of
Shakespeare; he troubled to read the original sources for Shakespeare's
plots (the old play *King Leir*, the Italian tale of Othello) and in every
instance found them more logical and plausible than the contorted, ambiguous plays that Shakespeare scribbled and that Goethe and other Germans
foisted off on the gullible nineteenth century as great works. Clarity and
naturalness were Tolstoy's touchstones; as his religious mission thickened,
he demanded patent moral purpose and sobriety, even abstemiousness. In
"Why Do Men Stupefy Themselves?" he asserts that "Kant's works
would not have been written in such a curious and bad style had he not
smoked so much." He came to believe, in a chilling approach to the
totalitarian view, that art must serve society with moral instruction, if it
is to exist at all.

Yet, as his life draws to a close in a tumult of private quarrels and public
causes and global celebrity, he wistfully notes in his diary a longing for
"literary work": "Yes, I would like some literary work. One can express
everything and unburden oneself without condemning anyone" (10/21/
09). A bit later, this man of eighty-one confides sadly, "I think I'm played
out as a writer of literary works. I can't concentrate on one thing. But
there's a lot I want to do." A year before his death, he notes, "I've been
reading through my books. I oughtn't to write any more. I think in this
respect I've done all I could. But I want to, I terribly want to . . ."
(11/2/09). Most of the ideas he jots down after completing *Resurrection*
never came to anything, as Mr. Christian's notes faithfully inform us. But
Hadji Murád, published posthumously, is as much a masterpiece as *Billy
Budd*, and the one passage in these two volumes that for me came alive
with the full Tolstoyan impetus, the racing pulse of truth, came very near
the end, when the old sage and patriarch, already in failing health, at long
last makes his escape from home, and sets out to be a pilgrim:

> Everything was packed somehow or other before 6; I walked to the stables
> to tell them to harness the horses; Dusan, Sasha and Varya finished off the
> packing. The night was pitch black, I lost my way to the outhouse, found

myself in a thicket, pricked myself, bumped into some trees, fell over, lost my cap, couldn't find it, made my way out again with an effort, went back home, took another cap and with the aid of a lantern made my way to the stables and ordered the horses to be harnessed. Sasha, Dusan and Varya arrived. I trembled as I waited to be pursued. But then we were on our way. We waited an hour at Shchokino, and every minute I expected her [Sonya] to appear. But then we were in the carriage, the train started, and my fear passed, and pity for her rose up within me, but not doubt about having done what I had to do. Perhaps I'm mistaken in justifying myself, but I think it was not myself, not Lev Nikolayevich, that I was saving, but something that is sometimes, and if only to a very small extent, within me.

This rapid succession of clauses unfurls the nervous clarity and concrete-ness, even the comedy, of the mind and body shown in slightly discordant action, of sensations and emotions constantly subject to a critique deliv-ered by a motionless, watchful, beautifully honest intelligence—the lucid partner in the Tolstoyan balancing act. Ten days later, Tolstoy was dead.

More threads than can be counted run through these journals. His remarks on art, for instance, range dramatically:

Literature is rubbish. [12/27/52]

Art is the ability to depict what ought to be, what all people ought to strive towards, what gives people the greatest good. [10/13/94]

Art is a microscope which the artist fixes on the secrets of his soul, and shows to people these secrets which are common to all. [5/17/96]

Happiness, like art and women, belongs to the realm of temptation; yet he can never quite turn his back on it:

Unhappiness makes man virtuous—virtue makes him happy—happiness makes him vicious. [March–May 1851]

Unhappiness is the best condition for improving oneself, for rising to a higher level; unhappiness is an indication of one's imperfection. [9/28/99]

There's much to note down, above all the joyful, steadfast, serene, almost always loving state in which I find myself. The question is: where does it come from? Why, given my vile life, do I have so much happiness? [12/13/04]

He preached asceticism but excelled in the portrayal of happiness; the concept figures in his work as prominently as that of truth, and seems to constitute the core of his genuinely religious, pantheistic intuitions; the hero of "Youth," lying awake on a moonlit night, beside a pond, amid birches and dew-coated flowers and gleaming, leaping frogs, confides, "All this assumed a strange meaning to me, signifying an excess of beauty together with a sort of uncompleted happiness."

It seems a sad paradox that the author who among male authors has given us unsurpassedly sympathetic and vital female characters, and whose literary career owed so much to the advice and secretarial labors of his wife and daughters, and who in "The Kreutzer Sonata" delivered a kind of feminist tract, should in his journals, under the stress of his struggles with Sonya, sink from casual chauvinism to dire misogyny:

Wenches have led me astray.   [6/23/53]

I want a woman terribly. A pretty one.   [6/27/57]

And it suddenly became clear to me what women's strong points are: cold- ness—and something which they can't be held responsible for because of their weak powers of thought—deceitfulness, cunning and flattery.
                                                               [8/31/84]

Yes, woman's kingdom is a disaster. Nobody but women (she and her daughters) can do stupid and dirty things in a clean and even nice manner, and be completely satisfied.   [3/3/89]

So to regard women as what they are—weaker creatures spiritually—is not cruelty to women; to regard them as equals is cruelty.   [6/13/91]

Women are people with sexual organs over their hearts.   [6/2/94]

For seventy years I've been lowering my opinion of women more and more, and I need to lower it still further.   [11/20/99]

Clearly all disasters, or an enormous proportion of them, are due to the dissoluteness of women.   [12/19/1900]

Women lie like children, without noticing it.   [5/11/01]

For the existence of a reasonable, moral society, it is necessary for women to be under the influence of men.   [7/31/05]

These strictures relate, perhaps, to the unreality of his own mother and the reality, even as he approaches death, of his need for her: "I, an old man, wanted to become a child, to nestle up against a loving creature, to snuggle up, to complain, to be caressed and comforted. But who is this creature I could nestle up against and in whose arms I could weep and complain? Nobody now alive." He never had a conversation with Marya Tolstoy; she was made into a silent immensity, a religious ideal:

> Yes, yes, my dear mother whom I never called by that name, since I couldn't talk. Yes, she is my highest conception of pure love—not a cold or divine, but a warm, earthly, maternal love. This is what attracts my better, weary soul. Mother dear, caress me.
> All this is stupid, but it's all true.

The words "true" and "truth" echo through these journals,* and the triumph of Tolstoy's art is the impression of truth it makes upon us, even when tinged by a cranky and stringent ideology. We assimilate the imagery, dialogue, and psychologies of his fiction as if they were already our own; the air we breathe within the books seems our natural air as well. Seeing exposed, in the journals, the scathing critical sourness with which Tolstoy regarded his own work, the work of others, and much of the world itself, one can only deduce that a supreme art can be achieved through a process largely negative, with a hypertrophied critical faculty pitted against an irrepressible creative urge. He was a terrific reviser; *War and Peace* was copied over and over by his patient wife, and was corrected so extensively in proof that his publisher, Bartenyev, wrote him: "God alone knows what you are doing! If you go on like that we will be correcting and resetting forever. Anyone can tell you that half your changes are unnecessary. . . . For the love of God, stop scribbling!" But Tolstoy answered, "It is impossible for me not to scribble the way I scribble." Very early in his career, at the age of twenty-four, he noted, "I must abandon for ever the idea of writing without revising." He achieved the vital concreteness and directness of his prose as if sculpturally, through a series of self-critical blows, a succession of energetic corrections. James Joyce, arguing about Tolstoy with his brother Stanislaus in 1905, intuitively couched his praise in negatives: "Tolstoy is a magnificent writer. He is never dull, never stupid, never tired, never pedantic, never theatrical!"†

Proust, the other modern novelist who approached Tolstoy's grandeur

---

*And through his writing in general, nowhere more rousingly than in the last sentence of "Sebastopol in May," dated June 26, 1855: "No, the hero of my story, whom I love with all my heart and soul, whom I have attempted to portray in all his beauty and who has always been, is now and will always be supremely magnificent, is truth."

†Letter to Stanislaus from Trieste, September 18, 1905.

of ambition, had this to say of him: "Every so-called stroke of observation is simply the clothing, the proof, the instance, of a law, a law of reason or of unreason, which the novelist has laid bare. . . . One feels oneself moving amid a throng of laws. . . . And for all that, in this apparently inexhaustible fund of creation it seems as though Tolstoi were repeating himself, as though he had no more than a few themes at his disposal, disguised and reshaped. . . . Might not the same memory have 'sat' for Kitty passing by in the carriage and Natasha in the carriage following the army?"* Indeed, part of Tolstoy's truth is a stubborn fidelity, in his fiction, to what his heart has verified; he refused to leave a certain emotional base, defined by Yasnaya Polyana. The scowling, bearded prophet, pronouncing on "the all-round development of everything that exists," looks out with the deepset live gray eyes of the overheated little boy, his cowlicks sticking up but the general expression "so lively, healthy and good-natured that I was pleased with myself." The year of his death, he wrote in his diary a sentiment stemming from childhood and more than once echoed in his youth: "What a strange thing: I love myself, but nobody loves me." Issued from the height of so long and victorious a life, the humble confession becomes epic.

Perhaps a word should be offered about this translation of the journals as an editorial production. Though admirable, it is not inviting and could have been, one suspects, nicer. Scribner's has done no more than serve up the English edition—big grim gray pages, numerous typos,† and all. The two volumes are a bit large to be handy, and making one's way from the index in the second, and back and forth to the footnotes in the back of each, is awkward. Mr. Christian has previously edited two volumes of Tolstoy's letters, and his knowledge of the minutiae of Tolstoy's life is impressively thorough. As in any selection, what was left out haunts what is in; triple dots swarm like mayflies, and a lot of the entries seem very snippety. As it happens, Professor Leon Stilman, of Columbia University, twenty-five years ago edited an edition of the diaries from Tolstoy's last year, 1910, and this single dramatic year of uncut entries made compelling reading. The entry of April 13 appears in the Christian edition (ellipses and brackets his) as:

Today is *13 April* Woke up at 5 and kept thinking how to escape, what to do. And I don't know. I thought of writing. Yet it's disgusting to write while

---

*"Tolstoi," in *By Way of Sainte-Beuve* (1908; English translation by Sylvia Townsend Warner).

†Including a persistent tendency to spell "worldly" "worldy" and that typographical classic "See p. 000."

continuing to live this sort of life. Should I speak to her? Go away? Change things gradually? [. . .] I think the latter is all I can and will do. But still it's depressing. [. . .]

The Stilman edition carries the section after the first ellipsis to a startling outburst:

It seems that the last is all I can and will do. But it is oppressive all the same. Perhaps, even very likely, this is good. Help me, help me, He who is in me and in everything, and who is, and whom I pray to and love. Yes, love. Now I weep, as I love. Very much.

Of the ten passages that I had noted, in the back of the Stilman book, as especially shrewd or poignant, eight were omitted by Mr. Christian, including this valuable and typically Tolstoyan insight: "I am conscious of myself in exactly the same way now, at eighty-one, as I was conscious of myself, my 'I,' at five or six years of age." If diaries are worth translating at all, an uncut version is perhaps best; it enables the reader to decide for himself what is important and to experience the drift of days somewhat as the writer did.

Mr. Christian's edition seems inadequate as a scholarly resource, while still intimidating to the general reader. Thus continue the ragged, unsystematic fortunes of Tolstoy's journals in English. The year 1917 saw published, by Dutton and Knopf respectively, two "first volumes" that turned out to be the last: *The Diaries of Leo Tolstoy: Youth—1847 to 1852*, translated by C. J. Hogarth and A. Sirnis, and *The Journal of Leo Tolstoi: First Volume—1895 to 1899*, translated by Rose Strunsky. Ten years later, Doubleday brought out the journals from 1853 to 1857, as rendered into English by the veteran Tolstoy translators Louise and Aylmer Maude. None of these volumes (all out of print) had a sequel, though sequels were implied; all of them, it might be said, were pleasanter to hold and peruse than Mr. Christian's big boxed pair. And all but Ms. Strunsky's carried the footnotes at the bottom of the pages, where footnotes, as the very word suggests, should be.

The Heartless Man

BERNARD SHAW: *Volume 1, 1856–1898, The Search for Love,* by Michael Holroyd. 486 pp. Random House, 1988.

COLLECTED LETTERS 1926–1950, by Bernard Shaw, edited by Dan H. Laurence. 946 pp. Viking, 1988.

Bernard Shaw, as he preferred to be called, was for so long a globally famous writer that it comes as a surprise to realize what a slow bloomer, in the world's gardens, he was. The third child and only son of an alcoholic Irish Protestant gentleman, George Carr Shaw, and a dedicated amateur singer, Lucinda Elizabeth "Bessie" Gurly Shaw, he was born into genteel poverty and raised in a curious *ménage à trois* rounded out by one George John Vandeleur Lee, his mother's singing teacher, a musical pedagogue of some small fame in Dublin society, and possibly (a rumor never confirmed) George Bernard's actual father. Sonny, as the boy was nicknamed, hated every school he attended, did poorly, and dropped out for good at the age of fifteen. The gawky, daydreaming youth then became an errand boy for a real-estate firm, rising to cashier and rent collector; in London, where he followed his mother and sisters and Vandeleur Lee at the age of twenty, he lived with his mother and sister Lucy, penned some music criticism under Lee's name, worked for the Edison Telephone Company until the company was disbanded, spent his days in the British Museum reading Marx and writing novels no one would publish, became a vegetarian and a Socialist, taught himself shorthand and foreign languages, applied unsuccessfully for a variety of lowly jobs, boxed, sang, suffered severe monthly headaches, wore broken boots and mended clothes, and felt himself to be, he wrote in his journal, "a complete outsider."

Only as he neared the age of thirty, with the help of his new friend William Archer, did Shaw find his niche as a journalistic critic—of music, of art, of novels, and finally, for Frank Harris's *Saturday Review,* of the theatre. By the age of forty-one, he had come to sign himself as "G.B.S." and to cut something of a figure in London; still, the available evidence for his self-proclaimed genius consisted in the main of four novels that had eventually been serialized in Socialist magazines, a great many superior and spirited columns in the back files of periodicals, a number of tracts and countless speeches for the Fabian Society, and a small and willful book on Ibsen. He did not seriously turn to playwriting until he was over thirty-five; his first drama, *Widowers' Houses,* was begun as a collaboration with

Archer, abandoned after two acts, completed by Shaw alone in 1892, and given two performances, at the first of which he was hissed. Five years later, he felt finished with the stage; of his eight plays, only one, *Arms and the Man,* was anything other than a complete financial failure, and most had not even been produced. Sir Henry Irving reneged on an agreement to star in *The Man of Destiny,* and *Candida,* conceived as a West End vehicle for Janet Achurch, was given instead an inglorious one-perform-ance run in Aberdeen. In 1896 Shaw had met Charlotte Payne-Town-shend, a plump Irish heiress six months younger than he. She possessed, Beatrice Webb wrote, "masses of chocolate brown hair," and in "flowing white evening robes she approaches beauty." Shaw, after two decades of mostly but not exclusively verbal philandering, married her. At the same time, his first volume of drama and prefaces, *Plays Pleasant and Unpleasant,* was published, and an American production of *The Devil's Disciple* proved a success and earned the playwright over six hundred pounds. By his wedding day—June 1, 1898—Shaw had solid ground under him at last, and there he is left standing by Michael Holroyd's scintillating and sus-penseful biography.

Mr. Holroyd's slightly pathetic subtitle derives from his premise that Shaw was unloved by his mother: "In her eyes he was an inferior little male animal tainted with all the potential weaknesses of her husband." Shaw himself, in his assorted autobiographical writings, is the primary source for this alleged maternal coolness: "She did not hate anybody, nor love anybody," and "We as children had to find our way in a household where there was neither hate nor love." Even when her son was arguing Bessie Shaw's case, he managed to sketch a bleak picture: "Poverty, ostra-cism, disgust, three children, a house rented at £30 a year or thereabouts, a drunken husband obviously incapable of improving the situation . . . it says a great deal for my mother's humanity that she did not hate her children." The biographer fastens firmly onto this initial deprivation as the clue to Shaw's stubbornly buoyant character:

> In a rare moment of emotion, G.B.S. wrote to Ellen Terry of his "devil of a childhood, Ellen, rich only in dreams, frightful & loveless in realities". But looking directly at such bleakness was too painful. Usually he put on the spectacles of paradox. This paradox became his "criticism of life", the technique by which he turned lack of love inside out and, by attracting from the world some of the attention he had been denied by his mother, conjured optimism out of deprivation.

If you like psychologizing biographers, you will like this and Mr. Hol-royd's other neat, brisk tracings of Shaw's limitations and perversities to the primal deprivation. If you harbor reservations about the reduction of a personality—and such a fertile, captivating personality!—to diagrams of psychic wiring, you may find some of the analysis pat and even condescending. "In his relationships with women Shaw was seeking a second childhood in which he could receive all the attention and happiness he had been denied by his mother." "He recoiled from searching for happiness in others because their rejection of him carried behind it the annihilating force of his mother's initial rejection." Even a rejecting mother, however, needs avenging: "In so far as they embodied these social conditions, both men [Shaw's father and Vandeleur Lee] grievously disappointed his mother. So Society became the dragon against which the fabulous G.B.S., armoured with tracts and speeches, would lead his campaign of lifelong knight-errantry." "As a polemicist he is marvellously convincing, but since he is fleeing from uncertainties his writings are studded with many brilliant evasions, and eventually, as doubt was beaten back, something human in Shaw diminished."

From his very debut as a playwright, perceptive critics agreed there was something missing in the dazzling Shaw. William Archer in *The World* cited *Widowers' Houses* as an example "of what can be done in art by sheer brainpower," and Max Beerbohm reviewed *Plays Pleasant and Unpleasant* witheringly: "Mr Shaw is not, as the truly serious dramatist must be, one who loves to study and depict men and women for their own sake, with or without moral purpose. . . . Flesh and blood are quite invisible to Mr Shaw. He thinks that because he cannot see them they do not exist, and that he is to be accepted as a realist." Even Shaw may have suspected something amiss within his imperturbable and magnanimous poise, his unstoppable energy and barrage of convictions. His title for his fifth novel, *An Unsocial Socialist*, was originally *The Heartless Man*. But should heartlessness be the biographer's leitmotif?

American reviewers have been rather churlish in the face of Mr. Holroyd's elegant feat—fifteen years in the making and not done yet—of research and synthesis. Just to have mastered the Shavian record, the copious oeuvre and the enormous posthumous harvest of letters and stray writings, warrants awed gratitude. But I have seen Mr. Holroyd faulted, in our American press, for not knowing enough about Irish class distinctions, English political movements, and the realities of the theatre, among other areas where his subject led him. Surely part of his achievement here, dealing with so heavily documented and quotably prolix a figure, is his compression; though not short, the book seems terse. Mr. Holroyd finds a few pages for everything, from a precise evocation of Shaw's youthful shabbiness to a comical account of his headlong adventures with bicycles. Such a marshalling of data demands briskness, and this reader sometimes longed for a less peremptory pace, and a stroll around the corner to investigate at leisure. My own nagging reservation concerning Mr. Holroyd's book is that he himself seems a bit too much in it, as a judgmental, sometimes tart, and rarely forgettable presence. The Shavian whirlwind has to compete with Holroydian breeziness. Shaw, writing to Frank Harris in 1930 about his relations with women, confided, "I was gallant in the old-fashioned Irish way, implying as a matter of course that I adored them; but there was nothing in it on my side." Mr. Holroyd appends the remark, "More probably there was nothing in it on theirs." Of Shaw's beard, which was grown partly to hide a scar, he writes, "Few people who had their attention arrested by this flagwaving at the head of the Shavian talking-machine would have known that Shaw was publicly concealing something." Holroyd is himself witty—he speaks of "Beatrice Webb's cephalous passion for Sidney"—but tends to get solemn over Shaw's little jokes, reminding us faithfully that the irony is a mask, a deceptive feint, as if the abrasive texture of flirtation in Shavian discourse, of droll hyperbole inviting contradiction, needs to be ground smooth. In the development of his you-can't-fool-me psychological portrait, the biographer gives short shrift to the quotidian facts; our strongest sense of how Shaw lived, what the streets and people looked like and what practical concerns occupied his days, comes from Shaw himself, in the epistles and prose quoted— quoted without, by a curious quirk of scholarly procedure, any source attributions. Mr. Holroyd explains in a bibliographical afterword, "To get round this difficulty [ongoing Shavian scholarship and publication] I have decided to print my sources separately after the publication of the third volume of my biography." So Shaw's voice hovers disembodied in this book, pronouncing out of the blue, and seems friendlier than the slightly chilly expository atmosphere. In 1936, besieged by would-be biographers, the great man wrote one of them, St. John Ervine, "I am not really a good subject, because all the fun that is to be got out of me I have already extracted myself." As long as Shaw was alive, it was his amiable habit to improve biographies, such as those by Frank Harris and Hesketh Pearson, by writing large sections of them himself. From now on, alas, Shaw studies are on their own.

Mr. Holroyd makes good on his subtitle and tells us more about Shaw's relations with women than we thought there was to know. That women interested Shaw no one could deny. The son of an independent woman and a cohabitant with her until past the age of forty, he created a raft of plummy, feisty female stage roles, and from *Mrs. Warren's Profession* (1898) to *The Intelligent Woman's Guide to Socialism and Capitalism* (1928) concerned himself with feminist issues. The dramatist in him awakened, as it were, when Nora slammed the door at the end of Ibsen's *A Doll's House*. In his young manhood, Shaw teased, adored, upbraided, and excited women. Mr. Holroyd formulates it in a jiggle of metaphors: "Shaw took the body away from women and addressed their minds. His own mind was astonishingly fast, but emotionally he was lame. The result was that women found themselves continually out of step with him. When Shaw looked at a woman, he appeared to turn his back on her and raise a mirror. It was a disconcerting stare, positive, remote, and appearing so bold while actually in retreat." Though he was an arresting figure of a man, and a frequenter of bohemian circles where "liberated women" were not uncommon, G.B.S. kept his virginity until his twenty-ninth birthday, when the widow Jenny Patterson, his mother's friend and singing student, graciously relieved him of it. She was fifteen years older than he, and the journal entry in which he noted the signal event seems to peel his seductress delicately away from the figure of his mother: "So, on the corner of Montpelier St. Mother went on by herself, and I returned to the Square with JP, and stayed there until 3 o'clock on my 29th birthday which I celebrated by a new experience." *The Search for Love* does not quote the droller descriptive sentence Shaw wrote to Frank Harris in 1930: "I escaped seduction until I was 29, when an enterprising widow, one of my mother's pupils, appealed successfully to my curiosity." In a letter to Harris four days later he characterizes "the heroine of my first adventure" as "sexually insatiable." Shaw himself was not so easily sated, and noted many a three o'clock return in his Pepys-like diary, as his affair with Mrs. Patterson survived eight years of ups and downs. Forty years later, he reflected in tranquillity that "Sexual experience seemed a natural appetite, and its satisfaction a completion of human experience necessary for fully qualified authorship." It is not said that the comfortably off widow wished to marry the young litterateur, but she was passionately possessive, and they broke up, finally, over the other named woman with whom he enjoyed humanizing sex, Florence Farr, a less-than-brilliant but considerably experienced actress married to an absent husband called Edward Emery. Shaw's diary of February 4, 1893, describes a scene he transcribed straight into *The Philanderer:*

> I went to FE; and JP burst in on us very late in the evening. There was a most shocking scene, JP being violent and using atrocious language. At last I sent FE out of the room, having to restrain JP by force from attacking her. . . . Did not get to bed until 4; and had but a disturbed night of it.

There were other conquests, too, Shaw boasted to Harris: "Some were prepared to buy friendship with pleasure, having made up their minds that men were made that way. Some were sexual geniuses, quite unbearable in any other capacity." But in this pre-marital period much of Shaw's sexual energy was diverted by his chronic attachment of himself, in the manner of Vandeleur Lee, to a married couple, playing piano duets and games of innuendo with the wife, and by his quasi-professional attempts to seduce a gifted actress away from her manager-consort and into one of his plays. He admired Ellen Terry, and wrote *The Man of Destiny* for her and Henry Irving, and at the same time ruthlessly undermined Irving, in his public reviews and private letters: "Is H. I. blind, is he deaf? . . . Has he ever loved you for the millionth fraction of a moment?" Or is it simply that "he is without exception absolutely the stupidest man I ever met?" Similarly, he wooed Janet Achurch under the nose of her husband, the actor and theatrical manager Charles Charrington, presenting himself with a predatory Platonism: "Do you know who will buy for twopence a body for which I no longer have any use? I have made tolerable love with it in my time; but now I have found nobler instruments—the imagination of a poet, the heart of a child, all discovered through the necessity—the not-to-be-denied inmost necessity—of making my way to an innocent love for Janet." Even as his entanglements with Jenny Patterson and Florence Farr were coming to a boil, he deluged Janet Achurch with such stuff, trying to woo her away not only from the spendthrift Charrington, who had her on a steady diet of *A Doll's House,* but from alcohol and drugs, on which she was also dependent. These curious courtships, aimed at a theatrical consummation with an actress shaped up by Shaw and starring in a Shaw play, show G.B.S. at his most wearyingly meddlesome— a word-machine that just won't quit, and one that is trying to make words do everything. Irving's last communication with Shaw, Shaw recalled in writing to Ellen Terry's son, was "in his own not very literary style (like Queen Victoria's) a sincere little letter, the gist of which was 'For God's sake, leave me alone!' " Mr. Holroyd adds in one of his saturnine asides, "How much more human this seemed than all those Shavian acrobatics."

And yet Shaw's inability to let the world alone, his wish to direct its every detail, from the distribution of wealth to the typeface and ink used in printed books, his endless hectoring and lecturing of actors, actresses, producers, professors, and politicians are aspects of his superhuman generosity and abundance of spirit. He was the last writer with a fused social and aesthetic program—the last artist in whom strong political views were more of a help than a hindrance. How noble, really, was his prodigious effort to make of the frivolous English stage an instrument of radical reform, and how invigorating his professed belief that the playwright's business, like the politician's, was "to strive incessantly with the public; to insist on earnest relations with it, and not merely voluptuous ones."

How fortifying, in the teeth of all the discouragements Shaw suffered before 1898, must have been his sense that reality was on his side: "My comedy will not be unactable when the time comes for it to be acted. . . . I have the instinct of an artist, and the impracticable is loathsome to me. But not only has the comedy to be made, but the actors, the manager, the theatre, the audience." How beautiful this credo, in which the young Shaw speaks as a disciple of William Morris:

> Art should refine our sense of character and conduct, of justice and sympathy, greatly heightening our self-knowledge, self-control, precision of action, and considerateness, and making us intolerant of baseness, cruelty, injustice and intellectual superficiality or vulgarity. The worthy artist or craftsman is he who serves the physical and moral senses by feeding them with pictures, musical compositions, pleasant houses and gardens, good clothes and fine implements, poems, fictions, essays and dramas which call the heightened senses and ennobled faculties into pleasurable activity. The great artist is he who goes a step beyond the demand, and, by supplying works of a higher beauty and a higher interest than have yet been perceived, succeeds after a brief struggle with its strangeness, in adding this fresh extension of sense to the heritage of the race.

Bernard Shaw: Collected Letters 1926–1950, the fourth and final massive volume of his letters masterfully edited by the American scholar Dan H. Laurence, takes us to the other end of Shaw's long life. Between 1898 and 1926, the great work—*Caesar and Cleopatra, Man and Superman, Major Barbara, Pygmalion, Heartbreak House, Back to Methuselah,* and *Saint Joan*—was done; the world's "brief struggle" with Shaw's strangeness gave way, if not to universal approbation, then to inescapable celebrity. Has any writer, ever, been more famous than Shaw in his last decades? In New Zealand in 1934, he confided to a correspondent, "My reception was overwhelming. The dockers cheered us as we came down the gangway; the Governor General entertained us; the cities invited us to civic receptions; the universities invited me to give one of their annual orations; the Maoris serenaded us with their native music, which turned out to be 'Just a song at twilight'; my broadcasts were carte blanche without a hint of censorship: in short, I escaped by the skin of my teeth from dying of my vogue." In India in 1933: "I have been hung with flowers in the temples and drenched with rosewater and dabbed with vermilion in the houses; and the ship is infested with pilgrims to my shrine." In Moscow in 1931, he was met by a brass band, a military guard of honor, and thousands of Russians shouting, "Hail Shaw"; he asked for, and received, an interview with Stalin. His dying, like Tolstoy's, was heavily attended by reporters, with Nancy Astor taking Sonya Tolstoy's role as chief mourner. Only Shaw's formidable reserves of crustiness prevented his ninetieth birthday from smothering him. "Dear Sister Laurentia," he wrote his favorite nun, "For the past week I have had over 100 congratulations a day. But for two strong men who have worked hard tearing them up for me I should never have been 90." To the two strong men, his instructions, reproduced in this volume in his shaky but ever-legible handwriting, were simple: "Throw away all the birthday ones. They make me sick." He had spurned the Crown's offer of a knighthood when he was seventy, and when sounded out about the Order of Merit at ninety, responded, "Deeply grateful as I am for the award of the highest distinction within the gift of the Commonwealth, yet the nature of my calling is such that the Order of Merit in it cannot be determined within the span of a single human life. Either I shall be remembered as long as Aristophanes and rank with Shakespear and Molière, or I shall be a forgotten clown before the end of the century."

The world, like women, found it difficult to keep in step with Shaw. He courted fame, creating in "G.B.S." a persona scarcely needing caricature, yet hid in the hamlet of Ayot St. Lawrence and avoided London literary society. To give himself relief from his mail and his admirers, he and Charlotte in the Thirties took to long ocean voyages, from each of which he emerged with a new play or two. He seemed to enjoy celebrity up to the point where it kept him from working; he thrashed to maintain a certain space around himself. To receive a letter from Shaw could be as soothing as a cold shower. Between 1926 and 1950 he advised various correspondents:

> I think you ought to leave your head to the College of Surgeons to ascertain what wonderful impressionable substance it contains instead of brains.

> What a tiresome idiot you are! . . . To the British Post Office the name G.B. Shaw means nothing. Bernard is the trade mark; and if you had been intelligent enough to use it (you really *are* an idiot) your letter would have reached me.

> Tell the Committee with my compliments that they are sentimental idiots, and have grossly overstepped their function in this business.

> You certainly are a jumping sillybilly.

> Politically you have the brains of a grasshopper.

As illustrations to a story they must surely be the very worst on record from an artist of your calibre.

You are always readable; but you have no intellectual conscience.

To save you from being written off as the stupidest woman on earth I must give you a testimonial.

You really are a pack of duffers.

It is amazing how players of genius, like you, can be such hopeless idiots as they mostly are when they try their hands as playwrights.

Devotion to an old crock like me is sentimental folly.

He was gruff with himself, too: in the course of these letters he tells Mrs. Pat Campbell, "Of course we are a pair of mountebanks," assures Frank Harris, "I am really a detestable fellow," and instructs the prospective founder of a Shaw Society, "I am old, deaf, and dotty. In short, a Has Been." To the friends of his Dublin boyhood, his clownish self-characterizations go somewhat deeper. In the year of his death, he wrote Ada Tyrrell, a surviving childhood playmate: "You and I will soon be the oldest inhabitants of the globe. It is perhaps as well that we cannot meet. . . . I had rather be remembered by you as Sonny than as the ghastly old skeleton of a celebrity I now am." Twenty-two years earlier, in 1928, he had written this same old acquaintance an unusually thoughtful and melancholy account of himself:

> My life has rushed through very quickly: I have seen very little of anyone who has not worked with me. Except with my wife I have no companionships: only occasional contacts, intense but brief. I spring to intimacy in a moment, and forget in half an hour. . . . Those who see me now are those who shove and insist and will not take no for an answer, with, of course, the great people who must be seen because they have earned a right of entry everywhere.

And to Matthew Edward McNulty, a friend made at the Dublin Commercial School and the only sharer of his youthful ideas and dreams, Shaw wrote the same year, "How are you? I have come through the shadows and am enjoying a hardy and unscrupulous old age in insufferable celebrity."

Seventy years in England did not shake Shaw's Irishness; his voice falls into a deeper resonance when addressed to these Irish survivors from his boyhood. When he decided to marry, it was to an Irishwoman. The relentless mischief and provocativeness of his public persona can be understood, in part, as a colonial's hostility toward the occupying power. British hypocrisy, snobbishness, inefficiency, and illogicality never ceased to animate his pen; twitting the English was his favorite sport. He would not get into step with them. No sooner did they, after his seventieth birthday, decide to accept him as an avuncular old genius with cranky views on vivisection and spelling than he announced himself an admirer of Mussolini and Stalin. As late as 1942, with German bombs falling around Ayot St. Lawrence, he was finding good things to say about Hitler. To Nancy Astor he wrote:

> I have been reading Hitler's Mein Kampf really attentively instead of dipping into it. He is the greatest living Tory, and a wonderful preacher of everything that is right and best in Toryism. Your Party should capture him and keep him as a teacher and leader whilst checkmating his phobias. On the need for religion, on the sham democracy of votes for everybody, on unemployment and casual labor, he is superb.

Shaw shared with the Fascist and Communist dictators a deep contempt for parliamentary democracy, which he saw as a mere bumbling front for the rapacious workings of capitalism. As a young man educating himself in the British Museum, he was caught up in the same Marxist radicalism as Jack London on the other side of the English-speaking world. But his political education had begun in his exposure to the Dublin slums, where, Mr. Holroyd's biography tells us, his nurse would take him while she visited her friends and even, possibly, prostituted herself to soldiers. His experience of the actual poor, from which his family's precarious gentility held him at no great distance, was a genuine inspiration among his many facile inspirations. In 1932 he lectured Margaret Haig Thomas, Viscountess Rhondda of Llalanwern:

> Are you sure you haven't a family habit of classing "poor devils with only ten thousand a year" as the poor? The submerged nine tenths dont all consider themselves poor. Most of them hate the poor. The real poor hate the poor. *I* hate the poor. That I prefer them, on the whole, to the rich, doesn't affect the case in the least.

"Oppression, starvation, compulsory prostitution and all the villainies of capitalism" were more than rhetorical concepts to Shaw; to Harold Laski he wrote, apropos of William Morris's social conscience, "No theories could get over the simple fact that the rich lived by robbing the poor and got nothing by it but ugly unhappy lives."

The heartless man came out of Dublin with two real passions: a love of music, and a hatred of poverty. The second emotion steels his realpolitik in some brutal assertions: "The danger is that Capitalism, instead of crashing, may peter out without ever producing a revolutionary situation. We may get no further than a succession of Kerenskys or Macdonalds trying to make omelettes without breaking eggs." This was written in 1932, when millions felt desperate about capitalism, and totalitarianism had not yet given the world a real taste of its omelettes. But till the end of his days Shaw, though never a card-carrying Party member, called himself a Communist, and in the 1940s, after the Moscow show trials, the nonaggression pact with Hitler, the campaign against the kulaks, the assassination of Trotsky, the Siberian gulags, and the enslavement of the once-progressive Soviet arts had all become history, Shaw could boast of the "Russo-Fabian state" and write to Alfred Douglas, "Why do you recommend me to go to Russia? I've been there. It is a paradise: no ladies and gentlemen there." Of Stalin he claimed, "When I met him in 1931 I knew that I was face to face with the ablest statesman in Europe; and the personal impression he made on me did not change my opinion. I still rank Stalin first, Roosevelt second, and the rest nowhere." And at the age of ninety-two he troubled to chastise the London *Times:* "A most discourteous practice is beginning to call the chief Russian statesman Mister Stalin. This is inexcusable. He is Marshal D[z]hugashvili or Generalissimo Vissionarovich; but under no circumstances should the soubriquet which he has made famous be mentioned or written with a prefix, as if he were a small shopkeeper."

The Man of Destiny, the philosophical Caesar creating and controlling a government like a work of art—these were the Shavian ideal, rather than an inglorious scramble of contending petty interests. It was the style, after all, in which he had launched and managed his imperial career. To Gabriel Pascal, negotiating for a Shavian film in Hollywood, he wrote, "No American feels safe until he has at least five other Americans raking off him, most of them contributing nothing except their entirely undesirable company. They get so settled in that way of doing business that they do not understand how a European with a cast iron monopoly under his own hat can play his game singlehanded." That Stalin appeared to exert such a cast-iron monopoly argued for him, as Mussolini's success in Italy argued for him against liberal and Socialist "atrocity mongering" that would preclude "common sense and common civility in dealing with a foreign statesman who had achieved a dictatorship in a great modern state without a single advantage, social, official, or academic, to assist him." As both political observer and playwright, Shaw loathed the impracticable, and to the "Libertarian Impossibilists" posed the question of "why both the workers and the Liberals were so hopelessly incompetent that Italy gave Mussolini carte blanche to extirpate them." In 1927 he was sternly writing Friedrich Adler, "We must get the Socialist movement out of its old democratic grooves. . . . We, as Socialists, have nothing to do with liberty. Our message, like Mussolini's, is one of discipline, of service, of ruthless refusal to acknowledge any natural right of competence." In a lesser matter, discussing his cherished project of a phonetic alphabet with I. J. Pitman, whose grandfather had invented the system of shorthand Shaw employed, he revealingly wrote, "There is one exception to my statement that there would be no squabble about details. There would be if the alphabet were thrown open to discussion. A few master spirits must decide it and get it designed by an artist both for print and handwriting. . . . It must be presented to the mob of spelling cranks as a fait accompli, as the Pitman alphabet was."

For all his political speaking, writing, and—in his six years as an elected municipal vestryman in the London district of St. Pancras—participation, Shaw's model of governmental procedure was artistic: the autocratic decisions of a "master spirit" with a monopoly over his own creation. While the hope of a political revolution eased his pain at what he perceived as a cruelly mismanaged world, it was art, in almost all its shapes, that had actually comforted his formative Dublin years. In 1948 he remembered in an advisory letter to Margaret Wheeler:

> I never wanted to be a writer. I wanted to be a painter. I wanted to be a musician. But I couldnt draw. I couldnt compose. If anyone had taught me I could have been a mediocre artist or painter or actor or singer or pianist. But nobody taught me; and I was a born writer. You must use the talent you have, not the talent you have only a taste for.

His taste was for music, and throughout these letters, even when the weariness of old age is shortening his replies, the subject of music excites him to bursts of fondness and specificity—recalling how a singer he heard in the 1870s weighed "19 stone at the least I should say" and how she damaged her voice "by attempting Donizetti's Favorita, and forcing her chest voice up to [he draws the note]"; and how his uncle played the ophicleide; and how only "celibate male singers after years of practise together can do [Palestrina's] polyphony justice"; and how as a boy he learned music theory by studying the texts of Day, Ouseley, and Stainer. He writes in his most respectful, least chaffing tone to the contemporary composer Edward Elgar, and takes the motto of his old age from Verdi's

Iago—*La morte è nulla* ("Death is nothing"). In writing for the stage, he was "only reviving the old operatic declamatory technique," Shaw told the actor O. B. Clarence. "There is nothing I like better than composing arias, cavatinas, and grand finales for good actors. My technique I had learnt, not in the cup and saucer school, with its 'reserved force' which was so welcome to actors who had no force to reserve, but from Salvini and Ristori, and from Barry Sullivan, last of stage supermen." After travelling to Peking, he advised Elgar, "The Chinese will reveal to you the whole secret of opera, which is, not to set a libretto to music, but to stimulate actors to act and declaim." The extraordinary loquacity of Shavian characters is a convention, like the impromptu melodiousness of operatic performers, which gives voice to the inner being: "What makes my plays unlike others is that my characters say what they feel and would not say in real life." In his letters and prefaces Shaw always stressed the "essentially aesthetic" nature of his education, and his professional dependence upon inspiration rather than conscious thought: "As I write plays as they come to me, by inspiration and not by conscious logic, I am as likely as anyone else to be mistaken about their morals."* To Virginia

---

*In the preface to *Buoyant Billions* he hyperbolically reiterates the point, and casts a wondering glance back over his life:

"There is nothing in my circumstances or personality to suggest that I differ from any other son of a downstart gentleman driven by lack of unearned income to become an incompetent merchant and harp on his gentility. When I take my pen or sit down to my typewriter, I am as much a medium as Browning's Mr Sludge or Dunglas Home, or as Job or John of Patmos. When I write a play I do not foresee nor intend a page of it from one end to the other: the play writes itself. I may reason out every sentence until I have made it say exactly what it comes to me to say; but whence and how and why it comes to me, or why I persisted, through nine years of unrelieved market failure, in writing instead of in stockbroking or turf bookmaking or peddling, I do not know."

The play at hand (he claims) illustrates his lack of control over his own activity: "I commit this to print within a few weeks of completing my 92nd year. At such an age I should apologize for perpetrating another play or presuming to pontificate in any fashion. I can hardly walk through my garden without a tumble or two; and it seems out of all reason to believe that a man who cannot do a simple thing like that can practise the craft of Shakespear. . . . Well, I grant all this; yet I cannot hold my tongue nor my pen. As long as I live I must write."

Shaw kept remarkably busy in his nineties: he contributed several hundred articles, messages, and self-interviews to journals; kept up his correspondence of several thousand letters and postcards a year; expanded *Geneva* to four acts for the Standard Edition; with the help of F. E. Loewenstein compiled and edited and provided fresh matter for the autobiographical *Sixteen Self Sketches;* resurrected a play, *The World Betterer,* left incomplete in 1936 and finished it as *Buoyant Billions* in late 1946; cheerfully grappled with the issue of global annihilation in *Farfetched Fables* (1948); and accepted the Malvern Marionette Theatre's invitation to write a puppet play about himself and Shakespeare, *Shakes Versus*

Woolf (perhaps the only one of the many correspondents in this volume who could give Shaw back language as fluent, arch, and winning as his own) Shaw wrote, "As a matter of fact I am an artist to my finger tips." William Butler Yeats, after attending the first night of *Arms and the Man,* famously dreamed "a nightmare that I was haunted by a sewing-machine, that clicked and shone, but the incredible thing was that the machine smiled, smiled perpetually." But G.B.S. came out of the same *fin de siècle* as Yeats and Wilde, and was in his fashion an acolyte of art as devoted as they; Shaw describes himself and William Morris as "both Aestheticists." His aestheticism subsumed his ethics and never failed to supply him with innocent enthusiasm and courage. His gaiety and naïveté, in the perpetuation of airy stage spectacles and handsomely, idiosyncratically printed books, distinguish him from a contemporary like H. G. Wells, whose work, but for the early fiction, has faded with the timeliness of his opinions and expertise. Shaw's musicality—and an Irish element, the wryness and self-mockery of a nation that has known repeated defeat—subverts his own opinions even as he announces them, leaving us with irreducible images of human vitality.

Although the fourth volume of his collected letters can be comfortably read only when propped up on one's chest in bed, and one's eyes sometimes weary of assimilating Dan H. Laurence's fact-packed editorial head-

---

Shav (1949)—"this in all actuarial probability is my last play and the climax of my eminence, such as it is." In 1948 he described himself as "this poor old crock, overworked to the limit," and on the verge of ninety wrote Sidney Webb: "The bachelor life with nobody to consult but myself—eat when I like, go to bed when I like, work when I like, order the house and garden as I fancy, and be solitary (or social) all to myself—suits me very well; it actually develops me at 90!"

Lest, however, he be thought unaffected by Charlotte's death in 1943, here is the description of her last hours that Shaw wrote to H. G. Wells: "Charlotte died this morning at 2.30. You saw what she had become when you last visited us: an old woman bowed and crippled, furrowed and wrinkled, and greatly distressed by hallucinations of crowds in the room, evil persons, and animals. Also by breathlessness, as the osteitis closed on her lungs . . . But on Friday evening a miracle began. Her troubles vanished. Her visions ceased. Her furrows and wrinkles smoothed out. Forty years fell off her like a garment. She had thirty hours of happiness and heaven. Even after her last breath she shed another twenty years, and now lies young and incredibly beautiful. I have to go in and look at her and talk affectionately to her. I did not know I could be so moved."

The tone takes us back to a letter he wrote Ellen Terry in 1897, evidently after making love to Charlotte: "And now, dear Ellen, she sleeps like a child, and her arms will be plump, and she is a free woman, and it has not cost her half a farthing, and she has fancied herself in love, and known secretly that she was only taking a prescription, and been relieved to find the lover at last laughing at her & reading her thoughts and confessing himself a mere bottle of nerve medicine, and riding gaily off."

notes to almost every missive, Shaw's company is invigorating to the end. We are moved through this accumulation by the certainty that every letter will be, in some fashion, honest, confrontational, and amusing—the sheer impudent efficiency of the prose is exhilarating. Shaw's prose, however amply supplied in this multitude of casual, hasty paragraphs, rarely feels padded or hedged; its enlivening and elusive essence is caught in his typically loyal praise of another writer and old friend, Frank Harris: "his power of assertion and readability will carry the day with posterity if posterity ever troubles itself about any of us." "Power of assertion" is what brims in Shaw's transparent-seeming prose, with its fearlessness of flat statement and its instinctive, swift recourse to the concrete. The power is so great as to overflow into recklessness, tumbling about with comic effect. His tonic purity of unimpeded assertion can be sampled at virtual random:

> Lady Cockerell keeps her good looks magically. Many many years ago she went to bed; found it comfortable; and has lain there in a sort of glory ever since. I have never pretended to believe that there is or ever was anything the matter with her.

> So I began with a prejudice against him [Henry Irving] through the disappointment of a strong fancy for him.

> As a Socialist it is my business to state social problems and to solve them. I have done this in tracts, treatises, essays and prefaces. You keep asking why I do not keep repeating these propositions and principles Euclidically in my plays. You might as well ask me why I dont wear my gloves on my feet or eat jam with a spade.

> As the raiders are highly scientific, and fly blindly by their instruments, they begin every night by bombarding us in the firm conviction that they are making direct hits on Churchill's hat.

The phrase "Churchill's hat" may have been current in wartime Britain, or Shaw may have invented it; in either case, it arises from a source in the language that only living slang or a born writer can easily tap. Shaw still "plays," though his estate has been most enriched by what he stoutly resisted when he was alive—a musical version of *Pygmalion*. Even if all the plays come to seem too declamatory and farcical for the contemporary stage, and all his brusque propaganda for a saner world sinks into the dust of discarded tracts, he will linger as a lightsome spirit whose heart, these private communications from his old age indicate, was in the right place.

The Virtues of Playing Cricket on the Village Green

COLLECTED ESSAYS: *Volume 2, The American Novel and Reflections on the European Novel,* by Q. D. Leavis, edited by G. Singh. 280 pp. Cambridge University Press, 1985.

As novelists sometimes comfort themselves by marrying other novelists, filling adjoining rooms with the hesitant clatter of two typewriters, critics can marry critics. Think of the Trillings. Think of Edmund Wilson and Mary McCarthy. Queenie (not a nickname) Dorothy Roth, born in 1906, was a literary adept before she married F. R. Leavis, in 1929, and she continued on her own, though in striking harmony with her celebrated husband's convictions and crotchets, to practice the critic's art, at the lecterns of Cambridge University and in the pages of his influential quarterly journal *Scrutiny.* Since the death of Q. D. Leavis in 1981, Cambridge University Press has been assembling a three-volume collection of her essays, published and unpublished, of which the second volume, *The American Novel and Reflections on the European Novel,* especially recommends itself to our attention. Though not so frantic in style or pugnacious in homage as D. H. Lawrence's *Studies in Classic American Literature,* Mrs. Leavis's observations have the same value, of the generalizing external glance. The Americans and the English share a language and a long historical interaction, but their literatures indicate a difference between them as great as that between Hawthorne and Trollope, or between *Moby-Dick* and *Middlemarch.* Mrs. Leavis was, like her husband, one of that vanishing breed of critics who can feel they have read all the novels that matter—who have been enough saturated in the all-too-copious genre of prose fiction to make brisk and authoritative assertions that cover the field and, in the guise of literary criticism, characterize whole nations. Whereas her husband organized his confident estimations into a number of book-length studies of poetry and fiction which systematically distinguished the sheep from the goats, Mrs. Leavis's opinions must be gathered piecemeal, from reviews and essays and lectures she did not bother to collect or, in the case of eight of the fourteen pieces in this volume, to publish in any form.

Ghan Shyam Singh, a Professor of Italian Language and Literature at The Queen's University in Belfast, and a friend of the Leavises, is to be thanked for seeing these specimens of her acute and spirited criticism into print. He is to be chastised, however, for the "minimal editing" (his phrase) that has left her hitherto unpublished lectures so full of erratic punctuation and grammar, with many run-on sentences and a few virtually inscrutable ones:

> Yet it is this social life which James had elected to share, evidently not without psychological strain, as a work that approaching never to perfection, yet does not strike cold.

> I would suggest that it is James's sense of not being on sure ground and his lack of any deeper knowledge of and response to the whole English subject than aesthetic or prejudiced that makes him so prone to make use of other novelists, truly English novelists, to provide a scaffolding from which to work or a framework within which to construct with a difference.

A more merciful editor, surely, would have silently corrected Mrs. Leavis's spelling "Nabakov" to "Nabokov," added the omitted definite articles to the titles she cites as *Grapes of Wrath* and *Cancer Ward,* given the post–Civil War epoch of American culture that she terms "the Gold Age" its usual name "the Gilded Age," restored William Dean Howells's own title *A Hazard of New Fortunes* to the novel that she with misplaced wifeliness calls *A Husband of New Fortunes,* and rectified the egregious misquotation of Huck Finn's pivotal declaration "All right, then, I'll *go* to hell" as the nonsensical "All right then, I'll go to hide." Professor Singh might also, editorial minimalist through he is, have considered deleting the sentence (concerning Henry James) "He tried and often succeeded in doing his duty as a novelist" one of the two times it appears, in identical form, in the same essay.

In 1980 Professor Singh persuaded Mrs. Leavis to come to Belfast and perform the Herculean task of giving, during a one-week stay, "five lectures—one each on the English, the American, the Anglo-Irish, the French, the Russian and the Italian tradition of the novel." I count six lectures there, but in any case it was a huge assignment, which, though she was a few months short of her death, she performed heroically, with a lavish dispersal of provocative ideas. The French, Russian, and Italian lectures close this volume, and the American one begins it, describing a complex cultural situation with a bracing simplicity:

> I see the American novel as resulting from two conditions. The first is the reaction of a former colony having emancipated itself successfully by war from the mother-country, determined to show it then stood on its own feet culturally as well as politically. . . . The second condition which gave the American novel its unique character was the naïve *Utopian* theory on which their settlement of the new continent was originally based. . . . Hence the American novelist was characteristically both a patriot and a dissident and the failure to achieve the intended (moral and spiritual) goal could not be

blamed on the English, but, as these writers recognized, was innate, owing to the facts of human nature. Hence a radical bitterness from loss of faith in man characterized the American novel from its early days and up to the present day, so that its prevailing and indeed inevitable style has always been ironic—ironic not only in tone but in essential structure.

Without quite knowing what an ironic structure is, this American reader can feel in his Utopian bones the justice of that supposed "radical bitterness" generated by a background of unreal expectation, a bitterness to be felt behind the tortuous verbal churning of Faulkner as well as beneath Hemingway's surface of taut facticity—a naïve, unending surprise and indignation that life is as it is. We cannot, unlike the Europeans, quite get over it.

Our two opposed attitudes toward the Old World are epitomized by men called Henry James: the father scorned the English as "an intensely vulgar race, high and low," and wrote that "American disorder is sweet beside European order: it is so full of promise," while the son found an artistic life impossible to live in America and settled in England. Eight of Mrs. Leavis's essays touch on the younger Henry James, and, composed over a span of forty years, they vary in degree of admiration. He saw his duty and frequently did it, we are twice assured, and the essay lengthily titled "The Fox Is the Novelist's Idea: Henry James and the House Beautiful" concludes in the tone of a guest tersely thanking his host after a quarrelsome evening: "In his *Notebooks* he exhorted himself 'Be an artist, be distinguished, to the last.' And I must say, I think it evident that he was." Yet Mrs. Leavis, despite the affection with which she recalls reading her first Henry James as a girl, sketches a rather devastating portrait of a foreigner in England who "was largely dependent on English literature for his usable knowledge of the English people," who as "an American novelist peculiarly dependent on Old World novelists for techniques, themes and patterns" borrowed wholesale and wrongheadedly from Trollope and George Eliot, and who through the decades of exile lost his ear for American speech:

> As regards language, the novelist's essential medium, we can see (as James apparently never did) that instead of having an advantage in having two closely related languages at his disposal he hadn't a really sensitive mastery of spoken English, while his native ear for American, at first so fine and sharp, gradually dulled, so that later American heroines like Maggie and Millie speak insipidly.

Further, James was not, as Americans see him, an Anglophile and imitation Englishman, but—in line with his father's patriotic views and his

Irish grandmother's animus—downright anti-British. "James's accounts of the English gentry, while becoming increasingly confident, are always hostile and external, and they are used for propaganda. His English lords and gentlemen are satisfyingly cut down to less than American size." James is "susceptible" to the charms of English country houses; however, "he sees them as beautifully desirable but in degenerate or unworthy hands. This is what makes it all right for them to be taken over by American money." His well-known short story "The Real Thing," generally understood to concern the paradoxical relations of art to reality, seems to Mrs. Leavis full of "anti-English hostility," vented when the American painter-hero "brutally" turns his two models, Major and Mrs. Monarch, "out to starve" even though "there is almost nothing to be said against [them] except that they are upper-class English." Their evident virtues, as she sees them—their "dignity in humiliating circumstances," their "touching magnanimity to the Cockney female model"—do not placate their creator's "uncertain and sometimes unmanageable anti-British drives," which hopelessly blind him to the fine balances and shadings of "the whole English subject."

It is a pretty picture that Mrs. Leavis paints of the eighteenth-century English society in which the English novel developed:

> It was a very fluid society where the middle class, unlike Germany and other European countries, constantly married into or otherwise rose into the aristocracy and where the younger brothers of aristocratic families were traditionally, ever since the Middle Ages, able to enter all professions and become merchants, without incurring social disability, and where the landowners traditionally lived on their estates for most of the year and in contact with their tenants of all grades, making local communities centring on the great house and parsonage complex, ideal for a novelist needing a microcosm of society for his purposes. But this was the English system.

Needless to say, "this inter-penetration of classes in England was a great asset to the novelist," and the established Protestantism added to inter-penetration "the compassion for the underdogs so unfailing in Fielding's novels, as later in Dickens's and George Eliot's." Mrs. Leavis waxes panegyric: "One sees why England, where the squire played cricket on the village green with his tenants, the blacksmith and the villagers, was the envy and astonishment of Europe." In contrast to the French—whose novels were aristocratic in origin and remained locked into "spiritually desiccating" studies of amorous psychology and thorough disillusion— the British in their novels, of which her favorite instance is *Middlemarch*, took as their province "a society revealed from top to bottom and all characters shown as mutually dependent and as affected by the rest, and all equally seen with respect and compassion." Whereas even "Stendhal's great novel, *Le Rouge et le Noir*, is utterly unEnglish in its absence of respect for social order and in being without any idealistic weakness for human nature or natural ties."

While this vision of a peaceable kingdom where the squire and the blacksmith play cricket together may seem rather rosy to those who are still struck by England's ineluctable stratifications and class antagonisms (which Thatcherism has done little to assuage), Mrs. Leavis does confront the central issue, in fiction, of accessibility. The class-bound British fiction writer would appear to have imaginative access to a broader, livelier range of human types than his democratic American rival. Hawthorne, the first of our writers resoundingly to strike the oddly hollow American note— the first to make apparent in the quality of his imagination that an American is not simply an Englishman on another continent—gave the case an indelible phrasing in a letter to his publisher, James Fields, in 1860, on the eve of the publication of his last novel, *The Marble Faun*. As he nears the end of his distinguished yet rather crepuscular career, Hawthorne makes the piquant observation that he is not really a popular writer. "Possibly I may (or may not) deserve something better than popularity; but looking at all my productions, and especially this latter one with a cold or critical eye, I can see that they do not make their appeal to the popular mind. It is odd enough, moreover, that my own individual taste is for quite another class of works than those which I myself am able to write."

A disconnection is observed between the artist as himself part of the populace and what he is able in good conscience to produce. No such disconnection yet exists in England, apparently, for Hawthorne goes on, illustrating the "quite another class," to ask Fields, "Have you ever read the novels of Anthony Trollope? They precisely suit my taste; solid and substantial, written on the strength of beef and through the inspiration of ale, and just as real as if some giant had hewn a great lump out of the earth and put it under a glass case with all its inhabitants going about their daily business, and not suspecting that they were made a show of."

This memorable and gracious confession of artistic envy is as penetratingly diagnostic of the American imagination as the oft-quoted sentences Melville wrote, a decade earlier, in Hawthorne's praise: "He says NO! in thunder; but the Devil himself cannot make him say *yes*" and "Certain it is, however, that this great power of blackness in him derives its force from its appeals to that Calvinistic sense of Innate Depravity and Original Sin, from whose visitations, in some shape or other, no deeply thinking mind is always and wholly free." Almost in spite of himself, Hawthorne was a seminal author. Melville likened him to Shakespeare and from his example took the courage to revise *Moby-Dick* with a new reach of ambition. Hawthorne—his flowing, delicate, ironical style, his tendency to work on the edge of allegory—was never far from the mind of Henry James, as a father to surpass. Hawthorne's fantastications, by way of the homage and emulation of Jorge Luis Borges, have even helped liberate Latin Americans into magic realism, unlocking thereby the colorful inner demons of the New World's southern half. It was Hawthorne who began in artistic earnest to investigate our peculiar American gift for unhappiness, and Mrs. Leavis points out that he was, in his investigation, a realist and a historian:

> Hawthorne's sense of being part of the contemporary America could be expressed only in concern for its evolution—he needed to see how it had come about, and by discovering what America had, culturally speaking, started from and with, to find what choices had faced his countrymen and what they had had to sacrifice in order to create that distinctive 'organic whole'. . . . He prepared himself for the task by study, though Providence had furnished him with an eminently usable private Past, in the history of his own family, which epitomized the earlier phases of New England history; this vividly stylized the social history of Colonial America, provided him with a personal mythology, and gave him an emotional stake in the past, a private key to tradition.

By her lights, even the slightest of his sketches of the colonial past have a certain intensity, a guilty searchingness, and more rounded and imaginative accounts like "The May-Pole of Merry Mount," "Young Goodman Brown," and "My Kinsman, Major Molineux" have a definite majesty; she compares "Young Goodman Brown" favorably with Coleridge's "The Rime of the Ancient Mariner" and the "Walpurgisnacht scene in Joyce's *Ulysses,* which smells of the case-book and the midnight oil." In her fondness for Hawthorne's historical stories, with their own smell of case-book archives, Mrs. Leavis ignores a number of, to my taste, more compelling and less parochial tales, such as "The Birth-mark" and "Rappaccini's Daughter." Hawthorne was not only and always a Puritan. According to Mrs. Leavis, the peculiarities of the Puritan inheritance—its forcible habit of introspection and its suspicion of worldly pleasures—drove our seminal novelist to poetry, and weakened him for Trollopeian earth-hewing. "Declining to be, perhaps incapable of being, a naturalistic novelist, he was true to his best perceptions of his genius when he did the work of a dramatic poet," she states. She quotes Henry James: "Hawthorne is perpetually looking for images which shall place themselves in picturesque correspondence with the spiritual facts with which he is concerned, and of course the search is of the very essence of poetry." But James, too, in the era of Zola and Howells, was by temperament condemned to the subtle search for such correspondences; another critic is chastised for failing his "duty" (a frequent word with Mrs. Leavis) to "warn the innocent reader off any attempt to take James as a naturalistic novelist." His novels are "in a tradition of medieval and Elizabethan drama transmitted through Shakespeare, Ben Jonson and Bunyan (and so Hawthorne)."

Indeed, it would seem that the nineteenth century saw a general poeticizing of prose fiction; Mrs. Leavis cites a passage from *Middlemarch* as "*the* example I should choose to illustrate what we mean by declaring that in the nineteenth century the novel took over the function of poetic drama." In another essay she tells us:

> While the novels of the eighteenth and nineteenth centuries, with a few exceptions, were descended from Addison and Defoe, with some admixture of a debased stage comedy, there is quite another kind of novel, created by Emily Brontë, Melville, Conrad and Henry James, among others, which makes use of the technique of the dramatic poem.

We are approaching, in such judgments, the moot question "What is poetry?" For if Defoe's image of Robinson Crusoe on his island, with his umbrella made of animal skins (with "the hair upwards"), finding Friday's footprint on the sand isn't poetic, what is? And what novel goes further in the direction of the purely verbal than Sterne's *Tristram Shandy?* Yet there does appear to have been a basic slow displacement of energy from one genre to the other. Browning was the last poet to write dramatic poems, with characters and dialogue and a plot, to major effect. In discussions of the poeticism and insubstantiality of the American novel, Trollope is usually named as the foil; the greater figure of Dickens is left out of account, perhaps because he is too much of a poet, with an extravagance and surrealism almost American.

Mrs. Leavis's willingness to read a novel as a poem, in the image-by-image New Criticism fashion, and to cheerfully allow Americans their cultural deficiencies, leads her to overvalue, I think, Melville's *The Confidence-Man* and, to a degree, all the products of his last gasp as a publishing writer, in the mid-1850s:

> To the modern English and American reader, well trained in practical criticism and knowing with regard to myth, symbol, allegory and imagery, the writings of the great 1853–6 phase are of more interest than the earlier novels, evidently more accomplished as art, more varied . . . and are noticeably more condensed, controlled and mature than either *Moby Dick* or *Pierre*.

The pairing of Melville's acknowledged masterpiece with his most abject failure is curious, and curiouser still her implicit belief that breaking down *The Confidence-Man* into its allegorical parts and apparent intentions will make it run. Training in "practical criticism" does not overrule, in the reading experience, readerly sensations of suspense, coherence, *jouissance*, and recognition, and Melville's *Confidence-Man*—all the more poignantly for those acquainted with the youthful exuberance of *Typee* and the irresistible virtuosity of *Moby-Dick*—is painful to read: crabbed in style, misanthropic in sentiment, arthritic and repetitious in movement, the work of a formidable writer on the edge of breakdown. Mrs. Leavis, fond of categorical statement and eager to find in fiction an "idealistic weakness for human nature," sometimes brushes past that elusive but essential something, that sense of music, of voice, of phrase-by-phrase unexpectedness, of constantly retuned attentiveness, which makes some texts wine and whose absence leaves the rest watery. Where she does settle to a text, as to the George Eliot passage mentioned, she can be thrilling, in explication and appreciation.

What thrilled us about her husband's dicta, in the easy-to-thrill Fifties, was his regal power of vast exclusion. "The great English novelists," his *The Great Tradition* begins, "are Jane Austen, George Eliot, Henry James and Joseph Conrad." Fielding, Richardson, Sterne, Thackeray, Dickens, Trollope, the Brontës, Meredith, Hardy, Joyce, Virginia Woolf—all excluded. It was thrilling to think that somewhere a principle of exclusion so decisive existed, that standards so exalted were being somehow maintained. In exactly what quality virtue so stingily distributed resided remained a bit general, a bit stiff-sounding—"the realized concreteness that speaks for itself and *enacts* its moral significance," Leavis said. His wife, in her slightly less unbending criticism, offers clues to the Leavisite principle nowhere more emphatically than in the last piece in this collection, "The Italian Novel."

The Italian novel, to be frank about it, won't do at all. Manzoni's *I promessi sposi*, generally considered Italian fiction's first classic, "belongs to the infancy of art." It is a historical romance, but "the romanticism does not get, as in Scott's better novels, a corrective in realistic sociological analysis." It "really tells us nothing about Italy" in the course of a "picturesque melodrama with a happy ending provided by Providence and not achieved logically by events." Giuseppe di Lampedusa, whose novel *The Leopard* was much admired, "spent goodness knows how many years on his one novel but he never even unified it in style and tone, much less integrated the parts." He is a poor Proust spin-off, "a willing victim of nostalgia." Svevo: "It is hard to understand Joyce's enthusiasm for Svevo,

who, though more Austrian than Italian in feeling, has none of the intellectual and imaginative power of Mann or Kafka" and, though dissatisfied
with the petty bourgeois life he portrays, shows "no imaginative grasp of
any other kind of life." Most interestingly: "His Freudian preoccupation
is a disability rather than a strength or a help—for psychoanalysis is
inevitably reductive." Moravia is a mere compiler of "clinical accounts of
sexual experience, pathological rather than pornographic." And so on,
except for Verga, who writes about peasants without sentimentalizing
them, in the way of George Sand and Tolstoy, and who in some novels
at least is "possessed by a genuine sense of the tragic nature of the life of
the poverty-stricken South of Italy." Like the French, the Italians tend to
be raised as Roman Catholics, and "having lost religious faith they have
no positives, other than the hope that once lay, apparently, in Communism, soon lost by novelists like Silone and Vittorini." To make matters
worse, Italians go to too much opera: "One concludes the frequentation
of opera as a national entertainment is inimical to the effort of grappling
with and possessing a serious novel." Another handicap is a national
incapacity, noticed long ago by Stendhal, for moral reflection: "No one
who reads Italian fiction of any period can fail to notice this absence of
conscience or awareness of moral values, in the characters. It makes Italian
fiction less interesting than that of every other country I know, giving its
novels characteristically a heartlessness and meaninglessness that only the
exceptional Italian writer avoids." As if all this weren't bad enough, in
modern times Italian writers have read and even, in the cases of Vittorini
and Pavese, translated "the American novelists who had such an unfortunate effect on post-war Italian writers . . . whose coarseness and crudity
and their simplification of people and issues and brutalizing cult of violence made them undesirable and misleading models." Oh, dear! No, what
is needed is not Roman Catholicism and opera and American fiction but
"firmly human values and outward-going sympathies."

Mrs. Leavis asserts, in connection with Edith Wharton, that a complete
writer must offer something "in the way of positives." Failure to do more
than complain prevents Wharton from being, for all her talent, a great
novelist like Jane Austen or George Eliot:

> She has none of that natural piety, that richness of feeling and sense of a
> moral order, of experience as a process of growth, in which George Eliot's
> local criticisms are embedded and which give the latter her large stature.
> Between her [Wharton's] conviction that the new society she grew up into
> was vicious and insecurely based on an ill-used working class and her convic-
> tion that her inherited mode of living represented a dead-end, she could find
> no foundation to build on.

And where does one find such a foundation? Presumably by playing cricket with the blacksmith or, if one is a blacksmith, with the squire. *The American Novel and Reflections on the European Novel* ends on a lofty admonitory note: "Unless men and women are capable of relationships which include loyalty, confidence, mutual interests, and there are people of integrity who can act disinterestedly sometimes, which of course requires courage and faith—people, in short, capable of respect for themselves and each other, I don't see how one can expect that novels worth consideration could be written."

Mrs. Leavis does not entertain the possibility that even in a world thoroughly debased and unrelational novels might still be written, describing conditions. Or that authenticity in rendering the actual condition of mankind is the *sine qua non;* without it, fiction becomes mere escapism, mere castle-building in air. She devotes a page to Camus's *L'Étranger,* complaining that the hero, Meursault, "has no feeling for his mother" (not quite the case, actually) and that "he refuses to admit that love is more than sex or that religion and morality are real." Well, does this disqualify him from being a character in a novel? Suppose religion and morality, conventionally understood, are not real to the novelist, or real, as for young Camus, only in the moral stand that abstention from false pretense involves? Mrs. Leavis claims, "Meursault's quarrel is really with the conditions for living as a human being anywhere and at any time." Insofar as Meursault is condemned to death by society in the novel, *L'Étranger* does acknowledge the coercive power of a social consensus, and insofar as the novel is a child of Western bourgeois culture, it may be true that where that culture dissolves or has never penetrated the novel cannot be found. But to elevate its satisfying forms into an argument for social order and human decency (as the critic understands them) is to ask the cart to drag the horse.

What is "moral"? The Leavises' pet word derives from the same Latin root as "mores"—*mos,* meaning "custom." Much of what we call moral is merely customary. Customs and convictions change; respectable people are the last to know, or to admit, the change, and they are the ones most offended by fresh reflections of the facts in the mirror of art. Hawthorne and Camus both presented stripped-down prose forms to do justice to the diminished worlds they saw around them and felt within themselves. *Middlemarch* was situated, we might notice, in an English era when the author was a child, so that a sense of "experience as a process of growth" could be readily grafted onto nostalgia; the author is exultantly "on top of" her material, lavishing upon it an affection and analytical zeal the novel will scarcely see again until Proust. However much we admire

Middlemarch, it cannot be written again, weighted by the same residue of Christian moral passion. As Borges showed with *Don Quixote,* the same words wouldn't have the same meaning. Q. D. Leavis, in her engaging and invigorating desire to read a positive humanism into the novel, seems to ask that this art form exempt itself from the negative and desolating effects of the modern age and thus surrender its right to bear credible witness.

AMERICANS

Twisted Apples

SHERWOOD ANDERSON'S *Winesburg, Ohio* is one of those books so well known by title that we imagine we know what is inside it: a sketch of the population, seen more or less in cross-section, of a small Midwestern town. It is this as much as Edvard Munch's paintings are portraits of the Norwegian middle class around the turn of the century. The important thing, for Anderson and Munch, is not the costumes and the furniture or even the bodies but the howl they conceal—the psychic pressure and warp underneath the social scene. Matter-of-fact though it sounds, *Winesburg, Ohio* is feverish, phantasmal, dreamlike. Anderson had accurately called this collection of loosely linked short stories *The Book of the Grotesque;* his publisher, B. W. Huebsch, suggested the more appealing and neutral title. The book was published in 1919, when Anderson was forty-three; it made his fame and remains his masterpiece.

"The Book of the Grotesque" is the name also of the opening story, which Anderson wrote first and which serves as a prologue. A writer, "an old man with a white mustache . . . who was past sixty," has a dream in which "all the men and women the writer had ever known had become grotesques."

> The grotesques were not all horrible. Some were amusing, some almost beautiful, and one, a woman all drawn out of shape, hurt the old man by her grotesqueness. When she passed he made a noise like a small dog whimpering.

Another writer, an "I" who is presumably Sherwood Anderson, breaks in and explains the old writer's theory of grotesqueness:

> . . . in the beginning when the world was young there were a great many thoughts but no such thing as a truth. Man made the truths himself and each

truth was a composite of a great many vague thoughts. . . . It was the truths that made the people grotesques. The old man had quite an elaborate theory concerning the matter. It was his notion that the moment one of the people took one of the truths to himself, called it his truth, and tried to live his life by it, he became a grotesque and the truth he embraced became a falsehood.

Having so strangely doubled authorial personae, Anderson then offers twenty-one tales, one of them in four parts, all "concerning," the table of contents specifies, one or another citizen of Winesburg; whether they come from the old writer's book of grotesques or some different set to which the younger author had access is as unclear as their fit within the cranky and fey anthropological-metaphysical framework set forth with such ungainly solemnity.

"Hands," the first tale, "concerning Wing Biddlebaum," introduces not only its hero, a pathetic shy old man on the edge of town whose hyper-active little white hands had once strayed to the bodies of too many schoolboys in the Pennsylvania town where he had been a teacher, but also George Willard, the eighteen-year-old son of the local hotelkeeper and a reporter for the *Winesburg Eagle.* He seems a young representative of the author; and there is also a "poet" suddenly invoked in flighty passages like:

> Let us look briefly into the story of the hands. Perhaps our talking of them will arouse the poet who will tell the hidden wonder story of the influence for which the hands were but fluttering pennants of promise.

A cloud of literary effort, then, attends the citizens of Winesburg, each of whom walks otherwise isolated, toward some inexpressible denoue-ment of private revelation. Inexpressiveness, indeed, is what above all is expressed: the characters, often, talk only to George Willard; their at-tempts to talk with each other tend to culminate in a comedy of tongue-tied silence.

> Elmer tried to explain. He wet his lips with his tongue and looked at the train that had begun to groan and get under way. "Well, you see," he began, and then lost control of his tongue. "I'll be washed and ironed. I'll be washed and ironed and starched," he muttered half incoherently.   ["Queer"]

> Darkness began to spread over the fields as Ray Pearson ran on and on. His breath came in little sobs. When he came to the fence at the edge of the road and confronted Hal Winters, all dressed up and smoking a pipe as he walked jauntily along, he could not have told what he thought or what he wanted.   ["The Untold Lie"]

Anderson himself had taken a long time to express what was in *Wines-burg, Ohio.* Raised in the small Ohio town of Clyde, he had worked successfully as a Chicago advertising man and an Elyria, Ohio, paint manufacturer, and had acquired a wife and three children, but remained restless and, somehow, overwrought. In late 1912, in the kind of spasmodic sleepwalking gesture of protest that overtakes several of the pent-up and unfulfilled souls of Winesburg, he walked away from his paint factory. He was found four days later in Cleveland, suffering from exhaustion and aphasia, and, more gradually than his self-dramatizing memoirs admit, he shifted his life to Chicago and to the literary movement that included Dreiser, Sandburg, Ben Hecht, and Floyd Dell. Already Anderson had produced several long novels, but, he later wrote, "They were not really mine." The first Winesburg stories, composed in 1915 as he lived alone in a rooming house in Chicago, were a breakthrough for him, prompted by his reading, earlier that year, of Edgar Lee Masters's *Spoon River Anthology* and Gertrude Stein's *Three Lives*.* Masters's poetic inventory of a small Midwestern community, just published that year, stands in clear paternal relation to Anderson's rendering of his memories of Clyde; but perhaps Stein's own elevation of humble lives into a curious dignity, along with her remarkably relaxed and idiomatic style, was the more nurturing influence in releasing Anderson into material that he *did* feel was really his and that gave him, for the first time, as he later related, the conviction that he was "a real writer."

Both the godparents of *Winesburg, Ohio* had a firmness and realism that was not part of Anderson's genius. Masters was a practicing lawyer, and his free-verse epitaphs state each case almost in legal prose; many have the form of arraignments, and a number of criminal incidents are fleshed out as each ghost gives its crisp testimony. Stein, before her confident and impudent mind went quite slack in its verbal enjoyments, showed an enlivening appetite for the particulars of how things are said and thought, a calm lack of either condescension or squeamishness in her social view, and a superb feel for the nuances of relationships, primarily but not only among women. For Anderson, society scarcely exists in its legal and affective bonds, and dialogue is generally the painful imposition of one monologue upon another. At the climax of the unconsummated love affair between George Willard and Helen White which is one of *Winesburg*'s continuous threads, the two sit together in the deserted fairground grandstand and hold hands:

---

*Both, as it happened, distinctly prompted by European models: Masters's poems by *Epigrams from the Greek Anthology*, which the editor of the St. Louis publication *Reedy's Mirror* gave him in 1913, and Miss Stein's trilogy, written in Paris, by Flaubert's *Three Lives*, which her brother Leo had urged her to translate.

In that high place in the darkness the two oddly sensitive human atoms held each other tightly and waited. In the mind of each was the same thought. "I have come to this lonely place and here is this other," was the substance of the thing felt.

They embrace, but then "mutual embarrassment" overtakes them and like children they race and tumble on the way down to town and part, having "for a moment taken hold of the thing that makes the mature life of men and women in the modern world possible."

The vagueness of "the thing" is chronic, and only the stumbling, shrugging, willful style that Anderson made of Stein's serene run-on syntax affords him half a purchase on his unutterable subject, the "thing" troubling the heart of his characters. Doctor Reefy, who attends and in a sense loves George Willard's dying mother, compulsively writes thoughts on bits of paper and then crumples them into little balls—"paper pills"—and shoves them into his pocket and throws them away. "One by one the mind of Doctor Reefy had made the thoughts. Out of many of them he formed a truth that arose gigantic in his mind. The truth clouded the world. It became terrible and then faded away and the little thoughts began again." What the gigantic thought was, we are not told. Another questing medical man, Doctor Parcival, relates long tales that at times seem to George Willard "a pack of lies" and at others to contain "the very essence of truth." As Thornton Wilder's *Our Town* reminded us, small-town people think a lot about the universe (as opposed to city people, who think only about each other). The agonizing philosophical search is inherited from religion; in the four-part story "Godliness," the author, speaking as a print-saturated modern man, says of the world fifty years before: "Men labored too hard and were too tired to read. In them was no desire for words printed upon paper. As they worked in the fields, vague, half-formed thoughts took possession of them. They believed in God and in God's power to control their lives. . . . The figure of God was big in the hearts of men." The rural landscape of the Midwest becomes easily confused in the minds of its pious denizens with that of the Bible, where God manifested Himself with signs and spoken words. Jesse Bentley's attempt to emulate Abraham with Isaac so terrifies his son David that the boy flees the Winesburg region forever. Anderson writes about religious obsession with distaste but also with respect, as something that truly enters into lives and twists them. To this spiritual hunger sex adds its own; the Reverend Curtis Hartman breaks a small hole in the stained-glass window of his bell-tower study in order to spy upon a woman in a house across the street as she lies on her bed and smokes and reads. "He did not want to kiss the shoulders and the throat of Kate Smith and had not allowed his mind to dwell on such thoughts. He did not know what he wanted. 'I am God's child and he must save me from myself,' he cried." One evening he sees her come naked into her room and weep and then pray; with his fist he smashes the window so all of it, with its broken bit of a peephole, will have to be repaired.

There are more naked women in Winesburg than the census declares. "Adventure" shows Alice Hindman, a twenty-seven-year-old spinster jilted by a lover ten years before, so agitated by "her desire to have something beautiful come into her rather narrow life" that she runs naked into the rain one night and actually accosts a man—a befuddled old deaf man who goes on his way. In the following story, "Respectability," a fanatic and repulsive misogynist, Wash Williams, recalls to George Willard how, many years before, his mother-in-law, hoping to reconcile him to his unfaithful young wife, presented her naked to him in her (Dayton, Ohio) parlor. George Willard, his chaste relation to Helen White aside, suffers no lack of sexual invitation in the alleys and the surrounding fields. Sherwood Anderson's women are as full of "vague hungers and secret unnamable desires" as men. The sexual quest and the philosophical quest blend: of George Willard's mother, the most tenderly drawn woman of all, the author says, "Always there was something she sought blindly, passionately, some hidden wonder in life. . . . In all the babble of words that fell from the lips of the men with whom she adventured she was trying to find what would be for her the true word." *Winesburg, Ohio* is dedicated to the memory of Anderson's own mother, "whose keen observations on the life about her first awoke in me the hunger to see beneath the surface of lives."

The author's hunger to see and express is entwined with the common hunger for love and reassurance and gives the book its awkward power and its limiting strangeness. The many characters of *Winesburg*, rather than standing forth as individuals, seem, with their repeating tics and uniform loneliness, aspects of one enveloping personality, a circumambient bundle of stalled impulses and frozen grievances. There is nowhere a citizen who, like Thomas Rhodes of Spoon River, exults in his material triumphs and impenitent rascality, nor any humbler type, like "real black, tall, well built, stupid, childlike, good looking" Rose Johnson of Stein's fictional Bridgepoint, who is happily at home in her skin. Do the Winesburgs of America completely lack such earthly successes? Does the provincial orchard hold only, in Anderson's vivid phrase, "twisted apples"? No, and yet Yes; for the uncanny truth of Anderson's sad and surreal picture must awaken recognition within anyone who, like this reviewer, was born in a small town before highways and development filled all the fields and television imposed upon every home a degraded sophistication. The Protestant villages of America, going back to Hawthorne's Salem, leave a spectral impression in literature: vague longing and monotonous, inbred satisfactions are their essence; there is something perilous and maddening in the accommodations such communities extend to human aspiration and appetite. As neighbors watch and murmur, lives visibly wrap themselves around a missed opportunity, a thwarted passion. The longing may be simply the longing to get out. The healthy rounded apples, Anderson tells us, are "put in barrels and shipped to the cities where they will be eaten in apartments that are filled with books, magazines, furniture, and people." George Willard gets out in the end, and as soon as Winesburg falls away from the train windows "his life there had become but a background on which to paint the dreams of his manhood."

The small town is generally seen, by the adult writer arrived at his city, as the site of youthful paralysis and dreaming. Certainly Anderson, as Malcolm Cowley has pointed out, wrote in a dreaming way, scrambling the time and logic of events as he hastened toward his epiphanies of helpless awakening, when the citizens of Winesburg break their tongue-tied trance and become momentarily alive to one another. Gertrude Stein's style, so revolutionary and liberating, has the haughtiness and humor of the *fausse-naïve;* there is much genuine naïveté in Anderson, which in even his masterwork flirts with absurdity and that elsewhere weakened his work decisively. *Winesburg, Ohio* describes the human condition only insofar as unfulfillment and restlessness—a nagging sense that real life is elsewhere—are intrinsically part of it. Yet the wide-eyed eagerness with which Anderson pursued the mystery of the meagre lives of Winesburg opened Michigan to Hemingway and Mississippi to Faulkner; a way had been shown to a new trust in the native material, a fresh passion for its elusive emanations. Though *Winesburg* accumulates external facts—streets, stores, town personalities—as it gropes along, its burden is a spiritual essence, a certain tart sweet taste to life as it passes in America's lonely spaced-out homes. A nagging beauty lives amid tame desolation; Anderson's parade of yearning wraiths constitutes in sum a democratic plea for the failed, the neglected, and the stuck. "On the trees are only a few gnarled apples that the pickers have rejected. . . . One nibbles at them and they are delicious. Into a round place at the side of the apple has been gathered all of its sweetness." Describing a horse-and-buggy world bygone even in 1919, *Winesburg, Ohio* imparts this penetrating taste—the wine hidden in its title—as freshly today as yesterday.

The Sinister Sex

THE GARDEN OF EDEN, by Ernest Hemingway. 247 pp. Scribner's, 1986.

The heirs of Ernest Hemingway—his widow and three sons are all listed on the copyright page—and the staff of Charles Scribner's Sons have produced yet another text out of the morass of unfinished manuscripts which bedevilled the writer's last fifteen years. *The Garden of Eden* was begun, according to the Carlos Baker biography, "in the early months of 1946," and was "an experimental compound of past and present, filled with astonishing ineptitudes and based in part upon memories of his marriages to Hadley and Pauline, with some excursions behind the scenes of his current life with Mary." Within a year, "more than a hundred pages of *The Garden of Eden* were . . . in typescript, with nine hundred pages still in longhand." Baker, not generally given to harsh criticism of his subject's work, blames this "long and emptily hedonistic novel of young lovers" for contaminating with its fatuity and narcissism the published novel *Across the River and into the Trees* (1950). In the early Fifties, a cut-down version of *The Garden of Eden* figured as the first part of Hemingway's projected sea trilogy, under the title *The Sea When Young*. In 1958, while working on the Paris sketches that would become *A Moveable Feast*, the author revised the recalcitrant novel down to forty-eight chapters and roughly two hundred thousand words; Baker still complains, "It had none of the taut nervousness of Ernest's best fiction, and was so repetitious that it seemed interminable." The lamentable opus, still not publishable, is last glimpsed as Castro is wresting Cuba from Batista, in late 1958: "The situation . . . was a constant worry. [Hemingway, off in Idaho,] tried to forget it by rewriting parts of the Paris sketchbook and revising three chapters of *The Garden of Eden*."

The propriety of publishing, as a commercial endeavor, what a dead writer declined to see into print is, of course, dubious. The previous forays into the Hemingway trove have unfortunately tended to heighten our appreciation not of his talent but of his psychopathology; even the charming and airy *Moveable Feast*, the first and most finished of the posthumous publications (1964), had its ugly flashes of malice and ingenuous self-serving. *Islands in the Stream* (1970) was a thoroughly ugly book, brutal and messy and starring a painter-sailor hero whose humanity was almost entirely dissolved in barroom jabber and Hollywood heroics. The letters (1981), too, which Hemingway had wisely tried to safeguard from the scavengers, provided insights more alarming than appealing into his bellicose, infantile, sexist, and at the end paranoid nature. Among the published letters is one addressed to an early scavenger, Charles A. Fenton, saying, "Writing that I do not wish to publish, you have no right to publish. I would no more do a thing like that to you than I would cheat a man at cards or rifle his desk or wastebasket or read his personal letters." Well, such old-fashioned gentlemanly thunder rings pretty hollow in this hustling era of professional desk-riflers. The second-wave Hemingway biographies proliferate, whispering to us that Oak Park was not the forest primeval and that three weeks of distributing candy bars do not a warrior make; soon the old poser will have been stripped down to his Freudian bones, much like Santiago's great dead marlin in *The Old Man and the Sea.*

However: Hemingway, after a semi-eclipse in the Sixties, when his fascination with violence and war seemed desperately unworthy, now stands as a classic as surely as Hawthorne, and twenty-five years after his death his bearish claims to privacy are perhaps superseded by the claims his literary personality makes upon our interest. There is every reason—its hackneyed title, Baker's scorn, the forty years of murky fiddling that have passed since its conception—to distrust *The Garden of Eden;* yet the book, as finally presented, is something of a miracle, a fresh slant on the old magic, and falls just short of the satisfaction that a fully intended and achieved work gives us. The miracle, it should be added, does not seem to be Hemingway's alone but is shared with workers unnamed in the prefatory note, which blandly admits to "some cuts in the manuscript and some routine copy-editing corrections." Some cuts. Some Chink, as Harry Morgan says to himself of the mysterious Chinese gentleman in *To Have and Have Not.* When last heard of, *The Garden of Eden,* according to Carlos Baker, consisted of over two hundred thousand words of lacklustre dialogue and eerie trivia. It is no secret—indeed, it has been widely reported—that last July a certain Tom Jenks, a thirty-five-year-old editor newly hired by Scribner's, was presented with over three thousand pages of *Garden of Eden* manuscripts—all three versions that Hemingway had struggled with, enough to fill two shopping bags—and was invited to find a publishable book in all that verbiage. He managed. In the trim published text of sixty-five thousand words, a daily repetition of actions remains (wake, write, drink, lunch, siesta, drink, eat, make love, sleep) but the dialogue never covers exactly the same ground and the plot advances by steady, subliminal increments, as situations in real life do. The basic tensions of the slender, three-cornered action are skillfully sustained. The psychological deterioration of the heroine, Catherine Bourne, the professional preoccupations of the hero, the young writer David Bourne, and the growing involvement of the other woman, Marita, are kept in the fore, interwoven with but never smothered by Hemingway's betranced descriptions of the weather, the meals, the landscape, the chronic recreations.

A chastening, almost mechanically rhythmic order has been imposed, and though an edition with a scholarly conscience would have provided some clues to the mammoth amounts of manuscript that were discarded,* this remnant does give the reader a text wherein he, unlike the author in his travails long ago, never feels lost. Endearingly, many of Hemingway's eccentricities have been defended from copyeditors—the commas omitted by ear rather than by sense ("driving the machine up the short hill feeling the lack of training in his thighs"); the commas tossed into a run of six adjectives (a "good light, dry, cheerful unknown white wine"); the stubbornly awkward word order ("the girl put the one she was reading down"); the English as spoken ("Feel it how smooth"); the idiosyncratic spellings ("god damned," "pyjama tops," "self conscious"); and a sentence containing no fewer than eleven "and"s.

The Garden of Eden adds to the canon not merely another volume but a new reading of Hemingway's sensibility. Except in some of the short stories and that strange novel *To Have and Have Not,* he avoided describing the life that most men and women mostly lead, domestic life. *The Garden of Eden* confronts sexual intimacy, marriage, and human androgyny with a wary but searching tenderness that amounts, for a man so wrapped up in masculine values and public gestures, to courage. What stymied him, while he was still in his mid-forties, from completing and publishing the novel must be idly conjectured. One possibility is that the material embarrassed as well as possessed him, and another is that he knew he was in over his head. His head was not quite right; his behavior in World War II had been strange, and in his work methods he was developing (and had just barely rescued *For Whom the Bell Tolls* from) the Papa-esque logorrhea, the fatal dependency upon free-form spillage, of which *The Dangerous Summer* was to be the disastrous climax—*Life*'s request in 1959 for ten thousand words producing a dizzying twelve times that amount. Perhaps, in *The Garden of Eden,* he pulled back from the snake pit of male-female interplay and sought to reconstitute the old impervious, macho Hemingway persona, whom women attend as houris attend the blessed immortals in the Islamic paradise. This is the plot solution the Scribner's editors have used—perhaps the only one available to them in the uncontrolled manuscript—and it is a feeble one, compared with the dark soft power of the opening sections.

In his other novels, Hemingway seems to me hobbled by his need to have a hero in the obsolete sense, a central male figure who always acts

---

*For an indignant account of the complete text, by someone who has perused the manuscripts at the Kennedy Library in Boston, see "Ernest Hemingway's Real Garden of Eden" in Barbara Probst Solomon's *Horse-Trading and Ecstasy* (North Point, 1989).

right and looks good, even when, as in the cases of Harry Morgan and Jake Barnes, the cruel world has externally mutilated him. David Bourne, as initially presented, is an oddity, an inwardly vulnerable Hemingway hero, mated with a woman who, very upsettingly in this narrow stoic universe, *wants*. "I'm how you want but I'm how I want too and it isn't as though it wasn't for us both." Catherine is David's three weeks' bride of twenty-one; like Eve, she has long hair and is generally naked. They are honeymooning at Le Grau-du-Roi, a Mediterranean town on a canal that runs to the sea; they bicycle and swim and eat and drink, everything they consume and do described with that liturgical gravity which Hemingway invented. "It had been wonderful and they had been truly happy and he had not known that you could love anyone so much that you cared about nothing else and other things seemed inexistent. . . . Now when they had made love they would eat and drink and make love again. It was a very simple world and he had never been truly happy in any other." She begins her wanting by wanting a haircut; she has her luxurious long dark hair cut short as a boy's. David is taken aback yet has no choice but to acquiesce. Also, she wants to get a very dark tan. "Why do you want to be so dark?" he asks. Her excited answer is "I don't know. Why do you want anything? Right now it's the thing that I want most. That we don't have I mean. Doesn't it make you excited to have me getting so dark?" "Uh-huh," he answers. "I love it." She wants the two of them to travel through Europe for months and months on her money; she does not much want, it develops, David to read his clippings or to work dutifully on his stories. To dramatize her tan she gets her short hair dyed as pale as ivory, and to dramatize their marriage she seduces David into also dyeing his hair and parading about Cannes with her. Penetrating more deeply into his feminine side, she does unspeakable "devil things" in bed that actualize the sex change she wants, whereby she becomes a boy called Peter and he a girl called Catherine. "You're my wonderful Catherine," Catherine tells David. "You're my beautiful lovely Catherine. You were so good to change. Oh thank you, Catherine, so much. Please understand. Please know and understand. I'm going to make love to you forever."

It is possibly a pity that Hemingway's own inhibitions, if not those of the changing postwar times, prevented him from telling us exactly what is going on here. How casually specific fiction has become about polymorphous sex we can estimate from a new novel like Carolyn See's *Golden Days*, where it is recounted of a typical contemporary woman, "Husband number three had been a Jamaican musician named Prince Le Boeuf who dressed all in white. He too had been great in the sack, at first, but liked, Lorna found out, to bugger his gentleman friends—all in the spirit of fun. Lorna found out there were limits to her tolerance: 'I told him, bugger

me! I've got an asshole like everyone else in this great democracy! I'll speak
in a deep voice, you shut your eyes, and who'll know the difference?' "
For Hemingway, there is no spirit of fun; the "devil things" lead David
to call his wife "Devil," and poison their Eden even before Catherine
decides, in her rampage of wanting, to introduce another, bisexual
woman, called Marita, into their honeymoon household. When it comes
to having men turned into women, or being overrun with them, Hemingway is a moralist of the old school; quaint words like "sin" and "right"
and "wrong" and "remorse" and "perversion" come into earnest play.
Evil is, evidently, feminine in gender: David reflects of his father, "He
treated evil like an old entrusted friend . . . and evil, when she poxed him,
never knew she'd scored." Having feminized David in bed, Catherine
now seeks to unman him as a writer. "Why should I shut up? Just because
you wrote this morning? Do you think I married you because you're a
writer? You and your clippings." It gets worse: she scornfully tells Marita,
"He writes in those ridiculous child's notebooks and he doesn't throw
anything away. He just crosses things out and writes along the sides of
the pages. The whole business is a fraud really. He makes mistakes in
spelling and grammar too."

"Poor David. What women do to you," commiserates Marita, who as
Catherine's feminine perversity blooms into madness turns increasingly
sympathetic and heterosexual. Having begun as a hardened, though attractively blushing, lesbian, she rather incredibly becomes a perfect man's
woman, who adores David's writing and his lovemaking and wants only
what he wants—that is, escape from women into the salubrious companionship of other men: "I want you to have men friends and friends from
the war and [*sic*] to shoot with and to play cards at the club."

Though *The Garden of Eden,* like the other Hemingway remnants, has
its psychopathological aspect, the pathology is caught up into a successful
artistic design. The author's heartfelt sense of women as the root of evil
enforces and energizes the allegory. Catherine's transformation from sexually docile Eve into caustic and destructive bitch makes her the most
interesting of his heroines; unlike the martyred Catherine Barkley of *A
Farewell to Arms,* she does things instead of having them done to her, the
perpetrator rather than the victim of "a dirty trick." Her advancing derangement, with its abrupt backslidings into affection and docility, produces some of Hemingway's sharpest pages of dialogue; like Bellow's feral
females, she becomes vivid and flashing in antagonism. And Hemingway's
pristine prose furnishes a natural innocence to fall from. What is his style
if not Edenic, an early-morning style wherein things still have the dew
of their naming on them?

The waiter brought them glasses of manzanilla from the lowland near Cádiz called the Marismas with thin slices of *jamón serrano,* a smoky, hard cured ham from pigs that fed on acorns, and bright red spicy *salchichón,* another even spicier dark sausage from a town called Vich and anchovies and garlic olives.

In the Buen Retiro in the morning it was as fresh as though it was a forest. It was green and the trunks of the trees were dark and the distances were all new.

. . . when he had finished for the day he shut up the room and went out and found the two girls playing chess at a table in the garden. They both looked fresh and young and as attractive as the wind-washed morning sky.

This same notation of simple large elements, with its curious surging undercurrent—"the sinister part only showed as the light feathering of a smooth swell on a calm day marking the reef beneath"—also serves to evoke the tidal mystery of matedness, the strangeness of sharing our sleep:

In the night he woke and heard the wind high and wild and turned and pulled the sheet over his shoulder and shut his eyes again. He felt her breathing and shut his eyes again. He felt her breathing softly and regularly and then he went back to sleep.

Hemingway's own innocence, surviving decades of aggressively courted experience, enabled him to reach back from his workroom in Cuba, through all the battles and bottles and injuries and interviews, into his youth on another continent and to make mythic material out of his discovery that sex could be complicated. He is able, he who so thoroughly hid behind assertiveness and expertise, to express sexual ambivalence, to touch upon the feminine within himself, the seducibility from which only his writing (for a time) was safe, and to conjure up, if only to exorcise, the independent, masculine will within women, of which he doubtless knew more than his typical heroes let him express. The mannered, scarcely articulate exchanges of Maria (a name echoed in *The Garden of Eden*) and Robert Jordan in *For Whom the Bell Tolls*, and Dorothy Hollis's masturbatory monologue in *To Have and Have Not* are Hemingway's nearest previous approaches, in a novel, to sexual realism. Lesbianism, or at least a male view of a woman deserting him for lesbianism, was the subject of the short story "The Sea Change," which takes place in one of the sparsely occupied cafés, with its typical angelic bartender, that dot the tasteful hedonist paradise of Hemingway's Europe. The story's nameless heroine, like Catherine Bourne, is well tanned, with pale and short-cut hair; like the Bournes, she and "Phil" are "a handsome young couple" being destroyed by a devilish tug of desire, of *wanting*, within the woman, whose exterior is impeccable: "He was looking at her, at the way her mouth went and the curve of her cheek bones, at her eyes and at the way her hair grew on her forehead and at the edge of her ear and at her neck." The story is intense and strange and one wonders, reading it, if the woman really existed in Hemingway's life. Asked about it, he explained, according to Baker, "that the prototypes of his people were a couple he had once overheard in the Bar Basque in St.-Jean-de-Luz."

But the woman has returned in *The Garden of Eden*, with her tan and her so fascinating hair. The story dates from 1931, and in the summer of 1929, in Spain, to celebrate her thirty-fourth birthday, Hemingway's second wife, Pauline, Baker tells us in a footnote, "had her hair dyed blond as a gesture of sexual independence and a surprise for EH. . . . Much is made of this gesture in EH's later unpublished novel, *The Garden of Eden.*" It was in the summer of 1926 that Hemingway lived, more or less, with two women: his first wife, Hadley, and the hotly pursuing Pauline Pfeiffer, who had befriended Hadley. In *A Moveable Feast* he tells it thus:

> Before these rich had come we [he and Hadley and their son, Bumby] had already been infiltrated by another rich using the oldest trick there is. It is that an unmarried young woman becomes the temporary best friend of another young woman who is married, goes to live with the husband and wife and then unknowingly, innocently and unrelentingly sets out to marry the husband. When the husband is a writer and doing difficult work so that he is occupied much of the time and is not a good companion or partner to his wife for a big part of the day, the arrangement has advantages until you know how it works out. The husband has two attractive girls around when he has finished work. One is new and strange and if he has bad luck he gets to love them both.

In Carlos Baker's description of the weeks that the *ménage à trois* spent living in two rented rooms at the Hôtel de la Pinède in Juan-les-Pins, the routine is much like that in *The Garden of Eden:*

> Each morning they spent on the beach, swimming and taking the sun. After lunch in the garden and a long siesta, they took long bicycle rides along the Golfe de Juan, returning at evening yardarm time for cocktails. . . . At the hotel there were three of everything: breakfast trays, bicycles, bathing suits drying on the line. . . .

Pauline was smaller and darker than Hadley, as Marita is relative to Catherine; and Hemingway lays on Catherine a malevolent version of the famous incident in which Hadley, with the best of wifely intentions, lost a suitcase of his early manuscripts. In the memoir version of the triangle composed toward the end of Hemingway's life, the wife is blameless and the mistress "innocently" tricky and unrelenting; in *The Garden of Eden*, the wife turns bad and the mistress good—i.e., an acolyte to the writer and his writing.

All thirteen years of Hemingway's marriage to Pauline (and most of his briefer marriage to Martha Gelhorn) were behind him when he sat down in 1946 to write a version of that traumatic period, twenty years earlier, when, as *The Sun Also Rises* set the seal on his celebrity, he was seduced away from his first wife. Hemingway, only twenty-seven at the time, felt with his desertion a remorse and grief nothing personal would give him again, and he remembered it as a fall, the end of an idyll he and Hadley had created in Austria and Spain and Paris. Pauline, then, provides the evil that undermines his *Eden;* her ghost is both Eve and serpent, and she contributes elements both to Catherine (her bleached hair and her Catholicism, which is lightly mentioned at the outset) and to Marita (her petiteness and her money; Marita's nickname is "Heiress," though Catherine, too, is tainted with independent wealth). The slow disenchantment of a longish marriage, plus Hemingway's constant battle, which extended through the boozy Key West years, to combine the labor of writing with what he once called his "fiesta concept of life," is compressed into a fictional honeymoon—as well as much else both imagined and recalled. In one regard, Hemingway's actual situation in 1926 is conspicuously falsified: Catherine is a mere twenty-one, and Marita no older, whereas Hadley and Pauline were both in their thirties, older than he by eight and four years respectively.* A liking for older women is not part of David

---

*In another regard, the cast of characters has been simplified; the summer of 1926 was complicated by young Bumby Hemingway's persistent whooping cough, which led to the family's being placed in quarantine by Sara and Gerald Murphy's British doctor (for this was also the fabled Riviera summer of the Murphys, the MacLeishes, and the Fitzgeralds at Cap d'Antibes, memorialized at the outset of *Tender Is the Night;* it was this summer when Hemingway showed Fitzgerald the carbon copy of *The Sun Also Rises* and received the criticisms that decisively improved the text). Pauline wrote from Paris that she had had whooping cough and invaded the quarantine, joining the little family first at the rented villa, Villa Paquita at Juan-les-Pins, borrowed from the Fitzgeralds, and then in the rooms at the nearby Hôtel de la Pinède. The fourth and fifth members of the *ménage à trois,* the Hemingways' ailing two-year-old Bumby and the so-called *femme de ménage* Madame Rohrbach, lived in a separate bungalow and presumably joined them on the beach. The sensations of a father about to desert his toddling son were understandably not added to David Bourne's welter of mixed feelings. Hadley's own nice description, as of 1967, to Baker of this interval (which ended in July, when the Hemingways, Pauline, and the

Bourne's vulnerability as he lets himself be led into the "devil things"—
into the possibility that male and female are less than absolute conditions.

An uncharacteristic ambivalence of feeling is also expressed about hunting. Drawing upon the African safaris whose carnage is so matter-of-factly
extolled in *Green Hills of Africa* (1935), Hemingway shows David Bourne
writing about an elephant hunt he experienced as a child with his father.
The fictional episodes, which come to occupy a place at the outset of each
hag-ridden day and chapter, develop a momentum and an interest of their
own. The boy and his dog Kibo spot the old elephant, with his fabulously
big tusks, by moonlight, and this starts his father, a hunter, and his father's
African sidekick, Juma, on the trail. As the days of tracking go by, the
tired child comes to love the doomed elephant and dislike his father and
Juma: "They would kill me and they would kill Kibo too if we had ivory."
The description of the shooting of the elephant is horrendous and moving
and also a fall from innocence. "Fuck elephant hunting," the boy tells his
father, and thinks: "He will never ever trust me again. That's good. I don't
want him to because I'll never tell him or anybody anything again never
anything again. Never ever never." The splicing and counterpoint of the
African story-within-a-story are managed quite brilliantly—by the author
himself, Mr. Jenks assured this reviewer. Some of the pages in *The Garden
of Eden*, as the elephant lumbers toward death and Catherine dips in and
out of madness and David speaks his goodbyes in his heart, are among
Hemingway's best, and the whole rounded fragment leaves us with a
better feeling about the author's humanity and essential sanity—complex
as sanity must be—than anything else published since his death.

Cohn's Doom

GOD'S GRACE, by Bernard Malamud. 223 pp. Farrar, Straus & Giroux, 1982.

God's Grace may seem a surprising book for Bernard Malamud to have
written; but each of his novels, beginning with that intensely stylized
baseball myth *The Natural*, has been surprising, a departure achieved, the

---

Murphys went to Pamplona) perhaps should be given in her words, as they appear in
Bernice Kert's *The Hemingway Women* (1983): "Here it was that the three breakfast trays,
three wet bathing suits on the line, three bicycles were to be found. Pauline tried to teach
me to dive, but I was not a success. Ernest wanted us to play bridge but I found it hard
to concentrate. We spent all morning on the beach sunning or swimming, lunched in our
little garden. After siesta time there were long bicycle rides along the Golfe de Juan."

reader is made to feel, after considerable contemplative effort and calculation of risk. Malamud is among the more ascetic and self-controlled of
postwar American novelists—controlled not by shifts of literary fashion
or vicissitudes either personal or national but by a dedication bordering
on severity, an artistic intent palpable on every resilient and economical
page of prose, a comic sense rooted in sorrow, and a capacity for passion
that, transferred to his characters, shocks even his most studied and seemingly flat narratives into sudden life. His earnestness leads him into parable
but never more than reaching distance away from the spontaneously,
helplessly true emotion. His heroes, for instance, fall in love with a tender
wonderment that neither age (as in *Dubin's Lives*) nor unlikelihood (in
God's Grace the beloved is a chimpanzee) diminishes. The tension in his
fiction between naturalistic instinct and symbolizing tendency seems to
give an alternating texture to his well-spaced succession of novels: following the interracial fantasy of *The Tenants, Dubin's Lives* was all too generously domestic and earthbound, and now *God's Grace* swings higher than
ever toward abstraction, toward the indubitably big but dubiously real
subject.

Calvin Cohn, a paleontologist studying microfossils at the bottom of the
sea during the nuclear holocaust, is the only human being left on earth.
Son and grandson of rabbis, he holds some direct discourse with God,
drifts on the "swollen seas" (God has seen fit to inflict a second Flood on
the scorched and depopulated earth) in a hundred-and-fifty-two-foot
oceanography vessel with no other company than the laboratory chimpanzee, and lands on an island where more primates (eight chimpanzees, a
single gorilla, eight baboons, an albino ape or two) mysteriously appear.
Cohn proceeds to re-create civilization as best he can, lecturing to the
unevenly receptive chimps on history, art, science, and religion. The book
reminds us of *Lord of the Flies* and *Robinson Crusoe* and Pat Frank's *Mr.
Adam,* whose hero was deep in a lead mine during a nuclear catastrophe.
But Malamud makes the terrain his own, mostly by uncannily humanizing, with touches both humorous and sinister, the primates. Among the
chimpanzees, there is Buz, the original companion of Cohn and an acolyte
to the memory of Dr. Walther Bünder, who taught him to speak and
converted him to Christianity; Mary Madelyn, a lissome young female
with silken hair and a heart-shaped face, whose arrival at sexual maturity
predictably causes trouble; Esau, a bully ("His face was large, his teeth
unsettled and wandering in the mouth") who boasts of being "the Alpha
Ape"; two oldsters, Melchior and Hattie; a pair of young twins, Luke and
Saul of Tarsus; and two supporting actors named Esterhazy and Brom-
berg. If this sounds cute, it is, and the phonetic transcription of chimp

English imparts a further frivolity to the proceedings; yet Malamud's curious sensual searchingness bestows upon the apes such individuality that soon the reader can almost tell them apart by smell. When the restraints of Cohn's civilizing efforts fall away, the chimpanzees' savagery is sickeningly believable—sickening from the human point of view, liberating from theirs. In a note of acknowledgment, Malamud mentions Jane Goodall's *In the Shadow of Man;* he has well benefited from her field studies of primate behavior.

God's Grace, however, as its title conveys, is less primatological than theological. It contains God as a character, speaking in quadruple quotation marks and a kind of vers libre:

> " "Why do you contend
> with Me, Mr. Cohn? . . .
> Who are you
> to understand
> the Lord's intention?
> How can I explain
> my mystery
> to your mind?
> Can a cripple ascend
> a flaming of stars?" "

Cohn quarrels with God but also says kaddish and observes seder and promulgates a set of seven commandments, of which the second reads, "Note: God is not Love, God is God. Remember Him." The fatal schism in Cohn's island community stems not only from sexual rivalry but from doctrinal dispute; Buz alters this admonition to read "God is   love." The chimpanzees end as barbaric Christians, making a blood sacrifice; only the gorilla, wearing a yarmulke he has found in the forest, is left to chant the ancient words of Judaism. God's (rather parsimonious) grace also surfaces in Cohn's sudden awareness of his own long white beard— " 'Merciful God,' he said, 'I am an old man. The Lord has let me live my life out' "—and in the many signs that the Creator, for all His wrath, is regenerating the world, with new kinds of vegetation and, it may eventually be, with a new form of primate civilization. Not that Malamud's fable is not bitter and pessimistic; but its darkness remains, as it were, orthodox, and does not spill out of those presumptions which tend to be, for Malamud characters, coterminous with their own identities. Jewishness, he and other fiction writers (Singer and Ozick more than Bellow and Roth) seem to say, is in part a religious condition but is not negated by irreligion, as, say, a disavowal of faith removes a person from the lists of Christianity or Islam. A Jew does not merely choose, he is chosen; like Jehovah Himself, Jewishness sticks in some realm beyond argument and dethronement. Adversity merely confirms the Jew's distinctive condition. Leo Finkle, the hero of "The Magic Barrel," draws from his misery "the consolation that he was a Jew and that a Jew suffered." In *The Assistant*, Frankie Alpine takes up Morris Bober's ordeal by grocery store and seeks out the pain of circumcision: "The pain enraged and inspired him. After Passover he became a Jew." The customary round of dutifulness, abasement, failure, and obdurate ritual with which Malamud's Jews define themselves in a world of woe rattles a little loosely, however, in a world swept clean: a gigantic stage of desolation in one corner of which Cohn plays his old 78s of a cantor's melodious lamentations and chimpanzees lisp answers to the seder's Four Questions. The allegory, with its random sprinkling of Biblical names and with Buz doubling as Jesus and Judas, seems confused, and our reaction to it is further confused by the historical Holocaust that did occur and that has attached itself to the very meaning of Jewishness. A Jew reasserting his faith in the wake of Hitler's Holocaust is a Judaic hero, a son of Abraham; Cohn in the context of global annihilation seems no more or less brave and quixotic than a Mormon or a devout animist in the same dire circumstances.

An instructive contrast with the eschatology of *God's Grace* is provided by Stanley Elkin's supernatural triptych *The Living End* (1979). The writers are in many ways similar; Elkin's cadences often remind us strikingly of Malamud's, at a slightly tougher pitch, corresponding perhaps to a generation's deterioration in the inner cities where both are most at home. Elkin has chosen to burlesque, by taking it literally, a specifically Christian version of heaven and hell: eternal fire is rendered with savage verve; the delights of heaven are mercilessly trivialized in the cataloguing; the sacred intimacies of the Holy Trinity are served up as family comedy. The cosmic indictment—Why is there suffering? Why is Creation such a cruel botch?—is delivered, not once but often, against a flip, side-of-the-mouth Creator who could be played by George Burns. The indictment, of course, has already appeared in the Book of Job, and God replies to Malamud's Cohn and Elkin's protagonist, Ellerbee, in the gist of the reply Job received: "Where was thou when I laid the foundations of the earth . . . Hast thou commanded the morning since thy days?" Job responded docilely, "Behold, I am vile." Ellerbee stridently keeps demanding "an *explanation!* None of this what-was-I-doing-when-You-pissed-the-oceans stuff, where I was when You colored the nigger and ignited Hell." Even Cohn shakes his fist and demands, "You have destroyed mankind. Our children are all dead. Where are justice and mercy?" Yet Cohn continues to be a Jew, idealistic and pious, leaving behind him the ragged start of a new world, while Elkin's characters cannot rest until they have goaded God into annihilating *"everything"* (author's italics).

Elkin, drawing on some deep heat of indignation, has composed the purer protest, a litany of scorn and incredulity directed against the images of conventional popular Christianity. None of his sufferers confess to any religious experience prior to their afterlives; we guess they are Jews— some of them—only from the way they talk. Perhaps in Elkin's Midwest (he teaches in St. Louis; *The Living End* is set in Minneapolis–St. Paul) Christian evangels are less ignorable than in Malamud's Manhattan and Bennington haunts. Christians and apes seem about equally remote from the essential humanity of Calvin Cohn. Yet he wishes the world well. Small miracles surround him. Begun, one guesses, in a fury at a world that can include the possibility of its own destruction, *God's Grace* goes on to sing such precarious pleasures as intercourse with a chimpanzee: "There was an instant electric connection and Cohn parted with his seed as she possessed it. He felt himself happily drawn clean of sperm." Happiness, usually sexual, peeks through the tatters that Malamud's humble sufferers wear and is often what we remember best—Frank Alpine's glimpse of Helen Bober naked through the bathroom window of *The Assistant;* in *A New Life* Levin's lovemaking with Pauline "in the open forest, nothing less, what triumph!" As a cosmic fable, *God's Grace*—a tender retelling of Noah's or Lot's shame and a comic sketch of final horror—is a muddle; but therein lies its mercy.

Summonses, Indictments, Extenuating Circumstances

A Summons to Memphis, by Peter Taylor. 209 pp. Knopf, 1986.

Peter Taylor's *A Summons to Memphis* is not quite the distinguished short-story writer's first novel; thirty-six years ago he published *A Woman of Means,* which, little more than forty thousand words long, might be called a novella. The two books have much in common: a narrator who was moved from a bucolic Tennessee childhood to a big house in a river city (Memphis, St. Louis), a handsome and strong-willed father recovering from a business setback, a witty but somehow incapacitated and mentally fragile mother-figure (a mother, a stepmother), two older and wearingly vivacious sisters or stepsisters, a psychological core of ambivalent and ruminative passivity, and a lovingly detailed (architecturally, sociologically) portrait of life in the upper classes of the Upper South between the two world wars. This last is Mr. Taylor's terrain, and he rarely strays from it. The narrator of *A Summons to Memphis,* Phillip Carver, lives in Manhattan, on West 82nd Street ("one of the safer neighborhoods on the Upper West Side, but still we have to be very careful"), with a woman fifteen years younger, Holly Kaplan. New York, that raucous plenitude, is felt as a kind of blissfully blank limbo, and the principal charm of his mistress seems to be that she, from a prosperous Jewish family in Cleveland, shares with the forty-nine-year-old Southern refugee a rueful, guilty obsession with the tribal reality left behind. "She felt they had a real life out there in Cleveland that she didn't have, had never had, would never have now." Both Holly and Phillip are in publishing, and their consuming activities seem to be reading galley proofs and discussing their families:

> Suddenly, with a sigh, Holly blew out a great billow of smoke and said irritably that I *was really* absolutely obsessed with my family!
> This was an accusation which Holly and I frequently hurled at each other. In the beginning our complaints about our families had been perhaps our deepest bond. We had long since, however, worn out the subject.

So worn out, indeed, that in the course of the novel they separate, only to be reunited on the firm basis of more family talk: "During the days and weeks that followed Holly and I talked of almost nothing but our two families. . . . And we sat there in the twilight and sipped our drinks while we talked our own combined nonsense together, each his or her own brand of inconclusive nonsense about the reconciliation of fathers and children, talked on and on until total darkness fell. . . ."

In the course of this meandering account it is possible to feel like Holly when she blew out the impatient billow of smoke. After a lifetime of tracing teacup-tempests among genteel Tennesseeans, Mr. Taylor retains an unslaked appetite for the local nuance. The rather subtle (to Yankees, at least) differences between the styles of Memphis and Nashville are thoroughly and repeatedly gone into, with instructive side-glances at Knoxville and Chattanooga. "Nashville," an old social arbiter of that town explains, "is a city of schools and churches, whereas Memphis is—well, Memphis is something else again. Memphis is a place of steamboats and cotton gins, of card playing and hotel society." The narrator puts it, "Memphis was today. Nashville was yesterday." His own temperamental preference, as we could guess from his leisurely, laggard prose, is for yesterday: "As one walks or rides down any street in Nashville one can feel now and again that he has just glimpsed some pedestrian on the sidewalk who was not quite real somehow, who with a glance over his shoulder or with a look in his disenchanted eye has warned one not to believe too much in the plastic present and has given warning that the past is still real and present somehow and is demanding something of all men like me who happen to pass that way." When Phillip moves to Memphis, just turned thirteen, he reports to school "in knee britches and wearing a sort of Buster Brown, highly starched collar" and discovers that (this is 1931), not only is his costume retrograde but his hair is cut too long, and he even fails to carry his books the Memphis way—"alongside my hip or thigh, with my arm hanging straight down from shoulder to wrist" rather than (evidently Nashville-style) "like a girl, in the crook of my arm." The accents are different, and men play golf instead of ride to hounds and don't wear cutaways downtown to the office: "Unlike other Memphis business-men [George Carver, Phillip's father] frequently went to his office wear-ing striped trousers and a cutaway jacket—a morning suit, no less—along with a starched wing collar and a gray four-in-hand silk tie." He comes to adopt the Memphis way of dressing: "in Manhattan or even in Nash-ville or Knoxville or Chattanooga people on the street might have turned and stared at Father and remarked on the peculiar cut of his jacket and the width of his hat brim." A hat alone will send Mr. Taylor into a rhapsody of Southern social history:

It seems that when a local gentleman was on the courthouse square of Thornton or when he was walking his own land in that part of the world, a hat was a very important item of apparel. Father's father and his grandfa-ther always ordered their hats from a manufacturer in St. Louis, and Father did so too, wherever he might be living. Even I can remember, as a small child, seeing my father and my paternal grandfather and great-grandfather, for that matter, in their hats walking the farm roads on the Town Farm, as we called it, or crossing the wide, wooden blocks in the streets on the courthouse square. In their law practice and even in their wide-ranging farm dealings (they also owned cotton farms in western Kentucky as well as in southern Illinois and southeastern Missouri) there were various occasions in the year when it was necessary for them to visit St. Louis and Chicago. Whether those visits related to their law practice or their landowning I don't know. Anyhow, it was always in St. Louis that they bought their hats and in Chicago whatsoever sporting equipment they owned. They shopped there in person for those articles or they ordered them through the mail from "houses" where they were known. They spoke of St. Louis as their "hat place," and Father continued to do so always. I am sure it was in a St. Louis hat that he met me that near noonday when I arrived at the Memphis airport. On the other hand, his shoes would always be Nashville shoes.

Now, this is admirably circumstantial and, within the generous space demanded by the unhurried tone, elegantly turned; but it is talk, not action. Direct dialogue in *A Summons to Memphis* is sparse, and the plot feels skimped, even snubbed. Although Mr. Taylor tells us a great deal about costumes, furniture, and civic differences, there is much he avoids showing. Indeed, he almost cruelly teases, with his melodious divagations and his practiced skill at foreshadowing and delaying climaxes, the reader of this novel. Its kernel of action—Phillip Carver's trip to Memphis at the summons of his sisters, in 1967—does not occur until well after midpoint. He at last boards the plane on page 132, arrives at the Memphis airport on page 135, and by page 153 is back on a plane, winging his way into more cloudy retrospect after having refused (implausibly, I think) to spend a single night with his father and sisters. And the events while he is briefly there seem oddly betranced; though his vital if elderly father has been frustrated in an attempt at marriage, the old man submits without a peep, and though his son has been summoned a thousand miles for a family conference, he says hardly a word. Concerning an earlier frustration, it is not made clear why or how the father covertly wrecks the romance between Phillip, who is a soldier and all of twenty-three, and Clara Price, who sounds lovely and, even if she does hail from far-off Chattanooga, would appear to be socially acceptable; she and her family live "in a splendid Tudor-style house atop Lookout Mountain"—presumably above bribery and bullying persuasion. Some nuance, no doubt, escaped me, just as, in trying to grasp the scarcely-to-be-forgiven trauma of being moved from Nashville to Memphis, I fastened on the tragic fact that the two girls thereby "came out" in the wrong city and wasted their debutante parties: "Young ladies in present-day Memphis and Nashville cannot possibly conceive the profound significance that the debutante season once held for their like or imagine the strict rules that it was death to disobey." In any case, one might argue that the action of the novel is not so much the doings, past and present, of the Tennessee Carvers but the struggle by the self-exiled Phillip, staged in "these very irregular notebooks" of his which we are mysteriously reading, to come to terms with his past—the magnificent, crushing father, the "cluttered-up, bourgeois life," the tenacious, static idyll of the South. As the boy rode behind his father, outside of Nashville, "the foliage of the black gums and maples and oaks often met overhead on those lanes, and it seems to me that every morning somewhere on our ride there would be an old Negro man bent down beside one of the walls, making repairs. It was a timeless scene. I could not imagine a past time when it had not been just so or a future time when it would not be the same." From this South, with its omnipresent past, Mr. Taylor, like Faulkner, draws endless inspiration; he stirs and stirs the same waters, watching them darken and deepen, while abstaining from Faulkner's violent modernist gestures. He stirs instead with a Jamesian sort of spoon.

In praise of *A Woman of Means* thirty-six years ago, Robert Penn Warren claimed for it "the excitement of being constantly on the verge of deep perceptions and deep interpretations." Peter Taylor keeps us on the verge much of the time. *A Woman of Means* did plunge, with the empathy of a James Agee or a William Maxwell, into the frightening dark of boyhood, when one is able to observe so much and do so little. Its evocation of a child's helpless, sensitive world seemed to close hastily, but not until our essential loneliness and the precariousness of even the best-appointed home were made painfully clear. In *A Summons to Memphis,* though the canvas is broader and adorned with fine comic splashes, some of the narrative churning brings up only what is already floating on the surface: "And I grasped at once that my not having other luggage meant to him that we would not be delayed by waiting at the baggage-claim window." Or, a perception still more hard-won:

> But as we turned between the boxwoods at the entrance to Father's two-acre plot, I at once became aware of a large rectangular object, somehow inimical to the scene, drawn up to the house and visible at the end of the two rows of old cedars that lined the driveway. The house was set back some three hundred feet from the road, and when we had traversed half that distance I recognized the unlikely object as a commercial moving van. I was able to identify it immediately then by the name of the local storage warehouse which was writ in large red letters on the side of the van.

James's heavily mirrored halls of mutual regard seem but feebly imitated by reflections like "I knew always that the affair referred to was pure fantasy but I do not know even now whether or not they knew I knew." The diction at times is so fastidious that a smile at the narrator's expense must be intended: "If slit skirts were the fashion, then my sisters' would be vented well above the knees, exposing fleshy thighs which by this time in my sisters' lives were indeed of no inconsiderable size." Some sentences can only be called portly: "But about Alex Mercer himself there was something that made him forever fascinated by and sympathetic to that which he perhaps yearned after in spirit but which practically speaking he did not wish himself to become." Such measured verbal groping among the shadows of morality and good intention has suffered a diminishment since James; he had no commerce with God but had retained the religious sense. In Phillip Carver's world, no religion remains, just an old-fashioned code of behavior, and its defense is hard to distinguish from snobbery or, to use a word he uses of himself, lethargy. He is so imbued with lethargy that he speaks of "debating the question of how many angels could sit on the head of a pin" when in the conventional image, of course, the angels dance. He registers for the draft as a conscientious objector (in peacetime, early in 1941), but when the draft-board clerk fails to understand and sends in his form with the others, "this was *so* like a certain type of Memphis mentality . . . I could not even bring myself to protest"; he indifferently puts on his uniform and goes off to Fort Oglethorpe. When, six years later, he flees Memphis for New York, "it was as though someone else were dressing me and packing for me or at least as though I had no will of my own." And when, in 1967, he discovers himself in the same restaurant with his long-lost love, Clara Price, he doesn't trouble to get up from his chair and present himself; like those angels on the pin, he just sits. During his visits home, the dynamism of his ambitious father and animated, vengeful sisters oppresses him; it seems that they don't share his knowledge of "how consummately and irreversibly life had already passed us by." His narrative can scarcely bring itself to describe present events, and comes to life only when recapturing some moment or fact from the buried past. The prissy, circuitous language (confided to "notebooks" yet elaborately explanatory and in one spot openly concerned about "the reader") is flavored with anachronisms like "for the nonce" and "lad."

And yet this language, with its echo of old usages and once-honored forms, delivers things a less quaint diction could hardly express. Explaining the ugly second-hand furniture he and Holly have in New York, Phillip writes, "It was not the kind of furniture either of us had grown up with, but we felt that the presence of such plain objects in our rooms was proof of our not having succumbed to the sentimental aesthetics of domesticity." A beautiful fittingness develops whenever the father is the subject. "And what I must confirm is that this man, my father, this Mr. George Carver, did care more about clothes than any other man of his very masculine character and temperament that I have ever been acquainted with there in Memphis or here in Manhattan or in any other place at all." Balked by his dim sight from finding an empty table in a nightclub, the old man "simply stood still and waited for events to develop in his favor." His manner of posing and dressing, Phillip comes to see, was "his most direct means of communicating his aspirations and his actual vision of how things were with him." A page of reminiscence about his father's two cumbersome and cherished wardrobes culminates when, arriving at the Memphis airport and unexpectedly greeted by his elegantly clad progenitor, Phillip feels "as though someone had thrown open the double doors to one of those wardrobes of his and, figuratively speaking, I was inhaling the familiar aroma of his whole life and being. Only it wasn't like an aroma exactly. For one moment it seemed I was about to be suffocated. For one moment it was as if I had never left Memphis." Phillip's virtually morbid interest in costume delivers, too, a telling and vivid portrait of his two sisters, who into their fifties dress with an embarrassing rakishness, partly as parody of the Memphis (as opposed to the sedater Nashville) style and partly in protest at having been denied marriage and "frozen forever in their roles as injured adolescents." The father and sisters are old-fashioned characters, with costumes and settings and histories and psychologies; Phillip, by leaving the hinterland where clothes make a statement and the family "things" are worth inheriting, has become a non-character, a sensate shade dwelling in the low-affect regions of Don DeLillo and Donald Barthelme, a human being who assigns only a limited value, hedged about with irony, to himself. Some day, Phillip Carver fantasizes, he and Holly will simply fade away in their apartment—"when the sun shines in next morning there will be simply no trace of us." The lovers will not have been "alive enough to have the strength to die."

Peter Taylor's ingrown, overdressed Tennessee world is bleaker than Henry James's transatlantic empyrean, for it is a century more drained of the blood of the sacred. The sacred, Mircea Eliade has written, "implies the notions of *being*, of *meaning*, and of *truth*. . . . It is difficult to imagine how the human mind could function without the conviction that there is something irreducibly *real* in the world." For James, the real constituted the human appetites, mostly for love and money, that flickered beneath and secretly shaped the heavily draped society of late-Victorian times. By Mr. Taylor's time, appetite has shrivelled to dread— dread of another's aroma, of being suffocated by one's father's appetites. For all the fussy good manners of his prose, the ugly war between parents and children has been his recurrent topic; one thinks of the short story "Porte Cochere" (the house in *A Summons to Memphis* has a porte cochere), which ends with that old father, in the darkness of his room, while his adult children noisily besiege his door, taking out the walking stick "with his father's face carved on the head" and stumbling about "beating the upholstered chairs with the stick and calling the names of children under his breath." In *A Summons to Memphis*, Phillip Carver wins through to a real, non-trivial insight when he accepts "Holly's doctrine that our old people must be not merely forgiven all their injustices and unconscious cruelties in their roles as parents but that any selfishness on their parts had actually been required of them if they were to remain whole human beings and not become merely guardian robots of the young." The wrongs of the father are inevitably visited upon the son and daughter, as part of the jostle of "whole human beings" sharing the earth. Beneath his talky, creaking courtesies, Peter Taylor deals bravely with the primal clauses of the social contract.

Back in Midland City

DEADEYE DICK, by Kurt Vonnegut. 240 pp. Delacorte, 1982.

The latest of Mr. Vonnegut's bemused pilgrims is Rudolph Waltz, born in Midland City, Ohio, in 1932, and destined to fire, at the age of twelve, on random impulse, a bullet that strikes a pregnant woman right between the eyes while she is blamelessly running a vacuum cleaner eight blocks away. The young murderer thenceforth must bear the nickname of Deadeye Dick. He does not go to jail, being too young, but his father, a flamboyant would-be painter named Otto Waltz, does, and lawsuits by the dead woman's family wipe out the Waltz fortune. Rudy waits on his helpless parents in lieu of servants, and eventually becomes a druggist and writes a play, *Katmandu,* which runs one disastrous night Off Broadway. And oh yes, while Rudy and his brother, a reformed methaqualone addict and former network president, are in Haiti a neutron bomb accidentally or on purpose wipes out all the people in Midland City but leaves the buildings and machinery nicely intact. These and many more curious circumstances are related in Vonnegut's familiar and cherished voice of laconic ingenuousness. The moral outrage that lit up *Slaughterhouse-Five* and *God Bless You, Mr. Rosewater* has dimmed to a fireside glow, and a kind of valentine to the small-city Midwest is delivered. The author has smuggled a fair amount of feeling into this cartoon of a humble life (Rudy never marries, and rarely complains); less intellectually festive than *Slapstick,* more persuasive than *Jailbird,* the tale has its odd beauty and a middling place in a unique oeuvre.

Last Blague

THE KING, by Donald Barthelme. 158 pp. Harper & Row, 1990.

This short novel was completed by the author three months before his death, and for all its farce it wears a melancholy tinge. King Arthur and the other figures of the Round Table legends have gotten mixed up with England's last finest hour, the grim early phase of World War II. The book is written almost entirely in dialogue, and is concerned more with the sexual interplay between knights and ladies than with the inscrutable military action. Barthelme's magical gift of deadpan incongruity seems muted here by a puzzled diffidence too deep to shake. "This is not my favorite among our wars," Guinevere complains. "One has to think about so many different sorts of people one never thought about before. . . . Croats, for example. I never knew there was such a thing as a Croat before this war." Similarly, King Arthur "can't imagine what it would be like to be a churl. The country's full of them, yet I have no idea how they think." The Red Knight is a Communist, the Black Knight is an African, and the Grail is the atomic bomb:

> "There's a race on," said the Blue Knight, "to find the Grail. The other side is hard at it, you may be sure. Myself, I'm partial to cobalt. It's blue."

Arthur renounces the Grail-bomb as immoral, and with his faithless but loyal Queen placidly waits the tragic end needed to make his name "resound in song and story." Death is in the air: Launcelot has sat down with a reporter from the *Times* to settle the details of his obituary, and Arthur keeps wondering if he hasn't lived too long. For all the eschatological gloom, there are some unrestrained Barthelme riffs of pure light-fingered nonsense: Lord Haw-Haw is made to say in one of his traitorous broadcasts, "Wake up, Englishmen! This war is not your war. If you believe you'll win, you will also believe that featherbeds grow on trees and sneezing increases the size of the female bust." A pacifist tract, a rueful travesty, a bumptious "feast of blague," and a dazzlement of style both minimal and musical, *The King* has been elegantly produced, with fifteenth-century ornamental initials and nine of Barry Moser's customarily superb wood engravings.

What You Deserve Is What You Get

You Must Remember This, by Joyce Carol Oates. 436 pp. Dutton, 1987.

Joyce Carol Oates, born in 1938, was perhaps born a hundred years too late; she needs a lustier audience, a race of Victorian word-eaters, to be worthy of her astounding productivity, her tireless gift of self-enthrall-ment. Not since Faulkner has an American writer seemed so mesmerized by a field of imaginary material, and so headstrong in the cultivation of that field. She has, I fear, rather overwhelmed the puny, mean-minded critical establishment of this country; after the first wave of stories and novels (most notably, *A Garden of Earthly Delights* and *them*) crashed in and swept away a debris of praise and prizes, protective seawalls were built, and a sullen tide set in. Many of the critics began to treat Miss Oates as one of her many scholar heroines, Marya Knauer, is treated by her eighth-grade school instructor, Mr. Schwilk:

> Finally, Schwilk said airily, "You have a most *feverish* imagination," and handed the story back; and that was that.

The author could have been offering a self-caricature when the hero of her third novel, *Expensive People,* wrote, "Now that I'm started, now that those ugly words are typed out, I could keep on typing forever. A kind of quiet, blubbering hysteria has set in." Throughout the Seventies, the five-hundred-page novels piled up numbingly; *Do With Me What You Will* followed *Wonderland* and was followed by *The Assassins,* and in the Eighties, a trilogy of mammoth volumes in imitation of popular nine-teenth-century genres—*Bellefleur, A Bloodsmoor Romance, Mysteries of Winterthurn*—blurred to near invisibility the line between Miss Oates and the scribblers of gothic romances. Her move, in the late Seventies, from an address in Windsor, Ontario, across from Detroit, to a position in Princeton also helped demythologize her; New York critics were in awe of anyone who could live near Detroit, but felt they owed nothing to a resident of bucolic New Jersey. Through these vicissitudes of repute, and some of the harshest scoldings ever administered to a serious talent, Miss Oates has continued to devote her energy to literature in almost all of its forms. Her short stories seem to be everywhere, from fledgling quarterlies to *Esquire* and *Playboy.* Her one-act plays have been produced Off Broad-way. Her poems are being readied for a collected edition. Her criticism is generous and wide-ranging. With her husband, Raymond Smith, she edits the handsome *Ontario Review* and its line of books. Single-minded-ness and efficiency rather than haste underlie her prolificacy; if the phrase "woman of letters" existed, she would be, foremost in this country, enti-tled to it.

As reader and critic I have been as overwhelmed as the next, and cannot offer to lay out for dissection the hydra-headed monster of Miss Oates's oeuvre. But I can, and do, report that her latest novel, *You Must Remem-ber This,* rallies all her strengths and is powerful—a storm of experience whose reality we cannot doubt, a fusion of fact and feeling, vision and circumstance which holds together, and holds us to it, through our terror and dismay. While some of her fiction appears to be built almost entirely out of projected anxieties, this book has a sentimental substance; its title (from, of course, the lyrics of "As Time Goes By," of *Casablanca* fame) might be addressed by the author to herself. *You Must Remember This* is a historical novel of sorts, centered on the mid-Fifties, with traces of research in its passing references to Adlai Stevenson, Senator McCarthy, the Korean War, the Rosenberg executions, bomb shelters, and the popu-lar songs and prizefights and automobiles of the time. Some of the glimpsed headlines seem a touch opportune, and some of the historical themes (such as that of bomb shelters) feel rubbed into the plot with a bit too much determination, but the background events of the period are by and large feelingly translated into subjective experience, by an author who was there. The advent of television, for instance, into the American home comes back with a rush:

> Now the machine hummed nightly in the shadowy living room, its small screen glowed with an eerie atomic radiance, pale, bluish, ghostly, flickering. During the daytime Mrs. Stevick set up her ironing board so that she could watch whatever chanced to be on. . . . Her sister Ingrid came over once or twice a week to watch, Lizzie stayed home more often or met her boyfriends at other times, Mr. Stevick sat in his old leather chair, a magazine or a book open on his lap, yes he really was reading though he glanced up now and then to see what was going on, what sort of foolery the studio audiences were in an uproar about, there was Uncle Miltie simpering in a woman's taffeta evening gown, staggering in spike-heeled shoes, there was Lucy fluttering her inch-long eyelashes at Desi, there was Phil Silvers in his army officer's uniform smirking and leering, there was Ed Sullivan rubbing his hands together—like a funeral director, Mr. Stevick said. . . . Evenings that winter Enid did her homework with the door to her room ajar so she could hear the sound of the television downstairs. . . . Sometimes she looked up from her work, stricken with a curious kind of happiness. Hearing laughter down-stairs—downstairs at 118 East Clinton! It was amazing. It was unprece-dented. It would not have been possible without television.

The stale little Stevick household—father and mother and three daughters, Geraldine and Lizzie and Enid Maria—is the core of *You Must Remember This,* and its central action is the affair between Enid Maria and her half-uncle, Felix, a former prizefighter who is sixteen years older than she. The setting is one that has figured in Oates's fiction from the start—a tough small upstate city, here called Port Oriskany and situated, like her native Lockport, on a canal. Her authority within this city, her ability to move through its schools and streets and stores and bars, evoking a social grid on which individual lives and dreams and passions bloom and quickly wilt, is grimly absolute. A shifty wheeler-dealer called Al Sansom, in bad trouble with both the IRS and his gangster colleagues, insists that Felix meet him at a tavern and then talks drunkenly about flying saucers:

> Wide dark nostrils more prominent than usual, waxen sheen to the nose, a light coating of sweat on his forehead and Felix supposed he was tasting fear like scum in the mouth—Felix knew just how that tasted. He interrupted Al, saying abruptly, "Did you want us to get together to talk about that shit?" and while Al stared hurt he felt the impulse to laugh, adding, "or some other kind of shit?"

Al, with "the look . . . of a man in a rapidly falling elevator," decides against confessing his soon-to-be-fatal troubles, and they step out onto the "snowy cindery" parking lot. "There was a hard stiff wind from the lake tasting of cold, of snow, an underlying chemical smell from somewhere close by." The olfactory detail seems simple, but in the context of what has gone before—a ruined man groping for sympathy and getting none— the chemical whiff amid the snow and cold goes through us like a verdict of execution, and seems the breath of a majestically indifferent environment. Naturalism, the tradition that nurtures Miss Oates's best instincts, always reports this indifference in our environments. What is compelling here (as in some of Jayne Ann Phillips's work) is the avidity with which the characters' spirits attempt to feed on this basically inedible stuff, making dreams of machines and canals and railroad bridges, or staggering with a pitiable softness ("As Al Sansom got drunker his skin got softer, pulpier, like whitish dough") out into the cinders and snow and chemical smells.

Miss Oates knows her protoplasm. She sees our dark softness churn like flame. The novel begins with one of her ominous prologues, all in italics (her publishers, by the way, should find a better italic face for her; it is so much lighter than the Roman face that the words whisper when they mean to shout)—a string of one-sentence paragraphs describing fifteen-year-old Enid Maria Stevick happily attempting suicide by ingesting forty-seven aspirin tablets. In these days of frequently reported teen-age suicide, this fictional example, dated June 7, 1953, enlightens us; we are admitted to the seethe of passion, delusion, and calculation that rages behind the façade of a bright middle-class girl, and are shown how thin the membrane is between her erotic and her self-destructive compulsions. When she masturbates, it is felt as a flirtation with death: "How hard the heart could kick yet not burst: a muscle gone mad. Like the secret muscles between her legs frenzied and racing, contracting against her fingers. Each time Enid Maria thought she would die but she never died. There would be no end to it." She flirts, too, on the trampoline at school, bouncing "high and higher still, risking her neck," so that the gym teacher rebukes her; and in the swimming pool, "a place where Death was possible," diving and swimming underwater to exhaustion, so that afterwards "nothing could startle or hurt, for hours"; and by shoplifting downtown; and by losing herself in contemplation of her room's intricately patterned wallpaper, "feeling her soul slip thinly from her into the wallpaper where there was no harm, never any danger"; and by being drawn to the steep-sided canal that flows through Port Oriskany, and the narrow footbridge that crosses below the railroad trestle—"the footbridge was maybe five feet wide and shaky and if a train came by the noise was deafening, terrifying, the planks of the footbridge vibrated and it was natural to think the bridge would fall apart and you'd fall into the canal far below and drown. . . . The canal walls were thirty feet high just solid rock face and nothing to grab hold of except scrubby little trees that would break off in your hands. It had the look of a nightmare and Enid dreamed of it often."

Her affair with her uncle, too, is a flirtation with nothingness, beginning with a clumsy assault in a deserted Adirondacks hotel:

> Still he said nothing. He seemed hardly aware of her except as a presence, a body giving him some small unwitting resistance, his will was dominant, all-obliterating. Enid understood that he was detached from her and from the rather anguished mechanical act he had performed, even as he stood swaying drunken against her, his arm crooked around her neck locking her in place, his hot shamed face in her hair, still he was somehow separate from her, saying her name, her name, so sweet so sweet so sweet—he swallowed a belch and Enid smelled beer.

She accepts the obliteration, writing him, *"Anything you do to me—it's what I want."* Her attempted suicide, insofar as it is a romantic stratagem, demonstrates to him her toughness and places them on a plane of equality as death-defiers, as familiars of violence. Felix recognizes this: "He didn't love her but there was this connection between them now, this bond. A blood bond as if between two men who'd fought each other to a draw." He was, when younger, a promising boxer; Enid, at the age of nine, was taken to see him box, "a man in a white silk robe trimmed in gold his face cross-hatched with blood whom she didn't know and who didn't know her." With a child's sharp eyes she sees amazing things at the prizefight: "Enid, squinting through her fingers, transfixed, saw a blow of her uncle's strike the other man on the side of the head, a terrible blow so that sweat flew like sparks in the bright lights." She sees Felix's opponent hit by the knockout left hook, "lifting his chin from beneath, shaking free a rainbow of moisture, a flying skein of blood." She "felt her bowels cramp thinking it was something you shouldn't see but there it *was*," and afterwards in her dreams she "could taste the trickle of blood, the back of her tongue was coated with something slimy and red, she couldn't swallow."

Violence is not just the projection of inward tumult and fear; it *exists*— "there it *was*." Joyce Carol Oates, both the writer and the person, is drawn to boxing as a curiously intimate, visible, regulated, caged yet living specimen of the nightmare that surrounds our fragile shelters and delusively peaceful lives. Like Hemingway and Mailer, she suggests that violence is uniquely authentic. But Mailer's writing on boxing is sports journalism compared with the fight descriptions in *You Must Remember This*—especially the terrific pages (246–52) that show the destruction of young Jo-Jo Pearl by an older fighter, Byron McCord. Miss Oates's comma-stingy, onrushing style pays off in such runs as "and there suddenly was Jo-Jo staggering back into the ropes unable to fall and McCord hammering away at him to the heart to the gut to the head slicing him open around the eyes and mouth in a matter of seconds as if he's taken a razor to the flesh." A dreadful beauty, an illumination of what men can endure, attaches to a sentence like "Jo-Jo continued to circle him bouncing on his toes and feinting as if his body performed by rote while his head rang, aglow with pain so intense it had no name." We learn that a boxer goes for the other's eyes, with the thumbs and laces of his gloves; we learn that a hazard of ringside seats is having your camel-hair coat spattered with blood; we experience a boxer's childlike daze as he sinks toward death of "subarachnoid hemorrhaging." As far as this reader is concerned, the sport could be outlawed on the strength of this single horrendous, yet relentlessly factual, fight scene.

Sex, too, in Miss Oates's telling, is a nightmare come true. "She heard herself cry out helplessly, crazily—the delirious words *I love you I love love love you* or no words at all, only frightened sounds like those of a small child being beaten." Unblinkingly the processes are detailed whereby an adolescent girl is loosened up by red wine and vodka and enjoyed in a succession of motels, and initiated into the full range of sensual possibility, and so habituated to lying that she comes to like it, and kidnapped from her high-school lunch hour by her jealous older lover in his cream-colored Cadillac Eldorado, and impregnated in their erotic fury, and then subjected to an abortion. The abortion is as harrowing, and as calmly detailed, as Jo-Jo's fight. All earthly experience, it comes to seem, except for Enid's homework and her piano lessons, is founded on some basic desecration. Not only chemical smells haunt Port Oriskany but Roman Catholicism, a creed shunned by most of the characters but present in whiffs, as when Enid thinks, "Whatever happened she deserved. She knew she deserved it because it happened." This echoes a saying of Nietzsche's that appears in *Marya*, a recent book of linked short stories which presents, as it were, the academic, intellectually achieving aspect of Enid: "Marya noted a chilling aphorism of Nietzsche's. *Terrible experiences give one cause to speculate whether the one who experiences them may not be something terrible.*" Victim and criminal, death and love, dream and reality can fuse when subjectivity, instead of being regarded as a mere epiphenomenon within objective reality, is granted a power of its own. Miss Oates, her earlier jacket flaps told us, majored in English at Syracuse University and minored in philosophy; quotes from Heraclitus, Spinoza, William James, and others offer to orient us in her seething fiction. Something Neoplatonic, of Berkeley's *esse est percipi*, licenses her visionary outpouring. Her fictional worlds exist to be consumed by her characters' passions and perceptions; the universe has no meaning beyond its uses by the feverish human spirit, and does not receive, therefore, the kind of artistic homage that imitates its enduring structure. Her plots suggest not architecture but cloud formation, beginning and ending in air; there is rarely a sentence that arrests a moment for its own cherishable sake, in a crystallization of language. All is flowing, shifting context. Her worlds refuse to enclose, to be pleasant. Prayers arise from them, but no praise.

You Must Remember This, away from its consummate portraits of two violent wills, is relatively thin, but solid enough to frame those portraits. Lyle Stevick's tatty second-hand-furniture store and his jumbled timorous mind convince us; his obsession with a backyard bomb shelter seems somewhat allegorical. His three daughters neatly enact, as in a fairy tale, three possibilities open to girls in the Fifties: Geraldine marries into a local life of chronic pregnancy and domestic drudgery; Lizzie becomes a singer, an entertainer, and possibly a hooker in New York City; and Enid goes off to college.* Their brother, Warren, a Korean vet and an early anti-

---

*Whereas the heroine of *Marya* goes to college *in* Port Oriskany, from a city "two hundred-odd miles to the west," Enid Maria leaves Port Oriskany for the Westcott School of Music in Rochester. Higher education, not marriage, constitutes the post-feminist novel's

nuclear protester, becomes almost interesting enough to warrant a novel of his own. In this novel Miss Oates does a daring amount of male stream of consciousness: she lets us know how men feel battering at each other in a prize ring, lusting after hat-check girls, watching each other sink or swim, speeding along in their fancy cars, and struggling against their wandering thoughts to maintain an erection during lovemaking. A very full model of Port Oriskany is clairvoyantly, affectionately constructed, so that we can watch it burn.

Beattieniks

LOVE ALWAYS, by Ann Beattie. 247 pp. Random House, 1985.

Ann Beattie, though there has always been a kind of fond humor in her deadpan, delicate stories of languishing young lives and her willingness to transcribe the grotesquer details of American popular culture, has not hitherto been satirical. Satire must stand outside a world and its values; it implies a better way of doing things, a certain doctrinal position, whether it be Waugh's Catholicism, Orwell's anti-Communism, Twain's rough-neck skepticism, or Beerbohm's hermetic dandyism. There must be some energy of indignation, of rejection. Miss Beattie's power and influence, on the contrary, arise from her seemingly resistless immersion in the stoic bewilderment of a generation without a cause, a generation for whom love as well as politics is a consumer item too long on the shelves and whose deflationary mood is but dimly brightened by the background chirping of nostalgia-inducing pop tunes and the faithful attendance of personable pet dogs; in the now-swollen chorus of minimalist fiction, it was she who first found the tone for the post-Vietnam, post-engagé mood, much as Hemingway found the tone for his own generation's disenchantment with all brands of officially promoted importance. Both authors remade reality out of short, concrete sentences and certifiable if small sensations; in the absence of any greater good, the chronic appearance of food on the table became an event worth celebrating: "Edward made them tabouli burgers

---

absolving fadeout and happy ending. Enid walks the paths of her campus as if treading Heaven's golden streets: "Did she deserve this, any of it, this place of cobblestone paths and green quadrangles, Gothic buildings, soaring arches . . . ? Wave upon wave of happiness washed over her. *You don't deserve it,* she knew but she didn't care."

for lunch. He had brought these, frozen, in a cooler that said It's Miller Time!, from Los Angeles."

In *Love Always*, Miss Beattie seems to be on the attack, though her targets dissolve so quickly that she keeps popping new characters into the gallery. The scene is Vermont; some additional developments, along with frozen tabouli burgers, arrive from Los Angeles. The time is the summer of 1984, with nostalgic references to Walter Mondale, the porn-tainted Miss America, and the mass murder at McDonald's. Most of the characters are about thirty-five. The hero, called Hildon (like Madonna and Hildegarde, he has only one name), two years earlier founded an unlikely magazine called *Country Daze*, which has purportedly caught on with the nationwide tribe of aging Baby Boomers:

> Hildon was quite up front about telling his friends that the magazine's success was proof positive that the entire country was coked-out. Hundreds of readers wrote in every month—readers who had caught the slightest, trendiest in-jokes. . . . Thousands of people had filled out a request form, in the last issue, to have the psychmobile come to their houses. This was one of Hildon's new concepts; it was modeled on the idea of the bookmobile, but instead of books to check out, there was a staff of psychologists to evaluate people's mental condition and see whether they should be checked in.

Though this joke seems broad, the novel offers no evidence to contradict Hildon's fundamental diagnosis of the nation as "coked-out" (not to be confused with a later locution, "tranqued-up"). *Country Daze*'s most successful feature is Cindi Coeur's advice column, giving flip answers to flaky questions. E.g., "Boxstep Betty" writes in to complain that her fiancé "loves to dance" and "wants us to do the hand jive at our wedding and have break dancing at the reception"; "Cindi Coeur" advises "Box" to have her fiancé checked for pinworms. A literary device that in Nathanael West's *Miss Lonelyhearts* served to frame a furious protest against the world's pain has become, fifty years later, callous, freaky chatter, a kind of talk show in print.

Yet Lucy, who writes both questions and answers, is our heroine; amid all the incidental static and jokiness of the novel she emerges as its most sympathetic figure—"solid," her fourteen-year-old niece, Nicole, comes grudgingly to perceive. Nicole lives in Los Angeles with Lucy's truly coked-out sister, Jane, and is an actress on a soap opera called, with an allusion to Yeats we are not allowed to overlook, *Passionate Intensity*. While her mother carries on with a twenty-four-year-old tennis player, Nicole is shipped east, and brings to the merry band of Green Mountain Yuppies her Hollywood style of cultural imbalance: she is very up on television-serial personnel but has never heard of Jonah and the whale. Ms. Beattie is at her warmest with precocious and lonely children; Lucy's developing maternal feelings toward her spacy, famous, yet not invulnerable niece form one of the novel's few traceable themes. The novel holds a dazing wealth of anecdote and attributed eccentricity: Noonan, a homosexual writer for the magazine, likes to steal things; Peter, his lover and a specialist in *in utero* surgery, drives a refurbished Checker cab with leopardskin jump seats and a black bear rug; Piggy Proctor, Nicole's agent, communicates with her by taping antic TDK cassettes; Hildon likes to make love while viewing videotapes from other moments of his life and further enhances his existence by disguising himself, in a "Born to Lose T-shirt, torn jeans, pointed-toe boots with spurs," as a "shit kicker"—that is, a normal, local person. These locals, however, seem as prone to personality tics and infestation by media-think as the Manhattan émigrés, and the Forest of Arden called Vermont offers little contrast to the play of imported dissatisfaction that serves, in *Love Always*, for comedy.

The author's view of the world is not comedic: no conceivable social order could be drawn firm, in Shakespearean style, when her romantic hurly-burly exhausts itself. Marriage, the traditional end of comedy and of Jane Austen novels (Austen and Scott Fitzgerald haunt this book along with Yeats), ranks here as a disaster area: Lucy and Jane's father deserted them, Jane's husbands are wildly loserish, Lucy helps to break up Hildon's marriage without a flinch of compunction, and she, momentarily considered as wife-material by a long-time suitor, is rejected for the fey reason that "She was wonderful, but she wasn't right." The changing nature of heterosexual relations and, particularly, the Protean unsatisfactoriness of men prompt Lucy's most extended meditations:

> Whatever crazy thoughts men had about other people, they would eventually have about her. If they distrusted the whole world and trusted her implicitly, they would come to distrust her; if they were not close to anyone and they attached themselves to her, one day they would just remove themselves. If you demonstrated, day by day, that you were not the person they feared, they would be confused for a while, but gradually they would stop trusting logic and become frightened.

There is, in short, no pleasing men, on any kind of substantial basis; indeed, they have no substance, they are all pose and fantasy. Lucy accuses Les Whitehall, a previous beau: "When I tried to deal with you as a real person instead of idolizing you, you left." She reflects that, for all Les's charm, "in reality he did not approve of himself or of anyone else. Anyone who had less than he had wasn't worth his time, and anyone who had more was a threat." Hildon ends by perceiving that "nobody was his type." Les has written Lucy claiming of Hildon that he is in Vermont "in hiding from being a serious person." Hildon is an editor, though we never see him edit; Les is a teacher, though we never see him teach; Hildon hates Les. These two are rivals, the two romantic leads of Lucy's inner video-tape, yet are so interchangeable that Les finally slips into Hildon's job, while Hildon sinks into an ending as bitter and smoky as that of a Don DeLillo novel.

Unreality, insubstantiality, interchangeability: these make up the novel's agenda, and are built disturbingly into its texture. Many of the characters seem superfluous, but then perhaps they all, and we all, are superfluous. Several introduced early with a promising flourish, like Nigel the photographer and Cameron Petrus the Bostonian and Matt Smith the new publisher of *Country Daze,* fade away as if forgotten by their creator; others, such as Myra DeVane the investigative reporter, have a continuing presence in the novel but no defined personality. A second interviewer, Andrew Steinborn, enters the novel to illustrate, as if we doubted it, that a man can be an aspiring writer and still be a fool and a lout. His girlfriend, Lillian, finds his gift for empathy wearisome: "He wanted them to be very close, so whenever they had a disagreement, he would later say out loud what he intuited that she felt. It was scary; he would become her—when he spoke from what he thought to be her mind, even his face took on her likeness. It made her hate every thought she had, rational or irrational." Yet, eighty pages later, it is Les whom we witness performing this trick, with Lucy:

> He . . . jutted out his chin the way Lucy did when she was angry. "So you've got a new car, Les," he said. "Big deal . . . And the women are a notion pretty much like cars to you, aren't they? Turn one in, get another one. When you do these things, aren't you embarrassed? Or can you really pretend, pretend so well that you convince yourself?"

The characters are oddly transparent—jellyfish through which one keeps seeing the same saltwater. Myra DeVane has a tryst at the Plaza, after Andrew Steinborn has been extolling its *chic* to Lillian. Nicole tries to read *Pride and Prejudice,* the same book Lucy's mother read to her as a girl. Are these connections, or symptoms of a presiding carelessness? The events do not feel consecutive, scenes that we want to witness are left out, scenes developed at length come to little, and the plot is twitched back and forth as if in mimicry of *Passionate Intensity*'s episodes.

"The best lack all conviction," Yeats wrote, "while the worst / Are full of passionate intensity." These best and brightest lack conviction and with it the coherence that make fictional characters in the old-fashioned sense; they are not so much round or flat, in E. M. Forster's geometrical terminology, as on or off. Images on a cathode-ray tube are produced by a bombardment of electrons; a pointillist bombardment from the culture at large seems to conjure up Lucy and her friends, who wink out in their own minds as readily as in our own. Too much self-consciousness evaporates the self. All pursuits end up trivialized. Take away the brand names, the slogans, the nicely worked-out costumes and postures, and you have blank tape. Lucy intermittently looks around her, at what she imagines is Vermont:

> From where Lucy sat, she couldn't see the trickle of muddy river below. The farmhouse with the blue roof she had always loved was visible on the hillside, and people hardly larger than dots were moving around it—people and cows—more of those mysterious people who thought something and felt some way Lucy couldn't fathom. People who lived in a house in a valley.

Yet the reader has no reason to suppose that the house in the valley holds anything different; it is just another blip, a few more jiggling dots, on a screen called Lucy.

Leaving Home

THE ACCIDENTAL TOURIST, by Anne Tyler. 355 pp. Knopf, 1985.

Anne Tyler's tenth novel manages to leave Baltimore; its hero, Macon Leary, writes a series of travel guides under the pseudonym of "Accidental Tourist," and his creator, whose many virtues have not hitherto included cosmopolitanism, provides for him convincing, characteristically perky versions of London and Paris, Edmonton and Vancouver, as well as some vivid airplane rides. Transatlantic jet travel is authoritatively sketched:

> There was the usual mellifluous murmur from the loudspeaker about seatbelts, emergency exits, oxygen masks. He wondered why stewardesses accented such unlikely words. [Macon] angled his book beneath a slender shaft of light and turned a page. The engines had a weary, dogged sound. It was the period he thought of as the long haul—the gulf between supper and breakfast when they were suspended over the ocean, waiting for that lightening of the sky that was supposed to be morning although, of course, it was nowhere near morning back home. In Macon's opinion, morning in

other time zones was like something staged—a curtain painted with a rising sun, superimposed upon the real dark.

Real morning and real life are restricted to Baltimore, where Macon is one of four middle-aged siblings. His two brothers, Porter and Charles, after their marriages failed, moved in with their spinster sister, Rose, who still lives in the large house where they were raised by their grandparents; and Macon, after his wife leaves him and he breaks his leg, moves in also. There, they complete their daily routines by playing a card game, Vaccination, which they invented in their childhoods and which is too complex for outsiders to learn. The point of Macon's guidebooks is to provide the unadventurous, "accidental" American traveller with information that minimizes the trauma of leaving home: where in Stockholm to get Kentucky Fried Chicken, what restaurants in Tokyo offer Sweet'n Low, how to avoid conversation in airplanes ("Always bring a book, as protection against strangers. Magazines don't last"). His guides are manuals of cautious, systematic self-protectiveness; Ms. Tyler's lovingly detailed, lively procession, from novel to novel, of mild-mannered agoraphobes and habit-hugging families has in Macon produced its theorist and its critic. The novel explores more forthrightly than any of its predecessors the deep and delicate conflict between coziness and venture, safety and danger, tidiness and messiness, home and the world, inside and outside, us and them.

Anne Tyler never fails to produce a fluid, shapely story sparkling with bright, sharp images drawn from the so-called ordinary world. Her Baltimore, though a city of neighborhoods and ingrained custom, is also a piece of the American Northeast and of Western culture; her fiction readily relays the brand names and pop tunes and fashions of the moment, with special attention paid to shoe styles. Yet, unlike some younger writers, she does not imply that these flitting fads and headlines are all the culture there is. She is a Southern writer in her sense of the past; her old people have a fine vitality, and some of her most moving pages reconstruct an older time, as in *Searching for Caleb* and *Dinner at the Homesick Restaurant*. In her run of fiction since *The Clock Winder* (1972),* she has made Baltimore, as a site for imaginative construction, her own—John Barth tends to stick

---

*A novel in many ways similar, and in some ways superior, to the work under discussion—more boldly ranging in its characters, and with a livelier ambivalence in its attitude toward home and homeboundness. Its Emerson family, like the Learys, enjoys comfortable wealth and the rapport of conspirators, but it is a quarrelsome rapport, and the mother, like the one in *Homesick Restaurant,* is husbandless and regarded by the children as tyrannical and tiresome. Mrs. Emerson and her son Andrew are among the author's most notable domestic monsters. Her gifts as a carver of gargoyles have been perhaps underindulged.

to the water and Maryland's Eastern Shore, and Mencken's city belongs
to the Rooseveltian past. As a site, Baltimore is rich in characters and
various in locale, yet with a cloistered and backwards-gazing quality like
that of a less drastic Yoknapatawpha County, with the same convenience
to a microcosm-maker.

Ms. Tyler's free rein there, with her artistic version of the metropolis
unchecked by any other (compare the multiple shadows New York writers cast upon each other, or the way that Bellow must repeatedly shoulder
aside Dreiser's and Algren's and Farrell's ghosts in dealing with Chicago),
abets our impression of a toy city, manipulated a bit lightly. Her generous
empathy and distinguished intelligence run toward moments of precious
diminishment. In the course of this novel, the Learys, all in their forties,
fall to making together a dollhouse extension, and the author's own delight breathes over their shoulders:

> The garage was convincingly untidy. Miniature wood chips littered the floor
> around a stack of twig-sized fire logs, and a coil of green wire made a perfect
> garden hose. Now they were working on the upstairs. Rose was stuffing an
> armchair cushion no bigger than an aspirin. Charles was cutting a sheet of
> wallpaper from a sample book. Porter was drilling holes for the curtain rods.

Her characters whittle away at playful hobbies, and tinker at witty inventions. The cuteness of the names invented, in *The Accidental Tourist,* for
fictional businesses savors less of mimesis than of literary foolery: Doggie,
Do is an outfit that trains canines; Re-Runs names a second-hand-shoe
store. Some of the Learys' behavior seems unlikely even for reclusive and
order-obsessed eccentrics. Macon treads underfoot each day's dirty laundry while giving himself a shower, mounts a washbasket on a skateboard,
and sleeps in "a giant sort of envelope made from one of the seven sheets
he had folded and stitched together on the sewing machine." His sister,
Rose, "had a kitchen that was so completely alphabetized, you'd find the
allspice next to the ant poison," which gives the reader a laugh but keeps
Rose at a distance. And are we seriously to believe of the Learys that four
prosperous adults enjoy such tenuous connections with the world at large
that they casually agree not to answer the telephone in their house, ever,
day after day? They just let it ring.

The Accidental Tourist is lighter than its wholly admirable and relatively
saturnine predecessor, *Dinner at the Homesick Restaurant.* Ms. Tyler takes
her time developing her story and fills much of the novel's first third with
domestic slapstick of the alphabetized-kitchen, treading-the-wash variety.
The story is a basic one of break-up and break-out. A year before the
novel's first scene, the rude outside world has dealt Macon and his wife

of twenty years, Sarah, a cruel blow: Ethan, their twelve-year-old son—"a tall blond sprout of a boy with an open, friendly face"—was senselessly murdered in a Burger Bonanza by a nineteen-year-old holdup man. Now Sarah announces that Macon has been no comfort and she is leaving him. Living alone, he breaks his leg and returns to his grandfather's house, where he and his three siblings play Vaccination and ignore the telephone. However, the misbehavior of his pet dog, an irritable Welsh corgi called Edward (and up to midpoint the novel's most sympathetic and intelligible character), brings into this airless situation a rasping breath of oxygen— dog-trainer Muriel Pritchett, who is younger, poorer, more vulgar and dynamic than Macon. That her brash and open world-view shakes up the careful Leary ways is predictable, as is the revival of Sarah's interest when Macon makes himself at home with this new woman. But the turns and climaxes unfold with many small surprises, and after a high point (liter- ally) where Macon panics at the revelation of distance afforded from what appears to be the top of the World Trade Center ("He saw the city spread far below like a glittering golden ocean, the streets tiny ribbons of light, the planet curving away at the edges, the sky a purple hollow extending to infinity") the book becomes a real page-turner. This susceptible reader, his eyes beginning to blur, stopped twenty pages short of the end, fell into a troubled sleep, woke before dawn, read to the end, and only then relaxed. It is a happy ending, as happy as one can be in a world where "After a certain age . . . you can only choose what to lose."

In a time when many women writers find themselves quite busy enough proclaiming the difficulties of being female, Anne Tyler persistently con- cerns herself with the moral evolution of male characters. Though mild, passive Macon is not exactly macho, we live in his masculine skin for three hundred and fifty pages and see through his eyes what he sees in both women—plump, solid Sarah with her "calm face, round as a daisy," skinny Muriel with her "spiky, pugnacious fierceness" and her eyes "very small, like caraway seeds." The wife is rather more winningly portrayed than the girlfriend, and Macon loves her with less effort, but he gropes beyond that: "He began to think that who you are when you're with somebody may matter more than whether you love her." With Sarah, he has been, as she herself charges, "muffled." She tells him, "It's like you're trying to slip through life unchanged." Yet she herself confirms the basis of the Leary caution: the world is a terrible place. "Ever since Ethan died," she tells him, "I've had to admit that people are basically evil. Evil, Macon. So evil they would take a twelve-year-old boy and shoot him through the skull for no reason. I read a paper now and I despair; I've given up watching the news on TV. There's so much wickedness, children setting other children on fire and grown men throwing babies out second-story windows, rape and torture and terrorism, old people beaten and robbed, men in our very own government willing to blow up the world, indifference and greed and instant anger on every street corner."

Muriel takes Macon outside himself. And distinctly beneath his own social level. *An Accidental Tourist* is about, in part, crossing class boundaries. One doesn't have to be a Baltimorean to perceive that Singleton Street, where Muriel lives with her sickly and repulsive seven-year-old son, Alexander, and Timonium, where her parents dwell in a development called Foxhunt Acres, are a far socio-economic cry from North Charles Street, where Macon and Sarah had their home, and the unnamed avenue where Macon's grandfather, a factory owner, reared his four grandchildren. Macon went to Princeton, and nothing about Muriel exasperates him more than her solecisms—"eck cetera," "nauseous" when she means "nauseated," "enormity" when she means to talk of size, "da Vinci" when she should say "Leonardo," and (very subtle, this) "a nother," as in "I wish I was just a totally nother person."

It is Macon, however, who becomes another person: "In the foreign country that was Singleton Street he was an entirely different person." An accidental tourist within Baltimore, "he was beginning to feel easier here. Singleton Street still unnerved him with its poverty and its ugliness, but it no longer seemed so dangerous." The hoodlums hanging out, he perceives, are "pathetically young and shabby," and children and women bring a constant cleansing wind of "good intentions." The scruffy society of neighborhood women that collects in Muriel's kitchen comes to feel as cozy to him as a game of Vaccination; one wonders, indeed, whether he truly adjusts to this tawdry neighborhood or whether it has been simply annexed to the gaily colored, miniaturized precincts of Tylerville. "Macon saw Singleton Street in his mind, small and distant . . . and full of gaily drawn people scrubbing their stoops, tinkering with their cars, splashing under fire hydrants." A mugger accosts them, but Muriel swats him with her purse and tells him to run on home. Can Baltimore's underworld really be this easily disarmed? When Mrs. Soffel, in last year's movie of the same name, left her safe quarters in the warden's end of the Allegheny County Jail for disgrace and likely doom with an escaping criminal, that was de-domestication with a price tag. Macon doesn't so much leave home as change homes; retaining his money, he, like many before him, finds the slums more fun than the proper neighborhoods.

But yes, people are not evil. Or not *only* evil. And they prove more responsive and entertaining than a stay-at-home would suppose. Muriel has never travelled. When she tells Macon, "If I could go anywhere I'd go to Paris," he quickly informs her, "Paris is terrible. Everybody is impolite." Yet in the eventual event (not to give away Ms. Tyler's slam-bang denouement) Paris for Muriel abounds with polite, helpful, English-speaking persons, who guide her toward fantastic bargains in second-hand clothes. Throughout the book, people spontaneously open up and talk about themselves—taxi-drivers, airplane pilots, neighbors, camp directors. Anne Tyler's mankind is a race of compulsive fabulists: everybody in motion, talking. Looking out of a plane window as he takes Muriel for her first flight, Macon has "an intimate view of farmlands, woodlands, roofs of houses. It came to him very suddenly that every little roof concealed actual lives. Well, of course he'd known that, but all at once it took his breath away. He saw how real those lives were to the people who lived them—how intense and private and absorbing." Though not every mug-ger can really be chased away with a swat, and not every Parisian is in fact polite to American yokels, an assumption to the contrary offers a basis for moving ahead. We should credit strangers and outsiders with a self-interest as intense and complex as our own—not an obvious fact to the initially timorous and solipsistic human organism—and with a benignity to match our trust. If Anne Tyler strikes us as too benign, too swift to tack together shelter for her dolls, it may be that we have lost familiarity with the comedic spirit, the primal faith in natural resilience and the forces of renewal. Like the older, graver Iris Murdoch, Ms. Tyler believes in love and art and the usefulness of a shaking-up. The constructive, tinkering, inventive, systematic side of our selves is not enough; he who would save his life must lose it.

"It occurred to [Macon] that the world was divided sharply down the middle: Some lived careful lives and some lived careless lives, and every-thing that happened could be explained by the difference between them. But he could not have said, not in a million years, why he was so moved by the sight of Muriel's thin quilt trailing across the floor where she must have dragged it when she rose in the morning." He cannot say, but the book itself slyly spells it out: Macon's mother, Alicia, glimpsed but rarely in the novel, is herself of the party of the careless. A woman of tempestu-ous and fleeting enthusiasms, she had been widowed in World War II and in 1950 remarried, to "an engineer who travelled around the world build-ing bridges," and settled her four children with their grandparents in Baltimore. "They were met by their grandparents, two thin, severe, distinguished people in dark clothes. The children approved of them at once." Henceforth, "like some naughty, gleeful fairy," their mother "darted in and out of their lives leaving a trail of irresponsible remarks." When Rose marries, Alicia, now on her fourth husband, startles Macon by being at the wedding, displeases him with her gaudy outfit ("a long white caftan trimmed with vibrant bands of satin, and when she reached up to hug him a whole culvert of metal bangles clattered and slid down her left arm"), and links arms with Muriel. "Macon had a sudden appalling thought: Maybe in his middle age he was starting to choose his mother's style of person, as if concluding that Alicia—silly, vain, annoying woman—might have the right answers after all. But no. He put the thought away from him." But the thought is a good one. We are all, however careful, the children of chaos. Leaving home can be going home.

No More Mr. Knightleys

SUPERIOR WOMEN, by Alice Adams. 368 pp. Knopf, 1984.

Take a group of female college friends. Simmer them in the post-graduate decades, tossing in timely headlines and fashions to taste. Add lovers, husbands, fathers, deaths, and at least one lesbian relationship. Bring to a boil close to the present time, and serve. This recipe, or something like it, seems to be a popular one; Rona Jaffe can't stay away from reunions, and Mary McCarthy's *The Group* put Candice Bergen in the movies. Now Alice Adams has come up with *Superior Women*, which takes five Radcliffe students—Megan Greene, Lavinia Harcourt, Peg Harding, Cathy Barnes, and Janet Cohen—from their first meeting in June of 1943, in Cambridge, to a June exactly forty years later, in northern Georgia. Readers of Ms. Adams's short story "Roses, Rhododendron" will be reminded of it—it, too, tells of female friendship dating from the Forties and sustained by letters, though the girls are ten instead of seventeen. As in the pairing of Lavinia and Megan, the one girl is cool and Southern and the other is needy and "hot," with an eccentric mother and the antique business in her background; superficially antithetical, both girls are intelligent and bookish and become, somehow, one. Such female alliances repeat throughout *Superior Women*, in a number of forms, across an American landscape of great breadth and sharp detail. Cambridge and Boston, New York and White Plains, Fredericksburg and Chapel Hill, Palo Alto and San Francisco, West Texas and northern Georgia are some of the locales knowingly evoked; as the characters become ever more mobile, erotic trysts take them to momentarily vivid hotel rooms in Alaska and Hawaii, so that a survey of our American vastness, not omitting the newer states, appears to be in progress. As happened in *The Group* twenty years ago, a natural short-story writer's avidity for the telling detail becomes, extended over a wide-ranging plurality of characters and events, rather actuarial; a certain bleakly notational texture overtakes the survey, and the reader feels that he is not so much enjoying vicarious experience as sampling data.

The first hundred pages of *Superior Women* move slowest and least skimmingly; they take place at Radcliffe between 1943 and 1946. Megan, back home in Palo Alto, has been smitten by "a post–prep school boy from New England," George Wharton, whose "compellingly exotic" looks, clothes, and accent excite her to a lifelong romance with things Eastern. She comes to Radcliffe—a bold, continent-spanning move—and meets the four other superior women of the title, all bright, we are somewhat insistently assured, and all resident in Barnard Hall; Janet Cohen, because she is Jewish, stands apart from her three housemates, of whom Lavinia is outspokenly anti-Semitic. The intricacies of remaining "technical virgins," the degradations of dating drunken and inept college boys, the rise and fall of romantic passions, the subtle but intensely felt shifts of closeness among the young women are lovingly and expertly laid bare. Megan, the most full-bodied and ardent of them, surrenders her virginity to a Jewish section man, Simon Jacoby, while her original heartthrob, George Wharton, defects to a girl of his social class; Lavinia crosses her own class lines to love the Irish Gordon Shaughnessey, who inconsiderately dies of a burst appendix; Peg unexpectedly collapses into pregnancy and marriage; Cathy is whirlwind-courted by her fellow Catholic "Phil-Flash" Flannigan; and Janet remains the patient admirer of the exuberant, foulmouthed, gifted, and Marxist Adam Marr. Graduation Day arrives and they go their separate ways, if they haven't already gone. Janet marries Adam, and Lavinia, done mourning Gordon Shaughnessey, marries the uninspiring but presentable Potter Cobb. Megan, after a year in Paris with the Marrs and others, travels to New York, carries on with a gorgeous black trombonist called Jackson Clay, works in publishing, and becomes a prosperous literary agent. She lives on West Twelfth Street; uptown, Lavinia settles into an East Sixties life of parties, interior decoration, and creeping discontent. Peg endures four children and the Texas climate until fondness for her Negro cook, Cornelia, leads her into social consciousness and rebellion. Cathy attends graduate school at Stanford and sees a fatherly priest a few times too often. As to the Marrs, Adam makes a great splash as a playwright and goes from being obnoxious to atrocious, while the divorced Janet heads for the haven of a medical degree. And that's not the half of it; the book in its latter stretches has so much plot, so summarily relayed, that it reads like the class notes crowded at the back of an alumnae magazine. Children and traumas and political movements are reduced to rumors that pop up in letters or conversations among the rapidly aging old friends; it all bounces along so briskly that the author seems to assign no importance to these events save a demographic one: this is what tends to happen to you if you graduated from Radcliffe in 1946. Typically, you marry, are miserable, have some miserable children, and take comfort in pills and affairs (Lavinia) or communal living and liberal activism (Peg).

Though there is a good deal of ethnic cross-reference in the text of *Superior Women*, its many characters fall almost entirely into four groups: blacks, Jews, Irish Americans, and upper-class Wasps. The Wasps are the heavies, with their ghastly clubbiness and haughty prejudices; just their melodious names—Lavinia Harcourt, George Wharton, Potter Cobb, Connie Winsor, Cameron Sinclair, Price Christopher—would make even a middle-of-the-road reader see red, and when the toniest name of them all, Henry Stuyvesant, turns out to have no money and to have once joined the Communist party, we still find it hard to love him. Whereas the blacks are beautiful people: Jackson Clay a great musician, if a little stoned in his later, Hawaiian phase, and Cornelia loyal and gentle and so intelligent that just a perfunctory sprinkling of money turns her from a cook into a schoolteacher, and Vera, who is Mexican and only *looks* black, the perfect match at last for dear, big, good-hearted Peg. The Jews, too, are beyond reproach. Whatever the job set before them, they do it: Janet Cohen Marr becomes a good intern ("Considered very able, I believe," Dr. George Wharton grudgingly admits), and her son Aron has written "a very good novel," about a gay relationship; Barbara Blumenthal, the literary agent who hires Megan, "is a very successful woman, who manages at the same [time] to be quite simply *nice*"; and Simon Jacoby, to whom Megan entrusts her defloration, does it ably and nicely. Blacks and Jews, in this book, are invariably figures of comfort. Wasps represent privilege and power; their hegemony, covertly asserted in a conspiracy of correct schools and addresses, of intertwining acquaintanceships and similar family antiques, becomes overt in the sinister figure of Harvey Rodman, a crippled and fantastically rich insider in the administration of Richard Nixon. He boasts to Lavinia, "It's exciting how few people we've managed to get it down to, just a very few, in total control. There's not much spreading around these days, baby doll, in terms of real power." And, somewhat like Fu Manchu in bygone days, "he laughs, excitingly." Only the Irish have in them the potential to be good or bad—to be human, in short. Adam Marr, though he doesn't seem—"light brown curly hair, a big nose, thin face, and large, intense blue eyes"—very Irish, is labelled as such and clearly designed, with his sensitivity and outrageousness, to arouse ambivalent feelings in the reader; Cathy Barnes, too, remains mysterious, as her wit turns to bitterness, and her austerity to martyrdom. Megan Greene, the heart and heroine of the novel, oscillates between her "strong, eager needs" and her habit of getting top marks, between her sexual and her intellectual prowess, between her passion for the circumspect Henry James and her headlong falls into love.

Lavinia and Megan are, like the two little girls of "Roses, Rhododendron," matched opposites: "tall thin blond, impeccably expensively dressed Lavinia—and plump dark Megan, in her slightly wrong California clothes." The compounded attraction and repulsion between them should be the axis of the novel, around which its many lesser worlds turn. If this doesn't quite work, it is not for any failing of vitality and believability on Megan's part but because Lavinia doesn't get, as a character, a fair shake. Her purported intelligence ("Actually, perhaps surprisingly, Lavinia herself has a remarkably high IQ; in those numerical terms the two girls are identical") is buried under the reflexive snobbery, the feral schemingness, the ossified narcissism that the author loads upon her, for political reasons: she symbolizes the sterility of the haves. Too rarely is Lavinia allowed to shed the accoutrements of her class. Toward the end, she and Megan have parallel breakdowns, and for a moment, dreadfully feeling her fifty years of self-indulgent, wasted life, she stands naked and confused: "But then she begins to cry again—crying, shivering, everything out of control, nothing as intended, as meant. She is an ugly white old woman, all gooseflesh, crying, crying, and every single minute getting older, uglier." Momentarily rescued, by Megan's lover, from this ugliness, she uses the rescue to perpetrate ugliness of her own design; the author restores her to her formal status as "rich and beautiful and rich and wicked" and drops her from the novel like a used-up poppet. She has amounted to less than we might have hoped from the Radcliffe pages. Megan, self-described as "poor and innocent and slightly simple," is intended to command our sympathy, and does; but are we supposed to feel something lamely collegiate about her life's culmination, in 1983, at a feminine dormitory in the Georgia hills, meddling in good works among the Atlanta underclass and snuggling into her weekend visitations from a Chapel Hill professor? Are we supposed to suspect that her tried-and-true beau, his physical charms detailed down to (or up to) his giraffelike eyelashes, is just a senior wimp? They once intended to marry, but put it off for one of the strangest reasons in romantic fiction: they were depressed by the election of Richard Nixon as President. "Both Megan and Henry find it surprising that this event should be a factor in their personal lives, but the truth is that they are both so depressed by Nixon that they are stunned into a sort of immobility."

Superior Women, indeed, makes much of Nixon, who may end by finding his way into more works of the literary imagination than any executive since King Arthur. World War II whisks by in a hazy flecking of uniforms, and of Korea and Kennedy's assassination there is not a mention, but Nixon and Watergate get right into bed with Ms. Adams's characters, causing impotence in one instance and celibacy in another.

Internal references indicate that the author had in mind, as models for this narrative, the schoolgirl novels of Jessie Graham Flower and Jane Austen's novels of female education and (as a graduation prize) marriage. The superior women, at college, entertain no expectation higher than the materialization of "the knight (ah! Mr. Knightley!), the perfect figure of romance." As Nina Auerbach, in her fine *Communities of Women: An Idea in Fiction,* has pointed out, the women in Austen are waiting for the door to open, and the gentlemen to enter. Elizabeth Bennet of *Pride and Prejudice* can scarcely stand the suspense: "Anxious and uneasy, the period which passed in the drawing-room, before the gentlemen came, was wearisome and dull to a degree, that almost made her uncivil. She looked forward to their entrance, as the point on which all her chance of pleasure for the evening must depend." Over a century later, the girls of Barnard and Bertram Halls are still pinning their chance of pleasure on the male visitors, though the dates as described are horror shows of compulsory drunkenness and frantic fumbling. The girls stagger back to the dorm like shell-shocked soldiers from the front, and even good-natured Megan is hard-pressed to find the bright side of being pawed on the cold dirt underneath a Charles River bridge. And yet, though four of the five become career women of a sort, their lives are chronicled in terms of amorous discovery and conquest, of multiple orgasms and helpless heartbreak. Looking back on the college years, Megan reflects, "The fact that Phil-Flash was on the whole a jerk now seems less important than that with him Cathy was confident, and happy. As she so visibly now is not."* As the novel progresses, the reader's heart learns to sink whenever a white heterosexual male enters the scene, for to a man they are crude, exploitive, and ultimately feckless. The black Jackson Clay doesn't disappoint, of course, nor do Megan's Paris pal Danny and her New York pal Biff; both are homosexuals. Naturally Megan asks herself, "Are gay men really nicer than so-called straight men?" Adam Marr, for whom she has always felt an unaccountable sneaking fondness, turns out to have been a closet homosexual, which explains the fondness. The plight of the superior

---

*Anne Tyler's Macon Leary came to the same conclusion: "Who you are when you are with somebody may matter more than whether you love her."

woman, as he once explained it to Megan, is that "Just any old guy won't do. You wouldn't like him, and even if you did your strength would scare him. . . . Inferior men are afraid of you." Since, on the evidence marshalled here, all men are inferior, the plight is universal. Stop watching the door, ladies, and ask yourselves to dance.

The novel, written in a swifter and less parenthetical style than Alice Adams sometimes employs, reads easily, even breathlessly; one looks forward, in the chain of coincidences, to the next encounter, knowing that this author always comes to the point from an unexpected angle, without fuss. Momentous scenes are dispatched in a page; Cathy's life, especially, seems more rumor than reality. Though not short, the book feels edited, by a racing blue pencil that leaps the years. One would have liked to spend more time with these people, who seem even visually underdeveloped. There are too few eye-opening descriptions like this, of Megan's mother, a carhop waitress grown old:

> Her hair, for so many years bleached and dyed a brassy bright blond . . . now has grown out several inches, at least two, past blond to white, a bright clean white, as startling in its way as the blond hair was. Her face is weathered, tanned. "Rain or shine, I walk my five miles a day, and sometimes more. I like it outdoors," Florence has explained. "May have ruined my skin, though. Doctors tell us everything too late, it seems like to me." Her skin is less ruined than it is intensely wrinkled. With her small nose and round brown eyes, and the violent band of white hair, she has the look of a monkey, an impression increased by the animation, the energy involved in all her gestures, her facial expressions.

And this reader would have gladly absorbed even more bits of specifically feminine wisdom than are granted. We learn, for example, that sex is good for your skin and that "it is extremely important, always, to pretend to believe whatever a man is saying . . . never accuse them of lying." These insights are courtesy of Lavinia; Megan perceives that men who dislike women express it by marrying a lot of them, and that, sadder still, there is "a connection . . . between crippledness and romantic extremity." Only the deformed and self-loathing can really love—that is, idealize—another. To such stark but not unbearable conclusions Megan's pilgrimage brings her, and to a relationship in which, we are assured, the man and she "exchange a small smile, of the most intense affection." The traditional joys of motherhood find no place in *Superior Women;* the children are forlorn and deplorable where they are not mercifully absent. Megan's main discovery, as she approaches sixty, is herself as a daughter; her path has led back to that basic superior woman, her (or anybody's) mother.

Louise in the New World, Alice on the Magic Molehill

IN SEARCH OF LOVE AND BEAUTY, by Ruth Prawer Jhabvala. 251 pp. Morrow, 1983.

ALICE IN BED, by Cathleen Schine. 228 pp. Knopf, 1983.

The title of Ruth Prawer Jhabvala's new novel evokes that of Proust's great opus in search of lost time, and much else about the novel is also Proustian: its aristocratic milieu, where there is always enough money to finance romance; its multi-generational scope; its free movements back and forth in time; its frequent scenes of sexual spying; its interest in Jewishness and homosexuality as modes of estrangement; and its insistent moral that human love will always find an unworthy object. Louise Son-nenblick, the handsome, robust heroine, born a German (like all of the first generation of these love-and-beauty-seeking characters) and a Protestant, is in love with Leo Kellermann, a pudgy blond pseudo-psychologist who manages in his fifty years of American residency to establish himself as a shady kind of guru. Bruno, Louise's dapper, dutiful, dainty German-Jewish husband, a wealthy thread-manufacturer in the Old World, is in love with his brazenly faithless wife. Marietta, their daughter and only child, briefly loves and unfortunately marries Tim, the alcoholic scion of an old Hudson Valley family. Mark, their son, a homosexual, loves Kent, a pretty but sluggish American roughneck. Natasha, a homely and prodi-giously passive "one-hundred-percent-guaranteed Jewish child" whom Marietta has adopted, loves Mark. Marietta also loves Mark and India—both of them hard to control. And Leo, charmer though he has been, as an old man loves the spacy Stephanie, with whom he is impotent. As if this roll of poorly requited passions were not extensive enough, Mrs. Jhabvala has adorned her elaborate monument to quixotic cathexis with accessory figures like Janet, one of Leo's many unhappy and befuddled clients, who is so in love with "an Iranian—or was she an Iraqi?—girl who claimed to be a princess and certainly looked like one" that she slashes her wrists, and Anthony, a middle-aged homosexual who is so in love with Kent that he tries to stab Mark with a carving knife. It is Janet's story that yields the phrase of the title, "in search of love and beauty," and it is Anthony's face that epitomizes our lovelorn misery: "His eyes, when they met Mark's, were pale and drained of color as though washed by nights of tears." Later, Natasha sees "that his eyes were washed and dimmed not only by these recent tears but by days and nights and years of them."

These last quotations indicate one respect wherein this novel does not resemble Proust—a certain hurried flatness of the prose; the authorial voice assumes a tone of gossip and summation before the characters have earned our interest and, briskly racing around the ambitious territory staked out, does not always provide the specificity of which this fine writer is capable. In Proust's interweave of romantic delusions, the glory of the descriptions, as the narrator strives to recapture the past, redeems everyone, even characters as tawdry as Jupien and Morel; in *In Search of Love and Beauty* no one is redeemed.

Yet the novel contains a world of knowing and many vivid scenes that in sum yield a colorful picture of what America meant to the upper-class Germans who immigrated here during the Thirties, and what they made of it. Like the Russians who came to Berlin a decade before, they retained as much of their social and actual furniture as possible. Bruno, who goes walking in Central Park in spats and a dove-gray homburg, feels most at home in his "large, lofty" West Side apartment: "not only was it filled with his family furniture but it also had the same high ceilings, vestibule and corridor, and sliding doors between the living and dining rooms as [his ancestral] house in the Kaiserallee." Louise's chic friend Regi, in contrast, has a Park Avenue apartment "done up in the Bauhaus style she had brought with her as absolutely the latest thing," with glass-and-chrome furniture and white wolf rugs. As Leo Kellermann charms both women into aiding his nebulous enterprises, both apartments are called into service: "Since Regi's apartment was starkly modernistic with a lot of empty space, it was more suitable for the physical expression classes; while the theoretical lectures remained at Louise's." To cater to the German refugee community, a posh restaurant called the Old Vienna opens— "the deep-blue buttoned banquettes, the velvet curtains with gold-fringed valances over panels of white lace, the chandeliers hanging down as thick and fast as paper lanterns"—and here at the center row of tables Louise and Regi, in girlhood called The Inseparables and now, like the century, in their thirties, make a splendid impression: "Their legs were too long to fit under the table, so they kept them crossed outside, long and smooth in silk. Both were elegantly dressed—Louise in one of her sober, well-cut suits of very expensive material with a fox-fur piece around her neck; and Regi much more flamboyantly in a long-skirted, clinging crêpe de Chine dress with masses of jewelry hung like booty all over her." With this vision indelibly in mind, the reader follows the two Teutonic beauties back and forth over the years, until the grisly last scenes of senility and death are attained.

Marietta, of the second generation, had no European girlhood to shape her, and in her American unease turns toward India, the site of most of Mrs. Jhabvala's previous fiction. A sure affection relaxes and lifts the prose when it describes Ahmed, the musician (he plays the sarod) whom Marietta takes as a lover, and Sujata, the huge female singer who, raised as a courtesan, supports a typically extensive Indian household where Marietta becomes a guest. Sujata, too, has had a career of painful loves—her son's father "had been a pimp and occasionally a pickpocket, an unworthy youth in every way"—and her son is a replica of his father and "now, what was worst of all, worse than anything, Sujata was in love again." But Indian philosophy, unlike that of German Americans, can accommodate these ruinous lurches of the heart:

> Then she grew very serious and very seriously she asked Marietta, as though expecting her to have the answer, that if it was so wrong to have these feelings, then why were they sent? If it was wrong, if it was shameful, then why was it there? And why was it so glorious?

The third generation, with its credit cards and drugs and religious sects overseen by charlatans, lacks the concept of glory. Mark, a conscientious child much leaned upon by his husbandless mother, becomes a successful realtor and a suave invert, but runs a constant low fever of depression: "He remembered Anthony's eyes and a sense of his own future passed through him in a shudder." Natasha, seeing that Leo, so shrewd a manipulator of others, is helplessly in love himself, is depressed by the thought, "for it seemed to her that there just wasn't enough love to go round and never would be—not here, not now—with everyone needing such an awful lot of it." And so dispirited a conclusion dulls the brilliance of this novel, wherein the characters possess intelligence and ardor but never a sense of choice or a motive for self-sacrifice, and are condemned, even the ebullient Louise, to figure in the universe as no more than witnesses of the inexorable dissolution that time achieves. The permutations and incidents of this chronicle are like Bruno's displaced and eventually lacklustre furniture: "The convoluted carvings of screens and furniture had an accumulation of dust that seemed to add to their ponderous weight."

The title of *Alice in Bed*, a sprightly first novel by Cathleen Schine, evokes another Alice, and in truth our nineteen-year-old heroine does seem to be frequently in Wonderland:

> At that moment, Alice lay on her stomach on a table. Her legs were trussed behind her and hung from the ceiling like a ham. "Get me outta here," she called occasionally.

"Leave it to me," the staff nurse said, and Alice was pulled up in bed, her feet were put on footrests, and the rest of her was twirled until her shoulders pressed against the back of the chair. She seemed to be sitting, but was actually several inches above the seat.

The nurse said, "There!"

Alice, rigid, resembled the figure in the middle frame of a film strip depicting "The Ejector Seat in Action."

A light glared from above. She could see her reflection in the aluminum shade: an expanse of crumpled blue sheets, at one end a little white face, at the other white legs. People in green bustled around her. They all had shower caps on their shoes.

The rabbit hole that this Alice, a Sarah Lawrence sophomore from Westport, Connecticut, has fallen down is the chasm of disease—her legs have suddenly ceased to function, her hips have agonizingly fused—and her adventures take place in the madcap underworld of a Manhattan hospital and then a rehabilitation center farther downtown. The marvels of modern medical treatment are scarifyingly, if nonchalantly, portrayed as a farce of brutality and noncomprehension, a kind of *M*A*S*H de luxe*. Though Alice is given all the expert attention her very rich father can afford, no diagnosis, not even a name, is bestowed upon her affliction. "My doctors have finally come up with a possible diagnosis," she writes a friend. "I may have osteomyelitis, which means my hips are rotting from an infection. Or I may have aseptic necrosis, which means my hips are rotting, but *not* from an infection. Well! You can imagine how relieved I am to know what's wrong." The tall and handsome Dr. Witherspoons ("He took care of famous football teams and was famous himself") pays a daily visit in which he twists her feet so that she shrieks and sometimes passes out. "The hips never actually moved and neither foot could possibly turn out toward the edge of the bed or in toward the other foot—her joints were unyielding blocks of bone. Why did he insist on twisting this inflamed solid mass? . . . She thought about it and thought about it, and finally decided Dr. Witherspoons was determining the degree of inflammation from the decibel of her screams." An especially callous and incompetent nurse, Mrs. Trawling, lets Alice suffer an entire night with worsening phlebitis of the arm rather than pull the I.V. A broken machine would get more care and understanding than Alice, as she describes it. Later, at the rehab center, some of her physical therapists are at least seen as torturers with a purpose, and the nameless surgeon who finally operates on her hips is spared, by way of thanks, being characterized at all.

If the title also suggests one of those demure-appearing "adult" books toward the rear of the paperback rack, this isn't entirely wrong, either, for our heroine, at the height of her misery and incapacitation, manages to perform what used to be called an unnatural act upon two men both old enough to be her father. When she becomes a bit more able-bodied, she seduces a boy with a broken spine and, to test her new prostheses, "a friendly aide, who brought along a bottle of Ripple." Not too much is made of any of this, and it is probably realistic. "In the mist of pain and drugs, her thoughts waxed pornographic. . . . These two men and their organs seemed to be the only things she had any control over, and she would wait in her bed like a despot to exercise her power." Beneath its gossamer-light prose and schoolgirl jokiness *Alice in Bed* is a saga of the body; as a portrait of *une femme sensuelle moyenne,* a bright upper-class Jewish girl abruptly plunged into a physical nightmare, it is hard to fault. Alice is more than anything bewildered, and focuses on the immediate. She doesn't aspire to a saint's fortitude, but she is no Job, either, troubling the heavens with her complaint. Her suffering doesn't tie into anything bigger; it is big enough in itself. Ms. Schine creditably solves the curiously technical literary problem of how to represent pain. Since pain, like music, is virtually indescribable, there is little to do but carve a kind of empty space on the page where the impalpable entity would fit:

> Her legs, which barely bent at all, were pushed until her knees were as close to her chest as possible. An aide held them there, straining against them, while strange geometric pieces of foam rubber were placed around her hips, knees, and legs. The aide let go, and Alice realized she was wedged into the horrible position by the innocent-looking triangles, circles, and squares. The pain was so intense that she felt nothing but a kind of huge, spilling heat.

Alice in Bed bears comparison with another tale of a cruelly hurt young person, Denton Welch's *A Voice Through a Cloud;* both works leave icy shards in the mind.

Ms. Schine writes in short, cool takes that in their innocent juxtapositions are often funny. She has a real caricaturist's flair; of Alice's two middle-aged lovers, Simchas Fresser, a hypnotist from Israel, is sketched as having hair that "when he had taken off his sheepskin hat . . . rose off his head like a wedge of cake" and the diminutive, playful Dr. Davis as "sitting lightly on the chair, elegant as an egg in a nest." Alice's letters to her friend Katie, who is incarcerated in a mental institution, and to her father, who has left her mother and moved to Vancouver, are sassy and sad in exact late-adolescent proportions. Alice has a smidgin of literary ambition:

Then Alice read an article announcing that everyone was writing screen-plays, so she began her own. "I Was a Teenage Gimp," she wrote at the top of a sheet of paper. She crossed that out and wrote "The Magic Molehill."

But Ms. Schine's glancing, skipping style, while it makes Alice's year-long ordeal bearable to read about, does not do well at creating the weave, the thickening circumstance, of a novel. Alice's parents, though her mother is in constant attendance and her father's inopportune defection is a source of pain to rival osteomyelitis, remain minor characters, bundles of identi-fying tics more than felt presences in Alice's world. Their separation and divorce, though simultaneous with Alice's illness, never merges with it in a way that would indicate a novelist in charge. Things just happen in this book. Characters—visitors, nurses, fellow invalids—come and go, appear and disappear. Dr. Davis, to whom much drolly honed description is devoted, vanishes from Alice's life without a farewell, and Simchas Fresser gets a one-line kiss-off: "Simchas Fresser went into a deep depression and they had to stop seeing each other." Alice's year of agony and rehabilita-tion is a kind of clothesline on which incidents and characters dangle and dry. Even the central questions that keep us reading—what is wrong with Alice? will she be cured?—are answered in a manner offhand and skimped; a wry, skittish, female lie-down comic vies for our attention with Alice the agonist.

Both this and Mrs. Jhabvala's novel show a world without guilt, one in which nobody makes a mistake. Whether your hips freeze or you fall in love with a rotter, it's beyond your control, it happens to you. Without the possibility of a mistake, there can be nothing to repent of, and no tragedy—just the flow of what Freud called common human unhappiness, bearing along with it moments of exceptional health. Louise Sonnen-blick's happy moment occurs when she is about Alice's age, a young woman skating on the frozen pond of the Gruenewald: "She glided around on the ice with the same ease as she danced, not thinking of her feet at all. Her eyes were half shut so that the bright crystal sunlight came to her dimly, and so did the voices of the other skaters." She has not seen Bruno standing there admiring her. He treats her to a cup of hot chocolate; while her attention is intent upon keeping a chocolate-and-froth mustache from appearing on her lip, he begins to propose. Still very much a girl, "she wanted to get back to her drink—she loved it so—but desisted, for she realized this was a very solemn moment." And a moment handsomely realized in fiction, a moment worthy of Thomas Mann in its corporeal radiance and latent irony. Both these novels, so unlike in their textures—

the one Germanic and musty, the other American and breezy—have their moments and epiphanies, but all somehow displayed behind glass, like beautiful objects that can no longer be handled. The reader never quite ceases to be an audience, of human lives that offer those who live them no alternatives and therefore pass as sheer glossy spectacle, like the existences of animals.

Back to Nature

SEVEN RIVERS WEST, by Edward Hoagland. 319 pp. Summit Books, 1986.

REINDEER MOON, by Elizabeth Marshall Thomas. 338 pp. Houghton Mifflin, 1987.

Once upon a time in the Fifties, before words like "ecology" and "counterculture" had any circulation and when the phrase "back to Nature" comfortably implied that there would always be a Nature to go back to, there were in Cambridge, Massachusetts, two young literary persons destined to spend an unusual amount of their future out-of-doors, in faraway places, seeking rapport with animals and so-called primitive peoples. Edward Hoagland and Elizabeth Marshall, of the Harvard-Radcliffe class of 1954, precocious as writers (he wrote an eventually published novel, *Cat Man*, while still an undergraduate, and she had a short story printed in Martha Foley's *Best American Short Stories of 1953*), have trod the less trodden ways in the decades since, and have become known for their non-fiction—his essays and travel books and her anthropological studies of African tribes. Now, within a few months of each other, both have produced novels—he, *Seven Rivers West*, and she, *Reindeer Moon*. Both books describe (and include maps of) perilous treks in a reconstructed past—his, the Canadian Rockies of 1887, and hers, central Siberia twenty thousand years ago. And both are excellent books, wonderful in the root sense: they renew our sense of wonder. They revive that elemental awareness dulled in the all-but-suffocatingly urbanized America of our tired century.

Hoagland's fiction, though he followed *Cat Man* with two other novels, has been quietly received. Readers of *The New Yorker* may recall from seventeen years ago a curious gem of a short story, "The Final Fate of the Alligators," about an aging sailor who kept a fully grown alligator in a bathtub in his apartment on Twenty-first Street. It and two other tales of

Manhattan were published last year under the title *City Tales*, by the Capra Press of Santa Barbara. The two non-alligator stories display a tough wisdom, a poetic slant, and many superb sentences but also an elusive grittiness—a faint abrasive pugnacity to the prose—and an impatient, sporadic way of moving that interferes with their forward glide. The longer of them, "The Witness," is, Mr. Hoagland's introduction confides, "about as autobiographical as fiction gets," and has much the tone of the boldly discursive and frank essays that have made his reputation. "I found at the end of the 1960s," the introduction continues, "that what I wanted to do most was to tell my own story . . . without filtering myself through the artifices of fiction." The change of genre came with a change of milieu. The nameless hero of "The Witness," after detailing the varieties of urban brutality visible from the windows of his workplace on Lafayette Street, and permitting glimpses of a doomed and dingy affair he is conducting with a married woman on the floor below his apartment on the Lower East Side, announces, "I needed a vacation badly, needed to get to the country; I was irritated simply by humans and human activity." To the far country, then, be it Alaska or British Columbia or northern Vermont or the Sudan, Mr. Hoagland has gone, with his avid yet somehow bleak attentiveness. His first non-fiction book, *Notes from the Century Before*, had begun, he tells us, "as a diary intended only to fuel my next novel." Though the journal was kept in the summer of 1966, it seems as though his observations of the lonely mountains and rivers and men of western Canada have, after twenty years, fed into the majestic panorama of *Seven Rivers West*.

The front matter holds an epic disclaimer: "This novel is an invention. No people or tribes, no rivers or mountains, no villages or events are drawn from life." A map shows the seven titular rivers (plus nine or so others) and the numerous, quaintly named mountains (Shipshape, Muckaboo, Belly, Tooth, Many Berries, Mother, Mad Me) of the invented territory; it contains two features, the Continental Divide and the tracks of the fictional Winnipeg and Pacific Railroad, that place it on the British Columbia–Alberta line not far from what is now Banff National Park. The map also traces the novel's story: the trip, by horseback, foot, and raft, that Cecil Roop, a young man from the Massachusetts Berkshires, took up north into the Rockies and back down again, in search of a bear to tame and carry east to the vaudeville circuit. In this adventure, which begins as the ice is breaking up in the rivers and ends a few moons later, Cecil is accompanied by Sutton, a stout, older man from Louisiana with hopes of a gold strike and a circus trick of diving into shallow water and landing on his belly; Margaret, a middle-aged Crow squaw widowed by one white man but left with a taste for more; Charley Biskner, a true leather-clad "mountain man," with some gold dust kept in "a buffalo's or a moose's scrotum" and a tight cabin high on the Memphramagog River; Left-Handed Roy, a shaky old "desert rat" who lost one arm in a sawmill accident; and more horses and dogs (not to mention a mule, cat, and kitten) than I could count, though Mr. Hoagland particularizes and cherishes them all. This ungainly crew swims rivers and climbs mountains and encounters the sparse human and rich animal population of an almost virgin land. Though the buffalo herds have been decimated, and a few settlers established, this is still the frontier. The railroad is just coming to the newborn town of Horse Swim as Cecil leaves; the river has recently been named Margaret in honor of one of our characters; and the Indian tribes are acquainted with white men but, in the mountains, far from subdued.

With a mysterious offhand assurance the novel conveys the unsettled, improvised, ragged state of the Wild West, as the wary and growingly demoralized but still-savage redmen intermingle, in these vast areas, with the forward edge of white adventurers, eccentrics, romantics, and entre-preneurs—a huge anthropic event that, though often sung in film and story, acquires a startling freshness through Mr. Hoagland's details. The sexual interaction, for instance, between white men and Native-American women, downplayed in the textbooks, is here bluntly and tenderly ex-plored, via the persons of two squaws—the hardened and somewhat whor-ish Margaret, who joins up with Sutton, and the quite unassimilated Lizzie, a young Sikink widow and captive with whom Cecil reaches a tussly and insecure accommodation. "Lizzie" is his version of "Xingu," meaning "Young Basket." The warmth of her vibrant though alien life and, as their courtship progresses, of a common human nature breaking through language and cultural barriers is vividly rendered: "To his nose she smelled no different from the Thloadennis—a sort of mixture of pikefish, smoke, charcoal and tamaracks. . . . He found he didn't care that she was as tall as him and her arms nearly as muscular. He liked her quizzing eyes and the planes of her face, which were less hefty than the Thloadennis' crowded cheeks, and the bulge of her hank of hair under her hat, and her strong hips." In the various tense encounters that the white wanderers have with local Indians, we feel the poignance of this moment of continental mixing. The Native Americans are neither implacably hostile nor stupidly gullible; their actions and attitudes are shaped by the very human question "What's in it for me?" Not much, it turned out in the long run; but in the short, many deals were struck, that permitted traffic and an uneasy co-existence. As Charley says, "The West is a great place for turnover."

Along with his keen and non-judgmental intuitions into human arrangements, Mr. Hoagland provides a wealth of tactile details about the tools, costumes, sights, and usages of the frontier. The tops of a horse thief's ears were clipped, as a stigma; cowboys wore rattlesnake skins as neckties; pioneers arrived deafened by the screeching of their wagon wheels; a sun hat could be kept stiff by washing it in starchy potato water—just the first chapter yields these facts, along with such strongly flavored old words as "navvies," "platted," "hightailed," and "quinsy."* Remarkably precise sentences revive vanished sights:

> He was elegant in his tan shirt and pants, trailed by a lovely blond matched pair of trotters hitched to a democrat, with cheesecloth screening over their noses to ward off the flies.

> Last year's onions were still stored in his house, braided in chains by their dried tops, the chains looped across the low ceiling beams, along with split string beans, which were strung up by the many hundreds like tiny two-legged dried-leather britches in walking postures all around.

Man's old-fashioned agriculture and husbandry are thus vivified, but it is the timeless—the animals and rivers and mountains—that excites Mr. Hoagland's noblest style. His particularization of the successive rivers, in terms of tint and surge and bottom quality, is as intimate and loving as his naming and description of the various animals, domestic and wild—the dog "Smoky, who was smoke-colored and affectionate but suffered from epilepsy"; a billy goat "with its brisk, fastidious gait, cowlicky beard, bald knees, and deep-thinker's forelock"; a grizzly bear "as purple-colored as a plum"; a moose "with his brown bell swinging and two upside-down chairs on top of his head." The animal world yields to the author's anthropofugal eye incidents of a human strangeness and fallibility:

> A kingfisher dashed out in pursuit of a fish hawk and actually rode on its neck for a hundred yards, sitting like a broncobuster, while underneath their conjoined, monstrous shadow a groundhog on the riverbank took such fright it bumped its head and stunned itself in diving for its den.

The effort to render precisely the vast mountainscapes drives Mr. Hoagland's prose to a kind of sprung rhythm, a Hopkinsesque compression:

> The mountains mobbed into a jumble of slopes and pitches, gun-metal heights and gunstock-colored gorges which didn't separate into isolated

---

*I did wonder, though, if "hog heaven" and "zoo" in the slang sense of mass confusion were in the language a century ago, and if one could speak of a "Czechoslovak" language before Czechoslovakia was founded, in 1918.

EDWARD HOAGLAND : 361

cones but ran together in multiple masses connected by short, cloud-stuffed plateaus as cold as the snow in the saddles not far above or the blade-edged crestlines that were an icy blue.

This jumble is good; at times the mimetic effort becomes perhaps too muscular and colorful, as in this version of northern lights:

These were as pink in the night sky as the salmon she was splitting open by firelight, and glowed like antler tines, vibrated like a dozen tuning forks, fanned high into an arch of organ-pipe columns, and blanketed the sky with orange sheets that turned to a diaphanous white chiffon before sweeping upward into instant oblivion.

We are given, in any case, a great deal to visualize, and relatively little to hear and to feel. The travellers are laconic with one another, though some pungent things are said. The motives of the central two, Cecil and Sutton, are rather lightly indicated. Both, as if escaped from the author's youthful circus novel, *Cat Man*, are circus-minded, with stunts they now and then perform. Cecil hopes to catch a bear, a squaw, and a Big Foot in these Rockies, and Sutton to settle down and mine gold, but rather fantastically: their quests don't communicate excitement, and in the end Cecil's bear seems to be both captured and forgotten. Perhaps this thinness of sympathetic motive holds a truth: the men of the far frontier were more concerned with getting away than going to, and the trip to the edge was its own mystical purpose. The foreground figures stand in this lovingly wrought homage to a stupendous terrain much as the little figures are planted in a great wilderness canvas by Frederick Church or Albert Bierstadt, to supply a sense of scale. Mr. Hoagland is better at "characters" than character; walk-ons like Ouddo, a deaf and affable old killer ensconced in eremetic luxury, and Switzer, an unarmed, Bible-quoting pilgrim carrying a bag of appleseeds, crackle with an authentic American crankiness. Among these vital, humanoid eccentrics should be included Big Foot, or Sasquatch, who turns out to be an apparition of hypnotic reality, smelling of "a mustardly piquancy or the vanilla scent of joe-pye weed" and after a while becoming just one more of the fauna in this remoteness, with "its peacock or parroty scream, . . . its baboon muzzle and bearish set of teeth, its body haired all over like a shaggy pony's, its hands like a giant man's or an ominous ape's, its forehead and face more spiritual than intelligent but more human than animal." Like Moby-Dick, this creature (whose presence makes Cecil feel woozy) reifies the murky and ominous meaning that gazes at man out of the external world in all its impervious magnificence. By setting himself in pursuit of this meaning,

Mr. Hoagland joins cause with the Transcendentalists, and wilderness mystics like John Muir (in whose praise he has written a rapturous essay), and that long line of American novelists who have attempted in one gorgeous grab to say it all. He has come closer than most.

Elizabeth Marshall Thomas's *Reindeer Moon* has the one thing missing from *Seven Rivers West*—a lovable protagonist, whose travels and travails we follow with continuous concern. Her heroine, Yanan, tells her story in a limpid, unassuming voice that engages us from the start:

> My story isn't big like the stories some of the mammoth hunter men could tell. Mine doesn't end with a huge pile of meat. My story has no captured women, only the gifts of a marriage exchange, and no battles, only arguments about the gifts. My story isn't very long, and perhaps lacks wisdom, since the beginning was told me by other people and the end came sooner than I wanted. I was still a young woman when I left the world of the living and became a spirit of the dead.

Such a voice—firm and direct yet afloat in an indeterminate subjective space—avoids the two aesthetic perils of third-person ventures into the Paleolithic like Jean Auel's best-selling volumes: the peril of sounding like animated anthropology, and that of sounding like one more querulous, ego-ridden modern novel. Yanan's people feel, as do we, anger, fear, love, and jealousy. But their sense of personal possessiveness is qualified by a clan solidarity more intense than ours; they know hunger as a constant companion; their relationship with animals is close and murderous; and their religion is interwoven with earthly survival.

On the earthly level, *Reindeer Moon* tells of Yanan's maturation, from a child to mother, in the space of perhaps four years. The years are harrowing but typical, for these semi-nomadic hunter-gatherers of the subarctic steppes, save for the winter when the cruel deaths of her mother and then her father isolate the still-girlish Yanan, with her little sister, Meri, in a wild world bare of clan protection. In the tale's most compelling and alarming episode, the two children manage to survive with the help of a similarly isolated female wolf and her one cub, and eventually make their way, living like animals in burrows and crevices, off roots and frogs, to a lodge of their kin. On the unearthly level, Yanan, as her opening sentences announce, dies young; yet she continues, as "a spirit of the dead," to experience and to function in the life of her clan, as a guardian of her people's lodge. In its matter-of-fact interlarding of a brief life with its wide-ranging afterlife *Reindeer Moon* is something of a tour de force, but rarely feels strained, or cute. Partly under her own volition and partly under the magical influence of the tribal shamans, Yanan as spirit takes the form of a number of creatures—a wolf, a deer, a raven, an owl, a bustard, a lion, even a mammoth—and re-enters reality from their angles. The novel gains thereby an entrancing variety and airiness of texture, while deepening its basic theme, which I took to be the terms upon which we human animals enjoy our place in nature.

Mrs. Thomas's writing runs smooth and almost colorless and rarely thickens into one of Mr. Hoagland's poetic knots. But our awareness of such a basic comfort as shelter is exquisitely sharpened by a simple sentence like "As we reached the middle of the woods in the early evening, tiny, grainy snowflakes began to fall." Yanan and Meri have that day abandoned the lodge where their father's corpse lies—he has died, after days of delirium and coma, of an infected wolverine bite—and the tiny, grainy snowflakes, falling into their hopeless trudge through this vast inhuman wilderness, have the weight of terror, of our young species' terrible frail loneliness. Food, too—what it means to be a carnivore—is comprehended anew, through the dozens of pitiless killings described in the novel with a coolly detailed accuracy. And the necessary tightness of the social weave that holds hunger and cold and predators at bay is illustrated by the cunning shape of the plot: Yanan's fatal sin, her break with the clan, comes during a fight precipitated by her stealing and destroying, to spare her sister's feelings, what she takes to be the pelt of the wolf cub who became a brother to her sister during the winter they were forced to live with wolves. And they had come to that pass, really, through an impetuous decision of their father's to remove his family from the larger clan because of an imagined slight. From one breach of order, others flow; no violation of taboo or mutual trust goes without its disruptive effect, and all must be repaired.

The incessant mending of the tribal consensus includes placatory rites directed at the gods—the Bear and the Woman Ohun. Man has extended his social net upward into the air, and rising smoke carries offerings of blood and meat to the spirits. The urgency of these natural and supernatural interconnections lends *Reindeer Moon* an intrinsic coherence and suspensefulness that modern novels, describing a world where the social unit is relatively loose and diffuse, must grope for. In *Seven Rivers West,* the deaths and matings, as set down by Mr. Hoagland's modern male sensibility, have a disjunct abruptness, as if to point up the cosmic indifference that frames such dramatic animal moments; in *Reindeer Moon,* the pace feels softer—each crisis rounded in the telling so that we can follow its curve, each event a fruit held and pulled from the tree of life.

As Yanan tells us at the outset, hers is a woman's tale. Its feminist overtones are audible but not strident. Since, from the pharaohs on, women have been assigned a back seat in history, there is a tendency to claim prehistory as their turf. "Men own the meat," Yanan tells us, but "Women own the families, the lineages." Her cousin Teal instructs her, "You came from a strong lineage, a Fire River lineage. If you're afraid of initiation or coitus, you mustn't show it." The implied moral of Yanan's heroic trek with Meri is that *women can do it*. Wielding the heavy spear taken from beside her father's corpse, she hunts with the men. She fights being beaten by her husband and, when the time comes, proudly attempts to give birth to her child away from the lodge, with only little Meri in attendance. She overreaches: women in the time of *Reindeer Moon* still must be creatures of endurance and submission. They less make things happen than have things happen to them. "What is happening to me?" Yanan asks herself when she first makes love, echoing the exact words her mother uttered when she found herself dying of a hemorrhage. Teal tells Yanan, "These women's things—menstruation, initiation, childbirth— they aren't very difficult and don't need skill or knowledge. . . . They just happen. You need only to keep quiet." When Yanan asks, "Why must I?" Teal answers grimly, "We must. It's the Woman Ohun's plan." Yanan's, and Mrs. Thomas's, vision of triumphant femininity is endearingly em- bodied in the hulk of an old female mammoth, the leader of a herd that Yanan joins in her spirit form—the most remarkable in a delightful, hu- morous, and scrupulous series of empathetic animal portraits:

> The elderly leader waited for me to come near. With her head high and her eyes squinting, her chin tight, her cheeks sucked in, and her lips pressed firmly together, the large mammoth seemed strong-minded. Her ears were small and tattered as if they had been frozen when she was young. Her tusks were long, sweeping out and down, then curving inward and upward, with grooves and scratches on them—tusks far older than mine, which were still growing into their downward curve. By the early light her shedding, patchy hair looked black; it was matted on her flanks but sleek on her chest where her summer coat parted over her breasts, which showed behind her forelegs as the breasts of a woman on her hands and knees show behind her arms. When the gathering light shone through this mammoth's hair, I saw its red color.

This monstrous yet not unfriendly vision, with its womanly breasts and blood-colored tint, corresponds to Mr. Hoagland's affecting, quizzical portrait of Sasquatch and to Melville's great picture, in the eighty-seventh chapter of *Moby-Dick*, of "The Grand Armada," the whale society, com- plete with nursing mothers and amorous couples, "suspended in those watery vaults": a vision, that is, of something quite *other* in nature, beyond the confines of human culture, that yet gazes back at us with eyes not so unlike our own.

PHILIP ROTH

Doing His Thing

ZUCKERMAN UNBOUND, by Philip Roth. 225 pp. Farrar, Straus & Giroux, 1981.

In this episodic sequel to *The Ghost Writer,* the fledgling writer Nathan Zuckerman now struggles with the wealth, fame, intrusions, and estrangements bestowed upon him by the enormous success of his fourth novel, *Carnovsky.* Zuckerman's parents, his thoroughly Jewish Newark, his discardable shiksa consorts, his pangs of guilt and impatience, his love for the classics of Western thought, and his fondness for Forties trivia may be already familiar to chronic readers of Mr. Roth, who has evolved from the broad-shouldered realist of *Letting Go,* the frenzied fantasist of *The Great American Novel,* and the unbuttoned psychodramatist of *Portnoy's Complaint* into something of an exquisitist, moving, in his last four novels, among his by now highly polished themes with ever more expertness and care. The comic diatribes seem almost engraved, they are so finely tuned, and the polarities between id and superego, Jew and goy, artistic honesty and human decency are as beautifully played upon as the themes in a Bach fugue. Always one of the most intelligent and energetic of American authors, Roth has now become one of the most scrupulous, and the grateful, amused, enlightened reader would be a churl indeed if he complained at the narrowing, almost miniaturized, scope of Roth's bejewelled and frisky world.

Warning: this short work, already thoroughly pre-published by a trio of magazines, bears on its jacket flaps a plot summary almost as long and gratuitous as a master's thesis. Ignore it or forfeit all surprises, pleasant and unpleasant.

Yahweh over Dionysus, in Disputed Decision

THE ANATOMY LESSON, by Philip Roth. 291 pp. Farrar, Straus & Giroux, 1983.

Nathan Zuckerman, the hero of Philip Roth's new novel, has been met by faithful Roth-readers twice before. In *The Ghost Writer* (1979), as a twenty-three-year-old just-published writer, he visited the Berkshire home of the revered older author E. I. Lonoff; Zuckerman had lately composed a short story entitled "Higher Education," based on some family incidents, which had occasioned his father considerable unhappiness and produced an unctuous letter and questionnaire from the highly respected Newark judge Leopold Wapter. Judge Wapter's concluding questions were:

> Aside from the financial gain to yourself, what benefit do you think publishing this story in a national magazine will have for (a) your family; (b) your community; (c) the Jewish religion; (d) the well-being of the Jewish people?

And:

> Can you honestly say that there is anything in your short story that would not warm the heart of a Julius Streicher or a Joseph Goebbels?

Lonoff (who died in 1961; this episode occurred in the Fifties) had his own hands full with a frolicsome houseguest who may have been really Anne Frank. But he took a moment to reassure Zuckerman that niceness is not of the essence in being a writer, and, demonstrating the social embarrassments of creativity, galloped off in pursuit of his wife, Hope, who had just decamped "in search of a less noble calling." By the time of *Zuckerman Unbound* (1981), our ethically troubled young writer had suppressed his desire to please the respectable Jewish citizens of Newark long enough to produce an uninhibited novel, *Carnovsky,* which in the scope of its success and scandal can be compared only to Mr. Roth's own *Portnoy's Complaint.* Success brought its misadventures, of which the most distressing was Zuckerman's father, on his deathbed, calling his son a "bastard." Nathan's younger brother, Henry, confirmed the epithet in a sudden diatribe as they, having buried their father, parted at the Newark airport:

> "You *are* a bastard. A heartless conscienceless bastard. What does loyalty mean to you? What does responsibility mean to you? What does self-denial mean, *restraint*—anything at all? To you everything is disposable! Everything is *ex*posable! Jewish morality, Jewish endurance, Jewish wisdom, Jew-

ish families—everything is grist for your fun-machine. Even your shiksas go down the drain when they don't tickle your fancy anymore. Love, marriage, children, what the hell do you care? To you it's all fun and games. *But that isn't the way it is to the rest of us.*"

The Anatomy Lesson finds Zuckerman mired ever deeper in his ill-gotten gains and the problems of conscience posed by Judge Wapter's questions and Henry's accusations. The time is 1973, Watergate time, and Zuckerman watches Nixon on television—"the dummy gestures, the satanic sweating, the screwy dazzling lies"—with fellow-feeling, for the President is "the only other American he saw daily who seemed to be in as much trouble as he was." Watches him, it should be explained, through prism glasses, for Zuckerman is flat on his back with excruciating, mysterious, undiagnosed, and uncured neck and shoulder pains. "Just having a neck, arms, and shoulders was like carrying another person around." He cannot walk more than a few blocks at a time, lift grocery bags or open windows, cook or make his bed or write. He has three ex-wives, four mistresses, and is furious with a critic, Milton Appel, who has spoken and written unkindly of his work. To kill the pain he takes Percodan, drinks vodka, and smokes marijuana, all in increasing quantities. He gradually comes to think that what he really wants, at the age of forty, is to be a doctor; in order to enroll in medical school he travels, heavily self-medicated, to Chicago, where he was once a happy student. But happiness is not so easily come by for Nathan Zuckerman now. With the help of Percodan he attains new heights of self-analysis and self-abasement, as his spirit apparently craves.

The Anatomy Lesson is a ferocious, heartfelt book. Materials one might have thought exhausted by Roth's previous novelistic explorations, in-flammations one might have thought long soothed burn hotter than ever; the central howl unrolls with a meditated savagery both fascinating and repellent, self-indulgent yet somehow sterling, adamant, pure in the style of high modernism, that bewitchment to all the art-stricken young of the Fifties. Zuckerman's admonition to himself, "Drive pain out with your battering heart the way a clapper knocks sound from a bell," could come straight from Kafka. Beckett also figures in: "Percodan was to Zuckerman what sucking stones were to Molloy." Writing has been his life and religion: "He used to wonder how all the billions who didn't write could take the daily blizzard—all that beset them, such a saturation of the brain, and so little of it known or named. If he wasn't cultivating hypothetical Zuckermans he really had no more means than a fire hydrant to decipher his existence." But this cultivation of hypothetical selves has become an endgame:

Either there was no existence left to decipher or he was without sufficient imaginative power to convert into his fiction of seeming self-exposure what existence had now become. There was no rhetorical overlay left: he was bound and gagged by the real raw thing, ground down to his own unhypothetical nub. He could no longer pretend to be anybody else, and as a medium for his books he had ceased to be.

Zuckerman wants out of his weary, overannotated, aching self; but, "if Zuckerman wrote about what he didn't know, who then would write about what he did know?" The postmodernist writer's bind is expressed in flat authoritative accents reminiscent of Hemingway's unbuttoned late-night letters: "If you get out of yourself you can't be a writer because the personal ingredient is what gets you going, and if you hang on to the personal ingredient any longer you'll disappear right up your asshole." Zuckerman is willing to sacrifice his writerly vocation; to be a harried emergency-room doctor promises "an end to the search for the release from self." He thinks, "Other people. Somebody should have told me about them a long time ago." Ministering to the pain of others promises release from personal discomfort. "Had he kept a pain diary, the only entry would have been one word: Myself."

A text so self-aware and self-referential suggests the torture-machine of Kafka's "In the Penal Colony," which inscribed, over and over, an unintelligible lesson upon the victim's skin. As well as tireless superscription a constant flanking motion seems in progress; the repeated self-indictments leave the critic little to say. One can scarcely complain of the novel's frenzied solipsism when frenzied solipsism is its chosen and announced topic. One should certainly not confuse Zuckerman's creator—the gracious and generous-spirited editor of a Penguin series devoted to the undervalued writers of Eastern Europe, a man who wears with an exemplary dignity and reserve the American writer's motley—with the abject Zuckerman himself, who differs from Philip Roth in as many biographical particulars as he happens to share. (Zuckerman has in twenty years of work produced a meagre four books, as contrasted with Roth's baker's dozen. Zuckerman has had three wives, Roth only one. Zuckerman's father has died; Roth's, as of 1983, flourishes.) One might venture to say that, like a goodly number of Roth's previous works, *The Anatomy Lesson* revolves around the paradox of incarnation—the astonishing coexistence in one life of infantilism and intelligence, of selfishness and altruism, of sexual appetite and social conscience—and has the form and manner of a monologue conducted under psychoanalysis, whose termination in this case seems premature.

Portnoy, at least, in arriving by way of strenuous sexual pilgrimage at a state of impotence in Israel, brought his complaint to a climax from which, as the intruding psychiatric voice at the end proclaimed, we might begin. Zuckerman, at the end of his trilogy, seems, though battered by some circumstances, still unimpaired in his basic mechanisms; his basic astonishment at being a person, once he gets his breath back, will continue to feed his indignation and ravenous rage of discourse, of "self-conscious self-miming." He is free from neither his pain nor his vocation, if I read correctly the novel's last, rather Jamesian sentence. Nothing, amid all the verbal fury, has happened, any more than David Kepesh, at the end of *The Breast*, ceased to be a breast. This unforgettable novella was published in 1972, in the era when *The Anatomy Lesson* takes place. Like the present work, *The Breast* begins with an inexplicable somatic assault—not in-capacitating neck pains but a "massive hormonal influx" that in a night of "agony" ("as though I were being repeatedly shot from a cannon into a brick wall") transformed a young professor of English into a six-foot-long breast with the end without a nipple "rounded off like a water-melon." Both works seek resolution in an orgiastic vision: the giant breast intends to be constantly caressed by naked twelve- and thirteen-year-old girls, "greedy wicked little girls, licking me and sucking me to my heart's content," and Zuckerman in Chicago reels off to his female chauffeur an extensive Dionysian fantasy about being a pornography king named, by a weird blow of his drug-loosened mind, Milton Appel. *The Breast*, follow-ing upon the best-selling *Portnoy*, baffled many readers, but has improved with age, and was honored by its author, in 1980, with a revision of its text. Comparing the two *Breast*s, this reader detected little improvement—just rearrangements of elements within paragraphs, a diminishing of aca-demic satire in connection with the character named Arthur Schonbrunn, and a subtle overlay of commas and dashes, producing a slightly more professorial tone. The fable's inner meaning has been softened and blurred at spots; in the first version, Kepesh cries out in his agony of immobility and blindness,

> "What do any of you know about grotesque! What is more grotesque anyway, but to be denied my little pleasure in the midst of this relentless nightmare! Why shouldn't I be rubbed and oiled and massaged and sucked and licked and fucked, too, if I want it! Why shouldn't I have anything and everything I can think of *every single minute of the day* if that can transport me from this miserable hell!"

This *cri de sein* was much shortened in the later version, and on the next page the descriptive phrase "spasms of illogic or infantilism" deleted. But infantilism is certainly what it is all about; Roth's message, driven home in book after book, is what infants men are. The infant, Freud has told us, is the prototypical human being, the fundamental stewpot: a "cocky little ogre," according to Auden (in "Mundus et Infans"), and, according to Wordsworth, heavenly spirit freshly planted in the flesh. Habituation dulls us to the "relentless nightmare" of our embodiment; but essentially it is no more grotesque to be conscious within an enormous breast than within the body one *does* have, with its hair and fingernails and teeth, its symmetrical limbs and asymmetrical internal organs. The helpless infant in his deep discomfiture limitlessly *wants,* as David Kepesh slung in his hammock wants, as Nathan Zuckerman wants while he lies immobilized on a playmat he has bought "in a children's furniture store on Fifty-seventh Street." As our hero lies on his playmat, his head supported by a thesaurus his father had given him with the inscription "From Dad— You have my every confidence," his four mistresses come and lower their orifices upon him. Kepesh's dream of attentive "greedy wicked little girls" has come true, with some unforeseen wrinkles; but still Zuckerman, sucking and sucked, is not satisfied; he wants the real thing, the original mother lowering her breasts upon him. "Zuckerman finally realized that his mother had been his only love." When she dies, in Florida, he takes away from her effects an old book of hers called *Your Baby's Care;* on the page headed "Feeding," which prescribes emptying the breast by hand every twenty-four hours, he finds a stain that he believes to have been left by a drop of her milk, expressed in 1933, and he closes his eyes and puts his tongue to the dry page. Adult infantilism can go no further.

It is the familial milieu of those early infantile gratifications that Zuckerman and his predecessors in Roth's fiction unforgivably violate, first by masturbation and then by sexual traffic with the dirty girls of the goyim and finally by the production of a "hate-filled, mocking best-seller" that, poisonous with "the tastelessness that had affronted millions, and the shamelessness that had enraged his tribe," kills the father and brings down his curse. The curse is reinforced by the adverse literary verdict of Milton Appel, against whom Zuckerman rages with an obsessive passion that amazes and bores his sensible Wasp girlfriend Diana. He explains, "I'm a petty, raging, vengeful, unforgiving Jew, and I have been insulted one time too many by another petty, raging, vengeful, unforgiving Jew." Roth, though accused, like Zuckerman, of writing anti-Semitically or at least in mockery of middle-class American Jewry, seems in this book the most Jewish of Jewish-American writers; Bellow can take pleasure in contemplating the gentile bohunks of Chicago, and Malamud can enjoy a Thoreauvian jog in the woods, and Mailer can get turned on by astronauts and Marilyn Monroe and Utah low life, but for Zuckerman as Roth has imagined him there is *no* authenticity away from the bosom of Abraham. If Milton Appel weren't Jewish, who would care what he says? Zuckerman's shiksas are so much nicely designed wallpaper on the walls of his cell; blacks have moved into his old Newark neighborhood and he feels as thoroughly exiled as Nabokov from Russia.

Jewishness figures as the one conceptual thread woven into the primal Newark nest, and *The Anatomy Lesson* contains a number of sociological reflections upon it, from "Jewish mothers know how to own their suffering boys" to "The disputatious stance, the aggressively marginal sensibility, the disavowal of community ties, the taste for scrutinizing a social event as though it were a dream or a work of art—to Zuckerman this was the very mark of the intellectual Jews . . . on whom he was modeling his own style of thought." More instinctively and symptomatically, the tenderness that bestows liveliness breaks into the narrator's monologue whenever an elderly Jewish male—Dr. Kotler, Mr. Freytag—makes an appearance; these are really the only characters, as distinguished from apparitions and interlocutors, that this novel has, the only bringers of life separate from the hero's tortured vitality. Roth has been preëminently a celebrant of a son's world. Who else has given us so many vivid, comical, shrewdly seen but above all lovingly preserved mothers and fathers in fiction? Or has so faithfully kept fresh as moral referent the sensations of childhood? Rousing from a doped stupor, Zuckerman sees from his limousine windows that it has begun to snow, and thinks, "There was nothing that could ever equal coming home through the snow in late afternoon from Chancellor Avenue School." "I am not an authority on Israel," he protests when approached to write a *Times* Op-Ed column in defense of the Jewish State, "I'm an authority on Newark. Not even on Newark. On the Weequahic section of Newark. If the truth be known, not even on the whole of the Weequahic section. I don't even go below Bergen Street."

John O'Hara was equally localized by the streets of Pottsville, but showed no disposition to linger; indeed, he once advised an old friend to "write something that automatically will sever your connection with the town." Nothing in Irish tribal sense asked the torment that Zuckerman visits upon himself. A diagnosis of his complaint comes early in *The Anatomy Lesson* and is not improved upon by his medical researches later on. "The crippling of his upper torso was, transparently, the punishment called forth by his crime: mutilation as primitive justice. If the writing arm offend thee, cut it off and cast it from thee. Beneath the ironic carapace of a tolerant soul, he [Nathan Zuckerman] was the most unforgiving Yahweh of them all." Zuckerman does not forgive himself, either, for spilling his seed upon the ground; he has had three childless marriages and, in his fantasy life as Milton Appel the messianic pornographer, assigns himself a fourth wife and a seven-year-old son—whom he names Nathan! His rage and pain peak in a scene, fabulous as a holy crisis out of Malamud or Singer, wherein the hallucinating author, chanting the praises of the Lord "who bringeth forth from the earth the urge to spurt that maketh monkeys of us all," attempts to strangle one more tenderly, comically rendered Jewish father, and comes up against the "Gestapo boots" of his female, pigtailed, Lutheran chauffeur. And the author, no mean Yahweh himself, contrives to smash Zuckerman on his offending part, his babbling, mocking, pleading mouth.

The Chicago scenes are visionary, and stay with the reader. Throughout, a beautiful passion to be honest propels the grinding, whining paragraphs. Yet, though lavish with laughs and flamboyant invention, *The Anatomy Lesson* seemed to this Roth fan the least successful of the Zuckerman trio, the least objectified and coherent. The pages devoted to Zuckerman's mental, epistolary, and finally telephonic quarrel with Milton Appel especially manifested a disproportion between the energy expended and the area of expenditure. True, there *are* shrewd, intelligent negative reviews which an author has to fight against as if fighting for his life; but by the age of forty a writer should be rising above the home-town beefs and metropolitan bad notices that go with the job, and perhaps by the age of fifty a writer should have settled his old scores. Zuckerman's babyish reduction of all women to mere suppliers eclipses much of Roth's engaging characterization of the mistresses, who are each set before us never to appear again. The book is elegant action writing, a hyperaware churning full of observations but thin (unlike *The Ghost Writer*) on characters the author respects; instead of characters *The Anatomy Lesson* has demons, and these are powerfully agitated but not exorcised. Neither Zuckerman nor his creator seems quite to realize that by aspiring to become a nice good-doing doctor the author of *Carnovsky* is at last knuckling under to Judge Wapter.

Bound to Please

ZUCKERMAN BOUND: *A Trilogy and Epilogue*, by Philip Roth. 784 pp. Farrar, Straus & Giroux, 1985.

To the previously published short novels *The Ghost Writer, Zuckerman Unbound,* and *The Anatomy Lesson* Mr. Roth has added an epilogue, "The

Prague Orgy," which shows his protagonist, the American literary man Nathan Zuckerman, involved with some raffish Czech counterparts in an attempt to smuggle out of Prague a manuscript of short stories by an unknown Yiddish writer slain by the Nazis. The painful contortions of human art and spirit under Communism are sketched with a bleak abruptness, in a strange mood of wistful farce; here, as for the perennially homeless Jews, the chief activity is "the construction of narrative art out of the exertions of survival." In toto, *Zuckerman Bound* shows the author's always ebullient invention and artful prose at their most polished and concentrated, the topic of authorship clearly being, to this author, a noble one. His repeated hints that his hero's misadventures connect with wider historical sufferings fail to persuade us, however, that they amount to significantly more than those of a gifted male child oppressed first by his fond parents and then by other admirers. Described as "the American authority on Jewish demons," Zuckerman counters the pangs of apprenticeship, success, and writer's block with a mounting irritability and a frantic, hilarious, anguished eloquence that leaves little air for any other characters to breathe; indeed, except as irritants and as display windows for Mr. Roth's great powers of mimicry, characters other than Zuckerman scarcely exist. Though a number of biologically complete females add to the hero's embarrassments, the nearest approach to a heroine, in nearly eight hundred pages, is Anne Frank's ghost. Proust, the author of another epic of the self striving to bear fruit, by comparison gave us Albertine, Odette, and Marcel's grandmother. But perhaps an analogue closer than *Remembrance of Things Past* would be Melville's *Pierre*, in which another driven young writer tortuously struggles with the besieging shadows of a feminized, claustrophobic America.

Wrestling to Be Born

THE COUNTERLIFE, by Philip Roth. 324 pp. Farrar, Straus & Giroux, 1987.

Philip Roth's new novel takes many turns and treats of many topics, including, for some especially fine pages, that of impassioned dentistry; but it is mostly about Israel, erections, and writing fiction. In this it resembles much of the author's post-*Portnoy* fiction—and one of Portnoy's complaints, you may remember, was that he became impotent in the state of Israel. Impotence is the starting point of the present novel of surging self-explanation, -exploration, -excoriation, and -justification, this time voiced by Nathan Zuckerman, whom we have met before. The Zuckerman trilogy-plus was preceded by the appearance of Zuckerman in the first third of *My Life as a Man* (1974), as the hero of two "Useful Fictions" written by the novel's real (whatever that means) hero, Peter Tarnopol. In the first of these stories, "Salad Days," the twice-fictional Zuckerman has an older brother, Sherman—a pianist who runs a high-school band, goes off to the Navy in 1945, and returns to marry "some skinny Jewish girl from Bala-Cynwyd who talked in baby talk and worked as a dental technician somewhere" and to become an orthodontist. The brother is absent from the second useful fiction, "Courting Disaster," and from *The Ghost Writer,* but in *Zuckerman Unbound* he reappears as a *younger* brother, named Henry, a dentist with a wife, Carol, and three children in New Jersey—"the good son," flawed only by a weak heart and an occasional extramarital affair. He is "the tallest, darkest, and handsomest by far of all the Zuckerman men, a swarthy, virile, desert Zuckerman whose genes, uniquely for their clan, seemed to have traveled straight from Judea to New Jersey without the Diaspora detour." Nathan looks at Henry over their father's deathbed and thinks:

> Softest, gentlest, kindest. Responsibility. Generosity. Devotion. That's how everybody spoke of Henry. I suppose if I were Henry with his heart I wouldn't jeopardize it, either. It probably feels very good being so good. Except when it doesn't. And that probably feels good in the end too. Self-sacrifice.

At the climax of *Zuckerman Unbound,* however, this softer and gentler Zuckerman turns on Nathan and furiously tells him that his writing is what has killed their father and that the old man's last utterance had been to call his older son a bastard. These accusations rankle throughout *The Anatomy Lesson,* but Henry and his family remain estranged from Nathan and scarcely appear in the book.

Now, in *The Counterlife,* Henry returns, as co-hero. It is he who, as a side effect of a beta-blocking medication taken to relieve his coronary disease and hypertension, is rendered impotent; it is he who, caught up in torrid liaisons with a German-Swiss patient called Maria and then with a dental assistant called Wendy, suffers the pangs of Portnoy's Complaint, clinically defined in the novel of the same name as "a disorder in which strongly-felt ethical and altruistic impulses are perpetually warring with extreme sexual longings, often of a perverse nature." The disorder, displaced onto Henry's conventional, dutiful, family-bound existence, regains intensity and interest. Explosion requires constraint. The trouble with the other Zuckerman as an agonist was that he had become too free:

a rich writer, thrice married but usually a bachelor when we see him in Roth's fictions, Nathan is able to fly where he wants, have whom he wants, analyze and clown away whatever he doesn't like, and concentrate entirely upon his own psyche and anatomy. If he is less than heroic, it is because the task he keeps setting himself and keeps being unable to perform—to break out of self-obsession enough to establish a family and become a father—is, for most heterosexual males, ridiculously easy.* In fact, biology and inertia usually do it for you. But for Zuckerman the writer, nothing comes, or goes, easy; he has been stewing over the mixed critical reception of his best-selling *Carnovsky* (1969) for nearly ten years (*The Counterlife* occurs in 1978) and rehashing his boyhood ever since it happened. "Tell me something," his exasperated brother, Henry, asks him, "is it at all possible . . . for you to have a frame of reference slightly larger than the kitchen table in Newark?" For Zuckerman the dentist, father, and husband—"a young man still largely propelled by feelings of decorum that he had imbibed and internalized and never seriously questioned"—lust is still an unhackneyed, majestic disruption subject to no mitigating literary uses and deformations. This five-part novel's first section, "Basel," describing Henry's affairs and his decision to undergo a life-threatening coronary-bypass operation that will restore his potency, has the vital freshness, the vivid minor characters, and implied communal pressure of *Goodbye, Columbus* (1959), Roth's first bracing dip into the surging waters of Newark Jewishness and sexuality.

The four remaining chapters give back, I think, some of the bright life borrowed from this shift of interest onto the brother. Unlike James Joyce and Thomas Mann, to whom the theme of competitive fraternity was objectively, oppressively present, Roth conceives brotherhood as another exercise in egoism. Nathan says of brothers, "How they know each other,

---

*This impasse is more painfully illustrated, because less obscured by writer-consciousness and intellectual slapstick, by David Kepesh, the hero of *The Breast* and its prequel *The Professor of Desire*. Perhaps Portnoy's Complaint—the disease—is merely a contemporary form of the Victorian pathology, pondered by Freud, that prevented men from loving their sexual partners. "The Most Prevalent Form of Degradation in Erotic Life" is both a paper by Freud and a chapter title from *Portnoy*. Roth's women, like Hemingway's, tend to be virgins or whores: solid, cool, boringly sensible Wasp women or devilish wet dreams, the Monkeys and Sharon Shatskys of the world, who, incredibly, "do it" as perversely and avidly as the hero's dark side desires. For this they win small thanks. Their lovers are, from the neck up, high-minded, public-spirited, squeamish. Altruism, of course, is a method of loving without contamination by sexual contact and its concomitant disgust: the Monkey accurately tells Portnoy, "You mean, miserable hard-on you, you care more about the niggers in Harlem that you don't even know, than you do about me, who's been sucking you off for a solid year!"

in my experience, is as a kind of deformation of themselves." Indeed, almost all the characters in *The Counterlife,* including the women, exist as deformations of the hero, or as curved mirrors giving back an exaggerated aspect of him. As if to proclaim imaginative distortion as the heart and soul of fiction (and to plead Not Guilty to charges of indecent exposure and invaded privacy), the novel incorporates discontinuous variations of its central situation. The plot bifurcates, revises itself, cross-examines itself, tries things several ways. In the first chapter, Henry dies during the heart operation; in the second, "Judea," Henry has survived and has fled his family and practice by going (as if in fulfillment of that "desert" quality casually ascribed in the earlier novel) to Israel and taking up with a Zionist zealot. In the fourth chapter, it is Nathan who has the heart problem, the impotence, and the mistress called Maria. In pursuing these variations, the virtuoso imaginer rarely falters; satisfying details of place and costume, astonishing diatribes, beautifully heard and knitted dialogues unfold in chapters impeccably shaped, packed, and smoothed. No other writer combines such a surface of colloquial relaxation and even dishevelment with such depth of meditating intelligence. Nathan, pondering the Hebraized, suntanned Henry, reflects "about this swift and simple conversion of a kind that isn't readily allowed to writers unless they wish to commit the professional blunder of being uninquiring." Inquiring the writing certainly is; the way in which yet one more insight, one more psychological wrinkle, is visited upon an already thoroughly explicated situation (Henry's resentment of Nathan, Nathan's condescension to Henry) is as thrilling as, in another sort of novel, one more body discovered in the library. The narrator is always striving to surmount his feelings, pains, animosities, rages; the narrative suggests two fast-moving, slippery wrestlers constantly breaking each other's holds, the wrestlers matched with an interminable equality because they are really one wrestler.

Israel means "he who wrestles with God." From Genesis 32:

> And Jacob was left alone; and there wrestled a man with him until the breaking of the day. . . . And he said, Let me go, for the day breaketh. And he said, I will not let thee go, except thou bless me. And he said unto him, What is thy name? And he said, Jacob. And he said, Thy name shall be called no more Jacob, but Israel.

Even the interchangeability of "he"s in this epochal passage seems pertinent to *The Counterlife.* Nathan's Maria, who also writes fiction, in a genteel/gentile fashion, says to him, "You didn't seem to realize that writing for me isn't everything about my existence wrestling to be born." In the modern absence of Jacob's ghostly opponent, Jews wrestle now with such ghosts as the id and the superego, and with the question "What is a Jew?" Nathan asks, "What is a Jew in the first place?" The question has taken on fresh dimensions in Israel—"a whole *country* imagining itself, asking itself, 'What the hell is this business of being a Jew?' " Here, where every cloud and tree and acre can be said to be Jewish, the pacific and pushed-around Jew of the Diaspora, at the mercy of his Christian or Islamic host nations, is superseded. Here Jews can live "a life free of Jewish cringing, deference, diplomacy, apprehension, alienation, self-pity, self-satire, self-mistrust, depression, clowning, bitterness, nervousness, inwardness, hypercriticalness, hypertouchiness, social anxiety, social assimilation—a way of life absolved, in short, of all the Jewish 'abnormalities,' those peculiarities of self-division whose traces remained imprinted in just about every engaging Jew I knew." Thus thinks Nathan, having gone to rescue Henry from his frontier settlement in Judea, among the West Bank Arabs. In his three-day visit, he talks with disillusioned, almost anti-Israeli Jews, with rabid expansionist Jews, with doggedly religious Jews, with Jews as crazy as those he meets in New York. He is less than enchanted; the pervasive social challengingness, the gun his brother totes, and even the terrain disturb him: "Judea . . . could have passed for a piece of the moon to which the Jews had been sadistically exiled by their worst enemies rather than the place they passionately maintained was theirs and no one else's from time immemorial." Aggressive, unapologetic Israel represents the timorous and massacred Diaspora Jew's "construction of a counterlife." At first, most of the non-Arab world cheered: "All over the world people were rooting for the Jews to go ahead and un-Jew themselves in their own little homeland."* Now, with the little nation convincingly tough in its Begin-led militance, anti-Zionism has crept into respectable

---

*Bernard Berenson at the time of Israel's first war for survival in 1948 wrote to the Baroness Liliane de Rothschild, "The complaint made by even the most friendly disposed gentiles has been that Jews would neither till the soil nor fight. The proof to the contrary, given by the Israelis, is perhaps the most important revaluation of Jewry that has happened in my time. It is the prime reason why we should not only be proud of Israel but give it support." Berenson would have preferred to ignore his own Jewishness; he converted to Episcopalianism in Boston at the age of twenty and, five years later, to Catholicism in Italy. But in the years after the Holocaust, the aesthete, in his letters, made observations not unlike some made in *The Counterlife*. Pondering his own narcissism, and the works of Kafka, Bergson, and Proust, Berenson reflected, "Hunted, always insecure, our ancestors must have developed unusual gifts of inner as well as outer observation, which nowadays turns us into psychologists, scientists, novelists, critics." In his nineties, he wrote, "I am more and more amazed to discover how seldom I meet an interesting thinker, scholar, or writer who does not turn out to be a Jew, half-Jew, or quarter-Jew. . . . How easy and warm the atmosphere between born Jews like Isaiah Berlin, Lewis Namier, myself, Bela Horowitz, when we drop the mask of being goyim and return to Yiddish reminiscences, and Yiddish stories and witticisms."

intellectual circles, as Nathan discovers in his adopted land of England.
As he is forcibly told on the plane back, "You think it's the Jewish
superego [the goyim] hate? *They hate the Jewish id!* What right do these
Jews have to *have* an id? The Holocaust should have taught them never
to have an id *again.*"

The Israel sections are interesting but perhaps in too journalistic a way;
the variety of possible opinions is paraded past almost as brutally as stand-
points on Communist Czechoslovakia, from anti through antic and anarchic to stolidly pro, were marshalled by Roth in "The Prague Orgy." The
conversations deteriorate into blocks of *talk,* one babbled essay after another. As the novel goes on, the topic of Jewishness overrides plausibility:
airplane security thugs allude to T. S. Eliot's symbolic, cigar-toting Bleistein, and sisters-in-law in church crypts give quick seminars in the anti-
Semitism of John Buchan. In England, with its faded but distinctly
Christian heritage, Nathan encounters anti-Semitism as if for the first
time, and becomes an American patriot. "To say Jew and goy about
America is to miss the point, because America simply is not that." Affronted repeatedly, he tells Maria, "I didn't run into this stuff there—
never." (He has evidently forgotten how, as related in "Salad Days," his
superior in the Army, the Southerner Captain Clark, would aim cotton
golf balls at his most Hebraic feature, saying, when successful, "Ah, they
we go, Zuckuhmun, rat on the nose.") Zuckerman, who loves to hear his
shiksas screech, finally succeeds in goading his English wife into admitting that even she sometimes asks herself, "Why do Jews make such a
bloody fuss about being Jewish?" and into delivering a three-page tirade
that ends by advising him: "Go back to America, please, where everybody
loves Jews—you think!" Tirades, philippics, self-expositions: reading a
Roth novel becomes like riding in an overheated club car, jostled this way
and that by the clamorous, importunate crowd of talkers while glimpses
of the outside world tantalizingly whip past the steamed-up windows. The
train slackens momentum and clanks to a halt, and we press our forehead
to the glass only to see that we already *were* in this station, an hour or
two ago.

Roth's inquiringness, the fervid delicacy of his subdividing investiga-
tions of mental and moral and emotional states, produces novels of sentiment as lacy, in their way, as a Victorian romancer's. In this novel, the
decisive events take place on operating tables and the actors are surgeons
we never meet. Otherwise, all is thought, feeling, second thought, and
speech. And like a Victorian the author takes us into his confidence with
a flattering concern for our good opinion. Roth has never written more
scrupulously or, in spots, more lovingly. The portrait of the English Maria

is a gorgeous, long-limbed, indolent Gainsborough, complete with horses and towpaths and gray stone walls in the background. The English in-laws are as perfectly "done" as bit parts in *Masterpiece Theatre.* Henry's final revenge on his brother stirs up a stunning anthropological metaphor: "Henry, like a cannibal who out of respect for his victim, to gain whatever history and power is there, eats the brain and learns that raw it tastes like poison." Henry not only eats Nathan's brain but has his number; he is the writer's sharpest critic—the writer as social animal and devious psyche—and an entire anthology of scathing and penetrating remarks about writ-ing and writers could be extracted from their fraternal by-play. The novel as a whole is a performance to cap performances, a defiant round-up and topping-up of the hang-ups and obsessions that wearisome critics like the undersigned have been shyly suggesting Roth has perhaps sufficiently exploited. Nathan himself claims, "As a writer I'd mined my past to its limits, exhausted my private culture and personal memories, and could no longer even warm to squabbling over my work." But, going to the same old well with a vengeance (and with some new geography), Roth shows that more can be still more; this is Zuckerman's most rousing outing since *The Ghost Writer,* and one in which the inspirational value of personal resentment seems blessedly reduced. Do we dare hope it will be Zucker-man's last ride? As Henry might ask, Who *cares* what it's like to be a writer? Having now pushed confessional fiction into meta-fiction, Roth might trust himself as a simple realist, a superbly alert witness of what is; the fringe characters—landladies and taxi-drivers miles removed from the claustral travail of a writer's self-impersonations—have a blunt humorous actuality that patiently waits for Prospero's undivided attention.

I wish I had liked the ending better. It seemed inflated and coyly Pirandelloian. And Zuckerman's concluding vow to have his son, if any, circumcised moved me as much as would a richly nuanced plea, in a novel by a Kikuyu, in favor of tribal scars and clitoridectomy, or an old Chinese poem hymning the symbolic beauty of bound feet. That a narrator so scornful of church and synagogue ends by praising ritual mutilation is a strange twist, in a tale of strange twists. Perhaps the author, who has repeatedly managed to offend Jewish sensibilities, set out in his last chap-ter, "Christendom," to give gentiles a rub of his abrasive satire. British anti-Semitism certainly exists—British anti-everything-un-British exists —but here it appears too bald and savage; it primarily testifies, as Maria observes (the characters get to read the book and complain about it), to Zuckerman's own "great verbal violence" and "aggression." At one point in his concluding stream of self-awareness he expresses dread and revul-sion during an Anglican service of Christmas carols. Christmas carols!

Christianity at its absolute sweetest!! No, that Nathan Zuckerman is definitely not a nice boy.

And Nothing But

THE FACTS: *A Novelist's Autobiography,* by Philip Roth. 195 pp. Farrar, Straus & Giroux, 1988.

The creator of Neil Klugman, Gabe Wallach, Alexander Portnoy, David Kepesh, Peter Tarnopol, and Nathan Zuckerman here bares the actual life behind these variously animated and anguished alter egos. The younger of two sons of a Newark insurance agent, Roth attended Weequahic High School, Newark Colleges of Rutgers, and Bucknell University; baseball, literature, and sex concerned him, each in its season. While studying for his Ph.D. at the University of Chicago, he met and married a gentile divorcée with two small children; he is still licking the psychic wounds left by their unhappy relationship. Another wound has been inflicted by critics, amateur and professional, who absurdly find his exuberant portrayals of Jewish-American life anti-Semitic. The autobiography would seem merely a thinner version, simultaneously dry and watered-down, of the author's droll, explosive, and fearless novels did not one of his characters, Nathan Zuckerman, contribute a long epistolary epilogue that lifts *The Facts* into the liberating uncertainties and revisionary cross-references of fiction. "Sure," Zuckerman portrays himself telling his charming English wife, Maria, "he [Roth, his creator] talks so freely about all his soft spots, but only after choosing awfully carefully which soft spots to talk about." Not so brilliantly convolute and argumentative as the author's last novel, *The Counterlife,* this new raid on Roth's private reality shows, once more, that what interests a good enough writer will interest us. "You don't necessarily, as a writer, have to abandon your biography completely to engage in an act of impersonation," he told *The Paris Review* in 1983. He also told it, "Writing for me isn't a natural thing that I just keep doing, the way fish swim and birds fly. It's something that's done under a certain kind of provocation, a particular urgency. It's the transformation, through an elaborate impersonation, of a personal emergency into a public act."

FRENCHMEN

Art and Artillery

THE POET ASSASSINATED *and Other Stories,* by Guillaume Apollinaire, translated from the French by Ron Padgett. 139 pp. North Point Press, 1984.

Guillaume Apollinaire is the poet who, in *Calligrammes* (1918), reinvented the emblematic or pictographic poem and, in going over the proofs of his first collection, *Alcools* (1913), airily banished all punctuation, thus giving modern verse its distinctive look and syntactical freedom. He wrote prose as well—art criticism, pornographic novels, gossipy journalism, and short stories. In 1968, Holt, Rinehart & Winston published, in the format of a small coffee-table book, a translation, by the poet Ron Padgett, with sinister photographic illustrations by Jim Dine, of Apollinaire's long, surreal story, "The Poet Assassinated." Now, sixteen years later, Mr. Padgett and North Point Press, of Berkeley, California, have come out with an unillustrated translation of the full text of the collection, *Le Poète assassiné,* which Apollinaire published in 1916 and which contained fifteen shorter pieces in addition to the title story.

Mr. Padgett, however scrupulous in his translation—it reads well, and captures Apollinaire's lazy lightness—and in thanking the many who have helped him in his prolonged labor, has not sullied this volume with any bibliographical or biographical information, whether in the form of introduction, afterword, or footnotes. Apollinaire's eccentric and by now rather antique fictions, the implication is, speak clearly for themselves; I am not sure this is the case. The poet's prose inventions were spontaneous and personal yet also fantastic and cunning. "The Poet Assassinated," for instance, was much revised and added-to, as real life altered the veiled autobiographical content, and a more thorough edition than Mr. Padgett's might have favored us with, in footnotes or an appendix, some of the excised paragraphs and altered phrases, which are a matter of French scholarly record and have been cited in such English-language biographies as those by Margaret Davies and Francis Steegmuller. The volume entitled *The Poet Assassinated* was assembled by Apollinaire while recuperating in a Paris hospital from a head wound suffered in battle on March 17, 1916; it included stories and sketches composed since the publication of his previous collection of short fiction, *L'Hérésiarque et Cie.* (1910; English version by Rémy Inglis Hall, *The Heresiarch and Co.*, 1965). A number of the pieces had previously appeared in such magazines as *Le Matin* and his own *Soirées de Paris;* the dates of their magazine publication and of, where known, their composition would have been welcome information. If Apollinaire's fiction deserves translation at this late date, it deserves what frame of scholarly clarification can be provided, rather than the chic starkness of this North Point edition, which gives us two pages' worth of Mr. Padgett's "friends and colleagues" and nothing of Apollinaire's circumstances, motives, or models.

The story "The Poet Assassinated" runs to sixty-nine pages here; in eighteen titled episodes, or chapters, it presents a highly distorted autobiography of the author in the guise of the frenzied rise and fall of Croniamantal, "the greatest living poet." Apollinaire was born in 1880, the illegitimate son of Angelica Alexandrine de Kostrowitzky, a twenty-two-year-old renegade daughter of a minor Polish nobleman; Apollinaire's father, it is probable if not certain, was her lover of many years, the aristocratic Italian officer Francisco Flugi d'Aspermont, who disappeared not only from Angelica's life but from the world at large after 1885. These muddled beginnings are outrageously parodied as the casual roadside mating of Viersélin Tigoboth, an itinerant Walloon musician, and the voluptuous and impulsive Macarée, "a dark young woman, shaped with pretty globes," who bares her breasts at the musician, copulates "under love's power, behind the blackthorns," and gets back on her bicycle and pedals away. She finds herself pregnant, debates abortion with herself, and ends, after rapturously apostrophizing her own "stretchy, bearded, smooth, bombed, dolorous, round, silky, ennobling belly," by having the child. Unlike Angelica de Kostrowitzky, Macarée gets rich at gambling, marries a baron, and dies in childbirth. The child is christened Gaétan-François-Étienne-Jack-Amélie-Alonso Desygrées, scarcely more fantastic than the string of names with which Apollinaire's mother, at the Roman Municipal Records Office, saddled her fatherless infant—Guillaume Albert Wladimir Alexandre Apollinaire de Kostrowitzky. She always called him Wilhelm. He spent his early years in Rome with a foster family; when Guillaume was six, his mother, he, and a younger, also illegitimate brother, Alberto, moved to Monaco. There, in several schools along the

Côte d'Azur, he became a good and enthusiastic student; his language became French, and his poetic vocation was well developed by the time, in 1899, that the Kostrowitzkys left Monaco and made their way, with many a detour, to Paris.

When Croniamantal's foster father, the Baron des Ygrées, commits suicide as a consequence of gambling debts, the boy is adopted by an erudite Dutchman, Janssen, and is educated by him. When Janssen dies, Croniamantal takes his inheritance and goes to Paris "so he could peacefully indulge his taste for literature, because for some time now, and secretly, he was writing poems which he kept in an old cigar box." The young poet is described running up the rue Houdon: "His eyes devoured everything they saw and when his eyelids came together rapidly like jaws, they engulfed the universe which was endlessly renovated by him as he ran along imagining the smallest details of the enormous worlds he was feasting his eyes on." He visits the atelier of a painter called the Bird of Benin, and experiences the bliss of paint: "In the atelier there were joys of all colors. A big window took up the northern side and all you could see was sky-blue, like a woman singing." The Bird of Benin announces that he has laid eyes on the perfect girl for Croniamantal: "She has the somber, childlike face of those who are destined to cause suffering. I'm telling you, I saw your woman. She is ugliness and beauty; she is like everything we love today." This closely parallels a real incident: in 1907, Picasso, having just met Marie Laurencin in an art gallery, told Apollinaire, "I have a fiancée for you." He introduced them, and shortly thereafter the poet moved out of his mother's apartment to pursue the affair, which lasted until 1912. Revising "The Poet Assassinated" after the break-up with his mistress, Apollinaire substituted the phrase "destined to cause suffering" for the original "made for eternal loves," and inserted a passage including the sentences:

> Six months passed. For the last five of them Tristouse Ballerinette had been Croniamantal's mistress, and she loved him passionately for a week. In exchange for this love, the lyrical boy had made her immortal and glorious forever by celebrating her in marvellous poems.
>
> "I was unknown," she thought, "and now he's made me illustrious among all living women.
>
> "They used to think I was generally ugly with my thinness, my oversized mouth, my horrible teeth, my asymmetrical face, my crooked nose. But now I'm beautiful and all the men tell me so."

Though Picasso and Marie Laurencin have been firmly related to these fanciful incidents, no one has unambiguously identified Paponat, the rich "fonipoit" (in the French, *"fopoîte"*; that is, *"faux poète"*) who becomes

Tristouse's new lover, or Horace Tograth, the German who, from the unlikely launching pad of a French-language newspaper in Adelaide, Australia, inaugurates a world-wide anti-poet crusade to which Croniamantal falls victim. The poet's assassination is a savage, though farcical, business:

> And raising his cane, [a man whom the charismatic Tograth has cured of baldness] thrust it so adroitly that it burst Croniamantal's right eye. He fell backwards. Some women fell upon him and beat him. Tristouse was prancing around with joy, as Paponat tried to calm her down. But with the point of her umbrella she went up and poked out Croniamantal's other eye, which saw her doing it. He cried out:
> "I confess my love for Tristouse Ballerinette, the divine poetry that consoles my soul."
> . . . The ladies stepped quickly aside and a man wielding a butcherknife laid in his palm threw it so that it stuck right in Croniamantal's open mouth. Other men did the same. The knives stuck in his belly and chest, and pretty soon there was nothing left on the ground but a corpse spiked like a big sea urchin.

The literary analogy is with the death of Orpheus, torn to pieces by the Thracian women in a Dionysian orgy; the episode also foreshadows Apollinaire's war wound, in which several shell splinters pierced his skull. Uncanny prophecy does not end there: the Bird of Benin, announcing that he is a sculptor as well as a painter, executes a memorial for the poet—a hole in the ground!—and in fact, forty years after Apollinaire's death, a memorial statue for him by Picasso—the head of a woman!—was placed in the garden beside Saint-Germain-des-Prés.

The primary interest of "The Poet Assassinated" lies in its masked revelations of Apollinaire's life. As a narrative, in its cold violence and clattering burlesque, it functions under the malign influence of Alfred Jarry, a self-destructive visionary whose extravagances fascinated bohemian Paris and who, toward the end of his short life, generously partook of conversation and of absinthe with the young Italian, seven years his junior. Certain rhapsodies and stretches of cultural satire show Apollinaire's softer, irrepressibly fluent touch. A fantasy on female fashion, for instance, is put into the mouth of Tristouse:

> "This year," said Tristouse, "fashions are bizarre and common, simple and full of fantasy. Any material from nature's domain can now be introduced into the composition of women's clothes. I saw a charming dress made of corks. . . . A big designer is thinking about launching tailor-made outfits

made of old bookbindings done in calf. It's charming. All the ladies of letters would want to wear them, and one could approach them and whisper in their ear under the pretext of reading the titles. Fish bones are being worn a lot on hats. . . . Dresses embellished with coffee beans, cloves, cloves of garlic, onions, and bunches of raisins, these will be perfect for social calls. Fashion is becoming practical and no longer looks down on anything. It ennobles everything. It does for materials what the Romantics did for words."

A reader at all acquainted with Apollinaire's biography will be struck by what is suppressed, in this fantasy version, of his formative years. Angelica (or Olga, as she called herself in Monaco) de Kostrowitzky was a mother more flamboyant and tenacious than the obligingly doomed Macarée; aristocratic in bearing, with nothing of the demimondaine about her appearance, and with no sympathy for her elder son's career in the arts, she had been a rebel against conventions since the age of sixteen, when she was expelled from an exclusive convent-academy run by French nuns for the children of the Roman nobility. She took up with the dashing Francisco, then in his forties, and after his defection became a virtual courtesan, who paraded a succession of "uncles" before her two boys and who—as revealed by documents published for the first time in Steegmuller's biography in 1963—was ordered expelled from the principality of Monaco shortly after she arrived in 1887. She was named in this official order (which she somehow evaded, staying in Monaco for twelve years) as a *"femme galante"* and mentioned in a memoir of the time as an *"entraîneuse"*—one who "leads men on" at the gambling tables and is financed partly by the proprietors thereof. One of her admirers, a Lyonnais silk-manufacturer with bookish tastes, perhaps contributed to the shadowy persona of Janssen, Croniamantal's protector. Her most sustained liaison, contracted in Monaco but continued in Paris until her death, was with an Alsatian gambler named Jules Weil. She herself was a devoted gambler. The insecurities the sons of such a mother endured, the deceits and pretenses forced upon them, must be mostly imagined, though in 1899 the young "Russians," as the Kostrowitzkys were called, made the newspapers and the court records; in a case of considerable local interest in the Ardennes town of Stavelot, the two teen-aged boys (their mother and Weil having returned to Paris) were hauled into court for sneaking out of a *pension* without paying the bill, causing the proprietors to postpone their daughter's wedding. Something evasive and too volatile remained part of Apollinaire. His handwriting was so changeable that his bank required him to file five or six specimens of his signature. His mother, in the months after his birth, had recorded him under three different sets of names with the Rome registry, and he ended by naming himself. Yet Olga never relinquished the role of mother, nor Apollinaire that of son. He lived with her off and on well into adulthood, and they kept in close touch. His shabby and unsettled upbringing left scarcely a shadow on his sunny, energetic personality, and almost the only complaint he committed to print is the line (from a poem, "Le Larron," written when he was about nineteen) *"Ton père fut un sphinx et ta mère une nuit"* ("Your father was a sphinx and your mother a night"). "A night," the poem goes on to say, "which charmed with its glow Zacinth and the Cyclades." The fictive Macarée's sexy glow is the most vivid thing about her, and she dies in a mixture of laughter and tears convenient moments after "giving the world a healthy, masculine child."

Apollinaire emerged from childhood with the imaginative writer's basic tool—a need to lie. His fancy served to transmute and dismiss his past. Of the fifteen shorter stories in *The Poet Assassinated*, a few give refracted glimpses of this past. "Giovanni Moroni" presents, as the memories of an Italian-born Parisian bank employee "of no great culture," a sumptuous child's Italy: "I had all kinds of toys: horses, Punches, swords, bowling pins, puppets, soldiers, wagons. . . . These feast days for the Three Kings, when I ate so many candied orange peels, so many anise drops, have left me with a delicious aftertaste!" Nothing is known of the Roman foster family with which the two little "Russians" were left in the pre-Monaco days, but Giovanni Moroni's recalled household of Beppo the toymaker and his superstitious wife, Attilia, with its delicious foods, its cockroaches exterminated with boiling water ("the unfortunate bugs, whose final agitation, running, and chaotic jumping enchanted me"), its murky encounters with a young monk who is naked beneath his dirty habit and with a gang of masked carnival celebrants who leave behind a corpse, has a resonance, an unliterary richness of feeling rather rare in Apollinaire's inventions. His first set of stories, *The Heresiarch and Co.*, had more of this earthiness, more anecdotal force and Mediterranean color, including an obsessive interest in Catholicism and blasphemy; it was published before *Alcools* and *Les Peintres cubistes*, and it may be that, with his roles as poet and as chief propagandist for modern painting relatively undefined, the young Apollinaire tried harder as a short-story writer.

Not that some of these later pieces, tossed off though they feel, are not accomplished; the poet—who wrote many of his letters in perfect verse, it came to him so easily—was also a prolific journalist and an editor. He could do a literary job. "The Favorite," though it ends on the note of slightly crazed misogyny that lurks like a sinister clown in Apollinaire's imagination, begins with the sunstruck bluntness of Hemingway or Unamuno, with a symbolist touch:

> It was in Beausoleil, near the Monacan border, in that part of Carnier called Tonkin and inhabited almost exclusively by Piedmontese.
> An invisible executioner bloodied the afternoon. Two men were bearing a stretcher, sweating and breathing hard. From time to time they turned toward the sun's slit throat and cursed it, their eyes almost closed.

The stories, generally no longer than three or four pages, are smoothly built about a single idea, and slide quickly toward their shrug of catastrophe. Some—"The Departure of the Shadow," "The Deified Invalid"—are so Borgesian in tone and form that one wonders if Borges, in his continental sojourn of 1914–21, ran across them. The Borgesian theme of mental simultaneity—of all phenomena concentrating to a single point—occurs several times, and the word "atrocious" in this sentence has the Argentine's ring: "We were walking along without talking, and, after a while, when I felt the desire to see our shadows again, I saw with a singularly atrocious pleasure [*un plaisir singulièrement atroce*] that Louise's had left her." Sometimes, Apollinaire can think of little to do with his characters but kill them ("The Meeting at the Mixed Club," "The Eagle Hunt"). His cruel fables have a double face, of Gothic relish and Latin stoicism. Unlike some poets launched into prose, he seems in firm control of his effects. "The Talking Memories," as a story, is almost slick, with a satisfying "twist" at the end, like a Saki or a Roald Dahl, and "Little Recipes from Modern Magic" could appear in a contemporary humor magazine:

> *Incantation for beating the stock market*
> Every morning you will eat a red herring while uttering forty times before and after: "Bucks and plug, clink and drink." And after ten days your dead stock will become live stock.
> *Recipe for glory*
> Carry with you four fountain pens, drink clear water, have a great man's mirror, and often look at yourself in it without smiling.

One small story, originally dedicated to his mother and believed to be based upon her reminiscences of the girlhood years she spent in the Roman convent, is a gem of psychologically plausible hallucination: a group of twelve-year-old convent girls hears beyond the walls the sound of a hunter's horn, and in the following days they all encounter in the corridors a disembodied blue eye, "making a beautiful azure splash in the darkness." Gradually, they cease to be frightened of it, and coquettishly seek to be seen: "None of us would have wanted to be seen by the blue eye with our hands spotted with ink. Each did her best to look her best when going down the halls." The convent holds no mirrors, but some of the doors have panes of glass, and "a section of black apron flattened behind the pane formed an improvised mirror, where quick, quick you'd look at yourself, arrange your hair, and ask yourself if you were pretty." The blue eye slowly disappears from the halls, having been conjured up by a group need and having served to objectify the first intense flash of budding vanity and sexuality in old-fashionedly cloistered females: "You have never seen the blue eye go by, O little girls of today!"

The last story, written in 1916, caps a half-hearted and ragged collection with a startling burst of terrible beauty; only a poet could have written it. "The Case of the Masked Corporal, That Is, the Poet Resuscitated" contains some pictographic verbal arrangements like the shaped poems in *Calligrammes* and also an attempt to round up the characters of the preceding stories, a hurried grab at unity. Like Borges's Funes the Memorious, the resuscitated Croniamantal, now a soldier, sees everything at once: "He saw the battlefields of eastern Prussia, of Poland, the quiet of a little Siberian town, fighting in Africa, Anzac, and Sedul-Bar, Salonika, the stripped and terrible oceanic elegance of the trenches in Barren Champagne, the wounded second-lieutenant carried to the ambulance, baseball players in Connecticut, and battles, battles. . . ." The battlefield is evoked with a passion beyond protest: "And the Front lit up, the hexahedrons were rolling, the steel flowers were blossoming out, the barbed wire was growing thinner with bloody desires, the trenches were opening like females before males."

Apollinaire had eagerly enlisted. As a foreigner—and one, furthermore, in his mid-thirties—he could have sat the war out in Paris, as did Picasso. His first application to the army, in August 1914, was ignored; he successfully enlisted in Nice, and jubilantly punned, "I so love art that I have joined the artillery. . . ." Later, he was to leave the relative safety of his artillery unit to become an infantry officer in the front-line trenches. Thus he demonstrated his courage and his loyalty to France, as if these had been in question. His mother, the daughter of a Polish-Russian colonel, approved of his soldiering as of no other aspect of his career. "How beautiful are the rockets that light up the night," he was to proclaim, in faint echo of *"ta mère une nuit."* The Italian Futurists, to whom Apollinaire the critic was attracted after cubism, had a theoretical thirst for violence; though he once wrote, *"Ah Dieu que la guerre est jolie,"* the letters he poured out as a *"soldat de la douce France"* show him shedding whatever naïve illusions he held concerning "the simple horror of the trenches." Yet his war injury, in its fictional rendering, is ennobled by a myth: "The corporal in the blind mask was smiling amorously at the future, when a fragment of a high caliber shell hit him in the head, from which sprang, like pure blood, a triumphant Minerva. Stand up, everybody, to give a courteous welcome to victory!"* Croniamantal has gone from being torn Orpheus to fruitful Jupiter; Apollinaire, who was never quite himself after his head wound, and who weakly succumbed to disease a few years later, has among his laurels a claim to being the last poet to write of war as a theatre of glory.

Between Pinget's Ears

BETWEEN FANTOINE AND AGAPA, by Robert Pinget, translated from the French by Barbara Wright. 83 pp. Red Dust, 1982.

THAT VOICE, by Robert Pinget, translated from the French by Barbara Wright. 114 pp. Red Dust, 1982.

The brave little publishing house called Red Dust, which operates out of a postal box at Gracie Station, keeps issuing, along with the new poetry from Peru and other such bulletins from the scattered legions of the avant-garde, the works of the esteemed contemporary French novelist Robert Pinget. Recently published, in translations by the indispensable Barbara Wright, are Pinget's first prose work, *Between Fantoine and Agapa,* and a novel from 1980, *That Voice.* What can one say of Pinget, as he comes through in Ms. Wright's loving translations, except that he conveys, amid much willful murk, an impression of integrity, intelligence, and power? He is a dark author, placidly settled amid his favorite village odors of damp stone and rotting wood (anybody who has stepped into an old French farmhouse will recognize the aroma), and mysteriously content to churn and rechurn the chronic garbled rumors of perversion and homicide that make up his plots, if he can be said to have plots. This reviewer had hoped that a consecutive reading of a work Pinget produced in 1951 and one published in 1980 would clarify what the author has

---

*Amorousness in Apollinaire takes many forms. In the title of this piece, for instance, the "Case" of the title is a pun on the French *cas,* slang for the penis, and the concluding exhortation has a jubilant phallic connotation, echoing the World War I cry *"Debout les morts!"* The name Croniamantal was, the poet told Marie Laurencin, a blend of "Cro-Magnon" and "Néanderthal," in boast of his stone-age priapic powers. I am indebted for these racy tidbits to a letter from Professor Scott Bates.

been "up to"; and indeed certain differences in texture and machination are apparent. But it cannot be said that Pinget began as anything but oddly, opaquely himself; his surrealism has been constant, though its field of operation has become more rural and, as it were, medieval and hellish.

One might suppose *Between Fantoine and Agapa* to have a certain geographical focus and to lay claim to the imaginary territory of provincial France where the later fictions—preëminently, *The Inquisitory,* still Pinget's most impressive and cogent work—more or less take place. Alas, one is fooled again, for the little book is a collection of disconnected pranks, or prose poems, which take place not so much between Fantoine and Agapa as between Pinget's ears. The first chapter, or sketch, or whatever, "Vishnu Takes His Revenge," deals with the curé of Fantoine, who is bored. "He subscribes to theater magazines. He dips into the fashionable authors. He gleans in learned vineyards. He passes for a scholar, but he's a rotter." His parishioners don't provide much amusement for him: "The inhabitants of Fantoine are hopeless. They drink. They work. They drink. Their children are epileptic, their wives pregnant." But, then, "luckily, someone from Agapa-la-Ville takes an interest in him and sends a book on Cambodia." The curé grows interested; he teaches himself the Khmer language; he thinks all day of the ancient temples and sees royal dancing girls in the local population. "The forest of Fantoine becomes populated with yak demons, with Mrinh Kangveal spirits, with Banra trees. Paddy-fields cover the country." Saying mass, he mistakenly intones, "Hic est enim corpus Yak"; and a gigantic demon "sprang out of the Host, dispatched the curé, and pulverized the church. And Vishnu the Eternal deigned to smile." In the title story, "Between Fantoine and Agapa," a man, his wife, and their child prepare to picnic between these two fictional towns when a sign in a field proclaims, "Alopecia-impetrating [patchy-baldness-obtaining-by-entreaty] prohibited"; this makes them so frightened they skip lunch. Later that night, the child vomits jam and the wife's hair stands on end. "But not for long, because half an hour later she was as bald as a coot." But for these two tales, there is no mention of Fantoine or Agapa, and the subject matter gravitates toward the mythic and the facetiously geographic—episodes take place in Manhattan, Menseck, the Forest of Grance, and Florence, and characters include Don Quixote, a parrot called Methuselah, Aeschylus and his maidservant Aglaia, and the Persian King Artaxerxes. As he roams through these prankish fancies, the young Pinget reminds us of various comrades in surrealism. Of Alfred Jarry and his frenzies of mechanical precision:

Everything that touches him, from near or from far, cucurbitaces—I mean: belongs to the gourd family, like the pumpkin—starting with the spirals in shells, cow pats, and velodromes, and ending with his own body, which pullulates with oblate spheroids.

Of William Burroughs and his gleeful wars and plagues:

In short, civil war. And one of atrocious cruelty. Once the steak-tracts had been launched, an epidemic of the bacteria of contradiction broke out. Every individual affected by the microbe considered that his arm and his head, his eye and his foot, his navel and his spleen, were irreconcilable. He destroyed himself by tearing out, burning, or vivisecting the contradictory organ.

Pinget also shows something of the antic sunniness of Raymond Queneau and of Beckett's clownish desolation. His playful dabbling with history and myth suggests a host of experimental modernists, from Borges to Barth, from the *Fabrications* of the late Michael Ayrton to the *Eclogues* of our contemporary Guy Davenport. Literary experiment and surrealism have certain natural channels into which to run, it would appear, not so unlike the well-worn grooves of realism; nonsense, being an inversion of sense, is condemned to share a certain structure with it, and a finitude of forms. Pinget, even in this early, rather frolicsome and eclectic work, does look forward to what is to become his mature tone. The last and longest piece in *Between Fantoine and Agapa* is titled "Journal," and, though concerned with such absurdities as snowstorms of fingernail clippings and dwarfs sold at auction to be used as candelabra by religious communities, it foreshadows the sinister cruelty and gloom of the later work. An inbred, joyless, cannibalistic sexuality is a recurrent theme in Pinget, and occurs here: "They mate among themselves, without the slightest desire, and give birth to edible daughters who are a kind of saprophyte." A dreamlike restlessness in the forms of things makes itself felt with a shudder: "Their agricultural work is backbreaking. They . . . tread down the excrescences that tend to form on the fences. I tried this, with the help of a peasant. But just as I was making an oblique movement over the unexposed part I let go my hold, the excrescence came and knocked on my foot, and the man only just had time to push me back out of the way." Pinget's preoccupation with the menace of the organic and with the Stygian stirrings of the dead emerges side by side with characteristic flashes of aesthetic theory: "In a work of art we do not try to conjure up beauty or truth. We only have recourse to them—as to a subterfuge—in order to be able to go on breathing." And the prose, though indeterminate in its significations, is chiselled in its cadences—so deliberate in its bewildering effects that the intimidated reader, coming upon alphabetical formations like "This has been goiñQHQfor so long" and "hnd he passes the laundry again," doubts whether he is in the presence of a misprint or of an especially refined, albeit obscure, intention.

That Voice concerns . . . well, what *does* it concern? The phrase *"manque un raccord"* ("a missing link") is used seventeen times in the French text, the translator claims on the jacket's back flap, and a phrase rendered as "impossible anamnesis" ("anamnesis" = "recalling to mind") returns a number of times also, as do "invincible fatigue," "traces of effacement," "psspss," "take a hair of the night that bit you," and "an invisible mani-tou." The author, in a special preface to the American edition, assures us that "the structure of the novel is precise, although not immediately apparent. The different themes are intermingled. One cuts into another point-blank, then the other resumes and cuts into the first, and so on until the end." The two themes named are "the theme of the cemetery" and "that of the gossip at the grocery." In the cemetery, evidently, at the intersection of alleys numbered 333 and 777, on All Saints' Day, near the tomb of the minor belletrist Alexandre Mortin, a young man called Théo-dore, coming to arrange and leave some chrysanthemums, meets a ghost, or walking dead man, who identifies himself as Dieudonné, or Dodo for short. Dodo, it slowly dawns, is Théo's uncle. Maybe Théo killed him, for his money. Alexandre Mortin has a brother, Alfred, who perhaps is also called the Master; he seems to be keeping little Théodore in his house by force, according to gossip down at the grocery store, where "that otiose, never-ending story" acquires ever more characters (the servant Magnin, Mademoiselle Passetant, Madame Buvard, Monsieur Alphonse, many of whom we have met before in other Pinget novels, or imagine we have) and effaces itself as it goes, like a slate being covered over and over with new versions, until with the best will in the world the reader starts to feel sandy-eyed and itches to turn on the eleven o'clock news, where things are said once or at worst twice. As we grind along in hopes of things coming clearer or of Pinget's making one of his graveyard jokes ("Just imagine the state of our necropolis, hygienewise, that'll discourage the All Saints' Day fans"), the tale appears increasingly to talk about itself:

> And little by little, just like that, with the passing days, a sort of stupid litany which took the place of a chronicle for us, you see how very backward we were.
> For indeed, the dead do answer.

Indeed, in such a close-knit village, the dead are not allowed to die; they continue to hold their place in the fabric of gossip, of remembrance, their deaths incidental within the pervasive dissolution of life erasing itself as it goes. The atmosphere is deadly, dank, musty: "Old formulas, old papers, old filth, old chimeras, everything is disintegrating." Rural France is Catholic France, and on this ground modernism joins hands with the pious macabre, with the supernatural's Gothic underside, "in touch with putrefaction and decomposition, hence oriented toward the future." Here voices matter-of-factly proclaim, "I went back into my tomb, where I'm awaiting the resurrection of the dead," and what may be the author's voice murmurs, "The life to come, it conditions, it contorts, it confuses, it's just life."

Pinget locates us in the gently moldering, nowhere solid hell* of communal remembering, of mutual awareness, never exact, never erased. "Something else is being prepared beyond people's consciousness, it had to be reshaped first, we have been at pains to do so." And we, it must be admitted, have been at pains to read the result. Could the impression Pinget creates be conveyed less exasperatingly, less numbingly? Perhaps not, since its theme, to a degree, is the exasperation and numbingness of our human, social, forgetful, banal existence. But why speculate as to the author's purposes when he has recently been in New York City and spelled them out? To a crowd gathered at New York University last October, Pinget, reading his lucid French text in a hard-to-hear monotone, explained (as translated by Barbara Wright), "My attachment to the technique of the intermingling of themes and their variations is due to the admiration I have always felt for so-called baroque music." He is also attached to the concept of the collective unconscious:

> In my eyes, the share allotted to the irrational is one of the ways that may help me to arrive at a personal "truth," which is only to a very limited extent present in my awareness of it. This is a kind of open provocation to the unconscious.... We are all, indeed, more or less dependent on the collective unconscious, whose nature we can only glimpse by examining as best we can those manifestations of it which we perceive in ourselves.

Later in this address he mentioned Jung, in connection with his own "approach to the dark face of language, in order to make it easier for unconscious values to break through." He spoke of his "declared intention, from the very first book, to extend the limits of the written word by replenishing it with the spoken word." Confusion, contradiction, "all the suggestions, refutations, prolongations and metamorphoses of fragments

---

*The word stems from the Germanic root meaning "concealed" and originally, like Hades and Sheol, had less to do with punishment than simple bleak survival in a vague netherworld.

of speech" are intrinsic to this intention; his reader will have "the impression that the book is being composed, and decomposed, under his very eye." Not that the books are written for the eye; they are "to be listened to, rather than read."

We are put in mind of *Finnegans Wake*, Jungian in its attempt to show the world-mind in its sleep, and also employing a tone of unremitting gossip, of multiple murmur. Language is, at bottom, a spoken thing. From the overthrow of Latin by Dante's Italian and Chaucer's English to the modernists' rejection of Georgian prosodic proprieties in favor of jagged colloquial rhythms, written literature has deferred to the evolving reality of speech. Defoe, Addison, Wordsworth, Mark Twain, Joyce, Hemingway, Henry Green—all refreshed themselves at the springs of the demotic idiom, and forged their styles in conscious opposition to "literariness." But the chronic shucking of tired literary conventions is itself a literary maneuver, and in Pinget's case a heavy escort of cerebration and deliberate experiment marches with his "fragments of speech." On the excuse of Alexandre Mortin's being a minor poet, many abstruse theoretical remarks are interwoven with the voices of *That Voice:* "And analyzed the whys and wherefores, and finally decreed that poetry had no existence outside a certain system or method." In his address at New York University, Pinget announced, "I have great respect for the present-day critical methods." And, moreover, behind his work, with his persistent rumors of the old religion, lies a less orthodox religious impulse:

> The *homo religiosus*, linked to the essential—if we admit his presence in every one of us—rebels against the lacerations produced by the succession of days, and seeks refuge in the time which knows neither succession nor laceration, that of the Word.

This comes from a beautiful statement given to the Mainz Academy of Sciences and Literature on the subject of "literary baggage." "The sole 'baggage,' " Pinget says, "that helps us to conquer chronological time and to participate in the other, absolute time, is a bouquet of texts. . . . Light baggage, buzzing with words, which, ever since the world has been the world—and there are many legends that vouch for it—has ensured our passage, without let or hindrance, over on to the other bank."

In the meantime, we are on this bank of earthly clay, and this reviewer would be doing less than his duty if he did not admit that he found *That Voice,* as an experience of readerly immersion in a fabricated world, less compelling and more mannered than, say, Pinget's *Libera Me Domine,* which it resembles in ambition and milieu. The sinister, shifting rumors of dark deeds done amid rural stagnation had a force there that here weakly tinges the pleasures of a self-professedly intricate counterpoint. A perfected artistic method can serve, unfortunately, to insulate the artist, to dull his recourse to the ever shifting, ever fructifying actual. *Between Fantoine and Agapa,* for all its buffoonery, was a venture into the unknown; *That Voice* is a demonstration of a mastered method, in a territory thoroughly subdued.

Illuminating Reversals

FABLE, by Robert Pinget, translated from the French by Barbara Wright. 63 pp. Red Dust, 1980.

From this French writer of strange integrity, a work of surpassing strangeness. The hero—"this Miaille or whatever his name is"—finds himself sleeping overnight in a hole in the hay of a barn he seems to recognize. Someone is watching him, but who? The countryside has been devastated by a disastrous war, or has it? Bands of naked men roam around eating corpses. There are allusions to the Crucifixion and the Fall, and overtones of blasphemy, which, the translator tells us in a curt afterword, "the author now disapproves of." The prose is resolutely abstruse, sibylline, and laconic; it's a rare paragraph that has more than a single sentence in it. "To move words around, a sublime game," the author (or an approximation) confides. "To inhabit every utterance so as to give it its own meaning." After a while, the hero puts out his eyes with a knife, and his name changes slightly, to Miette. The atmosphere of futuristic cataclysm yields to a gossipy lament for the past simplicities of country life in Pinget's fictional village of Fantoine. His bleak riddling is distinguished from his mentor Beckett's by a vivid sense of communal voice and surreally filtered regional authenticity. Not for every taste, this fable yet has its resonances, deriving from "these sorts of reversals that throw light on things in depth."

Michel Tournier

THE WIND SPIRIT: *An Autobiography*, by Michel Tournier, translated from the French by Arthur Goldhammer. 259 pp. Beacon Press, 1989.

GILLES & JEANNE, by Michel Tournier, translated from the French by Alan Sheridan. 126 pp. Grove Press, 1990.

THE GOLDEN DROPLET, by Michel Tournier, translated from the French by Barbara Wright. 206 pp. Doubleday, 1987.

At around the time, in the Sixties, when the intellectual innovations of Roland Barthes and Claude Lévi-Strauss and Fernand Braudel began to achieve international influence, French fiction ceased to export well. Alain Robbe-Grillet and his *nouveau roman* suddenly seemed just an idea, and a superficial one at that, producing novels as depthless as movies but on a much smaller screen; simultaneously, it began to appear that Françoise Sagan was not quite another Colette. Though the French literary industry has kept humming away, pinning prizes on itself and generating fodder for the wildly popular bookchat show *Apostrophes*, the reverberations carry but feebly across the Atlantic. Perhaps, having so heavily imported the ideas of Braudel and Michel Foucault and Jacques Derrida, we have no spare change for the light goods of fiction. It is symptomatic of a depressed market, in any case, that Michel Tournier, arguably France's foremost living novelist ("France has produced no novelist of real importance in twenty years, except Michel Tournier," quoth Raymond Sokolov in *The Wall Street Journal*), has come to be published so marginally here. The English version of his autobiography, *The Wind Spirit*, has been brought out by Boston's little Unitarian publishing house, Beacon Press, and Grove Press has performed a very skittish dance with Alan Sheridan's English translation of a 1983 novella, *Gilles & Jeanne:* Grove sent bound galleys to prospective American reviewers, then cancelled publication on the ground that the translation was riddled with errors, then turned around and produced an edition after all.

The Wind Spirit, prettily printed, and jacketed with a nineteenth-century German painting of a little shepherd lying on a dune stargazing, would be a good book for the stranger to Tournier to start with. In six lively, digressive, aphoristic chapters, the author presents his life mostly in terms of his opinions and inspirations; only in the first chapter, which sketches his origins and childhood, do biographical facts dominate. This chapter is titled "Born Under a Lucky Star," Mr. Goldhammer's translation of "L'Enfant coiffé"; he explains that *coiffé* means to be born with a caul, a piece of luck equivalent to being born with a silver spoon in one's mouth, and that the word ties into the epigraph by Saint-John Perse, which runs, "When you stop grooming me / I'll stop hating you." Throughout, the translator has added explanatory footnotes to the footnotes provided by Tournier, intensifying the somewhat stern pedagogic atmosphere of *The Wind Spirit*. It appeared in France in 1977, when Tournier was fifty-three years old. The curious but presently widespread autobiographical impulse in men still enjoying middle age possibly stems from a desire to set the record straight before senility muddles it, and a hope of lightening the ballast for the homeward leg of life's voyage.

Tournier was born, in 1924 in Paris, in the comfortable upper reaches of the bourgeoisie. His father was "the founder and director of something called the BIEM," the Bureau International des Éditions Musico-Mécaniques, which "orchestrated the complexities of rights and contracts pertaining to recorded music sold outside the right-holder's country of origin." The business was lucrative and complex, involving branches in many countries and feeding with many spare records a small boy's phonograph. Well-off, immersed in music, and further blessed with "an old-fashioned apothecary" for a grandfather, in the friendly village of Bligny-sur-Ouche, the little boy gathered a surprisingly grim impression of life:

> Stripped from his mother's womb like a fox cub from its lair, the child finds tenuous and temporary shelter in his mother's arms, nourished by capricious and parsimonious breasts. Subsequently he must abandon this refuge as well, after which he will be allowed only a few minutes a day in that last haven, his mother's bed, a vast ship, white and shadowy, in which for the briefest of intervals his body again clings to the body from which it sprang. Then comes the final expulsion. Grown "too big," the child can no longer "decently" lie in its parents' bed. Thereupon begins a long trek across a vast and terrifying desert.

At the age of four, Michel was "an extremely nervous child, subject to convulsions, hypersensitive, and perpetually ill." One morning, two white-coated strangers burst into his room and pulled out his tonsils, a bloody deed he has never forgiven: "During the last war prepubescent girls were raped by soldiers. I maintain that they were less traumatized than I was by having my throat slit at the age of four." The doctor became "the only man in the world whom I have ever hated without reservation, because he did me incalculable harm, having branded my heart at the most tender age with an incurable distrust of my fellow human beings, even those nearest and dearest to me." By the age of six, Michel had become "a child with an enormous head upon a sparrowlike body, and [he] neither slept nor ate." Nor was his physical frailty made up in mental brilliance: "I was an execrable student, and rarely did I finish a school year in the same institution in which I began. . . . I read little and late." And yet at some point in his resisted education he took a shine to the rarefied *Monadology* of Leibniz and to Anselm's ontological proof of God's existence: "From earliest childhood I had a yen for the constructs of the mind, for subtle proofs, for a rare and technical vocabulary."

The other unusual yen in Tournier's developing mind was his *Germanistik*, a fascination with German culture inherited from both parents: "My father and mother met at the Sorbonne when he was studying for a doctorate in German and she for a master's." His father's qualifying exam had been scheduled for August 1914, and he went to war against the Germans instead, incurring serious facial wounds. But Tournier's mother—whose uncle, a priest, taught German—"kept faith with her family tradition, and we grew up with one foot in Germany." As a child, Tournier went on Black Forest vacations with his family. As an adolescent, during World War II, he improved his German while living with twenty-two German soldiers in his parents' occupied house in Saint-Germain—"I will never forget the smell of the Wehrmacht, a compound of tobacco and boot polish. For me this was the fragrance of happiness." As a young post-graduate student, he studied for four years (1946–50) at the University of Tübingen, in the French Occupied Zone of what is now West Germany. At the age of twenty, he translated Erich Maria Remarque's novel *All Quiet on the Western Front*, and did not scruple at improving passages of it. Remarque, meeting him, said, "This is the first time that I have been able to converse in my own language with any of my translators. The others . . . spoke German as though it were a dead language, like Latin or Greek." Tournier's enthusiasm for things German is, of course, the animating passion behind his best-known novel, *The Ogre* (1970), which tells the tale of a French automobile mechanic who finds fulfillment and doom as a German prisoner of war in East Prussia. In his own persona Tournier can seem an alarmingly keen Germanophile:

Dream a little: had there been no Nazi madness, no war and no defeat, Germany and its outposts in Vienna, Zurich, and Prague would have formed an economic and cultural unit comparable in power and influence to France in the seventeenth or England in the nineteenth century. With the barbarians of the East and West held at bay, the world would have continued to be European, and it would have been German. . . . Because the Americans had won the war, it was their language that one had to speak to become a hotel porter or an airline pilot. But we were not really cheated, for the twentieth century was still built upon a German foundation, or at any rate upon works written in the German language. . . . There are few places where one can scratch the earth without coming upon the soil of old Germany. . . . "Old Germany, mother of us all!"

One could almost resent being called a barbarian while the perpetrators of Buchenwald are so rhapsodically extolled.

Tournier's chapter on *The Ogre* is the longest, and in the four remaining chapters he discusses his early professional years as translator and radio broadcaster; his growing determination to write apparently naturalistic stories that "would secretly be set in motion by ontology and logic"; his belief that humor and celebration are essential to literature; his first published novel, *Friday* (1967), "into which I hoped to pour the essence of what I had learned while employed at the Musée de l'Homme, especially under the tutelage of Claude Lévi-Strauss"; his novel *Les Météores* (1975; translated into English as *Gemini*), a tangled tale "inspired by a fascination with the super-flesh of twins" and crowned by the formula "twinship untwinned = ubiquity"; and the topic of wisdom itself. These connected autobiographical essays are brilliant and possibly wise, though a certain dark and teasingly perverse streak beclouds the sense of even and impersonal illumination that we expect from wisdom. We cannot ignore the saturnine personality projecting itself in such epithets as "that whining female monster, the crowd," such epigrams as "ontology when tossed into the crucible of fiction undergoes a partial metamorphosis into scatology," and such assertions as the one that circumcision keratinizes the epidermis of the glans and makes fellatio "so laborious that it loses all its charm."

Like Pangloss and Candide, Tournier ends up by cultivating his garden, which he describes in cosmic terms:

Every summer morning, as I toast my bread and steep my tea by an open window through which I can smell the grass and hear the wind in the linden branches, I suddenly become aware that time has been compressed, that space has shrunk to those few square feet enclosed by a stone wall, and that a single living thing—my garden—flourishes in the exorbitant immobility of the absolute. . . . The present lingers on eternally in a divine improvidence and amnesia.

There is no chasing all the hares that Tournier's energetic mind starts during the survey of his personal garden. His theories have a glittering

Hegelian intricacy that only a formidable patience could subdue to art. He was over forty when he published his first novel; he creates slowly, he tells us, devoting four or more years to a book, and lets the work in progress send him upon mysterious errands of research. "The writer who labors on a book for four years becomes that book and assimilates all its alien elements, which add up to a structure far more impressive, vast, complex, and learned than their author. . . . The work produces itself and the author is only its byproduct." The author and his work exist within a matrix of large and ancient forces: "Man is nothing but a mythical animal. He becomes man—he acquires a human being's sexuality and heart and imagination—only by virtue of the murmur of stories and kaleidoscope of images that surround him in the cradle and accompany him all the way to the grave. . . . That being the case, it becomes easy to describe the social—one might even say biological—function of the creative artist. The artist's ambition is to add to or at any rate modify the 'murmur' of myth that surrounds the child, the pool of images in which his contemporaries move—in short, the oxygen of the soul."

After formulations so spacious and humane, the actual work risks appearing minor. A glance at Tournier's recent fiction does suggest the limits of determined mythicization, of ontology and logic as prime aesthetic movers. *Gilles & Jeanne* sets itself to construct a connection between the two apparently diverse aspects of Gilles de Rais's fame: as the devoted comrade-in-arms and royally appointed protector of the saintly Joan of Arc, and as the black-mass orgiast and sodomizing slaughterer of children whom legend has transmuted into Bluebeard, slaughterer of wives. A premise of structuralist thought is that opposites (black/white, good/bad, up/down) share the identity of the conceptual structure that holds them and hence are basically aspects of the same thing. It is, for the adroit and learned Tournier, a matter of little more than a hundred pages to demonstrate that Gilles, possessed by the vision of simple goodness embodied in Joan and revolted by her body's horrible end at the stake in Rouen, logically seeks her and the absolute in satanism. As Joan, burning at the stake for witchcraft, cries out, "*Jesus! Jesus! Jesus!,*" so Gilles, burning for sorcery nine years later, calls out, "Jeanne! Jeanne! Jeanne!"

This stylized equation—Jeanne is to Jesus as Gilles is to Jeanne—forms the bare bones of the novel. What is its meat? The era and its cosmology offer Tournier many convenient ambiguities: Joan's voices might be angels or devils, Satan is "the image of God," a town square contains "a statue that was in such a sorry state that it would have been difficult to tell whether it was a Virgin or a Venus," alchemical experiments are conducted on "the fundamental ambiguity of fire, which is both life and death, purity and passion, sanctity and damnation." The book's alchemist, the Tuscan abbé Francesco Prelati (a historical figure, de Rais's assistant in his diabolical dabblings), construes his master's psychology in terms of "inversions." Prelati testifies to the court that a "malign inversion" occurred when Joan was captured and condemned, and then a satanist antidote: "To drive the Sire de Rais to the blackest edge of wickedness, then, by the igneous operation, to subject him to a benign inversion, like the one that transmutes ignoble lead into gold. He was becoming a saint of life!" Prelati's fancy thinking and talking rather sap Gilles's and Jeanne's tale of human interest. The little novel becomes, atrocious as the facts behind it are, bloodless, with nothing in its arch paradoxes as visceral and memorable as Lucifer's blunt pentameters in *Paradise Lost:*

> So farewell hope, and with hope farewell fear,
> Farewell remorse: all good to me is lost;
> Evil be thou my Good.

Along with Milton's epic of elected sin, the English language holds a play, Shaw's *Saint Joan,* that juggles ideas at the fifteenth-century crossroads with an impudent facility that makes Tournier seem relatively hard-breathing. Shaw's drama includes, amid its abundance of historical sidelights, a small part for Gilles de Rais, whom he calls Bluebeard and decorates to suit the name. He characterizes him thus: *"Gilles de Rais, a young man of 25, very smart and self-possessed, and sporting the extravagance of a little curled beard dyed blue at a clean-shaven court, comes in. He is determined to make himself agreeable, but lacks natural joyousness, and is not really pleasant."* The mild suggestion, regarding this legendary sadist, that he lacked "natural joyousness" brings us closer to the mass murderer than Tournier's schematic religious pathology. But as a cultural critic, the French author can be dazzling. Here, for instance, is what perspective in drawing and painting meant to a French priest travelling for the first time in Italy:

It seemed to him that the flat, edifying, worthy image of his pious childhood was suddenly exploding under the impetus of some magic force, was being undermined, distorted, thrown beyond its own limits, as if possessed by some evil spirit. When he stood in front of certain frescoes or pored over certain engravings, he thought he could see opening up in front of his eyes a vertiginous depth that was sucking him in, an imaginary abyss into which he felt a terrifying temptation to dive, headfirst.

Our modern abyss, as experienced by another unfortified sensibility, is the subject of Tournier's *The Golden Droplet.* Published in France two years later than *Gilles & Jeanne,* it tells of Idris, a fifteen-year-old Berber dwelling in the Algerian oasis of Tabelbala, who is one day suddenly photographed by a scantily dressed blonde who leaps out of a desert-cruising Land Rover. In pursuit of the photograph, Idris travels to Paris. If psychological structuralism shaped *Gilles & Jeanne,* semiology is the name of the game here. On all sides Idris is confronted by images and signs—which are not, it develops, the same thing. Images—"the opium of the Occident"—bind us to the world, and signs release us from it:

> These Moslem adolescents, submerged in the big occidental city, were subjected to all the assaults of the effigy, the idol, and the figure. Three words to designate the same servitude. The effigy is a door bolt, the idol a prison, the figure a lock. Only one key can remove these chains: the sign. . . . The sign is spirit, the image is matter. Calligraphy is the algebra of the soul craved by the most spiritualized organ of the body, its right hand. It is the celebration of the invisible by the visible. The arabesque manifests the presence of the desert in the mosque. Through the arabesque, the infinite is deployed in the finite. For the desert is pure space, freed from the vicissitudes of time. It is God without man.

Calligraphy lessons form the happy ending of *The Golden Droplet:* the child of the desert, lost in the evil land of images, of cinema and advertising and hair dyed blond, reclaims his semiotic heritage of pure emptiness. A complicated fable of the "Blond Queen," whereby a bewitching human portrait is reduced to a salutary pattern of calligraphed quotations, cinches the moral, which would seem to be that words are better than things.

The Golden Droplet has a denser texture than *Gilles & Jeanne:* the oasis, the trip north through progressively larger and more Westernized cities to Oran, the boat trip to Marseilles, the African quarter of Marseilles, and then the Maghrebi worker environment in Paris are all conscientiously presented. So conscientiously, indeed, that each chapter feels like a discrete essay. In a postscript the author acknowledges his many sources, from Dominique Champault's study *Tabelbala*—"a model of what the ethnological monograph should be"—to Hassan Massoudy, author of *Calligraphie arabe vivante* and a "master calligrapher . . . who enabled me to approach a traditional art whose beauty is indistinguishable from truth and wisdom." It is edifying and pleasing, of course, to be guided by Tournier from one oasis of research to the next, and to view, on our tour, sights that range from a traditional Berber wedding, complete with "a troupe of dancers and musicians from the High Atlas Mountains," to the grisly, exotic insides of a Parisian sex shop, peepshow, pinball palace, mannequin factory, and abattoir. As so often on an educational tour, though, the sights pile up but do not accumulate into an adventure. Idris, our Berber Candide, remains innocent and blank throughout—himself a mere sign, with a significance special to France, where a long involvement with North Africa and a large immigrant population of North Africans form a hot, recurrent issue. The novel's French title, *La Goutte d'or,* is also the name of a neighborhood of Paris, in the Eighteenth Arrondissement, populated by Africans and full of *l'ambiance africaine.* Like William Styron's *Confessions of Nat Turner,* Tournier's book is a bold attempt to empathize with an underclass, but it is carried out (unlike Styron's) behind an impervious screen of intellectual play.

There are, in the stretches of description and sociology, few events in the sense of happenings that invite suspense and pose an outcome which can grieve or gratify us—few moments when the narrative acquires a mind of its own. In one of them, Idris's nomad friend Ibrahim abruptly falls into an old well, which collapses and buries him alive: this sudden non-academic development startles us, and breaks Idris's last emotional link with his desert life. In another, Idris, having fallen under the spell of the filmmaking magus Achille Mage, is stuck with a camel used in a television commercial for a beverage called Palm Grove, and wanders Paris with the signal creature. In the fashionable districts, people pretend not to see him; only the lower classes allow themselves to express curiosity—"Once again, as the tissue of social relationships became less compact, the camel had become visible." The animal finally, to the reader's considerable relief, finds a haven in the zoo, a collection of living emblems where it is greeted by a female of its species ("Their morose, disdainful heads met very high up in the sky, and their big, pendulous lips touched") and is outfitted for children's rides by "adolescents dressed as Turks." In general, however, even mild emotional involvement is forestalled by the bristle of forked signifiers, and Tournier's pageant of incidents seems not so much a novel as a cunningly wrought image of one—calligraphy aping portraiture aping appearances.

These books made out of other books—are they what the future holds? To "read up" on an area of geography or history and then be clever and cool about it—is this all the postmodern novelist can do? Italo Calvino managed to include something of himself in the intricate package, a self that in his last novel, *Mr. Palomar,* became poignant, almost pleading. But of Michel Tournier, or of Patrick Süskind, the author of the much-admired *Perfume,* or of Julian Barnes, the concocter of such elegancies as *Flaubert's Parrot* and *Staring at the Sun,* we can guess a little but have, as it were, nothing. Joyce and Mann did their research also, but left a palpable weight of personal impulse if not confession in their constructions, whether as elaborate as *Finnegans Wake* or as limpid and light as

Royal Highness. Their fictions have a presence and a voice that are humbly human; their books give off the warmth of a proximate body. To be fair, Tournier did show warmth in such earlier novels as *Friday,* his anti-colonialist gloss on the Robinson Crusoe story, and *The Ogre,* his master-piece. *The Ogre* is a thick outpouring of arcane facts and involved feelings, a complex but sensual fable of loneliness and desire and perception that seems, as Roland Barthes said of classic literature, "replete"—a book satu-rated in its own completely fulfilled tendencies. Like *Gilles & Jeanne,* it is concerned with inversion and pedophilia; like *The Golden Droplet,* it equates purity with nothingness and points out that "the human soul is made of paper." Unlike both these flimsy fictions, it compels interest and arouses dread and pity. But how much of its engaging warmth, I wonder, derives from the entwinement of its intricate parable (a gloss of Goethe's poem "The Erl-King") with its fascinating facts about World War II? Göring's sybaritic hunting-lodge in *The Ogre,* and the four hundred child-warriors martyred to Hitler's fanaticism, and the East Prussian mud that the Ogre treads belong to an epic we never weary of hearing, and Tour-nier's peculiarly intense mental inhabitation of France and Germany en-abled his matter, for once, to make an equal contest with his mind. The trouble with the French love of pure thought is that thought must operate upon *something*—the world as it impurely exists, an apparently ill-thought-out congeries of contradictory indications and arbitrary facts. The novelist must be thoughtless, to some degree, in submitting to the world's facts: he must be naïve enough, as it were, to let the facts flow through him and unreflectingly quicken recognition and emotion in his readers. And this the French find difficult to do.

Small Packages

PIERROT MON AMI, by Raymond Queneau, translated from the French by Bar-bara Wright. 159 pp. Dalkey Archive Press, 1988.

THE PIGEON, by Patrick Süskind, translated from the German by John E. Woods. 115 pp. Knopf, 1988.

THE MUSTACHE, by Emmanuel Carrère, translated from the French by Lanie Goodman. 146 pp. Charles Scribner's Sons, 1988.

In an era when nobody has enough time to read and the world is running out of trees, you would think small novels would be the thing.

But the popular, or folk, sense of the novel is that to earn its keep it should be big, and, with few exceptions, the front tables at Waldenbooks groan under opuses thicker than a strong man's wrist. The three short novels about to be reviewed all come from Europe, and all, oddly enough, take place in France, though one is written in German. Perhaps France, with its fast trains, topless bathing suits, and habit of aphorism, is the last country in the West where anything can happen in less than two hundred pages.

A great deal happens in Raymond Queneau's *Pierrot Mon Ami*, and yet as far as the inner development of the hero is concerned nothing happens. But this is Queneau's perennial point: the banality and cheerful nullity of experience. We always feel good reading a Queneau novel; he is the least depressing of the moderns, the least heavy, with something Mozartian about the easy, self-pleasing flow of his absurd plots. *Pierrot Mon Ami* (what sort of translation is that? what would be wrong with *Pierrot My Friend* or *My Pal Pierrot?*) is centered, fittingly, on an amusement park; Uni Park lies in the northwest of Paris, toward Argenteuil, near the Seine, in a drab region of factories and vacant lots. Pierrot, when we first meet him, has been newly hired to work in the Palace of Fun, where his principal duty, and that of his colleagues Petit-Pouce and Paradis, is to steer young women over the vents that blow their skirts up, to the edification and delight of paying voyeurs called "philosophers." Queneau's preening, rather professorial language puts a strange glaze on this rude material:

> [In the Palace of Fun] maliciously-calculated indignities pursued the buffs' every step: staircases whose steps collapsed horizontally, planks that jumped up at a right angle or curved in and became a basin, a conveyor belt that moved in alternate directions, floors that consisted of strips shaken with a Brownian movement. And more. Pierrot's job was to get the people out of this impasse. With the men, it was enough to give them a hand, but when a woman, terrified by this difficult passage, came along, you grabbed her by the wrists, you lugged her, you tugged her, and you finally plunked her down over an air vent that sent her skirts billowing up—the first treat for the philosophers, if this flurry revealed enough thigh.

Pierrot's task encounters obstruction, however, when some pimps accompanying their women cagily hold the billowing skirts down, to the enragement of the philosophers, producing a small riot, with the result that the Palace of Fun is closed by the police. That same evening Pierrot falls in love with a girl, Yvonne, who turns out to be the daughter of Uni Park's proprietor, Eusèbe Pradonet; our smitten hero offends Pradonet by run-

ning him over with a bumper car, and is thereupon fired. His next unsuccessful job is as assistant to a fakir, Crouïa Bey, whom Pradonet's mistress,
Madame Prouillot, recognizes as the brother of her long-lost love, Jojo
Mouilleminche. Our hero faints when Crouïa Bey/Sidi Mouilleminche
begins to pierce his cheeks with hatpins, and so he loses *that* job. His next
involvement is with the mysterious Arthème Mounnezergues, who owns
a piece of land, in a corner of Uni Park, on which he has erected a chapel
to the memory of a Poldevian Prince, who might, it turns out, be the
reputedly dead Jojo Mouilleminche, who also seems to be a Monsieur
Voussois, an animal-trainer in the Midi to whom Pierrot, once again
gainfully if briefly employed, is trucking a wild boar called Pistolet and
an ape named Mésange. There's much more to the story, too, such as an
affair between Yvonne and Paradis, and the machinations of Pradonet to
obtain for Uni Park the plot of land Mounnezergues has consecrated to
the alleged Poldevian Prince, but all these intrigues and coincidences
generate in their whirl no more heat than a swarm of fireflies. Queneau,
without cracking a smile or dropping a stitch of his parody of a plot,
demonstrates—Q.E.D., *Queneau est demonstrator*—how futilely feverish
human activity is.

Not only our outer but our inner lives are genially reduced to absurdity.
The French have traditionally prized the life of the mind, and Queneau
attentively reports Pierrot's mental states:

> Leaning comfortably on his elbows, Pierrot was thinking about the death
> of Louis XVI, which means, specifically, about nothing in particular; his
> mind contained nothing but a mental, light, and almost luminous mist, like
> the fog on a beautiful winter morning, nothing but a flight of anonymous
> midges.

> Pierrot continued on his way and thought about nothing, which he
> managed to do with some facility, and even without meaning to; in this way
> he reached the embankment.

> During this journey, he thought, among other things, that it was high time
> he got his skates on and found a job. This thought was quicker than a flash,
> though, and he didn't dwell on it; and the rest of the time he thought a little
> about Yvonne and a lot about nothing.

The vagueness and triviality of thought extend to memory, whose powers
were so impressively extolled by Proust. Pierrot brings Proust down to
earth when he reflects upon his past: "He was thinking that it isn't funny
to have had a childhood like his, it goes sour on you, it goes mouldy, and

the good bits where you can look back and see you were so nice and so full of hope are forever tarnished by the rest." Madame Pradonet tells her daughter, "When *you* have a past, Vovonne, you'll realize what an odd thing it is. In the first place, there's whole chunks of it that have caved in: absolutely nothing left. Elsewhere, there's weeds that've grown haphazard, and you can't recognize anything there either. And then there's places that you think are so beautiful that you give them a fresh coat of paint every year, sometimes in one color, sometimes in another, and they end up not looking in the least like what they were."

Such deflationary psychological realism is temperamentally one with Queneau's scrupulous inventory of a shop window: "Gathering dust . . . were sticks of licorice, ceramic figures sitting on chamber pots, spools of thread, and illustrated publications, both Gallic and juvenile. Crippled tin soldiers threatened one another with their sabers or their buckled rifles, while authentic old Épinal prints were yellowing to the point of turning russet." Like James Joyce, Queneau recognized that the texture of daily life for Western man has become predominantly commercial; the contents of shop windows excite his characters to thought in the way flowers and stars prompted exclamation in Romantic poets. Pierrot is fascinated by a ball-bearing manufacturer's display of "little steel spheres mathematically rebounding on drums made of the same metal," and Étienne, the meditative hero of Queneau's first novel, *The Bark Tree* (1933), broods over "two little ducks floating in a waterproof hat that had been filled with water in order to demonstrate its primary quality." Without his oddly ardent precision, Queneau's playfulness and sly rigor would not hold us; along with the anti-intellectual intellectualism that dubs rowdy voyeurs "philosophers," he has a real affection for the surface of life as it is, in its sweet vapidity and farcical appetites.

One might add that *Pierrot Mon Ami* was published in 1942, in an occupied France surrounded by a war alluded to only, and very obliquely, by the destruction of Uni Park, which is consumed in a conflagration spread by fiery planes flung from the "chairoplane" tower. And that Queneau's frequent translator, Barbara Wright, has waltzed around the floor with the Master so many times by now that she follows his quirky French as if the steps were elementary.

Patrick Süskind, born near Munich in 1949, became a writer of international note with the publication of his first novel, the widely successful *Perfume.* As a performance, *Perfume* was dazzlingly expert and thrillingly cold: a tough act to follow. His new offering, *The Pigeon*—a long short story prettily gotten up as a book by Knopf—though certainly destined for nothing like *Perfume*'s success, deepens my affection and respect for this author; he shows here, after his brilliant exercise in eighteenth-century monstrosity, a willingness to work within the range of the normal and contemporary, and to derive startling colors from a freshness of angle rather than from another century's susceptibility to fabulation.

Freshness remains the fiction writer's problem; in an age when the old romantic and moral largenesses are so worn and coarsened as to be fit for little but parody and best-sellerdom, the microscopic offers fresh territory. The massive minutiae of Proust and Joyce and the circling, semi-paralyzed sensibilities of Faulkner and Kafka offer ample modernist precedent for a fiction of magnification. The story of *The Pigeon* is almost nothing: Jonathan Noel, an unmarried Parisian bank guard in his fifties, encounters a pigeon in the hall outside the tiny room he has occupied since 1954, and for the next twenty-four hours wrestles with the terror that this modest disturbance of his life of seclusion and routine causes him. The hundred pages in which Süskind traces his obscure hero's overreaction are crowded with enlarged details:

> [The pigeon] laid its head to one side and was glaring at Jonathan with its left eye. This eye, a small, circular disc, brown with a black center, was dreadful to behold. It was like a button sewn onto the feathers of the head, lashless, browless, quite naked, turned quite shamelessly to the world and monstrously open; at the same time, however, there was something guarded and devious in that eye; and yet likewise it seemed to be neither open nor guarded, but rather quite simply lifeless, like the lens of a camera that swallows all external light and allows nothing to shine back out of its interior. No luster, no shimmer lay in that eye, not a spark of anything alive. It was an eye without sight. And it glared at Jonathan.

We murder to dissect, Wordsworth said; and under the scalpel of Süskind's sharply observant prose all objects yield a redolence of death, even the bodies of the young girls whom the hero of *Perfume* kills to extract their complex, enchanting aromas. The pigeon's lifeless button-eye makes almost understandable the bank guard's hysterical fear; and the fraction that we do not quite understand leads us to read on. The guard's day of standing on the bank steps is full of suspense, as the sensations of standing still are rendered with an ominous, half-humorous exactitude:

> After only a few minutes he could feel the burden of his body as a painful pressure on his soles; he shifted his weight from one foot to the other and back again, sending him into a gentle stagger and making him interpolate little sidesteps to keep his center of gravity—which until now he had always held on classical plumb—from slipping off balance.

When he eats lunch, his tense mood inflames the simple act of swallowing:

> It took an eternity before the bite got to his stomach, it crept down his esophagus with snail-like slowness, sometimes almost sticking there and pressing and hurting as if a nail were being driven into his chest, till Jonathan thought he would choke to death on this nauseating mouthful.

And when, in his distraction, he rips his trousers on the back of a park bench, the little tear becomes a crevasse:

> It also seemed to him that the *rip*—it was still echoing in his ears—had been so monstrously loud that more than his trousers had been torn, that the tear had ripped right through him, through the bench, through the whole park, like a gaping crevasse during an earthquake, and it seemed as if all the people roundabout must have heard it, this terrible *rip*.

As with the contemporary work in German of Peter Handke and Thomas Bernhard, rage lurks beneath the taut surface of Süskind's world. Jonathan, as the sun climbs higher, spitefully exults in his sweating and itching: "The suffering suited him fine, it justified and inflamed his hate and his rage, and the rage and the hate in turn inflamed the suffering, for it set his blood surging ever more fiercely, continually squeezing new ripples of sweat from the pores of his skin." The bank guard has not always lived insulated from the agonies of his times; we are told at the outset that his parents disappeared in World War II, he became a farm laborer in the tyrannical care of an uncle, and as a young man he served and was wounded in Indochina. But, more than Handke and Bernhard, Süskind balances his dark side with a healing, comedic tendency: *The Pigeon* ends not unhappily, after Jonathan's recognition that even he needs people and his return, "on the wings of bliss," to the rain-puddled innocence of his childhood. In the course of its tiny adventure, the novella seems to run through most of the relations a man can strike with the world, and, by virtue of Süskind's acute powers of focus, achieves a surprising largeness.

The young French writer Emmanuel Carrère is also a formidable magnifier, at least in *The Mustache*. It is his third novel; his second, *Bravoure*, won two prizes, the Prix Passion and the Prix de la Vocation, and this one comes to translation into English bedecked with Franco-American praise. The tale's point of departure seems as trivial as a pigeon in the hall: a young Parisian architect, left nameless, decides to shave off the mustache he has been sporting for ten years. Like the bank guard of Süskind's tale, he is a man of routine, who shaves twice a day, the second time while luxuriating in his bathtub, which is surrounded by mirrors. "He'd prepare a drink, kept within arm's reach, then lavishly spread the shaving cream on his chin, going back and forth with the razor, making sure not to come too close to the mustache, which he would later trim with a scissors." Any fictional character with a razor in his hand makes a reader nervous, and our hero's impulsive, impish decision to surprise his wife, Agnes, by shaving off his mustache feels like a dangerous violation of the quotidian order. So it proves. Returning to their apartment and to her husband, she notices nothing different, though his upper lip is not only bare but paler than his ski-vacation-tanned face. When pressed, she claims that he never *had* a mustache. His friends and colleagues, too, assert he never wore a mustache, and Agnes maintains this fiction or delusion even while staring at vacation photographs of her husband's mustached self or when confronted with the mustache's remnants, rescued from the garbage.

What has happened? We never quite know, though the permutations of progressively malignant confusion are exquisitely described; in a sense, the book offers a paradigm of marital misunderstanding, with its volatile alternations of tenderness and rage, quarrel and lovemaking, empathy and bafflement. Agnes, who works at a publishing house, does have a history of willful and stubborn lying, even in the teeth of contradictory evidence, but this does not explain the apparent blindness of his colleagues at work and of the café-owner across the street to the hero's newly clean-shaven condition, or her perfectly enacted appearance of distress at what she construes as *his* loss of sanity. At one point, when he confronts her with a mustached identity photo of himself, she rubs a wet finger across the mustache and shows him a spot of ink on her fingertip, accusing him of doctoring the photo with Magic Marker. Then she produces a razor blade from her pocketbook and scrapes away the mustache in the photo. As their grapple approaches full-fledged "conjugal guerrilla warfare," each suspecting the other of insanity, what had been a loving relationship and a thriving conventional marriage reasserts itself in painful oscillations of mood:

> He vacillated between anger and a nauseating tenderness for Agnes, poor Agnes, his wife, Agnes, totally fragile, delicately put together, a sly fox, with a fine line between an active mind and the irrationality that had begun to consume her. . . . Through the power of love, patience, and tact, he'd tear her away from her demons, row with all his strength to get her to shore. He'd hit her if he had to, for the sake of love, just like you'd knock out a struggling swimmer to keep him from drowning. A wave of tenderness swept over him, facilitating this sudden burst of terrible and disturbing metaphors.

Agnes's denials of her husband's reality grow in scope: she denies that they have ever been on vacation in Java, though a blanket bought there hangs on the wall, and she tells him his father is dead, though he has just heard his father's voice on the answering machine. Yet the spreading irrationality is not only in her—an old Cary Grant picture that the couple watch together on television turns into a preposterous mélange—and *The Mustache* is not simply *Gaslight* with a female Charles Boyer. The irrationality lies in the tale itself, and the author has a nimble job of it to keep his hero away from a character who might restore order. The architect flees, for instance, from a scheduled appointment with a psychiatrist, and he unaccountably cannot find the apartment building where his parents live and where he himself lived for ten years. *The Mustache*, fine and glossy and inexorable, like a machine with one lost gear-tooth, processes reactions and emotions within a universe whose laws have slipped. The only rational explanation—if one is demanded—is that somehow, at the moment of his shaving off his mustache, the hero and his wife enter parallel universes, which one respectable contemporary school of cosmology holds are generated with every ambiguity of quantum measurement. In the words of physicist Bryce DeWitt, "Every quantum transition taking place on every star, in every galaxy, in every remote corner of the universe is splitting our local world on earth into myriads of copies of itself."

But *The Mustache* is not science fiction; it is a fantasy located just to one side of our world and an alarming commentary upon it. The stability of our personal lives rests upon a consensus of perception and memory that in fact has no guarantee. We are solipsists who in uneasy conjunction with other solipsists construct a society and a shared world. The apparatus and conventions of modern bourgeois life—the credit cards, the answering machines, the vacations by jet, the matter-of-fact sensuality, the days beginning with a shave and a "hiccuping coffeepot"—glitter familiarly through the slats of Carrère's subtly distorting, abruptly lowered blind. The relatively exotic settings of Hong Kong and Macao are realistically rendered, with plenty of tourist information, when the maddened hero flees there. The denouement is drastic but, then, so is any dislocation, however apparently minor, in our structure of shared perceptions. The book gets under one's skin; more than once, I turned to the back of the jacket to ponder, in the photograph of the boyish-looking author, the naked expanse of his prominent upper lip, to see whether something was growing there, or had been recently removed. *The Mustache* has been likened to "The Metamorphosis," but in Kafka's fable, once we accept that Gregor Samsa awakes in the body of a large insect, everything proceeds sturdily, dependably, knitting itself like a healing wound around this

initial violation of the ordinary, whereas Carrère's mise-en-scène deteriorates more and more; it melts away until nothing remains but the hero's
French determination to think, in a world where thought no longer
works. Gogol's "The Nose" offers a closer parallel, since the world of the
eccentric Russian master is also slippery and inconsistent. But Gogol's
nonsense is forgiving: he conjures up a Russia so brightly tinted and
primitive as to casually permit physical miracles—a nose in a loaf of bread,
a blank space where a man can no longer take snuff—and the nose reappears on its proper face one morning as if its interval of absence were a
dream. A much grimmer effort is necessary in *The Mustache* to put everything "back in place."

The book's ending shocks us, and we are additionally shocked to read,
in a notation under the last line, that it was written in five weeks—
"Biarritz-Paris / April 22–May 27, 1985." This is an arrogant miniaturiza-
tion of Joyce's dating of his majestic labor on *Ulysses*—"Trieste-
Zurich-Paris, 1914–1921." But *Candide*, it is said, was written in three
days, and perhaps *The Mustache* could only have been rapidly improvised,
a nightmare of slippage the author pulled quickly from the placid yuppie
trivia of the life around him. His book is, to risk a rather devalued word,
stunning—stunning in the speed and agility with which it slices through
to its underlying desolation, and stunning in its final impact. In less than
a hundred fifty pages, it packs a punch.

IRIS MURDOCH, PAIRED WITH OTHERS

Baggy Monsters

THE NAME OF THE ROSE, by Umberto Eco, translated from the Italian by William Weaver. 502 pp. Harcourt Brace Jovanovich, 1983.

THE PHILOSOPHER'S PUPIL, by Iris Murdoch. 576 pp. Viking, 1983.

Henry James wrote deprecatingly of novels he deemed to be "baggy monsters"; by way of illustration he cited—a grouping that would not occur to many critics these days—*War and Peace, The Three Musketeers,* and Thackeray's *The Newcomes.* But how, this very assortment of titles begs us to ask, can the novel *not* be somewhat baggy, as its heritage of roles as historical chronicle, adventure saga, social panorama, and personal confession descends to it and ever more self-consciously complicates and thickens? The masterpieces of this century, as represented by *Remembrance of Things Past, Ulysses,* and *The Magic Mountain,* yield nothing in farraginous ambitious bulk to those of the nineteenth cited by James, and the admired American careers of Saul Bellow, Norman Mailer, and Thomas Pynchon show that bagginess, if not esteemed as a virtue in itself, is nevertheless deferred to and indulged, like prankishness in young men, as a sign of vitality. For is not the novel a progeny of the epic, by way of medieval romances and *Don Quixote?* To its already vastly stretched potentialities modernism has added, from Flaubert on, the option that the novel form a marvellously extended prose poem. As philosophy has withdrawn from the epic mode of Hegel and Schopenhauer into an academic language of inscrutable nicety, philosophical messages further bulge the novel's bag. Indeed, prose fiction has become the one podium where philosophy can speak not in the mincing accents of semantics but in commentary upon our existential lives, along the lines laid down by Plato and Aristotle and Christian theology. The characteristic question of modern philosophy has become "Are we speaking clearly?"; but an atavistic element in us still asks, "How shall we live?" and "Is there Something Else?" When philosophers ask these questions now, it would seem they must ask them away from their lecterns, within that permissive genre which since the Renaissance has offered sanctuary to the otherwise inexpressively, unofficially, less-than-respectably human. The past summer's airy reading fare has been varied by two baggy and brilliant novels, totalling over a thousand pages, by teachers of philosophy in European universities.

One of them, Umberto Eco's *The Name of the Rose,* in fact has attained, for all its convolution and erudition and blithely untranslated Latin, the top reaches of the best-seller list here, as it has in Italy, France, and Germany. A many-branched murder mystery set in the Middle Ages, it has won as well a number of literary prizes; not since *One Hundred Years of Solitude* has there been such a consensual success on the Continent. The fifty-one-year-old Professor Eco is, the American book jacket tells us, "a world-famous specialist in semiotics, a distinguished historian, philosopher, and aesthetician, and a scholar of James Joyce. He teaches at the University of Bologna and lives in Milan." Now that Roland Barthes is dead, the popularization of semiotics triumphantly continues in this novel, whose title refers to a medieval aperçu: *"Stat rosa pristina nomine, nomina nuda tenemus."** The novel purports to be an Italian translation of a nineteenth-century French transcription, by "a certain Abbé Vallet," of a fourteenth-century manuscript written by one Adso, a Benedictine monk in the Austrian monastery of Melk, recounting events that occurred late in November of 1327 at an Italian abbey situated in "a vague area between Pomposa and Conques, with reasonable likelihood that the community was somewhere along the central ridge of the Apennines, between Piedmont, Liguria, and France."

Eco's introduction, heaped with intricate and musty references, pays

---

*The Latin source, I have learned from Jay Laughlin, is a twelfth-century poem, *De Contemptu Mundi,* by the monk Bernard of Cluny—not to be confused with the famous Saint Bernard of Clairvaux, or with the scholastic Bernard of Chartres. The line gathers intelligibility from those that precede it, a catalogue of the bygone like some of Villon's ballades:

> Nunc ubi Marius atque Fabricius inscius auri?
> Mors ubi nobilis et memorabilis actio Pauli?
> Diva Philippica, vox ubi coelica nunc Ciceronis?
> Pax ubi civibus atque rebellibus ira Catonis?
> Nunc ubi Regulus? aut ubi Romulus? aut ubi Remus?
> Stat rosa pristina nomine, nomina nuda tenemus.

open homage to Jorge Luis Borges, mentioning his native city as well as imitating his mock-scholarly style: "But then, in 1970, in Buenos Aires, as I was browsing among the shelves of a little antiquarian bookseller on Corrientes, not far from the more illustrious Patio del Tango of that great street, I came upon the Castilian version of a little work by Milo Temesvar, *On the Use of Mirrors in the Game of Chess.* " And one of the monks in the unnamed abbey that serves as the novel's mise-en-scène is named Jorge of Burgos. Other such punning allusions are woven into *The Name of the Rose,* and other literary influences than Borges's can be detected— Joyce's Thomistic rigor of organization, for instance, and the playful bookishness and maze-making of Eco's compatriot Italo Calvino. Calvino's recent novel, *If on a winter's night a traveler,* included a character strongly suggestive of Ian Fleming, and Eco is represented in the recently published critical anthology *The Poetics of Murder* by his analysis of "Narrative Structures in Fleming." Another structuralist represented in the anthology is Barthes, with two excerpts from *S/Z* entitled "Delay" and "The Hermeneutic Sentence"; these set forth the principle of suspense behind all "classic" narrative, of which the most stylized form (and the one most readily available to structuralist analysis and avant-garde manipulation) is the detective novel. Borges, Calvino, Robbe-Grillet, and Michel Butor are among the modernist writers who have come to the detective novel from on high, as it were—out of a certain theoretical attraction, as opposed to those practitioners like Graham Greene, Dorothy Sayers, and Simenon, who have lifted it toward literary status from below, with no initial condescension. Eco now joins *en haut* the former ranks, but without disregarding the main requirements of the popular form, and indeed managing to achieve popular success.

The Name of the Rose, twice as long as the conventional mystery, marshals these conventional ingredients: an eccentric detective given to inscrutable swoops of deduction, an amiable but naïve sidekick who narrates the tale, a closed setting wherein a succession of ghastly murders take place, a restricted array of characters that must include the murderer, an unsympathetic and bumbling official detective, maps and codes and secret passageways and hidden latches and missing documents, and a final, cleansing elucidation and denouement. The detective is a "learned Franciscan, Brother William of Baskerville"; like the hero of *The Hound of the Baskervilles* and its companion narratives, William is English, tall, thin, beak-nosed, and takes dope:

> On . . . occasions a vacant, absent expression appeared in his eyes, and I would have suspected he was in the power of some vegetal substance capable of producing visions if the obvious temperance of his life had not led me to

reject this thought. I will not deny, however, that in the course of the journey, he sometimes stopped at the edge of a meadow, at the entrance to a forest, to gather some herb (always the same one, I believe): and he would then chew it with an absorbed look.

In the manner perfected by Conan Doyle, Eco has William astound his "clients" at the calamitous abbey with an instant feat of apparent clairvoyance: "Come, come, it is obvious you are hunting for Brunellus, the abbot's favorite horse, fifteen hands, the fastest in your stables, with a dark coat, a full tail, small round hoofs, but a very steady gait; small head, sharp ears, big eyes." He never quite says, "Elementary, my dear Adso," though he does patronize his disciple in Holmesian fashion: "My good Adso, during our whole journey I have been teaching you to recognize the evidence through which the world speaks to us like a great book."

Young Adso (who is recalling these events in highly circumstantial detail toward the end of his life, over half a century later—a medieval miracle of sorts) has been assigned, as a young Benedictine novice, to accompany Brother William on a complicated mission that involves seeking a reconciliation between the Holy Roman Emperor Louis the Bavarian, to whose court William is attached, and the Avignon Pope, Jacques of Cahors—"an old man of seventy-two who took . . . the name of John XXII, and heaven grant that no pontiff take again a name now so distasteful to the righteous." Along with the intricacies of the deepening and increasingly gory murder mystery, a strong dose of the multifarious ins and outs of fourteenth-century politics is administered to the reader. The official detective who arrives at the seething abbey is an inquisitor, the venerable bishop Bernard Gui, to whom the Pope has entrusted the command of French soldiers assigned to protect the papal legation that is to meet, at the abbey, with Michael, minister general of the Minorite Franciscans, a body whose resolution in 1322 emphasizing the poverty of Christ had displeased the money-minded Pope and therefore pleased the excommunicated Emperor. Gui succeeds in unearthing some heretics in the lower regions of the abbey's personnel and leaves satisfied, though crime still rages. "Bernard is interested," says William ruefully, "not in discovering the guilty, but in burning the accused. And I, on the contrary, find the most joyful delight in unraveling a nice, complicated knot."

No doubt those who like their history lessons wrapped in colorful fiction have joined mystery aficionados in swelling this novel's international audience. As a paradigm of bloody turmoil and scintillant rot, of the cruellest cynicism confounded with the most extravagant religious passion, the fourteenth century is inexhaustibly fascinating, as Barbara Tuchman recently showed, and Jacob Burckhardt and Johan Huizinga before her. A hot issue of the time, according to *The Name of the Rose,* was the poverty of Christ and by extension that of Christ's by now notoriously wealthy and corrupt church. The Franciscans were part of a widespread protest movement, which included heretical sects such as the Fraticelli or Friars of the Poor Life, who broke off from the Franciscan order and supported themselves entirely by begging, and the even more radical Pseudo Apostles of Gherardo, who preached disregard of the laws of private property and discounted marriage vows. A disciple of Gherardo, Fra Dolcino, founded a roving band that practiced free love and banditry and urged the complete destruction of the church. When, under Bernard Gui's interrogation, the cellarer of the abbey confesses to having been a Dolcinian, he cries out:

> We burned and looted because we had proclaimed poverty the universal law, and we had the right to appropriate the illegitimate riches of others, and we wanted to strike at the heart of the network of greed that extended from parish to parish. . . . We killed to punish, to purify the impure through blood. Perhaps we were driven by an overweening desire for justice. . . . We had to kill the innocent as well, in order to kill all of you more quickly. We wanted a better world, of peace and sweetness and happiness for all, we wanted to kill the war that you brought on with your greed, because you reproached us when, to establish justice and happiness, we had to shed a little blood.

The parallel with the rationale of modern terrorism, which has afflicted Italy above all Western nations, is as clear as the sly allusion to Pope John XXIII quoted earlier. Eco spells out the revolutionary impulse behind heresy, and the oppressive poverty of the "simple" that lies behind the impulse: William of Baskerville tells the conservative, jewel-loving abbot, "I say that many of these heresies, independently of the doctrines they assert, encounter success among the simple because they suggest to such people the possibility of a different life." Yet he is frightened by the cellarer's outburst of radical fervor, the cellarer's lust for purity. When Adso asks, "What terrifies you most in purity?," William answers "Haste," and seems the very voice of the modern liberal paralyzed between the system's enforcers and its unappetizing would-be revisers.

Though a cleric and an imperial envoy, William of Baskerville is presented as an incipient modern man. He wears reading spectacles, concocts a magnet, and knows how to use—another fresh invention—a fork. He is an intellectual follower of the empiricist Roger Bacon and the nominalist William of Occam, both of whom he has known at Oxford, where,

Jorge of Burgos accuses him, he has been taught to idolize reason. He foresees a future when "the community of the learned will have to propose this new and humane theology which is natural philosophy and positive magic." Yet he also enters vigorously into medieval debate, with its stupefying mix of idle analogy, scholastic chop-logic, and reverent quotation from the Bible and its sainted commentators. Eco's picture of late-medieval intellectual life is one of the richest aspects of this richly worked book; where we tend to imagine a gray monochrome like that of the era's limestone cathedrals, he gives us splashes of brilliant debate upon issues still fundamental, in lurid colors taken from such now-faded sources as the apocalyptic Revelation of St. John and the *Coena Cypriani,* a kind of rhyming underground joke-book that flourished beneath the stern surface of orthodoxy and turned its images upside down. Eco even manages to give us a sex scene, bejewelled in quotations from the Song of Solomon; Adso, having been seduced by a young peasant girl from a village near the abbey, is thereby provoked to a noble philosophical examination of the nature of love:

> My intellect knew her as an occasion of sin, my sensitive appetite perceived her as the vessel of every grace. . . . I understood why the angelic doctor said that amor est magis cognitivus quam cognitio, that we know things better through love than through knowledge. . . . And I believe that the nighttime love had been concupiscent, for I wanted from the girl something I had never had; whereas that morning I wanted nothing from the girl, and I wanted only her good . . . and I wished her to be happy.

Yet it cannot be said that Umberto Eco immerses us in the Middle Ages as, say, Zoé Oldenbourg or a host of lesser historical novelists have striven to. We are always aware of—indeed, the very lavishness of his displayed erudition serves to remind us of—the play of his detached, very contemporary mind across the reflecting surfaces of his brittle invention. The book is semiotic in essence, a glittering assembly of signs vacant at the center; or, rather, at the book's center is its own bookishness, of which dozens of bookish references remind us. The preface is elaborately bibliographical. The first sentence posits the primacy of the Word. The central mystery involves the abbey's library and scriptorium and a certain priceless volume therein. "Here we are trying to understand," William explains, "what has happened among men who live among books, with books, from books." For William, Adso observes, "every book was like a fabulous animal that he was meeting in a strange land," and, a semiotic scholar before his time, he tells Adso, "Books are not made to be believed, but to be subjected to inquiry. When we consider a book, we mustn't ask ourselves what it says but what it means." Borges's beautiful parable of "The Library of Babel" has been here monstrously expanded, with the aid of the medieval belief that *"omnis mundi creatura, quasi liber et scriptura"*—"every creature of the world is as a book and scripture." A world composed altogether of signs, however, wears thin: medieval probability is strained as Eco smoothly leads his pious young narrator into what seems limpid late-twentieth-century atheism. "But how can a necessary being exist totally polluted with the possible?" Adso is made to ask. "What difference is there, then, between God and primigenial chaos? Isn't affirming God's absolute omnipotence and His absolute freedom with regard to His own choices tantamount to demonstrating that God does not exist?" As an old monk near death, he prepares to sink into a God who *"ist ein lauter Nichts"*—"a pure Nothing," a "silent and uninhabited divinity where there is no work and no image." Even granted that the Age of Belief had considerable daring in its thought and mysticism, and like our own was haunted by the void (St. Thomas discusses God, for instance, almost entirely in terms of what He is not), these stately stoic negations do seem forced upon our fourteenth-century monk from afar—from the University of Bologna, to be exact.

A murder mystery is the most bookish of novels, with its characters made to be killed and its puzzles knotted to be unravelled. As Eco observed in connection with Fleming, a mystery "seems to be built on a series of oppositions which allow a limited number of permutations and interactions." The reader/writer contract is plainly drawn up; after the hermeneutic delay, as Barthes wrote, "everything falls into place, the sentence can end." But an abrupt deflation accompanies the resolution of mysteries so formally limited, and a novel thus constructed ends by seeming terribly much smaller than while in progress. Indeed, the reader feels he has earned the right to have it disappear entirely; Agatha Christie fans hope for the total forgetfulness that will enable them to read her works all over again. I do not think (as did the distinguished Boston critic Robert Taylor) that *The Name of the Rose,* as a historical exploration, would be better without the murder mystery in it; it is the mystery which keeps us going through all the history. But once a code has been broken, it becomes a trinket. Once this novel is set down, it feels more miniature and toylike than it should, considering the large amount of passionate wit and learning poured into its pages.

Henry James had no use for the "fatal *cheapness,* " the "mere *escamotage,* " of the historical novel; if, after the exotic adventure of *The Name of the Rose,* we long for what James called "the palpable present *intimate* that throbs responsive," we can turn to no more reliable purveyor of intimacy than Iris Murdoch, whose new novel, *The Philosopher's Pupil,* is one of her biggest and best. It opens with a whirlwind of an argument between husband and wife, and its first paragraph is the most vivid description of driving a car in the rain—a "palpable present" sensation *par excellence*—that I have ever read:

> A few minutes before his brainstorm, or whatever it was, took place, George McCaffrey was having a quarrel with his wife. It was eleven o'clock on a rainy March evening. They had been visiting George's mother. Now George was driving along the quayside, taking the short-cut along the canal past the iron foot-bridge. It was raining hard. The malignant rain rattled on the car like shot. Propelled in oblique flurries, it assaulted the windscreen, obliterating in a second the frenetic strivings of the windscreen wipers. Little demonic faces composed of racing raindrops appeared and vanished. The intermittent yellow light of the street lamps, illuminating the grey atoms of the storm, fractured in sudden stars upon the rain-swarmed glass. Bumping on cobbles the car hummed and drummed.

Let this evocation stand as typical of Miss Murdoch's magic when it works: the blunt successive sentences, with scarcely a dependent clause among them, yield up the superb "little demonic faces composed of racing raindrops" to remind us that not all is as simple and declarative and breathless as it seems—that a highly symbol-prone intelligence presides behind this hurrying actuality. In twenty-one unstinting novels now, this writer has mined her imagination and the world around her for philosopher's gold. With rare concern and knowing, she writes, in a post-religious age, about spiritual activity, as it sparks along that interface where human perception breeds demons out of raindrops.

The quarrelling couple is George and Stella McCaffrey; the McCaffreys—Alexandra, the sixty-six-year-old doyenne of this wealthy family; George and Brian, her sons, in their forties; Tom, the twenty-year-old offspring of Alexandra's dead husband, Alan, and a runaway, now also dead, named Fiona Gates; and Adam, the eight-year-old son of Brian and his wife, Gabriel—are at the center of the saga, which has so many other characters they seem to constitute the entire population of Ennistone, the small English city, "not exceedingly far from London," where the action takes place in a busy period of about three months. The compressed time-span, the device of a disappearing and reappearing first-person narrator who knows impossibly much, and the emphasis upon a certain family and a provincial community, feel reminiscent of Dostoevsky's later novels. If Miss Murdoch has deliberately refreshed her reading of these, it is a happy move; the Russian's theatricality, wild humor, and troubled spiritual urgency are all up her alley. Like Dostoevsky, she is interested in people's influence over one another—their *sway;* the bogies we make in one another's minds; the gravitational permutations as spiritual bodies plunge on in their self-centered orbits.

The seminal event in *The Philosopher's Pupil* is the arrival back in Ennistone of Professor John Robert Rozanov, who, after a humble youth in one of the city's less fashionable districts, has found in the wider world fame as a philosopher and in America, where he teaches and lectures, some wealth. He has brought in his wake his granddaughter, Hattie Meynell, and her paid companion, Pearl Scotney, who by no great stretch of coincidence is half-sister to Alexandra's venerable servant, Ruby Doyle, and cousin to George McCaffrey's longtime mistress, Diane Sedleigh; Rozanov installs Hattie and Pearl in the Slipper House, an elegant little Art Deco residence on Alexandra McCaffrey's property, and, oddly keen to find a suitable mate for his seventeen-year-old ward, settles upon happy and innocent Tom McCaffrey. Tempestuous, demon-driven George, in the meantime, is ferociously obsessed—in one of those apostolic obsessions that torment Iris Murdoch's characters and that all seem descended from a primal schoolgirl crush on Teacher—by Rozanov, whose unsuccessful pupil he once was. John Robert's Olympian indifference to him rankles George to the point of murderous rage. The novel's title, incidentally, is somewhat ambiguous. Though George would seem to have foremost claim to be the titular pupil, his wife, Stella, was also a student of Rozanov's, and a more favored one; and Father Bernard Jacoby, a disbelieving Anglican priest, claims in a letter that "I was his last pupil and I failed the test." And, in a droll final twist, a prize younger pupil of Rozanov's, the American Steve Glatz, shows up in Ennistone and carries off the town prize, the rich and beautiful Anthea Eastcote, great-niece of the saintly Quaker philanthropist William "The Lizard" Eastcote—who, you should know, makes the first of several flying-saucer sightings reported in the novel. Another character worth mentioning is Emmanuel "Emma" Scarlet-Taylor, Tom's androgynous young Irish friend, a brilliant student on his way to be a historian but distracted by Pearl Scotney and his own magnificent counter-tenor voice. The peekaboo narrator calls himself "N" and names the town after himself—N's town, Ennistone. He is, we gradually learn, middle-aged, unmarried, something of a voyeur, and Jewish. Jewish also are Stella McCaffrey, Father Jacoby, and, one surmises, Steve Glatz. Enough plot, surely. There is plenty more of it, all sumptuously cloaked in Miss Murdoch's unfailing and seemingly effortless provision of faces and costumes and hairdos, of furnished rooms and architectural façades, of histories personal and local, of delightfully individual toads in botanically specific gardens. She is the happiest imaginer in the English-speaking world, fearless and fresh whether she bares a night of homosexual initiation or a music lesson, a Quaker meeting or a murderer's exalted frenzy, a dog's impression of a fox or an old woman's dream of dispossession.

This reviewer found *The Philosopher's Pupil* more involving and satisfying than the previous, equally energetic and knowledgeable novels by Miss Murdoch that he has read lately—*The Sacred and Profane Love Machine* and *Nuns and Soldiers*. Why? For one thing, love has been given something of a vacation here, or at least romantic infatuation shares with other sorts of steam the propulsion of the characters. A certain friendly grit coats this little industrial town, with its "strong and long-standing puritan and non-conformist tradition." Away from the dreaming spires of Oxford and the verdant squares of London, Miss Murdoch shows a bracing grasp of plain unpleasantness. In George McCaffrey she has created a fascinatingly nasty man—conceited, disappointed, muddled, and outrageous and destructive with a smugness that perhaps only an Englishman could muster. His brother, Brian, is saner but otherwise no great improvement; nor is tyrannical, corpulent John Robert Rozanov a very appealing apparition. Unless we call love George's mad desire to impress Rozanov, or Stella's aloof loyalty to her cruel and slovenly mate, erotic passion scarcely enters the plot until halfway through, and then in the ironic form of a knightly quest openly allegorized. Until then, and throughout, we are in the grip of a type of murder mystery, in which the question is not "Whodunit?" but "What did he do?" Did George try to kill Stella? And the psychological mystery the author has set herself to examine is not that of amorous affect but that of human destructiveness, bilious and incorrigible. Miss Murdoch, in short, has given her darker side some rein and her broad and shrewd perceptions of human nature some breathing space away from the doctrine of omnipotent Eros. *The Triumph of Aphrodite* is a masque rehearsed in the novel, but the reader is excused from seeing it performed.

Moreover, in the so thoroughly and affectionately constructed setting of Ennistone she has given her volatile spiritual dramas a solid stage. The town is distinguished by the presence of famous and ancient hot springs. The waters, dating back to Roman times and rumored to have medicinal and aphrodisiac qualities, are housed in a set of pools and Victorian structures called The Bath Institute. Almost all the citizens of Ennistone swim the year round, and the gatherings and encounters of the characters at this watery forum as they stand about in the near-nude like figures on

one of Dante's penitential terraces make a recurrently resonant image—
souls and not bodies seem to be assembled. Miss Murdoch, with her
painterly eye and theatrical sense, is a deviser of tableaux, of meaningful
environments. When, during an impromptu revel outside of the Slipper
House, a drunken Emma lifts the lid from his hidden gift and sings, the
crowd freezes like a throng in Mallory: "And they stood where they were,
as still as statues, some even in the attitudes in which the music had
surprised them, kneeling on one knee or holding up a hand." The Ennistone baths, with their constant steam and rumble issuing from an unfathomable underground source—the earth's subconscious, as it were—afford
the novel's vapors and machinations a hot center that yet is quaintly,
sturdily actual. Tom, in his role of knight errant, descends into the heart,
forbidden to the public, of the bath's mechanism, a "mass of gleaming
pipes, some very small, some enormous . . . a light silver gilt in colour,
a very very pale gold, and covered with tiny droplets of moisture which
glittered here and there like diamonds." We are thrilled, and simultaneously acknowledge the symbolic dragon's cave and the pragmatic
marvel of Victorian plumbing. Water has often figured in Miss Murdoch's
work as the outward emblem of the amorous power that suffuses and
overwhelms us; by enhousing it at the center of her city she has tamed and
channelled and strengthened the symbol. Things fit; the novel's furniture
is irradiated by feeling, and functions as thing and sign both. When,
toward the end, a UFO swoops low and blinds a character, we are not put
off as if by whimsy; we know by now what is meant, and in what sense
such things do happen. "The inner is the outer, the outer is the inner: an
old story, but who really understands it?"

Of course, fault can be found, as with any free and generous production.
In a field of characters so panoramically wide, not all ripen as perhaps was
intended. Adam and his dog Zed rather fade away; Ennistone's crowd of
"bright young things" do little more than swell the scene. Though Father
Bernard was mistaken for the main character by the person who writes
up the *Times Book Review*'s "And Bear in Mind" section (for this novel
was no best-seller), in fact the priest is flimsy, and a victim of the author's
tendency to hit and run, to fling scarecrows into her gardens. At one point
during an electric-power cut, this faithless but compassionate cleric is
ministering to a Miss Dunbury, who is near death, frightened, and deaf;
so she can read his ritual consolations, he has her train a flashlight on his
lips. What pathos and terror Bernanos or Graham Greene or even, in his
clipped way, Evelyn Waugh would have extracted from this inspired
tableau! But here it glances by, somehow campy. In a later scene the priest
is found meditating to the sound of Scott Joplin's "Sugar Cane." Though

he thinks, "But oh the desire for God, the desire, the desire," it is "Sugar Cane" that gets, and keeps, our attention. The novel's evident moral haphazardly falls to the priest to pronounce, in a letter penned from Greek exile: "Metaphysics and the human sciences are made impossible by the *penetration of morality into the moment to moment conduct of ordinary life:* the understanding of this fact is *religion.*"

Miss Murdoch has long been trying to rescue religion from an intellectually embarrassing theism. A headless chicken may flap about for a while, but it does not lay eggs; a Godless Christianity is scarcely more viable. Yet she continues to give us atheistic priests and nuns and patiently to record the subtle shades of disbelief and lapsedness—John Robert Rozanov is an unrepentedly lapsed Methodist, Diane Sedleigh a churchgoing but incredulous Anglican, Brian McCaffrey a Quaker in the same condition, Emma an Irish Anglican a bit envious of Catholicism, and so on. There is something dilute and wavering and flirtatious in all this that has enraged stout post-Christian critics like George Stade. But her rendering of these dim religious halftones is realistic, it seems to me, and for a literary artist very much to the point well put nearly forty years ago by Graham Greene:

> After the death of Henry James a disaster overtook the English novel. . . . For with the death of James the religious sense was lost to the English novel, and with the religious sense went the sense of the importance of the human act. . . . Even in one of the most materialistic of our great novelists— in Trollope—we are aware of another world against which the actions of the characters are thrown into relief. The ungainly clergyman picking his black-booted way through the mud, handling so awkwardly his umbrella, speaking of his miserable income and stumbling through a proposal of marriage, exists in a way that Mrs. Woolf's Mr. Ramsay never does, because we are aware that he exists not only to the woman he is addressing but also in a God's eye. His unimportance in the world of the senses is only matched by his enormous importance in another world.

The Philosopher's Pupil considerably resembles an early Murdoch novel, *The Flight from the Enchanter.* There the philosopher is in the dedication (to Elias Canetti) rather than the title; but both deal with teen-age females awakening to love and with the spell exerted upon a circle of characters by a charismatic shaman- or father-figure. The plots share small things in common: gypsies, carved netsukes, foxes—the Enchanter is named Mischa Fox, and Alexandra McCaffrey's grounds are haunted by a beautifully actualized family of foxes. Reading these two books with their affinities, one is struck by the glittering edge possessed by the younger writer, a jaunty farcicalness reminding us that Miss Murdoch came of age in the days of Waugh and Huxley and Rose Macaulay and Nancy Mitford, that she cut her teeth on a novelistic style of savage brightness and superior, heedless romp. One misses, in the later Murdoch, that unbaggy feminine sharpness—feminist, indeed; *The Flight from the Enchanter* is really about female uprisings—and the non-theoretical, "palpable present" bite to the heroines' amours. Hattie Meynell, in *The Philosopher's Pupil*, is vivid in quarrel but almost wordless in love, the inert object of a quest rather than a quester herself. Men have taken over the center of Miss Murdoch's novels—the opposite of what happened in the oeuvre of Henry James—and a certain heavy scent of last night's after-dinner cigars flavors the less dazzling pages. But all in all the earlier novel is greatly surpassed by the later, a book that seems as large as life, so large and various that no two people will read the same story in it. *Omnis mundi creatura, quasi liber et scriptura:* a book as replete as this one reverses the equation.

Expeditions to Gilead and Seegard

THE HANDMAID'S TALE, by Margaret Atwood. 311 pp. Houghton Mifflin, 1986.

THE GOOD APPRENTICE, by Iris Murdoch. 522 pp. Viking, 1986.

Margaret Atwood is a Canadian, a poet, and a woman; all three identities have contributed to her quizzical, delicate, and ultimately moving anti-Utopian novel, *The Handmaid's Tale.* It takes place, my best estimate is, some time just before the year 2000, in what is unambiguously Cambridge, Massachusetts, which has become the capital of a totalitarian, troubled, theocratic state named Gilead. Our heroine is known as Offred, because she is a Handmaid, a sort of combination nun and concubine, assigned to a Commander, that is, a government higher-up, named Fred. The principal duty of the Handmaid is to submit to a once-a-month shot at impregnation by the Commander, while she is being sacramentally clasped from behind by his post-menopausal Wife. Wives, with a capital "W," wear blue; Handmaids wear red habits that completely cover their bodies, and white-winged headdresses that restrict their vision as they, always in pairs, shop and stroll the streets. If they do not conceive after three "postings" of two years each, they are declared Unwomen and shipped off to the dreaded Colonies, where the main and fatal pastime seems to be cleaning up toxic wastes. Other well-defined castes in the new, cartoon-medieval society are Marthas (housekeepers, who wear habits of dull green), Aunts (female enforcers and instructors, who wear paramilitary khaki), Econowives (women who belong to the poorer men; in signification of their multiple roles they wear striped dresses, "red and blue and green and cheap and skimpy"), Angels of Light (soldiers), and Eyes (the secret police). The details of the brave new world, as they drift in through Offred's offhand, dreamlike monologue, often seem droll: stores called Soul Scrolls sell computerized prayers, printed on machines called Holy Rollers, and prostitutes wear the ragtag leftovers of the pre-Gilead days—not only risqué bathing suits and nighties but cheerleader outfits and exercise costumes. Serious enough, however, are the claustrophobia and outrage of Miss Atwood's visionary future; its features constitute a living checklist of a feminist liberal's bugaboos—rampant pollution, the Christian fundamentalist New Right, sexism, and racism (the "Children of Ham" have been resettled in North Dakota, and the "Sons of Jacob" turned into disenfranchised "boat people"). The contemporary allusions worked into the texture of Gilead range from the CIA to Romania's anti-birth-control policies, from the Vietnam aftermath to the Ayatollah's Iran, from "Think Tanks" to the "privatizing" of government operations. Historical allusions include "early Earth-goddess cults," "an English village custom of the seventeenth century," and this country's pre–Civil War Underground Railroad—which ended, of course, in Canada.

To Canadians we must seem a violent and somewhat sinister nation. It is a long way, atmospherically, from Toronto to Detroit. Though sharing a continent, an accent of spoken English, and many assumptions with the United States, and afflicted with its own domestic divisions and violence, our friendly northern neighbor stands above, as it were, much of our moral strenuousness, our noisy determination to combine virtue and power, and our occasional vast miscarriages of missionary intention. With some bemusement, no doubt, Canada let its Scotch be smuggled across the border during Prohibition, and over the same border received our Vietnam draft evaders fifty years later. Bemusement, mixed with dread, detachment, and a sense of superiority, animates Miss Atwood's spirited caricature of conditions south of the forty-ninth parallel. Her attitude has softened since her novel *Surfacing* (1972), wherein "the Americans" are the enemy, a malevolent force-field, a veritable plague of crassness and greed—"the pervasive menace, the Americans." She took her master's degree at Radcliffe, and, we are told on the dust jacket, finished *The Handmaid's Tale* in Alabama; like most of her countrymen, she knows the United States better than we know Canada. But what native of this republic, however politically thin-skinned, takes the New Right seriously enough to conceive of it rising up and machine-gunning the President and the Congress? Or would imagine the various contemporary "pro-life," anti-abortion, anti-pornography protests finding their logical conclusion in a murderous patriarchy wherein women are reduced to the status of slaves? Or would be so tactless as to make a major point of the low birthrates among Caucasians as opposed to those among non-Caucasians? Or so perverse as to locate "the heart of Gilead" in Cambridge, that present-day capital of liberal thinking, and to hang the bodies of executed political criminals from hooks embedded in the barb-wired brick walls of Harvard Yard? Or so careless as to propose a fundamentalist ruling elite that yet openly drinks and smokes? These strange notes add a charming dissonance to Miss Atwood's bravura improvisation upon observable trends in these United States. To the females of Gilead as to the fugitive slaves of the Old South, Canada is safe haven, the blameless north. Offred and her husband, Luke, and their five-year-old daughter almost make it over the border, when Gilead's monstrous reforms are still new. But the three are captured, and Luke and the girl are taken away, never to be seen again, and Offred is made into a woman in red, a Handmaid.

This novel could have been a humorless, strident tract; but the poet in the author renders it quite otherwise. The narrative is light-handed, fitful, and gradually compelling; it assembles its horrid world with a casual meditative motion, and saves most of its action for the last few pages. Certain small things remain unchanged and unpoisoned in Gilead. "Dish-towels are the same as they always were," and buttons with smiling faces on them are still being manufactured, and flowers still bloom: "Tulips are opening their cups, spilling out color. The tulips are red, a darker crimson towards the stem, as if they have been cut and are beginning to heal there." Even the pervasive pollution is described with a certain poetry: "The air got too full, once, of chemicals, rays, radiation, the water swarmed with toxic molecules, all of that takes years to clean up, and meanwhile they creep into your body, camp out in your fatty cells. Who knows, your very flesh may be polluted, dirty as an oily beach, sure death to shore birds and unborn babies." When a baby is born, there is celebration and holiday. Wives and Handmaids together gather in the birthing room, with its ancient smells: "The smell is of our own flesh, an organic smell, sweat and a tinge of iron, from the blood on the sheet, and another smell, more animal, that's coming, it must be, from Janine: a smell of dens, of inhabited caves, the smell of the plaid blanket on the bed when the cat gave birth on it, once, before she was spayed. Smell of matrix." And, amid the grim deprivations of Gilead, the small details of ordinary free life as it once was rise up in memory: "It's almost like June, when we would get out our sundresses and our sandals and go for an ice cream cone." Deprivation has turned tiny black-marketed items from those luxurious olden days into potent talismans: perfume, cigarettes, hand lotion, even a single kitchen match. When Offred becomes the Commander's mistress, they play Scrabble and he lets her look at illegally preserved copies of fashion magazines:

> Staring at the magazine, as he dangled it before me like fish bait, I wanted it. I wanted it with a force that made the ends of my fingers ache. At the same time I saw this longing of mine as trivial and absurd, because I'd taken such magazines lightly enough once. I'd read them in dentists' offices, and sometimes on planes; I'd bought them to take to hotel rooms, a device to fill in empty time while I was waiting for Luke. After I'd leafed through them I would throw them away, for they were infinitely discardable, and a day or two later I wouldn't be able to remember what had been in them.
>
> Though I remembered now. What was in them was promise. They dealt in transformations; they suggested an endless series of possibilities, extending like the reflections in two mirrors set facing one another, stretching on, replica after replica, to the vanishing point. They suggested one adventure after another, one wardrobe after another, one improvement after another, one man after another. They suggested rejuvenation, pain overcome and transcended, endless love. The real promise in them was immortality.

Any futuristic novel, of course, is about the present: what has struck the writer as significant and ominous in the world now. Such an enlargement of topical issues and phenomena tends to date faster than a novel, incidentally contemporary, that describes more or less perennial human adventures. What saves *The Handmaid's Tale* from a timely datedness is that, among its cautionary and indignant messages, Miss Atwood has threaded a poem to the female condition. Offred's life of daily waiting and shopping, of cautious strategizing and sudden bursts of daring, forms an intensified and darkened version of a woman's customary existence, a kind of begrimed window through which glimpses of Offred's old, pre-Gilead life—its work and laughter and minor dissipations, its female friends and husband and child, its costumes and options—flicker with the light of paradise. The phrase "woman's novel" is not a happy one—better, surely, for a writer male or female to attempt a "person's novel." But *The Handmaid's Tale* does feel purposefully feminine, and beneath the grim but also transparently playful details of its dystopia glows the vivid and intimate reality of its heroine.

Not until halfway through her tale do we learn that Offred is thirty-three years old, with brown hair, and stands five seven without shoes. We never do learn her pre-Gilead name. She is an American. Scattered clues tell us that she was raised by her mother, was a child in the Seventies, and went to college in the Eighties. After graduation, she lived in a run-down apartment near the Charles River, "worked a computer in an insurance company," and began an affair with a married man called Luke. By this time, the world has taken on a futuristic tint; her second job is that of "discer" for a library—transferring books to computer discs and then shredding the books. Paper money, also, is being phased out, in favor of accounts kept in a Compubank. The Gilead revolution occurs, and its first acts are not especially threatening: Pornomarts are shut down, and Bun-Dle Buggies and Feels on Wheels vans no longer shamelessly circle Harvard Square. Identipasses are issued. It has taken Luke two years "to pry himself loose," and the lovers are already married and their daughter is "three or four, in daycare," when Offred, stopping at the corner store for a pack of cigarettes, is told that her credit card is no longer valid. The credit cards of all females, it turns out, have been invalidated, and the money in their accounts has been turned over to their husbands or male next of kin. That same day, she and all other women are fired from their jobs. Luke, informed of these disasters, tells her he will always take care of her and wants, that night, to make love.

> He kissed me then, as if now . . . things could get back to normal. But something had shifted, some balance. I felt shrunken, so that when he put his arms around me, gathering me up, I was small as a doll. I felt love going forward without me.
> He doesn't mind this, I thought. He doesn't mind it at all. Maybe he even likes it. We are not each other's, anymore. Instead, I am his.

Offred's stream of experience and reflection, as the next year or two takes her to the unsuccessful escape attempt and then three more bring her to her abject condition as Fred's official Handmaid and unofficial Scrabble companion, is nowhere more interesting, at least to this male reader, than in how she sees men. The Commander at first is hardly seen: "I glimpse him only for an instant, foreshortened, walking to the car. He doesn't have his hat on, so it's not a formal event he's going to. His hair is gray. Silver, you might call it if you were being kind. I don't feel like being kind." In slightly better focus, he becomes a composite, middle-aged man: "The Commander has on his black uniform, in which he looks like a museum guard. A semiretired man, genial but wary, killing time. But only at first glance. After that he looks like a midwestern bank president, with his straight neatly brushed silver hair, his sober posture, shoulders a little stooped. And after that there is his mustache, silver also, and after that his chin, which really you can't miss. When you get down as far as the chin he looks like a vodka ad, in a glossy magazine, of times gone by." As this generalized male makes his move and invites her to visit his room illicitly, his image complicates, becomes "daddyish"; at moments he looks *"sheepish . . .* the way men used to look once," and when the time for their official monthly copulation comes "he was no longer a thing to me. That was the problem."

All the subtleties of Fred's and Offred's involvement play about this central perception of hers, achieved at their first interview: "But there must be something he wants, from me. To want is to have a weakness. It's this weakness, whatever it is, that entices me. It's like a small crack in a wall, before now impenetrable. If I press my eye to it, this weakness of his, I may be able to see my way clear." To want is to have a weakness, and by this weakness the powerless obtain a hook into the powerful. And by guilt, also; Offred learns that the Handmaid before her hung herself when the Commander's Wife discovered *their* affair, and she calculates, "Things have changed. I have something on him, now. What I have on him is the possibility of my own death. What I have on him is his guilt." Offred "goes along" with Fred in his whims—she learns a prostitute's tolerance and detachment—but power, power that is the basis of freedom, is her only ardor. When he asks for more than submission she cannot respond; she lies there "like a dead bird"* and tries to stir herself with vain

---

*She is wearing a feathered costume he has offered her for an illicit night out on the town: "He brings his hand out from behind his back. He's holding a handful, it seems, of feathers, mauve and pink. Now he shakes this out. It's a garment, apparently, and for a woman: there are the cups for the breasts, covered in purple sequins. The sequins are tiny stars. The feathers are around the thigh holes, and along the top. . . . I wonder where he found it. All such clothing was supposed to have been destroyed. . . . He must have come by this in the same way he came by the magazines, not honestly: it reeks of black market. And it's not new, it's been worn before, the cloth under the arms is crumpled and slightly stained, with some other woman's sweat." She is not entirely repelled: "Yet there's an enticement in this thing, it carries with it the childish allure of dressing up. And it would be so flaunting, such a sneer at the Aunts, so sinful, so free. Freedom, like everything else, is relative."

A fetishistic intensity clings to this bootlegged garment, with its old sweat stains and outlawed naughtiness; nothing is more winning about Offred than her willingness, with a mixture of curiosity, squeamishness, and Moll Flanderish good nature, to put it on: "I take off my shoes and stockings and my cotton underpants and slide the feathers on, under the tent of my dress. Then I take off the dress itself and slip the thin sequined straps over my shoulders. There are shoes, too, mauve ones with absurdly high heels. Nothing quite fits; the shoes are a little too big, the waist on the costume is too tight, but it will do." And, so costumed, she accompanies the Commander to the city bordello, which seems to occupy

encouragements: "He is not a monster, I think. I can't afford pride or aversion, there are all kinds of things that have to be discarded, under the circumstances."

But there is yet more to the relations between the sexes than this squalor of mutual exploitation. Female heterosexual desire, a terrible beclouder of pure feminist thinking, must be counted in; Offred, when she and we least expect it, falls in love (not with Fred). She becomes reckless and avid in the pursuit of lovemaking. "It wasn't called for, there was no excuse. I did not do it for him, but for myself entirely." And, in the plot's last swift turns, this heedless abandon turns out to be the shrewdest, most self-saving thing she could have done. The reader, suddenly dropped out of her life and inner voice into a humorous lecture upon Gilead delivered in the year 2195, experiences that shocking sensation of time overwhelming life which the reader of *The Age of Innocence* feels when the young lovers are suddenly discovered as old, or that Marcel felt at the final party in *Remembrance of Things Past*, or that we feel when realizing that everybody in a photograph we have been admiring is now dead. *The Handmaid's Tale* casts a chill, but is almost the reverse of the frozen blackness of *Nineteen Eighty-four*. Both books predict corrupt and claustrophobic totalitarianisms.* In *Nineteen Eighty-four*, however, the underground turns out to be the regime in disguise, and there is nowhere to escape; whereas in *The Handmaid's Tale* the regime turns out to be pitifully human and escape

---

what is now the Hyatt Regency Hotel. The reader, having known her so long in her nunlike condition, feels as prickly as she in her exposed, hypersensitive skin: "He puts an arm around my shoulders. The fabric is raspy against my skin, so unaccustomed lately to being touched." She is paraded and ogled; she encounters her old friend Moira, who though enrolled in whoredom can still give the feminist line: "They [men] like to see you all painted up. Just another crummy power trip." But the costume, and the sexiness of which it is the sweat-stained symbol, deepens when, with her true lover, Offred thinks, "For this one I'd wear feathers, purple stars, if that were what he wanted: or anything else, even the tail of a rabbit." The trashy and absurd costume, then, without being absolved of its sexist and mechanical aspect, also represents something tender—the female (and, differently costumed, the male) willingness to amuse the love object, to actualize the opposite other's erotic whims and fantasies. Iris Murdoch's love-obsessed novels suffer, I think, in the rareness, for all their talk, with which they present sexual images as concrete and redolent as this "garment, apparently, and for a woman."

*Both founded, too, upon global stalemate and formalized spheres of influence: "the splitting up of the world into three great superstates [that] prop one another up, like three sheaves of corn" (Orwell); "the superpower arms stalemate and the signing of the classified Spheres of Influence Accord, which left the superpowers free to deal, unhampered by interference, with the growing number of rebellions within their own empires" (Atwood). Odd, that this peaceable idea, the idea now called "détente," appears so distasteful to progressive minds.

is right around the corner. Orwell's book is suffused with his awareness of his approaching death; Atwood's, by life—the heroine's irrepressible vitality and the author's lovely subversive hymn to our ordinary life, as lived, amid perils and pollution, now.

Iris Murdoch cannot be accused of writing "women's novels"; her portly fictions, in later years, lean heavily toward male protagonists, while the female characters become ever more fey and glimmery will-o'-the-wisps—sex objects, or quest objects, of an ethereal sort. Or else they are brisk masculine professionals, who matter-of-factly say things like "I can't stand these prophets of doom, gloating over the collapse of civilisation, they're almost always anti-women. I think Harry despises women, well I suppose most men do." Thus speaks Dr. Ursula Brightwalton, without indignation and on the verbal run like most Murdoch characters, in this prodigious author's latest epic of England's educated classes, *The Good Apprentice.* It seemed to me to be, though nearly as long, considerably less spacious and vigorous than its predecessor, *The Philosopher's Pupil.* The earlier novel's fictional spa of Ennistone gave the author's imagination room to roam amusingly through the social scale and met it, at many turns, with the stimulating physicality of public baths, underground pipes, and canals winding through a thoroughly mapped town plan. In *The Good Apprentice* (a title I never came to understand; who is apprenticed to what?), water takes the form of a vague-making fog, of flooded boggy fens, and of a sea that, like the moral of this book, seems near at hand but is rarely glimpsed.

We must applaud the attempt to cross, in imagination, the sexual dividing line; but I do miss the certain edge Miss Murdoch's books had when their protagonists were young women, with their harassed acuity and nimble irony. She has chosen here to locate the action of the novel all too exclusively in the minds and mental turmoil of two rather priggish and self-centered young men: Edward Baltram and his so-called brother, Stuart Cuno. Though they grew up in the same household, they are not blood brothers. Edward is the son of the famous painter Jesse Baltram and his mistress, Chloe Warriston, and Stuart of the famous writer Casimir Cuno's son Harry, who married Chloe when she was pregnant with Edward, and Harry's first wife, Teresa *née* O'Neill, a Catholic from New Zealand who, like Chloe, died young, having produced one male child. Both young men have put their education (Edward in French, Stuart in math) on hold while they puzzle through the spiritual crises brought about, respectively, by Edward's feeding a friend, Mark Wilsden, a drug that caused him to jump out of a window, and by Stuart's deciding to renounce sex and devote himself to goodness, a step considered all the more extraordinary because he does not believe in God. In Miss Murdoch's long gallery of Godless saints and seekers, Stuart is one of the dimmest; he takes no significant actions and interacts with the other characters mostly by submitting to their astonishingly vehement abuse. His severest critic is his father, who is having a turbulent affair with Midge McCaskerville, Chloe's sister and the wife of Thomas McCaskerville, a well-known psychiatrist, and the mother of Meredith, a dignified pubescent who goes jogging with Stuart. Edward, meanwhile, has sought surcease from his Marconian grief and guilt by trying to find his father, the recessive Jesse, in the castlelike place called Seegard, which turns out to be inhabited by an elfin trio of women in (perhaps Miss Atwood's outfitter clothed them) pseudo-medieval dresses—Mother May, Jesse's wife, and her two daughters, Bettina and Ilona. All of these characters seem to mean more than words can easily tell; their activity consists of talking at one another, falling suddenly in and out of love with one another, and now and then looming to one another as the answer to his or her problems. The enchanter-figures in Miss Murdoch's work have so multiplied as to exist in hierarchies; Harry ranks lower than Thomas, and Thomas lower than Jesse, who is dying and deranged and has extraordinary "wet jelly-like . . . reddish brown" eyeballs that protrude far out of his head "as if . . . lightly resting upon the surface of the face." Potency manifests itself as magic and grotesquerie; the novel festively abounds with visions, hallucinations, poltergeists, omens, coincidences, and other paranormal thrusts of mental energy.

Miss Murdoch's own energy, as ever, verges on the exhausting; her fluidity in dialogue, her luxuriant conjuring of excited emotional states, and her descriptive zeal rampage through these pages, as wistful, ruminative longueurs alternate with brilliantly realized scenes. She jumps into any consciousness that pleases her, even entertaining, as a very minor character, a plant that has been fed a liquid love potion and pines into a wilt of unrequited passion. Love batters the air from all directions and attaches to insane and frigid men more enthusiastically than to responsive, romantic ones. Homosexual attraction among young males seems a more considerable factor than formerly. Of the female characters only Midge is given much of an inside, and some—most distinctly, Elspeth Macran, a horsy and vindictive feminist—are spurned with a virtual harshness by this author of protean sympathy. Introducing her large cast of characters goads Miss Murdoch to a frenzy of specification, and as their eyes, noses, clothes, and hair speed by the art of the novel veers close to the method of the checklist. Hair! Edward has "limp dark straight hair which flopped across his face"; Harry has "thick lively hair, skilfully cut, which had only lately faded a little from being 'golden', standing up in a crown above his unlined brow"; Stuart's hair is "golden like his father's used to be, but cut shorter"; Thomas has "a square-cut fringe of wiry light grey hair"; Meredith has "straight fairish brownish hair like his mother, which he wore combed down in neat lines to his collar, and with a fringe like his father"; Ursula's "dark greying hair was cut in a sensible bob"; Willy, her husband, "continually, even in the middle of dinner, combed a long lock of his gingery hair over his bald patch, but as often the lock fell away, depending awkwardly over his ear, giving him a slightly mad look"; Midge's "copious fairish brownish hair, which contained many tinges, including red here and there, disposed itself in a decorous graceful mop about her head, tossed mane-like from time to time." Each description excellent, and no two heads and haircuts alike, but the very profusion, in less than a dozen pages, seems comically manic and overtaxes that part of the brain designed to retain visual images. And when we move away from London to Seegard the hair thickens yet again, in three kindred but differentiated shades and states of tidiness: Bettina's "hair, of a rather disconcerting dark reddish colour, was elaborately pinned up, but trailing curly wisps drew attention to the transparent whiteness and smoothness of her neck"; Mother May's "reddish-blonde hair, lighter in colour than Bettina's, was more neatly piled"; and Ilona's "red hair, even untidier than Bettina's, had partly collapsed down her back." One wonders whether Miss Murdoch's narrative gifts, in the beginning so incisive and kinetic that her early novels read like scripts and one of them, *A Severed Head*, was made into a play, haven't settled into the descriptive to the point that she asks primarily of her characters that they stand still and allow themselves to be groomed, and have their portraits painted. Painting has become, for Miss Murdoch, the enchanter's true art; Jesse's weird paintings are set before the mind's eye one by one, and those of the characters here who turn to writing (Harry, Mother May, Thomas) do so, one feels, as a form less of art than of self-therapy. The painterly treatment extends to the characters' psychologies, which are rich and colorful but stagnant. Edward's decision, at the end of the novel and of all "the spiritual journeys, the redeeming ordeals, the healing draughts, reconciliation, salvation, new life" he has endured, to reread Proust, and Stuart's to go into teaching at the elementary-school level, but feebly echo Faust's resolution to drain the German swamps, or Stephen Dedalus's to forge in the smithy of his soul the uncreated conscience of his race.

As a landscape painter Miss Murdoch is superb. The scenery of her novels often outlasts, in the memory, the characters—the heavy, shadowy suburban gardens of *The Sacred and Profane Love Machine,* for instance, and the mucky riverside Thames of *Bruno's Dream* are indelible in a way not true of the feverish passions enacted in their settings. In *The Good Apprentice,* the flooded flat fens around Seegard—"I've never seen such an utterly pointless landscape," Harry exclaims—have a beckoning, eerie actuality. Those solemn, numbing, wordless moments when landscape penetrates the human spirit speak for themselves:

> The sky had by now become quite dark and the stars were hidden by clouds. Great grey balls of mist, illumined by the torches, moved slowly by, nudging the walkers and obscuring the way ahead. Harry took Midge's hand and pulled her along, keeping the torch-light fixed upon Sarah's muddy shoes and the frayed ends of her jeans. Midge stumbled, trying to make out where to put her feet, her high-heeled shoes sticking in the thick moist grasses which the torches vividly revealed. A chill wind was blowing, there were a few spots of rain. Midge began quietly and surreptitiously to cry.

Time and again reality does thus burn through the frightful talkiness of this novel, its breathless miasmic hurried (so to speak) series of adjectives—"that deep rhythmic heartbeat of perfect joy," "in wild lonely very beautiful country," "a universe of rich harmonious endlessly various and ever renewed happinesses"—and its helpless predilection for such witless modifiers as "awful," "terrible," and "wonderful." Not that Miss Murdoch never rises to her own occasions: the long-delayed confrontation scene between Edward and Jesse is handsomely understated, and a brief two pages in which Edward watches Ilona do a striptease in Soho are quite, well, wonderful. And let it be additionally said, in fairness to this great-hearted author, that the questions with which she so persistently grapples in her fiction are the very ones upon which the interest of all fiction depends. Our lives are momentous: all of her tremendous novelistic energy is bent to sustaining that faith. Our lives have meaning, there is such a thing as goodness: the head supplies little evidence to support these traditional assumptions, but the heart keeps insisting. The question is phrased in *The Good Apprentice* as one of "depth." Harry shouts at Stuart, "Modern science has abolished the difference between good and evil, there isn't anything deep, that's the message of the modern world." His creator, unable to locate depth in the external cosmos where God once reigned, turns, in the paradoxical gesture of Christian humanism, toward Man himself to supply the depth that Man demands. The prose cries, "But oh how crazy the mind is, ingenious, histrionic, wicked and deep." And Ursula flatly asserts, "The human mind is a bottomless mystery."

Bottomless? That seems extreme. And the bog of the quasi-supernatural a dubious proving ground. Miss Murdoch's central male triangle of Harry, Edward, and Stuart, while treated at length, does not illustrate much in the way of depth, though it does show the endless self-dramatization and internal histrionics of which educated, financially comfortable English males are capable. The novel ends with its heroes only incrementally chastened and fortified, and with the author wildly chatty as she fusses at all her loose ends, her bundle of animated signifiers. Her tale has rarely, unlike Miss Atwood's, outrun its proclaimed significances, and its moral (I have just glimpsed it) came in the middle: "Where there are people there's mess."

Back to the Classics

THE APOCRYPHA, by Robert Pinget, translated from the French by Barbara Wright. 143 pp. Red Dust, 1986.

ACASTOS: *Two Platonic Dialogues,* by Iris Murdoch. 130 pp. Viking, 1987.

The Summer 1983 issue of *The Review of Contemporary Fiction* was devoted dually to Jack Kerouac and Robert Pinget. Kerouac's fame has reached all the way back to Lowell, Massachusetts, which is dedicating a downtown park next spring to its wandering native son, but Pinget remains, in the United States, the all-but-exclusive property of college French departments and fanatic buffs of literary pre-postmodernism. His recent slim works, faithfully translated by Barbara Wright and published by the way-out firm of Red Dust, are printed in American editions of a thousand copies. Nevertheless, Pinget bulks large in the present rather fey world literary scene—a determinedly experimental and unfettered writer whose education in music, painting, and the law help give his curious oeuvre range and penetration. A considerable delay attends the publication of his books in English; the most recent to appear, *The Apocrypha,* came out in France in 1980. Like its predecessors *The Libera Me Domine* (1968 in France; Red Dust, 1978), *Passacaglia* (1969; 1978), *Fable* (1971; 1980), and *That Voice* (1980; 1982), it is an extension or variation of an established though unsettlingly fluid world—a rural village world of circling gossip, moldering architecture, lurking atrocity, and (ever more centrally) botany, both in the wild and in the garden. From book to book, characters overlap—especially that of a reclusive "Master," who inhabits a mansion with his servant and brother or nephews or uncle, depending on how the forgetful, restlessly revising dominant voice phrases it at the moment. An atmospheric reality emerges all the more forcefully for the vibrant uncertainty of details; the decay and banality of provincial rustic life blur, at their margins, into something hellish, and also something redeeming. Pinget has said, in a note to *The Libera Me Domine,* that "the interest of my work up to the present has been the quest for a *tone of voice.*" The voice of his books (never quite the same) mitigates the sudden incidents of murder and madness with a comedy of expression, a garrulous patience, an onrolling indifference, a kind of cheerfully brute communal transcendence.

The Apocrypha seems to me not only an extension of Pinget's world but a consummation of it, his best (if comparative terms can be applied within a created microcosm so consistently indeterminate) novel since his best-known and most popular work, *The Inquisitory* (1962; Grove Press, 1967). The Apocrypha (a plural term whose root sense of "hidden" was applied by the Church to non-canonical works, which in time became magical in the popular imagination) are being composed by the Master—tortuously annotated and revised notebooks that he is keeping, and that his heirs are trying to edit. "Unravel the intricacies of these chronicles which delight in getting in a tangle, there's a secret plan somewhere there. . . . Upsurges of fervor which soon flag and leave him prostrate in his chair, his manuscript scattered all over the room, monologuing on the theme of the book to be written, of the adventure of art, and of the chaos in his mind." The Apocrypha are, among other things, the pages we hold in our hands. Pinget's recurrent method becomes a metaphor for its subject here: "The essential often seems to be brushed aside in favor of the adventitious as if some occult tyrant has adjured the scriptor only to approach the truth at a tangent." The Master's notes to himself become Pinget's self-admonitions: "Beware literary tone"; "Clarify terms." The elusiveness of the endlessly complicated text serves as a metaphor, too, for decay—the Master's decaying mind, the erosions of anamnesis, the loss of circumstance within memory. His notebooks, often called "gramarye"—an archaic word associated not only with grammar but with necromancy—are, then, "secret wellsprings of this fight against nothingness." And, as the book moves toward its climax, its texture merges with the revisions of the annual natural cycle, the variations from year to year: "The work would take shape according to the rhythm of the year, a forgotten arcanum." The years are almost interchangeable: "Leafing through the book he finds that the words he'd underlined aren't on the same pages, they've been displaced from where they were the previous year. . . . Convinced that in the country things barely change from one year to the next, the first memorialist out of either laziness or lassitude might have confined himself to copying some of the passages dealing with the June of the previous year."

The temporal structure of *The Apocrypha* is clear enough: the year, marked by its seasonal weather and flowers and holy days, goes by twice, revolving about the figure of a shepherd most vividly seen in December. Stephen Bann, in a critical article of thirteen pages appended to this novel of not quite one hundred thirty, explicates the pattern and also establishes clear textual links between *The Apocrypha* and Virgil's *Eclogues* and the Psaltery. The figure of the Good Shepherd, of course, is where paganism and Christianity overlap; early statues of Christ show a beardless youth with a lamb on his shoulders, and lines from the Fourth Eclogue were interpreted throughout the Middle Ages as Virgil's magic prophecy of Christ's birth, out of a virgin, in the reign of Augustus. The prettified shepherds of classic eclogues, the Good Shepherd, and the shepherds who came to the Nativity in Luke's Gospel all blend into one another while the *image* of a shepherd, in the Master's roving purview, migrates from a shattered cup to a zodiac-rimmed picture printed in an ancient book, "an old book he found at a junk dealer's, a modern mind would be ill at ease with it the subject matter is so jumbled up, commentaries on this or that work of Virgil." Mr. Bann, with his sometimes bristling critical vocabulary ("plunged in his pettifogging apocalypse . . . is a vivid example of this reiterated catachresis"), pounces on Pinget's increasing use of Christian symbolism and sees the author as "anticipating the concerns of an important direction of French thought and criticism" and helping to establish "a claim for the seriousness of theological tradition in a post-psychoanalytic culture." This comes too close to making of Pinget a kind of latter-day Bernanos. Pinget's fiction has always been haunted and obsessed with the past, and Christianity is Europe's crumbling past: "the whole shebang of the centuries which now they're old project a terrifying shadow into their enfeebled hearts in what they're looking for something that ought to be the soul, which was it exactly, a precious gift now confused with the fear of death." On the other hand, the image of the shepherd does appear, in the course of *The Apocrypha*'s double annual round, to become whole. The imperfections repeatedly noted in both its ceramic and printed forms ("a tiny shard wrongly glued," "a bit of mould obliterates the original contour of the face and hands, just look how clumsily this ink line has been drawn to try to restore it") have by the last paragraph been, as if miraculously, absorbed into the perfection of an icon simultaneously Christian and humanist:

The halo crowning his head is the heart of a masterly composition in which each extended line at an equal distance from the other joins the ecliptic of the heavenly body that governs the system.

Iris Murdoch, too, toys with a classical model in her new book. *Acastos* binds together two Platonic dialogues, one of which has actually been produced in London as a short play. Miss Murdoch has taught philosophy at Oxford and published a book, *The Fire and the Sun: Why Plato Banished the Artists;* her own Platonism informs the intellectual and erotic seethe of her tireless novels, whose characters reside half in a solidly realized England and half in a translucent realm of immaterial passions and ideas. "Yes," she and her favorite characters seem to keep saying, "the Good and the True and the Beautiful *do* exist, compellingly, bafflingly, absolutely." Plato himself, as a somewhat minor character in these two dialogues, asserts, "People know that good is real and absolute, not optional and relative, all their life proves it," and, when challenged by Alcibiades, gets quite sputtery about it: "Good must be pure and separate and—absolute— and—only what's completely good can—save us—"

Alcibiades scoffs, "But your perfectly pure good thing does not exist, that's the trouble, dear, all the world proves *that!*" And Plato cries, "It *does,* it *must*—it's *more real*—I can't explain—" Plato, here a callow youth of only twenty, has already developed a lot of bullying mental maneuvers. God, too, *must* exist: "Religion isn't a feeling, it isn't just a hypothesis, it's not like something we happen not to know, a God who might perhaps be there isn't a God, it's got to be necessary, it's got to be certain, it's got to be proved by the whole of life, it's got to be the magnetic centre of everything—" Miss Murdoch is the philosopher, and knows better than I how true to Plato's mature thought is this rather Kantian or Kierke-gaardian sense of God's stern obligation to exist. Socrates gently says, "Then your 'ground of things', your 'it must be so', is really 'I want it to be so', it's a cry of fear?" Plato begs off, and even Socrates seems to concede more than a strictly materialistic and relativist standpoint would warrant: "The most important thing in life is virtue, and virtue isn't a mystery, it's truthfulness and justice and kindness and courage, things we understand. Anybody can *try* to be good, it's not obscure!"

Yet of course goodness *is* obscure, to an age that has heard it said that the state is organized violence, that humility and submission help perpetu-ate the powerful in their crimes, that altruism is a kind of neuroticism, that a repressed "drive" (Freud) becomes self-destructive, and that "slave mo-rality" (Nietzsche) should be despised and supplanted. Miss Murdoch has the aesthetic problem, in contriving these new Platonic dialogues, of how many of modern thought's dark chaotic voices to admit to the forum: to stay entirely within the intellectual frame of Periclean Athens would be a pointless tour de force, and yet her exercises would be hopelessly campy did they feel any more up-to-date than they do. "Public morality . . . *is* breaking down" no doubt expresses a timeless complaint, but "love is energy" seems more a contemporary formulation, put into Plato's mouth: "You see, love is energy. The soul is a huge vast place, and lots of it is dark, and it's full of energy and power, and this can be bad, but it *can* be good, and that's the work, to change bad energy into good. . . . All right, it's sex, or sex is it—it's the whole drive of our being and that includes sex." A distinctly modern view of the evangelized lower classes as well as a West Indian accent creep into a servant's refreshing testimony on these great matters: "Like little fish in sea am I in God's love! All I eat, sleep, work, do, inside his love. . . . I am not good man, I have many sin, many fault, many, many. I need my God. I am all bad, he is all good, I have bad thoughts—"

But religion and its conundrums are enduring enough to straddle epochs, and the dialogue on religion is much the livelier one. The dialogue on art, which was the one to enjoy performance (in the National Theatre, in 1980), seems relatively insipid, in part because its argumentation is confined to examples of art no later than the fifth century B.C. Even as a provisional definition, Miss Murdoch's Callistos could never, had he seen a single Rauschenberg construct or Pollock painting (or read a Pinget novel), have described art as "copying into a world where everything looks different and clearer, and there's no muddle and no horrid accidental things like in life." After Céline and Kafka, can we still, as Socrates urges, "thank the gods for great artists who draw away the veil of anxiety and selfishness"? Plato is made to say, "Art softens the demand of the gods. It puts an attractive veil over that *final* awful demand, that final transformation into goodness, the almost impossible *last step* which is what human life is really all about." This is thrillingly put, and in tune with the relevant chapters of *The Republic*—but is, say, a fur-lined teacup or a latrine displayed on a museum wall such an attractive veil? The phrase hardly seems true even of *Oedipus Rex,* or of the satyrical activities painted onto Greek vases.

When we turn to *The Republic* or to any of the authentic Platonic dialogues, we realize how much a novelist and sentimental *Neo*platonist Miss Murdoch is in her adroit and charming imitations. The original atmosphere was much more Spartan: in *The Republic,* Socrates proposed to ban poets because human emotion, which poetry indulges, is "irrational, useless, and cowardly." Poetry "feeds and waters the passions instead of drying them up; she lets them rule, although they ought to be controlled, if mankind are ever to increase in happiness and virtue." Dry reason and manly endurance should rule "the sympathetic element." Callistos's babbling suggestion that art is "exciting and sexy" would have fallen on stony ground in the fifth century. The element of homoerotic byplay* pervades Miss Murdoch's dialogues and verges on making them farcical playlets. As if in one of her irrepressible novels, each character strains to rattle off in his own direction; Socrates is a kindly presiding tutor but a shadow of the remorseless logical engine who bulldozes his way through Plato's dialogues, reducing all others to yes-men. Plato wrote in a time when truth was thought to be attainable, when permanent conclusions could be achieved and built upon; this live possibility, so near the beginnings of reasoned thought, throws a white light upon the stylized figures of his debates. Miss Murdoch writes in a time of multiplying shadows, of built-in indeterminacy and ambiguity, when Eros is the only apprehensible god. Her animated but highly inconclusive dialogue on art ends with Socrates claiming, "In truly loving each other we learn more perhaps than in all our other study." The excitable young Plato tells his teacher, "I'm so happy. I don't know why. I love you so much," and, runs the stage direction, "*Socrates puts his arm round him and leads him off.*" This note of affectionate fellowship among high-minded men and boys also ended Miss Murdoch's last novel, *The Good Apprentice,* and seems strangely satisfying to her. She and Pinget are almost exactly the same age, and in their different ways show a high tolerance for ambiguity. Models of creative integrity in a slack age, they sing perversely rapturous hymns to muddle.

---

*Not entirely absent from the originals: in the *Phaedo*, Phaedo relates how Socrates "gathered the hair on my neck" and stroked his young disciple's head while discussing his own imminent death.

BRITISHERS

Genius Without a Cause

CYRIL CONNOLLY: *Journal and Memoir,* by David Pryce-Jones. 304 pp. Ticknor & Fields, 1984.

THE SELECTED ESSAYS OF CYRIL CONNOLLY, edited by Peter Quennell. 307 pp. Persea Books, 1984.

The aura of disappointment, of failed promise, that surrounded Cyril Connolly was to a large degree his own creation. It was he who, in *Enemies of Promise* (1938), capped adverse diagnoses in all the sickrooms of contemporary literary endeavor with a ruthless self-portrait of his schoolboy self—a study in callow cleverness, romantic dither, permanent adolescence, cowardice, snobbery, and sloth. Though this least flattering of autobiographical sketches ends with Connolly's leaving Eton at the age of eighteen in 1922, his subsequent career is adumbrated as a continued "useless assignment, falling in love, going to Spain and being promising indefinitely." It was Connolly who began his other book of note, the suavely melancholy "word cycle" called *The Unquiet Grave* (1944), with the famous assertion "that the true function of a writer is to produce a masterpiece and that no other task is of any consequence." By the bald light of this harsh lantern readers would have no trouble perceiving that the little Diogenes holding it on high, at that time editor of the magazine *Horizon* and afterwards to become the lead reviewer of the London *Sunday Times,* was himself engaged in inconsequent tasks and, according to language farther down the page ("Writers engrossed in any literary task which is not an assault on perfection are their own dupes"), was his own dupe. Any subsequent critic wishing to write earnestly of Connolly finds himself, therefore, somewhat disarmed, facing a choice between sheepish agreement with these low opinions and disagreement that might seem merely mulish.

David Pryce-Jones, assigned the awkward task of presenting for publication a dishevelled, abjectly self-critical, and at the same time insufferably self-absorbed journal that Connolly kept between 1928 and 1937, seems on balance to agree that Connolly disappointed, while finding something successfully strategic in the pose of *maître manqué:* "The depiction of himself as some sort of royal failure was the foundation of his success. . . . Playing the leading part in this comedy of his own devising, he was imitating failure. Advantage came from it. Here was the way to avoid making hard choices or sacrifices, here was the way to have everything all at once and all the time, to be artist and critic, powerfully realising ambition while claiming not to be doing so." In the long biographical sketch that follows these judgments, Mr. Pryce-Jones tends to side with the school authorities so deftly mocked by Connolly in his memoir. The Wilkeses, who under the nicknames of "Flip" (Mrs.) and "Sambo" (Mr.) ran St. Cyprian's school, had been, we are told, "consistently well-disposed towards Cyril. . . . Within their capacities, they had done their best for a boy much cleverer and more sophisticated than usual."* At Eton, we are told, the Master in College, J. F. Crace, wrote with "some prescience" of the sixteen-year-old Cyril, "He is in danger of achieving nothing more than a journalistic ability to write rather well about many things." Connolly's "A Georgian Boyhood," in *Enemies of Promise,* is concerned for most of its pages with Etonian social and political intrigues; of these Mr. Pryce-Jones sniffs, "What had actually been storms in College tea-cups were exaggerated into grandeurs and miseries."

In the journal itself, the little storms pitter-patter on. Of Robert Longden, an Oxford crush of Connolly's with whom he continued to correspond and travel, the diarist breathily confided:

My sadism is very subtle with regard to Bobbie, I do not want to cause him any kind of pain or to hurt him, but I should like to storm him unprepared by a fire and sympathy of conversation, to glow right into his personality by a kind of corrosive imaginative beauty so that he feels he has never lived nor understood anything before as he has on this wild probing caress of words—to give him vitality that is greater than his vitality, to teach him a sensibility finer and surer than his own, to send an intolerable current down

---

*St. Cyprian's, under the pseudonym of Crossgates, was also the subject of George Orwell's scathing "Such, Such Were the Joys . . ." Mr. Pryce-Jones blandly assures us that "Actually nothing outside the normal run of schoolboy experience happened to either of them"—as if the horrors of the "normal run" weren't what they were protesting.

to light his heart's globe and to lap him all the time in a gentle warmth of tenderness, humour and understanding, that is my ambition, for if I succeed nothing else that he does will give him back his honeydew, nor will he taste the milk of paradise from other cups than mine.

Though now well into his twenties and not entirely innocent of post-graduate reality and of heterosexual contacts, Connolly continued school-boyishly to draw up graded lists of his acquaintances ("Friends," "In storage," "The old," and "*à la carte*" are the categories of one such inventory), to set questionnaires for himself and others ("Are you a sadist or a masochist?" "Are there as many grades of lesbians as of womanisers?" "What are the oddest circumstances in which you have made love?" "Would you drink a pint of blood to save your sister?"), and to pen self-admonishments like "Be more ruthless, and less flabby, cease being influenced by charmers and gentlemen." Though Connolly himself had little money, "on all branches of his family tree were large houses and private incomes," as Mr. Pryce-Jones puts it. His taste for the soft life was full-blown and cheerfully confessed: "O the joy of lingering over port and brandy with men in red coats telling dirty stories while it snows outside." A not untypically posh entry runs, "Enjoyed the rich patina of the Cunard soirée, the lovely women, the vacant faces of the extroverts, the expression of envy on Clarence Marjoribanks and the incredible stupid air of luxuri-ous abandon on Lady Cunard's face as she danced with the Prince of Wales." The young would-be writer rarely dined alone, and his strata-gems were directed less toward accomplishing work than toward making a social impression. In *Enemies of Promise* he was parenthetically to ob-serve how "all charming people have something to conceal, usually their total dependence on the appreciation of others." To his journal in 1928 he confided, "There is no finer sense of power than the power of one's own imagination over that of other men, no more exciting and impossible task than that of making oneself indispensable to one's best friend." In Zagreb, having spent the night mostly under the stars with a teen-age prostitute, he wondered as he walked home in the dawn "how my friends would see me." Of another occasion, when he had taken a gramophone onto a Channel-bound train, Connolly noted, "I played slow foxtrots in my empty carriage and felt that at last I had become an interesting person again." His obsession with his own image, whether as "an interesting person" or as "the most unlovable mug in England," certainly got in his way as a writer, and gets in our way as we try to read these youthful jottings, both pompous and plaintive, with sympathetic attention.

An Englishman of Connolly's class had to pursue literary ambition through social mists much thicker than any on this side of the Atlantic. One's schoolmates, slightly reshuffled, had become the rising elite, and there were, all around, maddening examples of gentlemen—that is, men supported by unearned income. Logan Pearsall Smith, the Anglicized Philadelphian who employed the young Connolly as a secretary, led a thoroughly aesthetic life thanks to what he called "the unfailing fountain of my little annuity." Connolly in his diary exhorted himself about the need to have a steady thousand pounds a year, or, better yet, three thousand pounds. His financial reality consisted of grudging doles from relatives, eight pounds a week from Pearsall Smith, and what he earned doing proofreading and unsigned reviews for Desmond MacCarthy at the *New Statesman*. This last sum went up to ten pounds a week when, in 1927, he became a regular contributor of signed reviews. In his journal he wrote this "advice to a reviewer": "So you wish to take up reviewing—but this is no easy matter. To begin with, you must be sure that writing is your vocation, next you must be convinced that reviewing is not writing, hence the conclusion that your vocation is not reviewing. Well, once you feel that, you can start." At the same time, Connolly had a decided taste and aptitude for the literary seethe—the old-boy snake pit of London literary life. "Desire for literary intrigue, power, influence, struggle," he noted in one of his self-accountings. If Eton turned out to be all politics, then literature must be also. *Enemies of Promise*, indeed, deals less with works than with reputations, to whose rise and fall it shows a sensitivity almost morbid. The portrait of the artist as a young man which emerges from these journals enhances one's admiration for the stubborn creative resolves of Lawrence and Joyce, who disdained the London critical establishment and in willful isolation composed their fierce provincial novels. Nottingham and Dublin pressed upon these two authors as no body of material apparently did on Connolly; nor did he have the savage humor or the uncanny empathy that enabled, respectively, his peers Evelyn Waugh and Henry Green to put worlds onto paper. The outer world interested Connolly as the means to his own comfort—a not entirely ignoble preoccupation but one more likely to produce philosophy than fiction.

After 1930, when he married Jean Bakewell, a young American with some money and a cheerful habit of "easy surrender," the journals pick up pace and interest and become less anxiously narcissistic. Jean's Americanness, so surprising to Connolly's friends, may have helped release him from what he called his "inferiorities and persecutions from Yeoman's Row." She was outside the English class system, mercifully, as was Europe. The couple had met in Paris and spent all the time they could on the Continent; for years Connolly had been complaining about England's stuffiness and ugliness in his journals. "England is a problem—parts of it so beautiful—a few people in it so intelligent and quite a good many extraordinarily nice—yet I can't ever manage to fit into it. . . . I hate colonels and I hate the people who make fun of them."

While married to Jean, he wrote his one novel, *The Rock Pool* (1936). A downbeat comedy of raffish expatriates in a Riviera town, it suggests the early novels of Waugh and Aldous Huxley yet has a spontaneous candor, a poetic sensuality, and a vulnerable air all its own. A few years later, Connolly wrote his one book-length critical work, *Enemies of Promise,* which became in its last third an essay in autobiography. On the wave of nostalgia and depression that followed his marriage's breakup in 1940, he assembled that curious scrapbook, *The Unquiet Grave,* like Eliot's *Four Quartets* a testament of solace for wartime London. The mild creative surge that produced these three disparate, odd, yet haunting works has to be associated with Jean, who shared his fondness for southern Europe, late nights, and pet lemurs. "Without your help, advice, love, and enthusiasm I am a mutilated person, a genius without a cause," he wrote her, seeking a reconciliation. He persisted in both the infidelities that had driven her back to America and in his attempts at reviving the marriage; they were not divorced until after the war. Henceforth he was to be a London pundit and character merely, though a foremost one, and one who brought to his reviewing and journalism considerable diligence and an ineradicable verve and fineness of mind. Connolly, who died in 1974, had become an interesting person, and remains one. All three of the books named above are in print in this country, recently reissued in paperback by Persea Books, which has also now published in hardcover *The Selected Essays of Cyril Connolly,* edited and with an introduction by Peter Quennell.

Mr. Quennell, whom Connolly knew at Balliol, figures in his journals as an especially respected friend, "my only contemporary interesting in himself and not because I choose to make him so." Yet the old friend has done a rather casual job of extracting this volume from Connolly's three miscellaneous collections—*The Condemned Playground* (1945), *Ideas and Places* (1953), and *Previous Convictions* (1963). There is no index. Most of the pieces bear no dateline, so that only stray internal evidences offer to orient us within four decades of composition, and a word like "beatnik" jumps up from an essay on "The Grand Tour" with the impudence of an anachronism. The allotment of three hundred seven pages seems rather meagre for a posthumous omnibus, with too pronounced a tilt away from Connolly's book reviews. The literary articles included are either general statements or else deal with major writers. I would have enjoyed a bit less caviar and a bit more bread and butter, in the form of Connolly's treatment of the minor and ephemeral works that necessarily come a constant reviewer's way—the feeblest works sometimes provoke the freest flights. Instead, there is a long section devoted to "Satires & Parodies." Though Connolly's parody of Huxley, "Told in Gath," is an anthology standard, his burlesque of Ian Fleming, "Bond Strikes Camp," seems grotesquely overextended, and the two "Felicity" pieces are parodying I don't quite know what; the writer's frustrated impulse to make fiction seems vented in these flights, and they overcarry the satiric point. And it would have been interesting to know, of the travel pieces, where they appeared, since they vary significantly in tone and were doubtless produced, like most travel pieces, for a market.

What can one say, critically, about a critic without seeming hypercritical? Cyril Connolly, at least in this selection, is no Edmund Wilson, burrowing with implacable brow through shelves of books in our behalf, nor a T. S. Eliot, offhandedly overturning reputations and bestowing a phrase that a thousand assistant professors can feed upon. Connolly lacked the trenchancy, the will to penetrate, that distinguished these two more determined minds. Novels honestly pained and bored him; no wonder he wrote only one. "The reviewing of novels is the white man's grave of journalism; it corresponds, in letters, to building bridges in some impossible tropical climate. The work is grueling, unhealthy, and ill-paid, and for each scant clearing made wearily among the springing vegetation the jungle overnight encroaches twice as far." He proposed a closed season— "no new novels to be published for three years, their sale forbidden like that of plovers' eggs." He advocated that no one under thirty should be allowed to write one, that "words like Daddy, love, marriage, baby, birth, death, mother, buses, shops" all be banned, plus "all novels dealing with more than one generation or with any period before 1918 or with brilliant impoverished children in rectories." The typical English novel "consists either of arranged emotional autobiography or a carefully detached description of stupid people to show that the author is too clever to be clever." Whereas "the typical 100 percent American novel has almost invariably a group hero, and is usually a monument of wasted energy, sentimentality striving after realism, and an admirable talent for description being thrown away on life that is quite unworthy to be described." The giants of modern literature pained him little less: Virginia Woolf, the journals aver, wrote lush and cliché-ridden prose and "does not care for human beings"; Proust, we read in *Enemies of Promise,* was "often repetitive and feeble" and "a reactionary writer"; and Joyce, it is said in *Selected Essays,* "fed his queen bee of a mind with inferior jelly" and produced

massive works "fundamentally uninteresting." Connolly further says of
Joyce, "His life is one of the saddest and one of the emptiest except in so
far as it was filled by the joys of artistic creation." He condemns Oscar
Wilde on an opposite count: "Perhaps what emerges from his letters is his
fatal indifference to the real demands of a talent. No one talked more about
art and artists or worked less."

On the evidence of these *Selected Essays,* what did Connolly approve of?
Travel, food, France, lemurs, the Latin elegists, Surrealism, and the
rococo. The essay "Living with Lemurs" is one of the most delightful:
"Their plaintive cry, their eyes of melting brown under long black lashes
. . . a terrier's head on a furlined Pharaoh's body . . . If the ribs or armpits
are tickled they are compelled to purr, to abandon any other posture and
to start licking whatever lies in front of them." "The Elegiac Temperament" treats Tibullus tenderly and Propertius as a soulmate: "He was a
weary and precocious adolescent in a tired world." The essays on the
Greek and Roman classics, on Surrealism ("the greatest artistic commotion of the twentieth century and one of the few enlargements of sensibility in the last thirty years which stand to the credit of humanity") and the
rococo conspicuously display Connolly's two strengths as a critic: his
surprising erudition and his energy of response and phrasing. He was
especially enthusiastic about those artistic topics that took him out of
England into the general European experience. "The rococo was an
explosive affirmation of the private life, an escape from Versailles. . . . In
fact, the whole of Europe needed liberation from heroics and the rococo
is an art sponsored by leading personalities . . . which caught on immediately with the humblest of their subjects and united all in a masquerade
of gaiety and pleasure terminated (as is every European aesthetic movement) by an internecine war." To a dazzling inventory of rococo masterpieces he characteristically adds the personal, elegiac note: "Even as I
write some facade is crumbling; a ceiling flakes, paneling is being stripped,
plasterwork crushed, chimneypieces torn out, a Chippendale lookingglass cracks and innumerable pieces of china are thumbed and shattered.
. . . So hurry, before the last cartouche, the fading arabesque, the final
cul-de-lampe goes the way of Sans-Souci and Schönbornslust, Belle-Vue
and Bruchsal." This reluctant critic's sudden bursts of specific information
should not surprise us; as a schoolboy Connolly won the Harrow History
Prize, a national cramming contest, and he worked up his successful
scholarship exam for Balliol on a subject, medieval history, not offered at
Eton. In *Enemies of Promise* he recalled, "I had an excellent memory, I
could learn by heart easily, gut a book in an hour and a half of arguments,
allusions and quotations, like a Danube fisherman removing caviare from
the smoking sturgeon."

He had a rococo, even at times surreal, gift for the unexpected image. Startling similes dot his critical prose and keep us charmed:

> When success permits them, both writers and painters prefer to barricade themselves deep in bourgeois country, like those birds which we admire for their color and song but which have divided our woods into well-defined gangster pitches of wormy territory.

> Edmund Wilson seems to have returned to the conception of the artist as an isolated wounded figure, as different from the social realist as is a huge lightning-stricken oak from a Government conifer plantation.

> Kitchener's Island, the perfect garden, Assuan Dam, the largest and loveliest of waterworks . . . they are relics of our art and altruism for which we receive scant credit. One day they will go the way of the lines of Suez or El Alamein or of the Edwardian novels and proconsular memoirs which sleep like papyri behind the locked grilles of the hotel library.

> [John William Mackail's] Christian attitude to paganism, that it was consciously pathetic and incomplete, like an animal that wishes it could talk, infected everything which he translated with a morbid distress.

His language at times can be too figurative, as when he writes of "the lilt of transience which is the breath of readability" or of Joyce as "this literary anti-Pope, this last great Mammoth out of whose tusks so many smaller egoists have carved their self-important ivory towers." But his profusion, and those sudden, almost madcap evocations to which his prose could rouse itself, enliven his criticism and lend great color and warmth to his remarkable travel pieces. Eight of these open Mr. Quennell's selection, and the best of them—about Bordeaux, the Dordogne Valley, and Switzerland, all regions that cater assiduously to the inner man—are studies in rapture and hymns to civilized hedonism:

> Latour, Lafite, Margaux, Cantenac; each vineyard marked out by an army of knotted green bushes whose powdery clusters dangle among the pebbles, whose wine gives out the most delicate of civilized aromas; fragrant, light, and cavernous as myrtle-berries from an Etruscan tomb, the incomparable *bouquet du vieux Médoc*, offspring of sunshine and hard work, parent of warmth, wit, and understanding.

The austerities and embarrassments of travel also entertained Connolly. In one brief sketch, a tourist's-eye version of an abortive revolution in Greece, we taste something Olympian, both in the gusto of the descriptions of boredom ("Sleeping late to shorten the day, one went to the window and found the Acropolis and the Parthenon blocking the horizon.

A thing of beauty, that is a joy once or twice, and afterward a standing reproach") and in the calm humor with which violence is described: "The machine guns began again. The street, in normal times so straight and dull, became an enormous affair of shadows and relief, of embrasures and exposed spaces. The kiosk at the corner seemed as far away as it would to a baby who could just walk, or to a very lame old man." Such sharp photographs of sensation are like something in Hemingway, but without the tense and consciously heroic surface. Inside the hotel, as an armored car roved outside, "all was cheerfulness and commotion; everyone felt important and with a reason for living." When the trouble had blown over, the onlookers, "while secretly admitting the futility of the eye-witness, the meaninglessness and stupidity of all that had happened, knew also that they had tasted the intoxication and the prestige of action, and were soon rearranging the events of the day on a scale, and in an order, more worthy of the emotions which had been generated by them." The cadences are Gibbon's, and along such grand lines of illusionless gaiety, of dispassionate and scrupulous witness, Connolly's gifts might have extended themselves, if the times had been more propitious, and his purposes more fixed.

Among the Masters

THE MYTH MAKERS, by V. S. Pritchett. 190 pp. Random House, 1979.

Nineteen essays—book reviews revised into less timely and more harmonious shape—gaze upon as many major fictionists, ranging from Stendhal and George Sand to Solzhenitsyn and Gabriel García Márquez, with not an Englishman or an American among them. Mr. Pritchett shows a marvellous acquaintance with literature as both a body of works and a branch of professional activity, and he walks among the mighty spirits with the benign authority of an investigating angel, taking puckish notes. Of the Tolstoys' marriage he writes, "Like the Lawrences and the Carlyles, the Tolstoys were the professionals of marriage; they knew they were not in it for their good or happiness, that the relationship was an appointed ordeal, an obsession undertaken by dedicated heavyweights." Of Dostoevsky's characters: "Life stories of endless complexity hang shamelessly out of the mouths of his characters, like dogs' tongues, as they run by." Great compression and wit attend these observations; e.g., "A scene of Oriental luxury was indispensable to the Romantics: the looting of Egypt was Napoleon's great gift to literature." Mr. Pritchett's ease in the ballrooms of history is absolute. He greets each master by the hand and, while seeming to make small talk, elicits from all the essence of their personalities; for García Márquez, he sees, "life is ephemeral but dignified by fatality," and the nineteenth-century Spaniard Perez Galdos is complimented, "The fact is that Galdos accepts human nature without resentment." Criticism this humane, precise, and unpedantic freshens the classics like a morning breeze.

To the Arctic

CHEKHOV: *A Spirit Set Free,* by V. S. Pritchett. 222 pp. Random House, 1988.

In this terse yet tender book Sir Victor leads the reader through Chekhov's fiction, in chronological order, allowing the biography to be background music. Glints of confident opinion highlight his rapid survey: "The danger [of a collected edition]—as we know from Henry James's revisions—lay in the temptation to elaborate, but Chekhov was a cutter, sensitive to the musicality of simple language." But the critic's voice is subordinate to the tale-teller's, as the marvellous stories and plays are recapitulated in a tone of delight and wonder. Two impressions emerge: the extent to which Chekhov's brilliant literary activity was mingled, in his forty-four busy years, with medical practice, good works, family concerns, and impulsive travel; and the poignant paradox that as his health got worse his art got even better, producing "The Bishop," "In the Ravine," "The Lady with a Dog," "The Darling," *Three Sisters,* and *The Cherry Orchard* in his last five, Yalta-bound years. The acceptingness at the heart of his humanity and his limpid realism seemed to widen as his body wasted: he let himself fall in love with Olga Knipper and, a few weeks from his death, talked of joining an expedition to the Arctic! *A Spirit Set Free* is this invigorating study's subtitle; Chekhov's declared "holy of holies" was "love and absolute freedom—freedom from force and falsehood."

Lost Among the Romantics

MARY SHELLEY, by Muriel Spark. 248 pp. Dutton, 1987.

Muriel Spark's first book, published in England in 1951 as *Child of Light: A Reassessment of Mary Shelley,* is now at last, retitled and thoroughly revised, published here. Mary Shelley, not quite seventeen when she eloped with the twenty-one-year-old poet (who had eloped with his first wife, Harriet, when she was sixteen and he three years older), was the daughter of intellectually eminent parents—the political philosopher William Godwin and the pioneer feminist Mary Wollstonecraft—and herself proved to be a considerable author, writing *Frankenstein* before she turned twenty and a good deal of fiction and non-fiction afterward. Her biographer sees her as a fundamentally intellectual, eighteenth-century, "classical" personality in conflict with the Romantic turmoil of teen-age romance, illegitimate children, *ménages à trois*, fantastical idealism, Alps, sailboats, scandal, blackmail, and premature dying. Mrs. Spark picks her way through the tangle of domestic and literary history with her usual unblinking firmness. Part of the book's pleasure lies in its shrewd and sympathetic reëvaluation of a shadowy reputation; another part lies in the sweet sting of such epigrammatic Sparkian judgments as

> Her [Mary's] infatuation, her jealousy, her panic, her remorse, and her childish pleasure at the happy issue of the affair—all might resound the experience of any woman at any time; no social accent of Godwin's, no spiritual effluvium of Shelley's, no choice literary dish, adulterates, as it were, the purity of the situation

and

> *Ladore* (successful in its time) represents . . . an effort to fit the unorthodox facts into an orthodox moral system; and as a creative work it has no health.

A Romp with Job

THE ONLY PROBLEM, by Muriel Spark. 179 pp. Putnam, 1984.

Muriel Spark's writing always gives delight; the sentences march under a harsh sun that bleaches color from them but bestows a peculiar, invigorating, Pascalian clarity. Her new novel, *The Only Problem*, begins:

> He was driving along the road in France from St. Dié to Nancy in the district of Meurthe; it was straight and almost white, through thick woods of fir and birch. He came to the grass track on the right that he was looking for. It wasn't what he had expected. Nothing ever is, he thought.

The thinker is an English clergyman-turned-actor, Edward Jansen; he is going to visit his brother-in-law, Harvey Gotham, a very rich Canadian who has left his elegant wife, Effie, in order to live in a shabby stone cottage in France and compose a monograph upon the Book of Job and the problem of suffering:

> For he could not face that a benevolent Creator, one whose charming and delicious light descended and spread over the world, and being powerful everywhere, could condone the unspeakable sufferings of the world; that God did permit all suffering and was therefore, by logic of his omnipotence, the actual author of it, he was at a loss how to square with the existence of God, given the premise that God is good. "It is the only problem," Harvey had always said. Now, Harvey believed in God, and this was what tormented him. "It's the only problem, in fact, worth discussing."

Mrs. Spark, she has confided to interviewers, composes her novels in small lined notebooks that she orders from Edinburgh, where she was once a schoolgirl. A scholastic mood of nicety and stricture controls her sentences; notice, for instance, in the long sentence above, how the second half manages to parse, "he was at a loss how to square" picking up the earlier "that God did permit." Unlike all but a few modern writers, Mrs. Spark uses the verb "comprise" correctly, as synonymous with "comprehend" rather than, as often supposed, with "constitute"—"Love comprises among other things a desire for the well-being and spiritual freedom of the one who is loved." Sentiments so firmly phrased issue steadily from the mouths of her characters, who yet never sound pedantic—merely concerned with main things, and efficient in expressing this concern. It is Harvey who tells Edward about love: "If there's anything I can't stand it's a love-hate relationship. . . . The element of love in such a relation simply isn't worthy of the name. It boils down to hatred pure and simple in the end. Love comprises . . ." etc. The author herself can put a moral paradox in a nutshell of an image. A flashback recalls the critical moment, a year before the opening events of *The Only Problem*, when Effie offended Harvey by stealing two chocolate bars from a snack-bar on an Italian autostrada:

> Effie said, "Why shouldn't we help ourselves? These multinationals and monopolies are capitalizing on us, and two-thirds of the world is suffering." She tore open the second slab, crammed more chocolate angrily into her mouth, and, with her mouth gluttonously full of stolen chocolate, went on raving about how two-thirds of the world was starving.

The problem, perhaps the only problem, with Mrs. Spark's novel is that her habit of pithiness squeezes all softness of feeling from her story, and leaves us with a skeleton of plot that dances to little but comic effect. Harvey Gotham is meant to be a modern Job, but he doesn't seem to suffer. He has no boils; his wealth never departs; and his feelings toward Effie, though indicated as belatedly fond ("Are you still in love with Effie?" "Yes." "Then you're an unhappy man. Why did you leave her?" "I couldn't stand her sociological clap-trap"), do not affect the rather sulky waiting game he plays. While ensconced in his cottage with his research materials on Job, he is visited by a number of comforters, beginning with Edward Jansen in April, and including by August Edward's estranged wife, Ruth, and an infant, called Clara, whom Effie, while away from Harvey, conceived with a lover named Ernie Howe, "an electronics expert." Ruth persuades Harvey to buy the château on whose property the cottage sits, and by Christmas they are visited there by Nathan Fox, a young, educated, and unemployed man previously attached to the Jansens. As Effie's offstage activities heat up, policemen and a policewoman join the throng, not to mention Harvey's London lawyer and his Auntie Pet, all the way from Canada.

Yet, somehow, nothing builds. For instance, Nathan Fox is carefully described at the outset ("He was a good-looking boy, tall, with an oval face, very smooth and rather silvery-green in color—really olive. . . . He had a mouth like a Michelangelo angel and teeth so good, clear, strong and shapely it seemed to Edward, secretly, that they were the sexiest thing about him"), and one expects he will blossom into one of this author's great leeches, along the lines of Hubert Mallindaine in *The Takeover* and Patrick Seton in *The Bachelors;* but Nathan manifests few machinations and little presence, and quickly becomes, with Effie, an offstage character. Again, Harvey is said to have developed a fondness for the baby Clara, but she is never shown as anything other than a background squalling, a tiny bundle of greed and noise. Most of Mrs. Spark's characters tend to be such bundles, in varying sizes, and perhaps her overriding message is—to quote Harvey—"the futility of friendship in times of trouble." Her comforters do not comfort, her lovers do not love. And her actors, though she suggests that much of life is "putting on an act," do not, in this book, often act. A number of characters are intently described only to drop utterly from sight: "a lean-faced man with a dark skin gone to muddy grey, bright small eyes and fine features" in "a black suit, shiny with wear; a very white shirt open at the neck; brown, very pointed shoes" is studied by Harvey in a police station, but "Who he was, where he came from and why, Harvey was never to know." On the other hand, many pages are consumed by stark and repetitive police grilling. So gappy a narrative fabric allows Mrs. Spark's supernatural to peek through; a reality so diminished

proves the existence of a great Diminisher. Modern Catholic novelists—
Graham Greene, Flannery O'Connor, Evelyn Waugh, François Mauriac—commonly present human interplay as unrewarding: as arid,
desultory, futile, and frequently farcical. One answer to "the only problem" which lurks unstated in Mrs. Spark's novel of ideas is that we human
reeds are such flimsy, dirty bits of straw we deserve all the suffering
we get.

Another answer is offered by Harvey, when he asks himself, "Is it only
by recognizing how flat would be the world without the sufferings of
others that we know how desperately becalmed our own lives would be
without suffering? Do I suffer on Effie's account? Yes, and perhaps I can
live by that experience. We all need something to suffer about." This
insight comes late in the novel, and presumably represents an advance
over his earlier proposal that "the only logical answer to the problem of
suffering is that the individual soul has made a pact with God before he
is born, that he will suffer during his lifetime. We are born forgetful of
this pact, of course; but we have made it. Sufferers would, in this hypothesis, be pre-conscious volunteers." Harvey jeers at the solution to the
problem apparently advanced by the Book of Job: "God as a character
comes out badly, very badly. Thunder and bluster and I'm Me, who are
you? Putting on an act." Harvey ignores what seems to me God's crucial
challenge, presented in verse 40:8: "wilt thou condemn me, that thou
mayest be righteous?" That is, God, the creator of Leviathan and Behe-
moth, Who laid the foundations of the earth and each day shows the dawn
its place, will not accept moral subordination to Man; He declines to take
instruction from His creature and to be graded by him (A+ for sunsets
and flowers, C— for insects and deserts, F for plagues and earthquakes).
Expressed non-theologically: existence, including our own, is a mystery,
and a critical attitude toward it is not fruitful. The immense notion of
Atonement, foreshadowed in Isaiah and enacted in the New Testament,
whereby the Creator involves Himself in suffering, does not intrude upon
the speculations in *The Only Problem*, nor does the possibility that an
afterlife rights all earthly imbalances. The world, for Mrs. Spark as for the
whirlwind God of Job, is somewhat bigger than hypothetical balances of
justice. Harvey and Ruth have this exchange:

> "A matter of justice. A balancing of accounts." This was how Ruth put
> it to Harvey. "I'm passionate about justice," she said.
> "People who want justice," Harvey said, "generally want so little when
> it comes to the actuality. There is more to be had from the world than a
> balancing of accounts."

And Effie is specifically linked—by way of a painting by Georges de La Tour, *Job visité par sa femme,* which Harvey studies in the museum at Épinal—to Job's wife; Effie strikingly resembles de La Tour's representation of the Biblical woman, who advised her husband, "Curse God, and die."* Social protest, whose extreme form is terrorism, is equated thus with cursing God. The opposite, the holier alternative, is acceptance, even when affluence—the curious state of being rich, more central to Mrs. Spark's later novels than the state of grace—is what must be accepted. Harvey might be speaking of himself when he says of Job, "His tragedy was that of the happy ending."

A good and profound novel lies scattered among the inklings of *The Only Problem,* but the author seems distracted and abrupt and to be gazing, often, at other problems. Her first novel, *The Comforters,* alluded to Job in its title and was about distraction and the need to write. The heroine heard a typewriter clacking in her head; so does this novel's closest approach to a heroine, Ruth. "Ruth's mother was a free-lance typist and always had some work in hand. . . . Ruth used to go to sleep on a summer night hearing the tap-tapping of the typewriter below, and wake to the almost identical sound of the woodpecker in the tree outside her window. Ruth supposed this was Effie's experience too, but when she reminded her sister of it many years later Effie couldn't recall any sound effects." Such differences in hearing make the difference between a terrorist and an artist. Mrs. Spark's last novel, *Loitering with Intent,* focused on the heroine's literary vocation; the religious issue of vocation underlies much of her fiction, more so than the problems of suffering and belief. Suffering and belief are settled matters; vocation requires an active search. Ruth seduces Harvey into buying the château because a woodpecker outside a bedroom window reminds her of a typewriter. To its happy sound she wakes every morning. We are never out of touch, in a Spark novel, with the happiness of creation; the sudden willful largesse of image and epigram, the cunning tautness of suspense, the beautifully firm modulations from passage to passage, the blunt yet dignified dialogues all remind us of the author, the superintending intelligent mind. Though her characters are often odious, and given so parsimonious a portion of sympathy as to barely exist, the web they are caught in is invariably tense and alive.

---

*What she actually says in Hebrew, I have learned from Frank Kermode's sermon "The Uses of Error," is "Bless God and die." Kermode explains, "But it has long been understood that 'bless' is a euphemism. It would have been improper for the author or a scribe to write the words 'curse God', and so here, as in the first chapter of the book, the difficulty is avoided by using the exactly opposite word, 'bless'." However, St. Jerome, who should have known better, in *The Vulgate* translated the command as "*benedic Deo*." You figure it out.

Spark but No Spark

A FAR CRY FROM KENSINGTON, by Muriel Spark. 189 pp. Houghton Mifflin, 1988.

In her eighteenth chiselled and quizzical novel, Mrs. Spark returns to that drab, homey, and somewhat spooky postwar London that figured in such early tales as *The Comforters, The Bachelors, Memento Mori,* and *The Girls of Slender Means,* and that she nostalgically revisited in her recent *Loitering with Intent.* The nostalgia, however, seems less warm this time, and the spookiness perhaps a bit threadbare. Her narrator, Nancy (a.k.a. Agnes) Hawkins—desultorily involved in publishing, on the verge of conversion to Roman Catholicism, and given to an aphoristic certainty of pronouncement—is a heroine from the Sparkian mold, but the eccentric and weakly creative spirits among whom she so decisively moves seem perfunctorily limned. Her lover, William, is a brilliant young medical student raised in such dire poverty that he never learned any nursery rhymes, and her enemy, Hector Bartlett, a grubby literary operator whom she scornfully dismisses as a *"pisseur de copie."* One thing leads to another with the usual snap and aplomb, and Mrs. Spark's prose is as always intensely composed, but it all seems a bit cut and dried. Mrs. Hawkins complacently states, "It is enough for me to discriminate mentally and leave the rest to God"; one wishes that Mrs. Spark, as a novelist, might leave a little less to God and be a bit more indiscriminate in what she chooses to animate. However, she remains *sui generis,* with an aloof, factual rigor that anticipates the Last Judgment.

Bad Neighbors

THE HANDYMAN, by Penelope Mortimer. 199 pp. St. Martin's Press, 1985.

NOTHING HAPPENS IN CARMINCROSS, by Benedict Kiely. 279 pp. Godine, 1985.

Penelope Mortimer's new novel is, to make no bones about it, a superb book—fierce in its disillusion, poetic and carefree in its language, comic and horrifying and deeply familiar all at once. Concerning three years of widowhood as experienced by sixtyish, conventional Phyllis Muspratt, who must cope with two grown children, two grandchildren, an oddly bouncy handyman, and a handful of churlish neighbors in the sinister village of Cryck, the novel shows the deft social weave at which English fiction excels, but presents its events with a terse fury the opposite of sociable complacence. An undercurrent of desperation presses against every harsh, droll detail. Phyllis's husband dies in the first paragraph with a stunning lack of fuss: "Gerald Muspratt gave no indication of what he was about to do. He walked over to the french windows in the dining room to inspect the weather and, without even turning round, died." Saki or Evelyn Waugh might have begun with such icy inconsequence; but neither could have so impressionistically given us, a few sentences on, the churn of a distraught woman:

> At first she trembled with shock, all of a dither; swivelled on her haunches, not knowing which way to turn, panting little gasps which sounded like oh dear, oh dear God, oh; her hands fluttered, patting, pulling at his hairy tweed jacket then flying away as though stung. She saw the table from an unknown angle, the packet of Bran Flakes blocking the ceiling, the heavy arches of the toast-rack tarnished on the inside, the shadow beneath the rim of the plate over which the dead man's marmalade oozed. What to do?

At this height of distress and dishevelment, the cleaning lady arrives, and impartially tidies up. "Mrs. Rodburn took over. By lunchtime Gerald had been removed, the table cleared, the breakfast things washed up and put away." Life goes on, in an atmosphere of harrowing triviality.

The light-handed speed and offhand knowingness of the prose could have been achieved only by a highly skilled writer impatient with mere skill. From such exquisite, charmingly placed phrases as "swivelled on her haunches" and "flying away as though stung," the prose can descend into the telegraphic, as when Phyllis's daughter encounters marital trouble:

> The impossible had happened. Sophia and Bron had talked about his affair. About all his affairs. She had left him. Walked out on Selina and Jasper. That was it. That was the end.

These fragmentary and breathless sentences tell us all we need to know, and the grim comedy of Sophia's violent reaction (she runs to her mother, who unbeknownst to her has plenty of her own troubles) lies in the prodigious importance this standard, casebook event has for her, to whom it appears unique. Sobbing into paper towels, she spills to her distracted mother all day long the young wife's classic litany of wrongs:

> Bron had been having these affairs, these things, for some time. Well, Sophia didn't blame him. It wasn't that. She knew she wasn't, well, perhaps she

wasn't much fun in bed but she was so worried all the time, it was all right
for men but of course she wouldn't take the pill—you didn't go out of your
way to get cancer, did you?—and she hated the idea of having some foreign
body inside her, she meant the coil of course, and she was terrified of getting
pregnant again, terrified. . . . No, what she couldn't stand, what really upset
her, wasn't the actual *sex*, it was—well, she didn't know how to explain it—it
was the *nice time* he had with these women, it was the fact that he talked
to them and went to discos with them and took them to the movies, and they
had no children to worry about, they could go out any time they liked, they
could spend hours over their hair and their—well, it was all that. It was so
bitterly unfair. . . . Well, she had put up with it so long as it didn't *interfere*.
She had settled for it. That was the way things had to be, she had told herself,
and so long as he kept quiet about it she could manage. But he had actually
expected her to *discuss* the situation, as though it were, as though it were
something *else* he expected her to deal with.

The reader's laughter at this long winding plaint isn't altogether heartless;
it is congratulatory, honoring the author for the prototypical perfection
of the imagined discourse, and the *virtuosa* deftness with which the requisite notes are played. Mrs. Mortimer's ear is as keen as her eye; again and
again the distances behind ordinary banal exchanges open up, and all our
troubles are put in the withering perspective of human repetitiveness—of
authentic sorrow seen as chronic cliché: "Isabel [Broune] watched her
mother approach with a familiar sense of doom. When she finally arrived
after this arduous journey up the path, she would certainly inflict some
punishment. 'How did you sleep?' she might ask, inferring that it was
Isabel's duty to sleep soundly; 'Have you had breakfast?', implying that
if she hadn't, she was deliberately starving herself to annoy; worst of all
would be 'How do you feel?', a question so unanswerable that to ask it
was a deliberate gibe."

Rebecca Broune, an antisocial, burnt-out writer, is the only even
remotely companionable neighbor for the widow Muspratt in her lonely
Cryck cottage. Rebecca is lovingly described, in sentences of breezy compression and verve. "Her three marriages and countless love affairs had all
ended in disaster; so, on numerous occasions, had she herself, or very
nearly, snatched back by stomach-pumps, blood transfusions, electric current, medications of the most dubious kind and enough psychiatrists to set
up a small symposium. All this had not made her the happiest of women,
but had given her insight of a kind." The kind of insight, we may infer,
that enables Mrs. Mortimer to cover so much psychological terrain with
such rasping authority, from the menace grandchildren hold for a grandmother ("their merciless eyes, which weren't turned inwards, like

Sophia's, their greed, their ruthless clamping on to her old love") to the bachelor blankness of a son who has loved his father too well, and from the jaunty effrontery of a country con-man and pervert to the style in which a prospering Jewish banker husband shines in the eyes of his for-mer, and now sadly deteriorated, wife:

> Ralph had always been a handsome man, but uxoriousness had perfected him. As he came out from behind his desk and glided rather than walked across the enormous drawing room of his private office toward her, Rebecca felt a spasm of admiration and regret, cruel as a wet winter. . . . He was tall, and had never been slim; she knew that a considerable belly must be con-tained somewhere between the massive chest and spare hips, but there was little sign of it—his dark suit gave him the line and grace of an old race-horse, lovingly groomed. . . . They were not just an old divorced couple. He had moved back to his Hebrew origins, entrenched himself in law and legend; from this inviolable position he saw her, she felt, at a great distance, a trivial, despicable creature, physically repulsive and morally unsound.

Rebecca's physical ugliness is rather doted upon: "Her ugliness gave her a curious satisfaction. It protected her against upstarts and repelled nui-sances. In case anyone should see through it she reinforced it with wild, greying hair, baggy denim, shapeless clod-hopping shoes; what remained of her fingernails were ridged with earth; through constantly holding a cigarette in the corner of her mouth, one eye had become smaller and redder than the other." Her daughter, timid, suicidal Isabel, has an even more fearful view: "Isabel, thinking herself camouflaged in the shade of the plum tree, imagined her mother as an old dog, scarred and moth-eaten, its yellow teeth still able to tear flesh, its hydrophobic little eyes like red-hot cinders in dark places." Rebecca has ceased to write, is rude to everyone, and gives all her love and energy to her roses. In the end, she returns to the typewriter, to tell the story of Phyllis Mustrapp, as if to atone for having been an indifferent neighbor; Rebecca's revival as a writer turns out to be the hidden thread of this many-sided, relentless chronicle of the way in which parents and children, husbands and wives fail, frustrate, and fascinate one another. We are all indifferent neighbors. I don't know when I have last read fiction that gave me such an exhilarat-ing sensation of being scoured by the brisk, bleak truth of our human condition and human interrelations. The long-silent Penelope Mortimer (whose last novel, the equally remarkable but quite different *Long Dis-tance,* appeared in 1974) has made a brilliant return to print.

The Irishman Benedict Kiely, a year younger than Mrs. Mortimer, has also produced a novel tinged by the bitter wisdom of late middle age and raked by sore disenchantment; but his book, *Nothing Happens in Carmincross,* is lamentably diffuse, as muddied and meandering in its execution as the Englishwoman's is crisp and direct. Mr. Kiely has always been a garrulous writer, most winningly so in such lilting short stories as "A Journey to the Seven Streams," where the easy, talking prose tumbles along as brightly as a mountain brook. He has, Thomas Flanagan informed us in his introduction to Kiely's collection of stories *The State of Ireland* (1980), a mind spectacularly stocked with quotations and songs; echoes drawn from this mental treasure have often deepened the run of his heroes' meditations and enriched our awareness of Ireland's complicated, incessantly verbalized history. But through his present hero, the historian and college teacher Mervyn Kavanagh, Mr. Kiely has provided himself with too smooth a conduit to his own erudition and has drowned his tale in recollected words.

The tale is a slight one: in the summer of 1973, Professor Kavanagh, who has been teaching at a girls' college in Virginia, returns to Ireland to attend his favorite niece's wedding; accompanied by an overweight and complaisant barmaid named Deborah, and pursued by phone calls from his estranged wife in New York City, he drives north from the vicinity of Shannon Airport to his home village of Carmincross, in Northern Ireland, where terrorist mischief mars the wedding. On this journey I clocked the literary allusions at two and a half per page, and braced myself every time the dialogue veered into the thudding rhymes of Celtic balladry:

—Up from the south, Deborah, at break of day bringing to Winchester fresh dismay. The affrighted air . . . what's after that?
—You're asking the right woman.
—Was it with a shudder or like a shudder bore, like a herald in haste to the chieftain's door, the terrible grumble and rumble and roar. . . .
—Rhymes with whore.
—. . . telling the battle was on once more and Sheridan so many miles away. Deborah, how many miles away was Sheridan?
—Don't know, Merlin. Don't care, Merlin.

She calls him Merlin and her pursuing husband Mandrake, and Mervyn repeatedly indulges the fancy that the three of them parallel the legendary triangle of King Fionn, Queen Gráinne, and her lover, Diarmuid. Another character, helpfully called Jeremiah, wields Biblical verses with a vengeance. "Quotations. Quotations," Mervyn's wife complains to him over the phone, and he himself reflects that "the mind of a reading man cursed with a plastic memory, who also goes to the movies, and watches television, is a jumble sale, a lumber-room." Irish history is discussed by the board foot, and a whole scrapbook of terrorist atrocities, Irish and other, is presented by way of conversation, rumination, and daily newspaper reading. Several long letters to the absent Mrs. Kavanagh are indited in a style quite as leisurely and farraginous as the narrative method itself. Italics are never used to distinguish levels of reality; third person and first swing back and forth from sentence to sentence in Mervyn's stream of consciousness; and Mr. Kiely's Joycean loyalty to the dash as the means of signifying speech (a typographical preference whose only conceivable utility is to brand the work at a glance as stubbornly, honorably avant-garde) further clouds the raddled flow. When the author does have an immediate, potentially affecting event to relate—and he has several, toward the end—he tends, Faulknerishly, to skim right past it and then reel it in by flashback. Though not quite incoherent, the novel appears to place coherence low on the list of aesthetic virtues. References to the Falklands War, Karmal's Afghanistan, and the Ayatollah's Iran dot the 1973 scene, and an afterword blithely acknowledges such anachronisms with the question "Does it matter?"

Not that Mr. Kiely's fine native style is altogether suppressed. Individual sentences flash out smartly:

> The plane shudders, shakes him out of the brandy torpor, and Ireland is there below him, flat and marked in fields, green and brown, bog and marsh by the silver estuary. One small cloud, cast out of the herd, limps and melts away toward the northeast.

> He is blocky in build and low to the ground: with a tonsure of hair of no particular color, a ruddy, pear-shaped face with the plump end of the pear to the top, billiard-ball eyes, and a slow sinister smile.

> The sun is shining. The river now and again spits silver into the air.

But the narrator's eye rather rarely focuses on external appearances. An extended wayward process of self-recrimination and consolation takes that eye inward and backward. The private aspect of Mervyn's journey, his sexual fling with Deborah, feels wishful and recalls Colonel Cantwell's amour with the Contessa in Hemingway's *Across the River and into the Trees* even in its cadences: "She stands close beside him, breathing like a young girl. It is a lovely morning over the glen. She is with a man she likes to love with." "Tell me about Ninon who made love until she was ninety," Deborah begs, in much the same tone in which the Contessa requested, "Kiss me once again and make the buttons of your uniform hurt me but not too much." The barmaid assures her erudite lover, "I like how you look. Old and fat and bald and all . . . Your fabulous face. It's like a sunset seen from the clifftops." The lady, indeed, is so purely the servant of Mervyn's desires and echo of his thoughts that when, late in their travels, she develops an individual decisiveness and a misfortune of her own the author and the hero both hurry, unchivalrously, to drop her.

The public aspect of *Nothing Happens in Carmincross* is of course the Ulster wars, the vicious pollution that Northern Ireland's competing terrorist factions have worked upon the beautiful land where Mervyn was reared, as a Catholic with Protestant neighbors. Carmincross is another version of Mr. Kiely's native town of Omagh, in County Tyrone. The bucolic scenes of his early fiction, to which war and violence travelled only as rumor and as legends spun by Ireland's adventuring sons, now are given over to the "Bombomb Yahoos" of both religious persuasions, whose explosives, home-made (a new cottage industry) of gelignite, fuel oil, and ammonium nitrate, are thrown into pub doors, dropped into letter boxes, delivered by teen-age girls pushing baby prams. The gangs, whether IRA (Irish Republican Army) or UDF (Ulster Defence Force), extract "black rent"—protection money—from shops and businesses, pour appropriately colored paint (orange or green) over the shaved heads of girls suspected of collaboration with the opposite side, and murder farmers in their fields and children in their beds. The centuries of Irish struggle against British rule have come, in Mervyn's view, to the triumph of "thuggery and blaggery" and the destruction of mutual trust and of every decent institution from the neighborhood pub to the public schools.

This is a somber and mighty theme. And no living writer is better equipped than Benedict Kiely, out of the depth of his feeling and knowledge, to dramatize it. But Mervyn Kavanagh offers a poor handle on the situation. He has always been, he tells us, an odd man out among his own fellow Irishmen: "Coming home to his own people he realises with a more painful intensity what he is always conscious of: his oddity, the *éan corr*, the one bird that slipped out of the nest." Our empathy with Mervyn feels obstructed; we want to like him better than he likes himself. Even as he visits the old sites and drives along the old ways his heart hangs back in America, with his unhappy, tenacious wife and "dogwood visions of slim girls like white fish in a blue pool." "They're a happy people," he says, of Americans. To the unhappiness of his own people he has returned as a tourist. Grieve though he does, Mervyn is merely visiting the distressed areas of Ireland; he does not have to live there, and the end of the novel sees him safely tucked back into the anesthesia of the New World. Having drunk thirteen brandy alexanders before boarding the plane to Ireland, he rejoins New York by having several more.

One would feel more diffident in expressing reservations about this novel's treatment of a topic so momentous and heartfelt had not Mr. Kiely, in the short story "Proxopera" (1979), already handled it consummately. In that fifty-page story, which concludes *The State of Ireland* and is dedicated "In Memory of the Innocent Dead," the hero, Granda Binchey, like Mervyn a teacher with a mind full of quotations, is, unlike him, a lifelong resident of his tormented village and has achieved all his ambitions there. Also unlike him, he is the protagonist of a dramatic action: with his son, daughter-in-law, and two grandchildren held hostage, the elder Binchey is forced to drive a car laden with a time bomb into the heart of town. This action, shown entirely through the old man's fluctuating observations and resolves, better conveys the agony of Northern Ireland than all the news items, horrific and deplorable though they are, that are strung on the crooked line of Mervyn's boozy peregrinations. At its most effective, *Nothing Happens in Carmincross* shocks us as a newspaper does: this happens out there. In "Proxopera," it happens within us, as fiction makes things happen. Compared with the circumstantial, suspenseful flight of the shorter work, the novel rushes ponderously about, feathered in quotations and wildly glowing, like an angel beating its wings but not quite getting off the ground. In this failure to rise we feel the heaviness of its theme.

The Jones Boys

ON THE BLACK HILL, by Bruce Chatwin. 249 pp. Viking, 1983.

Bruce Chatwin, an Englishman who worked some years for Sotheby & Company, as auctioneer and director of the Impressionist department, and who then became a traveller into such outré lands as Patagonia, writes a clipped, lapidary prose that compresses worlds into pages. *In Patagonia*, an account of his wanderings in southern Argentina, won high praise five years ago for its witty obliquity, suavely economical descriptions, wealth of curious historical and paleontological data, and perky word portraits of the drunken gauchos and homesick Scotsmen he encountered in this vast, raw region. The one virtue *In Patagonia* did not conspicuously possess was momentum; the traveller so deliberately minimized his personality and obscured his motives that the prose seemed to move on ghostly legs of its own, snacking on scenery and bits of dialogue where it pleased, and hopping about so airily between past and present, between experienced incident and researched document, that the exotic reality was half eclipsed by the willful manners of the invisible guide. Mr. Chatwin writes in such short paragraphs that he seems to be constantly interrupting himself. His narratives must be savored in short takes, like collections of short stories. His third book and second novel, *On the Black Hill,* also skips, scintillatingly, across a vast terrain—a stretch of time: the eighty years that the Jones twins, Lewis and Benjamin, have lived in Radnorshire, a rural county of Wales bordering that of Hereford, in England.

Amos Jones, the twins' father, is a red-haired Welshman, the son of a "garrulous old cider-drinker, known round the pubs of Radnorshire as Sam the Waggon." Their mother, Amos's second wife, was Mary Latimer, the only child of "the Reverend Latimer, an Old Testament scholar, who had retired from mission work in India and settled in this remote hill parish to be alone with his daughter and his books." This clergyman drowns one day in a peat bog (the first of many violent deaths that stud Mr. Chatwin's bucolic chronicle), and, Amos having been smitten by the sight of Mary in church, a courtship ensues which overcomes their awkward differences of education, class, and race—for she is English, or as they say in Wales "Saxon." They marry in the year 1899 and lease, with money realized from the sale of some of her father's books, a farm named The Vision, where "in 1737 an ailing girl called Alice Morgan saw the Virgin hovering over a patch of rhubarb, and ran back to the kitchen, cured." Mary Jones is pregnant "by the time of the first frosts," and twin boys are born in August of the new century. The boys never leave, for long, The Vision. Two global wars rumble by at a distance, and new machinery enters the world, from airplanes and automobiles to video games, but the important events of the twins' lives are strictly local, if not familial—the deaths of their grandparents, the birth and eventual flight of their sister Rebecca, the feud with their neighbors the Watkinses, the financial flurry when the Joneses must buy their farm from their aristocratic landlords. Benjamin is carted off to Hereford Detention Barracks for refusing to fight in World War I, and is cruelly treated there, and Lewis makes several attempts to find a woman for himself; yet both return always to the same house, the same chores, the same land. Weather, labor, loyalty, and other people's scandals make up the fabric of these two lives so intertwined as to be one life. They both live to be eighty, and Benjamin is last seen staring at his own reflection in his brother's shiny black tombstone.

The author lays out this tale of country narrowness in a mosaic of sharp and knowing small scenes. Though Mr. Chatwin was born in 1940, the details of daily life early in the century seem an open book to him. Here is how a sleeping farmer looks to his young wife in 1900:

Amos was asleep in his calico nightshirt. The buttons had come undone, and his chest was bare. Squinting sideways, she glanced at the heaving ribcage, the red hairs round his nipples, the pink dimple left by his shirtstud, and the line where the sunburned neck met the milky thorax.

It is "the pink dimple left by his shirtstud" that seems miraculously recovered. Here is how a recruitment speech sounded in 1914. Colonel Bickerton, the local squire, eases himself to his feet after a patriotic slide show climaxed by "an absurd goggle-eyed visage with crows' wings on its upper lip and a whole golden eagle on its helmet"—the Kaiser—and orates:

> "When this war is over, there will be two classes of persons in this country. There will be those who were qualified to join the Armed Forces and refrained from doing so, and there will be those who were so qualified and came forward to do their duty to their King, their country . . . and their womenfolk. The last-mentioned class, I need not add, will be the aristocracy of this country—indeed, the only true aristocracy of this country—who, in the evening of their days, will have the consolation of knowing that they have done what England expects of every man: namely, to do his duty."

We learn that the hall—the Congregation Hall of the Rhulen Chapel—is heated by a coke stove, that the squire's daughter wears a hat bearing a "grey-pink glycerined ostrich plume," and that there is considerable resistance on the part of the Welsh to fighting in behalf of the English, whom they still see, after centuries, as enemies and occupiers. Mr. Chatwin tells us what this bygone world is made of: the oilcloth hoods of the horse cabs, the reek of Jeyes Fluid in the Town Hall committee room, the sable coat Queen Mary wears onto the balcony of Buckingham Palace on the "drizzly November morning" of Armistice Day. So, too, persuasively and solidly enough, are rendered the accents, the sermons, the festivities, the gossip, the types of conflict and satisfaction in a Radnorshire whose "leafy lanes [were] unchanged since the time of Queen Elizabeth." To be sure, one is reminded of Hardy. As if to placate the spectre of his mighty predecessor, Mr. Chatwin has Mary Jones read Hardy: "How well she knew the life he described—the smell of Tess's milking-parlour; Tess's torments, in bed and in the beetfield. She, too, could whittle hurdles, plant pine saplings or thatch a hayrick—and if the old unmechanized ways were gone from Wessex, time had stood still, here, on the Radnor Hills." And if Radnorshire out-Hardys Wessex, a long scene of the Rhulen peace celebrations seems self-consciously to out-Flaubert, for satire and counterpoint, the agricultural fair in *Madame Bovary*. Yet by and large Mr.

Chatwin re-creates the past out of what seem not paper souvenirs but living memories, with an understated mastery of period detail and a loving empathy into the inner lives such detail adorned.

To what purpose? Why undergo what Henry James, in a letter to Sarah Orne Jewett in 1901, referred to as the "inordinate" difficulty, the "humbug" of the " 'historic' novel"? Mr. Chatwin might answer, "In order to display at full length the lives of my heroes, my magical twins." The Jones twins are his centerpiece, and the mysterious, infrangible connection between them somehow his moral. From toddlerhood on, they share the same sensations, and Lewis, the older and stronger, feels the pain that mishaps inflict upon Benjamin. Their earliest memories are identical, and even in old age they can dream the same dream. When Benjamin is at Hereford Detention Barracks and Lewis is still at The Vision, "from the ache in his coccyx, Lewis knew when the N.C.O.s were frog-marching Benjamin round the parade-ground. . . . One morning, Lewis's nose began to bleed and went on bleeding till sundown: that was the day when they stood Benjamin in a boxing ring and slammed straight-lefts into his face." Whenever Lewis, who likes girls, ventures into sexual experience, Benjamin telepathically feels it, and hates it, and does what he can to discourage the attachment. He succeeds; Lewis remains single, and after their mother's death the two sleep together in their parents' bed as they had slept together when children.

Now, Mr. Chatwin, a demon researcher, must have a basis for these supernatural connections that the twins enjoy and suffer; but this tale of what Michel Tournier has called "the super-flesh of twins" feels allegorical, and strains belief. Their twinship is in fact a homosexual marriage, with Benjamin the feminine partner and Lewis the masculine. Benjamin's love is painted plain: "On days when he was too sick for school he would lie on Lewis's half of the mattress, laying his head on the imprint left by Lewis on the pillow." "Benjamin loved his mother and his brother, and he did not like girls. Whenever Lewis left the room, his eyes would linger in the doorway, and his irises cloud to a denser shade of grey: when Lewis came back, his pupils glistened." "At nights, he would reach out to touch his brother, but his hand came to rest on a cold unrumpled pillow. He gave up washing for fear of reminding himself that—at that same moment— Lewis might be sharing someone else's towel." Lewis's feelings about towel sharing are less clear, and Mr. Chatwin's ingenuity at posing obstacles and long blank intervals is fully needed to suppress our wonder that a robust and prosperous male goes eighty years with no more than a few scratchy and aborted romances. Stranger still is the mother's role in this celibacy:

As Amos's widow, Mary wanted at least one daughter-in-law and a brood of grandchildren. . . . There were times when she chided Benjamin. "What is all this nonsense about not going out? Why can't you find a nice young lady?" But Benjamin's mouth would tighten, his lower lids quiver, and she knew he would never get married. At other times, wilfully displaying the perverse side of her character, she took Lewis by the elbow and made him promise never, never to marry unless Benjamin married too.

"I promise," he said, slumping his head like a man receiving a prison sentence; for he wanted a woman badly.

Since Mary has been portrayed as as happily heterosexual as one could be with a sometimes brutal husband, and her character in no way perverse but instead kind, lively, patient, and perfect, the devil that possesses her in regard to Lewis's mating may be an imp called in to enforce a fundamentally implausible conceit.

Nevertheless, the apparition of the linked twins chimes with much else that is slightly fabulous in their Welsh surround; we seem to see through them into a hilly, antique landscape drenched in flowers—dozens and dozens of botanical allusions are woven into the text—and overshadowed by dramatic clouds. There are many paragraphs as vividly atmospheric as this, at the moment when the twins' birth begins:

On the 8th of August the weather broke. Stacks of smoky, silver-lidded clouds piled up behind the hill. At six in the evening, Amos and Dai Morgan were scything the last of the oats. All the birds were silent in the stillness that precedes a storm. Thistledown floated upwards, and a shriek tore out across the valley.

Though weather and growth pursue timeless cycles, culture and history irrevocably unroll, and this novel begins in the era of the horse and ends with the "electronic warbling" of a computer game in a pub and the sight of men hang-gliding from a Welsh precipice: "A stream of tiny pin-men, airborne on coloured wings, swooping, soaring in the upthrust, and then spiralling like ash-keys to the ground." A sense has been conveyed—and this only a novel to some degree "historic" can do—of the immensity of time a human life spans, a span itself dwarfed by the perspectives of history. Proust piled up his volumes toward this abysmal sensation, this visceral realization of the abstractly known, and Lampedusa achieved it in *The Leopard,* and Anne Tyler last year in *Dinner at the Homesick Restaurant.* It is a measure of Mr. Chatwin's compression that *On the Black Hill* achieves it in less than two hundred and fifty pages. His studied style—with something in it of Hemingway's determined simplicity, and something of Lawrence's inspired swiftness—encompasses worlds.

Seeking Connections in an Insecure Country

THE RADIANT WAY, by Margaret Drabble. 406 pp. Knopf, 1987.

This novel forms a panorama, in its glancing way, of life in England from 1980 to 1985. Beneath its many personal incidents we feel not so much the triumph of Thatcherism as that dubious triumph's underside, the decline of the Labour Party—the ebb and fall of an idealistic socialism that for generations of British intellectuals and workers served as a quasi-religious faith. *The Radiant Way* titles not only the novel but a television series produced by one of its characters, Charles Headleand, way back in 1965—a "series on education . . . that demonstrated, eloquently, movingly, the evils that flow from a divisive class system, from early selection, from Britain's unfortunate heritage of public schools and philistinism. *The Radiant Way* was its ironic title, taken from the primer from which Charles had learned at the age of four to read at his mother's knee." At the novel's revelatory climax, there materializes an actual copy of the primer called *The Radiant Way,* discovered by Charles's ex-wife, Liz, on her mother's shelves—"She had no recollection of it, at first sight. She gazed intently at its jacket: two children, a boy and a girl, running gaily down (not up) a hill, against a background of radiant thirties sunburst." The children running down the hill, while "behind them burned forever that great dark dull sun," symbolize not only the mortality of each individual life but some innocent educational hope left behind by the nation. Education, both the enforcer and surmounter of the English class system, lies at the novel's heart: the novel's three heroines—Liz Headleand, Alix Bowen, Esther Breuer—all met at Cambridge, as bright scholarship girls, and in adult life Alix teaches English to young women in prison, Esther lectures on Italian art, and Liz is a psychiatrist, dispensing self-knowledge.

Though Liz, of the three, bulks largest in her complicated vitality, and in the closeness with which the author renders her thoughts and tears and panic and lust, Alix most plainly bears the novel's political burden, moving from an undoubting Socialist activism to a political despair that finds comfort in sifting through the papers of an old avant-garde poet, a friend of Joyce and Pound, Duchamp and Man Ray. "It is, like all her jobs, a dead-end job, but at least it is not socially useful; in that, at least, it is a new departure, and she takes some pleasure in this. She has had enough, for the time being, of trying to serve the community. . . . There is no hope, in the present social system, of putting anything right." She is the child of old-fashioned Socialists—"not left-wing political extremists, not loony vegetarians (though they were vegetarians), but harmless, mild, Labour-voting, CND-supporting, Fabian-pamphlet-reading intellectuals." Her father, called Dotty Doddridge, taught French at a Yorkshire boarding school whose history traces a revolution in reverse:

> It had offered a liberal, secularized, healthy coeducation, and had on its foundation in the 1860s set out to attract the children of vegetarians, Quakers, free-thinkers, pacifists, Unitarians, reformers. Its academic success had been such that it had become progressively less progressive, its original zeal swamped by the fee-paying prosperous solid northern conservatism of parents and offspring: it had become a bastion of respectability, its one-time principles upheld by stray survivors like Doddridge, who appeared blithely not to notice that at election time the entire school, with one or two flamboyant exceptions, howled its enthusiasm for the Tory party.

Alix's first husband died young, and in her widowhood, in Islington, she got to know the London poor: "She discovered the art of sinking. She sank. Not very deep, but she sank." She began to teach, moving from private tutorials to courses at a College for Further Education and a prison called Garfield Centre. Her second husband, Brian, is from the industrial city of Northam, "that figurative northern city," where his father worked as a circular-saw polisher and his grandfather as a furnaceman in the mills. Brian once apprenticed at the plant and would have followed his father into saw polishing but for the Army, which discovered his intellectual aptitude and sponsored his education; now he teaches English literature at an Adult Education College in London. "Alix Bowen is a sentimentalist about class, it has been alleged. . . . Lying in your arms, Alix said once, not very seriously, to Brian, I am in the process of healing the wounds in my own body and in the body politic." His working-class solidity and "firm grasp of the material world" warm her body; she thinks she is happy. But as the union strikes of the early Eighties grow more savage and desperate, Brian's hard Labour line and emotional attachment to the bygone machine age begin to alienate Alix; a friend, the émigré Otto Werner, becomes a founding member of the new, middle-of-the-road political party, the Social Democrats, and Alix finds herself drawn to Otto's thinking, and to Otto as a man. Coming back on the bus from a romantic lunch with Otto, she sees her husband on a corner of Oxford and Bond Streets soliciting money, holding a yellow plastic bucket and a handwritten sign reading "HELP THE WIVES AND FAMILIES OF THE MINERS":

> He stood stolidly, cheerfully, smiling when anyone threw in a coin. The brotherhood of man. Most people smiled at Brian, even the hardbitten shop-

pers of Bond Street and Oxford Street smiled. But Alix did not smile. Brian and his bucket were more than she could bear. She bowed her head and took out her handkerchief, and all the way to Wandsworth Bridge she wept.

But England—the boy and girl running downhill, the reduction of Fabian visions to a yellow begging bucket on a hardbitten shopping street—is the site and background of *The Radiant Way* and not its essential theme. Miss Drabble is ever less a political theorist than an anthropologist, and the sprawling, dazzling pluralism of her novel is meant to illustrate the glimmering interconnectedness of all humanity. Alix "had been encouraged (in theory at least) by her education and by her reading to believe in the individual self, the individual soul, but as she grew older she increasingly questioned these concepts—seeing people perhaps more as flickering impermanent points of light irradiating stretches, intersections, threads, of a vast web, a vast network, which was humanity itself; a web of which much remained dark, apparently but not necessarily unpeopled; peopled by the dark, the unlit, the dim spirits, as yet unknown, the past and the future, the dead, the unborn. . . . We are all but a part of a whole which has its own, its distinct, its other meaning; we are not ourselves, we are crossroads, meeting places, points on a curve, we cannot exist independently for we are nothing but signs, conjunctions, aggregations." The novel abounds with subtle connections, with names that recur after many pages, with coincidental meetings after many years, with semi-hidden threads between the South of England and the North, between the upper and the lower classes, between the public and the private realms, between individual lives and the great archaic rhythm of the national holidays. On New Year's Eve, "all over Northam, all over Britain, ill-remembered, confused, shadowy vestigial rites were performed, rites with origins lost in antiquity; Celtic, Pict, Roman, Norse, Anglo-Saxon, Norman, Elizabethan, Hanoverian, Judaic rites." An old custom in Northam calls for a lump of coal to be brought into the house at midnight, so Steve Harper, a haulage contractor, "taking with him a jar of Marmite in a garden trowel as a substitute for coal in a shovel . . . stood outside alone for a grateful crisp smokeless moment of silence, and when they opened the door to him a strange shadow of the night sidled in with him from prehistory. . . . Something was absent, yet something was present. The shadow filled the corners of the broad bright hallway."

Esther Breuer, petite and Jewish and Berlin-born, is the least English of the three central women, and the one about whom the most mystical lights glimmer in the vast human web. Her scholarship consists of flipping back and forth between books pursuing stray connections—e.g., "a connection between the nature of quattrocento pigmentation, and lichenology as a method of dating the antiquity of landscape"—and her lectures are known for "making startling, brilliant connections, for illuminating odd corners, for introducing implausible snippets of erudition." Esther claims that "all knowledge must always be omnipresent in all things." Her life as it develops bears witness to a connection between the Harrow Road Murders and the quiet young man above her flat in Ladbroke Grove, and to a link between her long-standing love for a married Italian anthropologist, Claudio Volpe, and the faltering vitality of a potted palm he has entrusted to her. Claudio, too, believes in a web, in an overarching world of spirit, in a hidden league of demonic powers: "He spoke . . . of the *spiritus mundi,* the *anima,* the *stella marina,* the *deus absconditus* . . . of Gorgon and the Medusa and Géricault and Demogorgon and Salome and the Bessi of Thrace." He believes that Esther has powers she does not recognize, and, uncannily, on an airplane, she meets and befriends a handsome wild Dutchman with whom Liz, long ago, had sexual intercourse on a North Sea crossing, in a Force 9 gale. Esther is the spookiest of the three heroines, the most detached and exotic, the least heterosexual and, to this reader, real. She is a lovingly assembled bundle of bohemian costumes and odd facts about Italian painting but her charm is more ascribed than conveyed.

It is not easy to dramatize the comforting fascination that some women have for each other. The increasingly frequent novels about the friendship between three or four or five women (for instance, this year's *Hot Flashes,* by Barbara Raskin) tend to be thin where thickness is alleged; the women, and the female author, keep *saying* how intense and meaningful the companionship is, but few actions actually illustrate it. The contacts are intermittent, giddy, and chatty, and leave each woman, in the end, alone with her life—her love life and her family life. On the very morning in which I tentatively type out this male impression, the Boston *Globe* quotes Marlo Thomas, the wife of the talk-show host Phil Donahue, as proclaiming, "Women have . . . started trusting each other and they have found a mutuality and community." That is good news; but novelists bent on illustrating it with a multiple heroine commit themselves to an effortful program of keeping a number of independent life-stories going, and of summing up the high moments of mutuality and community with word pictures like "They [Liz, Alix, and Esther] would eat, drink, and talk. They exchanged ideas" and "They eat, drink, talk, lie there in the sunshine."

Another triangle of women exists in *The Radiant Way:* Liz Headleand; her sister, Shirley Harper; and their mother, Rita Ablewhite. Interest, psychological and narrative, so naturally gathers about this blood-related threesome that one suspects that Miss Drabble's youthful instinct in her joyous, prattling first novel, *A Summer Bird-Cage*, was sound when she placed her sisters in the center of the narrative and let the female friendships be peripheral. In *The Radiant Way*, the unbreakable kinship between Liz and Shirley serves to connect the two Englands—the thriving, entrepreneurial south and the depressed, working-class north. Liz, the older sister, slaved at her schoolbooks, got a scholarship to Cambridge, and escaped to London and her radiant big house on Harley Street; Shirley, the more rebellious as a girl, "trusted sex," seduced a boy and married him, and stayed in Northam, becoming "a middle-aged housewife, mother of three . . . with nothing before her but old age." Yet Shirley, in the very constriction of her life, is somehow more vivid and sympathetic than Liz, who is half lost in her larger but more amorphous and shallow world; the London scenes are full of chatter asserted to be delightful, while the scenes of Northam have that stony authenticity of something loved in spite of itself. To Shirley, the rebellious child, has entirely fallen the task of caring for their peculiar mother, who for as long as the girls can remember almost never ventured out of her house in Northam, fed her daughters on stale bread and fish paste, and perpetrated a fictitious tale about their absent father. This father, of whom Liz, throughout most of the novel, has no conscious memory, and the strange round silver object, in the front room, engraved with the monogram SHO, are mysteries—connections not yet uncovered. They make Rita Ablewhite, lying in her bed and listening to the radio and cutting up her newspapers, the most fascinating character in the book, the keeper of its secret.

The initials SHO, we slowly discover, are those of three intertwined aristocratic families, the Stocklinches, the Hestercombes, and the Oxenholmes, members of which are dotted throughout the book. This glint of silver in the lowly, gloomy house, together with the many brisk socioeconomic biographies offered in these pages, informs the novel's noblest attempt at interconnection: the attempt to show, in the manner of, say, *Bleak House*, that no Englishman is an island, that the classes and regions are so woven together that manor house and palace impinge on rural hovel and urban slum, and the fates of a junkman like Krook and an orphaned street-sweeper like Jo can touch and alter those of Sir Leicester and Lady Dedlock. Alix Bowen gropes after a democratic unity when she reflects, "sometimes she had a sense . . . that there was a pattern, if only one could discern it, a pattern that linked these semi-detached houses of Wanley with those in Leeds and Northam, a pattern that linked Liz's vast house in Harley Street with the Garfield Centre towards which she herself now drove." But in the grand attempt to illustrate the pattern Miss Drabble labors under a certain artistic embarrassment, which has set in since Dickens, about melodramatic coincidence and two-dimensional psychologies. For all the talk of connection, her novel portrays disconnection—between husbands and wives, parents and children, government and governed.

The Radiant Way is exasperatingly diffuse. Scores of characters are named and never recur; dozens of scenes we would like to witness are relayed second-hand or tersely alluded to; a modernist jumpiness and diffidence undermine the panoramic ambition. The novel feels both scattered and boiled-down—as if an editor had stepped in to speed things up when its first twenty-four hours took over eighty pages to recount. The marriage of Charles and the woman he leaves Liz for, the aristocratic Henrietta, is left almost entirely to our imagination. The Headleands' adult children are evoked but not, as it were, set in motion. Charming lively apparitions like the bosomy Irish cook Deirdre Kavanagh are not followed into any further adventures. A number of London characters seem to exist for no more urgent reason than that Miss Drabble knows people like them. Liz and Alix have suitors who are carefully groomed for leaps that never come; Alix's marriage heads for a crisis and veers away. Even Liz's cunningly foreshadowed confrontation with her mother's secret, when it occurs, seems cursory, ambiguous, and sour: the long agony of Rita Ablewhite is laughed off as the bad smell from a jar of old pickles, while her daughters clean her house:

> Shirley laughed. "I must say," said Shirley, "I do think you behaved appallingly to Mother." She opened a jar of pickles, sniffed.
> "She behaved appallingly to us," said Liz.
> "Smell that," said Shirley, handing over the jar.
> Liz sniffed. "Jesus," said Liz.

More than once in the novel, the banality of the human adventure, its every crisis so repeatedly charted and analyzed by novelists and psychoanalysts, dulls passion: "And as Liz spoke and listened she was aware of a simultaneous conviction that this was the most shocking, the most painful hour of her entire life, and also that it was profoundly dull, profoundly trivial, profoundly irrelevant, a mere routine."

Well, a creatrix must be true to her bent, and Miss Drabble's is for the deft hint, the impulsive surge, the shrugging surrender to shapeless life. Her novel has a luxurious texture and wears a thousand beauties of expression and insight. Charles's relation to the British establishment is thus encapsulated: "First he had mocked it, then he had exposed it, then he had joined it, and now he represented it. A normal progression." Progression of another sort afflicts the British soil:

No one had lived on that hillside for nineteen centuries. The Brigantes had held it once, against the Romans, but they had retreated to the mountains and left it to gorse and the bracken. And so it had remained until the scoops and cranes and bulldozers of 1970s Post-Industrial Man had moved in to uproot the scrub and to build the suburb known as Greystone Edge.

Liz's reaction to Charles's desertion warrants the novel's most extended and exploratory treatment; the interplay of her psychic and social and physical selves elicits details of a startling intimacy. "Ivan [a bearer of bad tidings] at last cornered her, and even before he opened his mouth she felt the smell of fear from herself: her pores broke open, she stood there panting slightly, her hair rising on the back of her neck in terror, her heated skin covered in icy sweat."

Miss Drabble is formidably bright: she received a double first at Cambridge and, in the five years coincidental with the era of this novel, edited and revised *The Oxford Companion to English Literature*. *The Radiant Way* makes self-conscious bows toward *Great Expectations* and the novels of Jane Austen ("three or four families in a country village," "a few families in a small, densely populated, parochial, insecure country"). Miss Drabble can be as chummy as Trollope with the reader: "But that is another part of this story, and not to be pursued here, for Brian is not a woman and reflections on his prospects . . . would at this juncture muddy the narrative tendency. Forget I mentioned him. Let us return to Liz, Alix, and Esther." All this would be coy and brittle were it not for her earthiness—her love of our species and its habitat, and her ability to focus on the small, sweaty intersections of mind and body, past and present. This latter gift is so much hers that she takes it a shade too casually. The maze of human interaction she creates has many paths she declines to explore, or explores with a peek. *The Radiant Way* is a rare thing—a long novel we would wish longer.

P.S.: In fact, it turns out to have been the first novel of a trilogy, still in progress. Of two other novels reviewed herein—Anatoli Rybakov's *Children of the Arbat* (553–56) and Abdelrahman Munif's *Cities of Salt* (563–67)—did this also turn out to be true. In each case, I felt cheated; part of a novel's job, and not the least part, is to end.

THE OTHER AMERICANS

Living Death

COLLECTED STORIES, by Gabriel García Márquez, translated from the Spanish by Gregory Rabassa and S. J. Bernstein. 311 pp. Harper & Row, 1984.

Harper and Row, which published Gabriel García Márquez in the United States until his most recent book, *Chronicle of a Death Foretold*, have now issued the Nobel Prize winner's collected stories. The publicational history of these twenty-six tales is not made abundantly clear, though a stab of sorts is attempted in a "Publisher's Note" that breathlessly lets us know "They are now published in one volume in the chronological order of their original publication in Spanish from the three volumes of short stories *Eyes of a Blue Dog, Big Mama's Funeral,* and *The Incredible and Sad Tale of Innocent Eréndira and Her Heartless Grandmother.*" Confusingly, the first two collections were translated and published here in reverse order, and under quite different titles, the stories of *Eyes of a Blue Dog* appearing with the novella *Leaf Storm* as *Leaf Storm and Other Stories* in 1972, and those of *Big Mama's Funeral* with the long story "No One Writes to the Colonel" under that latter title in 1968. These two title pieces are not present in *Collected Stories,* and though the stories that are have been each assigned a date at their end, we are not totally persuaded; one, "One Day After Saturday," which the jacket of *No One Writes to the Colonel* identified as winning a Colombian literary prize in 1955, is here dated 1962, as are all the eight stories of the *Big Mama's Funeral* section.

In any case: the stories are rich and startling in their matter and confident and elegant in their manner. For the reader who has exhausted the wonders of García Márquez's masterpiece, *One Hundred Years of Solitude,* they probably constitute (along with its fine precursor, *Leaf Storm*) the next best place to turn. They are—the word cannot be avoided—magical, though for this reader the magic sparkled unevenly through the spread of tricks, and was blacker than he had expected. García Márquez did not begin, as some of his interviews have suggested, as a realist who then broke through to a new, matter-of-fact method of fantasy. Interviewed by Peter Stone in 1981, for *The Paris Review*, he described the breakthrough:

> I had an idea of what I always wanted to do, but there was something missing and I was not sure what it was until one day I discovered the right tone—the tone that I eventually used in *One Hundred Years of Solitude.* It was based on the way my grandmother used to tell her stories. She told things that sounded supernatural and fantastic, but she told them with complete natural-ness. When I finally discovered the tone I had to use, I sat down for eighteen months and worked every day.

The tone was brick-faced:

> In previous attempts to write *One Hundred Years of Solitude,* I tried to tell the story without believing in it. I discovered that what I had to do was believe in them myself and write them with the same expression with which my grandmother told them: with a brick face.

Yet the first story collected here, composed when García Márquez was a mere nineteen, with quite characteristic aplomb details the thoughts of a young man's corpse as it lies in the coffin:

> His body rested heavily, but peacefully, with no discomfort whatever, as if the world had suddenly stopped and no one would break the silence, as if all the lungs of the earth had ceased breathing so as not to break the soft silence of the air. He felt as happy as a child face up on the thick, cool grass contemplating a high cloud flying off in the afternoon sky. He was happy, even though he knew he was dead, that he would rest forever in the box lined with artificial silk.

The mature García Márquez's gift of linkage, his way of letting implausi-ble threads intertwine and thicken into a substantial braid, already flour-ishes in these stories composed when he was a student and a youthful journalist in Colombia. The next in order of composition takes up the thoughts of the dead boy's twin: "The idea of his twin brother's corpse had been firmly stuck in the whole center of his life." There is so much spiralling Faulknerian indirection that it is hard to know who is dead and who is merely imagining it; pronouns float in and out of embodiments and a host of creepy sensations flicker by—"Death began to flow through his bones like a river of ashes. . . . The cold of his hands intensified, making him feel the presence of the formaldehyde in his arteries." Perhaps the parent of all these coffined boys is the corpse seen by the ten-year-old child at the beginning of *Leaf Storm*:

> I've seen a corpse for the first time. . . . I always thought that dead people should have hats on. Now I can see that they shouldn't. I can see that they have a head like wax and a handkerchief tied around their jawbone. I can see that they have their mouth open a little and that behind the purple lips you can see the stained and irregular teeth. . . . I can see that they have their eyes open much wider than a man's, anxious and wild, and that their skin seems to be made of tight damp earth. I thought that a dead man would look like somebody quiet and asleep and now I can see that it's just the opposite. I can see that he looks like someone awake and in a rage after a fight. . . . When I discover that there are flies in the room I begin to be tortured by the idea that the [now-closed] coffin's become full of flies. . . . I feel as if someone is telling me: *That's the way you'll be. You'll be inside a coffin filled with flies. You're only a little under eleven years old, but someday you'll be like that, left to the flies inside of a closed box.*

The ideas of living death, of a consciousness travelling within an immobilized body, of piecemeal dying within the garish trappings of Latin American burial, of "chemical adventure," of "that somnambulism where the senses lose their value," of "an easier, uncomplicated world, where all dimensions had been eliminated," dominate these early stories, with their disagreeable sweetish stench of precocity, of adolescent terror turned outward. Though this spectral field will be extended into a sociological realm of closed houses and frozen lives, a geographical limbo where only the bitter past animates thought, García Márquez's great theme of suspended motion is announced here at the outset, along with a smooth and dandified indifference to the conventions of realism.

He is not sure he had read Faulkner at the time of his first fictions; he told his interviewer, "Critics have spoken of the literary influence of Faulkner, but I see it as a coincidence: I had simply found material that had to be dealt with in the same way that Faulkner had treated similar material." The similarities are remarkable, not only in the climate of class-ridden, aggrieved torpor but in the music of obsessive circling, of a trapped yet unquenchably fascinated sensibility; Faulkner even, in such stories as "Beyond" and "Carcassonne," drones into the life beyond the grave. The author the young Colombian did read was Kafka: "At the university in Bogotá, I started making new friends and acquaintances, who introduced me to contemporary writers. One night a friend lent me a book of short stories by Franz Kafka. I went back to the pension where I was staying and began to read *The Metamorphosis*. The first line almost knocked me off the bed. . . . I didn't know anyone was allowed to write things like that. If I had known, I would have started writing a long time ago. So I immediately started writing short stories." One story in this first collection moves out of the surreal into the orbit of Hemingway. "The Woman Who Came at Six O'Clock" gives us a nearly empty restaurant, a lot of unadorned dialogue, a woman of shady habits, a courteous barman, a whiff of criminal violence. But even here, the sluggish tide of semi-death sweeps in, drowning reality: "Across the counter she couldn't hear the noise that the raw meat made when it fell into the burning grease. . . . She remained like that, concentrated, reconcentrated, until she raised her head again, blinking as if she were coming back out of a momentary death." Nonsense, of a somber sort, nibbles at the edge of many a sentence, the rereading of which threatens to plunge us into a hopeless world of glutinous, twisted time:

> That's the way she's been for twenty years, in the rocker, darning her things, rocking, looking at the chair as if now she weren't taking care of the boy with whom she had shared her childhood afternoons but the invalid grandson who has been sitting here in the corner ever since the time his grandmother was five years old.

Spatial disorientation also occurs within the unpredictable prose:

> Then the three of us looked for ourselves in the darkness and found ourselves there, in the joints of the thirty fingers piled up on the counter.

These three have just been rendered blind, so their disorientation has some rationale. Elsewhere, a woman's consciousness inexplicably wanders into that of a cat and hangs for no less than three thousand years over the desire to eat an orange, and a black stableboy kicked by a horse lies interminably in the straw while the death angels wait and a "little dead and lonely girl," who seems also to be mute and over thirty, keeps recranking a gramophone. The story about the stableboy, "Nabo: The Black Man Who Made the Angels Wait," ends with a monstrous run-on sentence in which García Márquez, at the age of twenty-three, in bravura fashion lays claim to his authorial power. A method of centrifugal revelation, whereby a set of images at first glance absurd or frivolous gradually cohere into a frozen, hovering world that we can recognize as the site of an emotion, of dread and pity: this is to become the method of *One Hundred Years of Solitude*.

The second, middle set of stories, all dated 1962, are more naturalistic, and but for the title piece and "One Day After Saturday"* are located not

---

*Wherein a character enters a hotel labelled "HOTEL MACONDO." Also many of the characters—Rebecca, Father Anthony Isabel, Colonel Aureliano Buendía—from *A Hun-*

in Macondo but in El Pueblo—"the town," and a town differing from Macondo mostly in the relatively straightforward, staccato style with which it is described. Evidently García Márquez's lush early style had been chastised by his fellow leftists. In his *Paris Review* interview he said of this period of his writing, "This was the time when the relationship between literature and politics was very much discussed. I kept trying to close the gap between the two. My influence had been Faulkner; now it was Hemingway. I wrote *No One Writes to the Colonel, The Evil Hour,* and *The Funeral of Mama Grand,* which were all written at more or less the same time and have many things in common. These stories take place in a different village from the one in which *Leaf Storm* and *One Hundred Years of Solitude* occur. It is a village in which there is no magic. It is a journalistic literature." He lived, in the late Fifties and early Sixties, abroad, in Europe, Mexico, and Venezuela; for a time he worked for Castro's news agency, Prensa Latina, in its New York bureau. Though his involvement with radical causes was enthusiastic, the stories of *Big Mama's Funeral* seem scarcely political, but for their convincing rendition of stagnation and poverty, and the rather farcical condemnation of Big Mama's empire. They are brighter-humored, with more comic touches, than the earlier stories; unreality breaks into squalor like the chickens of this tinted sentence: "It was a green, tranquil town, where chickens with ashen long legs entered the schoolroom in order to lay their eggs under the washstand." There is a new epigrammatic loftiness: "She bore the conscientious serenity of someone accustomed to poverty"; "She was older than he, with very pale skin, and her movements had the gentle efficiency of people who are used to reality." García Márquez, by now a well-travelled man of the world, is contemplating his remembered Caribbean backwater with a certain urbanity, preparing to make a totally enclosed microcosm, a metaphor, of it. The young author's eerie muddling of the concrete and the abstract, his will to catch hold of a terrible vagueness at the back of things, now works within single polished sentences: "But this morning, with the memories of the night before floating in the swamp of his headache, he could not find where to begin to live"; "When she finished the stems, Mina turned toward Trinidad with a face that seemed to end in something immaterial."

Several of these tales are García Márquez's best. "There Are No Thieves in This Town," the longest of the lot, with magisterial empathy

---

dred Years of Solitude figure in the story, despite García Márquez's claim to William Kennedy in 1972 ("The Yellow Trolley Car in Barcelona, and Other Visions," *Atlantic Monthly,* January 1973) that "*Leaf Storm* and *Cien Años* are in Macondo, nothing else."

describes the confused, self-destructive behavior of a handsome young idler, Damaso, and the love borne him by his considerably older wife, Ana, and the small-town boredom that stretches stupefyingly to the horizon. The town is so low on recreational resources that Damaso's theft of three battered billiard balls creates an enormous social vacuum; with no overt touches of the fabulous, an enchanted environment, shabby and stagnant yet highly charged, is conjured up. "Artificial Roses," showing how a young girl's love-secrets are detected by her blind grandmother, and "Tuesday Siesta," sketching the arrival in town of the mother of a slain thief, are smaller but not inferior in their purity and dignity of treatment. "Balthazar's Marvelous Afternoon," a parable of artistry in which the local plutocrat, José Montiel, defaults on paying for "the most beautiful cage in the world," sidles toward fantasy, and the prize-winning "One Day After Saturday" enters broadly into it, as the town suffers a plague of dying birds. "Big Mama's Funeral" (attended by the President of Colombia and the Pope) is firmly fantastical and celebrates Macondo, the territory of imagination where the author was to strike it rich. But not immediately: after 1962 García Márquez, living in Mexico City, undertook a new career as a screenwriter and wrote almost no fiction until January of 1965, when "the right tone" for his masterpiece came to him.

The third and last group of stories were mostly composed after the completion and triumph of *One Hundred Years of Solitude,* and they have the strengths and debilities of an assured virtuosity. One of them, "The Last Voyage of the Ghost Ship," is a single six-page sentence, and two of them, "A Very Old Man with Enormous Wings" and "The Handsomest Drowned Man in the World," are subtitled "A Tale for Children." For the first time, we feel a danger of cuteness: "They wanted to tie the anchor from a cargo ship to him so that he would sink easily into the deepest waves, where fish are blind and divers die of nostalgia"; "The house was far away from everything, in the heart of the desert, next to a settlement with miserable and burning streets where the goats committed suicide from desolation when the wind of misfortune blew." Such imagery has become a mere vocabulary, used a bit glibly, though with flashes of the old morbid magic. García Márquez's conception of an angel as a dirty muttering, helpless old man with bedraggled wings is ominous and affecting, and scarcely less so the drowned corpse so tall and beautiful and virile that "even though they were looking at him there was no room for him in their imagination." But the sea he keeps evoking has the unreality not only of sleep and dreams but of, in the words of the old song, a cardboard sea, a sea that indeed could be packed up and sold like the sea in his novel *The Autumn of the Patriarch.*

The longest and latest of these later stories, "The Incredible and Sad Tale of Innocent Eréndira and Her Heartless Grandmother," has been made into a movie, with a script by the author and under his control, so the two forms of illusion can be fairly contrasted. Having seen the film before I read the prose, I was struck by how much that had seemed obscure was easily clarified—the photographer, for instance, who in the film appeared wholly gratuitous and of unrealized significance, is explained in the story as a natural adjunct of the carnival that grows up wherever the prostituted heroine is encamped. The comings and goings of Eréndira's young lover, Ulises, baffling on the screen, make simple sense in print. On the other hand, Irene Papas, as the grandmother, cannot look "like a handsome white whale" with "powerful shoulders which were so mercilessly tattooed as to put sailors to shame"; but she does, unavoidably, put a human face on this implacable character, and makes her more disturbing than she is in the book, where her cruelty remains a matter of literary premise and verbal comedy. The scene of Eréndira's defloration, which in its written paragraph is swathed in subaqueous imagery, in the movie flays the eyes with its real girl, its real man with his three-day beard, its real shack, its real torrents of rain, its real brutality. The film, in short, had a power to stir and scare us quite unrelated to any cumulative sense it was making; its script was logically so loose that García Márquez could insert into it another story, "Death Constant Beyond Love," for the sake of its photogenic episodes of a painted-paper ocean liner and of peso notes that become butterflies. The one image in "Death Constant Beyond Love" that penetrates into our own experience and lends it a negotiable significance—the frightened yet captivating odor of the heroine (not Eréndira), like "the dark fragrance of an animal of the woods . . . woods-animal armpit"—could not, of course, be put on film. Thrown into real landscapes, with flesh-and-blood actors, the careless cruelty of "the incredible and sad tale" glared at the moviegoer confusingly, not quite action and not quite poetry. Seeing real human beings go through his motions, one realizes how much stylized dehumanization García Márquez offers his readers.

There is a surplus of sadism in these later stories. Eréndira is made to submit to masses of men and her grandmother is prolongedly slain by a lover whom then Eréndira spurns; the fallen angel is relentlessly abused and teased; and in "Blacamán the Good, Vendor of Miracles" a child is transformed into a miracle-worker by a diet of pain:

> He took off the last rags I had on, rolled me up in some barbed wire, rubbed rock salt on the sores, put me in brine from my own waters, and hung me

by the ankles for the sun to flay me. . . . When [he fed me] he made me pay for that charity by pulling out my nails with pliers and filing my teeth down with a grindstone.

The child has his revenge: when he becomes a miracle-worker, and his master is dead, he revives him in his tomb and leaves him inside, "rolling about in horror." He revives him not once but repeatedly: "I put my ear to the plaque to hear him weeping in the ruins of the crumbling trunk, and if by chance he has died again, I bring him back to life once more, for the beauty of the punishment is that he will keep on living in his tomb as long as I'm alive, that is, forever." Not a pretty tale, but, then, we might be told, neither is life in Latin America.* Nor were García Márquez's two post-*Solitude* novels, *The Autumn of the Patriarch* and *Chronicle of a Death Foretold*, pretty tales. The former seemed, to this reader eager for more tropical dazzlement, tortuous and repetitive, and the latter astringent and thin. Both left a bad taste.

Even before he won the Nobel Prize, García Márquez was worried about the effects of celebrity and fame: "It tends to isolate you from the real world," he explained to *The Paris Review*. "I would really have liked for my books to have been published after my death, so I wouldn't have to go through all this business of fame and being a great writer." Being a great writer is not the same as writing great. He writes slow: "On a good working day, working from nine o'clock in the morning to two or three in the afternoon, the most I can write is a short paragraph of four or five lines, which I usually tear up the next day." He writes, he informed the interviewer, "for my friends," and the knowledge of "millions of readers . . . upsets and inhibits me." The bold epic qualities of his masterpiece, his genial and handsome jacket photo, and his outspoken leftist political views combine to give a false impression of a robust literary extrovert; reading his collected stories suggests instead that his inspirations are extremely private and subtle. And, it may be, fragile. "The point of departure for a

---

*Colombia, the country from which the United States filched the land for the Panama Canal and which now supplies us with cocaine, has suffered two upheavals that impressed García Márquez: the generation of his grandfathers fought in the bloody civil war of 1899–1903, and in his own youth, in 1948, the assassination of the Liberal leader Gaitán brought on riots in which hundreds of thousands died. He told *The Paris Review:* "I was in my pension ready to have lunch when I heard the news. I ran towards the place, but Gaitán had just been put into a taxi and was being taken to a hospital. On my way back to the pension, the people had already taken to the streets and they were demonstrating, looting stores and burning buildings. I joined them. That afternoon and evening, I became aware of the kind of country I was living in, and how little my short stories had to do with any of that."

book for me," he recently told an interviewer from *The New York Times*, "is always an image, never a concept or a plot." He also confided, "When you are young, you write . . . on impulses and inspiration. . . . When you are older, when the inspiration diminishes, you depend more on technique. If you don't have that, everything collapses." To write with magical lucidity along the thin edge where objective fact and subjective myth merge is a precarious feat. Though he emphasizes technique—"Ultimately, literature is nothing but carpentry," he said to *The Paris Review*— there is much in the process beyond conscious control, however artfully monitored the promptings of the subconscious are. *One Hundred Years of Solitude* was a work of consummate ripeness. The author's sparse production in the eighteen years since its writing betrays the effort of fending off rot.

Latin Strategies

THE REAL LIFE OF ALEJANDRO MAYTA, by Mario Vargas Llosa, translated from the Spanish by Alfred Mac Adam. 310 pp. Farrar, Straus & Giroux, 1986.

THE OLD GRINGO, by Carlos Fuentes, translated from the Spanish by Margaret Sayers Peden and the author. 199 pp. Farrar, Straus & Giroux, 1986.

Mario Vargas Llosa, a fifty-year-old Peruvian, has replaced Gabriel García Márquez as the South American novelist for gringos to catch up on; the agreeable impression made here four years ago by the translation of *Aunt Julia and the Scriptwriter* was deepened by last year's awed reception of *The War of the End of the World*, which won the fifty-thousand-dollar Ritz Hemingway Award last year in Paris. His newly arrived novel, *The Real Life of Alejandro Mayta*, is a dazzling performance—perhaps, it might be offered in cavil, a bit too much of a performance. But never mind; Señor Vargas Llosa has all the moves, and the reader's awareness of the author's virtuosity is in this case woven right into the intricate and suspenseful texture of his tale. In Spanish, the novel is called simply *Historia de Mayta;* the English title reminds one of Nabokov's *The Real Life of Sebastian Knight*—and, whether or not the echo is intentional, Nabokov does keep coming to mind as Vargas Llosa ingeniously, incessantly shuffles past and present, writer and character, "I" and "he," a historical Peru and a futuristic Peru, a mock-documentary manner and the ingenuous camaraderie of the professed fictionist. He begins by describing himself (or a narrator very like him) jogging along Lima's Malecón de Barranco, and lamenting to himself the dumping of garbage in this fashionable district, down the cliffs that look toward the sea. "The spectacle of misery was once limited exclusively to the slums, then it spread downtown, and now it is the common property of the whole city, even the exclusive residential neighborhoods—Miraflores, Barranco, San Isidro. If you live in Lima, you can get used to misery and grime, you can go crazy, or you can blow your brains out." A new paragraph marks the next sentence: "But I'm sure Mayta never got used to any of it."

Alejandro Mayta was the narrator's classmate at the Salesian School. A pudgy, awkward boy of humble background, Mayta was unduly sensitive to the beggars and other unfortunates of the Lima streets, and once asked the priest of his Communion class, "Why are there rich and poor people, Father?" The question never rests for him; he goes on a hunger strike, loses his Catholic faith, and becomes a Communist revolutionary—for two decades, a purist of the left who finds doctrinal adequacy in a tiny, seven-man cell of Trotskyites, and then, at the age of forty, an incongruous man of action, a leader of an abortive uprising in the Andes town of Juaja, in 1958. (This chronology, we might observe, puts Mayta's birth in 1918, which makes him and his classmate a generation older than Vargas Llosa, who was born in 1936.) Now, twenty-five years after the uprising, in a Peru supposedly racked by guerrilla warfare and turned into a battlefield by a "Russo-Cuban-Bolivian invasion" and American Marines supporting the ruling junta (fiction, though the conditions to make it plausible exist), the narrator decides to explore the life of Mayta, and to compose a novel based upon the violent events long ago in Juaja. He interviews a number of people around Lima, and in the process gives a good walking tour of the once-beautiful viceregal capital, now an overcrowded, filthy, and run-down urban sprawl. These interviews—with Mayta's aunt, with former Trotskyite associates, with radical nuns and a former Stalinist whose paths have crossed Mayta's, and with a woman, Adelaida, whom Mayta, a homosexual, had persuaded to be his wife—all alternate, sometimes several times on a page, with scenes from, as it were, the novel in progress, from Mayta's life in 1958 as the writer imagines it. The double focus is expertly manipulated and sometimes—as when a present-day senator's smooth slanders are interspersed with scenes of his homosexual seduction by Mayta as a young man—provides a stunning stereoptical effect, of lives as they exist in the depths of time. On occasion, Vargas Llosa seems to have too much going all at once, as when the former wife's description of the sham marriage and the fate of the son she conceived with Mayta is played against not only her present marriage, middle-aged self, and dumpy surroundings but an apocalyptic background of the destruction of Cuzco in the imaginary Peruvian war. This science-fiction element, when the plain truth about Peru would be bizarre enough, unnecessarily confuses a novel already luxuriantly complex; also, in this chapter the narrator's "I" creeps over into Mayta's consciousness, slipping one more transparency into the overloaded projector. Still, having elected certain instruments, an artist is obliged to use them to the hilt, and all manner of interesting anticipations and retrospections are generated by Vargas Llosa's glinting devices. Generally, any sustained double focus—other examples are Ruth Prawer Jhabvala's *Heat and Dust* and Anne Tyler's *Earthly Possessions*—drains tension from the foreground action; the frequent interruptions emphasize the authorial presence and suggest that everything exists on an airier level than forward-plodding, one-day-at-a-time reality. However, this novel's climactic chapters, portraying the abortive revolution at Juaja, seamlessly blend the accounts of surviving eyewitnesses with the twenty-five-year-old events, and a fine cinematic momentum is achieved.

Even here, the reader can't ignore the novelist-reporter, a more volatile and accessible character than do-gooding, pedantic, flat-footed (literally) Alejandro Mayta. We are invited to admire, as spontaneously as we admire the handsome, pin-striped hidalgo on the back of the book jacket, the imagination that can conjure up, say, the comic fussiness of a tiny left-wing splinter group in solemn session, or the nauseated feelings of a young wife who discovers that her husband is a homosexual, or the numb exaltation of a citified idealist engaging, while beset with altitude sickness, in a gun battle in the Andes. All wonderfully done, though we are disconcertingly reminded that it might have been done quite otherwise, that art is as arbitrary as truth is relative. The last chapter, like one of those Nabokovian endings in which the scenery falls away and the cocky puppetmaster faces the audience directly, piles twist upon twist and should be left its provocative surprises. The author, all but naming himself Mario Vargas Llosa, engagingly confesses to his character, "This conversation is my final chapter. You can't refuse me now, it would be like taking a cake out of the oven too soon."

The question keeps arising, in the reader's mind and on the printed page, why did our hero, the author, take as his subject this obscure and defeated revolutionary, Alejandro Mayta? Because, the answer suggests itself, the subject is political, and it is the proper and inevitable task of the South American novelist to write politically. As the Vargas Llosa persona explains to an interview subject, "I think the only way to write stories is to start with History—with a capital H." Lima, the city founded by Pizarro, from which Spain administered a continent of gold and slaves, certainly has History; the riddle of Latin-American poverty and unrest and crisis has its answer here if anywhere. The physical degradation of the city is far advanced; ubiquitous garbage begins and ends the novel. The proliferating slums and even the horrors of the dreadfully over-crowded jail are remorselessly described. Nor is there a rural idyll to offer contrast or relief; the Indians still flock to the wretched shack cities, from Andean towns like Quero:

> All the houses in Quero had to be like that: no light, no running water, no drainage, and no bath. Flies, lice, and a thousand other bugs must be part of the poor furniture, lords and masters of pots and pelts, of the rustic beds pushed up against the daub-and-wattle walls, of the faded images of the Virgin and of saints nailed to the doors. . . . Yes, Mayta, millions of Peruvians lived in this same grime, in this same abandonment, amid their own urine and excrement, without light or water, living the same vegetable life, the same animal routine.

Some reviewers in the United States have taken *The Real Life of Alejandro Mayta* to be a satire on left-wing commitment. It is true, comedy and even farce are found in the ineffectuality of the seven-man Trotskyite cell—utterly isolated, with its strenuous jargon, from the masses it seeks to educate and liberate—and in the inadequacies of Mayta's uprising, whose main troops consist of seven schoolboys who, failing to learn "The Internationale," instead sing a school song and the national anthem as they bounce along in the revolution's solitary truck. But, Vargas Llosa seems to say, a revolutionary seed *is* planted that day, amid all the absurdity; and in any case the need for a change shouts out on all sides, in the circumambient misery and disorder. His is a model of the most that political fiction can be: a description of actual social conditions and a delineation of personalities motivated by political concerns. Such motivation, of course, comes mixed with sexual and other intimate, clouded motives; yet it exists. All of the political-minded interviewees are left-wingers; there are no junta spokesmen, no intransigent landowners, no fresh-faced *norteamericanos* insidiously urging the virtues of free enterprise. But in his shrewd and lively portraits of Peruvian lawyers and barbers and store-keepers Vargas Llosa catches well enough the tone of the cagey, improvising citizenry that makes do with a system and, having made do, resists sweeping change. The conservative inertia of a society is suggested, while its agitators are dramatized. The dozens of little anticlimactic careers sketched in the margins of Alejandro's own anti-climactic career persuasively imply the limits of human aspiration and the defeat that awaits each dreaming, idealistic organism. If the novel has a moral, it might be, as a

Peruvian bureaucrat tells the narrator, "When you start looking for purity in politics, you eventually get to unreality."

The intelligence of Mario Vargas Llosa plays above the sad realities and unrealities with a coolness that should be distinguished from Nabokov's hermetically aesthetic ardor and Gabriel García Márquez's surreal fever. These two write prose that crests in poetic passages; whereas Vargas Llosa, to judge from this translation, writes in a way that is always adequately evocative but never spectacular. In the three hundred pages there is scarcely a simile. We are told that Mayta's splayed feet "looked like clock hands permanently set at ten minutes to two," and the sound of rats in the ceiling stirs the prose to this flourish: "Just then, they heard above their heads tiny sounds: light, multiple, invisible, repugnant, shapeless. For a few seconds it seemed like an earthquake." Vargas Llosa is a great noter of the undermining sensation, the private crosscurrent: Mayta all through his day of violent revolution struggles against the dizzying, thumping symptoms of mountain sickness, and during his crucial hearing within his Trotskyite cell he "felt that the pile of *Workers Voice* he was sitting on had begun to tip over and he thought how ridiculous it would be if he slipped and took a fall." This is one of the few novels I have read where the characters, in the midst of fighting for their lives, catch colds, realistically. As to the translation, I wish that Mr. Mac Adam [*sic*] had suppressed the rhyme in this rendering: "Yes, the small man in his vest and hat, surrounded by guerillas, ducking bullets being fired by guards from up in the mountains, begins to sneeze. Trying to put the squeeze on him, I ask . . ." And he disturbingly translates *josefinos*—the small boys from the Colegio San José who are meant to run errands for Mayta's revolution and who end by carrying its rifles—as "joeboys," a word I found in no dictionary but one of American slang, where it is defined as "the male counterpart of a flapper," and ascribed to "subdeb use" circa 1941.*

. Almost the only rich character alluded to in the tangled history of Alejandro Mayta is called Fuentes. It may be a coincidence, but the real Carlos Fuentes is indeed rich in acclaim and honors, on both sides of the border; he is Mexico's best-known novelist. His commendable determination to comprehend both his native land and the United States (where he

---

*The latest Partridge dictionary of slang, I have been told, gives "joeboy" as Canadian Army slang for "someone detailed to perform an unpleasant task" (circa 1940). Still, it is not easy to come up with a better rendering. I can think only of "Joeys," the capital letter helping us to distinguish the *josefinos* from baby kangaroos.

now lives, in Boston) and his generous desire to explain one to the other make me regret my opinion that his new novel, *The Old Gringo*, is a very stilted effort, static and wordy, a series of tableaux costumed in fustian and tinted a kind of sepia I had not thought commercially available since the passing of Stephen Vincent Benét:

> . . . the others blindly remembering the long spans and vast spaces on both sides of the wound that to the north opened like the Rio Grande itself rushing down from steep canyons, as far up as the Sangre de Cristo Mountains, islands in the deserts of the north, ancient lands of the Pueblos, the Navajos and Apaches, hunters and peasants only half subdued by Spain's adventures in the New World, they, from the lands of Chihuahua and the Rio Grande, both seemed to die here, on this high plain where a group of soldiers for a few seconds held the pose of the Pietà, dazed by what they'd done and by an accompanying compassion, until the Colonel broke the spell.

Some spell. We are asked to believe that Ambrose Bierce—perhaps the least appealing figure of enduring worth in American literature—joined up with Pancho Villa in 1914; this has been often rumored, but the verifiable facts show only that he disappeared into Mexico in 1913. Bierce, in Fuentes's fantasy, crosses the Chihuahua desert and becomes an instant father-figure both to Tomás Arroyo, a young rebel general who has returned to destroy the Miranda hacienda where he, the illegitimate son of the owner, was raised as a peasant, and to Harriet Winslow, a thirty-year-old schoolteacher from Fourteenth Street in Washington, D.C., who has arrived to give English lessons to the Miranda children, not knowing that the entire family has suddenly and shrewdly departed. Harriet's biological father, we are often reminded, was an Army captain who supposedly died in Cuba but by another interpretation surreptitiously lived right over on Sixteenth Street, sleeping with a black woman in the basement of a derelict mansion. Bierce, meanwhile, the old gringo, just wants to die, if only to get away from William Randolph Hearst, who has been employing him off and on for forty years. He marches straight into enemy fire but it doesn't touch him; finally he has to court death by burning the precious papers—"papers as brittle as old silk," a grant from the Spanish Crown—that prove to Tomás Arroyo his legitimate claim to the hacienda and its acreage. While waiting for their sour spiritual father to rig this roundabout suicide, General Arroyo and Miss Winslow take note of each other, and she is not too much the embodiment of interfering North American Puritanism ("Look at them, what these people need is education, not rifles. A good scrubbing, followed by a few lessons on how we do things in the United States, and you'd see an end to this chaos") to do some fancy rutting in the general's railway carriage, while thinking sweet nothings like "damn him, damn the brown fucker, damn the ugly greaser." From these earthy moments (the lowest point comes when "he kissed her again, entombed in her mouth as in a cellar of menacing dogs") the prose beats upward to such flights as "If it is necessary, our atomized consciousness invents love, imagines it or feigns it, but does not live without it, since in the midst of infinite dispersion, love, even if as a pretext, gives us the measure of our loss." There is much similar rumination, leavened by a smattering of overheard Hemingway ("Harriet looked at the old gringo exactly as he wanted to be looked at before he died"), a neat trick or two ("Each closed his fists over the other's"; "From the middle of the silent throng of sombreros and rebozos emerged those gray eyes fighting to retain a sense of their own identity, of personal dignity and courage in the midst of the vertiginous terror of the unexpected"), lots of phlegm and ochre dust, and dialogue of the fruitiest wood:

> "No, I'll never forget," General Frutos García told his friends after the Revolution, after the former colonel was promoted, to make amends this way for Villa's defeat and unite the many factions of the Revolution. "The gringo had come looking for death, nothing more. What he was finding, though, was glory—and the bitter fruit of glory, envy."

The Greek chorus of talk about the central figure ("The old gringo came to Mexico to die"; "Yes sir, you could see 'farewell' in his eyes") doesn't bring Ambrose Bierce to life, nor does the occasional paraphrase of one of his stories. He doesn't even have a sense of humor, this writer of a thousand sardonic jokes. He remains a fist clenched upon nothing, upon the announced intention to die, as Harriet Winslow and Tomás Arroyo remain clenched around a few stylized, heavily insistent memories. The most vivid and least programmatic pages of *The Old Gringo* portray a middle-class Mexican woman's reaction to a sudden rebel onslaught; this passage kindles an unforced interest, as if taking by surprise Fuentes's stiff army of symbols. But generally the only thing moving in this dead landscape is the author's mind as it spiders among his checkpoints, thickening the web of mirrors and keys and Oedipal fixations.

On the back of the book jacket the author states, "I have lived with this story for a long time." He conceived it forty years ago, wrote the first ten pages in 1964, and took it up again for a month in 1970. He held the inspiration and its emblematic figures too long in his head, perhaps; they became petrified. Although the novel goes through the motions of establishing geographical and historical authenticity, we learn little about Mexico we didn't know after seeing *The Treasure of the Sierra Madre* and *Viva*

Zapata! The glimpses of Washington, and Harriet's life there, seem more animated, more exciting to the writer, than the horde of rebel Mexicans, with their slit eyes and terse mutterings. Revolution, which in Vargas Llosa's book figures as a refracted complexity of mini-events and psychological shadows, has become in *The Old Gringo* a stock phantasmagoria the writer has sought to enrich with portentous Freudianism. Apropos of international as well as personal relations, Fuentes makes a point—"Did you know we are all the object of another's imagination?"—not far from the point of Vargas Llosa's ambiguous mock-researches. But in the Peruvian novel, the details are seen in a constantly changing light, by a restless intelligence. Though Fuentes is certainly intelligent, his novel lacks intelligence, in the sense of a speaking mind responsively interacting with recognizable particulars. Its dreamlike and betranced glaze, its brittle grotesquerie do not feel intrinsic or natural; its surrealism has not been earned by any concentration on the real. Latin-American surrealism has enchanted the globe, but its freedoms cannot be claimed as a matter of course. Mere mannerism results.

The Great Paraguayan Novel and Other Hardships

THE STORY OF A SHIPWRECKED SAILOR, by Gabriel García Márquez, translated from the Spanish by Randolph Hogan. 106 pp. Knopf, 1986.

I THE SUPREME, by Augusto Roa Bastos, translated from the Spanish by Helen Lane. 438 pp. Knopf, 1986.

A FUNNY DIRTY LITTLE WAR, by Osvaldo Soriano, translated from the Spanish by Nick Caistor. 108 pp. Readers International, 1986.

THE LONG NIGHT OF FRANCISCO SANCTIS, by Humberto Costantini, translated from the Spanish by Norman Thomas di Giovanni. 184 pp. Harper & Row, 1985.

THE INVENTION OF MOREL *and Other Stories,* by Adolfo Bioy Casares, translated from the Spanish by Ruth L. C. Simms. 237 pp. University of Texas Press, 1985.

The Story of a Shipwrecked Sailor, beautifully produced by Knopf and given a bright, smooth-running translation by Randolph Hogan, is not, actually, fiction, but a "real-life" adventure—the account by a twenty-year-old Colombian sailor, Luis Alejandro Velasco, of his ten days adrift in a raft in the Caribbean without food or water. It happened in the winter of 1955, and Velasco briefly became a national hero for his feat of survival. At the time, Gabriel García Márquez was a staff reporter for the Bogotá daily *El Espectador;* interviewing the young sailor in twenty sessions of six hours each, he was pleasantly surprised to find that Velasco had "an exceptional instinct for the art of narrative, an astonishing memory and ability to synthesize, and enough uncultivated dignity to be able to laugh at his own heroism." Fifteen years later, in an introduction written for the first book publication of the resulting story, García Márquez recalled how he and his interview subject "put together an accurate and concise account of his ten days at sea. It was so detailed and so exciting that my only concern was finding readers who would believe it." The story, under the sailor's by-line, ran in fourteen consecutive installments, and "readers scrambled in front of the [newspaper] building to buy back issues in order to collect the entire series." The government was less enthusiastic, as Velasco's narrative revealed that he and seven drowned fellow crew members were swept overboard not due to a storm but because their destroyer, returning from eight months of repairs in Mobile, Alabama, was loaded with contraband American goods—refrigerators, television sets, washing machines—that spilled from the deck in heavy seas on a sunny day. The Rojas dictatorship denied the scandal, and *El Espectador* countered by printing sailors' on-board snapshots showing the illegal cargo in the background. Within months, *El Espectador* was shut down by government reprisals, and Velasco himself, who refused to change his story, had to leave the Navy. By 1957 the former national hero occupied the obscurity of "a desk at a bus company."

These unfortunate consequences—which helped precipitate García Márquez into a wandering exile and his eventual fate as a world-class novelist—add a mere footnote to the sorry history of Latin-American censorship and mendacious repression; what matters now is that the shipwrecked sailor told and the youthful journalist conjured into print an enchanting tale, quite thrilling in its lucid, unhistrionic, often comic revelation of human fortitude and ability to absorb hardship. In its exposition of suffering solitude it ranks with Admiral Byrd's *Alone* and Mungo Park's *Travels;* along with the stoic heroism, the succession of perils and extreme sensations, there is something rollicking and colorful, an ironic good humor, which we tend to credit to the author more than the narrator. The power of invention, of course, is also the power of discovery, and perhaps García Márquez's only contribution to the story's many vivid surreal touches was to hear them and put them down. Velasco's Alabama girl-friend, for instance, is named Mary Address, and the surname is so unusual it stops us cold and makes her as oddly real as Olive Oyl, or the bar called the Joe Palooka where the Colombian sailors congregate. Oddly real, too, is the fin of a shark as it glides past the little raft: "In fact, nothing appears more innocuous than a shark fin. It doesn't look like part of an animal, even less part of a savage beast. It's green and rough, like the bark of a tree. As I watched it edge past the side of the raft, I imagined it might have a fresh flavor, somewhat bitter, like the skin of a vegetable." The starving sailor, on the fifth day of his ordeal, manages to capture a small gull and to wring its neck; but his attempt to eat the bird raw proves a grisly failure:

> At first I tried to pluck the feathers carefully, methodically. But I hadn't counted on the fragility of the skin. As the feathers came out it began to disintegrate in my hands. I washed the bird in the middle of the raft. I pulled it apart with a single jerk, and the sight of the pink intestines and blue veins turned my stomach. I put a sliver of the thigh in my mouth but I couldn't swallow it. This was absurd. It was like chewing on a frog. Unable to get over my repugnance, I spit out the piece of flesh and kept still for a long time, with the revolting hash of bloody feathers and bones in my hand.

What he *can* chew and swallow, and what gives him courage to keep living, is a casually pocketed business card from a clothing store in Mobile: "I could feel a tiny piece of mashed-up cardboard move all the way down to my stomach, and from that moment on I felt I would be saved, that I wouldn't be destroyed by sharks." His attempt to disassemble and eat his shoes is less successful and produces, when he is safe in Colombia, his appearance in shoe advertisements—"because his shoes were so sturdy that he hadn't been able to tear them apart to eat them." The grinning gods of anticlimax hover above Velasco's entire adventure: having finally sighted land and swum to where his feet can touch ground, he is almost drowned in the undertow and then is driven nearly crazy by his frustrated attempts to open a coconut on the shore. His return to civilization has many macabre wrinkles: his rescuers feed him only sugar water, and he is escorted to the distant hospital by a parade of six hundred men, plus women, children, and animals—a procession out of one of García Márquez's thronged novels.

The starved, sun-baked, semi-delirious sailor, at last granted human contact, discovers within himself a primary aesthetic impulse: "When I heard him [the first man he meets] speak I realized that, more than thirst, hunger, and despair, what tormented me most was the need to tell someone what had happened to me." Throughout Velasco's narrative we feel the thinness of the difference between life and death—a few feet of heaving ocean separate him from his less lucky shipmates in the confusion after they are swept overboard, and a fragile cork-and-rope raft holds him afloat, through the black night and burning day, in "a dense sea filled with strange creatures." The closeness of the living and the dead is one of García Márquez's themes, but in this journalistic narrative it emerges without morbidity, as a fact among many. The factuality of the real sailor's direct and artless telling bracingly mingles with the beginnings of the writer's "magic realism."

I the Supreme, by Augusto Roa Bastos, is a deliberately prodigious book, an elaborate and erudite opus saturated in the verbal bravura of classic modernism. Its Paraguayan author, a professor at the University of Toulouse until his retirement last year, has lived in exile since 1947; he found haven in Buenos Aires until 1976, when—to quote an interview he gave the Madrid journal *Leviatán*—"the military dictatorship was beginning to deploy the hecatomb" and "it was necessary to escape the rather sinister climate which was incubating." A journalist and poet in Paraguay, he began to write fiction in Argentina, most notably a long novel centered upon the Guaraní Indians, *Hijo del hombre (Son of Man),* and *Yo el supremo,* published in 1974.

"El Supremo" was the popular nickname for the founder of independent Paraguay, José Gaspar Rodríguez de Francia, who, after the bloodless coup against Spanish colonial rule in 1811, went from being secretary of the ruling junta to being Supreme Dictator; he ruled the country possessively and absolutely from 1814 until his death in 1840. A lawyer and one-time postulate for the priesthood, he held the degrees of master of philosophy and doctor of theology; he never married, and lived austerely, in an isolation akin to that which he imposed on the country he had founded. He forbade immigration and emigration and maintained neither diplomatic nor commercial ties with foreign countries. Within the embattled, landlocked country, his policies were aimed at developing a sense of independence and solidarity; a follower of the French Enlightenment, he curbed the power of the church and the aristocracy, introduced modern methods of agriculture, defended the rights of the Guaraní Indians, and maintained a formidable army. He wore a black suit and red cape and was rumored to be something of a sorceror. Paraguay, known to Americans mostly as the remote domain of the long-lived dictatorship of Alfredo Stroessner, has had an interesting history. From its capital of Asunción the Spanish ruled a vast area and founded Buenos Aires. Its southeastern region was the site of communistic Jesuit missions—the eighteenth-century *reducciones,* which one writer on Latin America, Carlos Rangel, has described as "the best possible materialization of a *City of God* on earth." And in the War of the Triple Alliance (1865–70) Paraguay defended itself against its two mighty neighbors, Brazil and Argentina, at the staggering cost of over half its population, including three-quarters of its men.

The founder of this stubborn country, a George Washington with elements of Huey Long, Enver Hoxha, and Merlin, lies dying and raving, aloud and within his skull, through the over four hundred large pages of *I the Supreme,* whose texture is varied with double-column excerpts from historical works, some of which are imaginary.* The valor and labor and intelligence exerted in this novel and in its faithful translation (including bits from the Guaraní, Portuguese, and Latin) intimidate criticism; suffice it to say that, if a masterpiece, it is the sort one should read for academic credit, and that much of its charm and interest presumably lie bound up in its virtuoso use of the original language. Many books have gone into the making of this book: contemporary and historical accounts of Francia's Paraguay, government documents and the eighteenth-century sources of the dictator's own extensive erudition, and the crabbed modern works of Joyce, Borges, and García Márquez, among others—there is even a sharp whiff of contemporary French interest in the elusiveness of texts and the multiplicity of signs.

In books as in dinosaurs, however, largeness asks a strong spine, and *I the Supreme* holds no action as boldly intelligible as Leopold Bloom's peregrination or the hunt for the Great White Whale. The looming, and virtually only, human relationship exists between the dying Francia and his obsequious secretary, Policarpo Patiño; their dialogues are given not only without quotation marks but without dashes or indentation, so that the secretary and dictator (himself once a secretary) tend to merge, while allusions to Don Quixote and Sancho Panza thicken around them. The central issue of suspense—the authorship of an anti-Francia pasquinade nailed to the door of the cathedral—is never, that this reader noticed, resolved. Nor does the author's attitude toward his polymorphous, logorrheic hero come into clear view. Repulsion and fascination, clearly, but to what end? A kind of long curse concludes the novel—an enthusiastic descriptive catalogue of the insects and worms that will devour El Supremo's corpse, and some condemnatory sentences in the author's (or Patiño's) voice:

---

*". . . I didn't want to write an historical work. That's why I took it upon myself to completely distort all historical references, because I don't believe one can mix the two genres. History as the basic material of a work of fiction is a special matter. What in Latin America we call history, that is, the history of the official historians, has no value whatsoever. On the contrary, it is precisely this false reality which we who write fiction feel obliged to contradict in every possible way" (Roa Bastos, in the *Leviatán* interview, translated from the Spanish by Peggy Boyers in *Salmagundi*).

You fooled yourself and fooled others by pretending that your power was absolute. You lost your oil, you old ex theologian passing yourself off as a statesman. . . . You ceased to believe in God, but neither did you believe in the people with the true mystique of Revolution; the only one that leads a true locomotive-engineer of history to identify himself with its cause, not use it as a hiding place from his absolute vertical Person, in which worms are now feeding horizontally.

One is led, by this learned book bristling with quaint particulars and amiable puns and verbal tumbles ("Yet the genes of gens engender tenacious traitorous taints"; "the filigreed fleuron in the vergered-perjured paper, the flagellated letters"), into a spiritual dungeon, a miasmal atmosphere of hate and bitter recalcitrance. The fictional Francia is most eloquent in his inveighing against the others—the devilish ecclesiastics, the "Porteños" of Buenos Aires—who threaten his power. He knows no positive connections; all is betrayal and potential assault. The inanimate objects that inspire and console and fortify him—a polished skull, a fallen meteorite, his ivory pen—supplant human faces and voices and whatever humane motives inspired, at the forging of a nation, his polity. The static, circling quality of many modernist masterworks is here overlaid with a political rigidity, an immobilizing rage that seizes both the tyrant and the exiled writer. *I the Supreme* differs from García Márquez's *Autumn of the Patriarch* in that the dictator-hero of the latter is a coarse ignoramus, whereas Francia, in Roa Bastos's reconstruction, suffers, amid the trappings of omnipotence, the well-known impotence and isolation of the modern intellectual.

The muddy, murderous atmosphere of Latin-American politics is concentrated alarmingly in Osvaldo Soriano's short novel, *A Funny Dirty Little War*. "Dirty war" conjures up, a bit misleadingly, Vietnam ("It's a dirty little war but we have to fight it"—Dwight Eisenhower) and the campaign of domestic oppression carried on by the Argentine junta now on trial; the Spanish title, *No habrá más penas ni olvido,* is a line of a tango, "Mi Buenos Aires querido," and translates as "There shall be no more sorrow or longing." Soriano is an Argentinian who went into exile in 1976, when the junta took over, and returned in 1983, in which same year his book, written in 1980, could be published in Buenos Aires, having been previously published in Spain and, translated, in Italy and a number of other European countries. In 1984 it was made into a movie which won an award in Berlin—an action movie, presumably, since *A Funny Dirty Little War* is an absolute of sorts: it is virtually all action, and the action is virtually all ugly. In little more than a hundred pages, the attempt of one petty official to oust another farcically, inexorably, horribly sweeps a small Argentine town into a local holocaust of violence and murder.

Suprino, the Party Secretary, accuses Mateo, the Town Clerk, of being a Communist, and enlists Inspector Llanos and Deputy Inspector Rossi and Guzman, the local auctioneer, in an attempt to oust Fuentes, the Council Leader, who opts to defend the town hall with two local policemen, a released prisoner, and Moyano, a humble gardener abruptly promoted to Director of Parks and Gardens. All these men know each other as fellow villagers, and all claim to be loyal Peronists, yet real bullets begin to fly, and real deaths occur: "The Inspector, posted in a doorway, Guzman and the wounded policeman from the house, and Suprino from the rooftop all fired at the town-hall windows. The shutters and the glass were blown to bits. Moyano fell back. Everybody in the office threw themselves to the floor. . . . The floor was spattered with blood. There was no sign of movement from Moyano." The whirlwind of violence, fed by nameless youths on both sides, swirls on into the night, a Walpurgisnacht of rain and mud and confusion and torture given its perhaps too-symbolic capping when a drunken crop-duster drops a load of pig manure from his plane. It is slapstick in which people actually bleed: "Guzman the auctioneer threw himself underneath the Peugeot. Two of the men got into the car, and started off at full speed. Guzman felt its whole weight run over his right hand, and a stabbing pain shot the length of his arm. When he saw the blood spurting from his crushed fingers, he felt sick, and then fainted." The rapid interlace of dialogue and blundering encounters opens, with sickening quickness, into unbearable pain:

> The brass knuckleduster smashed into Ignacio's jaw. The Council Leader fell against the bank accounts filing cabinet, and vaguely realised that something was cutting into his back. He felt as though he was chewing his own teeth. . . . A shrill buzzing was spinning round inside his skull, and finally settled in his brain. He could hear a moaning sound coming from his throat. His own scream gave him a feeling of horror. He attempted to force his eyes open, but the lids seemed as heavy as lead curtains. Eventually, by gripping the edges of the desk, he managed to raise his eyelids. He saw a red, smoking tip. Solid fire pressed on his eyes. He felt as though his head were a chaos of pain which he could not fuse into a whole. He longed for death to rescue him from the nightmare.

When dawn at last comes, all of the insurrectionists but the instigator have been killed, and two survivors from the other side have this bleary exchange: "It's going to be a beautiful day, Sergeant." "A day . . . for Perón."

But Perón, the ultimate target of this horrific satire, did not create Latin-American authoritarianism, nor did his passing end it, even in Argentina. Soriano plausibly builds his civic nightmare upon basic human competitiveness and macho pride; he so persuasively shows how a sleepy town can descend into carnage, and its middle-aged officeholders turn into cruel civil warriors, that we ask ourselves what spell holds in harmless suspension the rivalries and ambitions of our own local governments. Not that the United States, especially in its frontier territories, has not known lawless feuds, lynchings, and criminality claiming to be guerrilla protest. But official power *is* transferred peaceably here, with a tolerance for dissent only sporadically and precariously observed in our sister continent's many constituted republics. We may dislike our government but are not, by and large, afraid of it, or afraid of its sudden collapse, and a book like *A Funny Dirty Little War* reminds us what a luxury this is, and how thin is the skin of social order.

Humberto Costantini, another Argentinian recently returned from exile, has written *The Long Night of Francisco Sanctis*, which also describes a single nightmarish period of less than twenty-four hours. And again, comedy turns deadly, with the difference that in Soriano's book it is as if the amiable little village world of Don Camillo were blackened by the laconic ugliness of Hemingway's war writing, while Costantini begins with a mild, musing, midlife protagonist like Italo Svevo's Zeno—who is, like him, preoccupied by giving up smoking. Soriano's is a style of brutal efficiency; Costantini's is ruminative, chatty, with humorously elaborate chapter titles, such as

> CHAPTER I. *In which, so as to keep the reader from raising his hopes too high with regard to the entertainment value of this little book, it is here stated without further ado that its subject matter is of a more or less psychological nature—or, in other words, that the prospect ahead is fairly humdrum. Thus forewarned, the reader can now be told something about a certain telephone call that came from out of the blue.*

Francisco Sanctis, the forty-one-year-old head accountant for a small Buenos Aires grocery wholesaling firm, happily married and economically prospering, is phoned one day (Friday, November 11, 1977) at his desk by a ghost from his past—Elena Vaccaro, who seventeen years ago was an overweight fellow university student, like the youthful Sanctis active in literary and left-wing circles. Though their relationship was casual and unconsummated, she now asks him to meet her immediately, on the flimsy excuse that an old student poem of his is being reprinted in a Venezuelan magazine. He very grudgingly agrees to rendezvous on a street corner, and she, grown unexpectedly lean and glamorous, drives him around in her Renault while explaining that what she really wants is for Sanctis to notify two men that they are going to be abducted by the goons of Air Force Intelligence that night. He is naturally reluctant to become involved, contented bourgeois that he is, and yet enough of his old idealism lingers to let this abruptly assigned mission nag at him; he spends the rest of the novel, far into the night, indecisively wandering the streets of Buenos Aires.

The exposition is leisurely, confident, urbane. The gently erotic comedy of Sanctis's encounter with his old semi-flame (she admired him, in her plump radical days) is almost Cheeveresque, as he mentally takes her sociological temperature: "Sanctis observes her closely and draws some hasty conclusions: solid economic background, a social life, a pitiless diet consisting of a small glass of grapefruit juice and such for breakfast, dance or body expression, swimming or tennis, beauty treatments and yoga, a very busy husband, independence, the odd lighthearted affair." In his own apartment, where he briefly alights after ten o'clock, he notices that his wife, María Angélica, has put a bottle of wine in the refrigerator and that her remarks to him are accompanied "by a certain tone and a sleepy smile that Sanctis knows well and that have to do with bed, with a certain French perfume that only now he's aware he's been smelling without being conscious of it." Nevertheless, torn between domestic bliss and political conscience, he goes out into the streets again.

We have been here before, in Argentine novels, in this double invisible net where the secret police and the revolutionary underground intersect on a street corner—for example, Manuel Puig's *Kiss of the Spiderwoman*. What struck me, following Sanctis's increasingly ominous perambulations, was how Borgesian this Buenos Aires is—the practically endless, undistinguished streets that gather to themselves a mysterious maziness wherein a specific address becomes charged with some unspeakable spiritual burden. For Borges, Buenos Aires is not just a city, or even his city, but all cities, a horizontal, paved embodiment of our human lostness. In an early poem, "Daybreak," he wrote:

> In the deep universal night
> scarcely dispelled by the flickering gaslamps
> a gust of wind coming out of nowhere
> stirs the silent streets
> with a trembling presentiment
> of the hideous dawn that haunts

like some lie
the tumbledown outskirts of cities all over the world.

As Sanctis approaches, at three in the morning, the second of his two addresses, the author asserts that "something is taking place here in these placid middle-class streets in Villa Urquiza, among old acacias, rubbish bins, pretty little houses, and the silent padding of some cat on the prowl— something serious, something we don't want to explain too closely." Beneath the surface of social order, something atrocious waits. As with Kafka's, Borges's allegories may be less cosmic and more political than we think. His favorite adjectives—"atrocious" and "labyrinthine"—touch on life in a totalitarian state, and what is the Minotaur who fascinates him but the Dictator, brute power lurking and waiting to consume those trapped in the maze of inscrutable prerogatives and prohibitions? Borges's curious theology of defective or malign gods and the terror that fringes his stately anecdotes merely give the news, it may be, about Latin-American absolutism. As Costantini's hero moves through "the labyrinth of his own city," he evokes other books surveyed here: "with the desperate gesture of a shipwrecked sailor," he beckons a waiter and reminds us of Luis Velasco adrift on the "dense sea filled with strange creatures," and in reflecting upon "this miasma of stupidity and violence in which we're plunged up to our necks" he sums up the viscid immersion of *A Funny Dirty Little War*. All three short narratives make us feel a desperate insecurity, a dreadful bottomlessness to things, a moral chaos in which a bland decent Everyman like Sanctis becomes, against the dark background, a saint.

Adolfo Bioy Casares has been known in the English-speaking world primarily as a friend and collaborator of Jorge Luis Borges, and the co-author of the ornate literary jokes of *Chronicles of Bustos Domecq* (1967). Bioy Casares, however, is a prolific and successful writer on his own, and nearly a generation younger than Borges—he was born in 1914, and Borges in 1899. (Gabriel García Márquez was born in 1928, Augusto Roa Bastos in 1917, Osvaldo Soriano in 1943, Humberto Costantini in 1924.) Bioy Casares's *The Invention of Morel and Other Stories* arrives with a double Borgesian stamp: a preface by the master to the long title story and pen-and-ink illustrations by Norah Borges de Torre, Borges's sister. The illustrations are clumsy and few and do little harm. The preface is a provocative and revealing critical document; like *The Invention of Morel*, it dates from 1940. It claims that this *Invention* is perfect ("To classify it as perfect is neither an imprecision nor a hyperbole") and represents a blow in the good fight against that deplorable nineteenth-century invention, the plotless "psychological" novel, which includes Balzac, the Russians, and Proust. Borges was, we might say, the first self-consciously postmodern writer; his rebellion against Proust and Joyce and Woolf and James took the form of preferring Shaw, Wilde, Wells, and Chesterton. His preface offers the detective story—at its peak in the Thirties—as an example of what "works of reasoned imagination" might be. He and Bioy Casares collaborated on detective stories as well as on film scripts, anthologies, and translations. In a sense, Bioy Casares—whom Borges called "really and secretly the master" in these collaborations—armed the Borgesian counterrevolution. He provided boyish bravado, a typewriter, and, in *The Invention of Morel*, a prime text; the little novel won a municipal literary award in Buenos Aires and impressed such rising literati as Octavio Paz and Julio Cortázar. Further, it came to the attention of another postmodern theorizer, Alain Robbe-Grillet, and inspired the betranced repetitions and overlaps of his film *Last Year at Marienbad*.

Read in 1986, *The Invention of Morel* entertains in the dated way of science fiction by Wells or Jules Verne. Technology betrays its own acolytes: Wells's Time Machine was a late-Victorian gewgaw, a "glittering metallic framework" with parts of nickel and ivory and crystal, a kind of idealized elevator cage, and Alfred Jarry went into futuristic raptures over the then-newest thing, the bicycle. Bioy Casares, as of 1940, was understandably struck by the inventions of the motion-picture projector and the phonograph, which preserve reality as seen and heard; he imagines an island where an obsessed inventor, Morel, has constructed machines, tirelessly powered by the tides, that over and over project, in three palpable dimensions, the same recorded scenes of a week among friends. Thus he has created a kind of paradise, an eternity of returns; the original objects captured by his superphotography unfortunately wither and perish, but this seems a modest price to pay. Onto this island blunders our nameless narrator, who slowly comes to understand the illusion and, eventually, to enroll in it. Movies can't *do* that, we want to protest, just as elevators and bicycles can't become time machines. Nevertheless, there are ingenious technological twists: doors that normally open freeze shut when they are being projected, and broken walls implacably heal, sealing our hero in. And there are poignant moments: one of the projected beings, Faustine, becomes a love object for the castaway, and, as he disintegrates, his early life in Venezuela, from which he is a political exile, becomes another frozen paradise, projected in his head. But our interest in this rather too intricate fable, and in the six accompanying short stories from a 1948 volume, *La trama celeste*, tends to be magnetized by the elements that are, with a striking distinctness, Borgesian.

What could be more like Borges than this dream: "When I slept this afternoon, I had this dream, like a symbolic and premature commentary on my life: as I was playing a game of croquet, I learned that my part in the game was killing a man. Then, suddenly, I knew I was that man"? Or the lilt of these sentences, with their lifted eyebrow of complicated disclaimer: "He said that he waved his hand, and immediately afterward the gesture seemed false"; "After an extended stay in Paris, Horvath had returned to his own country, almost famous and totally discredited"; "He treated love and women with a dispassionate scorn that was not devoid of courtesy"? Or these fey modifiers, so curiously vibrant: "I experienced an intimate heaviness in my arms and legs"; "She was wearing a dress that was extremely green"; "He had deep circles under his eyes and an expression of astonished fatigue"? Borges's favorite adjective, "atrocious," recurs in Bioy Casares, and the image of a labyrinth, and that Borgesian device of the heterogeneous list, shorthand for the inventory of the maddeningly infinite universe. Abrupt islands of mathematical and topological distinctness imply the surrounding vague vastness, and the paradoxes of philosophical idealism are pursued to their monstrous conclusions. A dandified Gnosticism speaks in such an epigram as "To be alive is to flee, in an ephemeral and paradoxical way, from matter."

The imitation is startling; who was imitating whom? Borges came late to prose fiction; his first collection, *The Garden of Forking Paths*, was published in 1941, the same year Bioy Casares won his prize for *The Invention of Morel*. The older man may well have learned from the younger, or at least acquired from him the courage of his own predilections. But to turn from even the best of Bioy Casares's short stories ("The Celestial Plot," say, or "The Perjury of the Snow") to those of Borges is to reënter the realm of literature; there is greater concision and concreteness, a superior richness of mock-erudition and arch cross-reference, a jauntier and more challenging style. A poetic vision has entered in, and— we do not readily associate this quality with Borges—a warmth, a heat such as is generated deep in the geological strata, a spontaneous combustion of compacted learning and sublimated feeling. Even in those Borges short stories—"The Garden of Forking Paths," "Death and the Compass," "An Examination of the Work of Herbert Quain"—closest to the detective story there is an expansiveness of allusion, an amused intensity of tone that liberates us into something new, a fresh atmosphere, a frontier. These few dense and quirky *ficciones* lifted the lid on Latin-American fantasy, as Gogol's "Overcoat" supposedly ignited the great explosion of Russian fiction. "Magic realism," then, can be seen to have a pedigree that reaches from Borges, back through the fantasy of Chesterton and Stevenson—circumventing the triumphs of the realist-psychological novel—clear to Hawthorne and Poe. Bioy Casares's tales sound like Poe; they employ the first-person voice of detective fiction (an omniscient narrator would have to give the mystery away) and of travellers' tales and journals—the voice of Robinson Crusoe and Arthur Gordon Pym, of European man in the menacing strangeness of the New World.

Resisting the Big Boys

WHO KILLED PALOMINO MOLERO? by Mario Vargas Llosa, translated from the Spanish by Alfred Mac Adam. 151 pp. Farrar, Straus & Giroux, 1987.

OF LOVE AND SHADOWS, by Isabel Allende, translated from the Spanish by Margaret Sayers Peden. 274 pp. Knopf, 1987.

CLANDESTINE IN CHILE: *The Adventures of Miguel Littín,* by Gabriel García Márquez, translated from the Spanish by Asa Zatz. 116 pp. Holt, 1987.

The Peruvian man of letters Mario Vargas Llosa is almost too good to be true; cosmopolitan, handsome, and versatile, he puts a pleasant and reasonable face on the Latin-American revolution in the novel, and, in such gracious public performances as his panel appearances in New York last year and in Washington this, makes everybody, even North Americans, feel better about being a writer. Yet his fiction has a gritty side, a mode in which the ugly native truths of poverty and brutality abrasively rub through his debonair inventiveness. His recent *Real Life of Alejandro Mayta,* while in a sense mocking the unreal aspirations and clammy psyche of its Trotskyite hero, also conveyed the sour taste and decaying texture of modern-day Lima and in some of its incidental episodes penetratingly savored of private, as well as political, squalor. Even his farcical love-romp, *Aunt Julia and the Scriptwriter,* has some authentically harsh touches among its antic, ironically fabricated episodes, and at the end returns the reader to reality with a bump. Vargas Llosa's newest fictional offering, *Who Killed Palomino Molero?,* is nasty, brutish, and short; its first words are "Sons of bitches,"* and its first page displays the body of a young man tortured to death:

> The boy had been both hung and impaled on the old carob tree. His position was so absurd that he looked more like a scarecrow or a broken

---

*"Holy shit" in the proof version. "*Jijunagrandísimas,*" in the original.

marionette than a corpse. Before or after they killed him, they slashed him to ribbons: his nose and mouth were split open; his face was a crazy map of dried blood, bruises, cuts, and cigarette burns.

The time is 1954, in the strongman Presidency of General Manuel Apolinario Odría, an era of Peruvian history in which Vargas Llosa has located most of his novels. The place is Talara, in northern Peru; the protagonists are two members of the Guardia Civil, Lieutenant Silva and Officer Lituma, who, with resources so slender they must take the town's one taxi on their investigative journeys, attempt to unravel the murder. The victim, they soon discover, was Palomino Molero, a young recruit at the local Air Force base, who was distinguished chiefly by his lovely voice and his skill at singing boleros. The Air Force is not coöperative, and Lieutenant Silva, who has some of Sherlock Holmes's uncanny gifts, persists in his investigation mainly as a favor to his Watson, Lituma, who has been touched and rendered indignant by the crime. Silva seems to know that the society will ill reward their successful police work, and his interest keeps slipping to an incongruous amorous pursuit of Doña Adriana, the hefty married proprietress—"old enough to be his mother"—of a local restaurant. Yet he and Lituma detect on, through a series of dusty and heated interviews that in sum sketch the meagre, furtive, and faintly menacing life of the Peruvian provinces. The ruling oligarchy of "the big boys" figures as a presiding apathy, an ominous airlessness in which the two policemen gasp for truth.

The Pacific coastal-desert towns are less cheerful in their torpor than Gabriel García Márquez's Caribbean Macondo. In Piura, the victim's home town, the air smells of "carob trees, goats, birdshit, and deep frying." Talara's principal recreational facilities are a whorehouse on the edge of town and an outdoor movie theatre whose screen is the wall of the parish church ("so Father Domingo determined which movies . . . could show") and whose projector needs to be reloaded after every reel: "The movies, accordingly, were strung out in pieces and were extremely long." The weather is hot, the nearby oil refinery's housing compound with its gringos and swimming pool keeps the locals aware of their lowly status, and an emphatic racism divides the society. Officer Lituma (who figures, at least in name, in one of the soap-opera episodes of *Aunt Julia*) is a *cholo,* a half-breed, and as such instinctively subservient to Lieutenant Silva, who is "fair-skinned, young, good-looking, with a little blond mustache." Palomino Molero was also a *cholo,* and Lituma sympathetically imagines him "in the half light of the streets where Piura's purebreds lived, beneath the wrought-iron bars on the balconies belonging to girls he could never love, captivating them with his pretty voice." When Molero and the daughter of the base commandant, Colonel Mindreau, fall in love, trouble is certain. In Lituma's view, the Air Force men "all thought they were bluebloods," and also thought "the Guardia Civil was a half-breed outfit they could look down on." "These damned whites," Lituma says to himself. Another character complains of being treated "like some damned nigger." Generally we credit our Latin-American neighbors with less racism than northern Europe and the United States. As the historian Allan Nevins rather grandly put it: "Aside from a small white ruling class, society in the greater part of Spanish America was comparatively level and devoid of racial antipathies. . . . Long before the Moorish conquests, before even Hannibal's invasions, the people of what are now Spain and Portugal had been familiar with their African neighbors, had intermingled with them, and had learned to attach no excessive importance to the color line. The burnished livery of the sun carried little if any stigma." But in Peru, where the sun-protected viceregal aristocracy lived and ruled and where a mining economy was based upon Indian slavery, distinctions of bloodline are still jealously observed, to judge from Vargas Llosa's fiction. The question of his title implies the answer "the society"—a society, we see in the flurry of idle gossip at the end of this detective novel, willing to believe anything but the truth.

Sherlock Holmes and his myriad successors in American and English mystery fiction had the satisfaction of social approval; the identified criminal was hauled off to justice, and the detective's ingenuity was richly remunerated, sometimes, by a grateful client. At the least, a significant clarification was achieved and the rule of law and reason reaffirmed. In the Peru of *Who Killed Palomino Molero?* the diligent detectives are demoted, and their findings dissolved in a babble of xenophobic rumor: "With all these murders there had to be Ecuadoreans in the woodpile." For the book's final words, Lituma again pronounces, "Sons of bitches," and such do seem to be running this corner of the New World as of 1954. What, then, impels our two officers of the Guardia Civil to serve, via rickety taxi and rough encounter, the cause of truth and justice? Claude Lévi-Strauss, in *Tristes Tropiques,* asks much the same question in regard to the chiefs of the nearly extinct Nambikwara Indians: why do men seek power when it offers next to no rewards? He concludes, "It is because there are, in every group of human beings, men who, unlike their companions, love importance for its own sake, take a delight in its responsibilities, and find rewards enough in those very burdens of public life from which their fellows shrink." Just as no society is ideal enough to erase our darker impulses, so our more noble and altruistic tendencies persist, it would seem, even in the worst-managed system.

* * *

Of Love and Shadows is Isabel Allende's second novel and is smaller, paler, and less magical than her first, *The House of the Spirits,* which transposed into an upper-class, Chilean key the dreamlike sweep of *One Hundred Years of Solitude.* Rather than the Trueba family living through eighty years of history, *Of Love and Shadows* tells of three families—the upper-class though no longer wealthy Beltráns, the middle-class Spanish émigrés the Leals, and the lower-class Ranquileos, whose mother, Digna, runs a farm and whose father, Hipólito, is a circus clown. One of the Ranquileo children, Evangelina (she is actually a Flores, but was switched with the real Evangelina Ranquileo in the hospital; the mothers, unable to buck the obdurate system, were compelled to abide by the mistake), becomes subject, at the age of fifteen, to noontime fits that are taken by some of the superstitious to signify sainthood. Irene Beltrán, a journalist, and Francisco Leal, a photographer, come together on assignment to cover this newsworthy phenomenon and then to investigate Evangelina's abrupt disappearance, and while investigating fall in love and into conflict with their unnamed country's military regime. Evangelina, during one of her trances, has struck Lieutenant Juan de Dios Ramírez and, with super-natural strength, thrown him out of the Ranquileo house. From this unconscious affront to military authority her own doom and that of Irene and Francisco flow. Evangelina is the only magical character in this some-what misty but basically realistic novel, and her fits, her curious swap with the Flores infant (also called Evangelina), and her alleged miracles consort uneasily with the book's burden of political protest. So-called magic real-ism I take to be basically a method of nostalgia: the past—personal, famil-ial, and national—weathers into fabulous shapes in memory without surrendering its fundamental truth. Fantasy, for García Márquez and his followers, is a higher level of honesty in the rendering of experiences that have become subjectivized and mythologized.* But in rousing the reader

---

*The author herself, in a charming essay, "A Few Words About Latin America" (trans-lated by Jo Anne Engelbert), claims that in Latin America "everything is so disproportion-ate that it borders on falsehood. The truth—when it exists—is found hidden in this tangle of multicolor threads with which we embroider reality, as if we were victims of a perpetual, collective hallucination." She claims a continental tendency "to walk along the borderline of fantasy, to incorporate the subjective into daily life," and traces it back to the first Spanish explorers: "Excited by what they saw, they tried to describe that new land, but the words of the Spanish language were not sufficient; they began to flounder desperately to express their ideas, inventing, exaggerating, creating fables. They thought they had seen cities of pure gold where children played jacks with diamonds, and human beings with a single huge eye in their foreheads and one leg in the middle of their bodies provided with a toe so big that at siesta time they raised it up and it gave them shade, like a parasol. The fantastic realism of Latin American literature began with the Chronicles of the Indies." The Guate-

to care about a contemporary evil—the thinly disguised Pinochet re-gime—fantasy intrudes as a softening veil; it allows us to take the protest more lightly. If Evangelina's miracles are merely a manner of speaking, then the cave of corpses that the lovers discover, and the good Cardinal to whom the lovers confide their discovery, and the ordeals and disguises to which they submit, also can be felt as a manner of speaking.

And speaking deteriorates into rhetoric. The diction suffers from prim-ness, of a radical rather than conservative bent. We read of Francisco's "black eyes shining with understanding; the boyish grin when he smiled; the different mouth, thin-lipped, hard, when he saw evidence of man's cruelty to man." A worker-priest is not merely described but posterized:

> Although José Leal did not claim to be the Cardinal's friend, he knew him through his work in the Vicariate, where often they worked side by side, united in their compassionate desire to bring human solidarity where divine love seemed to be lacking.

This sentence, with its concluding rap on God's knuckles, does help animate the worker-priest movement; but when it comes to a family parting, the mural style smears into lugubrious cliché:

> . . . and their voices and footsteps resounded dully in the desolate air like an ominous omen. . . . Tense, beyond words, they embraced for one last time. Father and son clasped each other for a long moment filled with unspoken promises and guidance. Then Francisco felt his mother in his arms, tiny and fragile, her adored face unseen against his chest, her tears at last overflowing. . . . When they turned the corner, a harsh sob of farewell escaped Francisco's breast, and the tears he had held back during that terrible evening rushed to his eyes. He sank to the threshold, his face buried in his hands, crushed by ineffable sadness.

Perhaps the translator should share the blame for "ominous omen" and "ineffable sadness"; in general the English seems stiff, compared with Magda Bogin's flowing version of the earlier novel.

Of Love and Shadows comes to life mostly in its corners: Professor Leal's quixotic vow never to wear socks until Franco is deposed, and Irene's fiancé's return from an Antarctic sojourn with "his skin burned almost

---

malen novelist Miguel Angel Asturias, in his Nobel Prize acceptance speech, traced magic realism back to the Popol Vuh, a compilation of ancient Mayan legends set down shortly after the Spanish Conquest. The phrase itself was coined by a German art critic, Franz Roh, in his book of 1925, *Nach-Expressionismus, Magischer Realismus,* which was published in Madrid in 1927 under the title *Realismo mágico.* The Cuban novelist Alejo Carpentier may have had this phrase in the back of his mind when, in 1949, he wrote of *"lo real maravilloso."*

black from the reverberating snow," and Señora Beltrán's old-age home full of senile dreamers and her young lover who lazes his life away in a far-off beach resort and her incorrigible taste for luxury and her vain armory of "little bottles of oil for her breasts, collagen for her throat, hormone lotions and creams for her skin, placental extract and milk oil for her hair, capsules and royal jelly and pollen of eternal youth." The senior Leals are unpredictable and vivid in the account of their escape from Fascist Spain and of their joint descent, when a son dies, into an abyss of mourning from which they jointly return. The mystery of why military dictatorships are repeatedly allowed to arise is illuminated in a phrase: Irene's soldier fiancé explains to her, "I thought the nation needed a respite from the politicians." A respite from politicians is what Oliver North, for his moment on television, offered enchanted millions; more tragically, it is what the Latin-American armed forces, from Bolívar on, have stood ready to offer the nations to our south.

A Chile both more real and more surreal than Isabel Allende's is fragmentarily glimpsed in *Clandestine in Chile: The Adventures of Miguel Littín*. Littín is a filmmaker who, in 1970, was appointed by President Salvador Allende to be head of the newly nationalized Chile Films. When, on September 13, 1973, the Allende government was toppled in a bloody coup led by General Augusto Pinochet, Littín just barely escaped with his life. Since 1973 he has lived with his family in Mexico and Spain, and his name has remained on the government list of exiles forbidden to return to Chile. In May of 1985, disguised as a Uruguayan businessman, he returned to Chile on a false passport, and for six weeks travelled throughout the country, directing a number of film crews in capturing, on over a hundred thousand feet of film, twenty-five hours of life under the Pinochet dictatorship. This footage was smuggled out and subsequently edited to make a four-hour film for television and a two-hour feature for movie theatres. In 1986, in Madrid, Littín described his feat to Gabriel García Márquez, and the novelist persuaded the filmmaker to undergo "a grueling interrogation, the tape of which ran some eighteen hours." Out of nearly six hundred pages of transcript García Márquez condensed the ten chapters of this short text, much as, over thirty years ago, as a young journalist in Bogotá, he produced from interviews with Luis Alejandro Velasco *The Story of a Shipwrecked Sailor*. Both narratives come to about a hundred printed pages, and in both cases the story and perhaps the words are another's but the élan is all Gabriel García Márquez's.

Just as the shipwrecked sailor, in his extremities of hunger, thirst, and isolation, manifested a fabulous poise and capacity for observation, the clandestine filmmaker, amid the perils and strangeness of his situation, shows a breathtaking insouciance. Coming into Santiago for the first time in twelve years, in a disguise that includes a fake Uruguayan accent, plucked eyebrows, a doctored hairdo, a twenty-pound weight loss, and the fancy, expensive clothes of a *momio* (a conservative bourgeois; literally, a mummy), and further equipped with a fake wife—a Chilean expatriate, called Elena, actively associated with the Chilean resistance—Littín endangered the whole scheme by impulsively hopping from a cab and mingling with the crowds:

> Elena tried to dissuade me, but she couldn't argue with me as vehemently as she would have liked, for fear the driver would overhear. In the grip of uncontrollable emotion, I had the taxi stop and jumped out, slamming the door. . . . I was weeping when I got back to the hotel a step ahead of curfew. The door had just been locked and the concierge had to let me in. Elena had registered for both of us and was in our room hanging up the antenna for the portable radio when I entered. She seemed calm, but the moment I was inside she blew up like a proper wife. It was inconceivable to her that I could have run the risk of walking the streets alone until the last minutes before curfew.

Further, while in Chile, he stares at policemen and attracts their attention, ignores the passwords the resistance has set up, takes spur-of-the-moment excursions, neglects to remove his notes from his suitcase and his true identity card from his wallet, and pays an improvised, after-curfew visit to his mother. He stays in the country to the very last minute, after his crews are gone; the police are closing in and the underground is signalling him to "Get out or go under," but he tries to arrange one more clandestine interview and comes within seconds of missing the plane out. He keeps pushing his luck, in short, like a good director upping the suspense in a movie.

His misadventures generate some gaudy imagery. Told to meet, at a certain street corner, "a blue Renault 12 with a sticker of the Society for the Protection of Animals on the windshield," he jumps into the first blue Renault that comes along, without checking for the sticker, and finds himself in the back seat of a chauffeur-driven car with a woman "no longer young but still very beautiful, dripping with jewels, provocatively perfumed, wearing a pink mink coat that must have cost two or three times as much as the car itself. She was an unmistakable but rarely encountered example of the Santiago upper crust." To this startled apparition he gives the password, "Where can I buy an umbrella at this hour?" Recovering her composure, the lady in pink mink obligingly asks her chauffeur to drop Littín off at a department store that is still open. On another confused occasion, a restaurant liaison with a member of the resistance is broken up by a punch-drunk ex-boxer, and, on a third, Littín hides from the police in a theatre where a spotlight suddenly hits him and he is made the butt of a stripteaser's lewd banter—a scene right out of Hitchcock. Moments of magic realism fringe our hero's hazardous travels: Pablo Neruda's house in Isla Negra ("this legendary place is neither an island nor black") trembles every ten or fifteen minutes throughout the day; and at Littín's boyhood home, his mother, "carrying a lighted candle in a candlestick, as in a Dickens novel," leads him to an exact reconstruction, complete with furniture and disordered papers, of his old study in Santiago, just as he had left it when he went into exile twelve years before. Glimmers of fantasy play, too, about his brave fellow conspirators; one wealthy, elderly woman who hides him talks like an old gangster film:

> She could not resign herself to the possibility that she had wasted her time bringing up children to be *momios,* playing canasta with moronic matrons, to end up knitting and watching tearjerkers on TV. At seventy, she had discovered that her true vocation was the armed struggle, conspiracy, and the headiness of audacious action.
> "Better than dying in bed with your kidneys rotting away," she said. "I'd prefer to go out in a street fight against the cops with a bellyful of lead."

Needless to say, both Littín and Isabel Allende see Pinochet as a monster and the Allende years as happy days when land was distributed, industries nationalized, and the masses given a break from centuries of oppression. Dying in the assault that partly destroyed the Moneda Palace, Allende became a holy martyr. Littín tells how the former leader's photograph was hidden, in one home, behind an image of the Virgin, and how in many homes floral offerings and votive lamps are placed before the small busts of Allende that were sold in the markets during his presidency. Such reported facts tell more of a story than the somewhat abstract romance and sugary socialism of *Of Love and Shadows.* Further, Littín's random encounters, as mediated through the ghost authorship of a great writer, afford us a politically unfiltered picture of life, a reality wherein the clandestine visitor keeps blundering up out of the underground and can entertain, concerning a beautiful rich woman who tries to help him buy a code-word umbrella, the passing thought, "She was as charming and warm as she was beautiful and one would have wished to linger in the pleasure of her company, forgetting, for just one night, repression, politics, even art." Without some anarchical openness to possibilities, the Latin-American novelist is in danger of writing whodunits wherein the government, invariably, did it.

THE EVIL EMPIRE

How the Other Half Lives

Moscow Circles, by Benedict Erofeev, translated from the Russian by J. R. Dorrell. 188 pp. Writers and Readers Publishing Cooperative and Norton, 1982.

The Joke, by Milan Kundera, translated from the Czech by Michael Henry Heim. 267 pp. Harper & Row, 1982.

The Polish Complex, by Tadeusz Konwicki, translated from the Polish by Richard Lourie. 211 pp. Farrar, Straus & Giroux, 1982.

Wouldn't it be nice to forget about the dreary old Iron Curtain and to read fiction from the Communist countries purely for its aesthetic and informational charms? In a few instances—Stanislaw Lem, for one, and the late Yuri Trifonov—political side-thoughts can be pretty well suppressed; we read a Pole's science fiction and a Russian's novellas of domestic distress much as if an Italian or a Canadian had written them. But this cannot be the case with the three novels at hand—the first published in samizdat in Russia; the second legally published in Czechoslovakia in 1967, to great success, but banned two years later, and the author eventually expatriated; and the third written by a well-established Polish author and filmmaker but denied official publication in Poland. All contain political grief. If fiction from Communist countries is to be read as prisoners' outcries, the first is a bellow, the second a complicated groan, and the third a lively shriek.

The bellow, or yelp, is Benedict Erofeev's *Moscow Circles.* * A strange stark photograph of "Erofeev" which might do for the face of a million young Russians appears on the jacket's back flap; a biography on the front

---

*Also published, in 1980, by Taplinger, and reprinted by Fawcett Books, as translated by H. W. Tjalsma, with the title *Moscow to the End of the Line.*

flap gives some plausible information (born in 1939 in the region of Vladimir, Erofeev was expelled from the University of Moscow for "exaggerated ideas," and worked for many years as an underground-cable layer) together with some that seems fanciful: "Written in one go in the autumn of 1969, this work was the result of a wager for two bottles of liquor. The loser forfeited not only the two bottles, but had to read the manuscript as well. . . . Animated by [his] success, Erofeev embarked on his *Dimitri Shostakovitch.* Unfortunately this manuscript was stolen on the Pavlovo-Moscow line—along with two bottles of vermouth, the object of the theft." The author's preface continues this jocular-bibulous tone, alleging that one chapter originally consisted of the words "And then I had a drink" followed by a page and a half of obscenities, which have been now deleted because "all readers, and especially young ladies," turned immediately to this chapter and skipped everything else. *Moscow Circles* describes the inner monologue and external encounters of Benny Erofeev, a hard-drinking cable layer, as he travels by train from Moscow to Petushki, a town in the Vladimir region where his white-eyed sweetheart and his three-year-old son, unknown to each other, reside. He is carrying chocolates for the one and walnuts for the other, but by the time his train gets there—a distance of about seventy miles—Petushki has become a nightmare Moscow, and the transcendentally drunken Erofeev is pursued by four ominous men whom the translator in a footnote identifies as Marx, Engels, Lenin, and Stalin. One of them carries an awl. Stalin's father was a cobbler. God, not infrequently invoked in the course of Benny's delirium, is silent. Angels who have been intermittently talking to Benny cruelly laugh. The book ends with the unconscious narrator's assurance "I have not come to since and I never shall."

Set forth in paragraphs with white spaces between, and in short chapters titled with the names of the railroad stations on the Moscow-Petushki line, the tale reads speedily and has the feverish, centrifugal verve of Gogol and Bely and that doctrinaire French alcoholic Alfred Jarry. In something of Jarry's spirit of berserk calculation, Benny offers cocktail recipes involving calibrated amounts of purified varnish, antiperspirant, verbena, and anti-dandruff shampoo. Weird efforts at precision approximate the spotty perceptions of drunkenness. Of a simpleton encountered on the train it is said, "He didn't speak with his mouth, because that was always peering and was somewhere at the back of his head. He talked with his left nostril, and with such an effort—as if he had to lift his left nostril with his right nostril to do so." Though its ambience is intoxication, the little novel has been soberly executed: a brisk pace is maintained, and the implication of an entire society soused and despairing is made to emerge gradually, with a certain force of horror. Everyone on the train accepts and gives drinks. The conductor is bribed with grams of vodka. Russian history is travestied as one immense, morose binge: "No wonder all Russia's honest citizens were desperate, how could they be anything but! They couldn't help writing about the lower classes, couldn't help saving them, couldn't help drinking in despair. The social democrats wrote and drank, in fact they drank as much as they wrote. But the Muzhiks couldn't read, so they just drank without reading a word. . . . All the thinking men of Russia drank without coming up for breath, out of pity for the Muzhiks." Soviet slogans and the Revolution itself are parodied amid the hazy vacillations of Benny's consciousness; early in his ride, he ironically echoes the claims for spiritual superiority that Soviet propagandists have adopted from the nineteenth-century Slavophiles:

> The passengers looked at me with something akin to apathy, eyes round and apparently vacant. That's what I like. I like the fact that my compatriots have such vacant and protruding eyes. They fill me with virtuous pride. You can imagine what eyes are like on the other side. There, where everything can be bought and sold. Over there eyes are deep set, predatory and frightened. . . . How different from the eyes of my people! Their steady stare is completely devoid of tension. They harbour no thought—but what power! What spiritual power!

Yet, though jokingly, *Moscow Circles* shares in that same power—a directness, a fury, a humor, a freedom from self-pity that seem Russian. There is nothing whining about this portrait of self-destructive muddle and descending alcoholic night: a dark exhilaration, rather. If Erofeev has indeed allowed a photograph of himself and biographical facts to be published here, for the KGB to take note of, then we must feel some exhilaration of our own at such bravado and at the courage still alive after sixty years of the Soviet system.

The picaresque hero—the rogue, the loser—is a traditional vehicle whereby an author conveys subversive thoughts. For Benny Erofeev, there is only a vague, unreachable "they" to blame: "Oh the bastards! They've turned my land into a shitty hell. They force people to hide their tears and expose their laughter!" But Ludvik Jahn, the hero of Milan Kundera's *The Joke*, was a student proponent of Communism when it came to Czechoslovakia in February of 1948, and a youthful Party functionary; so his disillusion with this system, and its with him, are traumatic matters that form a suitable central topic for a thoughtful, intricate, ambivalent novel. *The Joke* was Kundera's first novel, composed from 1962 to

1965, published in Prague in 1967 without a touch of censorship, and then banned (among many other books) when the Russians invaded Czechoslovakia in 1968 and crushed Dubček's brief "Prague spring." Having made and unmade Kundera's name in his native land, *The Joke* has enjoyed a considerable career abroad. Louis Aragon wrote a foreword for the French translation, calling it "one of the greatest novels of the century," and translations appeared not only in all the languages of "free" Europe but in Polish and (though banned as it came off the press) Hungarian as well. The first English translation, in Great Britain, was sufficiently abridged and, in the author's opinion, "mutilated" to warrant a letter of protest to the *Times Literary Supplement;* in spite of apologies and adjustments, the English versions have remained incomplete until the issue of this new translation, prepared by an American professor and overseen by the author, who since 1975 has been a resident of France.

It is an impressive work, if not altogether great yet with the reach of greatness in it. Like Kundera's most recent work of fiction, the widely admired *The Book of Laughter and Forgetting,* the novel contains a hero "fallen" from a socialist "paradise," a running imagery of angels (perhaps traceable to the wealth of Counter-Reformation statuary in Czechoslovakia), a robust and subtle eroticism, a fervent and knowledgeable musicality (extending to fugal ingenuities in the narrative's organization), and a philosopher's concern with the importance that illusion and forgetting have for man and his systems. Less flashy and etherealized than the later novel, *The Joke* seems to me more substantial—more earnest in its explorations and less distractingly nimble in its counterpoint. Written within and for a society controlled by Communists, *The Joke* contains none of the frivolous bitterness and nihilism common in the West; its bitterness has been hard-earned and is presented at risk.

Ludvik Jahn, a prize student, gifted musician, and rising Party loyalist, falls from official grace through a joke: he sends a girl he wishes to tease and impress a postcard reading:

> Optimism is the opium of the people! A healthy atmosphere stinks of stupidity! Long live Trotsky!

Such irreverence on a postcard does not go overlooked; inexorably Ludvik is investigated, summoned, and expelled not only from the Party but from the university. The military is the compulsory option left to him, and he is assigned with other suspect recruits to the penal battalion, which wears a black insignia and mines coal. The process of his disgrace and the life of the penal camp are described with a convincing calm realism, the emphasis laid less on their cruelty than on the victim's psychological adjustments. Ludvik's fellow soldiers in the camp of outcasts are given human variety and plausible raisons d'être; even the brutal, histrionic boy commander who heads up the camp is analyzed and excused: "The young can't help acting: they're thrust immature into a mature world and must *act* mature. . . . Youth is a terrible thing: it is a stage trod by children in buskins and fancy costumes mouthing speeches they've memorized and fanatically believe but only half understand." The one camp inmate who gets destroyed is the one fanatic Communist, pathetically determined to prove himself loyal. The others do what they must, slack where they can, and cope with their sexual frustration. They are paid for their labors and allowed some weekend leaves. Ludvik makes the acquaintance of a virtually mute, shabbily dressed girl of the people, Lucie, and his love for her, fed by the gifts of flowers she slips through the barbed wire that usually separates them, is the one pure note of his life. They never consummate this love. They fight when she denies him sex, and Lucie disappears. After five years of laboring, Ludvik manages to resume his studies and eventually rises to a high position in an unspecified research institute. (Kundera himself was a professor at the Institute for Advanced Cinematographic Studies.)

Ludvik Jahn's memory of his expulsion from the Party, of the meeting that decided it—"Everyone present (and there were about a hundred of them, including my teachers and my closest friends), yes, every last one of them raised his hand to approve my expulsion"—and of the former friend, Zemanek, who delivered the eloquent address recommending expulsion, has poisoned his life and his relation with humanity. "Since then, whenever I make new acquaintances, men or women with the potential of becoming friends or lovers, I project them back into that time, that place, and ask myself whether they would have raised their hands; no one has ever passed the test." An opportunity arises, after fifteen years, to avenge himself upon Zemanek; Ludvik seizes it, with complex and unforeseen results. All the plot's threads are wound around a busy three days Ludvik spends in his home town, an unnamed community in Moravia where, as it happens, Lucie has reappeared and the streets are filled with a collective enactment of the Ride of the Kings, an ancient folk ceremony that the Party now administers. The climax of the novel is too crowded, too freighted with symbolization and pronouncement, and aspects of the denouement border too closely on farce. But this terminal congestion testifies to the fullness of the material and the pressure with which it bore upon the author.

Two old friends Ludvik encounters are Jaroslav, first fiddle in the town's cimbalom ensemble and an ardent folklorist, and Kostka, a doctor in the local hospital and a Christian whose faith has cost him several official posts. Both men, in their individual chapters of monologue, articulate their master passions and relate them to the country's socialism with striking brilliance. Kostka believes that materialism is unnecessarily linked to socialism; he mentally addresses the atheist Ludvik:

> Do you really think that people who believe in God are incapable of national-izing factories? . . . The revolutionary era from 1948 to 1956 had little in common with skepticism and rationalism. It was an era of great collective faith. . . . In the end the era turned coat and betrayed its religious spirit, and it has paid dearly for its rationalist heritage, swearing allegiance to it only because it failed to understand itself. Rationalist skepticism has been eating away at it without destroying it. But Communist theory, its own creation, it will destroy within a few decades. It has already done so in you, Ludvik. And well you know it.

Jaroslav finds the collective essence in folk music, and entertains us with a rapturous evocation of the levels of history he hears in the melodies of southern Moravia: brass-band tunes from the last seventy years, syncopated gypsy czardas from the nineteenth century, the songs of the native Slav population in the seventeenth and eighteenth centuries, late-medieval Wallachian shepherd songs "completely innocent of chords and harmony," four-tone mowing and harvest songs from the great ninth-century Moravian empire, and, finally, songs analogous to ancient Greek music—"the same Lydian, Phrygian, and Dorian tetrachords." Jaroslav's dream, unrealized, is to give his beloved folk music the world-wide currency of jazz, for, like jazz, it is a music of improvisation and rhythmic originality. While such fascinating passages of exposition run on, Kundera's plot stands still, and his Ludvik, Jaroslav, and Kostka speak too much with one voice, so that a single erudite professor seems to be discussing from three angles how Marxism failed him. But the virtue of these passionate digressions, much as with Mann's spoken lectures in *The Magic Mountain,* lies in their dense enrichment of the novel's locus and the significant weight they add to its incidents. *The Joke* is not ultimately about Communism, or love, or misanthropy; it is about a patch of land called, in recent times, Czechoslovakia. Most novels that strike us as great, come to think of it, give us, through the consciousness of characters, a geography amplified by history, a chunk of the planet.

Czechoslovakia could well have become another Austria; the last of the satellite countries to fall into Russia's orbit, and the most progressive and industrialized, it had itself—that is to say, a powerful domestic Communist movement—largely to blame. The ideology in *The Joke* is discussed in a geopolitical vacuum, as an internal debate encapsulated within each thinking citizen. Poland, on the other hand, has for centuries defined itself against the encroachments of the Germans to the west and the Muscovites to the east, and the ideology of Tadeusz Konwicki's *The Polish Complex* is purely nationalistic. The novel's hero—who, like the hero of *Moscow Circles*, bears the name of the author—is standing in line in front of a state-owned jewelry store in Warsaw, with dozens of others, waiting for a promised shipment of gold rings from the Soviet Union, the purchase of which will convert their sheaves of thousand-zloty bills into something of solider value. It is the day before Christmas. The rings never arrive; instead, Russia sends Poland a shipment of electric samovars, with a promise of five free trips to the Soviet Union to "customers with lucky sales slips." But there is time in the waiting line for many conversations and encounters, and many reflections by the fifty-year-old, ailing, depressed author. He reflects that nations, like people, are lucky or unlucky:

> Russia always had luck. The tsars slaughtered their own people, established the stupidest and most ignorant laws, embroiled themselves in the riskiest of wars, set unreal political goals, and the foolish always became the wise, the reactionary the progressive, and defeat was changed to victory. . . . The ignorant, obscurantist despotism, the barbarity of the higher spheres, the people's poverty, the arbitrary, stupid, venal officials, the unbelievable indolence of the leaders, the most reactionary laws and customs, the savagery of human relations, all this, instead of inundating the state in disgraceful anarchy . . . went into the laborious building of old Russia's power, her supremacy, her greatness among the nations of the old continent.
>
> In Poland, the nobility of educated monarchs, the energy of intelligent ministers, the goodwill of the citizenry, the homage to mankind's lofty ideas, in Poland all these positive, exemplary, copybook values were, quite unexpectedly, devalued. Out of the blue, they were prostituted and dragged the venerable corpse of the republic straight to the bottom like a millstone.

The Polish Complex is as zany as *Moscow Circles* and as intellectual as *The Joke*. Konwicki, born near Wilno, which is now part of Soviet Lithuania, fought as a teen-age Partisan in 1944–45, and in his early writings supported the new Communist order. A screenwriter and director as well as a productive author, he, until *The Polish Complex*, expressed his disillusions obliquely enough not to rouse the censors. Here in this banned novel, which was published in the underground Polish press in 1977, he seems to express a personal crisis as well as political exasperation; the

Konwicki persona drinks too many "binoculars" (two tall hundred-gram glasses of vodka), has chronic pain in his chest, suffers a heart attack, and while recovering from the attack in a back room copulates with a voluptuous shop attendant who calls him "old man." "I've been through it all," he tells her. "I have no curiosity left, my curiosity's exhausted, or actually, it was never satisfied and now nothing will satisfy it." He sees himself as "a miserable creature with emphysema of the soul." He invites a man, who claims to have been on his trail since 1951, to kill him, and steps out on the railing of a ruined balcony to make it easy for his assassin. The invitation is not taken, the night fritters away, and Christmas morn approaches by the glow of the feeble hope that "there is some sense to all this senselessness."

The texture of the present-day, ostensibly autobiographical passages is airy, startling, disjointed, and deft—somewhat like that of Raymond Queneau, if Queneau had been a less happy man. Konwicki enjoys that easy access to the surreal noticeable in Polish writers as disparate as Lem and Witold Gombrowicz and Bruno Schulz, as Jerzy Kosinski and I. B. Singer. But our attention scatters amid these tipsy incidents and arguments; it is in two extended historical fantasies that Konwicki shows his imaginative strength and brings the reader into the continuing Polish agony. The first, over fifty pages long, describes the attempt of a twenty-three-year-old soldier, Zygmunt Mineyko, to lead, under the name Colonel Macidj Borowy, a section of the uprising of 1863, one of a number of unsuccessful nationalist rebellions in the long century (1795–1918) when Poland didn't exist on the map, having been partitioned among its three large neighbors; the second historical episode, in a later time of troubles, shows another young man, with the name of Traugutt, saying goodbye to his wife in a hotel room before going off to accept "the leadership of the People's Government" in Warsaw—an assignment certain to cost him his life. No doubt both these doomed heroes are enshrined in the collective Polish memory; for any reader the sense of circumambient oppression, of terror and futile daring and bravery amid the details of the daily are evoked with a masterly command of such sensory realities as the noises of drunken Russian officers in the adjoining hotel room and the singing sound of sand spinning from the wheels of a carriage. Of course, Communist writers have often sought breathing space in historical fiction, where dangerous contemporary issues can be avoided or disguised, and are at home there; nevertheless, the immediacy of these "old-fashioned" pieces of Konwicki's narrative oddly overpowers the whimsical, skittish rest. A sexy strain of imagery does link the Polish past and present: the desirable women all savor of grass and herbs. Colonel Borowy admires a young wife whose eyes "shimmered with the colors of moss and heather" and whose scent is mingled of "sleep, lovage herb, and impetuous love." Traugutt's wife "gave up her warm cloak, which smelled of heather," and, when she was further undressed, "her damp sweat . . . smelled like herbs." Our aging author joins these warriors whose "sweetheart [was] Poland, golden-haired Poland," when, rather ignominiously couched with his shop assistant, he finds "she smelled like the wild herbs of the earth." An earth that, in the Polish complex, floats underfoot, not quite possessed, parcelled out, dominated by others historically and now.

Estrangement—from earth, sky, and the ruling powers in between—is not absent from Western contemporary literature, either, and there is no assurance that under a capitalist system Erofeev would drink less, Ludvik would find it easier to locate what he calls "final beauty," or Konwicki would be spared the discomforts of turning fifty. Yet all three books have been outlawed in their respective homelands, and therefore must contain words judged dangerous by the authorities. The absurd cowering by Communist governments in the face of honest and questioning art is one of the wonders of the world, a fertile source of embarrassment to its enforcers and an apparent declaration of bad faith; for from such fear of the truth we can only deduce a power that believes itself to be based upon lies.

Out of the Evil Empire

ANOTHER LIFE *and* THE HOUSE ON THE EMBANKMENT, by Yuri Trifonov, translated from the Russian by Michael Glenny. 350 pp. Simon and Schuster, 1983.

WILD BERRIES, by Yevgeny Yevtushenko, translated from the Russian by Antonina W. Bouis. 296 pp. Morrow, 1984.

RUSSIAN WOMEN: *Two Stories,* by I. Grekova, translated from the Russian by Michel Petrov. 304 pp. Harcourt Brace Jovanovich, 1983.

THE ISLAND OF CRIMEA, by Vassily Aksyonov, translated from the Russian by Michael Henry Heim. 369 pp. Random House, 1983.

The Russians seem to be receding. It is not just that our President cracks jokes about outlawing them and calls them an evil empire; their own chiefs of state, from the sickly late Brezhnev to the sallow and infirm Andropov to today's far from entirely healthy Chernenko, have become wan, and the Russian global presence is signified by a muffled, stubborn war in Afghanistan and by non-appearance—at the Olympics, at the conference table. One remembers with a perhaps soft-headed fondness the old days of Khrushchev in America, banging his shoe at the U.N. and waggling his hips at Disneyland. And one turns to some contemporary Russian fiction with genuine curiosity as to life in our recessive fellow super-power's territory, on that portion of our planet's surface just about equal, in acreage, to what we can see of the moon.

Yuri Trifonov had emerged, in the last decade of his rather short life (1925–81), as the most sensitive and honest of officially published Soviet fiction writers. The son of an Old Bolshevik who fell from favor under Stalin and disappeared, Trifonov, when young, wrote a novel that won a Stalin Prize. In middle age he turned apolitical and became a first-rate writer; his chosen form was the novella, and his subject the private lives of white-collar Russians—professors, translators, theatrical people. Three of his novellas were translated and published here in 1978, under the title *The Long Goodbye*. Now two more, *Another Life* and *The House on the Embankment*, are available, in one volume. All take place in Trifonov's recognizable world, a dense world of edgily multi-generational families crowded into Moscow apartments, of dachas and seaside vacations as escape hatches into the romantic, of mysterious and ominous professional rises and falls, of admirable women and unhappy men, of nagging dissatis-faction and nostalgia, a world described in leisurely loops of flashback, with something of Chekhov's tenderness and masterly power of indirect revelation.

Another Life transpires in the reminiscing mind of Olga Vasilievna, whose husband, Sergei, has recently died. She and her teen-age daughter, Irinka, still live with Sergei's mother, Alexandra Prokofievna, who pos-sesses a law degree and whose husband, a mathematics professor, died in the 1941 defense of Moscow. She is a staunch Communist and forgiving neither of her granddaughter's typically adolescent behavior nor of her daughter-in-law's supposed guilt: "This woman firmly believed that the death of her son, in November of the previous year from a heart attack at the age of forty-two, was the fault of his wife." Olga's memories, as if searching out the justice of this charge, move back through her seventeen years of marriage, beginning with a sunny Black Sea vacation and ending under a Moscow cloud as Sergei, a historian, somehow offends the aca-demic higher-ups with his researches into the Czar's secret police. Throughout their relationship, Olga has been distressed by the other women whom her moody and elusive husband has attracted, and by his fickle professional enthusiasms. A successful biologist, reasonable and shrewd enough to see in Sergei and his family an "emotional ineptitude and a compulsion to do only what pleased them," she nevertheless is "psychologically dependent" upon him and fiercely defensive of what is consistently italicized as *"their life"*—"their life" as opposed to the "separate life" he keeps living during his mysterious escapes from domesticity and "another life" of which he often dreams. In the surprising ending, it is Olga who finds "another life," with a nameless man who sounds even frailer in health than Sergei and who, from his coy anonymity (in a narrative where even the most fleeting characters are named), might be a version of the author. Trifonov dedicated the book to his wife, Alla, and seems to have reaped the benefit of detailed female confidences. As a portrait of Olga in her stages of young beauty and mature weariness, in her moods of happiness and anger, in her conflicting roles as mother, lover, daughter, and worker, *Another Life* has been executed with an air of natural understanding and admiration. "Look at this woman!—she exists!" the book seems to exclaim, and only the warmth of the exclamation suggests that the creator and the creation are not of the same sex.

The House on the Embankment also describes balked academic careers, rotting but embowering dachas, heavy-drinking men with adverse cardiovascular symptoms, and deliberate efforts of reminiscence. For Trifonov, too, the novella seems to have been an exercise in reminiscence; it reworks many of the characters that appeared in his first novel, *Students* (1950). One of these seems to be a stand-in for the author: "Yura the Bear" narrates intermittent chapters of this tale of ambition and aging, and Trifonov spent much of his childhood in privileged housing like "the house on the embankment." The apartments within are spacious and the top stories have a view, across the Moscow River, of the Kremlin walls; its shadow cuts off sunlight from the shabby little house where lives Vadim Alexandrovich Glebov, with his father, grandmother, and Aunt Paula in one room, while six other families crowd into the other rooms. The Glebov boy's jealousy of those who live above him in the apartment house forms "a source of burning resentment from his childhood onward." The schoolboy episodes of this novella reminded me of the coarse nicknames and dangerous pranks of Günter Grass's *Cat and Mouse* and Shusako Endo's *When I Whistle;* they reflect a more Spartan youth culture than that sketched in, say, *Penrod.* The author's treatment of Glebov—who from his shabby beginnings rises to betray (slightly) his literature professor and to become a literary functionary with a spoiled and silly daughter and international travel privileges—reminded me of Chekhov's

"The Darling," or, rather, of Tolstoy's well-known commentary upon it, to the effect that Chekhov, setting out to satirize his character, "intended to curse, but the god of poetry forbade him, and commanded him to bless."

Trifonov, whose own father fell to the unanswerable workings of tyranny, and who as an author had to maneuver his realism into print through the ever-present maze of official scruples, must have had little use for characters like Glebov. He portrays him as timid, indecisive, and materialistic; yet the timidity and indecision are so empathetically limned, and the materialism (Glebov is a great noticer of clothing and furniture, with all the social resonance of such possessions) such a basically humble attribute, that the reader, like Glebov's betrayed fiancée, Sonya, loves him in spite of himself. An apparatchik could hardly be more tenderly dismantled. The boy in his poverty begins by trading on the one meagre advantage he has: his mother sells tickets in a movie theatre and can let him in free, with what friends he chooses to bring. He ends, successful and afflicted by arteriostenosis, by failing to buy an antique table he had his heart set on; further, he is snubbed by a workman at the furniture market, whom he has suddenly recognized as a once powerful and flamboyant old school friend. A bit later, this same friend's mother, a former aristocrat also fallen in the social scale, has snubbed him on a train to Paris. We never see Glebov oppressing others, but only Glebov oppressed—oppressed not least by the need to make decisions. A splendid turn in the plot occurs when, on the eve of a fateful meeting at his university, where he must testify on one side or the other, his grandmother Nila, whom he loves ("Who else was there to love, if not old Nila?"), dies as if to spare him, on his day of mourning, this crossroads:

> "What can I say to you, Dima?" She looked at him with pity, with tears in her eyes, as though he and not she were dying: "Don't upset yourself, don't aggravate your heart. If there's nothing to be done about it, then don't think about it. It will all sort itself out, you'll see, and whatever that may be, it will be the right way. . . ."
>
> And strange to say he fell asleep that night easily, calmly and free of nagging anxiety. At six o'clock next morning he was suddenly awakened by a low voice, or it may have been by something else, and he heard someone say, "Our Grandmama Nila has gone. . . ."
>
> . . . Quietly, for fear of disturbing the neighbors, Aunt Paula was sobbing on the other side of the partition. The sound she made was strange and chilling, like the clucking of a chicken whose neck was being wrung. Glebov's father came in, muttering something about the doctor, a death certificate and the need to go somewhere. So began that Thursday. And Glebov was unable to go anywhere on that day.

Glebov's melancholy rise in the world is traced among so many such vivid vignettes and small scenes as to summarize the general flow of Russian life from 1940 to 1974. He is described, by the first-person voice whose disquisitions rather jarringly interlard Glebov's story, as "a *nothing person*"; but into this nothing, this cautious acquisitor of things, so much observed life rushes that a less passive and more principled hero would have seemed less human. "He dreamed of all the things that later came to him—but which brought him no joy because achieving them used up so much of his strength and so much of that irreplaceable something that is called life": a moral for many a capitalist tale as well.

At a student party in *A House on the Embankment*, one guest is "a poet who had been deafening people at student parties with his crashingly metallic verses—in those days, for some reason, they were regarded as highly musical. . . . Nowadays, thirty years later, the poet is still grinding out his brassy verse, but no one any longer thinks it musical—just tinny." It is a compliment, of sorts, to Yevgeny Yevtushenko's fame and durability that a Westerner, without presuming to judge what verse sounds brassy in Russian, thinks first of him in relation to this unkind allusion. Born in 1933 and still going strong, Yevtushenko has managed to steer a daredevil course amid the perils of being a poet, a crowd-pleaser, a sometime protester, a travelling emblem of Russian culture, and lately a movie director and actor—all this within the Soviet system, which since Lenin has insisted on its right to supervise the arts. Khrushchev, whose sanctioning of the publication of Solzhenitsyn's *One Day in the Life of Ivan Denisovich* in late 1962 unleashed hope for freer expression, personally took it upon himself, a few months later, to bring Yevtushenko to heel. More recently, Yuri Andropov publicly complained that "Trifonov and others devote too much concern for the minutiae of daily life without sufficient regard for the good of the Party, for whom they are not doing their bit." The Party has continued to allow Yevtushenko access to print and audiences because, my guess is, for all his rakish and rebellious tendencies he is a sincere patriot and genuinely at home in the poster-bright, semi-abstract realm of global aspiration wherein the slogans of the Revolution make some sense. Gone are the days, in Russia and the West alike, when he and Andrei Voznesensky were glamour boys, bringing to stadiums and auditoriums on both sides of the Iron Curtain word of the new possibilities stirring under Khrushchev. But neither poet has been silenced in the airless decades since, and Yevtushenko, who had earlier composed some short stories and a banned memoir (*A Precocious Autobiography*, 1963), published in 1981 a first novel that sold two and a half million copies. This book, *Wild Berries,* is now published here, in a typeface that looks muddy and a sexy pastel dust jacket that depicts two haystacks.

Yevtushenko, as a fiction writer, woefully lacks Trifonov's quality of patient truth—of calmly accruing detail, of psychologies permitted to find their own definition in inconsequential and contradictory movements. In *Wild Berries* the author is ostentatiously in charge, putting an epilogue first and a prologue last and, in between, pouring on importance from an unctuous overview, staging symposia and meaty dialogues in the Siberian taiga, importing significance-laden scenes from as far away as Hawaii and Chile. As a poet, Yevtushenko has developed an irritating trick of self-echo, as if repeating things renders them profound. *Wild Berries* begins, for example, with a hail of berries, as symbols of succulence, Siberian freedom, and female charms. A seduced and spurned woman ponders, "He's picked all my berries, and now he's looking for new berry patches"; another, also seduced and spurned woman sports "red bilberry nipples" and "dark, berrylike birthmarks" "sprinkled" on her "soft but blinding white" skin; and still another, while being seduced preliminary to being abandoned, has a full basket of berries spilled over her (of course) "naked breasts." Nor are berries the only foodstuff subject to overutilization; mushrooms, too, come in for a workout. A proposal of marriage is stimulated by the discovery of a "solid white mushroom" that the lady cuts off neatly, "leaving the root in the ground"; a few pages later, the children of this union are seen as "sturdy as white mushrooms." A few chapters on, an old mushroomer extols the earthy virtue of his speciality and, when his extolling day is done, dreams of "some extraordinary forest, where giant mushrooms grew taller than a man." His dreamwork leaving no symbol unturned, he cuts a gigantic one down so he can take it "to Hiroshima and show all mankind, to make them ashamed of that other, terrifying mushroom, invented by man."

The translator has matched the overwrought prose with some extraordinary efforts of English:

A wave of grandeur swept over his beak-nosed, time-ravaged face and washed away the wrinkles.

He had a cautious attitude toward social initiatives, feeling that in the long run they broke up into droplets against the moss-covered cliff of human psychology.

"And only when the boat was right inside the rapids' open jaws, dripping foamy saliva from the boulders that sat as solidly as molars . . ."

"Screw all these artists and correspondents," roared the president, something he did very rarely.

The heavy ore that holds these nuggets is the story of a party of geologists looking for cassiterite and the meaning of life in the taiga of Siberia; since Yevtushenko was born and bred in Siberia, and his father was a geologist, some authenticity leaches through his nobly hulking intention to write a panoramic novel of ideas. The stylized characters (hard-driving, out-of-touch-with-himself Kolomeitsev, the leader of the expedition; young, impressionable Seryozha; humpbacked, softhearted, highly mechanical Kesha; all-wise, often-silent Burshtein; fawning, villainous Sitechkin; and many others, not to mention the interchangeably delicious, berry-breasted young females who pop up in the forest like, well, mushrooms) and the stilted conversations ("If man came from the apes, then why didn't all the apes turn into people?" one man asks another as they head into some thundering rapids; the answer runs, in part, "Once upon a time the magnetic equilibrium of the earth was destroyed. And then some of the weaker apes underwent mutation") do not totally smother the author's joy in the space and sweet wildness of Siberia. His willingness to entertain basic questions is awkwardly allied with his coarsely imagined tale of adventure and seduction, of peasants who are diamonds in the rough and women who are loose cannons: "Her mighty breasts surged menacingly out from the shiny picture like a battleship's guns." In the absence of a restraining verisimilitude, the tale branches into such unusual familial scenes as that of a one-time seducer, now grown obese and decrepit, being given a prostate examination by a forty-three-year-old doctor who is, her "malachite eyes" tell him, his long-lost illegitimate daughter, and that of the reunion of four young American rock stars with their mothers, after a tumultuous concert, on a beach in Honolulu, where "the pure breeze from the ocean seemed to blow away the sweaty stink of the concert's roaring crowd." The scenes involving Americans, though they show that Yevtushenko has been around, have a patent falsity, a benign corniness, that serves as index to the falsity of *Wild Berries* throughout: the book is a pastiche, an assemblage of outsides and signifiers with no real insides or unwilled significance. Yevtushenko's inner self, glimpsable in *A Precocious Autobiography* and such early poems as "Zima Junction," shows here only in the brash naïveté of the novel's ambition.

The numerous characters in Trifonov's novellas fall into a consistent pattern. There is the generation of the aged, who were exposed to the heat and excitement of the Revolution and still feel it. There is that of the young, the punks and softies, who have felt only the heat of the West and its corrupting consumerism. And there is the middle generation, which fought and endured World War II; its members lack their parents' political certainties yet are nagged, unlike their children, by a collective conscience, by the suspicion that the blessings of peace and its relative prosperity, achieved through heroic victories over the Czar and then the Germans, are not enough, and fall short of some ideal. Glebov, for instance, has done nothing very wrong; yet he and the narrator seem to suspect and to imply that he is terribly in the wrong. Yevtushenko has now reached fifty and, however young at heart, belongs to the middle generation. A sophisticated and restive spirit, frequently at odds with the Soviet establishment and a staunch protester against the anti-Semitism that is one of Russian ethnocentricity's uglier aspects, he is no Party-liner; but in his role as bard, and now as novelist, he comes up with Socialism's blandest pieties: "Cassiterite? What is it compared to human lives?" "But what good is honesty, physical courage, or diligence, if people are cynics?" "The only thing that could end war forever is changing the human psyche. Those who fly up above earth and see her in all her beauty and fragility will undergo a psychological change. At first only individuals, but then hundreds, then millions. It will be a different civilization, a different humanity." *Wild Berries,* set in the scarcely tamed spaces of the Soviet hinterland, should be a comfortable, rollicking book; but instead it is a book with a bad conscience, by a writer who wants to feel more than he does, and one that, whenever it might develop some natural momentum out of its own low impulses, is slowed to a halt by another injection of anxious high-mindedness.

There is little about the handsome but staid jacket of *Russian Women: Two Stories,* or the resolutely unglamorous photograph of the stout, elderly authoress on the back, or Maurice Friedberg's solemn introduction to prepare us for the adroitness of the text itself. "I. Grekova"—from the French, *i grec,* for the letter "y"—means something like "Ms. X" and is the pen name of Yelena Sergeyevna Ventsel, a mathematician born in 1907, whose first fiction was published when she was fifty years old and a full university professor. (Scientific training is far from uncommon among Soviet creative writers: Solzhenitsyn was a teacher of physics and mathematics; Voznesensky was educated as an architect; and a number of prose artists from Chekhov to Vassily Aksyonov have been accredited doctors.) However trained, I. Grekova possesses to a rare degree the fiction writer's necessary gift of getting her material to speak for itself, through actions, sensations, and images. For instance, a grieving woman at her husband's funeral:

Vera Platonovna, deaf and dumb from crying, sat next to the coffin. Her hands, always so nimble, hung down lifelessly. They seemed not to belong to her. She felt grief not in her heart, but rather in her ears. Her world seemed soundless. Perhaps the whole world had gone deaf, not just she. The chair on which she sat seemed both too small and too big—in any case, not meant to be sat on.

Yet, on the next page, some sound does break through to her:

And now, in the streaming light of the candles, he seemed frighteningly alive, truly alive, and displeased with his wife. The hands folded under his chest had a pink tint, and the watch on his wrist was still ticking. The watch was old, prewar, a gift from the People's Commissar, with an inscription: "For Outstanding Service." Shunechka never took it off, even slept with it.

This strangely (but not implausibly) ticking watch calling out from the coffin to this so recently widowed woman sitting in a chair that feels both too big and too small has just that oddness of specificity which puts us there, and which brings emotion out of images. The comical homeliness of death is evoked, and a bit of the horror—the watch will be buried alive! Further, the dead man has been in the habit of tapping his watch as a disciplinary gesture to his wife, and we know, though she still hears it, that the watch will soon run down. Throughout her two long stories, the author easily transforms real details into the intertwining, chiming stuff of narrative. Her prose is light, candid, and unforced. Her topic is the independent, professional female, amid the Soviet Union's throngs of career women.

The first, and much shorter, story of the two bound together here, "Ladies' Hairdresser," was published in the magazine *Novy Mir* in 1963. Though I. Grekova was in her fifties when she wrote it, it has the happy freshness, the light-handed confidence, of a writer newly come into her material. It tells of a middle-aged female mathematician's rather maternal relationship with a twenty-year-old male hairdresser called Vitaly. The mathematician, Marya Vladimirovna Kovaleva, directs a Moscow computer institute and has two sons, Kostya and Kolya, both in college; their impudent, slovenly, clownish behavior at home is enough described, in lively and droll dialogue, to indicate why she would develop a soft spot for this hairdresser of her sons' generation but without their educational advantages. Vitaly is a conscientious genius at his craft, and she goes to him often, to be beautified and to advise him in his self-education. Her dim but pretty secretary, Galya, admires Marya's hair, goes to Vitaly for her own hair, and has a fling with him. But he, like most standouts, runs afoul of the system—specifically, the bureaucratic Hairdressing Section of the Service Administration—and has to be snipped down to size. At the tale's end he tells Marya that he is quitting hairdressing to become an apprentice metalworker and to go to college. She replaces the receiver thinking, "There's something here I missed." Her relations with the younger generation have been consistently fond but bemused; when she attends a Komsomol dance, she stares in reverie at the girls' shoes:

> And the shoes—shoes, shoes, shoes—imported, weightless, thin, with pointed toes, and almost invisible heels. More power to those who walk unfalteringly on such marvelous inventions, I can't. And dancing with the shoes are the men's short boots, or open-toed sandals, or sometimes high boots. And there are many—oh so many—high heels with high heels, girls dancing with each other. They dance elegantly, aloof, as though they don't need anything else. Oh you girls, you poor girls. The war's long been over, another generation has grown up, and there are still too many of you.

Women with women is the theme, too, of "The Hotel Manager" (1976), the story of Vera Platonovna Butova, who was born in 1895 and at the age of eighteen was swept off her bare feet at the seashore by a stern-faced military officer called Alexander Larichev; she marries him and is his wife for twenty-seven years, and then becomes a hotel manager, with a lover and, at the age of sixty, an offer of promotion to Moscow. Though her marriage and subsequent affairs are convincingly described, a deeper warmth of interest is generated by Vera's relation with her mother (Anna), her sister (Zhenya), her best friend (Masha), her adopted daughter (Vika), her housemate (Margarita), and her female colleagues at the Hotel Salute. "The staff of the hotel consisted almost entirely of nervous, middle-aged women. . . . They were morbidly vain, hypersensitive, poorly paid, but how those women worked! . . . [Vera] demanded not a show of work but genuine work, and got it." For I. Grekova's women, love comes and goes, but work is always there. The details of Vera's homemaking, as an Army wife, and of her hotel-managing are set forth almost rhapsodically. Of her childhood we are told, "From her father Verochka learned to laugh, and from her mother to work." The other story's heroine, Marya Vladimirovna, describes her mathematical labors: "The solution to the problem was working. I checked the computations once more. It worked. Good God, perhaps it's for such minutes that life is worth living. I've lived a long life and can state authoritatively that nothing—neither love, nor motherhood—nothing in the world yields as much happiness as those minutes." Her protégé, young Vitaly, discourses for paragraphs on the challenges and nuances of hairdressing and, when beset, proclaims, "I don't care, because it's my work that matters to me and only my work." The seriousness with which work is taken distinguishes these Russian novels from most Western ones, where jobs are usually confined to the wings of the romantic stage and, in a writer like Henry James, reduced to rather comical rumors; in these examples of Soviet fiction, the work, whether that of a biologist, historian, military man, geologist, berry commissioner, or hairdresser, fills up the character and is inextricably involved with his or her personal travails.

I. Grekova's interest in the details of work exposes, without any editorial flavor of defensiveness or indignation, the exact workings of privilege and corruption within the system. In "Ladies' Hairdresser," we see how line-hopping occurs in beauty parlors ("I was ashamed of my privileges," the computer director confesses, "and my heart was on the side of those who shouted and got upset, but my body took its out-of-turn place in that chair") and just how labor officials skim graft from the government's allowances for tool depreciation. In "The Hotel Manager," we are given instruction on not only how to juggle the hostelry regulations but how the black market in goods and services arises and perpetuates itself in an atmosphere of benevolence:

> On the surface, all kinds of goods did not exist. But in the depths, they were circulating and could be called up by something resembling sorcery. . . . One had to go through sacred rituals of camaraderie, to engage in (almost sincere) declarations of mutual love, when a matter was being settled not in return for a favor or, God forbid, a large sum of money, but simply out of love for one's neighbor. . . . The businessmen of the secret world needed to believe in their selflessness. And to believe it one had to drown oneself in vodka.

The government is not criticized; it scarcely seems to exist, except as a superfluity of regulations and excuses for inertia. Vera, in her capacity as manager, thinks to herself, "If only she had more freedom to act!" Yevtushenko's yea-saying novel includes a curious document, half obliterated by water and eventually tossed into the fire, which contains among its "Thoughts on Order and Disorder" the apothegm "We have to help the government relax a bit." In Trifonov's miasmic world, the murk thickens at the top, whence something sinister emanates, blocking upward movement. Sergei's balked dissertation concerned the Czar's secret police, and though the novel never states it, most of its readers could be assumed to know the legend that the young Stalin was, for a time, an agent for this perfidious force. Such dark allusions seem mere muttering, however, compared with I. Grekova's candid, matter-of-fact glimpses into the Soviet system's imperfect workings. A professorial bigwig herself, she knows something of how power flows under Communism, and also sees where the system cannot reach and perennial human happiness and misery take their course.

Like Trifonov's characteristic work, the longer of I. Grekova's two fictions contains a great deal of flashback and summary. After the death of Vera's loving bully of a husband, "The Hotel Manager" runs rather low on suspense, in part because the heroine is unremittingly brave, sunny, and resourceful. Her husband was her only flaw, and though partings and deaths darken her path, it is all natural process, and every loss is redeemed by a gain in freedom. There are too many startlingly real and tender touches ("the rainbow eyelashes of the streetlamps," "the child's pillow which smelled of almond soap") for us to doubt the reality of what we read, but we read on because we care about Vera, and we care about her because the writer so infectiously loves her, with her happy nature, her wide-hipped health, her ability to nurture and improvise. After all lip service has been rendered to the socialist ideals of rational planning and mutual criticism, self-heedless energy is dearest to the Russian heart. Vera, at the age of sixty, does not look long in the mirror. "No use looking and pulling," her friend Margarita tells her. "Self-criticism for a woman is death. I have never suffered from that."

Twenty years ago, when this reviewer visited Russia, Vassily Aksyonov was to prose fiction what Yevtushenko and Voznesenky were to poetry— young, daring, a rallying point for those Soviet citizens who craved freedom in the arts. Aksyonov had become famous with a novella, *Ticket to the Stars* (1961), that portrayed Western-influenced urban youths, *stilyagi,* in their authentic idiom and mood. In the decades since, while Yevtushenko adjusted to the post-thaw refreeze that followed Khrushchev's ouster, Aksyonov—a prodigiously productive writer, for the stage and screen as well as the printed page—increasingly clashed with the authorities. He was a moving spirit in the creation of a literary anthology, *Metropol,* which, when published in 1979 in a tiny edition of one, defied official censorship; when two of his fellow editors were expelled from the country, Aksyonov resigned from the Writers' Union, and when, in 1980, his domestically unpublishable novel *The Burn* was published in Italy he was himself forced to emigrate.

The Island of Crimea was written within Russia in 1977–79 and published in its original language by the late Karl Proffer's Ardis Publications in 1981. It is a prodigious, overpopulated, futuristic fantasy based upon the premise of an island—rather than the actual peninsula—of Crimea that was successfully defended against the Red Armies by the Whites in 1920 and that thereafter developed, somewhat in the manner of Taiwan, into a thriving capitalist democracy, with skyscrapers, superhighways, packed supermarkets and luxury shops, sports-car rallies, a Yalta beachfront full of sunbathing girls in minimal bikinis, a theme park of artificial mountains, ubiquitous and untrammelled news media, and a multitude of competing political parties. At the time of our story—"late in the present decade or early in the decade to come (depending on when this book comes out)"— our hero, fabulously rich and handsome forty-six-year-old Andrei Arsenievich Luchnikov, son of Arseny Nikolaevich, one of the White Army founders of the Crimean nation, and father of Anton Andreevich, a vagabond saxophonist, has decided in his middle-generation unease to lead, from the podium of his Simferopol newspaper the *Russian Courier*, a campaign for Crimea's restoration of itself to the Soviet Union, democratic institutions, material prosperity, and all.

Why Luchnikov would want to do this dreadful thing, and why his movement (called the Common Fate League, or SOS) eventually captivates ninety percent of the voting Crimeans, forms the novel's central mystery and problem. A Westerner, clearly, is reading this book from the wrong end. For all its explosive inventiveness and muffled passion, *The Island of Crimea* seems strained, stretched-out, and emotionally opaque. As I read it, I was awkwardly conscious of allusions I was missing, from puns and pointed caricatures on up to the entire ambience, the bias of the satire. The novel, Pynchonesque in its gag names, multiplying conspiracies, and mechanical interconnections, wears an unremitting grimace; but what is being grimaced at? Crimea as an epitome of Western enterprise and decadence is plausible enough; Aksyonov has done his travelling, including a visiting lectureship at U.C.L.A. in 1975. He has also read his Ian Fleming, and the Bond tales are evoked specifically at least three times and generally in the souped-up environment of fast cars, underground cloverleafs, wigwam-shaped glass penthouses, instantly compliant young women, and armadas of bad guys. Yet satire of the West's "hysterical materialism" is not the point; the author clearly loves the idea of Crimea, "the idea of a miniature, tinselly Russia" and its "carnival of freedom." The novel's heroine, Tatyana, whose demanding roles include those of television broadcaster, Soviet sports hero's wife, Luchnikov's mistress, KGB spy, and Yalta hooker, does entertain some dire thoughts about "the capitalist jungle where the very air is pornographic" and yearns to get back from Crimea to "a world where you can't get anything you need and everybody's afraid of everything, the real world." But the island of capitalist unreality, a festive blend of southern California, Hong Kong, and Oz, inspires affection in most everybody, including Soviet officialdom. For this novel to have earned its breadth and complexity, one convinced Communist should have been represented; but all the Soviets are cheerful thugs or secret Crimeans, as baffled by Luchnikov's betrayal of his homeland as the reader is. Kuzenkov, a Kremlin higher-up, calls the Common Fate League "that sadomasochistic Idea, that snobbish guilt gone berserk!"

Some clues to "Looch"'s state of mind are offered. When visits by Crimeans to the motherland became possible, "a few of them did try to understand and immerse themselves in Soviet life, and the first was Andryushka Luchnikov." Many visits later, arriving from Paris, he still immerses himself:

> After the first glass of vodka the atmosphere changed completely. Moscow comfort. He never could quite understand how it worked. Here you were, primed to feel the prying eye of the KGB on your back, aware of the most heinous form of lawlessness going on all around you, and suddenly you were in bliss. . . . Even here in the lower reaches of notorious Gorky Street— where a look out the window gave you an unobstructed view of the stone giants of Stalinist decadence—even here after the first swallow of vodka you immediately forgot your Paris night fever and sank into it ecstatically: Moscow comfort. It was like the old family nurse massaging their heads.

He seeks out the shabby back streets that give him "a deceptive sense of the normalcy, sanity, sagacity of Russian life." After a three-day binge in the city, "he had lost so much weight that his jacket hung on him as if on a hanger. He felt great pity for the poor lost Moscow souls he met; he identified with them wholly. He was quite fond of himself as he was now: thin and full of pity." Hiding in the remote countryside, in the company of "foul-mouthed peasants," Luchnikov goes down on his knees in the mud and makes "a large, slow cross." Crosses multiply as the book heaves toward its apocalyptic end, and like a refugee from farthest Dostoevsky Luchnikov preaches to a crowd of Crimeans about his proposed "daring yet noble attempt to share the fate of two hundred and fifty million of our brethren who, through decades of gloom and untold suffering, relieved by only an occasional glimmer of hope, have carried on the unique moral and mystic mission of Mother Russia and the nations that have chosen to follow her path." This is not so much the voice of Luchnikov as a voice within him. His other voice says to Russia, "Your economy's falling apart, your politics are a pack of lies, your ideology's at a dead end." Luchnikov's contradictions and disagreeable slipperiness stem, I think, from his embodiment of ambiguity, of the ambiguous feelings of the author, who while writing this work was ever more imminently facing the prospect of exile.

"He was prepared for one vast bomb site, the smoky remains of a series of trumped-up trials and expulsions. . . . Instead he found an uncanny gaiety: loft parties all over town, amateur theatricals in private flats, concerts at scientific institutes and outlying clubs . . . poetry readings by the young and struggling, meetings of the Metropol group, all-night philosophy discussions over tea, samizdat discoveries, basement exhibits. . . ." Luchnikov, arriving from Crimea, is the vehicle of perception but the world perceived is Aksyonov's, down to the Metropol group—the vital, busy, "semiunderground" world of Moscow artists. "He was amazed to find so many new deviations from the ideal citizen. . . . Yet here they were, living proof that life went on." This is Russia as the working writer experiences it, a mixed bag but alive and actual. Luchnikov's scheme of reintegrating Crimea with the U.S.S.R. makes sense only as a metaphor for Aksyonov's wish to remain part of a nation that is inexorably rejecting him. He will lose his language, his cultural frame of reference, and the audience that understands his frame of reference; and Russia will lose one more bright spirit. Without knowing it, Russia needs him. The dissident has not only a desire but a duty to stay. In *The Island of Crimea*, Vitaly Gangut, the film director, who seems closer to being the author's alter ego than the playboy magnate Luchnikov, knows that "even the ever so slightly nonconformist film at home was worth more to the cause than ten or twenty Paris-based dissident journals," and Dim Shebeko, the jazz-rock bandleader, has refused offers from America because "Russia needs Russians playing here in Russia." And, it is true, figures like Solzhenitsyn and Sinyavsky, as long as they stayed in the Soviet Union, were heroes on a global scale; outside it, they became just a few additional decibels in the West's cacophonous Tower of Babel.

I have never met a Russian, here or there, loyal functionary or indignant expatriate, who did not think Russia was the most interesting subject in the world. On the lip of the Grand Canyon, in the midst of Manhattan, they will wrap themselves in Russianness, and take in nothing. In Paris, Luchnikov, seeing newspaper headlines about cosmonauts and Sakharov, thinks proudly, "Yet one way or another, Russia—decayed, demoralized Russia—continued to give the world its headlines." Baxter, a rich American, is made to complain, "The only thing anybody talks about any more is the goddamn Russian question." "I want to be Russian, and I don't care if they send us to Siberia," Luchnikov cries. A reflexive chauvinism is part of the Russian genius; the land, the language, and (in a non-political sense) the way of life imprint themselves indelibly. All four of these books, with their differing tones and degrees of persuasiveness, take warmth from the rub between Russian self-love and Russian reservations, stated or implied, about the presiding system. Yet, indisputably, the distrusted if not loathed system has sprung from the cherished land, and is part of it. *The Island of Crimea*'s Kuzenkov, the most sophisticated and sympathetic of Soviet officials, confronted with a snide opinion of Stalin, reflects that "only someone completely foreign to our way of life . . . would deal so basely with our history, with a man whose name for generations of Soviets has meant victory, order, power. And if it has meant violence and even obscurantism as well, then at least they were majestic and grandiose."

People will always hearken to any system that offers to give suffering a meaning, even at the cost of deepening that suffering. Luchnikov, bored and depressed in his tinselly little capitalist paradise, likes himself thin and full of pity, and longs for Siberia, if that is what it takes to give his soul value. And a sense of immaterial value, of life as intrinsically vicissitudinous but worth suffering, animates all these instances of fiction; there is nothing in them, even in Trifonov at his weariest, of a death wish, of any cultural equivalent to Werther's widely imitated suicide or the skulls that bloomed generations later on the caps of the SS. A life-loving trait, rather, informs the resilient characters of Soviet fiction, even where, as in *Wild Berries*, their presentation seems coarse or ingenuous; this same trait, it may not be too fanciful to extrapolate, has helped make the Soviets, for these forty years of ragged truce, tolerable partners in power.

Russian Delinquents

NOVEL WITH COCAINE, by M. Ageyev, translated from the Russian by Michael Henry Heim. 204 pp. Dutton, 1984.

KANGAROO, by Yuz Aleshkovsky, translated from the Russian by Tamara Glenny. 278 pp. Farrar, Straus & Giroux, 1986.

The possibility has been raised, by the Russian émigré scholar N. A. Struve, that *Novel with Cocaine*, by M. Ageyev (a pseudonym), is in truth by the late Vladimir Nabokov. The novel takes its youthful hero, Vadim Maslennikov, up to 1919, the year Nabokov left Russia; both Vadim and Vladimir were born in 1899; and, according to Mr. Struve, M. Ageyev's only other known prose work, a short story entitled "A Rotten People," appeared in an émigré magazine, *Vstrechi*, to which Nabokov had promised—but never, it seems, delivered—material. *Novel with Cocaine* first manifested itself as an unsolicited manuscript sent from Istanbul to the

Paris-based journal *Chisla;* it was serially published there, in part, and then issued as a book in 1936. Contemporary reviewers found it rather thrillingly decadent, and even pornographic, but its author's attempts to emigrate to Paris on the strength of its *succès de scandale* came to nothing. "Ageyev" vanished.* In 1983, his novel was published in French to such high praise as "Mr. Ageyev is a genius" *(Le Point)*, "A book in the league of Thomas De Quincy's *Confessions of an English Opium Eater" (Temps Économie Littéraire)*, and "Mr. Ageyev has thrown his life into this novel. Finally, he is rewarded by immortality" *(Vendredi-Samedi-Dimanche)*. *Novel with Cocaine* has its merits and becomes fascinating in its second half, but I very much doubt that Nabokov wrote it.

---

*After this review appeared in *The New Yorker*, I heard from a living witness to these distant events—Dr. V. S. Yanovsky, of Rego Park, New York. He wrote, "In the midthirties, the Paris (Russian) Union of Writers and Poets elected a literary collegium to organize publications by subscription. Two men constituted this collegium: V. S. Yanovsky (the writer of this letter) and Yuri Felsen (soon to be killed by the Germans). We published three books: 'The Other Love,' by Yanovsky, 'Letters on Lermontov,' by Yuri Felsen, and 'Novel with Cocaine.' The latter had been sent to Nicholas Otsup, editor of our leading magazine 'Chisla' (Numbers). The author, resident of Constantinople, signed himself Levi. Otsup wrote him that he would like to publish an excerpt (!) of *Cocaine* and suggested that the author's name be changed to Ageyev, to which the latter agreed. Eventually, we offered to publish Mr. Levi's novel in our series. In connection with the publication—in 1937, I believe—of *Roman s Kokainom*, Felsen and I exchanged several letters with Levi in Turkey. . . . One day, Levi sent his passport to Otsup with the request that someone prolong it at the Uruguayan consulate in Paris. He could not do it personally in Turkey. The fact was that Mr. Levi, a Russian refugee, had escaped from Berlin to Turkey on an Uruguayan passport. There were many such fantastic stories which poor humans had to face in those days (and which good Americans couldn't believe). Otsup, of course, understood, and he entrusted a leading poet of our émigré group, Lydia Chervinskaya, with the mission. She was the last person to be trusted with such a mission: running from one café to another, she somehow, somewhere forgot or lost her handbag with the precious passport inside. She told me this herself, in tears. Her parents lived in Constantinople and she saw Levi when she visited them. She is one of the few old-timers still alive in Paris and has also testified to this effect."

This account, though not without its own mysteries, seems to me to banish any possibility that Ageyev was Nabokov or that, as has been suggested by at least one American reviewer (Ronald K. Siegel, "M. Ageyev's *Novel with Cocaine:* Russian Fiction or Snow Job?," *Journal of Psychoactive Drugs*, Vol. 17, no. 1 [January-March 1985]), the novel is a modern fabrication, riddled with anachronistic drug usages. Dr. Siegel's other suggestion, that Ageyev plagiarized an earlier, Italian novel concerning cocaine addiction, by Dino Segre under the pen name "Pitigrilli" (*Cocaina;* Milan: Casa Editrice Sonzagno, 1921), is still possible, though his cited parallelisms did not persuade me. If, as Dr. Yanovsky's letter states, Lydia Chervinskaya is alive in Paris and visited Levi/Ageyev in Constantinople, more light could still be shed on the identity of the author of *Cocaine* than Michael Henry Heim's introduction shares with American readers.

On the practical level, Nabokov after 1960 used the luxuries of leisure and attention won for him by his best-selling *Lolita* to supervise, lovingly and pedantically, the English translation of his youthful Russian-language works, and there seems no reason, when even his old chess problems were sifted and selectively preserved, that such a large and significant souvenir as this novel would be ignored. Further, what Nabokov himself neglected to collect (such as his academic lectures and a number of plays), his estate, under the guidance of his widow and son, has been bringing into print. The Nabokovs steadfastly disown Ageyev and his work.

On the literary level, the novel is intensely, derivatively Dostoevskian; yet Nabokov loathed Dostoevsky. Vadim Maslennikov can't stop craving humiliation and demonstrating human perversity. Like Dostoevsky's Underground Man, he hops about absurdly from mood to anti-mood: "Thus, taking a clean shirt from the wardrobe, the only silk shirt I owned, I threw it to the floor after a cursory inspection—the shoulder seam had begun to come undone—and trampled it underfoot as if I had a dozen of them. When I cut myself shaving, I continued to scrape the razor over the gash, pretending I could not feel it in the least. . . . After a sip of coffee I pushed my cup aside like a spoiled brat, though the coffee was perfectly good and I wanted to go on drinking it." His own behavior constantly takes him by surprise: "But when, inwardly composed and wishing to say something trivial, I again raised my head, I surprised myself by leaping out of my chair instead." He is morbid and self-destructive and vortically introspective, whereas the young heroes of early Nabokov novels like *Mary* and *Glory* are characterized by a certain robust innocence, a healthy willingness to be enraptured by the world. On the stylistic level, Ageyev does now and then strike off images reminiscent of Nabokov's eccentric precision: a man is observed "cleaning the door handle with whiting, his free hand following the same pattern as the hand that was doing the work," and we see a "circus poster of a beauty in tights leaping through a torn hoop, her peach-colored thigh pierced by the nail holding the poster in place." The hero specifies, "I would stand at the window for long periods of time, a cigarette in the catapult of my fingers, and try to count—through the deep-blue smoke from the tangerine tip and the filthy gray smoke from the cardboard filter—the number of bricks in the neighboring wall." But such hyperrealism (the "catapult" of the posed fingers, the two shades of cigarette smoke) could be learned from Bely and the Symbolists. Ageyev often overdoes it:

> Immediately behind the door . . . stood a rickety upright with keys the color of unbrushed teeth. A pair of drooping candlesticks screwed directly into the

piano's bosom sported a pair of red, golden-flecked, white-wicked, spiral candles which, since the openings in the candlesticks were too large, pointed off in different directions.

My fingers tightened as they grasped the hot roots of his hair, and pulling his head out of the shell of his palms, I brought it up to mine, eye to eye. I peered into his small gray orbs. They were oddly distorted by the skin being drawn back to the point where I was holding his hair. For a moment they peered back into mine with a look of sullen suffering, but then, obviously unable to master the harsh male tears welling up inside them, they disappeared behind their lids on either side of the fierce cleft that had dug its way between his brows.

And there is a sentimental excess, too, that the dispassionate, ironic young Nabokov would have disdained. Vadim, having financially exhausted his mother, turns and shamelessly borrows from their faithful old servant, Nanny: "I knew she had accumulated that money through years of toil and was saving it for the almshouse to assure herself a corner in her old age when she could no longer work for a living—yet still I took it. As she handed me the money, she sniffled and blinked, ashamed of showing me her joyful tears of love and self-abnegation."

If there are many passages that even the immature Nabokov would never have let his pen slip into, there are some that lie outside his vision. Ageyev was at home in depths of suffering that Nabokov saw in aloof overview, reduced to a pattern. *Novel with Cocaine* is one of those youthful works wherein we can feel the writer getting better as he goes along. Its first and longest chapter, "School," seems labored and puffed-up compared with, say, the schoolboy parts of *Bend Sinister.* The next, "Sonya," rather more successfully diagrams the intricate vanity of an adolescent offered an adult love experience. Vadim refuses to tell Sonya he loves her, on this fancy reasoning:

> My experience in matters of love seemed to have convinced me that no one could talk eloquently of love unless his love was only a memory, that no one could talk persuasively of love unless his sensuality was aroused, and no one whose heart was actually in the throes of love could say a word.

Sonya's farewell letter to him couches with epigrammatic force a number of bleak truths about relationships. Theirs, she writes, has reached that point where "all one of the parties has to do is tell the other the truth—the whole truth, do you understand? the utter truth—for that truth to turn into an indictment." The longer such a relationship lasts, "the more persistently both parties simulate their former intimacy and the more strongly they feel that terrible enmity which never develops between strangers but often between people very close to each other." She ends, "Your relationship to me is a kind of unending fall, a constant impoverishment of the emotions, which, like all forms of impoverishment, humiliates more the more the riches it supplants."

The affair thus eloquently dismissed, and school over, the stage is bare for the astonishing chapter, "Cocaine," that gives this long-forgotten novel its modern relevance and enduring interest. The strained, gaudy style seems stripped to a new vividness even before Vadim encounters the drug: "The frost was hard and dry. Everything felt ready to crack. As the sleigh pulled up to the arcade, I heard high-pitched metallic steps on all sides and saw smoke rising in white columns from all the roofs. The city seemed to hang in the sky like a gigantic icon-lamp." When he comes to take cocaine, every detail—the purchase, the distribution among the party of users, the snorting, and the sensations—is rendered with a cool and edgy clarity:

> The bitter taste in my mouth was almost gone, and all that remained was an ice-cold feeling in my throat and gums, the kind of feeling that comes when, during a frost, one closes one's mouth after breathing with it open and the warm saliva makes it even colder. My teeth were completely frozen, and if I put pressure on any one of them, I felt the others follow painlessly, as if they were all soldered together.

The ups, the downs, the exhilaration and despair, and the brutal plunge into abject addiction follow in masterly fashion, capped by a fully developed theory on the psychology of self-ruin:

> During the long nights and long days I spent under the influence of cocaine . . . I came to see that what counts in life is not the events that surround one but the reflection of those events in one's consciousness. . . . All of a man's life—his work, his deeds, his will, his physical and mental prowess—is completely and utterly devoted to, fixed on bringing about one or another event in the external world, though not so much to experience the event in itself as to experience the reflection of the event on his consciousness.

Cocaine so affects the consciousness that "the need for any event whatever disappeared and, with it, the need for expending great amounts of work, time, and energy to bring it about." Slavic mysticism here shows a sinister anarchic face, and we are almost relieved to discover that, while Vadim hurries to his inevitable end, the Revolution has occurred, bringing its enforced order.

* * *

The dire results of that Revolution are, with the bewildering mixture of slapstick and rage that used to be called "black humor," tumbled before us by the expatriate Yuz Aleshkovsky in his novel *Kangaroo*. *Kangaroo* has waited not fifty years but over ten for its presentation to American readers; it was finished, Mr. Aleshkovsky tells us in a brief autobiography supplied by his publishers, in 1975, whereupon he realized "quite clearly the impossibility of continuing this double life [that is, writing for samizdat] and that I longed to devote myself to writing without compromise." He now lives in Middletown, Connecticut. His underground novel makes no compromise with the American reader, who is expected to know and care, without benefit of footnote or appendix, who or what Ordzhonikidze, the Chelyuskin, Mikhail Zoshchenko, Chekists, Ilya Ehrenburg, Ivan Pyriev, Radishchev, Zoya Fyodorova, Tukhachevsky, Kirov, Karatsupa, Kulaks, Zhdanov, Voznesensky, Yuri Levitan, Bukharin, Rykov, Zinoviev, Kamenev, Zelinsky-Nesmeyanov gas, Joseph Vissarionovich, and zeks are or were. Our daunted American reader is further expected to pick the serious satirical strands from a grotesque, scatological, backward-looping farrago involving the conviction of a Russian pickpocket and criminal by name of Fan Fanych, alias Etcetera, alias Cariton Ustinych Newton Tarkington, for "the vicious rape and murder of an aged kangaroo in the Moscow Zoo on a night between July 14, 1789, and January 9, 1905." The trial occurs in 1949; the charge was cooked up by a primitive computer and is substantiated by a film made of the reconstructed incident. KGB ruses of enormous complication seek to persuade Fan Fanych that he is (a) a kangaroo (b) in a spaceship. He spends six years in Siberia, killing rats with the aid of a third eye developed by sheer will power at the back of his head and enduring debates of Communist fine points with fervent Old Bolsheviks of whom the leader appears to be the famous Chernyshevsky (1828–89). Fan Fanych remembers while under durance or en route his earlier curious involvements with Hitler in 1929 and the Yalta Conference in 1945; he returns to a de-Stalinized Moscow in 1955, finds his apartment full of sparrow nests, and falls in love with a girl he glimpsed just before packing to go to the Lubyanka. Finally, he locates his old friend Kolya, to whom he is somehow telling all this, much as Portnoy is delivering his complaint to a psychiatrist. The analogy with Philip Roth's exuberant demolition of bourgeois inhibitions may illuminate why *Kangaroo* struck me as so grindingly unfunny, albeit prankish: to relish unrepressed prose, we must have had some experience of the repression, and we must be able to hear the voice. *Kangaroo* is told in that heavily slangy Russian which drives translators to revive such stale English expressions as "mug," "screwball," "shoot the breeze," and "off his [her, its] rocker." While a patriotic citizen of the free West must be politically flattered by so detailed and vehement a blasphemy against the Soviet system, it makes deadly reading if you've never been a believer and don't know the iconography.

Only when *Kangaroo* floats free of its political burden does it stir a smile. In inflation-plagued Germany, our down-and-out hero has his overcoat and suit "turned"—torn apart and resewn inside out, to show the unworn side of the cloth. His clothes take revenge, with an animation that recalls the bedevilled and bedevilling objects of the old Chaplin films: "For some reason my whole body's twitching inside the suit, as if there's a flea biting me, or a sharp little splinter scratching me. . . . I can tell my rotten jacket's doing it on purpose, just to make me look like an idiot, and my pants are giving it moral support. They're riding up my knees in creases, and keep rustling. And my pockets are moaning like seashells, 'Oo-oo-oo.' " Here the referent—wearing clothes—is generally human, and the absurd can be measured against the actual and its degree of exaggeration appreciated. But in this Soviet system conceived as sheer demonism— "sucking people's blood just for laughs, destroying innocent souls, wearing out their strength and keeping the human spirit humiliated for half a century"—we do not quite know where we are, and hardly dare laugh in the dark. *Kangaroo* translates a work whose intended readers can all read Russian.

Visiting the Land of the Free

ALONE TOGETHER, by Elena Bonner, translated from the Russian by Alexander Cook. 264 pp. Knopf, 1986.

For a period of several months about a year ago, residents of New England were now and then treated to the sight, on television, of a small iron-haired lady, with thick eyeglasses and a wary smile, being ambushed by reporters and cameras while trying to mind her own business. Her name was Elena Bonner, and her business was a mixture of medical and familial matters: she was getting her ailing heart, eyes, and right leg attended to at Massachusetts General Hospital in Boston, and she was visiting her aged mother, her daughter and son, and her three grandchildren in nearby Newton. Her husband would have liked to accompany her but could not; he is the Soviet Union's foremost dissident, the physicist Andrei Sakharov, and was at that time held in internal exile in the Russian city of Gorky. It was extraordinary, indeed, that Bonner had received permission to visit this country, for she had recently been convicted of slander against the Soviet state and social system and been sentenced to five years of exile in Gorky. Her husband, believing that Soviet medicine could not be trusted with her drastic health problems, had several times undertaken a hunger strike to secure her permission to travel abroad. The couple had together staged a seventeen-day hunger strike in late 1981 which did secure the freedom of Liza Alexeyeva, the wife of Bonner's son, Alexei Semyonov, to emigrate and join her husband, who had already left the U.S.S.R., in Massachusetts. But in 1984 and 1985 the Soviet authorities seemed determined to suppress both Sakharov's hunger strike and all publicity concerning it. In the Gorky Regional Clinical Hospital, they force-fed him, sometimes with painful and humiliating violence, and forbade visits to him from his wife; at the same time they contrived a number of films, distributed to the West through the agency of the West German newspaper *Bild*, showing the Sakharovs apparently healthy and happy in Gorky. In 1985, however, Alexei staged his own hunger strike, in Washington, right next to the Soviet embassy, and the new Soviet leader, Mikhail Gorbachev, was travelling in the West and promoting a fresh Soviet image. Word abruptly came down that Bonner could go abroad, provided she did not give interviews to the press. She was nevertheless an object of much interest to the television cameras; as it happened, she was usually shown smoking, with the unfiltered, reckless absorption of one to whom lung irritation is a relatively minor problem. Scandalized American viewers, no longer used to seeing even bad guys light up on the screen, wrote letters of concern and protest to the newspapers and the television stations. At least one of the many doctors ministering to her ills (she eventually underwent a six-bypass heart operation and an operation on the artery of her leg) felt obliged to make a public statement that she was being urged to stop. And I believe that, by the time her five-month stay in this country was over, she had given up smoking, to the satisfaction of many.

During her visit here, amid her operations and travels and maternal and grandmaternal activities, she wrote a book about herself and, especially, her recent years as the persecuted, isolated wife of Sakharov. *Alone Together* is understandably a hurried, fragmentary production. Footnotes by the translator clear up many minor mysteries of cultural allusion and personal history. An appendix of nine documents, including reproductions of Elena Bonner's father's death certificate and her own service record as a nurse in "the Great Patriotic War," sheds additional light— indeed, a reader might do well to begin this book with the eighth item, a letter from Sakharov to the president of the U.S.S.R. Academy of Sciences on October 15, 1984, which sets out the history of Bonner's health and the couple's travails more consecutively than her own account. The steps that led Sakharov himself from a privileged position high within the Soviet scientific establishment to that of a determined public dissident are not discussed. His letter states in a brief paragraph:

> The authorities have been greatly annoyed by my public activities—my defense of prisoners of conscience and my articles and books on peace, the open society and human rights. (My fundamental ideas are contained in *Progress, Coexistence and Intellectual Freedom*, 1968; *My Country and the World*, 1975, and "The Danger of Thermonuclear War," 1983.)

Nor does Bonner disclose much of the ideological journey that has placed her, at Sakharov's side, in such a marginal and precarious position within her society.

In refutation of a defamatory article that she quotes at length, she rather grudgingly offers a few pages of autobiography. She was born in 1923. Her father, Gevork Alikhanov, was a leading Armenian Communist, who was arrested and imprisoned as a traitor in 1937, officially died of pneumonia in 1939, and was rehabilitated in 1954, the same year that his death certificate was issued. Bonner's mother, Ruth Grigorievna Bonner—who at the age of eighty-six lives in Newton with her grandchildren—was also arrested in 1937. Elena Bonner and her younger brother thereafter lived with their maternal grandmother in Leningrad. She writes, "Never did I believe—either as a child or as an adult—that my parents could have been enemies of the state. Their ideals and their internationalism had been lofty models for me, which was why I joined the army when war broke out." She became a nurse; in 1941 she suffered a concussion and other wounds at the front and was hospitalized for some months before being reassigned. In 1945 she was promoted to lieutenant and demobilized as "a group 2 invalid," with almost total loss of vision in the right eye and progressive blindness in the left, as a result of the concussion. Despite her eye problems, she enrolled in 1947 at the First Leningrad Medical Institute and graduated as a doctor in 1953. She worked as a district doctor and pediatrician and in Iraq on assignment for the Ministry of Health of the U.S.S.R. Along with her medical career, she was active as a writer, a journalist, and an editor. Though a member of the young people's Komsomol, she did not join the Communist Party for many years. "Neither while in the army nor in subsequent years did I feel a psychological right to join the Party as long as my parents were listed as traitors to the homeland. . . . After the criticism of Stalin at the Twentieth Congress, and especially the Twenty-second, I decided to join the CPSU, and in 1964 became a candidate and in 1965, a member. After the invasion of Czechoslovakia in 1968

I considered this step a mistake and in 1972, in accordance with my convictions, I left the Communist Party." She dissents, then, from deep within the system—the daughter of an Old Bolshevik who has paid her full dues as a Soviet citizen.

She married Sakharov in 1971. Her love life up to the age of forty-eight had not been barren. She had had a girlhood romance with Vsevolod Bagritsky, who was killed in the war and whose poems and diaries she helped compile for a posthumous volume. One of her attackers accuses her, in print, of "a wanton life." Her own book includes a rakish photograph taken of herself in 1949, wearing a broad-brimmed hat: "I decided to publish the picture in this book, even though I know it smacks of middle-aged coquettishness! 'I was never beautiful, but I was always damned cute.' " At medical school she met Ivan Semyonov, the father of her two children, Tatyana (born in 1950) and Alexei (born in 1956). Bonner and Semyonov separated in 1965. She does not describe when and how she met Sakharov, but Sakharov's letter to the Academy president spells out a pattern of their marriage:

> As soon as Yelena Bonner married me in 1971, the KGB adopted a sly and cruel plan to solve the "Sakharov problem." They have tried to shift responsibility for my actions onto her, to destroy her morally and physically. They hope to break and bridle me, while portraying me as the innocent victim of the intrigues of my wife—a "CIA agent," a "Zionist," a "mercenary adventuress," etc.

The appendix includes extracts from the Soviet news agency TASS, which describe Bonner as a potential "leader of the anti-Soviet scum on the payroll of Western special services," a "NATO-ized provocateur," and a basically healthy person who has used the pretense of poor health to travel abroad and profitably engage in "out-and-out anti-Sovietism." She supposedly motivates her husband's hunger strikes and would willingly see him dead: "It was Bonner who planted the idea of Sakharov going on a 'hunger strike' in order to feed the propaganda organs of the U.S.A. About the health of her spouse she worried least of all, acting on the principle: the worse the better." Bonner is part Armenian and part Jewish, and anti-Semitism adds to the propaganda campaign against her. An article by Nickolai Yakovlev in a 1983 issue of the widely circulated magazine *Man and the Law*, entitled "The Firm of E. Bonner and Children," asserts that "One of the victims of the CIA's Zionist agents is Academician A. D. Sakharov. . . . Provocateurs from subversive agencies pushed him and keep pushing this spiritually unbalanced man. . . . A horrible woman forced herself on the widower Sakharov." Letters arrive in Gorky advising Sakharov to "divorce the Jewess" and "live by his own mind, not Bonner's." In a train compartment, she was once assailed by her fellow passengers: "They shouted things about the war and about Jews. . . . I kept wishing I had a yellow star to sew onto my dress."

She has written this book, her foreword states, "to tell about what has happened during the last three years. . . . I had to recall and write, not the way things seemed, but the way they were. All this will be of help to Andrei, so I consider it my duty. No one else was with him, and Andrei himself is so efficiently isolated in Gorky that he cannot tell this story." Much of her intent, then, is to contradict the official Soviet version of their joint ordeal, and to place on the record facts and documents that have otherwise been suppressed. The American reader who has not followed the Sakharov affair closely, and who places no great trust in Soviet press handouts anyway, may find her detailed protestations less interesting than her general picture of what it is like to be a distinguished political prisoner within the Communist system. I was struck by the solemn legality with which vengeful and disciplinary trials are conducted, by the brazen use of medical services as instruments of state intimidation and torture, and by the prodigious amount of manpower expended in surveillance. Not only did teams of KGB men accompany Sakharov and Bonner everywhere they went, leaping in whenever they attempted to pick up a hitchhiker or telephone a television repairman, but her mother's empty apartment in Moscow warranted round-the-clock guards. "Night and day—they even had a cot so they could rest in shifts." No one, however, troubled to close a window that had blown open, and when Bonner and her friends tried to make the place briefly habitable again they were forbidden the use of a cleaning service and of a man—any man. Only some female friends of Bonner's were allowed in to shove the furniture around. A certain prank-ishness flavors the state's chastisements. "Whenever the authorities did not like something, it was our car that suffered. Either two tires would be punctured, or a window smashed or smeared with glue." Sealed envelopes arrived empty at their Gorky residence, and out of one package of scientific reprints "a dozen huge cockroaches scrambled." In their apartment, books, toothbrushes, glasses, and even dental bridges disappeared and then reap-peared: "This whirlwind of moving objects creates a feeling of a Kafka-esque nightmare on the one hand and on the other that you are on a glass slide of a microscope, that you are an experimental subject."

The subjects of these particular experiments have not been broken, though both are in fragile health.* Bonner admits to a sharp tongue and

---

*Sakharov died of a heart attack, in Moscow, at the age of sixty-eight, on December 14, 1989, after a long day of debate in the suddenly contentious Congress of People's Republics,

a hot temper, and describes a number of shouting matches with her guards and judges; we can guess that in any society she would be constructively critical. She was not especially impressed by some of Sakharov's supporters in the United States: "Almost all are ready to sign something . . . and yet many know very little. And not only about Sakharov's problems." Intellectuals who "talk about nuclear winter, star wars, pollution [and] all the horrors that await mankind" appeared to her paradoxically confident and future-minded in their own prosperous lives. "And they sleep peacefully. They do not notice that they have depressed and ruined the sleep of millions of other people." For many Americans, her courageous and suffering husband is only "a symbol, a game, politics." At the White House, she is taken through a back door—"in Russian, we sometimes say a back alley"—and in a small room was received by three people, of whom the greatest, none other than Admiral John Poindexter, reassured her that the administration "was profoundly worried about the fate of my husband and many others, but at the present time it felt that the best way to help them was through quiet, nonpublicized actions." She expressed disappointment, and explains: "Quiet diplomacy in the defense of human rights is such an old song. . . . Academician Sakharov considers publicity the main weapon in the struggle for human rights." She did not see the President, nor did she ask to. But her book includes photographs of herself with Prime Ministers Thatcher and Chirac of England and France, and she writes wryly, "I'm sorry I didn't see the famous Oval Office, or the garden where the President signed a proclamation declaring Andrei Sakharov Day. I won't be able to tell Andrei what they look like, but I will certainly describe the backstairs to him."

Americans who imagine that just by being their well-intentioned, freedom-loving selves they have won the admiration of persecuted Communist dissidents will be disappointed by *Alone Together*. A reception at Stanford, even though it included "nice people, delicious hors d'oeuvres, flowers, grandiloquent words, Joan Baez singing about freedom," displeased Bonner because the university had recently also warmly received Marat Vartanian, who is "implicated as one of the chief figures in the misuse of psychiatry for political purposes." The organization of International Physicians for the Prevention of Nuclear War, which received the Nobel Peace Prize ten years after her husband did, arouses her ire: "Aren't some of the people who tortured my husband members?" Her standard of excellence and rectitude is very specific—Andrei Sakharov—and few measure up to it. Her recurring impression that Americans do not very

---

to which he was an elected representative. A year before, he had visited the United States, and been pronounced in no need of heart surgery.

well understand Sakharov's case, or very much care, is probably accurate. In these last years, even under a conservative administration and in spite of the usual Cold War spy cases and murderous international meddling, there has arisen the sensation that the Soviet Union is not the enemy. Its political religion has fallen flat; free enterprise is creeping in even into its own sluggish system; as a nation, it is soggy with internal problems, and some of them resemble ours. Perhaps radical Islam is the threat, or, from another angle, Japan; but Russia, like a gruff old chess foe who has grown corpulent and distracted over the years, seems an almost comfortable neighbor in the global village. This could change, but for now it seems, to quote Sakharov himself, that "The world is further away from war than it has been in a long time." War between the two superpowers, that is. And therefore Russia's internal victims, its silenced and incarcerated writers and artists, its captive refuseniks, its isolated and slandered Sakharovs, are less interesting than formerly to practitioners of quiet diplomacy and to purveyors of our own propaganda.

Dr. Bonner is independent-minded, and not sentimental even about her own grandchildren, who are American: "Perhaps because Gorky is so distant—not geographically, but distant in other ways—I had pictured them differently. I feel uncomfortable being with them, and a certain . . . not disappointment, but perhaps disillusionment in not finding what I had expected to find. They are not what I had imagined them to be—not worse and not better, just different. They need a lot of getting used to, but I don't have that kind of time." America itself she takes as it comes, making a few scattered observations about the seriousness with which people shop, the size of Los Angeles, the abundance of yachts off Miami. She celebrates her sixty-third birthday at Disney World, and says, "Music is playing somewhere, everything here seems to be carefree, and the flowering trees confuse me—where's the winter?" While sitting alone on the beach in Miami, she is approached by a twenty-seven-year-old bearded beach bum. They manage to converse, in spite of her imperfect command of spoken English and her growing suspicion that he is stoned, and have this concentrated exchange:

> We spoke about his country and mine. What was good and what was bad.
> I said, "We don't have freedom."
> "We do—to jump in the ocean."

So a victim of thought control and totalitarian oppression meets a victim of freedom—one who longs, his implication seems to be, for society to be more watchful and directive. He yearns perhaps for Russia, where there is much less ocean. Bonner does not go out of her way to flatter the United States, nor does she succumb to the commonly intense Russian nostalgia: "I find nostalgia a form of playacting. . . . I am returning. Why? It's not that I miss the birches, the *beryozkas*. . . . About émigrés. You see many living in difficult circumstances. Our close friends, almost total strangers, and many elderly émigrés—all sometimes speak of their hardships. But there wasn't one among them who wanted to go back." She does not look forward to the return; of her previous returns to the Soviet Union, she writes, "As soon as I crossed the border, such a heavy fog, such darkness befell my soul that it is impossible to describe. . . . It takes incredible willpower to force yourself to learn once again how to breathe without air, swim without water, walk without ground." She is returning, only, because her husband is there. And he, this book reveals, would leave if he could. Sakharov does not martyristically avoid foreign exile and its low-ered profile; when in 1983 the Norwegian government offered him per-manent residence, he accepted with gratitude. The Soviet authorities, however, claiming that his mind still holds military secrets from his work on nuclear weaponry twenty years ago, deny him exit.

Alone Together was written here and there—Newton, Cape Cod, Miami, New York—and moves back and forth between detailed pleading and terse reminiscence, between glimpses of her blithe momentary sur-roundings and reflections upon her likely fate of continued ostracism and harassment. As the prose goes along, it seems to gather confidence and *esprit:* "This book wrote itself, without resistance, so easily that these pages probably should not be called a book." Might we even say it grows more American in style, more breezy and concrete? After all, she was here for five months. One of her last chapters expands upon, in a virtually Thoreauvian manner, the discovery that she wants a house. She has ob-served that "what Americans want is a house." Elena Bonner has never had one, always sharing crowded quarters and awkward communal ar-rangements. "I think that the first time I was mistress of my own place was—it's hard to believe—in Gorky, in exile. I do not want that. I want a house. My daughter has a house in Newton, Massachusetts. It makes me so happy to think that she has a house. . . . But it's time for me to pack my bags."

Her heart was repaired here, and this testy, plucky document was left behind as testimony. Bonner returned to Gorky early last June and dropped from the news until recently, when the world was told that General Secretary Gorbachev, personally calling Sakharov on a telephone installed in the physicist's Gorky apartment just the day before, an-nounced that the couple would be allowed to return to Moscow. This is good news, though mixed with that of another dissenter, Anatoly Marchenko, who has died in Chistopol Prison, and of a psychiatrist, Anatoly Koryagin, who has been imprisoned for protesting the use of psychiatry for political purposes. Talking to *The New York Times* on his suddenly permissible telephone, Sakharov said he expects to go back to scientific research while continuing to speak out on human rights. His wife, he said, "although she has gotten no worse, is generally a very sick person. . . . She stays at home because she has a heart condition that does not allow her to go out of the house in this kind of weather." Back in Moscow, they have endured countless interviews, and *Newsweek* quotes her as saying that, "if Gorbachev wants to be consistent, then an amnesty for prisoners of conscience is necessary. I also think it is necessary for him to include human rights in the policy of *glasnost.*" She hoped her husband could visit America, and lamented that "a person with such global thinking has not seen the world, not a single country outside of Russia." *Alone Together* was published simultaneously in ten Western countries and, besides making Elena Bonner likable and real to its readers, seems to have done her no harm and perhaps some good. The relatively happy aftermath of its publication bears out her husband's point that the main weapon in the struggle for human rights is publicity.

Doubt and Difficulty in Leningrad and Moscow

PUSHKIN HOUSE, by Andrei Bitov, translated from the Russian by Susan Brownsberger. 371 pp. Farrar, Straus & Giroux, 1987.

CHILDREN OF THE ARBAT, by Anatoli Rybakov, translated from the Russian by Harold Shukman. 685 pp. Little, Brown, 1988.

Glasnost, like the sun breaking through, brings shadows. More, clearly, is to be permitted in the Soviet Union, but how much more? *Doctor Zhivago* can now be published, as being not sufficiently injurious to the health of the Revolution, and so can a smattering of formerly scorned émigrés such as Joseph Brodsky and Vladimir Nabokov. And not only Nabokov's chess problems, his youthful translation of *Alice in Wonderland*, and his little book on Gogol have been published but two novels with a strong taint of political content—*The Gift* and *Invitation to a Beheading*—have been judged fit to print in the nervous homeland of their language. Who, a few short years ago, would have thought it?

Two ambitious novels by Soviet citizens have been recently translated into English and published here after suffering misadventures on the way to their local printer's. *Pushkin House,* by Andrei Bitov, was written in the mid-Seventies, circulated in samizdat, was published in Russian by Ardis Publishers, in Michigan, and last year achieved publication in the Soviet Union. *Children of the Arbat,* by Anatoli Rybakov, was suppressed for twenty years before, in "one of the most daring steps of *glasnost*" (to quote the words of Yevgeny Yevtushenko on the back of the jacket), it was published in the U.S.S.R., "where public libraries have a readers' waiting list for it in the thousands." The jacket of *Pushkin House,* too, bears an encomium: Vassily Aksyonov writes, "Although *Pushkin House* has not been published in the Soviet Union as of yet, this novel has stood up for ten years as a firm part of the contemporary Russian artistic and intellectual environment. Andrei Bitov belongs to the St. Petersburg–Leningrad School of Prose with its ambitions to inherit the perfection of the Silver Age." On the other hand, Yevtushenko tells us, "*Children of the Arbat* is written in the tradition of the Russian social novel of the nineteenth century. It is a geological cross section of *terra incognita* revealing all the layers of society of the early 1930s in Moscow." The symmetry of the blurbists is striking: Yevtushenko is the most internationally conspicuous of those now-middle-aged writers who blossomed during Khrushchev's brief cultural thaw twenty-five years ago and have since elected to tough it out as Soviet artists; Aksyonov, his former confrere and almost exact contemporary, is the best-known child of the thaw to immigrate to the United States, and now resides, jogs, and gives interviews in Washington, D.C. Their respective endorsements suggest that Rybakov's novel is that of an insider ("One of Russia's most successful writers," the back flap tells us) working close to the edge, and Bitov's that of an outsider (though five books of his short stories were published in Moscow between 1963 and 1972) who would rather not think about the edge. Suddenly allowed, last year, to appear at a Washington conference on Western literature, Bitov—a tall, rather sedate man with thinning hair and a drooping, graying mustache—said of the new climate under Gorbachev, "Personally, I am tired of all the changes taking place because I no longer have time to sleep. . . . Change, even for the better, causes discomfort."

Pushkin House is a brilliant, restless, impudent novel, reminiscent of *The Gift* in that it refracts a sensitive young man's moral and aesthetic progress through a prism of allusions to earlier Russian literature, and of Andrei Bely's *Petersburg* in that it makes the city now called Leningrad a vivid and symbolically freighted presence and swathes a few hectic domestic events in a giddy whirl of metaphorically packed language. All three of these novels feel, to the American reader, as if they were losing a lot in translation. The Silver Age mentioned by Aksyonov has no exact equivalent in English prose; its peculiar shades of purple and playfulness and its close alliance with Symbolist poetry suggest distinctly minor writers like Ronald Firbank and Edgar Saltus, while there is nothing minor, in Russian, about Bely and Nabokov. Perhaps Nabokov's English-language novels *Pale Fire* and *Ada* and the more philosophically expansive Saul Bellow works like *Henderson the Rain King* and *Humboldt's Gift* better suggest the controlled explosions, the high-energy conflux of poetic language and way-out thought, that the Russian tradition generated before Lenin and Stalin shut it down. Pushkin House is a literary institute and museum in Leningrad, and in a broader sense the house of which Pushkin laid the cornerstone—classic Russian literature. Epigraphs from and allusions to (attentively footnoted by the translator) this literature abound in Bitov's text, whose three sections bear titles taken from four masterpieces: "Fathers and Sons" (Turgenev), "A Hero of Our Time" (Lermontov), and "The Humble Horseman" (combining Pushkin's "The Bronze Horseman" and Dostoevsky's *Humble Folk*, a combination reversed in the epilogue as "Bronze Folk"). There is also some pointed, mischievous parallelism with Chernyshevsky's seminal radical novel *What Is to Be Done?* It would no doubt help us to have read all these works, as even the mildly educated Russian reader has, but perhaps we can get the idea anyway—the idea, that is, of the superfluous man, the gentleman who floats above the depths of Russian society, and whose existence is especially problematical for literature, since in his superfluity he is nevertheless the principal bearer of culture.

Aristocrats in the dashing old style of Pushkin's Onegin and Lermontov's Pechorin no longer exist, but Soviet society has evolved new elites, and Bitov's hero, Lyova Odoevtsev, belongs to the professorial elite, as well as being a member, through his ancestors, of the nobility. Though Lyova's sensibility, coupled with the talkative author's, occupies the entire foreground of this novel, he is not terribly easy to picture, or to love. His face is not described until near the end, and then with cunning indeterminacy:

> His facial features were devoid of individuality; although his face was unique in its way and fitted no usual type, still—how should I put it?—even though one of a kind, it was typical and did not wholly belong to itself. An expert might have described these features as regular and large, almost 'strong,' but there was something so hopeless and weak in the sudden downward rush of this sculpted mouth and steep chin that it betrayed, within the Slav, the

Aryan with his irresolute courage and secret characterlessness—I would have pictured Mitishatyev [another character, the hero's rival and enemy] thus, rather than Lyova.

Vague as he is, Lyova serves as the focus of three extensive, jumbled episodes: the return from exile and scholarly rehabilitation of his grandfather, the oscillating amorous life he splits among three young woman, and the disastrous three days he spends as lone caretaker at Pushkin House while the rest of Leningrad is celebrating the fiftieth anniversary of the October Revolution. The first and last episodes include long scenes of drunkenness, wonderfully rendered in its colorful, fluctuating fog and torrents of mock-profound discourse; "Vodka is the plot's myrrh-bearer," we are told at one point. In the plot, things seem to happen and then unhappen; a lively character called Uncle Dickens dies and is revived at a moment when his assistance would be convenient. Alternative plot possibilities are freely discussed, and sometimes several are pursued. The overall movement is that of a "sluggish dream" lurchingly flowing toward a meaningless denouement: "And here at last is the sum, peak, crescendo-mescendo, apogee, climax, denouement—what else?—the NOTHING; here at last is that critical NOTHING, idol, symbol: a small, smooth, darkly glossy little thing, prolate, fits in the palm of your hands . . . ! now you see it; now you don't!" The novel not only is difficult but feels to be *about* difficulty, Russian difficulty. In the U.S.S.R., into which Lyova is born in 1937, at the height of Stalin's purges, and in which he is glimpsed thirty years later, concluding on the banks of the Neva that his life "exists only through error," nothing is easy or obvious. Family life is difficult, career choices, career politics, love life; what's more, writing a novel, in this post-Pushkin, post-Stalin, postmodernist world, is difficult, a procedure so tricky and tortuous that the difficulty (I confess) spreads even to writing a review of it.

Within the large and unappetizing inertia of this vodka- and doubt-propelled plot, this "always postponed story," Bitov contrives a microcosmic hyperactivity of phrase, sentence, and image which is, even through the hazy scrim of translation, engagingly vital. Dip in anywhere; small surprises crystallize. "He kept looking at the watch on Karenina's arm. The watch impressed him: golden and tiny on her wide puffy wrist, it had drowned in the folds and lay there smiling." "The swollen Leningrad ceiling hung like a heavy, veined belly. Not rain, not snow—a sort of torn sky-flesh was coming down now, and it plastered the wayfarer in an instant, smothering him like the hateful and nauseating mask of a faint." The novel opens with a startling swoop of authorial rumination:

Somewhere near the end of the novel we have already attempted to describe the clean window, the icy sky gaze, that stared straight and unblinking as the crowds came out to the streets on November 7. Even then, it seemed that this clear sky was no gift, that it must have been extorted by special airplanes. And no gift in the further sense that it would soon have to be paid for.

The sketch of Lyova's family is surprisingly prickly:

Since the chapter is titled "Father," we should mention this: it seemed to Lyovushka that he did not love his father. . . . Father didn't even seem capable of tousling Lyova's hair correctly—Lyova would cringe—or taking him on his lap—he always caused his Lyovushka some sort of physical discomfort—Lyovushka would tense up and then be embarrassed by his own embarrassment.

And yet when Lyova at last meets his grandfather, a linguistics scholar who was imprisoned for thirty years and who should by all liberal and sentimental logic be sympathetic, the old man is repulsive, with an elastic face that seems to be of two halves, and a number of eerie mannerisms: "He drank long, delved deeply, choking, sucking in, soaking in, breathing in, sinking in, withdrawing entirely into the mug, he bumbled over it like a bee over a flower, and when he leaned back with a happy sigh Lyova noted with horror that the beer had not actually diminished in the mug— there was as much left as ever." Lyova initially has trouble distinguishing his grandfather from the old man's former labor-camp commandant, Koptelov, who has become, in a grotesque bit of *perestroika*, a crony. Where Lyova expects familial warmth, a young poet, Rudik, has usurped a favorite's place. As vodka flows, Lyova is roughly teased and mercilessly harangued by his grandfather, who rails against "this affront of rehabilitation. They're not afraid of me anymore. I'm slag. They threw me out into retirement—I've served my time as a prisoner and I'm no good for anything else. That's how capitalist countries treat workers in textbooks." At last, Lyova is dismissed into the bitterly cold "failed space" of outer Leningrad, where his sensations mimic the pace of this novel: "He was oddly aware of time flowing through him. It was uneven and seemingly fitful: it dragged, stretched out, thinned like a droplet, forming a little neck—and suddenly broke."

A real writer's wheels are spinning, and a fine mind is trying to follow truth's rapid changes of direction. "Were they [Lyova's acquaintances] this many at the very beginning, I wonder, and did I, as author, fuse them into one Faina, one Mitishatyev, one . . . in order to give at least some kind of focus to Lyova's blurred life? Because the people who affect us are one thing, and their effect on us is quite another; very often the one has no relation to the other, because their effect on us is already ourselves." The women in Lyova's triangular romantic life pop free of his obsessive concern with his own feelings only for moments of feverish vision: "Now at last Lyova saw that Albina was beautiful, her lofty neck . . . that she might be desired and loved, though again, for some reason, not now, but by the remote Lyova who so generously had not loved her, by that Lyova, not this one still sitting beside her, still not leaving, and almost loving her." Thus we learn that Albina, the unloved, has a long neck. Bitov's authorial hesitations and apologies have a comic vivacity, often:

> In concluding our coverage of this gathering, we must confess that we've been somewhat carried away, somewhat too literal about out task, too ready to rise to the bait. This is all vaudeville, and not worth the trouble. Now it's too late. We have trampled this stretch of prose—the grass will no longer grow on it. We shouldn't have lost our temper.

As in one of Nabokov's layered intricacies, the hero begins to realize he inhabits a work of fiction and is allowed to exult in "the cracks in the scenery (wind blowing in) . . . the general negligence, the hack melodrama, of a dream." A work so energetically, intelligently self-deconstructive as *Pushkin House* must of course make literary commissars uneasy, while Communism's cardboard house shudders and rattles around them. But renewal emerges from disintegration, and Bitov's loving demolition of the grand Russian tradition forms a new installment in that tradition.

Anatoli Rybakov is a good generation older than Bitov, and his *Children of the Arbat* is, compared with *Pushkin House,* an old-fashioned novel— less psychologically and aesthetically dense, more bulky with characters and incidents. Indeed, it would have benefitted from that old-fashioned device, a list of characters in the front, with perhaps an appended brief history of the Soviet Union. It concerns a number of young people who grew up in the Arbat region of Moscow, a bohemian quarter west of the Kremlin, and the ways in which their lives intertwine and diverge between the fall of 1933 and December of 1934. In this period, climaxed by the assassination of Sergei Kirov in Leningrad, Stalin is seen as corrupting Lenin's idealistic revolution with his own paranoia and power lust, and preparing with his Byzantine machinations for the great Party purge and show trials of 1936–38. The novel's portrait of Stalin, intimate and lengthy, must constitute its central scandal from the standpoint of the Soviet censors, and the principal reason it had to wait for *glasnost* to see print. To the Western reader, who has long had access to a number of

unvarnished biographies of the dictator, as well as the scathing characterization in Solzhenitsyn's *The First Circle*, this aspect is less than sensational, though Rybakov's imagination does pull off some lively
strokes—Stalin's tearful identification of his father, the Georgian cobbler
Vissarion Dzhugashvili, with the Charlie Chaplin of *City Lights*, and the
aging tyrant's gingerly give-and-take with a young Jewish dentist, who
succeeds in making Stalin a plastic plate though the dictator insisted he
wanted gold. But Stalin's meditations on how to rule Russia, rewrite
history, and eliminate even a shadow of opposition within the Politburo
are less valuable—less purely Rybakov's to provide—than the sketches of
ordinary Russian life, in its surprising variety and flavor, during a time of
growing oppression and, as nearly everyone but Stalin can see, approaching war with Germany.

The children of the Arbat are called Sasha, Yuri, Lena, Nina, Max,
Vadim, Vika, and Varya. Varya, Nina's sister, is seventeen; the rest are
in their early twenties. Most are members of the Young Communist
League, the Komsomol, and their friendly little world is shaken when the
school's Komsomol secretary, Sasha, is arrested and sentenced to three
years' exile in Siberia. The reasons are obscure. He is headstrong and
outspoken but an ardent Communist; just before his arrest, he successfully
appealed his expulsion from the Transport Institute because of some
satiric verses in the student "wall newspaper." It turns out he is condemned because, during this fracas, he had some casual but subversive
conversation with Krivoruchko, a minor school functionary in disgrace
with the Party. Krivoruchko had merely said, in passing, that "this is a
chef [Stalin] who likes to make peppery dishes"; Sasha declines to recall
this remark for his NKVD interrogator. Though Lena's father, the Old
Bolshevik Budyagin, and Sasha's uncle, Mark Ryazanov, a rising Party
official who directs a Siberian steel plant dear to Stalin's heart, separately
intervene, their intervention does not deflect Sasha's fate; both Budyagin
and Mark, the novel makes clear in its proliferating dark hints, are in
precarious shape themselves, Kremlin-wise. The subtleties of Party organization are not easy to follow, nor are the names easy to keep straight,
but a sense of tightening control, pervasive spying, and irrationality descending from on high is conveyed so well that we feel relieved and even
exhilarated when Sasha reaches the underpopulated hinterland of the
Angara River, between Kansk and Bratsk.

The arrangements of exile are rather informal in these remote riverside
villages within the immense taiga, among primitive peasants, and men and
women already outlawed allow themselves a relative freedom of speech.
The author, who suffered such an exile, evokes the summer atmosphere

of Siberia's rough Eden with the tenderness of remembrance. Sexual deprivation was not necessarily among the exile's hardships: Sasha begins by admiring "the very beautiful, stately Siberian girls with light brown hair, strong bodies, and strong legs," enjoys an episode with a barefoot girl, Lukeshka, who emanates "a scent of the river and new-mown hay," and ends up sharing a bed, in his assigned village of Mozgova, with the local schoolteacher, a petite and passionate Tatar called Zida. The novel's central theme, if one can be identified, is Sasha's moral education: he arrives, amid the system's outcasts and low-priority citizens, at the conclusion that "human feeling has not been killed in people and it never will be."

Meanwhile, back in Moscow, people are coping. Sasha's mother copes by getting a job folding linens in a laundry, and becomes, after a docile life, independent and outspokenly anti-Communist. Yuri makes love to Lena, gets her pregnant, induces an abortion by pouring boiling mustard water around her feet, and joins the NKVD. He discovers that one of his jobs is to "run" Vika, who in the course of her promiscuous, glamorous life in cafés and art circles has become an informer, sleeping with foreigners and relaying tidbits about them to Yuri in a weekly assignation that Lena jealously confuses with a sexual kind. Varya, young as she is, falls into another ring of the Soviet underworld, taking up with a billiard player, shady operator, and big spender called Kostya, and becoming his common-law wife in what was Sasha's old room. She finally frees herself of him and finds a measure of peace and redemption in that officially endorsed panacea, work. She gets a job as a draftsman, and the stolid prose approaches the lyrical:

> She laid the drawing that was to be copied on her board, covered it with a pale blue linen sheet, and pinned them both down with thumbtacks. She then wiped a thin film of machine oil over the surface . . . in order to make the tracing linen transparent, allowing the drawing to come through clearly and preventing the ink from running. . . . Lyova and Rina were full of admiration for her ability, if ink did spill, to remove it with a razor blade without leaving a mark. And to their amazement she could draw a free-hand curve with a fine pen.

Rybakov's prose, though rather too journalistically quick on its feet to be called plodding, comes across as colorless and rarely gets off the ground (whereas Bitov's rarely touches the ground). Little, Brown reportedly hoped for another best-selling *Doctor Zhivago,* but there is in *Children of the Arbat* nothing of Pasternak's poetry and magical sweep of vision and coincidence. Both novels under review, in fact, induce sensations of claustrophobia: in Bitov's we are caught inside a human head, and in Rybakov's inside a totalitarian state. But Rybakov does show some modernist daring in the shape of the book: big as it is, it feels like a fragment, a ragged thick slice of life. Almost all the questions raised by its multitudinous soap opera are left unanswered. Will Sasha some day return to Moscow, or will he accumulate ever longer terms of exile with his rambunctious free spirit? Will Varya find happiness away from her drawing board as well as at it? Will Vika succeed in disentangling herself from the NKVD and make a go of her marriage with an unnamed famous architect? Why won't Zida tell Sasha why she has come to this wild taiga? What will lovelorn Lena do now that Yuri is posted to Leningrad? What will happen to Mark Ryazanov, who thinks he still enjoys Stalin's favor? Who knows? Only Kirov, who is assassinated, has his story rounded out; and Stalin's has been rounded out by history. A number of the children of the Arbat, introduced with considerable ceremony, do a single turn and then retire to the wings, waiting perhaps for the next act, or the next opera. Can this drastically unresolved large novel be the mere first installment of a giant *roman-fleuve* cascading in rough parallel to the author's own eventful life? It is, Rybakov declared in a *Time* interview last year; he plans two more installments of his saga, bringing the reader up through World War II, in which the author, rehabilitated after a stretch in Siberia, served as a much-decorated tank commander.

But *Children of the Arbat*—whose American publisher gives no hint of anything less than a complete novel—doesn't even tell us how Sasha survives his first Siberian winter. On the public level, a climax of sorts is reached in Kirov's assassination, which will set off the historical purges to come. On the private level, things stay up in the air. For all its wealth of characters, the novel feels light and thin. It lacks the increased gravity of history rounding a curve. It dares to enter Stalin's head, but it cannot climb outside of Stalin's heritage, and conceives happiness in the traditional Russian way, as something filched from the state—a kind of spiritual sneaking, a defiant privacy and individual freedom. "The state had always seemed to Sasha so all-powerful, all-knowing, and all-pervasive. In fact, it wasn't so. You could avoid the state." Might the state itself change for the better? This question lies well beyond the horizon of this novel, and we scan the daily newspapers for the answer.

OTHER COUNTRIES HEARD FROM

Chronicles and Processions

CHRONICLE IN STONE, by Ismail Kadare, translated from the Albanian anonymously. 277 pp. The Meredith Press, 1987.

BALTASAR AND BLIMUNDA, by José Saramago, translated from the Portuguese by Giovanni Pontiero. 336 pp. Harcourt Brace Jovanovich, 1987.

Albanians are known for their ferocity, isolation, and ultra-Communism, and not for their modern literature; yet Ismail Kadare, born in 1936, has a considerable European reputation, and the second of his works to be published here, *Chronicle in Stone,** is no mere curiosity but a thoroughly enchanting novel—sophisticated and accomplished in its narrative deftness and lyrical economy, yet drawing strength from its roots in one of Europe's most primitive societies. Kadare has been likened to Gabriel García Márquez, and both writers tell of towns still shimmering with magic and dominated by clannishness; Kadare's nameless mountain city, no doubt based upon his own native Gjirokastër, seems less whimsical than García Márquez's Macondo, less willfully twisted into surreality.

Kadare's is a city made entirely of stone, "from the streets and fountains to the roofs of the sprawling age-old houses covered with grey slates like gigantic scales," and so steep that "the top of one house might graze the foundation of another" and a drunk falling in the street winds up on the roof of a house. Though the narrative takes place during the Second World War, the city harbors timeless customs: brides' faces are decorated with "starlike dots, cypress branches, and signs of the zodiac, all floating in the white mystery of powder," and outbreaks of magic cause people to

---

*The first was *The General of the Dead Army*, published by Grossman in 1972.

lock up their hair clippings and fireplace ashes. The erection of a statue in the town square years before had seemed to the natives an alarming novelty:

A metal man? Was such a creation really necessary? Might it not cause trouble? At night, when everyone was sleeping as God had ordained, the statue would be out there standing erect. Day and night, summer and winter, it would stand. . . . To avoid trouble there was no unveiling ceremony. People stood and stared in wonder at the bronze warrior, hand on his pistol, who gazed severely down into the square as if asking, "Why didn't you want me?" That night someone threw a blanket over the bronze man's shoulders. From then on, the city's heart went out to its statue.

When a Greek soldier shoots the statue in the thigh, people "had the feeling they were limping. Others actually were limping."

The prevalent animism is doubly intense in the sensibility of the un-named child at the center of the novel. He anthropomorphizes the rain-drops talking in the gutter, and the cistern beneath the house that they flow into: "I liked the cistern a lot and often leaned over its rim and had long talks with it. It had always been ready to answer me in its deep, cavernous voice." In his mind the city is a stone creature clinging to its mountain, the streets creep and plunge and crash into one another ("a collision from which both streets emerged crooked"), and the warplanes that use the nearby air strip acquire vivid personalities. A child's self-centered, metaphoric way of seeing generates a constant poetry:

The little cloud in the sky lurched ahead drunkenly. It had turned long and skinny now. Life in the sky must have been pretty boring in the summer. Not much happened there. The little cloud crossing the sky the way a man crosses a deserted square in the noonday heat melted away before reaching the north. I had noticed that clouds died very fast. Then their remains drifted in the sky for a long time. It was easy to tell the dead clouds from the live ones.

The voice of innocence and gusts of gossip relay the tale, though the chapters are interlarded with fragments of newspaper, proclamation, and historical chronicle. The Italians occupy the city, bringing with them nuns, a brothel, and an airfield; the British bomb the city; the Greeks momentarily occupy it; the Italians return and retreat again; Albanian partisans of various political stripes descend from the hills; and, finally, the Germans occupy the city. Most of its inhabitants flee ahead of the yellow-haired invader, and then slowly return: "Again the tender flesh of life was filling the carapace of stone." With the German occupation, the chronicle ends, as if its marvellous tone of childish fable could no longer be supported by memory. An adult voice tells us at the end, "A very long time later I came back to the grey immortal city. My feet timidly trod the spine of its stone-paved streets. . . . Often, striding along wide lighted boulevards in foreign cities, I sometimes stumble in places where no one ever trips. Passers-by turn in surprise, but I always know it's you. Rising up suddenly out of the asphalt and then sinking back in, deep down."

One would like to know where these foreign boulevards were, and how Ismail Kadare was able to produce, under the notoriously repressive and xenophobic Hoxha regime, an art so refined and so free in its feeling. Hoxha is referred to in a late chapter, as a hunted resistance leader and a former, once "well-behaved" resident of the city, but without any flattery or obsequious emphasis. The waves of competing authority that move through the city are seen, like spells of weather, in terms of their local effects purely, and the Communist characters participate in the internecine brutality without rising above it. The bits of prose between the first-person chapters reduce history to a non-progressive flutter of old feuds and fresh slogans. The most ominous event is the execution, by the German occupiers, of old Kako Pino, the painter of brides' faces, who is seized by a patrol on her way to one of the weddings that have absurdly, miraculously persisted through all the bombings and invasions. Her picturesque magic is perfunctorily and, one feels, irretrievably erased from the world.

Of the author's status within post-war Albania, we know only what the copyright page tells us—that *Chronicle in Stone (Kronikë në gur)* was originally published in Tiranë, the forbidding little country's capital, in 1971. Kadare takes us into the bosom of a land where all but a few Westerners are denied entry, and makes little of Albania's Muslim-tinged exoticism—the mosques, the fezzes, the orthographically strange names like Xhexho, Selfixhe, and Vehip Qorri. Rather, his stone city emerges as a persuasive analogue for anyone's childhood—friendly even in its mysteries, precious even in its recollected hardships and barbarities. Nostalgic reminiscence, of course, is one of the safer havens for a creative writer under a totalitarian regime (others are translation, children's stories, and historical fiction). Ismail Kadare, the jacket flap tells us, after first finding fame as a poet, "has mined medieval and modern historical events, legend and reality," in the writing of nine novels. It will be interesting to see, as these novels are translated into English, whether they maintain the superb balance and unforced amplitude of this one or slip, under the pressures of a watchful regime, into false naïveté and prudent stylization.

* * *

Baltasar and Blimunda, by José Saramago, also comes from a small European country, and partakes of magic realism, that now widely available elixir. Admirable and sweetly melancholy as this ambitious, panoramic novel often is, its magical freedom from realistic constraints, bestowed upon events of the historical rather than remembered past, permits the author to indulge himself in a great many flourishes of rather baffling intent. Moving between present and past tense, and between the royal court and the plebeian realm of workmen and vagabonds, the novel seems to be telling us something about Portugal, its great inequalities and pious cruelties, with an undercurrent of outrage that an effervescent love story keeps diluting. Its time runs from 1711 to 1739, all during the reign of João V, and its central historical event is the King's agreeing to build, in accordance with a bargain struck with the Franciscans, a convent in the town of Mafra, provided the Franciscans' prayers induce his Queen, Maria Ana of Austria, to bear him an heir within a year. She does, and the labor of building the extensive convent begins, described by the author in the kind of zealous pro-labor-force detail we might find on a Mexican mural. The transportation of a giant flagstone, thirty-five spans long, fifteen spans wide, and four spans deep (bigger than a breadbox), and weighing thirty-one tons, from the quarry to the site where it will serve as the convent's portico takes six hundred men, four hundred oxen, eight days, and twenty-two pages to move three leagues. The point of all this logistical description seems to be that kings of old made their subjects perform onerous and vainglorious tasks: "The Convent of Mafra was built by Dom João V in fulfillment of a vow he made should God grant him an heir. Here go six hundred men who did not make the Queen pregnant yet pay for that vow by bearing the burden."

Amid this work force is our hero, Baltasar Mateus, nicknamed Sete-Sóis (Seven-Suns), whom we first meet when he is twenty-six years of age—a soldier returning from an engagement with the Spanish cavalry, his left hand having been so shattered by gunfire that it had to be amputated. While idly watching an auto-da-fé in Lisbon, he is accosted by a nineteen-year-old woman, Blimunda, with changeable eyes and a gift, when she has been fasting, of seeing into people, to their tumors and fetuses and essences. She is accompanied by a priest, Bartolomeu Lourenço—a historical figure, who is famous for having invented a flying machine named, since it resembles a giant bird, the Passarola. Blimunda asks Baltasar *his* name, takes him home with her, sleeps with him, and draws a cross on his chest with her virgin's blood. The idyll of their faithful love continues to the day of his death, twenty-eight years later. How it and the additional marvel of Padre Bartolomeu's flying device (it works on the principle of balls of sun-activated amber exercising attraction upon bottled quantities of human wills, which are small dark clouds; these then attract magnets that lift the metal body of the airship) fit into the novel's indictment of corruption and extravagance in all-too-Catholic eighteenth-century Portugal remains, so to speak, up in the air.

Saramago likes to describe ceremonies, pageants, and processions. His prose takes on a stiff, brocaded quality:

> The King arrived at half past eight after drinking his morning cup of chocolate, which the Visconde himself served. The royal procession then set out, headed by sixty-four Franciscan friars followed by all the clergy of the region; then came the patriarchal cross, six attendants dressed in red capes, the musicians, the chaplains in their surplices, and representatives from every conceivable order. Then there was a gap to prepare the crowd for what followed, the canons of the chapter wearing their cloaks, some in white linen, others embroidered, and each canon with his personal attendant, chosen from the nobility, walking before him, and his trainbearer behind; then came the Patriarch, wearing sumptuous vestments and a priceless miter encrusted with precious stones from Brazil. . . .

Such pomp crushes, enforcing the reign of the clerisy and the aristocracy. Yet men are equal, in many ways: bedbugs bite the King, and "His Majesty's blood tastes no better or worse than that of the other inhabitants of the city, whether blue or otherwise"; the Infanta "pouts and bites her lip" like "any other child her age, whether born in a palace or anywhere else"; death takes royal infants along with others; "Lent, like the rising sun, is a season for everyone"; and all men throw cherry pits on the ground—"It is little things like these that make us realize that all men are equal." The curiously wandering, disembodied authorial voice is now inside the King, thinking with him, and now far outside, delivering an anti-royalist diatribe. Is the author trying to incite the citizens of eighteenth-century Portugal to overthrow the monarchy? If so, he comes a bit late. Perhaps some modern indictment is implied, of Portugal as a national case of arrested development: "Foreigners find us an easy target for jokes. . . . Our stupidity is clear for all to see, without recourse to Blimunda's visionary powers"; "Never has there been a nation so staunch in its faith yet so disorderly." The glorious past, as conjured up, seems an incubus, an ornate burden, a procession of stately vanity and hypocritical piety.

The great convent at Mafra is not the only construction in the book: Padre Bartolomeu's mechanical bird is assembled and maintained and finally flown, and the common-law marriage of Baltasar and Blimunda is a marvellous contraption of another kind. Built upon that imperious encounter when she asks his name and then signs him with her blood, it endures by the magic of sex and the mutual strangeness of his one-handedness and her clairvoyant, volatile eyes—"their coloring uncertain, gray, green, or blue, according to the outer light or the inner thought. Sometimes they even turn as black as night or a brilliant white, like a splinter of anthracite." They are Adam and Eve before complications set in; the couple have no children, and no privation or parting ever calls them out of the garden of themselves. Even into decaying middle age they kiss with the ardor of young lovers: "Those poor mouths, their bloom gone, with some teeth missing and others broken, but in the end it is love that prevails." Since they undergo no failures but simply persist as an enchanting demonstration of erotic success, and since the work of building the great convent can only plod along, readerly suspense must attach to the Passarola, which is most amusingly evoked, in its spooky mechanics and in its one brief interlude of flight. However, it is never deliberately flown again; its inventor, harried by fear of the Inquisition, succumbs to depression and goes to Toledo and dies, and Baltasar and Blimunda, though privy to its operating principles, merely hide the Passarola and tend it year after year. The flying machine, like this finespun novel, has nowhere special to go, and stays earthbound, balls of amber and bottled wills and magic realism and all.

There is a powerful negative impulse pulling at José Saramago's airy, wry poetry. His strangest literary habit is to disown thoughts and words that have flown out of his characters: "Who knows why such thoughts should occur to these rustics, for they are all illiterate except João Anes, who has had some education"; "This couple can neither write nor read, yet they can say things that seem most unlikely at such a time and in such a place"; "These are similes invented by someone who is writing on behalf of a soldier who fought in the war. Baltasar did not invent them." And, most confessionally: "Blimunda was clearly incapable of such subtle thoughts; therefore, we are perhaps not inside these people and cannot tell what they are thinking." For all its lovely color and imposing panoply of historical detail, *Baltasar and Blimunda* does somehow lack an inside; King and Queen and priest and lovers and even Domenico Scarlatti are paraded past us without our quite knowing what we are supposed to make of their embellished opacity. In this the novel sharply contrasts with *Chronicle in Stone*, whose exotica are rendered, through a child's eyes, intimate and familiar. At one point, Blimunda looks clairvoyantly at the Sacred Host and sees not Christ but "a dark cloud." A dark cloud lurks at the center of this superficially buoyant and festive narrative: "Human existence is so miserable," the narrator reflects toward the end. Queen

Maria is shown counselling her daughter the Infanta: "The longer you live the more you will realize that the world is like a great shadow pervading our hearts. That is why the world seems so empty and eventually becomes unbearable." This emptiness translates into a novelistic inertness, a frozen tableau vivant.

Satan's Work and Silted Cisterns

CITIES OF SALT, by Abdelrahman Munif, translated from the Arabic by Peter Theroux. 627 pp. Random House, 1988.

ARABESQUES, by Anton Shammas, translated from the Hebrew by Vivian Eden. 263 pp. Harper & Row, 1988.

The most fabulous geological event since the explosion of Krakatoa surely was the discovery of oceans of petroleum beneath the stark and backward Muslim realms of the Persian Gulf. Sheiks whose wealth was previously measured in horses and camels soon ranked with the world's richest men; dusty remotenesses like Kuwait and Bahrain and Saudi Arabia became able, with scarcely a dent in their national revenues, to shower all the blessings of an advanced welfare state upon their sparse populations. According to *The World Almanac,* the highest per-capita income on the planet belongs not to the United States or Sweden or Japan but to Qatar. The Western view of this global caprice is expressed by resentful caricatures of dollar-glutted sheiks and by our nervous protective naval presence in the Persian Gulf. The Arab view receives less publicity; *Cities of Salt* performs a needed service in dramatizing the impact of American oil discovery and development upon an unnamed Gulf emirate in the 1930s. It is unfortunate, given the epic potential of his topic, that Abdelrahman Munif, a Saudi born in Jordan, appears to be—though he lives in France and received a Ph.D. in oil economics from the University of Belgrade—insufficiently Westernized to produce a narrative that feels much like what we call a novel. His voice is that of a campfire explainer; his characters are rarely fixed in our minds with a face or a manner or a developed motivation; no central figure acquires enough reality to attract our sympathetic interest; and, this being the first third of a trilogy, what intelligible conflicts and possibilities do emerge remain serenely unresolved. There is almost none of that sense of individual moral adventure—of the evolving individual in varied and roughly equal battle with a world of circumstance—which, since *Don Quixote* and *Robinson Crusoe*, has distinguished the novel from the fable and the chronicle; *Cities of Salt* is concerned, instead, with men in the aggregate. Its focus might be described as sociological, and its sociological point as the single insistent one that Arabs are discomfited, distressed, and deranged by the presence of Americans in their midst. In over six hundred pages, repeated illustration of this point wears thin.

The book begins by evoking the oasis of Wadi al-Uyoun, "an outpouring of green amid the harsh, obdurate desert." It is, for most of its residents, a kind home: "Wadi al-Uyoun was an ordinary place to its inhabitants, and excited no strong emotions, for they were used to seeing the palm trees filling the wadi and the gushing brooks surging forth in the winter and early spring, and felt protected by some blessed power that made their lives easy." Births and deaths, the arrival and departure of caravans, the seasons of rain and drought make a rhythm of events that is timeless; when three white foreigners, escorted by two marsh Arabs, camp on the edge of the village, curiosity runs rampant and the strong emotion of dread enters the breast of Miteb al-Hathal, a patriarch of the Atoum tribe:

> He sensed that something terrible was about to happen. He did not know what it was or when it would happen, and he took no comfort in the explanations offered him from all sides. The very sight of the foreigners and their constant activity all day, the instruments they carried around, the bags of sand and stones they had amassed after writing in their notebooks and drawing symbols on them, the discussions that lasted from sundown until after supper and the writing that followed, the damned questions they asked about dialects, about tribes and their disputes, about religion and sects, about the routes, the winds and the rainy seasons—all these caused Miteb's fear to grow day by day that they meant harm to the wadi and the people.

He confides to his son Fawaz, "They said, 'Wait, just be patient, and all of you will be rich!' But what do they want from us, and what does it concern them if we get rich or stay just as we are? . . . They're devils, no one can trust them. They're more accursed than the Jews." His unease drives him to address the emir: "By God, Your Excellency, we were as happy as we could be before those devils came along. But from the first day they came to our village life has been camel piss. Every day it gets worse." Miteb is foremost but far from alone in his agitation: "Fear gripped the wadi. The men grew more rash and nervous, and Miteb was considered indispensable—if he absented himself from the wadi a single day to sleep in Zahra the people missed him acutely; only he was capable of saying everything, of expressing their innermost thoughts." Increasingly, the oasis-dwellers feel blighted by this lawless visitation from the outside world. The American oil-prospectors sunbathe in their shorts in view of the women fetching water; the affront is hardly greater when, a little later, the entire village is bulldozed into rubble. Miteb al-Hathal takes to the desert to wreak some ill-defined vengeance, and Fawaz, who has been itching to leave the oasis anyway, goes to work for the oil company as it builds its port in the seaside town of Harran.

In Harran, there is more of the same: on the American side, construction and revelry; on the Arab, puzzlement, depression, and hard labor. The cruellest cut seems to be not that the American houses have fences and swimming pools, or that the emir becomes obsessed by such devil's toys as a telescope and a radio, or even that the American bosses drive the Arab workers right through the heat of summer, but that, occasionally, like a voluptuous mirage, a white boat appears offshore, laden with nearly naked white women. "The women were perfumed, shining and laughing, like horses after a long race. Each was strong and clean, as if fresh from a hot bath, and each body was uncovered except for a small piece of colored cloth. Their legs were proud and bare, and stronger than rocks. Their faces, hands, breasts, bellies—everything, yes, everything glistened, danced, flew."* The women come ashore and dance and entwine with the Americans, while the Arabs of Harran look on in an astonishment beyond words: "The men were mostly quiet now and slightly dizzy, feeling sharp pains throbbing in certain parts of their bodies. Some cried out, and most of them wished that they had never come to see what was transpiring before them." During this long and shameful night, one of the Arab men announces out of the darkness, "Say what you want, but I'm afraid we've lost our world and our faith."

The book continues for four hundred more pages, but the moral has been stated: the invasion of the oil exploiters has cost the native population its world and its faith. The money that petroleum brings the populace is no consolation: "True, the company was paying them now, but the next day workers paid out again what they had received. Prices went up every day, and their savings declined." Ibn Naffeh, one of Harran's spokesmen for Islamic righteousness, announces, "Foreign lands are corrupt, and foreign people bring corruption, and money corrupts worst of all." An-

---

*What is happening, actually? Would Thirties costumes look so scanty, even to Arabs? These women seem clad in the Sixties minimum. Also, at another point the Americans anachronistically seem to produce tape recorders—"small black boxes, which they pressed whenever they got into a conversation."

other such seer, a healer called Mufaddi, refuses to work for money, and proclaims, "Money enslaves, it subjugates, but it never brings happiness." The Americans themselves, their wild women and useless money aside, have infuriating personalities. Invited to a feast, they "looked and behaved like small children"—asking endless questions, taking many photographs, speaking Arabic with funny accents, and showing a pathetic inability to eat with their hands correctly. They are not invited to a wedding because they would have turned it into "an orgy of interviews and picture taking." On the job, they are "cruel" and "tough and bigoted." "At first the Americans had laughed and slapped them on the shoulders. Now they did not look at them or if they did, spat out words that could only be curses." They awaken self-hatred, resentment, and fear in the workers. As Ibn Naffeh says, "The Americans came and the demons came with them. Anyone who drinks their water or eats of their provisions will have a demon enter him."

The maledictory rhetoric of the Ayatollah Khomeini is nothing new. In *Cities of Salt*, the boat full of shining and laughing women is "Satan's ship," and the American projects are "Satan's work," culminating in "Satan's pipe project." The novel's language strains in trying to capture the peculiarly intense mental states induced by the advent of modern Western enterprise and mores. "The people were overwhelmed with pity and fear; these were obscure but powerful emotions." After the staunchly religious Mufaddi dies, "babies cried all night, as though afraid or in pain." A man with a grievance against the oil company feels "an urge to weep or scream. He had to do something to keep from falling down dead." He is "burning with anger, no, not only anger; it was mingled with something as black as pitch and oozy thick as old blood that had not dried yet."

The undrying wound is the loss of tribal and village unity, of effortless interaction and mutual consideration. "In spite of the crowds and the endless influx of new people"—as Harran grows—"each man became a world unto himself. Dealings between people from different and perhaps mutually hostile places were wary and full of apprehensions." Urbanization detaches and renders deaf. "Harran was no one's property, no one's city. So chaotic and crowded had it become that everyone asked and everyone answered, but no one heard or understood." As sociology, this has its interest, but it doesn't animate the characters. A few of the Americans receive names (Henderson, Middleton, Blackie, Fatso), but they remain indistinguishable. Miteb al-Hathal stays out in the desert, a mere rumor of redemption from the demons. The Arabs in the foreground are rarely seen from within but live mainly in the gossip of others and the author's gossipy, regretful voice; they are not so much persons as reputations. In a village, no one needs to be described, since everyone is known. Only slowly, as the novel settles into Harran and the town becomes more corrupt and crowded, does Abdelrahman Munif begin to give us what we can recognize as characterizations, with physical descriptions:

His face was like that of a child, with its bold eyes, loud, innocent laugh and large, gleaming white teeth, and his slim, lanky body seemed carved from smooth stone or wood.

But such visualizations, and portraits of such outsiders as the truck-driver Akoub the Armenian, begin to clarify the picture too late: the novel's people and events are seen as if through a sandstorm, blurred by a hopeless communal grief and sense of affront. Some authorities, too, were evidently affronted: the jacket flap tells us that *Cities of Salt* has been banned in Saudi Arabia. The thought of novels being banned in Saudi Arabia has a charming strangeness, like the thought of hookahs being banned in Minneapolis.

Anton Shammas, the author of *Arabesques,* shows no lack of sophistication in the ways of the literary West: his novel about Palestinians is intricately conceived and beautifully written, with epigraphs from Clive James, Bernard Shaw, and John Barth. A crisp, luminous, and nervy mixture of fantasy and autobiography, it has not one but two heroes called Anton Shammas and a number of scenes set in Iowa City, during a session of the International Writing Program. Yet this elegant example of postmodern baroque, like Abdelrahman Munif's long and muffled quasi-oral tale, repels our attempts to enter it whole-heartedly; we feel we are not getting out of the book nearly as much emotionalized information as the author put into it. Something gets stuck. Is the stickiness to be blamed on our lack of familiarity with the Arab world? Munif's Muslims seemed, until the demonic modern world scrambled their souls, familiar: they were the noble caftaned savages admired by T. E. Lawrence, Wilfred Thesiger, and other doughty British travellers. Shammas's people are of a type we rarely hear about: Palestinian Christians. Shammas himself is a walking paradox: a non-Jew who considers himself an Israeli, a poet in both Arabic and Hebrew, and a columnist in two Hebrew-language newspapers. He has told *The New York Times* that he feels he has more in common with the average Israeli than with the average Palestinian or Arab living in Jordan. One wonders how long he can maintain his balancing act in a land where, as of now, Palestinian Arabs are assassinating officials and doctors who are perceived as collaborating with the Israeli authorities. Already, for having presumed to chide the beloved mayor of Jerusalem, Teddy

Kollek, in a newspaper column, he has received death threats, and graffiti spelling "Arab vermin" have appeared on his apartment building. At present, Shammas—in his book-jacket photograph, a studious-looking young man pensively scratching his ear—resides in Ann Arbor, Michigan, where he has a Rockefeller Fellowship in Middle Eastern literature; a note on the translation tells us that he helped Vivian Eden produce this smooth English version of his "very allusive and layered kind of Hebrew with equally complex Arabic resonances, especially in the rhythm section."

We expect, perhaps, a Palestinian novel to be about the present Palestinian problem, much as some foreigners feel that an American novel has a duty to grapple with our race problem or the horrors of capitalism. But *Arabesques* is fundamentally nostalgic: its most affecting scenes render the narrator's childhood experiences in the small Galilean village of Fassuta, and its principal narrative thrust is toward the past, toward the unravelling of the tangled past lives of the boy's parents, aunts, and uncles. There is war in the background, but much of it is the war to drive out the British before 1948, and some of it is the old and continuing civil/religious war in Lebanon, where Anton's mother comes from and her family, the Bitars, still lives. There is scarcely a Jewish character in the book, nor is Jewish clout felt until the epilogue, wherein an Israeli demolition expert is called in, by Uncle Yusef Shammas's grandson Yusef, to blow up a rock that, village superstition has it, conceals the mouth of a treasure trove over which *djinn* have appointed a magical rooster called Ar-Rasad to stand guard. The explosion reveals no treasure, but a crimson feather descends from the sky, symbolizing, let's hope, bright future possibilities in this long-disputed land, and demonstrating, once more, the international appeal of Latin-American magic realism.

The author is an adroit and suave negotiator between the real and the unreal, between family legend and personal epiphany, between objective mystery and subjective illumination. He titles the book's sections either "The Tale" or "The Teller"; under the latter head come scenes in Iowa City, where the foreign writers are housed, amid the alien corn, in an eight-story student dormitory called the Mayflower. The writing program there, complete with a real-life Paul Engle, is done in the colorful strokes that befit the exotic:

> Across North Dubuque Street, on the banks of the river, workmen in blue overalls laid strips of sod over the black earth with muscular and precise movements. On the way to the center of town, we saw white houses on either side, their tiled roofs sharply pointed. Before them lay wide lawns, with a narrow walk extending down to the sidewalk and the tree-lined street.

Squirrels rushed about at the feet of the trees, their tails erect with midwestern pride.

Again colorfully, in the international writers' little Tower of Babel Anton finds himself caught between a venerable and touchy Jewish Israeli writer, Yehoshua Bar-On, and a Palestinian Arab, called Paco Rabanne, after the pungent cologne he wears. On the romantic level, Anton is caught between his beloved mistress back in Jerusalem, Shlomith, a red-haired Jewish woman married to an Army officer, and his inamorata in Iowa City, Amira, a dark-haired native of Alexandria who lives in Paris. All this seems much as it would be, but when Bar-On tries to strangle Amira because she tells him, in Hebrew, that it's an act of *chutzpah* for him to smoke in an Amish house they are visiting, or when a female university student, after a night of some festivity, abruptly takes off her clothes, climbs up on a table ("The ivory down of her young triangle is wonderfully precise in the middle of the small room"), and sings an old Irish song, either behavior in Iowa has loosened up since I was last there or a touch of Palestinian blarney has tweaked the telling.

More deeply felt images emerge from the teller's memories of Fassuta, and in their oddity they evoke a people queerly caught between the past and the present. When Anton's grandmother dies, his father lays an iron sickle on her stomach, to hold down its swelling. Every fourth Sunday, Anton's father ritually cleans their intricate kerosene lamp, with its "magical fragile mantle" and tiny jet hole. An uncle in Argentina sends by sea a wooden box of clothes and includes a pair of scissors, which in the three months' boat passage rust and wander among the clothes, leaving "crazy patterns" of rust stain. When a mother rebukes her son with how much she suffered when she nursed him, he calculates the quantity of milk he suckled and presents her with two full dairy cans. A man drags his mattress into the street and pelts it with stones, "cursing it for all the hours of sleep he had wasted upon it." A priest labors for years composing and calligraphing a "unique and unparalleled work, which would glorify the Catholic Church among all the Arabic-speaking peoples," only to have his cat push it into a crock of olive oil, where the calligraphy returns "to its liquid state." And Anton, at the age of ten, is lowered by rope into the family cistern to clean it; the village tomboy, Nawal, is sent down the rope after him, and while he is bracing her buttocks to help her scrape the sides of the round cistern she has an orgasm.

The world where these things happen lies on the edge of the modern, but its interconnections are not electronic; the threads of kinship and family legend hold the Shammases together. In this Holy Land where the

Jews, the Romans, the ancient Christian church, the Muhammadans, the Crusaders, the Mamelukes, the Turks, the British, and now the Zionists have all exerted hegemony, the threads are tangled and knotted. At the center of the tangle is the figure of Laylah Khoury, a blond village girl who in 1936 was placed with the Bitar family in Beirut, removed nine months later by the sinister, nunlike Mademoiselle Sa'da to another family, and brought back to Fassuta in 1948, only to be expelled by the Israeli Army to Jordan, where she converted to Islam and married the son of Al-Asbah, an Arab rebel leader. At a point in her youth, she lived with the Abyad family, whose adopted son, Michel, seems to be the son of Uncle Jiryes Shammas; the child was kidnapped from the hospital by agents of the Abyads, and his mother, Aunt Almaza, was told he was dead. Laylah (which means "night" in both Hebrew and Arabic and has the esoteric meaning of "poet's lady" in Arabic) unrequitedly loved this Michel, who is really the first Anton Shammas, after whom our apparent narrator was named and who now, under the name of Michael Abyad, is an American-educated doctor who works for the Palestinian Center for Research in Beirut and has written the book we are reading, about the Anton Shammas who resembles the fellow on the dust jacket. He, the second Anton, in 1983, at the age of thirty-three, embraces (perhaps merely with a magic-realist, wishful-thinking sort of hug) the blond Muslim convert, now a fifty-seven-year-old widow and the mother of mute twins, and the sexual cistern returns:

> This is the body that should have visited the dreams of the other Anton in Beirut, this is the body that should have covered him with its virginity. I go down on my knees and cup my hands around the two white buttocks, I bury my face in her triangle and breathe in the chill of the mildew, the ancient odor of the stones and the dark scent of the silt rising from the bottom of the cistern.

But it's been a long way around, and the English-language reader, wearied by the effort of keeping the names straight and bringing his slender knowledge of Near Eastern history to bear on the tumble of chronology, may be too exhausted to relish the epiphanic ambiguity and the ingenious play of recurring motif. Or maybe not. Perhaps primal nostalgia can be smuggled into us only by an elaborate cleverness; certainly an investigation, like *Arabesques,* into a writer's own being must be in honesty a layered affair, a tale with a visible teller. In a world whose political trend is always toward strident simplification and brute loyalty, this almost stiflingly complex confession of complexity is a brave attempt, all the braver for the adopted language in which it has been composed.

Three Tales from Nigeria

FOREST OF A THOUSAND DAEMONS, by D. O. Fagunwa, translated from the Yoruba by Wole Soyinka. 140 pp. Random House, 1983.

THE WITCH-HERBALIST OF THE REMOTE TOWN, by Amos Tutuola. 205 pp. Faber & Faber, 1981.

DOUBLE YOKE, by Buchi Emecheta. 163 pp. Braziller, 1983.

The shift from spoken to written narrative is nowhere complete; there is always a voice, and in the case of exemplary modern novelists like Proust and Henry James it seems sometimes there is *only* the voice, coaxing us on to another page and another brandy, in these readerly circumstances of strange nocturnal intimacy. When we turn, however, to works markedly nearer the beginnings of writing than the outpourings of these two elegant and highly self-conscious scribes, we experience a dismay, a disorientation, for which the lucid epics of Homer and the oft-retold chronicles of the Bible have not quite prepared us. We do not know the language, the code of mythology and tradition, and feel oppressively confused, as when we look at the Tibetan pantheon arrayed on a *thang-ka*, while an equally populous mural, say, of the Last Judgment or the Battle of Waterloo quickly sorts itself out. There is always a code, and oral narrative disconcertingly assumes that we know it.

Forest of a Thousand Daemons, by D. O. Fagunwa, was first published in 1939—just yesterday, on the calendar of Western literature. A man of this century, Fagunwa was born in 1903 and died in 1963. Yet this first of his five novels in the language of the Yoruba—a black people concentrated in southwestern Nigeria—takes us back to a time when narratives existed only in the memories and utterances of their tellers. The opening page instructs the readers how to read a novel: "Firstly, whenever a character in my story speaks in his own person, you must put yourself in his place and speak as if you are that very man. . . . In addition, as men of discerning—and this is the second task you must perform—you will yourselves extract various wisdoms from the story as you follow its progress." Even so, the narrative, as if to soften the strangeness of its existence as a text, is presented as an oral tale that the writer has taken from the dictation of another. The writer, on a morning of benign beauty ("A beatific breeze rustled the dark leaves of the forest, deep dark and shimmering leaves, the sun rose from the East in God's own splendour, spread

its light into the world and the sons of men began their daily perambulations"), is seated in his favorite chair, "settled into it with voluptuous
contentment," when an elderly stranger comes up to him, chats, sighs, and
then commands: "Take up your pen and paper and write down the story
which I will now tell. . . . I am concerned about the future and there is
this fear that I may die unexpectedly and my story die with me. But if I
pass it on to you now and you take it all down diligently, even when the
day comes that I must meet my Maker, the world will not forget me." So,
its double-edged reward established (for the reader, "various wisdoms";
for the teller, immortality), the tale begins.

The teller identifies himself as "Akara-ogun, Compound-of-Spells, one
of the formidable hunters of a bygone age," and relates how his mother,
a witch momentarily in the shape of an antelope, was fatally shot by his
father, who within a month himself died, of no named disease—he simply
"followed her." Akara-ogun, then, an orphan in his twenty-sixth year,
travels to Irunmale, the Forest of a Thousand Daemons, where he survives
a welter of horrific encounters, mostly with supernatural creatures called
ghommids, which the translator's glossary describes as "beings neither
human nor animal nor strictly demi-gods, mostly dwellers in forests
where they live within trees." A fair specimen is Agbako: "He wore a cap
of iron, a coat of brass, and on his loins were leather shorts. His knees right
down to his feet appeared to be palm leaves; from his navel to the bulge
of his buttocks, metal network; and there was no creature on earth which
had not found a home in this netting which even embraced a live snake
among its links, darting out its tongue as Agbako trod the earth. His head
was long and large, the sixteen eyes being arranged around the base of his
head, and there was no living man who could stare into those eyes without
trembling, they rolled endlessly round like the face of clock." The procession of such patchwork monsters at times aspires to be a version of *The
Pilgrim's Progress;* Akara-ogun comes to the city called Filth, "a city of
greed and contumely, a city of envy and of thievery, a city of fights and
wrangles, a city of death and diseases—a veritable city of sinners." What
strikes the reader, however, in these moralistic apparitions is the redolence
of certain details: many of these citizen-sinners "wore their clothes inside
out. . . . Every garment shone with filth, it was more like the inside of a
hunter's bag." Later, our hero wearily sits on a dead and bloated goat:
"The moment my buttocks hit the carcass, it burst, and the gall bladder
and intestines flushed my buttocks with their fetid fluids."

The earthy seethe toward which Fagunwa's imagination tends is
tugged skyward on nearly every page by a pious interjection: "evil cannot
fail but end a heart of evil. Thus did this woman die the death of a dog

and rot like bananas: even thus did the King of Heaven raise this righteous king in triumph above their schemes." When, in the last long episode, the hero finds himself privileged to spend seven days with the saintly and immortal Iragbeje in his sublime house with seven wings, the rigors of enlightenment wear out the narrator, who after two days of fable and preachment declares, "there remained five days of our stay with Iragbeje, but I cannot tell you all the marvels which our eyes witnessed and our ears heard during these five days, for time is flying." On the seventh day, in a room whose "floor, ceiling and walls alike and every furnishing or article . . . were all white as cotton fluff," Iragbeje talks about the Creator and concludes, "Therefore when it is good for us, let us remember our Lord." Morals leap into being at every level of the narrative. Akara-ogun offers this wisdom to his audience, which in the course of three days of public dictation has grown quite large: "If a man overreaches himself, he crashes to the ground. . . . If a nation is self-satisfied it will soon enough become enslaved to another; if a powerful government preens itself, before a bird's touchdown its peoples will disperse before its very eyes." And the author-scribe concludes with a prayer that "we black people will never again be left behind in the world."

The determined moralistic impulse consorts incongruously with the folkloristic elements; more erratically than Milton, Fagunwa identifies the old pagan gods with Christian devils. When Akara-ogun marries a lovely ghommid, she does allow, some time after their wedding, that she has a nephew whose name is Chaos. "That child," she goes on, "grew up and sought employment under Satan who is king of hell. I learnt later Chaos was a most conscientious worker and earned rapid promotion at his job, and it pleases me greatly to learn that he is at this moment foreman of those who feed the fires of hell with oil." But the non-Christian supernatural is elsewhere a pathway to religious revelation; the teeming world of the ghommids is felt as merely a slightly darker department of the real world. Modern Africa peeks through. The exalted Iragbeje advises Akara-ogun matter-of-factly, "Do not permit your child to keep bad company, that he start from youth to pub-crawl, insulting women all over town, dancing unclean dances in public places and boasting, 'We are the ones who count, we are the elite over others.' "

Fagunwa's frame of reference included, along with Yoruba folklore and the Biblical tales so frequently echoed and paralleled, contemporary terms and texts as of the late Thirties in a British colony. Passages in *Forest of a Thousand Daemons* build like pieces of a novel; the plot begins to yield moral complexities and to reveal inner lives. When Kako, a warrior who joins Akara-ogun's band, abruptly deserts a woman with whom he has lived for seven years and is, according to custom, about to marry, she pleads her case with the sentimental fullness of a bourgeois heroine: "Ah! Is this now my reward from you? When at first you courted me I refused you, but you turned on the honey tongue and fooled me until I believed that there lived no man like you. I gave you my love so selflessly that the fever of love seized me, that the lunacy of love mounted my head. . . ." Kako, a warrior of the old school, is in no mood for a moral dilemma; he curses his plaintive consort as "woman of death, mother of witchery seeking to obstruct my path of duty," and strikes her with his machete so that "it lacked only a little for the woman to be cloven clean in two." She had been obstructing as well the flow of adventure and wisdom-imparting; in shared relief, the narrator and Kako together make merry for the next nine days. Their companions tease Kako about his slain woman, saying, "Deal-me-death thrusts her neck at the husband—such was the wife of Kako." She is flattened into an allegorical name, and her disturbing outcry sinks back like a bubble into the two-dimensional, alternately hectic and pious narrative.

Much the same hurried and harsh texture is presented by Amos Tutuola's *The Witch-Herbalist of the Remote Town*, except that Tutuola is a Yoruba who writes in English, which brings the menacing, scarred masks of his devil dance closer to our faces. He is the author, of course, of *The Palm-Wine Drinkard*, whose publication in 1952 was urged by T. S. Eliot and hailed by Dylan Thomas, in a review that called it "a brief, thronged, grisly and bewitching story." The middle two adjectives still apply to this later work, Tutuola's first book in fourteen years. (There have been five others since the famous first.) *The Palm-Wine Drinkard* concerned the narrator's pursuit of his own private palm-wine tapster into the Deads' Town; the search in *The Witch-Herbalist of the Remote Town* is for relief from the hero's wife's barrenness. To the striking but on the whole amiable eccentricities of his early style Tutuloa has added several distracting tics; one is the very free use of the abbreviation "etc." ("the skins of various kinds of animals such as lions, tigers, leopards, crocodiles, boar, forest lizards, etc."; "the chief of pagan, idol, spirit, god, etc. wor-shippers"; "dressed in beautiful clothes, etc."; etc.), and another is the curious but consistent substitution of the word "twinkling" for "minute," on the ground that "in the Yoruba language, 'twinkling' means minute"— this produces such remarkable verbal formations as "a half-twinkling or thirty seconds," "one-twinkling intervals," "sixty twinklings" (an hour), "a few sixtieths of a twinkling" (a few seconds), and "two hundred and forty twinklings" (four hours). To confuse our computations further, the nameless narrator travels with four ghostly companions, or "partners":

Although I had left my town without human wayfarers or partners, my first "mind" and my second "mind" were my partners, while the third partner which was my "memory" had also prepared itself ready to help me perhaps whenever my two "minds" failed to advise or deserted me. And it was also prepared to record all the offences which the two "minds" might commit. Again, my fourth partner was my "Supreme Second" who was totally invisible and who was entirely supreme to the three of them, yet he had prepared himself ready to guide me throughout my journey.

Can the first of these inner subdivisions be based upon too literal a hearing of the phrase "being of two minds"? Or upon a prescient inkling of the distinction between the right and left sides of the brain? No clear personality difference between the first "mind" and the second emerged for this reader; they both seem cowardly and erratic advisers to our hero, compared with his "memory," the guardian-angel-like "Supreme Second," and his faithful bag of juju tricks as he does battle with such black hats as the Brutal Ape, the Abnormal Squatting Man of the Jungle, the Long-Breasted Mother of the Mountain, the Crazy Removable-Headed Wild Man, and the Offensive Wild People. The plurality of inner voices imposes the delay of consultation upon every encounter:

> So as my first "mind" and second "mind" could not tell me what to do to save myself from this fast-moving strange shadow at this time, I began to think of another way to remove the sadness and depression from my "memory." After a while, as this thick shadow was still taking me to a greater height in the sky, it came to my "memory" unexpectedly to use one of my juju which had the power to make me disappear suddenly. So without hesitation, I used this juju. But I was greatly shocked that when I used it, it had no effect at all. And it was later on I understood that it could not help if my bare feet were not on the ground.

There is a certain psychological realism in this subdivided hero as he keeps trying to rally his scattered inner forces and bring them, like a sulky committee, to the vote of action. We are all more persons than the unitary conventions of social proceedings acknowledge. And there is a certain eerie evocativeness in some of Tutuola's slippery dealings with the English language. Here is the Abnormal Squatting Man of the Jungle, who subdues his prey with his icy touch and breath:

> His head was bigger than necessary with two fearful eyes. The two eyes went deeply into his skull. . . . His beard was long to about forty centimetres, it was very bushy and stale, and hundreds of fleas were moving here and there in it. But his thick and twisted arms and legs were able to carry his over-inflated belly, from which he used to blow out the cold onto his victims. . . . The other parts of his body which were not covered by the muddled

dirty hair, were full of big smelling mumps. To my surprise and fear when he was aloof, he seemed a powerless, morbid, wild jungle man. . . . Some time when the day was lurid, and as the hair which covered his head and body was just like light brown weeds, he used to lurk in the weeds for his victim, and when the victim came near him, he jumped on him or her unexpectedly and then started to blow the cold onto his or her body as hastily as he could. Again, he pretended sometimes to be motley, or when he saw one at a distance he burst into silly laughter suddenly as if he was mad.

A number of the villains—e.g., the Crazy Removable-Headed Wild Man, with his luxurious wardrobe of "hundreds of various kinds of large heads, arms, short legs, broad ears, wild eyes, round black bodies, etc."— are amusingly imagined. But in general the wild imagery of *The Witch-Herbalist of the Remote Town* has neither the schematic coherence and heraldic crispness of literary allegory nor the felt depth and resonance of the surreal images in, say, Kafka or Lewis Carroll, who give us back our own dreams. Though it follows the exact plot curve of *Forest of a Thousand Daemons* and like it ends in a kind of heaven where instruction and therapy are dealt out in surreal mimicry of school and church, Tutuola's tale seems not instructive but, in its fantastic way, confessional. A personal passion for fragmentation and interchanging units generates the hero's many minds, the Crazy Removable-Headed Wild Man's many body parts, and the Witch-Herbalist's many voices: "She had various kinds of voices such as a huge voice, a light voice, a sharp voice, the voice of a baby, the voice of a girl, the voice of an old woman, the voice of a young man, the voice of an old man, the voice of a stammerer, the voice of boldness, the voice of boom, the voice of a weeping person, the voice which was amusing and which was annoying, the voice like that of a ringing bell, the voice of various kinds of birds and beasts." We are in the realm neither of legend nor of dream but of indulged imagination; in this regard Tutuola is a more modern writer than Fagunwa, whose imaginings were at the service of a social ethic. Though Tutuola's first novel marked the arrival of African fiction on the international stage (*The Palm-Wine Drinkard* has been translated into thirteen European languages), it has not been imitated, except by him; he is a writer *sui generis*. This new novel bears out Anthony West's verdict, thirty years ago in *The New Yorker*, that *The Palm-Wine Drinkard*, though affording "a glimpse of the very beginning of literature, that moment when writing at last seizes and pins down the myths and legends of an analphabetic culture," was "an unrepeatable happy hit."

Buchi Emecheta, though she moved to London in 1962, when she was eighteen, and continues to live there, is Nigeria's best-known female writer. Indeed, few writers of her sex—Ama Ata Aidoo, of Ghana, is the other name that comes to mind—have arisen in any part of tropical Africa. There will surely be more; there is much to say. Ms. Emecheta's novels, as their very titles indicate—*The Slave Girl, The Bride Price, The Joys of Motherhood*—concern themselves with the situation of women in a society where their role, though large, has been firmly subordinate and where the forces of potential liberation have arrived with bewildering speed.

The heroine of her new novel, *Double Yoke,* is an Efik girl, Nko, who must pursue her education at the cost of losing her boyfriend and sexually submitting to an instructor. The novel is dedicated by Ms. Emecheta to "my 1981 students at the Department of English and Literary Studies, University of Calabar," and takes place in the early Eighties, but for all of its topicality, and along with the professional finesse that helped make it a modest best-seller in England, it retains certain traces of the oral mode. Like *Forest of a Thousand Daemons,* the book sets up a narrative frame; who is telling the tale, and why, is not taken for granted, and the narrator is not the disembodied third person who relays so much Western fiction to us, as if prose were a camera. A "new lecturer" at the University of Calabar, Miss Bulewao, is introduced with a jaunty touch of self-carica-ture, and sets her all-male writing class an assignment—"an imaginary story of how you would like your ideal Nigeria to be." One of her students, Ete Kamba, mulling over this tall order, remembers that Miss Bulewao also said "that oneself was always a very good topic to start writing about" and decides to write about what is uppermost in his mind: "He was going to tell the world how it all had been, between him and his Nko, until Professor Ikot came into their lives." The chapters that follow have the form of a flashback, taking Ete Kamba and Nko back to their first meeting, at the thanksgiving celebration for a local girl's passing her examination in hairdressing—no educational advance is too modest to be honored in these villages. Ete Kamba and Nko live in nearby villages but not the same one; he is eighteen, she is two years younger. He goes to the university on a scholarship; she eventually follows. As the story of their involvement and of hers with Professor Ikot unfolds, the tale slips more and more into Nko's mind, and away from the talk in the male dormito-ries—handled creditably but without much zest—to more animated inter-changes within the female quarters. Yet it all stays somehow contained within Ete Kamba's flashback, which is delivered in the form of an essay to Miss Bulewao; she asks all the right questions and urges the difficulty toward a solution as happy, given the double-yoked condition of the educated African woman, as it can be. The scribe enabled Akara-ogun to relate his pilgrim's progress to the world; the act of writing still has a power of magical release in the University of Calabar.

And Ms. Emecheta's prose, like Amos Tutuola's though to a much smaller degree, has a shimmer of originality, of English being reinvented. At an early meeting with Nko, Ete Kamba "stood there slouching around, somehow refusing to sit down, and noticing that people around him were leaving him completely alone and not bothering to pressurise him to sit down. He followed Nko's busyness with the corners of his eyes. . . ." Contemplating taking her virginity, he yearns to inflict "a pain that would uninnocent her." And the confusions of crowded traffic are conveyed: "Impatient taxis in their yellow colouring with a splash of blue in the middle would meander in between the cars in a hurry to get on first." Such pleasant expressionism brings us close, perhaps, to the spoken Nigerian English that, while the main characters speak with ungainly and unlikely correctitude, is transcribed from the mouth of a cleaning girl, accused of not cleaning a toilet: "Watin' you wan make we do, when we no geti water, whey we go use for flush, abi you wan make ago geti water from me mama well?" This accent is imitated, in foolery, by the male students, as they discuss love. "A no de for disi una sweety belle stuff," one says, and another answers, "Na so for me ooo. One women be like anoder. Why ago go kill myself for one chick, that wan pass me." To this reviewer's previous knowledge that a Lagos traffic jam is called a "go-slow" he was delighted to add the information that a "been-to" is a Nigerian who has been to England and that female sexual charm can be called "bottom power"—"It is easier to get a good degree," one female undergraduate assures another, "using one's brain power than bottom power. They may try to tell you that your bottom power is easier and surer, don't believe them."

The fellowship of women, wherein confession and counsel can be given, is the home base of *Double Yoke,* as it was for *The Joys of Motherhood,* whose heroine, Nnu Ego, after a lifetime given to serving her patriarchal society with child-bearing, realizes that "she would have been better off had she had time to cultivate those women who had offered her hands of friendship." The female students at Calabar—some of them middle-aged—have mothers who had gone into "fattening rooms" to become suitably plump brides; now they gossip about anorexia nervosa. The sense of relief, of escape from misunderstanding and harm, that accompanies Ms. Emecheta's scenes of women together is like fresh air after prison. In the crucial scene of Nko's submission to Professor Ikot, the author in her distaste can scarcely bear to describe the event:

> They ate and the professor drank spirits. She made do with Pepsi, and like a wooden doll, she let the man have what he wanted. He thundered and pushed her around and promised heaven and earth, but Nko was very still.

That marvellous "He thundered and pushed her around and promised heaven and earth" would deflate even Don Juan. However, absolute feminist fury, the wish to do away with men altogether and make a female Utopia, is never expressed by Ms. Emecheta or her characters, and the phrase "double yoke" is extended to describe not just Nko's plight ("I want to be an academician and I want to be a quiet nice and obedient wife") but that of Ete Kamba and his fellow young Nigerian males. At the end Miss Bulewao tells her class that "many of you are bearing your double burdens or yokes or whatever heroically," and spells out "the community burden . . . and yet the burden of individualism." In a Third World country like Nigeria, a matter like sexual harassment is even more serious than in the West. Female virginity has a higher value, and so does education. The dropout of the educated elite back into the villages is precipitous; the options to "the system" are few, and the rungs on the ladder of success—constructed by the departed colonial power—are rigidly set. Nko, Professor Ikot tells Ete Kamba, is "made for the Commissioner or the Professorial class, you know those on salary level sixteen and over. You'll be lucky to get level seven when you finish here." Monsters and peril still rule in the new Africa, though they take the form of lascivious professors and loss of status. Buchi Emecheta does not have to manufacture suspense and seriousness; issues of survival lie inherent in her material, and give her tales weight even when, as in this case, they are relatively light and occasional. Africans still have something exciting to tell each other, which is that the path of safety is narrow.

Chinese Disharmonies

THE QUESTION OF HU, by Jonathan D. Spence. 187 pp. Knopf, 1988.

HALF OF MAN IS WOMAN, by Zhang Xianliang, translated from the Chinese by Martha Avery. 285 pp. Norton, 1988.

Jonathan D. Spence, born in England in 1936 and since 1966 a member of the Yale History Department, takes an arcane delight in resurrecting personalities out of the depths of Sinological archives. A long-lived monarch in *Emperor of China* (1974), a laborer's doomed wife in *The Death of the Woman Wang* (1978), a polymathic Jesuit missionary in *The Memory Palace of Matteo Ricci* (1984): these diverse individuals have all been hauntingly brought to life through scrupulous fidelity to details in the copious yet generally impersonal historical records of the sixteenth, seventeenth, and eighteenth centuries. John Hu, the nominal hero of *The Question of Hu*, would be quite lost to history had he not been hastily recruited as an assistant by a fifty-six-year-old Jesuit, Jean-François Foucquet, who in 1722 returned from Canton to France, with eighteen precious crates of books, after over two decades of scholarly and missionary activity in China. Foucquet believed, fervently and perhaps foolishly, that he could show, by careful textual analysis, that "the ancient Chinese religious texts, such as *The Book of Changes*," had been "handed to the Chinese by the true God," and that the Way—the Tao—preached by these texts led to the God of the Bible. If this could have been demonstrated, the conversion of the Chinese multitudes would have been greatly eased, and obdurate official resistance to the Christian mission wonderfully softened, but Foucquet's own superiors resisted an idea that bordered on the heretical. Further, his extraction of Christian glimmers from the Chinese classics required enormous efforts of transcription and translation. Even though, as Foucquet wrote, "In such an enterprise the act of labor becomes sweet, and even the harshest pains become in some way delicious," he needed help, and had at times employed Chinese clerical assistants. His superiors, however, claimed that his vow of poverty forbade him to employ anyone. One superior, in particular, Father Pierre de Goville, the procurator of the French mission in Canton, frowned upon Foucquet's enterprise, with its considerable expenditures for quantities of books, and upon Foucquet's plan to take a Chinese assistant with him back to Europe. So Foucquet was not disposed to be picky when one John Hu, the keeper of the gate at the Sacred Congregation for the Propagation of the Faith, volunteered to accompany the Jesuit to France. The two men quickly signed a five-year contract, even though Foucquet found Hu "physically ugly" and observed as well that he was "none too clean" and had "a despairing look to him." Foucquet wrote later, "It was either this Chinese or none at all."

Hu at the time was forty, a widower with a mother and one son. He had become a Christian in 1700, when he was nineteen. Foucquet judged a sample of his Chinese calligraphy "serviceable, if inelegant." Hu had his own agenda: he wanted to travel to the West in order to visit the Pope, as had Louis Fan, a Chinese recently returned from ten years in Europe, and Hu wanted to write a travel book, a book that would "make him famous among his countrymen" when he returned from Europe. The only trouble was that—it developed soon after they embarked, with the many crates of books, on the long ocean voyage—Hu was crazy. Or, at the least, his behavior is (to adopt the present tense of Professor Spence's narrative) highly erratic. He seems unable to learn the French language or French table manners, grabbing all the food he wants as soon as it appears on the table; his shipboard dining mates "try to explain the idea of portions to him," and, that failing, "use a measure of force to restrain him." Upon recovering from a long bout of seasickness, Hu becomes violently censorious of "the loud ways and uncouth manners of the soldiers and sailors aboard," and gets into a fight with a sailor. During an encounter with a Portuguese vessel off Brazil, he seizes a cutlass and, "waving it in the air with menacing gestures, he marches proudly round the upper deck." In mid-Atlantic, Hu has a vision in which angels tell him his task is "to seek out the Emperor of China and introduce him to the truths of the Christian religion." When their ship is delayed outside the Spanish harbor of La Coruña, Hu demands a lifeboat and insists to Foucquet, "I will persuade the governor to listen to our needs. I will make him grant us permission to come ashore."

Spurts of uncontrollable officiousness continue to characterize his behavior in France; for instance, at an audience that Foucquet has obtained in Paris with the papal nuncio Hu grasps the offered armchairs and pushes them into what he has decided are more honorific positions. His spectacular and repeated kowtows to any crucifix he sees are unsettling, as is his insistence on sleeping on the floor, with the window wide open. Forced to dine with their host's housekeeper, he "will not allow her near him. He makes faces at her, and gestures her away, or simply turns his back whenever she appears." In Port Louis, though he has never before ridden a horse, he steals one and gallops around the town, winning the name "Don Quixote" from the townspeople. The French populace are inclined to be amused by the antics of their exotic visitor; in Paris, Hu collects a "large and attentive" crowd in front of the Church of St. Paul when, after beating on a drum he has made and waving a banner inscribed with the four Chinese characters *"nan nü fen bie"* ("Men and women should be kept in their separate spheres"), he preaches lengthily in Chinese. He becomes harder to control, disappearing for a day and then for a week and suddenly showing up at the Jesuit residence in Orléans. From there Father Léonard Gramain writes Foucquet's friend Father Jean-Baptiste du Halde in Paris, "Neither with words nor signs can he make us understand why he left Paris and where he wants to go. . . . Since he often says the words 'China' and 'Peking,' and also the words 'Rome' and 'Pope,' we are assuming that he would like to go to Rome and from there to China." Foucquet responds with a letter to Hu in phonetically spelled-out Chinese, admonishing him to behave better. "Jumping at Father Gramain, Hu snatches the letter out of the startled man's hands. Before anyone can prevent him, he tears the letter to angry pieces." And when Foucquet receives his long-awaited invitation to Rome, and invites Hu to accompany him, Hu refuses, though seeing the Pope has been his dream. He is under the impression that Foucquet "kills people," and he hides in his bed: "If Foucquet or anyone comes to remonstrate with him, he pulls the covers over his head." The exasperated Foucquet goes to Rome alone, having arranged to have Hu committed in his absence to the hospital for the insane at Charenton. There Hu languishes for two and a half years, living in one of the cells for pauper inmates, his unchanged clothes disintegrating as he wears them. When he is given a warm blanket, he rips it to shreds. When Father Goville, Foucquet's old enemy in Canton, visits Charenton and talks to Hu in Chinese, Hu's first question is "Why have I been locked up?"

Some of the oddities of Hu's behavior—his compulsive kowtowing to the cross, his rigid sense of caste, his abhorrence of female company, and his hopping about to avoid stepping on the maze of crosses he sees in a parquet floor—could be construed as marks of Oriental acculturation muddled with a Baroque Catholic faith. But a number of other Chinese, such as Louis Fan and "a well-educated and courteous young man" whom Foucquet discovered studying for the priesthood in Rome, visited Europe in this era without going berserk. Hu's evident inability to learn even the rudiments of French, during five years of immersion in it, and his refusal to take lessons when they were offered him upon his release from Charenton, indicates an impaired mental balance, as do his failure to perform the work Foucquet hired him for, his unreal sense of lapsed time, his visions, his megalomania, his periods of depressed inactivity, his abrupt ventures into vagabondage and beggary, and his fitful posturing and clowning. Perhaps he suffered from manic depression, severe to the point of psychosis. Though the details of his case almost all come from Foucquet himself, in a "Récit Fidèle" he composed to clear his good name in the wake of rumors that he mistreated Hu, there is no reason to doubt their accuracy, or to deny Foucquet our sympathy as he attempts to cope with a deranged dependent whose "acts of folly"—he wrote despairingly to the lieutenant of the Paris police, Marc Pierre d'Argenson, who arranged for Hu's commitment—"are accompanied by a malevolence and an obstinacy that can not be relieved by prayers, threats, or generosity."

In its laconic, deadpan paragraphs and swift-moving chapters, *The Question of Hu* evokes the strangeness of human life altogether—the dubious claim of any of it to sanity. How sane is Foucquet, with his frenetic letter-writing and his strenuous conviction that "in the long-distant past the Chinese had worshipped the Christian God"? The French King's librarian, the Abbé Bignon, comments of Foucquet's theories, "Nothing in the world has ever been so ill-founded." The King's confessor, Father Linières, finds Foucquet "strident in his views, rash in his behavior, and over-critical of the former Jesuit colleagues with whom he is arguing about the rites." As their correspondence grows heated, he writes Foucquet, "It seems to me that you might have done better to have learned a bit less Chinese, and to have spent the time instead studying the sciences of saintliness." There is a touch of bewitchment in the Jesuit missionary's descent into the musty ancient Chinese texts, his "intense desire of finding some way to get inside the written relics of that nation." In the accents of Borgesian romanticism he writes to Abbé Bignon of the secrets "hidden by the holiest of the Patriarchs more than eighty centuries ago under the surface covering of these profound and mysterious hieroglyphs."

Jonathan Spence, in this book, as in *The Memory Palace of Matteo Ricci*, dwells upon the description of systems (the rigorous way, for instance, in which the accommodations are arranged at the Jesuit retreat at Vannes, and at the asylum of Charenton) as if to suggest delusional systems that were erected in vain against the erosions of universal chaos. How sane, from our late-twentieth-century standpoint, was the effort of a few celibate clerics, armed mostly with zeal and quaint erudition, to induce the xenophobic, anciently self-satisfied subcontinent of China to make the Christian leap of faith? For that matter, is there not something peculiar in the author's own zealous scholarship as it fanatically seeks out in the old scribbles of many languages the traces left by John Hu's rather dismal, historically inconsequential life? Professor Spence includes in his grateful acknowledgments his pet dog, Daisy, who "climbed the narrow wooden steps to my summer study countless times a day, and lay across from me during every word, sighing gently in her sleep over my endless attempts to draw some meaning out of the constantly vanishing past." What he has produced is, if not quite Dada history, history with a postmodern texture, minimalist and enigmatic—subtly fantastic history that in its very minutiae of research mocks our ability really to know another age or another person. We are disconcerted and charmed, rejoicing (not quite sanely) in the question of Hu as we rejoice in the face of all unanswerable but beautifully posed questions.

Though some of the oldest literary works that can be called novels are Chinese, and the humanistic religions of Confucianism and Taoism conduce to an equable observation of society and psychology, the Communist Revolution and then the rampant Cultural Revolution offered little encouragement to realistic fiction. *Half of Man Is Woman* was, its jacket tells us, published in China in 1985 "to great popular enthusiasm, and much controversy because of its unaccustomed frankness about sex." Less shocking, evidently, was its picture of the life political prisoners lead in labor camps, or *laogai*—the equivalent of Soviet gulags. Zhang Xianliang, like his narrator-hero, Zhang Yonglin, was condemned in 1957 for rightist tendencies displayed in his poetry, and remained in various labor camps for twenty years. He was "capped"—that is, made to wear a dunce cap— and thus launched with public humiliation upon the path of ideological correction. Martha Avery's brief introduction explains how from 1966 to 1976, the years in which the novel takes place, the Cultural Revolution, precipitated when Mao lost control of the Party apparatus in 1965, raged chaotically throughout the vast nation, obliterating intellectual life and robbing personal life of intimacy and trust. "This is a book about survival in an insane world," she tells us. "Zhang describes a country that went mad." An agricultural labor camp was not such a bad place in which to wait out the convulsions of the Cultural Revolution—"In the labor camps you still get something to eat," one character observes—and the novel curiously acquires the atmosphere of an idyll, of an austere and regulated Eden in which the primal mysteries of man-woman relations are re-enacted with fresh passion, wonder, and dismay.

In a southern camp where the watery cultivation of rice is the main business, troops of female prisoners share the work. No contact with male prisoners is allowed, but the women can be closely observed: "Lightly, the women walked by, their provocative movements seeming to invite our examination. . . . If we were to ignore that walk, however, and see them standing stiff as the haughty reeds, would we believe that they were women? . . . A baggy top like a cloth sack and a pair of pants stubbornly covered all that was specifically female. Sexless, these women had descended to a state even lower than ours. The term 'woman' was used only by habit. They had no waists, no chests, no buttocks, as one after another their dark red faces passed by." Zhang Yonglin, however, one day spies a woman bathing in an irrigation ditch: "With cupped hands, she teased the water up over her body, splashing her neck, her shoulders, her waist, her hips, her stomach. Her body was lithe and firm. From between the two walls of green, the sun shone straight on her, making her wet skin shine like stretched silk." The vision becomes mystical:

> She bathed intently, completely. She bathed as if to wash her very soul and make it clean.
> She forgot herself, and I also forgot myself. At the start, I couldn't help looking, indeed my eyes kept returning to that most secret of female places.

Then from it, and from the entire picture, began to emanate a feeling, the aura of a powerful force. Here was something magical, that escaped all that man abhorred. Here, almost, was a myth, an archetype that transcended the world itself. Because of her, the world now had colour. Because of her, I now knew grace.

Astoundingly, when the woman realizes that she is being watched she boldly poses in her nudity, challenging the voyeur to come to her. He cannot, but he does fall in love: "I didn't exist. All that remained was her image, standing with crossed arms in the midst of that sheet of whiteness: her beautiful, enticing, fertile, glistening body. All that was left in the world was her."

He learns her name: Huang Xiangjiu. With the improbability permissible in romances, they meet again, eight years later, at a labor farm to the north, in the bleak province of Ningxia, where the main business is raising sheep. They are thrown together in a task, the rebuilding of a sheep pen. This time, amid the relatively relaxed discipline of a pastoral camp, they talk, visit one another, and decide to marry. In marriage, the imprisoned intellectual, a virgin at the age of thirty-nine, proves impotent. This impotence, the translator's introduction and the hero's own expostulations agree, is the central metaphor of the book: "One of the main themes," Ms. Avery asserts, "is that China's political system has desexed its population." Zhang puts it more circumspectly: "Our world had lost its link with human society." No doubt, to readers who have endured China's recent history along with the author, the political meditations and the references to "The Stinking Nines" and "7 May Policy" and "The Gang of Four" and "One Hit Three Counters Movement" are meaningful and stirring. Availing himself of the fantastic, supernatural streak in Chinese story-telling convention, the author stages some lively discussions between the hero and his piebald horse, and then a most entertaining roundtable exchange among the spirits of Song Jiang (a character in the classic novel *All Men Are Brothers*), Zhuang-tz (a Taoist sage who used to be transliterated as Chuang-tsu), and Karl Marx, who briskly informs the impotent husband, "Right now, your productive power has essentially been neutralized. You're trying to scrape by with words and hot air rather than real action." But Western readers are most apt to be struck and moved by the novel's portrait of marriage and its tracing of the pathetic, even tragic, course of an archetypal relation between the sexes.

Huang Xiangjiu is something of a wanton: she has been sentenced for promiscuity, has gone through two marriages and divorces, and betrays Zhang with the local Party secretary, Cao Xueyi. But she wants this marriage to "work," as we capitalists say. Not only is she beautiful with her clothes off; she is thrifty, and skilled at the domestic arts:

> Xiangjiu exhibited an extraordinary ability to manage the decor of our living quarters. I was instructed where to nail in the bamboo holder for the chopsticks, where to place a little shelf to put the soap, where to build the platform for the bed, how to pile up crates so they made a handy cupboard, how to make the frame for the stove and the cutting board into one extended surface, where to put the cooking pans, bowls and spoons so that they would be both convenient and hygienic—and at the same time would not take up too much space.

To Zhang, a long-term dweller in abasement, domestic life, however meagrely furnished, has a dreamlike luxury and strangeness:

> Every so often, the tiny tinkling of a sound would reach me. The sound was distant, as though it were issuing from a dream. This sound was the sound of a wife—it could not come from the hands of any other person. . . . Life is made up of just things such as these: a bed, a bedcover, a bookshelf made from a door, a hook for clothes with its white paper underneath, "Snow-flower" skin-lotion. The world she had created was engulfing me, so that I had the feeling of losing my identity.

The most elemental things about life with a wife amaze him: "The kang [a heated brick platform that supports a bed] had only one bedcover, but two pillows had been placed at the head of it. How very extraordinary to have a woman's head on one of them. . . . She was here beside me. A pile of long black hair curled across a soft white pillow. Two shiny eyes looked upwards into the confines of a narrow space." The act of sex is rather *too* elemental; she becomes in bed "a beautiful nautilus, suddenly stretching out sticky tentacles from the walls, wrapping around me and trying to draw me down," and he realizes that "the first struggle of mankind . . . was that between man and woman. . . . It demanded not only strength, but a vital spirit, using emotions and some innate artistic sense in its struggle to find balance, to reach unity and harmony, to achieve wholeness while maintaining its own separate self. In this struggle, I had failed." He is impotent.

This reconstruction of the primordial relationship in the context of a drastically desexed culture has considerable freshness for us inhabitants of a culture wherein on all sides sex is implied, acknowledged, extolled, and analyzed. The story of Zhang and Huang should not all be told here, since it has more than one surprising turn. Most surprisingly and illuminatingly, when Zhang sheds his impotence—in the wake of a feat of heroism during a communal disaster, as if his manhood and civic spirit must be empowered together—he begins to think of leaving Huang. Sexual conquest bestows a vitality that enables him to conceive of escape:

> Since I had ceased to be "half a man", ceased to be a "cripple", a fire had burned in my chest. All my previous behaviour, including making allowances for her—"understanding" her—was not, as I had thought, the result of education, but the cowardice of a castrated horse. I now realized that the comfort and orderliness of her small household were designed to swallow me up. Now I wanted to smash it and escape: I had obtained what I desired, and now I rejected it. I thirsted for a bigger world.

And no amorous effort on his wife's part, no loving stitching of her husband's clothes or sacrifice of her own food ration to his male appetite, can assuage this broader, as it were political, thirst. A paradox that torments the relations of men and women the world over is caught in three lines of a poem:

> A woman is the most lovable thing on earth,
> But there is something that is more important.
> Women will never possess the men they have created.

The novel's virtues—its penetration, candor, and lyricism—are accompanied by some clumsiness and awkward reticence. The author and the hero almost never express the indignation to which their undeserved sufferings would seem to have entitled them. Concerning the cruel confusion of slogans and movements emanating from Beijing, the novel's strongest comment, put in the mouth of the piebald horse, is aloofly sardonic: "You arrive on this earth, you work, you see things, you eat, you hear all kinds of strange things, such as how in a moment a head of state can become an imprisoned criminal, how a small-time hoodlum can become Vice Chairman of the Party of tens of millions of people. . . . You are personally relatively fortunate, because you're living in times that are unprecedentedly ridiculous." Though the times are ridiculous, Zhang never abandons his puzzled attempt to become a good citizen, to find the harmony whereby "man and the world are in a unified continuum." The other political prisoners rather cheerfully make the best of having their lives ruined. The character of Party Secretary Cao Xueyi, groomed to be that of a villain, falls short of villainy, as if the author had respectfully lost his nerve. Only Huang achieves a vital complexity: she is "charmingly stupid, and laughably clever"; she is harsh, sexual, calculating, tender, superstitious, pathetic, and lovely. She is also, one should not forget, a peasant, and a loyal Maoist, not above threatening her husband with reporting his intellectual divagations to the authorities. Behind their marital disharmony lurks the deep and ancient class distinction between the intellectual and the peasant, bridgeable only in the dislocations of an absurd time. The novel ends after the death of Chou but before that of Mao; so big and red a sunset might have swamped Zhang's vague farewell to marriage and the *laogai*.

It cannot be easy to translate from a language as grammatically uninflected yet as compounded and forked as Chinese, beset with its ancient tension between the literary and the colloquial, between the spoken and the written. Ms. Avery has made a readable and at times graceful job of it, only occasionally falling into some English impossibility like "The wrinkles that had crawled all over her face bore smiles." Throughout the book, deftly painted bits of landscape open upon a world of nature that political oppression cannot touch. They serve as glimpses of serene order, signs pointing to the "right track" that follows the traditional injunction "Unite the inside and the outside":

> A small garden had been made by levelling the land around: the hollyhocks were already tall, though not yet blooming, sprouts of tomatoes, hot peppers and aubergines were pushing up, and between them the yellow earth had been raked fine until it looked as soft as a piece of carpet. Two white butterflies circled blindly in the light, and near the wall was a low apricot tree. This was a regular life.

In Love with the West

NAOMI, by Junichirō Tanizaki, translated from the Japanese by Anthony H. Chambers. 237 pp. Knopf, 1985.

One does not have to have read all the way through *The Makioka Sisters* to be persuaded that Junichirō Tanizaki was a great writer; even his small fictions have a relaxed rhythm and heft, a directness and simplicity suddenly condensing into poetry and symbol, an imaginative reach that even while encompassing twists of erotic oddity and self-destruction still seems, itself, robust. His is writing at home in its skin, as instinctively realistic and non-fanatical as, say, Defoe's. *Naomi* was, we are told in a helpful introduction by the translator, the author's "first important novel," the immediate first fruit of Tanizaki's permanent move to Osaka from Tokyo and Yokohama, where he had been "living a fast life" among "the Westerners who gave Yokohama its cosmopolitan reputation." The move was forced upon him by the devastating earthquake of 1923, but once he had taken up residence in the older, more conservative city, he seemed to find firm ground as an artist, and indeed became something of an antiquarian as a writer, frequently setting his novels in the Japanese past.

Naomi, however, composed and serialized in 1924–25, dealt with a very up-to-date issue, the Westernization of popular culture and the Japanese equivalent of the "flapper." The heroine's name and "Naomi-ism" became by-words for the modern woman, and government censors and conservative readers found the material so disturbing that the novel's serialization in an Osaka newspaper was halted in the sixteenth chapter, to be eventually resumed and completed in the magazine *Josei*. To a Western reader sixty years later, the story is still exciting and even shocking in its mixture of traditional proprieties and casual impropriety, and in its close rendering of the progress of love and corruption, which are seen as inextricably entwined. The hero, Kawai Jōji, is twenty-eight, an electrical engineer with quiet bachelor habits; he first encounters Naomi as a fifteen-year-old apprentice hostess in a café. He is struck by the girl's name, an odd name written with three Chinese characters: "A splendid name, I thought; written in Roman letters, it could be a Western name." Her looks, too, seem Western; in Jōji's eyes she resembles "the motion-picture actress Mary Pickford," even though she is also "a quiet, gloomy child" with a face "as pale and dull as a thick pane of colorless, transparent glass." He decides—in a move that combines elements of buying a pet, taking in a needy child, and undertaking a betrothal—to invite Naomi to come live with him. Her family raise no objection; they are shady folk who live behind the Hanayashiki Amusement Park, in the dubious district called Senzoku. The rest is, to a degree, predictable: she grows from a shy, grateful child and servant into a beautiful, slovenly, wanton tyrant and wife, with expensive tastes for Western-style restaurant meals, Western-style social dancing, and Western-style men. The moral would seem to be Nature Over Nurture, or You Can Take the Girl Out of Senzoku, But You Can't Take Senzoku Out of the Girl. When eventually informed that Naomi's kin run a brothel, Jōji concludes, "It's true, then; breeding determines all."

The theme of an older man infatuated with an unworthy love-object is no stranger to European fiction, and especially not in these between-the-wars years when New Women were testing their wings. Proust wrung his hands for hundreds of pages over Albertine's possible betrayals; Heinrich Mann's *Professor Unrat* became the classic, searing film *The Blue Angel*; and Nabokov's *Camera Obscura* cast the demonic young temptress as a movie usherette. Tanizaki pursues the theme, however, with considerably less of a vengeance than these Western romancers, and with more ambivalence and good humor. *Naomi* is as much about growth as destruction. Jōji, "like a new parent who keeps track of his baby's development," maintains a doting diary called "Naomi Grows Up." His early delight in his young ward's body, as he bathes and feeds and dresses it, has a paternal, almost a pediatric, focus on strengthening muscle and lengthening limb. His pride has the innocence, too, of a movie fan's, as he observes, when she is still only fifteen, her resemblance, in a bathing suit, to the "famous swimmer Annette Kellerman" as she appeared in the movie *Neptune's Daughter,* and he is enchanted by the un-Japanese way that "her trunk was short and her legs long," long and straight, so that, "as she stood with her thighs together, her legs, so straight there was no space between them, formed a long triangle from her hips to her ankles." On almost the first page he assures the reader that "her body has a distinctly Western look when she's naked." Naomi gradually comes to share his admiration and to use her sexual power; their life together is a mutual corruption, his descent into enslavement matched by hers into whorishness. But she is corrupted first, corrupted by his love. And the results, it is perhaps not too much to reveal, are less dire than a Western novelist would have felt obliged to make them.

Tanizaki writes with an unabashed and undogmatic sensuality rare in the often hectic, guilt-ridden annals of modernism. Jōji's adoration fastens onto curious details of Naomi—her nostrils, for instance, and her tears, immensely magnified:

> I wished for some way to crystallize those beautiful teardrops and keep them forever. First I wiped her cheeks; next, taking care not to touch the round, swollen tears, I wiped around her eyes. As the skin stretched and then relaxed, the tears were pushed into various shapes, now forming convex lenses, now concave, until finally they burst and streamed down her freshly wiped cheeks, tracing threads of light on her skin as they went.

Tanizaki understands the fetish-making fecundity of love, and the satisfactions it offers even while giving pain, and its perverse, inverse accountings ("I realized that a woman's face grows more beautiful the more it incurs a man's hatred"). Also, he suggests, the intensely cherished love-object embodies an idea and derives her power from a larger field than her own skin. In the best postwar American novel about love, Nabokov's *Lolita,* the immature love-object represents for both its hero and its émigré author something of the gauche, touching, and seductive New World. Naomi's Western redolence is most of her charm. "If I'd had enough money to do whatever I pleased," Jōji tells us, "I might have gone to live in the West and married a Western woman; but my circumstances wouldn't permit that, and I married Naomi, a Japanese woman with a Western flavor. . . . I'd be forgetting my place if I hoped for a wife with the majestic physique of a Westerner." A Westerner must smile at Jōji's overvaluation of things Western and at the many chapters devoted to the mysteries of that imported Occidental pastime, ballroom dancing. Tanizaki, rescued by an earthquake from the Western-flavored bohemia of Tokyo and Yokohama, clearly had some satirical purpose—his Japanese title translates as *A Fool's Love*, and Naomi's dancing and flirting, high heels and grammarless English are no doubt meant to be excessive, as is her pursuit of another Western import, personal freedom. But Jōji never renounces his love, any more than Japan ever abandoned its drive toward Westernization.

Far-Fetched

YUCATÁN, by Andrea De Carlo, translated from the Italian by William Weaver. 213 pp. Harcourt Brace Jovanovich, 1990.

THE SIGNORE: *Shogun of the Warring States*, by Kunio Tsuji, translated from the Japanese by Stephen Snyder. 197 pp. Kodansha International, 1989.

DOGEATERS, by Jessica Hagedorn. 251 pp. Pantheon, 1990.

Novels are not just news; we ask some stretch of imagination, some attempt to extend the author's witness into human possibilities beyond the edge of his or her experience. Three recently published novels—by an Italian, a Japanese, and an American born in the Philippines—each show a brave reach, geographic and otherwise.

Yucatán has as narrator a young Englishman, Dave Hollis; as central figure an internationally revered Yugoslavian film director, Dru Resnik; and as setting southern California and some way-out spaces in Mexico. Resnik and Dave fly from London to Los Angeles to meet Jack Nesbitt, a thick-necked millionaire who has lined up a meeting with Astor Camado, a never-photographed but best-selling author whose four books "tell the same story from four different points of view. . . . A young New York musicologist of South American extraction goes to Mexico to do some research and meets this Indian witch doctor, who little by little draws him into a vortex of magic practices, until he's brought into contact with a world beyond, or a parallel world, if you like." Nesbitt wants to produce a movie by Resnik based upon these books, and the author himself appears and speaks amiably of the world beyond ("A completely empty, dark room. There's nothing to recognize, nothing happens. There is only this absolute blackness") and the secret of life ("The secret is knowing that absolutely *everything* is insignificant: love and activity and relationships and feelings, landscapes, desires, plans, et cetera. They're nothing but bric-a-brac, little pieces of kitsch scattered around. The secret is *not to be there.* You understand what I mean?"). Thus unburdened, he hands Resnik his "stick of power" and disappears from the novel.

Advisers from the other, or parallel world, however, take over, sending messages by pencilled notes "written in a shaky and sprawling hand," messages like *"Attention, wrongly directed, is dangerous, because it rebounds. We are watching you."* The world is just one big fortune cookie to these mysterious others. They telephone, too, in voices that are "almost electronic, but not exactly," with "some kind of expression, underneath," and function as travel agents, sending our trio of movie makers, and the female companions they effortlessly accumulate, to specified parts of Mexico and back. The characters are not very real, and their actions seem inconsistent and implausible, but perhaps that is the point. We are somehow inside a movie being made, proceeding by jump cuts and changed camera angles, in an atmosphere of agitated stasis. Dave and the woman, Elaine, designated by the voices as "the spiritual girl," get into bed together in a steamy Mexican motel, but can't quite make love, because, explains Elaine, "Tomorrow we have to receive enlightenment in the positive place." Dave narrates:

> It's a kind of ridiculous, confused torture; it's not doing us much good. We move in fits, sweating, our legs incredibly nervous, tangled in the sheets of the two sagging beds, and it's clear that whoever the voice is and whatever he wants, we're involved in a game conducted by others, and there's no way we can get out of it on our own.

Frustrating as it is, this scene is one of the more comprehensible ones, and relatively loaded with feeling, or at least with itching.

Everything happens as if to tourists who can't shake their jet lag. People keep being speechless, and ordering food in restaurants without eating it. Dave is jealous of and irritated by Resnik, with his off-again-on-again charm, his habit of directorial manipulation, his "spoiled superstar" airs. Nesbitt tags along in this increasingly weird project, frequently exasperated but never visibly tired of shelling out money for hotels, plane fares, and, in the end, a battery of expensive musical instruments. The women, like many women in movies, are good-looking but toylike—magnetized toys, drawn to Resnik, whom even waitresses sense to be a starmaker. The dialogue at times seems straight from a B-movie, as do the tropical scenery and the feeble strain of science fiction. Our narrator keeps noting filmic effects, like synchronization and discontinuity: "as if synchronized, we get up"; "the preparation of the flambé seems to go in jerks, like a film sequence from which frames have been snipped at random." A wannabe director, Dave stands outside his own actions: "My head is incredibly confused, with overlapping images of three or four possible reactions. I see myself detached, allowing her to leave; dragging her back inside; going out and facing Nesbitt. None of these possibilities is a complete sequence." Caressing Elaine in a romantic tropical shower, he reflects wonderingly "that of all the situations that have ever happened to me in my life, this is the closest to a film." Elsewhere, he mentally scolds her for not staying in character: "It's incredible how little she cares about maintaining any coherence of character; even with respect only to last night, or this morning."

But Dave and his creator are less into character than into atmosphere, and as an atmospheric seismograph the novel registers some very delicate jiggles: "The abandoned film is in the air: a kind of vibration just below or just above the muffled sounds of the lobby." The great Resnik, to whose thoughts we are privy by way of italics, broods, *"The atmosphere is disjointed, not fluid, as I had imagined; neither attraction nor isolation is sufficiently strong to prevail over the other."* Waxing spookier, he lectures his entourage, "People don't realize how dangerous negative landscapes can be. If you cross them without any kind of shielding, on a motorcycle, for example, they can even destroy you. I'm sure there are people who are dissolved, never found again." And when the group visits, at the behest of the voices from beyond, the monumental Yucatán ruins at Tis Talan and Atsantil, the negative and positive vibes are exhaustively plumbed. At Atsantil:

> The equilibrium of the stones seems temporary, as if in the course of the night someone could come and pull a couple of buildings closer together, or move them apart, or even dismantle them to use their material differently. At the same time, the whole is curiously strong, not having to overcome great pressures or resistance. . . . The tourists are not made insignificant by the imposing ferocity of buildings or by the enormity of empty space, as at Tis Talan; the movements and sounds here are absorbed by the landscape, purified without the knowledge of those who produce them. It doesn't even seem to be hot anymore, though the sun is at its peak and the light is extraordinarily intense.

There is beauty in such a laid-back, entranced evocation of atmospheric nuance, and there is a curious authenticity in Andrea De Carlo's washed-out, flimsy, heartless little movie of a novel. This is how the world seems as the millennium evaporates: a series of hotel rooms and tourist sights at which we arrive numbed by the journey. If there is a woman in the hotel room, she blends right in, like the objects in Elaine's friend Rickie's slide show, "photographed as if their use or normal meaning were unknown." We have lost touch with the *why* of things, and what is left is fast food for the senses and the humming brain. Mr. De Carlo's native Italy is perhaps still too saturated with traditional meanings, too full of inhabited historical allusions, so he had to come to the New World, the empty opulence of southern California and Mexico's death-haunted poverty, for the atmosphere he needed, the flickering bleached shimmer of not-being-there-ness.

Kunio Tsuji, the author of *The Signore: Shogun of the Warring States*, has travelled far geographically—he studied in Paris for four years—and imaginatively, setting this, his first novel to be translated into English, in the sixteenth century and in the mind and voice of a European. The narrative is framed as a long epistle from a nameless Italian soldier of fortune who finds himself for a few years an intimate of the Portuguese missionaries in Japan and of a warlord whom he calls the Signore but whom any Japanese reader, the translator assures us in a preface, would recognize as Oda Nobunaga (1534–82). Nobunaga was a chieftain of the small province of Owari, who managed, by dint of his cleverness and ferocity, to subdue twenty of the provinces around the beleaguered imperial capital of Kyoto and thus to take the first and crucial step in the unification of Japan after two centuries of chaotic civil war. A kind of George Washington, we might say, who had to conquer and massacre rival forces in the states around Virginia, all in the nominal service of a powerless royal government. Nobunaga is not named in Mr. Tsuja's novel, but his successors in the unifying process, Toyotomi Hideyoshi and Tokugawa Ieyasu, are. The only fictional character is the narrator; he, we are concisely informed, murdered his wife and her lover in an alley in Genoa, fled to Lisbon, worked as a porter and lived as a vagrant, enlisted in an expedition to the New World, served as an officer under cruel conditions, joined a Spanish fleet sailing for the Molucca Islands, and spent ten years at sea. He landed in Japan in 1570, at a village where there existed a small Christian church and several Japanese friars. "My first impression of the Japanese," he writes his Italian confidant, "was of a fair-skinned, courteous people who smiled readily and were extremely clean in their persons. Nor later did I have much cause to revise this opinion, except insofar as the courtesy and affability of the Japanese is not infrequently tempered with a kind of contempt or condescension, a com-bination not generally seen among the peoples of Europe."

Mr. Tsuji, to judge by this stately and lucid translation, maintains his cultural contortion gracefully, viewing the Japanese and their military tumult through the eyes of a renegade Latin. The narrator's voice seems sometimes prim and pedantic for such a ruffian, but, then, the author has set himself a basically philosophical problem: the humanization of Nobunaga, who was considered brutal and vindictive by even the lenient standards of feudal Japan. George Sansom, in his *History of Japan 1334–1615,* after patiently trying to balance the accounts on this pivotal histori-cal figure, concludes, "He was a cruel and callous brute." In 1571, Nobunaga's forces stormed and utterly razed the Buddhist stronghold of Mount Hiei, a fortified complex of temples and shrines of incomparable artistic value; in the words of a contemporary writer, "The whole moun-tainside was a great slaughterhouse, and the sight was one of unbearable horror." At the siege of Nagashima, in 1574, he exterminated the inhabi-tants of five fortresses, despite repeated offers of surrender. Upon the conquest of Echizen, in 1575, Nobunaga dispatched a letter to Kyoto boasting that the streets were so crammed with corpses there was no room for more. The remaining fugitives, he wrote, must be searched out and killed *"yama yama, tani tani"*—"on every hill, in every valley." In his last campaign, against the family of his old enemy Takeda Shingen, he wiped out all the Takeda kin and roasted alive the monks of the temple unfortu-nate enough to have sheltered Shingen's remains.

The narrator of *The Signore* witnesses some of this horrendous carnage, and reports on the slaughter of the captured servants and children of a general who has defected from Nobunaga's service, on the burning alive of ten thousand trapped inhabitants of a fortress, on the severed hands of drowned enemies that still cling "stiff and pale as if carved from stone" to the rails of Nobunaga's fleet. Why does the Signore, with his pallid calm, his high-pitched voice, and his nervously twitching brow, persist in such butchery? Out of perfectionism and rationality, the narrator decides: "Among all the Japanese people I met during my stay in that land, I never knew one who believed as strongly as he that the greatest good was that all things should come about necessarily and reasonably." He extols the Signore as "a man who possessed a will to seek the limits of perfection in the work he had chosen for himself." With his own murders in his mind, the narrator goes on, "And it was in precisely this kind of will . . . that I myself found the only meaning of our life here on this earth."

So austere a conclusion, perhaps, belongs more to a twentieth-century Japanese than to an Italian of the time of the Counter-Reformation; Kunio Tsuji, a Japanese with memories of modern war and Japan's subsequent indoctrination in the virtues of peace, worries at the riddle of martial morality, giving it a religious tinge when he has the Signore think, "I was unwilling to mar the hallowed rites of battle with acts of kindness. . . . The only mercy in battle is to be merciless!" After the slaughter at Ishiyama, the Signore dismisses one of his own generals, "the scholarly Lord Sakuma," for his "humanity and restraint in the final phase of the battle." The novel quotes the edict, presumably authentic:

> The way of the warrior is not that of others. In a battle . . . it is incumbent on the commanders—for their sake and for mine—to choose the most opportune moment, then attack with all they have. In this manner, the troops are spared prolonged hardship and struggle. It is the only rational course. But you, with your persistent reluctance and hesitation, have followed a course that can only be judged as thoughtless and unmanly.

Mercilessness, then, is the swiftest route to merciful peace. The American reader, and presumably the Japanese author, can hardly not think of the two atomic bombs which, in a few blinding moments, killed more non-combatants than Nobunaga's thirty years of systematic mayhem, but did open the way to surrender and recovery. As the Signore hacks his way through his enemies, peace prettily descends upon Kyoto:

> Relief and happiness could be sensed in every quarter of the city. Ruined houses had been repaired, new ones were under construction, and the lively sound of hammering filled the air. Under the Signore's tutelage, a police force had been installed, and the watch in each street had been strengthened so that the work of burglars, vandals, and other mischief makers had become unprofitable. Merchants had returned to the boulevards in great numbers, and little theatres and tent shows were again attracting an audience. The women of the pleasure quarters came back from the provinces and could be seen in their bright *quimonos*, beckoning to customers.

On the mountainside of Azuchi the victorious Shogun builds his own castle, roofed in blue tile, and magnanimously decrees that the same roofing material be used for the Christian church to be constructed near the castle walls.

Assuming a Westerner's point of view, the Japanese novelist identifies with the fate of the precarious but thriving Portuguese Jesuit mission in sixteenth-century Japan, portraying the priestly leaders—Francisco Cabral, Luis Frois, Organtino Gnecchi-Soldi, Alessandro Valignano—and animating with particular warmth another historical Christian, the Japanese Brother Lorenzo, a virtually blind and lame convert who acted as translator and go-between for the missionaries. The murderous, rationalist Nobunaga and his allied *daimyos* extended to the Jesuits a degree of protection and friendship they would never again enjoy from the rulers of Japan. The reasons are not so paradoxical. The Japanese samurai admired in the Jesuit missionaries an austerity and discipline equivalent to their own. The Portuguese brought with them Europe's trade and advanced technology, of which the military technology was especially valued—our Italian narrator's intimacy with the Signore is based upon his expertise in arquebus manufacture and deployment, and in naval design and armor. The infant Christian community, which numbered close to three hundred thousand converts by 1600, at first posed no threat to the established social order, whereas the Buddhist monks and clergy, spearheaded by the militant Hokke sect, were among Nobunaga's chief enemies. Further, as the novel tells it, the Jesuits fed the Signore's thirst for rational knowledge and intellectual companionship, whereas the Buddhists were a force for obscurantism and stagnation. The alleged companionship is a bit of a stretch to imagine, and even the mediating device of the soul-searching Italian soldier does not quite make the Signore sympathetic. The sorrow on his "pale, sad visage" is repeatedly mentioned, yet we never feel sorry for him, or believe in him as a kind of Nietzschean superman, a martyr to "the loneliness that came of a determination to test the limits of human existence." For all the historical blood and struggle it contains, *The Signore* makes a papery effect not much different from that of *Yucatán*—fiction at one remove, the characters dimmed by the intervening medium. Kunio Tsuji, coming the long way around by way of a European education and a European point of view, attempts to surprise into life a great name of his national heritage, and produces a stir of old pages.

As far as news—human activity given the immediacy of personal witness—goes, Jessica Hagedorn's *Dogeaters* is the richest of our three exotic novels. The Philippines, to be sure, are not exotic to those who live there, and have been no strangers to our newspapers, from the islands' pious acquisition by McKinley, through their Japanese occupation and American reconquest in World War II, to the latest headlines concerning disastrous earthquakes, the perils of Corazon Aquino, and the trials of Imelda Marcos. *Dogeaters* begins in 1956 and ends with the unnamed Marcoses still uneasily in power. Ms. Hagedorn was born and raised in the Philippines, but has led a vivacious artistic life in the United States, as—the book jacket tells us—"performance artist, poet, and playwright." The jacket elaborates: "For many years the leader and lyricist for the Gangster Choir band, she is presently a commentator on *Crossroads*, a syndicated weekly newsmagazine on public radio." A member of Mr. De Carlo's generation, she is thoroughly imbued with postwar popular culture, and her characters perceive the world through a scrim of movie memories and radio soap operas and try to act in tune with song lyrics and poignant cinematic poses. In the multicultural welter of impoverished Manila, however, the poses don't always fit, and the movies, arriving some years late, don't always make sense. Our young heroine and part-time narrator, Rio Gonzaga, and her bosom (and bosomy) friend and cousin, Pucha Gonzaga, are sometimes puzzled by the American movies of the 1950s: Jane Wyman seems to them too old for Rock Hudson in *All That Heaven Allows* (it should have been Kim Novak) and they are bewildered and bored by *A Place in the Sun* (it was "probably too American for us"). Yet some images hit home:

> The back of Montgomery Clift's shoulder in giant close-up on the movie screen. Elizabeth Taylor's breathtaking face is turned up toward him, imploring a forbidden kiss. They are drunk with their own beauty and love, that much I understand. Only half of Elizabeth Taylor's face is visible—one violet eye, one arched black eyebrow framed by her short, glossy black hair. She is glowing, on fire in soft focus.

A world on quiet fire is arrestingly conveyed by Ms. Hagedorn's episodic, imagistic collage of a novel. A borrowed American culture has given Filipinos dreams but not the means to make dreams come true. As in the novels of the Argentine Manuel Puig, we are reminded how ravishingly Hollywood cinema invaded the young minds of the Third World, where the moviegoers did not meet the corrective reality of North America upon emerging from the theatre. The popular culture in *Dogeaters* is consumed, like the constantly described food, with a terrible honest hunger.

Rio Gonzaga's family is upper-middle-class and, amid country-club games and muffled adultery and anxious rumors from the society's power structure, feels like many well-off households portrayed in the fiction of young Americans and Europeans. Filipinos, however, seem to take their roles rather theatrically: Rio's beautiful mother, who tints "her black hair with auburn highlights, just like Rita Hayworth," lives in mauve rooms with all the windows boarded up and painted over, the air-conditioner running twenty-four hours a day. *Her* mother, Lola Narcisa, is a small brown woman from Davao, in the south, who eats with her hands, walks with a stoop, has a childish giggle, and fills her room with the "sweet gunpowder smell and toxic smoke of Elephant brand *katol*, a coil-shaped mosquito-repellent incense." Rio's paternal grandmother, Abuelita Socorro, is a thick-waisted widow who lives in Spain with her effete son, wears a scrap of the Shroud of Turin pinned to her brassiere, prays before and after eating, and owns a miraculous rosary that glows in the dark. Rio's maternal grandfather is an American, slowly dying in the shabby American Hospital, whose "melancholy American doctors" are, like him, "leftovers from recent wars, voluntary exiles whose fair skin is tinged a blotchy red from the tropical sun or too much alcohol; like his, their clothes and skin reek of rum and Lucky Strikes." He and the family friends the Goldenbergs are among the few non-movie Americans in the novel; Americans are not villains in this novel, though the Philippine atmosphere is villainous, and the government slithers through *film noir* shadows. Among the Gonzagas' network of upper-echelon friends is the charming "Nicky," General Nicasio Ledesma, who turns out to be a conscientious torturer and to have as his mistress a drug-addicted actress, Lolita Luna, adored by millions but unable to realize her dream of emigrating to the United States, where she "can study acting and stop playing so much." The interconnections in Manila society ramify as the novel ranges from the First Lady's dreams to the squalid world of "shower dancers"—young men who lather up and get it up for the delectation of a homosexual nightclub audience.

Dogeaters has a teeming cast of characters, and their multiplicity somewhat dissipates the reader's involvement. The book, prefaced by excessive thanks for help in its composition, feels a bit boiled down, as though its scattered high-energy moments were edited from a more leisurely paced panoramic work. The Avila family, representing Manila's liberal aristocracy, especially seems skimped, though Senator Avila's assassination is the book's political climax, bringing a number of threads together, and his daughter Daisy's triumph in a beauty contest is its most magic-realist moment. "Our country belongs to women who easily shed tears and men who are ashamed to weep," the chapter called "Epiphany" begins. "During the days following her extravagant coronation, something peculiar happens to Daisy Avila. . . . Each morning, as Daisy struggles to wake from her sleep, she finds herself whimpering softly. Her eyes are continually bloodshot and swollen. The once radiant beauty cannot pinpoint the source of her mysterious and sudden unhappiness." As the press and the beauty-contest sponsors clamor at the Avilas' door, she finally wakes with dry eyes and agrees to be interviewed on television. In the course of the interview she "accuses the First Lady of furthering the cause of female delusions in the Philippines." From this scandalous indiscretion it is a short step for her to marry a publicity-conscious English playboy who sees her on television. Without much delay, she separates from him, takes a rebel lover, and is captured by the government, interrogated, raped, and released; next, she smuggles herself back into the rebel terrain and is reborn as the heroic, dedicated Aurora. But her transformation takes place mostly offstage, glimpsed through a series of news items, and her surreal siege of weeping remains the image we treasure, a distillation of this sad land of beauty contests.

Ms. Hagedorn allows herself more space in the underworld of young male hustlers, and in her impersonation of the novel's other narrator, the nightclub d.j., homosexual prostitute, and cocaine addict Joey. Piercingly she brings off his jaunty voice of cheerful bravado and wounded scorn. Joey's father was a black American soldier, his mother a beautiful whore who drowned herself when he was small. He was adopted by, or had already been sold to, a petty crook called Uncle, who trained him as a pickpocket and arranged his sexual initiation at the age of ten. "I've had my share of women since, but they don't really interest me. Don't ask me why. To tell you the truth, not much interests me at all. I learned early that men go for me; I like that about them. I don't have to work at being sexy." During a week-long tryst with a German film-director brought to Manila by one of the First Lady's ambitious art-film festivals, Joey's interior monologue is a running illumination of how sexual traders scheme, fantasize, and suffer flares of desire and pity. Looking at the German, he thinks:

> He's around forty, who knows. Pale and flabby, baggy clothes, a drooping moustache and the smell of cigarettes, straggling reddish-blond hair. I'm not sure I can bear to see him naked. It's one thing if he was just an old man. I'd expect to see his flesh hang loose like an elephant; I'd be prepared. . . . The old man with elephant skin drools. Maybe he's God the Father, lost in paradise. He can't get over how perfect I am; he can't get over the perfection of his own creation. He falls in love with me. They always do. I'll admit, I can get off with some old man that way. I need my own movies, with their flexible endings. Otherwise, it's just shit. Most sex is charity, on my part.

In the end, he steals his lover's drugs and money, having already stoked up on a big breakfast: "Scrambled eggs over garlic-fried rice, side of *longaniza* sausages and beef *tapa*, *kalamansi* juice, and fresh pineapple for dessert. My last good meal for the next few days . . . The German is amused."

Food and romantic fantasies crowd these famished pages. Everybody wants to be loved, especially the torturing general. With little overt editorializing, Ms. Hagedorn sketches a nation that has never had much to be proud of, where even the natives feel like strangers. "Two generations, three generations, it really doesn't matter," Rio's father says. "What matters is I feel like a visitor." A humiliating poverty undermines the First Lady's dreams of cosmopolitan elegance. She dreams she is in the lobby of the Waldorf-Astoria, having just chatted with Cristina Ford: "The third elevator's door slides open without hesitation she steps in she holds up her long *terno* skirt to keep her precious beads from dragging on the floor she looks down at her bare feet the red polish on her toenails is chipped the skin between her toes is cracked and blistered streaked with dirt she is horrified." Though the narrative at the end flies off into a flurry of artiness, including a prayer to the Virgin and a letter from Pucha to Rio Gonzaga as the author of *Dogeaters,* Ms. Hagedorn's novel is generally dense with felt observation. Worried upper-class family life, seamy and hypnotic nightlife, suffocating and sinister and impotent political life—it is all here, set down with poetic brightness and grisly comedy. The author sees her native land from both near and far, with ambivalent love, the only kind of love worth writing about.

As Others See Us

THE TENNIS PLAYERS, by Lars Gustafsson, translated from the Swedish by Yvonne L. Sandstroem. 92 pp. New Directions, 1983.

MASKS, by Fumiko Enchi, translated from the Japanese by Juliet Winters Carpenter. 141 pp. Knopf, 1983.

A MINOR APOCALYPSE, by Tadeusz Konwicki, translated from the Polish by Richard Lourie. 232 pp. Farrar, Straus & Giroux, 1983.

Lars Gustafsson is a Swede who has read, among much else, Nietzsche; from the German rhapsodist he has learned to combine philosophy and play, a sense of *homo* as both *ludens* and *in extremis*. The first of his intricate, slim novels to be translated into English, *The Death of a Beekeeper*, took the form of a dying man's diary, and presented piquant apian facts and the soft gray winter landscape of rural Sweden intermingled with the drastic pain of terminal cancer. The second, entitled *The Tennis Players,* is also in the first person, a reminiscence by an affable professorial type who calls himself Lars. He remembers "a happy time" as a Visiting Professor of Swedish Literature at the University of Texas at Austin in the fall of 1974; besides edifying innocent young Americans in the dark ways of Strindberg, Brandes, and Nietzsche, our hero works hard on his tennis game and gets involved in a spooky doubles match whose other participants are: Abel, a former pro and tennis mystic in a wide-brimmed leather hat; Polly, a tiny girl who turns out to be a Texas princess in disguise; and a math whiz called Chris, who works part-time for the Strategic Air Command, monitoring the Southern Air Defense District's operations computer in Fort Worth. One of Lars's students, a "very tall, very skinny, and quite mad" black called Bill, has located, in the remote top reaches of the university library (housed, as it happens, in the nine-teen-story tower from which the deranged Charles Whitman shot and killed thirteen people one June day in 1966*), a book printed in Paris in 1899, *Mémoires d'un chimiste,* by one Zygmunt I. Pietziewszkoczsky; Piet-ziewszkoczsky's memoirs indicate that in fact Strindberg was *really* being poisoned and was not just paranoid during the crisis described in his well-known (in Scandinavia) novel of 1897, *Inferno.* At Lars's suggestion, Chris tries to collate *Inferno* with *Mémoires d'un chimiste* on the giant government computer, precipitating a brief crisis which coincides with a university strike over the political implications of performing *Das Rhein-gold* and not *Aida* in a campus production, and with a local bigwig's being caught committing an immoral act in the batter's box of the local ballpark.

It is farce, but underplayed, and swiftly over, leaving a certain reso-nance of the personal; the conjunction of sunstruck Texas realities with the intellectual murk of *fin-de-siècle* northern Europe—"a time of coal smoke and absinthe, when Europe starts to give up hope"—is of course one the author lived through. Such cultural simultaneity is a campus commonplace, here especially embodied in the person of Doobie Smith, a Lou Salomé look-alike from Dallas so immersed in her reading that for her "Berlin was still a city of gaslights and dark hansom cabs going through cobbled streets." Lars, who has been to Berlin, tells us, "She would get impatient with me because I didn't know literary coffee shops that now exist only as building materials for some hundred feet of the Wall." Doobie, with her blond hair and chubby hands, was "one of the most committed Nietzscheans I've ever met." It is always interesting to see yourself as others see you, and Mr. Gustafsson's impressions of Amer-ica, though not notably harsh, are bracing:

---

*These facts as given in the novel; in truth, the tower has twenty-eight stories, and Whitman shot and killed fourteen people, wounding thirty-one others, on an August day.

There are hundreds of Reserve Policemen in every American city. They carry a special kind of heavy, watertight flashlight that can be used as a nightstick. In the sixties, they always used to be called up every time there were racial disturbances: they were drawn from approximately the same group as the subscribers to those brightly colored gun magazines one sees on all the newsstands.

Some things about [the students] never cease to amaze me. Their emotional brittleness, their perfect tennis serves, their almost frightening capability of grasping things: Gunnar Ekelöf's Akrit poems, non-Abelian groups, and Nietzsche's *Beyond Good and Evil*, almost in the same breath; their strange conviction that the world outside of Texas is meant for war and tourism.

It is such postcards home, rather than the Nordic basketwork intertwining themes from Strindberg, Wagner, and Nietzsche, that catch the American reader's eye. Mr. Gustafsson is himself both affable and semi-opaque; he uses himself as a prism, deflecting light into unexpected corners. The net effect combines high seriousness and offhand charm. If Susan Sontag were to meet Woody Allen halfway, we might get *jeux d'esprit* of such gently skewed vision and good-natured intellectual effervescence.

Fumiko Enchi is, according to her American publisher's flap copy, "generally regarded by the Japanese as their most important woman writer." She was born in 1905, and *Masks* has waited twenty-five years for its publication here. The daughter of a well-known Meiji scholar and the author of a ten-volume translation of Lady Murasaki's classic *Tale of Genji*, Mrs. Enchi in this short novel describes "a crime that only women could commit" and sheds, in passing, considerable scholarly light upon Nō masks and "spirit possession in the Heian era." Psychological possession in the modern era enables Mieko Toganō, a poet and widow in her fifties, to manipulate her beautiful widowed daughter-in-law, Yasuko, in a simultaneous romance with two men—Tsuneo Ibuki, a gaunt, married teacher of literature, and Toyoki Mikamé, an overweight, unmarried psychologist. Akio, Yasuko's husband and Mieko's son, was killed in an avalanche on Mount Fuji four years before, a scant year after his marriage. Mieko, it develops, conceived Akio and his feeble-minded female twin, Harumé, not with her own late husband, Masatsugu, but with a nameless lover who died in 1937 with the Japanese Army in China. Other characters include: Sadako, Ibuki's businesslike wife (in whose honor he coins the epigram "A rational woman is as ridiculous as a flower held together with wire"); Yū, the elderly maidservant who has been witness to all that has transpired in the twisted Toganō household; Toé, the daughter of Yorihito Yakushiji, a dying Nō master; and the Rokujō lady, a sinister figure from *The Tale of Genji* who haunts Mieko's thoughts and the spectral level of this novel. Some of the Nō masks are almost characters in themselves, and the novel's three chapters are titled after masks: "Ryō no Onna," "the spirit woman" and emblem of female vengeance; "Masugami," a mask representing a young madwoman; and "Fukai," meaning "deep well" or "deep woman," a mask used in roles depicting middle-aged women.

"It's very Japanese," a character says at one point, and so *Masks* does seem. The descriptive prose sometimes has the evocative precision and quickly shifted perspective of haiku:

> Patches of snow a few days old lingered here and there in the shadows of buildings and around tree roots in hollows in the ground. The sight of the snow, frozen hard now in odd shapes, reawakened in his senses the soft chill of the new-fallen flakes.

Other passages have the flatness of Japanese paintings, full of carefully indicated textures and angles:

> Yasuko sat up so suddenly that the quilt fell back in a triangle, revealing Mieko's slim figure lying gracefully draped in a sleeping-gown of patterned silk crepe, her legs bent slightly at the knee.

> Viewed from the bathroom window, overlapping rooftops on a steep and narrow alleyway formed a succession of triangles tumbling down to where the sea (this, too, a triangle, standing on its head) lay softly blue and sparkling.

Sometimes the prose seems as hard-breathing as a sumo wrestler:

> Her expression was calm and unflickering as always, but beneath the chill weight of her sagging breasts her heart raced in a mad elvish dance, while from hips to thighs a powerful tension enveloped her, anchoring her to the floor.

Perhaps the translator should share the blame for the effortfulness of a sentence like

> The road down which she must blindly grope her way, helplessly laden with that unending and inescapable burden, seemed to stretch before her with a foul and terrifying blackness.

But the author alone has produced the overload of symbols and melodramatic insistences and *dei ex machina* lowered creakily out of the classic literature and drama of the past. Mrs. Enchi's interpolation of a ten-page essay on the character of the Rokujō lady and the frequent depiction of her own heroines' faces in terms of Nō masks—"[Mieko's] was a face like a Nō mask, while the impression it gave was one of even greater obscurity and elusiveness"—muffle rather than illuminate what is going on among Mieko, Yasuko, and Harumé. Our sense of human event fights through, as it were, the wraps of decreed meaning.

The life that this delicate, mysterious book does have emerges in startling, grotesque gestures and images:

> . . . Mieko patted and brushed back the cold sweat-soaked strands of hair along Yasuko's brow. At the same time her legs began a smooth, rotary motion like that of paddle blades, softly stroking and enfolding Yasuko's curled-up legs.

We read that Harumé suffered brain damage from the pressure of Akio's feet in the womb, that Akio's body when found after five months under the snow had been torn to the bone along one side of his face, that Yasuko's body after beginning her affair with Ibuki had in Mieko's nostrils a peculiar smell—"the sharp pungency of a fish just taken from the sea." Ibuki, after an interview with the mother and daughter-in-law, "recognized the viscid flow of emotion between Yasuko and Mieko as, he felt, unclean, yet he was aware also of his own paradoxical desire to enter that unclean moistness." The Japanese psyche, without significant prompting from Christianity or Freud, seeks its own underworld, the fervid unclean flow behind the impassive mask. This restrained culture has produced, in its novels and films of this century, an art of violent imagery and painful beauty. Yasuko remembers how, searching for her husband beneath the snows of Mount Fuji, she thrust down the long steel rod she had been given and how it left each time "a tiny deep hole of a blue that was so pure, so clear, so beautiful, it took my breath away"; and one night she dreams that she stabbed "his dead face straight in the eye."

The transaction among the women of *Masks* is tortuously complex: Yasuko under Mieko's spell causes Harumé to be impregnated by her own drugged lover, and the new life thus brought into the world in some way replaces and revenges the child that Mieko miscarried when she was tripped by a nail maliciously fixed at the head of a stair by her husband's jealous mistress, Aguri. Jealousy, grief, sensuousness, and passivity contribute in inscrutable proportions to this "crime that only women could commit"; the mask of Fukai conceals a deep well indeed. As in Mr. Gustafsson's brief novel, Americans are seen with a slant from another culture. Yasuko and Ibuki, about to commence their adulterous affair, observe a young American couple on a train—a woman with flaxen hair and a man whose hair "resembled the fur of a small animal." The couple caress each other fondly and then "They were asleep, leaning against one another like a pair of tame animals." To the Swede, as of 1974, we are killers; to the Japanese, as of 1958, we have the innocence of animals.

Tadeusz Konwicki is a Polish writer and film director, born in 1926, who has gone from being an officially approved Socialist Realist to being a dissident whose fiction can be published only in the underground magazine *Zapis* and in the West. A previous novel, *The Polish Complex*, appeared here last year; *A Minor Apocalypse* extends its predecessor's jaunty, picaresque manner deeper into desperation. In both novels, Konwicki's heroes have his name and personal history, as if the times are too ramshackle and weary for the conventional concoction of an alter ego. "Weariness and powerlessness were overcoming me. My life was repeating itself and I was repeating myself. . . . My art, like my life, could be sliced like a sausage."

In this novel Konwicki awakes with a hangover, though he has not been drinking, and is visited by two fellow writers, Hubert and Rysio, who tell him he has been chosen to set himself on fire at eight o'clock that evening, in front of the Party Central Committee building, as a protest. Our hero's friends explain to him that since he is a prominent but not indispensable writer, and long obsessed by death anyway, he is a natural candidate; in truth he does not reject their proposal out of hand but mulls it over during a long day of wandering, during which he allows himself to be equipped with a can of gasoline and Swedish matches (Swedish because Polish matches tend not to ignite). Warsaw is collapsing around him—bridges fall, electricity fails, slabs of sandstone fly from the Palace of Culture in the wind—and the city is in the grip of an immense drunken celebration of what on various pages is identified as the fortieth, fiftieth, thirty-fifth, and sixtieth anniversary of the Polish People's Republic, which dates from 1952. Not only the calendar but the weather is unsteady; the day begins as one of "autumn's hopeless days" but enjoys some summery intervals and ends in snow. Konwicki visits old friends, an uproarious restaurant called Paradyz, and a Polish film called *Transfusion*, which is advertised on the marquee as a Russian film called *The Radiant Future*. During his perambulations he has various companions, of whom the most constant are Pikush, a many-colored dog, and Tadzio Skorko, an ardent Konwicki fan and aspiring poet who also seems to work for the secret police. Konwicki is repeatedly stopped by different varieties of police and is tortured by one set of them. He makes love to a red-haired Russian beauty, Nadezhda, and attends a kind of witches' congress of the fifteen women whose lover he has been at various times of his life. He engages in a great many excited conversations, with representatives of both the establishment and the opposition; but, so long has the unhappy Polish situation been marinating, it is hard to tell one from the other, and no marked conflict exists, just a tangle of wry and futile palaver.

Like such other anarchic spirits as Flann O'Brien and Céline, Konwicki has a lovely light way of writing, that never clogs chaotic flow with self-pity and bestows upon the direst pages sentences of casual felicity. He is especially good with women, to whom all sorts of delicate fragrances cling. Here is Nadezhda, being seduced:

> She smelled like water that had been warmed by the sun, and she also had the sharp, enticing aroma of birch leaves . . . We could hear the desperate pounding of each other's hearts and the polyphonic cry of the birds, like some rising reminder. . . . She had closed her eyes so tightly the lids had turned white. Sharp, predatory teeth gleamed in the heathery pinkness of her mouth.

Konwicki is effortlessly witty, and dizzies the Western reader with the convolutions of the vitiated Polish situation as it drowns in its ironies. A Marxist philosopher explains to the author that Communism has saved Poland from being absorbed by a vital, enterprising Russia: "You should pray every day and thank your gods that the Russians have been rendered inert by that idiotic doctrine, depraved by that ghastly life, exhausted by that moronic economic system." A Party official, Comrade Kobialka, who sacrifices his career by undressing at a televised Party celebration appears no less absurd than the televised embrace of the two all-powerful secretaries: "two fat men were kissing each other on the mouth." The peculiar demeaningness of television has crept into Poland; all political gestures are aimed toward it, while it turns every event into a trivial flickering. Misery becomes trite, and happiness is absurd, whether it is Kobialka's happiness as he is hauled in a padded straitjacket to the security of the state insane asylum or that of the lusty retired minister, now a painter of nudes, as he rushes off to the outer regions where "you can still find girls who'll put out for good old Polish zlotys" (as opposed to the Warsaw whores, who demand hard currency). Even interrogation by torture is farcical; the police inject Konwicki with a drug that makes him so sensitive he can be agonized by the flick of a fingertip and the battering of a paper ball. At his ordeal's end, he thinks, "Some sort of confused play was over."

That Communist governments are atrocious is familiar news; less familiar is Konwicki's repeated point that dissidence has something weary, corrupt, and pointless about it. By now in Poland, evidently, the motions of opposition, like those of governing, are a kind of sleepwalking. A race has grown up of "dissidents with lifetime appointments. The regime has grown accustomed to them and they've grown accustomed to the regime." Konwicki notices of his young fellow conspirators that "They were all small, thin, shaggy. But it was in them alone that any resistance to the authorities had smoldered. Over the years, the authorities had grown ugly, too, but in a different way—they had turned into fat, growing sideways; they had become womanish."

No Americans are seen in this long Warsaw day—a blend of Bloomsday and, the reader is often reminded, the Stations of the Cross—but a "senior journalist with the Associated Press" telephones toward evening, saying, "I wanted to ask what was going on in Warsaw today." Konwicki tells him, "Nothing too interesting. The usual holiday commotion." The answer is accepted. The West in general, far from being seen as a superior system to that decaying in Poland, is involved in the same entropic deterioration. Kobialka claims, "The West . . . started running away when we started chasing them, and then they slowed down when we eased up. They're exhausted, too. They're straddling the fence, too." As of 1979, from the Polish slant, we are neither innocent nor dynamic. In regard to the captive plight of Eastern Europe the free world has proved helpless; capitalism has become not Poland's savior but her creditor. In Paradyz, "the disabled veterans' cooperative band was playing a medley of American tunes but, to disguise them, was playing them backward so they wouldn't have to pay any royalties in hard currency." Poland can only afford to import black humor. Instinctively Konwicki assumes the tone of absurdist fiction, that tone which says, "This happens, that happens, don't expect me to make much of it, because life is meaningless; don't expect me to work you, gentle reader, up into much of a tizzy of caring, either." When, at the very end of *A Minor Apocalypse,* we are expected to care, the rhetoric embarrasses us, so effectively has our responsiveness been lowered by the deflationary slapstick of Konwicki's hopeless world.

Studies in Post-Hitlerian Self-Condemnation in Austria and West Germany

WITTGENSTEIN'S NEPHEW, by Thomas Bernhard, translated from the German by David McLintock. 100 pp. Knopf, 1989.

NO MAN'S LAND, by Martin Walser, translated from the German by Leila Vennewitz. 160 pp. Holt, 1989.

Somewhere, I have seen Hitler's hold upon the German people explained by the fact that he addressed his audience in very much the shrill way in which a German husband speaks to his wife. The Austrian playwright, novelist, and poet Thomas Bernhard, by the time of his death last February, at the age of fifty-eight, had collected the chief literary prizes the German-speaking world offers, and his great critical and even (with his widely produced plays) popular success in that world perhaps derives from a similar trait: he was, in his writing, always on the verge of a shriek, and in the Germanic psyche shrieking constitutes proof of caring. One of the lines of Bernhard's last play, *Heldenplatz*, characterizes Austria as "a nation of 6.5 million idiots living in a country that is rotting away, falling apart, run by the political parties in an unholy alliance with the Catholic Church." In his novel *Correction*, the narrator spills a little of his spare bile on "a time such as ours when . . . every year hundreds and thousands of tons of imbecility-on-paper are tossed on the market, all the decrepit garbage of this totally decrepit European civilization, or rather, to hold nothing back, this totally decrepit modern world of ours, this era that keeps grinding out nothing but intellectual muck and all this stinking constipating clogging intellectual vomit is constantly being hawked in the most repulsive way as our intellectual products though it is in fact nothing but intellectual *waste* products." And in his latest work to appear in English, *Wittgenstein's Nephew*, we find the following admonishment: "Let us not deceive ourselves: most of the minds we associate with are housed in heads that have little more to offer than overgrown potatoes, stuck on top of whining and tastelessly clad bodies and eking out a pathetic existence that does not even merit our pity."

Bernhard, with his tyrannical repetitiousness and unpredictably placed italic emphases—like the blows of an impulsive fist—was a maestro of the music of the diatribe, its churning, its hammering, its omnivorous momentum, a music such that any note *not* of disprise seems a discord and a momentary weakening of the artist's strength. Even his typographical signature—a resolute lack of paragraphing, an unrelieved march of unindented lines—shows hostility, toward the reader and also toward the printer, for whom every alteration involves a vast displacement of type. An irascible fury runs so consistently through Bernhard's fiction that one is tempted to think it an involuntary trait, demonstrated in the author's behavior as well as in his prose. One certainly suspects there is another side to his story of the official contretemps that occurred when he accepted the State Prize for Literature in an audience chamber of the Ministry in Vienna. First, by way of tribute, according to *Wittgenstein's Nephew*, he listened to "utter nonsense" and factually erroneous "idiocies" read out by a minister with "stupidity . . . written all over his face." Then he responded:

> Just before the ceremony, in great haste and with the greatest reluctance, I had jotted down a few sentences, amounting to a small philosophical digression, the upshot of which was that man was a wretched creature and death a certainty. After I had delivered my speech, which lasted altogether no more than three minutes, the minister, who had understood nothing of what I had said, indignantly jumped up from his seat and shook his fist in my face. Snorting with rage, he called me a *curr* in front of the whole assembly and then left the chamber, slamming the glass door behind him with such force that it shattered into a thousand fragments. . . . And then the strangest thing happened: the whole assembly, whom I can describe only as an opportunistic rabble, rushed after the minister, though not without shouting curses and brandishing their fists at me as they went.

Bernhard's acceptance, later, of the coveted Grillparzer Prize, bestowed by the Austrian Academy of Sciences, went no more smoothly. No one met the prospective honoree either outside or inside the hall. Bernhard decided to follow the crowd in, and took a seat, with his entourage, in the middle of the auditorium. "The Vienna Philharmonic was nervously tuning up, and the president of the Academy of Sciences, a man by the name of Hunger, was running excitedly to and fro on the dais, while only I and my friends knew what was holding up the ceremony." When Bernhard was at last found and asked, by an Academy member, to come to his reserved seat up front, the author balked: "I did not obey, because the request was made in a rather disagreeable and arrogant tone, and with such a sickening assurance of victory that, to preserve my self-respect, I *had* to refuse to accompany him toward the dais." He yielded only when President Hunger himself descended from the dais and escorted him. Writers less honored than Bernhard can take comfort from his hard-won perception that "to award someone a prize is no different from pissing on him. And to receive a prize is no different from allowing oneself to be pissed on, because one is being paid for it." Prizes "do nothing to enhance one's standing, as I had believed before I received my first prize, but actually lower it, in the most embarrassing fashion."

Thomas Bernhard's embarrassments in life began early. He was illegitimate, born in 1931 in a Dutch convent that sheltered unwed mothers until their accouchement. His first year he spent mostly in a hammock suspended from the ceiling of a trawler lying in Rotterdam Harbor, while his mother worked as a domestic to pay for his foster care in this floating establishment. In his autobiography—from 1975 to 1982 he composed five short autobiographical works collected in English as *Gathering Evidence* (translated by David McLintock; Knopf, 1985)—he wrote of her weekly visits, "I am told that I cried miserably every time and that while I was on the trawler my face was covered with ugly boils, since there was an incredible stench and impenetrable fumes where the hammocks were hung." His mother, named Herta, was the daughter of the little-published Austrian writer Johannes Freumbichler; his father, Alois Zuckerstätter, was a peasant's son and a carpenter from Henndorf, in Austria, where Herta had been living with her aunt. Bernhard never met his father, who died, violently and mysteriously, in 1943. In 1945 he persuaded his paternal grandfather to impart a little information about Alois ("He spoke of my father as though he had been an animal") and to give him a photograph of the man: "It was so like me that I had a fright." Young Thomas took it home to his mother, who snatched it out of his hand and threw it in the stove. It was her unkind custom to send the child to the town hall to collect the five marks which the state paid monthly to illegitimate children, telling him, "This'll show you how much you're worth!"

After a year on the trawler, *Gathering Evidence* explains, Bernhard was taken by his mother to live with her parents in Vienna. *Her* mother was the offspring of a prosperous Salzburg family who had disgraced herself by leaving, at the age of twenty-one, her husband and three children to run off with Freumbichler to Basel; the couple lived together for forty years before marrying. In 1934 the "poor, fly-by-night family" moved to the rural village of Seerkirchen, near Salzburg, and there Herta met and married a hairdresser's assistant named Emil Fabjan. They eventually had a boy and a girl, in addition to Thomas. Unable to find work in Austria, Fabjan moved across the Bavarian border to the town of Traunstein, while the grandparents lived in nearby Ettendorf. Freumbichler, whom his grandson "loved more than anyone else in the world," was well born (in Henndorf) and a great "enlightener" but also, according to Bernhard's account, "an individualist, unsuited to living in a community, and therefore unfit for any employment." A one-time theological seminarian turned anarchist, he earned virtually nothing through his writings; he "lived off his wife and daughter, who believed in him unreservedly, and in the end he lived off his son-in-law as well."

His grandson, too, proved ill-suited to communal life; after a promising first year in school at the age of five, he became a hopeless student, a truant, and a bed-wetter. He found grammar school "a condition of continuous torment," was even more unhappy at a home for maladjusted children in Saalfeld, and detested most of all the National Socialist Home for Boys in Salzburg, where he spent a year, from 1943 to 1944, in an atmosphere of mingled Catholicism and Nazism so hateful that a number of the boys committed suicide and Bernhard contemplated it fondly every day, during his sessions of violin practice in a shoe closet. His autobiography rates this interval as "the darkest and altogether the most agonizing I have known," and its misery was varied but not lightened by the ferocious air raids to which Salzburg by now was subject. School became a shambles, and the thirteen-year-old boy had ample opportunity to sit in the rubble and "contemplate the spectacle of human despair, indignity, and annihilation." After the war, he returned to the school in its new guise as the Johanneum Gymnasium, now run by priests, and found it no improvement over the Nazi version: "Swallowing and gulping down the body of Christ every day . . . was essentially no different from rendering daily homage to Adolf Hitler." He detested school, bourgeois Salzburg, and most everything else that surrounded him: "My childhood and youth were difficult in every way."

Bernhard's description of his closeted violin sessions reminds one of his rhapsodically free-form writing, as it developed in his monologuist novels and his autobiographical excursions: "He plays with the utmost virtuosity, if not with the utmost precision, and as he plays he is totally absorbed in the idea of suicide. . . . According to Steiner [his teacher] his playing was, on the one hand, highly musical, and on the other . . . totally undisciplined when it came to observing the rules." This frenetic musical activity as a substitute for suicide evolved along with other kinds of activity: Bernhard became an unbeatable school runner, and at the age of fifteen, he quit school and apprenticed himself to a grocery store in the toughest section of Salzburg, the Scherzhauserfeld Project. "Most of my real qualities, the positive features of my character, came to the surface again . . . after being buried and stifled for years by the odious educational methods to which I had been subjected. . . . Right from the start I did not just wish to be useful—I really was useful, and my usefulness was noted." Here, laboring in a cellar store among outcasts, he felt perversely useful, free, and happy.

But the strains of the job—inhaling flour dust, lifting heavy sacks—eventually broke his health. Unloading a truckload of potatoes in a snowstorm, he caught a case of influenza that became severe pleurisy. In 1949, not quite eighteen years old, he was consigned to a hospital death ward, and at one point was given last rites. He then spent over a year in two different sanitoriums, with laboriously treated lung disease. To compound his misfortunes during this time, his grandfather and mother both died. Yet he recovered enough to attend the Mozarteum Conservatory in Salzburg, to study music and theatre arts, to serve as a court reporter for the left-wing *Demokratisches Volksblatt*, and to compose, before he eventually succumbed to his debilities, over thirty works of fiction, poetry, and drama, as well as his remarkable autobiography, the record of a furious will persevering amid the most abysmal isolation. Though his typical hero is an intellectual trapped in mental paralysis, he himself wrote with energy, daring, and a shrewd sense of the sensational.

Publishers love to call books novels. *Wittgenstein's Nephew* has been labelled as one by Knopf, but really it is an undisguised memoir. Exactly one hundred pages long, it wanderingly describes, without much of the heat of *Gathering Evidence*, Bernhard's friendship with Paul Wittgenstein, the famous philosopher's nephew and a mentally unbalanced dandy once conspicuous around Vienna. Like *Correction* (whose fictional Roithamer, with his aristocratic background and English residence, is plainly patterned on the philosopher), it concerns a verbose and fascinated narrator's entwinement with a Wittgenstein. The entwinement in the memoir is based upon a shared fondness for opera and music, for Schopenhauer and Novalis and Pascal and Velásquez and Goya, for sitting in the Sacher coffeehouse caustically observing the other customers, for sweeping castigations and "cosmopolitan fooleries." Bernhard and Paul Wittgenstein also shared, we are told, "the counting disease"—a compulsion to count windows and doors from a vantage like that of a moving streetcar—and a habit of stepping on paving stones not randomly but according to "a carefully thought-out system." They both suffered from the "disease" of "always travelling, simply in order to get away from one place and go to another [without] finding happiness on arrival." To their more serious diseases Bernhard gives a romantic coloring of willed rebellion:

> Paul went mad because he suddenly pitted himself against everything and lost his balance, just as one day I too lost my balance through pitting myself against everything—the only difference being that he went *mad*, whereas I, for the selfsame reason, contracted *lung disease.* But Paul was no madder than I am. . . . The only difference between us is that Paul allowed himself to be

utterly dominated by his madness, whereas I have never let myself be utterly dominated by my equally serious madness; one might say that he was taken over by his madness, whereas I have always exploited mine.

Similarly, the narrator of *Correction* deems himself "probably somewhat more of a survivor than Roithamer, for I always seem to find a way out, while Roithamer could no longer find a way out."

As Paul became madder, Bernhard distanced himself; the reminiscence undergoes a rueful turn: "Quite deliberately, out of a base instinct for self-preservation, I shunned my friend in the last months of his life, and for this I cannot forgive myself." Remembering Paul's grotesque, emaciated, deathly appearance in his last days leads the author to some perversely complacent self-condemnation: "Watching him, I felt ashamed. I felt it shameful that I was not yet finished, as my friend already was. I am not a good character. I am quite simply not a good person." Paul had predicted to Bernhard, *"Two hundred friends will come to my funeral and you must make a speech at the graveside."* In fact, only eight or nine attended the funeral, and his friend Thomas Bernhard stayed in Crete, writing a play which, he tells us, "I destroyed as soon as it was finished." He additionally confides, "To this day I have not visited his grave."

The memoir, which takes Paul's mortuary prediction as its epigraph, has been delivered instead of the graveside speech. It offers no moral save the one that, as Bernhard stated on another occasion, man is a wretched creature and death a certainty. Its most vivid episodes reveal the author engaged in some display of reflexive irascibility; relatively little of poor, elegant, underemployed Paul shows through the domineering personality of the bad-tempered prose, which as it runs along blasts the "unbearable" German press, the "unspeakably perfidious thespians" who performed one of Bernhard's plays, literary coffeehouses whose "foul atmosphere [is] irritating to the nerves and deadening to the mind," psychiatrists, who are "the real demons of our age," and, at some length, the "gross self-degradation" of fashionably moving to the country and smoke-curing pork and growing your own vegetables. Bernhard's curmudgeonliness here comes close to being as droll a shtik as W. C. Fields's; his ferocious misanthropy, capable of generating nightmares in the fiction, almost sinks to the lovable.

Martin Walser (not to be confused with the Swiss novelist, feuilletonist, Kafka precursor, and mental patient, Robert Walser [1878–1956]) is described, among the jacket quotes on his novel *No Man's Land*, as "the closest thing the West Germans have to John Updike." Really? *No Man's Land* seemed to this naturally expectant reader a joyless, terse, efficient small novel that manages an unforced flowering toward the end, in the inevitably theatrical milieu of a courtroom. Until then, the novel conscientiously occupies the heavily trafficked gray area between the two Germanys, wherein spying, conflicted loyalties, and domestic discontent are local industries. We have been there before, with John Le Carré and other jaded singers of the Cold War blues, and Walser's intellectualized spy story, infused with generous quotations from Schiller's poetry and Schumann's lieder, doesn't, for all its earnestness and compassion, quite shake the feeling of a slumming expedition. A lot of the details seem to enter the narrative backwards, with their symbolic import foremost, and the action is so telescoped as to rebuke rather than satisfy our appetite for suspense.

The hero, Wolf Zeiger, is an East German would-be pianist who gave his piano teacher a concussion and, before heading west in the wake of this gaffe, was enlisted by the Ministry of State Security for six weeks' training in spy school at Potsdam-Eiche. He is not too unhappily married to Dorle, who works at the West German Foreign Ministry. She doesn't have access to the NATO protocols, so Wolf sleeps with the secretary who does, Sylvia Wellershoff. Sylvia—"not fat, but fleshy. She had a bit too much of everything. Her mouth always hung open, as if the lips were too heavy"—is as giving erotically as she is intelligence-wise. Meanwhile, Dorle, approaching forty, wants a baby; and her superior at the office, smarmy Dr. Meissner, is casting a fond eye her way; and the Hungarian mathematician who lives in the apartment below has deduced, from the way Wolf plays Schumann only one hand at a time, that he is a spy; and Wolf is cooling on the idea of returning east at the end of his perfidious career.

If this exposition of the plot seems hasty, so is the book's: all the elements, including opaque bits of the West's high-tech electronics and metallurgy and some plausible quick portraits of spymasters from the Communist side, are in place, but packed too tight to move. The novel seems neither a parody of a thriller, like Robbe-Grillet's *Les Gommes* or Queneau's *We Always Treat Women Too Well*, nor the real, grim-lipped thing. Perhaps one difficulty, for an American reader, is that Wolf's justification to himself for treason against the West German state is the selfless aim of eroding the boundary between the two Germanys and thus helping to heal "this unhappily divided country." The cause of reuniting the pieces of Hitler's Reich, however dear to the German *Volksgeist*, is not one to touch heartstrings universally. Our President's* rhetorical call to

---

*Bush, though all his predecessors since Kennedy had issued the same call. Little did any of us dream that, within a few months of this review's publication, the Wall would come down, and East and West would be no more.

tear down the Berlin Wall is one thing, and the living memory of *Deutschland über Alles* another. In the absence of a motivation easier to empathize with, Wolf's fretful ambivalence seems scarcely to deserve such portentous pondering as "To what extent may one's thoughts contradict one's actions? How much irreconcilability can one bear within oneself?" His self-scorn—in the actual unsparing style, I believe, of contemporary younger Germans—is so withering as to leave the reader small space where sympathy can grab hold: "Now he felt that he was perceiving himself with a kind of disapproval of which he couldn't get enough."

However, a number of scenes where geopolitical unease is translated into intimate behavior—a vacation that Dorle and Wolf take to the South of France, and certain hotel moments between Sylvia and Wolf—leap free of the plot's mechanism, and in the book's last third the terse, elliptic manner pays off in a rapid, no-fuss denouement, brimming with surprises, including, if I read it right, the sly revelation that Dorle is pregnant but not by Wolf. Only the last pages, in which the Zeigers' suspended but not destroyed marriage is presented as a metaphor for the temporarily divided German condition, does Mr. Walser's fondness for larger issues again crowd out the characters' vital tendencies. The novel is studied to a fault, and even a minor, contemptuously casual offering of Thomas Bernhard's like *Wittgenstein's Nephew* seems to come closer to literature, to breathe the air of freedom that permits epiphany. Bernhard is stingy with images and generous with repetitions, but once in a while he dives deep into the appearance of things. While he and Paul Wittgenstein are patients in different pavilions of the same hospital, he tries to walk to see him, runs out of breath, and sits on a seat outside and watches the squirrels:

> They appeared to have one consuming passion—to snatch up the paper tissues that the chest patients had dropped all over the ground and race up into the trees with them. They ran in all directions and from all directions, carrying paper tissues in their mouths, until in the gathering dusk all one could see were the paper tissues, a multitude of white dots darting hither and thither. I sat there enjoying the sight and naturally linking it with the thoughts that it seemed to conjure up automatically.

The mind-quickening atomatism of this odd "multitude of white dots" is approached by Walser's low-affect prose here and there: Wolf feels peculiarly at ease on buses, where "everyone . . . lacked something. Perhaps they all lacked the same thing"; he and Dorle together feel happy and free on a desolate stretch of French beach at the mouth of the Rhône, beyond an industrial sump, with fishermen tending their rods and the mistral driving "the sand in sharp jets against every unprotected particle of skin."

Back home, as Wolf's bus crosses the Rhine, "it gave him a good feeling to see the Rhine churning along there so powerfully, as if it were being paid by the ton for mass transportation of water." In such unexpected feelings and details, life breaks through; we feel in touch with real people, whose dilemmas are only a part of their substance, and with real sensations, whose significance is not imposed but arises automatically.

Rational Faith

A LATE FRIENDSHIP: *The Letters of Karl Barth and Carl Zuckmayer*, translated from the German by Geoffrey W. Bromiley. 72 pp. Eerdmans, 1983.

Zuckmayer, a German dramatist and the author of, among other film scripts, that for *The Blue Angel,* in the spring of 1967 received, amid much mail apropos of his recently published memoirs, a fan letter from the great Swiss theologian. "Much more than you," Barth wrote disarmingly, "I am a child of the nineteenth century; and the modern world of letters, the theatre, the cinema and—how shall I put it—noble Bohemianism, has certainly affected me but never grasped or touched me closely." As disarmingly, Zuckmayer wrote back, "I am one of those for whom God is *not* dead and Christianity, when properly experienced and lived, is still the message of salvation." A remarkably lively and affectionate correspondence ensued between the two elderly and ailing men until Barth, by ten years the older, died in late 1968. Zuckmayer, a Catholic, received mildly admonitory lectures on the dangers of "worshiping God in the bark of a tree," on the low intelligence of King Frederick William IV, and even on how to write a play, but proclaimed in a subsequent essay on this "late friendship" that he had "found once again what all of us most need if we are to know ourselves: a father figure." He also wrote: "Never has any person in our day, with the possible exception of Albert Einstein, so convinced me by his mere existence that faith in God is rational." Zuckmayer died in 1979, making possible the publication of this slim but affecting record of a meeting of minds. Both men's letters show, as Zuckmayer said of Barth, "the intellectual vitality of one who is aging but by no means finished with himself."

Mutability and Gloire

THE EUROPEANS, by Luigi Barzini. 267 pp. Simon and Schuster, 1983.

The author of *The Italians* and *O America* here takes on the Continent; this book of wide-ranging observations and dazzling aperçus is given its focus by the theme of European unification, which Mr. Barzini believes to be highly desirable and far from imminent. Drawing upon fifty years' experience as an Italian journalist and world traveller, he presents in successive chapters vivid historical and psychological portraits of the major members of NATO and the EEC—England, Germany, France, Italy, and Benelux—with a fond and shrewd sketch of the United States added for good measure. He has little to say of Scandinavia, Iberia, or Eastern Europe, to the reader's loss, for he is a master geopolitical essayist. By his account, the immense British prestige of the nineteenth century changed the color of male dress to black, which percolated down from the continental aristocracy through all classes in homage to England's supremacy in the age of coal and iron and empire; this success, Mr. Barzini suggests, derived from the convenient circumstance that all Englishmen had a mere "seven ideas" in their interchangeable heads. The resilience of the constantly teetering Italian state is linked to an underlying longing for *buongoverno;* in recent decades the economically disastrous creation, at American urging, of a center-left coalition, was stopped short of collapse into Communism by prodigies of private enterprise: "Naples exported five million pairs of gloves a year, in spite of the fact that there was not one glove factory in the city." Smaller nations, like the Dutch, tend to favor a United States of Europe, but have grown unrealistically pacific under the American nuclear umbrella. The key to European unity, as Mr. Barzini sees it, is "the mutable Germans," who have shown their neighbors so bewilderingly many faces in the century since Bismarck; the central obstacle is the French insistence on living by the light of a vanished *gloire.* Whatever the author's conclusions, getting there, by a route mixed of personal reminiscence, historical learning, and debonair generalization, is a delight made all the more palatable by his elegant adopted English.

Dutchmen and Turks

THE ASSAULT, by Harry Mulisch, translated from the Dutch by Claire Nicolas White. 185 pp. Pantheon, 1985.

THE SEA-CROSSED FISHERMAN, by Yashar Kemal, translated from the Turkish by Thilda Kemal. 288 pp. Braziller, 1985.

The chance of birth gives a writer his language; if the language is a small one, like Dutch, which is spoken by scarcely more than twenty million people and sits squeezed between its big brothers English and German, the writer must be more than merely good to receive international attention. Though the Dutch are a busily literary people, the modern writer in their language whom Americans know best is a fourteen-year-old diarist, Anne Frank. Harry Mulisch was born in 1927 and is, we are assured flatly (and not without bias) by his jacket-flap biographer, "Holland's most important postwar writer"; but he has waited until now to be published in the United States. His debut, a short novel called *The Assault*, is a brilliant one. A kind of detective story emanating from a violent incident in World War II, the novel combines the fascination of its swift, skillfully unfolded plot with that of a study in the psychology of repressed memory. Its hero, Anton Steenwijk, is twelve years old when, in January of 1945 (Holland, we may need to be reminded, continued to be occupied by the Germans until their final surrender, in May), a collaborationist Dutch policeman is shot on the street where Anton lives in Haarlem with his parents and his older brother, Peter. The body falls in front of their neighbors' house, but these neighbors, mindful of the German tactics of reprisal, quickly move the body so it lies in front of the Steenwijks', and before it can be moved again the Steenwijks are taken prisoner and their home is burned down. The house was one of four in an isolated row on a quay, surrounded by vacant lots; the qualities and secrets of all four sets of inhabitants figure in the sudden events of that nightmarish night, which Anton, soon safely moved to Amsterdam in the care of his uncle, tries to forget. He attends *Gymnasium* and medical school and becomes—fittingly enough—an anesthesiologist; he marries twice, has two children, and acquires no fewer than four homes. But the postwar decades fitfully bring him reminders of "the assault" and cast new light on that night's confusion; not until a day in November of 1981, when all Amsterdam is demonstrating against nuclear arms, does Anton, now gray-haired and about to be a grandfather, at last come, through a chance encounter, to understand exactly what happened on the quay in 1945, when he was twelve.

Mr. Mulisch is identified, in reference works, as an "absurdist"; but there is nothing absurd about this economically and thoughtfully worked-out novel except, perhaps, the wartime reality that serves as its premise. The surreal abruptness with which fateful events develop is stunningly rendered. The family are sitting quietly in their cold, blacked-out house at seven-thirty in the evening: Anton is reading about the time capsule buried at the New York World's Fair; Peter is translating from the Greek; the father, a court clerk and an amateur classicist, is helping him; the mother is unravelling a sweater and soothing a toothache with a clove. Shortly before the eight o'clock curfew, they sit down to a board game, and while they are rolling dice six shots ring out. The tame little details of this last moment of domestic peace—the dice, the clove—reverberate throughout Anton's life, awakening the trauma. About ten years later, for instance, he becomes sick, "overcome by a sense of something dreadful," while attending a performance of Chekhov, "during a scene where a man sat at a table with bowed head while a woman outside on a terrace shouted at someone." He has repressed the memory, but a parallel configuration on a terrace was impressed upon him in the jagged, out-of-control sequence of images that followed the shots:

> Anton saw and heard everything, but somehow he was no longer quite there. One part of him was already somewhere else, or nowhere at all. He was undernourished, and now stiff with cold, but that wasn't all. This moment— his father cut out in black against the snow, his mother outside on the terrace under the starlight—became eternal, detached itself from all that had come before and all that would follow. It became part of him and began its journey through the rest of his life.

A quality seems evoked, of disconnection and eternity, that is present in all experience but noticeable only in crisis. As the night tumbles on, and the Germans arrive to exact their cruel and random vengeance, and the child is thrust here and there in the dishevelled machine of wartime administration, a remarkably rounded impression of occupied Holland accumulates. The German rule is harsh, but the soldiers are only human, and themselves rather desperate, as defeat closes in; the Ortskommandant of Haarlem, turning fatherly, confides to Anton, "The world is a *Jammertal*, a valley of tears. Everywhere it is the same. My house in Linz was bombed also. Everything kaput. *Kinder* dead." For an hour, Anton is placed in an utterly dark cell with a wounded female prisoner who strokes his face, leaving traces of blood from a wound she has suffered. Next morning, a kindly sergeant called Schulz feeds the boy and dresses him in cut-down Army clothes and is fatally strafed while escorting him to

Amsterdam. On this trip the texture of war dawns upon the child, torn from the stringent haven of his freezing, darkened house:

> On the left the overhead wiring of the electric train and the trolley hung to the ground in graceful curves. Here and there the rails stood upright like the horns of a snail. Sometimes even the poles were lying down. On all sides, the hard frozen ground. They drove slowly. It was impossible to hold a conversation because of the racket inside the cabin. Everything was made of dirty, rattling steel, which somehow told him more about the War than he had ever understood before. Fire and this steel—that was the War.

Of course, we have been through this war many times, in newspapers and newsreels and novels and movies whose clichés have preëmpted the fading reality. The author is put to the trouble of proclaiming cliché the truth: "The German was about forty years old and actually had that lean, hardened face with the horizontal scar beneath the left cheekbone—a type no longer used except by directors of comedies or grade B movies. Today only babyish Himmler faces are still artistically acceptable; but then it was not an artistic matter, then he really did look like a fanatical Nazi, and it wasn't funny." From *Hogan's Heroes* to *Gravity's Rainbow*, art has transformed World War II into something we too readily understand. As the Napoleonic convulsions gave the nineteenth century its epic, World War II, in its European theatre, has supplied our central saga, our one eruption and defeat of unambiguous evil, and its vast emergency measures the extremes of human possibility for us. Its black-and-white imagery—blackout, bursts of light, rubble and gritty faces, curved helmets and sweeping searchlights—and its costumes and accents haunt films down to *Star Wars* and its spin-offs; even the galaxies must be cleansed of the swastika, over and over.

Also, we have seen, in postwar movies beyond counting (Italian, German, Russian, Polish), the claustrophobic intensity and insane destructiveness of this conflict yield to the weirdly tranquillized terrain of peace, which the contrast somehow reveals to be another kind of absurdity—selfseeking, petty, quickly jaded, and self-despising. War's chasms of heroism and pain make other human behavior seem shallow, even phantasmal. "All the rest," the author of *The Assault* tells us, "is a postscript—the cloud of ash that rises from the volcano, circles around the earth, and continues to rain down on all its continents for years." Anton moves through the anti-nuclear march "as if each step raised clouds of ashes." He looks upon children raised in freedom and plenty, upon young men and women never asked to kill and be killed in the service of Dutch resistance, with something like incredulousness. He cannot take the politics of postwar Europe

and its protests seriously: "Everyone knew that atom bombs were produced as deterrents not to be used, but to safeguard the peace. If such
paradoxical weapons were abandoned, then the chances of conventional
warfare would increase and eventually lead to the use of atom bombs
anyway." His personal focus is upon anesthesia and order; he is a cross-
word-puzzle addict, and lets others accidentally fill in for him the puzzle
of the four houses on the quay, where one neighbor's reclusiveness and
another's pet reptiles turn out to be crucial clues to the shape imposed, in
one white-hot night of forging, upon his own life. With the cool passion
of a scientist, Mr. Mulisch scrapes rust from the Forties' steel hell and gives
violence its anatomy. May more of his work come into English.

On the other side of Europe, Turkish is spoken by forty-five million
people; Yashar Kemal, another jacket flap assures us, "is internationally
acclaimed as Turkey's leading contemporary writer." Opposite the title-
page of *The Sea-Crossed Fisherman,* ten other titles in English are listed, of
which *Memed, My Hawk* may strike a memory chord for bookish Americans. Mr. Kemal's present offering comes garlanded with picturesque
praise: A. B. Mojtabai calls him "a storyteller in the old style, and a very
grand and spacious style that is"; the London *Times* circumspectly asserts
that "the richness of writing and breadth of canvas have caused Kemal to
be compared with Hardy and Tolstoy"; and John Berger claims, "He
writes fearlessly, like a hero." Like a hero, however, who, in the manner
of an old-fashioned British explorer, has only the foggiest idea of where
he's going and takes few provisions save his bravery. One wants to like
The Star-Crossed Fisherman, for its exotic milieu and for its flavor of
headlong, open-air narrative. It begins with a gust of wind: "The rough-
hewn door was kicked wide open, letting in a dusty blast from the mad
south wind that was churning up the sea that day, and Zeynel appeared
on the threshold, a gun in his hand. He hesitated, but only for a moment.
Then, with slow deliberate aim, he pointed the gun at Ihsan and fired shot
after shot. The men in the coffee-house froze in their seats."
A tall fisherman called Selim stands up, takes the gun from Zeynel, and
repeatedly slaps him. We are off to the roaring start of nearly three
hundred pages tracing the intertwined destinies of Zeynel, who is to
become a criminal legendary throughout Istanbul, and Selim, who is
"sea-crossed" by his love for, first, a blond nurse from his youth and,
second, a friendly dolphin from his mature days fishing in the Sea of
Marmara. The author seems to have a good idea for the framing and
elevation of his material: the myth-making capacity of gossip—teahouse
gossip as refracted upwards into newspaper accounts, which magnify the

frightened and harried Zeynel into a national menace, a tabloid bogey-man. The Greek chorus seems reborn in the novel's pages of communal rumor, as it spirals and spins its own reality. And some of the novel's descriptive excursions, whether of the shifting colors seen from a boat at sea or of the congested modern Golden Horn, are worthy of a canvas by Delacroix or a diatribe by Céline, complete with Céline's mannerism of triple periods:

> The Golden Horn, a noisome, nauseating dark well, yellow, red, mauve, the many crude colours of the neon signs stirred by its swell . . . The Golden Horn, that deep well surrounded by huge ugly buildings and sooty factories, spewing rust from their chimneys and roofs and walls, staining the water with sulphur-yellow rust, a filthy sewer filled with empty cans and rubbish and horse carcasses, dead dogs and gulls and wild boars and thousands of cats, stinking . . . A viscid, turbid mass, opaque, teeming with maggots . . . A strange musty creature, the Golden Horn, a relic from another age, battered, agonizing, rotting away, yet still restless . . . Lengthening, undulating, weaving into each other, the neon lights danced over this dark fathom-less well.

The trouble is, the well remains fathomless; the events pile up but don't add up. Zeynel's adventures, as he becomes involved with a street urchin called Dursun Kemal, and Selim's, as he nurses the mad idea of assassinating a magnate and land-developer called Halim Bey Veziroğlu, diverge rather than converge, and the narrative becomes delirious and disconnected, like yards of randomly shot film hastily spliced together in a cutting room, or like one of those spoofs cooked up by a cocktail-sipping committee of Long Island writers, each one contributing a separate chapter. Where Mr. Mulisch's story keeps cinching tighter around its opening incident of violence, rendering it ever more intelligible, Mr. Kemal's expands so that things make less and less sense. Is Zeynel a vicious, addled tough or a poor lad we are supposed to pity? His erratic actions permit no empathy. By the time, more than halfway through the novel, the reason emerges for his shooting of Ihsan—Ihsan, a gangster, murdered the owner of a golden eagle who had supernatural significance for the boy—we are numbed by the intervening plethora of slaughter and impulsive behavior. Fisher Selim's relations with the evil Veziroğlu are inscrutable: Veziroğlu has some land Selim wants and has planted olive trees upon; Selim goes intending to gun him down, and Veziroğlu abruptly gives him the land; Selim no longer cares about the land but wants some other land; he buys this land with some ill-gotten gains and builds a lavish house, which he then totally neglects, still wanting, out of some belatedly acquired revolu-

tionary instincts, to kill Veziroğlu, who by now has become indistinguishable from Aristotle Onassis ("They are both of Anatolian stock, these two,
Halim Bey Veziroğlu and Onassis. Both playing mischief with the
world").

Guns flicker in and out of this verbal turmoil like mystical signs, and
murder seems to be the only outcome that the characters and the author
can think of. Violence in *The Star-Crossed Fisherman* is recurrent, rhythmic, and unreal; all intentions and consequences are alike mired in a
bloody glue, a paralysis of coagulated rage. By the time Zeynel and Selim
have their final encounter, whatever personalities and psychologies were
originally constructed for them have been quite dissolved in the pervasive
paranoia. Any sense of distinct human psyches moving in a tightening
pattern is overwhelmed by the narrator's indiscriminate appetite for the
marvellous and for rhetoric of a wild-eyed kind. "Stop, Fisher Selim, stop!
The crowd is closing in, trampling over the black-clad men, pressing them
like grapes. Furiously, the people crush and pound. And suddenly they
draw back and there is not a trace of the black-clad men. Only a few
scattered, broken machine-guns . . ." What has happened, in a circumstantial way? Nothing. The prose has entertained a vision. The prose
remembers its novelistic duty to show, to make us see and feel the texture
of things, only now and then, as when Zeynel, eluding a police hunt
dreamlike in its inefficiency, patronizes a *çöp kebap*–vendor. And what is
a *çöp kebap?* The prose tells us, and something of present-day, real-life
Istanbul springs into being:

> "Right away," the vendor said, pleased. He was a very old man with a
> short white beard, a long sallow face, shrivelled pouches under his eyes and
> a knife scar on his forehead. His wide shoulders were hunched, giving him
> a lopsided gait. Sprinkling the tiny little cubes of skewered lamb with salt
> and pepper, he laid them over the embers which he fanned with a piece of
> cardboard adorned with the picture of a naked woman. In a moment the
> odour of burning fat spread through the square and thick fumes smoked
> greenly in the neon lighting. Dextrously the man slipped the meat cubes off
> the sixteen skewers into a bread loaf and added half a tomato and a sprig of
> parsley. "Here you are, sir," he said.

And that is how we make a *çöp kebap.*

Levels and Levels

LAST CALL, by Harry Mulisch, translated from the Dutch by Adrienne Dixon. 288 pp. Viking, 1989.

The Dutch writer Harry Mulisch is best known in the United States as the author of a small, perfect novel, *The Assault*, about a brutal incident in World War II and its continuing reverberations. A surprisingly excellent movie was made from the book and won an Oscar for Best Foreign Film in 1987. The book was a detective story, a case history of repression, and a study in the workings of time, as the postwar decades gradually transform the physical settings and remove the living witnesses of the war. This last aspect, conveyed by visual images of a changing, modern Holland, came through even more powerfully in the movie than in the book, stunning the viewer with a sudden sensation of the abyss of the past, itself unchanging yet productive of ever fresh installments of emotion.

Mulisch's new novel, *Last Call*, in its best and clearest moments evokes this same awesome dimension of reality, as experienced by the seventy-eight-year-old hero, Willem "Uli" Bouwmeester, a long-retired cabaret performer—the ignominious last of a distinguished Dutch theatrical family—who is unexpectedly cast as the star of a contemporary play, *Hurricane*, to be performed by a modernist playwrights' collective that occupies the Kosmos Theatre in Amsterdam. The drama, which concerns a turn-of-the-century performance of Shakespeare's *Tempest*, has levels and levels, and so does the novel; still, like *The Assault*, it is rooted in a wartime incident—in this case, Uli's discreditable but not extraordinary collaboration with the Germans. The facts are set forth early, as if casually but with Mulisch's typical circumstantial precision:

> Like virtually everyone else in cabaret (and not only in cabaret) he registered with the Chamber of Culture and continued cheering up audiences until 1943, even playing for Nazi organisations such as Winter Help and Front Fare—also after his Jewish colleagues had been deported and gassed—and finally even in Germany. In the following year all German theatres were closed (the end of the beginning of the end); he spent the last winter of the war in Amsterdam with his wife and dog, and in May 1945 he was arrested. His life had run aground for good. After a few weeks in the House of Detention he spent about six months as a kind of political detainee in a number of internment camps. He was never prosecuted, not having been important enough (perhaps the fact that he had a German mother counted as a mitigating circumstance)—but nevertheless, he was finished and that at the age of forty-one.

In the fall of 1982, then, while living out a moldering senescence with his sister, Berta, in a housing estate in a recently reclaimed polder, he is called back by *Hurricane* to the stage and to the excitements of life; his triumph is spoiled by a television interview in which the young interviewer, whom Uli in too expansive an interview mood calls a "Jewboy," revives the buried wartime facts. A commotion ensues. A fellow actor attacks the interviewer: "You bastard, taking on a man of eighty! Who do you think you are, coming here to act the judge?" The answer is simple: "I'm not having myself called a Jewboy by someone who has entertained the SS."

The jacket copy of *Last Call* tells us merely that Mulisch was born in 1927 and is "regarded as Holland's foremost author," whereas that of *The Assault* revealed Mulisch to have been "born in 1927 to a Jewish mother whose family died in the concentration camps, and a father who was jailed for collaborating with the Nazis." A heritage of intensely conflicted feelings forms part of his artistic capital. *The Assault* extends sympathy not only to the son of parents killed by the German occupiers of Holland but to the son of the collaborationist policeman slain by the resistance. The page-by-page fascination and eventually excessive muddle of *Last Call* stem from the author's rich sense of moral ambiguity, his search for categories less simple than those of good and evil. We become thoroughly immersed in the consciousness of Uli Bouwmeester somewhat against our better judgment; there is much about him that is unpleasant, from his casual anti-Semitism to an impulsive ruthlessness, a "something malicious" that destroyed his modest postwar career as a director of working-class amateur theatricals. While a performance that he had purposely misdirected was collapsing onstage, a "suppressed fit of laughter finally burst out of Uli Bouwmeester, as an almost physical hurt, a thing that somehow no longer had anything to do with the show." His behavior both past and present has a self-defeating streak, a scornful recklessness. He takes a young actress, Stella, to dinner at a restaurant without telling her he has insufficient money and, indeed, refuses her repeated offer to pay; faced at last with the bill, he leaves in hock to the restaurateur a precious silver-plated wristwatch that is the only memento he has of his father. He then arrogantly comes to redeem it after the appointed time and finds that the restaurant has moved. Later, in a string of surreal nocturnal adventures, he loses an elegant art book he has just been given and, more crucially, loses a good night's sleep on the eve of his play's dress rehearsal. Meanwhile, the author mislays the issue of Uli's wartime collaboration: the television interview's threat to the success of the production and to continued state sponsorship of the theatre dissolves in life's own theatre of the absurd, as the geriatric actor is slowly exhausted and emptied by a welter of bizarre events and vivid memories. The graspable, suspenseful question of war guilt and its consequences gives way to an ambitious, all-but-chaotic attempt to find, in a barrage of images from every point of Uli's life and consciousness, an objective correlative for the experience of dying.

The attempt is magisterial, and equips itself from the full armory of modernism. As in *Ulysses,* many threads and characters are cunningly interwoven, and a perfect memory is demanded of the reader: a dog's death at the end is explained by a kick casually given on page 27. The novel is arranged in five so-called acts, some scenes are described like stage scenes, and the reader is not infrequently addressed directly: "Honoured spectators! Let us enter. The die is cast." Artifice is open and as complexly folded as a piece of origami; the skeptical and playful moods of Pirandello, Nabokov, and Calvino take on a certain Dutch solidity. The play within the novel, with its play within the play, has been thoroughly thought out, and its verse speeches are amply quoted, along with Shakespeare's. The double role Uli plays—Shakespeare's Prospero being acted by the turn-of-the-century thespian Pierre de Vries—possesses and annihilates him, and Pierre de Vries becomes the hero of a chapter of *Last Call,* the play within the novel popping up to the level of the novelistic reality. In what we take to be Uli's dying delirium, a lengthy allusion to Poe's *The Narrative of Arthur Gordon Pym* plunges Uli and an imaginary child called Pim together into the cosmic whirlpool. All this, and lots of information about Nō drama and downtown Amsterdam, too. It is too much, and there is even more, I don't doubt, than met my eye. The basic emotional action— an old, failed man is called back into life and crushed by the stimuli— seems itself crushed under the sheer multiplicity of arresting, studied effects. There are too many hallucinatory scenes, too many artistic characters, too many pointed hints that "we are such stuff as dreams are made on," as Prospero too famously says. *The Tempest* is an adventurous text for a European writer to elaborate upon, but in English its best-known speeches border on the hackneyed. It, and the world of theatrical illusion, and Amsterdam's civic carnival of freedom all seem too lush, too quick to yield symbolic fruit. The sum of *Last Call* seems less than its parts.

But what parts they are! Uli's memories of his life, preponderantly his sexual life, have a mythic size and savagery. As he remembers his first copulation, with a cabaret dancer: "The headboard falls on top of them, but they notice nothing, nor hear the furious shouting of the neighbours below," and when it is done "he is wet all over, including his hair, as if he had just come out of the sea, even the panes in the skylight are misted." A homosexual encounter, in an air-raid shelter in wartime Germany, leaves his hand "wet, as if he had dipped it into a bucket of wallpaper paste." Sweating and shaking, Uli escapes the shelter:

> Outside there is the suffocating night, aflame, frenzied, crackling, the firestorm, the shrieks of people and the sirens of ambulances and fire brigade, houses collapsing in towers of dust—he lets himself fall headlong in the grass: God almighty, what times were these!

Mulisch has said, "It isn't so much that I went through the Second World War; I *am* the Second World War." He was a teen-ager in the years 1940–45, and his reconstructions of those dreadful times have the glow of nostalgia, of reëntry into a hellish paradise. Just as the hero of *The Assault* is piecemeal led by the accidents of his postwar life back into the primal furnace of that winter assassination and conflagration, so Uli Bouwmeester is led, by a monstrous encounter with a transvestite whose male genitals have been surgically transformed into "something terrible, something not of this world," to recall the scene, which he witnessed as a three-year-old child hidden behind costumes and props in a dressing room, of his mother's death in childbirth: "with both hands she tries to hold something back that is coming out of her, a large thing that splits her apart in the crotch far too wide." The visceral, psychological core of *Last Call* splits apart, as it were, the folds of its stagecraft, its ultimately arid postmodern self-reflexiveness. Mulisch is a rarity for these times—an instinctively psychological novelist. He knows our psyches are spun of blood, and builds his plots with a dense and slippery architecture. The persistence of trauma, the rapacity of eros, the fragility of our orderly schemes, the something monstrous at the heart of being alive: "Whereof one cannot speak," his novel concludes, "thereof one sings."

ODD COUPLES

A Pair of Parrots

FLAUBERT'S PARROT, by Julian Barnes. 190 pp. Knopf, 1985.

PARROT'S PERCH, by Michel Rio, translated from the French by Leigh Hafrey. 88 pp. Harcourt Brace Jovanovich, 1985.

What is a novel? Increasingly, in these days of cavalier labelling, a novel seems to be whatever is called a novel, whether it is a collection of linked short stories (*Love Medicine,* by Louise Erdrich; *Sarah Phillips,* by Andrea Lee) or a pumped-up piece of reportage (*The Executioner's Song,* by Norman Mailer). If *Flaubert's Parrot* is, as its dust jacket shyly claims, "a novel in disguise . . . a novel that constantly surprises," it is the most strangely shaped specimen of its genre (that I have read) since Vladimir Nabokov's *Pale Fire.* On the other hand, if it is a biographical-critical treatise on a dead writer, it is the oddest and most whimsical such since Nabokov's *Nikolai Gogol.* Written by an English television critic in his late thirties, *Flaubert's Parrot* arrived on these shores heavily garlanded by British praise ("An intricate and delightful novel"—Graham Greene. "Endless food for thought, beautifully written"—Germaine Greer. "Handsomely the best novel published in England in 1984"—John Fowles) and quickly acquired a headful of American posies as well ("I read it with a continuing chuckle"—Leon Edel. "Delightful and enriching"—Joseph Heller. "A gem"—John Irving. *"Flaubert's Parrot, c'est moi!"*—Fran Lebowitz). The book is indeed conceived with a dashing originality and does impart a great deal of odd data about Flaubert: his statue in Trouville has lost some of its thigh and mustache, his brother Achille's doctoral thesis was titled "Some Considerations on the Moment of Operation on the Strangulated Hernia," his novel *Salammbô* provided the name for a new brand of *petit four,* he sent camellias to the Empress Eugénie in 1864, he was born in such sickly condition that his father had a small grave dug in preparation for his body, his saliva was permanently blackened by mercury treatment for syphilis, his play *Le Candidat* was such a flop that the actors left the stage with tears in their eyes, he found a business card from Rouen at the top of the Great Pyramid of Cheops in 1849, he detested trains, he couldn't dance, he assured Louise Colet that he was thinking seriously of becoming a bandit in Smyrna, he did not appear on a French stamp until 1952, and in 1876, to facilitate his writing of "A Simple Heart," which deals of course with a servant woman who in dying confuses a beloved pet parrot with the Holy Ghost, he borrowed from the Museum of Rouen a stuffed parrot, which can now be seen on exhibit in two separate sites, the Hôtel-Dieu in Rouen and Flaubert's writing pavilion in Croisset, both relics identified as the actual bird borrowed over a century ago. The novel consists, if "novel" and "consists" are not putting it too bluntly, of wide-ranging reflections tangential upon this curious parrot-doubling as they occur in the mind of a Dr. Geoffrey Braithwaite, a sixty-plus-year-old Essex physician, widower, and ardent amateur Flaubertian who likes travelling to France and who participated in the Normandy invasion. Dr. Braithwaite, though verbal and clever to a fault, does not like to talk about himself, and pieces of his meagre self-description are still falling into place after page 100.

As an inventive and erudite treatise on Gustave Flaubert, *Flaubert's Parrot* is praiseworthy, hilarious in many of its details and yet serious in its search for clues to Flaubert's elusive and repellent character. Some of its facts and correlations should be news even to professors of Romance languages. The late Dr. Enid Starkie, "Flaubert's most exhaustive British biographer," comes in for several whacks, at her French accent as well as her scholarship, and, though Jean-Paul Sartre's accent escapes criticism, his unfinished life of Flaubert does not. In a multiple send-up of academic techniques, Geoffrey Braithwaite, or his consonant creator Julian Barnes, finds an abundance of ways to skin the Flaubertian cat: various chapters consist of a three-hour examination paper, a "dictionary of accepted ideas" in echo of *Bouvard and Pécuchet,* three chronologies of Flaubert's life (each with a different moral), a thorough inventory of bird and animal imagery in Flaubert's life and work, a survey of trains as they impinged and still impinge on his world, a definitive essay on Madame Bovary's shifty eyes, an imaginary monologue by Louise Colet, an encounter with a mythical American college instructor who claims to have discovered and destroyed Flaubert's letters to the mysterious Juliet Herbert, and a listing of the numerous books that Flaubert thought of writing but didn't. In sum, all this scattered, avid attention fleshes out an image of "the first modern novelist" rather more heroic and lovable than the haughty customary daguerreotype; beyond that, a certain excitement over artistic workings is communicated by Mr. Barnes's elaborate, antic, clicking, shuddering apparatus of exposition.

But as a novel? What is, indeed, the story, with its beginning, middle, and end, of *Flaubert's Parrot*? The self-abnegation of the loquacious narrator ("Three stories contend within me. . . . My own is the simplest of the three—it hardly amounts to more than a convincing proof of my existence—and yet I find it the hardest to begin. . . . I hope you don't think I'm being enigmatic, by the way. If I'm irritating, it's probably because I'm embarrassed") implies shame, something to hide. Dr. Braithwaite's unspoken secret, the motive for his tantalizing coyness, presses behind his screen of Flaubertian trivia, and occasionally pokes through. He finds it suspiciously difficult to speak of his late wife, Ellen: "My wife . . . Not now, not now." His tongue teases the subject like a sore tooth: "As for my wife, she was not sensible. That was one of the last words anyone would apply to her. They inject soft cheeses, as I said, to stop them ripening too quickly." The story finally emerges, and shall be left unrevealed, except to say that Dr. Braithwaite's shame is not unlike that of another medical man, the *officier de santé* Charles Bovary. No doubt this helps account for his passionate interest in the French author and his masterpiece; no doubt we are meant retrospectively to see that his frantically resourceful discourse on Flaubert is a way of talking around his own life. A mask both hides the real face and yet conforms to it. Braithwaite's frequent denials ("Don't get me wrong. I'm not saying that Ellen's secret life led her into despair. For God's sake, her life is not a moral tale. No one's is") echo Flaubert's proud negations; Braithwaite's conspicuous shyness within his own narrative acts out Flaubert's famous dictum that "an author in his book must be like God in the universe, present everywhere and visible nowhere."

The artistic strategy of *Flaubert's Parrot* employs the ancient magical technique of substitution; just as in *Pale Fire* Kinbote reads his own mad life into John Shade's poem on quite another subject, Braithwaite smuggles his own tragedy into the facts about Flaubert. The effect is ingenious but not, quite, moving. The blatant forestallment of revelation begins to nag as well as tease; as one disparate chapter of mock-scholarship succeeds another—each chapter a fresh insult, as it were, to our natural curiosity concerning the shadowy Braithwaite—readerly fatigue and irritation set in. By the time the narrator comes clean, we are tired of his voice, by turns arch, quarrelsome, curt, cute, and implausibly literary. Braithwaite's wickedly witty list of types of novels that he wants banned is surely a London culturati's, not a provincial physician's, and some of the metaphors are foppishly spun out:

> The imagination doesn't crop annually like a reliable fruit tree. The writer has to gather whatever's there: sometimes too much, sometimes too little, sometimes nothing at all. And in the years of glut there is always a slatted wooden tray in some cool, dark attic, which the writer nervously visits from time to time; and yes, oh dear, while he's been hard at work downstairs, up in the attic there are puckering skins, warning spots, a sudden brown collapse and the sprouting of snowflakes.

Emma/Ellen; Bovary/Braithwaite/Barnes: the partitions between them are permeable; author and persona too smoothly merge. Too many epigrams on art and life—"The past is autobiographical fiction pretending to be a parliamentary report," "Books are where things are explained to you; life is where things aren't"—keep reminding us that we are only reading a book. While the novel as a form certainly asks for, and can absorb, a great deal of experimentation, it must at some point achieve self-forgetfulness and let pure event take over. In *Flaubert's Parrot,* that point arrives too late, and brings too little. The attempt, I think, is to remind us that, as our narrator insists, "Books are not life, however much we might prefer it if they were"; that is, his real-life misfortune remains raw and rough, and resists sublimation by literature. But so much artifice in establishing the priority of the "real" feels artificial, and leaves us cold. Whatever we want from novels, we want more than conversation with the author, however engagingly tricksome.

Parrot's Perch is, at eighty-eight pages of large print, too small to be called a novel, though it is called that on the dust jacket. Michel Rio is about the same age as Mr. Barnes. Born in Brittany, he lives now in Paris. He confesses on the jacket's back flap to "a special affection for Conrad and Chomsky," and his two previous novels both won French literary prizes. (How many of those prizes *are* there?) This is the author's first work to be translated into English. His version of the "real" looms at the outset, in an introductory page that explains the title:

> Parrot's Perch—Widely used torture technique in Latin America. The victim is hung upside down naked, so that the whole weight of his body rests on his forearms. Soon he becomes convinced that his fingers will explode. His arms seem to be breaking. The parrot's perch is usually only a starting point for other tortures.   (Commentary from the film
> *The Year of the Torturer*)

We brace ourselves, torture being the thing above all from which we wish to avert our eyes. The book begins with a sermon, a commentary on the Eucharist given in a French monastery near the Atlantic coast by a guest there, a young priest from Latin America, Joaquin Fillo. His remarks are announced as "about pain, about the cult of pain which is one of the bases of our religion." He begins with the Passion of Christ, an agony "indissolubly linked . . . to the greatest good, which is the Redemption and the Life. The two blend indistinguishably in a fabric woven of blood and love, suffering and joy, the garden of tortures and the garden of delights, the victim and the executioner; and these produce a breed of man who is both his own victim and his own executioner." He proceeds to a harrowing litany of the martyrs, with the specifics of their cruel deaths ("Quentin, who was placed on a rack, flogged, burned with oil, pitch, and quicklime, and impaled. Euphemia, who was beaten, hung by her hair, and run through with a sword. Leger, who had his eyes and tongue torn out, and was decapitated") and proceeds to the paradox of Christian cruelty in turn: "whoever the torturer, whoever the tortured, suffering remains the route to Redemption. And for centuries the Holy Inquisition considered it a charitable duty to torture, burn, and destroy bodies in order to save souls." Father Fillo briefly describes his own acquaintance with torture, after becoming a radical priest in his native land and then being "arrested and tortured by people who claimed to defend the values of Christianity." He ends by renouncing, before the assembled monastery congregation, Christianity: "I reject that religion, a religion in which love has mixed with too much blood. I reject in it what is despicable, and so must also reject its sublimity. It reeks of human cunning, of the didactic imagination. For me God is other, or He doesn't exist. . . . I want to make you feel the pointlessness of the pain and humiliation that gave rise to despair, to my despair—you who practice discipline and humility, in which you place your hope."

These are huge themes, and it is no very severe criticism of *Parrot's Perch* to say that the rest of the book isn't up to them. Michel Rio, like Dostoevsky and Bernanos, Graham Greene and Shusako Endo, has posed a question—the problem of pain, of God's apparent indifference to the pain of living—to which no novel can present a persuasive answer, though it may tend to confirm answers the reader has arrived at in the intimacy of religion and personal philosophy. There is no answer on earth, and the novel form is earthbound, properly and beautifully (as Henry James would say) confined to human perspectives. The body's answer to the problem of pain is brute endurance, mitigated by the numbness of shock and the eventual mercy of death; the average secular citizen's answer is stoicism, a narrow focus, and full use of the modern armory of anesthesia, ranging from alcohol to morphine. In *The Brothers Karamazov,* the troubled answer offered to Ivan's indignation over the death of children is the saintly life, as exemplified by his brother Alyosha. The Book of Job ends by appealing to the opaque, inimitable magnificence of Creation: the Creator will not be brought, philosophically, to heel. In *Parrot's Perch,* Father Fillo, having delivered his devastating homily, broodingly strolls in the countryside, enjoys several impossibly stilted conversations with people he encounters, gazes at the sea, and succumbs to his own creator's portentousness.

The language proceeds from stately to awful: "He had cut himself off from his own reasoning, whose calamitous progress had contained the seed of its own negation, the possibility of a return or at least a detour in his rationalized trudging to the abyss." The priest's considerations begin to savor of too many graduate courses in epistemology, and of Beckett's existential Gothic: "He also thought that consciousness might freeze forever in contemplation of its own absolute incapacity: not-seeing, not-tasting, not-touching, not-hearing. A total impotence that recognized itself as such. And in that paradox of a consciousness that would have to suffer because it could not experience, he sensed the ultimate melancholy." He is overtaken on his walk by the abbot, who cheerfully seems to believe rather less than Teilhard de Chardin, if a bit more than Jacques Monod. "I don't believe in original sin," says the abbot. "How can one believe in the guilt of amino acids and of protein, the origins of life and consciousness? . . . In denying the assumption of guilt, I logically deny its consequence, which is Redemption; and like you I admit the gratuitousness of suffering." Even burnt-out Father Fillo flares up, and asks what the abbot does believe in. "In the permanence, perfection, and universality of the Spirit" is the liberal answer. "And I believe in the morality of Christ, which is a morality of love." The young apostate is not coaxed back into the monastery, however; a little farther in his walk, past an old canal laboriously described as "straddling the line between the vulgarity of the functional and the nobility of ruin, between the moribund affirmation of its artificial character and its final submersion, by a kind of slow chromatic melding, into its natural surroundings," he encounters a nameless woman operating the canal lock. "Her whole being emanated a kind of contained generosity, a spontaneous warmth held in check by a willed reserve." She had been in the congregation and heard his disavowal, yet greets him and invites him into her house. "Here were a man lost in a dark, inner space and a lonely woman—uneducated, vivacious, and intuitive." Yet no dialogue, no exchange develops; she sits utterly mute while the disillusioned priest pours nihilism into her ears. As one of the book's better sentences puts it, "Her own, inarticulate hope had vanished in his void, and she saw now that she could expect nothing from this man save perplexity."

Father Fillo walks on. His progress has become too baldly a pilgrim's, a self-absorbed pilgrim who doesn't need a novel's furniture around him. The little book has the seriousness but not the movement and society of a novel. In the end, certain semi-abstract scenic effects do for an epiphany. The Atlantic Ocean and evening are approached: "the night, half day at the top, darkness at the base, seemed to have emerged from the ocean rather than from the sky." This black immensity of sea serves to emblematize the universe and prompts a page of cosmological meditation and such mind-twisters as: "He found himself in a hell he feared was eternal, which revolved around two poles: the relativity of nothingness and the absoluteness of the universe." His unrest now seems, like Hamlet's, centered on a faint doubt of oblivion: "In an odd return to prayer, he asked only that the God Whom he found guilty of creating pain should also create oblivion." The scene before him has "the palliative nightmare of reality, a peaceful mirror whose obverse was violence; and in it he saw himself." At last, in a final tortured twist of perception and of language, Joaquin Fillo sees himself as part of the landscape he often viewed from his window at the monastery, and this goads his thought and the hard-working translator to such terms as "topologic," "metonymy," and "alterity," and brings him peace. "Flight became possible through the transmutation of place into image, of reality into illusion. He could escape into the fiction he had pulled from the truth of the setting, vanish beyond the field, beyond all the fields of the canvas framed by the sash of his window. . . ."

Overwritten and underdramatized as it is, *Parrot's Perch* engages us, invites us into its strife, where the richer-textured and more skillful *Flaubert's Parrot* suavely puts us off. Neither gives us much action in the way of those nineteenth-century novels that assumed Man and his environment to be in opposition and men and women to be obliged to act in order to save themselves. The notion of the world as a testing stage has faded, and with it much that gave even the crudest adventure tale a certain dignity. Helplessness characterizes the typical modern hero; the most energetic and human acts that Dr. Braithwaite and Father Fillo perform are verbal acts of protest, registering, in their differing styles, their astonishment that, as Flaubert said, the function of the sun is not to help the cabbages along.

Memory Palaces

SEVEN NIGHTS, by Jorge Luis Borges, translated from the Spanish by Eliot Weinberger. 121 pp. New Directions, 1984.

THE MEMORY PALACE OF MATTEO RICCI, by Jonathan D. Spence. 350 pp. Viking, 1984.

For nearly four decades, Jorge Luis Borges has been delivering lectures in public, even though, being blind, he must speak and quote from memory. Seven talks he presented in the summer of 1977 at the Teatro Coliseo in Buenos Aires were taped without his permission, sold as pirated records, and printed in cut and mangled form; an approved version, edited with his help, was published in Mexico in 1980 and now appears in English, under the title *Seven Nights.* These lectures make an enchanting small book, more loose and open in texture, more affectionate and frank in tone than the gnomic written criticism collected in *Other Inquisitions* and in the Borges reader edited by Emir Rodriguez Monegal and Alastair Reid; Reid has provided a sensitive, informative introduction to *Seven Nights.* The seven topics will not be strangers to those readers who have already trod the narrow, circling paths of the Borgesian universe: in literature, "The Divine Comedy" and "The Thousand and One Nights"; in religion, "The Kabbalah" and "Buddhism"; and, in his most personal vein, "Nightmares," "Poetry," and "Blindness." His own blindness, he tells his audience, is "modest"—"Modest, because it is total blindness in one eye, but only partial in the other. I can still make out certain colors; I can still see blue and green. And yellow, in particular, has remained faithful to me. I remember when I was young I used to linger in front of certain cages in the Palermo zoo: the cages of the tigers and leopards. I lingered before the tigers' gold and black. Yellow is still with me, even now." A color he does *not* see is black, the color of night. "I, who was accustomed to sleeping in total darkness, was bothered for a long time at having to sleep in this world of mist, in the greenish or bluish mist, vaguely luminous, which is the world of the blind."

His blindness descended gradually. "That slow loss of sight . . . began when I began to see. It has continued since 1899 without dramatic moments, a slow nightfall that has lasted more than three quarters of a century." Mr. Reid's introduction states that by 1946, when Borges was dismissed from a suburban library post and first turned to lecturing for a means of livelihood, he was already "unable to read a written text."

Borges seems to put the crucial moment somewhat later: "In 1955 the pathetic moment came when I knew I had lost my sight, my reader's and writer's sight." Prior to that moment, he had managed to read with the passion and rapture of a cabalist. Attracted to the labyrinthine and duplicitous, to texts as enigmatic as nightmares and as infinite as mirrored mirrors, Borges the reader "had always imagined Paradise as a kind of library."

His own mind has become, in his blindness, a library, whose volumes he consults with a charming freedom of association, returning always to the allied sensations of enchantment—"Without enchantment, the rest is useless"—and of horror, of what Mr. Reid spells out as "*asombro* or *sagrada horror,* 'holy dread.'" Captured within the friendly vessel of Borges's discursive voice ("talking not to all of you, but rather with each one of you"), the genie of dread is less alarming than in the abruptly dizzying spaces of the poetry and fiction. An elderly stoic speaks in comforting accents: "A writer, or any man, must believe that whatever happens to him is an instrument; everything has been given for an end." In the role of teacher, Borges has tried to teach his students "how to love literature, how to see literature as a form of happiness." In his cosmology, literature replaces the ordering principle that used to be called Fate or Providence: "We are made for art, we are made for memory, we are made for poetry, or perhaps we are made for oblivion. But something remains, and that something is history or poetry, which are not essentially different." Bibliophilia satisfies his own deep needs: "I am a hedonist reader; I look for emotion in books." Will the foreseeable future yield another reader so passionately content within the echoing library walls? Listening, via the printed word, to these relaxed and yet highly explicit discourses, one realizes that never again will there be a mind and memory stocked in just this way, with such benign and extensive curiosity, such patient and expectant attention to ancient texts. Bent upon conveying treasure, Borges reveals himself as a treasure.

The Memory Palace of Matteo Ricci also leads us to reflect upon the immensity and perishability of minds, each of which constructs in the course of a lifetime a unique store of knowledge. Ricci was one of the first Jesuit missionaries to penetrate China, and he carried with him not only the Christian good news but European clocks, crystal mirrors, eyeglasses, and maps; a mental treasure of Ricci's, and one with which he hoped to beguile the mandarins into friendliness and receptivity, was the system of memorization which European scholars of the Middle Ages and Renaissance had inherited from antiquity. The system called for the attachment of each piece of information to a decoration, tableau, or piece of furniture within a visualized "memory palace," which could be as simple as a single room or as complex as an entire town, containing thousands of rooms. Purportedly this technique of mental storage was invented by the Greek poet Simonides, who, having luckily departed a hall which forthwith collapsed upon a large party of revellers, was able to recall where each had been sitting, and thus could identify the disfigured bodies. Pliny, Quintilian, and the author of *Ad Herennium* described and extolled the method, and twelve centuries later Thomas Aquinas advocated "corporeal similitudes" to fix devotional sequences. The idea of memory systems lurks behind cathedral layouts, Giotto's iconography, the highly structured afterworlds described by Dante, and the procedures of Ignatius Loyola's *Spiritual Exercises*. When Matteo Ricci was a Jesuit student in the early 1570s, *De Arte Rhetorica*, by Cypriano Soarez, was used to inculcate memory training. The adult Ricci, we are told, was capable of "running through a list of four to five hundred random Chinese ideograms and then repeating the list in reverse order, while Chinese friends described him as being able to recite volumes of the Chinese classics after scanning them only once." Toward the end of his life, after decades of living remote from the libraries of the West, he was able to recall and translate into Chinese numerous paraphrases of Epictetus and, almost word-for-word, Planudes's life of Aesop. In 1596, to curry favor with the Lu Wangai, the governor of Jiangxi, whose three sons were preparing for the advanced government examination, Ricci composed a brief book on the art of building memory palaces. On the basis of the four ideograms that he used by way of example, and of four religious illustrations that Ricci contributed a decade later to a collection of Chinese calligraphy and graphics entitled *The Ink Garden,* Jonathan D. Spence has constructed a beautifully intricate, boldly non-chronological portrait of the erudite missionary of whom *The Encyclopedia Britannica* states: "Probably the name of no European of past centuries is so well known in China as that of Li Ma-tou (Ricci Matteo)."

Professor Spence has published five other distinguished and original works on aspects of Chinese history. In each book he has sought, with a wide learning carried lightly, to rescue the Chinese from our hazy and stylized notions of them. He is a researcher with the flair of a novelist; out of the vast mounds of perennial Chinese documentation he manages to sift the surprising, humanizing detail. In *The Emperor of China* (1974) he took the rare personal threads in the voluminous imperial records left by the sixty years' reign of the Manchu Emperor K'ang-hsi and wove a remarkably smooth-flowing and affecting apologia, in the Emperor's own words.

In *The Death of Woman Wang* (1978) he brought to life an obscure and impoverished county of northern China, merging a local history of T'an-ch'eng, in Shantung Province, with the short stories of P'u Sung-ling, who wrote in an adjoining county. A certain woman Wang, who deserted her husband and then returned and was killed by him, found her way into a magistrate's memoir; out of discrete fragments of P'u Sung-ling's fiction Mr. Spence not only composed background music for the woman Wang's sad dim tale but assembled her stream of consciousness at the moment of her murder—his most daring work of collage. Even such a relatively straightforward historical study as *The Gate of Heavenly Peace* (1981) explores its period, the last, turbulent century of Chinese history, through the lives and personal testimony of individuals—intellectuals and writers—on the edges of the political stage.

Matteo Ricci, too, was in a sense peripheral: he arrived at Macao at the age of thirty, and the following year he and Michele Ruggieri became the first Western missionaries allowed to live within China. Beset by bribe-hungry officials and hostile commoners, confronted by the all-but-impregnable indifference of the Buddhist bonzes and Confucian mandarins, Ricci edged his way north toward Peking and the Emperor Wan-li, whose conversion was his fondest dream. By virtue of his dazzling intellectual accomplishments, which came to include a fluent literacy in Chinese, he did make a number of friends and a few converts among the ruling intelligentsia; but he never made his way into the Emperor's presence. In his closest approach, he was allowed, at one dawn audience in 1602, to prostrate himself before the empty dragon throne. Ricci did get to know, however, a number of the court eunuchs, through whose intermediacy he was permitted to give presents to the Emperor (three religious paintings, a large clock, a gilded breviary, prisms and hourglasses, a small harpsichord, a rhinoceros horn, and more), to contribute the lyrics to eight songs to be sung by court eunuchs accompanied on the donated harpsichord, and to reside in Peking. Wan-li (whose own rather stalemated history was recently related by Ray Huang in his *1587, A Year of No Significance*) appears to have been distantly amused by the missionaries: not willing to meet them, he had his court painters prepare portraits of the Jesuits in Peking and, glancing at the result, said merely, "They are *huihui*"—a xenophobic term generally used for the Muslims of western China. When informed, via his eunuchs, that the rulers of Europe "sometimes lived on the upper floors of their high buildings," the Emperor burst into laughter at such grotesque behavior. Ricci resided for nine years in Peking, and his rather early death, in 1610, at the age of fifty-seven, is ascribed by Mr. Spence to the strains of the hospitality he enjoyed there. "For Ricci the search for acceptance was now over, but exhaustion mounted under the press of social commitment and constant intellectual exegesis. One Chinese contemporary noted that the Jesuit 'ate and drank exuberantly' on these occasions, and there is little doubt that the ceaseless social rounds took their toll." On his deathbed, as he sank into delirium, Ricci spoke of the Jesuit Pierre Coton, who had become the confessor of the King of France after Henry IV renounced Protestantism. "It is probable that in his last hours Ricci dreamed of being confessor to China's long-lived emperor Wanli. Coton's seems to have been the last name Ricci uttered. On May 11, in the evening, he sat up straight in bed, closed his eyes, and died."

The winding yet winning way in which this biography covers the ground of Ricci's life almost defies description. In brief, each of the four ideograms discussed in the book on mnemonics that Ricci presented to Governor Lu and each of the four religious illustrations contributed to Cheng Dayue's *Ink Garden* inspires an essayistic chapter that deals with an aspect of Matteo Ricci's life experience. The first ideogram, *wu*, representing war and construed by Ricci to show two warriors grappling, leads Mr. Spence to discuss: the violent atmosphere of Macerata, an Italian town in the papal domain where Ricci was born and grew up, amid blood feuds and banditry and war refugees from the north and rumors of Turkish attack on the Adriatic coast; the changes in military technology during Ricci's youth and the political turmoil in these times of Counter-Reformation; the Spanish siege of Antwerp, the Ottoman defeat at the naval battle of Lepanto, and the disastrous battle between the Portuguese and the Moors at Alcazarquivir; the bustling, tawdry Portuguese settlements at Goa and Macao, where Ricci prepared for his mission to China; his impressions of China's indifferent warrior spirit and cruel corporal punishments; the competition among both missionaries and traders in the Far East; the Spanish slaughter of close to twenty thousand Chinese in the Philippines in 1603; and a personal incident in 1592 when a gang of youths invaded Ricci's compound in Shaozhou and was repelled by a bombardment of roof tiles, but only after Ricci suffered an ax cut and a twisted ankle, which ever after caused him to limp.

For another example, the third picture, showing an angel blinding the men of Sodom, leads Mr. Spence into fascinating disquisitions upon the moral and religious condition of Rome in the late sixteenth century, the same of Lisbon, the social make-up of Goa and Macao, Chinese slavery, Ricci's ambivalent attitude toward Chinese institutions, the Emperor Wan-li's colossal tomb, eunuchs in China, drunkenness and misery and poverty and prostitution in Peking, Chinese accusations of sexual immorality among the Jesuits, Oriental toleration of homosexuality as contrasted with Christian abhorrence and Inquisitorial persecution, Loyola's proposed exercises in the correct contemplation of sin, and Ricci's Chinese translation of "Thou shalt not commit adultery" as "Thou shalt not do depraved, unnatural, or filthy things."

Each chapter pursues its theme with a similar wandering through the palace of fact. Mr. Spence's powers of correlation and connection are dazzling. Ricci's limp returns in a later chapter as a counterpart of Loyola's crippled right leg, the surgery upon which gave rise through the pain to a vision of Mary and her Child that left his heart ever serene. These instances of lameness then suggest the limp that Dante seems to describe in the Infernal line "*Si che 'l piè fermo sempre era 'l più basso*" ("So that the firm foot was always the lower"). From these anatomical considerations Mr. Spence effortlessly hops to holy relics, to the relics Ricci carried with him, to Marian sodalities in China and elsewhere, to the Counter-Reformation cult of the Virgin, to the observation by a Chinese contemporary of Ricci's that "the image used for the Christian God is the body of a woman." Quite dazzlingly, Mr. Spence shows that Ricci's fourth ideogram (*hao*, meaning "goodness" and represented by a servant girl with a child in her arms) and his fourth religious picture (Virgin and Child) converge and embody the same unsatisfied longing, a longing obliquely exposed by a misprint that Ricci allowed to remain in the etching of the Virgin—"*plena*" became "*lena*," a noun meaning "a woman who allures or entices." To convey so much information about a man, a religious fraternity, and two globally opposite cultures three hundred years ago by means of eight images and the themes that ramify from them is a rare tour de force, achieved by a scholar determined to refresh not only our knowledge of the past but the very forms in which history is presented.

Yet *The Memory Palace of Matteo Ricci* does not feel like a tour de force: it feels simply like a life explored from within, in terms of a mind exposed to certain influences, hardened in certain convictions, subject to certain shocks, and retentive of vast amounts of information now preserved only in libraries. Freed from the restraints of chronology, a life reveals its inner veins, its pattern of threads. The image of the memory palace returns rhythmically, as each ideogram is placed at one of the four corners of the reception hall, which is "suffused in an even light"—the light, it may be, of a Platonic heaven, or of the mind's delicately impassioned glow. The sense of mentally created spaces stretching extensively is eerie and majestic. The brief concluding chapter has the memory palace, about to be closed, yield a selective inventory of its contents, one vivid item for each of the five senses:

He sees the eunuch Ma Tang, suffused with anger, grasp the cross of carved wood to which the bleeding Christ is nailed. He hears the shouts of warning and the howling of the wind as the boat keels over, flinging both him and João Barrados into the water of the River Gan. He smells the incense that curls up around his triptych as he places it reverently upon a pagan altar in the luxurious garden temple of Juyung. He tastes the homely food prepared for him by the poor farmers in their country dwelling near Zhaoqing. He feels the touch of cheek on cheek as the dying Francesco de Petris throws his arms around his neck.

If this is not quite as moving as the similar coda to Lytton Strachey's biography of Queen Victoria, perhaps being a queen is more poignant than being a missionary. A queen cannot help being one, but a missionary to some extent chooses his fate, his isolation and loneliness. The cool and evenly lit halls of the memory palace as rebuilt by Mr. Spence do not contain the flame of Ricci's vocation and will, which drove him to his slightly absurd though courageous pose as a pseudo-mandarin—"a heavy, bearded man, in his robe of purple silk trimmed with blue"—importunate outside the Emperor's walls in Peking. But perhaps the shadowless atmosphere of the memory palace is the historian's way of suggesting that China quenched that flame, that Ricci's intricate mission ended in limbo.

In Dispraise of the Powers That Be

CURFEW, by José Donoso, translated from the Spanish by Alfred Mac Adam. 309 pp. Weidenfeld & Nicolson, 1988.

ANTHILLS OF THE SAVANNAH, by Chinua Achebe. 216 pp. Doubleday, 1988.

It is sometimes urged upon American authors that they should write more politically, out of a clearer commitment or engagement or sense of protest. Two foreign novels, one by a Chilean and the other by a Nigerian, demonstrate that having a political subject does not automatically give a novel grandeur, urgency, or coherence. Curfew, by the Chilean José Donoso, takes place in 1985, in a crowded time span of less than twenty-four hours, centering upon the funeral of Pablo Neruda's widow, Matilde. The occasion collects a number of varied friends and admirers—Mañungo Vera, a folk-singer returned from twelve years in Europe; Judit Torre, a blond, aristocratic revolutionary who looks like the young Virginia Woolf; Fausta Manquileo, a matronly literary figure of distinction; Don

Celedonio Villanueva, her husband and a literary figure of perceptibly less distinction; Juan López, called Lopito, a former poet and present drunkard and abrasively obnoxious hanger-on; Lisboa, a Communist Party zealot; Ada Luz, his girlfriend and a docile handmaiden of the late Matilde Neruda; and Federico Fox, a corpulent cousin of Judit Torre's and the only significant character who actively works with the ruling Pinochet regime instead of hating and resisting it.

Pinochet (who is never mentioned in the novel's text) came to power in 1973, in a bloody coup that ousted and killed President Salvador Allende; by 1985 the dissidents have had time to go into exile and return, to be imprisoned and released, to grow middle-aged in their youthful fury and frustration, to lose faith and make ironical accommodations and die of natural causes. Lopito says, "All of us have retired from the political scene, even though we keep telling ourselves that the people united will never be defeated when for more than ten years they've had us more defeated than I can imagine, Mañungo. This is total defeat. . . . A bomb here, another there, but they don't do anything, like swearing by nonviolent protest or violent protest, or the opposition, or the people united, et cetera. They broke our backs, Mañungo."

Pablo Neruda, the triumphant embodiment of Chilean culture and left-wing conscience, "returned to Chile to die of sadness." Now his widow, Matilde, whom he had nicknamed "La Chascona, the wild woman . . . because of her tangled mop of hair"—Matilde, who had been "a young, desirable woman of the people, as juicy as a ripe apricot, who took long, wine-soaked siestas with the poet"—has died in a Houston hospital, after receiving last rites and confiding to Ada Luz that she wants a mass said at her funeral. The suppression of this request—by Lisboa, because the presence of a revolutionary priest at the graveside would detract from Communist domination of the ceremony—is the main political thread wound around the observance. The main cultural thread is Federico Fox's acquisition of control over Neruda's valuable papers and letters in exchange for his removal of bureaucratic roadblocks in the way of establishing a Pablo Neruda Foundation. The main romantic thread is the coming together again of Judit Torre and Mañungo Vera, who had first romanced in their student days. The principal moral event, I suppose, is Mañungo's decision to stay in Chile, with his seven-year-old French-speaking son, after his round-the-clock experience of life under the regime. In his youth, Mañungo was a rock star, a "guerrilla singer . . . possessed by the potency of his guitar-phallus-machine gun"; his career, pursued since the coup in America and Europe, has been lately bothered by a "softening of his politics" and a chronic tinnitus in his left ear, a subjective sensation of noise that he identifies as "the voice of the old woman"—a certain wheezing sound made by the sea on the coast of Chiloé, his native island, calling him home.

Among these many—too many—threads, the most interesting psychological one traces Judit Torre's peculiar form of political and erotic deadness, induced by a traumatic episode when she was being held for questioning with some other members of her shadowy little group of anti-regime women. Tied and hooded and naked, she hears in her cell the other women being tortured and raped; but *her* torturer merely tells her in his nasal voice, while he puts his warm moist hand on her knee, to shout as if she were being raped. She remembers:

> I waited for his hand to touch me again, my skin waited to be caressed by that viscous, tepid hand that never went further although the nasal voice whispered, Shout more, as if you were enjoying yourself, as if you wanted more, as if I were hurting you but you wanted more, and I shout my lungs out howling like a bitch because I'm reaching a shameful pleasure I'd never felt before, not even with Ramón [her lover, a slain resistance leader]. Shout, shout, he repeated, and I call for help because his whisper threatens me if I don't shout, and I shout with terror at myself, because in this totally unerotic situation I shout my shame at my pleasure while in the other cells my friends are howling like me, but because of tortures different from the torture of being exempted from torture. . . . I didn't shout because of the tragedy of the other women, I didn't take part in the feast of that majestic collective form, from which the soft hand excluded me in order to satisfy God knows what fantasies, this impotent monster who demanded I shout with greater and greater conviction without knowing that my shouts of terror and pleasure were real.

This moment of feigned torture evidently constitutes Judit's supreme orgasm and forms the novel's most intimate and meaningful vision of the relation between the regime and its enemies. It also warrants revenge. Judit is given a pistol by her women's group and goes forth in the night to find and slay the impotent torturer whose "complex humanity" robbed her of solidarity and unqualified revolutionary purpose: "Sensitive, the bastard with the nasal voice. His sensitivity tore away my right to hatred and revenge." This loss is cause, in the murky atmosphere of contemporary Chile, for murder.

Curfew packs a baggage of Dostoevskian ambition which its action and conversations do not quite carry. Judit seems not so much tormented as whimsical, in the way of well-born beauties. The novel in Spanish was titled *La desesperanza* ("Despair")—but the English title refers to a section of the narrative which shows Judit and Mañungo wandering the "green ghetto" of an upper-class Santiago neighborhood during the five hours of curfew, from midnight to five. The curfew, to judge from the number of people they encounter and noisy incidents that take place, isn't very effectively enforced. With her feminist pistol Judit shoots not her impotent torturer-savior but a skylight and a little white bitch in heat who has attracted a disgusting crowd of nocturnal dogs. This eerie section, called "Night," in which the hiding, sometimes sleeping couple haunts the empty streets and merges with the vegetation, is the one effortlessly magical passage of the novel. A luxuriant, dreamlike atmosphere is evoked: "On the sidewalk, in their pale clothes, their arms around each other, hidden by plants that were so strong they looked carnivorous, Judit and Mañungo resembled inhabitants of a strange universe which barely needed the flow of love and sleep." Latin-American writers have a way of seeing their major cities as desolate and powerful, as awesome wastelands—one thinks especially of Borges's Buenos Aires, but also of Vargas Llosa's Lima, Cabrera Infante's pre-Castro Havana, and the Buenos Aires meticulously traversed in Humberto Costantini's *The Long Night of Francisco Sanctis*. Donoso here does something like that for Santiago.

Elsewhere, however, his will to significance generates too much sticky, tangled prose. "The only sure way to eliminate his demons was to eliminate himself, to drown in the slow green waters of the Cipresales River that mirrored the vertigo of the air tangled with the vines of madness; waters in which the tops of the oaks and elms sank, and out of whose lazy current emerged trunks of tortured pewter, bearded with moss and covered with a cancer of lichens and fungus." Just across the gutter of the book, a shorter sentence also numbs the mind: "Five years ago, Bellavista seemed immersed in the anachronistic anorexia of oblivion." The translator, perhaps, should share the blame for such heavy-handed conjurations as "Sartre, with whose words he had fertilized the Chiloé dirt from which he'd sprung," and "She gave him only the scrap of her body, which she did not succeed in relating to herself, leaving Mañungo outside the tangle of her feminine failure." Donoso's touch has lost lightness and impudent ease since *The Obscene Bird of Night*, written during the democratic rule of Eduardo Frei and published in 1970, the year Allende took power. In *Curfew*, the dominant metaphor—a mythical " 'ship of art,' the *Caleuche*, which was manned by a crew of wizards"—fails to float. The symbols in the background of the book—Carlitos, the toothless lion in the Santiago zoo; Schumann and his attempted suicide in the Rhine; the floods and fogs and witchcraft of Chiloé—have more life than the foreground. The links between history and the novel's character disorders seem forced: "Nadja's coldness was gratuitous, an aesthetic, an experiment with her own limits and the limits of others, while in Judit it was a vertiginous destiny that someone else, or perhaps history, had established." Woolf-like Judit and Mañungo with his "rabbitlike smile" are rather pale and wispy posters to be blazoned with such portentous words as "the incarnation of the despair the current state of affairs was pushing them to." Most unfortunately, the novel's climax of political violence befalls a character, Lopito, so repulsive, verbose, adhesive, and tiresomely self-destructive that the reader is sneakily grateful when the police do him in. The surge of indignation and sympathy that the text indicates should greet his demise does not come. Lopito makes a poor martyr.

Jacobo Timmerman has written, in whole-hearted praise of *Curfew*, that in it Donoso "reveals that even those who fight against the dictatorship may be cowards and antiheroes. Most important of all, he shows that not everything in Chile is clear—there is also confusion and despair. . . . No individual act of political protest is more telling than the sad lives that Chileans are forced to lead." Perhaps in Spanish the novel is more persuasive, less wordy and diffuse and slack, than in English; but in any translation the unhappy revolutionaries must quarrel and drink and seethe and drone in a political vacuum. Donoso, who returned to Chile in 1981, after an absence of eighteen years, generously credits the personnel of the regime with "human complexity," and perceives that the anti-regime forces can sink into "a hatred of all for all." In his exposition, however, the regime has little face and less philosophy, and those who oppose it have no dream or memory of good government. How things came to this claustrophobic pass is not explained, nor is a way out indicated. What human virtue we see resides in the oldest characters, the two venerable writers, Fausta and Don Celedonio, survivors from a more gracious time; in the last chapter, they are taking care of the novel's children, since nobody else will.

In Chinua Achebe's novel, too, a fine writer's spirits and prose appear to have been dampened by the politics of his country. The novel's country is called Kangan, its capital Bassa, and its drought-stricken rebellious region Abazon, but Achebe's native Nigeria and his painful identification with the Ibo cause in the Biafran war supply the blood that flows through his fantasy nation. The sorry condition of contemporary Africa is his subject; drought and the situation of women have been added, as major African concerns, to those of official corruption, regional division, and the continuing legacy of colonialism. Like *Curfew,* though at less length, *Anthills of the Savannah* seeks to encompass too much. The author's first novel in twenty-two years, it shows signs of piecemeal composition and interrupted inspiration. Jaggedly told, from a multiplicity of viewpoints, it quite lacks the purposeful narrative flow of Achebe's masterpiece, *Things Fall Apart;* its voices fitfully range from poems and myths to cocktail gossip, from almost unintelligible dialogue in West African patois ("You think na so we do am come reach superintendent. Tomorrow make you go contravene His Excellency for road and if they ask you you say you no know am before") to equally opaque flights of literarese:

> It was perhaps the strong, spiritual light of that emergent consciousness that gave Elewa, carrying as it turned out a living speck of him within her, this new luminosity she seemed to radiate which was not merely a reflection of common grief which you could find anywhere any hour in Kangan, but a touch, distinct, almost godlike, able to transform a half-literate, albeit good-natured and very attractive, girl into an object of veneration.

In some sentences, the words accumulate like sandbags being piled up by a weary worker:

> Before his voice had impinged on my thoughts I had temporarily with-drawn into them while physically appearing to attend to the Commissioner of Works struggling overconscientiously with an almost casual comment from General Lango that our highways break up even as they are being laid unlike highways he had seen in Europe and America and even Kenya.

Nevertheless, from the fractured telling a number of truths about Africa emerge. African educated elites are smallish, and power struggles can involve old friends. The three main male characters—Ikem Osodi, the crusading editor of the *National Gazette;* Chris Oriko, its former editor and now government Commissioner for Information; and Sam, now called His Excellency, the President of Kangan—were classmates, disciplined and influenced by the same English masters at a colonial institution called Lord Lugard College. As Chris remembers those days, "Ikem was the brightest in the class. . . . Sam was the social paragon. . . . He was the all-rounder. . . . He never failed once in anything. Had the magic touch. And that's always deadly in the long run. He is paying the bills now, I think. And if we are not lucky we shall all pay dearly. How I wish he had gone to Medical School which had been his first ambition. But he fell instead under the spell of our English headmaster who fought the Italians in Abyssinia in 1941 and had a sword from an Ethiopian prince to prove it. So Sam enrolled in the first school cadet corps in the country and was on his way to Sandhurst." The military proved to be the post-colonial path to power, but Sam has kept in touch with Chris and Ikem, and has shared some of his power, uneasily. Chris explains, "Ikem may resent me but he probably resents Sam even more and Sam resents both of us most vehemently. We are too close together, I think. Lord Lugard College trained her boys to be lonely leaders in separate remote places, not cooped up together in one crummy family business."

If African government is a "crummy family business," it is also a chancy raffle. The author states, "In the absurd raffle-draw that apportioned the destinies of post-colonial African societies two people starting off even as identical twins in the morning might quite easily find themselves in the evening one as President shitting on the heads of the people and the other a nightman carrying the people's shit in buckets on his head." To those whom the caprice of the raffle has favored, "the people" are a distant reality, idealized and avoided. The President declines to meet with delegates from drought-stricken Abazon, and Chris's flight by bus into this province becomes a redemptive immersion in the suffering masses. He reflects, "The kind of people—local bourgeoisie and foreign diplomats—who sidle up to you at cocktail parties to inform you that Bassa was not Kangan are the very ones who go on behaving as though it was. Why? Because, like the rest of the best people, they have never travelled by bus out of Bassa on the Great North Road." Embarked on the dusty vast plains, coached in talking pidgin and evading policemen, Chris rejoices as "the ensuing knowledge seeped through every pore in his skin into the core of his being continuing the transformation, already in process, of the man he was." A parallel transformation, more ardently than convincingly described, is that of Ikem's lower-class mistress, Elewa, into a pregnant "object of veneration" and a Madonna of national hope. The realer woman in the novel is Chris's lover, Beatrice Okoh, a government official who has undergone the dispiriting ordeal of education and urbanization.

Though Sam, the dictator, is depicted as a schoolboy, his decline from good intentions into tyranny is barely sketched, as if Achebe expected us intuitively to understand the logic whereby an African government deteriorates, in a modern national setting, into graft, a blinding obsequiousness, and the panicky fiats of a power-holder who holds his power in the dark. No ideal of public service or noblesse oblige shelters high office from the rule of rapacity; everything devolves to the demonstration and retention of status. Chris, pondering the political intricacies of secretaries putting their bosses on the line to other bosses, wonders "why everything in this country turns so readily to routines of ritual contest." An anachronistic old man who administers the healing kola-nut ritual tells his little audience of coup-survivors, "We have seen too much trouble in Kangan since the white man left because those who make plans make plans for themselves only and their families." Such a stricture is more apt to be applauded by white men than by the black administrators and intellectuals of Africa's many independent states, and Achebe deserves credit for facing the fact, however obvious it is, that post-colonial Africa has been no paradise. He seems more bemused and depressed than indignant, and, like Donoso in *his* political misery, offers as guide only a fond look back at the past, fetching up a gracious figure or two from the old, displaced hierarchies. Though a number of deaths occur in *Anthills of the Savannah*—with a casual suddenness somehow more grievous than Lopito's strenuous dying—the end effect is not claustrophobic but strangely lively. Life, life persisting and seeking new combinations, is what emerges from the near-cryptic shuffle of scenes, reminding us that this country of Kangan, whatever else it fails to be, is a collection of people, hopeful people. The kola-nut ritual asserts, "If something pursues us we shall escape but if we pursue something we shall catch it." The novel takes its title from a phrase in a long prose poem of Ikem's: "like antihills surviving to tell the new grass of the savannah about last year's brush fires."

Ungreat Lives

VOICES FROM THE MOON, by Andre Dubus. 126 pp. Godine, 1984.

CONCRETE, by Thomas Bernhard, translated from the German by David McLintock. 156 pp. Knopf, 1984.

As a writer, Andre Dubus has come up the hard way, with a resolutely unflashy style and doggedly unglamorous, unironical characters. These characters have tended to live to the north of Boston's urbane suburbs, in the region of Massachusetts bordering southern New Hampshire, from Newburyport to Haverhill, the city where Mr. Dubus now resides. The Merrimack Valley was the New World's first real industrial belt, and has been economically disconsolate for decades; the textile mills moved south and then foreign imports undermined the leather and shoe factories. But life goes on, and life's gallant, battered ongoingness, with its erratic fuelling by sex, religion, and liquor, constitutes his sturdy central subject, which is rendered with a luminous delicacy and a certain attenuating virtuosity in his new, very short novel, *Voices from the Moon*.

The title comes from a poem by Michael Van Walleghen, mentioning "the several voices/Which have called to you/Like voices from the moon." The voices, presumably, are the six characters whose points of view and interior monologues the reader shares in the course of nine chapters. The action takes place in one day, and its principal event is the announcement by Greg Stowe, the forty-seven-year-old owner of two ice-cream stores, that he intends to marry his twenty-five-year-old former daughter-in-law, Brenda. Along with Greg's and Brenda's, we get to eavesdrop on the thoughts and perceptions of Joan, Greg's first wife; Larry, Brenda's first husband and Greg's older son; Carol, Greg's twenty-six-year-old daughter; and Richie, his twelve-year-old son. The story, really, is Richie's; we begin and end in his mind, early in the morning and late at night, and two more chapters trace, as the day progresses, his inner turmoil over this confusing proposed change within his family. He has been living with his father, visiting his mother in the nearby town of Amesbury and often seeing his brother, who will now, he fears, shun the new household. Richie is a normal-appearing boy—"a lean suntanned boy . . . neither tall nor short"—with the heart of a saint; he likes horseback-riding and softball and cross-country skiing well enough, but the Catholic Church forms his deepest preoccupation and solace. He attends mass, by himself, almost every morning, and hopes to become a priest:

> Now Father Oberti lifted the chalice and Richie imagined being inside of him, feeling what he felt as the wine he held became the Blood of Christ. My Lord and my God, Richie prayed, striking his breast, immersing himself in the longing he felt there in his heart: a longing to consume Christ, to be consumed through Him into the priesthood, to stand some morning purified and adoring in white vestments, and to watch his hands holding bread, then God.

On a different plane of attraction from Father Oberti stands Melissa Donnelly, who is three months older than Richie and, at barely thirteen, one of the youngest temptresses in fiction since Nabokov's Lolita. In the course of the never-violent events of this summer day—a day, like most, of modest revelations and adjustments—we see Richie's priestly vocation just perceptibly erode. Though the novel bares a number of hearts, in a range of tough, detached, and even perverse adult attitudes, its supreme and presiding achievement is its convincing portrait of this benign male child, from whom the trauma of parental divorce and the instruction of the church have elicited a premature manliness. When his father asks him his opinion of the coming marriage, Richie merely says, "I want you to be happy," and the gritty older man has the grace to blush and become momentarily speechless.

A dramatically versatile overview as in *Voices from the Moon* risks reminding us too much of the overviewer. Mr. Dubus has taken especial care with his three women, and has much to tell us about female sexuality and, contrariwise, the female lust for solitude: Joan, having "outlived love," rejoices in her manless apartment and the comradely after-hours company of her fellow waitresses. Carol and Brenda also live alone, but have not yet outlived love, and seem therefore a bit cursed; one of the novel's theological implications is that in seeking relief from solitude we sin, and fall inevitably into pain. Joan reflects that "Richie had always been solitary and at peace with it"; so it is with a distinct sense of loss that the reader sees him, at the end, turn toward a human comforter. All three women, though assigned different attributes, are given neither much physical presence nor a palpable distinctness at the core; all three are too ready, perhaps, to train their thoughts upon the bumbling, rugged wonder of the masculine. Brenda fondly marvels at the way male friends never really talk about their lives, standing together at bars for hours, and how they fight "like two male dogs" and how "also like dogs they would not hurt each other." And Carol, looking at her own father, comfortably sees "in his lowered face, and his smile, that look men wore when they knew they were bad boys yet were loved by a woman anyway." For Dubus's men, as for Raymond Carver's not dissimilar quasi-blue-collar, sixpack-packing heroes, women tend to loom larger than life and to merge into one big, treacherous, irresistible lap. Carol, whose daughterliness cuts across the great sexual division, and Larry, who by a twist in his nature somewhat straddles it, are relatively cloudy stops in Mr. Dubus's tour of the Stowe family. Of his nine chapters, too many end with an embrace, with or without tears, and sometimes the language becomes overemotional: "and in the sound of his expelled breath Greg heard defeat and resignation, and they struck his heart a blow that nearly broke him, nearly forced him to lower his face into his hands and weep." The language can also wax abstract: "Because when you fought so much and so hard, against pain like this as well as the knee-deep bullshit of the world, so you could be free to lie in the shade of contentment and love, the great risk was that you would be left without joy or passion, and in the long evenings of respite and solitude would turn to the woman you loved with only the distracted touch, the distant murmurs of tired responsibility." At the opposite pole, the simplicities of Hemingway intrude: "He crouched to lock the rear wheel and was very hungry and hoped his father was making pancakes." And there is an excess of procedural detail, relating not to catching fish in the Big Two-Hearted River but to food preparation along the Merrimack: pancakes and bacon, tequila, lunch for the diet-conscious, vodka with onions and pepper—we learn how to prepare and consume them all. These characters are well catered to.

Yet Mr. Dubus's willingness to brood so intently above his disturbed, divorced, mostly lapsed Catholics lends his survey an aerial quality, an illusion of supernatural motion, that reminds us of what people used to read novels for. How rare it is, these days, to encounter characters with wills, with a sense of choice. Richie and his father both muster their inner strengths, make resolves, and grieve over their decisions. The most threatening opponents, Greg believes, are spiritual: "self-pity, surrender to whatever urged him to sloth or indifference or anomie or despair." In this book the streams of consciousness are channelled by mental exertion; the mind is a garden where some thoughts and impulses should be weeded out and others encouraged. An idea of purity beckons everyone to a clean place described by the epigraph:

> No, there is
> Nothing left for you
> But to stand here
>
> Full of your own silence
> Which is itself a whiteness
> And all the light you need.

Greg daydreams of walking beside an unspoiled Amazon, "where each step was a new one, on new earth." Brenda renounces promiscuity, and Joan has walked away from motherhood, at enduring cost to herself; when the opportunity arises to "tell one of her children something she knew, and to help the child," she seizes it, spelling out for Larry—who feels humiliated by losing his ex-wife to his father—the way in which the wound will heal and life will go on. For Jack Kerouac, another Franco-American from the Merrimack Valley, Roman Catholicism had dwindled to a manic spark, a frenetic mission to find the sacred everywhere; for Mr. Dubus, amid the self-seeking egos of secular America, the church still functions as a standard of measure, a repository of mysteries that can give scale and structure to our social lives. The family and those intimate connections that make families are felt by this author as sharing the importance of our souls, and our homely, awkward movements of familial adjustment and forgiveness as being natural extensions of what Pascal called "the motions of Grace."

Motions of another sort, in another country and on another social level, are described in *Concrete*. Though short, the novel—the fourth by Thomas Bernhard to be translated into English—does not seem especially so. Bernhard's particular contribution to the armory of the avant-garde, and a daunting one, was the elimination of paragraphs, so that the bitter pill of his writing is administered as steadily as an IV drip, and solid page follows solid page as if in an album of Ad Reinhardt's black paintings.

However, his sentences make lucid sense. Trained as a musician, Bernhard wrote for the ear, and in *Concrete* the voice of the narrator flutters on and on, unravelling in a fascinating comedy of self-incrimination. The narrator's name is Rudolf, and he is writing these "notes," it turns out, in Palma, on Mallorca. But most of the action (if you can call it that) occurs in Rudolf's country estate of Peiskam, where his delicate nervous system is recovering from a visit by his sister and he is trying to sit down at last to "a major work of impeccable scholarship" upon the composer Mendelssohn. Rudolf, who lived in Vienna for twenty years, was active in musical circles there and may even have published a critical article or two but has long since retired to Peiskam, where he fulminates, takes medicine, stalls, and becomes more and more of a recluse, seeing on a regular basis only Frau Kienesberger, his housekeeper. He is, we eventually learn, forty-eight years old and for most of his life has been dependent on medicine: "I myself owe everything to chemicals—to put it briefly—and have done for the last thirty years." A life so fruitless and self-indulgent requires money: "Basically I have no right whatever to lead the life I do, which is as unparalleled—and as terrible—as it is expensive." His wealth is inherited, and rouses his prose to one of its few surges of enthusiasm:

> My sister's business sense, which is her most distinctive trait, though no one would suspect it without knowing her as well as I do, comes from our paternal grandfather. It was he who made the family fortune, in the most curious circumstances, but at all events, however he did it, he made so much money that my sister and I, the third generation, still have enough for our existence, and all in all neither of us leads the most modest existence. . . . In fact, even though I am the most incompetent person in all so-called money matters, I could live for another twenty years without having to earn a penny, and then I could still sell off one parcel of land after another without seriously impairing the estate and thus lowering its value, but that won't be necessary, and it's absurd to contemplate it in view of the fact that I have only a very short time left to live, thanks to the incessant and inexorable progress of my illness.

Devotees of modern literature have met Rudolf's type of neurasthenic, self-doubting, hypercritical, indecisive, and demanding personality often before—in the letters and works of Kafka and Proust above all, but also in the luxuriant nervous systems and imaginations of Henry James, Virginia Woolf, and Thomas Mann. These all, of course, got down to work, and it is doubtful that Rudolf ever will; but the artistic sensibility, and a certain power of fascination, are his. His diatribes have a swing to them—Austrian politics becomes "all the horror stories emanating from the Ballhausplatz, where a half-crazed Chancellor is at large, issuing half-crazed orders to his idiotic ministers [and] all the horrendous parliamentary news which daily jangles in my ears and pollutes my brain and which all comes packaged in Christian hypocrisy." The suggestion that he get a dog to relieve his solitude prompts a magnificent caricature, not without truth, of the global dog situation:

> The masses are in favour of dogs because in their heart of hearts they are not prepared to incur the strenuous effort of being alone with themselves, an effort which in fact calls for greatness of soul. . . . If the dog has to go out, I have to go out too, and so on. I won't tolerate this dog comedy, which we can see enacted every day if we only open our eyes and haven't become blinded to it by daily familiarity. In this comedy a dog comes on the stage and makes life a misery for some human being, exploiting him and, in the course of several acts, or just one or two, driving out of him all his harmless humanity.

Sudden aphorisms dart from Rudolf's free-wheeling discourse: "Everyone is a virtuoso on his own instrument, but together they add up to an intolerable cacophany." "Everyone wants to be alive, nobody wants to be dead. Everything else is a lie." His own maneuvers—changing rooms, arising at a certain hour—to minimize his discomforts and secure a foothold in which he can begin writing his book have the beguiling energy of Kafka's nameless hero's futile efforts to secure his "Burrow." These movements and the shifts of his monologue suggest less Pascal's motions of Grace than what Nathalie Sarraute described as "numerous, entangled movements that have come up from the depths," and whose "restless shimmer" exists "somewhere on the fluctuating frontier that separates conversation from sub-conversation." Rudolf's sister exists in his discourse as elusively as a sea-monster in deep waters: she first appears to be a vulgar ogress whom he detests, but as he goes on, and describes her active life as a real-estate agent among the very rich, we see her as a normally dynamic woman of a certain set and style, faithfully trying to tease and goad her neurotic little brother into something like her own health. He does not hate her; he loves her, with the resentful adoration the ineffective feel for the effective, an emotion given its classic expression in Kafka's "Letter to His Father." Rudolf goes Kafka one better, however, in finally identifying with his sister, for all his protests against her: "We're both like this: for decades we've been accusing each other of being impossible, and yet we can't give up being impossible, erratic, capricious and vacillating."

And, just when the reader has resigned himself to another Beckettian study of total inertia and claustrophobic captivity, Rudolf manages to get himself out of fogbound Peiskam and to Palma. There he describes the scenery, the relative warmth, his agonies of recuperation after the adventure of the flight, and a story told to him over two years ago, during his previous visit to Mallorca, by a stranger, a Bavarian named Anna Härdtl, whom he and a local friend met on the street. Her tale, of a young woman's rather pedestrian misadventures with marriage and an ill-advised appliance shop, was as relevant as a shaggy-dog story to Rudolf's normal concerns, but he listened and now relates it, briskly and circumstantially, in his normally self-obsessed "notes." On his present visit to Palma, his memory of Anna Härdtl causes him to visit the local cemetery, where all the tombs are of concrete, giving this book its title. The hardness of Palma concrete contrasts with the soft fog and musty furniture of Peiskam, and, though Rudolf ends in his usual, typically modernist state of "extreme anxiety," he has been brought, for an interval, to think of somebody else's troubles.

These two small novels of slight movements within the heart yield morals that are modest, even bleak. "In the end we don't have to justify ourselves or anything else," Rudolf writes. "We didn't make ourselves." And, in *Voices from the Moon,* Joan tells Larry, "So when I'm alone at night—and I love it, Larry—I look out my window, and it comes to me: we don't have to live great lives, we just have to understand and survive the ones we've got." Relief from what Ibsen, in *The Wild Duck,* called "the claim of the ideal" is being prescribed. "Oh, life would be quite tolerable, after all," Ibsen's Dr. Relling concludes, "if only we could be rid of the confounded duns that keep on pestering us, in our poverty, with the claim of the ideal." Clearly enough, Rudolf's ardent wish to write a great "life" of Mendelssohn is preventing him from getting the first word onto paper; perfectionism is the enemy of creation, as extreme self-solicitude is the enemy of well-being. But have the people of *Voices from the Moon* been trying, except for Richie, to lead "great lives"? Joan's statement has this context: Larry is a dancer, and his mother has just asked him why he doesn't leave the Merrimack Valley and throw himself at New York. He won't, she knows. So, since more people, through humility or inability, must live in the Merrimack Valleys of the world than on the heights, she says what she can, which isn't much—for what does it mean, really, to "understand" and "survive" your own life? Religious resignation without religion is cold comfort. Traditional preachments promised a better life, an afterlife, or a Messiah-led revolution. Joan promises nothing, and Mr. Dubus promises little more, though he does imagine Richie lying on his back on "the soft summer earth" and feeling himself sink down into a normal human life, still "talking to the stars." But, then, Richie is only twelve, years short of such concrete realizations as "Everyone wants to be alive, nobody wants to be dead. Everything else is a lie."

Old World Wickedness

Perfume: *The Story of a Murderer*, by Patrick Süskind, translated from the German by John E. Woods. 255 pp. Knopf, 1986.

The Enchanter, by Vladimir Nabokov, translated from the Russian by Dmitri Nabokov. 127 pp. Putnam, 1986.

There are no monsters like European monsters; they need Gothic nooks and crannies and the icy swirls and trompe l'oeil of the Baroque to give them their nurture and setting. Patrick Süskind's *Perfume* takes place in a beautifully researched yet fancifully ominous eighteenth-century France; its monstrous hero, Jean-Baptiste Grenouille, is born in July of 1738 into the redolence of the Cimetière des Innocents in Paris—"the most putrid spot in the whole kingdom." This is a fragrant era:

> In the period of which we speak, there reigned in the cities a stench barely conceivable to us modern men and women. The streets stank of manure, the courtyards of urine, the stairwells of moldering wood and rat droppings, the kitchens of spoiled cabbage and mutton fat; the unaired parlors stank of stale dust, the bedrooms of greasy sheets, damp featherbeds, and the pungently sweet aroma of chamber pots. The stench of sulfur rose from the chimneys, the stench of caustic lyes from the tanneries, and from the slaughterhouses came the stench of congealed blood. People stank of sweat and unwashed clothes, from their mouths came the stench of rotting teeth, from their bellies that of onions, and from their bodies, if they were no longer very young, came the stench of rancid cheese and sour milk and tumorous disease. The rivers stank, the marketplaces stank, the churches stank, it stank beneath the bridges and in the palaces.

Amid this crush of odor, the infant, delivered by his reluctant mother beneath the gutting table of a fish stall, is twice freakish: he himself is odorless, and (it will develop) his own sense of smell is preternaturally keen. A kind of olfactory superman, he rises from this humblest of beginnings amid the fish offal to become the greatest perfumer in the world and from there to distill, out of the aromas of slain adolescent beauties, a perfume so captivating that its wearer could rule the world.

Could, but of course does not, for history, until this brilliant fable by a young Munich playwright and former musician, bears no trace of Grenouille, whom the author ranks, for moral deformity, with de Sade and Saint-Just and Napoleon. Like the creator of any superman, Mr. Süskind has some trouble generating significant obstacles to his hero's progress: with his fabulous nose Grenouille can detect a thread of scent a half-mile away, can sniff his way through the dark, can mix masterly perfumes with the ease of Mozart scribbling divine melodies, and in the end can subject an enormous crowd to his will. He also, we are asked to believe, can entertain himself for seven years of utterly eremitic life in a cave on an extinct volcano, drugging himself with symphonies of remembered scent. True, he is a superman fearfully handicapped at the outset; since his refusal to die at birth exposes his mother's previous, successful attempts at infanticide, she is soon beheaded, and the orphan is cast on the mercy of a world that finds his bent body, inarticulate speech, and lack of human scent repulsive. Though his name means "frog" in French, the tick—"the lonely tick, which, wrapped up in itself, huddles in its tree, blind, deaf, and dumb, and simply sniffs, sniffs all year long, for miles around, for the blood of some passing animal that it could never reach on its own power"—is the creaturely image most frequently associated with Grenouille as he and his monstrous talent mature under a succession of harsh caretakers and taskmasters. The casual squalor and brutality of ordinary eighteenth-century life forms one of the tale's subtexts, and its opening portrait of the crowded, smelly, disease-ridden ferment of Paris ("Paris produced over ten thousand new foundlings, bastards, and orphans a year") plausibly blends with its unfolding savageries.

The authenticity, never belabored, of the historical background, and the fascinating elucidation of the procedures of perfume-making, as revealed first in a Paris shop and laboratory and then in the essence-extracting cottage industry of Grasse, carry us quite pleasurably along. The writing has the light-handed authority of Mr. Süskind's fellow Münchner Thomas Mann (in the mood, say, of *Royal Highness* and *Felix Krull*), and John E. Woods has produced a translation of exceptional verve and grace. The reconstruction of the world in terms of scent is a charming tour de force. Babies, we learn from a wet nurse, have a variety of smells: "Their feet, for instance, they smell like a smooth, warm stone—or no, more like curds . . . or like butter, like fresh butter. And their bodies smell like . . . like a griddle cake that's been soaked in milk. And their heads, up on top, at the back of the head, where the hair makes a cowlick . . . is where they smell best of all. It smells like caramel." For Grenouille, smells are subtle and numerous beyond reckoning: there is "the odor of glass, the clayey, cool odor of smooth glass," and "the cool, musty, brawny smell" of a brass doorknob, and the "moist, fresh, tallowy, and a bit pungent" aroma of a dog. His murderous activities have to do with capturing the delicate scent a very young woman exudes, which has "a freshness, but not the freshness of limes or pomegranates, not the freshness of myrrh or cinnamon bark or curly mint or birch or camphor or pine needles, not that of a May rain or a frosty wind or of well water . . . and at the same time it had warmth, but not as bergamot, cypress, or musk has, or jasmine or daffodils, not as rosewood has or iris. . . . This scent was a blend of both, of evanescence and substance, not a blend, but a unity, although slight and frail as well, and yet solid and sustaining, like a piece of thin, shimmering silk . . . and yet again not like silk, but like pastry soaked in honey-sweet milk." Generally, Grenouille hates the smell of human beings; fleeing Paris, he travels by night to avoid this oppressive effluvium, which pervades most of the world. "There were humans in the remote regions. They had only pulled back like rats into their lairs to sleep. The earth was not cleansed of them, for even in sleep they exuded their odor, which then forced its way out between the cracks of their dwellings and into the open air, poisoning a natural world only apparently left to its own devices."

Another subtext of *Perfume*, and perhaps the major one, is Sartre's aphorism that hell is other people. People stink, nauseatingly; when Grenouille, to help give himself a human personality and presence, mixes up the odor normal people have, "the scent of humanness," his ingredients are half a teaspoon of cat excrement, "still rather fresh," plus vinegar, salt, and some decomposing cheese. Then: "From the lid of a sardine tub that stood at the back of the shop, he scratched off a rancid, fishy something-or-other, mixed it with rotten egg and castoreum, ammonia, nutmeg, horn shavings, and singed pork round, finely ground. To this he added a relatively large amount of civet, mixed these ghastly ingredients with alcohol, let it digest, and filtered it into a second bottle. The bilge smelled revolting." Wearing dabs of this complex concoction, overlaid with perfume, he ventures into the street, timidly, "because he could not imagine that other people would not also perceive his odor as a stench." They do not. For the first time in his existence, he is favorably noticed; he exerts an effect on people; he casts a proper, customary olfactory shadow. Seldom since Gulliver described the Brobdingnagian women from up close ("They would often strip me naked from top to toe, and lay me at full length in their bosoms; wherewith I was much disgusted; because, to say the truth, a very offensive smell came from their skins") has our fleshly envelope been the object of such merciless comedy. Along with the existential nausea is the proposition, borne out by modern scientific studies, that we are more sensitive and responsive to odors than we realize—that the great buried language of smell is still being spoken, subconsciously, by our brains. Whether that language is loud enough to carry instantly to the back of a great crowd and disarm ten thousand people of their reason seems unlikely but, in a land and city mesmerized within living man's memory by the unprepossessing Hitler, perhaps worth imagining.

Having invented his monster and run him through society like a hot knife through butter, Mr. Süskind doesn't quite know how to finish him off, short of calling in armies; the ending is the weakest part, an abrupt and bitter whiff capping a delicious book. *Perfume* slightly disconcerts us in being, like Grenouille's fabrication of human odor, so bluntly a concoction: it seems a fiction in which all personal and involuntary elements have been sublimated, a book that animates, with readily summoned erudition and flair, only its ideas. It is characteristically cavalier of Mr. Süskind, in framing his fable, to assign his hero two physiologically quite unrelated attributes—a superkeen sense of smell, which pertains to the olfactory membrane high in the nose, and an utter lack of body odor, which the skin and the glands generate. We close the book with the presumably postmodern sensation of having been twitted. Calvino's fantasies, though more genial, leave something of this same impression, as does Umberto Eco's *The Name of the Rose*—that of an adroit and dazzling playing at novelwriting, which has become, in our age of deconstruction, a smaller art than it used to be, a trick almost contemptibly well within an intelligent man's reach.

Vladimir Nabokov was an inveterate concocter, who patterned his fictions on chess puzzles and butterfly wings, footnoted poems and scrambled maps. But also at work was a live personal impulse, that flared out in projected emotion, were it in the form of a pervert's misplaced love or an exile's hopeless grief. He dictated *The Enchanter* to his wife in Paris, late in 1939, six months before sailing to America and leaving his European phase of exile behind. One "blue-papered wartime night," he stated in the afterword to *Lolita*, Nabokov read this long story—the manuscript, partly reproduced on the book's endpapers, identifies it with the peculiarly Russian genre-term *"povest'"*—aloud to a small group of friends; "but I was not pleased with the thing and destroyed it sometime after moving to America." A copy, however, showed up when he and his wife, with their repacked trunks, were returning to Europe in 1959, and he wrote to G. P. Putnam's Sons, his publisher, that it was "a beautiful piece of Russian prose, precise and lucid, and with a little care could be done into English by the Nabokovs." The idea was not pursued and the manuscript settled back into its trunk, to surface yet again in the early Eighties, in the course of bibliographical researches conducted in the wake of the author's death in 1977. Now, at last, having first been run through a French edition, *The Enchanter* has been published in English, perhaps the final significant piece of the Nabokov oeuvre to fit into place—though his unfinished novel *The Original of Laura* is still out there somewhere.

The Enchanter arrives in the reflected glow of *Lolita*, and does, like it, deal with a middle-aged man's passion for a twelve-year-old girl. Its nameless heroine is first seen in a Paris park, on roller skates—"skates that did not roll but crunched on the gravel as she raised and lowered them with little Japanese steps and approached his bench through the variable luck of the sunlight." The nameless hero (whom Nabokov remembered as being called "Arthur" and hailing from Central Europe) is a rather pale monster, though at one point, we are told, he "flashed a tusk from beneath a bluish lip" and at another, as if with Grenouille's nose, he notes "the rancid emanations of . . . wilted skin." His profession, several times coyly alluded to, might be that of diamond-cutter. Unlike Humbert Humbert in *Lolita*, he is not the narrator of his love story, but we are made intimately privy to his heavy-breathing observations of the nymphet's "large, slightly vacuous eyes, somehow suggesting translucent gooseberries," "the summery tint of her bare arms with the sleek little foxlike hairs running along the forearms; the indistinct tenderness of her still narrow but already not quite flat chest," the way in which "her dress clung so closely in back that it outlined a small cleft," her "rosy, sharp-knuckled hands, on which shifted now a vein, now a deep dimple near the wrist," "the exact way the checks of her dress . . . tightened when she raised an arm," "the soft skin of her underside and the tiny wedge of her taut panties," and even "the tiny flecks of dandruff" in the "silky vertex" of her head. She is never more than the sum of such details, however, since events contrive to keep her elsewhere even when her admirer marries her mother. When the stepfather and the child are at last thrown together (by the mother's death, as in *Lolita*) nothing happens equivalent to the complex and robust mixture of seductiveness, defiance, filial dependence, and comradely cockiness with which Dolores Haze meets Humbert Humbert's desire. The great superiority of *Lolita* to *The Enchanter* resides, above all, in the rich character of Lolita—her Americanness, her toughness, her resilience, her touching childishness as it shades fitfully into treacherous womanhood. The pedophilia of *The Enchanter* seems nastier for having a limp and silent body as its object. The courtship of the mother seems grimmer than the acquiescent conquest of crass Charlotte Haze, and her death sadder. The hero's lust is less ethereal and more genital, and there is not the relieving circumstantiality, in the vague France of *The Enchanter,* of the later work's amazingly and uproariously well-observed Americana. And the redeeming, splendid, headlong, endlessly comic and evocative English of *Lolita*—the manic voice of Humbert Humbert—has no equal in this translation, though there are indications that the original Russian was heavily worked, toward a feverish jocosity that might make its central topic palatable. Nabokov may have been knowingly wrapping up, with a culminating flamboyance, his days as a Russian writer; already, while still in France, he had composed his first English-language novel, *The Real Life of Sebastian Knight.*

During the author's lifetime, his son, Dmitri, raised in the United States, was his best translator of the Russian works into English, producing versions which benefitted from the paternal author's additional touches and refinements. Here Dmitri had to work with an abandoned text whose "virtuosity," he says in his afterword (or "postface," as he puts it) "consists in a deliberate vagueness of verbal and visual elements" and wherein "VN, were he alive, might have exercised his authorial license to change certain details." In a few spots (such as the "high-speed imagery of the finale," which comes through smashingly) the translator has ventured away from "a totally literal rendering" that would have been "meaningless in English." Often enough, the English version feels unnatural and even unintelligible:

> Raising drawbridges might be an effective system of protection until such time as the flowering chasm itself reached up to the chamber with a robust young branch.

> Never before, though, had the subordinate clause of his fearsome life been complemented by the principal one, and he walked past with clenched teeth.

> He felt both sorry and repelled but, realizing that the material, apart from its one specific function, had no potential whatever, he kept doggedly at his chore.

In this last instance, the protagonist is drinking tea and looking at some snapshots of his wife-to-be, and perhaps "material" isn't quite the word, since it seems as applicable to tea as to snapshots. One doesn't know whether to blame the translator's Nabokovian insistence on rigorous fidelity or the author's Nabokovian fondness for "double- and triple-bottomed imagery" that may ripple along in the original Russian but rather clots the derived English. Dmitri elucidates some "compressed images and locutions" in his afterword, as well as indignantly repelling some recent trespassers upon his father's reputation; but "precise and lucid" seem odd words to describe *The Enchanter*. Not only is there a fog of namelessness and verbal overload but ambiguity enshrouds such turns of plot as whether or not the hero sleeps with his bride on the wedding night and whether or not he goes into a pharmacy to buy poison for her.

The Enchanter, in short, is a squirmy work whose basic idea was tenacious enough to inspire a masterpiece on another continent a decade later. It is remembered, in *Lolita*, by the name of the hotel, The Enchanted Hunters, where Humbert and Lolita first sleep together. Or, rather, she sleeps while he stays awake, in one of the most beautifully described of the many insomnias in Nabokov:

> My pillow smelled of her hair. I moved toward my glimmering darling, stopping or retreating every time I thought she stirred or was about to stir. A breeze from wonderland had begun to affect my thoughts, and now they seemed couched in italics, as if the surface reflecting them were wrinkled by the phantasm of that breeze. Time and again my consciousness folded the wrong way, my shuffling body entered the sphere of sleep, shuffled out again, and once or twice I caught myself drifting into a melancholy snore. Mists of tenderness enfolded mountains of longing. Now and then it seemed to me that the enchanted prey was about to meet halfway the enchanted hunter, that her haunch was working its way toward me under the soft sand of a remote and fabulous beach; and then her dimpled dimness would stir, and I would know she was farther away from me than ever.

In the same bedded situation where these magical sentences evoke the drifting Tristan and his underage Iseult, *The Enchanter* has its cruel, obscene, and cacophonous climax. The transformation is one of the miracles of modern fiction.

VN Again and Again

THE MAN FROM THE U.S.S.R. *and Other Plays,* by Vladimir Nabokov, translated from the Russian by Dmitri Nabokov. 342 pp. Harcourt Brace Jovanovich, 1984.

SELECTED LETTERS 1940–1977, by Vladimir Nabokov, edited by Dmitri Nabokov and Matthew J. Bruccoli. 582 pp. Harcourt Brace Jovanovich, 1989.

The Nabokov estate continues to come up with treasures; *The Man from the U.S.S.R.,* following the three posthumously published volumes of lectures by the great novelist, poet, and lepidopterist, contains two full-length plays, two short plays, two lectures upon the drama, and two introductions by the translator. All make entertaining reading; the elder Nabokov's famed trickiness, which often threatened to burst the bounds of prose fiction, fits nicely on the stage, where a high level of artifice is already established. *The Event,* a three-act play composed in 1938 and successfully produced in Paris that same year (and given subsequent performances, all in Russian, in such unthinkable locales as the Prague and Warsaw of 1941), with particular brilliance teases theatrical commonplaces like the unities of time and place, stage asides, "character" parts, twins played by the same actor, and melodramatic audience expectations.* Three years after writing *The Event,* Nabokov, lecturing in the Palo Alto of 1941, at Stanford University, set forth his shrewd criticisms of conventional stagecraft and his wish to see the "secret rhythm of chance . . . pulsating in the veins of the tragic muse." His farces flirt with desolation; his abiding sense of the deceptions of art within nature give a curious power to the fragile illusions of theatre. *The Pole* and *The Grand-dad,* one-act verse plays both written in 1923, poetically present terminal historical moments—the end of Scott's ill-fated polar expedition and the encounter of an intended victim of the guillotine with his now-senile would-be executioner. The title play, dating from 1925–26 and set in Berlin's émigré community, displays in five acts a jumble of actions from which nothing more clearly emerges than the young playwright's hopeless longing to be back in Russia.

---

*It also contains the most serious attempt in Nabokov's oeuvre to portray a marriage as a union neither laughable nor idyllic, and one of his few indications that the egoism of the artist is not an entirely sunny phenomenon. The painter-hero's wife tells him, "Oh, Alyosha, if only you weren't stuffed full of yourself to the exclusion of all air and light, you would probably be able to see what I've turned into during the past few years, and what a state I am in now."

* * *

The epistolary trove begins with a letter written in 1923, to his mother; it contains the lustrous paragraph (as translated by Dmitri Nabokov) "It is evening now, with touching cloudlets in the sky. I took a walk around the plantation, behind the grove of cork oaks, ate peaches and apricots, admired the sunset, listening to a nightingale's twees and whistles, and both its song and the sunset tasted of apricot and peach." The last letter, written shortly before his death, to his son, begins, "My dearest, your roses, your fragrant rubies, glow red against a background of spring rain." In general the letters are businesslike, as, from 1940 on, the American immigrant sets about reconstructing and surpassing in English the artistic achievements he had amassed in over twenty years as a Russian émigré in Europe. We find him tenaciously engaged in the awkward authorial tasks of seeking publication, bickering with editors, pursuing academic appointments, listing typos, and taking the properly aloof tone with un-comprehending readers, reviewers, and interviewers. Above all, *Lolita,* its gingerly rise to masterpiece status by way of a Paris pornography pub-lisher and its heady aftermath of notoriety, wealth, and film adaptation, queens it over these communications. Not so continuously interesting as the previously published correspondence between Nabokov and Edmund Wilson, and rather wearing in its eventually dominant tone of offended hauteur, this volume nevertheless holds many glints of pure verbal gold, sprinkled in spendthrift fashion by a diabolically (as he might say) viva-cious and poetic mind.

Nice Tries

LATECOMERS, by Anita Brookner. 248 pp. Pantheon, 1989.

A THEFT, by Saul Bellow. 108 pp. Penguin Books, 1989.

In a decade when the differences between the sexes are on the one hand being minimized (equal pay for equal work, males should learn to dust and cook, females are scoring better in spatial-relations tests all the time) and on the other schematized (women want relationships, men want achieve-ments, their wavelengths are so different the signals pass right through), it takes some nerve for an author to attempt a protagonist of the opposite sex. Tolstoy did it, George Eliot did it, but that was long ago, when classics walked the earth and women and men were simpler mechanisms, as their hoop skirts and stovepipe hats signified. Yet here, right on my bedside table, two bright, brave, bay-laden novelists whose names begin with "B" have boldly barrelled into the territory beyond the gender barrier. Anita Brookner's *Latecomers* concerns the enduring friendship of two men who as solitary boys escaped to England from Germany, and Saul Bellow's *A Theft* seizes upon the psyche of a middle-aged, four-times-married New York fashion editor from the Christian wilds of Indiana. The first sentence of each novel defiantly stakes its claim in alien turf: *Latecomers* begins, "Hartmann, a voluptuary, lowered a spoonful of brown sugar crystals into his coffee cup, then placed a square of bitter chocolate on his tongue, and, while it was dissolving, lit his first cigarette," and *A Theft* announces, "Clara Velde, to begin with what was conspicuous about her, had short blond hair, fashionably cut, growing upon a head unusually big." We get a decided picture, and although in the end both novelists appear more solicitous and knowing in regard to characters of their own sex, the novels have nevertheless gained the liveliness of exploration, and an energized scope.

Anita Brookner, who teaches at the Courtauld Institute of Art, has published seven other novels as well as four books on such artists as Watteau, Greuze, and David. She writes thrillingly well, in lucid, balanced sentences that owe something to the scrupulous qualifications and dry moral vigilance of Henry James. She sees human beings, if one may generalize, as most active in their own behalfs, and the ruthless drive of her characters, as filtered through the rueful sensibility of one of her female observers, can shock us into laughter. She is, in the English tradition, a thoroughly social novelist, for whom there lies beyond the human spectacle nothing but death and scenery, yet she brings to the English scene an outsider's precise eye. Her parents were born in Central Europe, and her characters tend to be, with the most delicate of exotic shadings, immigrants. Thomas Hartmann, our voluptuary, was sent as "a frightened boy" from Munich to London before the war, "to live with his father's sister, Marie, who had providently married an Englishman named Jessop." At a bleak boarding school in Surrey he encounters Thomas Fibich, who was even more abruptly severed from his past; Fibich has no childhood memories except of himself—very plump, though he has become a slender man—sitting in a large wing chair called "the Voltaire," and of his mother fainting in his father's arms as they see him off at a Berlin railroad station. The two war orphans, forbidden to speak German to each other at school, form a lifelong bond, "although their temperaments were diametrically opposed and they rarely thought alike on any matter." Hartmann's Aunt Marie informally adopts Fibich as well. Both young men enter the printing trade after the war and then, under Hartmann's inspiration, found a company producing "greeting cards, of a cruel and tasteless nature, which did very nicely for about twenty years, until Hartmann, who did little work but was valued for his *Fingerspitzengefühl,* his flair, his sixth sense, suggested that the market in this commodity was self-limited, and that there were fortunes to be made in photocopying machines." The prospering partners find mates who reinforce their aura of orphanhood: Hartmann marries an inept secretary for the company, Yvette, whose father met a mysterious end in occupied France and whose mother, to escape destitution at the end of the war, married in Bordeaux the representative of an English wine shipper; and Fibich, after considerable prompting from Hartmann, takes to wife Christine Hardy, whose mother, before her early death, had been Mr. Jessop's sister and thus established for Christine a tenuous link with Aunt Marie's household and its two young Germans named Thomas. The couples come to occupy two flats, one above the other, in Ashley Gardens; the Hartmanns are blessed with a beautiful daughter, Marianne, and, six years later, the Fibichs with a robust son, called Toto, for Thomas. If it has taken this reviewer a while to spell out these arrangements, rest assured that the book takes even longer, and that, indeed, their stately and witty spelling-out composes most of the plot.

The novel spans more than fifty years, and gently moves through an atmosphere thick with inertia and melancholy. Much is told, little is shown. Not until page 85 do we begin to get runs of dialogue, though an earlier brief spurt comically dramatizes Christine's brusque abandonment by her stepmother after her father dies:

> One day Christine came home to find four suitcases in the hall, and beside them Mrs. Hardy, in a fur coat that had belonged to Christine's mother, waiting for her.
>
> "Well, Christine, I'm off," she said. "You can stay here. He left you the flat. You'll have enough to manage on for life if you're careful."
>
> "But where will you be?" asked Christine.
>
> "I'm off to Bournemouth. I'll leave you my address, although I can't promise to be in touch. I'm going into the hotel business with my brother-in-law. My first husband's brother, that is. He's on his own, like me." The light of remarriage was already kindling in her eye.

The four principals' childhoods, just sufficiently populated with adults to keep them from being wards of the state, equip them with suppressed memories and an ineradicable desolation; the London they inhabit, despite Ms. Brookner's gift for lively visual details, feels like a ghost town. World

War II, with its millions of severances, spared their lives but left them not much ability to live, except by forced hedonism (the Hartmanns) and wan stoicism (the Fibichs). The latter's state is analyzed in a passage not untypical of the heavily expository prose:

> Both had been so deprived of childhood that in a sense they were both still waiting in the wings, unaware that, happy or unhappy, this state must be passed, that all beginnings are to a certain extent situated in limbo, and are only an introduction to the definitive actions to which they are a prologue. What, in [Fibich's] view, incapacitated both Christine and himself and constituted their inalienable but unwelcome bond, was that they had been deprived of their childhood through the involuntary absence of adults, that his own parents and Christine's mother had vanished without a trace, spirited away by a turn of events that wholly excluded their offspring, without being known, and that they had been left in the charge of strangers who, though tolerably well disposed, were uninvolved, uninterested. They had grown up, therefore, without true instruction, without the saws and homilies, the customs and idiosyncrasies, that, for children, constitute a philosophy.

"Definitive actions" are what don't forthcome, though the second half of the book abounds with aborted possibilities. Christine dreams of leaving and going to a land of sun, but doesn't. The couples talk of acquiring in common a Mediterranean retreat, and in the end don't bother. The possibility that their two children, of opposite sexes though of inconvenient ages, might unite their lines comes to naught; the Don Juanish Toto does try a little date rape on Marianne two days before her wedding, but the bruising moment does not save her from a frumpy marriage or himself from an isolated life of film stardom and self-centered celibacy. Climactically, Fibich at last dares his long-meditated return to Berlin, but he pursues no search for his lost family's identity or home, and experiences no revelation until back in Heathrow Airport, where a strange woman faints. In Berlin, he remembers afterwards, he felt "on the verge of a great discovery. But perhaps that was the discovery, quite simply that life brings revelations, supplies all the material we need. And if it does not supply it in the right order, then we must simply wait for more to come to light." A modest moral for a loving and expert but eerily tentative fiction. Like many excellent modern novels, *Latecomers* supplies everything but a catharsis.

Perhaps a more intrinsic moral is, as Fibich perceives during his five aimless days in Berlin, that "nobody grows up. Everyone carries around all the selves that they have ever been, intact." Ms. Brookner sensitively measures out emotional deprivation and traces its results in subtle bereavements and disappointments. She, as author, seems to set herself to give the characters the love they cannot give each other. The two male heroes are coddled to the point of remaining rather milky; their fussy self-regard and essential passivity begin to exasperate us, and we feel less spark between them than we would like to. They would seem to be Jewish, but this is never stated or used to illuminate their melancholy and grateful wonder at being alive. It is the women who really brighten the author's eye and pen: flashy and chattery and yet frigid Yvette; "shadowy" yet deeply feeling Christine; Hartmann's too-perfect mistress, Elizabeth, through whose ministrations both parties come "into contact with their lesser selves"; Aunt Marie, with her Germanic tweed cape and "pheasant feathers in the band of her brown felt hat"; Yvette's aged mother with "that hardy appearance of French women past the age of pleasure, still flushed, thin-lipped, the head held high, dour, unsmiling"; and even a passing monster like Rita Hardy on her way to Bournemouth, or Fibich's psychoanalyst, "Mrs. Gebhardt, with her transfixing but fallacious maternal aura and the kindly smile built on a foundation of indifference." The heroine of Anita Brookner's *Hotel du Lac*, a writer of romances, at one point thinks, "I have been too harsh on women . . . because I understand them better than I understand men. I know their watchfulness, their patience, their need to advertise themselves as successful." The world of the novel is usually a world of relationships and in this world women do star. Ms. Brookner's female characters glow by the light of her wry knowing, and fill the pages of *Latecomers* with a mood of helpless sympathy.

Saul Bellow's *A Theft* also bestows more love than the recipients seem to earn. A novella of scarcely a hundred pages, it is a curious work in several respects, not least the manner of its publication—in quality paperback, forgoing the hardcover profits that even a minor offering by our preëminent fiction writer would blamelessly generate. Bellow, at this point of his career, has sat atop the American literary heap longer than anyone else since William Dean Howells; it has been over thirty-five years since the publication of *The Adventures of Augie March* established him as our most exuberant and melodious postwar novelist, and as the most viable combination of redskin and paleface in our specialized, academized era. Street-smart and book-smart with an equal intensity, he has displayed, in a salty, rapid, and giddily expressive idiom, heroes grappling with, and being thrown by, the great ideas of Western man. Until *A Theft*, he has not presented a woman as an autonomous seeker rather than as a paradise sought; his women have tended to be powerfully tangible and distressingly audible apparitions warping his heroes' already cluttered intellectual horizons. This venture into the female soul has made both the redskin and paleface jumpy, the idiom becoming gruff and the great ideas sinking into a peculiar form of celebrity-consciousness.

For gruffness, take these sentences from the opening page, introducing Clara Velde: "So there she was, a rawboned American woman. She had very good legs—who knows what you would have seen if pioneer women had worn shorter skirts. She bought her clothes in the best shops and was knowledgeable about cosmetics; nevertheless the backcountry look never left her." Got that backcountry look? I'm not sure I did, nor did the hurried case history at the end of the paragraph fill my mental dossier: "A disappointing love affair in Cambridge led to a suicide attempt. The family decided not to bring her back to Indiana. When she threatened to swallow more sleeping pills they allowed her to attend Columbia University, and she lived in New York under close supervision—the regimen organized by her parents. She, however, found ways to do exactly as she pleased. She feared hellfire but she did it just the same." She has had, we are told, quite a life—four husbands and three daughters by the age of forty, and a meteoric career in journalism that has left her high and rich: "In the boardroom she was referred to by some as 'a good corporate person,' by others as 'the czarina of fashion writing.' " Who is confiding all this, with such aggressive breathlessness? A curious tone has been adopted, a gossipy tone, as if fictional characters were a subdivision of the rich and famous. These certainly keep fast company—for instance, Clara's third husband, Spontini, "Spontini the oil tycoon, a close friend of the billionaire leftist and terrorist Giangiacomo F., who blew himself up in the seventies." F. for Feltrinelli, in case you missed the news that day.

The celebrity parade doesn't begin to roll, however, until we meet Clara's true love, who bears the name, fit for an angel, of Ithiel Regler. "Ithiel Regler stood much higher with Clara than any of the husbands. 'On a scale of ten,' she liked to say to Laura, 'he *was* ten.' " He never got around to marrying her, we presume, partly because there's nothing, as the Princess of Cleves perceived long ago, like marriage to spoil a perfect love, and partly because he had been too busy chasing around in his curious profession of free-lance big shot, "a wunderkind in nuclear strategy," based in Washington but treasured and telegenic wherever he goes. "People of great power set a high value on his smarts. Well, you only had to look at the size and the evenness of his dark eyes." For all his "classic level look," Ithiel is, like Bellow heroes before him, subject to "brainstorms" and fitful explosions of geopolitical opinion. He jets about sharing his wisdom with Henry Kissinger, Anatoly Dobrynin, the late Shah of

Iran, "Betancourt in Venezuela," and "Mr. Leakey in the Olduvai Gorge." To Clara, at least, there appears no limit to Ithiel's abilities. She reflects, while doting upon him in a Washington restaurant:

> Why, Ithiel could be the Gibbon or the Tacitus of the American Empire. . . . If he wanted, he could do with Nixon, Johnson, Kennedy or Kissinger, with the Shah or de Gaulle, what Keynes had done with the Allies at Versailles. World figures had found Ithiel worth their while. Sometimes he let slip a comment or a judgment: "Neither the Russians nor the Americans can manage the world. Not capable of organizing the future." When she came into her own, Clara thought, she'd set up a fund for him so he could write his views.

If Ithiel's brilliance fails to flash out in the judgment above, and Clara's adoration boggles belief, we are persuaded beyond doubt that Bellow's fascination with the seriocomic world of international power has not abandoned him in the years since he penned *Herzog*.

Plot: The alleged countrywoman once upon a time induced the alleged wunderkind, at the height of their romance, to buy her an engagement ring, an emerald "conspicuously clear, color perfect, top of its class." The engagement founders, but the sentimentally priceless ring remains in her care, is stolen once, recovered (though she doesn't give the insurance money back), and then stolen again—by, Clara thinks, the sexy, slinky Haitian boyfriend of her solidly bourgeois but not unsexy *au pair* from Vienna, Gina Wegman, for whom she has strong motherly feelings. This is Bellow's first fictional visit since *Mr. Sammler's Planet* to New York City, which in *A Theft* he calls "Gogmagogsville"; in his updated view, Manhattan is still in the forefront of the decline of the West. "Unless heaven itself were to decree that Gogmagogsville had gone far enough, and checked the decline—time to lower the boom, send in the Atlantic to wash it away." Gina understandably elects to sample the racially mixed local society. "The city has become the center, the symbol of worldwide adolescent revolt." Clara comes into a party Gina is giving for her new friends: "The room was more like a car of the West Side subway. Lots of muscle on the boys, as if they did aerobics." But Gottschalk, the "minimal sleaze" private detective whom Clara hires, sums up Frederic, the Haitian boyfriend, as "Casual criminal. Not enough muscle for street crime." Frederic does do one plainly wicked thing, however: while petting on the sofa with Gina, he puts his combat boots up on Clara's silk pillows.

The simple story is told in a purposefully dishevelled way, much of it by means of Clara's confidences to an ill-defined Manhattan neighbor,

Laura Wang. We are often reminded of Ithiel's rather abstract wonderful-
ness and of Clara's loyalty, which she shares with her creator, to a theological perspective, but we learn almost nothing about Wilder, her present
husband and the father of her three girls, nor about her job, which seems
all glamour and no performance. The book is jumpy and skimpy, and feels
like a set of signals to someone offstage. The clearest thing about Clara is
her sparkling view of Ithiel; the murkiest, her maternal feeling toward
Gina.

For all this, *A Theft* holds a gallant intention and a great gift. Who else
but Bellow can swoop in with a coinage like "Clara found Ithiel in a state
of sick dignity" or unashamedly physicalize an emotion in such a trope
as "She felt as if the life had been vacuumed out of her"? A Biblical spirit
is in him, giving vitality a severe grandeur:

> Gina was shaken. Both women trembled. After all, thought Clara, a
> human being can be sketched in three or four lines, but then when the
> sockets are empty, no amount of ingenuity can refill them. Not her brown,
> not my blue.

The brain fever that races through a Bellow narrative can always catch
fire into poetry, a poetry present in the otherworldly names he bestows—
Odo Fenger, Etta Wolfenstein, Wilder Velde, Bobby Steinsalz. Marginal
characters suddenly flare into an arresting vividness: Clara, visiting her
psychiatrist, Dr. Gladstone, notes his "samurai beard, the bared teeth it
framed, the big fashionable specs," and while visiting Ithiel's lawyer,
Steinsalz, she "could not help but look at the lawyer's lap, where because
he was obese his sex organ was outlined by the pressure of his fat." The
pressure of an overflowing sense of life keeps Bellow adding touches to
his central characters—filling them in, adjusting old touches. In a taxi to
her last tête-à-tête in the narrative, Clara leans "her long neck backward
to relieve it of the weight of her head and control the wildness of her
mind." Her big head weighs on her; we hadn't known this, we are still
learning about her, she is still being created, she is unfinished, in process,
and perhaps that is the point. "Won't the dynamic ever let you go?" she
asks herself. Evidently not, if her lover is to be believed when he tells her,
"Well, people have to be done with disorder, finally, and by the time
they're done they're also finished."

HYPERREALITY

The Flaming Chalice

THE WORLD TREASURY OF SCIENCE FICTION, edited by David G. Hartwell. 1077 pp. Little, Brown, 1989.

So-called science fiction has been around long enough, abundantly and variously enough, to keep even a mega-anthology like this one from offering a launching platform broad enough for generalizations that will go into lasting orbit. David G. Hartwell, in assembling what his introduction calls "the largest and most ambitious collection of science fiction from all over the world ever compiled," limited himself to "the modern period, 1939 to the present." Even so, one doesn't have to be an expert to notice omissions. Of the pre–World War II "Golden Age," centered on the pulp magazines *Amazing Stories* (founded 1926) and *Astounding Stories* (founded 1930), selections by *Astounding*'s editor, John W. Campbell, Jr., and John Berryman (not the poet) are included, but nothing by A. E. Van Vogt, whom in one of his headnotes Mr. Hartwell calls "the wildest, least polished, and most aggressively creative of the 1940s Campbell writers." Another writer alluded to often enough to pique our interest but not represented in the anthology is the "New Wave" fantasist Roger Zelazny. Kurt Vonnegut is present, but not William Burroughs. Calvino and Borges are here, but not, of those with international literary reputations who have been attracted to science fiction of a sort, Nabokov and Doris Lessing. Though Arthur C. Clarke, J. G. Ballard, and Brian Aldiss are included, nothing is said of that vein of British dystopian prophecy that produced books famous far beyond the confines of SF devotees—Orwell's *Nineteen Eighty-four* and Aldous Huxley's *Brave New World*. C. S. Lewis's peculiar Christian strain of SF, which led to Tolkien's *Lord of the Rings* and a whole galaxy of mystical never-never lands, receives mention but no space here. And the transition from the sacred ancestors Poe, Verne, and Wells to the state of the art in the late 1930s is left to our already overexercised imaginations.

The fifty-two pieces chosen for inclusion range in date from 1937 (not 1939) to 1986; in length from brief gems by Calvino and Stanislaw Lem to a sixty-page saga by the Russian brothers Arkady and Boris Strugatsky; and in original language from English and French to Polish, Dutch, Norwegian, and Japanese. The order is not chronological, but describes a wandering course from the nuts-and-bolts adventure tales of the Campbell pre-computer era through assorted fancy software (transplanted consciousnesses, cloned identities, time travel, futures that look like the past, SF feminism, SF self-satire, etc.) back to nuts-and-bolts adventure, this time in Russian. One reads along, day after day, logging the light-years, noting the shifting angles of thrust, and curious as to the next coruscating comet to swing around the corner. There is some lumpy prose and strung-out dialogue in the penny-a-word pulp manner; see, for example, the tales by C. M. Kornbluth, Frederick Pohl, Isaac Asimov, and Henry Kuttner and C. L. Moore, or savor such sentences as "A kind of glazed incredulity kneaded his face into a mask of shocked granite wearing a supercilious moustache" and "It was not only that patina of perfection that seemed to dwell in every line of their incredibly flawless garments." The editor, however, has kept the overall literary quality respectable, and his knowledgeable headnotes convey enthusiasm. His categories—"Golden Age," "New Wave," "speculative fiction," "alternate universe SF," "post–New Wave," and even "post–New Wave hard science fiction"—ramify a bit luxuriantly, and his critic-ese can overheat:

> In the late 1960s Larry Niven appeared and held the center ground in science fiction just as the excesses and excitement of the New Wave were dominating critical discourse. . . . [His] traits have made him in a sense the sea anchor of the field at a time when storms of change have ravaged the surfaces of SF and the demand for rounded characterization and stylistic play has tended to devalue traditional approaches.

But we are in the hands of a loving expert, and his thousand-plus chosen pages constitute an excellent text to have in hand while asking oneself the crucial question: "What keeps science fiction a minor genre, for all the brilliance of its authors and apparent pertinence of its concerns?"

The short answer is that each science-fiction story is so busy inventing its environment that little energy is left to be invested in the human subtleties. Ordinary, "mainstream" fiction snatches what it needs from the contemporary environment and concentrates upon surprising us with details of behavior; science fiction tends to reverse the priorities. The crew of the spaceship of John Berryman's classic "Special Flight" could come from the mixed ethnic bag of the war movies that Hollywood, in 1939, was poised to crank out. Stoic, jokey, constantly puffing cigarettes, these spacemen seem to be in a rusty tough old tanker, dodging icebergs instead of meteors. They do not feel perilously poised within the extreme thinness of space; they never confront the real practical problem of space flight— weightlessness. Of course, we know from newspapers and television what space travel is like, and Berryman did not. The Soviet brothers Strugatsky, as of 1959, knew a thing or two, yet their space travellers in "The Way to Amalteia," amid all the beautifully worked-out technicalities of extricating themselves from the grip of Jupiter's gravity, and the titanic scenic effects its heavy atmosphere would likely make, are shopworn Socialist heroes, a touch too good to be true. Announcing their apparent doom, Captain Bykov bluntly tells them, "We've lived well, and we'll die well." They are heroes in a very special can—"a first-class photon freighter with a parabolic reflector that resembled a skirt, with a round living gondola and a disk-shaped freight section, with cigarlike emergency rockets on long supports"—but it is canned heroism nevertheless. The captain, our gruff but friendly Soviet superhero, will predictably pull us through, land the damaged ship, and save the population of J-Station on the planetoid Amalteia from famine, declaring with gallant understatement, "Comrade Kangren, the spaceship *Takhmasib* has arrived with its cargo."

Robert A. Heinlein's "The Green Hills of Earth" (1947) and Walter M. Miller, Jr.'s "The Lineman" (1957) offer American versions of good guys getting the dirty job done. It is perhaps not entirely accidental that a Czech, from a nation long subject to larger nations' heroisms, contrived, in Josef Nesvadba's "Captain Nemo's Last Adventure" (1964), an ironical version of the rocket hero. This tender parody, whose central adventure has a giant spaceship of protozoalike extraterrestrials frantically demanding of our aging, hag-ridden hero an "answer to the fundamental question of life," finds its resolution in poetry and music and an end of technical progress: rocketry and exploration are carried on in the new world by robots indistinguishable from flesh-and-blood heroes. It is true, many of the characters in science fiction might as well be robots.

And, of course, many are. In this anthology, robots figure as servants ("The Golem," by Avram Davidson), tutors ("The Fifth Head of Cerberus," by Gene Wolfe), constant companions and enforcers of social order ("Codemus," by Tor Åge Bringsvaerd), sexual partners ("Pairpuppets," by Manuel van Loggem), and implacable warriors ("Second Variety," by Philip K. Dick). Robots rebel against their human masters ("The

Proud Robot," by Lewis Padgett) and fall in love with them ("Stranger Station," by Damon Knight). The uncertain line between men and machines, one of our century's philosophical sore spots, fascinates science fiction. In Arthur C. Clarke's "A Meeting with Medusa," the hero is revealed to be a formerly human pilot so badly damaged in a crash that his body was almost entirely replaced with mechanical elements. In John Varley's "The Phantom of Kansas," human identities are preserved in recording cubes; an often-murdered woman is just as often reprogrammed into a new body and, discovering that her assailant is a male incarnation of herself, makes mad love with him: "We were made for each other, literally. It was the most astounding act of love imaginable. He knew what I liked to the tenth decimal place, and I was just as knowledgeable. . . . Call it masturbation orchestrated for two." In Ursula K. Le Guin's "Nine Lives," workers are cloned in multiple teams, with sex differences only; they make love as part of their pooled activity, and can hardly function apart from one another. In "The New Prehistory," by the Colombian René Rebetez-Cortes, a movie line becomes a kind of centipede, and urban clusters of people merge into giant organisms. The narrator protests in vain, "I don't want to find myself transformed into something shapeless like an amoeba or a glob of spittle, nor to become the last segment of a gigantic worm. I cling to my human identity, my own individual and separate personality." In Robert Bloch's "I Do Not Love Thee, Doctor Fell," a press agent who feels his head invaded by others' phrases—"I'm losing myself. There's no real *me* left"—becomes, or already is, his own psychiatrist, a certain Doctor Fell.

The alterations that psychiatry, geology, astronomy, evolutionary biology, anthropology, microscopy, theoretical physics, and computer technology have worked upon Man's self-image: science fiction is willing to face these head-on. Man inhabits history; human nature changes. "Advancing technology, fashion, frontiers, taste, or morals can make the best of us obsolete overnight," says the heroine of "The Phantom of Kansas." If a number of these hypothetical tales seem populated by old-fashioned characters, other stories do attempt to show humanity transformed, as well as the furniture of technology. Joanna Russ's "Nobody's Home" makes the point, with a Chekhovian casualness, that in the improved future there may be no place for the ordinary human being. A stocky, self-confessedly "stupid" female called Leslie Smith is assigned to an ethereal, playful commune in the Himalayas, a heightened version of the counterculture still thriving in 1972, when the story was written. This outsider's docile but unmistakable ordinariness is like a crack in a perfect crystal, leading the heroine, the lovely and brilliant Jannina, to tears:

"This life!" gasped Jannina. "This awful life!" The thought of death became entwined somehow with Leslie Smith, in bed upstairs, and Jannina began to cry afresh.

In "Vintage Season," by Henry Kuttner and C. L. Moore, the people of the future, clad in their "incredibly flawless" garments, have discovered the secret of time travel and become tourists in time, on a package that includes Chaucer's Canterbury in 1347, a cataclysmic meteor in the United States any day now, and the coronation of Charlemagne in Rome at Christmastime in 800. Forbidden to tamper with the past and thus possibly spoil their own pleasure-seeking present, they are as basically vapid and cruelly removed as geographical tourists now. Two separate stories, C. M. Kornbluth's "Two Dooms" and Keith Roberts's "Weih-nachtsabend," portray a grim future in which the Axis powers triumphed in World War II. Gene Wolfe's "The Fifth Head of Cerberus" and Brian Aldiss's "A Kind of Artistry" immerse us in futures of a medieval eeriness, of looming castles and riddling foreordinations. More regressive still, Boris Vian's "The Dead Fish" presents a glutinous future so degraded that nothing makes sense, at least to me; Vian, a French translator of A. E. Van Vogt, is likened by the editor to William Burroughs, and seems to take us into the savage world of Jarryesque farce:

> Then she tucked up her little pleated skirt, and from where she stood she saw the boss's face turn violet, then completely black, then begin to burn, and as he kept his eyes fixed on what she was showing him, he tripped over the garden hose that he used to drown the rats; he fell with his face against a large stone, which fitted itself precisely between his cheekbones, in place of his nose and jaws. His feet stayed behind on the ground and dug a double trench, where, little by little, according to the rate at which his shoes wore out, could be seen the trail of five clumsy toes, which served to keep his socks on.

The hallucinatory transformations in Anthony Burgess's "The Muse" are rooted, it would seem, in a slight unsteadiness whereby the past expresses its resentment at being invaded from the future. Paley, a Shakespeare scholar visiting the Elizabethan era, feels that even the stars "had done a sly job of refiguration, forming fresh constellations like a sand tray on top of a thumped piano." Shakespeare himself is the Droeshout engraving, with moving lips and then worse: "The face grew an elephantine proboscis, wreathing, feeling; two or three suckers sprouted from its end and blindly waved towards Paley."

The presence in the volume of such thoroughly literary imaginers as Burgess, Calvino, and Borges, with the faintly but distinctly different flavor their contributions afford, points up a qualitative limitation. In confronting Man's transformation by accumulating technology, and in enlarging upon such striking developments as the atomic bomb and computerization, science fiction makes us stop and reflect and identify theoretical issues but it rarely penetrates and involves us the way the quietest realistic fiction can. The writer of non-fantastic fiction, wishing to pique his reader's interest, naturally gravitates to "news," to incidents and details that seem novel. These details unprogrammatically trace the changes in the human condition from one generation to the next. The pieties that bind up the universe of Dickens and Trollope dissolve around the characters of Henry James, to their dismay and ours. Hemingway's hero discovers that *gloire* and other patriotic catchwords mean nothing to him, and that after a loved one dies one merely walks back to the hotel in the rain. Conventional morality, conventional propriety, conventional feeling are always being outgrown, and, with them, artistic conventions. "The writer," Edmund Wilson wrote, "must always find expression for something which has never yet been expressed, must master a new set of phenomena which has never yet been mastered." Those rhapsodies, for instance, which Proust delivered upon the then-fresh inventions of the telephone, the automobile, and the airplane point up the larger relativities and magical connections of his great novel, as well as show the new century breaking upon a *fin-de-siècle* sensibility. The modest increments of fictional "news," of phenomena whose presentation is unprecedented, have the cumulative weight of true science—a nudging, inching fidelity to human change ultimately far more impressive and momentous than the great glittering leaps of science fiction.

Speculative leaps, the spectacle of the never-seen: these are what attract and dazzle and in the end weary us in science fiction. Aristotle placed spectacle last in his list of the components of poetic representation, saying, "The Spectacle has, indeed, an emotional attraction of its own, but, of all the parts, it is the least artistic, and connected least with the art of poetry." What we tend to remember of science fiction is its amazing, astounding scenery. Slowly sinking into Jupiter, the heroes of "The Way to Amalteia" cannot but marvel at what they see:

> They saw broad motionless zigzags of lightning, running from the darkness above to the pink abyss below, and heard the lilac discharges pulsing with an iron thunder. They saw some sort of fluttering films that flew close by with a high-pitched whistle

and

> Enormous rainbow spheres rose up out of the yellow-pink abyss. They resembled soap bubbles and shone green, blue, red.

On Arthur C. Clarke's pre-Voyager Jupiter, envisioned in 1972, giant living forms adorn the vaporous vastness—mile-wide floating medusas and herds of arrowhead-shaped cattle browse upon "the cloud pastures . . . the dark, red-brown streaks that ran like dried-up river beds down the flanks of the floating cliffs." In Gérard Klein's "The Valley of Echoes," a smaller, harder planet is evoked: "The Martian sky was always like itself, very pure, a very dark blue with an occasional hint of gray, and with admirable pink efflorescences at sunrise and sunset." Horizons seem "short, curtailed," as tractors traverse the monotonous "gray sand and scattered lichens." Then: "Suddenly, we saw surge up and grow on the horizon translucent needles of rock, so thin and so high, with such sharp contours, that we did not believe our eyes." The human scenery, too, in science fiction strains optical belief; in "The Fifth Head of Cerberus," prostitutes of the future parade

> in costumes that displayed their rouged breasts in enclosures of twisted wire like birdcages, or gave them the appearance of great height (dissolved only when someone stood very close to them), or gowns whose skirts reflected their wearers' faces and busts as still water does the trees standing near it, so that they appeared, in the intermittent colored flashes, like the queens of strange suits in a tarot deck.

And when we come to extraterrestrial life-forms, the sky is the limit. Near to *Homo sapiens,* only a mutation away, is a comely female in Brian Aldiss's "A Kind of Artistry": "She was a velure, born of the dense y-cluster worlds in Vermilion Outer, and her skin was richly covered with the brown fur of her kind." In the middle distance, picturable in cartoon fashion, are Josef Nesvadba's macro-microscopic truth-seekers: "One was almost the size of a whale and looked something like a swollen ciliaphore; another was covered with flagella, while another featured eight feet. They were all transparent, and he could see a strange liquid pulsating through their bodies." At an extreme of strangeness, so strange that sheer proximity mutually gives man and creature a killing psychic pain, is the giant alien of Damon Knight's "Stranger Station," visible only in televised glimpses:

> a tangle of nameless limbs, whiplike filaments, claws, wings . . . the great clustered eyes were staring directly into the camera; the coiled limbs threshed in pain: the eyes were staring, asking, pleading. . . . The thick stems were like antennae, the leaves thoraxes, the buds like blind insect-eyes. The whole picture moved slightly, endlessly, in a slow waiting rhythm.

The seriousness of such conjurations rests upon the possibility that they are not impossible—that they might, somewhere, sometime, exist. But our improved knowledge of the solar system and beyond offers no confirmation; we seem to be stunningly alone. Science fiction finesses the paradoxical gap between the infinity and the vacuity of extraterrestrial space. Feasible travel to all but the nearest stars, even granting spaceships a speed near that of light, would consume human lifetimes. Robot exploration of the solar system has discovered no life, not even on Mars, with its polar frosts and ancient traces of a watery atmosphere. The astronomical facts, since the days of H. G. Wells's marvellously populated planetary fantasies, add up to chemical bleakness. Yet fantasy fiction wishes to provide escape into plenitude, wherein the dreadful thinness of space is magically enriched. Nathalie-Charles Henneberg, in "The Blind Pilot," unveils, in the visions of a hero bewitched by a manateelike alien, "the star spirals and the harmonies . . . oceans of rubies, furnaces of emeralds, dark stars, constellations coiled like luminous dragons. Meteorites were a rain of motionless streaks. Novas came to meet him; they exploded and shattered in sidereal tornadoes, the giants and dwarfs fell again in incandescent cascades. Space-time was nothing but a flaming chalice." Alas, the chalice appears empty, except for what we put into it. Stanislaw Lem, in his fairy tale "How Erg the Self-Inducting Slew a Paleface," parodies the universe as adventure site; his hero is lying when he tells of

lands unknown to anyone, such as that of the Periscones, who build hot sluices of corruption; of the planet of the Epoxy-eyed—these merged before him into rows of black billows, for that is what they do in time of war, but he hewed them in two, laying bare the limestone that was their bone, and when he overcame their slaughterfalls he found himself face to face with one that took up half the sky, and he fell upon it, to demand the way, but beneath the blade of his firesword its skin split open and exposed white, writhing forests of nerves. And he spoke of the transparent ice-planet Aberrabia, which like a diamond lens holds the image of the entire Universe within itself; there he copied down the way to palefaceland. He told of a region of eternal silence, Alumnium Cryotrica, where he saw only the reflections of the stars in the surfaces of hanging glaciers; and of the kingdom of the molten Marmaloids, who fashion boiling baubles out of lava, and of the Electro-pneumaticists, who in mists of methane, in ozone, chlorine and the smoke of volcanos are able to kindle the spark of intelligence, and who continually wrestle with the problem of how to put into a gas the quality of genius.

This marvellous spoof (marvellously translated from the Polish by Michael Kandel) goes on and on, a bejewelled memorial to our romantic expectations of space.

The future, too, feels deromanticized: more pollution, more population, more poverty on this pooped planet. It is touching, in Mr. Hartwell's world treasury, to discover that some of the futuristic tales now happen in the past; Alfred Bester's "The Men Who Murdered Mohammed," with its omniscient government and Professorships of Applied Compulsion, occurs in 1980, having been published in 1958. Now we know 1980 wasn't quite like that, nor was 1984. Fritz Leiber's parody of L. Ron Hubbard's scientism, "Poor Superman," locates its post-atomic-war wastelands and glitzy governmental towers in an "America approaching the end of the twentieth century," which in 1951 must have seemed fantastically remote. Are we, as the fabled twenty-first century approaches, still innocent enough to dream of escape into either the future or the realms of other stars? Or has the future come too close to escape to, and are the stars revealed as, in all their splendor, forever out of reach?

Ecolalia

TRAVELS IN HYPERREALITY, by Umberto Eco, translated from the Italian by William Weaver and others. 307 pp. Harcourt Brace Jovanovich, 1986.

One way to ensure loving attention from your publisher is to write a big best-seller the first time out. In the churning wake of *The Name of the Rose* (1983), by the previously obscure Italian professor of semiotics Umberto Eco, Harcourt Brace Jovanovich has brought out Eco's amusingly brief and scholarly *Postscript to The Name of the Rose* (1984) and now a collection of Eco's essays, entitled *Travels in Hyperreality*. Eco, it should be said, has *two* American publishers: the Indiana University Press has issued, from his more academic self, *A Theory of Semiotics* (1976), *The Role of the Reader* (1979), and *Semiotics and the Philosophy of Language* (1984). The general essays of *Travels in Hyperreality* verge, some of them, on the linguistically technical, and some on the fadingly topical, but the best of them recall the *jeux d'esprit* of the late Roland Barthes in his journalistic, foreword-writing mode. Eco does not quite convince us, however, as did Barthes, that he is in possession of a wholly new tool of perception, a cerebral instrument that by a quick process of reduction and reassembly gives familiar and commonplace matters a bright, freshly faceted aspect. Barthes had something of the puckish perverse, the smirk of the true provocateur, whereas Eco is relatively benign and earnest—he is the plump, cigarette-puffing tutor who sits across from us at his littered desk and gently conveys the rueful truth that our honors thesis would be much better if he could only write it himself. Barthes's agility was all mental;

enthroned in Paris, the capital of intellection, he had no need of research or legwork, though he might strangely find himself, as if by a blink of thought, in Japan. Eco actually travels, visiting voodoo rites in the out-skirts of São Paulo, sightseeing in the intellectual hinterlands of North America, and delving into some rarefied neighborhoods of history.

As an essayist Eco has two strengths, two areas where he is unusually knowledgeable and therefore especially interesting: the Middle Ages, upon which *The Name of the Rose* was an animated disquisition, and the New World, where he is a well-acclimated tourist. The title essay, the longest in this collection, ranges across the United States in search of instances of the native appetite for "the real thing" (to quote the Coca-Cola commercial) and (to quote many another) "more." Realer than real are Disneyland, Forest Lawn, the Movieland Wax Museum, Old Bethpage Village on Long Island (where changes in sheep produced by breeders flaw the otherwise perfect reconstruction of an early-nineteenth-century farm), and three-dimensional wax versions of Leonardo's *Last Supper*—Eco visited seven between Los Angeles and San Francisco, all of them claiming evident superiority to the fading, flaking original in Milan. In the Palace of Living Arts in Buena Park, for five dollars the dumb-founded tourist could (until 1982, when the Palace closed) view colored wax reproductions of famous marble statues like Michelangelo's *David* and the *Venus de Milo* (her arms considerately restored) and 3-D travesties of such celebrity paintings as the *Mona Lisa,* Ingres's *Grande Odalisque,* and Thomas Lawrence's *Pinkie,* complete with a concealed fan stirring her silk dress. This bold, if not commercially successful, attempt to bring closer to the American citizenry the wonders of European culture—"the fetishization of art as a sequence of famous objects"—is brother, Eco suggests, to such massive conglomerate appropriations as Hearst's San Simeon and the Ringlings' Venetian palazzo Ca' d'Zan in Sarasota; thence to the Getty Museum, with its authentic masterworks in a re-created Roman villa, is a short, if tastefully trodden, step. Eco is not insensitive to the pathos of our vulgar homages, the "something disarming about this search for glory via an unrequited love for the European past," nor quite unmindful of Old World wax museums and reliquaries that also strive for what he calls hyperreality. He takes a dainty philosophical delight in the paradoxes of such marriages of the synthetic and the actual as ecologically minded zoos and marine parks where "Nature has almost been regained, and yet it is erased by artifice precisely so that it can be presented as uncontaminated nature," and artificial Old West towns whose fake shops sell actual goods for real money. In the entertainment industry, he tells us, "when there is a sign it seems there isn't one, and when there isn't one we believe that there is. The condition of pleasure is that something be faked." He leaves few semiotic nuances of our recreational fakery unravelled, and rises to an insight into popular American theology:

> If you follow the Sunday morning religious programs on TV you come to understand that God can be experienced only as nature, flesh, energy, tangible image. And since no preacher dares show us God in the form of a bearded dummy, or as a Disneyland robot, God can be found in the form of natural force, joy, healing, youth, health, economic increment (which, let Max Weber teach us, is at once the essence of the Protestant ethic and of the spirit of capitalism).

We perhaps don't need the reference to Weber's well-worn teaching, and an American native, becoming the object of so lively and amused an anthropology, grows, like anthropologically considered natives the world over, rather restive with possible objections, such as that most of the hyperreal sites Eco surveyed are to a great extent aimed at the entertainment and edification of children. More than once, for light on our essence, he draws upon comic strips, with which he shows an encyclopedic acquaintance. Lyndon Johnson's enormous monument to himself in Austin is likened to Superman's Fortress of Solitude, and the market for kitschy hyperreality is "the America of Linus, for whom happiness must assume the form of a warm puppy or a security blanket, the America of Schroeder, who brings Beethoven to life not so much through a simplified score played on a toy piano as through the realistic bust in marble (or rubber). Where Good, Art, Fairytale, and History, unable to become flesh, must at least become Plastic." That hurts. Next we'll be told that Beethoven is plastic Beethoven if played on an American piano. Eco's tour begins with an exhilarating prospectus—"There is . . . an America of furious hyperreality, which is not that of Pop Art, of Mickey Mouse, or of Hollywood movies. There is another, more secret America (or rather, just as public, but snubbed by the European visitor and also by the American intellectual). . . . It has to be discovered"—but ends on a sour, somewhat Marxist note: "The ideology of this America wants to establish reassurance through Imitation. But profit defeats ideology, because the consumers want to be thrilled not only by the guarantee of the Good but also by the shudder of the Bad. . . . Thus, on entering his cathedrals of iconic reassurance, the visitor will remain uncertain whether his final destiny is hell or heaven, and so will consume new promises."

Semiology, the study of signification born from the semantic theories of Ferdinand de Saussure, is limited, as a tool of cultural analysis, by its necessary focus on propaganda—that is, the loading of discourse, visual or auditory, with messages of salesmanship and social reassurance. In Barthes's deft and beguiling essays, the "mythologies" of the French petite bourgeoisie are caught and held to analysis as they flicker past, all but subliminally, in the Paris press; he practiced an updated and more urbane version of Flaubert's satire of Bouvard and Pécuchet's conventional wisdom. Eco, as he reads the Italian newspapers of the Seventies and Eighties, finds grimmer matter—the death of Aldo Moro, the barbarities of the Red Brigades. In "Striking at the Heart of the System," Eco concludes that the terrorists' mythology, which he couches in rather recondite comic-strip terms—"their Disney-like mythology, in which on one side there was a wicked individual capitalist named Uncle Scrooge and on the other the Beagle Boys, a cheating rabble, true, but with a certain charge of crazy amiability because they stole, to the tunes of proletarian confiscation, from the stingy, egotistical capitalist"—has become obsolete, because Uncle Scrooge has gone multinational, and "the system" is now "headless and heartless." As such, it displays "an incredible capacity for healing and stabilizing," and "manages things in such a way that, except for the inevitable outsiders, everybody has something to lose in a situation of generalized terrorism." Eco, reading the signs, takes comfort in the conclusion that power has become unlocatably diffused. A photograph in *Corriere d'Informazione* shows a ski-masked terrorist brandishing his pistol alone on the street: "The collective element was missing," Eco's interpretation of this sign runs. "This image suggested other worlds, other figurative, narrative traditions that had nothing to do with the proletarian tradition, with the idea of popular revolt, of mass struggle." In "Language, Power, Force," citing Barthes, Georges Duby, and Michel Foucault, Eco proposes that power in today's world is, like language, subject to many small adjustments but never to revolution; change expresses itself as "progressive adjustment through slow, marginal shifts, in a centerless universe where all is margin and there is no longer any 'heart' of anything."

Our world, Eco believes, resembles the medieval world, with its intricate and shifting alliances between clergy and nobility, clergy and populace, national monarchies and monastic orders. The barons of multinational capitalism are observed "to medievalize their territory, with fortified castles and great residential complexes with private guards and photoelectric cells." Fantasy fiction and movies are riding a "neomedieval wave," and this nostalgia, the essay "Living in the New Middle Ages" explains, is really a search for self-understanding, as we traverse our post-imperial landscape of personal insecurity, wandering thieves and mystics, plagues and massacres, monasterylike university campuses, and a gaudy artistic culture pasted together from the flotsam of the past.

An art not systematic but additive and compositive, ours and that of the Middle Ages: Today as then the sophisticated elitist experiment coexists with the great enterprise of popularization (the relation between illuminated manuscript and cathedral is the same as that between MOMA and Hollywood), with interchanges and borrowings, reciprocal and continuous; and the evident Byzantinism, the mad taste for collecting, lists, assembling, amassing of disparate things is due to the need to dismantle and reconsider the flotsam of a previous world, harmonious perhaps, but by now obsolete.

Eco's belief—easier to entertain, perhaps, in semi-anarchic, picturesque Italy than on the tame plains of the United States—that we are living in a new Middle Ages gave urgency and weight to his fourteenth-century novel, and a "coded" quality that added to its detective-story pleasures. These essays, too, take life from his historical passion, whether he is praising St. Thomas Aquinas, describing Marshall McLuhan as "someone who writes the Canticle of Sister Electricity," or placing the Jonestown mass suicide in a dizzying context of medieval millenarian movements—the fraticelli, "the apostolics of Gherardo Segarelli, from which was born the revolt of Fra Dolcino," the "endura," the followers of Tanchelm and Eudes de l'Étoile, the Tafurs (hairy, dirty, cannibalistic), the Crucifers, "the secret Flagellants of Thuringia," and so on. But our neomedieval world is also the global village of mass communication, and Eco takes as topics pop songs, *Casablanca, 2001,* how to trick the phone company and how "the system" builds such technological thievery into its balance sheets, and the procedure whereby interest in sports becomes interest in media discourse upon sports: "Born as the raising to the nth power of that initial (and rational) waste that is sports recreation, sports chatter is the glorification of Waste, and therefore the maximum point of Consumption. On it and in it the consumer civilization man actually consumes himself."

In this self-consuming, heartless society of all margin, communication becomes an end in itself, a kind of floating brain without central content. The international exposition, as exemplified in Montreal's Expo 67, builds on communicatory style pure and simple. "A country no longer says, 'Look what I produce' but 'Look how smart I am in presenting what I produce.' . . . Each country shows itself by the way in which it is able to present the same thing other countries could also present. The prestige game is won by the country that best tells what it does, independently of what it actually does." The large temporary buildings at such an exposition function less "as structures to live in or pass through" than "as media of communication and suggestion"—the United States pavilion, a Buckminster Fuller geodesic dome, triumphed as a sign ("Mystical and technical, past and future, open and closed, this dome communicated the possibility of privacy without eliminating the rest of the world, and suggested, even achieved an image of power and expansion"), and in its triumph as container overshadowed its rather predictably American contents. The show *per se*, rather than the thing shown, matters more and more, whether the topic is sports discourse replacing sports, guerrilla publicity-seeking, or "the levels of institutional cultural showmanship that have been reached in the United States." By the same trend, these essays, shaped by the semiotician's interest in secondary meanings, have an air of removal that consorts awkwardly with their occasional reflex of Marxist terminology—e.g., "He [a visitor to a trade fair] has only accepted his role as consumer of consumer goods since he cannot be a proprietor of means of production."* Marx believed that the world in its true workings, in the structure of its layered power, could be analyzed and then actually altered; Umberto Eco's reflections, generally amusing and often brilliant, glint off of the surfaces of processes simultaneously elusive, inexorable, and feather-light. "Machines for communicating," as Eco says of clothes, make up the human world, a shell of sheer significations like a suit of armor with nothing in it. Such a suit, in the delightful novella *The Nonexistent Knight* by Eco's fellow countryman Italo Calvino, walks and fights and falls in love; but can there truly, we who are inside the world must ask, be nothing at all inside?

In Borges's Wake

THE ADVENTURES OF A PHOTOGRAPHER IN LA PLATA, by Adolfo Bioy Casares, translated from the Spanish by Suzanne Jill Levine. 169 pp. Dutton, 1989.

FOUCAULT'S PENDULUM, by Umberto Eco, translated from the Italian by William Weaver. 641 pp. Harcourt Brace Jovanovich, 1989.

The reputation of the Argentine writer Adolfo Bioy Casares is still associated, in the United States, with that of his friend and sometime collaborator Jorge Luis Borges. They wrote spoofs and parodies together, and worked on film scripts, anthologies, and translations; it might be said that Bioy Casares, though a generation younger, called the older man out

---

*The Marxism of Western European intellectuals itself must be taken as a sign, a bit of plumage whereby they recognize one another, since surely with the dismal example of Eastern Europe next door they can't really want to turn Italy into another Romania, or France into China.

of his shell, and inspired Borges's first and most mind-blowing book of prose, the collection *Ficciones*. Bioy Casares is known, on his own, as the author of the betranced science-fiction novella *The Invention of Morel*, and of a number of novels few non-Latin Americans have read. His latest novel to be published here, *The Adventures of a Photographer in La Plata*, is a slight and sly tale not apt to widen his local audience greatly, yet it has a charm and a sinister wit and a sudden sadness only an assured literary performer could deliver. It tells, in a terse and flat but not unfriendly style, of a young small-town photographer, Nicolasito Almanza, who arrives with his equipment in the city of La Plata, the capital of Buenos Aires Province. No sooner has Almanza emerged into the city from his all-night bus ride than he is hailed by a stranger—a tall, rosy-faced "older gentleman" who is leading an entourage consisting of two attractive young women, an infant in arms, and a little girl. These, it develops, are the Lombardos, also newly arrived in the capital, from the district of Magdalena. Before the novel is over, our hero will give blood to save the father, Don Juan, from dying, and will sleep with both of Don Juan's daughters—Griselda, the mother of the children, and Julia, who assists Almanza with his photography. The photographer is amply warned to disentangle himself from this family, who have evidently fled their native soil in some financial embarrassment, and whose patriarch is rumored to be none other than Satan, but a certain modernist glue prolongs entanglements, delays deliveries, and complicates arrangements in this plot, and Almanza extracts himself only when he moves on to photograph the sights of another city, Tandil. In fact no harm befalls him, except the loss of Julia, with whom he has, without the reader's much noticing it, fallen in love.

The pleasure and the discomfort the book affords derive from what we might call the comedy of daily intercourse—the great amounts of time (the characters') and words (the author's) expended in going back and forth among boarding houses and restaurants, explaining and fulfilling or missing appointments, chasing disappearing suitcases and delayed remittances, observing obscurely motivated conversational courtesies. Hastening from place to place, "Almanza remembered a dream situation: being in a hurry and walking slowly with tired legs that weigh him down. The truth was that everything that day was taking too much time." The grid of numbered streets whereon the characters pursue one another is indicated with a mathematical precision; upon the grid, however, human conduct oscillates unpredictably. Almanza and Griselda rent a hotel room for two hours for a tryst, but the electricity between them shorts out:

> Again she held him close. How strange, he thought, so slender and so strong. She looked beautiful but attracted him less than before, and at mo-

ments she irritated him a little. Perhaps because she had lied to him (not meaning any wrong, one must admit) and also, incredible as it seemed, because she had confessed her lie. He had discovered that he didn't feel at ease with nervous, complicated people. While he was thinking this, a hard arm held him by the neck. He felt some pain and couldn't move; meanwhile Griselda was rubbing against him. Suddenly, with noticeable force, she pushed him away. Almanza wanted to wipe his forehead with his handkerchief. He was still looking for it in his pant pockets and jacket, when he saw her fall as if she had fainted with her head hanging off the edge of the bed, looking up wildly, her mouth half-open and her breast bare. One is always being manipulated, he thought and got angry again. He reconsidered: It's not that bad.

The encounter ends oddly; Almanza obeys "an impulse that was familiar to him" and takes out his camera and photographs Griselda, no fewer than twenty times. "She looked up coyly and shook her hair. He photographed her again." The one thing that proceeds smoothly for him in La Plata is his photography of the city's buildings and monuments; his lens cuts through the maze, as art saves us from life.

Bioy Casares is a deadpan parodist, and what is parodied here seems to be the traditional novel itself—its solemn tracing of the psychological, erotic, perilous relational currents among "nervous, complicated people." No wonder that Almanza, caught in the web of the Lombardos' seductions, and beset by gossip from all sides, takes an interest, while in Griselda's bedroom, in a magazine article that tells "how the great powers and even your country were only a smoke screen and how everything that happens on God's earth—even what happens to you and me—depends on the decisions of a handful of men in dark suits sitting around a table." In our hunger for a pattern behind things we entertain fantasies of conspiracy. At several points in the book, Almanza senses an echoing: "Everything happens to me in pairs." When he and Julia part, she gives him a kaleidoscope, a toy that fetches symmetry out of accidental arrangements.

The novel's mood, laconic style, and mechanisms—the careful notation of happenstance, the plurality of ominous characters—are those of a mystery novel, but one whose minor mysteries (What do the Lombardos want? Is Don Juan the Devil or a garrulous old con man with two daughters at loose ends?) and major mystery (What do the photographer's seemingly aimless adventures add up to?) are left unresolved. The novel arrests our attention and wins our respect by the things it disdains to do: it does not overdramatize or moralize, it denies events a deeper meaning. A clean if desolate flatness results—the spookiness of the minimal, haunted by the absence of ghosts. Whodunit? Nobodaddy. In using the mystery-novel format to tease forth nihilist sensations, *The Adventures of a Photog-*

rapher in La Plata resembles, among many other modernist works, Robbe-Grillet's *Les Gommes,* Raymond Queneau's *We Always Treat Women Too Well,* Borges's story "The Garden of Forking Paths," and that surprising best-seller, Umberto Eco's *The Name of the Rose.*

Borges inspired a character, the blind Jorge of Burgos, in *The Name of the Rose,* and also the book's central image of a labyrinthine library, an essentially infinite library as a universal metaphor. Another Borgesian notion, that of a Cabalistic conspiracy running beneath things, staining and twisting history and putting men in touch with diabolical deities, informs Eco's second novel, *Foucault's Pendulum,* which, like his first, is bulky, recondite, intricate, and best-selling. Borges, in his short stories and in his highly individual literary criticism, could give us a shiver with the lightest, most offhand touch of his private supernatural. His stories often open with a creak of esoteric pedantry:

> I owe the discovery of Uqbar to the conjunction of a mirror and an encyclopedia. ["Tlön, Uqbar, Orbis Tertius"]

> No one saw him disembark in the unanimous night, no one saw the bamboo canoe sink into the sacred mud, but in a few days there was no one who did not know that the taciturn man came from the South and that his home had been one of those numberless villages upstream in the deeply cleft side of the mountain, where the Zend language has not been contaminated by Greek and where leprosy is infrequent. ["The Circular Ruins"]

> In Asia Minor or in Alexandria, in the second century of our faith (when Basilides was announcing that the cosmos was a rash and malevolent improvisation engineered by defective angels), Nils Runeberg might have directed, with a singular intellectual passion, one of the Gnostic conventicles. ["Three Versions of Judas"]

And, in fullest throat:

> Those who write that the sect of the Phoenix originated in Heliopolis, and make it derive from the religious restoration which followed the death of the reformer Amenhotep IV, cite texts by Herodotus, Tacitus, and inscriptions from the Egyptian monuments; but they ignore, or try to ignore, the fact that the denomination of the sect by the name of Phoenix is not prior to Rabanus Maurus, and that the most ancient sources (the *Saturnalia,* or Flavius Josephus, let us say) speak only of the People of Custom or the People of the Secret. ["The Sect of the Phoenix"]

In attempting to expand one of these Borgesian *frissons,* with their union of curious fact and macabre fancy, their solemn conspiratorial tone, their expert trafficking along that shadowy borderline where knowledge becomes arcane and thought becomes madness, into a six-hundred-forty-page, one-hundred-twenty-chapter saga of research and rumor in modern Italy, Paris, and Brazil, Eco has not reckoned with the possibility that *frissons* are not endlessly expandable. Borges was always brief; he wrote with a poet's ear; his own blindness and reclusive habits gave his mental explorations a peculiar and inimitable resonance, an earnest sorrow and uncanny repose. He had the voice of a sphinx. Eco, contrariwise, appears to be a postmodern intellectual as animated as he is intelligent, a mental extrovert whose cerebrations spill over into a number of disciplines. *Foucault's Pendulum* is a monumental performance, erudite beyond measure, and, insofar as Eco's brainy presence on the page is enjoyable, enjoyable. But as a tale of human adventure, erected upon the not quite interchangeable characters of three Milanese editors who prankishly cook up a secret sect called Tres (Templi Resurgentes Equites Synarchici) and are consumed by their creation, it totters and sags, and seems spun-out and thin.

The medieval characters of *The Name of the Rose* had at the least the solidity and color of their richly evoked fourteenth-century milieu. Those of *Foucault's Pendulum* belong to our era, and they seem, rather than creations of the author's erudition, victims of it. They are disposable plastic holders that pour out ribbons of information, of facts and quotations all looped around the central notion that the Templars—a monastic order of Christian knights founded in 1118 to protect pilgrims to the shakily held Holy Land and destroyed in 1314 by Philip IV of France, who wanted their money—in truth survived and, by means of a relay system of hidden initiates who are supposed to meet six times, in six different countries, at intervals of a hundred and twenty years, are invisibly progressing toward a secret concerning the earth's "telluric currents" that will enable its holders to rule the world. Why they didn't simply start ruling in 1314 may have escaped me—there is some tricky business about a map, and a beam of sunlight at a certain moment of the year on Foucault's pendulum, a non-imaginary object which hangs in the Conservatoire des Arts et Métiers in Paris. This great plot involves everyone from the Rosicrucians to the Jesuits, Francis Bacon to Cagliostro, the Freemasons (of course) to the Jews (perhaps), and was the real reason, it would seem, that Napoleon invaded Russia and Hitler perpetrated the Holocaust. If this last jest seems in dubious taste, a better joke is that the three editors reason from a cryptic document—entrusted to them by a prospective author who then vanishes—that is finally demonstrated to have been simply a merchant's delivery list. Better yet is the underlying jest that our human lust for conspiracy theories and secret organizations is so keen that a donnish parody of a cult becomes a murderously real one. There can't be too many hermetic stones left unturned in this ransacking of texts, this orgy of citation and paraphrase for which Eco, he told an interviewer for *The New York Times Magazine,* "pillaged the bookshops in at least 10 cities in Italy, France and America," acquiring "1,500 books on occultism plus 400 or so rare books." He could be describing his own researches when he has his narrator write:

> I found myself in a morass of books, in which it was difficult to distinguish historical fact from hermetic gossip, and reliable information from flights of fancy. Working like a machine for a week, I drew up a bewildering list of sects, lodges, conventicles.

The enterprising Italians have already published a dictionary of Eco's strange words and quotations—*Dizionario del pendolo di Foucault.* William Weaver has performed nobly (and with praiseworthy speed) in producing an English translation that hums imperturbably along, through tunnels of French and Latin and Hebrew, around ancient graven illustrations, in an emblematic variety of type styles. *Foucault's Pendulum* is a dense and inventorial novel that lacks, and needs, an index.

It also needs more blood, more human juice. It has some. Casaubon,* the narrator and the Templar expert who provides most of the scholarly

---

*The name, strange for an Italian, invites comment. Its most illustrious real possessor was Isaac Casaubon (1559–1614), a classical scholar born in Geneva of Huguenot parents exiled from France. As with Eco's hero, his intensely bookish life was beset by a certain international peril: the contest between Calvinism and Catholicism impoverished his youth in Geneva, and complicated his patronage first by Henri IV of France and then by James I of England. Reputed to be, after Scaliger, the most learned man of the age, he was sought as a prize by the Ultramontane Catholics and subjected to stern criticism by the anti-Papist Reformed theologians. His own taste was for a halfway position, which he read into the early church fathers and found in the Church of England; after the assassination of Henri IV, he went to England in 1610 at the invitation of the Archbishop of Canterbury, becoming a favorite conversational companion of the British monarch. He did not speak English, however, and encountered hostility from cockneys and Jesuits. In an age of violent religious contention, scholarship had no safe nook. Casaubon's chief scholarly monuments are his editions of Athenaeus and Theophrastus, with profuse commentary; his diary, edited and published by his son under the title *Ephemerides,* provides an unequalled record of the daily life of a sixteenth-century scholar.

A scholar mustier still, and perhaps more present to Eco's mind, is Edward Casaubon, the fictional cleric who marries Dorothea Brooke, the heroine of George Eliot's *Middlemarch.* A wealthy, prematurely aged man in his fifties, this Casaubon is engaged upon an interminable work of arcane research and learned controversy he calls the Key to all Mythologies. George Eliot, translator of Feuerbach and Strauss's *Life of Jesus* and well versed in the religious controversies of her century, with eerily intense comedy conjures up the cobwebbed maze of Casaubon's impossible endeavor to show "that all the mythical

ingredients of the three editors' witches' brew, fathers a baby in the course of the novel, and the birth inspires a few sentences striking in their unlayered simplicity, their humble celebration of the *Ding an sich*. Absorbed in an interview with a sinister taxidermist, Casaubon is late to the hospital, where his consort, Lia, has already delivered:

> Finally—I don't know how—I found myself in a room. Lia was pearly pale but smiling. Someone had lifted her hair and put it under a white cap. For the first time I saw Lia's forehead in all its splendor. Next to her was the Thing.
> "It's Giulio," she said.

Amparo, an earlier woman friend, a Brazilian mulatto, occasions some salty verbal exchanges, a little sexual heat, and an episode, in Brazil, that is psychologically interesting: attending a macumba ceremony as a disdainful, educated spectator, she is caught up in the dance and possessed by the she-devil Pomba Gira. Her lewd and rigid movements and her sweaty, breathless dismay afterward get Casaubon, as it were, to look at her. In general, even in bed, he is too busy reading to give his women enough attention to make them real to any reader but himself. Eco, who was born in 1932, has had experience of being a child, a university student, and an intellectual in these last, stormy years of Italian history; whenever he drops his occult texts and describes a village war between the resistance and the Fascists, or a student riot of the Sixties, or the bar where the idle wits of Milan gather, reality breaks through, a breezy sense of witness, suggesting what he might write a novel about if he could ever forgo his ingenious schemes of signification and self-deconstruction, of encyclopedic foolery.

The most bloodless of the three heroes is Diotallevi, a Piedmontese who thinks he is a Jew, and who exists only to waste away, infected by the

---

systems or erratic mythical fragments in the world were corruptions of a tradition originally revealed." (Cf. page 580, the similar endeavor of Father Jean-François Foucquet.) Though Dorothea initially "listened with fervid patience to a recitation of possible arguments to be brought against Mr. Casaubon's entirely new view of the Philistine god Dagon and other fish-deities," the youthful bride rather soon comes to feel that it is all a "sort of dried preparation, a lifeless embalmment of knowledge" and half-scornfully to pity her husband's "plodding application, rows of note-books, and small taper of learned theory exploring the tossed ruins of the world." In the end, she quails before the task, bequeathed to her by the dying scholar, of "sifting these mixed heaps of material, which were to be the doubtful illustration of principles still more doubtful," of "sorting what might be called shattered mummies, and fragments of a tradition which was itself a mosaic wrought from crushed ruins." This claustrophobic atmosphere, of littered labyrinths futilely searched for a key to "the tossed ruins of the world," is of course exactly that of Eco's Casaubon's demonstration, on behalf of Tres, of history as one gigantic, shadowy conspiracy—scholarship as dementia.

terrible sacrilege of the plot he has joined in concocting. He sees in the cancer that afflicts him the product of their intellectual tampering, a transposition in the DNA alphabet generated by the mock-conspiracy's devilishly clever transpositions of fact: "To manipulate the letters of the Book takes great piety, and we didn't have it. . . . If you alter the Book, you alter the world; if you alter the world, you alter the body. . . . I'm dying because we were imaginative beyond bounds." But Diotallevi at his liveliest has little vital presence, and Belbo, the most active of the pseudo-occultists, has a fitful and strained one. He is a generation older than Casaubon but draws what fictional life he has from the same roots: Milanese bohemia and an obsession with texts. He is an unpublished writer, and fills a word processor called Abulafia with abortive confessions and stories that add up to a psychohistory of avoidance and non-participation relieved only by a childhood love for the trumpet and what becomes an obsession with the Templar conspiracy he has helped embroider. His character is spelled out but doesn't quite read convincingly. His lady love, the flighty, promiscuous, pinball-playing Lorenza, exists only to symbolize the Gnostic goddess Sophia, and his word-processed effusions, brilliant jumble though they are, just add to the novel's crushing burden of textuality. Words, words: "You write using the alibi of a machine, telling yourself you are a spectator, because you read yourself on the screen as if the words belonged to another, but you have fallen into the trap: you, too, are trying to leave footprints on the sands of time. You have dared to change the text of the romance of the world, and the romance of the world has taken you instead into its coils and involved you in its plot, a plot not of your making." Though Belbo is shown as rising to a certain heroism before his demise, and his rustic boyhood is intently scanned for an epiphany, he becomes in the end just a toy on a string, and our patience with the novel's plethora of symbols snaps at the point where we are told, of his eccentrically twitching body, that "Belbo hanged from the Pendulum would have drawn, in space, the tree of the Sefirot, summing up in his final moment the vicissitude of all universes, fixing forever in his motion the ten stages of the mortal exhalation and defecation of the divine in the world."

Some rather sweet morals are extracted from this papery honeycomb. The "real secret," the dying Diotallevi avers, is "to let the cells proceed according to their own instinctive wisdom." "It's wrong," Lia tells the inventive Casaubon, "to add to the inventings that already exist." "Truth is brief," Casaubon tells the reader, near the conclusion of more than two hundred thousand words supposedly somehow confided to paper in the space of two days. He remembers the childhood bliss of biting into a peach, and says, "Like Belbo when he played the trumpet, when I bit into the peach I understood the Kingdom and was one with it. The rest is only cleverness."

Eco's tower of cleverness, which melts in the mind as it is climbed, is a remarkable intellectual phenomenon, however flimsy and lopsided as an imitation of human actions. One has to think back to the Brothers Grimm and Henry Wadsworth Longfellow to find an academic turning from scholarship to achieve such popular success. Eco is an initiate and an adept in the critical mysteries, whose magus is Jacques Derrida, that have deconstructed the hidden constructions of literature, revealing every page to have a conspiratorial dimension. Derrida-ism, however liberating its effect upon university English faculties, does not offer much encouragement to creative writing. Indeed, insofar as it has revealed the once-revered canon of literary classics to be largely a bag of dirty tricks played by imperialist white males upon minorities and women, it might be supposed to exert a depressive effect. For who wants to add to a bag of dirty tricks? And Eco's novel does come burdened by a complicated, if not downright guilty, conscience. His practical answer to the difficulties of making literature is to appropriate what he calls "dime novel" plots and pump them full to bursting of professorial learning. Belbo and Casaubon, those two faces of one post-structuralist coin, argue the case for "cheap fiction": "Maybe only cheap fiction gives us the true measure of reality. . . . Proust was right: life is represented better by bad music than by a Missa solemnis. . . . The dime novel . . . pretends to joke, but then it shows us the world as it actually is—or at least the world as it will become. . . . History is closer to what [Eugène] Sue narrates than to what Hegel projects. Shakespeare, Melville, Balzac, and Dostoyevski all wrote sensational fiction. What has taken place in the real world was predicted in penny dreadfuls." The inclusion of the canonical names muddles what I take to be the basic point: popular romantic narration, by seizing upon our dreams and manipulating our passions, presents the forces that shape the world—"the world as it will become"—as opposed to relatively inert and backward-looking highbrow realism. In this Eco echoes Borges's distrust of the modernist mandarins, his reiterated preference of Wells and Chesterton over Henry James and James Joyce. But of course mandarins distrust themselves, at least in the role of hero: Joyce's triumph was to move from the mind of Stephen Dedalus into that of Leopold Bloom—to put a dime-novel mentality in a narrative frame of Thomistic rigor and Homeric grandeur. Eco's strategy in *Foucault's Pendulum* is the reverse: to put his three Milanese bibliophilic polymaths in a dime-novel plot. The novel gothically begins with Casaubon hiding for hours in a kind of periscope inside a darkened museum, and ends with a scene of ritual revelry and sacrifice like something out of *Salammbô*. That cumbersome and punishing novel, indeed, is the nearest analogy I can think of for this *de luxe* cheap thrill, this million-dollar penny dreadful.

Modernist, Postmodernist, What Will They Think of Next?

Fancy Goods/Open All Night, by Paul Morand, translated from the French by Ezra Pound. 151 pp. New Directions, 1984.

Marcovaldo, *or, The Seasons in the City*, by Italo Calvino, translated from the Italian by William Weaver. 121 pp. Harcourt Brace Jovanovich, 1984.

John Barth, than whom there is no more aplomb-filled and equable theorist among contemporary practitioners of American fiction, five years ago tackled, in an address entitled "The Literature of Replenishment," the super-delicate distinctions between modernism, postmodernism, premodernism, and none of the above. John Hawkes, for example, came out as "fine late modernism," "most of" Saul Bellow as "comparatively *pre*modernist," Gertrude Stein and William Faulkner, among Americans, as unimpeachably "great modernists," and Barth himself, along with Donald Barthelme, Robert Coover, Stanley Elkin, Thomas Pynchon, and Kurt Vonnegut, Jr., as bona-fide postmodernists. To this last club, women and British need not apply, being evidently incorrigibly concerned with "the eloquent issuance of what Richard Locke has called 'secular news reports.'" So, whatever postmodernism is, it is not secular news reports. Nor is it, one may hazard, sacred news reports. It is not, really, news reports at all; it is, if I understand Professor Barth's paraphrase of several other professors, a kind of cartoon-cat version of modernism—the cat keeps running even though he has only air beneath him. Modernism's "self-consciousness and self-reflexiveness" keep "performing," but in a "spirit . . . of anarchy." The "anti-rationalist, anti-realist, anti-bourgeois program of modernism" is carried on, but without "a solid adversary," the bourgeois "having now co-opted the trappings of modernism and turned its defiant principles into mass-media kitsch." This may not be a totally bad thing, Mr. Barth concludes, since the postmodernist writer can now honorably appeal to a somewhat larger, more democratic audience than did the embattled hard-core modernists and can look back without contempt upon the nineteenth century and the novel's gnarled old roots in "middle-class popular culture." Mr. Barth cites, as both significantly appealing and adventurous, Italo Calvino and Gabriel García Márquez; he might add Umberto Eco* were he giving the speech now.

Such literary labelling is innocent fun, and helps not only us but, more to the point, college English majors to get a grip on things. Mr. Barth takes it no more seriously than he should. Categorization in these matters, of course, tends to excuse us from confronting each author in his or her intricate individuality, and to enlist artists in phantom armies—the modernists, for example, doing battle in a body with something called "the bourgeoisie." But who were their patrons and early readers but bourgeoisie? Whence were they recruited but from bourgeois families? To what did they aspire, these artists, by and large, but bourgeois comforts and the dignity of bourgeois craftsmen? And was modernism, with its extensive reclamations of lived life—life freed from clichés of morality and artistic convention—really empty of "secular news"? Residents of Dublin saw in *Dubliners* and *Ulysses* all too much local news. Don't even Mr. Barth's anfractuous exercises in postmodernism tell us, amid their many self-reflexive turns, a great deal about at least academic life in America, not to mention Maryland marsh fauna and the procedures of sailing? And what does one do with a writer like Hemingway, so impeccably modernist in his short stories and so grossly popular as a novelist and cultural personality? He is, in Mr. Barth's consideration of modernism and its aftermath, simply omitted, without even a "Terra Incognita" to mark his spot on the map of twentieth-century letters. Writers have awkwardly long lives, while artistic fashion swings in ever-quickening arcs, each swing needing a marketable label. I myself doubt whether "postmodernist" will acquire the canonical permanence of "Post-Impressionist" or "post-Kantian," for the reason that Impressionism and Immanuel Kant were phenomena more distinct and limited than modernism was. We still live in modern (from the Latin *modo*, "just now") times, and so will our descendants, until the dictionary falls to dust.

Two small books of recently published—though not recently written—short stories offer to impart some twists of specificity to these general considerations. *Marcovaldo, or, The Seasons in the City,* a set of twenty

---

*Who, in any case, discusses and quotes Barth's essay in his elegant little *Postscript to The Name of the Rose* (1984). Eco seems to agree that the postmodernist is free to offer the reader simple enjoyment and to revisit the past—"but with irony, not innocently." More interesting, to me, was Eco's parenthetical aside: "I wonder if postmodernism is not the modern name for mannerism as a metahistorical category."

linked tales by Italo Calvino, must be postmodernist, if Calvino is all that Mr. Barth claims. And *Fancy Goods/Open All Night,* by Paul Morand, fairly drips with old-fashioned modernist credentials: the jacket lists New Directions as the publisher, Ezra Pound as the translator, and Marcel Proust as the author of a preface.

What dark sun is this, who held such planets as Pound and Proust in his orbit? Morand had a long life, from 1888 to 1976, but his artistic celebrity rests upon the short stories he published in the first half of that classic modernist decade, the Twenties. A professional diplomat since 1912, he occupied a cosmopolitan variety of posts and served during World War II as minister at Bucharest and ambassador at Bern; in 1945 he was dismissed from the diplomatic service for collaboration with the Vichy government. For the same reason his candidacy for the Académie Française was opposed and defeated, though in 1968 he was at last elected a member. As Breon Mitchell sets forth in his excellent introduction—a model of clear and brisk elucidation of a bibliographical tangle—Morand was already known as a rising young writer when Pound arrived in Paris, in 1920. Before the year was out, Pound had taken upon himself the translation of a Morand story, "La Nuit turque," which was published, as "Turkish Night," in the September 1921 issue of *The Dial.* Pound's "Paris Letter" in the next issue praised Morand, for "with buddhic eye contemplating the somewhat hysterical war and postwar world and rendering it with somewhat hasty justness. . . . And he has surely the first clear eye that has been able to wander about both ends of Europe looking at wreckage, and his present news value need not fail ultimately of historical validity." By April of 1922, Pound and Morand had agreed that Pound would translate two of Morand's highly praised collections, *Tendre Stocks* (1921) and *Ouvert la Nuit* (1922). In Pound's first years after leaving London, then, while he was busily involved in such epochal middleman activities as the promotion and serial publication of *Ulysses* and the editing of Eliot's diffuse and rather foppish *Waste Land* manuscript into a masterpiece, Pound was also translating Morand—his most ambitious effort, ever, at prose translation. He submitted drafts of his version to the author, who knew England and English well, and to Victor Llona, a professional translator; but he took few of their suggestions, where style was concerned. An agreement for the two titles was signed with the London firm of Chapman and Dodd. However, when Pound submitted *Open All Night* in June of 1922, right on schedule, Guy Chapman found the translations "quite appalling" and was confirmed by an independent reader, A. B. Walkley, who told him in August that "You certainly cannot with credit, or indeed without ridicule, publish this translation." Pound responded to

Chapman's rejection with characteristic ill temper: "Your letter is an impertinent lie. . . . There was no question of a verbatim translation into stenographer's pidgeon English." Pound threatened legal action, and for a final settlement of twenty-five pounds the contract was cancelled; Morand's work found other English translators, and Pound's manuscript of *Open All Night* and the rougher but completed version of *Fancy Goods* found their way, when their author left Paris for Italy in 1924, into a trunk at the Paris office of William Bird's Three Mountains Press, for whom Pound had done some editing. In 1926, Bird sold his publishing house to Nancy Cunard; he took Pound's material with him in boxes as he moved to Chartres and then North Africa. He died in 1964, and twelve years later the boxes were finally opened, by Bird's heirs in Fairfax, Virginia. After much negotiation, the letters to Pound from his wife, Dorothy, went to their son, Omar; other manuscript material was fitted into the already extensive Pound collection at Yale; and the Lilly Library at Indiana University acquired the rest, including the Morand translations. So here at last, sixty-two years late, they are, edited by Mr. Mitchell with a nice postmodern reverence.

    Fancy Goods contains three stories—"Clarissa," "Delphine," and "Aurora"—and *Open All Night* six—"Catalan Night," "Turkish Night," "The Roman Night," "The Six-Day Night," "Hungarian Night," and "Borealis." Each story has a woman at its center and indeed seems designed to display her, by means of a glittering succession of scenes and anecdotes that yet leave ambiguous, often, her relationship with the narrator. He, though unnamed and passive, is a continuous presence, and by virtue of his ardent voice an emphatic one. In *Fancy Goods,* whose episodes take place primarily in London, during World War I, the narrator is younger than in the stories of *Open All Night,* where he has become a man-about-Europe, if not a roué. The women flit through his life like large, gorgeous, inscrutable butterflies. Some achieve unhappy ends: Remedios, a Spanish revolutionary, sets off an explosion and is arrested; Isabel, a French coquette in Rome, is found strangled; Anna, a Russian aristocrat reduced to being a waitress in Constantinople, announces her intention of spending two weeks in Paris and then committing suicide; and Zaël, a Jewish dancer in Vienna, demands to be taken back to Hungary and is kidnapped and presumably murdered there. Others simply vanish from view, like Aurora in London: "She makes a sign. Number 19 bus comes docilely to curb at her feet. She ascends the stair like a frieze unrolling itself."

    The writing is the thing. Whether the prose's confident oddity derives from Morand's original or from Pound's translation scarcely matters; the effect is luxurious, sharp, compressed, startling:

The caged sun went down between tree trunks, like a red slice of beetroot. The ferryboat came into dock. Two anchors fell from its nostrils.

In the street the cold came against my cheeks like the charge from a gun loaded with rock salt. I felt light as a pigeon and wholly soaked with electricity.

Her eye cast forth its scrutative beam to-me-ward, and it sank in like a grappling iron.

Her face, smooth as a porcelain bowl, sloped away in an even curve, holding level in its surface her two flat liquid eyes, but my memory hesitated before the softened mouth, weary at its corners and showing no pleasure in possessing its even teeth.

Irritated by the lights, the chandelier wallowed like a crystal porcupine in the midst of Venetian mirrors reflecting cerise damask hangings and rococo boxes copied from Schönbrunn.

The conversation is pasty. I go to the feeding room. The plates still offer a few dried sandwiches turned up at the corners like ill-stuck postage stamps; cigarette ashes, corks; the liquid level is low in the bottles; the guests' beards increase implacably. One's hands are sticky, and one's face is uncomfortable.

Such richness of imagery, so quickly folded and superimposed, feels cubist. The issues are circled rather than faced. Not so much the people as the spaces between them are exactly drawn. The spurts of dialogue, where they occur, are elliptical and Firbankish. A certain deliberate Gallic wit presides; the humorous rhetorical device of syllepsis occurs perhaps too often: "freshly caulked keels flaming with red lead and the sunset," "a small woman, excessively preserved by milk of cucumbers and egoism," "I . . . arose with satisfaction and with bleeding hands." The Zeitgeist is diagnosed in a kindred cadence: "It's the sacrificed generation, ma'am. The men have gone off to be soldiers, and the women have all gone crazy." The shattered, frenetic postwar Europe is described in language both jazzy and coldly detached; the scenes seem illumined by sliced moonlight:

At every start I found the pillow next to me swollen and cold and the boundless room lit only by the moon which an obliging mirror reflected into the dusty water of a fire-bucket.

Mr. Mitchell's introduction compares a few passages of Morand's French with Pound's and other translations in case we needed to be convinced that as a translator Pound was incomparably bold and energetic. Though linguistic scholars have always been pained by some of

Pound's liberties and etymological leaps, it was he above all others in the twentieth century who lifted translation to the status of an art. His translations are not transparent; they can be eccentric and flamboyant and more active than the original. *"Dans une atmosphère de tabac"* becomes "in this air freighted with tobacco," *"Atroce matin d'exécution"* becomes "A good day for a hanging" (as opposed to another translator's flat-footed "Atrocious morning for an excursion"), and *"Voilà une curieuse rencontre"* becomes, simply, "Mm." Modernist translation came to the fore, a proclaimed artistic medium, like thick paint. Even if a dozen cavalier extensions of the literal French exist on every page, Morand was well served by Pound, and perhaps his English reputation would be less negligible if this translation had been published when delivered.

Proust's preface to *Fancy Goods* aimed to serve in a different way: by blessing Morand in full view of French readers, much as Anatole France had, a generation before, provided a preface for the young Proust's *Pleasures and Days*. In 1921, Proust, like his hero Baldassare Silvande in that youthful collection, knew he was dying; his preface, in Pound's translation—the least worked-over, we are told, of Pound's manuscript—is a remarkable late efflorescence, an epic example of a gratuitous genre. Proust begins by telling the reader that "I should like to have undertaken the useless labor of doing a real preface for these charming brief romances"; but "a stranger has taken her abode in my mind." He gives the stranger's name: Death. "I was surprised at her lack of beauty. I had always thought Death beautiful. How otherwise should she get the better of us?" Then the invalid takes up the notion, once raised by his old patron Anatole France, that "singularity of style should be rejected," and in a grandly irrelevant delirium of quotation from memory discusses the past styles of Baudelaire and Taine, Sainte-Beuve and Stendhal ("a great writer without knowing it"), Madame de Sévigné and Racine ("doubtless in Racine an hysteric of genius was struggling in the control of a superior intelligence"). It all suggests a prima donna's fluttering farewells, though what Pound liked about the preface was how it "shoveled what one hopes is a final funeral clod upon the corpse of Sainte-Beuve." Of young Morand there is scarcely a word, though Proust does drop a valuable warning: "This new writer is usually fatiguing to read and difficult to understand because he joins things by new relationships. One follows the first half of the phrase very well, and then one falls. One feels it is only because the new writer is more agile than we are."

Since the death of Vladimir Nabokov, no writer has been more agile than Italo Calvino—and there was something gruff and abrasive about Nabokov, something modern as it were, which the Italian postmodernist

has smoothly shucked. Calvino's prose, though ingenious, is never difficult; though colorful, never opaque. The reader is charmed, not challenged. True, *Marcovaldo* is a minor work, untranslated into English for
twenty years. The author's note tells us that the first of these twenty
stories "were written in the early 1950s and thus are set in a very poor
Italy, the Italy of neo-realistic movies. The last stories date from the
mid-60s, when the illusions of an economic boom flourished." The sardonic Marxist tone of this note reminds us that Calvino was for twelve
years—up to the Russian suppression of the Hungarian revolt in 1956—a
Communist. Marcovaldo is a member of the working class in an unnamed
industrial city; he lives with his wife and six children in a half-basement,
and later in an attic apartment. While in a park, he longs to sleep "in the
midst of this cool green shade and not in my cramped, hot room; here
amid the silence, not amid the snoring and sleep-talking of my whole
family and the racing of trams down below in the street." In another story,
a snowfall mercifully masks the realities of his workday until a sneeze
disperses the flakes; then "to his gaze there appeared the familiar court-
yard, the gray walls, the boxes from the warehouse, the things of every
day, sharp and hostile." His family chops up roadside billboards for
warmth, and wants to cook a pet rabbit he has brought home to them. But
such grim proletarian realities are established primarily as the ground for
merriment, for the repeated demonstration of Marcovaldo's hopeful, generous, and dauntless spirit. He nurses a sallow potted plant into a flourish-
ing tree; he develops a thriving clinic based upon the healing properties
of wasp stings; he dresses up as Santa Claus and motorbikes about the city
delivering presents. The stories, as they play across potentially sombre
ground, reminded me of nothing so much as Giovanni Guareschi's *Little
World of Don Camillo* (1950) and its successor volumes of comic vignettes
about the jockeying between the priest and the Communist mayor of a
small Italian village—best-selling Cold War whimsy.

Yet *Marcovaldo* shows not only Calvino's fine fanciful hand and habit
of mathematical rigor (the twenty stories make a fivefold cycle of the four
seasons) but the concerns of his major fiction—Man in the universe, men
in cities.

> This Marcovaldo possessed an eye ill-suited to city life: billboards, traffic-
> lights, shop-windows, neon signs, posters, no matter how carefully devised
> to catch the attention, never arrested his gaze, which might have been
> running over the desert sands. Instead, he would never miss a leaf yellowing
> on a branch, a feather trapped by a roof-tile; there was no horsefly on a
> horse's back, no worm-hole in a plank, or fig-peel squashed on the sidewalk

that Marcovaldo didn't remark and ponder over, discovering the changes of season, the yearnings of his heart, and the woes of his existence.

Natural reality, for which natural man naturally hungers, emerges even in the cityscape, once men are eliminated. During the August holidays, when the streets are deserted,

> Marcovaldo's eyes peered around seeking the emergence of a different city, a city of bark and scales and clots and nerve-systems under the city of paint and tar and glass and stucco. And there, the building which he passed every day was revealed to him, in its reality, as a quarry of porous gray sandstone.

The little book carries a surprising message: Destroy. In the last story, a wealthy child smashes all his presents and burns down his house; the joy of the Destructive Gift dawns upon the spirit of Christmas Consumption, and the city in Marcovaldo's vision is replaced by a wilderness, "an expanse of snow . . . white as this page."

But there is a qualitative difference between such envisioned simplification—the reduction of experience to the page, the word, the book—and the actual shattered aftermath sketched by Morand, the Europe of crazy women and of men who ask, "Who [will] console me for the anonymous farce of creation?" Calvino is as much a postwar writer as Morand; indeed, he fought, in the Italian resistance, whereas Morand merely witnessed World War I from within the diplomatic service. Yet Calvino's work gives a consoling impression, of delectable self-entertainment in a world of deferred disaster. Whereas Morand's prose texture prickles with a thousand little tenacious claws of extra precision, of "reaching," Calvino's (as rendered in William Weaver's transparent translation) is smooth, even where its message is anarchic and subversive. One feels that personal outrage and bewilderment have been sublimated, that an insulating interface with the world has been developed. Calvino's experiments, though copious and tireless, lack the sense of emergency that Morand's nervous glimpses of café life convey. They are not, to use a term that has cropped up several times already, hysterical.

A certain light on the modernist-postmodernist problem was slantingly cast by the recent small squabble over the new frames in the renovated Museum of Modern Art's rehanging of its collection. The early "modern" paintings, from Cézanne to the Fauves, were shifted from their traditional bulky and ornate sculptured frames to thin flat gilded frames marked to ape bamboo. The Museum, according to *The New York Times*, says the new framing saves space and reduces visual clutter. Mark Davis, a professional framer, observed of the new framing, "I think it's silly, antiseptic, and somewhat hysterical. . . . The reductive idea is a tenet of hard-core Modernism, and we're not so concerned with orthodox Modernism today. Now that we've arrived at post-Modernism, things are much looser, more eclectic. Tastes have broadened, a lot more is acceptable." There are a number of adjectives that invite comment here, but "hysterical" is the striking one. Was modernism hysterical? In the dictionary sense of "emotional excitability" I suppose it was; and if you had inherited a century's worth of Victorian furniture, of overstuffed thrones and rococo priedieux, of peacock feathers and elephant's-foot umbrella stands, of ornate plaster picture frames and leatherbound uniform sets, of busts of Napoleon and Victor Hugo and Alfred, Lord Tennyson, of morals and rhymes and armor-plated pieties, you might be hysterical, too. The clutter of that compulsively accumulating nineteenth century goaded the modernists to great efforts of rejection and made them see reality, however bleak, as an invitingly open attic window. Webster's dictionary, helpful as always, defines "modernism" as "the philosophy and practices of modern art; *esp.:* a self-conscious break with the past and a search for new forms of expression." A requisite of modernism was disenchantment with past masters— Proust wrote "*contre* Sainte-Beuve," Pound trashed the Edwardians, etc. The good postmodernist, on the other hand, enjoys a respectful educated acquaintanceship with the moderns; indeed, he often makes his living by teaching them to students. As John Barth puts it, "He has the first half of our century under his belt, but not on his back." The moderns digested, the postmodernist looks relatively plump. He can go nimbly through motions that cost the moderns some agony. Instead of cleaning out an attic, he lives in one, among the smiling busts of Proust and Joyce, Kafka and Rilke and Pound. The window, for the time being, is closed.

States of Mind

MR. PALOMAR, by Italo Calvino, translated from the Italian by William Weaver. 130 pp. Harcourt Brace Jovanovich, 1985.

Italo Calvino, who began to write forty years ago in the shade of Italian neorealism, became in his fiction increasingly cerebral and schematic. But even in his early short stories, even in the grim little war anecdotes based on his youthful experiences as a Partisan in the Ligurian mountains, there was something fanciful and ideal, an underlying formalism. His new novel, *Mr. Palomar,* consists of twenty-seven small chapters, each describing observations by its hero, who is named after an observatory. Twenty-seven is three to the third power, and an afterword attached to an index of the chapters demonstrates that the possibilities for symmetry and modulation were lovingly weighed by the author:

> The numbers 1, 2, 3 that mark the titles of the index, whether they are in the first, second, or third position, besides having a purely ordinal value, correspond also to three thematic areas, three kinds of experience and inquiry that, in varying proportions, are present in every part of the book.
>
> Those marked "1" generally correspond to a visual experience, whose object is almost always some natural form; the text tends to the descriptive.
>
> Those marked "2" contain elements that are anthropological, or cultural in the broad sense; and the experience involves, besides visual data, also language, meaning, symbols. The text tends to take the form of a story.
>
> Those marked "3" involve more speculative experience, concerning the cosmos, time, infinity, the relationship between the self and the world, the dimensions of the mind. From description and narrative we move into meditation.

Such a grid rivals Joyce's intertwining schemata for *Ulysses,* which assigned each chapter not only a corresponding episode of *The Odyssey* but a particular color, an organ of the human body, an hour of the day, a dominant symbol, and a human science or art, and which furthermore carried forward this huge apparatus of multiple significance through a Thomistic system of contraries and coincidences, products and antidotes, not to mention parallels with various of Giambattista Vico's ages of mankind and a presiding metaphysics of space and time.

Joyce's encyclopedic and abstractifying ambitions were incongruously but fruitfully wedded to his love of life's small talk and petty grit, and to the passionate autobiography that his elaborate designs hold. Where the autobiographical, factual impulse is less powerful, schematization runs the risk of seeming playful and automatic; and Calvino did not always dodge this gentle danger. *Invisible Cities* (1974), amid all its airy machinery, was infused with his lively civic concern and cosmopolitan reach of imagination, but *The Castle of Crossed Destinies* (1977) seemed at times to be merely playing cards, to be filling in the scheme's blank spaces, and in *If on a winter's night a traveler* (1981) the overlays of cleverness and the charm of the literary parodies left an afterimage that melted in the mind like a Platonic pastille. *Mr. Palomar,* though short, is a more substantial and integrated book than these last two; it undertakes a description of existential man rather than literary man, and deals with issues of perception rather than of reading and narration.

Mr. Palomar—a man, we learn, of middle age and no definite occupation, with a wife and an apartment both in Rome and in Paris—sets himself to look at things, and focuses until he arrives at a conclusion, however small. "A nervous man who lives in a frenzied and congested world, Mr. Palomar tends to reduce his relations with the outside world; and, to defend himself against the general neurasthenia, he tries to keep his sensations under control insofar as possible." Chapter 1.1.1, for instance—the most intense dose, as we can gauge at a glance, of the visual, descriptive mode—finds our hero on the beach, viewing the waves with a determined precision:

> Mr. Palomar now tries to limit his field of observation; if he bears in mind a square zone of, say, ten meters of shore by ten meters of sea, he can carry out an inventory of all the wave movements that are repeated with varying frequency within a given time interval. The hard thing is to fix the boundaries of this zone, because if, for example, he considers as the side farthest from him the outstanding line of an advancing wave, as this line approaches him and rises it hides from his eyes everything behind it, and thus the space under examination is overturned and at the same time crushed.

He tries to use the waves as an instrument wherewith "to perceive the true substance of the world beyond sensory and mental habits," feels "a slight dizziness" instead, and goes off along the beach "tense and nervous as when he came, and even more unsure about everything."

With 1.1.2, we enter the anthropological mode: Mr. Palomar attempts to cope visually and socially with the sight of a naked bosom, "the bronze-pink cloud of a naked female torso," on this same beach. To stare is wrong, yet not to stare is also wrong; his reactions to this provocative sight swing from an "indiscreet and reactionary" looking away that reinforces "the convention that declares illicit any sight of the breast" to a liberal attempt to convey "detached encouragement" with a gaze that, "giving the landscape a fickle glance, will linger on the breast with special consideration, but will quickly include it in an impulse of good will and gratitude for the whole, for the sun and the sky, for the bent pines and the dune and the beach and the rocks and the clouds and the seaweed, for the cosmos that rotates around those haloed cusps." Thus he will signal that, "though he belongs to a human generation for whom nudity of the female bosom was associated with the idea of amorous intimacy, still he hails approvingly this change in customs." But in walking back and forth trying to achieve just the right political adjustment in his gaze he finally succeeds in driving the possessor of the bosom off in an angry huff. It is all funny, familiar, and sociologically thoughtful. The next chapter, 1.1.3, takes us into cosmic and philosophical considerations as Palomar swims toward the swordlike reflection of the sun on the sea and ponders the dependence of this blazing phenomenon upon his own witnessing of it. Persuaded that "the sword will exist even without him," he "dries himself with a soft towel and goes home."

Such a cycle of three is repeated three times three times; we see Mr. Palomar on the beach, in the garden, and stargazing; on the terrace, shopping, and at the zoo; travelling, in society, and meditating. He ponders the lovemaking of tortoises, the composition of lawns, the moon in daytime, Rome's plague of pigeons, Paris's plethora of cheeses, an albino gorilla, a Zen sand garden, a Mexican ruin, and why we get so angry at the young. When the book heads into its last third and the 3's pile up, the topics get increasingly heady: "The model of models," "The universe as mirror," "Learning to be dead." We learn, in the bargain, a bit more about Mr. Palomar: He does not love himself, we are told, and therefore "has always taken care not to encounter himself face to face." He thinks of death as benign insofar as it will eliminate "that patch of uneasiness that is our presence." The middle section, under the anthropological sign of 2 and the general head of "Mr. Palomar in the City," reads the easiest, and has a distinctly creaturely emphasis, from the colorful evocation of a butcher's shop—"Vast ribs blaze up, round tournedos whose thickness is lined by a ribbon of lard, slender and agile contre-filets, steaks armed with their invincible bone. . . . Farther on some white tripe glows, a liver glistens blackly"—to the close scrutiny of a gecko, lit transparently from underneath, as it swallows a large, live butterfly: "Will it all fit? Will he spit it out? Will he explode? No, the butterfly is there in his throat: it flutters, in a sorry state but still itself, not touched by the insult of chewing teeth; now it passes the narrow limits of the neck; it is a shadow that begins its slow and troubled journey down along a swollen esophagus."

Witty observation and artful phrasing are the rule in Calvino's subtly arranged sets and subsets of vignettes; some add up better than others, but none falls below a certain high level of intelligence and attentiveness. The world, as it were, is inventoried afresh, by this most generally (and genially) alert of postwar writers. Yet a melancholy, defeated tone seeps through the polish. The albino gorilla is pictured as discovering in an old rubber tire "a glimpse of what for man is the search for an escape from the dismay of living—investing oneself in things, recognizing oneself in signs, transforming the world into a collection of symbols. . . . We all turn in our hands an old, empty tire through which we try to reach some final meaning, which words cannot achieve." This collection of animated essays tricked out as a novel has a certain upper limit, too; Mr. Palomar's world offers itself as food for thought too meekly, without fighting back. As in Robert Benchley's old humorous pieces, the bemused hero can meet no worse fate than embarrassment—looking momentarily like a fool. It would be as if Mr. Sammler, in Saul Bellow's novel, were allowed to wander through New York thinking his thoughts and never having to cope with the menacing black pickpocket, the outrageous college radical, the distressingly sexy great-niece, the lethal Israeli son-in-law. Even in Paul Valéry's *Monsieur Teste,* a book *Mr. Palomar* considerably resembles, there is more sense of activity and contention; Monsieur Teste has had to hack out his clearing for pure intellection with a heroic, ascetic effort, and in the assembled texts he is seen from the outside, by an admiring friend and a loving wife. "He is tall and dreadful suddenly. The machine of his monotonous acts explodes; his face sparkles; he says things that often I only half understand, but they never fade from my memory. . . . It took all the energy of a great body to sustain in the mind that diamond instant which is at once the idea and the Thing, both the entrance and the end." Thus Madame Teste sees her amazing husband, whose name puns not only on the Old French *teste* for "head" but the Latin *testis,* meaning "testicle" as well as "witness." What Signora and Signorina Palomar make of their woolgathering protector is not disclosed.

Well, Calvino might have argued, the 1980s, when he wrote *Mr. Palomar,* are not the 1890s, when Valéry created Monsieur Teste, "the very demon of possibility." The demon of impossibility has replaced that of possibility. We live now in "the era of great numbers," when humanity "extends in a crowd, leveled but still made up of distinct individualities like the sea of grains of sand that submerges the surface of the world." If one such individuality chooses to pose on the sand and contemplate the waves, little will come of it for good or ill; in society, Mr. Palomar holds his tongue, and in solitude "no longer knows where his self is to be found." Can this diminished person be a portrait of today's Western European intellectual? Backed off from any doctrinal certainty, concerned with words and signs since things are now properly abandoned to science, mellowed by forty years of affluence and peace, his "patch of uneasiness" affably entertains the "dismay of living."

In this book's last chapter, the hero contemplates his own death: "The world can very well do without him, and he can consider himself dead quite serenely, without even altering his habits." The sadness of this modest reflection is deepened by Calvino's own death this month, of a stroke, at the age of only sixty-one. Presumably, he had many books still to write and honors still to reap; he had become, with the death (also premature) of Roland Barthes, Europe's leading litterateur. Thoroughly "up" on all the latest devices of thought and style, Calvino could neverthe-less immerse himself for years in Italian folktales; for all his love of compli-cation, his work had a timeless lucidity, a unique unclouded climate, like that of a fall afternoon whose coolness is the small price we must pay for its being so sunny and clear.

Final Fragments

SIX MEMOS FOR THE NEXT MILLENNIUM, by Italo Calvino, translated from the Italian by Patrick Creagh. 124 pp. Harvard University Press, 1988.

UNDER THE JAGUAR SUN, by Italo Calvino, translated from the Italian by Wil-liam Weaver. 86 pp. Harcourt Brace Jovanovich, 1988.

The sudden death of Italo Calvino in 1985 left a number of his ingenious schemata uncompleted. His intended 1985–86 Norton Lectures at Har-vard fall one short of the proposed *Six Memos for the Next Millennium*. The five literary values he did discuss, as exemplified in his own work and that of others, were "Lightness," "Quickness," "Exactitude," "Visibility," and "Multiplicity"; "Consistency" is the ghost of the sequence, the unfor-mulated final virtue. The lectures are marvels of charm, mental adroitness, and casual erudition, drawing upon literary instances in five languages and citing with special affection Italian masters such as Cavalcanti, Boccaccio, Leopardi, and Carlo Emilio Gadda, not to mention Dante. Calvino, the most civilized of postmodern creative spirits, saw his own working method as "the subtraction of weight" and spoke refreshingly of the stimulus exerted upon his imagination by science, comic strips, and folk-tales, along with modernist writers like Valéry, Musil, Queneau, and Jarry. Calvino read everything, and in his dazzling designs—nothing less than tours de force interested him—made the play of the mind sensuous.

Under the Jaguar Sun titles another unfulfilled scheme—an intention, from as long ago as 1972, to write a short story for each of the five senses. The three stories he finished, though each is brilliant, are quite dissimilar in texture and approach. "A King Listens" dramatizes hearing through the interior monologue of a timeless, isolated, rather Beckettian monarch. "The Name, the Nose" relates the olfactory sense to eros and death through three interwoven narratives, those of a nineteenth-century Pari-sian dandy, a Seventies rock musician in London, and a nameless human animal reminiscent of the generic creatures in *Cosmicomics*. "Under the

Jaguar Sun" deals with taste as a matter of Mexican cuisine—from *chiles en nogada* to ritual Aztec meals of human flesh—as it figures in the relationship of a middle-aged tourist couple; this story, the most realistic of the three, is a delicious fabrication.

Slogging Sammy

Worstward Ho, by Samuel Beckett. 47 pp. Grove Press, 1983.

These forty-seven small pages of very large type extend Beckett's wrestle with the void to the point where less would be nothing. A personless voice, uttering words of mostly one syllable in sentences of rarely more than five words, urges itself onward in a dim but resistant realm where humanoid apparitions fragmentarily loom and then fade. "So leastward on. So long as dim still. Dim undimmed. Or dimmed to dimmer still. To dimmost dim. Leastmost in dimmost dim. Utmost dim. Leastmost in utmost dim. Unworsenable worst." The dim shapes in this environment most minimal are called shades, and we probably would not be entirely wrong to think of it as an old-fashioned Hades that ends in new-style entropy ("Vasts apart. At bounds of boundless void. Whence no farther"). A sterile, dreadful exercise, it might be said, and one does not, as Dr. Johnson remarked of *Paradise Lost,* wish it longer than it is. And yet, the words—"How almost true they sometimes almost ring! How wanting in inanity!"

Still Stirring

Stirrings Still, by Samuel Beckett, illustrated by Louis le Brocquy. 25 pp. Blue Moon Books/John Calder, 1989.

Is Beckett selling out? The price of this latest of his minuscule later works—$1,700—suggests that he's angling for the big bucks, but its less than two thousand words of baleful text should repel any considerable excess over the two hundred purchasers that this joint British-American limited edition can provide for. One more of those nameless heroes sits around in a characteristically underfurnished universe and manages to make a move or two while longing for the end. The lulling bare-bones prose almost begs to be set to music: "Such and much more such the hubbub in his mind so-called till nothing left from deep within but only ever fainter oh to end. No matter how no matter where. Time and grief and self so-called. Oh all to end." There is an ashen beauty here, and a heroic willingness to dwell upon the guttering spiritual condition of human life amid our century's material blaze. More expansive than *Lessness,* less boisterous than *Worstward Ho,* and more easily followed than the segments of *Fizzles, Stirrings Still* will not disappoint hard-core acedia fans. It contains two proper names (Darley, Walther), nine inky lithographs by Louis le Brocquy, and not a single comma. If time is money, and shelf-space precious, this volume is the bargain of the year.

Still Staring

STARING AT THE SUN, by Julian Barnes. 197 pp. Knopf, 1987.

The tricky author of *Flaubert's Parrot* here takes as his subject the rather uneventful but long (ninety-nine years and still counting) life of an Englishwoman, Jean Serjeant. The men in her life—her prankish uncle, her boring husband, her timorous son, and an RAF pilot who boarded with her parents during World War II—are a rather cryptic lot who set her to musing over such marginal items as model airplanes, minks' will to live, and the five sandwiches Lindbergh took with him when he flew across the Atlantic (he only ate one and a half). Late in life, she flies to China and the Grand Canyon and is impressed by both. This wispy heroine is meant to be an instrument whereby the great existential questions are examined: life, which an epigraph from Chekhov likens to a carrot, and death, which the book's prevailing metaphor likens to the sun. As a manipulator of motifs, Mr. Barnes is assiduous and brilliant; recurring images weave a wonderful basketwork of implied meaning. But his heroine remains a cipher, and the basket more than half empty.

Writer-Consciousness

THE STORYTELLER, by Mario Vargas Llosa, translated from the Spanish by Helen Lane. 247 pp. Farrar, Straus & Giroux, 1989.

THE AFTERNOON OF A WRITER, by Peter Handke, translated from the German by Ralph Manheim. 87 pp. Farrar, Straus & Giroux, 1989.

THE WRITING LIFE, by Annie Dillard. 111 pp. Harper & Row, 1989.

Harold Ross, the founding editor of *The New Yorker*, was wary of "writer-consciousness," and would mark phrases and sentences wherein, to his sensibility, the writer, like some ugly giant squid concealed beneath the glassy impersonality of the prose, was threatening to surface. Writing, that is, like our grosser animal functions, could not be entirely suppressed but shouldn't be performed in the open. Yet fashions in aesthetic decorum change. Modernism, by the spectacular nature of its experiments, invited admiring or irritated awareness of the experimenting author. Intentionally or not, the written works of James Joyce and T. S. Eliot and Virginia Woolf and Gertrude Stein and Ernest Hemingway all were exercises in personality, each provoking curiosity about the person behind the so distinctive voice. Postmodernism, if such a thing exists, without embarrassment weaves the writer into the words and the twists of the tale. Philip Roth's *The Ghost Writer* and its brothers in invented autobiography, the mirrors and false bottoms of Vladimir Nabokov's *Pale Fire* and *The Gift*, John Barth's self-proposed and exhaustively fulfilled regimens of tale-telling—all place the writer right up front.

Mario Vargas Llosa, Peru's foremost novelist as well as the leading candidate for that country's Presidency, has never been averse to writer-consciousness; his early, extensive romp, *Aunt Julia and the Scriptwriter* (1977, English translation 1982), pursued its action through a series of parodic soap-opera plots somehow sprouting from the head of a character, the indefatigable scriptwriter Pedro Camacho, and the novel is framed by the relaxed voice of a young man whose literary ambitions, excursions to Europe, and pleasant success match with a breezy closeness those of Mario Vargas Llosa. More recently, *The Real Life of Alejandro Mayta* (1984, translation 1986) showed the first-person narrator piecing together, chapter by chapter, supposition by supposition, the life of a pudgy schoolmate who had turned into a violent leftist revolutionary. Now *The Storyteller* tells the tale of another schoolmate,* Saúl Zuratas, who went off to become a storyteller among the Machiguenga Indians, in the jungles of the upper Amazon. As in *Aunt Julia,* a tale-teller's voice alternates with the author's voice; as in *Alejandro Mayta,* a narrative relativity is invoked, and the imaginative act of speculation takes the place of unquestionable assertion. It *is* asserted that Saúl Zuratas is Jewish and has "a dark birth-mark, the color of wine dregs, that covered the entire right side of his face." He is nicknamed Mascarita—Mask Face. "The birthmark spared neither his ears nor his lips nor his nose, also puffy and misshapen from swollen veins. He was the ugliest lad in the world; but he was also a likable and exceptionally good person." We see him, through the nameless narra-tor's eyes, as a university student who becomes increasingly fascinated by the Indian cultures surviving on the Amazonian side of the Andes; later, at a greater distance, we hear of him, through an American missionary couple, the Schneils, as a nearly naked storyteller wandering among the small, widely separated units of the Machiguenga tribe.

The narrative's levels are multiple. In its foreground, the narrator, a writer in no way distinguished from the author, relates how he was diverted into his subject matter from an intended period of study and repose in Florence: "I came to Firenze to forget Peru and the Peruvians for a while, and suddenly my unfortunate country forced itself upon me this morning in the most unexpected way." An exhibit of photographs of the Peruvian jungle, taken by an Italian photographer, has been mounted near "Dante's restored house . . . and the lane where, so legend has it, he first saw Beatrice"; these photographs of "the wide rivers, the enormous trees, the fragile canoes, the frail huts raised up on pilings, and the knots of men and women, naked to the waist and daubed with paint," distract the writer from his plan "to read Dante and Machiavelli and look at Renaissance paintings for a couple of months in absolute solitude." The writer has frequently before, we are told, attempted to imagine and tell the curious story of Mascarita. So the composition of what we are reading presents itself as a feat, the fruit of a struggle. Two large literary spirits are conjured up to aid the telling: Dante, the singer of an otherworldly geography even more exotic than that of trans-Andean Peru, and Kafka, whose tale "The Metamorphosis," about a man turned into a giant insect, is the one classic cherished by Saúl Zuratas in his own helpless monstros-ity. Saúl's first name holds another literary reference: to the exemplary

---

*This habit of tracing the later career of schoolmates—could it relate to the opening of Vargas Llosa's favorite novel, *Madame Bovary,* in which the ill-fated Charles Bovary ap-pears as a shy "new boy"?

convert, whose namesake is similarly stricken—"I can say that Saúl experienced a conversion. . . . From his first contact with the Amazon jungle, Mascarita was caught in a spiritual trap that made a different person of him."

Vargas Llosa is a diligent researcher. Anthropology pervades *The Storyteller,* and since the Machiguengas are an actual tribe and the acknowledgments credit a number of scholarly and exploratory institutions, we can take the mythology and lore to be authentic. The Machiguengas call themselves "the men who walk": their survival tactics in the face of competing tribes and the incursions of the white men (called Viracochas) comprise constant migratory motion from one temporary settlement after another, in family groups of as few as ten. Amid a situation of potential total fragmentation, the wandering storyteller serves as a news bearer and oral historian, as "the memory of the community, fulfilling a function similar to that of the jongleurs and troubadours of the Middle Ages." "Storyteller" isn't quite exact: the Machiguenga word—"a long, loud guttural sound full of *s*'s"—more literally translates as *hablador,* or "speaker." The narrator of the novel, our modern Peruvian novelist enjoying his Florentine respite, is stirred to think that "storytelling can be something more than mere entertainment." He is, he confides,

> deeply moved by the thought of that being, those beings, in the unhealthy forests of eastern Cusco and Madre de Dios, making long journeys of days or weeks, bringing stories from one group of Machiguengas to another and taking away others, reminding each member of the tribe that the others were alive, that despite the great distances that separated them, they still formed a community, shared a tradition and beliefs, ancestors, misfortunes and joys.

The *habladores* are "the living sap that circulated and made the Machiguengas into a society."

The anthropology is more vivacious than the fiction, more plausible than the novel's premise that a white man could insert himself into a primitive tribe and take on the caretaking of its arcane cultural essence. But it cannot be said that the novelist dodges the difficulties; not only does Vargas Llosa, courtesy of the Summer Institute of Linguistics (real) and the American missionaries the Schneils (fictional), give us a thorough tour of the Machiguenga world as it survives in the state of Peru, but he takes upon himself, in the novel's tour de force, the voice of Saúl Zuratas as a Machiguenga storyteller. He mimics the concision and the hellish slipperiness of American Indian tales, as recorded and compiled by generations of anthropologists. Nothing quite makes sense or is purely nonsense. The Machiguenga genesis legends have a grandeur and pathos not unfamiliar to those of us raised with the Bible:

After, the men of earth started walking, straight toward the sun that was falling. . . . There was no evil, there was no wind, there was no rain. The women bore pure children. If Tasurinchi wanted to eat, he dipped his hand into the river and brought out a shad flicking its tail. . . . Those who went came back, and entered the spirit of the best. That way, nobody used to die. . . . After, the earth was filled with Viracochas tracking down men. They carried them off to bleed trees and tote rubber. . . . "It's no use trying to escape from the camps," said Tasurinchi. "The Viracochas have their magic. Something is happening to us. We must have done something. The spirits protect them, and us they abandon. We are guilty of something."

As retold by Saúl Zuratas as imagined by Vargas Llosa, the myths are gradually, cleverly infused with novelistic elements. Saúl's pathetic personal history begins to intrude, a process abetted by the pliable way that Tasurinchi, the god of good, takes, Vishnu-like, many forms, and bewilderingly becomes the hero of almost any tale that is told:

Alas, poor Tasurinchi! I'd changed into an insect, that's what. A buzz-buzz bug, perhaps. A Gregor-Tasurinchi . . . I've asked the seripigari [wise man] many times: "What does it mean, having a face like mine?" . . . Why did Tasurinchi breathe me out this way? Shh, shh, don't get angry. . . . Before, this stain used to matter a lot to me. I didn't say so. Only to myself, to my souls. I kept it to myself, and this secret was eating me alive. . . . We'd best be what we are. The one who gives up fulfilling his own obligation so as to fulfill that of another will lose his soul. And his outer wrapping too, perhaps, like Gregor-Tasurinchi, who was changed into a buzz-buzz bug in that bad trance.

Transformation is the novel's theme, as metamorphosis is the engine of primitive legend. Saúl, born disfigured, is born transformed, and his self-conversion into a Machiguenga corrects the wrong and completes the cycle. A "talking parrot" in the Zuratas household in Lima during Saúl's school days is changed, in the jungle, into Saúl's totem—a pet and guardian who travels on his shoulder, who conjures up a canopy of friendly parrots, and whom Saúl calls Mascarita.

These mock-primitive chapters are the novel's dark and tangled heart, and they reward a second reading with greater, though not perfect, intelligibility. Enough, perhaps, has been quoted to indicate the fervor and vigor of Vargas Llosa's powers of invention, and also the strain he has placed upon them. The smell of ink doesn't quite leave this tale of tale-telling. Little seems to fall into place lightly. When the novelist is being himself and not Saúl being Tasurinchi, he can drop vivid casual details, like the "dark pouches hanging from the palm-leaf roof" that disappear at daybreak and turn out to be "balls of hundreds of spiders that curled up together," or like the interviewed Spanish writer of romances who stores "thousands of novelettes" in her basement and "finishes one every two days, each exactly a hundred pages long." This novel could do with a little romance. Saúl Zuratas and the narrator, like the heroes of boys' adventure books, have no sex lives. And the notion, insistently repeated, that Saúl's being Jewish makes it easier for him to identify and merge with the persecuted Machiguengas comes to seem too simple. Vargas Llosa, if he has a fault, tends to be programmatic; his prose presents a blunt, masculine texture rarely varied by a touch of the spontaneously sensual, the off-handedly immediate. *The Storyteller* is an animated anthropological, eco-logical, psychological meditation, admirably intelligent and humane, but not much, strange to say, of a story.

Peter Handke, in *The Afternoon of a Writer,* presents a texture that is almost alarmingly immediate. Handke can be hysterical—indeed, hysteria is his métier—but this brief tale of the after-work hours of one of those nameless writers (he walks into town, out of town, has a drink or two, walks home, and goes to bed, alone) applies such an intense sensibility to the details that we seem to enter a supernatural dimension:

> It was early December and the edges of various objects glowed as they do at the onset of twilight. At the same time, the airy space outside and the interior of the curtainless house seemed joined in an undivided brightness. No snow had yet fallen that year. But that morning the birds had cheeped in a certain way—in a monotone suggestive of speech—that heralded snow.

> The snow settled first on the middle strip of grass; it looked as though birch branches had been laid on the road, one after another, and so on to the horizon. In a bramblebush, single crystals would balance on thorns and then encircle them like ruffs. Though there was no one to be seen, the writer had the impression at every step that he was walking in the traces of someone who had been there before.

And when the hero comes in his walk to a convex traffic mirror, and gazes into its bent reflections, we labor along with the translator to realize the precise evanescent shades of reported sensation: "The rounding of the image gave emptiness a radiance, and gave the objects in this emptiness— the glass-recycling center, the garbage cans, the bicycle stands—a holiday feel, as though in looking at them one emerged into a clearing."

Handke's hero is all eyes, all nerves. Being a writer gives his hypersen-sitivity a use, and also a professional alternation with insensibility. While he writes, he is all but oblivious to the outer world: "In his mind, it was only a moment ago that the midday bells of the chapel of the old people's home at the foot of the little hill had suddenly started tinkling as though someone had died, yet hours must have passed since then, for the light in the room was now an afternoon light. . . . At first he was unable to focus on anything in the distance and saw even the pattern of the carpet as a blur; in his ears he heard a buzzing as though his typewriter were an electric one—which was not the case." Preparing to leave the house, he returns to his study to make one last revision: "It was only then that he smelled the sweat in the room and saw the mist on the windowpanes."

In his few human contacts, too, he is able to turn off. A drunk in the bar addresses the writer at futile length:

> As he spoke, his face came so close as to lose its contours; only his violently twitching eyelids, the dotted bow tie under his chin, and a cut on his forehead that must have bled recently remained distinct. . . . Not a single word of what he was saying came through to the writer, not even when he held his ear close to the speaker's mouth. Yet, to judge by the movements of his lips and tongue, he was not speaking a foreign language.

The writer inwardly bemoans his deafness, his isolation, his "defeat as a social being." He asks himself, "Why was it only when alone that he was able to participate fully? Why was it only after people had gone that he was able to take them into himself, the more deeply the farther away they went?" Handke's writer suffers a Promethean, a Luciferian, isolation— that of the too greatly daring, the damned. "To write was criminal; to produce a work of art, a book, was presumption, more damnable than any other sin. Now, in the midst of the 'gin-mill people,' he had the same feeling of unpardonable guilt, the feeling that he had been banished from the world for all time." A translator of his (apparently an American), whom he meets in his day's one scheduled encounter, once wanted to be a writer but couldn't bear the onus: "My attempt to decipher a supposed Ur-text inside me and force it into a coherent whole struck me as original sin. That was the beginning of fear." Translation, while being sufficiently engaging, avoids the primordial fear: "By displaying your wound as attractively as possible, I conceal my own."

At his brief excursion's end, our wounded but resolute hero climbs into bed. Trying to recall the hours so vividly just passed, he can visualize only two small details, both of them distorted. Already, he is writing. He is an inscrutable stewing, a transmuter of world into word. "To himself he was a puzzle, a long-forgotten wonderment." To a cold-eyed reader, however, he is in danger of seeming a self-dramatizing solipsist. With a phenomenal intensity and delicacy of register, the little book captures the chemistry of perception and of perception's transformation into memory and language. We are *there* with the writer, behind his eyes and under his skin. But the cultural presumptions that make it worth our while to be there are perhaps more European than universal. These winter walks with reflective, misanthropic bachelors occur also in the brief contemporary novels of the Swede Lars Gustafsson and Handke's fellow Austrian the late Thomas Bernhard, and go back to Olympian strolls with Kant and Goethe and Nietzsche. To an American reader, so reverent an examination, by a writer, of a writer's psyche verges on the pompous and, worse, on the pointless.

The Afternoon of a Writer is dedicated to F. Scott Fitzgerald, who in 1936 published a short story called "Afternoon of an Author." Freshly available in Scribner's edition of *The Short Stories of F. Scott Fitzgerald,* the story offers a somber contrast with Handke's small, rapt novel. It has none of the Austrian's triumphant undercurrent; Fitzgerald's American scribe is in poor health and down on his luck. He wakes up after nine o'clock, gratefully observes that he does not feel distinctly ill ("better than he had for many weeks"), shuffles through "an annoying mail with nothing cheerful in it," chats desultorily with his maid, has to lie down for fifteen minutes, and then unsuccessfully tries to write: "The problem was a magazine story that had become so thin in the middle that it was about to blow away. The plot was like climbing endless stairs, he had no element of surprise in reserve, and the characters who started so bravely day-before-yesterday couldn't have qualified for a newspaper serial." He ends by going through the manuscript "underlining good phrases in red crayon," tucking these into a file, and dropping the rest into the wastebasket. The process, though dismal, seems more concrete than the creative processes in Handke's book, and there are phrases of mournful self-illumination, of a flickering romantic light. Looking into a mirror, the writer calls himself "slag of a dream." Out riding a bus, he comes into a district where "there were suddenly brightly dressed girls, all very beautiful . . . no plans or struggles in their faces, only a state of sweet suspension, provocative and serene." He observes within himself a sudden spark of life-force: "He loved life terribly for a minute, not wanting to give it up at all." A deflationary sentence immediately follows: "He thought perhaps he had made a mistake in coming out so soon."

After getting a shampoo at a barbershop, he rides the bus back to his apartment, reflecting on reviews he received when young, at "the beginning fifteen years ago when they said he had 'fatal facility' and he labored like a slave over every sentence so as not to be like that." He feels fatigue and the "growing seclusion" of his life; he thinks of himself as needing "reforestation" and hopes "the soil would stand one more growth." But, he further reflects, "It had never been the very best soil for he had had an early weakness for showing off instead of listening and observing." He makes it back home, chaffers bleakly with the maid, asks for a glass of milk, and lies down again: "He was quite tired—he would lie down for ten minutes and then see if he could get started on an idea in the two hours before dinner." The reader doubts whether he will get started; the atmosphere of creative exhaustion is thick. Death is not far off. Writer-consciousness, in Handke exhilarating and enviable, in Fitzgerald weighs like a disease, a gathering burden of guilt. We pity the fellow, while admiring the subtle slight strokes by which his plight is sketched. As so often in Fitzgerald, we have only the afterglow of a dream to see by. There is a strong sense of professional predicament and none of cultural mission; a weary clarity but no wonderment. The point is, we die.

A democracy of honest workmen, it may be, resists the idea that doing one kind of labor deserves more exaltation and excuses more self-indulgence than doing another kind. The shoemaker, for example, doesn't get moony and mock-heroic about pounding out his shapely, intricate product, and doesn't ask to be especially praised for sticking to his last. Yet shoes are more plainly useful than books. We all have chosen, in submission to the passions of childhood and accidents of adulthood, lasts to stick to, and the trade of writer is, with its unstructured hours, opportunities for self-expression, and possible rich rewards, sufficiently attractive so that there are far more applicants than positions available. The lucky few able to see their product into published, distributed, profitable form should be quiet about it, and exaggerate neither the hardships nor the glory of their achievement. Annie Dillard, the inimitable essayist and metaphysician, whose newest flirtation with the absolute is called *The Writing Life*, is able, in the course of her segmented, diverse disquisition upon her craft, to come up with an occasional modest shrug: "It should surprise no one that the life of the writer—such as it is—is colorless to the point of sensory deprivation." But more often she presents the writing life as a constant marvel of hazardous adventure and surging metaphor:

> When you write, you lay out a line of words. The line of words is a miner's pick, a woodcarver's gouge, a surgeon's probe. You wield it, and it digs a path you follow. Soon you find yourself deep in new territory. Is it a dead end, or have you located the real subject? You will know tomorrow, or this time next year.

The line of words fingers your own heart. It invades arteries, and enters the heart on a flood of breath; it presses the moving rims of thick valves; it palpates the dark muscle strong as horses, feeling for something, it knows not what.

Every morning you climb several flights of stairs, enter your study, open the French doors, and slide your desk and chair out into the middle of the air. . . . Your work is to keep cranking the flywheel that turns the gears that spin the belt in the engine of belief that keeps you and your desk in midair.

This is your life. You are a Seminole alligator wrestler. Half naked, with your two bare hands, you hold and fight a sentence's head while its tail tries to knock you over.

Some years ago in Florida, she goes on to tell us, an Indian alligator wrestler lost the struggle and his life. And her seventh and last chapter extols, as an implicit symbol of the writer's feat, the stunt flying of a pilot, Dave Rahm, who eventually crashed and died. Does writing, that most sheltered and stationary of occupations, whose principal hazards are alcoholism and eyestrain, warrant such flights of melodramatic mystique?

Dillard, in her determination to impress her reader, or an imaginary classroom of callow students, with the splendid difficulty of writing, introduces at the outset a couple of dogmas that struck me as not necessarily so. One: "It is the beginning of a work that the writer throws away. . . . The work's beginning greets the reader with the wrong hand." Two: "It takes years to write a book—between two and ten years. Less is so rare as to be statistically insignificant." Well, perhaps Simenon and P. G. Wodehouse and Trollope and Voltaire and Evelyn Waugh (who told *The Paris Review* that his early novels each represented "six weeks' work") and William Dean Howells and Agatha Christie are statistically insignificant, but they did produce books oftener than biennially, without, one suspects, throwing all the first chapters away. If these authors are not the most academically chic, and their books furthermore are often dismissably slim, consider how Stendhal composed *The Charterhouse of Parma* in seven weeks and Henry James belted out *The Ambassadors, The Wings of the Dove,* and *The Golden Bowl* at the rate of one a year. Not to mention Balzac and Dickens and that obliging hack Shakespeare, who never blotted a line. Styles and methods greatly vary; the kind of writing Dillard does—intense, poetic, inquisitive, philosophically ambitious—no doubt does proceed much as she describes, in the manner of an inchworm attaching its back feet to a grass stem and "in virtual hysteria" throwing its front end about in search of the next footing. As far as this reader is concerned, she *could* have thrown her first chapter here away, or at least lowered its pontifical tone.

When she describes herself writing, her dramatic and romantic propensities are usefully hitched to a personal narrative. She tells a good story on herself, as, for example, of the way she sometimes lays out her manuscript on a twenty-foot conference table: "You walk along the rows; you weed bits, move bits, and dig out bits, bent over the rows with full hands like a gardener. . . . You go home and soak your feet." Once, she solemnly avers, her typewriter (presumably electric, unlike Handke's writer's) erupted on her like a volcano. The time she spent on lonely insular terrain in Puget Sound working through the writing of her most nakedly religious book, *Holy the Firm,* is especially charged in her memory.

> The writing was simple yet graceless; it surprised me. It was arrhythmical, nonvisual, clunky. It was halting, as if there were no use trying to invoke beauty or power. It was plain and ugly, urgent, like child's talk. . . .
> Once when I opened my eyes the page seemed bright. The windows were steamed and the sun had gone behind the firs on the bluff. . . . By the time I left, I was scarcely alive. The way home was along the beach. The beach was bright and distinct. The storm still blew. I was light, dizzy, barely there. I remembered some legendary lamas, who wear chains to keep from floating away. . . . My thighs felt as if they had been reamed.

The reader cannot but be excited by her descriptions of nature and her way of examining its details as if they compose a script of the spirit. At her best, she writes like a giantess in love with infinity—a sister more of Melville than Thoreau, an Emersonian without a pinch of Yankee salt. Her writerly remarks are most illuminating when they are most incidental. She reveals in passing that to warm up her writing faculties she reads "pure sound unencumbered by sense"—Conrad Aiken's poetry, or "any poetry anthology's index of first lines." She relates how while writing her first book she let all the houseplants die—they "hung completely black dead in their pots in the bay window." A certain blackness and ruin also attend the finished result of inspiration: "The vision is not so much destroyed, exactly, as it is, by the time you have finished, forgotten. It has been replaced by this changeling, this bastard, this opaque lightless chunky ruinous work." She can be delightfully definite, in a regal manner reminiscent of Rebecca West:

> The novel often aims to fasten down the spirit of its time, to make a heightened simulacrum of our recognizable world in order to present it shaped and

analyzed. This has never seemed to me worth doing, but it is certainly one thing literature has always done. (Any writer draws idiosyncratic boundaries in the field.)

Surely we didn't need that anxious, academic parenthesis. A split exists in the personality of *The Writing Life.* On the one hand, the life, *her* life, is exhilaratingly scrutinized like any other natural phenomenon, as potent and numinous as the tides or insect behavior; on the other, weaker hand, a certain instructive, exhortatory tone seems to want to enlist us in a quixotic but good cause.

Good for what? Both Handke and Dillard present the writer as an eremitic, obsessed creature, whose saintly creative efforts barely brush the crude question of utility, of audience, of communication. Yet writing *is* communication, at least with oneself, in the faith that others are like-minded enough to get interested. Dillard says rightly, "In my view, the more literary the book—the more purely verbal, crafted sentence by sentence, the more imaginative, reasoned, and deep—the more likely people are to read it. The people who read are the people who like literature, after all, whatever that might be. They like, or require, what books alone have." But this class, never a majority, dwindles of late, and both these youngish writers describe encounters with readers or potential readers as comedies of incomprehension. Dillard suspects there is something wrong: "I was too far removed from the world. My work was too obscure, too symbolic, too intellectual. It was not available to the people. Recently I had published a complex narrative essay about a moth's flying into a candle, which no one had understood but a Yale critic." Handke's hero, in the course of his stroll, cringes from the passersby who recognize him as a literary celebrity, and reflects that, whenever an interview was published, he "would be seized with terror or shame—he would even feel guilty, as if he had broken a taboo." The mysteries the writer nurtures in his or her study are beyond explaining. Readership, a public, and public attention arrive as violations, embarrassments, beside the point. The writer's artifacts are like shoes that disdain actual feet.

Even Vargas Llosa's *hablador,* though he has an intent audience and an explicable social function, has obscurity problems, outside the small initiated circle. The anthropologist Edwin Schneil, privileged to audit two performances by a Machiguenga story-teller, had to fight against falling asleep in his boredom and bewilderment: "What a hodgepodge! A bit of everything, anything that came into his head . . . his travels, magic herbs, people he'd known; the gods, the little gods, and fabulous creatures of the tribe's pantheon. Animals he'd seen and celestial geography, a maze of rivers with names nobody could possibly remember." The rapture with which the Machiguengas hear the *hablador* and the interest with which we follow the sensitive revelations of our living authors require a cultural conditioning more extensive than we would like to think. The modern writer, perceiving that his reach is not wide, hopes that it is high. Priestly longings cling to writer-consciousness—pre–Vatican II priests, who kept their backs to the congregation while chanting in Latin. Perhaps what Harold Ross resisted was the imputation among writers that their shop talk is holy.

A Materialist Look at Eros

IN PRAISE OF THE STEPMOTHER, by Mario Vargas Llosa, translated from the Spanish by Helen Lane. 149 pp. Farrar, Straus & Giroux, 1990.

Literature owes a debt to the Peruvian electorate for their recently declining to elect Mario Vargas Llosa to the thankless position of being their President. So elegant, pessimistic, and Europeanized a literary performer's candidacy for this high office, amid the perils of terrorism and the sludge of daily speechifying, seems, at our distance, even more mysterious than Norman Mailer's campaign for the New York mayoralty or Gore Vidal's gracious offer, some years ago, to serve as a senator from California. Novelists presumably understand the workings of the world, and perhaps would govern no worse than lawyers, movie stars, or retired oilmen, but why anyone with an opportunity to create imperishable texts would want to exhaust his body and fry his brain in the daily sizzle of power brokerage lies quite beyond my own imagining. At any rate, the good people of Peru, with the masses' customarily sound instinct, turned from the novelist, once the odds-on favorite, to a Japanese-Peruvian agronomical engineer, thereby releasing Vargas Llosa to the contemplative solitude and part-time irresponsibility necessary for artistic creation. He has been prolific, producing plays and criticism as well as novels. While he was hiking the mountainous campaign trail, a naughty butterfly of a book by him was flitting from couch to couch in the lamplit dens of Spanish-language readers. Now this book, billed on the jacket as "a classic of eroticism," has been been published in English, as *In Praise of the Stepmother.* It is, in our erotically retrenched nation, a startling document: not only would an American Presidential candidate not have written it, but the National Endowment for the Arts wouldn't have given it a grant.

The stepmother is named Doña Lucrecia, and she lives in Lima and has just turned forty. Four months before her birthday, she married a widower, Don Rigoberto—a step taken with some trepidation, since "her first marriage had been a disaster and the divorce a nightmarish torment at the hands of money-grubbing shysters." Don Rigoberto is the prosperous general manager of an insurance company, collects erotic art, and has one small son, Alfonso, by his previous marriage. The ages of the two males are never given, but Rigoberto seems at least fifty, or a lusty fifty-five, and his son, insistently described as a "little boy," ten or so. Perhaps eleven or twelve, considering the sexual feats he comes to perform—but there is an artistic fudging here, tiptoeing as the writer is on the edge of the repulsively perverse. A comely black maid, Justiniana, rounds out the household, and devotees of erotica will perceive that this cast of characters allows for enough combinations to be satisfactory. Vargas Llosa, whose male-dominated fiction rarely possesses the aura of sensual saturation present in Gabriel García Márquez or Saul Bellow, has announced, in interviews, a liking for frank eroticism in fiction. In his superb homage to *Madame Bovary* and Flaubert, *The Perpetual Orgy*—an extended critical work which also serves Vargas Llosa as a self-description—he states, "If I am left to choose between unrealities, the one closer to the concrete has my preference over the one that is abstract: I prefer pornography, for example, to science fiction, and sentimental stories to horror tales." One of the traits he loves in Emma Bovary and in her novel is concreteness, an unashamed materialism, "something that she and I share intimately: our incurable materialism, our greater predilection for the pleasures of the body than for those of the soul, our respect for the senses and instinct, our preference for this earthly life over any other." He goes on:

> The ambitions that lead Emma to sin and death are precisely those that Western religion and morality have most savagely combated throughout history. Emma wants sexual pleasure, she is not resigned to repressing this profound sensual need that Charles is unable to satisfy because he doesn't even know that it exists; she wants to surround her life with pleasing and superfluous things, elegance, refinement, to give concrete form by way of objects to that appetite for beauty that her imagination, her sensibility, and her reading have aroused in her.

One wonders whether Flaubert would have ascribed to his heroine quite such nobility of rebellion; but the passion of his disciple rings out with clarion effect, calling us all to realism, atheism, sensuality, and consumerism. Later in *The Perpetual Orgy*, however, Emma's confusion of love and expenditure, which brings her down, is described in phrases that, though still enthusiastic, suggest a process gone awry:

When Emma is in love, she needs to surround herself with beautiful objects, to embellish the physical world, to create a setting for itself as lavish as her sentiments. She is a woman whose enjoyment is not complete unless it takes on material form: she projects her body's pleasure into things, and things in their turn augment and prolong her body's pleasure.

The reification of passion begins to feel like a mistake; so, too, *In Praise of the Stepmother*, exploring its sexual theme to rigorous, materialist extremes, brings the reader up against the possible limits of his or her own commitment to sensuality.

Don Rigoberto, in his systematic religion of bodily love, flirts with grotesquerie. He has large ears, and his weekly cycle of ritual ablutions includes, on Wednesdays, laboriously cleansing them of wax and stray hairs. Then he utilizes these perfected organs as instruments of bliss:

> "Let me hear your breasts," he would murmur, and amorously plugging his wife's nipples, first one and then the other, into the hypersensitive cavern of his two ears—which they fit into as snugly as a foot into a moccasin—he would listen to them with his eyes closed, reverent and ecstatic, his mind worshipfully concentrated as at the Elevation of the Host, till he heard ascending to the earthy roughness of each button, from subterranean carnal depths, certain stifled cadences, the heavy breathing, perhaps, of her pores opening, the boiling, perhaps, of her excited blood.

Anticipating further adventures in aural sex, he imagines his ears "avidly flattened against her soft stomach" and "could already hear the lively burbling of that flatus, the joyous cracking of a fart, the gargle and yawn of her vagina, or the languid stretching of her serpentine intestine." He anticipates, even, his marble tomb being engraved with the epitaph "Here lies Don Rigoberto, who contrived to love the epigastrium of his spouse as much as her vulva or her tongue." Behind this Rabelaisian comedy of organs a serious question is raised: What is love if it stops short at the beloved's digestive tract? Don Rigoberto's methodical and fanatical achievement is "to fall in love with the whole and with each one of the parts of his wife, to love, separately and together, all the components of that cellular universe." It is an achievement at which most mortals consciously or unconsciously balk, yet one which a thorough passion, in its fever of cherishing, seems to command. Vargas Llosa's materialism defies us to set bounds to love's rampage of possession, of sensory consumption. Ideal love is an omnivorous monster.

The chapters of narrative development in *In Praise of the Stepmother* alternate with chapters of pictorial meditation, each incorporating a rather dinky color reproduction of a painting. The author is fond of such layered fictions, which alternate a detached narrative voice with slices of another substance—radio soap operas *(Aunt Julia and the Scriptwriter)*, the hero's consciousness *(The Real Life of Alejandro Mayta)*, Amazonian Indian recitations *(The Storyteller)*. The added liveliness and the doubled perspective are obtained at the price of author-consciousness, a stilting awareness of deliberate experimentation. Here, the tale itself being fanciful and parodic, the art essays almost seamlessly blend into the gauze of artifice. The chapters on paintings of nudes by Jordaens, Boucher, and Titian seem a bit arch and mannered, but the one on a partially pink abstraction by Fernando de Szyszlo becomes a real poem on sexual merging, and the one on a bizarre head by Francis Bacon reawakens the central theme of erotic monstrosity. Bacon's expressionistically distorted head is imagined as a full-bodied freak, with stumps instead of arms and legs, a slit of an ear, a hideous mouth, an eye next to his mouth. Yet his sex organ is intact, and he does not lack for lovers: "Women even come to love me, in fact, and youngsters become addicted to my ugliness. In the depths of her soul, Beauty was always fascinated by the Beast." He gives his lovers "advanced instruction in the fine art of combining desire and the horrible so as to give pleasure"; they learn "that everything is and can be erogenous and that, associated with love, the basest organic functions, including those of the lower abdomen, become spiritualized and ennobled." The concept of spiritualization is a surprising one, especially on the same page as the blithe sentence "It is possible that God exists, but at this point in history, with everything that has happened to us, does it matter?" It matters in that spirit/body dualism continues to give sex its spice, its sense of movement from one realm to another: sex is, our lovable monster tells us, a "descent into filth," whereby we recognize ourselves.

No two erotic works are quite alike; each author comes to reveal, in the repetition that soon sets in, his or her fetishes and hot spots. Vargas Llosa, through his psychosexual anatomy of the stepmother, puts forth the idea that voyeurism is exciting not only to the seer but to the seen. Knowing that her enraptured young stepson is viewing her from the bathroom skylight, Doña Lucrecia determinedly displays herself and assumes poses of "indecent abandon," as "a subtle way of punishing the precocious libertine crouched in the darkness up above, with images of an intimacy that would shatter, once and for all, that innocence that served him as an excuse for his boldness." Afterwards, in bed, she experiences "hot flashes that, from time to time, electrified her nipples" and dreams a painterly dream of Titian's Diana and her attendant, named Justiniana, making love in the forest while a little goatherd, called Foncín, watches. His silent witness is stimulating: "As I descend through the tunnel of sensation and quiver in delicious little spasms, I divine the presence of Foncín. . . . His innocent little body, glistening with sweat as he watches me and takes his pleasure by watching me, contributes a note of tenderness that subtly shades and sweetens mine."

The notion that being watched is aphrodisiac implies that sexuality has a social dimension: though closeted, we make love in a crowd—of predecessors, of simultaneous entanglements, of romantic images the culture has provided, of personified superegos. A lot of sex is "showing" others, and not just those who are present. Without a surrounding society to defy, adulterous passion often wilts, and a daring elopement sinks into the ranch-house funk of socially approved marriage. Sixties-style sexuality, with its hot tubs and bustling crash pads, was on to something; promiscuity, at least until it turns into a quasi-religious, obligatory form of exercise, suits our interior multiplicity. Our complex psyches generate complex structures of gratification. Doña Lucrecia, having committed adultery, feels certain that the new involvement, "however obscure and complicated, however difficult to explain, enriched her marital relation, taking it by surprise and thus giving it a fresh start." She has attained, in a happy word, "sovereignty":

> One morning, on opening her eyes, the phrase "I have won sovereignty" came to her. She felt fortunate and emancipated, but could not have said what it was that she had been freed from.

Of course, like Emma Bovary, she is punished for her overreaching, and so is her unsuspecting husband; our erotic fabulist is a realistic novelist as well, and he does not exclude, as does the true pornographer, the tragic dimension. Yet we feel that Doña Lucrecia, by succumbing to the perverse and the dangerous, is more human than her husband, with his ridiculous, fussy, bowel-loving personal "utopia" of the body. She sins her way to sovereignty; he merely topples from paradise.

In Praise of the Stepmother is, like the author's other books, somewhat nasty. And its dramatization of corrupting innocence is not quite convincing—wicked little Alfonsito doesn't have the undeniable, quirky, heartbreaking sociological reality of Lolita. Vargas Llosa's moral—emphasized by an epigraph, from César Moro's *Amour à mort*—seems to be that innocence and beauty intrinsically have something sinister about them. To become human we must make the descent into filth, into time. God Himself, Christianity claims, descended into Mary's womb. The last painting Vargas Llosa weaves into his text is Fra Angelico's *Annunciation;* he imagines the young Mary, confronted with a shimmering youth of an angel, asking herself, "Why did he call me queen? Why did I discover a gleam of tears in his eyes when he prophesied that I would suffer?" Love is a labyrinth we must enter even knowing it contains the Minotaur of destruction and loss. We leave much behind: "altruistic sentiments, metaphysics and history, neutral reasoning, good intentions and charitable deeds, solidarity with the species, civic idealism, sympathy toward one's fellow." It is a rare candidate for President who can put civic idealism in its place; rarer still one who could hearken, in so impish and delicate yet fiercely serious a fiction as this, to the rumbling epigastrium of love.

LANDSCAPES AND CHARACTERS

A Long Way Home

BLUE HIGHWAYS: *A Journey into America,* by William Least Heat Moon. 421 pp. Atlantic–Little, Brown, 1983.

Hurling oneself more or less blindly at the highways of America would not seem a very efficient method of producing a book; but a surprising number of people have tried it. In recent memory, there have been John Steinbeck's *Travels with Charley: In Search of America,* Erskine Caldwell's *Around About America,* Jonathan Raban's *Old Glory: An American Voyage,* and Richard Reeves's *American Journey.* To be sure, the author puts some spin on himself as he hurls; there has to be an angle. Mr. Reeves had the excellent idea, which he carried out with purposeful, prearranged interviews, of following in the nineteenth-century footsteps of the supreme American-travel impressionist, Alexis de Tocqueville. Mr. Raban, with that brave English willingness to act out childhood fantasies, went down the Mississippi in a boat because he had read *Huckleberry Finn* at the impressionable age of seven—much as Bruce Chatwin journeyed to Patagonia because of a bit of *Mylodon* skin in his grandmother's dining-room cabinet. Steinbeck and Caldwell, native men of letters mature in age and rich in distinction, went forth to investigate their national turf. Steinbeck, for twenty-five years marooned by success in New York City, had come to feel that, as he wrote, "I did not know my own country":

> I, an American writer, writing about America, was working from memory, and the memory is at best a faulty, warpy reservoir. I had not heard the speech of America, smelled the grass and trees and sewage, seen its hills and water, its color and quality of light. I knew the changes only from books and newspapers. But more than this, I had not felt the country for twenty-five years.

What he *had* been feeling, and smelling and hearing, in the terrain between his apartment in New York and his summer home in Sag Harbor is left undescribed. Steinbeck was a Westerner and his soul breathed best in the wide open; in *Travels with Charley* he extolled the North Dakota Badlands and wrote, "I am in love with Montana." He travelled, with a poodle called Charles le Chien, in a small truck called Rocinante and fitted up like "a little house," with facilities for sleeping and cooking. William Least Heat Moon, author of *Blue Highways: A Journey into America*, also used a truck rigged like a camper, and gave it a fanciful name—Ghost Dancing, in salute to the "desperate resurrection rituals" whereby the Plains Indians tried to bring back the bison and the old warrior life—not unlike Steinbeck's allusion to the quixotic. The resemblance does not go much further. Heat Moon (Least seems to be his middle name) is an unknown, a mixed-blood Sioux who, when he was thirty-eight years old, was propelled outward from Columbia, Missouri, by a marital break-up and the sudden loss of his job teaching English at Stephens College. His Christian name is, or has been, William Trogdon. This is his first book. It has been launched toward success by kind words from Annie Dillard, Farley Mowat, and Robert Penn Warren. Mr. Warren not only has obliged with an ideal puff for the front of the jacket—"A masterpiece"—but has written the front-flap copy as well. It is he, and not the author, who tells us that William Least Heat Moon "set out to . . . write a book about America."

Heat Moon's own explanation is

> With a nearly desperate sense of isolation and a growing suspicion that I lived in an alien land, I took to the open road in search of places where change did not mean ruin and where time and men and deeds connected.

This seems disingenuously high-minded—self-dramatizing but not self-revealing. The author could, I think, have confided a bit more of his curriculum vitae to the reader in the course of over four hundred big pages. His third chapter, less than two pages long, announces, "I give this chapter to myself. When done with it, I will shut up about *that* topic." He does not tell us where he is from, where he has been, or what he has done. He does not tell us that, set adrift by spouse and employer, he has embarked on an odyssey determined to redeem his life with a literary feat, though this would appear, from the determined manner of his peregrinations and his prose, and from the tape recorder, journal, and cameras he took with him, a plausible conjecture. It is a shortcoming of his adventure that, though an immense thirteen-thousand-mile itinerary develops—a rough clockwise circuit of the boundaries of the forty-eight contiguous states along mostly back roads—no inner curve of feeling tells us if this grandly invoked search reaches or fails to reach its objective. Instead, thousands of miles and hundreds of incidents, conversations, and pieces of scenery bear in upon the reader with the numbing, glittering muchness of a very long car ride. Since Heat Moon writes a thoughtful, sharp-eyed, and evocative if not exactly dancing prose, and since he is a benign and shrewd though somewhat taciturn companion, one reads on, and on, out of a kind of courtesy to the author. But no Moby-Dick of an envisioned thesis surfaces on the horizon to pull the worlds of detail toward some gravitational center; the venture never quite becomes an adventure.

There are, it is true, encounters along the way: the pilgrim blunders mistakenly into a whorehouse in Nevada, nearly freezes while stuck on a snowy mountain pass in Utah, is hassled by police in Alabama and New York State, has his water pump replaced in North Dakota, gives a Seventh-Day Adventist vagabond missionary a ride across Idaho and into Montana, and goes out on a trawler from the coast of Maine. And there are facts: the former college instructor knows how to use local libraries as well as strike up local conversations, and the blue highways ("On the old highway maps of America, the main routes were red and the back roads blue") yield much odd information by the way. The Mississippi carries forty tons of topsoil every hour to the Louisiana delta. The word "turnpike" arose because the early toll roads were barred by revolving poles. Martin Van Buren's autobiography never mentions his wife, and he, Charles Dickens, Andrew Johnson, and James Polk all spent a night in Jonesboro, Tennessee, which was once the capital of a state called Franklin. The first Mason jar was made near Millville, New Jersey. Since 1930, while automobile traffic has gone up fifty percent, the miles of American streets and roads have increased only eighteen percent. The phrase "skid row" comes from Portland, Oregon, where the seedy wharf area was known as Skidroad, a logger's term for "a timber track to drag logs over." All this is interesting, and perhaps even more germane to his announced themes of change and connectedness are such incidental data as that the mine workers of Hachita, New Mexico, wouldn't move into a new company town because the location didn't get good TV reception, and that the slaves of old Kentucky built miles of precisely fitted limestone fences that now, when a car knocks down a section, are heaped back haphazardly: "Like the slaves, the skill and time necessary to build a good stone fence were gone."

We could have used more generalization. In de Tocqueville, the proportion of incident to generalized assertion and description is no more than one to ten; *Blue Highways* reverses the ratio. We hope for more from a travel book—especially when its terrain is the land where we live, and whose news we see nightly on television—than a heap of piquant facts, however nicely chiselled and arranged. "Reading my notes of the trip—images, bits of conversations, ideas—I hunted a structure in the events, but randomness was the rule." Heat Moon's inner quest keeps sinking out of sight; his *Weltschmerz* merges with road weariness, his muffled marital grief—his wife, also of mixed blood, is identified simply as the Cherokee—is relegated to a single long-distance phone call, which leads nowhere. His intermittent wish to pump significance into his material drives him toward tangled rhetoric like

> Maybe it was the place or maybe a slow turning in the mind about how a man cannot entirely disconnect from the past. To try to is the American impulse, but to look at the steady continuance of the past is to watch time get emptied of its bluster because time bears down less on the continuum than on the components.

He is a great believer in bars as forums of opinion, and we hear a good deal about café cuisine. Some of the conversations he has are good; others feel stagy and forced—forced by his need to produce them for his unac-knowledged companion, this book in embryo. It seems bookishness that tugs him toward towns bearing quaint names—Nameless, Lookingglass, Dime Box, Othello. His regional descriptions can be magical—such as that of the Palouse, a weirdly fertile area, in Washington State, of hills so steep that special machinery has to be built to harvest the crops—but sometimes feel as obligatory as postcards. There are too many pushed metaphors, including a peculiar type of pathetic fallacy, highway personification:

> Highway 260, winding through the pine forests of central Arizona, let the mountains be boss as it followed whatever avenues they left open.

> Utah 56 went at the sagebrush flats seriously, taking up big stretches before turning away from anything.

More might have been done with the author's partial Indianness; this was meant, perhaps, to provide the angle of vision, the spin on the pitch. Few stretches of land and pages pass without a reminder of some past battle or treaty whereby the first Americans were deprived of their conti-nental domain. Heat Moon takes along with him as literary companions Walt Whitman's *Leaves of Grass* and J. G. Neihardt's *Black Elk Speaks*. Black Elk even has some words on "the blue road": it is the route for "one who is distracted, who is ruled by his senses, and who lives for himself

rather than for his people." There is something Indian, too, about the
ordeal of Spartan travel that Heat Moon has imposed upon himself; James
Ferry, another Native American, has written in a recent short story, "My
grandfather once told me that there was a certain pain that purified.
Because of the pain, some Indian ceremonies may seem like mere torture
to outsiders. But beyond the pain there is something else, if only one can
get beyond the pain. The inside is reduced to ash, as the sun has touched
you, sanctified you." Yet William Least Heat Moon's actual encounters
with Indians, and his long drives through old Indian territory, fall rather
flat. In Texas, he picks up an elderly hitchhiker who turns out to be the
offspring of a *vaquero* (cowboy) and an Apache mother, and, though "he
was the only Apache, mestizo or otherwise," the author had ever talked
to, neither man can find much to say: "When the silence got noticeably
long, he said, 'Pretty good country.' " Driving on west, Heat Moon sagely
observes that "there's something about the desert that doesn't like man."
Visiting the Hopi reservation in Arizona, he has "no luck in striking up
a conversation," and among the Navajo is bluntly snubbed:

> Intimidated by my ignorance of Navajo and by fear of the contempt that
> full-bloods often show lesser bloods, I again failed to stir a conversation.
> After the storm blew on east, I followed the old men back outside, where
> they squatted to watch the day take up the weather of an hour earlier. To
> one with a great round head like an earthen pot, I said, "Is the storm finished
> now?" He looked at me then slowly turned his head, while the others
> examined before them things in the air invisible to me.

The old pothead has sensed, no doubt, that his interlocutor is part paleface—a literary man, an educator, an instinctive alluder to Henry Miller
and H. L. Mencken, Calvin Trillin and John McPhee. Heat Moon is a
fractional brave well enough assimilated to worry winningly about being
eaten by a bear while he sleeps in his steel truck. "I lay a long time, waiting
for the beast, shaggy and immense, to claw through the metal, its hot
breath on my head, to devour me like a gumdrop." Though he does get
a Hopi student at Southern Utah State College to talk about being Indian,
and to explicate the maze at the heart of Hopi philosophy, when the
author climbs back into his truck and drones through the monotonous
immensity east of where Sitting Bull at last surrendered it is not Whitman
or Black Elk that comes to his mind for quotation but one of Gertrude
Stein's incomparable epigrams: "In the United States there is more space
where nobody is than where anybody is. This is what makes America
what it is." Farther east still, he is insulted as "Tonto" and a "freak" by
a businessman in Michigan, though the photograph on the back of the

jacket shows a pale, fine-featured man with a studiously shaped haircut and beard. The only things that look Indian about Heat Moon are his dark eyes and his enviably flat stomach.

After being called "Tonto," the author seems to wake up, and to cease wishing to see the invisible things that full-blooded Indians see, and to exercise his eye more satirically, especially as upper-class Northeasterners hove into view: "In the piney taproom I sat near a table of two men and their wives who wore the colors for that spring: pink and Kelly green touched up with white. The women were in perfect trim like mortuary lawns, and the husbands wore clothes for the man who knows where he's going. . . . The conversation was about suitable gifts to take the children at home with grandmothers. The decision: volleyballs for the boys, stuffed kangaroos for the girls, brandied apricot cakes for grandmothers." And in Kennebunkport, Maine:

> The summer season was coming on, and already middle [*sic*] matrons in nonskid-soled shoes and wraparound skirts were leading middle-level husbands into shops rigged out in macramé and down counters of perfumed candles, stained-glass mobiles, Snoopy beach towels, brass trivets, ceramic coffee mugs from Japan, music box cheeseboards, ladybug jewelry. Clerks, a generation younger, watched with expressions stuck on like decals.

Smile though he will, Northeasterners, from Cheshire, New York, to Smith Island, Maryland, were the warmest people Heat Moon met—the most amusing and the least wary, the most giving. He was invited to eat dandelion salad and fried venison with an Italian family in the vineyard country of New York State, to tramp through an old-timer's sugar-maple farm in New Hampshire, to join a fishing expedition in Maine, to sing the praises of atomic submarines ("They're longer than the Washington Monument") in Connecticut, to have drinks and dinner in southern New Jersey, and to go on a private tour of a six-by-four-mile island in Maryland. The author has a few friends in this region, and some memories: he was once a sailor stationed at Newport. He walks Thames Street, sanitized and commercialized since the Sixties, when it was "still a dark little guttery thing filled with the odor of beer and fried food and dime-store perfume," and remembers an old fisherman he met in a tavern where a parking lot now exists:

> He'd lost a thumb to a kink in a line, but he believed he'd had a good life. Around his neck hung a small scrimshaw, showing a crude yet detailed image of the Holy Virgin, carved from the knuckle of his thumb. "Your own bone," he had said, "she's the best luck."

That carved bit of your own bone might have served better than the Hopi maze as the ruling metaphor for this book. By sticking to the back roads, Heat Moon by and large met Americans who have stayed put, where fate set them, gradually gathering dignity to their lives from the continuing history of places like Shelbyville, Kentucky, and Melvin Village, New Hampshire. Their talk, where they do not grudge it, is firm and, within the tiny given periphery, authoritative. One doubts if life has many lessons they would have learned better by moving around. And one doubts, when *Blue Highways* and all its passing sights have been traversed, if William Least Heat Moon learned much about himself or about America that he could not have discovered in Columbia, Missouri.

The Local View

CHARACTERS AND THEIR LANDSCAPES, by Ronald Blythe. 208 pp. Harcourt Brace Jovanovich, 1983.

This book in its original English publication was called *From the Head-lands*—a more suitably diffident title for a collection of essays, some quite brief, written over the years for various occasions. What the occasions were we are left to guess. Some, to judge from the acknowledgments, were introductions to paperback reissues of classics (Hazlitt, Tolstoy, Hardy); others have the tone of radio talks and were previously published in *The Listener*. Though Mr. Blythe's introduction, which naturally emphasizes the something heaven-sent and unifying in his sundry inspirations, claims, "A few of these essays have been previously published in the scattered way of such things, and quite a few of them have not," only three of the fourteen, in fact, escaped prior publication. One would be grateful to know what prompted the delivery of such relatively offhand and inconclusive accounts as "Dinner with Dr. Stopes" and "Interpreting the Shades." What has dictated their preservation in this volume, we are told, is "the native element," "a linkage of mood, thought and autobiographical facts," "writing which 'doubles' certain literary and personal reactions to readings and events." Mr. Blythe protests too much; he is a distinctive writer with a pervasive passion for rural England, and any collection by him would have unity enough.

He is best known, of course, for the exquisite assemblage of village testimony called *Akenfield* (1969); a somewhat lumpier but still remarkable set of interviews with the elderly, *The View in Winter* (1979), has followed.

As well as a good listener he is a keen reader, not so much a critic as a connoisseur, whose fresh enthusiasm would send us warmly back to the classics. In this volume, the essays on Hazlitt, on John Clare, on Tolstoy's "The Death of Ivan Ilyich," and on Hardy's *A Pair of Blue Eyes* and *Far from the Madding Crowd* are superb appreciations. Hazlitt he portrays as the unreconstructed radical among the Romantics, "cursed with everlasting youth," his writing marked by "ultimate defencelessness." Mr. Blythe does some writing of his own to describe Hazlitt's:

> The exposition of an idea would start out on the page in light, happy phrases which threatened no man's complacency, and then the skilful strengthening would begin, and intellectual involvement would bind the reader. Each essay shows the build-up of numerous small climaxes, such as are sometimes employed in the novel. Excitement and expectation mount. Hazlitt is the word-juggler who never misses; his almost casual use of ornament, epigram and fancy is hypnotic.

Hardy touches Mr. Blythe most deeply and touches off his highest praise. Of *Far from the Madding Crowd*, he writes:

> There is often a wonderful moment towards the beginning of a literary career after the pump has been substantially primed with "early works" when a book appears which is all morning brightness, inspiration and possibility, and no English novel so completely fulfils these fresh conditions than [*sic*] does this one. In it the big recurring themes of mortal existence, love, power, treachery, happiness, toil and transcendence, are played out on the farm. The rural scene isn't limited and hedged; on the contrary it is sumptuous. We are not looking into a midden or even to the stretching headlands, but at a landscape which satisfies every stir of the imagination and which ravishes the senses.

The word "sumptuous" recurs, in connection with the novel's sheep-shearing scene:

> It is a form of sumptuous reality. It challenges every view of the quaint and simple task, as Chardin did, and directs us towards a vision of fundamental labour that contains within it satisfactions that are usually searched for in poetry and religion. Scenes such as this are the permanent cliffs in his writing, stalwart headlands against which melodrama and suspense can fret and dash without any danger of their becoming a merely sensational movement.

Mr. Blythe is a partisan of those writers who have let the English countryside speak, Hardy foremost: "No one before or since has given the full village picture with such original authority, no writer conceded less to what it was generally held to contain, either socially or spiritually." The cultural assumptions that muffled the countryside and its villages in silence are sketched in the essay "The Dangerous Idyll," which begins, "Extreme though it may sound, any literary undertaking by an English villager has until quite recently, by which I mean the late nineteenth century, been received with much the same suspicion as novels and poetry written by English women. Each, by daring to produce literature, had broken through ancient orderly concepts of their functions." First cited, and fondly referred to throughout this book, is the unhappy case of John Clare—a ploughman of Helpston ("a gloomy village in Northamptonshire," in Clare's own description) whose poetic efforts were negligently destroyed by his mother and loudly ridiculed by his fellow villagers. "From about twelve years onward, Clare lived a furtive, aberrant existence, hiding in woods with his books, hoarding old sugar-bags to write on, muttering behind the plough." Yet, when literary London opened to him in 1820, upon publication of his first book of poems, Clare stuck to Helpston for his residence as well as his inspiration, and, according to Mr. Blythe, found the forced move to a village three miles away so traumatic he became mentally ill. Such sensitive attachment to the land was rare; the rural reality was grimmer than the bucolic poems of Pope and Thomson indicated, and a former bumpkin like George Crabbe, when once accepted in urban circles, quickly and totally severed all connection with the Suffolk farm-laboring class into which he was born. Robert Burns, we are told, published *his* ploughman's poems "not to celebrate his oneness with the village of Mossgiel but to make enough money to get off the land altogether and sail to Jamaica and work on a plantation."

Our author is so interesting on this subject of land and literature, and so clearly well informed, that one wishes he had abandoned his usual slanting, quotation-laden manner and written a systematic study. Taking as his clue the skittish attitude of the characters in Jane Austen's *Emma* toward venturing out of their own parks into the "ordinary agricultural background," he points up the gulf between what the Wiltshire diarist Francis Kilvert distinguished as the "gentle" and the "simple." Mr. Blythe explains, "When the long peace between the gentlemen and the peasants was broken by the rationalisation of what remained of the manorial system, the contrast between the two rural cultures was often so extreme that the baronet in his park could feel that he was surrounded, not so much by his countrymen as by savages." The agricultural laborers were from the genteel point of view not merely lowly but invisible: " 'Osbert,' remarked Sir George Sitwell, staring across Sheffield, 'do you realise that there is nobody between us and the Locker-Lampsons?' " A certain comedy of inattention attaches to Romantic celebrations of the countryside: Constable's "marvellous series of Stour Valley landscapes, each with its sprinkling of minuscule boatmen and field-workers," was serenely produced while "labourers rioted and were lighting bonfires on the hills." The intensified enclosures and the famine of 1815 had brought new waves of misery to the shires; Constable sent blankets from Soho but inveighed against the rural laborers' forming protective unions. Even Hazlitt, that champion of the downtrodden, despised country life in its particulars: "There is a perpetual round of mischiefmaking and backbiting for want of any better amusement. . . . There are no shops, no taverns, no theatres, no opera, no concerts, no pictures . . . no books or knowledge of books. Vanity and luxury are the civilisers of the world, and sweeteners of human life. Without objects either of pleasure or action, it grows harsh and crabbed. The mind becomes stagnant, the affections callous. . . ." As Sherwood Anderson said of the nineteenth-century farmers of Ohio, "Men labored too hard and were too tired to read." Or, as Hawthorne's Miles Coverdale observed while engaged in field work, "The clods of earth, which we so constantly belabored and turned over and over, were never etherealized into thought. Our thoughts, on the contrary, were fast becoming cloddish."

Pastoral illusions found little nurture in America; almost everybody was a farmer, and the Nebraska wheat fields were not dotted with manor houses and deer parks. The British situation combined an ancient feudal hold on land by the aristocracy with the existence of overseas colonies that for a time made domestic agriculture seem dispensable. From the Napoleonic Wars to World War II a state of depression hovered over British agriculture, descending with especial severity in the last third of the nineteenth century, as grain poured in from Canada, frozen mutton from New Zealand, and frozen beef from Argentina. The farm laborers, then, were not only culturally despised but politically slighted in a way that helps account for Mr. Blythe's sympathetic interest in Socialism. Two of his more enigmatic, though animated, essays deal with two forgotten stars of "alternative politics" in the 1880s, the American economist Henry George and the Scots Utopian Thomas Davidson. Both men are seen en route. "The Voyager" shows George as the foremast boy on a clipper ship bumping its way up a corpse-clogged branch of the River Ganges and then as steward of a steamer being chased around Montevideo Harbor by the bobbing casket of a shipmate who had ardently asked to be buried on land and not at sea. Mr. Blythe draws a moral from this spooky tale: "An ordinary man had demanded and finally claimed his elemental right and the steward . . . had been involved in a parable and had listened to a sermon." From here, the implication is, it was a quick step to George's once-famous "single tax" proposal. Thomas Davidson's pilgrimage is even obscurer; the young radicals of London, Havelock Ellis foremost, rather rapidly grew disillusioned with the inspirational Scotsman, who had a way of wandering off, and indeed wandered off to America, to found a commune of "New Lifers" in the Adirondacks, leaving behind in England the seeds, somehow, of the Fabian Society, which he disowned.

Mr. Blythe's anecdotes tend to raise more questions than they illuminate, e.g., "Lamb, for whom Hazlitt's sex life was the only thing about his friend he could never take seriously, laughed so much during [Hazlitt's] wedding that he was nearly turned out of church." Oh? The reader is addressed as an old chum who knows pretty much the same things the author does: "But, as we know, Sweet Auburn was Nuneham Courtenay, Oxfordshire." Mr. Blythe writes, "Lear said, 'At Christmas I no more desire a rose than wish a snow in May,' " without indicating whether this is Edward, King, or a third Lear speaking.* He flips startling specificities at us archly—"William Cory's own phot[ograph] shows a pale, rather formidable person. He has big thin ears like the emperor Augustus"—and cozily overloads a few of his polished sentences to the point of babble:

Not perp and dec but the all but rubbed from history creatures, human and divine, which they housed. A holy romance world, in its way, in which Felix, Gobban, Dicuil, Fursey, Foillan, Mindred (whose well at Newmarket is now in the possession of the Jockey Club), the Pied, White, Grey and Black friars, Tobias, Sir John Shorne (a medieval Dr Scholl who conjured the devil from a boot), Edmund, of course, Apollonia, cherubyn, sarafyn, potestate, principatus, Michael Arkeangelus *et al*, still faintly crowd.

Like the patient flint-pickers of his beloved East Anglian fields, this author collects and arranges; his receptive intelligence and his virtually angelic tenderness toward the anonymous and overlookable are well displayed in his first and last essays, the last, "Reading Other People's Diaries," a roughly chronological wandering through the private journals of Englishmen from the boy-king Edward VI to Virginia Woolf, and the first, "An Inherited Perspective," a celebration of "the local view" in art and life.

---

*The quote in fact is not from *King Lear* but *Love's Labour's Lost:* Act I, scene i, lines 105–7. Berowne says:

> At Christmas I no more desire a rose
> Than wish a snow in May's new-fangled shows,
> But like of each thing that in season grows.

Unlike all but a few modern writers, Ronald Blythe has worked and matured where he was born, and if he sometimes seems to speak in the code of local dialect, his words have the weight of things firmly fixed in his mind's eye. He remembers his childhood impressions of "the aged village relations who sat four-square in their lush gardens like monuments, as if growing out of the Suffolk clay itself, their bodies wooden and still, their eyes glittering and endlessly scanning leaves and birds and crops, their work done and their end near." Pinned to a certain space, he has witnessed the effects of time: "When I was writing *Akenfield,* and thinking of the old and new farming generations, it struck me that I was seeing the last of those who made landscapes with their faces hanging down, like those of beasts, over the soil." For all of his sometimes pawky historical knowingness, he affectingly communicates a sense of what lies beyond history's edge—our daily, animal lives persisting in their chronic cycles.

Hymn to Tilth

THE GARDENER'S YEAR, by Karel Čapek, translated from the Czech by Robert and Maria Weatherall. 160 pp. The University of Wisconsin Press, 1984.

Cooking up a calendar is one of the first things men do on the road to civilization, and literary celebration of the year's cycle is at least as old as lines 383–616 of Hesiod's *Works and Days,* from the eighth century B.C. Edmund Spenser's *The Shepheardes Calender,* with a bow to the eclogues of Theocritus and Virgil, ushered in the heyday of Elizabethan poetry; it takes the months and seasons, however, less as matters for description than as *points de départ* for a series of delightfully artificial rhymed dialogues. Similarly, *The Twelve Seasons,* by Joseph Wood Krutch, consists of a dozen essays very loosely linked to the turning year. The ties are much closer in Hal Borland's *Sundial of the Seasons,* a collection of three hundred sixty-five of his "outdoor editorials" from the *Times,* and in Mikhail Prishvin's *Nature's Diary.* Both Borland and Prishvin begin their years with spring, and both pleasantly roam in recording the anecdotes and observations that trace what Borland calls "the oldest continuing story known to man, the story of man and his natural surroundings." Prishvin's surroundings were central Russia, with its peasant lore (he began as an ethnographer), bears, lakes, forests, and immense winters; Borland's, the tamer but still woodsy southern Berkshires of Connecticut. Still another form of environment—European, damp, mild, domesticated—is lovingly chronicled in Karel Čapek's *The Gardener's Year*, a charming and curiously majestic survey, from January to December, of the writer's backyard garden and his activity therein.

The book was first published in 1929, and this English translation followed two years later, with an American edition by G. P. Putnam. It has not been reprinted here until now. Its Gluyas Williams–like illustrations by Čapek's brother, Josef, at first glance suggest a Benchleyesque account of comic bumbling and entrapment:

> One would think that watering a little garden is quite a simple thing, especially if one has a hose. It will soon be clear that until it has been tamed a hose is an extraordinarily evasive and dangerous beast, for it contorts itself, it jumps, it wriggles, it makes puddles of water, and dives with delight into the mess it has made; then it goes for the man who is going to use it and coils itself round his legs.

A tone of agricultural exasperation, as in S. J. Perelman's *Acres and Pains*, is struck: "This is one of Nature's mysteries—how from the best grass seed most luxuriant and hairy weeds come up; perhaps weed seed ought to be sown and then a nice lawn would result."

But we soon realize that Čapek comes not only to complain but to rhapsodize; his basic theme, however light his manner, is the primordial one of Man's reabsorption into nature. "Your relation towards things has changed. If it rains you say that it rains on the garden; if the sun shines, it does not shine just anyhow, but it shines on the garden; in the evening you rejoice that the garden will rest." In the plays which had made him famous *(R. U.R., The Insect Play)*, Čapek dealt with the mechanized horrors of modernity; through his garden, modern man relearns the ancient lessons of attentiveness. "If I ran as far as Benešov, I should see less of the spring than if I sat in my little garden. You must stand still; and then . . . you will hear the infinite march of buds faintly roaring."

Nor is this revelation of roaring confined to the growing season. In dark November, the gardener digs, and finds a teeming world:

> Every year we say that Nature lies down to her winter sleep; but we have not yet looked closely at this sleep; or, to be more precise, we have not looked at it yet from below. You must turn things upside down to know them better; Nature must be turned upside down so that you can look into it; turn her roots up. Good Lord, is this sleep? You call this a rest? It would be better to say that vegetation has ceased to grow upwards, because it has no time for it now; for it has turned its sleeves up and grows downwards, it spits in its hands and digs itself into the ground. Look, this pale thing here in the

earth is a mass of new roots; look how they push; heave-ho! heave-ho! Can't you hear how the earth is crackling under this enraged and collective charge?

Čapek, who was to die within a decade of writing this, at the youthful age of forty-eight, rhapsodically extols the ceaseless activity of Nature's year: "I tell you, there is no death; not even sleep. We only pass from one season to another. We must be patient with life, for it is eternal." Beginning like Benchley, he ends like Emerson.

Expert witnesses to wild nature such as Borland and Prishvin interact with it mostly on the plane of investigation or in the contest of hunting and fishing. The backyard gardener with his few square feet of Prague soil engages himself more intimately. He delves, and inventories the farraginous contents of the soil: "The garden—or cultivated soil, also called humus, or mould—consists mainly of special ingredients, such as earth, manure, leafmould, peat, stones, pieces of glass, mugs, broken dishes, nails, wire, bones, Hussite arrows, silver paper from slabs of chocolate, bricks, old coins, old pipes, plate-glass, tiny mirrors, old labels, tins, bits of string, buttons, soles, dog droppings, coal, pot-handles, wash-basins, dishcloths, bottles, sleepers, milkcans, buckles, horseshoes, jam tins, insulating material, scraps of newspapers, and innumerable other components which the astonished gardener digs up at every stirring of his beds." He observes how stones apparently "grow from some kind of seeds or eggs, or continually rise out of the mysterious interior of the earth." He enriches this earth with all his improvised means: "he hunts about at home for eggshells, burns bones after lunch, collects his nail-cuttings, sweeps soot from the chimney, takes sand from the sink, scrapes up in the street beautiful horse-droppings, and all these he carefully digs into the soil; for all these are lightening, warm, and nutritious substances." The proper gardener adores manure: "A cartload of manure is most beautiful when it is brought on a frosty day, so that it steams like a sacrificial altar." He is a connoisseur of earth: "it should crumble, but not break into lumps; under the spade it ought to crack, but not to squelch; it must not make slabs, or blocks, or honeycombs, or dumplings; but, when you turn it over with a full spade, it ought to breathe with pleasure and fall into a fine and puffy tilth."

Enough has been quoted, perhaps, to indicate the rhapsodic quality of the prose, and the felicity of its translation. The Weatheralls (she was herself Czech) had not only to produce a bouncy and flexible version of Čapek's style but to locate the English equivalents of hundreds of botanical names. Celebrant as he was of Nature's diversity, Čapek loved lists; I counted fifty flower names in a single, not untypical sentence. The catalogue, that definitive naming of names, is the gardener's hymnal, whose music can be played all winter long. In its torrential* specificity and devoted tone *The Gardener's Year* asks a place on the shelf near the embowering books of Eleanor Perényi, Katharine White, Thalassa Cruso, Ann Leighton, and Vita Sackville-West. Graceful words grow readily around garden subjects; the name of the rose has something of the rose's essence, and the arrangement of a bed and the timing of its blooms are somewhat syntactical. Much of the gardener's pleasure is in the head, in organization and anticipation. "We gardeners live somehow for the future; if roses are in flower, we think that next year will flower better. . . . The right, the best is in front of us. Each successive year will add growth and beauty." A deathless thought, from the last page of a gallant little book republished after half a century, in a cover as green as your thumb.

Damp and Dull

SAILING THROUGH CHINA, by Paul Theroux, with illustrations by Patrick Procktor. 64 pp. Houghton Mifflin, 1984.

Mr. Theroux, whose last travel book was a long and dour walk around the coast of the United Kingdom, here sails down the Yangtze with a group of American millionaires, with much less effort to himself. His account seems more a set of notes than a finished work, and has the charm of fragments. The millionaires played cards to win, and the famous gorges on the river lived up to their billing. The Chinese cities, however, were "poisonous-looking," and "the air of pollution gives China the look of existing in a permanent sunset," and "the land looked scraped—no trees, only tiny houses, or huts, and cultivation everywhere." Waxing apocalyptic, the Anglo-American traveller concludes that threadbare, overused, birdless China is everybody's future: "In a hundred years or so, under a cold uncolonized moon, what we call the civilized world will all look like China, muddy and senile and old-fangled. . . . Our future is this mildly poisoned earth and its smoky air. We are in for hunger and hard work, the highest stage of poverty—no starvation, but crudeness everywhere,

---

*Consider, speaking of lists, the sequential piling-on in this evocation of a shower: "strings of rain hiss on the pavement, the earth almost breathes aloud, water gurgles, drums, pats, and rattles against the windows, tiptaps with a thousand fingers in the spouts, runs in rivulets, and splashes in puddles, and one would like to scream with joy, one sticks one's head out of the window to cool it in the dew from heaven, one whistles, shouts, and would like to stand barefoot in the yellow streams rushing down the streets."

clumsy art, simple language, bad books, brutal laws, plain vegetables, and clothes of one colour. It will be damp and dull, like this." Enough to make one nostalgic for 1984.

Empire's End

THE EMPEROR: *Downfall of an Autocrat*, by Ryszard Kapuściński, translated from the Polish by William R. Brand and Katarzyna Mroczkowska-Brand. 164 pp. Harcourt Brace Jovanovich, 1983.

In September of 1974 the Emperor Haile Selassie I was deposed as ruler of Ethiopia by a committee of young Army officers called the Dergue; at that time the monarch had reigned for forty-four of his eighty-two years. The nature of his long rule and the circumstances of his deposition are enchantingly illuminated in *The Emperor: Downfall of an Autocrat*. Ryszard Kapuściński, who for many years covered the Third World for the Polish Press Agency, visited Ethiopia in 1963, when Haile Selassie was playing host to a conference of African leaders in Addis Ababa, "then a large village of a few hundred thousand inhabitants, situated on hills, amid eucalyptus groves." On this occasion the Polish reporter befriended a member of the Imperial Ministry of Information, "a tall, handsome, usually silent and reserved Amhara" named Teferra Gebrewold. Not long after the Emperor's fall, Mr. Kapuściński returned to Addis Ababa and with Teferra's help sought out in their hiding places surviving members of the Emperor's circle and interviewed them. "We were a couple of collectors out to recover pictures doomed to destruction: we wanted to make an exhibition of the old art of governing."

A stunning exhibit it is; the interviewed subjects, while the turbulent aftermath of the revolution and its frenzied nationwide *fetasha* (Amharic for "search") raged about them, enunciated their memories of the days of Haile Selassie in a magical reverie that frequently achieves poetry and aphorism:

> The Emperor slept in a roomy bed made of light walnut. He was so slight and frail that you couldn't see him—he was lost among the sheets. In old age, he became even smaller. . . . He had the habit of sleeping little and rising early, when it was still dark outside. He treated sleep as a dire necessity that purposelessly robbed him of time he would rather have spent ruling or at Imperial functions. Sleep was a private, intimate interval in a life meant to be passed amid decorations and lights. That's why he woke up seeming

discontented with having slept, impatient with the very fact of sleep. Only the subsequent activities of the day restored his inner balance.

The first of his activities, having risen at four or five, was to walk within the Palace grounds while a scheduled series of high-ranking informers poured news of the night's conspiracies into his ear. They walked a step behind the Emperor, who never made a comment or took a note: "Our monarch not only never used his ability to read, but he also never wrote anything and never signed anything in his own hand. Though he ruled for half a century, not even those closest to him knew what his signature looked like." During imperial audiences, a Minister of the Pen, when the Emperor spoke, "moved his ear as close as a microphone" and "transcribed his ruler's scant and foggy mutterings. All the rest was interpretation." In hourly segments rather picturesquely named—the Hour of the Cashbox, the Hour of the Supreme Court of Final Appeal—Haile Selassie moved through his day, expressionless, virtually inaudible, his every move framed by slavish attendance. One employee of the court had the sole job of wiping from the shoes of respectfully immobile dignitaries the urine deposited there by the Emperor's pet lapdog, Lulu; another was for twenty-six years "His Most Virtuous Highness's pillow bearer":

> His Majesty would take his place on the throne, and when he had seated himself I would slide a pillow under his feet. This had to be done like lightning so as not to leave Our Distinguished Monarch's legs hanging in the air for even a moment. . . . I had mastered the special protocol of this specialty, and even possessed an extremely useful, expert knowledge: the height of various thrones. This allowed me quickly to choose a pillow of just the right size, so that a shocking ill fit, allowing a gap to appear between the pillow and the Emperor's shoes, would not occur. In my storeroom I had fifty-two pillows of various sizes, thicknesses, materials, and colors.

The "keeper of the third door" also had his heavy responsibilities and his pride of expertise: "It was an art to open the door at the right moment, the exact instant. To open the door too early would have been reprehensible, as if I were hurrying the Emperor out. If I opened it too late, on the other hand, His Sublime Highness would have to slow down, or perhaps even stop, which would detract from his lordly dignity, a dignity that meant getting around without collisions or obstacles." And a high ceremonial official rejoiced in being called "His Distinguished Majesty's cuckoo"; his duty was, when the moment came "for the Emperor, in accordance with official protocol, to pass from one activity to another," to stand before him and rapidly bow several times, as a signal.

At the center of all this clockworklike apparatus of absolutism, the Emperor maintained, according to the testimony of these voices (identified simply by initials, for their own protection), an inscrutable poise, a trance of power that let scarcely an appointment or an expenditure take place within the entirety of the empire without his approval. His objective was peace, obtained by balancing factions: "The Palace divided itself into factions and coteries that fought incessant wars, weakening and destroying each other. That is exactly what His Benevolent Majesty wanted. Such a balance assured his blessed peace." He distrusted activists and fanatic enforcers of order: "Desirous of His Majesty's approbation, they tried to introduce absolute order, whereas His Supreme Majesty wanted basic order with a margin of disorder on which his monarchical gentleness could exert itself." What power he shared he shared on one basis: loyalty. "It didn't matter if a given dignitary measured up or not, as long as he showed unshakable loyalty." "I don't remember His Magnanimous Highness's ever demoting someone and pressing his head to the cobblestones because of corruption. Let him enjoy his corruption, as long as he shows his loyalty!" A certain Prince Imru "began to smell of reform, and without asking the Emperor's permission he gave some of his lands to the peasants. Thus, having kept something secret from the Emperor, in an irritating and even provocative way he violated the principle of loyalty. His Benevolent Highness, who had been preparing a supremely honorable office for the prince, had to exile him from the country for twenty years." The underlying rationale is expressed by one former courtier in a celestial metaphor:

> I'll come right out and say it: the King of Kings preferred bad ministers. And the King of Kings preferred them because he liked to appear in a favorable light by contrast. How could he show himself favorably if he were surrounded by good ministers? The people would be disoriented. Where would they look for help? On whose wisdom and kindness would they depend? Everyone would have been good and wise. What disorder would have broken out in the Empire then! Instead of one sun, fifty would be shining, and everyone would pay homage to a privately chosen planet.

One wonders how much of the elegant style of Abyssinian testimony— beautifully caught by this supple English translation—was smuggled in by way of Mr. Kapuściński's Polish. Certainly the editing and sequencing of these interviews is highly artistic, and creates a more than documentary effect, a Kafkaesque poetry and mystery. The events that led to the Emperor's downfall are, but for an occasional italicized interpolation, seen entirely from within the court, with the moist eyes of injured innocence:

I also took care of another bag, a large one that was filled with small coins on the eve of national holidays. . . . On such occasions our august ruler went to the most crowded and lively quarter of Addis Ababa, Mercato, where on a specially constructed platform I would place the heavy, jingling bag from which His Benevolent Majesty would scoop the handfuls of coppers that he threw into the crowd of beggars and other such greedy riffraff. The rapacious mob would create such a hubbub, however, that this charitable action always had to end in a shower of police batons against the heads of the frenzied, pushy rabble. Saddened, His Highness would have to walk away from the platform. Often he was unable to empty even half the bag.

Nowadays, all those who destroyed the monarchy point out that in each province His Most Worthy Majesty maintained a Palace always ready for his arrival. It is true that some excesses were committed. For instance, a great Palace was constructed in the heart of the Ogaden Desert and maintained for years, fully staffed with servants and its pantry kept full, and His Indefatigable Majesty spent only one day there. But what if His Distinguished Majesty's itinerary were such that at some point he had to spend a night in the heart of the Desert? Unfortunately, our unenlightened people will never understand the Higher Reason that governs the actions of monarchs.

The trivial event that set things off was a fashion show at the university, organized by the American Peace Corps even though all gatherings and meetings were forbidden. But His Distinguished Majesty could not forbid the Americans a show, could he? And so the students took advantage of this cheerful and carefree event to gather in an enormous crowd and set off for the Palace. And from that moment on they never again let themselves be driven back to their homes.

There had been an unsuccessful rebellion in 1960, led by Germame Neway, an aristocrat who had returned at the age of thirty from the United States, where an imperial scholarship had financed a university education. Made governor of the southern province of Sidamo, Germame began to turn uncultivated land over to landless peasants; Haile Selassie's characteristically mild reaction was to transfer the rash reformer to the governorship of Jijiga, where the only inhabitants were nomads uninterested in land. Germame's attempted coup, when it came, was efficiently quelled by the Army; the common people, lacking radios, were slow to realize that a revolution was in progress and the Palace had been taken. When they became aware, they pursued the rebels with sticks and stones. Nevertheless, from 1960 on "a sort of negativism started to flood over us. . . . you noticed it everywhere on people's faces, faces that seemed diminished and abandoned, without light or energy, in what people did and how they did it. . . . Even though the Emperor went on issuing decrees and striving to get things done, got up early and never rested, all the same the negativism was there, growing all the time. . . . People seemed unable to control things; things existed and ceased to exist in their own malicious ways, slipping through people's hands. . . . The Palace was sinking, and we all felt it. . . . We could feel the temperature falling, life becoming more and more precisely framed by ritual but more and more cut-and-dried, banal, negative."

Haile Selassie was not bloodthirsty or unintelligent. He perpetrated many actual reforms in his anachronistic empire, and to the last was going through the motions of "development." The fatal weakness of his rule—which he would not have outlived had he not lived so very long—was the rapacity of his officials, a rapacity he encouraged as a seal to their loyalty. As the collapse drew near, the corruption grew worse: "The closer it got to the end, the more horrible was the grabbing and the unrestrained snatching. Instead, my friend, of applying himself to the tiller or the sails as the boat started to sink, each one of our magnates stuffed his bag and looked around for a comfortable lifeboat."

The vessel sank, finally, under the weight of the Sahel drought, which had been afflicting northern Africa for a number of years. A British television journalist, Jonathan Dimbleby, who had previously made films flattering to the Emperor, in 1973 took cameras into the desolated north of the country and produced a film entitled *Ethiopia: The Unknown Famine*, "in which this unprincipled calumniator"—to quote the interview subject called "A. A."—"pulled the demagogic trick of showing thousands of people dying of hunger, and next to that His Venerable Highness feasting with dignitaries. Then he showed roads on which scores of poor, famished skeletons were lying, and immediately afterward our airplanes bringing champagne and caviar from Europe. Here, whole fields of dying scrags; there, His Highness serving meat to his dogs from a silver platter." An outcry greeted the film's showing in England, and the empire reluctantly had to admit foreign aid with its attendant personnel, including "correspondents disguised as male nurses."

It's never good to let so many foreigners in, since they are amazed at everything and they criticize everything. . . . When these missionaries, physicians, and so-called nurses reached the north, they saw a thing most amazing to them, namely, thousands dying of hunger right next door to markets and stores full of food. There is food, they say, only there was a bad harvest and the peasants had to give it all to the landowners and that's why they've got nothing left and the speculators took advantage and raised the prices so high that hardly anyone could buy wheat and that's where the misery comes from.

More scandalous yet, the Emperor's officials turned out to be appropriating the food shipments sent in aid. And with astonishing effrontery, the Finance Minister, Yelma Deresa, demanded high customs fees from the overseas donors; when they balked at payment, the loyal press hastened "to denounce the rebellious benefactors, saying that by suspending aid they condemn our nation to the cruelties of poverty and starvation." And:

> Amid all the people starving, missionaries and nurses clamoring, students rioting, and police cracking heads, His Serene Majesty . . . summoned the wretched notables from the north [and] conferred high distinctions on them to prove that they were innocent and to curb the foreign gossip and slander.

The well-placed Ethiopians had trouble understanding what the fuss was all about. "First of all," A. A. told Mr. Kapuściński, "death from hunger had existed in our Empire for hundreds of years, an everyday, natural thing, and it never occurred to anyone to make any noise about it. Drought would come and the earth would dry up, the cattle would drop dead, the peasants would starve. Ordinary, in accordance with the laws of nature and the eternal order of things . . . Consider also, my dear friend, that—between you and me—it is not bad for national order and a sense of national humility that the subjects be rendered skinnier, thinned down a bit." The Emperor, after all, had issued a statement upon the famine announcing that he "attached the utmost importance to this matter."

> For the starvelings it had to suffice that His Munificent Highness personally attached the greatest importance to their fate, which was a very special kind of attachment, of an order higher than the highest. It provided the subjects with a soothing and uplifting hope that whenever there appeared in their lives an oppressive mischance, some tormenting difficulty, His Most Unrivaled Highness would hearten them—by attaching the greatest importance to that mischance or difficulty.

Such celestial reassurances to the contrary, unrest and criticism continued to swell, there were riots and strikes, and the Army—the biggest in black Africa, and since the 1960 rebellion the mainstay of imperial power—began, in February of 1974, to mutiny. The Dergue came into being, and the Emperor consented to meet with it. The last surreal act of the drama was under way; acting in the Emperor's name, the Dergue gradually arrested all the Emperor's officials and favorites, emptying the

Palace around him. The grim farce was heightened by the arrival of some Swedish physicians who had been previously engaged to lead the court circle in calisthenics. "To prevent the rebels from capturing everyone at once, the grand chamberlain of the court pulled off a cunning trick by ordering that calisthenics be done in small groups." The Dergue relentlessly continued its arrests, "cutting off great hunks of dignitaries, until in the end the Palace was picked clean, flushed out, and there was nobody left except for His Most Extraordinary Majesty and one servant." This servant, like the Emperor, was an octogenarian. Through August the two old men held to routines of server and served in the vast void of the Palace: "It rained for days on end," Mr. Kapuściński tells us. "Mornings were foggy and nights cold. H. S. still wore his uniform, over which he would throw a warm woolen cape. They got up as they had in the old days, as they had for years, at daybreak, and they went to the Palace chapel, where each day L. M. [the servant] read aloud different verses from the Book of Psalms. . . . Afterward, H. S. would go to his office and sit down at his desk, on which more than a dozen telephones were perched. All of them silent—perhaps they had been cut off. L. M. would sit by the door, waiting for the bell to ring, summoning him to receive orders from his monarch." Delegations of young officers arrived, attempting to persuade Haile Selassie to yield up to them the millions of dollars he had secreted over the years in Swiss banks; he never did, though the Dergue did find the dollars he had hidden beneath his Persian carpet and in his great collection of Bibles. The night of September 11, 1974, was New Year's Eve according to the Ethiopian calendar, and the two old men in the Palace did not sleep; in observance of the holiday the servant lit candles in chandeliers throughout the deserted rooms. The next morning, three officers in combat uniforms arrived, and one of them read to the Emperor an act of dethronement that stated, "Even though the people treated the throne in good faith as a symbol of unity, Haile Selassie I took advantage of its authority, dignity, and honor for his own personal ends. As a result, the country found itself in a state of poverty and disintegration." They told the servant to pack his belongings and go home. The streets of Addis Ababa were still empty under a morning curfew; nevertheless, the Emperor waved his hand at the few people they passed as he was driven from the Palace in a green Volkswagen. He was held in rooms of the Menelik Palace on the hills above Addis Ababa, close to where his pet lions were caged.* According to a report from Agence France Presse, he was granted many signs of respect by his captors and on his side repeatedly proclaimed, "If the

---

*In 1960, he had ordered some of these lions shot, "because instead of defending the Palace they had admitted the traitors."

revolution is good for the people, then I am for the revolution." He died, according to a terse announcement in the *Ethiopian Herald*, a little less than a year after his deposition, of circulatory failure.

The Emperor is a parable of rule which offers a number of lessons. Foremost looms the inevitable tendency of a despot, be he king, ward boss, or dictator, to prefer loyalty to ability in his subordinates, and to seek safety in stagnation. One of Haile Selassie's problems, well managed as long as power was kept within court circles, was to balance the forces within his government so that no one branch or clique developed any initiative or momentum of its own. The price paid, of course, was a corruption and an inertia that broke the bonds between the monarchy and the nation. Another lesson, more elusive in its workings, is the fragile, even phantasmal nature of the connection between the ruler and the ruled. Haile Selassie was so accustomed to ruling, with its ceaseless pomp and protocol, that he displayed a sublime passivity—infuriating to some of his retainers—when the Palace began to sink. He allowed himself to be used by the military as its figurehead and through his non-resisting person permitted a transition to revolution. How much of this was intentional it would take another book to tell us. The courtier "C." explained to Mr. Kapuściński, "His Venerable Majesty wanted to rule over everything. Even if there was a rebellion, he wanted to rule over the rebellion, to command a mutiny, even if it was directed against his own reign." Perhaps, in his mind, as he conferred each day that summer with delegations from the Dergue and—himself always dressed in military uniform now—visited his terrified ministers as they awaited incarceration, he was still ruling. These procedures might have seemed no less real than those of the days when his Ministers of the Pen and the Purse would translate his murmurings into governmental action. "It's so very difficult," mused "M. W. Y.," "to establish where the borderline is between living power, great, even terrifying, and the appearance of power, the empty pantomime of ruling, being one's own dummy, only playing the role, not seeing the world, not hearing it, merely looking into oneself." For power, appearances to the contrary, flows upward from the governed: all the munificence of Haile Selassie's court derived from the exertions of desperately poor peasants. And in fact power can be eventually withheld. Ethiopia in 1960 was not ready for revolution; by 1974, it was.

Not that peasants, as such, revolted. The eloquent and philosophical A. A. observes:

> Up north there was no rebellion. No one raised his voice or his hand up there. . . . The usefulness of going hungry is that a hungry man thinks only

of bread. He's all wrapped up in the thought of food. . . . Who destroyed our Empire? Who reduced it to ruin? Neither those who had too much, nor those who had nothing, but those who had a bit. Yes, one should always beware of those who have a bit, because they are the worst, they are the greediest, it is they who push upward.

It is no paradox that the customary fomenters of modern revolution are young members of the middle class rather than of the oppressed masses. It is these who have had opportunity to think of more than bread, yet have not attained an entrenched position in the established order. Haile Selassie distributed scholarships and selectively encouraged education and thus helped create the class that brought him down. Both the leader of the failed coup of 1960, Germame Neway, and of the successful one of 1974, Mengistu Haile-Mariam, had spent time, at the imperial government's expense, in the United States, which continues to export, in the form of raised consciousness, more revolution than the Soviet Union.

Ethiopia is distinguished from most Third World countries by its ancient history of independence, on its craggy African plateau. It is typically Third World, however, in that its government is the nation's one significant accumulation of capital and therefore must serve as the main avenue to wealth. Mr. Kapuściński calls it "a poor country, in which the only source of property is not hard work and productivity but extraordinary privilege." The United States and the other industrial nations of the West are fortunate insofar as high political office is financially unattractive, except as a stepping stone to best-selling memoirs. When the most energetically entrepreneurial types are drawn elsewhere in the economy, a possibility of altruistic service enters officialdom. But until a society can generate superior economic opportunity elsewhere, government is apt to be a league of exploiters, a protection racket dearly selling the governed a modicum of peace. The jacket flap of *The Emperor* claims that when it was published in Poland, in 1978, "it was widely viewed as an allegory of dictatorship in general. Critics saw its publication as a key event in shaping the consensus for reform in Poland." Perhaps; but the Cold War moral that stands out is the orthodox Communist call to revolution against autocratic and elitist regimes. The intolerable extent of callously regarded misery allowed to flourish under Haile Selassie is firmly, though gracefully, indicated, in this book devoted to the melodious ghosts of his regime. The vivid charm of these voices—the courtesy, the irony, the rhetorical flair, a certain antique quality of dispassionate speculation amid timeless horizons—transports us to an atmosphere perfumed with the lingering scents of the Queen of Sheba. The Emperor himself, though he is the titular subject, remains less than vivid—something of a mystery to his court as he was to the world, a grave and soft-spoken king seen through the wrong end of the telescope, a man who became invisible when he went to bed. Yet his world, the abruptly abolished world of the Amharic aristocracy, lives in these pages, so curiously delicate, of remembrance collected amid danger and ruin.

Schulz's Charred Scraps

LETTERS AND DRAWINGS OF BRUNO SCHULZ, *with Selected Prose,* edited by Jerzy Ficowski, translated from the Polish by Walter Arndt with Victoria Nelson. 249 pp. Harper & Row, 1988.

This is a book of remnants—a scrapbook of those drawings, letters, and uncollected prose pieces that Jerzy Ficowski, no less devoted a posthumous executor for Bruno Schulz than Max Brod was for Franz Kafka, has been able to find in the forty years since World War II's horrendous work of destruction and scattering ceased. Schulz was born in 1892 in the Galician province of the Austro-Hungarian Empire, a territory that after 1923 became part of independent Poland; he was murdered by a Gestapo agent in 1942 during a minor—for those black days—massacre in the Jewish ghetto of Drohobycz. Here in this town (now Drogobych in the Soviet Ukraine) Schulz had spent all fifty years of his life, supporting himself as a teacher of drawing and crafts in the secondary school. His training had been in architecture, and his first artistic exertions had been in graphic art. He published, in his fifth decade, two small but amazing books, whose awkward American titles are *Sanitorium Under the Sign of the Hourglass* (1934) and *The Street of Crocodiles* (1937). In the few years before frail health, chronic depression, and the advent of the Holocaust silenced him, he enjoyed a modest literary celebrity and communication with the brightest spirits of the Polish artistic world. After the war, Schulz's works have found—what he vainly sought during his lifetime— translation out of Polish into the major languages of Europe. The fevered brilliance of his descriptive prose and the bold mythologization he imposed on his childhood impressions have generated, if not quite the universal impact of Kafka's or García Márquez's fantasy, an exalted reputation among other writers. I. B. Singer has called him "one of the most remarkable writers who ever lived," Cynthia Ozick has paid Schulz the homage of devoting a novel *(The Messiah of Stockholm)* to the supposed discovery of the Polish writer's lost work *The Messiah*, and the Yugoslav Danilo Kiš has said simply, "Schulz is my god."

Schulz was, as his critical essays and comments make manifest, a bold and profound literary theorist, whose program has a postmodern ring to it. He approached literary works, including his own, as above all texts, collections of words encoded with "polysemantic, unfathomable" significance. His most extended and rapturous review praises a novel few non-Poles will have read, *The Foreigner*, by Maria Kuncewicz; in Schulz's interpretation, the adventures of the heroine, Róza, all work to deepen for her the meaning of a nonsensical German verse—*"Diese, diese, o ja, wunderschöne Nase"* ("This, this, oh yes, absolutely lovely nose")—encountered in her girlhood, during her first romantic involvement. "This was the text of Róza's fate, the couplet she would recite endlessly, each time with a different intonation, each time closer to understanding." Until this understanding is reached, she will be terrified by death, "which is devoid of meaning when it does not seal a destiny fulfilled." She cannot "be redeemed except by the words uttered that single time, the couplet that was her curse." The couplet somehow returns in the mouth of a doctor, and she attains the grace of psychological healing: "Discrepancies of time, place, and person are irrelevant to the psyche, hence they vanish before the essential semantic identity." But more happens than one heroine's revelation: "Into the clinical case, the psychoanalytical interview, eternity steps unnoticed, and it transforms the psychoanalytical laboratory into eschatological theatre." Or, expressed with an image of characteristically Schulzian violence:

> So it comes to pass that, when we pursue an inquiry into a character beyond a certain depth, we step out of the field of psychological categories and enter the sphere of the ultimate mysteries of life. The floorboards of the soul, to which we try to penetrate, fan open and reveal the starry firmament.

To Schulz's mind, primed by a Germanic mixture of Freud and Rilke, "Language is man's metaphysical organ." His brief essay "The Mythologizing of Reality" argues, decades before McLuhan, that the medium, language, is the message, delivering "Meaning or Sense" like some archetypal memory: "the word in its common usage today is only a fragment, remnant of some former all-embracing, integral mythology." "Philosophy is actually philology," not in the reductive sense that the old philosophical questions can be reduced to semantic confusions, but in the expansive sense of "the deep, creative exploration of the word"—"the primal word, the word that was not yet a sign but myth, story, sense." We resist, perhaps, the mystical connotations of "primal word" (Schulz speaks of its "shimmering aura" and cites the Biblical "In the beginning was the Word"), but we should have no problem with the more pragmatic assertions that "the nameless does not exist for us" and "what is put into words is already half under control." This potent act of taming gives Schulz's language its reverent urgency, the solemn thickness of its magical conjurations. In an essay on himself written for the poet and editor Stanislaw Witkiewicz, Schulz said, "The role of art is to be a probe sunk into the nameless. The artist is an apparatus for registering processes in that deep stratum where value is formed." The difference between art and philosophy "is not that art is a crossword puzzle with the key hidden, and philosophy the same crossword puzzle solved. The difference lies deeper than that. In a work of art the umbilical cord linking it with the totality of our concerns has not yet been severed, the blood of the mystery still circulates; the ends of the blood vessels vanish into the surrounding night and return from it full of dark fluid."

The image is typically visceral: Schulz in his fiction everywhere strives to physicalize the immaterial, rendering atmospheres into "plasmas," showing skies to be weighty accumulations, thickening and slowing the passage of appearances so that the reader becomes sleepy with the heavy verbal richness. It is as in his "Autumn," published here for the first time in English:

> The vast cavernous beds, piled high with chilly layers of sheets and blankets, waited for our bodies. The night's floodgates groaned under the rising pressure of dark masses of slumber, a dense lava that was just about to erupt and pour over its dams, over the doors, the old wardrobes, the stoves where the wind sighed.

Images crowd toward virtual gridlock, a frozen carnival of gnarled accuracies:

> Autumn looks for herself in the sap and primitive vigor of the Dürers and Breughels. That form bursts from the overflow of material, hardens into whorls and knots, seizes matter in its jaws and talons, squeezes, ravishes, deforms, and dismisses it from its clutches imprinted with the marks of this struggle as half-formed hunks, with the brand of uncanny life stamped in the grimaces extruded from their wooden faces.

Schulz's drawings and *cliché-verre* etchings—over fifty are reproduced here, at a generally stingy size, in a busy, choppy format full of photographs and border lines—have relatively little of this passionate reification. They accept conventions of doll-like stylization in depicting women, and most of the men look like Schulz in his photographs—twisted and foreshortened as if by some unconscious evasive maneuver. Though skillful and earnest in their fashion, the drawings also seem wooden and constrained, falling short of the pornography implicit in their ambience of deshabille, whips, and greasy hatching. Juliusz Flaszen, an acquaintance, recalled of Schulz in the late Twenties, "He was morbidly shy; I was right, I think, in setting him down as suffering from an inferiority complex. One day he brought along his paintings and drawings and asked for my opinion. The great part of this work consisted of pen and pencil sketches which in their thematics and technique recalled [Félicien] Rops. The chief motif was male sexual enslavement to the beautiful contours of the female body." One etching, from a cycle titled *A Book of Idolatry,* shows a naked woman, attended by a winged minion and elevated upon a fanciful couch, pressing her bare foot down into the face of a male adorer in suit and shoes. Others show men crawling and crouching on the floor, and half transformed into beasts. Schulz's work was admired, and his exhibits nearly always sold out—"at wretched prices," Flaszen added. "His self-esteem was so low that he always feared to overcharge." Schulz's graphic skills continued to serve him in darker times. After Drohobycz was occupied by the Soviets in 1939, local authorities commissioned from Schulz, according to an editorial note, "portraits of Stalin and scenes symbolizing the joys of annexation, painted in the obligatory manner of Socialist Realism." When the Nazis moved in, his drawings were admired by a Gestapo agent, who hired Schulz to decorate his child's bedroom with murals. In one version of his death, "he was shot in the street by a Gestapo officer who had a grudge against another Nazi, Schulz's temporary 'protector' who liked his paintings."* He was killed out of spite, like a pet dog.

The horrors of German rule over Poland permeate this book of remnants; its scraps of salvaged correspondence smell of slaughter and incineration. Vast numbers of his letters perished in the Holocaust, as did most of his correspondents. Before the war, Schulz in his loneliness was a dedicated letter-writer. In 1936 he wrote to Romana Halpern, "It is a pity we didn't know each other a few years ago; I was still able to write beautiful letters then. It was out of my letters that *Cinnamon Shops* [the literal title of *The Street of Crocodiles*] gradually grew. Most of these letters were addressed to Debora Vogel." All of Schulz's letters to Vogel, an

---

*From the introduction to *Sanitorium Under the Sign of the Hourglass* by the translator, Celina Wieniewska. The sole eyewitness account of Schulz's murder comes from Izydor Friedman. His response to Jerzy Ficowski's appeal for information, as quoted in the footnotes to *Letters and Drawings,* does not contain the motivation offered above, though it does give the name of the Gestapo agent who killed Schulz—Guenther. Friedman buried the body that night at a site he could not later identify; the Jewish cemetery no longer existed.

avant-garde poet and novelist, have vanished, as have his letters to another early encourager, Wladyslaw Riff, and to Schulz's fiancée, Józefina Szelinska, and to "muses" (as Schulz called them) like Maria Chazen and Zofia Nalkowska, and to Thomas Mann, whom Schulz admired next only to Rilke and to whom he confided the manuscript of his one German-language narrative, *Die Heimkehr*. *Die Heimkehr* has vanished, as has *The Messiah* and all the trove of "papers, notes, and correspondence" which Schulz told Izydor Friedman he had deposited with a "Catholic outside the ghetto." Friedman, one of the few witnesses to Schulz's life to survive the war, claimed, "Unfortunately he did not give me the person's name, or possibly I forgot it." No advertisement or search has discovered the person, or the cache—though Ficowski has lately expressed to journalists his belief that *The Messiah* will still be found.

Only four letters survive of those written before the publication of Schulz's first book in 1934. The surge of epistolary energy that helped create this book ebbed after its publication, though there are still flashes of poetic extravagance, of Schulz's visionary materialization of feelings. To Tadeusz Breza he wrote in 1934, "People's weakness delivers their souls to us, makes them needy. That loss of an electron ionizes them and renders them suitable for chemical bonding," and, later in the year, "For you must realize that my nerves have been stretched thin like a net over the entire handicraft center, have crept along the floor, smothered the walls like tapestry and covered the shops and the smithy with a dense web." His powers of expression revived in his last extended correspondence, with Ania Plockier, a young painter killed at the age of twenty-six by the Ukrainian militia. "More and more I have occasion to realize," he told her, "that delight with the world, spasms of disinterested joy, are only forms of personal hope, generalized pictures of vitality projected onto the artist's sensitivity." And he managed now and then to toss off a Schulzian gem of description: "On one early autumn evening we wandered through the park in the rain and behind our backs the traffic of families, the most intimate family history, unfolded in lighted windows."

But generally the surviving letters show him as a working man of letters, rather abjectly currying favor with the better-known, hinting to peers of possible literary favors they might bestow, seeking to wangle a leave from his depleting teaching post, complaining of writer's block, lamenting his second book's cool reception ("No one besides you has had one good thing to say about it"). To Romana Halpern he confessed, "It seems to me I have swindled the world by some sort of flash or glitter when there is nothing inside me." His real writing—passionate, luminous, warped by its own density—he saved for publication, as in his almost absurdly original afterword to a translation of Kafka's *The Trial,* in an eloquent riposte to a challenge by Witold Gombrowicz's and a warm review of Gombrowicz's *Ferdydurke,* above all in the imaginative episodes waiting to take their place somewhere in the next book of fiction. The greatest letters, like those of Kafka and Keats, are written by those with few other outlets; the individual recipient becomes a public. The Schulz letters salvaged here are not, by and large, of this unstinted quality; he did, after 1934, have a literary public and a role to play—burdensome, perhaps, for one so basically private—within a vivacious, Polish cultural world that was about to be crushed.

BIOGRAPHIES

The Process and the Lock

THE NIGHTMARE OF REASON: *A Life of Franz Kafka*, by Ernst Pawel. 466 pp. Farrar, Straus & Giroux, 1984.

The Nightmare of Reason is full of information and intellectual energy and should be read by everyone who cares about Kafka; it fills in many of the gaps and firms up some of the soft spots in Max Brod's indispensable but unavoidably personal biography of his friend, and offers a more contoured, searching version of the life than Ronald Hayman's staccato *Kafka*, of two years ago. However, one wishes that Ernst Pawel had found a slightly different tone in which to write. His prose, like his title, comes on too strong; his literary voice, as it details the earthly adventures of his quiet, almost unfailingly tactful protagonist, echoes at times the "booming parade-ground voice" of that much-maligned father, Herrmann Kafka. There is something bullying and hectoring about Mr. Pawel's approach as he boxes the young Kafka into a rather too classically Freudian Oedipal mess, with a coarse, crass father, a distant, distracted mother, two younger brothers both dead in infancy, and three little sisters to reinforce Franz's emotional arrest. "The symbiotic entanglement with his family," the biographer states in no uncertain terms, "the haunted pursuit of a mother lost to him along with two rivals killed by his own lethal fantasies, the obsessive struggle against the omnipotent father, spawned a rage so overpowering that it all but crippled his instincts and left him firmly locked in guilt beyond understanding." Mr. Pawel is, in his early pages, a dues-paying member of the "must have" school of biography:

> As a mother, Julie no doubt did her best; but having never been mothered herself, her best was a kind of corseted tenderness that must have felt like ice to the touch.

By this time, however, he must—at least at the conscious level—have come to terms with his mother's emotional distance.

The mob that for some days took over the streets of the city and beat up anyone who looked like a "dirty kike" must have given him clues to his identity that were hard to miss.

Emotional health and even flitting happiness were strangers, in Mr. Pawel's schematization, to the Kafka household. If Franz, the first and only surviving son, was "a child hating his father to the point of murder," his amiable relations with his sisters did not bode well, either: "They were good to him, he was fond of them, but at bottom the mirror-smooth harmony of these blood relations, so seldom ruffled by even the merest wisp of rivalry or jealousy, points to cold blood and vast distances." A triad of boldly declarative sentences takes us deep into the scarcely knowable: "Kafka grew up hating his body. He dreaded physical intimacy. Sex to him was the quintessence of filth, the antithesis of love." To be sure, passages from the diaries and letters are cited in support of Mr. Pawel's stark analysis; yet his tone throughout seems more of a prosecutor's than an admirer's. Innocent bystanders are suddenly indicted: Robert Klopstock, who with saintly devotion nursed the dying Kafka and who eventually became a universally esteemed pulmonary surgeon in the United States, is described as having "an ego as fragile as a raw egg" and as bombarding Kafka with "near-paranoid reproaches followed by abjectly hysterical apologies." Brod, though given his due elsewhere, gets batted down for "sentimental twaddle, at best the aging, childless Brod's projection of his own pietistic feelings." The European statesmen of 1914 are "criminals and imbeciles"; the Austrian military command is made up of "hopeless clowns." Even a long-dead English author, alluded to in one of Kafka's letters, gets hauled into court: "Swift, with a love life considerably more muddled than Kafka's, kept his marriage a secret, had no known progeny, and his expertise in child-rearing was most convincingly demonstrated in 'A Modest Proposal.' " A certain exasperation tinges the characterization of Kafka himself; his two attempts at getting married, to Felice Bauer and Julie Wohryzek, especially quicken Mr. Pawel's impatience. As he tells it, Felice, "numbed by the mute pleas of her would-not-be lover, who looked and acted like a moonstruck teenager, realized that left to his own devices he would forever go on wallowing in self-pity." The vocabulary as well as the viewpoint of Herrmann Kafka colors the young Kafka's engagement to Julie Wohryzek: "The prospect of his son—a shlemiel in many ways, but still, a doctor of jurisprudence and a scion of the House of Kafka—marrying the daughter of a petty *shammes* doubling as shoe-maker was nothing less than a slap in the face, a direct assault on his own hard-won social status." Why, oh why, the text seems to sigh, can't Kafka be sane like us, and handle these women like a man?

> There can be no doubt that the obsessive fear of sex, or more specifically of wallowing in lustful filth and degradation not with a paid hooker or lower-class shopgirl but with the virginal mother image he secretly wor-shipped and wanted to love, did, in fact, account for much of the tension of the relationship.

A little more doubt, in dealing with the virtual embodiment of it, might have been becoming to the biographer.

Mr. Pawel's prosecutorial edge is no accident; he has a case to prove. He wants to rescue Kafka's Jewishness from those who, following Brod's lead, would make of him a crypto-Christian allegorist and saint, and from those who would simply enroll him in the Teutonic pantheon of German-language classics:

> . . . to read him as a latter-day Kleist, to trace his inspiration back to primordial *Angst* or Kierkegaard, and to invoke Goethe, Dickens, and Dos-toevsky is to confuse form and substance, is to miss the essence of who he was and what he was struggling to discover within himself. Kafka's true ancestors, the substance of his flesh and spirit, were an unruly crowd of Talmudists, Cabalists, medieval mystics resting uneasy beneath the jumble of heaving, weatherbeaten tombstones in Prague's Old Cemetery.

He quotes a letter from Kafka to Brod on the difficulties of assimilation:

> Most of those who started to write in German wanted to get away from their Jewishness, usually with their fathers' vague consent (the vagueness of it was what made it outrageous). They wanted to get away, but their hind legs still stuck to the fathers' Jewishness, while the forelegs found no firm ground. And the resulting despair served as their inspiration.

Mr. Pawel diagrams the peculiar position of Prague Jewry in Kafka's lifetime; compelled, under the Hapsburg regime, to identify with Bohe-mia's German minority, they were thus doubly distrusted, by the Ger-mans as Jews and by the Czechs as Germans. Kafka and his father were typical of the generational progress. Herrmann, son of a kosher butcher in the ghetto of the Czech village of Wossek, left home at fourteen as a peddler and, after Army service, came to Prague, married a wealthy brewer's daughter, and founded a successful drygoods wholesale business. Franz, raised in middle-class style by nurses and governesses, attended compulsory German-language schools whose student bodies were preponderantly Jewish. In 1900, some eighty-five percent of the roughly thirty-five thousand German-speaking citizens in the Prague population of 420,000 were Jewish. The Kafkas were unusual in bearing a Czech name—*kavka* means "jackdaw"—and in speaking Czech at home. In the Prague pogrom of December 1897, Herrmann Kafka's establishment was spared by the Czech mob, and Franz Kafka's charmed career at the Workmen's Accident Insurance Institute for the Kingdom of Bohemia continued when this bureaucratic organization was taken over in 1918 by the newly created Republic of Czechoslovakia: under the Hapsburg monarchy, he had been one of the Institute's two token Jews; under the Czechs, he became the token German. By Mr. Pawel's analysis, Kafka's generation of Prague Jews, minimally observant and trained for assimilation, found most paths barred by "an endemic anti-Semitism." "The fathers, smugly content with having overcome piety and poverty, groomed their sons for roles they could never hope to play. The sons, however, found themselves locked out of the show altogether; and trapped between promise and reality, they drifted into literature as a way out of the impasse." Indisputably, Kafka, from his exhilarated discovery of Yiddish theatre in 1911 to the dreams of moving to Palestine that lit up his last months in 1924, was a man in search of the Jewishness that he felt his father had failed or refused to transmit to him. And yet, turning from Mr. Pawel's brief to Kafka's own works, one is struck again by how submerged their specifically Jewish elements are, by how directly his parables apply to the whole Western spiritual condition. *The Nightmare of Reason* quotes Simone de Beauvoir, raised as a Catholic, on the effect Kafka exerted on the postwar French intelligentsia:

> Faulkner, all the others, told us remote stories; Kafka spoke to us about ourselves. He revealed to us our own problems, confronted by a world without God and where nonetheless our salvation was at stake. No father had embodied the Law for us, but the Law was inflexibly engraved in us just the same.

Mr. Pawel's insistent references to the coming Holocaust shadow his narrative of Kafka's life in a way that felt to this reader somewhat unnecessary and rhetorical. It is necessary and instructive to be told what anti-Semitic riots raged in Prague during Kafka's lifetime, and to be given samples of the widespread racist journalism and speechifying of the time. It is eye-opening to learn that Kafka, safely employed at the Institute, refused to sponsor the application of an Orthodox Jewish friend, on the grounds that "The institute is off limits for Jews," and to learn that he himself wrote of Jews, to Milena Jesenská, "Sometimes I'd like to stuff them all into the drawer of my laundry chest, wait a while, then open the drawer a little to see if they've all been suffocated, and if not, close the drawer again, and so on to the end." It is a piquant flourish, perhaps, to add, apropos of little Franz's first day at school, that, "Earlier that year, in the not too distant Austrian town of Braunau, one Clara née Plözl, wife of the customs inspector Alois Hitler, had given birth to another of the emperor's subjects, a sickly infant whose survival seemed doubtful. He survived." We are reminded as well, in connection with Kafka's move to Berlin in 1923, that that same year "an Austrian ex-corporal led a handful of crazies, ex-officers, and other thugs in a coup." Yet in these touches, and in the frequent authorial foretelling of the mass murder that in the 1940s overtook Kafka's three sisters, Milena Jesenská, Brod's younger brother, and many other characters in Kafka's story, there is a danger of making Hitler the hidden hero of that story, and the Holocaust its culminating event. It is a doubtful presumption that "the figure of the head torturer [in "In the Penal Colony"] is a prescient portrait of Adolf Eichmann, drawn from life." It is not true, as the biography's last paragraph claims, that "The world that Kafka was 'condemned to see with such blinding clarity that he found it unbearable' was our own post-Auschwitz universe, on the brink of extinction." Kafka saw his own world, which held the seeds of the future, the traces of the past, and the timeless dilemmas of human existence. To make him a prophet of the Holocaust or of the totalitarianism that has overtaken Prague is to turn his art into magic and into a magician a man who found everything difficult, problematical, fraught, almost impossible. He died in 1924, and his visions were entirely based upon evidence that had accumulated up to that year.

In the presentation of this evidence Mr. Pawel's book is most valuable. The basis, structure, and personnel of the schools Kafka attended; the coffeehouse society of Prague's Jewish intellectuals; the kind of work Kafka with such oft-disclaimed competence performed for the Workmen's Accident Insurance Institute; the life and death of the mysterious asbestos factory of which he was part-owner and reluctant manager (Kafka, in fact, had more real experience of industrialism than all but a few modern writers); the biographies of the succession of women with whom he was involved; the labyrinthine changes of address and sanitorium that make up his history of residence; the contribution that the flu epidemic of 1918 made to Kafka's debilitation and eventual demise; World War I as it reverberated in imperial Prague—all this is set down with clarity and authority. Further, Mr. Pawel is shrewd and vivid, though brief, in treating the works themselves, sidestepping most of the tortuous commentary with such observations as, of *The Castle,* that Kafka "worked when, and only when, the spirit was upon him, guided strictly by its dictates rather than by any preconceived ideological road map, translating the dilemmas of his life into the paradoxes of his fiction," and "From several tentative drafts of further chapters in his notebooks it seems clear that the novel's growing complexity had outrun the author's power to control it—as suitable a conclusion to this extraordinary work as any that could be imagined." Born in Germany, the biographer has translated all the quotations afresh, pointing out some nuances (*Der Prozess* = "the process" as well as "the trial"; *Das Schloss* = both "the castle" and "the lock"). He places in a perspective of reasonable doubt Grete Bloch's claim (which Brod accepted) to have borne Kafka's child and Gustav Janouch's claim to have accurately transcribed Kafka's remarks of twenty-five years before. All of Kafka's major works are fixed in the time and place of their creation, along with the fallow periods when Kafka was given over completely to distraction and exhaustion. The biography supplies, in short, the full context in which the Kafka phenomenon emerged. How a brutish father and ineffectual mother produced a sensibility so subtle and tender, and how the bustling, gossipy literary bohemia of Bohemia, whose typical talents were facile and prolix, like Brod's and Franz Werfel's, nurtured an artistic vocation so austere and fanatic, are mysteries that research can scarcely touch. What research *can* touch Mr. Pawel here displays, albeit with a brusqueness that might have made Kafka wince. Kafka's life, so closely bound up with his work, fascinates us, it may be, unduly, at the price of a certain coarsening. As Elias Canetti has written in his own violation of the Kafka enigma, his brilliantly probing essay on the *Letters to Felice:* "There are writers, admittedly only a few, who are so entirely themselves that any utterance one might presume to make about them must seem barbarous."

Eliot Without Words

T. S. ELIOT: *A Life,* by Peter Ackroyd. 400 pp. Simon and Schuster, 1984.

Peter Ackroyd, at the end of two solid pages acknowledging thirty-nine libraries, collections, and archives plus twenty-seven individuals who aided the extensive research on his life of T. S. Eliot, confesses:

> I am forbidden by the Eliot estate to quote from Eliot's published work, except for purposes of fair comment in a critical context, or to quote from Eliot's unpublished work or correspondence.

Again and again, in the chronological plod of Mr. Ackroyd's assertions, one longs for the confirming quotation, the enlivening snatch of poem or letter, that would prove his point. Instead, we get a number, which tantalizingly refers us, in over fifty columns of endnotes, to some library where Eliot's own words are still locked up safe from all but a few prying eyes. "Should he adapt an academic career and raise a family? Or should he plan eventually to live in Paris? What was he to do? These were some of the worries which he poured out in his correspondence.[20]" Fumbling our way to the proper back page, we find "20 Eliot to Conrad Aiken, 25 February 1915. Huntington." Again: "Their relationship was further impaired when in 1954 Pound criticized Eliot's Christianity as 'lousy'; Eliot wrote a caustic letter back.[79]" The reader who would like to see Eliot being caustic in defense of his religion must travel, "79" informs him, to New Haven, and presumably beg access from the stern guardians of the Beinecke Library. Even when the source is not the great man's correspondence but his first wife's diary, a superscripted number pinch-hits for specifics: "Certainly he was himself capable of violent emotions, and in her diary Vivien remembered an instance of his sudden and violent ferocity.[62]" "Vivien's diaries for this period[21] give an extraordinary picture of a woman who is tearing herself to pieces, and scattering those pieces in the sight of all those she had known." Even when the source has been placed by others into print, the habit of paraphrase rules Mr. Ackroyd's style: "Virginia Woolf had denounced *The Rock* and in April 1934 was arguing violently with him about his religious convictions;[32] three months later she told Stephen Spender that Eliot seemed to be turning into a priest.[33]" The first number refers us to the fourth volume of the published diaries of Virginia Woolf, and the second to the fifth volume of the published letters. Seek, and ye shall find. Mr. Ackroyd considers Eliot to have been an elusive, all-too-mimetic man, with something peculiar hidden at his core; the words "curious," "peculiar," "unreal," and "bizarre" recur. Yet some of the strangeness of Eliot as portrayed here lies in the unnatural silence imposed upon him by the restrictions of his estate; but for a few phrases from his letters and an odd line or two of his verse, the poet walks gagged through his own biography.*

As early as 1925, Eliot had announced he did not want a biography of him written; this has not totally discouraged Mr. Ackroyd, nor T. S.

---

*Since the writing of this biography and this review he has been lovingly, voluminously ungagged, in *The Letters of T. S. Eliot: Volume I, 1898–1922,* edited by Valerie Eliot (Harcourt Brace Jovanovich, 1988). The editing, footnoting, printing, and binding couldn't be more handsome; but the avid peak of our curiosity about Eliot may have passed. The tenor of the reviews, at any rate, was rather cool. No major revelations forthcame, and most reviewers seemed merely confirmed in their previous bad impressions.

Matthews, whose impudent *Great Tom* (1974) skates saucily over great tracts of confessed ignorance, or Lyndall Gordon, whose *Eliot's Early Years* (1977) quotes its subject with relative abandon and nevertheless received a helpful reading from Valerie Eliot, nor those several friends—Robert Sencourt, Joseph Chiari, William Turner Levy, Victor Scherle—who have added their personal memoirs of Eliot to the swelling bibliography, nor the armies of literary critics who must draw upon what facts are known about the tortuous and reluctant production of the Eliot oeuvre. Although Mr. Ackroyd is certainly superior to Mr. Matthews in the number of archives and informants he has visited, he is English and born in 1949, so an air of book learning hovers over areas where his American senior was effortlessly at home. Mr. Ackroyd oversolicitously tells his English readers, apropos of Ezra Pound's nickname for Eliot, "Old Possum," that "the opossum [is] an animal which shams death in order to escape predators," and he informs his younger readers, apropos of the Twenties, that "this was the age of 'flappers' and 'bright young people,' that irruption of the pleasure principle between the Great War and the Depression." New Englanders will be somewhat disoriented by his opening pages, in which "Beverly" is spelled "Beverley," Eastern Point is spoken of as the Eliot family's own summer house rather than as an extensive section of Gloucester, the Harvard *Lampoon* (or the Lampoon Building) becomes "the Lampoon Club," and young salts ungeographically "would sail in Eliot's catboat along the coast of Massachussetts [*sic*] up to the Canadian border." Though Mr. Ackroyd has been a Mellon Fellow at Yale, he tends to see us as little Puritan dears far across the sea: America is "marked by a vague spirituality and an inchoate civilization," Eliot's father "represented the American aspiration toward success, thrift and practicality," and his do-gooding mother "was, to use a convenient analogy, a Fabian of American life." And the biographer's grasp of Eliot's religious life seems gingerly, though he musters what sympathy he can: "If it were necessary to locate those elements of the Christian faith which impressed Eliot most deeply, they would surely be those of prayer and confession, balm and absolution for a soul deeply conscious of sin. . . . That self-imposed martyrdom which Eliot had dramatised many years before in his Harvard poetry . . . is the particular fate of those who associate the senses with sin and guilt; such an association is formed early in life, and its origins are not susceptible to investigation."

Within its limitations—another of which is a slightly unctuous stiffness of tone, as if Mr. Ackroyd were trying to make adequately stuffy conversation with an odd old type with whom he has been condemned to spend a fiendishly prolonged sherry hour—the biography has the virtues of solidity and fairness. In orderly fashion it arrays the stages of Eliot's pilgrimage: the comfortable upbringing in the St. Louis family of Unitarian Brahmins, the brilliant but not quite comfortable academic career at Harvard, the escape to England in 1914, the escape into marriage in 1915, the few unsatisfactory years of schoolteaching, the harried and overworked but artistically valuable years at Lloyds Bank, the pleasant and lasting change to a publishing job at Faber and Faber in 1925, his reception into the Anglican Church and British citizenship in 1927, his agonized decision to leave his first wife in 1932, his increasingly public and hyperactive bachelor career as editor, lecturer, churchman, playwright, and international personage, and, finally, when it would seem that Old Possum should be playing dead, his happy marriage, in 1957, to a woman thirty-eight years younger than he. Eliot died in 1965, at the age of seventy-six. He was never entirely healthy, having been born with a double hernia, an overwrought nervous system, and a constitutional fragility. A doctor once told him, "Mr. Eliot, you have the thinnest blood I've ever tested." The English winters regularly laid him low with bronchitis and high fevers and his teeth gave him much pain and trouble. In late middle age he developed tachycardia (like "harbouring some runaway machine," he said) and emphysema. He smoked cigarettes most of his life and was a surprisingly heavy, though rarely demonstrative, drinker.

His marriage to Vivien Haigh-Wood was a wedding of maladies, since she, even when young, was something of a nervous wreck, given to headaches, depression, and excessive self-medication. Even her skin looked unhealthy, as Virginia Woolf more than once observed in her journals. A large amount of Eliot's energy was deflected into humoring and nursing his neurotic wife, in the very years when he was working full-time at Lloyds Bank and writing those poems and critical essays that renovated English poetry. After he left her, she would remember in her diaries, according to Mr. Ackroyd, "how gentle he was with her during her illnesses . . . how 'handy' he was around the house." Whatever neuroses and inabilities the virginal twenty-six-year-old groom brought to the precipitate wedding, "Viv" was certainly sicker than "Tom," and for seventeen years he endured her demands and collapses and abuse with a fortitude and patience that, if not absolutely saintly, were about all that could be humanly expected. Mr. Ackroyd states flatly, "The decision to leave his wife was justified—and it is significant that no one, not even the members of Vivien's own family, criticized him for it at the time." Eliot's feelings of guilt, however, gave even his lectures at the time of the separation an undercurrent of despair and self-disgust; poetry is a "mug's game," he told the Harvard audience for the Charles Eliot Norton lectures of

1932–33, and a poet "may have wasted his time and messed up his life for nothing." His sore conscience can only have been aggravated by Vivien's pathetic attempts, on his return to London, to confront him and win him back, or by her permanent commitment to a mental institution in 1938, or by her death there in 1947, at the relatively young age of fifty-eight. "Any man might do a girl in," he had written in "Sweeney Agonistes," "Any man has to, needs to, wants to / Once in a lifetime, do a girl in." By one account, he was "shattered by grief and almost despair" by Vivien's death, and by another he cancelled a lunch on the day of her funeral with a cable saying he had to "bury a woman" and was subsequently "unusually relaxed . . . almost gay at times." Mr. Ackroyd says, "These accounts are contradictory but not incompatible."

The same even-handedness characterizes Mr. Ackroyd's treatment of two other sensitive points in Eliot's story: his anti-Semitism, and his political conservatism. Concerning the former, the best-known literary evidence, besides a few veiled phrases in the early poems, is the observation in *After Strange Gods* that in "the society that we desire . . . reasons of race and religion combine to make any large number of free-thinking Jews undesirable." *After Strange Gods* comprised three lectures given at the University of Virginia in 1933, and was published by prior agreement with the university; Eliot never permitted them to be reprinted in any form. The poems, including the lines from "Burbank with a Baedeker: Bleistein with a Cigar" that run "The rats are underneath the piles. / The jew is underneath the lot," stood unchanged, though he capitalized "jew" in later editions. These lines from the *Waste Land* manuscripts—

> Full fathom five your Bleistein lies
> Under the flatfish and the squids.
> Graves' Disease in a dead jew's eyes!

—did not see print in Eliot's lifetime. Mr. Ackroyd found some slighting references to Jews in the unpublished correspondence, but none of them of later date than 1929. Eliot had, of course, a number of Jewish friends, and one of them, Leonard Woolf, said, "I think T. S. Eliot was slightly anti-Semitic in the sort of vague way which is not uncommon. He would have denied it quite genuinely." Mr. Ackroyd proposes a connection with the misogynistic traces in Eliot's utterances of the Twenties: "it seems likely that his distrust of Jews and women was the sign of an uneasy and vulnerable temperament in which aggression and insecurity were compounded. This is an explanation, however, and not a justification."

Of Eliot's politics, and especially on his often-chastised refusal to take an anti-Franco position on the Spanish Civil War, the young biographer, removed from the heat of these ardent old issues, ventures, "His scepticism about his own motives as well as those of others, and his general belief that one should not comment on any situation until one understood it thoroughly, made him refrain from making the kind of easy judgment or fashionable 'stand' in which others indulged." In contrast to Ezra Pound and Wyndham Lewis, and in spite of a "peculiar" letter to the *Daily Mail* in 1923 praising a series of pro-Mussolini articles, "Eliot recognized very well that the reliance upon order and 'the state' alone was a form of escapism, a cover for unprincipled militarism and nationalism." Not that Eliot was an outstanding democrat or populist; in those aggressive Virginia lectures he asserted with stark elitism, "The number of people in possession of any criteria for discriminating between good and evil is very small." But not even the haziest undergraduate should be allowed to confuse Eliot's circumspect, if paternalistic, ideas of a Christian society* with the irrational and vicious fascism that Pound wound up espousing.

Eliot was, as his employers and co-workers all recognized, a reasonable and practical man: an effective and conscientious banker, and an even more able editor in a publishing house. Pound himself, in 1915, had written reassuringly to Henry Ware Eliot predicting to him that his son's progress in London would be smoother and swifter than Pound's own; and so it proved. Pound went to Paris, then Italy, and drove his great talent onto the shoals of fanaticism, disgrace, and despair. Eliot stayed in England, and in the postwar period reaped honors, popular success as a playwright, and virtually sacred cultural status. "Eliot had always been the subtler and more complicated man, shrewd enough to make his peace with an age to which he did not truly belong." As editor at Faber and Faber

---

*Some of the ideas, indeed, expressed in "The Idea of a Christian Society" (1939) have a surprisingly contemporary, ecological ring. From his peroration: "We are becoming aware that the organization of society on the principle of private profit, as well as public destruction, is leading both to the deformation of humanity by unregulated industrialism, and to the exhaustion of natural resources, and that a good deal of our material progress is a progress for which succeeding generations may have to pay dearly. I need only mention, as an instance now very much before the public eye, the results of 'soil-erosion'—the exploitation of the earth, on a vast scale for two generations, for commercial profit: immediate benefits leading to dearth and desert. . . . For a long enough time we have believed in nothing but the values arising in a mechanized, commercialized, urbanized way of life: it would be as well for us to face the permanent conditions upon which God allows us to live upon this planet. And without sentimentalizing the life of the savage, we might practise the humility to observe, in some of the societies upon which we look down as primitive or backward, the operation of a social-religious-artistic complex which we should emulate upon a higher plane."

and of *The Criterion*, Eliot usefully encouraged younger poets from Auden and Spender down to Ted Hughes and Thom Gunn. "Eliot's contemporaries, like Lewis or Pound, were generally quite unable to see the solid or objective merit in the work of the generation then emerging, but Eliot was able to get outside his own preconceptions and assumptions so that he could spot the real thing, even in work very different from his own." He was even, Mr. Ackroyd claims, something of a postmodernist: "it was Eliot who in the end loosened the hold of the 'modernists' on English culture—not only did he assert the public role and 'social usefulness' of the writer in an almost nineteenth-century manner, but he also announced that the principles he derived from his religious belief were more enduring than literary or critical ones." Where the typical modernist religion was private and revolutionary, like the arcana of Yeats or D. H. Lawrence's bombastic eroticism, Eliot found his own answer in a long-established institution, the Anglican Church, whose committees he did not spurn and whose ongoing existence in society instilled, as did the councils of publishing, the human lessons of compromise and adjustment. In temper Eliot was close to the eclectic Joyce: both men warmed their genius on old loyalties and demotic language, their heads a mix of music-hall tunes and medieval exemplars. Eliot, so long queasy at the feast of life, ended as a celebrant of domestic pleasures, his voyage like Bloom's come home to (as his last published poem, "A Dedication to My Wife," pungently puts it) "The breathing in unison / Of lovers whose bodies smell of each other."

Along with a freshly detailed impression of Eliot's hard-working worldliness—how many lectures he gave! how many cultural excursions across the Channel and the Atlantic he undertook, in ill health and good!—Mr. Ackroyd's biography affords a renewed appreciation of the immense difficulty with which Eliot pulled his few poems out of himself. The fitful and pained assembly of fragments into *The Waste Land*, and Eliot's diffidence in accepting Pound's editorial slashing and in affixing to the published text, at the last minute, the suavely owlish "Notes," have been well documented by the publication in facsimile of the manuscripts in 1971. One turns those facsimile pages reverently, noticing with what furious speed Eliot wrote when inspiration was upon him, as it was in the "Elizabeth and Leicester" and "water-dripping" sections. He was, for all his professed "classicism," a most unsystematic bard, given to long fallow periods and much advice-seeking from interested friends; not only Pound but Vivien annotated the *Waste Land* manuscripts, and John Hayward was to serve as consultant on *Four Quartets*. Between these two major poems, in nearly twenty years of what should have been his prime, there was precious little, notably "The Hollow Men" of 1925 and "Ash-Wednesday" five years later—poems of a suppliant thinness, affecting chiefly in their near approach to total silence, in their sense of utterance achieved out of a desert dryness. And *Four Quartets*, which renewed his reputation and gives ballast to his poetic oeuvre, was carried to completion, we are assured by Burton Raffel in his *T. S. Eliot* (1982), because of "the coming of World War II and the fact that it made further theater work for the moment impossible." From the unfinished music-hallish "Sweeney Agonistes" on, Eliot's heart belonged to the theatre; he had always been a poet of voices, of shifting impersonations. Mr. Ackroyd finds even in Eliot's Ph.D. thesis on F. H. Bradley proof of his "extraordinary ability to create a synthetic discourse; he is able to employ over an extended space a certain form of language while simultaneously remaining quite detached from it." Having read Eliot's letters to Pound, he marvels at "Eliot's extraordinary ability to mimic Pound's verbal mannerisms, as if he were willingly immersing himself in his personality. He even goes so far as to fabricate his signature in a way similar to Pound's, so that it forms a kind of hieroglyph." This propensity for mimicry Ackroyd relates to an inner vacuum, a central incoherence. Edmund Wilson found Eliot's personality "really rather incoherent." Wilson had heard Eliot read in New York in 1933 and wrote to John Dos Passos, "He is an actor and really put on a better show than Shaw. . . . He gives you the creeps a little at first because he is such a completely artificial, or, rather, self-invented character." V. S. Pritchett described him as "a company of actors inside one suit, each twitting the others." Wyndham Lewis saw him as "an inveterate *moqueur.*" Siegfried Sassoon referred to his "cold-storaged humanity" and once heard him claim that "all great art is based on a condition of fundamental boredom." Lady Ottoline Morrell wrote of her first encounter with Eliot, "I found him dull, dull, dull. He never moves his lips but speaks in an even, mandarin voice. . . . I think he has lost all spontaneity and can only break through his conventionality by stimulants or violent emotion." Before he perfected his impersonations of a banker and a clergyman, there was a latent extravagance in his dandified torpor; several acquaintances of the Twenties detected "green powder on his face"—"pale but distinctly green," the Sitwells thought, "the colour of forced lily-of-the-valley." Some of the japes and poses affected by the young Eliot sound quite mad. As he and Vivien thrashed through their *maladie à deux,* nervous collapse was held off by a grim will.

The private springs he drew upon for his poetry were exceptionally deep and difficult of access. A poet of Auden's preening fluency must have seemed to him a creature from another planet. He believed, as firmly as the Surrealists, in the crucial collaboration of the subconscious, of buried forces he hoped to call to the surface with a drumbeat of verbal rhythm. When he wrote the final sections of *The Waste Land,* he told an interviewer, "I wasn't even bothering whether I understood what I was saying." His imagination was thoroughly auditory, a matter of voices and repetitions; sharp visual images become ever more rare in his poetry as the cadence of utterance, increasingly pontifical and ruminative, takes over. After the example of Dante, he strove for simplicity and directness, to the point of baldness; in an unpublished address given in New Haven in 1933 he spoke of hoping to write poetry "with nothing poetic about it, poetry standing naked in its bare bones, or poetry so transparent that we should not see the poetry, but that which we are meant to see through the poetry." However lame and flat the thing being said (and his tranced way of composing admits much that seems flat and semi-conscious), the music is real, and seeks those ancient centers of awareness where incantation and lullaby merge.

Eliot was in his life a paradigm of modernism, a dutiful product of the nineteenth century who broke through his repressions with drumbeat, pastiche, and parody. Though critics still find much to fume at, his bare-bones, nearly transparent poetry will not go away; there will be no anthologies without him. His attempts to bring verse back onto the English stage are of irreducible literary interest, though perhaps they are better read than played. As a literary critic, he had the advantages of a superb ear and an outsider's irreverence; his essays up to about 1935 contain more ideas, more energizing and clarifying insights into the classics of the English language than anything since. Twenty years have passed since his death, and his claims to privacy need no longer be rigorously respected. As Henry James rollingly wrote of the posthumous publication of Hawthorne's journals:

> These liberal excisions from the privacy of so reserved and shade-seeking a genius suggest forcibly the general question of the proper limits of curiosity as to that passive personality of an artist of which the elements are scattered in portfolios and table-drawers. It is becoming very plain, however, that whatever the proper limits may be, the actual limits will be fixed only by a total exhaustion of matter.

Goody Sergeant; the Powerful Katrinka; K.S.W.

ONWARD AND UPWARD: *A Biography of Katharine S. White,* by Linda H. Davis. 300 pp. Harper & Row, 1987.

Those of us who knew Katharine Sergeant White only relatively late in her life learn a lot from *Onward and Upward.* We learn that, as a young lady from Brookline attending Miss Winsor's School in Boston, she was known as Goody Sergeant: an old classmate told her biographer, Linda H. Davis, "We called her Goody Sergeant behind her back, shortening it to Little Goody or simply Goody, because she was the goodest and the brightest in the class." We learn that her first husband, the lawyer Ernest Angell, would sometimes call her, after she went to work for *The New Yorker* in 1925, Katrinka, referring to the comic-strip character the Powerful Katrinka—Ms. Davis reveals her own youth in supplying a footnote explaining Fontaine Fox's "Toonerville Folks" as if few remain to remember that jaunty single-panel cartoon, with its rickety trolley car and highly comical figure of a super-strong woman. The nickname was bestowed, the biographer conjectures, with "perhaps some underlying resentment," and indeed each partner of the impressive couple, in fourteen years of wedlock, had acquired reason to regard the other with mixed emotions. Divorce in 1929 was followed later the same year by Katharine's marriage to E. B. White, and it was her second married name, with its forceful initials K.S.W. (attached to notes and memos in a hand of singular clarity and erectness), that she carried through most of her more than thirty-five years as an editor with *The New Yorker.*

To say that she took to her editorial work there like a duck to water would be an understatement, since heaven provides water whereas she to a marked degree had to create the element she prospered in. The magazine was six months old, predominantly humorous in content and masculine in personnel, and financially faltering when she was hired by its editor and founder, Harold Ross, as a first reader of manuscripts. Both she and he were thirty-two years old. Her two marriages to gifted and complex men come in for a good deal of scrutiny in *Onward and Upward,* but no less interesting, with its own veil of impenetrable privacy, was her professional mating with Harold Ross, a man as superficially coarse and bumptious as she was refined and dignified. It would appear that he needed her—her fierce Bryn Mawr education, her aristocratic sureness of taste, her instinctive courage and integrity—and she needed him; his almost inchoate energy and perfectionism created, in this fledgling weekly, an arena where, more than in any home, she felt important and active, useful and well compensated. She was hired for part-time work at twenty-five dollars a week; within two weeks she was working full-time at twice the salary. Women made Ross uncomfortable, and she would say that she "never felt any attraction to Ross as a male. In fact I couldn't see how anybody could bear to be married to him, but we were fond of each other and had complete faith in each other. When he died I felt I had lost my best friend." Mrs. White told her husband's biographer, Scott Elledge (in a statement only partially quoted by Ms. Davis), "Ross was furious that I was a woman but he soon came to depend on me and accept me." James Thurber, in his fanciful memoir, *The Years with Ross,* has the awed Ross say, of the then Mrs. Angell, "She knows the Bible, and literature, and foreign languages, and she has taste." It was she who persuaded Ross to publish not just light verse but poetry, and, though she disavowed it, she is generally given credit for pushing the fiction in the direction of greater seriousness and scope. Not only was her advice sought on every kind of editorial question, but Raoul Fleischmann, *The New Yorker's* owner, thanked her for helping form policy on advertising:

> Being a sensitive, cultured New Englander, imbued with the fine conscience characteristic of that famed rock-ribbed area, you had strong feelings involving honesty, decency and believability in the advertising we should accept, and you got Harold seriously interested. In spite of a few fumbles at the outset, when we got a bit educated, [we] were all for your ideas, and it evolved that our current acceptance of advertising is based solidly on certain musts and must-nots.

E. B. White thought that his wife and Ross "met at one point (they both thought the same things were funny)." Another point, surely, was the ethical ardor they both brought, from such different backgrounds and temperaments, to the business of getting out a weekly magazine.

Her determination to have a career was unusual but long-held: "I can hardly remember a time in my childhood, absurd a child as I must sound to admit it, when my plans for myself 'grown-up' did not include both marriage and a definite career." She wrote this in an essay of 1926, "Home and Office," addressing feminist issues that, sixty years later, are more alive than ever. "If honest, I must admit to a distinct personal ambition that is thwarted and an underlying cause for unhappiness when I cannot do the work of mind, not hands, for which I am best fitted." Katharine was the youngest of three daughters born to Charles Spencer Sergeant, the son of a grain merchant from Northampton, Massachusetts, and Elizabeth ("Bessie") Blake Shepley Sergeant, from Naples, Maine. The Sergeant side, especially, held a number of educated and independent-minded women; four of Charles Sergeant's five sisters remained single, and two became teachers following their graduation from Smith. As she approached the age of seventy, Katharine saluted, in one of her gardening essays, "my New England aunts . . . who cultivated their own gardens, and who had strong opinions on Rights for Women." On her mother's side, there was the redoubtable "Aunt Poo," an artist who, at the age of fifty-one, married a thirty-year-old Japanese, Hyozo Omori, and, after his untimely death, lived in Japan, translating Lady Murasaki and performing so heroically in the great earthquake of 1923 that she was awarded the Order of the Rising Sun. Katharine's older sister Elsie became a writer, and an uneasy rivalry between the two lasted until Elsie's death in 1965. Katharine followed her to Bryn Mawr, whose president, Martha Carey Thomas, the second woman in the world to receive a doctorate of philosophy (she had to go to Zurich to get it), urged a life of "intellectual renunciation" upon her students, and supervised a rigorous, classical education as free as possible from male distraction: "It is undesirable to have the problems of love and marriage presented for decision to a young girl during the four years when she ought to devote her energies to profiting by the only systematic intellectual training she is likely to receive during her life." Even if she were so ill-advised as to marry, the Bryn Mawr graduate should ideally be "both economically and psychologically independent" from her husband.

Some other factors possibly contributed to Katharine Sergeant's habit of independence and personal achievement. No brother was present in the Sergeant household, to hand the girls a second fiddle. Bosomy, unambitious Bessie Sergeant died, of maltreated appendicitis, when her youngest daughter was only six, so that Charles Sergeant thenceforth raised the girls in company with his sister, "Aunt Crully," an eloquent Smith graduate and former headmistress. Katharine went off to Miss Winsor's seventh grade well read and instructed, if (Ms. Davis suggests) insufficiently cuddled. Also, early in her marriage to Ernest Angell, when their infant daughter was not quite a year old, he enlisted in the Army and was not discharged until twenty-two months later—"Your grandfather was overseas longer than almost anybody I knew," Katharine would write to her granddaughter Callie Angell, with a rhythm as of relived pain. He came back decorated, debauched ("Soldiers who went to France, as your grandfather Angell did," Katharine wrote to Callie, "came back with the French idea that a wife and a mistress was the way to live"), and determined to leave Cleveland, where he had been raised and had joined his father's law firm. They came to New York, which suited his wife fine. In most of the years before she was hired by Ross, she had managed to find jobs, paid or volunteer—interviewing patients at Massachusetts General Hospital, conducting a door-to-door survey of handicapped people in Cleveland, lobbying for worker-protection laws, reading to children at Boston's Children's Hospital (this medical emphasis was perhaps related to her mother's painful and needless early death and certainly to her own notorious and uninhibited lifelong fascination with matters of health), raising money for Bryn Mawr, writing articles for *The New Republic* when she accompanied Ernest to Hispaniola, running errands for a decorator friend in Sneden's Landing. She was a doer. While in Nevada for three months, to obtain her divorce, she got involved in ranch life and round-ups to the extent of getting kicked by a horse—"a distinction," she wrote E. B. White, "of which I'm a trifle vain."

By the terms of the agreement, custody was joint. Nancy Angell, twelve, and Roger, nine, were to spend weekdays with their father and weekends, holidays, and summer vacations with their mother. Since she had a full-time job and the divorce, however provoked, was her desire, and since no account implies that Ernest Angell was anything less than a loving father, this might seem a civilized and enlightened arrangement; but, Ms. Davis tells us, without any corroborating quotation, "Katharine suffered terrible guilt feelings about the custody arrangement the rest of her life." This is but one of numerous places where the biographer, with surprising sharpness, ascribes guilt feelings to her subject or in her own voice criticizes her. Katharine was extravagant, she insists: she employed too many servants, refused to do housework and was "nearly incapable in the kitchen," bought the best for herself in clothes, and took the "opulent" Twentieth-Century Limited to Reno, where she stayed in "the town's new luxury hotel" and "put up at a ranch, the costlier way to wait out a divorce." As a person, we are told, she was unconfiding, hypochondriacal, relatively insensitive "to human needs and complexities," sometimes brusque and formidable, and work-centered. She trysted with E. B. White in Saint-Tropez and Corsica while still married to Ernest Angell, yet "always vigorously denied that Andy had had anything to do with the break-up of her marriage" and "was never comfortable . . . with the circumstances of her divorce." Well, we want at times to ask, so what? Nothing is obtained for nothing, and if her passionate involvement with *The New Yorker* sometimes detracted from her domestic performance, we can scarcely be as shocked as seems Ms. Davis, who in the course of writing this biography herself married and bore two children and was perhaps exceptionally sensitive to familial responsibilities. If Katharine Sergeant had heeded Carey Thomas's Amazonian advice, she wouldn't have married at all; when she confided to a classmate that she was engaged, her fellow Bryn Mawrtyr spontaneously exclaimed, "Oh, Katharine, how perfectly awful!"

In fact, what emerges from *Onward and Upward*, and from E. B. White's passing sketches of his wife in *One Man's Meat* and elsewhere, and from the overflowing letters of K.S.W.'s later years, and from the memories of most who knew her even slightly, is how much warmth she did convey, above and beyond as well as within her editorial duties. Her good humor and resilience were as conspicuous as her dignity and (when provoked) her hauteur. Not all of Ms. Davis's psychologizing takes the form of stricture; some of it is appraisal, and feels quite just:

> Katharine White's was a deeply private nature, her life, essentially creative. Much of her time was spent alone in a room—reading, writing, and editing. Her personality is perhaps finally understood in this context: as one who needed this kind of solitary activity, and consequently more replenishment than the ordinary person needs from the world outside.

Her creativity expressed itself not only in her own slight, though confident and lively, literary output, but in her endless editing. To the born editor, it must be, the mass of manuscripts looms as nature and experience do to the writer—as a superabundance to be selected from, and refined, and made shapely and meaningful. The attentive editor shapes, or at least pats, the writers. Katharine Angell's jobs before 1925 were almost all social work, of a sort; she liked to deal with people, on the terms work provided. "In her contact with writers, whom she endlessly reassured, counseled, encouraged, and comforted, and to whom she was always available, Katharine was essentially maternal; paradoxically, she was unable to mother her own children. She was compelled to express her maternity by leaving her family, as, years earlier, she had left Nancy in the care of a nurse so that she could do volunteer work with children. . . . Editing gave her the distance she required while simultaneously allowing her to free her abundant warmth and gregariousness." While her three children, who are all alive and well, might dispute the down side of this analysis, few of her innumerable correspondents could deny that "Katharine White's letters give no indication of her formidableness: one who knew her only through her letters would find there a freer and more openly affectionate person than the woman others knew in life."

Though she was able to deal affably with such prickly male authors as John O'Hara and Vladimir Nabokov, female writers like Jean Stafford and Mary McCarthy elicited her least guarded epistolary affection, making up, perhaps, for a lack she once confided in a letter to her husband: "All I need is a woman friend or two which seems to be my great NYC lack." Faith McNulty is quoted to the effect that the "impression of strength" Mrs. White gave may have tended to isolate her: "I suspect that she did a lot of understanding of other people who leaned on her in various ways, but she looked so capable that it would not occur to one that she might need any sort of support."

She did not lack, in the second half of her life, for loyalty and love from her husband, nor for family bustle, nor for grandchildren (nine) and, toward the end, great-grandchildren (six). Ms. Davis paints an engaging picture of the North Brooklin matriarch as she tries to impart to her proliferating descendants the severity of Maine's anti-marijuana laws and such old-fashioned customs as plum pudding for Christmas and dressing up for dinner. Her own girlhood, with its soft Brookline lawn and its summers of gathering water lilies by canoe on Lake Chocorua, returned in glowing paragraphs in her discursive, erudite gardening essays, posthumously collected in a lovely book that is sadly shy of its intended last chapter, about the gardens of her childhood, which her declining health didn't allow her to write. From almost the day of her retirement in 1961, her body was beset by a series of mishaps and illnesses: falls, faints, fears of a brain tumor, a blocked carotid artery that was misdiagnosed for eight months, and—most lastingly, painfully, humiliatingly, and expensively— a rare skin disease, subcorneal pustular dermatosis, which in its worst phases shed her skin like a snake's and precluded all but the lightest clothing. Cortisone side effects, shingles, a fractured vertebra, a kidney infection, osteoporosis, diabetes, failing vision, and congestive heart failure added to her Job-like plague of complaints, about which she was frank and animated—"I slop about all ungirdled and wearing loose cotton"—in the letters that she pushed out through the haze of drugs, often dictating and then emending in her shaky hand. She struggled on bravely to the age of eighty-four; though she was famous for her hypochondria, no one could quarrel with her last recorded words: "I'm sick."*

Linda Davis deserves our gratitude for bringing Katharine White back to life—for placing her career as woman and editor in perspective, for eliciting interviews from living witnesses of this career, for putting into print the subject's written views of herself, and for publishing such a delectable array of photographs, including the striking, rather melancholy near-profile of Katharine Angell used on the jacket. Her handsome looks were not those of a typical thin-skinned New Englander; there was some-

---

*Her mother's last words could also have been hers: Bessie Sergeant, dying at forty-one, had said to her sister from her bed of agony, "Nobody can say I didn't have courage."

thing exotic—Latin, or even Middle Eastern—about the thick hair pulled back in a big bun, the hook nose, the heavy lids and shadowed gray (not blue, as Brendan Gill to her vexation claimed in his *Here at The New Yorker*) eyes. *Fortune* in 1934 described her as "hard, suave, ambitious," and the suavity was there, the photographs, and an elegant caricature by Peter Arno, remind us.

Ms. Davis began this book as her master's thesis, and the many facts she had to marshal come on a bit jumpily. Her information, especially in the first chapters, seems crowded and scattered—we would like to know more, for instance, of Elsie Sergeant's writing and history of publication, and how Ernest Angell, having been "energetically, audaciously unfaithful," could have been so hurt and angry when Katharine decided to leave him. I have never before read a book-length biography in which the subject's date of birth is not given and even the year left somewhat ambiguous. Ms. Davis says "Katharine had been married only nineteen months when . . . she became pregnant with her first child"; in fact, Nancy, her first child, was *born* nineteen months after the wedding. The biography speaks of the Algonquin Hotel as being, in relation to *The New Yorker* office building, "conveniently located in the next block" when in truth, if you leave by the 44th Street entrance, as anyone would, it's the *same* block. "Lady Murasaki" is the name not of a book but of an author.* An occasion is described as dinner that I remember as lunch, having been there. And no doubt more nits could be picked, by those who know.

However, I liked and admired the biography's overall organization, in rather sweeping topical chapters that lift us above the plod of years, and the biographer's lack of timidity in dealing with her subject. She expresses her own literary opinions firmly ("Katharine . . . was blind to the strongest virtues in her own writing"), speculates boldly upon the thorny and delicate issues of Katharine's mothering, wiving, and formidability, and draws as close to the dead woman as she can, detailing her diseases and sleeping habits and cuticle-picking and even sharing with us what the Whites thought was the right amount of married sex (once or twice a week). Katharine White no doubt would have deplored some of these revelations. She scorned publicity, not out of shame but in aesthetic distaste. When, in 1937, she was invited to be included in a book called *Women of Achievement*, she declined, saying, "I can't see any reason for

---

*In E. B. White's wartime essay, "Aunt Poo," reprinted in *One Man's Meat*, he also italicizes the name of the author of the eleventh-century *The Tale of Genji*, as if she were a book herself, and gives the Japanese earthquake year as 1922, in which Miss Davis follows him.

such a book, other than to satisfy the vanity of the ladies described in it."
She and Ross agreed in regarding their magazine's workings as a purely
private matter; gossipy books by *New Yorker* insiders like Thurber and
Gill, as they began to be published, gave her pain, benign though they
generally were. Yet the truth-seeking spirit of *Onward and Upward,* even
where the tone turns combative and carping, is surely the right and
worthy one, and one suited to its honest, industrious, selflessly engaged
subject.

Katharine White's achievements—"the best woman editor in the
world," Janet Flanner called her—were by the nature of editorial work
largely invisible; an editor is like an actor or actress in that the performance leaves its traces mostly in hearsay and memory. The satisfaction
Mrs. White took in her work focused on the product and did not ask that
she herself be made widely visible. Still, it is nice to see her here, from little
beribboned bookworm to infirm great-grandmother; her life offers a
model, in its stresses as well as its surmountings, for the many women
now who bravely try to combine a full career with a full womanliness.

Witty Dotty

DOROTHY PARKER: *What Fresh Hell Is This?,* by Marion Meade. 459 pp. Villard,
1988.

It is hard to know what made reading this biography as enjoyable as it
was, since the writing is shoddy, the mood sour, and the subject rather
resolutely unsympathetic. Perhaps in my case it was a teen-age infatuation
with the Algonquin Round Table, or what I imagined of it with the help
of the late Bennett Cerf, who used to compile books of jokes (e.g., *Try and
Stop Me* and *Shake Well Before Using*) that drew heavily upon the alleged
ripostes and verbal barbs of Mrs. Parker, Robert Benchley, Alexander
Woollcott, Franklin P. Adams, George S. Kaufman, Marc Connelly,
Heywood Broun, and other "celebrated wits" of the Twenties, who,
legend assured me, liked nothing better than to have lunch together at
their own special table at the Algonquin Hotel and endlessly bask in one
another's banter. That such an angelic assembly, glorying in its own pure
being, objectively existed seemed proved by a fallout of books that reached
us provincial mortals—Mrs. Parker's slim volumes of poems and short
stories, F.P.A.'s copious verse and anthologies, and, above all, the humorous essays of Robert Benchley, packaged under such saucy labels as *My*

Ten Years in a Quandary and How They Grew and *20,000 Leagues Under the Sea, or David Copperfield.* The very titles bring back the sickly-yellow, pencil-gouged look of the old oaken high-school library tables where, trying to stifle my laughter lest I become known as a discipline problem, I used to read Benchley's collections, with their tidy illustrations by Gluyas Williams. It is fascinating, if a bit drearily so, to learn now, from Ms. Meade's book, that Benchley, the epitome in print of hilarious innocence, who never penned a word that stirred a licentious shadow in an adolescent's mind, was in his personal, New York life a priapic demon. Having settled his wife with a "Victorian divorce" in Scarsdale, he kept his own kimono at Polly Adler's brothel and "played backgammon with the madame for the services of her women." Outside the whorehouse walls, "the wife of a well-known banker was so eager to continue sleeping with him that she once crawled through the transom of his room at the Royalton Hotel," and he was praised for his phallic grandeur by no less a connoisseuse than Tallulah Bankhead. Nor were the other Round Table regulars models of monogamy:

> While most of Dorothy's wedded friends were less noisy about their troubles than the [F. Scott] Fitzgeralds, their marriages seemed no better. Benchley . . . was in a dreadful mess. George Kaufman had stopped sleeping with Beatrice. Frank Adams bedded a succession of young women, whose names he flaunted in his column for his wife and a million New Yorkers to read over their morning coffee.

Coffee, however, was not this crowd's beverage of choice; the Algonquin circle brimmed with alcohol. Heywood Broun "had a habit of fueling himself all day long from his hip flask." Charles MacArthur, soon after he arrived from Chicago in 1922, "was putting away a quart of Scotch every night." Benchley and Mrs. Parker came late to the joys of the bottle but became unshakable devotees. Benchley's father in Worcester, Massachusetts, had been an alcoholic, and his son was an "ardent prohibitionist," who hailed the ratification of the Eighteenth Amendment as "too good to be true." But on the night of the Dempsey-Carpentier fight, in July of 1921, a group of Round Tablers were celebrating Dempsey's victory at Tony Soma's speakeasy, on Forty-ninth Street, and Benchley, who usually drank coffee at the speakeasy, was persuaded to have an Orange Blossom. Within weeks, he had moved on to whisky sours and become a bibulous mainstay at Tony's, where liquor was served in thick white china cups. He favored rye, but was not above adding vodka to chocolate ice-cream sodas; the story goes—try and stop me—that when Scott Fitzgerald said to him, "Bob, don't you know that drinking is slow death?,"

Benchley responded, "So who's in a hurry?" Benchley died (like Broun and Woollcott) in his fifties—of a cerebral hemorrhage complicated by cirrhosis of the liver.

Dorothy Parker, up to her marriage, in 1917, to Edwin Pond Parker II, was alcohol-innocent: "She hated the taste of liquor herself and refused to touch it." Her husband, however, was a tremendous drinker, whose nickname in the ambulance corps was Spook, "because hangovers made him look pale as a ghost," and who returned from the war addicted to morphine as well. To make herself companionable to Eddie and to such sportive *Vanity Fair* colleagues as Robert Sherwood, she began to allow herself a cocktail or two, despite being warned by the then-abstemious Benchley, "Alcohol will coarsen you." Gin made her sick, but, "after a good deal of experimentation, she found that Scotch whisky, without water, was generally quick, safe, and reliable." Although both her marriages—to Eddie and to Alan Campbell, a fellow writer and rumored homosexual—dissolved in alcoholic brawls, and long stretches of her career were soddenly unproductive, she remained faithful to Scotch into her seventies: "Several times she went too far with Scotch and found herself in Flower Fifth Avenue Hospital. Whenever visitors appeared, she politely offered them a drink, then guessed she would pour one for herself." A friend of her old age, Parker Ladd, thought to reduce her dependence by emptying a bottle with her:

> One night shortly before Christmas 1965, he prepared highball after highball for them, swallowing a little of his own and dumping the rest down the sink. Finally he heaved a sigh of relief to find the bottle empty. To his amazement, Dorothy hauled herself up and began rummaging around on the closet floor among some old shoes. In triumph, she produced another bottle of Scotch.

For a time in Hollywood in 1951, she found a housemate with a thirst to match hers—James Agee, who, she told S. J. Perelman, had on one Friday evening "consumed three bottles of Scotch unaided." Perelman wrote of their ménage, which included Agee's twenty-two-year-old companion, Pat Scallon (whom Dorothy named Pink Worm), that they lived "in a fog of crapulous laundry, stale cigarette smoke, and dirty dishes, sans furniture or cleanliness; one suspects they wet their beds."

This is sad stuff, and Ms. Meade leaves little doubt, for those who might not have already heard, that the Algonquin wits and, for that matter, most of the literary lights of the Twenties carried forward their work under a fearful burden of booziness, at a cost of truncated lives and deflected ambitions. But since she is not, presumably, writing a temperance tract, one might ask what she *is* writing, in these four hundred nicely annotated and beautifully indexed pages. The biographer seems far from in love with her subject. Ms. Meade's previous heroines have been Eleanor of Aquitaine, Madame Blavatsky, and the medieval nun Héloïse (in a novel), and her prose keeps crinkling as if with distaste at having to touch on the twentieth century, and on this unhappy and conflicted modern woman. Her subtitle seems excessive and awkward. Her sentences snarl with unprovoked aggression:

> Despite her piety, there must have been times when Eleanor [Dorothy's stepmother, the second Mrs. Henry Rothschild] felt like strangling the miserable brat. Instead, she admonished lucky little Dorothy to count her blessings.

> [Alexander Woollcott's] literary style leaned heavily on the side of lavender and old lace, but he successfully resisted all impulses to improve it. If not one of the worst writers in America, he surely ranked among the top ten. Even his friends made fun of his style and were genuinely surprised to realize just how atrocious it actually was.

> Dorothy . . . viewed a ski slope with the same enthusiasm as she did an electric chair.

> She fell flat on her face in the hall and had to be scraped up and carried out feet first.

> He [David Susskind, after Dorothy appeared on his talk show] ushered her away with all the tact and delicacy of a funeral director exhibiting a decomposed corpse, and she rode back alone to Manhattan with her ego reduced to the size of a pea.

The curious seething undercurrent of scorn and a taste for vivid metaphors at times bizarrely stress Ms. Meade's syntax:

> Courageous Becky [Sharp], thumb glued to her nose, was able to confront and defy adversity head-on.

> For eight dollars a week, she received a room the size of a pantry and two meals—and the idea that perhaps she could become a famous writer.

> . . . the women deprived of maternal warmth and comfort who are condemned to seek love forever in the barren soil of husbands and children and even animals . . .

Nor does the biographer, while deploring the sins—alcoholism, promiscuity, bitchiness, indolence, inchoate neediness, fellow-travelling—admire the sinner for her talent and oeuvre. She gives Dorothy Parker's writings rather short shrift, ranging from the patronizing ("She was careful about rhyming the first and third lines of quatrains and fussed over masculine and feminine endings") to the forthrightly dismissive: her fashion-photo captions for *Vogue* were "drivel," and her work in the early Twenties consisted of "dozens of hokey verses and prose pieces." It is observed of her theatre reviews, "She was beginning to run out of nasty cracks and to repeat herself," and, disapprovingly, of her poetry, "Nearly everything she wrote found a buyer, in itself a comment on the quality of her work." Ms. Meade quotes from the fiction as if it were autobiography and displays antipathy to the, as she sees it, parasitic process of literary creation:

> While striking fancy poses and whipping herself into an emotional frenzy got her adrenaline moving, that white-hot heat also served a serious purpose; it generated salable verse and enabled her to deposit checks into her bank account. In this respect, she was no more calculating than Scott Fitzgerald who, in April, published his novel *The Great Gatsby*, which he had extracted from his and Zelda's eighteen-month residence in Great Neck. His characters were modeled on people he had met at the Swopes', who were some of the very same men winding up in Dorothy's bed at the Algonquin and, eventually, in her verse. Both Dorothy and Fitzgerald were adept at sucking the juices out of people.

Though in the course of this thorough survey of Dorothy Parker's seventy-three years there must be some words in her favor, they do not linger in the mind or prevail over the main impression of domestic misery and professional inconsequence. Even the quips she was famous for do not rise very high above the ambient sleaziness and fug, though some made me laugh. Of John McClain, an athletic and faithless lover, Dorothy said that "his body had gone to his head." After being told that Clare Boothe Luce was always kind to her inferiors, she asked, "And where does she find them?" She called her Southern mother-in-law "the only woman alive who pronounced the word egg as if it had three syllables." And after meeting Somerset Maugham she claimed that "whenever I meet one of these Britishers I feel as if I have a papoose on my back."

She was very American, beginning with her Jewish father's determination to put his Jewishness behind him. He married two gentile women, of whom the first, Eliza Marston, became Dorothy's mother in 1893, in stormy weather, at the New Jersey beach resort of West End. Eliza and Eleanor Lewis were both "Christian schoolteacher[s] . . . liberated from spinsterhood," and both died young—her mother when Dorothy was five, her stepmother before she turned ten. Dorothy, though she referred to herself, often deprecatingly, as Jewish, was given no Jewish religious instruction and attended a Catholic school near her home, on Manhattan's West Side; its influence may be detected in her work as the great frequency of the word "hell." J. Henry Rothschild, though not of the international-banking Rothschilds, was a wealthy clothier, an amateur versifier, and, his letters indicate, an affectionate father; but Dorothy, who under his protection had grown into a pert, piano-playing, dog-loving, largely self-educated minx less than five feet tall, was not grateful. Indeed, though she was to enjoy indulgent benefactions from New York publishers, Hollywood studios, and the Long Island rich, she does not seem to have been grateful for anything, except perhaps the friendship of Robert Benchley, with whom she never slept—which cannot be said of Elmer Rice, George Kaufman, Charles MacArthur, Ring Lardner, and Deems Taylor. She and Benchley, though, did spend hours and days together and for a time co-inhabited a midtown office so small that she claimed, "An inch smaller, and it would have been adultery." She thought of herself as an orphan. Her jokes, her poems, and her prose personae defy a cold world, a world of deaths and departures. Her hard-boiled gallantry, like Hemingway's, belongs to the generation from which World War I had stripped amiable illusions. She helped set a style, and perhaps a legitimate complaint about her as an artist is that she stayed set in that style; unlike her contemporary Rebecca West, or Mary McCarthy in the following generation, she did not let her edgy young brightness and irreverent sass deepen into an intellectual boldness and an expressive range. Her stories wear better than her poems, though some of her light verse will last as long as the genre is anthologized:

> Razors pain you;
> Rivers are damp;
> Acids stain you;
> And drugs cause cramp.
> Guns aren't lawful;
> Nooses give;
> Gas smells awful;
> You might as well live.

Her meticulous, Housmanesque neatness, especially fine in the second quatrain, redeems the sentiment from bathos. Within her conscientious quatrains, she sometimes, though rarely, compresses language to a lyric intensity:

> God's acre was her garden-spot, she said;
> She sat there often, of the Summer days,

> Little and slim and sweet, among the dead,
> Her hair a fable in the leveled rays.

In her stories, she captures the voice, above all, of neediness; the newly-weds in "Here We Are" and the disintegrating heroine of "Big Blonde" and the tipsy, haughty mother of "I Live on Your Visits" all demonstrate how need in its very urgency clogs and blocks its own satisfaction. Dorothy Parker was an expert on the lovers' quarrel, and her wasteful life afforded her a thorough education in the self-wounding perversity of the human heart.

A fonder biographer than Marion Meade might have discovered something to admire in how her subject, after her precocious infatuation with death, a number of suicide attempts, and the apparent suicide of her second husband, settled herself grudgingly to live. She outlived all the original Round Tablers except for Marc Connelly, and in her last burst of creativity—a handful of short stories and a play, *The Ladies of the Corridor,* written with Arnaud d'Usseau, which ran six weeks on Broadway and was called by her "the only thing I have ever done in which I had great pride"—she took lonely, aging women as her topic. Interestingly, in the late stories "I Live on Your Visits," "Lolita," and "The Bolt Behind the Blue," children vividly figure, though she herself had borne none. In "I Live on Your Visits," an adolescent boy observes with chagrin and precision the drunken mannerisms of a woman who, from her high-toned and arch way of talking, exactly matches what we know of Dorothy Parker. The consolations and detachment of art remained available to her, and it might also be said in admiration that neither alcoholic haze nor romantic distress cut her off from the pleasures of reading. She was, as her column for *The New Yorker* proclaimed long ago (1927–33), a Constant Reader, and the book reviews she procrastinatingly executed for *Esquire* toward the end of her life show the same enthusiasm for the written word that lighted up her girlhood as a mock-orphan. She treated books with a rectitude and a respect she could not muster for people. And her passion for left-wing causes argues a warmth for people in general if not in particular, though Ms. Meade sniffs, "She had a tendency to assume personal responsibility for world catastrophe," and reports that some observers considered Dorothy to be "playing amateur revolutionary, just as she once had played amateur suicide." Raised amid a wealth based upon the sweatshops of the Lower East Side, Mrs. Parker became an avid proponent of unionizing screenwriters in Hollywood. Having publicly marched for Sacco and Vanzetti in 1927, she travelled the extra mile with the Communist Party in the Thirties: in April of 1938 she signed a statement declaring that Stalin's infamous Moscow trials established "a clear presumption of the guilt of the defendants," and, unlike many radical intellectuals, she did not drop out of pro-Communist groups when the Soviets and the Nazis signed their nonaggression pact. Though no conclusive evidence or remembrance has emerged that would identify her and Alan Campbell as card-carrying members of the Communist Party, she took the Fifth Amendment when asked about her membership before a New York State legislative committee. However, viewed in the gentle twilight of the Cold War, her left-wing commitment and her active fund-raising for Spanish Civil War refugees show a generous and selfless spirit that otherwise had few opportunities to express itself as she fiddled away at unproduced scripts for a weekly salary bigger than most Americans' annual one. Scott Fitzgerald, writing from Hollywood to Gerald Murphy in 1940, considered her a "spoiled writer" and "supremely indifferent": "That Dotty has embraced the church [i.e., Communism] and reads her office faithfully every day does not affect her indifference." Perhaps we, a half-century later, can judge her more kindly.

To answer my own question: what makes *Dorothy Parker: What Fresh Hell Is This?* enjoyable is its deglamorized depiction of the literary and cultural world that hatched and to an extent smothered Dorothy Parker. The Algonquin wits, most of them, were under thirty when the Round Table first assembled, in 1919, and their blithe misuse of their time and bodily health, and their quick-fix approach to literary production, have the charm of youthful innocence. As in the Sixties, being young then was in itself an empowerment; writing under Harding and Coolidge was impudent fun. Dorothy Parker's life brushed against most of the strands of American literary life from 1920 to 1950, and the strands crackled with an energy not felt since. Yet in those pre-television days, when New York had a dozen newspapers and short stories were as hot as rock videos are now, making a living out of words still wasn't easy, even for those who became, like Mrs. Parker, celebrities. F.P.A.'s famous "Conning Tower" paid nothing to contributors, Harold Ross's fledgling *New Yorker* paid little, and Condé Nast—who was a man before he was a corporation—called the tune to his pipers. Few New York writers could spurn the summons to Hollywood when it came, though it condemned them to a virtually anonymous and utterly frustrating part in the manufacture of mass entertainment. Benchley, the irresistibly publishable, jumped at the chance to become a stage actor, and then a screen actor. Dorothy Parker was more strugglingly loyal to her ancient craft. Her life, even unsympathetically told, evokes the pulse of a spendthrift generation, whose promise sparkled in speakeasies and glimmered through a long hangover.

Was B.B. a Crook?

ARTFUL PARTNERS: *Bernard Berenson and Joseph Duveen,* by Colin Simpson. 320 pp. Macmillan, 1987.

BERNARD BERENSON: *The Making of a Legend,* by Ernest Samuels. 659 pp. Harvard University Press, 1987.

It is always a pleasure to see a reverenced reputation besmirched, and Colin Simpson works hard, in his flat-footed but roundly detailed account of a secret partnership between "the most successful art broker of the twentieth century" and the high-art-minded sage of I Tatti, to do some besmirching. His revelations, though, are somewhat less sensational than he and his jacket copy seem to think, and they hit at rather faded targets— Bernard Berenson's reputation, in the public mind, at its acme borrowed much of its gloss from an amiable confusion with that of Bernard Baruch, and Joseph Duveen has already been unabashedly portrayed as a rascal in S. N. Behrman's rollicking series in *The New Yorker* in 1958. *Artful Partners* on one hand takes a judgmental tone and on the other limns an international art world that had all the moral nicety of an underwater feeding frenzy. Between 1869, when Joel Duveen began to deal on the London antiques market, and 1939, when his son Joseph, titled Lord Duveen of Millbank, died, colossal American fortunes arose and uprooted hundreds of European artworks from their damp nooks in monasteries and palaces and the moldering great homes of the aristocracy; such a transatlantic surge required adroit fishers of men like Joseph Duveen and his uncle Henry and, to give some semblance of order and decency to the upheaval, experts like Berenson. That art experts received fees for their accreditations and recommendations, and that these were not always entirely disinterested shocks me rather less than it does Mr. Simpson, an English "popular historian." Indeed, for one of my nationality, severe moral repugnance might seem downright ungrateful, since the result of these genteel predations lies all about us, in the form of the great American collections, which have passed from flattering the vanity of plutocrats to withstanding the conscientious scrutiny of humble museum tourists. Thanks to the Duveens and their ilk, we have a National Gallery and masterpieces for the masses.

Mr. Simpson's freedom to quote from Berenson's correspondence has been legally hampered by Harvard University; it claims the literary rights in the letters Berenson willed to it and, in line with its motto of *"Veritas,"* wished to keep the texts for its own version of the truth, as offered in Ernest Samuels's sanctioned and bulky biography, of which one volume appeared in 1980 and another is at hand. Mr. Simpson, however, thanks to his ghost-writing the memoirs of Edward Fowles, the head of the Duveens' Paris office and their eventual successor, has had access to records, correspondence, and diaries that not even such noble researchers as Sir John Pope-Hennessy and the late Kenneth Clark were able to get at. It is Lord Clark, however, who, toward the end of *Artful Partners*, reminds us of what we quite miss in Mr. Simpson's inventory of old transactions: a stylistic verve, an animating personal touch. In a few quoted passages from Clark's autobiographical *Another Part of the Wood*, Joseph Duveen and his milieu are brought at last to life:

> [Duveen] was irresistible. His bravura and impudence were infectious, and when he was present everyone behaved as if they had had a couple of drinks. He worked entirely by instinct and was incapable of writing a letter or making a coherent statement; and he had rightly seen that, whereas in America it paid him to be very grand, in England he could get further by bribing the upper classes and playing the fool.

Clark had the advantages of having met the man and being himself a man of the world; Mr. Simpson can only retail others' anecdotes and censoriously reconstruct an unappealing and abstract monster of rapacity, who welcomed his father's failing health, shouldered his elderly uncle aside, ousted his many siblings from any effective role in the firm, and milked millionaires with outrageous mark-ups and canvases shamefully reworked and brightened and then slathered with carriage varnish.

Mr. Simpson's style, while it rarely vivifies, frequently sneers. There is a latently violent tone that produces such overwrought sentences as "[Charles Eliot] Norton saw the cozy nest his uncle had so kindly feathered for him about to be invaded by a vociferous cuckoo" and (of Pater's *Marius the Epicurean*) "Read slowly in small gobbets, it is easier to digest." We are assumed to be already privy to a great deal of gossip, so that Mary Berenson's "boundless sensuality" and "ever wayward affections" are taken for granted. Some of Mr. Simpson's sneers irresistibly invite us to smile along: "[Herbert Michelham] took the title of Baron Michelham of Hellingly, and settled down to enjoy a life of semi-retirement at Michelham Priory with his wife and the two sons with which she had presented him: Herman, born in September 1900, and Jack, who arrived on Christmas Eve 1903. What the happy baron did not know was that Jack, his favorite, had been fathered by Jefferson Davis Cohn." Mr. Cohn, with his strikingly hybrid name, is one of the more vivid of the many minor figures on the take from the Duveens; characterized as "a ubiquitous lounge lizard," he rose to great heights through his conquest of Lady Michelham (herself suitably named Aimée) and as precipitately fell. The sexual behavior of the upper classes forms all too sketchy a background to this mercantile tale; we just barely glimpse a wealth of personalities through the muck Mr. Simpson claims to be raking.

Of the Duveens, the most appealing is Henry. A mere twenty-three when dispatched by his brother Joel in 1877 to sell china in America, he made himself quickly at home. "I like America very well," he wrote back. "It is a fine rich country. It beats England in everything." He sniffed and savored the climate of the Gilded Age; "Money," he wrote Joel, "is what America is all about." The Duveens were Dutch Jews who became involved in the English porcelain trade; it was Joel who, by buying and selling the Hawthorn Ginger Jar, now in the Victoria and Albert Museum, moved up into antique furnishings and, finally, paintings. Uncle Henry handled the American side, and built up valuable friendships with Stanford White and, through him, with the likes of J. Pierpont Morgan, Collis Huntington, P. A. B. Widener, and Jay Gould. "There was something about Henry Duveen's rotund little figure and drooping walrus mustache that they found rather endearing."

Joseph Duveen was the oldest of Joel's twelve children and, according to Mr. Simpson, was possessed of unseemly haste to take over the firm. He was aided in his ambition by his father's fragile health, which made Joel a semi-invalid when Joseph was only twenty-two. Joseph ended as Lord Duveen, whose benefactions enlarged the Tate Gallery and the British Museum, but who was in the end rebuffed by the English aristocracy it had been his life's work to cultivate. We are told how Kenneth Clark, a brilliant art scholar born into elevated British circles, saw to it that Duveen, dying of intestinal cancer, was dropped from the Trustees of the National Gallery. "It broke Joe Duveen's heart": this is the first we hear that Joe had a heart. Before this sad end, he had smoked many a custom-made cigar and supervised many a lucrative purchase, and Mr. Simpson cannot forbear retelling some of the most notorious of the dealer's feats of salesmanship: how he sold the Chicago restaurateur John R. Thompson a million dollars' worth of paintings by implying that Thompson couldn't afford them, and how he, conniving with Andrew Mellon's secretary, David Finley, installed in the New York apartment just beneath that of his terminally ill and virtually bedridden client a gallery of paintings from which Mellon bought over six million dollars' worth, at a net profit to Duveen of five million.

Mr. Simpson, with his access to the Duveen accounts, sings a saga of thrilling mark-ups. The Hainauer Collection, sold to Duveen for a million dollars by a widow intimidated by the anti-Semitic currents of turn-of-the-century Berlin, was unloaded to American millionaires for five million, with dozens of items left over. The same cost-price ratio obtained when a tapestry bought for a bit over one hundred thousand was sold to Morgan for five hundred thousand, so he could lend it as decoration for the coronation ceremony of Edward VII in 1902. In 1911 a painting authenticated as a Verrocchio by Berenson was bought by the Duveens for $6,250 and sold to Bernhard Altman for $125,000. Four years later, another tapestry, which had cost the Duveens $8,772, including restoration costs, was sold to the shady financier Carl Hamilton for $150,000, and four paintings in whose purchase and enthusiastic accreditation Berenson had been active went to Hamilton for nearly ten times their cost. The banker William Salomon paid $650,000 in 1913 dollars for paintings that had cost the Duveens $145,000. Depreciations equally dramatic sometimes accompanied the resale of such acquisitions: Lady Michelham paid $70,000 for a painting attributed to Sir Thomas Lawrence that, after her death, was sold for $150. *Caveat emptor.*

The news this book purports to bring, however, is not that the Duveens were capable of sharp practice but that Bernard Berenson connived, fudged, and cheated along with them. Relatively little space, in this portrait of a partnership, is given to Berenson's side, and Mr. Simpson's indictment of him must be sifted from many pages of colorful art-market scramble. He begins by giving the early biography of a precocious boy, born in 1865 of a timber-worker and an eighteen-year-old mother in a Lithuanian town called Butrymanz. At the age of five the child suffered a revelation of the beauty of the world and was thereafter fired by a passionate (and, it is suggested, rather incongruous) taste for fine things. His father, Albert Valvrojenski, had studied to be a rabbi for two years but his college closed down and he was reduced to working in the forests. Tickets to America were secretly peddled in the Jewish villages of the Pale, and in 1874 Albert bought two and came with his cousin to Boston. His wife and three children followed the next year. They first lived in a cottage backing on the railway shunting yards; the father made a living pulling a peddler's cart, selling pots and pans for a local tinsmith, and the mother took in washing and sewing and served lunch to railway workers. Young Bernhard (the Germanic "h" was dropped during World War I) continued precocious, and spent much time reading in the Boston Public Library. His mother scraped up fees to send him, at fifteen, to the Boston Latin School, and at the age of seventeen he qualified for a free place at Boston University.

He was attractive as well as bright: "He still wore his hair in ritual locks but brushed and curled it so that he looked almost Byronic." As a freshman, he supported himself by coaching other students, including Harvard men like George Santayana and Charles Loeser, through whom he met the wealthy Ned Warren, who sponsored Berenson for Harvard. His tuition was paid—"very probably"—by Jack and Isabella Gardner; they were known to finance impoverished students whom the celebrated Charles Eliot Norton thought promising. Berenson's Harvard career brought him into proximity with the Gardners and such other swells as the openly homosexual Logan Pearsall Smith, but somehow he displeased Norton, who vetoed Berenson for a post-graduate travelling fellowship the young man sorely wanted. B.B. went to Europe anyway, and never looked back. He drifted about Europe on doles from his rich friends, studying art and becoming especially expert in the Renaissance Italians. He became known as a scholar, though his publications were at the least improved and at the most entirely written by his fellow traveller, devotee, and eventual wife, Mary Smith, Logan's sister, who had in transit married an Irishman called Costelloe and borne two children by him.

Berenson first came to the Duveens' attention as the author of a scornful, unsolicited catalogue of an 1895 London show of Venetian art from great English homes. Of thirty-three alleged Titians, only one seemed to him genuine; of nineteen paintings attributed to Bellini, only three passed muster. This was an impudent enough performance to cause the Duveens to run a check on Berenson; word came back that he was "difficult," "egotistical," "fiercely ambitious," and (from Columbia Professor George Rice Carpenter) "a charlatan." Uncle Henry opined, "It appears that he could be most useful to us, but I advise caution as all are agreed that he will never play the second fiddle." It was not until 1912, after Berenson had done a good deal of profitable business with Isabella Stewart Gardner and received commissions from a number of other dealers, that the Duveens signed him to a secret contract whereby "Doris," as Berenson's code name was, received twenty-five percent of all items of Italian origin sold by them. To deepen the skulduggery, the transactions were all to be recorded in a secret ledger kept by "X," a London accounting firm who didn't know who Doris was until 1927.

But what, exactly, did Berenson do wrong? To recommend artworks for purchase and resale is surely no sin, nor is asking a fee in exchange for scholarly expertise notably venal. Even a source as bland as the *Encyclopaedia Britannica* knows and admits that Berenson "was an adviser to Lord Duveen and his opinion was often sought in the purchase of paintings." The scholarly authenticator was a necessary part of a European art scene wherein the primal creators had seen no great distinction between themselves and studio assistants, and lordly owners had felt free to adjust artworks to their interior decoration, and good bright copies were thought better than deteriorated originals, and restorers blended into forgers and experts into dealers. Mr. Simpson's indictment of Berenson seems to include these specific charges: (1) Always clumsy with written English, he signed criticism that was Mary's work. (2) Operating on a five-percent commission from Isabella Gardner on paintings she purchased, he knowingly urged fakes and inferior imitations upon her—a pseudo-Cima, a "Titian" by a Portuguese copyist, a Sienese Annunciation that had been almost entirely repainted. Otto Gutkunst, the director of the art firm Colnaghis, wrote him during this pre-Duveen period, "Business is not always nice. . . . It is important for both of us to make hay while Mrs. G. shines." (3) He continued to deal with Colnaghis after Mrs. Gardner had instructed him not to. (4) He assisted in a fair amount of smuggling, which was sometimes the only way to get Italian works of art out of the country. (5) He and Mary supplied her brother's antique shop in London, called their "Iniquity Shop," with the products of "Icilio Frederico Joni," one of Italy's finest and most prolific forgers. (6) Berenson recommended in 1903 that the Metropolitan Museum purchase an El Greco and accepted eight thousand dollars of the profit from the dealer. (7) Such duplicity became commonplace after 1907, when he entered into an agreement with the Duveens. They paid him, at first, ten percent on Italian items and then, under the Doris agreement, twenty-five; between 1911 and 1937 his share of the profits, never less than a hundred thousand dollars a year, added up to $8,370,000—a gigantic sum in those days. (8) Angered because Joseph Duveen had tricked him out of his percentage of the Mellon purchases, Berenson unsuccessfully conspired with Louis Levy, the firm's lawyer, to become a partner when Joseph died. (9) When this plot backfired, Berenson tried to scuttle the dying man's last big sale, that of the "Allendale Nativity," supposedly by Giorgione, to Samuel H. Kress, by vociferously insisting that the work was an early Titian.

There may be more perfidy wound into Mr. Simpson's many accountings, but this is the gist. The victims were exceedingly rich, or frauds themselves, and even if only a third of the art they bought was genuine it was still the best investment of their lives. Whatever his misdeeds in Mrs. Gardner's service, she remained friendly with him until her death.* The smuggling and the flirtation with Joni's forgery were perhaps illegal. The

---

*Or, in Mr. Simpson's unwontedly rude language: "Isabella was to continue as an occasional milch cow until she died."

rest seems no more than slippery, in a slippery business, and none of it invalidates the rare passion and erudition that Berenson brought to his field, or his tutorial contribution to generations of art scholars and museum heads, or his bequest of Villa I Tatti, his Tuscan estate, to a New World university as a place where others could study the Old World culture of which he had been, in his fashion, an inspired votary.

Harvard *did* give Ernest Samuels, professor of English at Northwestern University, access to the Berenson documents and correspondence, and the bulk of these materials, his preface states, "outran all calculation." His wife, Jayne—listed on the title page as a collaborator—and he have "hewn a path" through mountains of paper that include letters from fourteen hundred correspondents plus six thousand letters Mary and Bernard Berenson wrote each other and, however disputatious and intimate their contents, scrupulously retained; this second volume of the Samuels biography covers the fifty-five years from 1904 to 1959, when B.B. died at the age of ninety-four.

Though an "official" biography, sanctioned by Harvard and by Nicky Mariano—the chief keeper, for forty years, of the Berenson flame—the book does not shy from showing its subject as vain, snobbish, ruthlessly romantic, and incorrigibly luxury-loving. Indeed, it provides, in a tone often of amusement if not reproach, ample context for the avarice that Simpson alleges to have been unscrupulous. Berenson's favorite term of praise was "life-enhancing," and the foremost life he sought to enhance was his own. He was greedy for exquisite sensations: he hobnobbed with the aristocrats of Europe, he travelled widely and in style, he bought himself a palatial establishment near Florence and kept expanding and improving it. He provided financial support, as well, for his wife's two daughters and his own parents and many relatives in America. In 1911, four years after their purchase of I Tatti, Mary wrote to a friend that it was "really rather awful to think how many people live off of B.B.'s interest in Italian art . . . seven servants, six contadini, two masons, one bookkeeper, one estate manager, and their wives and children and then me, with a mental trail behind me of all the things I do and the people who look to me. And then B.B.'s whole family. Really it is a lot for the shoulders of one poor delicate man." In the year he purchased the estate, Berenson had written to Isabella Gardner, "I have become a society lounger and money grubber and God knows what. It brings one in contact with the most distressingly odious people in the whole world, the dealers." Yet the "real inferno" of the dealers and their "squillionaires" constituted the only treasury where he could fund his appetite for fine things—for paintings and thousands of books and a mode of life suited to a latter-day Marius the Epicurean. At one point he considered dressing his footmen in livery; Mary balked at that. She, from a family of Philadelphia Quakers, disapprovingly but passively noted, "Evidently our feet are set upon the path of worldliness and riches and the devil take the hindmost." Berenson plaintively wrote to Duveen in 1912, "Whispers already are getting harsher and louder that for money I am sacrificing my gifts and my higher calling. . . . Not that I object to making money but I want to make it with scrupulous honesty and absolutely aboveboard."

And did he? The kind of pressure brought by art dealers upon experts is several times illustrated. In 1935 Baron Thyssen wanted to buy two paintings which were believed to be by the painter Cossa but which Berenson had previously identified as by Ercole Roberti. The baron did not want Ercole Robertis. From the Duveens' Paris office Edward Fowles wired Berenson, "Should we sell as Cossa would you flatly contradict?" Berenson responded, "Sorry, would have to." Again, the fracas over the Allendale Nativity and Berenson's refusal to call it a Giorgione began with Andrew Mellon's churlishly telling Duveen, "I don't want another Titian. Find me a Giorgione." What Mr. Simpson, so anxious to imply evildoing, perhaps fails to appreciate is that the value of Berenson's attributions rested upon the squillionaires' conviction that he was honest, even if on occasion inconveniently so. Asked by the Duveens to educate the tastes of the investment banker Jules Bache, Berenson cockily told his pupil, "Art criticism suffers from being the priesthood of the slimy and slippery realm. I have been trying for forty years to sanitate and rectify this priesthood. . . . If you can trust my honor as well as my judgment I shall be glad to help you." B.B.'s reputed integrity was his ticket to wealth, and neither the Simpson nor the Samuels book offers any evidence that Berenson ever deliberately falsified an attribution. Simpson, for all his sneers, in an appended list of relevant paintings leans away from any such charge: "Berenson and Duveen . . . sometimes sincerely over-estimated or indeed under-estimated the quality of their pictures. Attribution always has been and always will be a difficult business."

If B.B. badly cheated anyone, it was himself—his long old age was fretted by the thought that he had failed to produce what a reviewer of 1909 had asked for: "the great book he owes his generation." His studies and lists of Italian Renaissance painting were unsurpassed in their field but intellectually rather local, and a general work on aesthetics, though often contemplated, never came; his energy was diverted into "the frivolity of making money," into pursuing aesthetic pleasures in museums and in travel, into hobnobbing with the rich, who were "apt to be enjoyable works of art in themselves." Santayana, who shared with Berenson a Harvard education and an outsider's detachment, offered a contrast in this respect, and though Berenson called Santayana "cold" he always spoke of him with respect. Santayana, on the other hand, took a rather mordant view of the irrepressible aesthete, and wrote after an encounter in 1939, "Berenson surprised me by talking with juvenile enthusiasm about 'art' (as if we were still in the 1890s). . . . It's lucky for B.B., in one sense, that he keeps the old flame alive; but I can't help feeling that it was lighted and is kept going by forced draught, by social and intellectual ambition, and by professional pedantry."

Berenson loved people, as if finding in them the "tactile values" and "ideated sensations" that he preached should be sought in paintings. Many a stranger, writing Berenson a letter, became swept up in a prolonged correspondence and invited to come to I Tatti, where the old man, punctiliously dandified with his trimmed beard and boutonniere, presided over a constant swirl of the famous and rich and beautiful. His amorous affairs he flaunted as if they were masterpieces, and he invited his marital partner to share in the aesthetic experience. His and Mary's voluminous correspondence brims with startling confidences incongruously mixed with his spiritual attitudinizing and her quaint use of the Quaker "thee" and "thou." In one letter he gallantly made Mary one of a blessed trinity, avowing that all he would "take from this world to the next" would be the "memory of [her] young eyes, of Miss Greene's, and of Madame La Caze's . . . at a sexual crisis." In the margin of another she wrote, "My God, his conceit, selfishness, snobbishness. Good heaven, what a revelation of self-satisfaction and cruelty to me." Yet until middle age and avoirdupois overtook her, Mary was no slouch at open marriage; an especially intricate refraction of intimacy occurred when her lover, Geoffrey Scott, suddenly married Lady Sybil Cutting, a neighbor upon whom Berenson had often called; Mary, though heartbroken by Geoffrey's defection, soothed her ex-lover's doubts about his fiancée's sexual abilities with the assurance that Bernard had told her he found Lady Sybil "très accomplie au lit."

Like another disciple of Pater, Oscar Wilde, Berenson might lament that he had put too much of his genius into his life and not enough into his works. Looking back, the still mentally vivacious nonagenarian thought not of Pater but of Emerson as his teacher, who had "taught him the importance of 'becoming, of being rather than doing.' " He had taken Emerson's advice and hitched his wagon to a star. Though he lived in this country only from the age of eleven to that of twenty-two, he always thought of himself as an American, and perhaps only via America could an itinerant pot-peddler's son have risen to such posh eminence. Having become and been so flamboyantly, he yet wished to leave something "done" behind; he wrote essays for the newspaper *Corriere della Sera* almost to the last days of his life, and determinedly organized his bequest of an adequately endowed I Tatti, where students "should become ripe humanists and not mere teachers of facts about the arts." He paid dearly for his own marvellous ripeness, but not, I think, with stolen funds. His conception of how he earned his money was simplicity itself, as he explained it in 1922 to the Internal Revenue Service: "I earn it by enjoying such authority and prestige that people will not buy expensive Italian pictures without my approval."

The Bimbo on the Barge

CLEOPATRA: *Histories, Dreams and Distortions,* by Lucy Hughes-Hallet. 338 pp. Harper & Row, 1990.

This book, beneath its alluring jacket bedecked with Elizabeth Taylor and Cleopatras of bygone ages and, not the least glamorous, the pale-eyed English authoress, is a stolid dark green such as I associate with textbooks of first-year college math—analytic geometry and the foundations of calculus. I know the color well, for I lugged this naked tome, reft of its jacket, with me for over a month, everywhere I went. Amid the shimmering enchantment of Venice, and the grimy reality of Ravenna (that yet enhouses the most marvellous mosaics in Christendom), and the medieval ochre and stony lace of Verona, *Cleopatra* sat on my hotel table, waiting for me, jet-lagged or not, to brave another chapter. And on domestic trips as well, into Manhattan during its monsoon season, to rural fastnesses of Pennsylvania, and even into the dental offices of Boston's fabled North Shore did the volume accompany me, read and yet not completely read, as if I were paddling between its Nile-green covers only a snail's-pace faster than an opposing current. I say Nile-green, because this is what must have been intended, but for me it became the color of duty.

Why so? Lucy Hughes-Hallet writes very well, with a sometimes epigrammatic edge, and she has mulled her topic thoroughly and done perhaps all the Cleopatra research that can humanly be done. The "F" section of her index, for example, reveals not only Freud and Foucault, Flaubert and Anatole France, as one might expect, but Fulvia (Antony's first wife) and Ftatateeta (a character in Shaw's Cleopatra play), Antonia Fraser (author of *Warrior Queens* and *The Weaker Vessel*) and Eddie Fisher (third husband of warrior queen Elizabeth Taylor, father of warrior princess Carrie Fisher, and singer of "Oh, My Papa"). Relevant and revelatory quotations from Hegel and Tertullian and Ed Sullivan and the Marquis de Sade find space in Ms. Hughes-Hallet's text; Shakespeare and Shaw and Petrarch and Lucan of course have their say on the subject, but also consulted and cited are such out-of-the-way works as Giulio Landi's *La vita di Cleopatra reina d'Egitto* (1551) and Daniel von Lohenstein's *Kleopatra* (1661) and Fuzelier's *Cléopâtre: Ballet Héroïque* (1748) and Rider Haggard's *Cleopatra* (1889) and Jean Cantel's "gorgeously decadent romance" *La Reine Cléopâtre* (1914) and the Italian film *Due notti con Cleopatra* (1954), starring Sophia Loren. In addition, Ms. Hughes-Hallet has compiled a variegated sheaf of fifty art plates, from Old Masters to movie stills, which almost alone, with the help of her witty and well-turned captions, would carry the burden of her book.

Her thesis can be briefly stated: Cleopatra has presented many images down through the ages. Most of these images, the subtext runs, have been unfair. Winners get to write history, and Octavian, in the struggle for the Roman Empire capped by his defeat of Antony and Cleopatra at Actium, perpetrated a propaganda image of the Egyptian Queen as an enticing monster, wanton, extravagant, devious, spineless. "Cleopatra was Rome's enemy, and we in the West are Rome's heirs. The notion of Cleopatra that we have inherited identifies her primarily as being the adversary, the Other. Her otherness is twofold. She is an Oriental, and she is a woman. Even in her lifetime her legend was already shaped by the two overlapping chauvinisms of race and sex."

The author's feminist brief is most obtrusive in the early sections, as she paraphrases the macho Roman attitude: "Orientals, who are ruled by queens, are effeminate. To submit to them would be tantamount (oh, horror!) to submitting to a woman." She offers in opposition a picture of Cleopatra as a learned and loved ruler, a royal wheeler-dealer:

> It is known that Cleopatra came to an extremely profitable arrangement with the Natatean Arabs over the oil rights in some territory at the southern end of the Dead Sea and that, having persuaded Antony to grant her some land around Jericho that was valuable for its dates and balsam, she subsequently leased it back to King Herod of Judea, a deal that brought Egypt substantial revenues without any outlay of money or manpower.

This well may be, but the tenuous traces of the "working queen" pale before the remarkable, and historically irreducible, facts of her sexual alliances: she bore children to Julius Caesar and Marc Antony, and her liaison with Antony produced a war for control of the Roman Empire, ending in the lovers' joint suicide. With facts like these, who needs a legend?

Ms. Hughes-Hallet's purpose is not to grope for the historical Cleopatra in the impenetrable mists of the first century B.C., but to trace the permutations of her reputation in the documents of Western culture. "As Cleopatra receded from living memory, as new generations of writers took up her story, she acquired the melancholy glamour of something irrevocably lost." To the Middle Ages, surprisingly, she was a martyr for love; Chaucer included her in his *Legend of Good Women*, and her suicide, like those of Dido and Thisbe, appeared sublime by the traditions of courtly love. Behind this approval of her suicide stood the basic Christian disapproval of sex: "It is for sexuality—not her own, but man's—that woman must be punished." The Middle Ages did not make much of her role as an adulteress; medieval marriage was, away from the dynastic matches, so informal that Cleopatra was popularly accepted as Antony's woman and allowed the title of "wife" (the word derives from *wīf*, meaning simply, like *femme* in French and *Frau* in German, "woman"). With Protestantism's enthusiastic "valorization of marriage"—Calvin and Luther proclaimed that "monogamy was as 'chaste' as virginity"—Cleopatra aroused abhorrence and fascination as an "other woman," as a promiscuous harlot. Ms. Hughes-Hallet's analysis of the patriarchal-Protestant dread of female promiscuity seems especially acute: "A woman who had several lovers was not fully to be reached or understood by any one of them. . . . She had knowledge other than that which her husband had imparted to her." Cleopatra's two husbands, by the way, were both short-lived younger brothers called Ptolemy.

The eighteenth century involved the story of Cleopatra in its debate on monarchy, and the nineteenth century found in the exotic legend poetic justification for its imperialist penetration and possession of the languid, licentious nations of Africa and the Orient. Cleopatra as man-killer had a masochistic appeal for the Romantics and the Decadents: "The killer-Cleopatra's heyday lasted roughly from the defeat of Napoleon to the outbreak of the First World War, an era during which heroism, the willingness of young men to allow themselves to be killed, was at an unprecedently low premium in Europe . . . hence the proliferation of fictions in which death could be experienced vicariously at the hands of a monster, a villain, a *femme fatale.* " Ms. Hughes-Hallet does not make the point, but could, that whether as killer or suicide Cleopatra satisfyingly confirms our Judaeo-Christian suspicion that sex should be punished by death.

Our own century, in trying to make mental room for the uncomfortable idea of sexuality that Cleopatra embodies, has camped her up, or bimboized her. Ms. Hughes-Hallet, who until writing this book was known in print as a writer for *Vogue* and a television critic for the London *Evening Standard,* energetically connects the kittenish Cleopatra of Shaw's *Caesar and Cleopatra* (1898) with the childlike burlesque queens in such popular entertainments as the British film farce *Carry On Cleo* (1963): "Humour of this kind at least clears an imaginative space in which sex is possible, and friendly, but it does so at a high cost. All the participants must consent to be made foolish and the women, before they can be allowed their share of the jollity, must first sacrifice their claim to be fully grown-up people." When Elizabeth Taylor's Cleopatra, in the notorious film of 1963, winks, a new element of self-mockery, of complex devalorization, enters the game; quite brilliantly the author elicits from the publicized extravagance of the film's cost, and of Burton and Taylor's real-life, jet-set reprise of Antony and Cleopatra, an essay upon the spiritual worth of prodigality, seen as a Rabelaisian, Dionysian "holy foolishness" that liberates us from all those oppressive old Roman values.

The book concludes with the author's own vision of Cleopatra, as a Venus subduing Mars and producing, as the myth goes, Harmony, an end to all the simple oppositions—"right/wrong, friend/foe, east/west, man/woman, alive/dead"—that make our thinking so stressful and rancorous. A pretty vision, endorsed as yet by few artistic re-creations of Cleopatra, though the author digs up an Egyptian play, Ahmad Shawqui's *Masra' Kliyupatra* (1929), and a curious painting of a nude, hefty, sky-gazing Cleo, asp on nipple, by Giovanni Pedrini. "If the sexes could become one, if love and power could be reconciled, if Orient and Occident could combine, death would be defeated. That concord and that hope appear epitomized in the person of my last Cleopatra."

Well, with such a benignly cosmic conclusion, and so many insights, apt quotations, and provocative facts along the way, why did I have such a heavy time with this book, my distracting personal circumstances and possible Octavian resistances aside? Especially in its first sections, *Cleopatra* has the dogged, adviser-approved aura of a Ph.D. thesis, chewing up the centuries and spitting out word bites in a spirit of obligatory erudition. The appearance of so many plays, novels, and histories in chopstick-friendly fragments leaves one with an empty feeling that nothing, not even Shakespeare, could be a meal in itself. "The deconstruction of ancient narratives is a late twentieth-century practice," Ms. Hughes-Hallet says in her introduction. Deconstruction sets out to relieve literary works of their intended content, substituting instead the subliminal messages the author did not intend. The old-fashioned reader expects to confront, between the Nile-green covers, Cleopatra herself, the reality of her, or an earnest estimate of that reality, and what he gets instead are images of her, generated by the delusions and neuroses of bygone generations. This makes for a faintly monotonous flutter. "I do not know her," the author confesses cheerfully. "I, like all the other writers whose works I have dissected, know only her depictions and descriptions, masks made by others in her image."

The notion that an image might be "true to life," or some images less untrue than others, is not entertained. But surely there *is* something about the story of Antony and Cleopatra that was real, and is real, and accounts for its perpetuation these two millennia. Isn't it the story, in a sense, of every small-town boy who, at the moment when he plans to set out to conquer the world, falls in love with a local girl and stays, to reap the harvest of children, of drudging days, of relative failure? Biologically, a woman is a Venus's-flytrap of sorts, holding her Antony, for the moments of seduction and enthrallment, in what Ms. Hughes-Hallet nicely calls "a bewildering swamp of instinctual pleasure." Is Rider Haggard, hysterical old imperialist though he was, to be denied the element of truth in his remark "Woman, in her weakness, is yet the strongest force upon the earth . . . for Nature fights ever on her side"? Since Ms. Hughes-Hallet, out of the thousands of pages she read, chose that sentence to quote, she, too, must have quickened to something in it, something possibly that helps us see, that helps us grasp our condition, that helps us live. *Cleopatra*'s air of enervation stems from deconstruction's fatiguing premise that art has no health in it, it is all cultural pathology.

HARD FACTS

Something Substantial and Useful About It

THE PENCIL: *A History of Design and Circumstance,* by Henry Petroski. 434 pp. Knopf, 1990.

The history of the pencil has rather few highlights. The first picture of one appears in a book on collecting fossils, written in Latin by the German Swiss physician and naturalist Konrad von Gesner, and printed in Zurich in 1565; a woodcut depicts a rather ornately turned tube of wood holding a tapered piece of a substance Gesner terms "a sort of lead (which I have heard some call English antimony)." Before then, English shepherds in Cumberland had been marking their sheep with chunks of a black substance discovered, legend had it, in the roots of a large tree that a storm had felled. This substance, locally called "wadd," was also called "black lead" and "plumbago" after the metal (in Latin, *plumbum*) that for millennia had been used, for want of a better, to make marks on pale surfaces. Wadd—given in 1789 its current name of "graphite," from the Greek *graphein,* "to write"—was found in exceptionally pure form at Borrowdale, near Keswick. Until the deposit's final exhaustion, in the nineteenth century, "Borrowdale lead" was the by-word for quality in this matter of making a mark; the mine, operated as a crown monopoly, was closed for years at a time to conserve the precious mineral, and security precautions were taken worthy of diamonds, a more compact form of carbon. A mouthful of smuggled wadd, the miners used to say, was as good as a day's wage.

By the end of the seventeenth century, the substance was known all over Europe and used by artists and others. To keep the hands clean, black lead could be wrapped in string or vines or held in elongate holders called *porte-crayons.* The idea of permanently encasing a rod of wadd in wood is, like so much else about the pencil* industry, obscure in origin; some credit a joiner in Keswick, and others claim priority for the carpenters of Nuremberg. In the German city, one Friedrich Staedtler is identified as early as 1662 as a pencil-maker. The first pencil leads were square, cut from a slice of raw graphite to fit a grooved strip of wood; the "lead," commonly in a number of pieces laid end-to-end, was sealed in place by a glued strip of wood. The resulting implement, square in cross-section, could then be planed at the corners into an octagon, or fully rounded.

The pulverization, melting, and reconstitution, with sulphur added, of fragments of graphite is described as early as 1726, in Berlin; but the major breakthrough in pencil-lead technology occurred in France, where Nicolas-Jacques Conté (whose name is remembered by the Conté crayon), under pressure of the severe graphite shortage occasioned by the Napoleonic Wars, quickly developed, and in 1795 patented, a process for mixing powdered graphite and clay, shaping the paste in long molds and firing it at a high temperature, producing ceramic leads. Borrowdale wadd had been taken as it came, but now the hardness of pencil lead could be graded by the proportions of the clay-graphite mixture; the basic chemistry of pencil lead was established. Mechanical pencils, which needed extruded leads of very precise diameter, were first patented in 1822 but have never supplanted the wood-encased, repeatedly sharpened, disposable pencil. Red cedar was early recognized as the ideally strong, straight-grained, easily shaved pencil wood; no substitute quite matches slow-growing red cedar's pleasant tint and odor. As the cedar forests, mostly American, ran out, pencil manufacturers sent agents all through the South buying up fences, railroad ties, and log cabins made of the once-abundant wood. Rubber got its name (supposedly from the English chemist Joseph Priestley, in 1770) for its ability to rub out pencil marks. The first patent for an attached rubber eraser was issued in 1858 to Hyman Lipman, of Philadelphia. The pencil-sharpener as we know it—consisting of two revolving bevelled cutters—dates from the early twentieth century, thanks to the Automatic Pencil Sharpener Company (Apsco) of Chicago. Yellow became the favored color of paint for pencils with the Austrian firm of L. & C. Hardtmuth's introduction, in 1890, of the Koh-I-Noor model, exhibited at the Columbian Exposition in 1893. The rest is chemistry (most recently, polymerization) and forestry—what can pencil-makers cut down when all the red cedar is gone?—and corporate rivalry. Industrial competition pitted Faber against Faber—Johann against Lothar, the

---

*The word comes from the Latin *penicillum*, a diminutive form designating a little brush, made of hairs from animal tails, the Latin word for "tail" being, surprisingly, *penis*.

firm of Anton Wilhelm against that of Eberhard—and saw early English supremacy give way to French inventiveness and German organization and American mass production, all now threatened by the pencil-fabricating hordes of Japan. Present global production amounts to fourteen billion pencils a year.

Well, if the tale can be told, with but a few trifling omissions, so concisely, why has Henry Petroski, in *The Pencil*, given us a chubby book of over four hundred pages, including a twenty-two-page bibliography, an eighteen-page index, and five tightly printed pages of grateful acknowledgments? The answer, I think, belongs, like certain aspects of the standard pencil's scale and texture, to the subjective realm of marketability. A book of a mere two hundred pages entitled *The Pencil* might appear to be merely informative. A book twice that size, though not twice as informative, is a feat, a prank; it has a certain mysterious majesty, a material mysticism, like that fondly remembered best-seller of yesteryear, *Zen and the Art of Motorcycle Maintenance*. Such a swelling, looming, teasingly excessive book promises to lift us high from its quaintly specific base. With its striking blue jacket, which successfully imitates pencil sheen, and its unusual shape—tall, thick, but not wide—the artifact beckons. We want to seize it, to hold it. Mr. Petroski has an engineer's light touch upon his own pencil. He writes a relaxed, translucent, spun-glass kind of prose, with a not inconsiderable percentage of pure air betwixt its twirled filaments. A good deal of flourish accompanies his deliveries. Here is a fair specimen of a paragraph revving up:

> How does a lump of lead that draws a creditable line evolve into a modern pencil? How does a rounded rock turn into a wheel? How does a dream become a flying machine? The process by which ideas and artifacts come into being and mature is essentially what is now known as the engineering method, and the method, like engineering itself, is really as old as *Homo sapiens*—or at least *Homo faber*—and the process is about as hard to pin down and as idiosyncratic in each of its peculiar applications as is the individual of the species. But while each invention and artifact has its unique aspects, there is also a certain sameness about the evolutionary way in which a stylus develops into a pencil, a sketch into a palace, or an arrow into a rocket. And this observation itself is as old as Ecclesiastes, who may have been the first to record, but probably was not the first to observe, that "what has been is what will be, and what has been done is what will be done; and there is nothing new under the sun."

Beneath this long "Ahem" may be heard the hum of a theme—the nature of engineering, with the pencil as a paradigm of the process whereby men invent, manufacture, and improve things. Pencils, so lowly and common that antique dealers chuck them out with the shavings when they acquire a box of old tools, are yet put together with a hard-won precision. The two halves of the pencil case must fit tightly enough against each other and around the centered lead to form a bond that withstands warpage and the spasmodic pressure of writing; the woodworking machinery of pencil-making operates "to perhaps the highest tolerance of any woodworking equipment"—a tolerance as small as five ten-thousandths of an inch. The leads, extruded through sapphire or diamond dies to similarly strict tolerances, are composed of graphite and clay particles of a marvellous fineness; a sifting process through a series of tubs, usually six in number, is followed by a grinding together that, in the case of Koh-I-Noor leads, lasts for an average of two weeks. The proportions of clay and graphite and lesser, waxy constituents derive from formulae as jealously guarded as the secrets of alchemy. A pencil lead that writes smoothly, with a consistent darkness, soft enough to leave a mark yet tough enough not to break, is a mundane miracle that readers of *The Pencil* will never again take casually for granted.

Mr. Petroski's attempted dramatization of engineers as cultural heroes suffers from their professional habit of taciturnity; they figure and sketch with their pencils but rarely confide autobiography to paper. Like the heroes of old-fashioned Westerns, they solve the problem and ride on. Conté is the central figure in Mr. Petroski's posse of engineers, yet he scarcely leaps off the page. A portrait painter driven by the Revolution into science, he was said to have "every science in his head and every art in his hands." This paragon "promoted the military use of balloons, and he was apparently working on some experiments with hydrogen when an explosion injured his left eye." He was familiar with the use of graphite to make crucibles in which to melt metals, and from this experience, presumably, he reasoned and experimented his way to the baked, part-clay pencil lead that was his great innovation. Yet, oddly, his breakthrough was not soon disseminated through the pencil industry:

> While it has been said that German pencils made by the Faber family were the models that Thoreau was trying to emulate in the mid-1830s, there is some question whether many German pencils themselves were then being manufactured by the Conté process. . . . German pencils were not at all common in America when young Thoreau first sought to improve his father's product, and any German pencils that did exist may not even have been made by the superior Conté process. What Henry Thoreau may have been hoping to do was emulate a French pencil.

The designation of Henry David Thoreau (who was, we are told in one of Mr. Petroski's flourishes of fact, named David Henry up through his Harvard degree) as a significant pencil engineer will surprise those who know him only as a monument of American literature and libertarian thought. His father, John Thoreau, had been invited by his brother-in-law, Charles Dunbar, to join in the exploitation of a lode of graphite that Dunbar, his family's black sheep, had stumbled upon in Bristol, New Hampshire, in 1821. The senior Thoreau may have learned the rudiments of pencil manufacture from one of the first Americans in the business, Joseph Dixon, of Marblehead. Ceylonese graphite was brought back as ballast in New England sailing vessels and dumped; Dixon, the son of a shipowner, learned to utilize the graphite in crucibles, shoe polish, and pencils—the last so gritty and brittle that merchants told him "he would have to put foreign labels on them if he expected to make sales." Long after Conté, American pencil-makers "continued to mix their inadequately purified and ground graphite with such substances as glue, adding a little bayberry wax or spermaceti." Nevertheless, John Thoreau's pencils were superior to those of rival companies, and were sold under his own label—a photograph of a wrapped bundle of them appears in *The Pencil.* When David Henry graduated from Harvard in 1837, he began to teach at the Center School in Concord, but his resistance to applying corporal punishment led to his rapid resignation, which, "coupled with his insistence on reversing his names," earned him a local reputation for eccentricity. Like many another young individualist, he found refuge in the family business; at the Harvard library he set about a course of research to improve the product.

Mr. Petroski delves deeply into what was then available about pencil-making in existing reference works, and concludes that the *Encyclopaedia Perthensis,* published in Edinburgh, may have furnished the crucial hint at the concoction of ceramic lead. According to Ralph Waldo Emerson, Thoreau was enough of a pencil man to be able to pick up twelve at a grab (a trick common in the trade, since they were sold in packages of a dozen), and according to Emerson's son, Edward, it was Thoreau who invented and worked out the details of a machine for producing finer graphite, by means of encasing the grinder in a seven-foot-high box and trapping the finest dust at the top, to which only it would rise. Certainly Thoreau was capable of what we now call mechanical drawing, and the sensibility behind *Walden* relishes construction and quantification. Yet in the two million words of the journal that he began at the same time as entering his father's business Thoreau almost never mentions pencil-making. There is no mention of it in *Walden,* and pencils were so little on his mind that he left them off a list he prepared of everything needed for an excursion to the Maine woods. The humanistic poetry of invention and technology, though apparent to Benjamin Franklin and the French Encyclopedists, has waited until our century for its full due; the century of Romanticism may have sketched and made notes with pencils, but it reserved its odes for nightingales and untransmuted Nature. However, a fresh pointedness and a cedarish pungence characterize *Walden*, and by the time Thoreau retired to his cabin (where he purportedly invented raisin bread), his father's company was making the best pencils in America. Emerson sent some to a friend in Boston, and she replied, "The pencils are excellent,—worthy of Concord art & artists and indeed one of the best productions I ever saw from there—something substantial & useful about it." As opposed to, the implication is, most Transcendentalist productions.

The failure or refusal of a passionate self-describer like Thoreau to commit to paper anything about his own genuine engineering achievements is symptomatic of the elusive transparency of engineering in general. We see around us, as modest as pencils and as grand as bridges, the work of engineers, but their language is largely beyond us; it is like those sacred languages addressed to gods who respond only in the thumping vocabulary of earthquakes and thunderstorms. A popularization like Mr. Petroski's, taking as its field of interest the furtive advances of applied chemistry and the tidal shifts of competitive capitalism (one of his most charming episodes describes the American Armand Hammer's successful importation of an entire German pencil factory to Soviet Russia), is more of a tour de force than, say, a popularization of contemporary cosmology. Investigations of Nature fascinate us with their possibility of displaying, at the last peel of the onion, the Creator. "To see a World in a Grain of Sand, / And a Heaven in a Wild Flower" remains our romantic, quasi-theological ambition. An annual fourteen billion is the closest the pencil will bring us to infinity, and instead of Heaven we see, peering closely in, the rackety gray hell of the assembly line. *Homo faber* knows himself too well. Microcosms of which man is the creator rather repel our gaze, even as we hold them in our fingers. The green plastic garbage bag, for instance, is nothing but deplored these days, though hardly a household can manage without it. *The Pencil*, with its airy prose contortions—

> After the leaded slat of the modern process is covered with a mating slat of wood, the assembly is not ready for use until some of the wooden centering is cut away, to be discarded and forgotten, leaving the short pencil point to make a daring bridge between pencil and paper—a metaphorical bridge that

can carry from mind to paper the lines of a daring real bridge, which can
cause jaws to drop, or the words of a daring new philosophy, which can
cause eyebrows to arch

—asks us to face ourselves.

Bull in a Type Shop

FREDERIC GOUDY, by D. J. R. Bruckner. 144 pp. Harry N. Abrams, for Documents of American Design, 1990.

Typography presents a volatile, rapidly changing technology combined
with a highly conservative aesthetic. In the last hundred years, typesetting
has gone from painstaking hand distribution to Linotype and other metal-
manipulators to today's computer-setting, a process of pure imaging
whose virtually infinite resources have as yet done little to change the look
of the printed page. The letters that are still used are closely based upon
prototypes of roman and italic faces developed in the Renaissance by
printers imitating the calligraphy of manuscripts. Daniel Berkeley Updike, a leading American printer and the author of the classic *Printing
Types: Their History, Forms, and Use* (1922), saw no advance beyond the
fonts that the French-born printer Nicolas Jenson developed in Venice
over five hundred years ago: "Jenson's roman types have been the accepted models for roman letters ever since he made them, and, repeatedly
copied in our own day, have never been equalled."

In the narrow, nice, and conservative shop of typography Frederic
Goudy was something of a bull—big, boisterous, and overproductive.
Born in Bloomington, Illinois, the year the Civil War ended, and transplanted to the Dakota territory as a teen-ager, he was a roving businessman
who dabbled in the design of advertising layouts. By 1890 he was pushing
real estate in Chicago, then the largest printing center in the United States
and in 1893 the site of the Columbian Exposition; the ideas of John Ruskin
and William Morris, rejuvenating the arts and crafts, were in the air. The
year after the Exposition, Goudy founded, with C. Lauren Hooper, his
own press, the Booklet Press, which became the Camelot Press. His first
type font, cut in 1896, was an alphabet of capitals called Camelot; but
another fifteen years went by before he (now transplanted to New York
and running, with his competent wife, Bertha, the Village Press) became
in his own eyes a professional type designer. Having set the proof sheets

of an H. G. Wells volume in Caslon, he became dissatisfied enough to design, in a week's time, a face he called Kennerly, as well as an elegant capital face called Forum. His early types were taken up enthusiastically in England: the British typographer Sir Bernard Newdigate wrote of Kennerly that, "since the first Caslon began casting type about the year 1724, no such excellent letter has been put within the reach of English printers."

Goudy was off and running. Before his death in 1947 he designed a hundred fonts, counting the italic and roman faces as separate. He also was a prolific speaker and self-advertiser; in 1937, D. B. Updike wrote with a fastidious shudder to the British printer Stanley Morison, "You have put your finger on what ought to be the merit of many types and is the merit of very few, that is that it does not 'look as if it has been designed by somebody in particular' and you add that Mr. Goudy 'has designed a whole century of very peculiar looking types.' He certainly has. Poor man, I have never seen anybody with such an *itch* for publicity, or who blew his own trumpet so artlessly and constantly."

Even now, in this handsome volume (printed in Japan in a digitized version of Bodoni, a face Goudy despised) meant to be a tribute, D. J. R. Bruckner allows a mysterious note of cavil and reservation to sound when praise is called for. By way of tribute, he cites the barbed compliment with which George W. Jones gave Goudy a gold medal in 1921: "Fred Goudy never did any harm to typography." Mr. Bruckner, an editor of *The New York Times Book Review,* himself confides, "Goudy's printing and typography, his design of pages and magazines and books, would never have earned him a place in the history of design or printing." On the remaining matter of type design he asks, "Was Goudy the greatest American type designer or the most prolific?" and then after paragraphs of waffling says that "it seems merely silly to deny" that he was the former. On individual letter-forms Mr. Bruckner can be quite acerb ("incongruous," "hodge-podge, "open and rolling to the point of annoyance") and he relays what was the prevailing complaint about Goudy: "Critics of Goudy are fond of saying that all his types are advertising faces."

Bluff and entrepreneurial though he was, Goudy was aesthetically conservative. He favored a hand-drawn, relatively irregular and rounded look to his letters—in this he was loyal to the crafts tradition propounded by William Morris. He hit his full stride as a designer when he imported a German matrix-cutter that enabled him to translate his own drawings directly into metal. His most successful and widely used faces tend to be "old style." He disliked the look of "modern," regularized faces like Bodoni, and in his design of Goudy Modern "bravely [his word] increased

. . . the weight of the hairlines, bracketed the serifs slightly, and carried my curves more generously toward the stems." In an age when computers can not only set but design type, Goudy's bravely emphasized hairlines and curves, possessing what Mr. Bruckner calls "marked pen qualities," are worth prizing. He was not afraid of new technology, and one of his pet goals, a tighter fit of the letters, has become, with computer setting, all too easy to achieve. To withstand the pressure of the gracelessly computer-squeezed line, and the inhuman regularity of post-hot-metal type, the rounded, hand-wrought letter-forms he favored still serve.

Art's Dawn

THE CREATIVE EXPLOSION: *An Inquiry into the Origins of Art and Religion*, by John E. Pfeiffer. 270 pp. Harper & Row, 1982.

A mark, once made on stone, bone, canvas, or parchment, will remain until erased. Of all the unfathomable, intimidating, anonymous millions of men and women who have preceded us on this planet, the artists and artisans feel closest to us, where the marks made by their hands can still be inspected and still invite empathy. I have stood in the tomb of a pharaoh, in the remotest of many chambers hollowed out of solid rock, and seen the sketchy gray underpainting of an unfinished mural, the strokes of the brush as full of decision and nervous energy as if done the day before rather than three thousand years in the past. That artist, his very bones long dust, was present in that chamber, where his work had been interrupted. The oldest paintings are those that Cro-Magnon people left on the walls of the deep limestone caves of southern France and northern Spain during the Upper Paleolithic—a period from about thirty-five thousand to ten thousand years ago. Cro-Magnon man was, of course, *Homo sapiens sapiens,* as are we. Neanderthal man, Cro-Magnon man's predecessor on the European stage, had core-struck flint tools, and buried his dead with supplies for their afterlives, and arranged bear skulls and ibex horns in patterns; but he did not produce art. Art that has survived, at any rate—he may well have, like most primitive peoples, painted his body and decorated wood and hides. Some apprenticeship with perishable materials must underlie the sophisticated and vital animal portraiture preserved on the walls of the caves. But in the archaeological record art begins almost as abruptly as books of art history open with the famous wounded (or sleeping) bison from the cave at Altamira, the great frieze of bulls from

Lascaux, the Willendorf Venus, and the bison so artfully carved from reindeer horn and found near Les Eyzies. All these are dated "c. 15,000–10,000 B.C." in H. W. Janson's revised *History of Art.* What precipitated, after hundreds of millennia of rather stagnant human existence on this planet, the first outburst of painting and sculpture is the question John E. Pfeiffer undertakes to elucidate in *The Creative Explosion.*

Mr. Pfeiffer is a science writer rather than a scientist; he has worked for *Newsweek, Scientific American,* and CBS, and has to his credit a list of books whose titles include *The Human Brain, The Search for Early Man,* and *The Emergence of Society.* His strengths as an observer at art's dawn belong to the left, logical side of the brain: he has done his homework thoroughly, not only in viewing the art itself (no easy matter) and reviewing the considerable pertinent literature but in bringing to bear upon the Upper Paleolithic the latest information and speculation in anthropology. What seemed to me a certain right-brained weakness lies in his failure to make a persuasive intuitive connection with the art and the artists; the cave paintings are illumined by many lights brought from afar but not from within. The generally held impression that they were used in the conjurations of sympathetic magic in aid of the tribal hunt is subordinated to a rather abstract and trendy theory concerning the "chunking" of information necessary when a complication of society, with its informational increase, demands new feats and rites of mnemonics. Maybe so; but we have been taken far from the vivid animals themselves, many of which are shown wounded by arrows and scored by inverted "v"s and some of which "took quite a beating in prehistoric times . . . mutilated by repeated blows." A contemporary French investigator, Michel Lorblanchet, has closely re-created the materials of the Paleolithic artists (including their animal-fat lamps) and duplicated, stroke for stroke, on a blank wall, a number of the drawings in the cave at Pech-Merle. "For example, he knew that in the case of one bison the artist had started with a sweeping line at the head end, followed in clockwise direction by successive lines for the back, tail, legs, and then to the head end again, exactly thirty strokes in all. Most of the figures took him from one to four minutes to draw, except for a number of schematic figures which he copied in less than thirty seconds each." Such speed of execution, along with the cave drawings' random-seeming superimposition, discrepancy of scale, and frequently unfinished state, suggests an art created in the process of a ceremony—action painting, of a sort, like sand painting among the Navajo now—rather than the mural tableaux of "planned sequence" that Mr. Pfeiffer argues for. "Organization practically shouts at you in the Lascaux rotunda with its converging friezes, the great bison-dominated hall of Altamira, the

Salon Noir of Niaux, the Trois Frères sanctuary and its crouching 'sor-
cerer' or 'horned god.' " But to judge from the welter of superimposition
in the "sanctuary" at Trois Frères, or the bison in the Salon Noir at Niaux
with a tiny horse between his legs and two feet and a muzzle of two other
bison intersecting his back, the artist and the audience "saw" not the
drawings already on the wall but only the act of drawing, the conjuration
of the animal out of the wall.

However, one argues with Mr. Pfeiffer in a context he has provided
and splendidly furnished with facts and first-hand impressions. The extraordinary difficulty of physical access which many of the cave paintings
present, quite dissipated when they are reproduced in a book, is well
described here. The decorated caves are tortuous watery affairs miles long,
and not the shallow caves the Cro-Magnons did their daily living in. "The
art [is] located in utter darkness, far from daylight and twilight zones and
living places, on wide expanses of wall or doubly hidden inside tiny
chambers, caves within caves, secrets within secrets." Drawings are found
at the top of a slippery forty-five-foot limestone flow, on the sheer-drop
side of a stalagmite, at the end of passages reached only by squirming
through tight, panic-inducing "chatières." Mr. Pfeiffer intrepidly visited
two midget caves in the Les Eyzies region:

> One, located on a hillside along the road to Lascaux, has an opening
> smaller than a manhole cover and must be entered backward, a feet-first slide
> through a narrow hole down into a pit with just enough room for crouching.
> Then a twist around for another slide through a chatière to a place where
> it is possible to stand up and see a group of figures including an ibex and,
> off by itself, a fine 8-inch engraving of a reindeer. The other site also involves
> a slide into a pit and a squeeze through a chatière with two sharp bends to
> a dead end where you roll over on your back. From that position you see
> close to your face a red and black horse, the only figure in the cave.

The text makes clearer than any reproduction can the involvement the
drawings and paintings have with the surface of the wall: curves are fitted
into fissures, rocky protuberances are turned into bulging flanks. Visibility
is a real problem for investigators; it is common to mistake patterns of
cracks and hollows for engravings, and it is possible to miss even with
inch-by-inch inspection representations perfectly obvious on another occasion. It is even possible, this reviewer has found, to look at a photograph
of the oldest nude relief sculpture, the life-size carving from the Madeleine
cave, and see nothing but stone. The Abbé Breuil's watercolor copies of
cave paintings, by which the works achieved their first wide circulation
in the world, were marvels of simplification and clarification, executed

under conditions of heroic discomfort. The arcane locations of cave art compel a sense of connection with initiation rituals, with underground ordeal and symbolic rebirth.

The Australian aborigines still practice, in the fastness of their deserts, rock painting; Mr. Pfeiffer devotes several chapters to them, and persuasively interprets as mnemonic devices both their rock art (which is out in the open, not in caves) and their coming-of-age ceremony. The suspense, mysteries, terrors, and pain of the coming-of-age rite, climaxed by circumcision, are "all calculated to attach emotion to information," so that the imprinted initiates can maintain the tribe's collective memory, which is crucial to survival. The art, along with the tribal dances, riddles, and songs, relates to the sinuous, intertwining travels of the primal totem figures (Great Rainbow Snake, Blue-Tongue Lizard, etc.) as they roamed over a "dreamtime" earth, "when all the world was young and green"; the practical effect of the legends is to fix names and incidents to every location in the desert, spinning an immense and accurate mental map for people without scale maps or writing. Topographical information is not only stored on the rocks but carved into spear throwers and sacred boards. "It is no surprise that these people are never lost, that they know the locations of more than 400 possible water sources." The people of the Upper Paleolithic were never lost, either: "In all the galleries of all the art caves no one has ever found skeletal remains of lost individuals." By justifiable analogy, Mr. Pfeiffer extends the usages of the desert aborigines to the cave dwellers of the European Ice Ages. As bands of scattered hunter-gatherers united to exploit more efficiently the dwindling herds of bison, reindeer, ibex, and mammoth, more information needed to be absorbed and retained; ceremonies became more ornate, shamans more important and powerful. Art, as one of many instruments of indoctrination, was called into being. The creative explosion had taken place.

This thesis is developed with much demographic calculation. The amount of Ice Age territory needed to support a single hunter-gatherer is estimated as being from twenty to two hundred square kilometres. The optimum mating pool, or tribal group, is estimated at about five hundred. The mathematics of hostility and multiplying dyads (two-person relationships) is given in the formula $\frac{N^2 - N}{2} = D$, and we are told that "when the Yanomamo Indians . . . reach the 100 to 125 level, 4,950 to 7,750 dyads, the atmosphere becomes so charged with hostility that the group must split in two." Yet organized large-scale killing of animals is indicated by massive bone heaps and by the concentration of human habitations in river valleys, near natural fords where herds might cross and be ambushed. Neanderthal man lived on the plateaus; Cro-Magnon man moved into the valleys. After the peak of glaciation, around twenty thousand years ago, the ice receded and the Siberia-like climate of Europe warmed; as forests moved into the tundra, the herds thinned and drifted north. Late in the Upper Paleolithic, stone tools bearing "sickle sheen" indicate that the harvesting of cereal grasses had begun. Subsistence pressure may have been increased by the arrival in Europe of southern peoples driven to migrate away from the expanding deserts; so much water was locked up in glaciers that a land bridge existed across the Dardanelles. The numbers involved are poignantly small: "According to one estimate, 2,000 to 3,000 persons were living in France 20,000 years ago, and perhaps 6,000 to 10,000 more in all of Europe. The totals may have doubled or tripled during the next ten millenniums." Archaeological evidence suggests the rise of "seasonal villages" of bands of hunter-gatherers, akin to county fairs, and of extensive trade networks.

Still, does all this say more than that things became more complicated, and art was one of the complications? The style and intent of the art are still unexplained. Its naturalistic power and accuracy of observation, its submissiveness to natural contour, whether in the surface of the rock or in the anatomy of the animal—these are somewhat anomalous in the history of Western art. Nothing so vitally representational was to occur again until the classic art of Greece and Rome, and after that until the Renaissance. Abstraction and stylization are more the rule. The cave art that preceded the black-and-ochre herds of the Upper Paleolithic, and coexisted with them, limned enigmatic signs: "Claviforms or club-shaped, tectiforms or roof-shaped, scutiform or shield-shaped, tesselated or checkered, bell-shaped, tree-shaped, quadrangular, rayed, barbed, branched, serpentine scrawls . . . We do not know what they mean, but we know they were full of meaning for the people of the Upper Paleolithic." When the long Paleolithic period ended, about ten thousand years ago, with the recession of the glaciers and the herds and the rise of fishing as a transition to full-fledged agriculture, the Mesolithic people turned to "abstract designs painted on pebbles." This was art in search of an alphabet, headed toward Egyptian hieroglyphics. The figurative side of Paleolithic cave painting, however, was not an isolated episode; it had progeny. The rock murals of the Spanish Levant and the Sahara stylize and flatten its motifs and offer an apparent bridge to the art both of black Africa and of the Nile. In the Spanish Levant, human figures, daubed in lively silhouette, came to dominate the animals, and a calm flatness to supplant an evoked roundness. At the same time, the pain of impaled animals was first represented. The world had, Mr. Pfeiffer speculates, become "a more secular place, bright and sensual," after the somber "religious, mystical world" of the Cro-Magnons.

Surprisingly, having made a detailed case for the economic genesis of cave art, the author introduces in his last pages the idea of play—"Art seems somehow to have arisen from play, in a uniquely human spinoff process which has acquired a life of its own." It is true that modern artists, especially uninhibited types like Picasso, give the impression of being lucky individuals who, like professional athletes, have been licensed by society to continue being children. But play is a form of interplay, a social activity that, when solitary, is enacted among imaginary companions. Whereas the artist, like the shaman, is a solitary intermediary between the tribe and the non-human. Play is self-enclosing; art aims outward, and seeks to bring something forward out of invisibility and silence. Art is a transaction. It needs a market. What was the market that the artists of Altamira and Lascaux served? Mr. Pfeiffer must be right in locating it within the tribe's religious life, though he emphasizes initiation when a ritual of emboldening and solidarity for adult warriors seems no less plausible. His emphasis on memory-stocking is hard to reconcile with the simplicity, and even monotony, of the representations; from their realism one might conclude that their importance was not so much associative as illusionistic, in creating the impression of a living creature emerging from the womb of earth. Fertility and engendering are further suggested by the numerous sexually emphatic representations of women; as one investigator, Annette Leming-Emperaire, has written, "the association of the horse, the bison, and the woman appears to go deeply into Paleolithic beliefs. . . . We can gradually distinguish the broad lines of a theme by which woman, the universal principle of fertility, occupies a central place."

But the mystery abides. The abundant icons and crucifixes preserved in our museums would baffle anyone who knew nothing of Christianity. What future anthropologist could guess that the baby in the Virgin's lap and the gaunt man on the cross were the same divine person? Twenty thousand years is ten times the span of the Christian era: time enough for art to have a number of uses—as household decoration, tribal insignia, shorthand narrative, surrogate prey, invoked totem. Perhaps we are asking the wrong questions in these secret places. The abiding mystery is not what art is for but what force it is that seizes the artist and makes him exceed the strict requirements of the market. This excess, strangely, is what we value. Call it virtuosity, inspiration, dedication, the cave artists had it.

Computer Heaven

WHEN I RECENTLY VISITED the M.I.T. Laboratory for Computer Science, I felt much as when touring an old-fashioned factory: dazzled by the ingenuity of men, and somewhat dwarfed and dehumanized by men's works. But the old-fashioned mechanical factory at least produced a recognizable product, and the actions of its noisy machines were analogous to human actions and somewhat transparent to visual analysis. A computer center offers no such transparency to the layman: inscrutably the wheels spin, the screens flicker, the unseen electricity darts like lightning along its microscopic forked paths, and the product is labelled, again inscrutably, information.

A delicate opacity, as of a very finespun veil, is for the layman the computer's essence. When my word processor malfunctions, there is no part-by-part repair, no soldering or fine-fingered tinkering as with a machine of old, but, rather, the replacement of an entire sealed unit, in a few minutes of the repairperson's time, which is worth, a computerized bill later assures me, one hundred twenty dollars an hour. Today's high-school student, instead of laboriously performing a multiplication, extracting a square root, or resorting to a trigonometric table, presses a few keys of his hand calculator and copies down the answer that within nanoseconds is spelled out for him in numbers ingeniously formed of segments of a subdivided rectangle. The answer is achieved by methods radically different from the mathematics one is taught in elementary school—the little machine proceeds, in fact, in less time than we need to add six and seven, by a succession of narrowing approximations, as the algorithm submits numbers, broken into binary strings of zeroes and ones—offs and ons—to a loop again and again, until two results are identical to a specified number of decimals and thus the answer is reached.

The computer does not think as we do, though in its shining face and user-friendly dialogue it offers itself as anthropomorphic, as a relatively efficient and emotionally undemanding colleague. Our brains, we are told, are made up of long strings of electrical connection, just like *its* brain, and the gap between our intelligence and its is bound to narrow to the point where, and not far in the future, any difference will be in the computer's favor. Already, computers outthink us in every realm that is purely logical; what remains ours is the animal confusion—the primordial mud, as it were—of feeling, intention, and common sense. Common sense is noth-

Remarks at the celebration of the twenty-fifth anniversary of the Massachusetts Institute of Technology's Laboratory for Computer Science, in Cambridge, on October 26, 1988.

ing, after all, but accumulated experience, and computers, let us hope, will always be spared the bloody, painful, and inconclusive mess of human experience. Let them be, like the spoiled children of men who have fought their way up from the bottom, exempted from any need for common sense, and let their first and only emotion be bliss, the bliss we glimpse in Bach fugues, in elegant mathematical proofs, and in certain immortal games of chess.

I am here at your celebration, I believe, as a token humanist—a laborer on the arts-and-humanities side of the gulf that, we were assured decades ago by C. P. Snow, divides the realms of knowledge. The gulf is real. Just a few days ago, perhaps you saw, as I did, the item in the Boston *Globe* which revealed that twenty-one percent of adult Americans, according to a telephone poll, think the sun goes around the earth instead of the other way around, and seven more percent answered that they were undecided. Of the seventy-two percent who answered that the earth *does* orbit the sun, seventeen percent said that it takes one day, two percent one month, and nine percent could not guess at any time span. Lest we laugh too hard at such ignorance, let me confess that, though I myself follow in the newspaper such dramatic scientific revelations as the existence of gigantic bubbles of vacuity in the universe and of intricate coupling attachments on the surface of the AIDS virus, I have no more first-hand evidence of such truths than medieval men did of the widely publicized details of Heaven and Hell. Most science is over our heads, and we take it on faith. We are no smarter than medieval men, and science tells us that our brains are no bigger than those of Cro-Magnon men and women, of cave people; the contemporary assertions that our world is round and not flat, that it is a planet among others, that our sun is a star among others, in a galaxy among billions of others, that the entire unthinkably vast universe was compressed fifteen billion or so years ago into a point smaller than a pinhead, that for aeons before men appeared on this planet mountains have been rising and sinking and oceans and continents shifting about and extraordinary animal species arising and going extinct, that intricate creatures exist too small for us to see, that lightning and thought are both forms of electricity, that life is combustion, that the heavy elements we are made of all came out of exploding stars, that atomic bombs release energy inherent in all matter—all these assertions we incorporate into our belief system as trustingly as Cro-Magnon man accepted, from his shamans and wizards, such facts as the deity of the moon, the efficacy of cannibalism, and the practical link between real animals and pictures of them painted on cave walls. Scientists are the shamans and wizards, the wonderworkers and myth-givers of today.

So, in the context of our ignorance and wonder, what do we humanists make of the computer? What is our mythic image of it? We feel that it is silent and quick, like a thief. It is not quite to be trusted, since computer error and computer viruses crop up. We notice that the computer plays games with children. Though not as thoroughly domesticated as the radio and telephone, it has undergone a disarming regression in size, having been cozily shrunk since the days of ENIAC from roomfuls of vacuum tubes and wires to models that sit in the lap and fit in the hand. Computers, we know, store information and make it retrievable: somewhere, somehow, they hold our bank balances and those of all the other depositors, right to the penny; they make it possible to check our credit rating in an electronic twinkling; they aid and abet the police in keeping track of traffic tickets and once-elusive scofflaws. Indeed, their capacity for the marshalling of data seriously threatens our privacy, and conjures up the possibility of an omniscient totalitarian state where every citizen is numbered and every hour of his or her activity is coded and filed. Some corporations, we read in the newspaper, oppressively clock their employees' every fingerstroke.

And yet totalitarianism is not really the computer's style. Freedom is the computer's style. In a recent novel from mainland China, written by a veteran of that country's prison camps, I read these sentences: "Technology did not stop at the borders of our guarded country. It broke relentlessly through the steel bars of ideology. It held the world together in its net with invisible electronic waves, looping back inside pieces that had been sundered from the rest." The author is speaking of radios, but the language seems flavored with computerese, and the message—technology overwhelms ideology—is the reverse of that of *Nineteen Eighty-four* and those other dystopian visions wherein information-processing reinforces tyranny. The electronic revolution seems to expand the scale of interrelations beyond the limits at which tyranny can be enforced.

In regard to the iron curtain that exists between the humanities and the sciences, the computer is a skillful double agent. The production and the analysis of texts have been greatly facilitated by the word processor: for instance, programs for the making of indices and concordances have taken much of the laboriousness out of these necessary scholarly tasks. In my own professional field, not only does word processing make the generation of perfectly typed pages almost too easy, but computer-setting has lightened the finicky labor of proofs. Where once the game was to avoid resetting too many lead lines on the Linotype machine, now the digitized text accepts alterations in an electronic shudder that miraculously travels, hyphenations and all, the length of a perfectly justified paragraph.

In sum, the computer makes things light; the lead and paper of my craft are dissolved into electronic weightlessness, ponderous catalogues are reduced to a single magnetized disc, and in computer graphics a visual simulacrum of the world can be conjured onto a screen and experimented upon. Our human lightening of the world is an ancient progressive tendency, with an element of loss. Man, beginning as an animal among animals, hunted and hunting, once shouldered the full dark fatality of nature. Taming other beasts to his use, taming wild plants to a settled agriculture, inventing devices to multiply his own strength and speed, he has gradually put an angelic distance between himself and matter. It is human to regret this leavetaking; our aesthetic sense has earthy roots. Computer-set type, for instance, is faintly ugly and soulless, compared with the minuscule irregularities and tiny sharp bite that metal type pressed into the paper. In turn, manuscript inked onto parchment had an organic vitality and color that type only could weakly ape. But we cannot go back, though we can look back; we must swim, like angels, in our weightless element, and grow into the freedom that we have invented.

Evolution Be Praised

THE FLAMINGO'S SMILE: *Reflections in Natural History,* by Stephen Jay Gould. 476 pp. Norton, 1985.

"Evolution," writes Stephen Jay Gould in introducing his latest collection of essays, "is one of the half-dozen shattering ideas that science has developed to overturn past hopes and assumptions, and to enlighten our current thoughts." Shattering, indeed. The non-scientist's relation to modern science is basically craven: we look to its discoveries and technology to save us from disease, to give us a faster ride and a softer life, and at the same time we shrink from what it has to tell us of our perilous and insignificant place in the cosmos. Not that threats to our safety and significance were absent from the pre-scientific world, or that arguments against a God-bestowed human grandeur were lacking before Darwin. But our century's revelations of unthinkable largeness and unimaginable smallness, of abysmal stretches of geological time when we were nothing, of supernumerary galaxies and indeterminate subatomic behavior, of a kind of mad mathematical violence at the heart of matter have scorched us deeper than we know. Giacometti's eroded, wire-thin figures body forth the new humanism, and Beckett's minimal monologuists provide its feeble, hopeless voice. Yet still we beg of science, "Talk to us," and honor with sales and celebrity those practicing scientists willing to condescend to the general reader and to entertain us with the astonishing facts and even to share our atavistic awe and dread as the facts inexorably unfold. In recent years, the astronomer Carl Sagan has been the most conspicuous of American popularizers, but his relentless televised mooning after the stars, his tub-thumping for extraterrestrial life, and his willingness to extend his hyperactive speculative faculty into fields well beyond his own all give his information a certain gleam of vulgarity. Gould, his contemporary (and fellow alumnus of the New York City public schools), has contrived to write accessibly and amusingly of the natural sciences with no sacrifice of seriousness; he is the worthy successor, as naturalist and essayist, to Loren Eiseley. Gould is a less poetic writer than Eiseley, and hews closer to developments within paleontology and evolutionary theory; one suspects that he would consider "romantic" many of Eiseley's later, more brooding and personal essays, as well as the cheerful microbiological ruminations of Dr. Lewis Thomas, whom Gould must have in mind when he writes, "Siphonophores do not convey the message—a favorite theme of unthinking romanticism—that nature is but one gigantic whole, all its parts intimately connected and interacting in some higher, ineffable harmony."

For over ten years now, Gould has been writing a monthly column, "This View of Life," for the magazine *Natural History. The Flamingo's Smile* is his fourth collection of (with some few other essays) these varied, vivacious columns. The other three collections are *Ever Since Darwin* (1977), *The Panda's Thumb* (1980), and *Hen's Teeth and Horse's Toes* (1983). All have contained roughly thirty essays apiece, tidily grouped for consecutive reading; however, as the author points out, each collection has been longer than the last. He is not only writing more lengthily but, my faint impression is, more felicitously. Some of his earlier essays had a slangy, self-assertive tone and a tinge of the sensational—e.g., the one in *Hen's Teeth* speculating that the priest and philosopher Teilhard de Chardin assisted Charles Dawson in perpetrating the Piltdown hoax, paleontology's most notorious fraud. The tone of *The Flamingo's Smile* seems to be a mellowed one, more appreciative than assertive. A number of its essays sympathetically explicate what now seem to be preposterous scientific theories and patiently explain how learned and honorable men could hold them. One extended piece, the hundredth column Gould has composed for *Natural History,* is fondly devoted to his pet object of research and field work, the Bahamian land snail *Cerion* ("I love *Cerion* with all my heart and intellect"). And a number of crusading excursions into human history attempt to rescue from the mistreatment of their own times such dwellers on the social margins as Saartjie Baartman, a southern-African woman put on public display in early-nineteenth-century Europe as "the Hottentot Venus"; Carrie Buck, a Virginia woman whose legal sterilization in the 1920s was upheld in a decision by Supreme Court Justice Oliver Wendell Holmes, famously pronouncing, "Three generations of imbeciles are enough"; and Ernest Everett Just, a brilliant black biologist who died in 1941, at the age of fifty-eight, after a career frustrated by racism in the highest academic levels. Gould has written much of this book while battling cancer, and, his preface states, "I write these essays primarily to aid my own quest to learn and understand as much as possible about nature in the short time allotted." To "the plodding regularity of these essays" he credits some of his will to live: "Who can surpass me in the good fortune they supply; every month is a new adventure—in learning and expression. I could only say with the most fierce resolution: 'Not yet Lord, not yet.' I could not dent the richness in a hundred lifetimes, but I simply must have a look at a few more of those pretty pebbles."

Gould's prose pebbles make addictive reading in part because of his unabashed enthusiasm for evolutionary theory, which "beautifully encompasses both the particulars that fascinate and the generalities that instruct." In *The Panda's Thumb,* he explained, "[Evolutionary theory] is, in its current state of development, sufficiently firm to provide satisfaction and confidence, yet fruitfully undeveloped enough to provide a treasure trove of mysteries." His essays, far from being lecture notes recited out of a store of settled knowledge, have the fresh zeal of self-education. Footnotes cheerfully acknowledge demurs and amplifications that their magazine publication attracted. His titles are lively, even jazzy—"The Titular Bishop of Titiopolis," "Bathybius and Eozoon," "Death Before Birth, or a Mite's *Nunc Dimittis,* " "Of Wasps and WASPs," "Hannah West's Left Shoulder and the Origin of Natural Selection"—and our interest is further piqued by the illustrations, which have often been fetched from their obscure source like a paleontological treasure in their own right. The pages on Carrie Buck, for instance, reproduce the first-grade report card of Carrie's daughter Vivian, who was born just before her mother was sterilized (indeed, her birth prompted the sterilization) and who died at only the age of eight; the poor child, the third generation of alleged imbeciles, got A's in deportment and B's and C's in academic subjects. She even made the honor roll one term. The look of her homely old report card cries out like a wounded voice. Mr. Gould has a salutary ethical feel for the actual detail, the exact quotation. He firmly lets us know, "All these essays are based on original sources in their original languages: none are direct reports from texts and other popular summaries." Not only a historian of life, he teaches the history of science at Harvard, and is never more interesting (or ingratiating) than when he delves up some long-buried theory and dusts off its key paragraphs and makes it, as it were, still tick. Philip Henry Gosse, in his *Omphalos* (1857), argued that God had loaded the geological strata with "prochronic" indications of time-spans older than the Biblical Creation so as not to violate the cyclical integrity of natural processes, just as He fashioned animals with feces already in their intestines; the Reverend William Buckland (1784–1856) argued that the gravel and loam deposits found throughout England were evidence of Noah's Flood, but he had the grace and scientific wisdom eventually to see that they were in fact evidence of glacial ice sheets; the German Lorenz Oken and the British William Swainson, in the decades just before Darwin's *Origin of Species* (1859), propounded grandly fallacious taxonomic systems based, with cabalistic intricacy, upon the number five. These mistaken theorists were all excellent descriptive naturalists; but, until Darwin took the not unknown principle of natural selection (it had been expressed in 1831 by the Scots fruit-grower Patrick Matthew, in an obscure work called *Naval Timber and Arboriculture,* and even earlier by another Scotsman, William Charles Wells, in a posthumously published paper on skin coloration) and showed this fortuitous mechanism to be the creative force transforming organisms in the vastness of geological time, the nineteenth century was one of accumulating heaps of evidence being shuffled about along anthropocentric and quasi-theological lines. God the Master Mechanic died slow, with many a confusing deathbed word.

Gould's evangelical sense of science as an advancing light gives him a vivid sympathy with thinkers in the dark. The great Lord Kelvin, the discoverer of the second law of thermodynamics, for forty years proposed ages of the earth and sun too brief to allow organic evolution; but, then, how could anyone calculate the sun's thermal life before the discovery of radioactivity and nuclear fusion? How could the energetic debates over embryology carried on in eighteenth-century France, by such savants as Pierre-Louis Moreau de Maupertuis, be less than grotesquely simple-minded two centuries before DNA was analyzed, and fifty years before the jacquard loom offered the first analogous instance of programmed instructions? Science not only produces technology but must wait upon it. We forget how tangled things looked to those who first tried to sort them out; as the record of the strata emerged, catastrophism (which is now having a revival of sorts) was the logical conclusion to reach, as Gould has pointed out in an essay on Georges Cuvier:

> In the great debates of early-nineteenth-century geology, catastrophists followed the stereotypical method of objective science—empirical literalism.

They believed what they saw, interpolated nothing, and read the record of the rocks directly. This record, read literally, is one of discontinuity and abrupt transition: faunas disappear; terrestrial rocks lie under marine rocks with no recorded transitional environments between; horizontal sediments overlie twisted and fractured strata of an earlier age.

Gould chastens us ungrateful beneficiaries of science with his affectionate and tactile sense of its strenuous progress, its worming forward through fragmentary revelations and obsolete debates, from relative darkness into relative light. Even those who were wrong win his gratitude.

In a day of perhaps excessively professional and instrumentalized research, Gould loves with the ardor of a boyish amateur the dispassionate scientific method. This method, he keeps insisting, must be resolutely non-mystical and isolated from human wishful thinking—what he several times calls "hope." "Always be suspicious of conclusions that reinforce uncritical hope and follow comforting traditions of Western thought," he writes in a discussion of the "anthropic principle," which is a new name for the venerable human idea that things must have been designed for us, since here we are. It has taken new life lately from the realization of what extremely fine balances were apparently struck among the fundamental physical forces to provide a universe as stable and locally congenial as it is; but an earlier version was advanced in 1903 by Alfred Russel Wallace, who ranks alongside Darwin in the discovery of natural selection but who later drifted, unlike the ever-empirical Darwin, into spiritualism and anthropocentricism. Wallace, working with turn-of-the-century astronomy, demonstrated to his own satisfaction that "the marvellous complexity of forces which appear to control matter, if not actually to constitute it, are and must be mind-products." Mark Twain ridiculed Wallace's thesis ("According to these figures, it took 99,968,000 years to prepare the world for man, impatient as the Creator doubtless was to see him and admire him") and Gould tartly says of it, "I, for one, will seek my hope elsewhere." He does not say where, unless it be in the hope of ever-newer scientific ideas.

Though a devout disciple of Darwin, he is no slave to the gradualism that Darwin conceived to be the pace of adaptation and that makes the larger steps of evolution very hard to picture. Gould has written on, and written a new introduction to, the geneticist Richard Goldschmidt's controversial *The Material Basis of Evolution* (1940), which argues that, though Darwin's gradualism satisfactorily accounts for, say, the prevalence of white rabbits in snow country, the large mutations can only be explained by the hypothesis of the "hopeful monster"—the rare freak whose malformation has a survival value and who finds (here's a rub) another hopeful monster to mate with. Gould has offered, as a way of coping with the embarrassments of discontinuity in the paleontological record, a theory of "punctuated equilibria" that has, to his annoyance, given some comfort to creationists. As the last essays in *The Flamingo's Smile* show, he is considerably excited by the recent so-called Nemesis hypothesis, which holds that mass extinctions have been caused every twenty-six million years by the return of a star that comes close enough to the solar system to stir up the Oort cloud of comets and thus precipitate collisions and climate-altering dust-storms on earth. This might be called catastrophism with a heavenly face.

As he sifts through biological riddles, however, whether in the fossil record (conodonts, the banana-shaped *Tullimonstrum,* the pre-Cambrian Ediacaran fauna) or the living world (sexual cannibalism among insects, sequential hermaphroditism in *Crepidula,* identity problems in Siamese twins and Portuguese men-of-war), or fends off cladists and creationists, advocates of eugenics and of the anthropic principle, Gould has Darwin's example ever before him. He has read the books Darwin wrote in addition to the two notorious ones, *On the Origin of Species* and *The Descent of Man* (1871), and has written separate essays on *The Formation of Vegetable Mould, Through the Action of Worms, with Observations on Their Habits* (1881) and *On the Various Contrivances by Which British and Foreign Orchids Are Fertilized by Insects* (1862). Patient and scrupulous observation are as important to the naturalist as worms and pollination are to nature; Darwin's slowness to generalize and the detailed concreteness with which he substantiated his generalizations are of a piece with his unique powers of insight into the workings of nature. The proper observer must not be hasty to impose order, or to demand too much neatness of nature. Gould frequently delights in nature's intricate dishevelment, in the waywardness of adaptation:

> Our world is not an optimal place, fine tuned by omnipotent forces of selection. It is a quirky mass of imperfections, working well enough (often admirably); a jury-rigged set of adaptations built of curious parts made available by past histories in different contexts. Darwin, who was a keen student of history, not just a devotee of selection, understood this principle as the primary proof of evolution itself.

The word "evolution," with its connotation of onrolling or progressive development, was not favored by Darwin; he preferred for his theory the bleak string-phrase "descent with modification through variation and natural selection." The pure fortuitousness and physicality of nature's workings must not be polluted, Gould reaffirms, by human thought-habits or wishful thinking. "The human mind delights in finding pattern—so much so that we often mistake coincidence or forced analogy for profound meaning. No other habit of thought lies so deeply within the soul of a small creature trying to make sense of a complex world not constructed for it." To lock out old notions of divine planning and human singularity, the notions of randomness and fortuity and contingency are stressed as if themselves sacred: "Random processes do produce high degrees of order—and the existence of pattern is no argument against randomness." The shattering effect Darwin's theory had upon the Victorians did not concern its allegations of "nature red in tooth and claw," to which every farmer and soldier could already attest, but, rather, its description of how intricate organic design would arise without any divine intention. "Evolution," Gould stated with relish in the prologue to his first collection, "is purposeless, nonprogressive, and materialistic." In the essay upon Darwin's worm studies, he cited as exemplary "the materialistic character of Darwin's theory, particularly his denial of any causal role to spiritual forces, energies, or powers." Even such a mild, almost furtive suggestion of the supernatural as vitalism's hint that there exists in life a "spark" or "special something" must be rejected—even the plausible notion that *Homo sapiens*'s high intelligence crowns an evolutionary trend. "Human brains and bodies did not evolve along a direct and inevitable ladder, but by a circuitous and tortuous route carved by adaptations evolved for different reasons, and fortunately suited to later needs."

Mammals developed in size and capability because, in large part, the dinosaurs died out. But, one wonders, might not reptiles have developed superior intelligences? Gould's own essay "Were Dinosaurs Dumb?" discusses small, flesh-eating, necessarily quick and agile dinosaurs, such as *Stenonychosaurus*, heading in this direction. Is not intelligence so formidable a weapon for survival as to develop inevitably? In the sea, are not the cetaceans—the whales, porpoises, and dolphins—its newest considerable citizens and also its brightest? Gould does not entertain these questions, asserting instead that "Conscious intelligence has evolved only once on earth, and presents no real prospect for reëmergence should we choose to use our gift for destruction." This closed outlook comes oddly from the man who marvelled at how the panda, needing a thumb to grip his bamboo shoots, evolved one from a wrist bone, or who points out how flight has evolved four times on earth, the wing derived each time from different body elements. Gould regards human intelligence as in the same class—ornately evolved oddity—as the flamingo's upside-down beak, which gives him his title. Our brains are a kind of unintended smile on the surface of the *bellum omnium contra omnes*—the war of all against all, as Marx called Darwin's nature. A stark view, but a lucid and, it would appear, an invigorating one. As a constant writer (who has not in ten years, he tells us, missed a deadline), Stephen Gould is fortunate to possess an approach and a theme that cast a clarifying light upon such a wide variety of facts and texts. He is additionally fortunate in having, in Darwin, a hero to serve as a point of reference and a standard of honor.

Deep Time and Computer Time

TIME'S ARROW, TIME'S CYCLE: *Myth and Metaphor in the Discovery of Geological Time,* by Stephen Jay Gould. 222 pp. Harvard University Press, 1987.

TIME WARS: *The Primary Conflict in Human History,* by Jeremy Rifkin. 263 pp. Holt, 1987.

European man, who once dwelt with a certain unsanitary snugness on a flat world hedged in by Vikings and Saracens and enclosed by the chiming celestial spheres, has suffered a series of traumatic widenings of consciousness. First—and perhaps least unnerving, since it was accompanied by triumphs of conquest and trade—was the increased awareness of the earth's actual geography, as Italian merchants, Portuguese sailors, Spanish conquistadores, and British explorers brought back word of the vast Asian landmass, the long African coast, the two unsuspected continents of the New World, the watery vastness of the Pacific Ocean, and the icebound polar regions. Then there was astronomy, which showed the fixed nightcap of stars with its seven "wanderers" (the sun, the moon, and the five observable planets) to be the visible fraction of unthinkable extents of space and energy. The Copernican revolution removed the earth from the center of the universe but did not alter its scale; this the telescope, first used astronomically by Galileo, was to enlarge inexorably, until in the 1920s Edwin Hubble demonstrated that our Milky Way, with its billions of stars, was but one of countless galaxies, which are generally flying from one another like shrapnel in a gargantuan explosion. In the direction of the small, lenses, as microscopes were developed in the seventeenth century, revealed a teeming sub-world of animalcula and microbes, beneath which lay an even finer world of molecules, atoms, and subatomic particles—dizzying depths of active complexity beyond the reach not only of the eye but of all direct observational apparatus. And in the dimension of time another abyss was uncovered by the geological sciences, whose early theorists include Leonardo and Descartes: by the late eighteenth century it had become clear that only huge amounts of elapsed time could account for the stratified, folded, eroded, fossiliferous state of the earth's rocks, which the Bible had declared to have been created only at the outset of its own historical record, in a year calculated to have been 4004 B.C.

The blasphemous and dwarfing revelation of "deep time" forms the underlying drama of Stephen Jay Gould's *Time's Arrow, Time's Cycle: Myth and Metaphor in the Discovery of Geological Time.* In the monthly essays with which Gould has been amusing and edifying the readers of *Natural History* magazine, he now and then shows a surprisingly fond acquaintance with the debunked and forgotten theories that litter the history of science: the present book, an expanded version of lectures given at Hebrew University in Jerusalem, considers three early British geologists—Thomas Burnet (1635–1715), James Hutton (1726–1797), and Charles Lyell (1797–1875)—who he feels have been misrepresented in the contemporary textbook version of geology's progress. In "textbook cardboard," this progress is represented as the "victory of superior observation finally freed from constraining superstition"—the supplanting, that is, of fanciful, religion-tainted theories by the patient field work and inductive reasoning of true scientists. Yet, Gould argues, "scientists are not robotic inducing machines that infer structures of explanation only from regularities observed in natural phenomena. . . . Scientists are human beings, immersed in culture, and struggling with all the curious tools of inference that mind permits—from metaphor and analogy to all the flights of fruitful imagination that C. S. Peirce called 'abduction.' "

Among the cultural metaphors that shaped the searching out of deep time are those of time's arrow and time's cycle. Did the enigmatic evidence of the rocks show that the earth had a history proceeding from a beginning to an end, or was its geology a matter of endless cycles of erosion and repair, subsidence and uplift? The truth, Gould says, lies with both: the cycles move along an arrow. And Burnet, the textbook-deplored proponent of the Bible-inspired *Sacred Theory of the Earth* (1680–89) came closer to this double truth than Hutton's *Theory of the Earth* (first publication 1788) and Lyell's *Principles of Geology* (first edition 1830–33). "Hutton and Lyell, traditional discoverers of deep time in the British tradition, were motivated as much (or more) by . . . a vision about time, as by superior knowledge of the rocks in the field. . . . Their visions stand prior—logically, psychologically, and in the ontogeny of their thoughts— to their attempts at empirical support." Hutton, to be more precise, was so much under the sway of Newton's magnificent analysis of heavenly motion as to impose a similarly perpetual and ideal mechanics upon geology, and Lyell was so caught up in his combat with the "catastrophists" on behalf of "uniformitarianism" as to ignore, until late in his life, the fact that earth's fossils do trace an irreversible history, and that strata of rock can be ordered by them.

If this sounds technical, it somewhat is. But geology has the charm that we all walk upon its raw material, and Gould's lucid, animated style, rarely slowed by even a touch of the ponderous,* leads us deftly through the labyrinth of faded debates and preconceptions. His own contemporary engagement in the debate with evolutionary "gradualists" opposed to his and Niles Eldredge's theory of "punctuated equilibrium" lends verve to his exposition of old points of contention. Though gradual change, operating through great tracts of time, is now assumed to be the empirically proven mode of biological and evolutionary change, the evidence, Gould takes some pleasure in reminding us, favored and still favors the catastrophists:

> Read literally, then and now, the geological record is primarily a tale of abrupt transitions, at least in local areas. If sediments indicate that environments are changing from terrestrial to marine, we do not usually find an insensibly graded series of strata, indicating by grain size and faunal content that lakes and streams have given way to oceans of increasing depth. In most cases, fully marine strata lie directly atop terrestrial beds, with no signs of smooth transition. The world of dinosaurs does not yield gradually to the realm of mammals; instead, dinosaurs disappear from the record in apparent concert with about half the species of marine organisms in one of the five major mass extinctions of life's history. Faunal transitions, read literally, are almost always abrupt, both from species to species and from biota to biota.

To concede this abruptness, and to try to adopt a theory to fit it more closely than a dogmatic gradualism, does not make Gould a creationist, nor did it make Lyell's catastrophist opponents, such as Georges Cuvier and Louis Agassiz, any less empirical or scientific than he, and scarcely less right: "We must admit that current views represent a pretty evenly shuffled deck between attitudes held by Lyell and the catastrophists." Gould, with a passion that approaches the lyrical, argues for a retrospective tolerance in science and against fashions which would make heroes and villains of men equally committed to the cause of truth and equally immersed in the metaphors and presumptions of their culture and time.

---

*"Many great arguments in the history of human thought have a kind of relentless, intrinsic logic that grants them a universality transcending time or subject" perhaps contains such a touch.

The situation of cosmology now, as it floridly sprouts suppositions of superheavy "strings" and extra dimensions rolled into tiny tubes and violently "inflationary" or infinitely multiple universes, is perhaps analogous to that of nineteenth-century geology, where much hard evidence and sound reasoning existed intermingled with hypotheses that time would show to be, though no more fantastic than the truth, false. Gould implicitly asks that tolerance be extended to such contemporary guesses as the Alvarez hypothesis of asteroidal or cometary causation of the mass extinctions, and the theory of punctuated equilibrium, which merely proposes that speciation occurs in spurts—that evolution, like most terrain, is lumpy and uneven.

The book ends with a surprising burst of Christian art: cathedral windows and bosses, and James Hampton's great American folk sculpture, *The Throne of the Third Heaven of the Nations' Millennium General Assembly*. With these artworks Gould is saying more than that scientific theory is beautiful; he is emphasizing the Judaeo-Christian arrow of time, which flies from Creation to Apocalypse, from Adam's Fall to Christ's Second Coming, from Noah's Flood to Jesus's Baptism. The Old and New Testaments are in a sense two cycles, which echo one another and yet register an advance; and this is also the way of the earth, which lifts up mountains and flattens them and raises them up again, and allows species to perish and others to arise and fill the same ecological niche with similar forms, and yet also has a history, an overall change from a young, violent, oxygenless planet to the oxygen-rich and relatively stable one that supports our present unique chapter in the ongoing saga of life. The universe itself, which as recently as the 1950s could be plausibly imagined to exist in a "steady state" of perpetual atom-by-atom creation, also now seems, on its colossal scale, to be arrowing from a Big Bang fifteen billion years ago to an eventual end in total entropy. The seventeenth-century cleric Thomas Burnet, though without much in the way of facts and with little notion of how truly deep time was, more accurately combined the metaphors of arrow and cycle than his successor geologists Hutton and Lyell, who both, in wishing to lift their science above the "complex contingencies" of "just history," conceived of cycles without end or aim. Stephen Jay Gould, in his scrupulous explication of their carefully wrought half-truths, abolishes the unnecessary distinction between the humanities and science, and honors the latter as a branch of humanistic thought, fallible and poetic.

Time is tackled from a wider angle, and more pugnaciously, in *Time Wars*. Jeremy Rifkin, president of the Foundation on Economic Trends, in Washington, D.C., is not the scientist or the writer that Gould is, but he has produced a brisk book that in little more than two hundred pages covers a large territory. *Time Wars* seems at least three books in one. First, it is a survey of how men have considered time, from the hunter-gatherers' complete submission to the "migratory rhythms of the great herds of animals and the gestation and ripening times of wild herbs and roots," through the early agricultural societies' celestial reckonings and their invention of calendars, up to medieval man's invention of the daily schedule (first perpetrated by the Benedictine monks) and industrial, bourgeois man's exaltation of the clock and today's increasing domination by a "computime" measured in nanoseconds (billionths of a second). Second, *Time Wars* launches a cautionary jeremiad against the computer society, which compels men to interface with inhumanly rapid machines and invites them to treat reality merely in terms of proliferating information systems:

> The nanosecond culture brings with it a new and more virulent form of reductionism. The clockwork universe of the industrial age is being replaced, in fast order, by the computational universe of the postindustrial age. . . . We are entering a new temporal world where time is segmented into nanoseconds, the future is programmed in advance, nature is reconceived as bits of coded information, and paradise is viewed as a fully simulated, artificial environment.

In both these aspects, *Time Wars* seems an efficient rehash of other recent works of popular sociology and anthropology; its footnotes draw preponderantly upon books written in the 1980s (*Technostress*, by Craig Brod; *Turing's Man*, by David Bolter; *The Second Self: Computers and the Human Spirit*, by Sherry Turkle; *Silicon Shock: The Menace of the Computer*, by Geoff Simons; *The Discoverers*, by Daniel Boorstin; *The Dance of Life: The Other Dimension of Time*, by Edward T. Hall; *Hidden Rhythms: Schedules and Calendars in Social Life*, by Eviatar Zerubavel; *The Culture of Time and Space 1880–1918*, by Stephen Kern; *Clocks and the Cosmos*, by Samuel L. Macey; *The Information Society*, by Yoneji Masuda) and even when an older voice is quoted (Augustine, Swift, the Welsh bard Dafydd ap Gwilym) the notes give the source as an intermediate scholarly work.

A personal and original note sounds only in *Time Wars*'s third aspect, that of a sermon urging us to return to biological time and to dwell empathetically in the global ecosystem. There is on all fronts, we are assured, a surge in this direction; there are "the environmental movement, the animal-rights movement, the Judaeo-Christian stewardship movement, the eco-feministic movement, the holistic health movement, the alternative agriculture movement, the appropriate technology movement, the bio-regionalism movement, the self-sufficiency movement, the economic democracy movement, the alternative education movement, and the disarmament movement." Without denying that every little movement has a praiseworthy meaning all its own, I find it hard to grasp how all this New Age pietism relates to the concept of time that the computer has allegedly drilled into our heads. I use a word processor, and the appearance on the screen of the letter I just tapped seems no more or less miraculous and sinister than its old-fashioned appearance, after a similar action, upon a sheet of white paper in my typewriter. Has the fact that this electronic machine is designed in terms of nanoseconds affected my consciousness any more deeply than the minute calculations involved in the design of the carburetor that, when I simple-mindedly ask my automobile to go, mixes fuel and air so judiciously that the mixture explodes and the car does go? The capacity of human beings to absorb what they wish to and to ignore the rest seems to me almost limitless. The telephone, for instance, is a still-evolving technological marvel, and more pervasive than the computer: has it changed what people talk about? Not according to the television commercials urging us to reach out to sweetheart and mother. Television itself came heralded as the reshaper of global culture, and yet its staple content remains the primitive stuff of sporting events, shoot-'em-ups, car chases, and comedies as homely and inane as the plays we used to watch in high-school assemblies in the hoary days of Harry Truman.

Rifkin cites instances of professional "technostress" when computers replace older hardware, and quotes some "computer compulsives" and M.I.T. students who have acquired rather people-unfriendly attitudes, and discusses the spread of the "information" metaphor in such sciences as biology, psychology, and even astronomy. He did not prove, to me, that the computer as a culture-altering device is yet in the same league as the clock, the wheel, or the plow, or that its theorists will have the cultural impact of Newton, Darwin, Einstein, or Freud. A fever of overstatement vitiates many a sentence:

> It [the spiral] is the new symbol of creation captured in both the double helix and in the cybernetic vision where feedback loops simulate new worlds pulsing in the crevices of millions of silicon chips.

Rifkin's leaps into the cosmic sometimes leave us behind:

> The new universe resembles a giant computerlike mind, ever expanding, creating new information and new knowledge, filling the cosmos with higher and higher levels of consciousness. . . . Human beings reach out to

this new informational deity by interfacing with the evolving mind of the universe. Communion is the experience of gaining access to larger and larger stores of information, of simulating more complex programs, each reaching ever closer to the ultimate computerbank storage facility, the mind force of the cosmos.

Even on the more solid ground of the past, his prose overreaches:

> In just a few short centuries, the bourgeois class had managed to hoist the mechanical clock to the top of the town tower and then succeed in lifting its spirit up into the heavens where, like the angel Gabriel, it proclaimed the coming of the kingdom. The promised land, however, bore a strikingly secular imprint. God's countenance, which once shone brightly, now cast only a pale shadow. The sounds of divine rapture could no longer be heard. They were subsumed by the relentless ticking of the giant cosmic clock. Underneath its watchful gaze, the faithful scurried to and fro, frantic to keep up with the tempo of the times, anxious not to miss a single beat for fear that they might be forever condemned to that netherworld where no clocks existed and mayhem and confusion reigned supreme.

The torments of Hell, we learn, include the annoyance of not knowing what time it is.

That the clock was needed to regulate the factories and appointment books of industrialism, and that the calendar, with its religious and state holidays, is a prime enforcer of the prevailing culture, I do not doubt, and Rifkin's details on these matters (and on the remarkable biological clocks of insects and animals) repay the reading of *Time Wars*. But the computer, unlike the calendar and the clock, does not mark (or "keep") time; it and its programmers seek to minimize time. It is a time-saving device, meant to save clerical labor as its predecessor mechanisms saved physical labor, and as such it is the friend, not the enemy, of the biology-attuned slow-down Rifkin prescribes. He hymns "the new empathetic movements" that are "committed to the establishment of a social time order that is compatible with and complementary to the natural time order" without asking what the natural time order has entailed for most human beings. No workday is longer or harder than that of the agricultural worker, and any who think the hunter-gatherer led the life of Riley should read Elizabeth Marshall Thomas's brilliant neolithic novel *Reindeer Moon*. The most ringing quotation in *Time Wars* comes from John Locke: "The negation of Nature is the way toward happiness." Selective and tactful negation, let's hope, but there is no turning back, against time's arrow.

APPENDIX

Literarily Personal

LITERARILY PERSONAL

AN ARTICLE, *entitled "Writers as Progenitors and Offspring," written at the request of* Poets & Writers Magazine; *it appeared in the January-February 1987 issue, with a typically benign and evocative account by my son David of his own impressions, which do not contradict mine. I especially treasured this kindly glimpse from our shared past: "And at night, as he [I] sat reading books for review, or going over proofs with the same stubby golf pencil that had recorded his score that afternoon, he gave off an impression of leisure and repose, of doing exactly what he wanted to do."*

As both the son and father of a writer, I feel doubly qualified for this topic. My mother wrote in the front bedroom, beside a window curtained in dotted swiss. With a small child's eyes I see her desk, her little Remington with its elite face, and the brown envelopes that carried her patiently tapped-out manuscripts to New York City and then back to Shillington, Pennsylvania. I smell the fresh paper, the damp ink on the ribbon as it jerkily unfurls from spool to spool, the rubber flecks of eraser buried within the slanted bank of springy keys—an alphabet in the wrong order. We used to travel together to Hintz's stationery store in Reading, and there was beauty and power and opulence in the ceiling-high shelves of fresh reams, of tinted labels and yellow octagonal pencils in numbered degrees of hardness and softness, of tablets and moisteners and even little scales to weigh letters upon. Three cents an ounce it took in those days to send a story to a Manhattan magazine, or to *The Saturday Evening Post* in nearby Philadelphia, and what a wealth of expectation hovered in the air until Mr. Miller, our plodding, joking mailman, hurled the return envelope through the front-door letter slot! There was a novel, too, that slept in a ream box that had been emptied of blankness, and like a strange baby in the house, a difficult papery sibling, the manuscript was now and then roused out of its little rectangular crib and rewritten and freshly swaddled in hope. My mother's silence, at her desk, was among the mysteries—her faint aroma of mental sweat, of concentration as if in prayer.

I knew she was trying to reach beyond the street outside, where cars and people moved toward their local destinies as if underwater, toward a world we couldn't see, where magazines and books came from. That these magazines, with their covers by Norman Rockwell and John Falter, and the books of the world, some of them old and faded like pieces of nature and others shiny new and protected in an extra cellophane wrapper at the drugstore rental library, were written by our kind of people seemed unlikely to me; but now and then she got an encouraging pencilled note scrawled on the rejection slip, and in her fifties, I am happy to say, began to receive acceptances—enough to form her single published book, *En-chantment.* * Though there was much about her enterprise I didn't under-stand, I liked the smell of it, the silence, the modest equipment required, and the sly postal traffic with a world beyond; at an early age I enlisted in the enterprise myself.

My son David—what did he see? I wrote, when he was small, in a little upstairs room that, like my mother's room a generation before, overlooked a small-town street. The room had a door I could close, and he and his siblings used to scratch at the door, and have quarrels outside it. I moved to an office downtown, a half-mile away, and there they would come visit the confusion of papers, the faded Oriental rug, the bulletin board where jotted ideas and urgent requests slowly curled up and turned yellow, the pervasive stink of too many cigarettes and, after I gave those up, of nickel cigarillos. Dirty windows, without curtains of dotted swiss, overlooked the Ipswich River, and the chief wall decoration was a framed drawing that the great James Thurber had been kind enough to send me from Connecticut when I was a boy in Shillington.

I spent mornings and little more in the office. They were, David and his brother and two sisters, pleasantly aware, I assumed, that I had more free time than most fathers. (Though was I, when with them, entirely with them? A writer's working day is a strange diffuse thing that never really ends, and gives him a double focus much of the time.) My children enjoyed, I imagined, the little mild gusts of fame—the visiting photogra-pher and interviewer, the sudden box of new books in the front hall—that my profession brought into our domestic world. And they said little, tactfully, of the odd versions of themselves and their home that appeared

---

*Augmented, in November of 1989, by the narrowly posthumous publication of another collection, *The Predator* (Ticknor & Fields).

now and then in print. They never spoke to me of being writers themselves. So I was taken unawares when all showed distinct artistic bents and the older son, at an age earlier than his father, became published in *The New Yorker*. At the time I gave his Harvard girlfriend, who herself wrote, and Ann Beattie, who had accepted him into her writing course, more credit than any example I had inadvertently set. The writing enterprise seemed to me self-evidently a desperate one, and though my mother and I—both only children—had been desperate enough to undertake it, I thought my children, raised in a gentler, undepressed, gregarious world, would seek out less chancy and more orthodox professions. But I underestimated, it would seem, the appeal of the mise-en-scène, the matrix, that had charmed me—the clean paper, the pregnant silences, the typewriter keyboard with its scrambled alphabet. We are drawn toward our parents' occupations, I have concluded, because we can see the equipment and size up the effort; it is like a suit of clothes we try on for size and then discover ourselves to have bought and to be wearing for good.

IN ANSWER *to a question, in 1985, from the French magazine* Libération: "Pourquoi écrivez-vous?"

From earliest childhood I was charmed by the materials of my craft, by pencils and paper and, later, by the typewriter and the entire apparatus of printing. To condense from one's memories and fantasies and small discoveries dark marks on paper which become handsomely reproducible many times over still seems to me, after nearly thirty years concerned with the making of books, a magical act, and a delightful technical process. To distribute oneself thus, as a kind of confetti shower falling upon the heads and shoulders of mankind out of bookstores and the pages of magazines, is surely a great privilege and a defiance of the usual earthbound laws whereby human beings make themselves known to one another. This blithe extension of the usual limitations of space is compounded by a possible defiance of the limitations of time as well—a hope of being read, of being heard and enjoyed, after death. Writing is surely a delicious craft, and the writer is correctly envied by others, who must slave longer hours and see their labor vanish as they work, in the churning of human needs.

But, it will be said, must there not be some *content* to these books, some message? I suppose that, along with my selfless delight in the play of creativity, there was some selfish wish to express myself, to impose my reality upon others. The saga of my mother and father, the unique tone and color of my native region of Pennsylvania—these were the subject matter of my first books. Then, slowly grasped and formulated, certain scenes of my adopted New England and certain truths, surprising to myself if to no one else, concerning adulthood, family life, and American society. Always, to begin to write, I needed the sensation that I was about to reveal what had never yet been quite revealed—not by Sinclair Lewis or Faulkner or my adroit companions on the pages of *The New Yorker*. Always I have been drawn to dusty and seldom-visited corners—my one effort at historical fiction chose an obscure President, James Buchanan, sneered at in his lifetime and since his death nearly lost in the shadow of his successor, Abraham Lincoln. My one effort at a novel of global realities dealt with a part of the world, the African Sahel, quite remote from the consciousness of most Americans, though with its repeated famines growing less so. Such, at least, has been my notion of the novelist's duty to society—to publicize the otherwise obscure, and to throw a complex light, from many angles, upon issues that tend to be badly lit, from the right or left, with half the matter left in shadow. Our furtive yet not quite extinguished religious impulses and needs also, I suppose, fall into this category, of human "news" rare enough to be delightfully and flexibly packaged in the form of printed fictions.

A REMINISCENCE, *entitled "I Was a Teen-Age Library User," written for* Bookends, *the journal of the Friends of the Reading-Berks Public Libraries.*

Reading—the Pennsylvania city, not the activity—seemed a considerable distance from Shillington in the 1940s; you boarded a trolley car in front of Ibach's Drug Store and for twenty minutes jerked and swayed down Lancaster Avenue through Kenhorst and the Eighteenth Ward, up over the Bingaman Street Bridge, along Fourth Street. If you wanted to get off north of Penn on Fifth Street, you bucked one-way traffic for a block of Washington Street, with much honking of automobile horns and clanging of the trolley bell. If you were going to the public library, you could get off at Franklin and walk a block to where the stately building, one of sainted Andrew Carnegie's benefactions, was located along Fifth, with Schofer's sweet-smelling bakery on one side and the Elks on the other. The Elks had a bronze elk in their front yard. As a boy I was fascinated by the little sharp points that had been placed on the metal animal's back; the purpose was to prevent bad boys from sitting on the statue, but for a long time I thought they might be part of an elk's anatomy.

Inside the library, there was a whispering quiet and walls of books. The great central space now occupied by a big box of central shelves was empty, and to my young eyes the ceiling seemed infinitely far away, and the balconies cosmically mysterious. My mother was a keen reader and my early trips there were at her side. An attempt was made to enroll me in the children's library downstairs, but I found children's books depressing, with their webby illustrations of historical costumes and crumbling castles, and by the age of twelve, I think, I was allowed to have my own adult card, and to check out whatever books I wanted. Miss Ruth, who had been (I later discovered) a high-school classmate of Wallace Stevens, was the head librarian, and very kind. I used to check out stacks, and she never blinked.

Stacks of what? P. G. Wodehouse is the author that comes first to mind: the library owned close to all of the master's titles, around fifty of them at that time, and they all struck me as hilarious and enchanting. They admitted me to a privileged green world of English men's clubs, London bachelor flats, country weekends, golf courses, roadsters, flappers, and many other upper-crust appurtenances fabulous to think of in wartime Berks County. A real reader, reading to escape his own life thoroughly, tends to have runs on authors; besides Wodehouse, I pretty well ploughed through Erle Stanley Gardner, Ellery Queen, Agatha Christie, and Ngaio Marsh, whose mystery novels stood in long orderly rows on the library shelves. Books cost two dollars then, and must have cost libraries rather less, and in pinched times seemed in abundant supply. The libraries and the railroad stations were the monumental structures that a citizen of Roosevelt's America was most apt to enter, and the era of television and the airplane has yet to construct with a comparable dignity. The movies and the radio were offering their own styles of popular entertainment without seizing, as does television for its addicts, all the day, every day. Department stores like Whitner's and Pomeroy's and many corner drugstores ran their own rental libraries—the cellophane-wrapped books available for (can it be?) as little as two cents a day. The public-library books had shed their jackets and in many cases had worn out their covers, and the sturdy look of a book that had been redone at the bindery was so pleasing to me that, in my late teens, I had some collected pages of my own composition professionally bound, for some modest charge like five dollars.

I loved the peace and patience of the library. Now, amazingly, some libraries have music in the background, and permit animated conversations; but silence was a sacred rule then, and one could hear with the distinctness of forest sounds at night a newspaper page being turned, or the drinking fountain by the front door being operated. A young man is perforce a somewhat distrusted creature, full of noisy tendencies and inconvenient impulses, and what I remember of the library is its accept-ingness of me—tiny Miss Ruth's friendly smile, the walls of books wait-ing to be opened, the august long tables with their mellow green-shaded lamps glowing. When I went away to college, I discovered that the Reading Public Library functioned surprisingly well as a research cen-ter, and I was able to do at least one college paper (on Héloïse and Abélard) with the resources upstairs in the mysterious balconies, where the more scholarly books were stashed, unruffled by the greedy hands of collegiate competition.

Aside from my beloved mystery writers and humorists (have I men-tioned Thurber and Benchley, and the Mr. Tutt stories of Arthur Train?) I did now and then stab randomly toward higher culture: Eliot's *Waste Land* and Wells's *Time Machine* and Shaw's *Back to Methuselah* are three books that I pondered at those glowing tables, along with Edmund Wil-son's *Memoirs of Hecate County,* James Cain's *Serenade,* and something by Irving Shulman about New York teen-age gangs—all of them offering a stimulating glimpse into the strange realities of sex. It saddens me to hear of books being pulled from library shelves for their alleged lubricity or radicalism or racism; surely the great thing about books as instruments of education is that one reads no more than one is ready to understand. One is always free to stop and read a book of a different quality or an opposed opinion. A book doesn't trap a reader, it is there to be taken or left. I remain grateful to the Reading Public Library and its personnel for the freedom given me in those formative years, when we, generally speaking, become lifelong readers or not. A kind of heaven opened up for me there. As a writer, I imagine my books' ideal destination to be the shelves of a place like the Reading Public Library, where they can be picked up without prejudice, by a reader as innocent as I was, and read for their own sake, as ways out of reality and back into it.

MY CONTRIBUTION *to a photo-essay feature in the Knoxville magazine* Spe-cial Report, *involving essays of two hundred and fifty words "in which"—as the editor put it—"different writers from around the United States describe a region of that nation—or an element of that region—that's especially close to their hearts." I chose Harvard Yard.*

My seventeenth summer, it must have been, when my parents and I drove from Pennsylvania to New England to look at Harvard College. My father got lost in the middle of Boston, and when he asked another driver how to get out, the man said it was too complicated to explain. Instead, he led us, in his own car, through the maze of one-way streets and pointed us up Storrow Drive toward Cambridge. We parked next to Harvard Yard, beyond the Square, and wandered into what would become, and remains, the center of New England for me. The quadrangles, linked by gravelly walks and framed by buildings the oldest of which were colonial brick, seemed outdoor rooms, half open to the sky. Healthy elms arched overhead in 1949, and the vogue of sunbathing did not then litter the grass with supine flesh. Chastity, seclusion, venerability was the effect, salted by something open and light and cheerful. The old place was alive. I was to live in Hollis Hall, a brick, black-floored dormitory little changed since Henry David Thoreau had roomed there. I was to walk, every morning, noon, and evening, across the Yard to the Freshman Union for my meals, past the gray bulk of University Hall and its statue of our youthful founder, along the base of Widener Library's mountainous steps, past Richardsonian Sever Hall and neoclassical Emerson and modernist Lamont, up a little slope now regularized by the underground Pusey Library. A free-ranging variety unified by a tonic Puritan aura: that was to be my New England, and still is. Its bricks, its spires, its snows, its lacy late springs and fiery long autumns are still mine, all steeped in a sacred atmosphere of books.

A REMINISCENCE *for the* Harvard Gazette, *on the occasion of my thirtieth reunion in June of 1984.*

I had a lot to learn when I came to Harvard, which was fortunate, since Harvard had a lot to teach. College reminiscences tend to focus on friendship and foolery and the anxious bliss of being young; and there was that for me, too. But I loved, strange to say, taking courses—the pre-semester shopping in the crimson-bound catalogue, its aisles bulging with goodies from Applied Mechanics to Zoology, and then the concoction of the schedule, with due avoidance of any class meeting before ten, and then the attendance, the sedate amusement of going to an antiquated lecture hall, its every desk pitted with the initials of the departed, and being entertained for an hour with a stream of things one hadn't known before.

Of the thirty-two half-courses that made up my requisite sixteen credits, every one was a more or less delightful revelation, beginning with the person of the instructor. These men (not one class I took, it just now occurs to me, was taught by a woman) seemed heroic to the point of comedy, having devoted their lives to erudition. Math 1a and 1b (Introduction to Calculus, under a straw-haired section man whose name I have forgotten but whose innocently proud way of swooping an inscrutable equation onto the blackboard I still can picture) cured me of my freshman notions of being a math major; I turned to English, and concentrated earnestly.

Francis Magoun, raptly chanting the guttural language of his cherished Anglo-Saxons, his arms jutting out in imitation of clashing broadswords; Hyder Rollins, white-haired and dapper, with a beautifully unreconstructed Southern accent, calmly reducing the Romanticism of Byron, Keats, and Shelley to a matter of variorum editions; Walter Jackson Bate, bringing the noble agony of Sam Johnson to startling life at the lectern; Douglas Bush, with his bald bowed head and squeezed voice and amiable dry wit, leading us doggedly through the petrified forests of Spenser and Milton; Kenneth Murdoch, folding his arms just like Jack Benny and allowing with a sigh that the metaphysicals could be tedious—these were some of the giants of the department in those days. Of these only Harry Levin, who taught a course in Joyce, Proust, and Mann as well as one on Shakespeare, offered any sense of access to the world of modern, living letters—it was common undergraduate knowledge that he had written the sole contemporary review of *Finnegans Wake* that Joyce had much liked. His lectures on Shakespeare, delivered with a slightly tremulous elegance to a huge throng in Emerson, not only opened my eyes to our supreme classic but, with their emphasis on dominant metaphor, to a whole new way of reading. Some of the smaller courses were among the best—Edwin Honig's quizzical, softspoken survey of the modern poets; Robert Chapman's bouncy seminar in George Bernard Shaw; Kenneth Kempton's resolutely professional writing course, in which he read aloud to us those magical early stories by Salinger.

The early Fifties are now considered a politically torpid era, but we did have our excitements, that stirred reactions even within our heavy scholastic wraps—Joe McCarthy (against), Adlai Stevenson (for), the Checkers speech (against), the Korean War (for, as long as somebody else was fighting it). My most vivid civic memory is of holding up a pencil, in short-lived Allston Burr Hall, to signify my readiness to take a simpleminded test that would prove my fitness to be temporarily exempt from the draft. Nobody at the time, to my knowledge, questioned the justice of these procedures, or declined their deferment. It was a dog-eat-dog world, of doing your own thing before it was called that. It was, for us English majors, a literary universe—how we worshipped, and gossipped about, Eliot and Pound and those other textual Titans! Eliot and Frost,

Cummings and Stevens, Dylan Thomas and Carl Sandburg all made appearances at Harvard in those four years, and Thornton Wilder and Vladimir Nabokov taught courses. Literature was in. Pop music was Patti Page and Perry Como, the movies were Doris Day and John Wayne, and youth culture was something that happened, if anywhere, at summer camp.

We wore gray coats and narrow little neckties, like apprentice deacons, or would-be section men. Some English majors did in fact become section men and Ph.D.s and then professors, promulgating the great texts to yet younger generations. To me that seemed a frightening prospect; my capacity for other people's words was limited. I peaked, as a scholar, in my junior year and capped my academic career with a dull thesis and a babbling display of ignorance at my oral examination. Four years was enough Harvard. I still had a lot to learn, but had been given the liberating notion that now I could teach myself.

IN ANSWER *to* Harvard Magazine's *question, "What is your favorite spot in and around Harvard?"*

Well, that's not an easy question. My nostalgic heart flutters between the cavelike entrance to Sever Hall, the far recesses of the Fogg library, and the grand space of (as it was called thirty years ago) New Lecture Hall, now abandoned and nailed shut like a South Bronx tenement. Other vanished fond spots: the counter at the Midget Restaurant, up on Mass. Avenue, and the window tables at the Hayes-Bickford cafeteria, once known universally as the Hayes-Bick. But the spot I will name has not vanished, and indeed has only enriched and deepened with the passage of time. I mean the place on the fourth floor of the Widener stacks where everybody, exiting, has to turn around an inconvenient little set of metal shelves and thence with some more strides make his or her way to the door, the brief downward stairs, and the circulation desk. More than once, as an undergraduate, I missed this unmarked turn, and found myself faced with a blank wall or a doctoral candidate dozing like a fluffy owl in his nook.

How like Harvard, I thought at the time, to set us these incidental intelligence tests. The spot on the floor, where the vast shuffling hordes of stacks traffic must pivot, has in the not very many decades of the library's existence been worn into a distinct depression; the gentle tread of scholars has visibly troughed the marble. I hope that particular slab is never replaced, though it grow as deep as the similar spot on the stone threshold of the kitchen in Hampton Court, which generations of royal servants, stepping in and out, depressed to the depth of several inches. Here, where the Widener architect might have arranged a more convenient corridor, generations of Harvard students and instructors have all had to change direction in obeisance to the immovable primacy of books and their shelving; here word-weary, knowledge-burdened young men and women have carried each away a few mineral atoms on the soles of their shoes, and thus made their dent in the world of ideas.

FOREWORD *to* Jester's Dozen, *a book of twelve youthful poems, with contemporary illustrations by the author, published in a limited edition by Lord John Press in 1984.*

These twelve poems have been selected from the forty or so that I wrote for the Harvard *Lampoon* from 1951 to 1954, as an undergraduate member of that organization, which produced a more or less monthly magazine and a more frequent issuance of social frivolity. I also did many cartoons and a number of prose pieces; the drawings now give me pleasure to contemplate, the prose pieces pain, and the poems a guarded sensation in between. Callow though increasingly deft, they show assiduous study of the previous generation of American light-verse writers. The *Lampoon* had been founded in 1876 as an imitation of *Punch,* became in the earlier, roistering decades of this century an imitation of *Judge,* and by the 1950s was imitating, in format and tone, *The New Yorker.* Which suited me, since *The New Yorker* was where I wanted to be and where, a few scant months after the penning of the last, rather valedictory poem in this selection, I did appear, with four light-verse quatrains entitled "Duet, with Muffled Drake Drum." Though the *Lampoon* may have lent its affably dishevelled pages to many more talented and sophisticated juvenile spirits than I (George Santayana and Robert Benchley among them), none, I imagine, more eagerly played apprentice in the several categories of "humor" than young JHU, as I then was identified. The reader of this slim souvenir of a happy apprenticeship will find here a parody of Milton, an exercise in the meter of Ogden Nash, an extended mock-ballad in the manner of Phyllis McGinley, a ballade such as Arthur Guiterman and Louis Untermeyer used to write, and a threnody of sorts for a rival-college humor magazine, the Dartmouth *Jackolantern*—there once was a legion of college humor magazines, and now I believe scarcely any save the *Lampoon* are left. A pity, since, however modest (and modestly amused) their audiences, these magazines gave their staffs a healthy training in make-up, proof management, and the hard art of being droll. Four poems first printed in the *Lampoon*—"Poetess," "The Population of Argentina," "Why the Telephone Wires Dip and the Poles are Cracked and Crooked," and "Mountain Impasse"—I thought well enough of to include in my first book, the verse collection called *The Carpentered Hen*. Three others, including the lines on Helen Traubel included in this jester's dozen, made it into Max Shulman's *Guided Tour of Campus Humor* (Hanover House, 1955), my first appearance in a real book. In determining my selection here, I have tried not to embarrass my much younger self but, while keeping the undergraduate flavor, to pick those verses most apt to let a present reader share the pleasure with which they were, ever longer ago, composed. The joy of getting into print is one that, for me at least, never palls, and these poems were part of my first sweet taste of it.

IN RESPONSE *to a request from* The Independent on Sunday, *of London, for a contribution to their weekly feature "A Book That Changed Me."*

Every book I have read has changed me to a degree, if only to supply some new bits of information to my leaky brain, or to have aged me by the extent of one more vicarious emotional ordeal. A number of volumes that I can recall lighted my way to authorship, from the comic books of childhood, through the mystery novels and science fiction of adolescence, to those titles by James Thurber and Thornton Wilder and Ernest Hemingway that somehow held out the possibility of emulation, of joining their authors on the library shelves. At college, Shakespeare, of whom I had read but a few plays by the age of eighteen, offered an image of authorship with a vengeance—an insatiable impersonator, spouting language, ranging with a wild freedom from scene to scene, murder to murder, metaphor to metaphor. That a literary work could have a double life, in its imagery as well as its plot and characters, had not occurred to me until Professor Harry Levin's meticulously textual course in Shakespeare. And then, after college, as I have confided more than once to interviewers, my discovery of Henry Green's novels and of Scott-Moncrieff's translation of Marcel Proust served as revelations of style, of prose as not the colorless tool of mimesis but as a gaudy agent dynamic in itself, peeling back dead skins of lazy surface notation, going deeper into reality much as science does with its accumulating formulations. My intoxicated imitations of these two writers marked the beginning of a style of my own.

But when I search for a book that changed *me*, the me who lives as well as writes, I come up with Søren Kierkegaard's *Fear and Trembling*, bound with the shorter work *The Sickness Unto Death* in an Anchor paperback. I still have the book; it cost eighty-five cents, fit easily in the hand, and had a pumpkin-colored cover designed, as were all the early Anchor books, by Edward Gorey. It came out in 1954; I read it in 1955 or early 1956, as a nervous newcomer to New York City, husbandhood, and paternity. Amid my new responsibilities I felt fearful and desolate, foreseeing, young as I was, that I would die, and that the substance of the earth was, therefore, death. My quest for consoling contradiction of this syllogism had already led me to books. I remember standing in Blackwell's great bookstore, in Oxford, staring at the plain broad backs of a complete set of Thomas Aquinas and thinking that somewhere in there was the word I needed. I read the *Encyclopaedia Britannica* articles on "Jesus" and "Miracles"; I read Chesterton, Unamuno, Mauriac, Maritain, C. S. Lewis, and Eliot, to name a few—for in the Fifties a number of professed Christians still commanded intellectual respectability and even glamour—but it wasn't until I entered the Kierkegaardian torrent that my trepidation washed away, or at least began to erode.

Kierkegaard's torrential, mesmerically repeated evocation, at the outset of the book, of Abraham's setting forth to sacrifice Isaac, an incomprehensible act that marked the beginning of Judaic faith and God's stated covenant, established a feverish pitch that corresponded to my state of inner alarm. As Kierkegaard proceeded to discuss—to torment, as it were—the outrageous miracle of Abraham's faith, the fussy terminology of high German philosophy had a strangely reassuring effect on me. "The paradox of faith is this, that there is an inwardness which is incommensurable for the outward, an inwardness, be it observed, which is not identical with the first but is a new inwardness": such a sentence was music to my ears, balm to my soul, preconditioned as my ears and soul were by an earnest if rather sketchy Lutheran upbringing. Eagerly I took from Kierkegaard the idea that subjectivity too has its rightful claims, amid all the desolating objective evidence of our insignificance and futility and final nonexistence; faith is not a deduction but an act of will, a heroism. So I took courage and thumbed my nose, in a sense, at the world, in imitation of Kierkegaard's proud, jeering, disorderly tone. Reading *Fear and Trembling* relieved my dreadful solitude; his voice— luckily an abundant voice, which I pursued in volume after volume as they tumbled forth from the university presses in those postwar years— gave me back my right to live. After *Fear and Trembling*, I had a secret twist inside, a precarious tender core of cosmic defiance; for a time, I thought of all my fiction as illustrations to Kierkegaard.

A REMINISCENCE *of Alfred A. Knopf and myself, composed for a booklet honoring his firm's seventy-fifth anniversary in 1990.*

My reverence for Alfred A. Knopf was so great that I was always surprised by his willingness to treat me like a grown-up. I had never before met a man who was also a company. In his august, purple-shirted presence, in that baronial panelled office of his, I felt a bit like one of the slender arrows clutched, on our national seal, in the talons of the American eagle; my impulse was to fly. Yet in all our transactions he was amiable and equable and even kindly, the curve of his hussar's mustache reinforced by the beginnings of a smile.

Our relationship reached its peak of intimacy in 1960, at the time of the publication of *Rabbit, Run.* I had rushed to type up this my second novel before moving for some winter weeks, with my family, to the island of Anguilla, then a remote Caribbean outpost of the severely dwindled British Empire. Just before New Year's I mailed the manuscript down to New York and headed into the sun; after some weeks, a limp ten-cent air letter wandered into the Factory, Anguilla's breezy combination of a general store, town hall, and post office, and was brought, with some fanfare, to me. Its contents were pleasing but also slightly puzzling:

> Dear John:
>
> I have no idea whether this letter will reach you, or when, but I don't like to delay writing to you until your return the middle of next month.
>
> I have read your manuscript, so have Blanche and two others, and we all admire it greatly. There are one or two little matters to discuss in connection with it, as well as the question of terms so that we can draw up a proper agreement. It would be best, I think, not to correspond, so I am wondering when you could have a brief visit with us at the office. I will be here, etc.

When I paid my visit a month later, at the old Knopf offices at 501 Madison, Alfred told me, with a slightly ceremonious air, that his lawyers had advised him that, in view of some of the novel's sexually explicit scenes, its publication might land us both in jail.

The notion of sharing a jail cell with Alfred must have had its charms, for in the next instant of this conference he pulled his camera out of his desk and took a photograph of me remarkable in its serenity. My face, youthfully smooth and oval, looks lovingly into the lens, and a cigarette languidly smolders in my gracefully posed hand; the photo was used on the back flap of the jacket of *Rabbit, Run,* where it can still be admired. The author at peace with the world.

I think what Alfred captured at that moment was the relaxed visage of a man who has decided to sell out. Rather than grab the uncensored manuscript and stalk out onto Madison Avenue in search of a more daring publisher (this was 1960, mind), I agreed to go along with the legal experts, and trim the obscenity to the point where the book might slide past the notice of hypothetical backwoods sheriffs vigilant against smut. *Lolita* and the unexpurgated *Lady Chatterley's Lover* had rather recently been published, and in 1961 the publication of Henry Miller's *Tropic of Cancer* would make our delicate verbal surgery absurd, but for the moment we were on the cutting edge, snipping away.

None of the excisions really hurt, though I did restore them in later editions. The youngish, roundish, baldish lawyer who guided my scalpel, as we sat at the big table in the firm's windowless book-lined conference room, was especially leery of my lyrically developed description of a woman urinating, and of what he called "contact"—*le contact de deux épidermes,* as the French say, in definition of *l'amour.* The word "fucking" in itself bothered him less than I would have thought. Alfred, present for some of this lengthy operation, at one point exclaimed, in that voice of his that was, like that of a great boxer, somehow smaller than one expected, "How the hell can you have fucking without contact?"

But the lawyer knew, and I came to enjoy the editorial process at his side; having performed the requisite excision with his guidance, I would then stitch the sutures as tidily as I could, even prettily, endeavoring, as is the artist's habit, to make a virtue of necessity. Who knows?—now that the sexual revolution and its foul-mouthed verbal outriders are as old hat as orgone boxes and waterbeds, I might find that the expurgated version was the better. At any rate, a little less contact here, and a subdued urinary lyricism there, and the lawyer was, so to speak, satisfied. We put away our blue pencils and let the text run out to play.

He had been a gentle, word-sensitive adviser. Lawyers and writers after all are both dealers in language. I felt I had gotten off easy. Some of my most somatic rhapsodies had been left untouched, and even in the touchier parts sufficient textual evidence remained to indicate that my hero and his doxy weren't playing backgammon. This young lawyer, whose name escapes me and shall not be pursued, sadly died not many years after this consultation, of a heart attack on a golf course. He was my first dead collaborator.

It seemed worthwhile, in 1960, to give names to things and acts that formed a central part of human workings. I was fresh enough from college to have Catullus, Swift, and Rabelais in mind as models of untrammelled realism, and of course James Joyce's noble, unyielding modern example. And, since I didn't expect the novel to make me rich (it didn't), and had previously left a publisher who wanted, for different reasons, to tamper with another novel, *The Poorhouse Fair*, it would have been no great matter for me to have dug in my heels and taken my chances elsewhere, where less cautious lawyers might be called in, or, better yet, none at all.

But I trusted Alfred. I liked the way the books he published looked, and I liked his old-fashioned, no-nonsense way of working. My estimate— perhaps that is what I am doing in the contemplative photograph, estimating my chances—was that in this bind the best shake in town was likely to be given here, across the desk from me. I have never regretted sailing on with *Rabbit, Run* and its slightly trimmed sails. Many books followed. When *Couples'* turn came to raise eyebrows, it was 1968, and the text went to the printers just as I had submitted it. Alfred and, when he was gone, the firm that still bears his name have done for me all a writer can ask a publisher to do: they have made attractive packages out of my manuscripts and given the public a chance to buy them. Though he looked somewhat like a pirate—a pirate emeritus—there was nothing visibly piratical about the ship he ran, and he would be disappointed to see the cutthroat, money-mad mood that prevails in the book industry now.

To the young man I was, Alfred conveyed, with his costumes, his mustaches, and the twinkle in his unexpectedly blue eyes, the welcome notion that the book business was fun. Even dodging Southern sheriffs could be a kind of fun. "If it was just you and me, John, we'd fight it and have a helluva good time," he said at one point in the little *Rabbit* crunch, or so I remember. I was flattered by this spontaneous avowal of comradeship, across the gaps of years and eminence, and took it to heart. Though we didn't fight the sheriffs, we had a pretty good time together anyway.

IN RESPONSE *to a query from* Esquire *as to bad reviews one remembers receiving.*

Three reviews, all of early books, that have stuck in my craw were John Aldridge on *Of the Farm* in *Book Week*, the late Alfred Chester on *Pigeon Feathers* in *Commentary*, and *Commentary*'s editor, Norman Podhoretz, on *The Centaur* in some unlikely magazine like *Horizon*. The reviewers all seemed to my tender sense of it to be intent not so much on dismissing the book as on annihilating its author, who in some unwitting ideological fashion had given them deep offense. To find oneself assaulted like this in print is certainly a salubrious experience for a young writer, for in a world that does much to soften and conceal its basic dangers he is frankly invited to consider whether he intends to go on existing or not. My decision, after an initial flash of uncertainty, was to go on existing, even if everything these shrewd and inimical voices said was true. More recent reviews that have given me the same sensation—of a reviewer whom there could be absolutely no pleasing, and whose opinion therefore was a purely animal noise, marking an invasion of territory—are a short notice by a Dorothy Rabinowitz of *Museums and Women* in, I think, *The Saturday Review* and a strenuous put-down of *The Coup* in a Midwestern journal of the New Right (or was it the New Left?) which I would not have seen had not its editors kindly mailed it to me. Gilbert Pinfold, in Evelyn Waugh's novel about his ordeal, confesses to being unable to detect a particle of difference in intelligence between his favorable and his adverse reviewers; my own tendency has been to believe the worst and to find its proponents far cleverer than the poor fools who are more or less on my side. But in the end, the next day dawns with its sunburst of blank paper, and the enterprise of composition itself, with its grand intention of bringing a piece of reality over into print, overrules the keenest self-doubts and the most venomous sneers.

IN RESPONSE *to a query from* The New York Times Book Review *as to "important" books one has never been able to finish reading.*

Like many an autodidact I have taken simple-minded pride in finishing a book once I began to read it. With considerable pleasure I devoted a youthful summer to reading through *Don Quixote;* in my early twenties I made my blissful way, over several years, through all of *Remembrance of Things Past. War and Peace, Portrait of a Lady, Moby-Dick, Ulysses, The Iliad,* and *The Odyssey* all in their season fell to the buzzsaw of my reading. I had every expectation of relishing *Tristram Shandy,* by Laurence Sterne. My taste ran to prankish books, British books, and books of pivotal importance in the history of Western thought. *Tristram Shandy,* modernism's first masterpiece, triply qualified. Had I not, furthermore, read through *Ada* and Boswell's *Life of Samuel Johnson,* thus somewhat straddling the case? I remember well more than one summery occasion when my increasingly tired-looking Modern Library edition of Sterne's facetious, mind-addling classic was hauled down from its shelf into the sun and shade; once I took it with me to a week alone on Martha's Vineyard, thinking to force the issue. Alas, even the boredom of utter solitude was no match for the boredom that poured in waves off the chirping pages of this particular great book. I made it as far as page 428, a half-faded bookmark tells me; but, like Scott on his return from the South Pole, I did not quite have the stuff to complete the job. I should have eaten the sledge dogs, like Amundsen.

IN RESPONSE *to a query from* The Michigan Quarterly Review *for its Winter 1987 issue as to my preferences in contemporary American fiction.*

Though the alleged minimalists—Carver, Beattie, Bobbie Ann Mason, Barthelme the Younger—get all the publicity these days, my heart still belongs to the old-guard maximalists, those who risk the onus of overdoing: Ozick, who lets her metaphors and fancy mind take her as far as they wantonly will; Barth, who pushed through on his impossibly tricky scheme in *Letters* and tested the will of even his most faithful readers; Roth, who in the face of all friendly advice runs his sexy, conscience-stricken, vociferous all-purpose hero through ever more ornate and obsessive paces; Salinger, who has taken non-publishing to new heights of expressiveness; Oates, who publishes like crazy and can't ever get enough of fear and loathing in familiar surroundings; Brodkey and Pynchon and (not to overdo) other hopeful and earnest intellectual children of the Fifties, raised on *The Faerie Queene* and the Fisher King, on brinkmanship by John Foster Dulles and big, big fins out of Detroit.

REMARKS *in acceptance of the National Arts Club Award, in New York City on February 29, 1984.*

One does not have to be a member of an Arts Club to observe that great art comes in clumps, that there seem times when a culture conspires to produce artists. Greek drama in the Periclean era, Dutch painting in the seventeenth century, Elizabethan poetry, nineteenth-century Russian fiction, German music from Bach to Brahms—such episodes seem waves that lift to sublime heights the individuals lucky enough to be born in the right place and time. The energy and interest of a society focus upon certain forms, and the single, sometimes anonymous artist conducts the gathered heat and light into a completed work. A thousand years ago, crucifixes were foci of fervent attention, and for centuries what men knew of the nude male form and of human agony and dignity sought expression through the crucifix carver's hands. Something of the same concentration attaches to representations of Lenin in the Communist world; and a visitor to the Soviet Union must admit that its official painters and sculptors do wonderfully well with the expressive possibilities latent in the image of a short bald man wearing a three-piece suit and a goatee—though this visitor's rapture was slightly dulled, twenty years ago, when he was taken through a Lenin factory, a clattering place where identical busts of the sacred agitator came down an assembly line and where bins were filled with items of this manufacture that had failed, because of a chip or skin blemish, to meet quality controls.

In our own American culture, it seems clear enough where the highest pitch of artistic energy is presently focussed. After trying to watch the heavily hyped Winter Olympics, I have no doubt that the aesthetic marvels of our age, for intensity and lavishness of effort and subtlety of both overt and subliminal effect, are television commercials. With the fanatic care with which Irish monks once ornamented the Book of Kells, glowing images of youthful beauty and athletic prowess, of racial harmony and exalted fellowship are herein fluidly marshalled and shuffled to persuade us that a certain beer or candy bar, or insurance company or oil-based conglomerate, is, like the crucified Christ or the defiant Lenin in other times and places, the gateway to the good life. Skills and techniques developed in nearly a century of filmmaking are here brought to a culmination of artistry that spares no expense or trouble. For a split-second thirst-inducing image, herds of Bedouins are assembled and directed; to convey a thirst-quenching coolness, Antarctica is visited by the film crew. Miraculously, bulls tread lightly through china shops; immaculate dives and heart-stopping car crashes colorfully knife across our screens. Our entire earthly existence—our eating, our drinking, our whole magnificent cradle-to-grave *consumption,* in short—is here compressed upon an ideal iconic plane; one can only marvel, and be grateful, and regret that, except within narrow professional circles, the artists involved, like Anglo-Saxon poets and Paleocene cave-painters, are unknown by name.

Now, what of the rest of us, who huddle with our known names on the sidelines, practicing relatively retrograde and impoverished art forms while this great glowing pillar of polychrome flickering rotates at the hot center of our culture? Well, there are some consolations to being in the shade. It is cooler there, and people can't always see what you are doing. As Aldous Huxley pointed out, freedom thrives upon the inattention of the powerful. Those of us who are riding the inky old print media into its sunset have, like the last threadbare cowboys, a certain grimly jaunty independence. We *may* do what we *can* do, and in our friendly limbo are under no obligation to assert that Coca-Cola is beneficial for not only the physical but the spiritual health of the nation, or that Mobil is watching out for our best interests night and day. We are free in our obscurity to try to tell the impure truth. We are free from committee meetings, from story conferences; no banker invades our sound stage in his anxiety to protect his investment, no character will refuse to speak the lines we give him. We are free to explore and transmit complex sensations, to attempt that permeation of the ego's cell walls which empathy and love and altruism as well as art achieve. In a world where virtue and even the word "virtue" are hard to find, the hand-woven fictional or poetic text offers a boundless field for striving toward the excellent and the exact. Quite wonderfully, it can always be better, and only its end effect matters. There is a fair amount of folderol in a writer's life, but the proof, finally and deliciously, is nowhere but in the pudding. So, to be brief, I am well content at my desk, and grateful that the world has allowed me to stay at it. This kind award comes as something extra, which I take as a symbol of society's wish to cheer the imaginative writer on in his private task, as a caretaker of sorts, these last few centuries, of all of our cherished and threatened privacies.

PREFACE *to the catalogue of an exhibit of my own papers in Houghton Library at Harvard University in the spring of 1987.*

Coming into Cambridge last November to view the proposed contents of this exhibit, I had expected to greet old friends—yellowed manuscripts and elaborated proofsheets the sight of which, like so many retasted madeleines, would cause to well up fond memories of bygone moments and outgrown selves and faded sites, towns and houses and rooms, where I had once labored. Instead, I found myself facing a shuffled multitude of hostile strangers—aborted stories I had totally forgotten, tortuous changes that had utterly slipped my mind, old editorial tussles mercifully quite erased from recollection. Who was this writer? And what did he have to do with me? I was overswept by a panicky sense of the fundamental unseemliness of such an exhibition, such a display of the bedraggled gray underwear that literary enterprise wears beneath the plumage and silks in which it fancies itself trotting forth. The false starts, the misspellings, the factual errors, the repetitions, the downright ungrammar, the marginal chastisements severe and gentle, the craven thrift and cunning with which a pitifully slender store of inspirations is hoarded and recycled—all set out in cases, like the mummified bits gathering dust in Egyptian museums, crumbs of bandage and skin and bone and once-magical embalming honey proclaiming in their abject confusion and hapless desiccation the scarcely believable fact that once life, human life, had passed this way and striven for perpetuation.

Some writers, like the late Vladimir Nabokov, have made a point of destroying all manuscripts and intermediate stages of their works of art, thus presenting to posterity an implacably clean face. Others, like Theodore Dreiser, have been so solicitous of their remnants as to keep carbons of even their love letters. In a less self-conscious time than ours, before authorship was seen as a means of generating academic treasure, the accidents of the printshop and the attic were allowed to carry away the smudged and frayed by-products of the making of books; combustion and careless housemaids also relieved the world of much that might now be regarded as precious. Now, in an age unprecedented in its ability to generate "papers," an indeterminate potential value attaches itself to every scrap, and prodigies of storage and cataloguing are achieved. The egoistic fantasy that everything one does is, like the sparrow's fall, worth observing has been, in my case, rather wickedly encouraged by the Houghton Library, which twenty years ago suggested that I deposit in the library's meticulous, humidified care the refuse of my profession.

My gratitude goes to Rodney Dennis for proffering this suggestion and putting up with its messy aftermath, and my admiration goes to Elizabeth Falsey for selecting points of interest and making coherent cases of them. I myself find other writers' drafts and worksheets fascinating; one draws closer, bending over (say) Keats's initial draft of "Ode to a Nightingale" in the British Museum, to the sacred flame, the furnace of mental concentration wherein a masterpiece was still ductile and yielding to blows of the pen. But inspecting such material is (like most science) a form of prying; we should not forget that what we glimpse here is the long and winding middle of a human process whose end is a *published thing*—shiny, fragrant, infinitely distributable—and whose beginning is the belief on the author's part that he or she has something to say, something to deliver. The creative process is lit from two directions—by the remembered flash of the first innocent and thrilling vision, and by the anticipated steady glow of the perfected, delivered result, in its crisp trimmings of manufacture. It takes strong light and high hope to bring the writer through the dreary maze of writing. Most of writing is reading—reading again, to regrasp what is there. As writers go, I am not much of a reviser, but, seeing these numerous papers spread out, I quailed at how multiple and fallible are the procedures that work toward the straightforwardest of texts, which then when published is still not safe, as long as the author lives, from further revision. And after the author has died, in instances as worthy as those of Faulkner and Joyce, zealous scholars go on, removing alleged typos and restoring squeamishly deleted passages until no such thing as a final text seems to exist, and the very books on the shelf, though bound in thick leather with marbled endpapers, have a somewhat tentative air.

My pleasure in this exhibit depends upon my sensation of detachment; its items were typed and scribbled by a series of ever-older young men whom I no longer know well, but with whom I once evidently enjoyed a close relation. On the basis of that relation I have been invited to say a word in this catalogue, which I here do, and now have done. A parable: More than once, walking on a soft and nearly unpopulated beach, I have been frightened by my own footprints behind me. They seemed left by feet much bigger than mine, and there was no escaping them. Nevertheless, I kept walking forward, the fright built into the experience along with the sun, the sand, the lapping milky-green sea, and the pink cliffs ahead, where the pelicans were dive-bombing, their own bodies the bombs.

A "SPECIAL MESSAGE" *for the Franklin Library's First Edition Society printing of* The Witches of Eastwick *(1984).*

Next to the small Pennsylvania town in which I grew up there was an even smaller town called Grille, and in the middle of Grille, so I was told, a "witch doctor" practiced his mysterious arts. No shingle advertised the office, but the building was in plain sight; the sex of the supposed practitioner has been exorcised from my mind, but pow-wow doctors—makers of spells and animistic little cures—were an undoubted fact in Berks County not many decades ago, and may be yet.* It is a land of gloomy

---

*By a coincidence truly uncanny, my Shillington High School classmate Barry Nelson, in the April 1984 issue of *Governor Mifflin Area History,* wrote at length of "Pow-Wows and Faith Healers in the Mifflin Area" just as my novel was being published. The "witch doctor" in Grille was identified as Harry C. Ohlinger, a Reading native and weaver by trade who died in 1955 at the age of sixty-two; he had lived in Grille, opposite the Center Hotel, since 1938, and had begun to practice his healing arts before then, at a farmhouse near Angelica on Candy Road, in Cumru Township. He was a Bible-reading, prayerful man, some of whose cures were simply traditional faith healing. Some were a bit stranger: "A woman who ran a farm in Maxatawny thought she had a jinx on her. He told her to put an ace of spades in a milk bucket, and milk a cow's milk into it. This broke the hex or spell." People lined up on his porch to see him, waiting two or three hours; he never charged money and was instead paid with "donations, whiskey, food, or knick-knacks." One satisfied customer recalled, "He cured my wife's back in three visits. He put his hand on your body, said something, and you could feel something happening." In Shillington, the widow of the pow-wow doctor Ellsworth Mohn remembered, "Ells would sit in front of you and he'd cup his left hand and hold it out like he was receiving something, holding it palm up. He took his right hand in a sweeping move across the inflammation in a catching motion, blew into the right hand, and slapped it into his upper hand. He would do this three times." Mohn always said his spells in "Dutch" (Pennsylvania German) and had learned how to pow-wow from a Mammy Bitting, also of Shillington. A sexual curiosity of the art of

hilltop forests and abandoned quarries and barns bearing hex signs; my grandmother was a great one for observing the minor superstitions, involving cats and salt, ladders and umbrellas. The supernatural never seemed far off, especially after the sun had set, and the friendly street I walked to school on every day yet had its quota of mysterious old women peeking out from behind their curtains, ready to pounce upon the child so careless as to set a foot on their little carpets of front lawn. I wonder, now, if the famous German discipline—for the presiding spirit of the land was certainly German, though its language was English and many of the place-names were Welsh—isn't maintained in large part by threats from the spirit world. At any rate, as a boy I ran scared.

New England, land of clear thinking, welcomed me to college. One of the very few books I bought and read on my own, in my four years at Harvard, was a translation of the French historian Jules Michelet's *La Sorcière*, entitled *Satanism and Witchcraft*. Michelet's romantic vision of the witch as the persecuted perpetuator of pagan nature-worship and a gentle rebel against the medieval church's tyranny stayed with me. To Michelet the decades since have added the reading of Huysmans's *À rebours* and Sylvia Townsend Warner's *Lolly Willowes* and those several novels by Muriel Spark that confidently touch upon the demonic. The 1960s saw witchcraft hit the media and go political. War protesters chanted and "tripped" and tried to put a spell on the Pentagon, and self-anointed enchantresses and warlocks from London to Los Angeles advertised their satanic commitments and supernatural powers; the gruesome climax came with the Manson murders of August 1969.

It is a curious fact of witchcraft study that, though members of contemporary cults and covens readily pose nude for the tabloids and fill volumes with their philosophy (in which astrology and health diets dance hand-in-hand with worship of a Satan hard to distinguish from Santa Claus), and though such relatively recent episodes as the *fin-de-siècle* black masses in Paris that Huysmans described and the affair, in the 1670s, of the Marquise

---

pow-wowing is that only a woman can teach it to a man, and vice versa. "The prayers are passed on by word of mouth. They must be memorized. There is no hexerei involved. The prayers are from the Bible." Yet some of the cures cited are distinctly elaborate: to cure a sick baby, a mother is instructed "to take the baby's shirt off, turn it inside out, and pinch it in the attic door over night." And: "Another story involved a small baby that cried constantly. The mother tried to quiet the child, but the crying got worse. Finally, in frustration, she said, 'Enough! I'm going to do something about this!' She placed a bucket of hot water in the middle of the parlor and placed a burning hot poker into the water while reciting a prayer. The next day a woman in the same town was scalded to death. This woman had visited the mother and had given the mother and her family something to eat. She was really putting a hex on them."

de Montespan—a mistress of Louis XIV's who attempted to secure his love with obscene rites—are undoubtedly historical, a fog of unknowing descends as the alleged Dark Age heyday of witchcraft is approached. Modern scholars like Norman Cohn (in *Europe's Inner Demons*) strenuously argue that there were *never* any covens or organized Devil-worship, that all confessions to the contrary were the product of torture or demented delusion. His opponents in this argument include Michelet, who was carrying forward certain earlier suggestions among nineteenth-century historians that witchcraft was an underground survival of the ancient pagan religions, and Margaret Murray, the Scots anthropologist whose book of 1921, *The Witch-Cult in Western Europe*, with its successor, *The God of the Witches* (1933), claimed, by the light of Frazer's *Golden Bough*, an extensive historical reality for the perennial rumors of witchcraft. While scholarly debates raged, modern British and American women were founding covens along the lines of Miss Murray's anthropology, and by 1970 (roughly the time of my novel), a Witches' International Craft Association had come into existence, along with a Witches' News Service, a Witches' Lecture Bureau, and a Witches' Anti-Defamation League. My heroines are not members of these organizations; their witchcraft is an intuitive and fitfully articulated collusion, sprung from their discovery that husbandlessness brings power. Witchcraft is the venture, one could say, of women into the realm of power. What women in the Middle Ages besides witches and queens wielded power that men needed to fear?

The ideology of my portrait descends from the impression of pathos and heroic subversion that Michelet communicated to a college student in the early Fifties. Many of the details of ritual and of the Devil's hollow appearance (for from the testimony of witch trials he would seem to have often been a man in a mask, with an artificial phallus) come from Margaret Murray's assemblage of evidence. The business of feathers and pins emerging from the mouths of the bewitched was suggested by the strange case of Christian Shaw, as described in *Witch Hunt: The Great Scottish Witchcraft Trials of 1697*, by Isabel Adam. Books by Charles Williams, Richard Cavendish, Erica Jong, Pennethorne Hughes, Montague Summers, Colin Wilson, Peter Haining, Ronald Holmes, A. F. Scott, and others contributed to my picture. But I would not have begun this novel if I had not known, in my life, witchy women, and in my experience felt something of the sinister old myths to resonate with the modern female experiences of liberation and raised consciousness.

Moreover, I once moved to a venerable secluded town, not far from Salem, where there had been a scandal. I was never able to discover exactly what had happened—those old-timers who knew went vague and sly when pressed—but its aura, as it were, still hung in the air above the salt marshes, and haunted me. Among my literary debts let me acknowledge one to the French writer Robert Pinget; his novels admirably capture the spookiness of communities that hold in the crevices of faulty, shifting communal memory a whiff of sulphur, a whisper of the unspeakable. Emboldened by Pinget's example, I have tried here, in my own style, to give gossip a body and to conjure up human voices as they hungrily feed on the lives of others. The appetite is not trivial; we write and read novels to satisfy it.

A "SPECIAL MESSAGE" *for the Franklin Library's First Edition Society printing of* Roger's Version *(1986).*

A few years ago, yielding to the times, I bought a word processor, and one evening, in shutting it off, I saw on the screen a curious facelike configuration that sparked into sudden being and then slowly faded away. I had the impression of a mournful countenance gazing out through the scrambled numbers, a squared-off, green-on-green Veronica; and perhaps this was the seed of *Roger's Version.* To this seed adhered the new cosmology that was in the air and the newspapers not long ago, and my feeling that, after composing in *The Witches of Eastwick* yet one more novel cozily concerning a small town, I should attempt a city novel. And even an academic novel—for if with *The Coup* I dared essay an African novel without being an African, why not an academic novel without being an academic? Interviewers have often enough elicited from me my aversion to that particular vocation, and in truth I do think it cruel to ask a creative spirit to continue being creative while conforming to the needs of students, faculty committees, and the ingrown collegiate milieu. Yet I have been a student, pose now and then as a writer and creature from outer space within academic settings, and treasure learned professors among my friends. Also, teaching runs in my blood; not only was my father a high-school teacher, whose travails were embroidered in *The Centaur,* but, on my mother's side, my grandfather, the John Hoyer whose name I bear, taught at one-room schools in the Pennsylvania countryside. He walked miles each way, and (my mother recently told me) caught my grandmother's eye on those long walks, and (she says) carried his entire year's wages, in the form of the last century's thin gold coins, in his pocket. His long life overlapped with the first twenty years of mine, and his elegant, explaining, elocutionary voice still echoes in the language-processing part of my brain and no doubt modified some of its loops; indeed, all the people I grew up among aimed, with their various voices, to be instructive.

An academic novel must be, to an extent, about information, and this requires the ingestion of some by the novelist, who should have at least an inkling of how his characters' heads are stocked. For the sake of Roger Lambert, I delved into ecclesiology and the maze of early heresy, and betook myself to a seminary library to search out Tertullian's Latin in dusty, untouched volumes. For his antagonist and alter ego Dale Kohler, there was the tough nut of computer science to crack, or at least take a crack at: the binary electricity of it, and the overlay of Boolean math that shapes the adders and half-adders, and the mind-boggling elaboration of these relative simplicities into the various computer languages and the storms of computation that crackle behind such miracles as vector and raster graphics. Dale's supply of cosmological and evolutionary data represented long-standing interests of mine, and needed a mere brushing-up. But even relatively brainless Verna knows things about, say, pop music and the welfare system that I do not and that I had to grope my way toward, often by asking simple-minded questions of people in my vicinity. And the city itself, nameless and cavalierly distorted but perhaps not unrecognizable, had to be visited and paced off and viewed from above. All this self-education, of course, is pleasurable in itself; as Joyce Carol Oates once said to me, doing the research for a novel is so *blameless*. The novelist in the library stacks is safe, for the moment, from editors and critics and the intense embarrassment that attends the bringing of his brain-child into the cold light of publication.

The informational content of this novel had to be high; the debates between Roger and Dale are meant to be real debates, on issues that are, to me, live and interesting. And the book as a whole, in its novelistic life as an assembly of images, concerns information itself: the intersection of systems of erudition, and the strain of the demands that modern man makes upon his own brain. Pre-scientific hunting man, too, had a busy brain, extensively stocked with plant and animal lore and with memorized mythology—indeed, our utilized memory is surely inferior to his. But he was not oppressed, as are we, by torrents of freshly manufactured input (much of it televised trivia but importunate nonetheless) and by our nagging awareness of vast quantities of information, in books, films, tapes, and journals, that we should, ideally, master. We have surrounded our consciousness with vastness—vast libraries, vast galaxies, vastly complex molecular and atomic entities—and in the miniaturized guts of a computer the complication of God's (so to speak) world meets an equivalent complication we have created.

In reference to this intimidating vastness, the book was initially called *Majesty;* vestiges of the title can be seen in the epigraphs, and in the recurrence of the adverb "majestically," usually applied to the city's sky-scrapers. My novel might be mistaken, it was feared, for one more biography of the Queen of England, and I am happy with the new, though less resonant, title in that it makes clear this is *Roger's* version—that is, Roger Chillingworth's side of the triangle described in *The Scarlet Letter*, the one classic from the lusty youth of American literature that deals with society in its actual heterosexual weave. (Hawthorne, indeed, of our classic writers, seems to be, recessive and shadowy as he was, the one instinctive heterosexual—which suggests how uncertain, how vitiated by Puritan unease and the love of freedom, the mating part of the American character is.) I gave Dimmesdale's version, in an of course updated, askew, and irresponsible way, in *A Month of Sundays*, over ten years ago, and should no doubt some day try to confront Hester's version. Here, though, we have the villain of the piece, and also the character who encloses the others and modulates, with his arcane potions and malign remedies, their story.

In shaping this story with him, I might add, I have done more adjusting and fine-tuning than, if memory serves, for any other novel. Regulating the recurrence of adjectives and tinkering with the eye and hair color of characters, numbering the incarnations of Pearl,* meshing theology with pornography and fitting the segments of my imaginary city together, I felt at times like one of the mechanics hopelessly engaged on Charles Babbage's Analytical Engine, the first computer, whose visionary principles quite outraced the era's resources of machined metal and pasteboard, of cogwheels and jacquard cards. The word processor, in its magical ease of insertion and transposition, and computerized typesetting, in freeing the author from the old constraints of the Linotype's slug-by-slug replacements, invite the prosist to tinker, perhaps excessively. A novel is, like a computer, a system for the storage, manipulation, and retrieval of information; but its basic analog is the ancient interaction between the human voice and ear, and all our mechanical ingenuities aim at the hope of inducing in another brain a wave, an excitement, an emotion, a movement of the spirit.

UNSOLICITED THOUGHTS *on* S. *(1988)*.

By the time I came to write this third installment of what had developed into a trilogy of comic novels based on Hawthorne's *Scarlet Letter*, the set

---

*She seems to be present thrice: once as Richie ("of great price"), secondly as Paula, and thirdly—well, why *does* Esther's weight at last swell to over a hundred pounds?

had acquired certain formal characteristics: each book must be the first-person narrative of a spiritual pilgrim; American religion and its decay since Puritan New England would be a theme; the prose should be antic—"all out"—and bristle with some erudition; there must be footnotes. Marshfield's footnotes, in *A Month of Sundays,* were comments upon his Freudian slips, which were in most cases the actual typing errors of his creator; *Roger's Version,* in academic style, cited some original texts and references. I was well into *S.* before the Hindu and Buddhist terms, proliferating as I became an increasingly enthusiastic disciple of Indian religions, suggested the convenience of a glossary. This appended list served as the obligatory footnote; like any footnote, it forms part of the text, and should be read through. The accidents of alphabetization, if happy, are as legitimate as any of the other accidents we bind into a fictional narrative; from *abhayamudra* ("the gesture dispelling fear") and *abhinivesha* ("the will to enjoy; the will to live") to *yoni* and *yuganaddha* the glossary as I worked on it conspired with me, it seemed, to underline and echo the tangled, tinkling themes of the novel. The glossary became the novel's music, the poetic essence, mechanically extracted, of the preceding narrative, and its final entry, rather than the dying fall of Esther's last letter—her insincere/sincere "Ever"—to Charles, the book's true conclusion:

> **yuganaddha** a state of unity obtained by transcending the two polarities of *samsara* and *nivritti* and perceiving the identity of the phenomenal world and the absolute

O happy hovering last chord!—"the identity of the phenomenal world and the absolute." By *yuganaddha* the Sanscrit gurus meant either that there is no supernatural, or else (as in a novel's hyperspace) everything is supernatural. What is, is absolute. The net of religious and philosophical terminology leaves reality exactly where it was before. Or does it?

A "NOTES AND COMMENT" *for* The New Yorker, *published March 23, 1987.*

A writer we know writes:

An American visitor to a Communist country, if the visit partakes at all of publicity and official status, acquires symbolic values for which his native cultural conditioning has ill prepared him. As an American, be he or she fat or thin, conservatively contented or radically unhappy, he is looked upon, by the regime, as a potentially tricky mini-invasion of un-friendly forces, and, by those dissatisfied with the regime, as a symbol of freedom and opposition. It was as such a symbol, and not on the basis of my agricultural expertise, that I was invited to plant a "peace tree" on a scruffy slope in Prague last spring, in the company of a few American escorts from our embassy and of many more or less young and excited Czechs. They were members and devotees of the Jazz Section of the Czechoslovakian Musicians' Association, led by Mr. Karel Srp, who led me through the ancient and apolitical procedure of settling a scrawny young sapling (a maple, I think) into a muddy hole in the ground. The sapling erect and on its own, we went inside a very crowded small room in a drab but extensive housing project and drank a toast to something or other (perhaps simply one another) and dispersed, the Jazz Section members and followers to their various duties and fates and I to my next appointment and act of cultural display.

The ceremony, in my swift and distracted experience of it, reminded me of college days—the day when some hastily organized prank was being played. The Jazz Section offices were small rooms holding jazzy posters, flushed young faces, a jabber of hectic and ill-focused excitement, and the smell of white wine in paper cups. Without knowing the language, I could sense the joke in the air, that perennial young-people's joke of seeing "how much" they could "get away with," of "how far" things could "go." As a Western writer I was one of the prank's props, but not a terribly important one—the prank would go on, in its multitudinous improvised forms, whether I was there or not. Its perpetrators, however, were, some of them, much more than college age, and its possible cost for them was not just a scolding from the dean but years in prison and a life of jobless-ness. Yet such a reckoning seemed quite remote on the cloudy day of our innocent, amiable, mysterious little occasion.

At the end of the summer (during which the sapling presumably took root on its unpromising-looking slope, in the small thicket of trees previ-ously planted by such other momentary arborists as Kurt Vonnegut and Wendy Luers), Mr. Srp and four other directors of the Jazz Section were arrested, along with the group's treasurer and landlord, and charged with conducting illegal economic activities. Among their previous offenses, for which they had already been fined, was listed erecting a monument with-out a permit—a small stone commemorating the fortieth anniversary of the United Nations, set among the "peace trees." Repressive arrests of conspicuous cultural experimenters and symbol-cultivators are common enough in the Communist world, but this was surprising, because it went against the present tentative trend, set by the Soviet Union's First Sec-retary Gorbachev, of *glasnost*, of more openness and permissiveness in the Socialist world, and because the Jazz Section had for fifteen years been ingeniously functioning in a "gray area" of the government's cultural controls.

Jazz itself is not officially condemned and, as readers of Milan Kundera know, has a long and vigorous history in this very musical part of the world. The Jazz Section evolved, after its founding in 1971, from a union of dues-paying musicians to a kind of fan club for not only jazz but rock and the art of the capitalist West; it organized festivals and exhibits and—utilizing the printing privileges granted all official unions and clubs—published pamphlets and books; it became a gray-area purveyor of alternative culture. Its shaky semi-authorized status has been tenaciously maintained: when the musicians' union, under government direction, disbanded the Jazz Section in 1983, it immediately reconstituted itself, with the same officers, as a local, Prague section; and when, in the next year, the entire Prague division of the union was disbanded, the section responded that its charter allowed disbanding only after a two-thirds vote of its membership.

The government's piecemeal attempts at discipline, never addressing the issue of free speech, have had a flavor of desperation. In 1985, section member Petr Cibulka was sentenced to a seven-month prison term for "insulting the nation" after complaining that a restaurant failed to serve a low-cost meal as required by law. In 1986, section member Jaroslav Švestka was sentenced to two years' "protective supervision" for "harming the interests of the republic abroad." And a few days ago, I read in the papers, five of my comrades from that spring afternoon were pronounced guilty of "unauthorized commercial activity." The proceedings had some Kafkaesque touches; when Karel Srp, testifying in his own behalf, said he had written one hundred thirty letters to the Ministry of Culture requesting clarification of its anti–Jazz Section actions, a government witness explained that "We could not answer letters from an organization that does not exist." The judge, professing his admiration of their "contributions to Czechoslovak culture" and protesting that "we don't want in any way to limit cultural movements in our country," handed down sentences not only less than the maximum eight years' imprisonment but significantly lighter than those the prosecutor asked for. Karel Srp was sentenced to sixteen months, minus the six months he had already been in prison; the group's secretary, Vladimir Kouřil, was given ten months minus the six; and the three others received suspended sentences. While the judge delivered his verdict, a crowd of over a hundred people, most of them young, clapped hands in the corridors and afterward sang "Give Peace a Chance."

The Jazz Section has been punished, but with an awkward ambivalence, as the neo-Stalinist Czech regime, installed in the wake of a runaway liberalization twenty years ago, now tries to swing into line with the Soviet Union's turn toward openness. The Jazz Section has suffered, but not in silence; international protest has been joined by braver open protest within Communist Czechoslovakia. I am told that the unofficial monument, so subversively remembering the founding of the United Nations, has been removed; I don't know if the surrounding set of trees still stands. Trees can be cut down, but eventually others take their place. Eastern Europe is a forest where the growing will not stop.

ANOTHER "NOTES AND COMMENT," *published May 5, 1987.*

Birds do it. Bees do it. U.S. Marines in far-off lonely American embassies do it. Jim Bakker, evidently, did it. So, the strong implication is, did Gary Hart. Why do we care? Recent news developments demonstrate, if we ever doubted it, that we do care, out of all due proportion—nocturnal pairings and a ride to Bimini in the good ship *Monkey Business* easily eclipse such grave questions as whether or not the President of the United States, in his zeal to see hostages released and the Sandinistas deposed, knowingly broke the law. A startled young woman, gouged from her private life by a storm of publicity (which also brought to light many old photos taken of her wearing a bikini), is a more interesting object than the Constitution, even in this year of the Constitution. The affair (so to speak) is not merely, however, a testimony to the cheesecake in our hearts. Something new was injected into Presidential politics early in the administration of Harry Truman: the President has his thumb on the red button. The man we elect can push us into nuclear war and sudden death. Eisenhower's was a slow and experienced old thumb we trusted; but the Presidents since, search as the electorate will, have been nervous-making: Jack Kennedy was bright and handsome and jaunty but young, with a thing about "Cuber" and Khrushchev; Lyndon Johnson groaned with good intentions but seemed only to know Texas-style arm-wrestling; Nixon was a bundle of suspicions and tics; Ford kept tripping over himself; Carter had that high twangy voice and a scary way of popping his eyes during press conferences; Reagan . . . well, Reagan has been soothing, but has he been minding the store? The issue was not whether Lee Hart could trust Gary but whether *we* could: he had an unsteady glitter to his eye, and maybe his hair was a little too long over his ears. We have to look these men over. With the limited accommodations the world has to offer nowadays, we all, more or less, get into bed with the President.

REMARKS *intended for the May 1989 ceremonial of the American Academy and Institute of Arts and Letters, left undelivered in deference to a fire scare that interrupted the proceedings, and published, three months later, with a timely new first paragraph, in, yes,* The Wall Street Journal.

We live in a nation where art rarely impinges upon the realms of government and power, aside from musical entertainment at White House dinners and the design of postage stamps. Americans are therefore naïve about government sponsorship of the arts, as if shown by the shocked indignation in culture-bearing circles at some Congressmen's shocked indignation at the Mapplethorpe photograph exhibit and the NEA-sponsored image of a crucifix suspended in a container of the artist's very own urine. The ancient law that he who pays the piper calls the tune has not been repealed even in this permissive democracy, and the cultural entrepreneurs so eager to welcome NEH and NEA money into the arts may now be aware that they have invited a dog—woolly and winsome but not without teeth and an ugly bark—into their manger.

The most dramatic government-sponsored event in arts and letters in the last year has been the promulgation by a head of state, the late Ayatollah Khomeini, of a death sentence upon a writer, Salman Rushdie, who was not then and had never been a citizen of Iran, but who instead was writing postmodernist fiction within the United Kingdom. The affair at worst may yet result in murder; at the least it has achieved, for Rushdie, a severe and apparently permanent impairment of his personal freedom. What are American artists to make of this astounding event? The concept of blasphemy seems quaint here, and almost as quaint the notion that artists might have to pay a price in blood for what they write, paint, or compose. But it is perhaps salutary and, in the root sense, encouraging to be reminded that art is a significant activity, with possibly grave consequences, and that our freedom to be artists as best we can is not one that all societies automatically grant.

Nor, even in a society as generally indulgent as ours, is the artist asked to pay no price whatsoever for the delightful, cathartic exercise of his creative faculties. Neglect and relative poverty, to begin with, are the likely prices we pay for embarking upon the cloudy path of artistic self-expression. Further along that path, critical attack from one's differently persuaded colleagues in art may await, and boycott, banning, and blame from the larger society's enforcers of decency and positive values. In a capitalist society, art is expected to pay its way, and the demands of the marketplace work their own constraints. To reach market, one must negotiate with middlemen and envision a consumer, with his needs and prejudices. Friendly censors, in fact, offer guidance at almost every turn of a professional artistic career, and even the most amiable artist must at some point choose between an inner imperative of private vision and the outer imperatives of group acceptance. In America little appears sacred, in the sense that the Koran is sacred to the spokesmen for Islam, but success is sacred and tempts many to an insincere conformity.

None of this, of course, compares to Rushdie's ongoing ordeal, or to that of Václav Havel and Frantisek Stárek in Czechoslovakia, or Albert Mukong in Cameroon, or of hundreds of artists under totalitarian regimes around the globe. But in all cases the artist's defense against a society's impositions and seductions must be the same—the problematical but deeply felt subjective answer to Pilate's ancient question, "What is truth?" Each individual holds an impression of life, and the discourse of the arts attempts to revise the art consumer's impression by the light of the artist's impression. It is perhaps in the nature of modern art to be offensive: it wishes to astonish us and invites a revision of our presuppositions. A crucial offense that *The Satanic Verses* gave its enemies, indeed, concerns, precisely, revision—the possibility that the Koran itself was in a few verses revised.

One attitude to art, and not purely an old-fashioned one, construes it as a voice of the gods, flowing out through momentarily inspired mortals. It is magic, and the truth it proclaims is absolute, and mankind's duty is to defend and repeat what it has thus received. The other attitude expects revision in the arts, experimentation in the sciences, criticism in the public forum, and frequent change in the personnel if not the forms of government. All change, all revision, is something of an affront, and it leaves certain sacred securities behind. However, it contains not only destructive and dismissive tendencies but an optimism, a faith that the human sensibility can suffer revision and survive and even be the healthier for it. No doubt Rushdie knew his book would offend Muslim orthodoxy, just as James Joyce expected in *Ulysses* to offend the Irish Catholic Church, and Nabokov in *The Gift* to offend the orthodoxies of Russian Communism, and Hawthorne in his gently polemical works to offend the lingering representatives of Puritan theocracy. No doubt the artists who offended Senators Helms and D'Amato hoped to offend someone. But in this century, if we are not willing to risk giving offense, we have no claim to the title of artists, and if men and women are not willing to face the possibility of being revised, offended, and changed by a work of art, they should leave the book unopened, the picture unviewed, and the symphony unheard.

I would see art and government kept separate not to protect government funds but to protect the arts, for even the most enlightened patronage still exerts a controlling effect, and even the most well-intentioned and subtle control nevertheless contaminates the freedom of exploration and expression that we require from the arts, a purity of inner determination that distinguishes their enterprise from all others.

FOOTNOTES *to* Self-Consciousness *(1989)*.

For one of our performances, she had been quite ill with a stomach flu.
                                                                —page 38
Maryann Stanley Moyer reports that in fact she had food poisoning, from, of all things, some canned grapefruit juice.

My mother tells me that up to the age of six I had no psoriasis; it came on strong after an attack of measles in February of 1938, when I was in kindergarten.   *—page 42*
My mother sometimes kept carbons of letters that she had worked especially hard on, and among her papers I found a blue carbon of a letter from May 2, 1939, to her sister-in-law, Mary Ella Updike, on the occasion of the death of my grandmother Virginia Blackwood Updike. It begins, "On Sunday night a soldier quit fighting and all our lives will have a new emptiness because your mother loved life enough to fight for it," and goes on to mention me—"Now and then one of our neighbors tells me that John is a 'good boy'. They always say it with an exclamation point, as if hard to believe"—and concludes with this medical description:

> John came out last November with the worst case of psoriasis I ever saw outside of a book on skin diseases. It's like mine except that it doesn't even try to confine itself to his scalp as mine did but parades in all its flaming scabbiness from head to toe. He had a very sore throat in March and an increase in the skin disease which may indicate a chronic infection of the tonsils. So, we think of selling John a tonsillotomy. How I'll make a convincing sales talk with all my scabs and no tonsils to cause them I don't know. Yet chronic infections do add to the horrors of psoriasis. And, of course, we want to do whatever can be done to keep the thing within the limits of decency. Bad as it sounds and looks, the children and teachers have treated him so humanely that (so far) there have been almost no mental complications and I'm mighty thankful. What the thing would do to his personality worried me most because, physically, there is little discomfort. But it has left him sane as far as I can tell and Wesley and I are trying to keep our heads too.

Louris Jansen Opdyck came to New Netherland before 1653, at which time he resided in Albany and bought land at Gravesend, Long Island.

—page 192

David M. Riker, of the Holland Society of New York, wrote me early in 1990, "You might be interested in the enclosed record from the Van Rensselaer Bowier manuscripts which shows that Laurens (Louris) Jansz and his wife (Stijntje) Christina, were recorded as living on a Rensselaerswyck farm in January of 1650." Thus my Dutch-American roots were deepened by several years. Rensselaerswyck was the second-most-populous settlement in New Netherland; a large tract granted in 1629, by the Dutch West India company, to Kiliaen Van Rensselaer, a diamond merchant of Amsterdam, it extended on both sides of the Hudson and included Beverwyck, which was renamed Albany when the English took over the Dutch colonies in 1664. Thanks to this genealogical chapter addressed to my two (now three) African-American grandsons, I have joined the Holland Society, a body of less than a thousand male descendants of the solid settlers of New Netherland.

I hear my mother turn and breathe in her bed. The sleet sprinkles in the fireplace and a mouse scrabbles behind the baseboard beneath the table and the picture of me as a pretty child. My mother knows this mouse; she has told me that in the darkest of her post-fall, bedridden days, he used to come into her bedroom and, standing right there on the floor beside the baseboard, would vigorously make noises, trying to tell her something. His attempt to offer advice amuses her in the telling and she does not yet have the heart, nor perhaps the muscular strength, to set a trap for him.   *—pages 241–42*

My mother died on October 10, 1989, alone, in the house she wanted to be in, where she had been born eighty-five years and four months before. She was dressed to drive her car to a garage in New Holland, first thing in the morning, and a heart attack felled her as she stood behind the kitchen sink. Her doctor had told her not to drive, and the excitement of the trip ahead of her, ten miles down Route 23 with its tricky mix of trailer trucks and horse-drawn Amish buggies, may have stressed her frail heart that extra, fatal amount. Since a day passed before her body was found, the date is officially recorded as October 11, an everlasting inaccuracy that bothers me more than it would have her. She had always been one for the big picture, with a sometimes surprisingly relaxed attention to details. Even as a young woman she had had high blood pressure, and this gift for intermittent relaxation—for laughter when you least expected it—may have enabled her to live so long. Toward the end, her blood pressure dropped, along with her appetite and weight, and it was clear to those who knew her that she was no longer herself.

Cleaning out the house in the course of several solitary visits that fall, I encountered, in drawers and behind cupboards, hoards of sunflower-seed husks her pet mice had built up, as well as caches of old cleaning supplies—furniture polish, silver polish, floorwax of several sorts—that testified to her high domestic hopes when we moved to this house in October of 1945. Decades, it seemed, had passed since these signifiers of good "Dutch" cleanliness had been touched. There were, even deeper under the kitchen sink, pre-war food-grinders, potato-mashers, cake tins, muffin pans, all savoring of the Shillington kitchen as it had been, with an oak icebox and a stone sink and oilcloth shelf-liners, in my childhood fifty years before. Everywhere, I found a stifling wealth of souvenirs—a pocketbook with two pairs of navy-blue gloves mildewed within, liniments for my grandparents' aches and pains, lotions and lace and brooches, vases and crystal and figurines wrapped in tissue paper and boxed toward some loving resurrection, every object freighted with its years and a whiff of appeal to my memory, to some once-living self long layered over. Suddenly the tenderly musty old house was ripped open as if by brutal winds. My children and I divided up the best furniture and hauled it away in a rented truck; an auctioneer was engaged to dispose of the rest. Still, there were awkward leftovers: the stray cats my mother used to feed, now starving, and pounds of aging cold cuts in the refrigerator—the caterer had greatly overestimated the number of mourners.* In my frenzy of efficiency, on the last afternoon of a visit in early November, happening upon several mousetraps neatly tied together in a drawer, I set a trap with a bit of funeral cheese and went out for dinner.

The ex-wife of an old college friend had invited me; she and her second husband had a weekend house in Chester County, not an hour away. Philadelphia Avenue, the street of my boyhood in Shillington, extended east, past what had been the poorhouse property, toward Birdsboro, and became Route 724, running along the south side of the Schuylkill as it flowed from Reading through Pottstown toward Philadelphia. In all my years here, and in twice that number as a returning native, I had never driven this way, that I remembered, and was struck, as the autumn sun sank from gold to red amid the thin clouds of late afternoon, by the beauty of the road, the soft tall yellowy vine-laden trees of the riverine woods, the hopeful stone houses and tawny shorn cornfields of Pennsylvania. The

---

*Not the first such overestimation in my mother's life. A child when her grandfather died, she remembered in her short story "Translation" how "The church was strangely warm and empty, as railroad stations sometimes are after a train has passed, and much of the food that the caterer had brought to our house to make a feast for my grandfather's friends had to be taken away."

dinner, at my hosts' authentic yet, compared with my mother's rugged place, cosseted and chic Chester County farmhouse, took me back to a college mood, for my old Harvard friend's wife was a literary scholar, and to her all those majestic modernist presences that haunted the Fifties, Eliot and Pound and Stevens and William Carlos Williams and H.D. and Marianne Moore, were still living presences, occasioning gossip and titillation. Their antique celebrity, and the reverent precisions of the New Criticism, and the old faith that books make a proudly self-sufficient world animated the evening and brought back to me the cloistered, ivied warmth in which my awkward countrified ambitions had expanded and acquired sophistication. I drove back in the dark by another, faster route and found, turning on the kitchen light, that my trap had caught a mouse: *the* mouse, I was certain, that had kept my mother company during her long vigil of bodily decline and growing helplessness, while I pursued my life hundreds of miles away.

I felt sick, guilty, exhilarated. I removed the downy little body, curled up in death like a fetus, and tossed it by the tail into the swampy area between the backyard and the old spring. To be alive is to be a killer. That night I slept in the house for the last time. The guest bed, with its cover of white dotted swiss and its rounded cherry bedposts, had startled me, entering the bedroom with my suitcase a few days before, by being so crisply made, so welcoming amid the parallels of sun rays and soft floorboard, so innocently unknowing of its changed status, on the edge of dismantling and auction. Things have such crisp faces, such clear consciences.

The next morning I loaded the car with the last furniture and souvenirs to be saved and drove to New York, where I had to attend a meeting, in city clothes. Always, in driving away from the farm, the hour on the Pennsylvania Turnpike, skimming through Valley Forge, had been a green and shaggy limbo, where the Jersey Turnpike was a kind of inferno and yet a path of freedom. I stopped finally at the Admiral William Halsey Service Area, beyond the Newark airport, amid junk dumps and tatters of marshland. Though it was November, the asphalt of the parking lot still exuded a swampy heat, a mugginess that reminded me of Updike family reunions in a hot summer meadow near Trenton. My father had come from New Jersey. I was on his turf now. In the roadside cafeteria—Roy Rogers having displaced Howard Johnson—I treated myself to a cinnamon doughnut and a Styrofoam cup of coffee. I had given up coffee years before, in deference to my own high blood pressure. Through the smeared big windows I looked out at the many slanting levels of the exit ramps, the steady murmuring stream of the traffic beyond, and thought of the mouse, and the bed, whose dotted-swiss bedspread was folded in the trunk of my car, and felt in my daze of loss and ragged sleep an old emotion, that I used to feel when an adolescent and stranded, for an hour or two, in a booth of the luncheonette near the high school where my father was working after hours. Soon he would finish, and come and pick me up, and drive me home to our farm. But for now, I was an orphan, full of the triumphant, arid bliss of being on my own.

AN ANSWER *to the question "Why Are We Here?," posed for a* Life-*sponsored book shamelessly titled* The Meaning of Life.

Ancient religion and modern science agree: we are here to give praise. Or, to slightly tip the expression, to pay attention. Without us, the physicists who have espoused the anthropic principle tell us, the universe would be unwitnessed, and in a real sense not there at all. It exists, incredibly, for us. This formulation (knowing what we know of the universe's ghastly extent) is more incredible, to our sense of things, than the Old Testament hypothesis of a God willing to suffer, coddle, instruct, and even (in the Book of Job) to debate with men, in order to realize the meagre benefit of worship, of praise for His Creation. What we beyond doubt do have is our instinctive intellectual curiosity about the universe from the quasars down to the quarks, our wonder at existence itself, and an occasional surge of sheer blind gratitude for being here.

A "SPECIAL MESSAGE" *for the Franklin Library's First Edition Society printing of* Rabbit at Rest *(1990).*

When I am asked—least welcome of questions—which of my novels is my favorite, I grope for the answer but never name any of the Rabbit books. They have enough friends; they have gone out into the world and made their mark. They are not, it may be, the kind of novel I most like to read: my taste is for crotchety modernist magicians like Joyce and Nabokov and Calvino; of my own, I prefer the trickier novels, with several layers in different colors, like *The Centaur* and *The Coup,* or narratives that have a nice informational abundance, like *Roger's Version* and *S.* Plain realism has never seemed to me enough—all those "he said"s and "she said"s, those obligatory domestic crises and chapter-concluding private epiphanies. Novel-readers must have a plot, no doubt, and a faithful rendering of the texture of the mundane; but a page of printed prose should bring to its mimesis something extra, a kind of supernatural as it were, to lend everything roundness—a fine excess that corresponds with the intricacy and opacity of the real world.

Yet Rabbit's world is not perfectly plain. Rereading the first three novels in preparation for this fourth and final one, I was struck by the oddities perpetrated by my younger self thirty years ago, when he, in *Rabbit, Run,* laid down the basic elements of the Angstrom saga. Rabbit's old nemesis, Ronnie Harrison, for instance, the embodiment of physical vulgarity to my somewhat squeamish Swede—why that name? There are two "son"s in the continuing cast of characters, Nelson and Harrison. And some other names that I felt obliged to impose upon my phantoms are odd, surely, from Marty Tothero (death[*Tod*]-hero, an assiduous critic has explained to me) to Fern and Bernie Drechsel. Webb Murkett? Ollie Inglefinger? In this present novel, I couldn't rest, for some reason, until I had given Joe Gold's wife a name, even though she scarcely exists as a character. After a number of meditation sessions I arrived at it: Beu, short for Beulah. Not to be confused with another character of mine, Bea Latchett, who grotesquely became, in her marriage to my other revival-prone hero, Bea Bech.

And Harry's search for a daughter—what is going on here? In the first novel, his infant daughter drowned; in the next novel, *Rabbit Redux,* a kind of adopted daughter, Jill, dies by fire. In the third of the sequence, *Rabbit Is Rich,* my hero becomes obsessed with the notion that a girl who wanders into the car lot is his illegitimate daughter by his mistress in *Rabbit, Run,* and spies upon her in her rural home—the closest he and I ever came to *Rural Rabbit,* a title I once tossed off in a self-interview. It would seem that the novels as a whole trace Rabbit's relations with the opposite sex, which have two principal aspects, the paternal and the erotic. In each novel—this much was a conscious decision—his sexual experience is deepened, his lifelong journey into the bodies of women is advanced. Fellatio, buggery—the sexual specifics are important, for they mark the stages of a kind of somatic pilgrimage that, smile though we will, is consciously logged by most men and perhaps by more women than admit it. In *Rabbit at Rest,* he has very little further to go, just a bit of incest and impotence, while his old bed partners are joining the dead.

A Rabbit novel has certain traits. For one, the present tense, taken up when it was a daring novelty and sustained into this present period, when it has become a cliché. It is a delightfully apprehensive tense, quick on the pickup and easy to ride between external event and inner reflection. For another trait, a sprinkling of news items, following the precedent of the March 1959 radio news faithfully transcribed during the course of Rabbit's first southward flight. America—its news items, its popular entertainment, its economic emanations—is always a character. And there is a gauzy, accidental quality to these books. Taking place in the present, they are disturbingly open to accidents, to the random promptings of contemporary event, national and personal. In *Rabbit, Run*, a number of the Pennsylvania details—the rhododendron gardens, the Episcopal rectory—were suggested by features of my new New England environment. While writing *Rabbit at Rest*, I walked in a summer parade, and hence so does Harry; I subscribed to a Florida paper, and the local adventures of Deion "Prime Time" Sanders joined my hero's stream of experience, and Hurricane Hugo supplied the last chords of his *Götterdämmerung*.

Rabbit, Janice, Nelson, Mim, and the four grandparents, which last are all alive in 1959 and even 1969, but by 1979 are reduced to Ma Springer and by 1989 all dead and reduced to vivacious memories—this is the family. The city of Brewer and its suburban outriggers Mt. Judge and Penn Park and its rural satellites Galilee and Oriole and Maiden Springs compose the environment, whose name, once given as Brewer County, came to be Diamond County, after the diamond shape of my native county of Pennsylvania, Berks. When, at the age of twenty-seven, six years married, five years a published writer, and two years a New Englander, I sat down to write my fable of an ex–basketball player gone off the rails, I drew haphazardly on the geography of my native turf, getting most of it rather wrong. To a child raised in Shillington, Reading was an ominous great city; its geography consisted of scattered eminences and glimpses, and in cooking up Brewer I twisted its orientation by ninety degrees, making what was east north, and jumbled real route numbers like 422 with unreal ones like 111. The fictional geography has solidified during the subsequent novels, but only up to a point; the mind's eye in the end overrules the surveyor's transit. Rabbit experiences his Pennsylvania milieu much as I did mine—as a series of impressions, whose interconnections and historical background dawn but raggedly, if at all.

For this novel—the fourth, and the fourth that the Franklin Mint has honored, in one or another of its series, with publication in elegantly tooled leather—I transplanted Rabbit to Florida, for six months of the year, as a natural extension of his week-long sally into the Caribbean in *Rabbit Is Rich*. Americans have gained mobility in thirty years, and so has Harry. Exercising my own mobility, I travelled to Florida several times to scout out the landscape. But Deleon, like Brewer, is fictional and must not be held to strict geographical account; it lies roughly where Juan Ponce de León, the discoverer of Florida and the hero of a frequently revised and never-published novel by my mother, was slain by Indian arrows. Using the materials and to some extent the maps and newspapers of our real world, fiction locates its characters in a cloudland where they can find the freedom to fulfill their tendencies. I wanted, in *Rabbit at Rest*, while plausibly portraying a specimen American male's evolution into grandpaternity, frailty, lassitude, sensations of dispensability, and even inklings of selflessness, to allow the thematic tendencies, conscious or unconscious, of the three other novels to run to their destination, to wind up. I wanted to cap my series and make it a tetralogy while I still had most of my wits about me, and before my living connections with Pennsylvania quite ceased.

As long as my parents and then, after 1972, my mother lived in Pennsylvania, I had opportunity to visit and keep tabs on Rabbit's changing world. Two weeks after the completion of the first draft of *Rabbit at Rest*, my mother died; her decline, long forestalled but unignorable in her last year, contributed to the hospital scenes of this book and to its overall mortal mood. For me 1989 was a year of goodbyes, to the real and the unreal. During my many visits to Reading and its environs in this year—my most intense dose of Pennsylvania since the Fifties—I was conscious of how powerfully, inexhaustibly rich real places are, compared with the paper cities we make of them in fiction. Even after a tetralogy, almost everything is still left to say. As I walked and drove the familiar roads and streets, I saw them as if for the first time with more than a child's eyes and felt myself beginning, at last, to understand the place. But by then it was time to say goodbye.

Index

A Note About the Author

John Updike was born in 1932, in Shillington, Pennsylvania. He graduated from Harvard College in 1954, and spent a year in England on the Knox Fellowship, at the Ruskin School of Drawing and Fine Art in Oxford. From 1955 to 1957 he was a member of the staff of *The New Yorker*, to which he has contributed poems, short stories, essays, and book reviews. Since 1957, he has lived in Massachusetts. He is the father of four children and the author of fourteen novels. His fiction has won the Pulitzer Prize, the American Book Award, and the National Book Critics Circle Award. His previous collection of essays and reviews, *Hugging the Shore*, won the National Book Critics Circle Award for criticism in 1984.

A Note on the Type

The text of this book was set in a digitized version of Janson, a typeface long thought to have been made by the Dutchman Anton Janson, who was a practicing type founder in Leipzig during the years 1668–1687. However, it has been conclusively demonstrated that these types are actually the work of Nicholas Kis (1650–1702), a Hungarian, who most probably learned his trade from the master Dutch type founder Dirk Voskens. The type is an excellent example of the influential and sturdy Dutch types that prevailed in England up to the time William Caslon developed his own incomparable designs from them.

Composed, printed, and bound by
The Haddon Craftsmen, Inc.,
Scranton, Pennsylvania